June 22–25, 2015
Glasgow, United Kingdom

**Association for
Computing Machinery**

Advancing Computing as a Science & Profession

C&C'15

Proceedings of the 2015 ACM SIGCHI Conference on
Creativity and Cognition

Sponsored by:
ACM SIGCHI

Supported by:
The Glasgow School of Art, City of Glasgow College, and NSF

**Association for
Computing Machinery**

Advancing Computing as a Science & Profession

The Association for Computing Machinery
2 Penn Plaza, Suite 701
New York, New York 10121-0701

ISBN: 978-1-4503-3598-0 (Digital)

ISBN: 978-1-4503-3878-3 (Print)

Additional copies may be ordered prepaid from:

ACM Order Department
PO Box 30777
New York, NY 10087-0777, USA

Phone: 1-800-342-6626 (USA and Canada)
+1-212-626-0500 (Global)
Fax: +1-212-944-1318
E-mail: acmhelp@acm.org
Hours of Operation: 8:30 am – 4:30 pm ET

Printed in the USA

Welcome: Céad mile fáilte

As Conference Chair it is my great pleasure – on behalf of all those who have prepared for this event – to welcome you to the 2015 Conference on Creativity and Cognition, here in Glasgow, Scotland.

Glasgow – in gaelic the "dear green place" – is arguably the UK's most vibrant city. In the past it has played a major role in the Industrial Revolution and in the Scottish Enlightenment. Currently it is a city of some 800 thousand people known for their hospitality, generosity, love of the arts and great good humour. You are sure of the most warm welcome (fáilte).

The 2015 Conference is hosted jointly by the Glasgow School of Art and the City of Glasgow College. The Glasgow School of Art has had an eventful year. On 21st May 2014 a massive fire damaged part of the world renowned building designed by Charles Rennie Mackintosh; a few months earlier the GSA celebrated the opening of the great Reid building designed by Stephen Holl Architects that faces the Mackintosh building and in which the main events of the Conference will take place. The City of Glasgow College will shortly occupy a brand new campus on a city centre site; this will bring together a number of prestigious, and previously disparate, colleges.

The Glasgow School of Art will host the three days of the main Conference and the Workshops, Posters, Performances and the Graduate Symposium. The City of Glasgow College will host the Art Exhibition in its splendid "Gym" space.

The Monday evening Reception will be hosted by the Lord Provost of the City in the marvellous City Chambers. The Conference Dinner will be held on Tuesday in the wonderful Oran Mor, in the city's West End. The Wednesday Party, with Performances, will be held in the "Vic", on the GSA campus. Thursday see the Workshops and the Graduate Symposium.

Conference titles are always difficult and often contentious. The 2015 theme is Computers | Art | Data – sufficiently descriptive, inclusive and stimulating. The objective of all those involving the selection of academic papers, workshops, performances, posters and graduate papers has been to live up to the very high standards of previous conferences in 2009, 2011, and 2013. As currently planned there will be some 27 Academic Papers during the Monday to Wednesday conference in the Reid auditorium; some 20 Art Exhibits in the CGC Gym space over the 4 days of the event; some 4 Workshops on the Thursday in the Reid building; some 5 Performances during the Party in the Vic on Wednesday evening; some 14 Posters in the foyer of the Reid building; and some 10 Graduate Student presentations on Thursday in the Vic. A real feast of activities in the theme of Creativity and Cognition!

Of course, such success as C+C/15 may have is largely due to the efforts and judgement of all those involved: very many thanks for the difficult selection of submissions are due to Andruid Kerne, Ellen Do, David Shamma, Brian Bailey, Michael Smyth, Paul Cosgrove and Erin Cherry. We are particularly privileged to have Marcos Novak, Steve Benford and Stephen Scrivener as Keynote Speakers.

As Conference Chair my weekly contact over the last 9 months has been with the local operations/arrangements team – Inga Paterson of the Glasgow School of Art and Andrew Welsby and David Eaton of the City of Glasgow College. In particular, David and Inga have been a tower of strength – so my grateful thanks to them.

Above all, very many thanks to Ernest Edmonds for trusting us to be your hosts.

Tom Maver, *Glasgow School of Art*
Conference Chair, June 2015

Preamble

ACM Creativity and Cognition 2015 will serve as a premier forum for presenting the world's best new research investigating computing's impact on human creativity in a broad range of disciplines including the arts, design, science, and engineering. We are interested in how computing can promote creativity in all forms of human experiences. Thus, we value research that address new, synergistic roles for computing and people in creative processes. We also acknowledge that computing, as contextualized in sociotechnical systems, may sometimes have an undesirable impact. These phenomena also warrant investigation.

Creativity and Cognition 2015 will be hosted by The Glasgow School of Art and the City of Glasgow. The C&C'15 conference theme is **Computers | Arts | Data**. The theme will serve as the basis for a curated art exhibition, as well as for research presentations.

Creativity is the cornerstone and the fundamental motive of both the aesthetic and engineering disciplines. According to the U.S. National Academies of Science and Engineering, creativity is the strategic key to economic success. Creativity, at the personal (mini-c), social (little-c), and societal (big-C) levels, is fundamental to human satisfaction, happiness, and progress.

Despite its identification with ineffable aspects of human experience, much has been accomplished in the study of creativity. Powerful methodologies are based in art and design. One set of valuable methodologies comes from creative cognition. Another set comes from social psychology. Yet another beneficial mode of inquiry comes from ethnographic and sociological studies of human experience. All of these diverse approaches are used to fruitfully investigate the impact of computing on human creativity. Investigation of creativity and computing thus involves and connects the arts, the humanities, and social sciences, in addition to science, technology, engineering, and mathematics.

ACM Creativity and Cognition 2015 invited papers, posters, and demonstrations investigating how interactive computing systems and sociotechnical processes affect creativity. We cherish creativity as a wonderful aspect of human experience, transformative and potentially transcendental. Creativity is the partner of inspiration, of moments when we seem to go beyond ourselves to reach new heights. Creativity is the font of innovation.

Creativity and Cognition papers address the impact of computing on individual creative experiences, as well as social and collaborative contexts. In all cases, we seek for the presentation of work to include forms of validation featuring data about people, in order to show how computing environments impact human creativity. The data can take many forms, including qualitative, quantitative, and sensory. Creativity and Cognition 2015 will present papers addressing: (1) creativity support environments, (2) studies of technology, people, and creativity, (3) evaluation methods, (4) theory, and (5) creative works that utilize computing to engage, stimulate, and provoke human experience.

Numbers

Creativity and Cognition 2015 Conference will present a wide variety of work selected through the peer review process. As in the CHI conference, reviewers were asked to focus on the significance of the submission's contribution, originality and validity, the quality of the presentation, and the benefit others can gain from its results.

Full papers are up to 10 pages. Notes are up to 4 pages. Poster submissions are to be a maximum of 4 pages in length. Demonstrations are to be a maximum of 2 pages in length. Papers, posters, and demonstrations were reviewed independently. Graduate Student Symposium submissions are to be a two-page paper. We also called for proposals for artworks, music, performances and installations to be presented in conjunction with the conference, in a two-page format.

We received 103 paper submissions. Of these, 88 were full paper submissions and 15 were notes. After the review, we accepted 23 full papers and 6 notes, for a combined 28% acceptance rate.

The conference will also include technical demonstrations, posters, and the graduate student symposium. Submissions to these tracks were selected through a peer review process. Five technical demonstrations will be showcased at the conference, selected from eight submissions. From 27 submissions, 14 posters were selected for display at the conference. The graduate student symposium is a one-day workshop held after the main conference. The symposium received 23 submissions of which 14 were accepted for presentation. The symposium was also funded in part by an award from the U.S. National Science Foundation.

In addition to the main conference there will also be an exhibition of artworks and performances that relate to the conference themes. The exhibition will be held in the original gymnasium that sits on top of an iconic 1960s Glasgow City College building. As a city, Glasgow has a tradition of using alternative "pop up" spaces. There were a total of 49 submissions from which 23 were chosen for inclusion. The selection was completed through peer review. The criteria for acceptance focused on both the quality of the submission and the suitability for display in the designated exhibition space.

Organizing a conference is no small feat. With the tireless efforts from the Organizing Committee members, reviewers and volunteers, C&C'15 will be a unique experience of the gathering of the minds. We thank Lisa M. Tolles for the impossible tasks of herding the cats to produce this volume to document the excitements of the event for your enjoyment and contemplation.

Ellen Yi-Luen Do
Technical Program Chair
Georgia Institute of Technology & National University of Singapore

David Eaton
Local Organising Chair
City of Glasgow College

Andruid Kerne
Papers Chair
Texas A&M University

David A. Shamma
Papers Co-Chair
Yahoo Labs & Flickr

Brian Bailey
Poster & Demo Chair & Graduate Student Symposium Chair
University of Illinois

Erin Cherry
Poster & Demo Co-Chair
Northrop Grumman

Danilo di Mascio
Graduate Student Symposium Co-Chair
Northumbria University

Paul Cosgrove
Art Program Chair
Glasgow School of Art

Sue Gollifer
Art Program Co-Chair
University of Brighton

Papers Introduction

Aw'rite Glasgow! We are excited to present the Papers of ACM Creativity and Cognition 2015. We sought to create a truly interdisciplinary site for presenting human-computer interaction research, putting artistic and scientific methods on equal footing, and promoting synergetic syntheses. While following in the tradition of Creativity and Cognition, we introduced several new procedures and processes; our aim was to improve the review process, the feedback to the authors, and the overall diversity of the papers' program. To do this, we introduced a more distributed reviewing process, new keywords for describing Creativity and Cognition research, and emphasized thoroughness and compassion in the reviews. We recruited 25 expert Associate Chairs — some identified as artists, some consider themselves scientists, some technologists, some cultural theorists — from a broad and intentional blend of fields and methodologies. We matched 3–6 papers to each AC, based on their expertise, ensuring all conflicts were marked and help blind to anyone affected.

We overhauled the keywords that authors use for describing papers and reviewers use for describing their expertise. Along with a bidding process by ACs, who could also upload papers indicative of their research interests, the keywords played a major role in matching ACs with papers. We organized the keywords around 5 conceptual dimensions: Fields, Media of Expression, Interaction (Modalities and Components), Evaluation Methodologies, and Users. We hope the community will find this conceptual space useful in years to come.

We developed a clear specification for what constitutes a good review. In addition to identifying aspects of intellectual merit, the specification includes guidelines such as to be kind as well as clear, to be thorough, and to be explicit when identifying missing prior work. We integrated the instructions to reviewers and ACs directly into review forms, to keep reminding reviewers.

In practice, the Associate Chairs were the heart of the reviewing process. Each AC was responsible for recruiting 3-4 appropriate external reviewers for each of their assigned papers. Each AC was responsible for writing her own review of each paper, and then writing a meta-review synthesizing all the reviewers' positions. In some cases, where a consensus was not easily arrived upon, we recruited an additional 2AC review. The ACs also nominated the best paper candidates.

Following other SIGCHI conferences, we increased the length of full papers to 10 pages, we introduced a Notes designation, for 4 page papers, and we used the Precision Conference System (PCS). We received 103 valid submissions. Of these, we accepted 23 full papers and 6 notes, for a 28% acceptance rate. We are proud to certify the integrity of the process. We believe we have fostered an excellent papers program. We look forward to the excellent discussions to come.

We would like to thank Tom Erickson, of the SIGCHI Executive Committee, for supporting our keyword endeavors, James Steward for his support with PCS, and Bill Hamilton for helping in the initial organization of the paper's track. And finally, much thanks to our ACs and Reviewers who made this program excellent as evident by many of the authors, both accepted and rejected, who have reached out to us in thanks for their high quality reviews.

We hope that you will enjoy the papers, that your interests will be piqued, imaginations tickled, and discussions stimulated. We hope that the through the papers program and the rest of the conference, the Creativity and Cognition community will grow through 2015 and beyond.

Andruid Kerne
Papers Chair
The Interface Ecology Lab, Texas A&M University

David A. Shamma
Papers Chair
HCI Research Group, Yahoo Labs & Flickr

Table of Contents

Keynote Address 1
Session Chair: Tom Maver *(Glasgow School of Art)*

Paper Session 1: Textiles and Objects
Session Chairs: Andruid A. Kerne *(Texas A&M University)* and David Shamma *(Yahoo Labs)*

Paper Session 2: Tools and Interfaces
Session Chair: Will Odom *(Simon Fraser University)*

Paper Session 3: Finding
Session Chair: Andrew Webb *(Texas A&M University)*

Keynote Address 2

Session Chair: Tom Maver *(Glasgow School of Art)*

Paper Session 4: Moments and Movements

Session Chair: Celine Latulipe *(University of North Carolina, Charlotte)*

Posters and Demos Session 1

Session Chairs: Brian Bailey *(University of Illinois)* and Erin Cherry *(Northrop Grumman)*

Posters and Demos Session 2

Session Chairs: Brian Bailey *(University of Illinois)* and Erin Cherry *(Northrop Grumman)*

Paper Session 5: Working and Learning

Session Chair: Ellen Do *(Georgia Tech & National University of Singapore)*

Paper Session 6: Ideation Play, and Experience

Session Chair: Eva Hornecker *(Bauhaus-Universität Weimar)*

Paper Session 7: Places of Creativity
Session Chair: Steven Dow *(Carnegie Mellon University)*

Graduate Student Symposium
Session Chairs: Brian Bailey *(University of Illinois)* and Danilo Di Mascio *(Northumbria University)*

Art Exhibition

Performances

Workshop Summaries
Session Chair: Michael Smyth *(Napier University)*

Keynote Address 3
Session Chair: Tom Maver *(Glasgow School of Art)*

C&C 2015 Organizing Committee

Conference Chair: Tom Maver (Glasgow School of Art)

Program Chair: Ellen Yi-Luen Do (Georgia Tech, USA/NUS, Singapore)

Papers Chair: Andruid Kerne (Texas A&M University)

Papers Co-Chair: David Ayman Shamma (Yahoo Research)

Local Organising Chair: David Eaton (City of Glasgow College)

Treasurer: Andrew Welsby (City of Glasgow College)

Poster and Demos Chair: Brian Bailey (University of Illinois)

Poster and Demos Co-Chair: Erin Cherry (Northrop Grumman)

Graduate Student Symposium Chair: Brian Bailey (University of Illinois)

Graduate Symposium Co-Chair: Danilo di Mascio (Northumbria University)

Art Program Chair: Paul Cosgrove (Glasgow School of Art)

Art Program Co-Chair: Sue Gollifer (University of Brighton)

Papers Organizer: William Hamilton (Texas A&M University)

Workshops/Tutorial Chair: Michael Smyth (Napier University)

Local Organising Co-Chair: Inga Paterson (Glasgow School of Art)

Website Chair: David Eaton (City of Glasgow College)

Associate Chairs for Papers:

Anne Balsamo (The New School,
    University of Amsterdam)
Winslow Burleson (NYU)
Linda Candy (University of Technology, Sydney)
Pablo Cesar (CWI)
Erin Cherry (Northrop Grumman)
Sally Jo Cunningham (University of Waikato)
Steven Dow (Carnegie Mellon University)
Rebecca Fiebrink (Goldsmiths, University of London)
Sara Jones (City University London)
Eva Hornecker (Bauhaus-Universität, Weimar)
Hayley Hung, (Delft University of Technology)
Boriana Koleva (University of Nottingham)
Charlotte Lee (University of Washington)
Patrick Lichty (University of Wisconsin - Milwaukee)
Kurt Luther (Virginia Tech)
Mary Lou Maher (University of North Carolina, Charlotte)
Will Odom (Simon Fraser University)
Steven M. Smith (Texas A&M University)
Andrea Polli (University of New Mexico)
Stuart Reeves (University of Nottingham)
Orit Shaer (Wellesley College)
Andrew Webb (Texas A&M University)
John Zimmerman (Carnegie Mellon University)

Steering Committee:

Nicholas Bryan-Kinns
Ashok Goel
Tom Hewett
Samuel Ferguson
Celine Latulipe
Ernest Edmonds
Linda Candy
Nagai Yukari
Ben Shneiderman
David England

Additional Reviewers

Ragaad AlTarawneh	Eric Baumer	Erin Bradner
Morgan Ames	Ben Bedwell	Erin Brady
Salvatore Andolina	Ben Bengler	Katharina Bredies
Fabien Andre	Laura Benton	Jo Briggs
Michelle Annett	Sven Bertel	Barry Brown
Lisa Anthony	Allen Bevans	Quincy Brown
Ahmed Arif	Joan-isaac Biel	Scott Brown
Ruth Aylett	Paul Booth	Amy Bruckman
Chris Baber	Nis Bornoe	Patrick Brundell
Liam Bannon	Cati Boulanger	George Buchanan
Jeffrey Bardzell	Simon Bowen	Daniel Buzzo
Louise Barkhuus	Karen Bradley	Francesco Cafaro

Licia Calvi
Pasquina Campanella
Kristin Carlson
Alejandro Catala
Marc Cavazza
Daniel Cermak-Sassenrath
Daniel Cernea
Teresa Cerratto Pargman
Joel Chan
Sanjay Chandrasekharan
Jack Shen-Kuen Chang
Abon Chaudhuri
Xiang 'Anthony' Chen
EunJeong Cheon
Marshini Chetty
Harshit Choudhary
Eunki Chung
Luigina Ciolfi
Adrian Clark
Rachel Clarke
Enrico Costanza
Brigid Costello
Tim Coughlan
Lynne Coventry
Donna Cox
David Coyle
Michael Crabb
Bronwyn Cumbo
Martyn Dade-Roberstson
Florian Daiber
Peter Dalsgaard
Nicholas Dalton
Sheep Dalton
Areti Damala
Andreea Danielescu
Sandra Danilovic
Nicholas Davis
Alwin de Rooij
Mustapha Derras
Audrey Desjardins
Heather Desurvire
Sebastian Deterding
Nicoletta Di Blas

Danilo Di Mascio
Tawanna Dillahunt
Anke Dittmar
Afsaneh Doryab
Graham Dove
Ruofei Du
Sarah Eagle
Claudia Eckert
Chris Elsden
Gwenn Englebienne
Jonathon Epstein
Ingrid Erickson
Clay Ewing
Neta Ezer
Haakon Faste
Yuanyuan Feng
Sam Ferguson
Ylva Fernaeus
Bruce Ferwerda
Casey Fiesler
Flavio Figueiredo
Martin Flintham
Angus Forbes
Sarah Fox
Michael Frantzis
Christopher Frauenberger
Göttel Funke
Timo Göttel
Krzysztof Gajos
Jérémie Garcia
William Gaver
Gretchen Gelke
Hans Gellersen
Elizabeth Gerber
John Gero
Kiel Gilleade
Berto Gonzalez
Elizabeth Goodman
Danny Goodwin
Nitesh Goyal
Kazjon Grace
Colin Gray
Michael Greenberg

Mick Grierson
Mark Gross
Shad Gross
Leman Gul
Rebecca Gulotta
Hatice Gunes
Kristina Höök
Joshua Hailpern
Julia Haines
John Halloran
Sarah Hamilton
William Hamilton
Mark Handel
Lane Harrison
Björn Hartmann
Tracy Harwood
Christin Henzen
Luis Hernan
Luke Hespanhol
Alexis Hiniker
Jason Hockman
Axel Hoesl
Trevor Hogan
Jonathan Hook
Simo Hosio
Yu-Chun Huang
Julie Hui
Shah Rukh Humayoun
Lilly Irani
Germaine Irwin
Petra Isenberg
Nils Jäger
Christian Jacquemin
Ajit Jain
Yvonne Jansen
Sampath Jayarathna
Carolina Johansson
Andrew Johnston
Judith Kahn
Andrea Kanneh
Karrie Karahalios
Kerstin Keil
Patrick Kelley

Aisling Kelliher
Sarah Kettley
Jaejeung Kim
Jeeeun Kim
MiJeong Kim
Nam Wook Kim
Sunyoung Kim
Alan Kimball
mc Kindsmueller
Reuben Kirkham
Clemens Klokmose
Søren Knudsen
Naveen Kolla
Joke Kort
Ilpo Koskinen
Ted Krueger
Stoffel Kuenen
Bill Kules
Stacey Kuznetsov
Edward Lank
Martha Larson
Walter Lasecki
Celine Latulipe
Shawn Lawson
Michael Lee
Sang Won Lee
Uichin Lee
Mike Leggett
James Lester
Catherine Letondal
Samantha LeVan
Meng Li
Shuowei Li
Hai-Ning Liang
Youn-kyung Lim
Rhema Linder
Joseph Lindley
Siân Lindley
Silvia Lindtner
Agnes Lisowska Masson
Peter Ljungstrand
Kiel Long
Pedro Lopes

Andrés Lucero
Christopher Lueg
Joanna Lumsden
Nic Lupfer
zhihan lv
Michael Lynch
Dale MacDonald
Christopher MacLellan
Brian Magerko
Thor Magnusson
Roger Malina
Gary Marchionini
Jennifer Marlow
Jane Marques
Andrea Marshall
Joe Marshall
Paul Marshall
Christina Masden
Michael Massimi
Kohei Matsumura
Nolwenn Maudet
Jon McCormack
Lorna McKnight
Nemanja Memarovic
Eleonora Mencarini
Rada Mihalcea
Amon Millner
Roger Mills
Chulhong Min
Alex Mitchell
Manas Mittal
David Monaghan
Jonathan Morgan
Fabio Morreale
Robert Morris
Christiane Moser
Stefanie Mueller
Michael Muller
Frank Nack
Kumiyo Nakakoji
Kher Hui Ng
David Nichols
Kristina Niedderer

Anton Nijholt
Valentina Nisi
Mobina Nouri
Jasminko Novak
Kenton O'Hara
Ian Oakley
Hyunjoo Oh
Johanna Okerlund
Leif Oppermann
Andrea Paciotto
Yue Pan
Nadia Pantidi
Andrea Parker
Paul Parsons
Evan Peck
Isabel Pedersen
Claudia Pederson
Lucas Pereira
Sarah Perez-Kriz
Daniela Petrelli
James Pierce
Thammathip Piumsomboon
Katrin Plaumann
Beryl Plimmer
Niberca Polo
Sarah Poon
Ronald Poppe
Manoj Prasad
Larissa Pschetz
Michael Punt
Andreas Pusch
Yin Qu
Robert Racadio
Andrew Raij
David Randall
Sue Rau
Vikas Rawat
Arockia Xavier Annie Rayan
Johan Redström
Dennis Reidsma
Katharina Reinecke
Christian Remy
Stefan Rennick-Egglestone

Sean Rintel
Scott Robertson
Jennifer Rode
David Rosen
Daniela Rosner
Thijs Roumen
Mark Rouncefield
Rebecca Rouse
Silvia Ruzanka
Alan Said
Bahador Saket
Albert Salah
Huda Salman
Antti Salovaara
Rob Saunders
Yann Savoye
Marie-Monique Schaper
Florian Schaub
Thecla Schiphorst
Holger Schnädelbach
Marc Aurel Schnabel
Bertrand Schneider
M.C. Schraefel
Sue Ann Seah
Hartmut Seichter
Mark Selby
Monika Sengul-Jones
Jami Shah
Amy Shannon
Renata Sheppard
Patrick Shih
Victoria Shipp
Buntarou Shizuki

Pao Siangliulue
Ricardo Sosa
Katharina Spiel
Preethi Srinivas
Anna Ståhl
Norman Su
Wu-Chen Su
Joshua Tanenbaum
Karen Tanenbaum
Alex Taylor
Robyn Taylor
Michael Terry
Alexander Thayer
Phyo Thiha
Jakob Tholander
Seth Thompson
Claire Timpany
Martin Tomitsch
Cesar Torres
Zachary Toups
Meredith Tromble
Deborah Turnbull Tillman
Ilyas Uyanik
Heli Väätäjä
Remko van der Lugt
Doug Van Nort
Andrew Vande Moere
Noé Vargas Hernández
Tony Veale
Dan Ventura
Victoria Vesna
Fernanda Viégas
Rohan Vijay

John Vines
Simon Voelker
Gualtiero Volpe
Romain Vuillemot
Chat Wacharamanotham
Ron Wakkary
James Wallace
Hao-Chuan Wang
Yulin Wang
Thomas Ward
Colin Ware
Henry Warwick
Garry Wei-Han Tan
Carolyn Wei
Christian Weichel
Jens Weppner
Ryen White
Chris Willey
Amanda Williams
David N. Wilson
Max Wilson
Heather Wiltse
Paweł Woźniak
Donghee Yvette Wohn
Sarita Yardi Schoenebeck
Svetlana Yarosh
Jude Yew
Xiaojun Yuan
Konstantinos Zachos
Haimo Zhang
Lin Zhong
Kening Zhu
Arkaitz Zubia

C&C Sponsor & Supporters

Sponsor

Supporters

THE GLASGOW
SCHOOL OF ART

CITY OF GLASGOW COLLEGE

The Graduate Student Symposium is supported in part by a grant from the U.S. National Science Foundation under award no. IIS 15-21215

Of Guitars, Stories, Luthiery and Hybrid Craft

Steve Benford

Mixed Reality Laboratory, School of Computer Science
The University of Nottingham, Nottingham, NG8 1BB, UK
steve.benford@nottingham.ac.uk

Abstract

Every guitar tells a story, from the provenance of its tonewoods, to the craft of its making, to the players that own it, to the places it visits, to the many songs that it plays. I will tell you the story of a unique guitar, one that has been created with the express purpose of telling its own life story. My guitar is called Carolan in honour of the legendary composer Turlough O'Carolan, the famous itinerant harper who roamed Ireland at the turn of the 18th century. Like its namesake, Carolan is a roving bard; a performer that passes from place to place, learning tunes, songs and stories as it goes and sharing them with those it encounters along the way. This is made possible through interactive decorative patterns that are inlaid into the instrument's wood and that can be scanned using mobile devices in order to reveal different facets of Carolan's digital footprint.

By reflecting on how Carolan was constructed by a luthier and graphic designer and subsequently experienced by players, I will explore the relationship between a valuable physical artefact and its digital footprint. What does such a footprint comprise? How might it add value to the artefact? And how can this digital footprint become permanently associated with the physical artefact?

By reflecting on the challenges of making Carolan's interactive decorative inlay, I will explore the wider relationship between digital interactivity and traditional craft skills such as luthiery. I will draw on these reflections to inform an emerging research agenda for hybrid craft – the skillful interleaving of physical materials and digital interactions to create valuable handmade artefacts.

You can follow Carolan's story at: www.carolanguitar.com

ACM Classification

H.5.2 User Interfaces (D.2.2, H.1.2, I.3.6)
J.5 ARTS AND HUMANITIES **Subjects:** Music

Author Keywords: Musical Instrument; Guitar; Digital Footprint; Augmented Reality; Mixed Reality; Materiality; Craft; Design; Aestheticodes.

Figure 1. Steve with the Carolan Guitar

Short Bio

Steve Benford is Professor of Collaborative Computing at the University of Nottingham where he is Director of the EPSRC-funded Horizon Centre for Doctoral Training. He has been an EPSRC Dream Fellow, Visiting Researcher at Microsoft Research Cambridge and a Visiting Professor at the BBC. He received best paper awards at the ACM's CHI conference in 2005, 2009, 2011 and 2012 (with honorable mentions in 2006, 2013 and 2015). He won the 2003 Prix Ars Elctronica for Interactive Art, the 2007 Nokia Mindtrek award for Innovative Applications of Ubiquitous Computing, and has received four BAFTA nominations. He was elected to the CHI Academy in 2012. His book Performing Mixed Reality was published by MIT Press.

Acknowledgements

I am grateful for the support of the Engineering and Physical Sciences Research Council through the Fusing Semantic and Audio Technologies for Intelligent Music Production and Consumption (grant EP/L019981/1).

Imagining Future Technologies: eTextile Weaving Workshops with Blind and Visually Impaired People

Emilie Giles, Janet van der Linden
Dept of Computing and Communications
The Open University
Walton Hall
Milton keynes MK7 6AA
emilie.giles@open.ac.uk, j.vanderlinden@open.ac.uk

ABSTRACT

The traditional approach for developing assistive technologies for blind and visually impaired users is to focus on problems and to try and resolve them by compensating for the loss of vision. In this research we took the approach of involving blind and visually impaired people, from a range of ages, in a hands-on making activity using an eTextile physical computing toolkit. Our aim was to create an environment where people could both make and learn form each other, but also where they would share their thoughts and imagine future scenarios for the technologies they were developing. We observed highly creative ways of working at all levels, from unique weaving techniques to choices in fabrics and materials, as well as expressions of personal preferences. We discuss the 'in-home enjoyment' scenarios sketched by the participants and point to the role of creative workshops and eTextile toolkits as a tool for imagining future technologies.

Author Keywords

eTextiles; weaving; visual impairment; dual impairment; future technologies; participatory design; accessible technology; haptic technology.

ACM Classification Keywords

H.5.2. [Information Interfaces and Presentation]: User Interfaces - Haptic I/0, Prototyping, Input devices and strategies.

K.3.1[Computers and Education]: Computer Uses in Education - Collaborative learning.

K.4.2. [Computers and Society]: Social Issues - Assistive technologies for persons with disabilities.

C&C '15, June 22 - 25, 2015, Glasgow, United Kingdom
© 2015 ACM. ISBN 978-1-4503-3598-0/15/06$15.00
DOI: http://dx.doi.org/10.1145/2757226.2757247

INTRODUCTION

The increasingly ubiquitous touch screen, as used in smart phones, tablets and interactive touch tables enables us with a flick of a finger to be in touch with the latest sources of information, the music we want to listen to and to see the whereabouts of our friends. However, for many blind and visually impaired users these touch screens form a hurdle as they are difficult to navigate and interact with. Various efforts have been made to ensure people with visual impairments are not cut off from the rest of society by this technological divide, by creating voice over work-arounds [22], or haptic Braille [7] input devices that can work alongside a range of mobile devices and touch-based screens. These approaches have certainly helped some users to participate in text-based interactions, listening to their emails while on the go and using texting as a form of communication. However, for blind people using these devices requires a lot of effort, is limited to being text based and hasn't quite got the feeling of fun and aesthetics that most sighted people experience when using such devices.

In our research we wanted to explore, together with blind and visually impaired users, how technologies could be developed that would be comfortable to hold, easy to work with and provide an aesthetically pleasing and fun interaction. Rather than taking an approach that focuses on problems and needs, by compensating for the lack of vision, we sought for ways that blind people could take delight in new technologies. We also wanted to create an environment where they could start to imagine how or where they might want to make such technologies a part of their life.

To explore these issues we organised creative workshops which focused around electronic textiles, or eTextiles, in which components are created by combining ordinary fabrics and materials together with a range of conductive materials, allowing technology to be directly integrated into textiles. eTextiles are fabrics, yarns and threads that are integrated with metals such as silver and steel and electronic components to create garments or other textile based objects which are conductive. Small groups of blind and visually impaired people were encouraged to create their own small samples of woven fabrics, which could then be interacted with by touching and squeezing providing a range of different sound effects. The workshops were organised to enable people to creatively explore the use of a range of different materials and sounds, but were also framed as a place to have a shared discussion on where and how such technologies could become part of their lives. We discuss the various creative ways of working that participants developed throughout the workshops, outline the 'in-home enjoyment' scenarios sketched by the participants and point to the role of such creative workshops as a tool for imagining future technologies.

RELATED WORK

Many different technologies have been developed for blind or visually impaired users to use for everyday actions and tasks. These range from devices that support text reading that are worn on a person's finger [18] to iPhone apps that allow for users to write braille on a smooth touchscreen [19]. The focus of these technologies is to compensate for the poor levels of vision, and to replace the visual aspects of the environment through other sensory mechanisms, with many of them focusing on reading or writing. VivWiz [2] is an iPhone app which also revolves around solving visual issues but with a slightly different twist to it. The app works by blind users taking a photograph on their iPhone of something that they have a question about; this could be the colour of a piece of clothing, the precise cooking instructions on a product they have bought or whether their child has a rash. Users then send their photo and question to 'the crowd', this either being crowdsourced workers, their Facebook friends or Twitter Followers or they can email it to contacts. Brady et al explored what kinds of questions were frequently asked to try and further understand the challenges blind people face as well as to motivate research into new assistive technologies that provide independence. Whilst VizWiz clearly focuses on resolving visual problems, it also has a directly social angle by connecting people together. In some instances, for example, blind users were encouraged by the crowd to make photos from different angles to make sure the image was usable. One of the questions in the research was *do blind people become better photographers as they use VizWiz Social?'*, pointing to issues more related to creativity than pure functionality.

Whilst these technologies hold a lot of potential for people with sensory impairments, they still revolve around a touch screen or something which ultimately feels hard and cold to the touch. There are now increasingly technologies around which are more physical and tactile, such as a vibrating belt for finding your way [13] and gloves for deafblind people that assist with translating the hand-touch alphabets, as in the work by Gollner et al. [10] and Caporusso et al. [5], also through vibrations. What is interesting about these gloves is that they are not just for the benefit of the user but also sighted people with whom they might be communicating with, opening up the possibilities for two people to communicate who might previously not have been able to speak to each other.

eTextiles are another form of technology with interesting haptic, i.e. touch-based interaction possibilities. eTextiles are gaining ground in various domains, including health, in particular for their potential in sports and fitness applications or physiotherapy [23]. eTextiles have strong tactile properties and act as soft sensors - sensors that can pick up on movement through the way the fabric stretches, or touch, as people hold, squeeze or press against fabric layers to activate electronics. It is therefore likely that they can also play a bigger part in technology for blind and visually impaired people, with possibly more creative uses as well as functional.

Touching fabric is a pervasive element of human perception and many more people are familiar with the touch and feel of fibres, threads and yarns as opposed to wires and PCBs. They are also more likely to have some traditional craft skills such as knitting or sewing, as opposed to soldering or building circuits. Workshops in eTextiles are a popular method to introduce people to these materials and encourage them to use them in their own making [11]. Although a lot of these workshops are targeted towards sighted people, often focusing on how STEM subjects can be more engaging [9], there is also the potential for them to open up conversations and encourage people to be interested in technology who might not otherwise be so or who might lack confidence. Kobakant's workshops focus on more visceral outcomes, embracing the materials and their qualities [14], whilst the work by Kuznetsov et al focuses on reaching young people at risk [15]. Micha Cárdenas's work combines eTextile workshops with a range of other activities such as performance or self defence with vulnerable communities [6]. What all of these studies and projects have in common is that due to the open source nature of the hardware used, such as a the LilyPad Arduino, how it can be programmed and the different choices of materials that can be combined, participants are able to be creative and explore how it might be used in a more personal way, rather than constructing a pre-designed kit that only has one outcome.

Between its research phase and becoming a product to buy, the LilyPad Arduino itself was used in hands-on making workshops with different participants to see what creative choices they would make in using it for textile based projects [3]. Buechley et al. found that the workshops attracted a lot of girls, a very positive finding as women are statistically less likely to study computer programming or engineering based subjects. They also found that aesthetics certainly played a key part in its success [3].

For people who might be in danger of being excluded from mainstream activities, due to having an impairment or disability, hands-on making workshops can be very beneficial. Vogelpoel and Jarrold outline how these benefits include improving self confidence and mental wellbeing but that such workshops can also encourage participants to carry on with their own making in their own time, often with each other [21]. Similarly, in their research around how older people can engage with technology and creativity using the MaKey MaKey toolkit [16] Rogers et al. [17] explore how collaborating on short projects can empower people and question what more could be done to involve people in the design and uses of creative technologies. Their research highlights that people can be encouraged to think about new design ideas for technologies by them directly engaging with such open creative toolkits in settings where they can play and explore. Such workshops can open up a creative flow, in contrast to an approach of asking people for their needs and having to come up with ideas, out of the blue - which is particularly difficult when confronted with novel ubiquitous technologies that they may not be familiar with.

AIMS

We wanted to explore whether eTextile workshops could not only be a creative hands-on experience for blind and visually impaired people but also stimulate creative ideas for future technologies. For our study we had three aims: firstly, to see how blind and visually impaired people would go about making their own eTextile objects, secondly, what creative choices they would make during this making process and thirdly, whether they would find eTextile objects engaging, and whether they could imagine them being used in their own and other people's lives.

METHODOLOGY

Our research approach was ethnographic, focusing on participatory design where we have been learning from the participants about their ideas on the wider use of eTextiles as a technology that could be very accessible to them. The workshops were designed around weaving with conductive materials, using capacitive sensing as a way for people to create various sound effects when handling a piece of fabric. The emphasis was therefore deliberately not on the programming and electronics aspects, but instead focused on the felt experience of different materials and how to interact with them.

We organised three workshops for blind and visually impaired people spread out over two months: two with an art gallery and blind people's charity as part of their outreach activities to make art accessible to wider audiences; and one with a day centre where deafblind people would come and spend the day to participate in a variety of social, music making and craft activities. The workshops had a making part to them, but there was also plenty of time to talk and discuss with the participants, and the various support workers and volunteers who helped in running the sessions.

Technology for Interaction

The wooden looms that we chose for participants to work with are small, measuring approximately 20cm in length and width, with 36 pegs on them (see Figure 1). We deliberately chose simple lateral looms that could be easily used by beginners, allowing them to focus on making and feeling their way as opposed to worrying about the tool itself as may have happened with more advanced looms using shafts, shuttles and foot pedals. Whilst weaving is a popular activity with a number of blind and visually impaired groups [4, 12] - where they use large complex looms - this is a skill that takes many years to master and in consultation with occupational therapists we settled for this

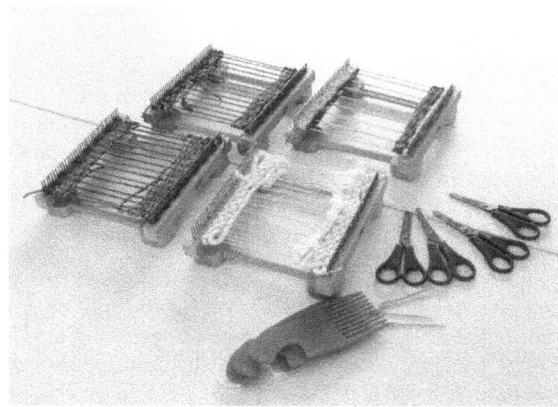

Figure 1: Looms set up on the workshop tables with the warp on them and a bit of the weft as a starting point.

particular shape loom as one in which all aspects of the loom could be readily felt and understood.

We set up the looms with the warp already on them (this is the yarn which goes around the pegs that the participants had to weave through), using both non-conductive and conductive yarn to ensure that their work would end up

Figure 2: The technology set-up: a laptop running the SuperCollider application, an Arduino board with capacitive sensing and eTextile woven swatch connected by crocodile clip.

being interactive even if a participant did not choose much conductive material to use in their weft (the part that is woven through the warp to make a finished piece).

The interaction with a finished woven piece, i.e. a swatch, was accomplished through capacitive sensing. For this we had uploaded a capacitive sensing sketch onto an Arduino Uno board [1] which communicates with a patch in SuperCollider [20] (see Figure 2). The circuit is very simple, with the woven swatch (connected through a crocodile clip) acting as a sensor that the Arduino takes readings from as it is touched. These readings differ depending on the type of touch, whether it be squeezing, stroking or rubbing and is also dependent on the type of materials used with some being more conductive than others. SuperCollider takes in the sensor readings from the

Arduino board and from them changes the sound output in line with the changing values, which makes the music responsive and interactive. The sound files ranged from wind chimes to crunching leaves; and we were able to change the sound file even as the interaction was happening, to find out which sound was of most interest to a participant, and adjust the responsiveness of particular music files by changing some numbers in the file.

We chose to use Arduino and SuperCollider, as opposed to using the inbuilt sound circuit on the Arduino board itself which has a more crude sound output, in order to be able to pick up on the smallest changes in readings associated with very light touching, and with fine differentiations in the type of materials used.

Materials

For the actual weaving activity, we chose a variety of different materials, conductive and non-conductive, for the participants to use, all of which varied in their texture, colour, thickness and sometimes in smell too (see Figure 3). The intention was that by including such a variety of different yarns and fabrics that participants could express some of their individual preferences, and make choices. This was not only to observe if these different materials evoked different reactions, emotionally, but also how this impacted on how they were handled.

Figure 3: The different materials participants could use in the workshops.

The Participants

The three groups attending were quite varied and we did not know until the day of the workshops who exactly would be there, nor how many participants to expect, as our partner organisations were responsible for the recruitment and sign-up process. The first group contained three older people (50+), two of whom had been sighted all their lives but became visually impaired as they aged. The third participant went completely blind in his thirties. Their workshop took place after an audio descriptive tour at the gallery space, so the creative weaving workshop was linked to the artist's work on show.

Material	Qualities
Conductive	
Stainless steel fibre	Resistance of 740 nΩ.m, smells metallic, has heaviness to it, difficult to tear, good for felting, grey.
Stainless steel and polyester yarn	80% polyester 20% stainless steel, soft to touch, not very elasticy, surface resistance: < 104 Ω, good to make sensors with, light grey.
Stainless steel thread	Resistance of 1.4 Ohms per linear foot, smells metallic, thick, has heaviness to it, tricky to sew circuit with, grey.
Silver plated thread	Resistance of 40 Ohms per metre, soft to touch, good to sew circuits with, very thin, grey.
Tin copper tap	Knitted metal tape, resistance of 14 ohm/meter, grey.
Conductive fabric - 3 layered tin, nickel and silver over nylon - Ripstop	Resistance of < 1 ohm/sq, very papery to touch, light grey, frays when cut.
Conductive fabric - silver plated nylon	Resistance of < 1 ohm/sq, 180 Ag Nylon single directional stretch, 78% nylon & 22% elastormer, dark grey.
Non-Conductive	
Jute fibre	Straw like to touch, slightly rough, sandy coloured.
Milk protein tops fibre	Extremely soft, easy to tear apart, white in colour.
Merino wool tops fibre	Soft, easy to tear apart, different bright colours.
Cotton yarn	Soft, cream coloured.
Linen yarn	Rough, rope-like, thick, 2/1.3 nel., copper coloured.
Unwashed wool fibre	Smelly, greasy, hard to tear, very matted bits, dirt in it, brown in colour.
Acrylic yarn	Soft to touch, almost elasticy, different colours.

Table 1: Materials used in the workshops and their qualities.

The second group consisted of 12 young people, with different visual impairments and learning disabilities, some of them being completely blind as well as autistic. This workshop was also at the gallery space and so like the first workshop took place after an audio description tour. They attended through a community youth programme which has monthly outings - on this occasion to the gallery.

Every participant in the third group had learning disabilities, some severe, as well as being blind, visually impaired or deafblind. They needed a significant amount of help with their weaving with some of them also having no speech.

For groups 1 and 3 we had access to specific participant information (see Table 2), but for group 2 we did not. Participant's names were changed for confidentiality.

Age	Participant	Impairments/ Disabilities
GROUP 1		
50 - 60	John	Completely blind, is comfortable with making things and is an artist.
65 - 80	Shelley	Visually impaired, knows a lot about materials and crafts, was a teacher.
65 - 80	Liv	Visually impaired and chairs quarterly meetings for blind and visually impaired people.
GROUP 2		
15 - 25	Jennifer Dave Jim Zo Nazmeen Will Andy Tariq Moh Sabine Tamina Zina	Most participants were visually impaired, with three being completely blind, three being autistic and one with learning disabilities.
GROUP 3		
29	Heather	Completely blind and uses her right ear as a preferred side to hear out of. Has a learning disability, enjoys talking and is interested in singing.
25 - 29	Nicolette	Has bi-lateral hearing impairment, a visual impairment, left arm is absent from below the elbow. Has not much speech and has mobility issues but can walk. Has learning disabilities.

Age	Participant	Impairments/ Disabilities
20 - 29	Tanya	Blind (sees bright light), has good hearing, wheelchair user, learning disabilities, cerebral palsy, no speech. Enjoys making continual vibrational sounds with fingers and lips.
20 - 29	Anna	Almost completely blind but with tunnel vision in her right eye, profoundly deaf, cerebral palsy. Enjoys craft activities and has good manual dexterity.

Table 2: Profile of participants who took part in our workshops.

The Workshops

Each workshop differed very slightly in our approaches due to the variety of participants. The workshops also varied in time from two to five hours, depending on whether they had to fit in with other activities, such as touch based audio tour of the art gallery (workshop one and two) or a long extended lunch break as part of a fun day out.

We began each workshop by briefly discussing eTextiles followed by passing around an example eTextile woven swatch for everyone to explore with their hands and demonstrating how it can be interactive. This immediately allowed for the participants to understand how this was an object that can create interaction as opposed to just being normal textiles. This was then followed by participants working on their own swatch using the materials that they chose. We developed a style where all materials that could be used for weaving were put together on a separate table, and we encouraged participants to walk up, feel the various textures and fibres and select the ones they wanted to use so as to make them feel in control of that part of the process.

In each workshop the participants were guided by a variety of support workers and volunteers who showed them the process by guiding their hands (see Figure 4). Once this was demonstrated to them, participants carried on with their work independently, occasionally being helped to find the scissors or to be guided to the table with materials to make further choices; while in the case of people with severe learning disabilities, assistance was on hand continually and adapted to the individual needs of the participant.

Once participants had finished their work we helped them lift their weave off the loom and connect it to the Arduino board to interact with the audio in SuperCollider. We either carried the laptop around and brought it to the participants or participants walked over to us to take their work off the loom and interact with it. People were given a choice of audio to experiment with, being playfully encouraged to look for the sound they liked best or that provided the best effect for them.

Figure 4: Participant weaving.

During the first and third workshop we had discussions with participants about the possible uses of eTextiles during the activity itself but with the second workshop we did this at the end, as a brainstorm discussion with the whole group. The first workshop was more informal and so these discussions happened naturally; due to many of the participants in the third session having little to no speech, it was more about observing their interest in the activity and their response to it.

DATA ANALYSIS

Following a participatory research approach we were immersed in the workshops as people who would provide hands-on support and guidance to participants and the volunteers. All workshops were documented through informal notes from various observations jotted down by the researchers, transcriptions of recorded conversations and discussions where these were audible, and study of photos and video materials of the sessions. Through sharing these various notes and in-depth discussion within the team a number of themes were identified under which we report our findings.

FINDINGS

Whilst there were a lot of differences between the participants, in terms of their age, their background, their health issues, cognitive abilities as well as their level of visual impairment - it was surprising how all experienced creative and exciting moments from doing the activity. People worked in a concentrated, focused way - taking pride in their work and keen to complete their sample in order to experience the sound interaction. There was a relaxed atmosphere in the group, with people showing their progress to each other and sharing associations about what they were doing and aspects of their personal their life.

From Apprehension to Confidence and Enjoyment

Initially participants expressed a sense of apprehension about the task they were embarking on, but this apprehension gradually disappeared as they started to work on their piece. John, during the first workshop, explained that as a blind person he felt quite anxious being asked to do weaving - as he felt that this was clearly not something

he could be expected to succeed in doing without being able to see. However, as he started to work on his piece and realised he could feel with his fingers where the warp and weft were, and that there was no right or wrong way of weaving the thread, he relaxed into a focused style of work clearly enjoying the regularity of the patterns he was creating. Liv, also from workshop one, initially treated the idea of eTextile technologies with great suspicion, reflecting on all its possible evil purposes '...*you could put in people's number, you can give them a number 649786, and press a button, and then they die...*". Her thoughts were echoed by Shelley "*This is all a bit scary. This is all a brave new world that we're into now*". It is possible that their suspicions were caused by a similar anxiety as mentioned by John about the task itself as Liv was initially keeping her loom close up to her eye, using a strong lens, in order to use the glimmer of sight she still had, to see the weaving pattern. Once she realised she'd be able to feel the weaving pattern with her fingers she also relaxed into the work, explaining how this reminded her of the tapestry work she used to do and that she hadn't been able to do for some years now.

In one of the other groups, Jennifer, who is autistic, was seen anxiously flinging her arms around, pushing all the materials far away from herself as if scared to touch them. A volunteer explained that Jennifer was fearful of the prospect of '...*connecting things to a computer...*' but we noted that once she got over her initial hurdle through the patience of the volunteer working with her, she was seen cooperatively pulling wool as well as milk protein tops, her favourite material, through the warp on the loom. She never went as far as wanting to hear her piece through the computer software, but was happy for others to demonstrate their pieces to her and indeed, for others to demonstrate the sound of the piece she had worked on to her. We understood from the carers who knew her well and were better able to interpret some of her behaviour, that she was clearly enjoying herself and would go home talking excitedly about the event she'd been to that day.

It appears therefore that some of people's initial anxieties were related to their not being able to see what they were doing and that this was an unfamiliar task. However in each workshop we saw examples of people rising to the task and what they were making.

Responding Creatively

There were many examples of people working creatively, giving their own meaning and personal touch to the piece they were making. The materials themselves provided much opportunity for people to express themselves, with participants having clear favourites among the range of materials available. One very peculiar type of fibre, milk protein, has a very smooth, super soft feel to it, and Nazmeen, from workshop two loved using it, saying "*It feels like marshmallows*". In workshop three, Nicolette, who has a little bit of vision but is unable to speak, had carefully selected a blue bobbly yarn to work with, brought it to the table, and was seen enthusiastically banging the bobbin on the table to emphasise that this was the yarn she wanted to work with. Tanya also enjoyed plucking at this blue bobbly yarn, and went on to tasting it in her mouth, rocking herself forwards and backwards, being clearly excited about the unusual feel of this material.

There were mixed reactions to the smelly unwashed sheep wool. In workshop one Liv excitedly exclaimed *"My God he's a smelly old animal that this came from!...My God he's a smelly beast!"* while several participants in the third workshop kept holding it up to their noses in order to smell it and holding it out to others for them to smell. For Heather, also from workshop three, the sheep wool brought up happy associations with her favourite story about Peter Rabbit (a story set in the countryside) and she was clearly excited about this connection between the wool and her story. In workshop two, interestingly, none of the participants wanted to use the sheep wool as it was seen as filthy and smelly.

We observed how many participants developed their own techniques with regards to weaving. Using the loom provided enough constraint for people to have a framework in which to work, making it a task with clear boundaries, but it also allowed for many different creative approaches to complete it. Jim and Nazmeen, from the second workshop, developed a technique where they would go back on themselves with each weave before going forwards again, wrapping the yarn or fibre around the last one (see Figure 5). This is an unusual weaving style, not dissimilar to a hand-manipulated style known as 'Brooks Bouquet' [8] but clearly the participants were not aware of this style and had made this up themselves. Sabine, also in the second workshop, and who is completely blind, clearly had been struggling with the issue of threads escaping from the warp when it was being pulled through, and so she and her support worker developed a style of knotting a thread to the warp before starting to weave it. They were sharing their insight with others around them at their table and Sabine was pleased to show others how well this worked *"Look, I am racing through this!"*, showing how her needle was swiftly going up and down through the warp.

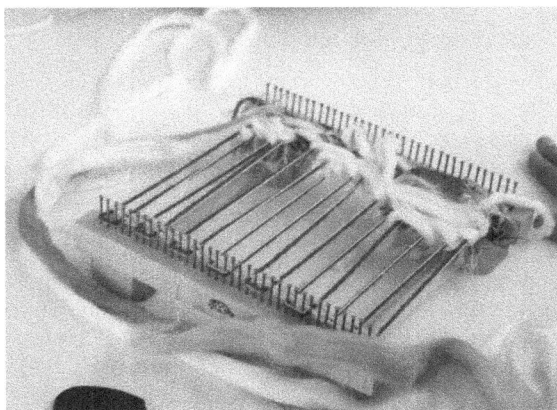

Figure 5: Nazmeen's 'Brooks Bouquet' weaving.

Once people had finished weaving their swatch, it would be taken off the loom in order to connect it to the laptop,

through a crocodile clip and Arduino board. The moment of taking the swatch off the loom in each case caused some consternation - as people were eager to feel their piece, but they were also worried it might fall apart at this point. As Sabine felt her piece just as it came off the loom she exclaimed, with clear delight, 'Oh, *this feels so creative!*'.

Not only had people developed their own technique, but by each person choosing their own yarn, as well as choosing in which order to use the different yarns and fibres, how long to use each yarn for, what type of weave pattern to follow (if following one at all) the overall effect was one of huge variety (see Figure 6). Each piece was quite distinct from the others and people were seen stroking their own piece, as well as that of others to get a sense of what each person had made, with people being delighted by their own effort and

Figure 6: Different eTextile swatches created by workshop participants.

feeling how it differed from other people's.

Interacting with the Electronic Textiles

While weaving with a variety of the materials, participants had to be reminded to make sure they would include conductive materials as well as ordinary fibres in order to make sure the piece would end up as an interactive piece. This aspect was of particular interest to the participants in the first group who, after their initial apprehension, were keen to really understand the conductive properties of some of the fibres. Liv spent some time exploring the silver plated nylon conductive fabric, which was a tricot fabric, only stretchy in one way, and Shelley who was very surprised about the properties of silver plated conductive thread, saying:

"This is an electronic kind of wire? Oh I see, so this is really plastic in its way. It feels silky, but it's plastic. It's a viscose of some sort and, if this is electronic, what are you sewing into your clothes then?"

When Liv's piece was finished and connected to the Arduino board's capacitive sensing circuit, she squeezed and felt her woven piece describing one of the sounds it produced as being like 'glass' or 'raindrops' and thought it was as if the textiles were 'speaking'. Another sound (the 'MusicBox' sound) made her very excited *"Ah, this is a very nice thing, it's beautiful"*. While gently swaying her fingers across her piece, she also wondered if different materials and colours might trigger a different volume of sound:

"I want to see what the blue sounds like...now what does the sheep's wool...and this is the jute. So it has changed because this is the one which is electrified or whatever you call it, and this one is conductive. That's interesting as it's not as loud, this is much louder. This to that, it's musical. So you could compose with this! It could almost tell you if it's dark or light in colour 'cos it goes up and down..."

The technology clearly sparked her imagination and she was able to draw various creative links between the felt experience of the fibres, their colours (some of which she was able to see and others she imagined were there) and their interactive behaviours. It was particularly remarkable to see her work the piece with such curiosity and delight, having put aside her initial reservations, and being able to speculate about what such textile pieces would be able to do. She also speculated how these effects could be even further enhanced through other felt effects, such as vibration, which she had come across as a participant in other research projects.

With all participants the moment of taking the woven piece from the loom and connecting it to the Arduino board for interacting with it - was a special moment, and something they much enjoyed. Participants were quite different in the way they would handle their piece - some hesitantly touching it, with careful fingers feeling it - while others had a more robust style of squeezing and folding it. We made sure that participants could feel how the computer was connected to the Arduino board and the crocodile clip to their piece - by running their hands across the cables - and most seemed satisfied with that explanation. However Sabine, from the second workshop, who is completely blind and autistic, clearly wanted to understand the entire set-up in some detail. She kept feeling not just her woven piece, but also the Arduino board, and the cabling to the laptop, its keyboards and mouse. Although she was familiar with laptops, the various hardware components involved in this experiment clearly intrigued her, not having come across Arduino boards and various other electronics previously. Another participant in workshop one, Tariq, developed a particular style of sounding his woven piece, by pulling at the crocodile clip and its cable. He played it as a base guitar, pulling at the strings, rather than handling the woven piece itself. He enjoyed the effect as even with this unusual style of touching the piece, it still provided a good range of sounds.

For some of the very disabled participants in the third workshop it was the sounding of their piece that made them particularly pleased. Some of them, including Tanya and Heather had not been able to do much of their own weaving, and for them hearing the sounds was when the activity became alive. Tanya wiggled her entire body as an indication that one sound was more her favourite than the

other, while holding the piece in her hand and mouth. While Heather was delighted with a particular sound, the 'Jew's Harp' sound, which is very bouncy and reminded her of a rabbit, bringing up again her favourite story character Peter Rabbit and causing her to react quite physically to the

Figure 7: Heather interacting with her eTextile swatch.

sound, clearly excited by it (see Figure 7). She said she would call her woven piece 'Rabbit'.

We thus noticed that people were engaged with different aspects of the technology. Some people particularly focused on how different conductive materials had potential for different interactive effects, including projecting connections between colours and sound, whilst others were intrigued by the hardware components of the set-up, and wanting to understand how it all fitted together. For others sound was something that spoke to them, giving a chance to associate between their textile piece and souznds that they enjoyed. For one of the very deaf participants, Anna, the sound effect was inaccessible, but she was made aware of the changing lights in the SuperCollider application and while she also had limited vision, we believe she was able to make a connection between her gestures and the flickering lights, which she studied with intense concentration.

Imagining Future Technologies

As people had relaxed into their weaving, creating interesting sounds and helping each other with various techniques, the workshop setting was clearly a fruitful environment to generate a range of imagined further uses of eTextile based technologies. An initial suggestion by one person had been that eTextiles might be useful to create garments to detect the onset of a stroke - whilst later these participants moved away from such serious applications towards more playful examples that they could imagine having in their home. The musings about associations between colours, fibres and different sounds left one participant thinking about larger displays in her home, that would give off various playful sounds when you walked up to them and felt them. She also reflected how she would enjoy making those sorts of displays herself. Several ideas for new musical instruments were voiced - either to compose pieces using eTextile displays, or as suggested by another participant not so much using textile elements but using the underlying notion of capacitive sensing with other metal based materials. Participants also talked about carpets with conductive properties that would make sounds, perhaps to play tricks on visitors, or other jokes, while for one younger girl it was more something she imagined being surrounded by, perhaps as she would fall asleep in bed.

Several of the care workers articulated that this type of technology also comes close to how they work with sensory rooms, where people with sensory impairments get a chance to explore a rich variety of sounds, lights and other felt experiences. This sentiment was echoed by the girl who had likened her woven patch to Peter Rabbit, as she wanted her piece to be part of story telling - an activity she much enjoys.

All the examples that were brought forward were positive, creative ideas, that would liven up one's sitting room or surprise visitors in a fun and lighthearted way. From not knowing anything about eTextiles at the start of the session, and never having worked with Arduino or other toolkits, the success of their accomplishments had given participants the confidence to propose new design ideas. Many of the design ideas were not particularly practical, or functional, but were more inspired by aesthetics and about creating playful encounters as part of their daily environment.

DISCUSSION

The creative workshops with blind and visual impaired participants were enjoyed by all, forming a creative experience. Creativity was apparent at a number of different levels throughout these workshops: from the choices made around materials, the techniques used for the weaving and in the way participants responded to using physical computing with a woven eTextile swatch. As a stand-alone activity without the interactive element, participants found much joy in their making, as it was a concrete and focused activity. But the steps of combining the non-conductive materials with the conductive, followed by connecting their work to the Arduino board and hearing the sounds was, for all who participated, the moment where many of their amazing ideas were realised.

There is something special about combining a traditional crafting activity like weaving to a computational one, using it in an environment which is untraditional, and transforming it into a creative technology toolkit. Bringing the two together has made this experience accessible for different people on different levels, whether it be giving them a better understanding of how technology might work or how hands-on making need not be fiddly or require sight. Using touch, the participants found their own way around the loom in a way personal to them.

Previous work with eTextiles has tended to emphasise the visual aspects that can be achieved with such creative toolkits - by creating interesting glowing effects with LEDs, that blink on and off, or that shine through thin layers of fabric creating intriguing effects. In this workshop we demonstrated that eTextiles can be very effective as a purely haptic medium, where the regularity of threads, the patterns that can be achieved, the bobbliness of some fibres versus the rougher feel of others, and even their smell all add to an intriguing surface with an interactive potential.

Technological toolkits such as Arduino and the vast array of conductive yarns and fabrics have endless opportunities for exploration. By not being bound to specific configurations but having the freedom to combine all types of material and applying any number of crafty making skill, there are endless opportunities for people to put their personal stamp on what they are making and to express something of who they are.

As an approach to imagining future technologies we found the creative workshop, similar to the findings by Rogers et al [17], to provide a safe environment in which people could come out with their own ideas. From hesitant beginnings they had grown in confidence and through their own making efforts, understood that their ideas and notions were valued. The design dimensions that they sketched, through their examples of interactive carpets to pull jokes, blankets to hide under and wall hangings to walk up to and touch, clearly indicate that there is room for more pleasurable technological experiences that go beyond having to compensate for the lack of sight. They indicate that eTextiles can form part of a new form of designing for accessibility that actually goes beyond accessibility, by putting the sensation of touch at the core of the experience - as something that is fun, inspiring and accessible to all.

CONCLUSION

eTextile pieces, simply put together by people using their own hands and imagination, can form a powerful way to tap into people's creativity and raise their curiosity. While many accessible technology approaches for blind and visually impaired users focus on resolving problems around reading and writing, our creative workshop approach demonstrated that a simple but open-ended physical computing toolkit can give people the opportunity to express themselves and develop something aesthetically pleasing to hold. Particularly at a time when the largely inaccessible touch screen has come to pervade all aspects of our lives, it is important to explore the potential of other, more tactile oriented surfaces and objects for people with different sensory characteristics. The interactive woven pieces produced during these workshops showed that eTextiles can create interfaces that are graspable, squeezable, stroke-able and that are surprising. They inspired participants to think wider, beyond the immediate problems of the here and now, towards technology designs that are about delight and enjoyment.

ACKNOWLEDGEMENTS

We want to thank Sense, the Whitechapel Art Gallery, the Royal London Society for Blind People and all the participants for working with us.

REFERENCES

1. Arduino (2013) *Arduino homepage* [Online]. Available at http://www.arduino.cc/ (Accessed 23 December 2013).

2. Brady, E., Morris, M.R., Zhong, Y., White, S., Bigham, J.P., (2013) 'Visual Challenges in the Everyday Lives of Blind People', Proceedings of the SIGCHI Conference on Human Factors in Computing Systems, Paris, 27 April - 2 May, New York, NY, ACM, pp. 2117-2126.

3. Buechley, L., Eisenberg, M., Catchen, J., Crockett, Al., (2008) 'The LilyPad Arduino: Using Computational Textiles to Investigate Engagement, Aesthetics, and Diversity in Computer Science Education', Proceedings of the SIGCHI Conference on Human Factors in Computing Systems, Florence, 5-10 April, New York, NY, ACM, pp. 423-432.

4. Camphill Families and Friends (2014) *Camphill Foundation's World Wide Weave* [Online] Available at http://camphillfamiliesandfriends.com/camphill-foundations-world-wide-weave-extraordinary-lives/ (Accessed 22 December 2014).

5. Caporusso, N., (2008). 'A Wearable Malossi Alphabet Interface for Deafblind People', Proceedings of the working conference on Advanced visual interfaces, Napoli, 28-30 May, New York, NY, ACM, pp. 445-448.

6. Cárdenas, M. (2014) *Local Autonomy Networks* [Online] Available at http://autonets.org/background/ (Accessed 22 December 2014).

7. Chandrika, J., Acuario, C., Johnson, W.A., Hollier, J., Ladner, R.E., (2010). 'V-braille: haptic braille perception using a touch-screen and vibration on mobile phones', Proceedings of the 12th international ACM SIGACCESS conference on Computers and accessibility, Orlando, FL, 25-27 October, New York, NY, ACM, pp. 295-296.

8. Dixon, A. (2007) *The Handweaver's Pattern Directory*, Fort Collins, CO, Interweave Press.

9. Glosson, D. and Peppler, K. (2013) 'Learning about Circuitry with E-Textiles in After-School Settings', in Buechley, L., Peppler, K., Eisenberg, M. and Kafal, Y. (eds) Textile Messages: Dispatches From the World of E-Textiles and Education, New York: Peter Lang Publishing, pp. 71-83.

10. Gollner, U., Bieling, T. and Joost, G (2012) 'Mobile Lorm Glove - Introducing a Communication Device for Deaf-Blind People', Proceedings of the Sixth International Conference on Tangible, Embedded and Embodied Interaction, Kingston, ON, 19-22 February, New York, NY, ACM, pp. 127-130.

11. Hartman, K (2014) *Make: Wearable Electronics*, Sebastopol, CA, Maker Media Inc.

12. Henshaws (2014) *Arts and Crafts* [Online] Available at http://henshaws.org.uk/what-we-offer/arts-and-crafts-centre/workshops/arts-crafts/ (Accessed 22 December 2014).

13. Heuten, W., Niels Henze, N., Boll, S., Pielot, M., (2008) 'Tactile Wayfinder: A Non-Visual Support System for Wayfinding', Proceedings of the 5th Nordic conference on Human-computer interaction: building bridges, Lund, 20-22 October, New York, NY, ACM, pp.172-181.

14. Kobakant (2014) *Technical Intimacy Workshop* [Online]. Available at http://www.kobakant.at/DIY/?p=5301 (Accessed 23 December 2014.

15. Kuznetsov, S., Trutoiu, L., Kute, C., Howley, I., Siewiorek, D., & Paulos, E. (2011). 'Breaking Boundaries: Mentoring with Wearable Computing.' Proceedings of the SIGCHI Conference on Human Factors in Computing Systems, Vancouver, BC, 7-12 May, New York, NY, ACM, pp. 2957-2966.

16. MaKey MaKey (2015) *MaKey MaKey - An Invention Kit for Everyone.* [Online]. Available at http://www.makeymakey.com/ (Accessed 3 January 2014).

17. Rogers, Y., Paay, J., Brereton, M., Vaisutis, K., Marsden, G., Vetere, F., (2014) 'Never Too Old: Engaging Retired People Inventing the Future with MaKey MaKey', Proceedings of the SIGCHI Conference on Human Factors in Computing Systems, Toronto, ON, 26 April - 1 May, New York, NY, ACM, pp. 3913-3922.

18. Shilkrot, R., Huber, J., Liu, C., Maes, P., Nanayakkara, S.C., (2014) 'FingerReader: A Wearable Device to Support Text Reading on the Go', Extended Abstracts on Human Factors in Computing Systems, Toronto, ON, 26 April - 1 May, New York, NY, ACM, pp. 2359-2364.

19. Southern, C. Clawson, J., Frey, B., Abowd, G.D., Romero, M., (2012) 'An Evaluation of BrailleTouch: Mobile Touchscreen', Proceedings of the 14th international conference on Human-computer interaction with mobile devices and services, San Francisco, CA, 21-24 September, New York, NY, ACM, pp. 317-326.

20. SuperCollider (2013) *SuperCollider homepage* [Online]. Available at http://supercollider.sourceforge.net/ (Accessed 23 December 2014).

21. Vogelpoel, N and Jarrold, K. (2014) 'Social prescription and the role of participatory arts programmes for older people with sensory impairments' *Journal of Integrated Care*, Vol. 22 No. 2, pp. 39-50.

22. VoiceOver for iOS (2014) *Accessibility* [Online]. Available at https://www.apple.com/uk/accessibility/ios/voiceover/ (Accessed 1 January 2015).

23. XelfleX (2014) [Online] *Next-generation wearable tech threads optical fibres through sports clothing* [Online] Available at http://www.ibtimes.co.uk/next-generation-wearable-tech-threads-optical-fibres-through-sports-clothing-1478812] (Accessed 3 January 2015).

Challenges for Creating and Staging Interactive Costumes for the Theatre Stage

Michaela Honauer, Eva Hornecker
Bauhaus-Universität Weimar, Fak. Media. Bauhausstr. 11, 99423 Weimar, Germany
michaela.honauer@uni-weimar.de, eva.hornecker@uni-weimar.de

ABSTRACT

In this paper, we discuss the requirements and critical challenges for creating and staging interactive costumes in the theatre. Different to other types of performance, theatre costumes are secondary to acting. Our investigations are based on two practice-based case studies: a self-directed design research within a student project, and a collaboration with a local theatre house, where interactive costume elements were developed in a real-life setting. These reveal requirements and challenges for the design process as well as the effective staging of interactive costumes, the biggest challenge being how to integrate these into existing structures of traditional theatre houses, and requirements for the costumes themselves. Because interactive costumes integrate technological features and traditional analogue crafts, they require interdisciplinary collaboration and transcend established boundaries between departments in theatre houses, challenging established work processes and structures.

Author Keywords

Theater Performance; Design Research; Wearables; Interdisciplinary Collaboration; Crafts.

INTRODUCTION

The evolving potential of e-textiles and wearable computing is a growing topic in HCI and related areas. There are dozens of examples but many are technical demos [6, 19], proofs of principle [3], or fashion prototypes [15] and art pieces [4, 28]. Beyond these, the potential of computational clothing for specific applications still needs to be demonstrated; in particular we need to ensure that it can integrate into existing practices and infrastructures. Such practices are highly situated [26], requiring us to engage with specific real world application areas and scenarios.

Currently, there are only such few case studies, most of which focus on healthcare and fitness, where wearable gadgets (e.g. the fitbit) are more dominant than interactive

clothing itself [12], and a few research projects are related to gaming [6]. In our own work we are interested in the potential aesthetic and creative uses and role of interactive clothing as a new medium. This has led us to explore its use within the context of theatre. Theatre is one of the oldest entertainment forms, and from early-on costumes were an element of performance. It is an interesting application area because theatre organizations create their own costumes, relying on existing practices and crafts. This allows us to investigate what challenges interactive costumes might pose for these practices and for theatre infrastructures.

In this paper we discuss critical challenges and requirements for creating and staging interactive costumes for theatre stages. In this context, we understand interactive costumes as theatre costumes that are enhanced with computational components that can be controlled by their wearer. Our interest here is less in the technology as such, than in the (creative) design process for interactive costumes, and in how these could fit into the practices of professional theatre to fulfill their potential as a new medium in this domain. As this is still a novel topic for theatre houses and for research, there are a number of larger scale research questions that our work is beginning to address: How do we best go about designing/developing interactive costumes? How do their users (wearers = actors) adopt them and what needs do they have? How can such costumes and their development become an integral part of the routines and organizational structures of professional theatre houses?

Our findings are based on the experiences made in two projects, each employing a different approach. The first is an interdisciplinary student project at the Bauhaus-Universität Weimar using a *research-in-and-through-design approach*. It aimed at arriving at an ensemble of costumes that can be imagined by their end users (actors) to be used on stage. The second project, a collaboration with a local theatre house, the Theaterhaus Jena, used an *ethnographically oriented action-research approach*, where we assisted in developing electronic components for costumes for two productions. This allows us to compare the student project's self-directed development process, which could explore how to best go about developing interactive costumes, with the practices and institutional constraints of a theatre house. We describe our experiences and findings regarding the aforementioned research questions regarding the creation process for interactive costumes and their adaption by actors. In particular, various frictions in the theatre collaboration highlight the critical role of the application context's socio-technical-organizational infrastructure.

BACKGROUND

Interactive Theatre and Performance Arts

While visions of *interactive theatre* have emerged in the literature [8, 21, 24, 27], these mainly refer to stage design and predominantly utilize visual projections. A noticeable number engage the audience to influence the outcome of a piece [8, 21]. But in our literature overview we did not find any projects that integrate *interactive costumes*.

This is different in *performance arts*, where computational systems often relate to the performer's body [1, 4, 16, 28]. The majority attaches technologies to the performer and generates audio feedback from movement [4]. Such examples can be categorized as *wearable computing*. Wearable sensors have been used in digital music performances for 30 years [23]. Many projects make use of costume-like elements, e.g. "helmets with mirrored eyepieces that allow the wearer to shift her focus onto herself" [23] that can be categorized as technical wearables although no computational components are included. Nowadays, artists use the human body as a surface for projections [1] often relying on camera-based tracking. A few projects integrate light output into the performers costumes, usually with LEDs and light-strips [16]. The light-arrays suit [28] goes beyond this with integrated laser beams that dynamically project into the environment. A number of specialized performance groups utilize electronics as a key artistic feature and core of performance, typically in dance, acrobatic, or music shows.

Other research investigates how spectators perceive interactive elements of a performance. Benford and Giannachi reflect on how the boundaries of the stage disappear as well as those between spectators, actors and other participants/players in participatory performances [2]. Spectators may experience interactions as secretive, expressive, suspenseful or magical, depending on the visibility of interface manipulations and their effects, which each may be hidden, partially or fully revealed, and amplified [22].

New Challenges for Traditional Theatres

One of our primary interests lies in how traditional theatre houses can incorporate interactive costumes into their production processes. These differ from performance art and specialized troupes in their professional practice. The organizational structures in theatre houses have developed historically and tend to clearly separate different creative responsibilities (e.g. costume/stage design) from technical areas (lighting technician, sound engineering). Many departments produce a piece in a coordinated process but their work is only integrated in the final rehearsals [14]. All responsibilities in the production are separated by departmental competencies and professional expertise. The process seems optimized to enable parallel work on different components with minimal interdependency and maximal autonomy for each department [17]. This constitutes the in-

frastructure, embedded in social structures and taken-for-granted organizational arrangements [14, 17] that any attempt to introduce interactive costumes to traditional theatres will have to integrate into [11]. How much of a challenge this poses was revealed by our theatre collaboration.

TWO CASE STUDIES OF INTERACTIVE COSTUMES

In this section we describe our experiences and insights from creating and staging interactive costumes. These were gained from two parallel studies in different contexts. The first is a four month student project supervised by the authors, where interdisciplinary teams developed interactive costumes. The project goal was to explore the creative process and to evaluate the prototype costumes in a workshop with 'real' actors. This self-directed development can be characterized as a *research-in-and-through-design process* [7], as our research concerned the design process itself while the results (the costumes) were the base for further knowledge generation [29]. The other study combined *ethnographic-oriented participant observation with an action research approach* [9, 13]. One member of the research team worked one month as intern at the Theaterhaus Jena, a theatre house interested in integrating interactive technologies into their program and continued to collaborate as external designer over the next five months. Here, interactive costume elements were developed in a real-life theatre setting, in collaboration with its staff, and our experiences highlight frictions with existing organizational structures and professional practices. In the following, we present the student project, followed by the theatre collaboration and discuss the ideation, development, and deployment/staging phases for each study, as well as the lessons learned.

A Self-Directed Design Process in a Student Project

In this research project, students from *Applied Computer Science, Media Arts/Design,* and *Product Design* developed costumes for the story *Twenty Thousand Leagues under the Sea* by *Jules Verne* (figure 1). At the onset, they were organized into three teams of one product/media design and two technology students each in order to work from the start in small interdisciplinary teams so technology and design ideas could be developed hand in hand. Design should push technical possibilities and technology ideas influence the designs. In hindsight, it also turned out that this helped teams to quickly figure out whether an idea was feasible. We first give an overview of the costumes created, before detailing the design process and the insights gained.

- *Captain Nemo* is the captain of the *Nautilus* submarine. His 'living' robe is made of sea creatures such as anemones (figure 1B). It can glow in the dark underwater world, and vibrates if enemies approach. A simple light sensor activates the lights. A distance sensor controls vibrating motors under the robe. All features can be dis-/enabled by the actor by pushing a button hidden in the costume.

- The *Diving Suit* is worn by the *Nautilus Crew* (figure 1D). Its jacket has a fin- or rib-like pattern that glows

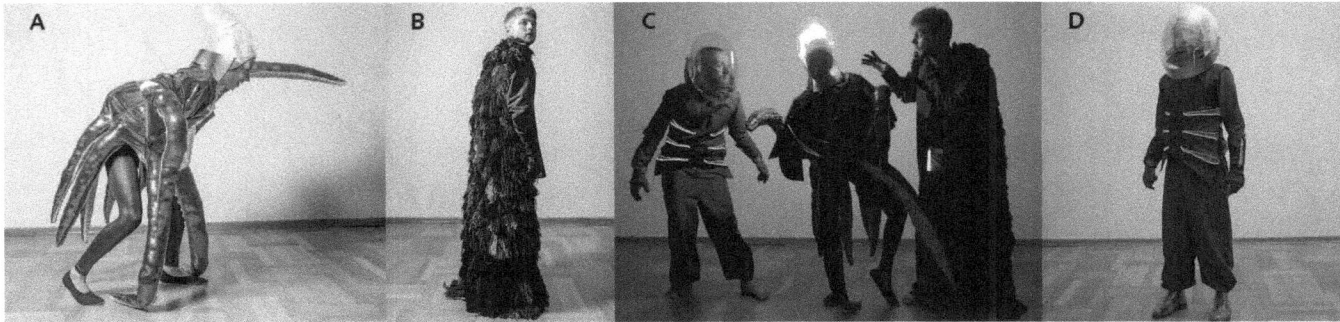

Figure 1. Octopus (A), Captain Nemo (B), and all costumes together (C), Diving Suit (D)

blue in water and white on land. These modes indicate whether the helmet is open or closed and are activated via a button on the jacket at chest height. The diver wears an oxygen tank with two chambers, one delivering air while the other chamber regenerates. The tank is controlled via a display on the suit's glove. LEDs show the active fill level and a button allows switching chambers.

- The *Octopus Sea Creature* is the antagonist living alone and roaming through the deep sea. It can move two tentacles at its front (motorized skeletons are integrated, operational mode see figure 3). As an animal cannot talk, the octopus' brain glows according to its moods – green when relaxed, yellow when attentive and red if aggressive. Two dials control these functions, both hidden in the costume sleeves that the actress puts her arms into.

Ideation and Background Research (ca. 4 weeks)
As most of the students had no prior experience with theatre, it was important to first gain a better understanding of the domain. This included a sense of what it is like to be acting, and understanding the role of costumes in theatre. This phase therefore included field observation and hands-on activities as a form of background research. In parallel, the students decided on a general theme for their work, picking the deep sea and then quickly settling on the Captain Nemo story and the three characters. Some basic ideas for the costumes emerged in this phase, such as using EL wire and the living robe. Working in interdisciplinary teams from the very start, technology and design ideas came from both sides, as technology students explained aesthetical concepts and designers described technological features.

To learn more about the role of costumes, we visited two different plays at a local theatre, focusing on three costumes. From observations, it became clear that the costumes often conveyed cultural, social or historic meaning, such as social status and emotional state. For example, a dirty corset and overlong multilayered but torn skirt worn by a poor woman indicated that she had once been affluent. The dirty and torn garments of another character meant he had problems. When his clothes were clean, his condition was more stable. Moreover, the mentioned corset and overlong skirt affected the actress' postures and movements, embodying the restrictions of societal conventions: she could not run

and had to lift up the skirt to turn around. In another play the actors changed clothes very often on or behind the stage. We concluded that costumes should be very robust as they are typically worn and cleaned repeatedly, or need to be changed quickly. Furthermore, hairstyle, hats, shoes, and jewelry also influence a character's appearance and hence are part of costume. Overall, costumes emphasize a character's status or mood, while influencing actors' movement and behavior [14], as well as supporting (non)verbal communication to other actors or the audience.

We also attended a two-day design-acting workshop run by a drama educator/ theatre pedagogue practitioner. This introduced students to a range of acting techniques, such as improvisation and role-play. Students improvised based on their initial character ideas. We further experimented with costumes, using a few objects (rope, scarf, coconut, wooden sticks, aluminum foil). Overall, this workshop gave students deeper insights into the practice of acting and some first-hand experience. We realized that playing a role is an actress' main task on stage demanding full concentration. Thus, the costume is subordinate to the activity of acting and it should never require full or focused attention.

Development Phase (10 weeks)
The development phase included a synthesis of design and technical development. It began with a 2-3h bodystorming [25] and tinkering session in which students constructed simple costume prototypes from cheap everyday materials, put them on, and experimented what kind of garments might fit with their character. From this activity, students identified solutions for integrating technical elements into the costumes. For instance, the octopus should be able to move the motorized front tentacles. In this session we decided to hide the technical construction under a cape (figure 2A/B). Similarly, bodystorming the diver suit (figure 2C) had the students imagine wearing a helmet and inspired the idea of making it retractable (figure 2D). Experiencing early costume prototypes with our own body and movements was helpful to understand and improve costume concepts.

Following this, student teams began to work on the detailed prototypes. All teams investigated materials and fabrics that evoke the deep-sea theme. The students experimented with different physical phenomena (e.g. the behavior of flexible

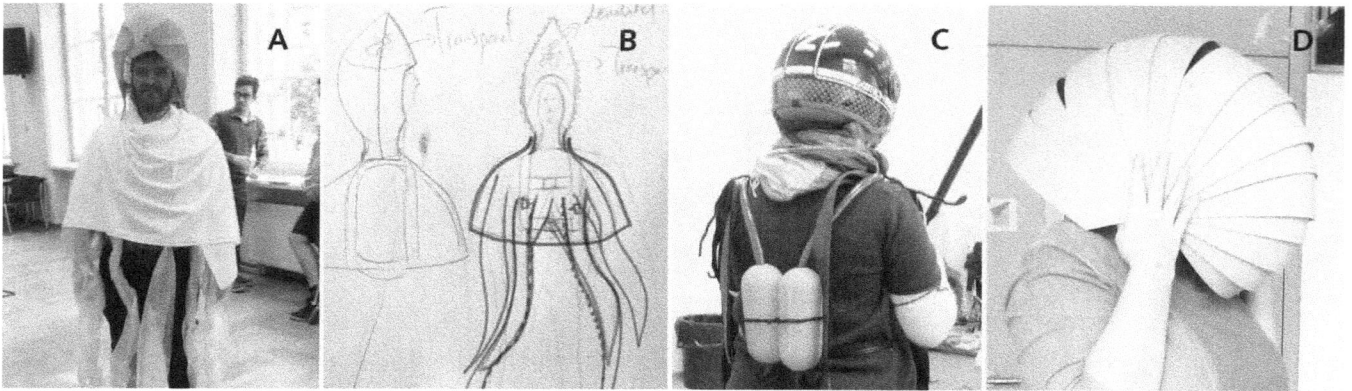

Figure 2. Octopus – lo-fi prototype (A) and early sketch (B). Diving Suit – bodystorming (C) and cardboard mockup of helmet (D).

shafts for the octopus arms) and hacked electronic components (e.g. connecting electroluminescent wire to an Arduino) to realize their concepts. Technical and design ideas developed step by step. For instance, the captain's costume has lots of fringes on the shoulders that are to glow and move. The test of an early prototype (figure 4) revealed this was hardly visible from a distance. The audiences' point of view needs to be considered when designing interactive costumes. While the audience does not need to understand how an effect works, it needs to see, hear or feel it. The students thus created a longer robe (figure 1B) and inserted a second textile layer with ten vibration motors underneath.

During this process, we repeatedly discussed how much feedback the wearer would need for their actions. Some costumes create light effects outside of the wearer's visual field – the actor inside the octopus costume cannot see her glowing head and the diver has a two-chambered oxygen tank on his back. A feedback display was added to the diver's glove, with LEDs showing the fill level of the active chamber and a button to switch chambers. In contrast, the octopus team decided for purely haptic interaction via a dial with a tangible start and end value, and visual feedback provided from the environmental reflection of the glowing head in the dark (see figure 1C where the environment is green from the head's glow).

Towards the end of this process, we visited a professional costume designer at a theatre. We explained some of our concepts and how we had realized these to the costume designer. She provided elaborated feedback and sewing and tinkering tips. In retrospect, meeting her complemented the final production phase with aesthetical aspects. Furthermore, she provided insights into her daily work, and explained her work routines with the director, tailor or dresser (who helps the actors to dress). It turned out that her creative process hardly ever overlaps with technical staff. She thus was impressed by our cooperative work. We had found that establishing working routines between design and technology students early-on ensured a fruitful collaboration. Most confirmed that they gained insights into the other discipline. Design students developed costume ideas that were unfinished until the engineers in the team merged the technical features into the textiles.

Deployment/ Staging

The last phase involved having the users' (i.e. actors) encounter and wear the costume prototypes in a one-day workshop. This revealed benefits and critical factors for introducing interactive costumes to the stage. The drama educator supported us again in the preparation and during the workshop itself, for which we invited actors that would improvise, rehearse and then perform a short play while wearing our costumes. With the drama educator, we developed a short plot for the play, designed the workshop procedure and prepared interview questions. We chose a mix of observation, interviews and group discussion to analyze how the actors appropriate the costumes.

Three semi-professional actors took part in the workshop. The first hour was reserved for getting to know each other, and letting the actors explore, put on, and experience the

Figure 3. Octopus' skeleton: Sequence of smooth movements.

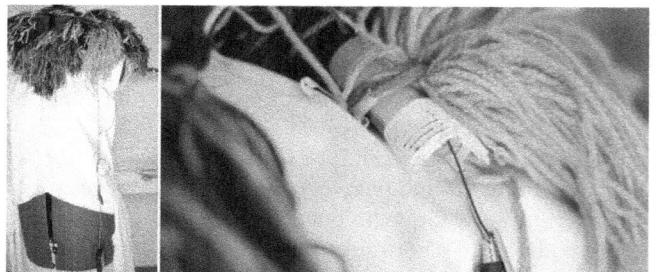

Figure 4. Early working prototype of Nemo's costume

costumes. We first withheld from explanations. Then, our teams explained all interactive features step by step. Next, the drama educator introduced the story plot, and guided the improvisation, rehearsals and a final performance for the next few hours, while we helped organizing, made notes, and held the interviews with the actors. We video-recorded everything from first contact over rehearsals to final performance and interviews.

From the initial first exposure on, the actors reacted very open-minded and positive. They were curious to discover all features and immediately understood most explanations. They seemed impressed by simple features, such as LED light. For instance, once the actress wearing the octopus costume was familiar with changing the color of her head, she showed it to a colleague who was very surprised. This may be because the manipulation mechanism is invisible, hidden in a costume sleeve (Reeve et al.'s magical spectator experience [22]). Moreover, all actors confirmed it was the first time they ever had contact with interactive costumes.

In this workshop, our user group tested our prototypes, but subordinated to their task of improvising and performing a new play. They started moving as if floating under water, in slow motion, to get into 'living in the sea'. Our observations indicate that the shape and appearance of the costumes supported the actors in their task. For instance, when in the 'deep sea' Captain Nemo stooped, ducking his head into his wool-tentacled shoulder as if listening to his 'living robe' (figure 5). The weight and size of the robe seemed to facilitate this posture. Also, over time the actors became more confident using the interactive features. This means rehearsing with the technology is just as necessary as rehearsing the text and choreography of a play.

Furthermore, the computational components only had a minor role while the actors learned to play a character. They never stopped the rehearsals because of technical problems. Any technical issues were solved in the breaks or between scenes. A reason for this could be the basic rule that an actor should always continue acting despite of whatever happens. This relates to our earlier observation at the local theatre house. In other words, costumes support an actress in playing a role, but she should express her role primarily through her performing skills and not rely on a costume.

The final individual semi-structured interviews with all actors asked their opinions about the costumes, ranging from aesthetical aspects over technical understanding to usability. In general they liked the costumes and thought their features enhanced the performance. A central theme emphasized by all actors concerns wearability and freedom of movement. The diver felt the rigidity of the backpack-helmet construction and captain Nemo felt the weight of his robe (figure 5). Yet both seemed to be comfortable and explained this helped them immerse into their role, as this would be what the character experiences. This verifies our observation from the rehearsals. There thus is a tradeoff for wearability, as it can be the cumbersomeness of a costume

and the restrictions it poses for movement that support the actor in immersing themselves in a role.

The answers to how much feedback is needed differed for all costumes. The actress wearing the octopus said she got a feeling for the colors in her head after training with the dial, and, as assumed, could see the light reflections in the environment. She stated an additional feedback would probably distract her from acting. On the other hand, the actor with the diving suit thought the display in his glove suited playing a diver who would probably want to check and control his oxygen tanks. Again, we conclude that interactive costumes should support actors in expressing their character instead of distracting them, and hence the amount of feedback provided depends on individual role-related decisions.

A last finding concerns inhibition of technology and worries about lack of control. All actors offered diverse thoughts on where control should be located. The diver actor thought that sometimes it might take too much concentration to act and simultaneously control the costume features. Rehearsing would improve this to an extent, but it likely also depends on the complexity of actions on stage. The actor wearing Nemo's costume told that he was irritated if the light in his robe worked and didn't the next moment because of technical issues. While this was not noticeable from a spectator's viewpoint, he did not feel comfortable. Thus, interactive costumes need to work reliably before giving them to actors. Also, it could be helpful to tell an actress beforehand what kind of technical issues could arise and pre-plan how to deal with these. Finally, the octopus actress raised concerns over the motorized tentacles. She was afraid to loose control or activate the mechanism accidentally and said that she needs to test this feature often enough to get familiar with it. All of this points to the need for substantial rehearsing with interactive costumes.

Moreover, all actors made suggestions on how to improve the costume concepts or designs, either during rehearsals or interviews. For instance, the octopus actress pointed out that having the motorized tentacles on her back would give her more liberty than at the front where she needs space for her own gestures. This suggests that one should involve actors at an early stage to ask for their ideas and feedback

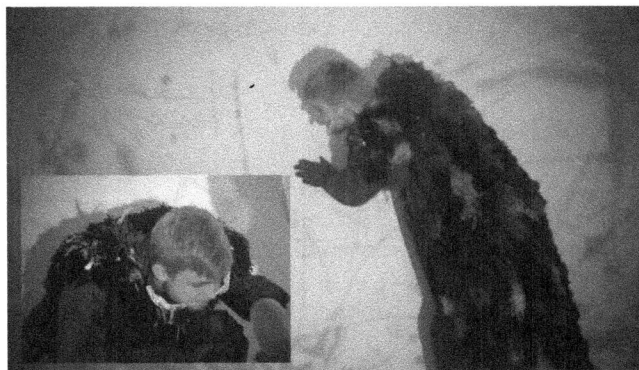

Figure 5. Nemo stoops, caused by the robe's shape and weight.

when designing interactive costumes, thus following a more *user-centered* or *participatory approach* [13].

Lessons Learned
In general, costumes support actors in playing a role; they underline a character's appearance and status, influence movement and posture, but are subordinate to acting. Seen as a working garment, they must be very robust to withstand excessive use over at least a season. From a spectator's perspective, effects should be perceivable independent of their location in the audience.

Most actors are not used to deal with computational clothes. That's why the user (actor) needs background knowledge to handle this easily and requires appropriate feedback on their actions. This means we need to carefully introduce them to the new possibilities of interactive costumes. These should provide easy and intuitive input, appropriate feedback, and ensure enough freedom for acting and moving, while supporting immersion into the role. Above all, an actress should gain basic knowledge about a costume's technical operation as well as potential breakdowns, and should learn how to deal with these. Actors should rehearse early and often enough in the interactive costumes to get familiar with its features.

Moreover, our interdisciplinary collaboration ensured successful development. It is advantageous for designers and engineers to develop interactive costumes together from the start for ideas to be brought in and get reflected by both sides. Activity-based work, collaborative development and testing support teams to come up with individual design solutions for interactive costumes and to deal with functional issues. Finally, involving actors during the creation process would enable designers and engineers to get early user feedback and include these insights into their designs.

Collaboration with a Theatre House
In parallel to the student research project, one of the authors contributed to two productions at a local theatre house that was interested in exploring interactive elements. The Theaterhaus Jena is small (< 50 staff) but has traditionally structured departments, as most theatres do [14], with clearly defined responsibilities. This collaboration enabled us to experience professional theatre structures and outline further requirements for interactive costumes. In the following, we outline our role in the two productions, before detailing the design process and the insights gained.

(Panda Show) One of the authors spent a month as intern at the theatre to get an overview of the workflows behind stage and the different professional roles and viewpoints. Her task was to support the technical staff and produce video content for plays. She also became involved in creating an interactive costume for *The Panda Bear Show* where a panda mask was to have 'red-glowing eyes' (figure 7). The production of this play took six weeks whereof she was involved the last four; the premiere was in March 2014.

(King Ubu) The same author continued to participate as external designer in the production of *King Ubu* where the main character was to wear a fat-man suit that can 'smoke from its armpits and rear' (figure 6). This play was produced in around three months but we started discussing ideas a few weeks earlier; the premiere was in July 2014.

Ideation Phase
We started discussing ideas for both productions processes based on the costume designer's initial visions. In both cases, we brainstormed potential solutions for characters and costumes that were already defined. This means the technical components had to be integrated into existing costumes. Once the costume designer had agreed on an initial proposal, we began discussing potential solutions with the other staff. We held separate meetings with the creative (e.g. tailor, design assistants) and technical (e.g. light technicians, engineers) employees. Shared meetings were not feasible due to busy schedules. It was our task to bring design and technology together while mediating all interests.

The *Panda Show* production had already started and the intern entered the ideation process when hearing that the costume designer wanted to have the eyes in the panda head glow red. She proposed to the costume designer and director to enable the actor to switch it on and off. Both were open to this initiative. Normally the light technicians would have installed the red eyes.

Before the production of *King Ubu* started, the costume designer told the researcher she would like to have this character smoke out of his armpits and rear because this fits with his vulgar demeanor. She personally would not know how to realize this and would normally speak to the light technicians about such ideas. We started investigating potential technologies for smoke (e.g. tiny fog machines inside clothes, tube connections to a big machine backstage, ultrasound fog machines, smoke pellets or dry ice). After talking to the technicians we decided to integrate a tiny fog machine into the fat man suit because this seemed to be the most safe, elegant and effective solution.

Development Phase
In this stage, we first created low-fidelity prototypes to examine whether the technical concepts had the desired effect. We showed these to the creative and technical department before developing the final interactive prototypes that had to be integrated into the costumes. In this phase we still mediated between creative and technology interests. We mostly met separately with staff from each department to discuss aesthetical/design-related or functional/technical issues. Despite this separation, it was notable that both areas placed a major focus on robustness and safety of the costumes as a main requirement. In particular, discussions with the creative departments revealed that robustness of costumes is the most important issue. The tailor and the costume designer made clear that the audience's overall im-

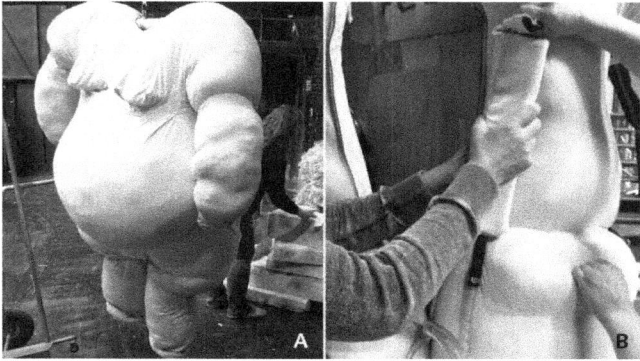

Figure 6. Fat suit (A) - integrating pipes and fog machine (B).

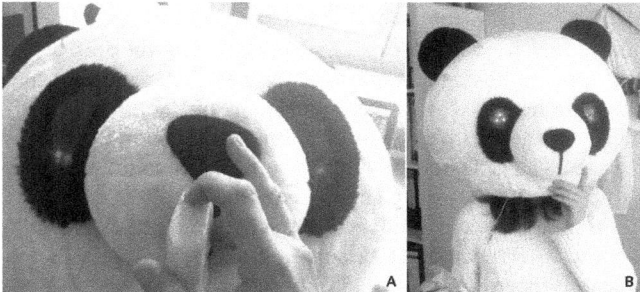

Figure 7. Panda mask – LEDs position before (A) and after (B).

pression of a play is central for a theatre house. If a costume breaks on stage, any positive effects are jeopardized.

When creating the red glowing *Panda* eyes for the *Panda Show,* there was no direct collaboration between technical and design development. This was surprising because the creative staff lacked knowledge of how to light up a LED. They only wanted the lights to be integrated well enough to outlast lively jumping, and to allow for quick changes of costume. The technicians, not being very interested in creating such a simple and not technically challenging feature, deferred the task to the intern and supported her only after repeated requests. After having finished a prototype with a 3-LED matrix per eye wired to a button hand piece that could be hidden inside the costume sleeve, the intern (and not the tailor who argued it was not in her work responsibility to work with technological elements) integrated the technology into the head. But because design and technology did not work together, the development was not really successful. It took three weeks to realize, and was finished only a day before the premiere. We believe it could have been done much earlier if both departments would have worked closer together. The director finally decided to not use the interactive eyes on stage. We therefore removed the button and installed an on-off switch that had to be en-/disabled before the actor put the head on.

In contrast, the development process of *King Ubu*'s smoke costume was more collaborative. After producing a low-fidelity prototype that resulted in a pipe system for safely distributing smoke, we conducted several technical tests

where different persons responsible took part (costume designer, tailor, assistant, light technician, engineer). For testing there were shared meetings with creative and technical staff. For more specific technical questions, we only met the technicians who had relevant expertise. Simultaneously, we continued communicating individually with the costume designer and tailor that developed a solid solution for including the pipes and the tiny fog machine into the fat suit (figure 6B). The fog machine was integrated into a pocket consisting of an inner layer of fire-safe fabrics and an outer cover from skin-colored fabrics. Robustness was a major requirement because Ubu goes wild during the performance, and the integrated fog machine needs to be refilled and recharged after every performance. We mediated the process and, together with the tailoring department and the technical staff, solved how to integrate the components into the fat suit. We believe this resulted in a robust interactive costume, and consequently, collaboration with all departments was essential. Nevertheless, the process took a long time, for several reasons. Firstly, the production was large. Once a year, the theatre house produces a large open air play, with more than 50 background actors and a stage about three-times larger than for ordinary. Thus, the human resources of this institution were at their limits and creating this interaction never had priority. Secondly, it was a challenge to find a robust, safe and invisible solution for integrating the machine into the suit. The safety checks had to be done with the technicians and the integration into the textiles was carried out with the tailors. Both tasks took time when the staff was busy with many other things.

Deployment/ Staging Phase – Revealing Frictions
The advantage of collaborating with the theatre was that we received stakeholder feedback at various points during the design, so we could improve designs and interaction concepts early-on. Here, the actors as wearers of the costumes were involved, bringing us towards deployment. Since rehearsals already ran in parallel to the development, there was an overlap between both phases. In both productions, we visited the early rehearsals to understand the characters and how the actor plays (as it is common in costume design [14]). Costumes were not worn in these early stages, but both actors much later had rehearsals where they wore the costume and thus inhabited another body format (both costumes had an extraordinary shape). After confirming the actors handedness, we decided with the costume designer to integrate the triggers for activating interactive features next to their left hands, so that the actors were still able to use their right hand freely.

Unfortunately, in both production processes, the creative direction finally decided against staging the interactive features since the actors were not fully familiar with them, and therefore the effects were not deemed useful enough for the play. The actual staging of interactive costumes thus is another challenge next to the development process. While the actors (who are the 'end users'), as professionals are used to wear any kind of garment and trained to assume various roles, wearing interactive costumes is a novel experience for them as they have to act intentionally with these. The actors need time to experiment with these novel costumes to explore how they can enhance their role. But in our case, the actors were hardly involved in the creation and rehearsing with the interactive costumes started very late (in both cases just a week before the premiere, which is normal [14]). Next to technical problems, these are the main reasons why the interactive elements were not staged. We assume that early rehearsals with the interactive features would have allowed for their successful staging. Overall, while in both cases the costumes ended up not being staged, analysis of the causes led to valuable insights.

For the *Panda Show*, director, stage and costume designer seemed to be very open to the idea of integrating interactive features into the *Panda*'s costume whereas the actor remained skeptical. Initially, while rehearsing with the costume on, he criticized the integration of the interactive eyes; then the cable was too short, then he said the position of the LEDs obstructed his view. Thus, we moved them to keep his field of view free (figure 7A/B). He also provided critique without trying on the panda head. Feedback from the director, stage and costume designer was more helpful because they exactly explained what to improve, e.g. using more LEDs to intensify the glowing eyes. Early-on we discussed the idea of interactive control with the actor who thought it would be sufficient to switch the red eyes on or off before coming on stage. But the director supported our idea. Yet one day before the premiere, he nevertheless decided for a non-interactive solution. We assume the main reason was that the actor did not have enough rehearsals with the interactive costume and therefore was neither familiar nor comfortable with the feature. The costume designer, when talking about the interactive costumes to the researcher, said: "it's always good to test things with [the actor], so that he immediately knows how it works", which indicates that actors generally need time to rehearse with a costume. This is very likely even more important if a costume contains novel interactive features.

The actor of *King Ubu* raised safety concerns after seeing the pipe system for distributing the fog inside the suit for the first time. He was afraid the synthetic wool in the suit could burn or melt and hurt him. We decided to run a safety test with the actor to address his concerns. A light technician who is an expert for fog machines explained how it works and that nothing is flammable since the machine works with steam (not smoke). We could only relax the actor's worries with an extended test, letting the fog machine smoke directly into the wool and fabric for several minutes. Nothing happened. Another challenge concerned other stakeholders: The fog machine inside the costume had to be refilled and its battery recharged after every show and it was not clear whose responsibility this task was – the light technician who normally cares for the larger fog machines or the dresser who sorts and cleans the costumes after every

show? We finally found a compromise and planned to position a chair next to the costume's backstage location where the handover of the fog machine should always took place. The technician should refill and charge the device, and the dresser's task was to insert it into the costume and take it out again. Unfortunately, there were only two rehearsals with the interactive costume that then worked not properly. We could not attend these, but later-on, we talked to the costume designer and light technician to find out what happened, and why the smoke feature had not been staged. The costume designer reflected on this from a socio-political viewpoint. She said that in both rehearsals the effect was not properly visible from the audience viewpoint, even though the actor had activated it. As the costume designer also had to care for many other issues during and after rehearsals, there was no capacity to check why the smoke did not appear. Also, the actor already was under pressure because he had to wear a heavy fat man suit in summer. Furthermore, he seemed to not feel comfortable with the smoke feature. The decision of the director and costume designer to not stage the smoke effect was due to all of this. The lighting technician analyzed the situation purely from a technical perspective. He assumed that the fog machine was possibly inserted in too many fabric layers and did not get enough air supply, and that laying the device vertically instead of the usual horizontal position may have led to dysfunction. He was right; we had lacked the time to test the machine in these conditions, and had only done component testing, but not tested the integrated final system.

Lessons Learned
Though the creative department had hardly any technological knowledge and totally relied on the technical staff, they were open-minded, especially when interactive effects could expand expressive abilities of a role. During a production, the processes of designers and technical staff are strictly separated by traditional organizational structures as well as definitions of responsibilities and competences that do not support early collaboration or border-crossings. Nevertheless, an early cooperation can create synergy effects and result in a time-/content-efficient production. A person/group with a bridging role can be instrumental when interactive costumes are to be developed with several departments. Beyond that, individual meetings are necessary to solve smaller problems related to specific expertise.

Besides creating interactive costumes, staging them is another challenge and potentially risky, especially since actors are not used to wear computational clothes even though they are trained to adapt to new situations. They may have concerns or fears that make them feel uncomfortable or unsafe. Thus, we need to help them overcome these at an early stage by discussing and testing everything. Rehearsing with interactive costumes is important and should commence early-on. Robustness and security are major requirements for crafting and staging costumes. Moreover, creative and technical departments can provide helpful feedback for construction of and workflow with interactive costumes. Also, staging interactive costumes can result in novel situations that do not fit the normal workflow of traditional theatres and therefore demands new tasks from the staff. Then it needs mediation between the different interests.

DISCUSSION AND CONCLUSIONS

Integrating technology into costumes is a challenge for theatre houses. The studies presented here – conducted in the very different contexts of a self-directed student project and a collaboration with a local theatre house – illustrate this. The main findings concern the lack of integrated collaboration processes between designers and engineers in theatres, the actors as users who need knowledge on interactive costumes as well as more time for dress rehearsals, and continuity of conventional costume requirements (role-support, robustness, security, perceptibility).

A general function of theatre costumes is to support the actors in playing a role, in particular by affecting appearance, movement and posture [14]. Interactive costumes need to do this as well. Gonzales et al., who studied interactive projections, suggest the design principle *Augmented Expression* [10]: "technology should enrich the mediums of expression" (which is also relevant for other stakeholders e.g. choreographers). But, as we further found, costume tends to have a minor function in theatre and is subordinate to playing a role, and the overall performance. Individual effects are secondary to this. In contrast, Gonzales et al. argue for *Aesthetic Harmony*, where performer and manipulated effects should "complement each other to create an integrated aesthetic" [10]. This may be relevant for dance, but based on our experiences we believe this is rarely necessary for theatre performances. To support acting and not interfere with the overall play, interactive costumes need to be intuitive and easy to use and to provide adequate feedback on interaction. Moreover, while the student project had already revealed the importance of robustness, the theatre collaboration revealed this to be even more crucial, and pressed safety as a core issue for staging interactive costumes.

Furthermore, we found that perceptibility of interactive effects from a spectator's perspective is crucial to successfully stage interactive costumes. Arguing with Reeve's magical spectator experience [22], we think for theatre plays the audience does not need to understand how manipulation works. In contrast, Gonzales et al. pose the *Connected Kinetics* principle, which means the audience should be able to understand not only effects but also manipulations [10].

Both our studies suggested that actors should have sufficient time to train with the interactive features and rehearse while wearing the costumes and possibly should also be included in the creation process. While the student project only indicated this to be useful, the collaboration with the theatre house revealed it to be essential, as actors can be the show-stopper if they do not feel comfortable and safe, or their ability to act is hindered. Early rehearsals are not only important for actors in learning to deal with technology issues and errors, but also provide an opportunity to gain their feedback to improve the costume design. This is similar to what Latulipe et al. [18] found for dance performances with interactive projections.

From our second study we conclude that for creating, staging, and maintaining interactive costumes, professional theatres would have to adapt to enable more direct collaboration between departments. The self-directed student project had developed its own interdisciplinary routines in a tightly connected process. This shows how design and technology can go hand in hand. Gonzales et al.'s principle *Integrated Process* [10] also argues for a tight connection, in particular for the involvement of engineers in design. Latulipe et al. further argue that all stakeholders should be involved in all rehearsals and that interactive costuming "may actually require a longer production cycle" [18]. The integrated processes that interactive costumes require, challenge the traditional organizational structures of theatre houses. As we saw in our projects, technology features need to be considered in the early costume design, but also in staging and maintaining costumes. Interactive costumes integrate technology and art/craft and thus concern several departments, when these are all historically different responsibilities and the departments only rarely interact (cf. [14]). It is not easy to change these structures, as this interferes with established skill sets, professional roles, and might even create new workflow problems elsewhere. One solution, exemplified in our external designer, would be the creation of a new responsibility and role that mediates between departments. This has also been suggested by Ha and Kim [11], who explore the design process of wearable computers for performances. However, this is a pragmatic solution and may be more of a work-around. A suggestion for a long-term solution would be to train both creative and technical staff in the other areas for a better mutual understanding. Our student project showed that collaborative creative work not only supports mutual understanding, but also results in shared (creative) ownership. We found the early activity workshops to be highly important, where all sides brought in ideas, and then wanted to contribute to their realization. While for a teaching project approaches such as the design-acting workshop are useful, other activities might be more appropriate within the theatre process.

One of our suggestions for future research is to involve actors early-on in iterative design. But how would we go about this? For a fully *user-centered* or *participatory process* they should be involved already during ideation. This may not be straightforward, as actors tend to be very busy, rehearsing several plays in parallel to staging others, may not be used to being involved in such decisions, and in general we do not yet know much about the actors' viewpoint. Another limitation of our work is that we only collaborated with one theatre. Plans for future work include attaining insight into other theatre houses of different size, investigating the viewpoints of producers and actors, as well as studying the audience perception of interactive costumes. Longer-term studies could focus e.g. on costume maintainance. Finally, an open question is whether the organizational structures of Ballet or Opera provide similar challenges.

Concluding, we have provided real-world case studies of wearables in the theatre domain. These revealed requirements and challenges for the design process as well as the effective staging of interactive costumes, the biggest challenge being how to integrate these into existing infrastructural structures of traditional theatre houses. We also suggested initial solutions to these challenges

ACKNOWLEDGMENTS
Special thanks goes to Theaterhaus Jena, in particular costume designer V. Bleffert, our project students (H. Abitz, G.D. Acay, M. Al-Hallak, S. Gottschlich, S. Luge, W. Müller, T. Rückert, H. Sahibzada, M. Schmandt), the theatre pedagogue (J. Hahn), and the actors (C. Kneisz, M. Oehlke, R. Ecker). The Frauenförderfonds of Bauhaus-Universität Weimar supported the student project with funding.

REFERENCES
1. Barnett, A. The dancing body as a screen: Synchronizing projected motion graphics onto the human form in contemporary dance. *Computers in Entertainment (CIE) 7*, 1 (2009), Article No. 5.

2. Benford, S., Giannachi, G. Interaction as Performance. *interactions 19*, 3 (2012), 38-43.

3. Berzowska, J., Memory Rich Clothing: Second Skins that Communicate Physical Memory. *Proc. C&C 2005*, ACM 2005, 32 - 40.

4. Birringer, J., Danjoux, M. The Sound of Movement Wearables. *LEONARDO 46*, 3 (2013), 232-240.

5. Buechley, L., Eisenberg, M. Fabric PCBs, Electronic Sequins, and Socket Buttons: Techniques for E-Textile Craft. *Pers. Ubiq. Computing 13*, 2 (2009), 133-150.

6. Cheng, S.H., Kim, K., Vertegaal, R. TagURit: a proximity-based game of tag using lumalive e-textile displays. *Proc. CHI 2011 EA*, ACM 2011, 1147-1152.

7. Dalsgaard, P. Research In and Through Design – An Interaction Design Research Approach. *Proc. OZCHI 2010*, ACM 2010, 200-203.

8. Friedrichs-Büttner, G., Walther-Franks, B., Malaka, R. An unfinished drama: designing participation for the theatrical dance performance Parcival XX-XI. *Proc. DIS 2012*, ACM 2012, 770-778.

9. Gobo, G. *Doing Ethnography*. SAGE, London, UK, 2010.

10. Gonzalez, B., Carroll, E., Latulipe, C. Dance-Inspired Technology, Technology-Inspired Dance. *Proc. NordiCHI 2012*, ACM 2012, 398-407.

11. Ha, Y.-I, Kim, Y.-K. The Design Process of Wearable Computers for Extending the Performer's Expression. *HCI International 2014 EA*, 2014, 421-426.

12. Harrison, D., Marshall, P., Berthouze, N., Bird, J. Tracking Physical Activity: Problems Related to Running Longitudinal Studies with Commercial Devices. *Proc. UbiComp 2014*, ACM 2014, 699-702.

13. Hayes, G.R. The Relationship of Action Research to Human-Computer Interaction. *ACM TOCHI 18*, 3 2011, Article No. 15.

14. Holt, M. *A Phaidon Theatre Manual – Costume and Make-Up*. Phaidon Press Limited, London, UK, 2012.

15. Juhlin, O., Zhang, Y., Sundbom, C., Fernaeus, Y. Fashionable shape switching: explorations in outfit-centric design. *Proc. CHI 2013*, ACM 2013, 1353-1362.

16. Ka, W. Man in lelspace.mov / Motion Analysis in 3D Space. *Proc. MULTIMEDIA '05*, ACM 2005, 590-593.

17. Kittleson, H., McCarthy, M. Pert and Plays: Project Management in the Theatre Arts. *Educational Theatre Journal 25*, 1 (1973), 95-101.

18. Latulipe, C., Wilson, D., Huskey, S., Gonzalez, B., Word, M. Temporal Integration of Interactive Technology in Dance: Creative Process Impacts. *Proc. C&C 2011*, ACM 2011, 107-116.

19. Mauriello, M., Gubbels, M., Froehlich, J.E. Social fabric fitness: the design and evaluation of wearable E-textile displays to support group running. *Proc. CHI 2014*, ACM 2014, 2833-2842.

20. Olsson, T. *Arduino Wearables*. Apress, New York, USA, 2012.

21. Owen, C.B., Dobbins, A., Rebenitsch, L. Theatre Engine: Integrating Mobile Devices with Live Theater. *Proc. MoMM 2013*, ACM 2013, 378-386.

22. Reeves, S., Benford, S., O'Malley, C., Fraser, M. Designing the Spectator Experience. *Proc. of CHI 2005*, ACM 2005, 741-750.

23. Salter, C. *Entangled: Technology and the Transformation of Performance*. MIT Press, Cambridge, 2010.

24. Saltz, D.Z. Live Media: Interactive Technology and Theatre. *Theatre Topics 11*, 2 (2001), 107-130.

25. Schleicher, D., Jones, P., Kachur, O. Bodystorming as Embodied Designing. *interactions 17*, 6 (2010), 47-51.

26. Suchman, L. *Plans and situated actions*. Cambridge University Press, New York, USA,1987.

27. Torpey, P.A., Jessop, E.N. Disembodied performance. *Proc. CHI 2009 EA*, ACM 2009, 3685-3690.

28. Wilde, D., Cassinelli, A., Zerroug, A. Light Arrays. *Proc. CHI 2012 CHI EA*, ACM 2012, 987-990.

29. Zimmerman, J., Forlizzi, J., Evenson, S. Research through design as a method for interaction design research in HCI. *Proc. CHI 2007*, ACM 2007, 493-502.

The Textility of Emotion: A Study Relating Computational Textile Textural Expression to Emotion

Felecia Davis
Stuckeman Center for Design
and Computation
Pennsylvania State University
121 The Stuckeman Building
fadav@psu.edu

Figure 1. Five still and moving textile textures used in the study. From left to right, Textures 1-5.

ABSTRACT

Computational textiles are textiles that respond to computer programming commands through embedded electronics. The purpose of this study is to determine what still and shape-changing, textural expressions of computational textiles can communicate emotionally to people. The central hypothesis is that for both kinds of textiles, there will be differences depending on whether the study participants experience the textiles via vision alone or via both vision and touch.

If designers could begin to understand the nature of what various textile expressions communicated, and what computational textiles communicated in transformation then it would be possible to more clearly understand the role that texture of a computational textile plays in communicating emotion through a computational object.

Author Keywords

Aesthetics; emotion in design; design process; computational textiles; e-textiles, computational materials; material expression; somaesthetics, shape-changing textiles

ACM Classification Keywords

H.5.m. Information interfaces and presentation (e.g., HCI): Miscellaneous.

INTRODUCTION

Computational textiles are textiles that respond to commands through computer programming, electronics, and sensors over time. The computational quality and transforming expressivity of these textiles augment the choices designers have in regard to communicating in a non-verbal, sensual way through the textiles themselves.

Modeled on animal skin, fur, or feathers the shape-changing textiles used in this study are designed to elicit emotional responses. But what is communicated emotionally to people via the transforming textural expressions of computational textiles? And, how do the aesthetic textural expressions of still and moving computational textiles communicate emotion to people through vision and touch?

This study explores the hypothesis that different emotions are communicated through textile expressions of still and transforming (i.e., shape-changing) textile samples when a person experiences them via vision alone than via both vision and touch. The study uses three very different methods to obtain people's responses to textile expressions: one that focuses on a qualitative or free-word association to obtain rich information about experience with the textile, one that maps stimulation versus sentiment to a dimensional grid of affect, and one that uses graphic facial expressions, which participants are asked to match to what they understand the textile to be communicating. These methods help show which emotions are elicited from people in response to the still and shape-changing textile expressions.

This methodology can be combined with design methods from urban design, architectural design, and industrial design, etc., to help designers and others understand how textiles can be used to communicate emotion. The study's results suggest a *textility*—an ability to create an emotional communication through the body's relationship to the material/computational expression [20, 21, 23]. There are also implications for creating a large-scale computational textile designed to communicate a range of emotions.

BACKGROUND

This section is organized around two related concepts that are important to this study. The first concerns research through material, the second research on human emotional responses whereby the body relates to the environment. Very little research has connected the two issues explicitly.

The Material Itself

Much of the recent research on design that investigates the relationship between emotion and material expression focuses on materials in an already-designed object, such as a building façade, clothing, or home furnishings. Yet, any given material has its own qualities before it is contextualized and made into something. These qualities change according to context. Research into the qualities of the material itself can lead to new ways to communicate through that material—new ways that cannot be imagined when only the need to solve a specific user problem is in focus [33]. In fact, research into materiality has introduced a new paradigm whereby computation occurs through the material itself and whereby material in general is not set up as something for a user to manipulate via a tool, i.e., a computer [35].

In "SKIN: Designing aesthetic interactive surfaces," Jung et al. look at surfaces as a way to address materiality understood through exploration rather than use. They argue that the standard HCI-user study and behavioral modeling are "not optimized for investigating emerging concerns [… in regard to] experience and engagement with interactive objects" [24]. Their design examples, an inflatable cup, a tactile mouse, and an interactive lampshade, refer to a process of design based on natural references. In considering the material (i.e., the material itself) used to develop each of these examples, the researchers reflect that "the surface in tangible computing is no mere superficial design feature sitting on top of the 'real interaction.' Rather, it can be essential to the generation of different meanings and experiences" [24]. This is especially true for computational textiles where interaction is embedded in material.

In seeking examples of materials and looking at emotion in relationship to those materials, researchers would benefit from working across disciplines, as materials are often classified according to their use in a specific discipline. For example, Addington and Schodek [3], Brownell [8], and Fernandez [19] all discuss transitive and emergent materials in ways that try to break out of the categorization system proposed by the architectural profession (material for walls, material for windows, material for interiors, etc.) to offer a more open system focusing on material properties. Addington and Schodek introduce temporal,

phenomenological perception to the categorization of transitive or smart materials [3]. For, Fernandez the transient nature of these materials means that their use requires considerable experimentation and playing on the designer's part to understand what the materials can do [19]. Similarly, Bergstrom et al. defy any rigid categorization of materials. Instead, in their words, materials are "becoming" or "point to potentials not currently realized" in time and context [6].

Dumitrescu's computational textile projects *Tactile Glow*, *Touching Loops*, *Designing with Heat*, and *Repetition and Textile Forms in Movement* provide a useful framework through which textile designers can consider the expression of materials as transforming and relational [17]. Dumitrescu discusses the blending of design methodologies from textile design and architecture in relation to making textiles for architectural use. Such a process requires design at the micro-scale of fibers and yarns to design at the macro-scale of architecture. Further, Dumitrescu addresses emotion in *Knitted Light* as a human response often overlooked in architectural design and to which more attention should be paid [16].

Coelho et al., Raffle et al., and Valgarda and Redström discuss composite materials into which computing is incorporated as a transitive element [9, 30, 34]. Robles and Wiberg consider the idea that computing should not disappear into materials, suggesting instead "new ways of thinking about the aesthetics of calm computing" [31]. And, they use the term "texture" to connect appearance and feel as a way to think metaphorically and to address a gap in the HCI literature in which thinking is generally organized according to the categories of (1) material, digital space and (2) physical, symbolic space [31]. For Wiberg and Robles, this method ensures that the materiality of digital objects makes sense on a broader scale. Further, in Wiberg and Robles's usage, "appearance" "refers to the way in which the underlying infrastructure is communicated to an observer" [31]; thus, "appearance" communicates material properties via both the visual and the haptic senses. And, "feel" refers to the immaterial aspect of a surface [31]—"a way to address the effect or consequence of a material" [31].

Relating the Body to the Environment

Emotions have been understood as a way of relating bodily responses to an environment. To neglect non-verbal bodily responses as a designer, therefore, is to diminish the communicative possibilities of the body in that space [2, 10, 12, 20, 22, 23, 29, 36]. Ingold, for example, connects the human body to material itself with his term the *textility of making*, whereby textility is understood as weaving the body with material in a feedback loop of forces that shape the material, the body, and the environment [21]. In Ingold's reading, any kind of communication or reading from the material, the body, or the environment is interwoven and created from moment to moment [21].

Gibson's concept of the body's sensing of the environment also reflects the idea of the body related to material and environmental forces. Accordingly, "There are poles of experience that place in a continuum the concepts of subject and object. If you want, you can focus on the dent made in your hand or focus on the edge of the table. The same equipment we use to explore, feel and alter our environment is the same equipment we use to feel and produce emotional experience" [20]. Similarly, Johnson claims that "emotions are both *in us* and *in the world* at the same time … they are one of the most pervasive ways we are continually in touch with our environment" [23].

In the fields of architecture, computational clothing, and product design, Desmet and Ugur have modeled human behavior in context to elicit a specific emotional value [14, 33]. Their study is useful in the HCI-user paradigm, but it does not explore the potential of material itself, rather the focus of these studies is on the wholeness of the completed object.

On the quantitative side, methods designed to understand emotional responses to the environment are being created and used in an ongoing way in the fields of psychology, computer science, and neuroscience. In psychology, for example, Russell has proposed a 2-dimensional model that maps emotions along a positive–negative dimension and an excited–calm dimension [32]. His Circumplex Model of Affect is central to the present study.

In design and computer science, Davis et al. in "Actuating mood: Design of the textile mirror," use the Mechanical Turk to obtain feedback to photographs relating emotion to texture from over 600 people using questions graphed to Russell's Circumplex Model of Affect [13]. And, in computer science, Kim et al. in "Emotion-based textile indexing using colors, texture and patterns," developed a textile-image-indexing system based on human emotion [25]. Using machine learning and neural networks, their system can predict human emotional responses to a textile image's specific color and pattern. The researchers used machine learning to develop fuzzy rules to address color and texture in pairs, such as warm/cold, gay/sober, cheerful/dismal, light/dark, strong/weak, and hard/soft. Neural networks were used to address pairs of emotional aspects such as natural/unnatural, dynamic/static, unstable, stable, and gaudy/plain. Kim et al. focused on images of textiles rather than on the material itself; however, they also used a dimensional analysis based on opposites to determine each textile's place in the index.

In computer science, Akshita et al. in "Towards a multimodal affective feedback: Interaction between visual and haptic modalities," created a dataset for designers to draw on in endeavors to shape emotions. This work is based on the International Affective Picture System (IAPS) and a haptic actuator, which provides different rates of vibration [1]. The researchers discuss the inter-modality between vision and touch, and their results show that vision dominates the affective feedback and sets the sentiment or valence of visual-haptic cues. Touch raised the stimulus of an experience but did not really affect the sentiment or whether people felt positively or negatively toward the stimulus. If one wanted to raise the visual-haptic affect of a low rated sentiment image only a very high-rated haptic stimulation could raise the stimulation level of the low-sentiment image. Although their study does not specifically address affective feedback relating to material qualities, the results relating to vision and touch are pertinent to the present study.

In computer science, Picard's agenda is for computers to read and express human emotions. Specifically, Picard has used voice, facial expression, heart rate, and perspiration as methods to measure human affect, and he has used values obtained by sensors to train computers to use models of emotion to recognize human emotions [29]. Computers can be trained by categorizing human physiological changes on the model of emotion through observation over time, and computers can be programmed to understand the model in different environmental, cultural, and social conditions [29]. The relevance of Picard's work to the present study relates to determining which physiological states map to which specific expressions as a basis for creating designs to elicit given emotions [1].

In neuroscience, Damasio posits that patterned responses to different things or events in the environment are mapped to specific cells in the brain, which create the feeling of a body being in a particular way [10, 11, 28]. His work focuses on mapping response patterns to regions of the brain using positron emission tomography (PET) scans [10, 11, 28].

In the emerging field of neuroaesthetics, neurologists look for patterns of responses to art that activate specific perceptual regions of the brain [5, 7]. Scientists in this field are working to understand which colors, shapes, textures, and material expressions communicate to people, and a key method is to take neurological images of the brain when exposed to different aesthetic artifacts [5, 7]. Balachander's dissertation, *Sculptural Aesthetics and Neural Representation of Surface Curvature*, deals explicitly with what is communicated to people through the aesthetics of 3D sculptural expressions using vision alone. Based on 3D computer-modeled shapes, shown on computer screens to study participants, Balachander's results showed that people preferred smooth, broadly curved shapes and reacted negatively to sharp, jagged-edge shapes. Balachander argues that the attraction to broad smooth curves or "plumpness" may relate to desirable characteristics seen in nature indicating "fertility, health, and edibility" [5].

MAPPING EMOTIONS TO STILL AND MOVING TEXTILES USING VISION AND TOUCH

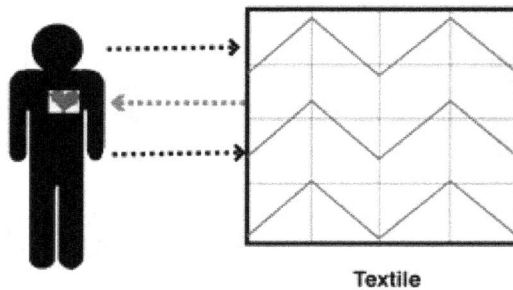

Figure 2. Person using vision and touch (black arrows) to receive affective feedback (red arrow) from a textile.

Outline of Study

The purpose of the present study is to obtain feedback from people regarding the emotions textiles communicate to them (1) through vision alone and (2) through both vision and touch. The textiles are presented in both conditions as still and then as moving. The study outline is as follows:

1. Textiles are Still
   a. Looking **[ROUND 1]**
   b. Looking & Touching **[ROUND 2]**
2. Textiles are Moving
   a. Looking **[ROUND 3]**
   b. Looking & Touching **[ROUND 4]**

Design of the Computational Textile Samples

The reactions of animals were used as inspiration in the design of five textiles of various textures. This inspiration, which was not shared with the study participants, was selected as likely to elicit emotional responses. It was expected that the movement of each animal's fur, feathers, or skin would communicate a different emotion [11]. The animals used to develop the textures for the study, were (A) a cat for its raised fur, indicating fear, alarm, or shock; (B) a bird for its raised feathers, indicating a disturbed or angry state; and (E) an elephant whose skin wrinkles could indicate a number of emotions depending on how a participant manipulated it. (The animals used as models in the present study can be viewed at this link: https://www.pinterest.com/pin/489625790714066530/.)

In order to keep the focus on the transforming textural expression rather than on the color or indeed, the material, a cream-colored felt was used for all five samples. These were 9" x 9" [23 cm x 23 cm] in size. Each texture was selected with the idea of eliciting an emotional response ranging from excited to calm that would be either negative or positive. The samples included smooth textures, rough

and triangulated textures, rounded textures, and textures with superimposed formal systems. The samples (Figure 3)

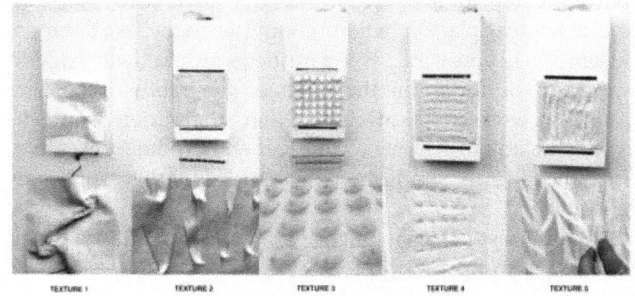

Figure 3. Top: textiles displayed on boxes. Bottom: close-ups of textiles.

were mounted on a box, which hid the motors used to actuate the textures. (Some of the samples' textures (2, 3, and 4) required weights to pull the fabric back to the starting position.) Each sample had a different motion and speed, which changed the texture of the textile. The motor speed for each textile was set so that the textures would transform in a way that mimicked a relaxed breathing animal. (Here is a link to a posting of a video that shows the five textures and their range of motion and speed: http://vimeo.com/85620116   ).

Hypothesis about Textility

This study explores four hypotheses, each of which is addressed in one of four rounds constituting the study's structure. Hypothesis 1 (explored in Round 1) is that by using vision alone, people consistently associate particular emotional states with specific characteristics of textiles in a still state. Expectations for the study were based on the results of a study by Davis et al. in which Mechanical Turk users were shown black-and-white photographs of textile textures and on the results of neurological work with computer images of 3D digital sculptural shapes by Balachander [5, 13]. Crisp curvilinear shapes and textures were associated with positive, excited, and happy feelings [2, 4, 13]. Smooth curvilinear shapes were associated with positive and calm feelings [2, 4, 5]. Triangulated shapes, textures, and facial expressions were associated with negative and angry feelings [2, 4, 5, 13, 26]. Smooth triangulated and superimposed systems or poorly defined combinations were associated with negative, depressed, and calm feelings [13]. In Round 1, Texture 1, which was floppy, curvy, and droopy, was expected to communicate calmness and happiness. Textures 2, 3, and 5, highly triangulated, sharp, or pointy-looking, were all expected to communicate agitation/anger, with Texture 4, a smoothly wrinkled skin, communicating calmness, which could be either a negative sentiment communicating depression and sadness or a positive sentiment communicating happiness and serenity.

Hypothesis 2 (explored in Round 2) is that when people use vision and the haptic senses together the emotional associations change as compared to the emotional associations when only vision is used. It was expected that when the participants could see and touch a still texture that a negative emotional association using vision alone would change to a positive emotional association using both vision and haptic senses. It was expected that all the textures would communicate positively because they were made of soft felt and that the haptic expression would override the visual expression. Texture 5 was expected to communicate excitement/agitated happiness.

Hypothesis 3 (explored in Round 3) is that when people use vision alone to observe moving textile textures that the stimulus rating of what is communicated will increase. It was expected that once the textures were seen in motion that each would communicate happiness and excitement and stimulate the participants.

Hypothesis 4 (explored in Round 4) was that when people can view and touch a moving textile that the stimulus rating would be raised for all of the textiles.

Methodology of the Texture and Emotion Study
The study took place at M.I.T. in January 2014 with 19 participants (15 women and 4 men) aged from 18 to 55 years. Each participant interacted with the textiles in a one on one session with the principal investigator (PI) for about an hour, during which four rounds of questions were completed. All the participants were able to see the textiles and touch them with their hands, and all the participants were able to speak and write in English. The interviews were recorded by video with sound, and the PI also took handwritten notes. All the textile samples were mounted on foam board boxes, which hid servo motors, and hung on a wall at the same height, i.e., at about eye level for adults or 4–6 ft. [137 cm]. The participants viewed the textiles from a standing position, and the PI interviewed each participant at each textile separately. All the textiles were uncovered for the entire interview. Figure 4 shows a photograph of the room's appearance for the duration of the 1-hour sessions.

Each of the four rounds consisted of a series of the same four questions. After the participants had been given the opportunity to see or see and touch a textile, they were asked to free-associate for the first question.

The PI asked some questions to begin the conversation: What are some words that describe some emotions that you could attribute to this textile? What are some adjectives that you could use to describe the mood of this textile? The PI told the participants that the free association should focus on what the textile communicated to them in terms of emotional attributes. The participants were also told that it was OK to talk about things that the textile reminded them of and to talk about any particular associations or memories

that they attached to the textile. Their responses to this question were recorded in notes and on videotape.

Figure 4. Set-up of room for texture and emotion study.

After this first question, the participants answered the questions presented on stapled 8.5" x 11" [A4] sheets of paper. The next two questions were as follows:

1. What does the texture communicate to you?
   [Negative Mood] 1 2 3 4 5 [Positive Mood]
   The participants were asked to circle a number between 1 and 5. This question provided the x-axis coordinates for Russell's Circumplex Model of Affect.
2. What does the texture communicate to you?
   [Relaxed] 1 2 3 4 5 [Stimulated]
   The participants were asked to circle a number between 1 and 5. This question provided the y-axis coordinates for Russell's Circumplex Model of Affect.

Lastly, the participants were shown a sheet of faces/words projecting emotions and asked to pick a face from the sheet to answer the question. (The faces can be seen here: https://www.pinterest.com/pin/489625790714066693).

Then, they circled the face/word that described one of the faces on their sheet. The participants were told that they could circle as many of the faces/words as they wished.

3. **FACE:** What mood would you associate with this textile texture? Happy, Cross, Scared, Sad, O.K., Horrible, Worried, Excited.

After completing the four questions for the first textile, the participants were asked to proceed to the next textile until they had reviewed all five textiles for Round 1. Then, the participants were asked to start at Textile 1 for Round 2, then Round 3, and, lastly, Round 4.

ANALYSIS AND RESULTS

Free-association Word Analysis

The free association introduced individual personality and experience into the account of what each of the textiles was taken as communicating. Memory and analogy played a large part in terms of how the participants related to the textures. Further, the participants tended to provide more than just descriptive emotional words. The participants' words were drawn from descriptions of previous experiences. The free-association question showed the least consistency in terms of producing a reading of either a positive or negative sentiment or valence. The author hypothesizes that as the participants were not expected to select from a limited range of sentiments and stimuli that were this data analyzed quantitatively for sentiment, the results would be more neutral than those of either the Circumplex models or of the face/word test.

The results from this question for Texture 3 showed some of the strongest reactions: the participants either loved it or hated it. The participants' comments are marked with a code [P] so that the comments can be connected to specific participants. In Round 1, many of the responses related to memories. For example, the textile "reminds me of a Dali piece or Indian Shiva sculpture [P9]; "reminds me of a sweater with the balls popping up; calls to mind a bath mat" [P10]; "scales or armor" [P7]. Analogies were another type of response. For example "uh, scary, looks like aliens with boobs; cow's breasts; got scared too many breasts; do not want to touch it; makes me tense" [P9]; "like pores" [P12]; "thinking about [the] nose of an animal; see pointy nose, full of animals personified in an animal realm; like trophies and war medals; inquiring noses sniffing the world around them" [P16]; "feeding; lewd" [P12]. Emotional-word reactions included "My gut reaction is fear; negative; what it evokes is negative; it looks relaxed but if I get close to it[,] it would throw water at me" [P12]; "disgusted by biomorphic holes; hesitant to touch it; sensation does not look subtle; rollercoaster have weird anticipation" [P13]; "scary; disturbing" [P9].

Round 2 also elicited similar memory- and analogy-type responses: "Reminds me of [an] advent calendar [P4 and P5]; "reminds me of seaweed pods in water" [P6]; "thinking of an animal like a snake or reptile" [P7]. However, it was possible to change the texture by petting or stroking, which changed the reactions: "I do not have a good feeling. I'm scared petting it" [P10]; "They don't move they sleep. I don't like the texture. I like it better flattened after petting it" [P11]. Or, "When I run my hand through it they all change; cause[s] you to want to engage with it; not thorny as expected" [P18]. Also, "Now I can see how it is constructed which is a relief; looks very planar and stiff but loss of mystique after I touched it" [P9].

Round 3 elicited memory- and analogy-type responses as well. However, the motility of the texture caused the participants to quickly decide if it was going to harm them

or not. For example "It's timid only when it lifts its head up like when a mouse lifts its head up and has shakiness" [P6]; "It's not moving the whole time so it's not going to attack; looks like cannons that shoot; anxious climax [P7]; "a warning sign [P8]; It's gross; reminds me of different substances that would be bad for you if it were living; if you were in a forest you would stay away, walk away" [P10].

In Round 4, when the participants were asked to look at and touch the moving textile, there was more concern about harming the "creature" that the textile represented or even fighting with it. For example, "It's breathing and feeling and you are petting something that [is] breathing and friendly" [P16]; "like having a naked body that you're not familiar with" [P19]; "I have a feeling of being overwhelmed as I touch it if it cannot breath[e] or move" [P8]; trying to fight it; it's asking for a fight; but when you actually touch it[, it] is no match; like to play with it" [P9]; "Don't like heads rearing up in [an] angry way, a defense mechanism; forcing my hand off it; it moves with vigor; it is irritated within; I am cross with it; who are you to tell me to get off?" [P13].

The comments also showed that the speed and size of the texture had a strong influence on many of the participants' reactions, many of whom wanted a texture to go faster as if they were expecting an already-learned reaction. One participant noted that "Imagining it as a large wall you would be irritated because you would expect it to move *all the time*" (my italics). Thus, distance from the textile mattered, as details were lost from far away, which had a bearing on the communication.

The results here show that what people bring to the textile influences what is communicated. The results also show that manipulation makes it possible for people to change what is communicated and, more specifically, that if something is acting like a living thing they will be worried about harming it or being harmed by it.

Russell Circumplex Analysis

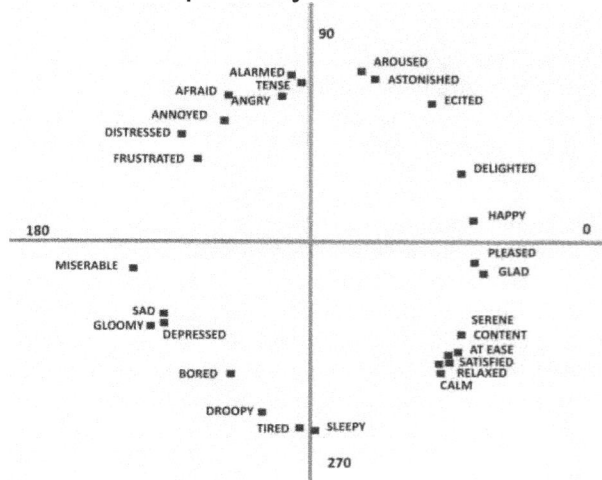

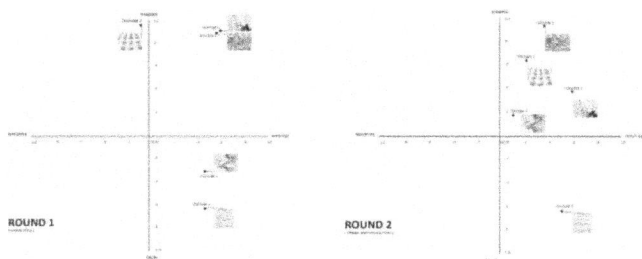

The first results of the study were mapped onto Russell's Circumplex Model of Affect where values along the x-axis denote a sentiment of negative on the left side of the axis and positive on the right. The values along the y-axis denote a valence ranging from "pumped" at the top and "calm" at the bottom. An example of Russell's Circumplex Model is shown in Figure 5, which maps the affect of each of 28 words onto the model.

In Round 1 (plots seen to the left in Figure 6), the participants were asked to view the textures while these were in motion. The results from Round 1 differ somewhat from what was expected. As expected, Texture 1 elicited calm/happy, Texture 3 starts in the upper left quad, communicating negative, anger; and Texture 4 confirms calmness and starts in the lower left side of the quadrant communicating boredom/depression. Yet, unexpectedly, Textures 2 and 5 start in the upper right quadrant, communicating excitement/happiness, not agitation/anger.

In Round 2, when the participants touched the still textures, all but one of the textures moved up in valence or up the y-axis. Texture 3 in Round 2 actually changes in sentiment from negative to positive and happy.

In Round 2 (plots seen to the right in Figure 6), the participants were asked to see and touch the textures while these were still. All the textures were expected to be on the positive half of the grid or sentiment axis for this round, which was confirmed once Texture 3 moved to the right. Texture 4, started with a low visual valence or stimulus and did not move at all in Round 2, which supports Akshita et al.'s results whereby there were both low visual and haptic stimulus ratings [1]. This is perhaps because Texture 4 looked how it felt. Texture 1, which also started with a low visual valence, moved up in stimulus because the participants could readily manipulate the flaps of this texture. This result supports results reported by Akshita et al. whereby a very high haptic stimulation can raise a low visual stimulus level [1]. However, Texture 5 rather than eliciting excitement read as more subdued, indicating that it was visually more interesting to see than to touch.

In Round 3 (plots seen to the left in Figure 7), the participants were asked to view the textures while these were in motion. All the textures were expected to be in the upper right half of the Circumplex. This was confirmed by

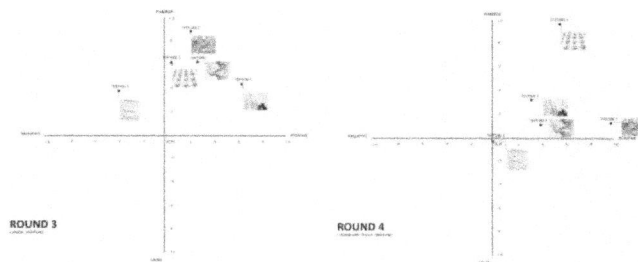

However, surprisingly, Texture 4 moved to the upper left quadrant, communicating agitation/anger.

In Round 4 (plots seen to the right in Figure 7), the participants were asked to see and feel the textures while these were in motion. As expected, the textures stayed in the upper right half of the quadrant. Yet, most lost excitement or had lower y coordinates. However, Texture 3 moved up considerably in terms of excitement.

Graphical Face and Word Cloud Analysis

Word cloud data was prepared using the free online software program Wordle. The word count list next to the word cloud was prepared using the free online software program WriteWords [18, 37].

The information from the face/word question showed much less correlation than seen in the Circumplex Model. The participants had the option of selecting more than one face/word in response to question 4. As a result, there was much less correspondence with the Circumplex. However, it was expected that answers to this question would show more nuanced communication. Many of the participants added their own words to the faces to express what they saw the texture as communicating.

For Texture 1 (Figure 8), the strongest overall reading was neutral or O.K. for all four rounds. However, the word "worried" either matched O.K. or came in second in the count with the exception of Round 4, where it came in 3rd. The expected position on the Circumplex Model for a texture communicating "worried" would have been to the left side of the y-axis in the negative region. It is hard to correlate the position of Texture 1 in the Circumplex Model because the words "worried," "sad," "excited," and "calm" all received the same count. Some of the divergent words attributed to this texture in Round 1 may have come from the different starting positions of Texture 1 on the wall, as the texture was quite floppy. Despite efforts to return it to the same place each time, the texture's shape varied from person to person. Also, for Rounds 1, 2, and 4, the word "happy" is used, suggesting that the texture can be found on the positive side of the Circumplex Model. In Round 3, the word "cross" received a relatively high count. Therefore, it was reasonable to expect that the position of Texture 1 on the Circumplex would move farther left than in Round 2. However, Texture 1 moved to a slightly more positive position.

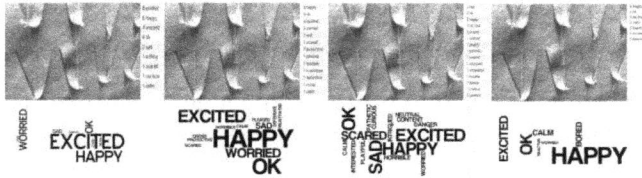

Figure 9. Word cloud and word counts for Texture 2, Rounds 1-4, left to right.

Texture 2 (Figure 9) showed a stronger correspondence between the words selected and its position on the Circumplex grid. The words "excited" and "happy" exchanged 1st and 2nd place in the word counts for Rounds 1, 2, and 4. In Round 3, the words "sad" and "o.k." have equal counts to "excited" and "happy." Therefore, Texture 2 could have been expected to move a bit to the left on the Circumplex grid, but Texture 2 remained in the same place.

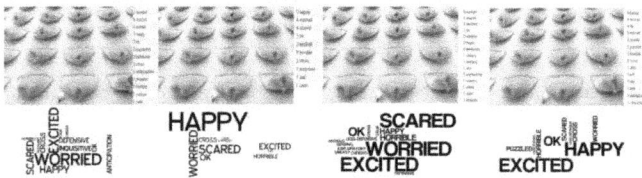

Figure 10. Word cloud and word counts for Texture 3, Rounds 1-4, left to right.

Texture 3 (Figure 10) showed varied responses from round to round, exhibiting a similar range to that of Texture 1. This range should imply that the texture moved a lot over the Circumplex grid, which it does. As expected, with "worried," as the highest word count in Round 1 the texture starts in the negative side of the grid to the left of the y-axis. In Round 2, "happy" received the highest word count, and the texture moved to the right side of the y-axis. In Round 3, however, "scared," "worried," and "excited" are the next highest count words. Therefore Texture 3 would be expected to move to the left side of the y-axis. Instead, Texture 3 remained in a similar position to its position in Round 2, on the right side of the y-axis. In Round 4,

"happy" and "excited" lead the word count, which corresponds to Texture 3's location on the Circumplex grid.

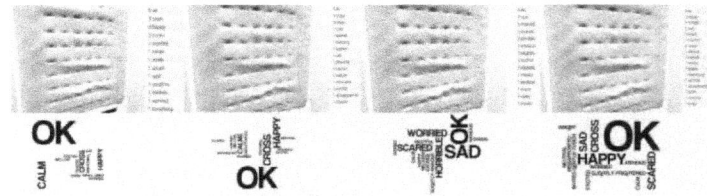

Figure 11. Word cloud and word counts for Texture 4, Rounds 1-4, left to right.

Texture 4 (Figure 11), "o.k." consistently had the highest count in all four rounds. However, in Rounds 1 and 2, this count maps to the lower right quadrant of the Circumplex. In Round 3, "sad" has the next highest count, and as expected Texture 4 moves to the left side of the y-axis on the Circumplex. Lastly, in Round 4, "happy" has the next highest count, and as expected Texture 4 moves toward the right. However, the word counts for "sad," "cross," and "scared" appear to balance this, as Texture 4 lands in the nearly neutral position, i.e., close to where the x- and y-axes cross. It appears that "o.k." can be inflected by the words that have the next highest count. It also appears that two words which would be located in opposite quadrants of the Circumplex with the highest but equal counts can cancel each other, such that the word with the third highest count, for example, "calm" in Round 2, would most influence the position of Texture 4 on the Circumplex.

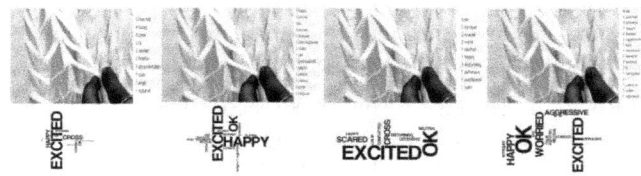

Figure 12. Word cloud and word counts for Texture 5, Rounds 1-4, left to right.

The results for Texture 5 (Figure 12) indicated "excited" as the most important expression communicated to participants in Round 1. In Round 2, the result was highest and equal counts for "excited" and "happy," and, as expected, Texture 5 moved down and slightly to the right in the Circumplex Model. Round 3 shows "excited" and "o.k." as having the highest and equal counts, and Texture 5 did not move its position. Round 4 shows "o.k." as having the highest word count, which suggests that Texture 5 would move to the left on the grid, as expected. Another factor that should be mentioned here is that toward the end of the study, numerous technical difficulties arose with Texture 5 such that it moved more slowly than it should have, which may have affected the results. The results from the face/word question showed less correspondence and often did not correlate with the Circumplex grid, suggesting that Texture 5 elicited a range of emotions.

DISCUSSION AND CONCLUSION

The most useful results herein for designers is the information mapped to the Circumplex Model of Affect. The word cloud information is not as useful as expected. A future research direction would be to perform a quantitative sentiment analysis on the data from the free-association and face/word questions to compare to the Circumplex results.

For Round 1, the expectation was that using vision alone, participants would consistently associate particular emotional states with specific expressive characteristics of the textiles in the still state. This hypothesis received some support from the results of the Circumplex Model of Emotion. Three of the five textures or 60% received the expected feedback. The difference between these results and the previous results from the studies by Davis et al., Balachander, and Akshita et al. can be attributed to the fact that the present study done was live rather than based on photographs and computer images showing one view of the texture or shape. The most useful aspect of the free-association question was that it offered some insight into the participants' reasoning, thus providing a meaningful way to get at the textility of the experience. For example, quite a few participants said that Texture 3 reminded them of an animal, specifically a small animal, an animal's face, or a mouse's face. When the shared experience was visual information, any difference between feedback about the affect of the experience related to the participants' views of their own experiences with small animals. Some participants found the texture cute and friendly; others were disgusted or even a little scared.

In Round 2, the participants could use vision and the haptic senses together so that it could be determined whether the emotional associations would change as compared to when only vision is used. The negative sentiment using vision alone was expected to give way to positive sentiment using both vision and touch. The Circumplex Model results supported this hypothesis, and the free-association analysis showed that the participants changed the texture by stroking or moving it if they did not like it. The free-association question showed why the ratings changed. The second hypothesis, as explored in Round 2, is valid.

In Round 3, most of the participants considered the textures to be more stimulating than in Round 2. And, the third hypothesis, as explored in Round 3, is valid.

In Round 4, as the participants could both see and touch the moving textiles the ratings for the valence and sentiment were expected to rise. Yet, this was not the case. It may be that by Round 4, the participants had lost interest in the exercise itself. The fourth hypothesis was not supported.

Some lessons from this study are that the sequence in which the textiles were presented influenced what the participants felt was communicated because they compared the textures to each other, as the study proceeded. And, the emotions communicated by one texture changed over time, as the participants interacted with this texture.

A second lesson was that the use of animal reactions as a design method helped to communicate the emotions because the participants understood and even referenced animal reactions in their answers. Yet, the participants' own responses to these animal reactions were highly personal and experience-dependent and so varied accordingly.

Preliminary guidelines from this study include these:

- Visual feedback from live textures versus photographs can greatly affect the sentiment and stimulus reading of a texture, i.e., whether it is joyous, serene, angry, or sad.

- Feedback from touch can override visual feedback about sentiment (i.e., positive or negative) if the touch and visual sentiments are not in accord.

- The motion of the texture seen and/or touched raises the stimulation level of the affective rating compared to a still texture.

- The motion of a texture seen and/or touched can change the sentiment rating of a texture compared to a still texture.

For designers wishing to communicate emotions via transforming computational textiles, the study results can be used in combination with other design methods. In architectural design, for example, a space could be mocked up by integrating computational textiles, and the scale, size, lighting, sounds, colors, and uses of the space could all be considered in communicating via transforming textiles. It is difficult to quantitatively map the expressive qualities of materials to specific emotions, as communications are both very personal and created in time and place. The most valuable result herein then is that these qualities depend on textility, a reading of body, place, and material [21]. It is possible that as the computational textiles were materials, not particular things, the participants conceived through each textile. Its meaning and place was not fixed. Such ambiguity is an opportunity: any material has the potential to be imagined and created as many things.

Finally, this study makes a contribution to neuroaesthetics and perception in design. By considering computational textiles as communicating via seeing and touching, this study frames a new avenue for computational material research wherein emotional communication from a material is a source of creativity in humans' interactions with computing. Furthermore textility is shown as foundational to this endeavor [21].

REFERENCES

1. Akshita, S. A.H., Indurkhya, B., Lee, E., et al. Towards multimodal affective feedback: Interaction between visual and haptic modalities. In *Proc. CHI 2015*. ACM Press (2015), 2043-2052.

2. Arnheim, R. *Art and Visual Perception: A Psychology of the Creative Eye*. University of California Press, Berkeley, CA, USA, 1974.

3. Addington, M., and Schodek, D. *Smart Materials and Technologies: For the Architecture and Design Profession*. Routledge, Oxford, England, 2005.

4. Aronoff, J. How we recognize angry and happy emotion in people, places, and things. *Cross-cultural Research 40*, 1 (2006), 83-105.

5. Balachander, N. *Sculptural Aesthetics and Neural Representation of Surface Curvature*. PhD Diss., Johns Hopkins University, 2012.

6. Bergström, J. Clark, B. Frigo, A., Mazé, R., Redström, J., and Vallgårda, A. Becoming materials: Material forms and forms of practice. *Digital Creativity 21*, 3 (2010), 155-172.

7. Chatterjee, A. Neuroaesthetics: A coming of age story. *Journal of Cognitive Neuroscience 23*, 1 (2011), 53-62.

8. Brownell, B. *Transmaterial: A Catalog of Materials that Redefine Our Physical Environment*. Princeton Architectural Press, New York, NY, USA, 2005.

9. Coelho, M., Sadi, S., Maes, P., Oxman, N., and Berzowska, J. Programming reality: From transitive materials to organic user interfaces. In *Proc. CHI EA 2009*, ACM Press (2009), 4759-4762.

10. Damasio, A. R. *The Feeling of What Happens: Body, Emotion and the Making of Consciousness*. Random House, New York, NY, USA, 2000.

11. Damasio, A. R. *Looking for Spinoza: Joy, Sorrow, and the Feeling Brain*. Random House, New York, NY, USA, 2004.

12. Darwin, C. *The Expression of the Emotions in Man and Animals*. Oxford University Press, New York, NY, USA, 1872/1998.

13. Davis, F., Roseway, A., Carroll, E., and Czerwinski, M. Actuating mood: The design of the textile mirror. In *Proc. TEI 2013*, ACM Press (2013), 99-106.

14. Desmet, P.A, *Designing Emotions*. PhD Diss., Delft University of Technology, 2002.

15. Dewey, J. *Art as Experience*. Perigee Trade Press, New York, NY, USA, 2005.

16. Dumitrescu, D. Knitted light–Space and emotion. *The Nordic Textile Journal, Special Edition* (2008), 158-169.

17. Dumitrescu, D. *Relational Textiles: Surface Expression in Space Design*. PhD Diss., University of Borås, 2013.

18. Feinberg, J. Wordle. http://www.wordle.net/.

19. Fernandez, J. *Material Architecture: Emergent Materials for Innovative Buildings and Ecological Construction*. Elsevier, Ltd., Oxford, England, 2012.

20. Gibson, J. J. *The Senses Considered as Perceptual Systems*. Houghton Mifflin, Oxford, England, 1966.

21. Ingold, T. The textility of making. *Cambridge Journal of Economics 34*, 1 (2010), 91-102.

22. James, W. What is an emotion? *Mind 9* (1884), 188-205. http://psychclassics.yorku.ca/James/emotion.html.

23. Johnson, M. *The Meaning of the Body: Aesthetics of Human Understanding*. University of Chicago Press, Chicago, USA, 2008.

24. Jung, H., Altieri, Y.L., and Bardzell, J. SKIN: Designing aesthetic interactive surfaces. In *Proc. TEI 2010*, ACM Press (2010), 85-92.

25. Kim, S., Kim, E.Y., Jeong, K., and Kim, J. Emotion-based textile indexing using colors, texture and patterns. In *Proc. IVSC 2006*, ACM Press (2006), 9-19.

26. Larson, C.L., Aronoff, J., and Stearns, J.J. The shape of threat: Simple geometric forms evoke rapid and sustained capture of attention. *Emotion 7* (2007), 526-534.

27. About Maketon. https://www.makaton.org/.

28. Mallgrave, H.F. *The Architect's Brain: Neuroscience, Creativity, and Architecture*. John Wiley and Sons, Hoboken, NJ, USA, 2010.

29. Picard, Rosalind W. *Affective Computing*. MIT Press, Cambridge, MA, USA, 2000.

30. Raffle, H., Joachim, M.W., and Tichenor, J. Super cilia skin: Textural interface. *Textile: The Journal of Cloth and Culture 2*, 3 (2004), 328-347.

31. Robles, E., and Wiberg, M. Texturing the material turn in interaction design. In *Proc. TEI 2010*, ACM Press (2010), 137-144.

32. Russell, J.A. A Circumplex Model of Affect. *Journal of Personality and Social Psychology 39*, 6 (1980), 1161-1178.

33. Ugur, S. *Wearing Embodied Emotions: A Practice Based Design Research on Wearable Technology*. Springer, Dordrecht, Germany, 2013.

34. Vallgårda, A., and Redström, J. Computational composites. In *Proc. SIGCHI 2007*, ACM Press (2007), 513-522.

35. Wiberg, M. Methodology for materiality: Interaction design research through a material lens. *Personal and Ubiquitous Computing 18*, 3 (2014), 625-636.

36. Wölfflin, H. Prolegomena to a psychology of architecture. *Empathy, Form, and Space: Problems in German Aesthetics, 1873-1893*. Getty Publications, Santa Monica, CA, USA (1994), 149-190.

37. Writewords http://www.writewords.org.uk/word_count.asp.

Intersecting with Unaware Objects

William Odom[1], Ron Wakkary[1,2]
Simon Fraser University, Surrey, British Columbia, Canada[1]
Eindhoven University of Technology, Eindhoven, Netherlands[2]
{ wodom , rwakkary }@sfu.ca

ABSTRACT

We adopt a design-oriented approach aimed at motivating and expanding the notion of everyday creativity beyond explicit interactions to also include the implicit, incremental and, at times even, unknowing encounters that emerge among people, technologies, and artifacts over time. We explore these ideas through the design and investigation of two interaction design research artifacts: the Photobox and table-non-table. Through analyzing and synthesizing insights that emerged across our studies, we describe a related set of concepts in support of a more implicit form of everyday creativity, which includes: unaware objects, intersections and ensembles. We conclude by interpreting findings in context of prior implications for everyday creativity and outline considerations for future work.

Author Keywords

Unremarkable Creativity; Unawareness; Interaction Design.

ACM Classification Keywords

H.5.m. Information interfaces and presentation (e.g., HCI): Miscellaneous.

INTRODUCTION

Investigating people's practices of transforming and adapting design artifacts in everyday life is an important and ongoing focus in HCI and interaction design research. A range of observational studies over the past several years have revealed how people engage with everyday objects in creative, innovative, and emergent ways that often extend well beyond what they were originally designed for. These empirical works are diverse and grounded in different conceptual framings, such as appropriation [3], customization [12], everyday design [26,2], and organizing systems [24]. They nonetheless share the goal of describing and analyzing people's actions to make design artifacts better situated to their evolving practices and desires through what may be described as everyday creativity.

A core aim of this paper is to investigate further the idea of everyday creativity, a notion that has been of growing interest in the Creativity & Cognition community [e.g., 2,18,26]. Our approach builds on the assumption that creativity is at the heart of the dynamic changes of people's everyday experiences and actions [23,24]. However, in contrast to earlier efforts, we take a research-through-design approach [21,27] that explores everyday creativity through the making and situating of interaction design artifacts. Through this approach, we focus on a radically reconfigured understanding of the relations between users and design artifacts that finds creativity to be a quality shared in the emergent configurations among people, artifacts, and the environment they are situated in.

Our goal is to take a step toward expanding the notion of everyday creativity beyond explicit interactions or purposed manipulations to also include the implicit, incremental and, at times, unknowing encounters and relations that emerge among people, artifacts, and environments over time. In our view, investigating such considerations can contribute new insights into design strategies that might better support the meaningful and situated integration of interactive technology in everyday life.

To support our investigation of everyday creativity, we describe the design of a type of interaction design artifact that emphasizes actuality over functionality, which has neither an explicit interface nor computational awareness of its owners presence or actions. We refer to these interaction design artifacts as *unaware objects*. As a result of studying these objects in-situ we developed a notion of post-functional engagement with design artifacts, which we term as *intersections*. We found that as intersections accumulated around a unaware objects, unique and dynamic configurations of artifacts, contexts and human actions emerged, which we refer to as *ensembles*.

Specifically, we examine two interaction design research artifacts, named Photobox and table-non-table, which aim to explore the notion of a more implicit everyday creativity. We individually deployed and studied each artifact in several households to gain rich accounts of people's experiences of living with them over time. The ways in which unawareness manifested in Photobox and table-non-table differed, but nonetheless opened both artifacts up to being understood, resourcefully drawn on, and incorporated into people's lives on their own terms.

In the sections that follow we synthesize insights that emerged across our experiences of developing and studying these design artifacts. Based on our analysis, this paper concludes with a discussion of the key features of unaware objects as creative resources, unique ensembles, and unremarkable creativity. We also explore implications for emphasizing actuality and post-functionality as a means of creating new design artifacts to support everyday creativity.

BACKGROUND AND RELATED WORK

Related work falls into three areas: everyday creativity; human-technology relations; and emerging works in the materiality of interactive technologies.

Within the Creativity & Cognition community, the notion of everyday creativity is strongly rooted in prior research related to everyday design. The basic premise behind everyday design is that everyone is a designer and, in this way, people creatively and constantly appropriate and transform objects around them. The term everyday design originated from a study of families where a type of emergent, shared creativity supported household members' navigation of daily activities through the routine repurposing of common objects—a process described as *design-in-use* [26]. Here, the notion of 'design' is comprised of a shaping of their worlds in an ongoing fashion to better address their unique needs. Some aspects of this study resonate strongly with Taylor and Swan's [24] research on families' evolving development of domestic systems that bring order to their lives. They argue that technologies ought to be designed as resources to support the complex ways people socially organize their homes. Tolmie et al. [25] also observed the social organization of families at home and articulate the need to make technologies as unremarkable as the domestic routines themselves. These related concerns have also surfaced in movements in the humanities to conceptualize everyday life as an essential site for sociomaterial creativity [e.g., 23].

Later studies in everyday design expanded focus beyond routines to a diverse activities, such as analyzing the materials, meaning and competences that comprise everyday design [e.g., 2] as a form of social practice [20]. A range of other works also shares some of the same core commitments to supporting everyday creativity that everyday design holds. Dix [3] champions designing for appropriation, noting: "whilst you cannot design for the unexpected, you can design so that people are more likely to be able to use what you produce for the unexpected" (p. 28). Relatedly, Gaver et al. [6] articulate ambiguity as a worthwhile strategy for fostering personal relationships with technologies in ways that "provide rich resources for experience that can be appropriated by users" (p. 233).

We aim to extend this research further by articulating nuanced and often indirect or incremental forms of everyday creativity in relation to notions like ambiguity, appropriation, the unremarkable, and design-in-use.

The need to foster creative, self-determined uses of design artifacts reflected in the works above is emblematic of a broader shift in the HCI community toward taking more seriously the complex ways technology shapes everyday life and, ultimately, mediates between humans and their actions in the world. Various works have migrated to perspectives outside of HCI, such as the philosophy of technology [4,16], to critically explore the nature of relations that form between humans and technology. Drawing on the works of Albert Borgmann, Don Ihde, and Peter-Paul Verbeek, Fallman [4] advocates for the design of computational objects that are more open to people forming relations to them that reach beyond explicit purposes or utility. This imperative is well articulated through Maze and Redstrom's [13] assertion that crafting computational objects requires researchers to "investigate what it means to design a relationship with a computational thing that will last and develop over time—in effect, an object who's form is fundamentally constituted by its temporal manifestation" (p. 11). On a high level our work aims to generatively engage philosophical notions of human-technology relations in ways similar to Maze and Redstrom's proposal. We aim to explore how the design strategy of unawareness and the concepts of intersections and ensembles might offer constructive ways of expanding how researchers and designers approach creating interactive technologies that might persist in people's lives over long periods of time.

In parallel to growing interest in adopting philosophical and temporal framings to understand computational objects and their social effects, there has been a growing turn within the HCI community toward critically considering the material basis of interactive technologies. While these works are diverse and surface in and outside of the creativity literature, they are united by a central concern to unpack the complex ways that materiality—the things computational objects are made of—shape experiences and interactions with them. Jacucci and Wagner [10] reveal how material features of interactive technologies speak to people's "multiple senses" and shape the character of creative actions with them. Rosner and Ryokai [18] have illustrated that materials in technology can blur the boundaries between digital and physical interactions in the context of creative material practices, such as knitting. Gross et al. [8] have argued for the need to refocus attention on how materials mediate relations to tangible interaction artifacts in the service of better leveraging their creative potential in design. More broadly, there exists a growing number of works investigating how materiality shapes interaction with design artifacts [7]. Our work aims to modestly extend this discussion of actuality and materiality in computational artifacts by analyzing design exemplars, like the Photobox and table-non-table. These exemplars emphasize materiality to support lived-with qualities and emergent engagements that are implicit, incremental, direct and reflective.

CONCEPTS AND EXPLANATIONS

The concepts of unaware objects, intersections, and ensembles developed from our studies of the Photobox and table-non-table. Importantly, these are not *a priori* concepts. They emerged through critical reflection on the conceptualizing, designing, and analysis of our two design artifacts. Thus, this paper provides a space to consider findings emerging across the Photobox and table-non-table from a higher-level perspective to articulate these related concepts. However, for readability, we briefly describe each concept upfront to preface our subsequent reporting and analysis.

Unaware objects are intentionally designed to enact their respective behaviors without requiring nor demanding the attention of their owners. They execute preset computational processes and, in this sense, operate entirely unaware of their owner's presence or actions. These objects have no explicit output functions based on interaction with them and they lack any kind of traditional 'interface' or control mechanisms. Our use of the term unaware in this context owes specifically to the fact that these objects are designed to be computationally unaffected by direct interactions (unless of course if they were to be unplugged).

Intersections refer to people's ongoing incremental encounters with a design artifact in which a modification or transformation may or may not occur. While interaction often involves direct manipulation of an artifact, intersections can range from experiences of being mindful of the artifact, to subtle uses of the artifact that may be only briefly noticed (or go unnoticed), to piecemeal re-situations of the artifact within its physical context. Intersections can be treated as complementary to interaction, but are notably more general in their aim to account for the broader range of known and unknown, incremental and ongoing encounters that unfold with computational and non-computational objects alike in everyday contexts.

Ensembles manifest through cumulative intersections. As intersections accumulate, qualities emerge that go beyond the individual artifact, often becoming experienced among an ensemble of things and people within their local environment, such as the home. This concept is influenced in part by Alexander's [1] earlier discussion of the notion of ensemble, where he writes: "when we speak of design, the real object of discussion is not the form alone, but the ensemble comprising the form and its context." (p. 16). In this sense, the quality of everyday creativity is achieved at the level of ensembles through the holistic relationship of artifacts, contexts, and human actions. In this way, an ensemble is a dynamic collection of social and material elements within an environment that can become increasingly unique and nuanced over time.

THE PHOTOBOX AND TABLE-NON-TABLE

The Photobox and the table-non-table are two interaction design research artifacts developed through a research through design [21,27] approach that embodies *unawareness*. While they differ in terms of their materials and behaviors, they both draw on familiar forms of actual objects: a chest and a table. In conceptual terms, analogue objects like a chest or table can be seen as cousins of unaware computational objects. Like almost all analogue objects, a chest or a table does not have the computational processes to sense or detect data, nor do they provide interfaces or control mechanisms to interact with another thing (or a representation of another thing). Like most analogue objects, unaware objects are designed with people in mind and, so while unaware, they are not independent of people. However, unaware objects differ from their analogue cousins in that they have computational features. Furthermore, these features and their effects are often distinct from more traditional or common computational artifacts in that they offer people no control over the computational processes that are enacted. These design qualities may seem counter-intuitive to supporting everyday creativity. However, as we describe, the Photobox and table-non-table emerged as significant objects once they accumulated a range of intersections and became embedded within unique ensembles in people's homes.

Photobox

The motivation for the Photobox emerged from research on the rapidly growing generation and use of personal digital content to capture life experiences (e.g., photos and videos). This primarily included qualitative studies of people in their homes with an eye towards their practices and workarounds to construct meaning with these digital materials (see [15] for an overview). One overarching theme across the studies was that the rapid proliferation of digital materials was leading to experiences of overload. As digital archives grew larger, it became difficult for people to get a grasp on what they contained and how to engage with them as an everyday resource. A secondary motivation centered on the growing need to investigate designing new forms of technology that are potentially more capable of having a more enduring presence in everyday life [9,13,16].

Motivated by these observations and issues, the Photobox was developed as a conceptual artifact to theoretically and practically explore how a computational object could critically intervene in experiences of digital overload. We targeted digital photos because they remain one of the most enduring forms of digital content, and they continue to rapidly proliferate. Inspired by the *slow technology* design philosophy [9], we wanted to explore how slowing down the consumption of digital photos might support experiences of reflection on people's digital materials and also on the Photobox itself as a domestic technology. A portion of findings from research on the Photbox appears in an earlier article [14] that emphasized future opportunities for digital photo consumption. In this paper, we move beyond our original motivations to articulate how intersections and ensembles were evident in people's experiences of the Photobox.

The design and deployment of Photobox
The two main components of Photobox are an antique oak chest and a Bluetooth-enabled Polaroid Pogo printer (which makes 2x3 inch photos). We decided to use an oak chest as it presents a familiar form with a simple interaction (i.e., it can be opened and closed; things can be kept inside of it and taken out). We decided to use a printer because it produced a simple material form (i.e., a paper photograph) that was open to a range of potential uses. All technological components were embedded in an upper panel in the chest. The printer was installed in an acrylic case that secured it to a small opening in the panel to allow a photo to drop onto the central platform of the box (see Figure 1).

Photobox's behavior is enacted through a .NET application, which runs on a laptop that wirelessly connects to the embedded printer via Bluetooth. At the start of each month, Photobox indexed its owner's Flickr archive and randomly printed four or five photos that month. In similarly random fashion, it selected four (or five) photos and generated four (or five) selected timestamps that specified the print time and date for each photo; at print time, the matching photo was printed. Photobox's behavior was designed to make it difficult for the owner to anticipate when it would 'act' next and what might be that action. The computational process never changes and Photobox as an interaction object is extraordinarily simple.

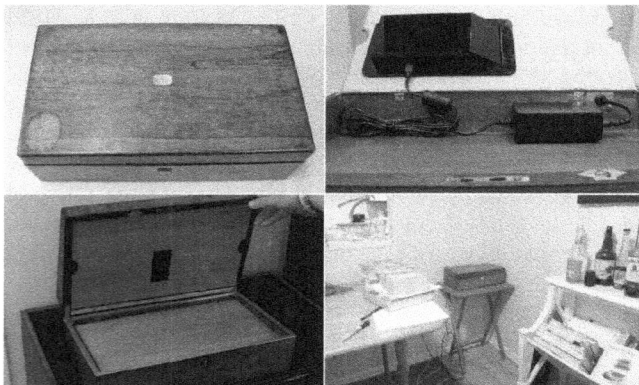

Figure 1. Clockwise from top left: An oak chest before it was augmented; Upper panel (open) where printer components are hidden; Photobox can be opened to see if a photo has been printed; Photobox lived in the corner of Samuel and Shelly's livingroom.

Three Photobox design artifacts were deployed in three households for fourteen months respectively. Household A consisted of a married couple in their mid-40s Tim and Britt; Household B of five roommates in their 30s: Heather, Zack, Thomas, Jenn, and James; and, Household C of a couple in their mid-30s Samuel and Shelly. Each Photobox was tied to a household member's Flickr account, which ranged from 2500-4500 photos. Few details were provided about the Photobox when it was installed other than it will occasionally print the owner's Flickr photos. Bi-monthly

interviews were conducted with households to record participants' experiences with Photobox (during these times additional paper was loaded into the printer). All of the field data presented in this paper are taken from in depth final interviews when participants reflected in depth on the range of experiences they had with the Photobox.

Photobox: experiencing unawareness
After initially being installed and syncing with its owner's respective Flickr archive, the Photobox operated on its own, unaware of the actions of those around it. Nonetheless, it led to intriguing and unexpected experiences across households. When describing Photobox, participants often contrasted it to other digital technologies in their homes: *"It doesn't look like technology, I can't do anything to it, there's no buttons, but it is connected to Heather's* [Flickr] *account on the web and occasionally does something. It is very peculiar. It definitely grew on me over time."* (Zack). Similarly, Samuel describes how the unawareness of Photobox gave it a sense of 'otherness' compared to more familiar devices: *"With technology, it's either on or off. If it's on, you're probably using it. ...When it's off, it's basically worthless. It's not doing anything. ...In the end* [Photobox] *never really seemed that way. Since it's doing what it wants when it wants. It's hard to even tell when it actually is printing. It feels different and that's what makes it easy to open up or forget about for a while. It stayed mysterious the whole time* [we had it]."

Additionally, Tim reflects on how unawareness produced a less constraining, even somewhat relieving effect: *"My Phone is always pinging me. ...someone's tagged me, or I got a new GroupOn. ...it keeps going and I do feel compelled to check so I don't miss anything. ...*[Photobox] *didn't try to change for us. No matter how many times I opened it, it's not going to affect it. ...It's awesome to find new photos, but* [Photobox] *doesn't make me crazy to run over and check it every time I get home. ...I can walk past it. I can come back later. ...in that way it has quite a different character."*

Collectively, these reflections help illustrate how Photobox's lack of any control mechanisms paired with a difficult to anticipate yet ultimately enjoyable behavior helped distance it from the kind of relations its owners associated with other computational technologies in the home. Interestingly, Tim's statement highlights how Photobox could be noticed and interacted with, or fade into his material and perceptual background, which imbued it with a distinctly 'different character.' In the next section we expand more on how a variety of intersections to accumulated around Photobox.

Intersections with Photobox
Intersections with Photobox ranged from simple material actions (e.g., opening and closing the chest, or rearranging in relation to other domestic artifacts or places) to purely reflective actions (e.g., contemplating the Photobox as a

thing and its meaning in one's life, or simply glancing at it and moving on). These actions occurred on a mundane basis, and as Photobox became absorbed into its local environment, it would shift in and out of perceptual view of household members. For example, Tim described how, after returning from a trip, his Photobox became obscured by various objects on and around it: *"I set down a stack of magazines on it. ...it* [Photobox] *had become just another thing. ...Three, four weeks later we finally moved everything back to their proper places. All of a sudden I realized I should check it and I found three photos. ...from different times in our life. ...It was delightful to happen across it like that."* Later Shelly remarked: *"...we can leave it for a while and stumble across it and then there's these snapshots. ...It's surprising* [that] *the feeling of living with it is really pretty natural."*

What we want to highlight here is how the Photobox emerged as a computational object capable of triggering a spectrum of experiences. These ranged from simple, at times unrecognized, actions that happened on and around the design artifact to extraordinary direct encounters. This range of intersections supported the Photobox's emergence as a fixture that could be resourcefully drawn on within households when desired. Eventually, it developed into a computational object with natural, lived-with qualities, like "just another thing" in the home.

Figure 2. From left to right: Britt's Photobox brought an ensemble of artifacts "into harmony." Heather reflected on Photobox in relation to other domestic technologies in her home.

Another important dimension of the concept of intersections is that as they accumulate, the computational object itself can become embedded within an ensemble. One of the most striking examples of an ensemble involved Britt's eventual actions to move and arrange a ceramic pitcher made by her father and a framed picture of her parents close to the Photobox (see Figure 2). She described the ritual that emerged around these things: *"Whenever it'd* [sic] *print a photo of them* [parents], *I'd take a little time, look at it and the* [framed] *photograph and put* [the printed photo] *in the pitcher Dad made. Kind of as a ritual to remember them and to keep all those memories together. ...it brought all these things that belonged together into harmony for a moment. ...Getting one of them* [a printed photo of parents] *was always wonderful. ...But, after a few months all of them* [objects] *together, just being there, made that part of the living room much more significant than it was before. ...over time it came together into something that left quite an imprint on our home."*

This instance is exemplary of Photobox's emergent capacity to draw other artifacts into relation within an ensemble, which in Britt's case, led to an emergent ritual that was well situated within her home.

Photobox also led to intersections with ensembles in less direct, unexpected ways. In this example, Heather described how the Photobox's juxtaposition to gaming systems provoked her to consider her relation to them: *"...the GameCube itself doesn't matter that much. There's no value in it aside from playing games. ...Sometimes, sitting in here, I'll be thinking* [Photobox] *is unusual around these systems. ...Like, it being there can be inviting, I can look in it. ...or sit on the couch, think about what already* [printed] *or what could* [be] *printed. ...Or that it's a bizarre thing but also a very intriguing thing. Sometimes it catches my attention and I get lost thinking about this stuff. ...The point is that it's not used in the same way like the* [GameCube]. *It can't be. ...it feels like it can settle in down there. The other stuff around it, feels like they'll be gone sooner than later."*

Heather's reflection helps illustrate how Photobox became integrated into an ensemble in her living room. Its unawareness and material presence opened it up to be mindfully intersected with, which led Heather to curiously consider her relations to other devices in the ensemble. On a deeper level, her statement revealed how, once situated within the ensemble, Photobox started to be perceived as a distinct computational object—one that she could imagine persisting beyond other technologies whose value was largely associated with their utility.

table-non-table

The motivation for the table-non-table emerged from research on everyday design, which primarily included ethnographic studies of people in their homes and various other everyday practices [e.g., 26,2]. In an attempt to move beyond this empirical work, the table-non-table was developed to theoretically explore, from a design perspective, what could comprise an everyday design computational artifact and what its effects might be. The design of the table-non-table was also informed by theories of social practice [20]. Given this, we aimed to create a computational artifact that could be aligned with the competences, materials, and motivations of everyday home life practices. Stacked paper was used as a core design element due to its familiarity as a material, its flexibility in terms of potential uses, and because the simple practice of stacking paper were extremely simple assembly and disassembly techniques. Lastly, we aimed to explore how computation embedded within this simple artifact could help mediate the resourcefulness and social practices of people—everyday designers—in their daily lives.

The design and deployment of the table-non-table
The table-non-table is a slowly moving stack of paper supported by a motorized aluminum chassis. The paper is common stock (similar to photocopy paper). Each sheet

measures 17.5 inches by 22.5 inches with a square die cut in the middle to allow it to stack around a solid aluminum square post that holds the sheets in place. There are approximately 1000 stacked sheets of paper per table-non-table, which rest on the chassis about one half-inch from the floor. The chassis itself rests on four small steel balls. Set toward the center of the chassis hidden from view are two wheels attached to motors that are connected to and controlled by a customized Arduino board. The chassis and motors are strong enough to support stacking heavy objects on it including a person sitting or standing on it. The paper sheets can easily be removed and manipulated like any sheet of paper. We experimented with several variations of movement from a continuous and slow movement (1 revolution per minute) to short periods of movement (5-12 seconds) occurring once during a longer period of time (a random selection between 20 to 110 minutes). We settled on the latter version for its final form. The movement pattern is random yet it stays within an initial radius of less than half a meter square. The movement can be almost imperceptible, taking up to several days to a week to notice.

The table-non-table became part of one household for five months, became part of two households for six and three weeks respectively, and became part of two households in a preliminary deployment for several days. The households included thirteen people in total (eight male and five female) ranging in ages from early teens to mid-50s. In the longer deployments, households were recruited by word of mouth and knew nothing of the project. In the preliminary study, households had some prior knowledge of the project. In the longer deployments, participants were given the table-non-table and a card with instructions on how to post photos and comments about their experiences to a blog on tumblr.com. In the table-non-table deployment we adopted a speculative approach rather than a formal user study or evaluation. Our aim in the deployments was to bring our concept artifact into existence in lived-in environments. Methodologically, our interests were in the reporting of people's subjective encounters with the table-non-table. We were less interested in conducting an analysis of their behaviors with the artifact. As a result, our interpretations rely on photos of encounters and commentary that participants shared with us on tumblr.com and also in home interviews. The table-non-table deployment differed to some extent from the Photobox study in terms of methodology, yet mirrored many of the findings in terms of unawareness, intersections, and ensembles.

table-non-table: experiencing unawareness
The table-non-table required no attention after finding a place for it in participants' homes and plugging it in. Regardless if its movement was noticed, it continued to move as it was programmed. The stacked paper was free to be removed, however this too had no impact on its behavior. This apparent incongruity between the materiality of the table-non-table and its computational features emerged in a participant's attempt to connect the stacked paper with an interface function: "*The whole electricity feature is pretty strange. The thing is after all a pile of paper. Paper involves a type of use that is somehow incompatible with being electric. ...It's almost like removing a sheet of the pile 'unplugs' the piece of paper. Which doesn't make much sense.*"

This statement highlights how the table-non-table's materiality created ambiguity and a sense of unfamiliarity around its expected behavior and, more generally, around it as a computational object. In an attempt to make sense of the table-non-table, the participant speculates, although doubtfully, that the stack of paper could be a tangible interface to turn the table-non-table on and off. On a higher level, the rejection of the table-non-table as a tangible interface can be attributed to the perceived unequivocal actuality of the table-non-table in which it is "after all a pile of paper." This helps illustrate that the table-non-table is an unaware object in that its qualities are independent of human attention, and further, the actuality of its material composition problematizes its potential role as a user interface in any kind of traditionally recognized sense.

Similar to the Photobox, the table-non-table has no awareness of its environment. It has no sensors and no input functions. Its movement is very circumscribed in terms of area, which prevented it from colliding with furniture and walls. In essence, the table-non-table was a benign and unintelligent object. Despite this, participants assigned it with distinct and unique perceived qualities. For example, in one household when it was found under furniture the participants described it as "*The thing slowly hiding under the couch.*" In another instance, when the table-non-table was placed under a Christmas tree: "*The prototype is pretending it's a gift under the Christmas tree.*"

What we want to draw attention to in these statements is that while the table-non-table was unaware of its environment in having no computational sensing capabilities, and it was designed to not require human attention, it developed a deeply textured relationship within households as it was perceived to have abilities such as to "hide" and "pretend". Like the Photobox, the table-non-table's unawareness counter-intuitively created qualities of interactions, perceptions, and relations that were rich and, at times, distinctly different in comparison with other computational objects.

Intersections with table-non-table
The table-non-table led to several intersections in terms of simple material actions and everyday reflections. The table-non-table was particularly open to simple actions that people may not have been fully aware of when the intersection occurred. Many instances emerged that consisted of simply placing objects on top of it. For instance, the simplicity of stacking a glass and ceramic mug in Figure 3 is a good example of this common intersection.

Unaware objects are designed with intersections in mind rather than being incidental outcomes. In this way, both in form and behavior the table-non-table easily accommodated simple actions like objects being placed on top of it.

Similar to the Photobox, as intersections accumulate over time, the artifact may become embedded in an ensemble of artifacts. For example, figure 3 illustrates how intersections emerged among the ensemble of things brought together by the table-non-table, which included a stack of books, and a coffee thermos. In this simple ensemble, removing a book or shifting the thermos to one side was as much an intersection with the book, thermos and table-non-table together. Within ensembles, the computational artifact is seen in relation to other things, including analogue objects.

Figure 3 (from left to right). Stacking a glass and mug on the table-non-table is a simple intersection; A collection of objects considered together within an ensemble.

These documented examples help further illustrate the material nature of intersections, which are simple and demand little attention, and that the table-non-table achieved its goal of supporting these kinds of simple actions. Like the Photobox, intersections with the table-non-table also cumulatively developed into intersections with ensembles of things. The examples above show an ensemble in which the table-non-table directly interacts within an ecology of objects that must be considered and made sensible together.

Figure 4. The table-non-table within an ensemble that triggered mindful consieration of its relation to other artifacts in the home.

Many other examples of ensembles emerged as the table-non-table settled into an easy cohabitation with other material artifacts in the home (Figure 4). While there was an understandable peculiarity about the table-non-table, participants reported it generally called no more nor less attention to itself than the other objects nearby. Here, we describe the table-non-table within an ensemble to show not only the nature of this type of intersection, but also to

further emphasize that intersections are as much reflective in nature as they are action-oriented. For example, it was within the broader context of an ensemble that caused one participant to notice for the first time that the table-non-table moves. He noted that his "*architect eyes were unhappy to see that the thing was always crooked and not parallel to the couch!*" He soon realized that despite his efforts to align the table-non-table parallel to the edge of the couch, it would move itself out of alignment.

Interestingly, intersections emerged among non-human members of households too. For example, a family's cat found the surface of the table-non-table inviting and familiar, making good use of it as a bed. Yet simultaneously it became an artifact of curiosity and worthy of exploration (see figure 5). One participant noted that the "*cat noticed before us*" that the table-non-table moved. Soon after the cat played with the table-non-table, family members used the paper to make large snowflake Christmas decorations.

Figure 5. The family cat uses the table-non-table as a bed; The cat plays with the paper in the table-non-table; A large paper snowflake is made from table-non-table.

This example illuminates several key aspects of intersections. First, we saw in our households that intersections with unaware objects are not exclusively by humans. This particular instance is exemplary in how it shows simple intersections by a cat catalyzed richer and more involved intersections and, ultimately, creative actions by people in the home. Despite the simplicity of intersections, the cumulative and collective experiences of them can lead to rich complexities. Further, in this example, we can see how simple computation, like the random movement of the table-non-table mediated a level of curiosity that led to a chain of intersections, first by the cat and then by people that grew in richness and complexity with each link in the chain.

DISCUSSION AND IMPLICATIONS
Through a design-oriented approach we aimed to build on and extend prior research on everyday creativity by exploring how it emerges over time as a type of implicit relationships, incremental encounters and engagements.

While we acknowledge the broader context of research on everyday creativity, we found the implications for interaction design articulated in earlier works on everyday design and creativity [e.g., 2,25] to be a useful point of reference for further analysis of our findings. The relevance of this approach is that these earlier works resulted from empirical analyses that anticipated the challenges and opportunities in designing interaction design artifacts that better leverage everyday resourcefulness and creativity. In our own design efforts, we found resonance with key aspects of these implications including artifacts as creative resources, uniqueness, and the unremarkable. Our current work extends these implications through a generative, design-oriented perspective with added precision, nuance, and utility for interaction design.

Unaware objects as creative resources—The quality of unawareness paired with careful choices in form and materials set the stage for intersections to accumulate around our design artifacts and for ensembles to emerge. The lack of an interface and control mechanisms in our design artifacts catalyzed broader concerns that reveal how they operated as creative resources. We found unaware objects led to direct creative engagements, such as the ensemble Brit created in configuring a framed photo and an ceramic pitcher near the Photobox to commemorate her father, or the chain of encounters that resulted in the making of snowflakes from the paper of the table-non-table.

In other cases, reflective engagements that were interpretive illustrated a form of creative rethinking of everyday encounters, such as Tim's reflections on the relief he found in how Photobox's subdued background quality produced a distinctly different character compared to his phone that frequently "pings" him and demands a level of constant attention. Or, how a participant curiously queried the electronic aspect of the table-non-table's stack of paper, which had no obvious switch or interface. We also found mindful intersections led to considerations of creative juxtapositions and self-determined understandings in interpreted relationships among things, such as Heather's momentary attentive reflections on the differences between the Photobox and the nearby gaming consoles. Or, participants' acts of endowing anthropomorphized qualities to the table-non-table as a thing 'hiding' under a couch or 'pretending' to be a present under the Christmas tree.

Ultimately, the unaware nature of Photobox and table-non-table enabled them to be lived-with yet remain open-ended over time. These resulting higher-level qualities appeared crucial to their ability to facilitate routine intersections that eventually accumulated into creative actions and encounters. In earlier empirical work, we saw that common objects could be recast as creative resources to be appropriated [26]. Through our design-oriented approach we have articulated engagements with our design artifacts that go beyond appropriation in ways that are more nuanced and multi-dimensional including creativity that is reflective, mindful, direct, and emergent across complex connections of things and things, and things and people.

Unique ensembles—The creation of ensembles in themselves are a series of intersections that can lead to a unique ecology of computational and analogue things within the home. This occurred as design artifacts became situated to other people, things and the environment through ongoing reconfigurations. We highlighted several such ensembles with the Photobox and table-non-table that were distinct and particular, whether momentary or longstanding. These ensembles exemplified how everyday creativity developed over time as social systems, routines and practices emerged around design artifacts and, in several cases, they became sedimented fixtures in daily life.

Earlier work has focused on a more human-centric notion of uniqueness in which systems and routines formed uniquely as a result of *explicit* human actions [2,16,24,26]. We see our work as expanding this perspective by incorporating the complexities of ensembles and a more distributed set of relations that gives equal prominence to artifacts and the surrounding contexts they help construct and occupy, as it does to human actions. More broadly, the notion of unique ensembles extends works illustrating the value in crafting interaction design artifacts that can drift in and out of perceptual view in the home as relations to them evolve slowly and subtly over time [5,9,14].

Unremarkable creativity—Combining the quality of unawareness with relatively common forms and materials enabled the Photobox and table-non-table to oscillate between being perceived as alien and familiar. Striking this balance was essential in enabling people to creatively speculate on and determine the meaning(s) of these things and their situation to everyday life in an ongoing, unselfconscious manner. Unremarkable creativity in this case led to a range of intersections that spanned the unknowing, the mundane, and the extraordinary.

This feature relates strongly to earlier work that referred to unremarkable affordances as an implication to follow in interaction design [26]. In this prior work the term 'unremarkable' was borrowed from Tolmie et al. [25], who argue for unremarkable computing for everyday routines. The difference with our current work is that while we can design unremarkable attributes into unaware objects, the *unremarkability* often extends beyond the artifact to include the intersections and ensembles that exemplify the type of implicit everyday creativity we aimed to explore and develop. We see the broader relational nature of unremarkable creativity as a means to catalyze future design efforts where choices in form, materials and behavior can be framed in terms of their capacity to be situated to and resonate in a lived-in environment over time.

DESIGN CONSIDERATIONS

Collectively, our findings suggest several considerations for the design of new interaction design artifacts. In what follows, we detail two opportunity areas that emphasize actuality and post-functionality as higher-level strategies to guide future generative work aimed at supporting everyday creativity in the interaction design community.

Emphasizing the actuality of computational objects– As a result of this research we found that designing to emphasize the *actuality* of computational objects presents an intriguing and underexplored strategy for supporting everyday creativity. In referring to the actuality of computational objects we aim to emphasize the material existence of an object. Here the object is not an interface to something else, but an actual thing itself. In fact, unaware objects point to the incompatibility of viewing an artifact simultaneously as an actual thing and as an interface. This was evident in one participant's perception that it was nonsensical for a "pile of paper" to require electricity. Without knowing at the time that the table-non-table moved (hence the electricity), he considered the stack of paper as an interface to turn it on and off. However, this made no sense to him since the table-non-table already existed as an actual thing, "a pile of paper" that did not mediate a reference to anything else. It was also clear that Photobox's lack of a traditional interface shaped its emergence as a distinct material entity that, across households, attained a unique character often perceived as qualitatively different from other domestic technologies.

These examples and others illustrate how emphasizing the actuality of computational objects extends the potential for various kinds of human-technology relations to emerge and shift over time. In our view, a key reason for this is that as a computational object is recognized as a distinct thing in-and-of-itself, the nature of a person's relation to it may extend beyond being predicated solely on its utilitarian value or practical purpose. Over time a person might leverage her competences to draw on the design artifact as a creative resource by putting it to use, or mindfully appreciate the history it's accumulated, or merely consider how it situates within the home, or, forget about it entirely as it fades out of perceptual view within an ensemble.

In designing for the actuality of computational objects we found it was crucial to integrate analog and computational components into a cohesive whole. Our decisions to use common materials and forms were successful in enabling the Photobox and table-non-table to stay relatively within the realm of their familiar analogue cousins, the chest and table. They also catalyzed a range of intersections and engagements that other computational objects in our participants' homes often fell short of achieving.

Collectively, these findings suggest there is a strong need for future research to investigate various ways in which emphasizing actuality in the design of unaware objects (and other interaction design artifacts) can enable them to be drawn on as creative resources over time. Strongly resonant with this direction are recent works that foreground the careful crafting of computational objects such that they bring attention to the objects as distinct material entities [e.g., 5,11]. There is a significant opportunity to build on this research and others that explore materiality more generally [e.g., 8,7, 18] to articulate further the role of actuality as a generative framing mechanism for designing computational artifacts. Our hope is that these related threads of research will nurture future investigations into how materials, form, interaction, and computation come together into fully realized things that mediate relations among objects, environments, and humans (and even non-humans) in rich and ongoing ways. On a deeper level, this opportunity area explores the material basis of computational objects that might lead to more critical consideration for the complex and dynamic nature of human relations to technology in contexts of everyday life and, as we explored, everyday creativity.

Leveraging post-functionality in unaware objects–The design of contemporary domestic technologies is often tied to their functional means to support people, often in terms of circumscribed purposes or applications. While unaware objects are designed with people in mind, their functionality differs significantly and is not dependent on human interaction, attention or presence. They do function, yet in ways that provoke people to work towards their own understandings or uses of unaware objects within their own everyday lives and environments. In this way, they exhibit a type of post-functionality that critically contrasts more traditional human-centric approaches.

Nonetheless, the post-functionality embodied in our unaware objects produced complex effects as evidenced by how they were intersected with, contemplated, reconfigured, and drawn on in implicit yet growingly unique and creative ways. The decision to create design artifacts devoid of any discernable interface that inhibited people's control over their computational behaviors proved to be a viable strategy. It provided a means for avoiding over-determining the artifacts' computational use, purpose, or place among the households they were situated in.

Additionally, the conceptualization of computation as intermittent and infrequent in our unaware objects brought issues of temporality to the forefront—it emphasized that 'functionality' was emergent over time rather than on demand. As intersections accumulated, our design artifacts were continually reconfigured and their character became expressed through their temporal form [13]. Unaware objects take a modest step toward giving shape to the design space of post-functionality as a resource for everyday creativity. We see this opportunity area as in parallel to other critical approaches in interaction design, including counterfunctionality [17] and zensign [22] and, more broadly, the rich history of leveraging ambiguity as a resource for provoking dynamic, varied, and speculative interpretations of a design artifact [6,19]. The works on ambiguity and openness reveals how usability is independent of the meaning of artifacts similar to how functionality in unaware objects can serve indeterminate variations of everyday creativity.

CONCLUSION

This paper has described and synthesized details of the design and deployment of the Photobox and table-non-table. Our aim was to build on and move beyond prior empirical works on everyday creativity through the making and situating of these interaction design research artifacts. An array of tightly related concepts were surfaced and articulated through our analysis in support of this goal. These include *unaware objects*, *intersections*, and *ensembles*. We interpreted these notions in the context of prior works' implications for everyday creativity, which highlighted how, over time, unaware objects can function as creative resources, accumulate intersections, manifest unique ensembles, and, ultimately, support unremarkable creativity. We concluded with two opportunity areas that emphasized *actuality* and *post-functionality* as strategies for critically framing future design-oriented research in the HCI and interaction design communities. As focus in the C&C community increasingly expands to everyday life, we hope this research will inspire future investigations into a more implicit and incremental type of everyday creativity.

ACKNOWLEDGMENTS

Many thanks to Abigail Sellen, Richard Banks, David Kirk, Tim Regan, and Mark Selby for their help on the Photobox project, and the Everyday Design Studio for its work on the table-non-table. This work is supported in part by a Banting Fellowship, and grants from SSHRC and NSERC.

REFERENCES

1. Alexander, C. (1964). Notes on the synthesis of form. Harvard University Press.

2. Desjardins, A., Wakkary, R. (2013). Manifestations of everyday design: guiding goals and motivations. *Proc. of C&C '13*, 253-262.

3. Dix, A. (2007). Designing for Appropriation. *Proc. of BCS-HCI '07*, vol 2., 27-30.

4. Fallman, D. (2011). The new good: exploring the potential of philosophy of technology to contribute to human-computer interaction. *Proc. of CHI '11*, 1051-1060.

5. Gaver, W. et al. (2013). Indoor weather stations: investigating a ludic approach to environmental HCI through batch prototyping. Proc. of CHI '13, 3451-3460.

6. Gaver, W., Beaver, J., Benford, S. (2003). Ambiguity as a Resource for Design. *Proc. of CHI '03*, 233-240.

7. Gross, S., Bardzell, J., Bardzell, S. (2014). Structures, Forms and Stuff: the materiality and medium of interaction. *Pers Ubi. Comput*, 18, 637–649.

8. Gross, S., Bardzell, J., Bardzell, S. (2013). Touch Style: Creativity in Tangible Experience Design. *Proc. of C&C '13*, 281-290.

9. Hallnäs, L., Redström, J. (2001). Slow technology–designing for reflection. *Pers. Ubi. Comput.*, 5 201-212.

10. Jacucci, G., Wagner, I. (2007). Performative Roles of Materiality for Collective Creativity. *Proc. of C&C '07*.

11. Jarvis, N., Cameron, D., Boucher, A. (2012). Attention To Detail: Annotations of a Design Process. *Proc. of NordiCHI '12*, 11-20.

12. Marathe, S., Sundar, S. (2011). What drives customization? control or identity? *Proc. of CHI '11*, 781-790.

13. Maze, R., Redström, J. (2005). Form and the computational object. *Digital Creativity*, 16, 1, 7-18.

14. Odom, W., Sellen, A., Banks, R., Kirk, D., Regan, T., Selby, M., Forlizzi, J., Zimmerman, J. (2014). Designing for Slowness, Anticipation and Re-visitation: A Long Term Field Study of the Photobox. *Proc. of CHI '14*, 1961-1970.

15. Odom, W., Zimmerman, J., Forlizzi, J. (2014). Placelessness, Spacelessness, and Formlessness: Experiential Qualities of Virtual Possessions. *Proc. of DIS '14*, 985-994.

16. Odom, W., Pierce, J., Stolterman, E., Blevis, E. (2009). Understanding Why We Preserve Some Things and Discard Others in the Context of Interaction Design. *Proc. of CHI '09*, 1053-1062.

17. Pierce, J., Paulos, E. (2014). Counterfunctional things: exploring possibilities in designing digital limitations. *Proc. of DIS '14*, 375-384.

18. Rosner, D., Ryokai, K. (2009). Reflections on Craft: Probing the Creative Process of Everyday Knitters. *Proc. of C&C*, 195-204.

19. Sengers, P., Gaver, W. (2006). Staying open to interpretation: engaging multiple meanings in design and evaluation. *Proc. of DIS '06*, 99-108.

20. Shove, E., Pantzar, M., Watson, M. (2012). *The Dynamics of Social Practice and How it Changes*. Sage.

21. Stolterman, E., Wiberg, M. (2010). Concept-driven interaction design research. *HCI Journal*, 25(2), 95-118.

22. Tatar, D., Lee, J., Alaloula, N. (2008). Playground games: a design strategy for supporting and understanding coordinated activity. *Proc. of DIS '08*, 68-77.

23. Tanggaard, L. (2013). The sociomateriality of creativity in everyday life. *Culture and Psychology, 19*, 1, 20-32.

24. Taylor, A., Swan, L. (2005). Artful Systems in the Home. *Proc. of CHI '05*, 641-650.

25. Tolmie, P., Pycock, J., Diggins, T., MacLean, A. and Karsenty, A. (2002). Unremarkable computing. *Proc. of CHI '02*, 399-406.

26. Wakkary, R., Maestri, L. 2007. The resourcefulness of everyday design. *Proc. of C&C '07*, 163-172.

27. Zimmerman, J., Forlizzi, J., Evenson, S. (2007). Research through design as a method for interaction design research in HCI. *Proc. of CHI '07*, 493-502.

Building Support Tools to Connect Novice Designers with Professional Coaches

Daniel Rees Lewis, Emily Harburg, Elizabeth Gerber, Matthew Easterday
Delta Lab
Northwestern University
Evanston, IL 60208, US
{daniel.rees.lewis, eharburg}@u.northwestern.edu, {egerber, easterday}@northwestern.edu

ABSTRACT

Creativity support tools help learners undertake creative work, such as facilitating coaching by creative professionals. How might we design creativity support tools that increase learners' access to coaching by creative professionals? This study took place in an extracurricular project-based learning program where students were co-located, and met professional coaches face-to-face once a week but otherwise communicated online. To test an online creativity support tool called the Loft and investigate coach-student communication we collected data from 47 interviews, online log data and field observations. We found that (a) explicit help-seeking was rare outside of meetings, (b) help from professionals was highly-valued but not sought out, and (c) online systems could surface learner struggles and trigger help-giving. Our findings suggested that online creativity platforms can support professional coaching through: (1) structured virtual updates (2) coach thanking, (3) Computer-Supported Group Critique, (4) disclosure of expertise, and (5) help-seeking training.

Author Keywords

Help-seeking, novice teams, coaching, mentoring, networked learning

ACM Classification Keywords

H.5.3 [Group & Organization Interfaces]: Computer-supported cooperative work, Web-based interaction

INTRODUCTION

Learning to do creative work is challenging. Creativity entails individual creating something they have never created before [1]. A vital component in supporting learners in creative endeavors is to foster help-giving and receiving with those who have relevant experience – peers, teachers, and coaches. While teachers and peers are on-hand within crea-

C&C '15, June 22 - 25, 2015, Glasgow, United Kingdom
© 2015 ACM. ISBN 978-1-4503-3598-0/15/06···$15.00
DOI: http://dx.doi.org/10.1145/2757226.2757248

tive support environments at schools and universities, connecting creative professionals (who have relevant experience) to learners is far more challenging because of issues of proximity, scheduling, and differing expectations. Creativity support tools can help connect learners with creative professionals, and draw upon their expertise.

Creative support tools offer the chance for more learners to have a higher level of support for the same educational resources. While MOOCs have successfully increased access to educational resources, such as bringing lectures to large numbers of learners [26], learners undertaking creative tasks also need support through collaboration and connection with those with relevant expertise. The history of educational technology shows that increased access does not necessarily increase learning. Bain argues that despite promises of "dramatic improvement in teaching and learning for all students" and the largely successful efforts to bring about 1:1 student-to-computer ratio in schools, the movement "failed to demonstrate attributable, scalable and sustainable learning effects in education" (p. 7) [2]. Rather, what is important is for creativity support tools is to promote successful educational practices for creative learners.

Two such effective educational practices include project-based learning [4] and receiving help from an expert human coach [16]. Pedagogical approaches, such as project-based learning, recommend building longer term help-giving and -seeking relationships between learners and expert human coaches, as the coach can give higher quality help if they have knowledge of the project [4, 5, 32].

In this study we look to build on existing literature on creative support tools by focusing on the interactions between students and professionals acting as project coaches. We believe that this is an important area to pursue as professionals can bring valued expertise to learners, but are a different type of stakeholder with different set of motivations than teachers or peers. As such this brings a different set of considerations when designing creativity support. Following this, we ask h*ow might we create online tools that support help-giving and -seeking practices between learners and professional expert coaches in project-based creative learning environments?*

BACKGROUND

Orchestrating Project-based Learning Environments

Project-based learning (PBL) is a resource-intensive educational approach [5, 6]. Learners work in teams to create an original solution to a problem. The solution takes the form of "advice or a product that answer a - research or practice - question" (p. 62) [16]. Project-based learning is an organizing principle for the design of learning environments [4], and gives educators the chance to challenge learners with authentic problems to encourage experience and modes of thinking aligned with real-world creative work [27]. Teams are paired with coaches who help the team throughout the project. One challenge of scaling project-based learning environments is building capacity in educational institutions [4]. In this work we examine the challenges and propose solutions for building creativity support tools that foster connections between learners and coaches who are paired together over the course of a project.

Coaching

Receiving help from an expert coach is one of the most powerful educational interventions [3]. In educational institutions, teachers traditionally play the role of help-giver. Creativity support tools offer the chance to include professional coaches who typically cannot be included in educational institutions [9, 28]. By professional coaches we mean industry professionals who are not the primary educator in a given learning environment. That is, professionals whose expertise is relevant to the project team (e.g. user researcher or product designer), rather than those whose primary job is to work as a coach in industry. Tapping into a network of professional with relevant industry experience can widen the pool of expertise available in learning environments. Professional coaches have expertise that peers and many teachers do not. It is important to note that professional coaches are different from teachers, in that they don't hold power through grades, or other performance reviews. Rather, coaches provide help when prompted through routine meetings or learner-initiated help-seeking. Coaching is a form of "on demand" and "adaptive" education, helping a learner complete a project that may otherwise be too hard [32]. Coaches and learners meet to review work, and create a plan for future work [32]. In recent years a number of innovative pre-professional educational programs for creative work that provide learners with expert coaches have emerged. Examples include robotics competitions and civic innovation clubs [15].

Help Tools

A number of other approaches have used technology to create more effective pedagogical help-giving approaches, such as peer formative feedback and cognitive tutors. In peer formative feedback similar-status learners consider and comment on the work of their peers in order to improve work and increase learning [30]. While socio-technical systems have been shown to gather valued feedback [11], and improve learning [8], peers by definition have limited knowledge in comparison to professionals. Likewise, cog-

nitive tutors provide step-level feedback and have shown to produce learning gains rivaling that of one-on-one human coaching across many domains that do not initially seem well-defined [31]. However, cognitive tutors are unable to support learners in many aspects of creative work, such as when it is not possible to predict the activities that learners will undertake, such as in non-specific goal tasks [32].

The HCI community has created many tools that support help-seeking and -giving in multiple contexts. Prior work has demonstrated that online help-seeking tools can assist learners sourcing relevant examples of others' work. For example, Blueprint, an interface that provides sample code to programmers, was shown to help users write code [6]. Other web-based technical support tools, such as Lemon-Aid, assist learners with finding help through asking them to select elements of a task that they are confused about and connect them with answers to frequently asked questions [7]. This work provides help by tailoring search to specific needs. Other tools, such as Aardvark, have been created to pinpoint specific people within the user's network who can answer questions [18]. However, these systems either cannot help learners outside a narrow domain, and so cannot be adaptive to the vicissitudes of creative projects, or take into account that learners don't always seek help as they don't know to or feel comfortable asking for help.

Help-Seeking

Tools can connect learners to currently untapped expertise. Individuals are often willing to provide help when they know they have relevant and rare knowledge to contribute [22]. To enlist professional coaches creativity support tools must support (academic) help-seeking and -giving.

Help-seeking is defined by Nelson-Le Gall [14] as having the following stages in which individuals:

1. **Recognize the Need for Help:** by realizing that their available resources are insufficient to achieve a task.
2. **Decide to Seek Help:** which may *not* occur. For example they may decide the costs of help-seeking are too high (e.g. loss of face), which is affected by the availability of online channels and self-esteem [20].
3. **Choose Type of Help Sought:** such as advice on how to conduct user testing on an educational design.
4. **Identify and Select Helpers:** including both person or informational resources [25] that can provide help.
5. **Enlist Helper:** by persuading the helper to provide help, a form of "social problem solving" [14].
6. **Evaluate Responses:** by judging the success of the help-seeking. May result in further help-seeking.

Nelson-Le Gall's framework gives an overview of help-seeking. Work from Hrastinski [19] shows that experienced peer coaches often find it hard to gauge learner expertise, and as a result how to help them. If we are to integrate expert coaches in creative support environments, we need a more complete understanding of the help-seeking and -giving relationships.

DESIGN MOTIVATION

In this study we aimed to: (a) test a novel professional coach-learner communication tool, (b) investigate coach-learner interactions, (c) develop a model to describe what mechanisms affect help interactions, and (d) begin to develop design principles based upon this model to inform future creativity support tools. This work contributes to the design of creativity support tools that support coach-learner interactions in creative support environments.

To start we wanted to examine how the following set of established design principles succeeded or failed to support help-seeking (both on- and offline) in a creative project-based learning environment. In this environment learners were all co-located in the same physical design studio space, typically meeting coaches face-to-face once a week, but otherwise communicating with coaches online. As our goal was exploratory for the purpose of building theory, this implementation represents a minimally designed system:

a) **Making Project Thinking Visible: Project Storyboards:** Making learner thinking visible is an established way to support help-givers such as teachers [9]. Storyboards are templates that prompt learners to summarize key aspects of the project (e.g. the challenge, key stakeholders, context, proposed creative solution) to help educators and peers understand the learners project [21]. Software that organizes learner work allows educators to browse (e.g. [21]) and supports their ability to give feedback more frequently [12,13]. For example, Kolodner [21] used storyboarding software to help middle-school students share their vehicle design projects in a physical sciences class. Motivated *a) Design Canvas* (see Systems, next section).

b) **Making Project Thinking Visible: Computer Supported Formative Feedback Routines:** Feedback routines are another way to make learner thinking visible. Formative feedback is a powerful form of help that can assist with learning [16]. We define feedback as a specific form of help directed at specific work [16], especially when iterating on creative work. Giving learners the opportunity to pose questions to direct the help they want on work in progress can illicit a great deal of feedback [11]. Project teams of learners in educational institutions [11] and practitioners [10] value these feedback routines. One advantage of these socio-technical systems is that they can structure interactions and create a record that supports review by help-givers [17]. Motivated *b) Computer-Supported Group Critique* (see *Systems*, next section).

c) **Making Plans and Actions Visible: Computer Supported Task Setting:** A key role for coaches is to both monitor and suggest learner activities [32]. Understanding what learners are doing is an additional challenge for professional coaches who, unlike teachers, are rarely in the same location as learners. Regularly reflecting upon and setting project goals is a vital task in projects. Motivated the *c) Workbench* (see Systems, next section).

In this paper we focus on how these design principles might work with a coach-learner rather than teacher-learner or learner-learner relationship. While both coaches and teachers give help to learners, coaches are under less obligation to ensure work is completed and do not have formal power over the learner in the form of grades and reports. We predicted that implementing these principles would lead to profitable coach-learner interactions.

SYSTEM

We implemented the design principles described above using an exploratory online creativity support platform, the Loft, designed to support project-based learning environments. The Loft platform currently has over 1000 active users. To support creative learners, the Loft attempts to distribute the pedagogical tasks associated with project work (e.g. critiquing and help-seeking) amongst learners, while maintaining the depth of practice, thus reducing the orchestration challenge faced by educators. To support communication between coaches and learners we created the Loft Project Page that included the following features:

a) **Design Canvas (Project Storyboard):** the Design Canvas is an online page that outlines the key aspects of the project, created to help make learners thinking visible (influenced by the Business Model Canvas [24] and Storyboards [21]). The page is available to browse by all members of the program. Based upon reviewing project-based learning literature, the research teams own expertise in teaching and researching, and expert review, we selected ten key aspects for the teams to define. These aspects were: a 'How can we' statement (framed the creative challenge the team were solving), Team (expertise), Context, Partners and Stakeholders, Users, Design Process they were applying, Project Goals, User Experience (how the team envisage users interacting with their solution), Potential Solutions (descriptions of the creative solutions being considered), and Testing (testing plan or results).

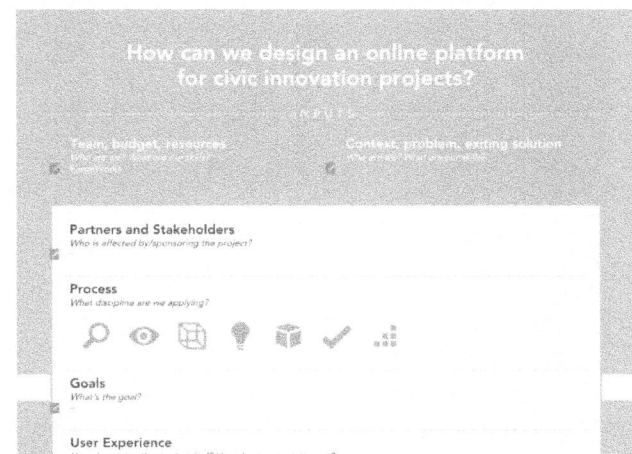

Figure 1: Design Canvas

b) **Computer-Supported Group Critique:** Computer-Supported Group Critique is a facilitated routine and system designed to give learners project feedback and make learner thinking visible. The critique system includes: (a) a write-first script (those giving feedback write their feedback into a system during a short presentation, and before a following verbal feedback session); (b) question prompts written by the project team; (c) written comments; (d) public, near-immediate, threaded commenting; and (e) anonymous up- and down-voting [11]. The critique interface contained question prompts (prepared by the team) relating to the presenting design team's work. Each question prompt allowed threaded commenting (depth of 1 reply) that was public to everyone in the program. Participants could up or down vote the comments of others.

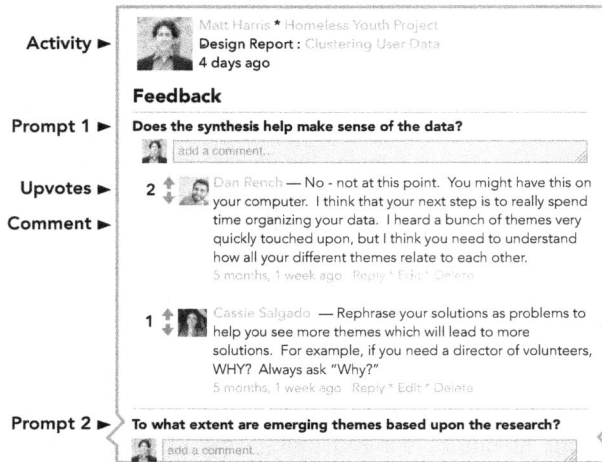

Figure 2: Computer Supported Group Critique

c) **Workbench:** A space for teams to post high-level goals ["Initiatives"] paired with short-term goals ["Tasks"]. For each task, learners could outline the location, owner, and due date for each task. Coaches could view these goals to understand the team's activities.

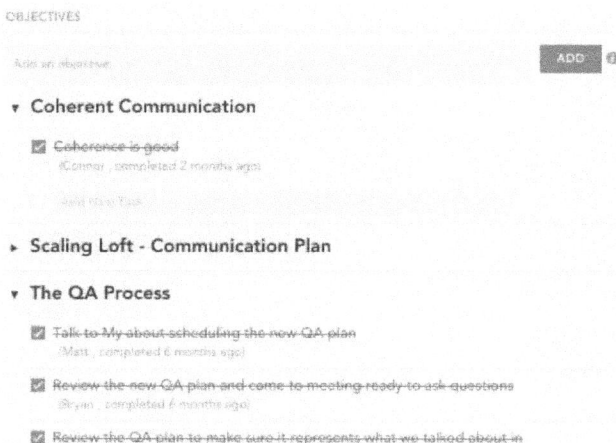

Figure 3: Workbench

METHODS

This study is part of a larger design-based research initiative to design creativity support tools to teach design to students throughout the US. The purpose of this stage was to create a working model that supported coach-learner

interactions. To this end we conducted an observational study to investigate the context and how learners and coaches responded to the tool. In this section we describe the research *setting*, the *intervention*, and the *data collection* and *analysis* we conducted throughout the study.

Setting. The study took place at one location within the Design for America (DFA) network. DFA is an extracurricular program at 21 universities across the US [15], with 5 full-time members of staff, and 800 university student members who participate in teams each year. Learners work in project teams to identify local challenges and design products or services to meet these challenges. In the previous year, DFA received 127 offers to coach teams from creative professionals via their online interest form. However, they only engaged 9 of these coaches because the time it took staff to orchestrate the coach-learner relationship.

We conducted this research at one DFA site in which students undertook an intensive 6-week extra-curricular summer program located at a university design institute. All student teams worked within the same physical studio, and coaches typically came to the space for 2 hours each week for coaching sessions, but otherwise communicated with teams online. Students received no course credit or pay. An experienced undergraduate served as the program facilitator and was available 9am-5pm each day. This site was rare in the network, as the program engaged professional coaches, but had no full-time staff member orchestrating the program or the coach-learner relationship. However the lack of full-time teaching support made this site an ideal setting for studying how creativity support tools function with minimal orchestration.

In the DFA teams of 4-5 university students create solutions (products and services) that solve real-world social challenges selected by program developers. The project teams' challenges were animal rights in animal shelters, bed-bugs in low-income housing, and under-utilized school gardens in education. Teams are not restricted to a particular solution, rather are expected to create an original solution based on their investigations and understanding of the problem and context. The undergraduate program facilitator paired each team with 1-to-2 professional coaches and with a local non-profit client organization.

The undergraduate program facilitator coordinated weekly skills training workshops led by professional designers from the community for all design teams. Teams met (primarily face-to-face) with their coaches for two hours each week over the six-week period. Coaches also agreed to give an extra 2 hours per week in communicating (online) with teams as needs arose. Team members worked approximately 40 hours a week on their projects.

Participants. The study involved thirteen undergraduates between 19-23 years old at a private Midwestern university. Participants majored or double majored in engineering (10), social sciences (3), and humanities (2), and included 5 freshmen, 4 sophomores, 3 juniors, and 1 senior (54% female). Twelve of the 13 student participants had no formal training in design or similar creative fields. All participants used the Internet daily.

Coaches: The study involved 5 creative professional coaches who worked in the neighboring city to the research site (40-60 minutes travel time). Coaches were between 35-60 years old. All coaches had over 10 years of relevant professional experience (design research, product design, service design), and their primary job was in industry. Coaches also had a range of experience as adjunct professors (1, 3, 4, 6, and 11 years). None of these adjunct positions were at the university where the study took place. All coach participants used the Internet daily. Coaches were recruited by the student facilitator from a roster of volunteers from the program's interest form.

Intervention. We conducted a face-to-face demo of the Design Canvas and Workbench to each team of students for 30 minutes on the first day of the program. A researcher sat with the each team around a laptop, presented functionality, and answered questions.

Design Canvas. On the first day of the program and two days before both mid- and final- review presentations, one of the researchers advised teams to update the design canvas. They were also advised to have weekly conversations with their team to define and re-define the key categories as their project developed.

Computer-Supported Group Critique Sessions. The student facilitator ran critique sessions. Critique sessions involved all student participants, the student facilitator, and members of the design community (between 0-1 design professors and between 5-6 design undergraduates and graduate students). There was no expectation for the coaches to attend. Only one coach attended a critique session in-person during the first week. During weeks 4-6 the Loft sent out email notifications from the site to the coaches when feedback was given online.

Workbench. On the first day of the program a graduate student researchers advised teams that (a) they could use the Workbench to set and assign goals, and (b) the Workbench was one way to keep the coach up-to-date.

Data collection. We conducted observations and in-person interviews to understand what occurred within the environment (both off- and online). We observed the studio for 5 hours each week, taking notes on how the designers and coaches interacted with each other and the system. We kept in close contact with the student facilitator to understand the challenges the teams were facing.

We conducted 38 semi-structured individual face-to-face interviews (30-55 minutes) with students on their project work, experience interacting with coaches and use of the

system. Each student was interviewed 3 times, other than one student who was interviewed twice. We conducted 9 semi-structured individual face-to-face interviews (45-65 minutes) with coaches on their coaching strategies, interactions with their team, and use of the system. Each coach was interviewed twice, other than one coach who was interviewed only once. We amended our protocol as themes emerged. An example theme was coaches monitoring team (non-)actions following coach advice. For part of each interview we returned to the online system to clarify responses and aid the recollection of the participants. We scheduled interviews with each student every 2 weeks for students, and each coach in the 2nd and 6th (final) week of the program.

We transcribed all interviews immediately following the interview, resulting in more than 800 pages of transcripts. We used the field notes, transcriptions, and data log to crosscheck emerging themes.

Analysis. We treated the design of the system as a *pre-structured case* [23], meaning we derived categories in our coding scheme based on existing theories (for help-process and systems motivation) and then added nuance to, amended and developed new categories as we analyzed the data. We analyzed the interview transcriptions for themes based around Nelson-Le Gall's help process [14], while also looking for other themes that might compliment or contradict this process. Analysis occurred during data collection, allowing us to alter our data collection to better capture emerging themes that we had not predicted. First level coding identified 550 instances of 27 codes describing how the system provided and failed to provide support. We then iterated between first level coding and open coding to cluster these codes into 17 conceptual categories pertinent to learner-coach communication. We formalized our findings as a process diagram (see *Figure 4*) with descriptive narrative. To refine our theory and resolve researcher disagreement we checked the model against our data and existing research.

RESULTS

Systems that connect learners with professional coaches must support complex help interactions that can break down in a number of ways. The first aim of the study was to build on existing models of help-seeking by extending these models to the realm of online creativity support tools. We found that help seeking interactions occurred primarily through two routes: (1) highly explicit help-seeking, and (2) unsolicited help giving in response to learner disclosure about their project, as well as by mixtures of the *two. We describe the process model and related evidence in this section.* The titles A)-Q) in italics correspond with *Figure 4*. Table 1 summarizes the Participant IDs (PIDs) across roles and teams.

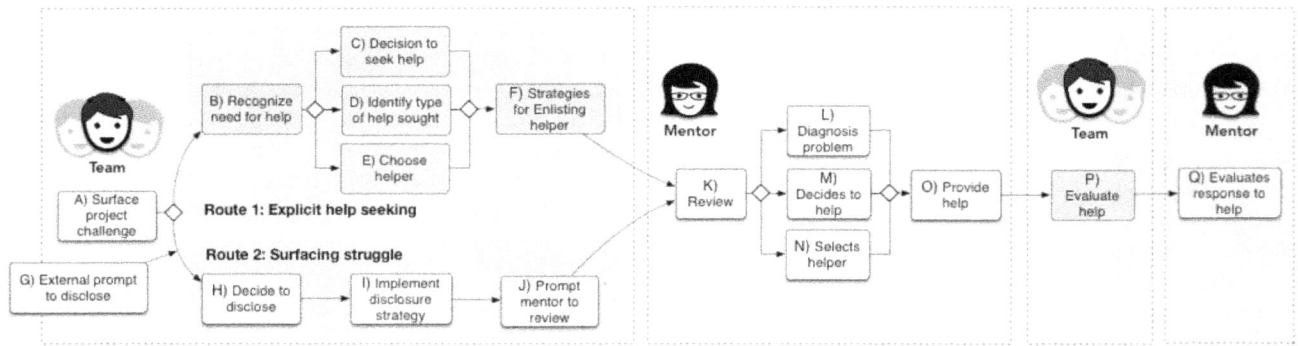

Figure 4: Help-seeking and –giving model

	Team 1	Team 2	Team 3
Challenge	under-utilized school gardens in education	Animal rights in animal shelters	bed-bugs in low-income housing
Student PIDs	11, 12, 13, 14	21, 22, 23, 24, 25	31, 32, 33, 34
Coach PIDs	41	42.1, 42.2	43.1, 43.2

Table 1: Summary of Participant IDs (PIDs)

(A) Surface project challenges (learners): As learners worked on their projects they would surface aspects of their project that they perceived needed attention. This was a different state than *awareness for need for help* described by Nelson-Le Gall's process [15]. Teams would work together and discuss these issues. For example, PID 22 reported on the discussion the team had when they realized older cats weren't reacting to their pet care device as expected: *"We've started to hit some bumps in the road … …I think there have been a lot of conversations we've had as a team there and we've just kind of been working through and trying to come up with a landing point that we all feel competent in."* All teams reported having these types of discussions between two (PID 23) and five (PID 31) times a week.

Route 1: Explicit help-seeking

(B) Recognize need for help (learners): As expected, learners and coaches did not always agree that learners needed help. *Learner awareness for need for help* can be thought of as a learner generated prompt that they should seek help from a source outside of the team. Learners reported that outside of meetings they didn't need the coach's help (PID 11, 13, 14, 21, 22, 25, 32, 33). When discussing contacting coaches outside of the meeting PID 32 stated that: *"I feel just because we don't need it too much in the end."* Conversely, coaches reported that learners were often not aware that they needed help (PID 41, 42.1 42.2, 43.1). As PID 42.1 states: *"they don't even always recognize that they need help."*

(C) Decision to seek help (learners): While learners might recognize they need help, this does not guarantee that they will seek help [15]. The coaches perceived that learners

were sometimes aware that they needed help, but found it difficult to ask (PID 41, 42.1, 42.2, 43.1). PID 43.1 reported *"I think [the learners]… …don't like to fail, they don't like to admit it."* A number of learners stated that they didn't ask for help on an issue that the team had discussed and had differing views on (PID 11, 12, 22, 24, 25, 31, 32). Specifically, they felt that asking for help from the coaches could create divisions within the team. PID 22 described this situation: *"But I feel like I don't necessarily want to be asking for advice [from the coach] …because I feel like then it gets into this like debate where whoever presents the information in the best way or makes the most compelling or convincing argument kind of wins there… …it feels like an 'us' versus 'them' type situation".* The majority of learners also expressed that they were very comfortable reaching out to the coach outside of meetings (PID 13, 14, 21, 22, 23 25, 31, 34).

(D) Identify type of help sought & E) Identifying helpers (learners): Help-seekers have a sense of the type of help that they need, and who or what can help them. Both coaches (PID 41, 42.1, 43.1) and learners (PID 11, 12, 25, 31, 34) reported that learners struggled to articulate questions to coach. PID 41 (coach) noted: *"I want them to have more specific questions prepared but I know that like that's hard."* (Coaches can however diagnose problems and give help based on these less complete questions, expanded upon in *L) Coach Diagnoses Problem*).

Learners were at times unaware of coach expertise, and reported discounting coach as a source for help. For example, learners in one team reported that their coach could not help them in testing their product, when in fact one of their coaches had 22 years experience in user product testing. Learners in another team perceived that their coaches could not help them with their educational intervention designed to train and bring a sense of trust in community housing affected by bed bugs, while their coach had 18 years experience as an educator and 12 years as a community organizer.

(F) Strategies for enlisting helper (learners): When asked most learners did not report using strategies for help seeking. Some learners (PID 11, 12, 23, 34) reported preparing questions for the coach before they met. In terms of the

channel for enlisting help, learners favored asking for help in meetings. They reported perceiving asynchronous forms of communication (email and Loft) as feeling "inefficient" as it would take too long to write an email and wait for a reply (PID 11, 12, 14, 25, 31).

P) Evaluation of help (learners): All learners reported that interactions with their coach(es) were helpful. They identified that meetings reduced the anxiety they were feeling [PID 11, 21 24, 25, 34], increased confidence they felt in their project because of coach expertise [PID 11, 12, 31, 32, 34], and helped the team to be motivated and "energized" (PID 22) after meetings (PID 23, 33, 25). Teams noted that they had a clear plan of action after coach meetings thanks to coach help, leading to the team being more effective (PID 13, 22, 23, 24, 31, 32, 34). As PID 12 stated *"after meeting with her we have like such a clear sense of like objectives and we have like her expert opinion on like what to do next, so we have like a lot of momentum."* Furthermore, learners reported that coaches helped them think through what they perceived as challenging and important decisions (PID 11, 12, 14, 21, 22, 25, 31, 32). As PID 32 notes *"sometimes when we have conflicting ideas… …and they'll help us like work through it. So yeah, the coaches have been pretty helpful with that."*

Help Giving Process

(G) External prompting to disclosure: In meetings all coaches would prompt learners to talk about their project. As PID 42.2 (coach) stated: *"so they're [meetings] really about sitting down, getting an update, what happened between this time and last time? What today are your big burning issues? Where do you need help?"* Discussing how long coaches would ask questions for, PID 41 (coach) reported: *"So that I would say, me kind of driving it for the first I don't know maybe 45 minutes into an hour of just like "then what?", "then what?", "then what?".* Coaches also encouraged learners to contact them outside of these meetings in two forms. Firstly, at the start of the program all coaches and teams agreed that teams should send out weekly "update emails". Secondly, coaches all encouraged their teams to contact them if they needed help. PID 42.2 (coach) explained he reiterated this each week as he *"never want[s] the team to be like they couldn't reach out to one of us if they needed something".* Learners all reported understanding there was an open invitation to contact their coaches.

(H) Decision to disclose (learners): Learners disclosed significant details about their projects in face-to-face meetings and in update emails. Learners by-and-large rejected the Design Canvas as a prompt for communicating their project with coaches. Teams filled out the Design Canvas on two occasions, in the first week, and in the final week. The Design Canvas was perceived as a summative communication device that felt *"final"* (PID 11, 21, 25, 31, 32, 34), and *"formal"* (PID 14). When discussing why they didn't use the Design Canvas PID 13 *"I feel like [our project] is like a work in progress like we're not fully sure…I want to like put something that's like definite."* This resulted in

learners feeling unmotivated to regularly use the Design Canvas as a communication channel with their coaches.

Similarly, learners largely rejected the Workbench as a way to communicate with the coach. While all teams did use task lists to organize their work, they preferred to do so on paper (PID 11, 12, 13, 12, 22, 32, 33) and did not perceive value in the coach seeing what they did (PID 14, 23, 33).

(I) Implement disclosure strategy (learners): Once learners decided to communicate information about their project they would employ a certain strategy. In face-to-face coach meetings all learners stated that they would report on their recent activities and their current plans. As PID 23 states *"we catch her up on what we've been doing and then we kind of end our spiel with, "And this is what we have planned for today."* In meetings learners would also sometimes prepare questions regarding what course of action to take (PID 12, 14, 22, 33, 34) and describe the pros and cons of different options they were considering. This report differs from how the how coaches describe meetings (as expanded upon in *Prompting Disclosure from coach*) as coaches reported that they were the chief drivers or face-to-face interactions (PID 41, 42.1, 42.2, 43.1) As expanded upon in *Coach Diagnosis* and *Coach Help Strategies*, this disclosure led to interactions that learners found useful (see *P) Learner Evaluates Help*).

Email and Loft disclosure differed from face-to-face disclosure. Teams sent coaches "update emails" 2 or 3 days after their weekly meeting. PID 25 described update emails as explaining *"what we've done this week, this is what we're going to do next week…. …for example like last week it would have been you know, we continued working on the heating and cooling element."* Update emails would not include questions or descriptions of what the team was struggling with (PID 11, 12, 25, 31, 32, 34, 41, 42.1, 43.1). As PID 24 said the emails were *"more of a status update like I don't think we ever really ask questions to them like specific questions."* Rather, learners saw it as a way to keep the coaches aware of what they were doing (PID 11, 12, 13, 14, 22, 24, 25, 31, 33, 34). Analysis of teams update emails found 1 question pertaining to the project out of the 15 emails. As expanded in *(L) Coaches Decision to Help*, these emails did not trigger coach help giving. For Computer-Supported Group Critique teams also prepared 3-7 questions and associated files (e.g. personas, sketches) that they wanted feedback on (when prompted).

(J) Prompt coach to review (learners) & K) Review (coach): Help-givers need to have some prompt to review information, and once prompted can decide whether or not to review. Coaches all reported that they would always review anything that teams disclosed. In the final three weeks of the course when coaches received email notifications to review team Computer-Supported Group Critique (CSGC) online PID 42.1, 42.2, 43.1, and 43.2 reviewed every critique. Coaches also browsed Loft without the team prompting (PID 42.1, 42.2, 43.1, 43.2). However, away

from the meetings coaches did not view it as their responsibility to seek out information about the project. PID 41 stated: *"my role is a responsive one… …if they need me I will respond because that's kind of what I signed up with them… I definitely won't, I mean, you know, seek it out."*

(L) Diagnoses problem and *(M) Decides to help (coach)*: In theory it is not always certain that help-givers will always give help. For example, helpers might decide that they don't have time to help. In meetings coaches diagnosed a range of problems, such as: (a) teams being emotionally "down" (b) lack of clarity around goals (all coaches).

When reviewing team disclosure on the Loft, participants had mixed reactions to the different channels (see Table 1). Coaches reported that reviewing the Design Canvas did not help with diagnosis, or trigger help giving (PID 41, 42.1, 43.1). When discussing the Design Canvas PID 41 reported *"I mean, this is sort of like what we did on day one… …I mean there's nothing here that's like, I need to know. Sort of like, a little bit basic.".* Likewise, on reviewing the Workbench coaches noted that while it gave them more detail about the project (PID 42.1, 43.1), it didn't give the type of information that the coach would be looking for to give help (PID 41, 42.1, 43.1). Furthermore, PID 42.1 also noted that she wouldn't know if her help was needed as if teams didn't use the Workbench daily it would be out of date: *"So it feels like it's outdated. Just because they move so quickly… …every day they have different stuff".*

Communication Channel	Team Use	Coach Use
Design Canvas	Limited use as it felt too "final" and "formal" for the to use regularly.	Did not trigger help interactions as felt too "basic", even when up-to-date.
Computer Supported Group Critique	Generated questions each week around areas they wanted help on.	When prompted by the system gave team help either on line, or followed up during face-to-face meeting.
Workbench	Limited as no perceived value of coach seeing specific goals.	No use due to lack of team use. Coaches felt information was "outdated".
Update email	Sent weekly emails but rarely included questions or details of team struggles or decisions	Did not trigger coach replies. Emails viewed as "non-actionable".

Table 2: Summary of communication channel use

Update emails also failed to trigger coach help-giving. No coach reported responding to these emails by giving the team help. Referring to one email PID 43.2 said: *"It was not specific questions. It was here we put up some new things interesting your thoughts, but no it was more of a passive role [for him], I felt."* Similarly PID 41 (coach) noted: *"They sent me that email and I was kind of like, it just wasn't an email that even been merited to response. I was so busy I was like "okay, great to know". But if they had added a question I would have totally responded. But it was like a non-actionable".*

(N) Selects helper (coach): While coaches mostly reported only their own help-giving activities, they also reported considering others who could help their team. Coaches who worked in pairs reported that they would were aware of their partners expertise, and so they took over help-giving accordingly (PID 43.1, 43.2, 42.1, 42.2). As PID 43.2 said: *"[PID 43.1] and I seem to work just very comfortably… ….if she is strong in that area, I could kind of sit back and let her be strong in that area. And if I have something to offer to your show probably reciprocate so there were certain areas that I was more engaged."* There was also evidence that coaches were ready to connect their teams with other experts. PID 42.1 and 42.2 offered to connect their team with professional contacts they had should the team want to create a higher fidelity prototype.

(O) Provide help (coach strategies for help): Coaches reported using a range of strategies. In meetings coaches: (a) encouraged teams by praising their project and progress (PID 41, 42.1, 43.1, 43.2), (b) stated choices teams had to help decision making (PID 41, 42.1, 42.2), and (c) helped teams organize and prioritize all the tasks they need to do (all coaches). While doing this coaches also reported that they had an opinion of what they thought the team should do (PID 41, 42.1, 42.2). Throughout the session coaches entered into a dialogue with the learners and expressed "working through it with the teams" (PID 43.2). All coaches reported spending time reaching a consensus with the teams over project plans.

Outside of meetings coaches also gave help on the Computer-Supported Group Critique. Between weeks 4-6 (after automated email notifications were implemented) PID 42.1, 42.2, 43.1, and 43.2 all commented on the system after having seen team questions and peer comments.

(Q) Evaluates response to help (coach): Coaches monitored the help they gave learners. In meetings coaches would ask questions to see if teams had followed their advice (PID 41, 42.1). Coaches reported feeling good about help that was appreciated and improved the project (PID 41, 42.1, 42.2, 43.1). PID 41 (coach) reported on advice she gave a team to recruit teachers to test their educational design: *"They were like "That's a good idea" and then they did it and they were like "Yeah, that was great, everyone signed up" So I was like "Yes"… .. but also like [the help] moved them along and I felt like great about that."* The coaches also recognized that they have limited power with learners in persuading them to follow the advice. As a result when coaches saw teams not following their advice they stopped persuading them and recalibrated their advice.

DISCUSSION
In this study we have sought to illuminate ways to build successful creativity support tools that encourage interactions between learners and professional coaches.

	Feature	Description	Rationale	Evidence
1	Structured Virtual 'Update' Routine	Teams regularly write short report in structured form that prompts disclosure about current challenges and decisions.	Prompts that lead teams to disclose questions and information about project challenges elicit more coach help. Could make help more timely (addresses Route 2).	Learners *were* capable of disclosing information about their project that triggered help giving. See *(J) Prompt coach to review (learners)* & *K) Review (coach)*. They were also prepared to write emails, that served limited purpose, but the coaches did review. See *(H) Decide to disclose*
2	Computer-Support Group Critique (CSGC)	See Systems Description.	The team generated questions and peer feedback could trigger coach help-giving when they reviewed this disclosure. Coaches reviewed.	Once coaches were made aware of CSCG they reviewed it, gave help on the system, and used this to inform help given in meetings. See *(J) Prompt coach to review (learners)* & *K) Review (coach)*
3	Explicit Expertise Disclosure	Coach platform profiles that list expertise, and introduction routine.	The system and related routines should support learners in relating the tasks they are taking on with the expertise of the coach.	Teams struggled to know who they could use their coaches, and were often unaware of their expertise. See *(D) Identify type of help sought & E) Identifying helpers (learners)*
4	Coach thanking & help-review (routine & functionality)	System prompts team to report successful help to coach. Teams inform coaches of result of coach help - system notifies coach.	Coaches monitored the results of their advice, and reported a positive emotional response when their advice was useful.	Coaches monitored the success or their help, and *were* motivated by knowing their help was successful. See *(Q) Evaluates response to help (coach)*
5	Help-seeking instruction	Teams are provided with written instruction on how to work with coaches, including how to prepare for meetings, how to generate questions, and peer examples of questions that trigger help.	Preparation for meetings could significantly improve the quality and quantity of questions for the coach. Furthermore, seeing examples of peers asking for questions could help teams feel more comfortable about help seeking.	Teams struggled explaining the help they wanted. This led to coaches spending a significant amount of time asking questions about their project. Furthermore, some coaches reported teams as unwilling to initiate help seeking. See *(B) Recognize need for help (learners)*, *(C) Decision to seek help (learners)*. Coaches wanted more specific questions from teams. See *(D) Identify type of help sought & E) Identifying helpers (learners)*

Table 3: Suggested directions for future creativity support tools for connecting professionals and students

Most importantly, through this study we found that:

• *Explicit help-seeking outside of face-to-face meetings was ineffective.* Learners face significant barriers to effective help-seeking, especially outside of a face-to-face meeting with coaches. Specifically, learners' greatest challenges were diagnosing the need for help, overcoming the perceived shame of asking for help, formulating help requests, and recognizing that help-givers have relevant expertise. This explains the seemingly paradoxical situation of students reporting that they value coach interactions highly, but do not seek any coach interactions outside of face-to-face meetings. Without coach guidance they did not communicate in ways that triggered coach help-giving. Furthermore, existing online tools did not sufficiently overcome these barriers, even tools designed specifically for project-based learning.

• *Online systems can promote help-giving by surfacing problems and notifying* coaches. When learners used the online peer-critique systems (which automatically notified coaches), coaches were able to diagnose problems from the critique questions written by teams, discussion which triggered help-giving. This shows that prompts for online disclosure can promote help-giving by coaches. It demonstrates how social-technical systems can expand the possible help-seeking routes. These routines need to support student disclose that triggers coach help giving. Such disclosure could include highlighting important team decisions, as well as current team struggles.

The model suggests a number of features that future designs and research might pursue. We present descriptions for these features, rationales, and evidence related to our findings in *Table 3*.

Limitations

The participants in this study were undergraduates, so the issues that arise may differ across age groups. Some of the data in this study was taken from self-reporting from on-going use. Advantages of this approach include collecting both reflective and in situ data; disadvantages include biases from self-report [29]. As an observational study, the causal relationships remain speculative. However, as a theory building exercise, this study provided us with a richer model of the help-giving and help-seeking between learners and coaches that offers detailed and plausible explanations for how and when different systems can support critique.

CONCLUSION

We examined how creativity support tools might allow us to incorporate professional coaches – a currently untapped resource – to provide help. This study contributes to our understanding of creativity support tools in three ways. First, we tested a novel online creativity support platform for student-professional coach interactions. Second, we extended existing help-seeking models by developing a new model that: (1) identifies the challenges learners face in explicit help-seeking that actually arise in creativity support tools, (2) shows how online critique can surfacing problems. Third based on this model, we suggested principles for creativity support tools that scaffold help-seeking that future work might pursue.

Using an existing creativity support tool, this model shows how a range social and software factors influence the help-giving and -seeking process and interventions that can be applied to creativity support environments to support the coach-learner relationship.

ACKNOWLEDGEMENTS
This work supported by the National Science Foundation Grants No. IIS-1320693 and No. IIS-1217225.

REFERENCES

1. Amabile, T.M. *Creativity and innovation in organizations*. Harvard Business School Boston, 1996.
2. Bain, A. *The learning edge: What technology can do to educate all children*. Teachers College Press, 2012.
3. Bloom, B.S. The 2 sigma problem: The search for methods of group instruction as effective as one-to-one tutoring. *Educational researcher,* (1984), 4-16.
4. Blumenfeld, P., Fishman, B.J., Krajcik, J., Marx, R.W. and Soloway, E. Creating usable innovations in systemic reform: Scaling up technology-embedded project-based science in urban schools. *Educational Psychologist 35,* 3 (2000), 149-164.
5. Blumenfeld, P.C., Soloway, E., Marx, R.W., Krajcik, J.S., Guzdial, M. and Palincsar, A. Motivating project-based learning: Sustaining the doing, supporting the learning. *Educational psychologist 26,* 3-4 (1991), 369-398.
6. Brandt, J., Dontcheva, M., Weskamp, M. and Klemmer, S.R. Example-centric programming: integrating web search into the development environment. In *Proceedings of the SIGCHI Conference on Human Factors in Computing Systems.* 2010, 513-522.
7. Chilana, P.K., Ko, A.J. and Wobbrock, J.O. LemonAid: selection-based crowdsourced contextual help for web applications. In *Proceedings of the SIGCHI Conference on Human Factors in Computing Systems.* 2012, 1549-1558.
8. Cho, K. and Schunn, C.D. Scaffolded writing and rewriting in the discipline: A web-based reciprocal peer review system. *Computers & Education 48,* 3 (2007), 409-426.
9. Collins, A., Brown, J.S. and Holum, A. Cognitive apprenticeship: Making thinking visible. *American educator 15,* 3 (1991), 6-11.
10. Cross, N. *Designerly ways of knowing*. Springer, 2006.
11. Easterday, M.W., Rees Lewis, D., Fitzpatrick, C. and Gerber, E.M. Computer supported novice group critique. In *Proceedings of the 2014 conference on Designing interactive systems.* 2014, 405-414.
12. Edelson, D.C., Pea, R.D. and Gomez, L. Constructivism in the collaborator. *Constructivist learning environments: Case studies in instructional design,* (1996), 151-164.
13. Fogarty, J., Au, C. and Hudson, S.E. Sensing from the basement: a feasibility study of unobtrusive and low-cost home activity recognition. *In Proceedings of the 19th annual ACM symposium on User interface software and technology,* (2006), 91-100.
14. Nelson-Le Gall, S. Help-seeking behavior in learning. *Review of research in education,* (1985), 55-90.
15. Gerber, E.M., Marie Olson, J. and Komarek, R.L. Extracurricular design-based learning: Preparing students for careers in innovation. *International Journal of Engineering Education 28,* 2 (2012), 317.
16. Hattie, J. and Timperley, H. The power of feedback. *Review of educational research 77,* 1 (2007), 81-112.
17. Hoadley, C.M. and Bell, P. Web for Your Head: The Design of Digital Resources to Enhance Lifelong-Learning. (1996).
18. Horowitz, D. and Kamvar, S.D. The anatomy of a large-scale social search engine. In *Proceedings of the 19th international conference on World wide web.* 2010, 431-440.
19. Hrastinski, S. and Stenbom, S. Student--student online coaching: Conceptualizing an emerging learning activity. *The Internet and higher education 16,* (2013), 66-69.
20. Kitsantas, A. and Chow, A. College students perceived threat and preference for seeking help in traditional, distributed, and distance learning environments. *Computers & Education 48,* 3 (2007), 383-395.
21. Kolodner, J.L., Owensby, J.N. and Guzdial, M. Case-based learning aids. *Handbook of research on educational communications and technology 2,* (2004), 829-861.
22. Ling, K., Beenen, G., Ludford, P., Wang, X., Chang, K., Li, X., Cosley, D., Frankowski, D., Terveen, L. and Rashid, A.M. Using social psychology to motivate contributions to online communities. *Journal of Computer-Mediated Communication 10,* 4 (2005), 00-00.
23. Miles, M.B. and Huberman, A.M. *Qualitative data analysis: An expanded sourcebook*. Sage, 1994.
24. Osterwalders, A. Business model canvas. (2008).
25. Puustinen, M. and Rouet, J.-F. Learning with new technologies: Help seeking and information searching revisited. *Computers & Education 53,* 4 (2009), 1014-1019.
26. Serverance, C. Teaching the world: Daphne koller and coursera. (2012).
27. Shaffer, D.W. and Resnick, M. Thick" Authenticity: New Media and Authentic Learning. *Journal of interactive learning research 10,* 2 (1999), 195-215.
28. Sloep, P. Redes de aprendizaje, aprendizaje en red. *Comunicar 19,* 37 (2011), 55-64.
29. Spradley, J.P. *Participant observation*. Holt, Rinehart and Winston, New York, 1980.
30. Topping, K. Peer assessment between students in colleges and universities. *Review of Educational Research 68,* 3 (1998), 249-276.
31. VanLehn, K. The relative effectiveness of human tutoring, intelligent tutoring systems, and other tutoring systems. *Educational Psychologist 46,* 4 (2011), 197-221.
32. Van Merriënboer, J.J. and Kirschner, P.A. *Ten steps to complex learning: A systematic approach to four-component instructional design*. Routledge, 2012.

Evaluating TweetBubble with Ideation Metrics of Exploratory Browsing

Ajit Jain[1], Nic Lupfer[1], Yin Qu[1], Rhema Linder[1], Andruid Kerne[1] and Steven M. Smith[2]

[1]Interface Ecology Lab, Dept. of Computer Science and Engineering, Texas A&M University

[2]Dept. of Psychology, Texas A&M University

ajit, nic, yin, rhema, andruid@ecologylab.net, stevesmith@tamu.edu

ABSTRACT

We extend the Twitter interface to stimulate exploratory browsing of social media and develop a creative cognition method to establish its efficacy. *Exploratory browsing* is a creative process in which users seek and traverse diverse and novel information as they investigate a conceptual space. The TweetBubble browser extension extends Twitter to enable expansion of social media associations—`@usernames` and `#hashtags`—in-context, without overwriting initial content. We build on a prior metadata type system, developing new presentation semantics, which enable an integrated look and feel consistent with Twitter.

We show how exploratory browsing constitutes a mini-c creative process. We use prior ideation metrics as a basis for new ideation metrics of exploratory browsing. We conducted a mixed methods crowdsourced study, with data from 54 participants, amidst the 2014 Academy Awards. Quantitative and qualitative findings validate the technique of in-context exploratory browsing interfaces for social media. Their consistency supports the validity of ideation metrics of exploratory browsing as an evaluation methodology for interactive systems designed to promote creative engagement.

Author Keywords

information-based ideation; social media; browsing

ACM Classification Keywords

H.5.2. Information Interfaces and Presentation (e.g. HCI): UI

INTRODUCTION

We develop an exploratory browsing interface for Twitter, *Tweetbubble*, and a creative cognition method to evaluate it. Exploration, be it of the moon or the World Wide Web, is a fundamentally creative endeavor. Creativity researchers identify a spectrum of creative acts, spanning from mini-c to Big-C [21]. They define *mini-c* creativity as, "the novel and personally meaningful interpretation of experiences, actions, and events" [3]. They consider empirical studies of mini-c creativity as essential to supporting learning and expression.

Likewise, according to Boden, exploratory creativity arises through traversing a structured conceptual space [4]. We thus define *exploratory browsing* as a creative process through which users seek and traverse diverse and novel information as they use the web to investigate a topic or conceptual space. Exploratory browsing of a structured conceptual space helps users develop new perspectives [4, 44, 27]. In this paper, we investigate mini-c creativity that arises through experiences with exploratory browsing interfaces.

Evaluation of exploratory browsing interfaces is an interesting research challenge. Kerne et al. derived ideation metrics of curation for measuring creativity in the curation products people assemble through engagement in information-based ideation tasks [22]. They took a creative cognition approach [14], extending methods developed for engineering design [35]. They developed elemental metrics—Fluency, Flexibility / Variety, and Novelty—for measuring creativity in the digital objects that people collect, and holistic metrics—e.g., Emergence and Exposition—for measuring creativity in the whole. Their research addresses the spectrum of mini-c to Big-C ideation activities and resulting creative products.

The present research alternatively investigates processes of mini-c creative ideation in exploratory browsing. As the user does not assemble a whole curation in exploratory browsing, only Kerne et al.'s elemental ideation metrics are applicable. We reformulate these elemental metrics to address creative processes and so derive *ideation metrics of exploratory browsing* for evaluation of exploratory browsing interfaces.

Twitter constitutes a conceptual space for exploratory browsing. The Twitter microblogging service is a vital medium for news, politics, scholarship, and other social discourse [25]. Twitter provides mechanisms for making *social media associations* within a tweet: `#hashtags` are used to collectively organize and categorize social media content on topics, spontaneously creating *folksonomy* [29]; `@username` references enable user-to-user exchanges [18]. Hashtag and username references provide a basis for exploratory browsing.

To support exploratory browsing, we developed the Tweetbubble Chrome extension, which subtly transforms the prior Twitter interface. While the prior interface (Figure 1a) replaces initial content on activating a social media association, Tweetbubble's new affordances (Figure 1b) enable in-context expansion (Figure 2). We *hypothesize* that through this technique, users will explore significantly more diverse and novel perspectives than default Twitter interface users. Compari-

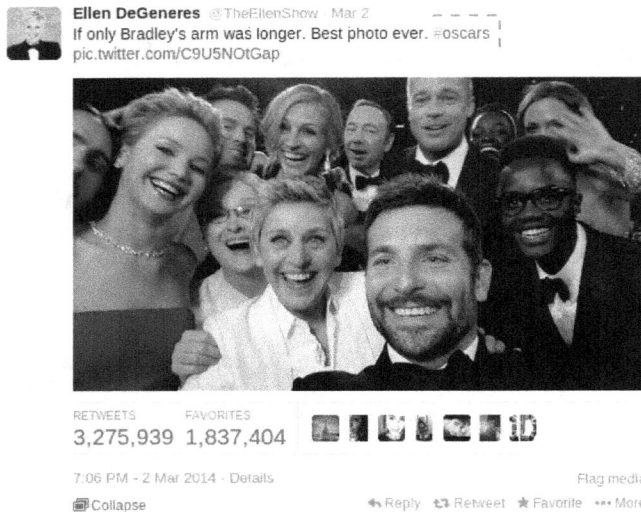

Figure 1. Social media association interfaces for Twitter. (a) Prior Twitter interface. Clicking @username and #hashtag overwrites content in the current window. The user experiences a loss of context. (b) TweetBubble interface prepends expansion affordances (+ sign in circle) to @username and #hashtag associations. Cursor arrow points to Ellen's @username feed association. Dashed lines delimit the hashtag #oscars. Clicking would afford in retrieval and presentation in the current context, without overwriting initially rendered content.

son is performed by applying ideation metrics of exploratory browsing to data from a crowdsourced study.

The present hypothesis and interaction technique are based on recent findings by Qu et al. [33]. Their metadata type system enabled dynamic exploratory browsing interfaces, which simultaneously present multiple web pages as connected metadata summaries. This allows traversal of hyperlinked associations while maintaining context. In their study, computer science students preferred to browse research papers using the exploratory interface, in comparison to traditional browser tabs and windows. The exploratory interface also helped deal with disorientation and digression and supported comparison. The present study alternatively investigates the impact of dynamic exploratory browsing interfaces, on mini-c creativity, in everyday engagement with social media.

Measures of diversity and novelty have previously been utilized in studies of various creative contexts: e.g., prototyping web ads [11], collaborative ideation [24, 37], and game modding communities [16]. Flexibility and novelty in exploration and engagement are key factors in various creativity models [14, 35, 8]. Flexibility of thought processes is vital in exploratory browsing of Twittersphere, as people develop mutual understanding of a topic. We provide further basis for Fluency, Flexibility, and Novelty metrics in the next section.

Our contributions include: (1) validation of in-context exploratory browsing as an interface technique for social media; (2) ideation metrics as an evaluation methodology for exploratory browsing interfaces; (3) new presentation semantics to enable mimicking the look and feel of diverse, yet specific social media in generalized exploratory browsing interfaces; (4) the use of browser extensions for evaluation of interface design.

We begin with a survey of prior work across fields. We then show how the TweetBubble exploratory browsing interface

system is developed by extending a prior metadata type system [33]. Next, we motivate and present a crowdsourced study, with data from 54 participants, conducted amidst the 2014 Academy Awards. We gather mixed methods data. We derive ideation metrics of exploratory browsing. We find that the TweetBubble exploratory browsing interface results in increased Fluency, Flexibility, and Novelty. We draw on grounded theory methods to also show how our interface promotes creative exploration of social media. We discuss implications for exploratory browsing interface design and evaluation of their support for mini-c creativity.

BACKGROUND
We first consider prior work on evaluating information-based ideation, focusing on ideation metrics relevant to exploratory browsing. We follow with brief surveys of (1) interfaces and design principles for exploring associations, and (2) technologies for injecting scripts into web pages.

Evaluation of Information-Based Ideation Environments
Information-based ideation (IBI) is a paradigm for investigating open-ended tasks and activities, in which people generate and develop new ideas while browsing, searching, and collecting information [22]. Users perform exploratory browsing and search as part of engagement in IBI.

For evaluating exploratory search systems, White and Roth [44] suggested measuring information novelty, encountering sufficient information, and extent of topic space covered. However, they did not provide methods for these measures.

Building on Guilford's factors of creativity [17], engineering design researchers measured ideation in solutions to design problems [35]. Extending this, Kerne et al. derived a quantitative methodology for evaluating IBI support tools through a battery of *ideation metrics* [22]. Among these are elemental ideation metrics:

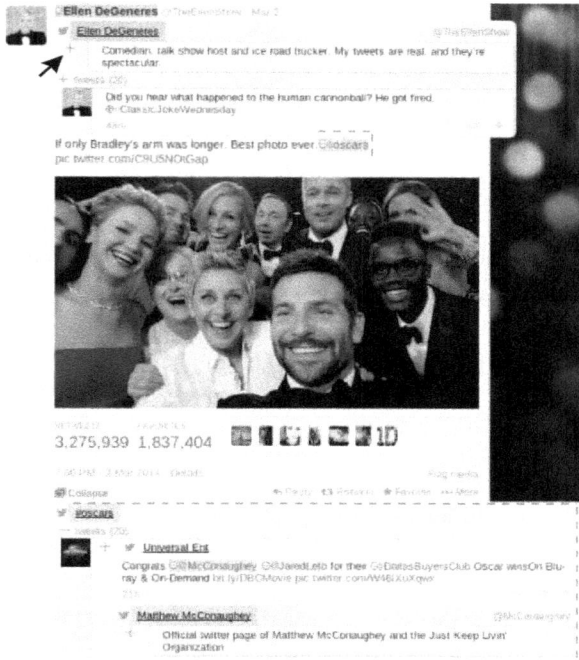

Figure 2. **In-context expansion of social media associations with the TweetBubble Chrome Extension. @username and #hashtag feeds are now rendered without replacement of initial content. Cursor arrow is now pointing to the expansion of Ellen's @username feed. Dashed lines delimit the #oscars association and the expansion of its feed.**

Figure 3. **Presentation semantics enable highly detailed metadata expansion. The rendering of Ellen's @username feed is customized with concatenates_to, navigates_to, hide_label, use_value_as_label, show_expanded_as_always, and label_at (See Tables 1 and 2).**

Fluency is the number of ideas. According to Darwinian theories of ideation, the more ideas a person considers, through survival of the fittest, the more likely it is that one idea will survive and grow to achieve creativity.

Flexibility / Variety is the number of categories of ideas. It addresses exploration of alternative interpretations. Flexibility measures the span of the solution space explored during ideation. Flexibility in thinking describes the cognitive process of trying out a Variety of different ways of looking at a problem. Variety provides opportunities for more remote associations, and more remote analogies, both of which are likely to lead to creativity.

Novelty is the rareness of an idea. It can be measured with statistical infrequency, which requires an appropriate norm for the space of possible ideas. While potentially difficult to assess globally, Novelty is straightforward to measure in the context of a controlled experiment, by building a master list and inverted index of all ideas generated by all participants. Then, count the number of participants that presented each idea. The lower the count, the higher the Novelty. The Novelty metric is analogous to information retrieval's inverse document frequency (IDF) measure [34].

Kerne et al. applied ideation metrics to measure creativity in the curation *products* that people author through engagement in IBI activities, by collecting, organizing, and annotating. The present research applies these metrics instead to creative *processes* of exploratory browsing.

Interfaces for Exploring Associations

We survey interfaces and design principles for supporting users in exploring associations. We pay particular attention to Twitter.

Wilson et al. found that in knowledge discovery tasks, interfaces that visually present associations help users assess how individual elements fit into a domain [45]. Web Summaries [9] extract and present metadata summaries from hyperlinked web pages. However linked summaries are presented in a separate Web Summaries window. Consistent with Wilson et al.'s findings, Web Summaries users reported spending too much time switching between regular browser and summary windows [10].

Fluid links [47] is an interface technique that presents brief representations of linked content below hyperlink anchors through interline expansions. The present in-context exploratory interface also interjects linked content.

We observe that Twitter's @username and #hashtags links are a lightweight mechanism for providing what Chi et al. call 'distal information scent' [7] in tweets, based on emergent trending topics and social networks. Suh et al. found that tweets containing #hashtags are often retweeted [40]. We interpret this to mean #hashtag content is significant to users' exploration, thus contributing to mini-c creativity.

TweetDeck [43] is a popular Twitter interface that can concurrently present multiple @username and #hashtag feeds in separate columns. Associations among Tweets are not visually presented across feeds.

Injecting Scripts into Web Pages

We developed a Chrome web browser extension to customize Twitter. Chrome extension technology enables selective injection of "content scripts" into web pages. This is similar to Greasemonkey [1], but enables broader deployment. Chrome plugins are self-contained packages, which users, such as the microtask workers in our study, install through the Chrome Web Store. Chickenfoot [5] also enabled end users to automate, customize, and integrate web applications.

Semantics	Description
layer	order of the metadata field; higher value means higher in order
hide / always_show	visibility of the metadata field; always_show is used to override the hide attribute
navigates_to	hyperlink metadata field to the specified destination
style_name	css class name to be applied to the metadata field
shadows	show this metadata field instead of the specified field
is_facet	metadata field can be used as a facet

Table 1. Presentation semantics previously defined in the Meta-Metadata language for metadata types.

Semantics	Description
label_at	positioning of label w.r.t. value of metadata field
concatenates_to	concatenate the metadata field to another
use_value_as_label	use value of another metadata field as label for this field
hide_label	visibility of the label of metadata field
show_expanded_initially	show the composite / collection field expanded initially
show_expanded_always	show composite / collection field expanded without affordance for collapse
style	element-level directive for conditional application of presentation semantics, based on these properties: is_child_metadata, is_same_metadata, is_only_element, is_top_level

Table 2. New presentation semantics in Meta-Metadata provide finer-grained control of rendering to enable seamless integration of exploratory browsing of @usernames and #hashtags social media associations within the Twitter interface.

EXPLORATORY BROWSING SYSTEM DESIGN

We briefly present the the TweetBubble exploratory browsing interface system design. The TweetBubble runtime, as a *Chrome extension*, is constituted by a content script that transforms the Twitter interface. In order to help users understand, work with, and think about conceptual spaces formed by Twitter social media associations, a dynamic exploratory browsing interface requires multiple feeds to be rendered within a single web page. TweetBubble uses the browser's JavaScript's XMLHttpRequest to retrieve social media association web pages in the background.

To facilitate extraction and presentation from associated @username and #hashtag feeds, we extend the *Meta-Metadata* language for metadata types, a component of the open-source *BigSemantics* framework [20]. Metadata types defined with Meta-Metadata integrally describe data models, extraction rules, and presentation semantics, for semantic representation of linked web pages [33], such as Twitter feeds. We used the types to build a look and feel consistent with Twitter. *Presentation semantics* enable detailed customization of the visual interface for particular metadata types.

We present a small use case, including details of new presentation semantics that enable customizing the look and feel of Twitter social media in the exploratory browsing interface. We follow this with the details of present interface design.

Mini-Scenario

We develop a small use case to demonstrate how user experience is facilitated through the type system's integration of presentation semantics. Janet clicks on the @TheEllenShow's expansion affordance (Figure 1b). Presentation semantics for the twitter_microblog type direct the in-context rendering of the @username feed (Figure 2, Figure 3: detailed). Janet then expands the newly rendered Twitter account information, to see details such as description, number of tweets, fol-

lowing, and followers. Presentation semantics again direct rendering. Likewise, Janet continue to expand the @username and #hashtag contained within the newly rendered tweets.

Prior presentation semantics provided important fundamental constructs (see Table 1). However, our goal was to seamlessly integrate TweetBubble into Twitter, mimicking its look and feel. This required us to provide more fine-grained control in Meta-Metadata. We developed new presentation semantics: positioning, expanding, collapsing, concatenating, and changing labels of the fields (Table 2). Figure 3 shows how TweetBubble is able to mimic @username feeds using the presentation semantics from Table 1 and 2.

The navigates_to directive hyperlinks the title to the URL value, affording press, to browse the original web page in a new tab (Figure 3). The hide directive eases the user's visual load by specifying to not directly render the URL field. We position labels below values, Twitter style, using the label_at directive in conjunction with the tweets, following, and followers fields. Meanwhile, concatenates_to renders these fields in the same horizontal span. The show_expanded_always directive renders complete metadata for each tweet, without any expand / collapse affordance. Applying the use_value_as_label directive renders the twitter microblog's photo as the label of each tweet.

Interface Design

TweetBubble interjects affordances for in-context expansion of @usernames and #hashtags into Twitter. Affordances also get interjected in the expanded @usernames and #hashtags metadata; their activation creates nested metadata expansion branches (Figure 4). This provides the ability to simultaneously view multiple feeds, form associations, and make comparisons. A palette of related colors is used to connect a social media association and its expansion as metadata.

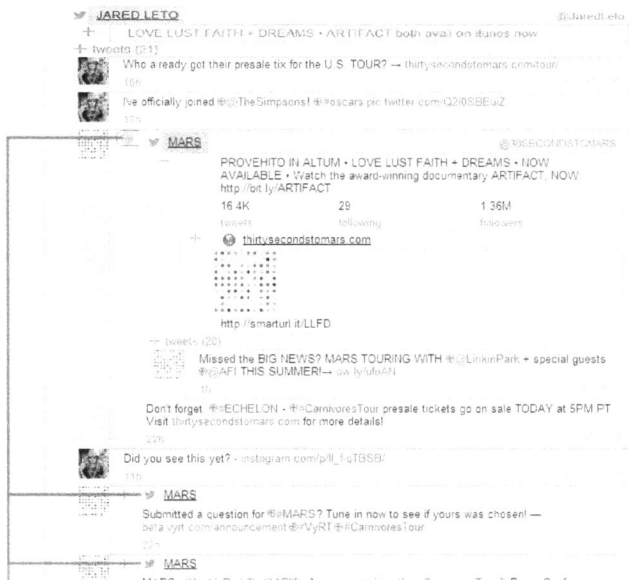

Figure 4. Nested in-context expansions of @usernames, JARED LETO and, in his retweet, MARS, facilitate understanding of associations and seeing the big picture. Redundant tweeter name and handle information within tweets rendered in these expansions are suppressed by presentation semantics: the style, hide, and is_child_metadata (see Tables 2 and 1). When social media associations recur, (here, those from the retweet of MARS), connection lines visualize recurrences.

Repetitive information becomes a problem as Twitter feeds and tweets are recursively expanded. More feeds are presented at once than in default Twitter. TweetBubble addresses the repetitive information problem by using presentation semantics, on each tweet, to suppress otherwise redundant display of tweeter name and handle. Further, to help orient the user, when s/he activates an @username field in a retweet, the interface draws red lines to visualize recurrent references to that @username in other retweets (Figure 4).

TweetBubble provides interaction consistent with Twitter. In Twitter, after expanding a tweet to see prior social discourse actions—*reply, retweet,* and *favorite*—pressing the background collapses. TweetBubble extends the mapping of press background to collapse all expanded information, streamlining navigation. Consistent interaction also includes affording social discourse actions with each tweet. We form tweet action URLs, using Twitter's unique ~18-digit tweet identifier, extracted via metadata types.

EVALUATION: ACADEMY AWARDS

We chose the 2014 Academy Awards as a context, or domain, for study of TweetBubble's support for creative exploratory browsing of social media. Baer and Kaufman develop the case for conceptualizing creativity 'as something that transcends content domains' [2]. Their Amusement Park Theoretical Model of creativity connects work in specific domains to general assessment and investigation.

With regard to general phenomena of creativity, ideation metrics, especially Flexibility / Variety, make sense for measuring creative exploration. The basis for this lies in the definition of

mini-c creativity, which involves meaningful learning and understanding. In social media, as in life, understanding diverse points of view provides a cognitive basis for comparison, synthesis, and mutual understanding. This constitutes the basis for a general assessment and investigation of creativity, in the Amusement Park Theoretical Model.

Various domains provide specific meaningful contexts for general investigation into mini-c creativity. People invest time and energy into that which they experience as meaningful. Learning and understanding about the Academy Awards is no more or less meaningful than domains more useful to society, such as citizen science and molecular biology.

Thus, the popularity of engagement in social media during the Academy Awards identifies this domain as a site for the investigation of support for mini-c creativity by an exploratory browsing interface. During the 2014 Academy Awards, over 5 million people sent 19.1 million Tweets and over 37 million people viewed those Tweets [15]. The mix of who tweeted included movie and fashion participants, press, and fans. Twitter users could experience large and diverse cross-sections of tweets. Encountering diverse and novel perspectives in a domain, such as this, results in mini–c creative ideation.

Study Design

We conducted a between-subjects study with Twitter interface as independent variable. As described, the TweetBubble extension condition offered affordances to expand @username and #hashtag social media associations. The control condition was the default Twitter interface, in which clicking a social association link overwrites initial content. Across conditions, the apparatus logged how users explored encountered information.

The study asked users to browse a trending Twitter topic for 15 minutes, based on their own interests, starting from the #ERedcarpet or #oscars2014 page. The Red Carpet event attracts a fashion-oriented audience. Celebrities walk up to the Oscars, wearing outfits from prominent fashion designers. We first published 12 Mechanical Turk HITs with #ERedCarpet, around 3pm PST, when the TV broadcast of Red Carpet started. This was followed by 38 more HITs for #ERedCarpet, a couple of hours later. As the main Academy Awards event began, around 7:30pm PST, we published 50 HITs with the topic #oscars2014. Overall, there were 59 male and 41 female participants in the 3 sets. Participants were given pre- and post-questionnaires.

The HITs specified that participants should be regular Twitter users (having used Twitter at least once in last one week). We didn't strictly validate this, instead relying on participants' self-reports. We took care in the study design to eliminate confounds. We included sanity and attention checks [30, 23], independent of the Twitter interface condition.

In the pre-questionnaire, sanity check questions validated participants' interest in the topics. The sanity check questions were: (1) Who of the following is not nominated for Best Actress or Best Supporting Actress? Response choices were (a) Meryl Streep (b) Jennifer Lawrence (c) Miley Cyrus (d) Sandra Bullock; and (2) Which of the following is not known as a

Metric	TweetBubble μ	SE	Control μ	SE	p <
Fluency	8.76	2.007	1.137	0.431	.0000186
Flexibility	6.84	1.614	1.103	0.421	.0000746
Flexibility (User Type)	3.6	0.881	0.759	0.267	.00000352
Novelty	0.599	0.118	0.288	0.096	.001744

Table 3. Ideation metrics of exploratory browsing for `@username` associations. All were significantly higher in the TweetBubble condition.

Metric	TweetBubble μ	SE	Control μ	SE	p <
Fluency	5.6	1.473	1.517	0.755	.00397
Flexibility	3.32	0.888	1.068	0.509	.008859
Novelty	0.269	0.065	0.16	0.064	.084316

Table 4. Ideation metrics of exploratory browsing for `#hashtag` associations. All except Novelty were significantly higher in the TweetBubble condition.

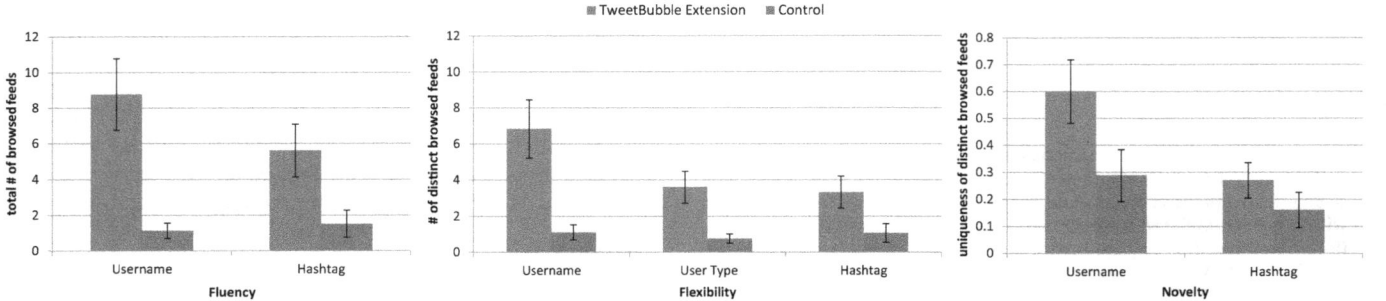

Figure 5. Mean Fluency, Flexibility, Novelty of `@username` and `#hashtag` feeds that users browsed. The TweetBubble Extension interface condition (in blue) resulted in significantly more creative exploratory browsing than the Control condition (in red) for 6 out of 7 ideation metrics. Error bars show standard errors of the mean.

dress designer? Choices were (a) Vera Wang (b) Estee Lauder (c) Alexander McQueen (d) Christian Dior. For the Red Carpet study we wanted fashionistas. Through sanity check questions, we weeded out more average people. We discarded 17 and 15 responses respectively from the TweetBubble extension and control conditions, based on the responses.

In the post-questionnaire, an attention check question and an open-ended summary question served to validate participants' engagement. We followed prior practices in formulating the attention check: 'How many times in the last 5 minutes have you had a heart attack while riding a unicycle in the Alps?' [30]. Based on these responses, we discarded in total only 1 participant, from the TweetBubble extension condition. We also eliminated 13 participants post hoc because of logging problems—7 in the TweetBubble extension condition and 6 in the control. This leaves 25 participants in the TweetBubble condition and 29 participants in the control.

We gathered and analyzed mixed methods data. We developed and applied a quantitative method for measuring the creativity of exploratory browsing engagement with Twitter. We collected and analyzed qualitative data about users' social media experiences.

Method: Ideation Metrics of Exploratory Browsing

Exploratory browsing of Twitter is a mini-c creative process, involving personally novel interpretation of social media associations. We thus derive new ideation metrics of exploratory browsing by recontextualizing Kerne et al's elemental metrics of curation [22]. We shift application of the

metrics from the products of information-based ideation to its processes of exploratory browsing. We rework prior methods for computing elemental ideation metrics—Fluency, Flexibility, Novelty—to derive new ideation metrics for creative engagement in exploratory browsing of Twitter social media.

Define the the set of types $M = \{username, hashtag\}$ of Twitter social media associations. Using type m from this set, $o_{m,i}$ refers to each feed a user browses, of each type.

Then, we express the set of all social media `@username` and `#hashtag` associations traversed in a user's exploratory browsing process, which corresponds to Kerne et al.'s set of all found digital media objects in the product that a user curated [22]:

$$c = \{o_{m,0}, o_{m,1}, ...\}; \forall m \in M \quad (1)$$

Then, $Fluency_m(c)$ will be the total number of feeds the user browsed, of type m

$$Fluency_m(c) = ||o_{m,i} \in c||; m \in M \quad (2)$$

Note that recurrent browsing of any particular feed is aggregated in this Fluency measure.

Flexibility will be the total number of distinct `@usernames`, `#hashtags` browsed. This means that instead of becoming aggregated, any recurrences of browsing a particular feed do not contribute to the Flexibility measure. To compute Flexibility, form the set of all distinct feeds of type m, $DistinctFeeds_m(c)$, from collection c of all the

`@usernames`, `#hashtags` a user browsed.

$$DistinctFeeds_m(c) = \bigcup_{o \in c} o_{m,i}; m \in M \quad (3)$$

$$Flexibility_m(c) = ||DistinctFeeds_m(c)|| \quad (4)$$

We also categorized user feeds into types. We compute $Flexibility_{user\_type}$, drawing on Kerne et al's site type granularity. For this purpose, we extend the categories of Twitter users established by Wu et al.: *celebrities, media, organizations, and blogs* [46], adding: *fashion, professional*. We separate *organizations* into categories: *community, activist*. We performed manual classification to assign types to the 179 `@username` feeds browsed by study participants. The resulting mapping is defined by a *UserType* operator.

$$Flexibility_{user\_type}(c) = || \bigcup_{o \in c, m=username} UserType(o_{m,i})|| \quad (5)$$

To compute Novelty, build an inverted index that shows for each feed f, of type m, the number of users who browsed it.

$$Occurrences_m(f, C) = \{c | c \in C \wedge f \in DistinctFeeds_m(c)\} \quad (6)$$

$$Novelty_m(f, C) = \frac{1}{||Occurences_m(f, C)||} \quad (7)$$

Then, Novelty of feeds browsed by each user, of type m, can be computed as aggregated mean of Novelty scores for `@username` or `#hashtags` feeds that the user browsed.

$$Novelty_m(c, C) = \frac{\sum_{f \in DistinctFeeds_m(c)} Novelty_m(f, C)}{||DistinctFeeds_m(c)||} \quad (8)$$

Results: Ideation Metrics of Exploratory Browsing

We used this method to compute ideation metrics of exploratory browsing. Results across conditions of the Twitter interface independent variable were compared with t-tests, assuming unequal variances. We found that all ideation metrics of exploratory browsing were significantly higher for `@username` social media associations in the TweetBubble extension condition (Table 3). For `#hashtag` associations, Fluency and Flexibility significantly increased in the TweetBubble condition (Table 4). Figure 5 graphs the results.

Qualitative Results

TweetBubble condition participants were asked, via questionnaire, how clicking on related content, seeing it on the same page, and thus simultaneously browsing multiple feeds affected their experiences. Drawing on grounded theory methods [6], we performed a qualitative analysis of resulting data. We first performed open coding of a set of participant responses. This resulted in 25 codes. We followed with focused coding of remaining responses. We aggregated codes into 5 categories: 'Reduces Disorientation and Digression',

'Helps Explore Related Content', 'Connecting Perspectives to Gain Broader Understanding', 'Fluid and Effective', 'Too Much Information?'.

Reduces Disorientation and Digression

Participants reported that TweetBubble helped them focus. They liked that the original context of reading is maintained when browsing related content. This helped them stay oriented and on topic. They reported having more information at their fingertips. Participants were able to decide whether or not they want to further explore linked content. These findings match those of Qu et al. [33] and Zellweger et al. [47].

P99: *"Being able to see everything on one page kept me much more focused."*

P5: *"I liked the pop outs with more info without losing my place in the feed."*

P3: *"It made it more cohesive and allowed me to keep a train of thought instead of getting so hopelessly sidetracked by having new windows constantly."*

P47: *"It gave more information as to what that person or group was about, this is a very nice feature as it allows one to determine whether or not they may be interested in checking out someone."*

Helps Explore Related Content

Without going back and forth between windows, participants found themselves more engaged. They reported easily and efficiently viewing and discovering more content, exploring more Twitter users' feeds, following online conversations better, and building more in-depth understanding of topics. TweetBubble introduced them to more diversified content, often missed when using the default interface.

P37: *"...the more you have to go back and forth, the less interested I am in staying and learning/reading about topics, because it is too time consuming. So having everything all together made me interact a lot more than I would've before."*

P99: *"It helped me delve into the subjects more. It also kept me more engaged in browsing the Twitter feed."*

P91: *"It allowed me to see more of the conversation and subject."*

P67: *"It made my experience so much quicker, with so much more content. I was amazed by how easy it was to see tweets between two of my favorite celebrities."*

Connecting Perspectives to Gain Broader Understanding

Participants reported new ability to see relationships across topics and perspectives. They more readily saw diverse viewpoints. Exposure to contrasting viewpoints enabled them to connect perspectives, and so gain broader understanding. This corresponds directly to mini-c personally novel and meaningful interpretation.

P47: *"This allows one to understand how the system connects related topics and to see how and why they are linked together"*

P21: *"You get to see many different points of view, professional and civilian. You could get quick quips or detailed facts. It allows for a much broader reading experience."*

P33: *"It gave me a broader view of the topic all in one area, instead of being segmented across several pages. Made it a lot easier to understand as a whole."*

Fluid and Effective

Users found the experience of the TweetBubble interface to enable more fluid and effective navigation of Twitter.

P41: *"You could see more viewpoints and different opinions on it more readily."*

P69: *"...the fluidity of the page was really nice."*

P75: *"It made it easier to just see the tweets in a descending ladder format."*

Too Much Information?

A few participants felt overwhelmed, as the number of expansions increased.

P59: *"The extension made the @usernames and #hashtags open up a tree menu which ended up being confusing and cluttered. I understand how it can link topics and users together, but it is too messy."*

P61: *"I still jumped between pages a lot, but I am still only getting used to TweetBubble."*

DISCUSSION

We frame investigation of exploratory browsing by delineating the everyday contextual role of social media in society. We derive implications for design and evaluation of exploratory interfaces: social media interfaces, exploratory browsing as mini-c ideation, ideation metrics of exploratory browsing, browser extensions as design laboratories, and metadata types integrating presentation semantics.

Everyday Contextual Role of Social Media

Popular social media, particularly Twitter and Facebook, have attained such a pervasive role in the conduct of society, that, drawing on the work of Linder et al. [26], we call them *everyday*. An indicator is how the medium of television—e.g., The Tonight Show, news, and sports—positions Twitter in leading roles, framing discourse. Similarly, personal lives and business relationships are extensively built and expressed through Twitter and Facebook. Everyday use refers to people's engagement with these platforms for a panoply of meaningful events in their lives. Thus, how people engage in exploratory browsing of social media is very significant, on a societal level. We compare interfaces for everyday exploratory browsing of social media.

Exploratory Browsing Interfaces for Social Media

According to Marchionini, browsing is an approach to information seeking that is informal, opportunistic, and iterative [28]. One respondent in Lindley et al.'s study addressed this for social media: "There's always something" engaging to

pursue [27]. Users iteratively compare, analyze, and synthesize information. They develop new perspectives. Our qualitative and quantitative study data validate the present approach to social media exploratory interface design and development. Qualitative study data matches the findings from prior work, corroborating the suitability of interaction technique for exploratory browsing.

An exploratory browsing interface should provide means to explore related content, while maintaining originating context. It should depict browsed chains of association. The role of information visualization here extends beyond that of providing 'insights': it enables synthesis and ideation [22, 41]. In the study, users began from the same #hashtag search pages: #ERedCarpet or #oscars2014. With the TweetBubble extension, they discovered significantly more diverse and novel content, as compared to the participants using the default Twitter interface. This shows that the TweetBubble's in-context expansion of social media associations promotes users' exploratory browsing. It provokes discovering associations, stimulates users to learn about diverse perspectives on a topic, and so promotes flexibility in thinking.

Exploratory Browsing as *mini-c* Creative Ideation

Exploratory browsing of @username and #hashtag social media associations constitutes a form of mini-c creativity, because people encounter and learn about new perspectives. Beghetto and Kaufman emphasize the importance of mini-c creativity in education, in K-12 and beyond [3]. The Amusement Park Theoretical model [2] connects domain specific creativity to general assessment and investigation. In the present research, the domain is the Academy Awards, as experienced through Twitter social media. We use these established models of creativity to motivate generalization of our findings of the significance of exploratory browsing interfaces, which maintain context, to support creative experiences in diverse forms of education and social media.

Fallon and Timberlake demonstrate how widely used hashtagging has become in popular culture [13]. The preponderance of @username and #hashtag references in meaningful tweets (such as those retweeted [40]), highlights their role. The diversity and novelty of people's exploration, through @username and #hashtag social media associations, constitute measures of the extent of their mini-c creativity. Diversity and novelty are central in creativity models [17, 31, 42, 14, 38, 35]. We thus took a creative cognition approach [35] and reworked ideation metrics of curation [22], to compare interfaces designed for exploratory browsing of social media.

Ideation Metrics of Exploratory Browsing

For evaluation of systems for casual information seeking, Elsweiler et al. demand new metrics [12]. We found that ideation metrics [22] provide a means to measure efficacy of an interface in stimulating creative exploration. To measure creative exploration in browsing social media, we recontextualized prior ideation metrics, in terms of the @username and #hashtag associations that Twitter users explore. This methodology can generally be applied to interfaces designed for exploratory browsing, exploratory search, and information visualization, to compare interface conditions based on diversity and novelty in experiences of creative exploration.

Previously, think-aloud protocols, double stimulation, and microgenetic methods have been used to gather and analyze data to evaluate mini-c creativity [3]. Like microgenetic methods, our approach captures incremental contributions to each user's creative ideation. Ideation metrics aggregate units of mini-c creative engagement. With TweetBubble, the aggregated measure correlates to the synthesis of different perspectives in context of each other, valuable towards creative cognition and visual analytics research of developing new ideas by combination of individual elements [22, 41].

We recall that exploration, of the moon or the web, is by nature creative. In tandem with ideation metrics of exploratory browsing, the present mixed-methods research collects qualitative data in order to categorize user experiences and connect them with measurable effects of mini-c creativity. This cross-validation confirms the methodology of recontextualizing ideation metrics from products to processes, a novel quantitative approach to evaluation of exploratory browsing interfaces' support for mini-c creativity.

We investigated a particular everyday social media context, the 2014 Academy Awards, in order to study how interfaces support people in creative exploratory browsing. To engage typical users with TweetBubble dynamic exploratory browsing interface, we directly embedded it into Twitter. Users of the TweetBubble interface performed significantly higher on 6 out of 7 ideation metrics of exploratory browsing (the 7th was close). Qualitative data mirrors the quantitative results. This grids the claims of validity both for the exploratory browsing interface, and for the method of using ideation metrics of exploratory browsing as the basis for interfaces.

Browser Extensions: A Technique for Design Evaluation
Browser extensions serve as *interface design laboratories*. In conjunction with recruiting micro-task workers, validated by reliability measures [30, 23], the browser extension approach facilitates elicitation of feedback on interactive system design, utility, and performance of an interactive system's design. Both quantitative and qualitative data can be fruitfully gathered in browser extension ideation laboratories. Users become involved in the design of new technologies, while researchers gain valuable insights from their feedback. Browser extensions have the capacity to serve as technology probes [19], when their use is open-ended and extended. Researchers can study new interaction techniques via browser extensions to enable data collection over extended time periods.

Metadata Types Integrating Presentation Semantics
The metadata types in the Meta-Metadata language integrate data models, extraction rules, and presentation semantics, providing a strong foundation for dynamic exploratory browsing interfaces. Presentation semantics enable customizing generalized exploratory browsing interfaces to match the look and feel of specific websites. This integration enables construction of a consistent and integrated user experience through detailed visual reproduction of linked web pages.

The present research extends these semantics to enable mimicking Twitter social media. The type system's re-use of data models and presentation semantics will facilitate future work that extends this technique to other social media, such as Facebook, Reddit, Pinterest, and Google+.

CONCLUSION
TweetBubble stimulated exploratory browsing of the Twitter social media associations during the Academy Awards study. We derived new ideation metrics of exploratory browsing, extending prior research, which enable quantitative comparison of the interfaces, in how they support users' mini-c creative experiences. We found that the TweetBubble dynamic exploratory browsing interface users performed significantly higher on 6 out of 7 metrics of Fluency, Flexibility, and Novelty. Users reported that with the TweetBubble interface, the gaining of perspectives, introduction to new people and topics, and following of conversations becomes more easy, engaging and efficient. The metrics match the user experiences.

What is the significance of these findings? Social media, particularly Twitter, have attained an international transformative impact, playing a catalytic role in social movements, such as Arab Spring, [39] and politics, such as U.S. presidential debates [36]. They cut across individuals, communities, and organizations, redefining participation, communication, and awareness. Social media content is vast and fast moving. With increased exploratory browsing of Twitter, not only will users make more connections across @usernames and #hashtags, tweeters will also get better reach for their social media posts. Both the producers and consumers of information gain as diverse and novel perspectives are shared, growing mutual understanding. We identified the Academy Awards as a meaningful cultural context for this purpose. The Amusement Park Theoretical Model can similarly be invoked, to interpret and generalize mini-c meaningful learning and mutual understanding in contexts of crowdsourced community participation, such as expressions of solidarity and mutually supportive content filtering during Arab Spring.

Using Boden's notion of exploratory creativity, and Kaufman et al.'s mini-c creativity, we identified exploratory browsing as a form of creative experience, and so of information-based ideation. Creativity is vital to personal well-being [4, 21]. Creative innovation is vital to economic growth and national interests [32]. Ideation is a cornerstone of participatory democracy. Thus, techniques for building interfaces that promote creative engagement in exploration of social media, and methods for evaluating these interfaces, have great potential to significantly impact how social media transforms the world. Ideation metrics of exploratory browsing are applicable in visual analytics, where exposure to diverse and novel perspectives contributes to novel and meaningful interpretation, and so to creative synthesis. Exploratory browsing interfaces have the potential to play a leading role, as humans engage in information-based ideation activities, which, in turn, are the heart of humanity's potential to transform the raw material of our digital society and super-abundant information resources into connectedness, well-being, and success.

ACKNOWLEDGEMENTS

This material is based upon work supported by the National Science Foundation (NSF) under grants IIS-074742 and IIS-1247126. Any opinions, findings, and conclusions or recommendations expressed in this material are those of the authors and do not necessarily reflect the views of the NSF.

REFERENCES

1. Greasemonkey add-on for firefox. `http://mzl.la/1cdCxOR`. Last accessed: 01/12/2015.

2. Baer, J., and Kaufman, J. C. Bridging generality and specificity: The amusement park theoretical (APT) model of creativity. *Roeper Review* 27, 3 (2005), 158–163.

3. Beghetto, R. A., and Kaufman, J. C. Toward a broader conception of creativity: A case for "mini-c" creativity. *Psychology of Aesthetics, Creativity, and the Arts 1*, 2 (2007), 73.

4. Boden, M. A. *The creative mind: Myths and mechanisms*. Psychology Press, 2004.

5. Bolin, M., Webber, M., Rha, P., Wilson, T., and Miller, R. C. Automation and customization of rendered web pages. In *Proc UIST* (2005), 163–172.

6. Charmaz, K. *Constructing grounded theory: A practical guide through qualitative analysis*. Pine Forge Press, 2006.

7. Chi, E. H., Pirolli, P., Chen, K., and Pitkow, J. Using information scent to model user information needs and actions and the web. In *Proc CHI* (2001), 490–497.

8. DeYoung, C. G. Higher-order factors of the big five in a multi-informant sample. *Journal of personality and social psychology 91*, 6 (2006), 1138.

9. Dontcheva, M., Drucker, S. M., Wade, G., Salesin, D., and Cohen, M. F. Summarizing personal web browsing sessions. In *Proc UIST* (2006).

10. Dontcheva, M., Lin, S., Drucker, S. M., Salesin, D., and Cohen, M. F. Experiences with content extraction from the web. In *Proc UIST* (2008).

11. Dow, S. P., Glassco, A., Kass, J., Schwarz, M., Schwartz, D. L., and Klemmer, S. R. Parallel prototyping leads to better design results, more divergence, and increased self-efficacy. *ACM TOCHI 17*, 4 (2010), 18.

12. Elsweiler, D., Wilson, M. L., and Lunn, B. K. Understanding casual-leisure information behaviour. *Library and Information Science 1* (2011), 211–241.

13. Fallon, J., and Timberlake, J. "#hashtag" with Jimmy Fallon & Justin Timberlake. https://www.youtube.com/watch?v=57dzaMaouXA. Last accessed: 07/30/2014.

14. Finke, R., Ward, T., and Smith, S. *Creative Cognition: Theory, Research, and Applications*. MIT Press, 1992.

15. Fleischman, M. The reach and impact of oscars 2014 tweets. `https://blog.twitter.com/2014/the-reach-and-impact-of-oscars-2014-tweets`. Last accessed: 01/12/2015.

16. Grace, K., and Maher, M. L. Towards computational co-creation in modding communities. In *Proc AIIDE*, AAAI (2014).

17. Guilford, J. Creativity. *American Psychologist 5* (1950), 444–454.

18. Honey, C., and Herring, S. C. Beyond microblogging: Conversation and collaboration via twitter. In *Proc HICSS*, IEEE (2009), 1–10.

19. Hutchinson, H., Mackay, W., Westerlund, B., Bederson, B. B., Druin, A., Plaisant, C., Beaudouin-Lafon, M., Conversy, S., Evans, H., and Hansen, H. Technology probes: inspiring design for and with families. In *Proc CHI* (2003), 17–24.

20. Interface Ecology Lab. BigSemantics Framework. `https://github.com/ecologylab/BigSemantics/wiki`. Last accessed: 01/12/2015.

21. Kaufman, J. C., and Beghetto, R. A. Beyond big and little: The four c model of creativity. *Review of General Psychology 13*, 1 (2009), 1.

22. Kerne, A., Webb, A. M., Smith, S. M., Linder, R., Lupfer, N., Qu, Y., Moeller, J., and Damaraju, S. Using metrics of curation to evaluate information-based ideation. *ACM ToCHI 21*, 3 (2014), 48.

23. Kittur, A., Chi, E. H., and Suh, B. Crowdsourcing user studies with mechanical turk. In *Proc CHI* (2008), 453–456.

24. Kohn, N. W., and Smith, S. M. Collaborative fixation: Effects of others' ideas on brainstorming. *Applied Cognitive Psychology 25*, 3 (2011), 359–371.

25. Kwak, H., Lee, C., Park, H., and Moon, S. What is twitter, a social network or a news media? In *Proc WWW* (2010), 591–600.

26. Linder, R., Snodgrass, C., and Kerne, A. Everyday ideation: all of my ideas are on pinterest. In *Proc CHI* (2014), 2411–2420.

27. Lindley, S. E., Meek, S., Sellen, A., and Harper, R. It's simply integral to what i do: enquiries into how the web is weaved into everyday life. In *Proc WWW* (2012), 1067–1076.

28. Marchionini, G. *Information seeking in electronic environments*. No. 9. Cambridge University Press, 1997.

29. Marlow, C., Naaman, M., Boyd, D., and Davis, M. HT06, tagging paper, taxonomy, flickr, academic article, to read. In *Proc HYPERTEXT* (2006), 31–40.

30. Marshall, C., and Shipman, F. Experiences surveying the crowd: Reflections on methods, participation, and reliability. In *Proc WebSci* (2013), 234–243.

31. Mednick, S. A. The associative basis of the creative process. *Psychological Review* (1962), 220–232.

32. National Academy of Engineering. *Rising Above the Gathering Storm, Revisited: Rapidly Approaching Category 5*. The National Academies Press, 2010.

33. Qu, Y., Kerne, A., Lupfer, N., Linder, R., and Jain, A. Metadata type system: Integrate presentation, data models and extraction to enable exploratory browsing interfaces. In *Proc EICS*, ACM (2014), 107–116.

34. Salton, G., and Buckley, C. Term-weighting approaches in automatic text retrieval. *Information Processing and Management 24*, 5 (1988).

35. Shah, J. J., Smith, S. M., and Vargas-Hernandez, N. Metrics for measuring ideation effectiveness. *Design studies 24*, 2 (2003), 111–134.

36. Shamma, D. A., Kennedy, L., and Churchill, E. F. Tweet the debates: understanding community annotation of uncollected sources. In *Proc SIGMM* (2009), 3–10.

37. Siangliulue, P., Arnold, K. C., Gajos, K. Z., and Dow, S. P. Toward collaborative ideation at scale-leveraging ideas from others to generate more creative and diverse ideas. In *Proc CSCW*, ACM (2015).

38. Simonton, D. K. Creativity as blind variation and selective retention: Is the creative process darwinian? *Psychological Inquiry 10*, 4 (1999).

39. Starbird, K., and Palen, L. (how) will the revolution be retweeted?: information diffusion and the 2011 egyptian uprising. In *Proc CSCW* (2012), 7–16.

40. Suh, B., Hong, L., Pirolli, P., and Chi, E. H. Want to be retweeted? large scale analytics on factors impacting retweet in twitter network. In *SocialCom, IEEE* (2010), 177–184.

41. Thomas, J. J., and Cook, K. A. Illuminating the path: The research and development agenda for visual analytics. Tech. rep., Pacific Northwest National Laboratory (PNNL), Richland, WA (US), 2005.

42. Torrance, E. P. The nature of creativity as manifest in its testing. *The nature of creativity* (1988), 43–75.

43. Twitter. About TweetDeck. `https://about.twitter.com/products/tweetdeck`. Last accessed: 01/12/2015.

44. White, R. W., and Roth, R. A. Exploratory search: Beyond the query-response paradigm. *Synthesis Lectures on Information Concepts, Retrieval, and Services 1*, 1 (Jan. 2009), 1–98.

45. Wilson, M. L., Kules, B., schraefel, m., and Shneiderman, B. From keyword search to exploration: Designing future search interfaces for the web. *Foundations and Trends in Web Science 2*, 1 (2010), 1–97.

46. Wu, S., Hofman, J. M., Mason, W. A., and Watts, D. J. Who says what to whom on twitter. In *Proc WWW* (2011), 705–714.

47. Zellweger, P. T., Chang, B.-W., and Mackinlay, J. D. Fluid links for informed and incremental link transitions. In *Proc HYPERTEXT*, ACM (1998), 50–57.

You're the Voice: Evaluating User Interfaces for Encouraging Underserved Youths to Express Themselves through Creative Writing

Frederica Gonçalves
Madeira-ITI
Polo Científico e Tecnológico
da Madeira. Piso -2
9020-105 Funchal, Portugal
+351 291 721 006;
frederica.goncalves@m-iti.org

Pedro Campos
Madeira-ITI
Polo Científico e Tecnológico
da Madeira. Piso -2
9020-105 Funchal, Portugal
+351 291 721 006; pe-
dro.campos@m-iti.org

Julian Hanna
Madeira-ITI
Polo Científico e Tecnológico
da Madeira. Piso -2
9020-105 Funchal, Portugal
+351 291 721 006; julianhan-
na@gmail.com

Simone Ashby
Madeira-ITI
Polo Científico e Tecnológico
da Madeira. Piso -2
9020-105 Funchal, Portugal
+351 291 721 006;
simone.ashby@m-iti.org

ABSTRACT

Minority groups are the fastest growing demographic in the U.S. In addition, the poverty level in the U.S. is the highest it has been in the last 50 years. We argue that the community needs more research addressing this user segment, and we present a novel study about how underserved youths react when presented with different UI designs aimed at promoting creative writing. The act of creative writing *per se* can become the driver of change among underserved teenagers, and researchers should strive to discover novel UI designs that can effectively increase this target group's productivity, creativity and mental well-being. Using MS Word as baseline, our contribution analyzes the influence of a Zen-like tool (designed by the authors and called Haven), a nostalgic but realistic typewriting tool (Hanx Writer), and a stress-based tool that eliminates writer's block by providing consequences for procrastination (Write or Die). Our results suggest that the Zen characteristics of our tool Haven were capable of conveying a sense of calm and concentration to the users, making them feel better and also write more. The nostalgic Hanx typewriter also fared very well with regard to mental well-being and productivity, as measured by average number of words written. Contrary to our initial expectations, the stress-based UI (Write or Die) had the lowest productivity levels.

Author Keywords

User Studies; User Experience Design; Creative Writing; Creativity Support Tools; Civic Media.

ACM Classification Keywords

H.5.m. Information interfaces and presentation (e.g., HCI): Miscellaneous.

C&C '15, June 22 - 25, 2015, Glasgow, United Kingdom
© 2015 ACM. ISBN 978-1-4503-3598-0/15/06...$15.00
DOI: http://dx.doi.org/10.1145/2757226.2757236

INTRODUCTION

"We have the chance to turn the pages over / We can write what we want to write / We gotta make ends meet, before we get much older"

– John Farnham, "You're the Voice"

Creative writing is often used as a pedagogical tool to increase literacy. It can also be used to build positive relationships and encourage dialogue across diverse communities. Creative writing gives a voice to marginal groups in society, helping them to tell their stories. In this sense, new tools for creative writers can be used to support community-based writing projects and encourage people from all backgrounds to find their voice and tell their unique stories. But we also believe that creative writing can be used not only for the mental well-being of underserved populations but also as a way to empower people to tell their unique stories and thereby increase society's awareness of their situations and challenges.

The problem, however, is that there are very few studies about what makes a good user interface design for creative writing, as there is no consensual approach to evaluating them. In this paper we propose an approach that addresses, for the first time, a minority user group of underserved youths, by evaluating how they write using different user interfaces. We triangulate data from different sources to assess productivity, creativity and mental well-being of users writing in four different user interfaces: MS Word (the baseline), Haven (our own tool), Hanx Writer (a nostalgic retro-futuristic typewriter), and Write or Die, a stress-based tool that combats writer's block by providing consequences for procrastination.

The remainder of this paper is organized as follows: in the next section, we review related work about research targeted at empowering minority groups, creative writing user interfaces, and supporting creativity. We then present a section describing our own tool for creative writing called Haven, as well as the other tools we used in our experiments. Thereafter, we detail the participants, methods, procedures and results of three studies. We wrap up with a qualitative discussion that also includes some reflections on the entire experience, as well as the overall conclusions.

RELATED WORK

Empowering Minority Groups

Broadly speaking, our research addresses the needs of minority groups, such as underserved youths, working on the premise that creative writing can empower people in these demographics by allowing them to better express themselves, thus enabling them to share their specific challenges with the larger society. In addition, the simple act of creative writing can improve mental well-being, a problem that is more and more prominent in today's world.

Yardi and Bruckman [1] show that minorities are the fastest growing demographic in the U.S., and note that the poverty level in the U.S. is the highest it has been in 50 years. Their results show that socioeconomic differences both reflect and reinforce technology use at home. Our work builds on this growing user segment, a segment that is often overlooked both in research and product design.

Other researchers have studied the role of digital storytelling for the empowerment of marginalized youth through a series of workshops conducted in the context of Palestinian refugee camps in the West Bank and East Jerusalem [4]. Among other relevant conclusions, they note that the most challenging part of all youth workshops is the story development phase, which needs greater focus from educators and more effective tools and processes to be successful [4].

Researchers have also targeted other types of underserved groups. For instance, Cooper et al. [5] observed that the enrollment and interest in Computer Science (CS) at the university level has not increased in proportion to the rise in demand for computing technologies, which has been very rapid in recent decades. They identified key success factors, such as the value of strong partnerships, clear establishment of roles, accomplishment of needs assessment, field-testing, and effective team communication. However, this study was focused on a multidisciplinary effort targeted at improving CS interest among global underserved youth and showing how to make a difference. Minority groups have also been the subject of studies regarding participation of women in the Information Technology workplace [6], career development of minorities, ensuring that a greater number of women and minorities progress to a full career in cyber security [7], and even more specific cases, such as using statistical means and survey data to analyze the success in Germany of ethnic Germans (the majority group) in relation to four different minority groups [8].

To our knowledge, however, there are no studies dealing with bringing the power of creative writing UIs into the hands of underprivileged youths. These users make up the core group of our research.

Creative Writing User Interfaces

The second, and perhaps most important, perspective of our work revolves around creative writing user interfaces and tools. Perhaps surprisingly, there is relatively little research performed around creative writing tools, but some research-

ers, e.g. Magnifico [9], have investigated how to improve the creative writing *process*. Giving students the opportunity to interact with real readers of their work may motivate them not only to write, but also to take on new literacies and to regard themselves as writers in new contexts. Advances in tool support have been mostly made in very specific areas. For example, Yannopoulos [10] proposed a symbolic language intended to express the content of films (motion pictures) much as notes provide a language for the writing of music, therefore bringing a new approach to the creative process of filmmaking.

Since writing is frequently a collaborative activity, some researchers, such as Magnifico [9], chose to study the use of tools and resources for computer-supported collaborative writing. They implemented a custom-made, computer-supported environment that enables pairs of high school students to collaborate in writing an argumentative essay. They concluded that the tools analyzed reflected the writing strategies adopted by the students. Other authors focused on computer writing tools used during the production of documents in a professional setting [11]. They report on a focus group conducted with professional writers, in which writers narrated their experiences using computer tools to write documents, describing their practices, pointing out the most important problems they encountered, and analyzing their own needs. Based on this work, they describe LinguisTech, a reference website for helping language professionals. Keeping in mind that one goal of digital tools for creative writing is to help users produce greater quantities of writing, some researchers note that the productivity expectations placed on writers are, at present, higher than ever before [9]. Therefore, there is a need for tool support that can promote not only writers' creativity but also their productivity levels.

Coughlan and Johnson [12] present three perspectives on creative interaction that have emerged from four years of empirical and design research. They argue that creative interaction can be usefully viewed in terms of *Productive Interaction* – focused engagement on the development of a creative outcome; *Structural Interaction* – the development of the structures in which production occurs; and *Longitudinal Interaction* – the long-term development of resources and relationships that increase creative potential.

The ultimate goal of our research is to design and build novel user interfaces for creative writing that can be used not only by minority groups but also by as many people as possible. Unleashing the hidden potential of creative writers is, therefore, an essential objective to achieve. Mobile narratives can be one way to reach this goal [13]. This concept allows creative writers to exploit knowledge of the reader's context, by intensifying the user experience and integrating that knowledge into the writing process [13]. Another approach is to use crowdsourcing, as in the case of Soylent, a word processor that integrates crowdsourced human contributions directly into the user interface [14]. Other tools support the more general concept of creativity. Adventure Author is a learning environment that supports the creative design process that occurs during game design [15].

Finally, it is important to note that creative writing can be regarded as a means to achieve certain goals. For instance, our particular goal is to discover the most relevant user interface design characteristics in order to improve mental well-being of underserved youths, a minority group that can also use creative writing as a way to build positive relationships. But other goals are possible. Jones et al., for example, use creative writing as a means to teach introductory programming [16].

Supporting Creativity

The third dimension of our work is related to supporting and measuring creativity, generally speaking. Today there are many different approaches to measuring creativity: one of the most famous is Flow Theory [2]. Csiksentmihalyi defines flow as *"a state in which people are so involved in an activity that nothing else seems to matter; the experience is so enjoyable that people will continue to do it even at great cost, for the sheer sake of doing it"* [2]. As the author argues, we all experience flow from time to time and we recognize its characteristics. When we are "in the flow" we typically feel strong, alert, in effortless control, unselfconscious, and at the peak of our abilities.

Csiksentmihalyi posits seven stages that combine together to bring a sense of deep enjoyment and full energy in the flow state:

1. *Focused and concentrated* – completely involved in what we are doing;
2. *A sense of ecstasy* – feeling outside of everyday reality;
3. *Great inner clarity* – knowing what needs to be done, and how well we are doing;
4. *Goals and feedback* – knowing that our activity and skills are adequate to the task;
5. *Serenity* – a sense of having no worries about oneself, and of growing beyond the boundaries of the ego;
6. *Timelessness* – being thoroughly focused on the present, as hours seem to pass by in minutes;
7. *Intrinsic motivation* – whatever produces flow becomes its own reward.

In this paper, we were particularly interested in the following dimensions of Flow Theory: concentration, sense of control, losing track of time, and loss of self-consciousness.

Despite significant efforts spent on creativity research, there is no consensual methodology for evaluating how much creative support a given tool can provide to its users. This is problematic because a solid evaluation is paramount to the design of new creative support tools as well as the improvement of existing ones [17]. One approach to dealing with this problem is the use of *triangulation methods*, which involve several temporal metrics, self-report ratings, external judgments, and physiological measurements [17]. Silva and Read [18] selected and defined four metrics to evaluate their creativity method: Mass of Ideas generated

(MI), which is the number of ideas generated by a group divided by the number of participants; Quality of Ideas generated (QI), the average novelty rating (from three creativity evaluators) multiplied by the average appropriateness rating (from the same three evaluators); Enjoyment of Participants (EP); and Learning of Participants (LP). The five ratings are combined into a single calculable value metric, given by a formula. As the authors mention, HCI is not particularly strong when it comes to the evaluation of methods, especially with regard to creativity and innovation. However, evaluation and comparison are needed not only when one is required to select a specific method to work with, but also when one wants to compare the results of different methods [18].

CREATIVE WRITING USER INTERFACES

We are all writers, the difference is that some of us write, and others don't.

– J. Saramago, Nobel of Literature

This work addresses the general research question of how to design user experiences where the creative side of people is fostered by the peculiarities and elements of the user interface. We started out by addressing the study, design and evaluation of novel user interfaces for supporting creative writing. Our initial goals included the design and evaluation of a new application, which supports creative writers by helping them shape and articulate their thoughts, review texts, and become more creative and productive, as compared to using the currently available tools. After completing the design and development of this tool, called Haven, we selected two more, in different categories: Hanx Writer and Write or Die. In this section, we describe these three different UIs.

Haven: a "Zen" Creative Writing UI

Haven, which was developed previously by our team based on creative writing techniques and the needs of writers, is one of the user interfaces we evaluated during this research.

Figure 1: Snowy writing theme.

Haven includes: a plot generator, a writing prompts generator, background soundtracks, typewriter sounds, and other elements. Most importantly, it features a "Zen-like" design with different writing "themes", as illustrated by Fig.1 and Fig. 2, which show, respectively, a "snowy white" theme and a "moonlight writing" theme.

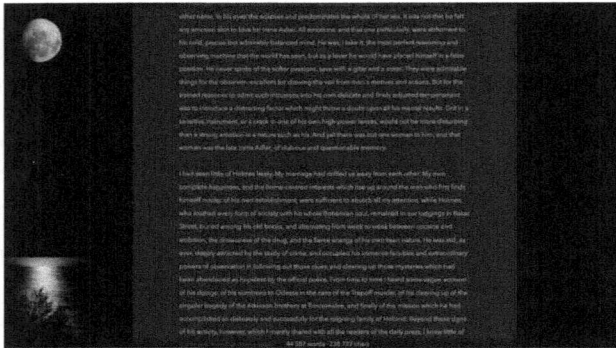

Figure 2: Moonlight writing theme.

The writing prompt is a popup window that displays dozens of different story triggers that can be used to spark the writer's imagination. Fig. 3 shows an example of this.

Tell this story:

He turned the key in the lock and opened the door. To his horror, he saw...

Figure 3: An example of a writing prompt.

The plot generator is similar, but in this case it structures a story plot around two random characters, sets them in a random place (e.g. a river, a university, etc.), in a given situation (e.g. a marriage proposal, a blind date, a love triangle), and suggests a theme for unifying the story (e.g. vengeance, rebirth, opportunity, etc.).

Hanx Writer: the Return of the Nostalgic Typewriter

Just like the cachet of vinyl in an mp3 world, some facets of the typewriter can instill hipster appeal in a writing interface for a post-media user group. After some research, we chose to evaluate the impact of Hanx Writer[1]. This tool was recently launched by Tom Hanks, the actor, and gained momentum due to the solidness of its design, which realistically mimics the mass and metal of a real typewriter.

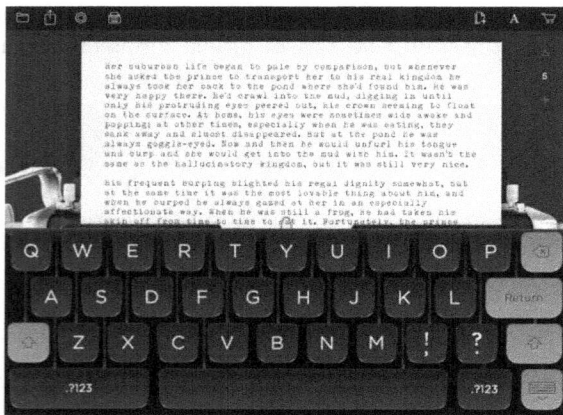

Figure 4: Hanx Writer.

Hanx Writer has a proper sheaf-rolled-in typewriter interface complete with ribbon color choice and margin measurements. Figure 4 illustrates its look. We hypothesized that

the retro analogue appeal could positively influence the creativity, productivity and even mental well-being of our target group of youths.

Write or Die … no tagline needed!

Write or Die[2] aims to eliminate writer's block by providing consequences for procrastination. The users write to avoid annoying sounds and alarm warning colors, i.e. if a certain threshold of time passes by without any new words being added to the manuscript, a visual stimulus is triggered and coupled with annoying sounds. Figure 5 illustrates this UI, taken at a time when the background was becoming more and more red in color.

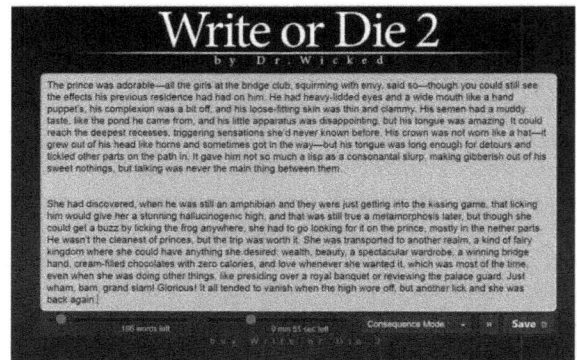

Figure 5: Write or Die.

We hypothesized that our target user group would enjoy the excitement and gaming aspect of this tool, and would be more productive due to the challenge this particular UI brings.

As an introduction to the following experiments, we will first focus on what they have in common: the participants we chose. Since we were interested in empowering marginalized groups by providing them with creative writing tools, we targeted teenagers with learning difficulties, cognitive deficits, and problems of socialization. These teenagers (aged between 12 and 18 years old) were taken from their family environment for various reasons: suffering physical, sexual, or mental abuse; lacking the care and affection appropriate to their age and personal situation; being forced into age-inappropriate conditions such as excessive work; and so on. They currently live and study in a full-time formal education institution at Estabelecimento Vila Mar in Funchal, Madeira. Figure 6 illustrates the environment where they study.

In the next three sections, we will describe the evaluations: including the participants, method, procedure and results of each. All the data taken from the experiments was made completely anonymous.

---

[1] http://www.hitcents.com/b2b/work/hanx

[2] http://writeordie.com

Figure 6: The youths in the educational establishment.

FIRST STUDY: ZEN UI VS. BASELINE

Words were not given to man in order to conceal his thoughts.

— J. Saramago

Our first evaluation study included a two-week experience in the previously mentioned educational institution for underserved youths. We addressed the following research questions:

RQ1: Can a "Zen-like" creative writing UI positively influence the productivity of users?

RQ2: Can a "Zen-like" creative writing UI positively influence the mental well-being of users?

RQ3: Can a "Zen-like" creative writing UI positively influence the creativity of users?

Participants

This preliminary experience involved 14 students from the institution's population, aged between 12 and 18 years old. There were five females and nine males. We conducted fifteen sessions and used two Mac Minis and eight PCs. As a prerequisite, the participants had to have some interest in writing and a basic amount of computer and Internet experience.

Method

Our experimental design was based on a between-subjects design, in which two groups of students were randomly assembled according to different conditions such as gender, age, computing experience, and Internet experience, to ensure that the groups were similar as possible. The conditions to compare were two tools: MS Word (as baseline) and Haven (a Zen-like tool). The control group used MS Word, a tool without any explicit creative writing features, and the experimental group used the Zen-like creative writing user interface Haven.

Setting

Before starting the experiment the scope of the study and the rules were explained. Each group was instructed to start by answering the daily challenges and then responding to a daily survey. During the challenges, the two groups were separated in different rooms. Since we were using our tool, Haven, we introduced them to the tool and then left them to try it for a few minutes before they began on the first day.

Procedure

Participants were given a daily writing challenge, and were asked to fill in a very short Likert scale survey about how that daily experience made them feel. No time limit was set for completing the writing tasks.

Examples of the daily writing challenges included: "Write about a time when you used your inner strength to get through a tough situation"; "Write about the bravest thing you have ever done"; and "Write about when someone hurt your feelings". These were conceived by one of the authors (a creative writing instructor), who also took into account the age of the participants.

The daily survey was based on the following Flow Theory dimensions: (i) intense and focused concentration on the present moment, (ii) sense of personal control or agency over the situation or activity, (iii) loss of reflective self-consciousness, and (iv) distortion of temporal experience. Participants ranked a 7-point Likert scale based on questions such as: "I felt very concentrated during this challenge" and "I lost track of time during this challenge".

Results

We analyzed the results from a perspective that triangulates the words written, the data from the surveys, feedback from the teacher, interviews with the students and the stories themselves.

Productivity was measured using the average number of words as an estimate. Creativity and mental well-being were measured using subjective, quantitative (Likert scale-based) daily surveys which were constructed from the Flow Theory's concepts [2]. Note that each student completed a daily writing challenge during the period of 15 days in a row, for a total of 43 data points, as the average number of participants, per day, was around 9 (not all students participated every day).

RQ1: *Can a "Zen-like" creative writing UI positively influence the productivity of users?*
To analyze the deviation data normality we used the Skewness and Kurtosis and Kolmogorov-Smirnov tests ($p<0.05$). We concluded that our sample had a deviation of normality as showed in Figure 7.

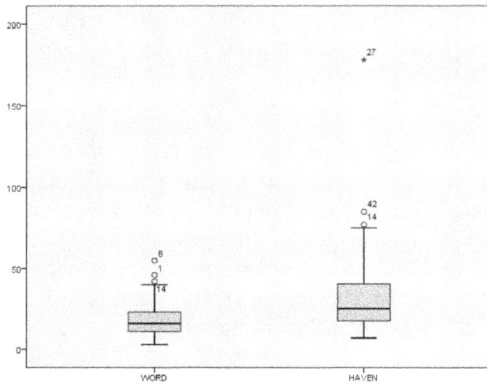
Figure 7 - Box plot

Regarding data dispersion, users in the experimental group (using Haven) wrote more words (M=34.3, SE=4.3), than those in the control group using our baseline MS Word (M=18.3, SE=1.7). The non-parametric Wilcoxon test was applied to evaluate MS Word and Haven deviation differences. For students using Haven the results were significantly higher than students using MS Word (T=9, z=-3.7, p<.05, r=-.56).

RQ2: *Can a "Zen-like" creative writing UI positively influence the mental well-being of users?*

In order to assess the participants' mental well-being as well as its evolution along the two weeks of this study, we asked them to select up to three adjectives from the following list: Surprised, Delighted, Laid back, Depressed, Pacific, Happy, Tired, Bored, Sad, Satisfied, Frustrated, Angry, Serious, Animated, Distressed, Creative, and Frightened.

Figure 8 shows all the word clouds automatically generated according to each daily writing challenge (the numbers indicate the corresponding day). We can see that Happy and Creative were increasing slightly along the weeks, although the most relevant observation is simply the confirmation that most adjectives indicated a positive mental well-being.

Figure 9 displays the total count for each adjective selected by the participants. We can see that Happy, Animated, Laid back, Satisfied, and Creative are the most chosen adjectives, especially when using Haven.

Figure 9: Total count for the adjectives chosen by participants.

We proceed using repeated measures such us Friedman's ANOVA approach to testing differences between each tool from the answers in the survey based on the dimensions of Flow Theory and ranked by participants in a seven-point Likert scale.

The dimensions (ii) sense of personal control or agency over the situation or activity, (iii) loss of reflective self-consciousness and dimension, and (iv) distortion of temporal experience did not have statistical significance when compared with each tool.

For the other dimension, (i) intense and focused concentration on the present moment, $Fr(1)$=4.00, p<.05 was statically significant. Therefore Wilcoxon tests were used to display if there were any differences between the control group using MS Word and the experimental group using Haven. The results showed that for the participants in the experimental group, concentration levels were significantly higher than in the control group (T=24, z=-2.05, p<.05, r=-.25).

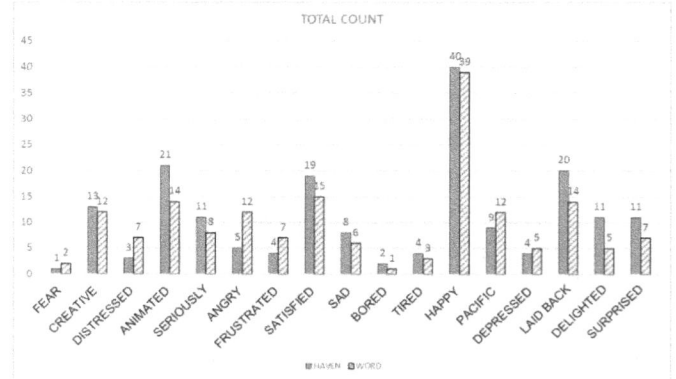

	Adjective	
Day	Happy	Creative
D1	3	4
D2	3	2
D3	4	3
D4	3	5
D5	4	4
D6	5	4
D7	4	4
D8	6	5
D8	5	6
D9	4	5
D10	7	6
D11	7	5
D12	6	6
D13	8	7
D14	10	8
D15	10	7

Figure 8: Word clouds for the adjectives that participants selected at the end of each daily challenge. Numbers indicate the day.

RQ3: *Can a "Zen-like" creative writing UI positively influence the creativity of users?*

Regarding the stories written, and from a creativity perspective, we found some differences between the control and experimental group, with Haven apparently allowing for greater levels of creativity. However, it was not possible to establish this difference with sound confidence. In the remainder of this section we include excerpts taken from the students' writings.

"In the place where I grew up, there were many, many trees, some more pretty than others, but they all had their particular enchantment, an enchantment that leaves me nostalgic now that I don't live there anymore. I am now an adult, but I am nothing but a problem for people around me. The only thing I have left is the memory of those beautiful trees living in freedom, dancing in the wind, freeing their leaves during the Winter so that children like me could play in them." –User4-Haven

"Three wishes? I just wish for my family to be happy, that would be a real dream." –User7-Haven

"I hit my father hard. Yes it's true. And it was all because of fighting over school. If I had the power to make something disappear, I would vanish the terror I have from the possibility of being arrested and put into prison." –User9-MSWord

None of the users had ever taken an experiment such as this one. In the beginning, we found a slight initial resistance to meet the first daily writing challenge, as they were not very familiar with this kind of exercise. Later, students were curious to know what challenges would be proposed next, and that increased their desire to write. Note that the challenges were the same for both the control and experimental groups, and there was no transfer of learning as we were using a between-subjects experimental design. Triangulating the results with semi-structured interviews allowed us to corroborate some of these results and observations. When interviewed, all expressed genuine interest in creative writing and most users emphasized that the background soundtrack in the Zen UI was very helpful in making them relax and thus respond better to the writing challenges. Many of these underprivileged students have had very difficult lives, but we should highlight that some of them aspire to become amateur or even professional writers in the future, and showed great interest in the writing challenges we proposed. Some students claimed to use personal diaries in their daily lives, in which they would record their most meaningful and deeply felt experiences.

SECOND STUDY: NOSTALGIC TYPEWRITER VS. ZEN UI

In our second evaluation, we investigated whether Hanx Writer's nostalgic, retro appeal could positively influence the students' creativity, productivity and even mental well-being, as compared to the Zen UI of Haven. In this context, the second study addresses our research question 4.

RQ4: What is the influence of the typewriter UI on the participants' productivity and mental well-being, when compared to the Zen UI of Haven?

Participants

In this experiment, the participants were 8 students (five male and three female) of a similar age as the same group from the first experiment. We conducted one session and used two iPads running Haven and Hanx Writer.

Method

We employed a within-subjects experimental setup, where we divided the students into two groups: one using the Haven iPad app and another group using the iPad with the Hanx Writer app, randomizing the order. When they finished, we switched the tools and gave them a different challenge, also randomly picked.

Procedure

In this evaluation, we gave the same writing challenge to all students and conducted the sessions in the same room. Each group of participants was instructed to start by answering the challenge in 10 minutes and completing a short survey in the end. The survey was basically the same as in the first study.

Results

We evaluated the overall impact of both the Zen features and the nostalgic, realistic, retro-futuristic typewriter. Again, productivity was estimated as the average number of words produced, and mental well-being was estimated through the Flow Theory survey (the same as in the previous study). We used the Skewness and Kurtosis and Kolmorov-Smirnov tests *(p<0.05)* to analyze the data normality. Results show that our data was normal. T-tests were used to compare the statistical significance of the samples using a 95% level of confidence.

Tests of Normality

	Kolmogorov-Smirnov[a]			Shapiro-Wilk		
	Statistic	df	Sig.	Statistic	df	Sig.
HANXWRITER	,228	8	,200[*]	,896	8	,266
Haven	,196	8	,200[*]	,859	8	,117

[*]. This is a lower bound of the true significance.

a. Lilliefors Significance Correction

Figure 10 - Test of normality

From observation, both tools aroused the curiosity of the participants. The most effective elements were the keystroke sounds and realistic animations in Hanx Writer, and the background soundtracks of Haven. Haven does not allow writing in landscape orientation (we used iPads) and that created some disappointment with users, since they felt it would be easier to write in that orientation. Note that, for these students, anything that does not make them achieve their objectives immediately creates a great sense of anxiety and frustration, as the teacher told us when interviewed:

"For these students, when we give a different type of routine other than the ones they are accustomed to, and if for some reason they do not achieve their objective, they tend

to react in a frustrated manner, much more than the average teenager or student."-Teacher.

A threshold of ten minutes was set in this experiment, but only three participants used the time in its entirety. The remaining participants wrote their short stories in less time. Using Hanx Writer, participants wrote on average more words (M=41.3, SE=6.5) than using the Zen UI of Haven (M=38.5, SE=9.6). However, this difference was not found to be statistically significant (t(14)=0.22, p<0.41). Both tools were effective in putting users into a good mood, selecting the adjectives that reflect this attitude: animated, happy, creative, and so on.

We also used repeated measures such us Friedman's ANOVA approach to test differences between each tool when compared with Flow Theory. In all dimensions, (i) intense and focused concentration on the present moment, (ii) sense of personal control or agency over the situation or activity, (iii) loss of reflective self-consciousness, and (iv) distortion of temporal experience, results were not statistically significant when compared with each tool.

We complemented this information with semi-structured interviews performed after the experiment, which suggest that both Haven and Hanx Writer were equally pleasing and effective.

THIRD STUDY: WRITE OR DIE

Finally, we hypothesized that our target user group of marginalized youths would enjoy the excitement and pressure brought by Write or Die, and would be more productive due to the challenge element of this particular UI.

RQ5: *Can the pressure and stimulus provided by Write or Die positively influence the productivity of participants?*

Participants

In this experiment, 10 students participated (eight males and two females) with a similar age to the same groups before. We conducted one session and used 10 PCs.

Procedure

In this case, we did not divide the participants into groups. Instead, they were all together in the same room. The writing challenge was solved using the tool Write or Die. All participants began responding to the challenge at the same time and were given 10 minutes as a max timeout. They finished the experiment and then answered a short survey (the same as the second study survey). The experimental setup and procedure were thus exactly the same as in the second study.

Results

This experiment was based on a premise taken from our observations of previous experiments: we wondered whether the student would write more if presented with a UI that used pressure as a motivation tactic.

Results showed that the participants using Write or Die wrote an average of 26.6 words (SE=5.7), which contrasts clearly with both Haven (M=38.5, SE=9.6) and Hanx Writer

(M=41.3, SE=6.5). For exactly the same conditions and experimental setup, the difference was not statistically significant when comparing Write or Die with Haven (t(14)=1.22, p<0.12), but was significant when comparing Write or Die with Hanx Writer (t(14)=1.87, p<0.05).

Semi-structured interviews conducted after the writing challenges suggest that participants did not find the auditory stimulus (an alarming noise that Write or Die produces when the user is not writing, not to be confused with Haven's calming soundtrack) to be a productive influence; in fact almost all participants found it too stressful, which is particularly significant since they were very excited with this new tool at the beginning of the experiments. Figure 12 plots the total count of adjectives selected by the participants at the end of the experiment's survey. We can see that users' mental well-being was also very good, as most of the adjectives selected were positive (happy, animated, satisfied, and creative). In fact, the downside of Write or Die was lower productivity, as measured by average number of words written.

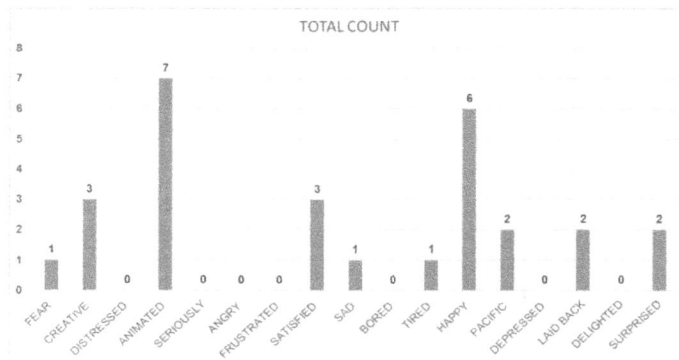

Figure 12: Total count for the adjectives selected by the participants when using Write or Die.

COMPARING CREATIVE WRITING USER INTERFACES

Finally, it is possible to combine productivity (as measured by the average number of words written) with the Flow Theory dimensions into a single radar chart, normalizing the results (average number of words written) into the 7-point Likert scale. This allows a fast and useful comparison of different tools.

Figure 13 shows the combined results for our experiments and the different tools involved. By looking at the figure, one can see that the sense of control was not a significant issue for any of the tools we evaluated. MS Word, Haven, Hanx Writer and even Write or Die exhibited high Likert-scale values in this dimension. The same observation is valid for the Concentration dimension. The greater difference between the tools was found to be in the Loss of self-consciousness and Distortion of time dimensions. According to the survey, participants reported feeling less self-conscious while using Hanx Writer and Write or Die. The same happened when asked about losing track of time.

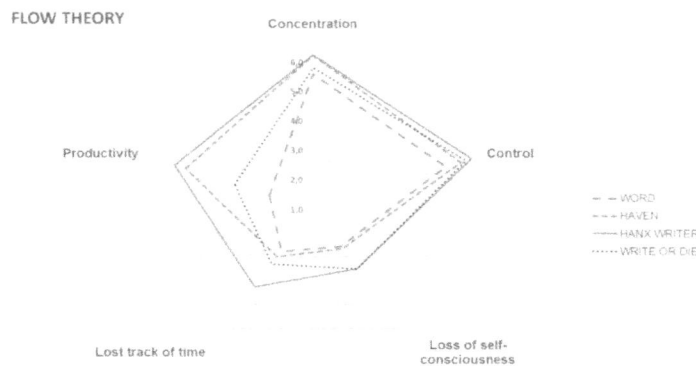

FLOW THEORY

Concentration

Productivity

Control

Lost track of time

Loss of self-consciousness

– – WORD
- - - HAVEN
—— HANX WRITER
······ WRITE OR DIE

Figure 13: Framework and chart for plotting and comparing creative writing tools.

DISCUSSION

During all of the experiments, it was clear that the participants became intensely focused in the writing moment. A loss of reflective self-consciousness was also reported. From a qualitative perspective, some users described their experiences, usually emphasizing the tool and writing challenges they felt better with. For instance: "*In the story we had to write about a man sitting on a park bench, that's when I felt most creative, because having that jump start a lot of things came into my mind and I felt in the mood for writing, forgetting about everything else. It was my longest text.*" (User9-Haven). Therefore, the writing prompts were observed as effective tools for kickstarting the creative writing process. Another effective feature was the background soundtrack: "*With the music, so many things started to come to my mind ... without the music my thoughts got lost*" (User5-Haven).

It was clear that all participants felt somewhat empowered and creative during the experiments, especially when using Haven. "*I thought about things I had never imagined before, I felt very creative*" (User11-Haven). According to the teacher who observed later, if one considers the low levels of education, socialization and problematic past experiences and behaviors of the test subjects, then both Haven and Hanx Writer were effective user interfaces for getting these users writing. The students became more creative and even felt better, happier and more relaxed. Finally, regarding the users' intention to adopt the tools, it was clear that they exhibited a positive attitude towards using them, for example: "*We should use this tool during class or to do our homework. It makes me want to write more.*" (User 4-Haven).

One limitation of our study is that it does not consider the long-term usage of these tools. Therefore, conclusions are limited to an incipient (two-week) usage of the different creative writing user interfaces. However, it is still very useful to have this data, since overcoming initial resistance is the key to unleashing the creativity and writing skills that these teenagers possess.

CONCLUSION

Public access to culture, especially literary culture, is one of the greatest achievements of modern civilization. Writing is among the oldest human activities and creative writing is an essential activity in many industries and professions. Creative writing is also often used as a pedagogical tool to increase literacy and can be used to build positive relationships and encourage dialogue across diverse communities. Creative writing gives a voice to marginal groups in society, allowing them tell their stories.

In this paper we presented a novel approach that addresses, for the first time, a minority user group of underserved youths and evaluates how they write using different user interfaces. Specifically, we described three experiments that analyzed the impact of different creative writing user interfaces on the productivity and mental well-being of underserved youths. We compared MS Word (our baseline), a "Zen" user interface (Haven), a nostalgic typewriter (Hanx Writer), and a stress-based tool called Write or Die. From a productivity perspective, our results suggest that the typewriter UI was the most effective, followed closely by the Zen UI. From a mental well-being perspective, it was clear that this marginalized group felt more inspired, more focused and more immersed when using the Zen UI and the typewriter UI. Contrary to our initial expectations, the stress-based UI (Write or Die) showed the lowest productivity levels.

We have addressed these somewhat sensitive issues and tried to empower underserved youths with user interfaces that help them to find their inner voices and express themselves. Moreover, our results have a practical utility for interaction designers who are interested in devising new interaction styles and designs that can promote positive relationships and even encourage dialogue across diverse communities. Our tool Haven is a first step, but certainly there is plenty of room for advancement and many discoveries to be made. By presenting a perspective on how underserved teenagers use creative writing tools, we hope this paper might inspire the design and development of novel and empowering digital tools.

ACKNOWLEDGMENTS

We would like to thank the students who participated in this research, as well as the teacher Rosário Antunes. The institutional support from Vila Mar was generously provided by the director Patrícia Branco and pedagogical director José António Banganho.

REFERENCES

1. Yardi, S. and Bruckman, A. (2012). Income, race, and class: exploring socioeconomic differences in family technology use. In *Proceedings of the SIGCHI Conference on Human Factors in Computing Systems* (CHI'12). ACM, New York, NY, USA, pp.3041-3050.

2. Csikszentmihalyi, M. (1990). *Flow: The Psychology of Optimal Experience*. New York, NY: Harper and Row.

3. Carroll, E. and Latulipe, C. (2012). Triangulating the personal creative experience: self-report, external judgments, and physiology. In *Proceedings of Graphics Interface 2012* (GI'12). Canadian Information Processing Society, Toronto, Ont., Canada, 53-60.

4. Sawhney, N. (2009). Voices beyond walls: the role of digital storytelling for empowering marginalized youth in refugee camps. In *Proceedings of the 8th International Conference on Interaction Design and Children* (IDC'09). ACM, New York, NY, USA, pp. 302-305.

5. Cooper, Y., Bernardine Dias, M., Teves, E., Belousov, S., and Dias, F. (2011). Enhancing participation and education in CS through guided research projects in underserved communities. In *Proceedings of the 42nd ACM technical symposium on Computer science education* (SIGCSE '11). ACM, New York, NY, USA, 577-582.

6. Tapia, A. and Kvasny, L. (2004). Recruitment is never enough: retention of women and minorities in the IT workplace. In *Proceedings of the 2004 SIGMIS conference on Computer personnel research: Careers, culture, and ethics in a networked environment* (SIGMIS CPR '04). ACM, New York, NY, USA, pp. 84-91.

7. Shumba, R., Ferguson-Boucher, K., Sweedyk, E., Taylor, C., Franklin, G., Turner, C., Sande, C., Acholonu, G., Bace, R., and Hall, L. (2013). Cybersecurity, women and minorities: findings and recommendations from a preliminary investigation. In *Proceedings of the ITiCSE-WGR'13*. ACM, NY, USA, pp. 1-14.

8. Spaiser, V. (2011). Young people's political participation on the Internet in Germany: empowered ethnic minority groups? In *Proceedings of the 12th Annual International Digital Government Research Conference: Digital Government Innovation in Challenging Times* (dg.o '11). ACM, New York, NY, USA, 307-316.

9. Magnifico, A. (2010). "Getting others' perspectives": a case study of creative writing environments and mentorship. In *Proceedings of the 9th International Conference of the Learning Sciences - Volume 1* (ICLS'10), Kimberly Gomez, Leilah Lyons, and Joshua Radinsky (Eds.), Vol. 1. pp. 1151-1157.

10. Yannopoulos, A. (2013). DirectorNotation: Artistic and technological system for professional film directing. *Journal of Computing and Cultural Heritage* 6, 1 Art. 2.

11. Goulet, M., Duplessis, A. (2012). Focus group on computer tools used for professional writing and preliminary evaluation of LinguisTech. In *Proceedings of the EACL 2012 Workshop on Computational Linguistics and Writing*. Association for Computational Linguistics, Stroudsburg, PA, USA, 39-47.

12. Coughlan, T. and Johnson, P. (2009). Understanding productive, structural and longitudinal interactions in the design of tools for creative activities. In *Proceedings of the seventh ACM conference on Creativity and cognition* (C&C'09). ACM, New York, NY, USA, pp.155-164.

13. Wiesner, K., Foth, M. and Bilandzic, M. (2009). Unleashing creative writers: situated engagement with mobile narratives. In *Proceedings of the 21st Annual Conference of the Australian Computer-Human Interaction Special Interest Group: Design: Open 24/7* (OZCHI'09), ACM, New York, NY, USA, pp.373-376.

14. Bernstein, M., Little, G., Miller, R., Hartmann, B., Ackerman, M., Karger, D., Crowell, D., and Panovich, K. (2010). Soylent: a word processor with a crowd inside. In *Proceedings of the 23nd annual ACM symposium on User interface software and technology* (UIST'10). ACM, New York, NY, USA, pp. 313-322.

15. Robertson, J. and Nicholson, K. (2007). Adventure Author: a learning environment to support creative design. In *Proceedings of the 6th international conference on Interaction design and children* (IDC'07). ACM, New York, NY, USA, pp. 37-44.

16. Mary Elizabeth "M.E." Jones, Melanie Kisthardt, and Marie A. Cooper. 2011. Interdisciplinary teaching: introductory programming via creative writing. In *Proceedings of the 42nd ACM technical symposium on Computer science education* ACM, NY, USA, 523-528.

17. Carroll, E. and Latulipe, C. (2012). Triangulating the personal creative experience: self-report, external judgments, and physiology. In *Proceedings of Graphics Interface 2012* (GI'12). Canadian Information Processing Society, Toronto, Ont., Canada, Canada, pp. 53-60.

18. Silva, P. A. and Read, J. C. (2010). A methodology to evaluate creative design methods: a study with the BadIdeas method. In *Proceedings of the 22nd Conference of the Computer-Human Interaction Special Interest Group of Australia on Computer-Human Interaction* (OZCHI'10). ACM, NY, USA, pp. 264-271.

MetaMorphe: Designing Expressive 3D Models for Digital Fabrication

Cesar Torres   **Eric Paulos**

Electrical Engineering and Computer Sciences
University of California, Berkeley
{cearto, paulos}@berkeley.edu

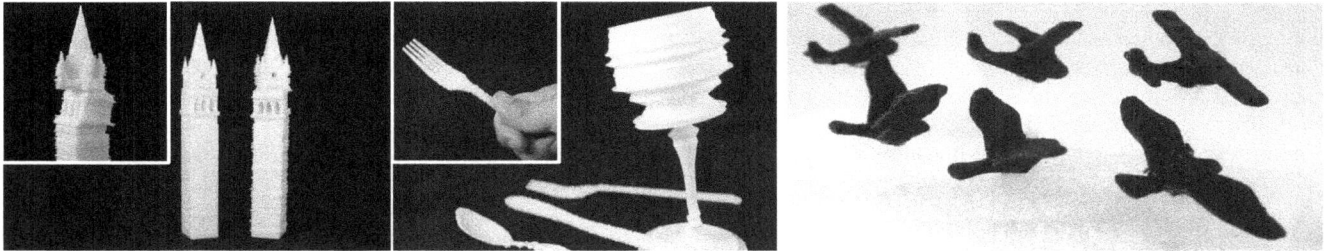

Figure 1. a) the UC Berkeley Campanile embedded with audio data from Marco Savio's "Bodies upon the gears" speech, b) *EarthquakeWare*, utensils and tableware expressing seismograph data near you, c) small multiples of airplane and bird forms reformed and retargeted using a MetaMorphe style.

ABSTRACT

The creative promise of 3D digital fabrication tools is tremendous. However due to the wide range of tools and interfaces, a common static file format called STL is used for sharing designs. While customization tools add creative handles to these digital models, they are often constrained to pre-configured parameters limiting the creative potential of shared digital models. We introduce MetaMorphe, a novel digital fabrication framework that uses a common web-programming metaphor to enable users to easily transform static 3D models into re-formed, re-made, and re-imagined customized personal artifacts. We demonstrate the compatibility of Meta-Morphe with three well-established design interfaces, direction manipulation, scripted-CAD, and generative design. Through a user study with design experts, MetaMorphe reveals that decisions that physically produce bespoke artifacts or encode unique metadata actively affect perceptions of authorship, agency, and authenticity. We discuss how expressive model-building tools such as MetaMorphe enable a cultural shift in 3D design in terms of participation, personalization, and creativity.

Author Keywords

digital fabrication; creativity support tools; design; DIY;

ACM Classification Keywords

D.2.2 Design Tools and Techniques: User interfaces

INTRODUCTION

"The authenticity of a thing is the essence of all that is transmissible from its beginning, ranging from its substantive duration to its testimony to the history which it has experienced"
- Walter Benjamin (1936)

Just as Benjamin noted how objects are fundamentally transformed through *mechanical* reproduction, the way we see and make objects is being challenged by today's *digital* fabrication (DF) technologies. Even now grassroots innovation in the Maker Movement is addressing critical themes in education, manufacturing, and health care [4, 17]; more opportunities exist for design technologies to be even more accessible.

Currently, artists and hobbyists freely share their designs on online repositories like Thingiverse [20]. However in order to span modeling tools and for convenience, files are shared in a lowest-common-denominator format called the STereoLithography (STL) which unfortunately only encodes a static mesh. Emerging tools such as Thingiverse Customizer[1] expand the variety of forms from a single design; however such parametric designers have been found to be less than engaging. In a quantitative analysis of digital models on Thingiverse, Oehlberg, et al., observed that Customizer objects make up 74% of remixed objects, yet rarely elicit subsequent user activity or contribute additional content to Thingiverse [23]. Other sites such as GrabCAD[2] provide original CAD files, however altering these models depends on a user's ability to use more sophisticated CAD tools. Thus for a novice user, designing a model quickly breaks down to finding the "correct" pre-made model, downloading it, and printing it. While initially satisfying, this static design practice generally prevent users from critically engaging with either the form or function of a printed object.

---

[1] http://www.thingiverse.com/apps/customizer/
[2] https://grabcad.com

The current state of 3D modeling tools and sharing practices encourage *designs to favor replication and sameness*. While this "copy exact" is indeed a strength of 3D modeling, we argue that design tools are needed that actively engage users and invite new creative opportunities for variation, personalization, derivation, and versioning (Figure 1). We imagine models that are encoded with multiple forms, easy to derive and extend, and incorporate new digital practices. We term this metamorphic design, and introduce MetaMorphe — a DF design framework for modifying static, digital meshes and creating customized, personal artifacts. This paper makes two contributions to DF design tool research.

First, we introduce a JavaScript framework which takes a new look at CAD, and separates modeling into structural, style, and interactivity concerns. This allows developers to flexibly interact with a mesh in a form similar to web programming and quickly create engaging modeling interfaces that are tailor-fit to different creative practices.

Second, MetaMorphe presents a "meta-design" space through a parallel interface (Figure 4) consisting of multiple interaction styles. This interface allows users to engage with *form* through direct manipulation, inspect and modify *functionality* through scripted CAD, and produce multiple variant *styles* of a single design through a generative interface. By using a common underlying framework, MetaMorphe provides a fluid transition between each interface style, allowing users to move between and reflect on different design priorities.

This paper first motivates the design of MetaMorphe through related work. We then outline the rationale behind our web-inspired framework, provide a grounding example of interaction with the tool, and present supported design practices. Lastly, we evaluate the MetaMorphe interface through a workshop study with creative experts, and conclude by discussing implications of our findings for digital fabrication.

RELATED WORK
MetaMorphe is inspired by emerging DF design tools and concerns arising from communities of artists, makers, and industry. We also examine creative design practices that are redefining digital interactions with physical media.

Sharing models
As digital fabrication matures, a revised STL format is proposed to support new techniques such as multimaterial printing [9]. Similarly, Reprap hosts a forum[3] for discussing improvements to the STL format. Such proposals include adding functional metadata, altering data structures, or encoding a voxel representation. Eschewing a static file altogether, OpenFab proposes a GPU-like pipeline for supporting multi-material prints; geometries are procedurally evaluated thereby reducing the memory footprint and startup time [34]. Autodesk has incorporated iPart and iAssemblies, a parametric design widget that allows designers to specify dynamic components and generate derivative parts. MetaMorphe suggests the need to incorporate multiple design instances in model representations in order to encourage derivative work.

[3]http://reprap.org/wiki/A_community_specification_for_an_improvement_to_STL_files

Crafting interfaces
Several studies examine how modeling tools can be made more accessible to users outside mechanical design. Most relevant to our work, Jacobs, et al., *Codeable Objects* is a tool that enables novice users to produce personal and functional objects through parametric models and generative patterns. In her study, Jacobs confronted a tension between the inherent dissimilarity between traditional fabrication techniques and computational design tools [11]. Such dissimilarities have traditionally been absolved by incorporating more traditional craft processes in the design of digital tools [19]; this continues to be a current trend:

In software, MeshMixer engages with physical forms through mesh mixing, or the collage and hybridization of multiple models. Sculpting metaphors (e.g. pinch, tug) are widespread in tools like Autodesk Sculpt. Hybrid techniques such as Nervous System[4] sculpt a mesh topology by subdividing geometries using a brush interaction. A proprietary online community has developed from these tools centered around model sharing, demonstrating that this type of customization is highly desired by users. MetaMorphe further extends these sharing practices to include models that are encoded with multiple designs, and provides a mechanism for users to "source" a design's history that is often lost.

Tangible interfaces are more akin to the physical making process. *FreeD* [39], a reductive sculpting tool, provides tactile feedback to novices and interactively guides them as they sculpt a digital model freehand. Alternatively, real world objects are collaged and digitized into new forms and shapes [7, 8]. MixFab, a mixed-reality CAD interface, allowed users to carry out CAD operations using gestural manipulation [35]. Similarly, sketch-based editing in *ModelCraft* is enabled by capturing physical annotations and converting them to operations on digital models [31]. While these types of tools enable more natural interactions for constructing and manipulating objects, the space of operations is more restricted to those already present in the equivalent physical media [10]. In work on digital tool building for maker communities, Jacobs, et al., suggests CAD tools should enable designers to "reconfigure virtual and physical modular parts through a small number of operations that are derived from the topology of the parts themselves" [12] as an alternative to a full-featured *tabula rasa* CAD interface. Through parallel interfaces, MetaMorphe supports both *crafting* interfaces with direct manipulation and *computational* interfaces with generative design and scripted-CAD interactions on *existing* designs.

Scripted CAD
Open initiatives like openSCAD [16] and openJSCAD [21] are gaining footholds within the scripted-CAD community. In particular, these tools allow programmers to produce end-user interfaces for customizing models which allow users to alter features such as width, curves, or text. These customization tools engage novice users by providing creative handles to otherwise static designs. However the programming scheme for developing these interfaces still relies on domain knowledge of computational geometry. To the end-user, their choice

[4]http://n-e-r-v-o-u-s.com/

of parameters is already fixed by the interface designer. A large number of authors (42%) on Thingiverse only produce generated designs and never contribute other content, suggesting that many authors lack the technical expertise necessary to modify designs using CAD tools [23]. While these tools provide some customization, they do not go further to explore more expressive and creative design a user might envision. Autodesk's Project Dreamcatcher [1], an experimental generative modeling tool, proposed a higher-level shape descriptor for specifying function and form. While not as abstracted, MetaMorphe exposes customization code through human-readable style sheets, providing a scaffold for users alter and build upon existing designs.

Bespoke Fabrication: Outside the "copy-exact" paradigm

Though "copy-exact" is a major benefit of mechanical reproduction, DF design tools have opened new opportunities for customization. However in the rush to "copy exact", there has been little attention to modeling tools that value personalized or unique artifacts. Below we detail the emerging role of bespoke fabrication in practice and production.

One-off designs
The introduction of chance and meaning in the design process has been used to digitally fabricate unique artifacts. For instance, Zoran et. al. incorporated history by adding breaks and repairs into the form of digitally fabricated artifacts [38]. Different forms of data have been used to add personal meaning: stories and memories are used to shape knitted crafts [27], environmental data is used to shape artistic sculpture [37], or even a life-logged relationship is embedded in the design of matrimonial rings[5]. Other approaches manipulate the fabrication process. *FreeD* allowed users physical control of the DF process leaving impressions of "the hand of the artist"[39]. Willis et. al. used interactive audio and gestural input to give form to artifacts in a series of *Interactive Fabrication* tools [36]. Our paper aims in foregrounding these unique and bespoke interactions in the design of metamorphic models.

Digital Fabrication as an Artistic Medium
Artists have shown that digital fabrication is a critical disruptive medium that can promote a new class of designs. For instance, Tarik Sadouma's *nike town 2* utilizes the rubber treads of a shoe to create dynamic urban landscapes [28], while *DERRICK* [33] features *digital* IKEA furniture models which have been hacked and "infected" to produce misshapen forms that materialize a *biological* phenomena. Engaging directly with 3D printing aesthetics, Artist LIA subverts the layer-by-layer DF process with *Filament Sculptures* [18] by producing custom g-code, or printhead instructions, to produce continuous free-form lines to form a type of 3D thread art. Plummer-Fernandez explores a different sharing practice in *Disarming Corrupter*, a protocol which encrypts and corrupts digital models [26]. MetaMorphe provides an open method for artists and designers alike to explore the physical language of artifacts in order to critically engage with everyday forms.

[5] http://www.diarings.com/

SYSTEM DESIGN

As we developed methods for designing dynamic digital models, we quickly realized that we needed a flexible way to create and iterate on different design interfaces. In this section, we cover the design rationale behind the MetaMorphe framework and how this enables developers to quickly create interfaces for manipulating a mesh.

MetaMorphe is a web-based framework written in JavaScript and extends the THREE.js[6] WebGL library. As the *lingua franca* of the web, building the framework using JavaScript provides easy access to several external APIs (e.g., weather data, webcam, microphone, and GPS) that can enable novel interaction techniques. The framework uses Separation of Concerns (SoC) — a common software pattern used in computer science to separate a program into distinct sections. This pattern appears prevalently in web architectures as HTML/CSS/JS and in HCI at the Model-View-Controller. Inspired by the Web SoC, we incorporate "view-source", a functionality known to encourage open cross-disciplinary design practices driven by learning from the work of others [24]. As an added benefit, SoC implicitly creates disciplines, allowing users to develop specialized skills using a subset of concerns (e.g., visual design, interaction design), and enables a scaffold for specialized users to adopt complementary skills gradually. The MetaMorphe framework is divided into three concerns: *structure*, *dynamic style*, and *interactivity*.

Structure concern - Mesh selection
Moving individual points on a mesh is a tedious process; selecting elements in a design based on a higher-order arrangement or relationship aligns with many traditional design tasks. For instance, similar elements in a design can be grouped together, breaking down complex design problems into modular pieces. This enables interactions like "select all limbs" or "select sibling finger". In particular, hierarchical structures have proven as effective selection schemes, allowing users to focus on smaller conceptual components.

Using STL models from the Princeton Benchmark [5], and segmentations and labels provided by [13], we decomposed a mesh into an XHTML tree (Figure 2). The mesh is separated into *regions* based on form semantics (e.g. **chair** → ⟨**support**, **backsupport**, **leg**⟩). This allows designers to custom-annotate and group components to suit their specific needs. Similar to HTML, attributes such as **id** and **class** can be used to group and identify regions.

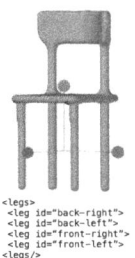

```
<legs>
  <leg id="back-right">
  <leg id="back-left">
  <leg id="front-right">
  <leg id="front-left">
<legs/>
```

Style concern: 3D Modeling Style Sheets
An iterative design process requires the ability to prototype quickly and interchangeably. Using a stylesheet paradigm similar to CSS, we specify a concise language for controlling how an artifact's form changes.

For each structural element, or region, in a mesh, we impose a simple parametric model described by Kho et.al. [14]. This technique binds vertices on a mesh, or skin, to a reference curve, or bone. This allows simpler deformations to the bone

[6] http://threejs.org/

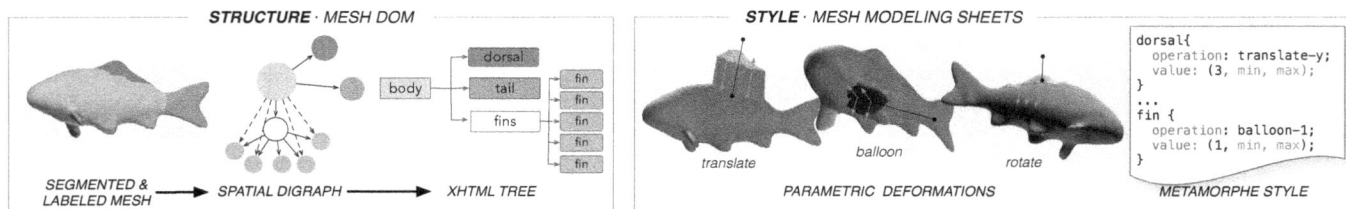

Figure 2. MetaMorphe Framework. Extracting structure (left) begins with segmenting the mesh, and then using the regions (colored circles) to construct a directed graph. Dummy nodes (white circles) can be used to group regions with similar volumes (e.g., fins); the minimum spanning tree (solid arrows) provides a hierarchy served to the user as XHTML. Applying styles (right) consists of constructing a MetaMorphe style to specify the parameters of one of three deformations and the mesh region it will affect.

to deform the skin while preserving local geometry. For out-of-the-box interaction, bones are specified as a region's principal component. We implement the following common deformations on each region:

1. *translate* moves a region along a selected axis,
2. *balloon* scales a region relative to a selected axis,
3. *rotate* moves a region about a selected axis.

A region can be deformed by specifying the following parameters through a *style* (Figure 2) described by the following properties:

- **operation** - [translate, rotate, balloon]
- **axis** - direction of deformation
- **value** - strength of the deformation
- **value-type** - unit of measurement (length, angle, volume)
- **min**, **max**, **distribution** - constraints on value
- **smooth** - controls deformation propagation
- **texture** - displaces vertices based on a heightmap

These properties are chosen to provide the basic functionality of direct manipulation, such as the conversion of a chair to a bar stool (Figure 3). In shorthand notation, the style translates

```
legs{
    operation: translate-y;
    value: (1, min, max); // meter
    distribution: uniform;
}
```

Figure 3. A bar stool style for Princeton Benchmark #120 - Chair

the legs of a chair by one meter relative to the y-axis. More dynamic design properties enable users to specify ranges with the **min** and **max** property, as well as how values are sampled from the range using the **distribution** property. Lastly, not depicted, **texture** specifies a displacement map for encoding values on the surface of the mesh, described in §§ Designing with Data. We leave out traditional graphics properties such as specifying: **material, reflectance**, etc.., to focus on styles that alter form.

Interactivity concern: Feature representation

Designing how a digital model responds to a condition or input and produces a relevant output is difficult due to the cost of loading and rendering new geometries. To allow for a flexible way to alter designs quickly, we convert each set of applied styles into a feature vector. This feature representation captures mesh properties at a specific *style-instance* akin to a *key frame* or *morph target* in traditional animation. The feature vector can be decomposed into two-parts:

- *Metadata* - this represents non-real values, such as the type of operation (e.g. translate) used. This allows a given feature vector to be backwards-compatible, i.e. can be parsed back into style treatments.
- *DNA* - this represents the appearance of the mesh and contains the real-valued properties of each style. This DNA has both a phenotype (i.e. the actual external physical representation) and a genotype (i.e. a range of potential but unexpressed physical traits). When phenotype subvectors of different designs are averaged, it generates a new subvector which represents the "mixture" of those two *style-instances*. In comparison, a genotype subvector needs only itself to generate new vectors based on values encoded by **min, max** and **distribution** style properties.

We describe example interactions with feature vectors in §§ Generative Interface and §§ DNA as a Metaphor.

METAMORPHE INTERFACES

Using MetaMorphe we created three parallel interfaces (direct manipulation, scripted, generative) to showcase the compatibility of this SoC framework with interaction techniques used by different creative practices.

Direct Manipulation Interface

Due to the natural translation from physical design and the need for realtime feedback, direct manipulation is the current *de facto* standard for 3D modeling. Especially for users without a programming background, direct manipulation offers the shortest learning gap. In order to utilize the natural exploratory property of this interface, we utilize the *generator* design pattern — whereby specific design tasks (e.g., choosing a color) are streamlined and produce only the relevant information needed to achieve the task (e.g. a RGB value).

The interface is decomposed as follows: an STL model is loaded onto a central screen (Figure 4A). Following conventions of industrial CAD interfaces, three operations are exposed to the user as noun-verb actions: balloon, rotate, translate. Axis handles used to control the strength of an operation. A form on a separate pane holds all possible values for a *style*, and is brush-and-linked such that any direct manipulation to the mesh updates the relevant values in the form. Lastly, an "export" button generates MetaMorphe style text.

Scripting Interface

A programmatic representation provides expert control of the mesh and foregrounds interactive design, however it also introduces the largest semantic gap for novice users. To provide

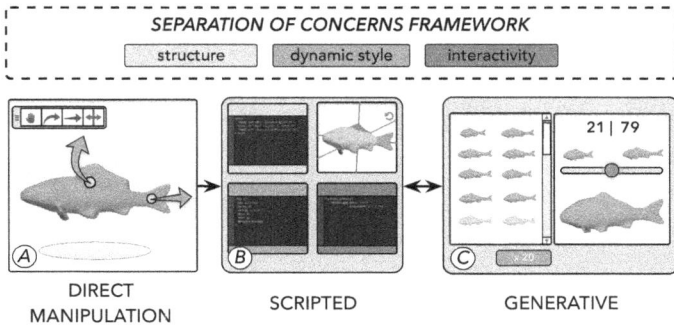

Figure 4. Makers explore form with direct manipulation (left), express dynamic styles and interactions with scripted CAD (center), and evaluate and refine dynamic models in a generative interface (right). These interfaces use a common SoC framework.

a quick iterative coding environment, the MetaMorphe scripting interface is inspired by the rapid prototyping online IDE jsFiddle[7], whereby the screen is divided into four partitions: style, structure, script, and an output mesh (Figure 4B).

We extend this pattern by adding data access widgets to use data from existing datasets or live data feeds. For our user study, we incorporated an interface to the Aeris Weather API[8], and an interface to a hardware microphone to record 2 seconds of audio. A compile button executes the appropriate script, links styles to their appropriate regions, and generates a set of parametric sliders for each style. These scripts are logged per user in a SQL database and are used to a) supplement other interfaces, and b) share code with other users.

Generative Interface

MetaMorphe also extends a user's ability to explore a design space more explicitly through a multiples view. This view divides the screen into two areas: a live view of the mesh, and a gallery of small multiples (Figure 4C). For a set of styles applied to a mesh, the framework allows us to extract a feature vector which can be used as follows:

- Applied to the mesh. This is done to generate an image and populate the gallery.
- Used to generate new feature vectors. A new set of styles is generated via the **min**, **max**, and **distribution** constraints in each respective parent style. More sophisticated design space search algorithms exist [25]; we show its feasibility under a web programming paradigm.
- Mixed with multiple feature vectors. In this interaction, a user specifies two or more parent styles and "mixes" these two models by applying a weighted sum to the parent feature vectors. In the MetaMorphe interface, we expose a slider as a method of interpolating between two models.

METAMORPHE DESIGN SCENARIOS

MetaMorphe leverages well established modeling principles like parametric design, but also supports a range of new interaction metaphors detailed in this section. To situate our framework we outline an evolution of several envisioned usage scenarios. These illustrate the power and novelty of how

---

[7]http://jsfiddle.net/
[8]http://www.hamweather.com/products/aeris-api/

MetaMorphe facilitates creativity, sharing, and co-design across the landscape of 3D digital fabrication.

First, Patricia, a hobbyist baker, has perfected her grandmother's cookie recipe and needs to produce several batches for her new small business. Since she uses non-standard ingredient quantities, measuring has become the bottleneck. Using MetaMorphe, she decides to develop a custom measuring cup in order to streamline her process. As a starting point, she finds and loads a cup model from an online repository.

Using the *manipulation view*, she explores different deformations on the cup's body (Figure 5). She quickly realizes that applying a balloon deformation effectively changes the cup size. She switches over to the *scripted view* to add a *style*, She names this **cup-size**, selects the **value-type** of interest as the volume (milliliters), and sets the volume to a fixed **value**.

She further sees the option for specifying the **distribution** property that allows her to specify a set of allowable values apropos to her recipe. In the *generative view*, she sees the **cup-size** style expressed as five cups with differing capacity and prints the set to start her baking empire.

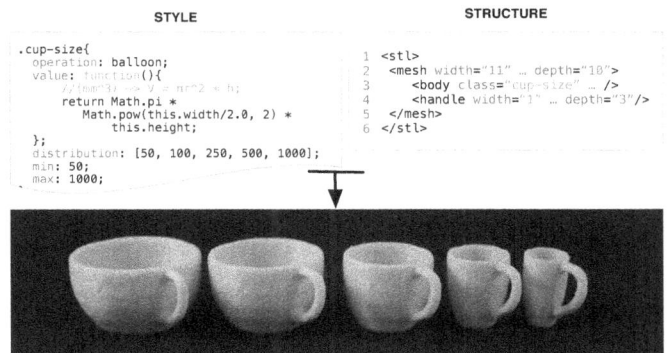

Figure 5. In this example, a cup model is applied a ballooning deformation and parametrized to produce a set of measuring cups.

Weeks later after growing her business, she decides to revisit her design to incorporate her newly developed brand. She is inspired to use a 3D scan of her two cupped hands. She loads it into the framework and using direct manipulation selects the parts of the hand that form the "cup". Looking back at her previous design, she copies the **cup-size** style and applies it to the hand model. She then switches over to the *generative view* to see the different small multiples of the hand cup models expressed by the **cup-size** style. She then compares each model and narrows down to the one that looks the most aesthetically pleasing. She decides to submit her creation to the MetaMorphe repository for others to view and extend.

SCRIPT

```
1  // obj is user-submitted stl file
2  // returns screenshots of five generated models
3  var canvas = document.getElementsByTagName("canvas");
4  MM(obj).load(function(stl, canvas){
5      stl.addStyle("cup-size")
6          .generate(5);
7  }
```

Figure 6. A simple measuring-cup script for a ad-hoc model using the MetaMorphe framework. The script is implemented in Javascript cascade-syntax.

Later, Alex, a web developer, comes across Patricia's clever measuring cup design and views its source. She decides to make it an app, and using the MetaMorphe interactivity script writes a short "Measuring Cups" widget (Figure 6) that takes a user-submitted model, applies the **cup-size** style, and renders images of the generated measuring cups. Lastly, she adds a download mechanism for a user to print their creation.

While an end-user might accomplish the same operation with a traditional CAD modeling tool, either by scaling a cup model or making one from scratch, we claim that the Meta-Morphe's framework provides a richer and more creative user experience for rapid and flexible design exploration and collaboration. The **cup-size** style can be transferred and extended to other structures while needing to minimally alter code. As designs become even more complex, we expect increased benefit from providing semantic information to create templates for more complex or custom uses.

Designing-with-data
The increased control from scripting enables a novel design capability: *the ability to incorporate data as a primary design element in the creative process*. Incorporating data into artifacts has been explored as physical data visualizations [32], as physical activity artifacts [15], and as a means of creating reflective, meaningful objects [22]. However, designing with data is not only useful as a visualization, but as an exercise in understanding how structures and forms can change. The MetaMorphe framework provides methods for not only encoding data as a surface texture but also for using data to *conditionally* alter an artifact's form. The former utilizes the **texture** property in the style treatment as a heightmap and alters the surface of the mesh. The latter uses conditional Javascript programs to selectively toggle styles. We detail a few powerful examples of *designing-with-data* in practice.

Data-driven design
Medical information from sensor data is becoming increasingly accessible through wearable devices. Linking and adapting to a patient's changing medical statistics, symptoms, and anatomy can be used to influence the design of a digital model. For instance, as someone heals they may want or be allowed or encouraged to increase movement of a joint or limb as it heals. MetaMorphe could be used to easily specify a design that allow more and more flexibility in each iteration of a cast. Since each design has an associated feature representation, at scale, failed designs can be leveraged to revise existing designs based on new understanding of use cases.

Digital editioning
In another scenario, an digital artist creates a model of an object and publishes the STL file for others to use. Countless users download and 3D print this design, yet they are all identical. Limited supply is already a common practice amongst digital practitioners; a designer can choose to allow access to certain types of designs at a certain time and under certain conditions. The artist can "design in" uniqueness such that for each person, and each print, the artifact can exhibit some guaranteed uniqueness. These variations can act as a patina based on the time it was printed, the location, political conditions, or a host of other factors. These objects could

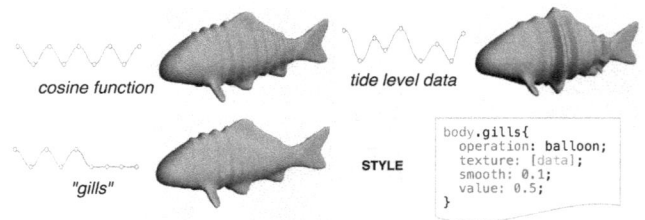

Figure 7. Designing-with-data. The body of a fish model is applied a non-uniform balloon deformation. The weight of that deformation is controlled by a cosine function to create a texture along the body, a tapered cosine function to add the appearance of "gills", and a NOAA tide levels feed is encoded into a "live" data sculpture.

serve as cryptographic encodings, or act as markers for large scale manufacturing inventory control. Figure 1b displays everyday objects (tableware) with conditional forms subject to seismograph readings tied to a specific region (2014 Napa Earthquake). John Simon's 32 by 32 pixel permutation grid *Every Icon* [29] is an example of such an object that exists in multiple instances, yet each instance embodies a unique variation with added value.

Designing a public art installation
In this example, an environmental artist has been commissioned to create an art and science public installation on tides (Figure 7). While an interactive visualization could be used to "show the numbers", the artist decides to instead create a data sculpture that can appeal to a wider audience, does not require a electronic display, and still maintains fidelity to the data. She selects a fish model and perturbs its surface structure as a function of location and tide levels retrieved from a national database. Placing these along beaches can attract visitors curiosity and provide a link for them to provide their own GPS coordinates (supplied from a browser) and view a constantly changing, unique model relative to their location. Similar to photographs, printed artifacts can serve as snapshots *linked* to certain times and places.

DNA as metaphor
Evolution as algorithm has historically been a powerful design strategy for incorporating chance and uniqueness [30], and most recently 3D objects have been evolved using biological morphologies to create unique forms [6]. Akin to keyframing in animation, we use the *DNA subvector* to mix, reproduce, and search through a design space. This allows users to essentially manipulate more than one parameter at a time; users can selectively assign different styles, and weight how much each style influences the final offspring design.

Getting the right wearable design
A hardware designer is making a data glove with wearable snap-on sensors worn on the finger tips. Their end-goal is to produce a design that feels un-obstructive, but also holds the hardware in place. The designer specifies places of the model that should not change (the hardware footprint), and specifies a few styles that change the center of mass, angle of the clasping mechanism, and the tip width. Using the *generative interface* to produce variant designs, she chooses a few possible candidates, and prints them in an array (Figure 8).

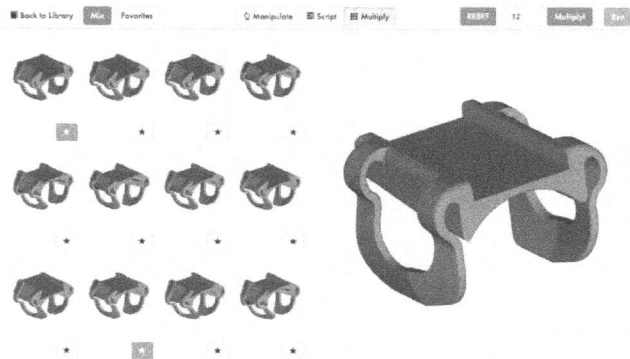

Figure 8. A high-poly finger-worn IMU distal ring design (149K faces, 7.6MB). Twelve multiples were generated and rendered in 7.2 seconds. Four styles were applied to the model: swivel and expand-out to the IMU footprint, and clasp-sides to both claspers.

Especially in the case of fitted items such as wearables, optimal designs require physical testing. By generating these multiples, the designer can use designs at the fringe, or at the extremes of certain parameters to gain critique and feedback. After testing each design, she finds that two designs which fit the criteria. She then references each design's object-DNA and reproduces an additional four "in-betweens" to refine the final model. This example highlight how generating design alternatives with current CAD tools is laborious, requiring manually altering each derivative model, and keeping separate files for each prototype. MetaMorphe enables iterating and refining designs as a part of the tool workflow.

EVALUATING METAMORPHE

We conducted a user study with creative experts from digital and traditional practices to provoke discussion on how themes in the MetaMorphe interfaces affect the design of digital models. We focus on *new design techniques and approaches* in the context of digital fabrication, rather than strictly modeling. The focus in expertise within our user study was designed to expose many of the issues faced by designers, such as learning new design tools, creatively exploring a design space, and selecting a final design. As such, our different user groups were chosen to diversify the feedback, and provide insight for how future interfaces can be designed to support multiple creative practices. Creative practices across our selected users were grouped into three categories: 3D traditional (e.g., sculpture, assemblage), 2D digital (e.g. graphic design), and 3D digital (e.g. mechanical design, 3D animation, architectural design). For the purposes of this paper, we will refer to participants in the above groups as **Sculptors (S)**, **Designers (D)**, and **CADers (C)**, respectively.

Recruitment and Selection

We submitted messages through local listservs within the Art, Architecture, and Engineering departments at our local university and advertised through *craigslist* to the surrounding community. Participants were selected on a 3-quota sampling, where each participant was asked to complete a survey. The survey consisted of three 10-point Likert scales where participants self-reported proficiency within each creative practice. Only participants with self-reported ratings

above intermediate expertise ($\geq$ 7) in at least one of the creative practices were asked to participate. Our final study group consisted of nine creative experts (3 female, 6 male) with the following years of experience: **Sculptors** (4, 16, 17), **Designers** (4, 6, 25), and **CADers** (3, 5, 29). Only two participants report 3D printing experience (**C1, C2**).

Study Design

For each session, participants were asked to individually meet with us in our digital fabrication studio. Participants were paid $20/hr; each session lasted two hours and consisted of a warm-up tutorial, three design tasks, and lastly a card sort. We also conducted interviews before and after each session. Participants were also asked to reflect out-loud their reflections on tools and design process as they went through the workshop. The experimenter aided solely on interface issues.

Each participant engaged in three separate modeling tasks using any of the three MetaMorphe interfaces. The modeling tasks required participants to search for an existing STL model from the Princeton library and engage with the model as follows: a) a *technical* task: add styles to a model to describe multiple forms, d) a *transfer* task: design a style that can be applied over a class of models, and lastly c) a *context* task: design a model intended for someone else. We instructed participants that one of the digital models made would be 3D printed for them to keep. Due to long 3D printing times, objects created during this study were later fabricated and mailed to users; participants were interviewed several days after receipt of their artifacts.

Findings

Each participant completed the three design tasks and engaged with the "designing with data" paradigm through either of the two provided feeds of weather or voice. Five participants chose to have their context task model printed, while four chose to have the transfer task model printed (Figure 9).

MetaMorphe as Creative Tool

Several novel design trends emerged from using MetaMorphe: *Exaggerated Anthropomorphism* where we observed several individuals adding emotion to animal and human models by exaggerating or anthropomorphizing appendages such as the case of a *muscle* class for an action figure (**C2**) or a pig caricature designed to the likeness of **C3**'s landlord. *Remixing* where metaphors were remixed within a single object such as **D1**'s hip sunglasses applied a rippled effect from Los Angeles weather patterns on the lens (Figure 9A) or **D3**'s beer glass encoding of Tokyo's weather data, designed for her sister. Her inspiration, she reflected, was that the hot temperatures in Tokyo called for a shared beer (Figure 9D).

We also observed direct *Nostalgic and Memento Mappings* using voice or sound to enhance visual form and personalize models such as **S3**'s "BeatTable" that encoded one of his experimental music compositions or **S2**'s homage and remembrance of Masaru Emoto's writings and water experiments through a conceptual diptych of two simple forms perturbed by "positive" and "negative" sounds (Figure 9C). When searching for a context task model, **C1** encountered a donkey which reminded her of a humorous shared memory

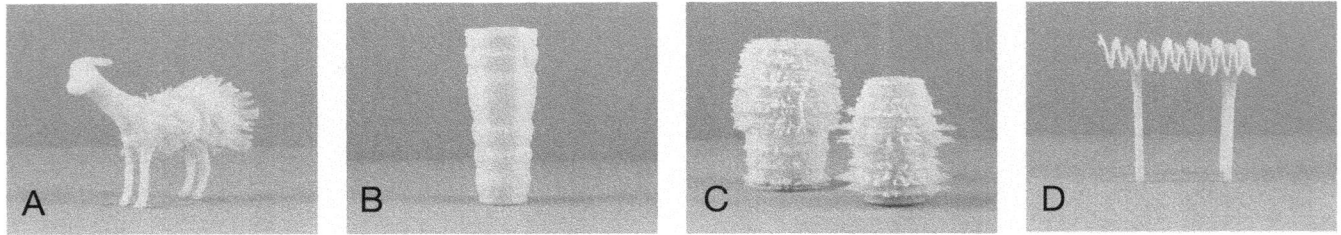

Figure 9. Models 3D printed from the user workshop. A) *Iron burro* - a nostalgic shared memory is encoded on the body of a donkey as sound (C1), B) Tokyo weather data is mapped onto the side of a glass (D3), C) Masaru Emoto-inspired positive and negative forms (S2), D) flexible table structure made from convoluted weather and tide data (S3).

between her and her father; in her piece christened *Iron Burro*, she encoded a soundbite of that personal story onto the torso of the donkey (Figure 9A). Finally, many of the designs explored *Improved Functionality* over form such as a *grip* class style designed as a non-slip texture for tool handles. However, the designer also conceptualized the texture as a means of artistically encoding an artist signature (S3).

Many of these designs would be extremely difficult if not impossible to achieve using traditional 3D modeling tools. However, many of our participants readily engaged with these creative and expressive new forms using MetaMorphe.

MetaMorphe as Computational Literacy Tool
Making system mechanisms transparent through a visual interface promoted learning and computational literacy. Amongst study participants, three were regularly coders (C1, C3, D1) while several described failed or continuing attempts at picking up programming (D2, S1, S3). Although not a requirement for participation (and not elicited) all participants revealed familiarity with the HTML/CSS markup style. While initially apprehensive about the scripting environment, it became a central point of interaction for these designers. During the transfer style task, several participants stated that they experienced a learning moment. Furthermore, participants expressed having a multiplicity of views and realtime visual feedback enhanced their experience and helped them understand the underlying mechanism of the system and adjust their conceptual model:

> **D2:** The image and the code help people see something physical and see how [the code] changes these values... to see that this [code] is equated with this [model] when people play with it. I see it as a way to understand computer science, coding, and language by breaking it down based on visual exploration.

This corroborates the concept of a Web framework as a platform for learning, as users are able to establish a programming metaphor through practice as they iterate on their work and re-enforces the value of the view source function. This is an early indication that MetaMorphe affords scaffolding and learning within 3D design and perhaps DF design literacy.

MetaMorphe as Facilitator of the Design Process
Sites of exploration evolved as users became familiar with the MetaMorphe framework. In general, initial frustration of specifying a style in the *scripting view* led participants to concentrate most of the exploratory design process in the *manipulation view*. However, once interface mechanisms were understood, participants found that they enjoyed the control

from the *scripting view* and shifted the majority of their design time to this view. In fact, designers desired more control to lock parts of a design as they drilled into more fine grain manipulations (D1, D2, C3).

We noted that more experienced participants incorporated a bidirectional flow (C3), returning to the *manipulation view* and iterating regularly with the small multiples in the *generative view*. Several **Designers** recognized the role this software process had in defining their workflow, such as *layering* in Adobe Photoshop (D2). While not originally part of their design process, the software-defined process gradually began to mirror their analog design processes:

> **S2:** [MetaMorphe's interfaces] mirrored my creative process enough that I could easily start following into its parameters. It's slightly different from menu selects, and once you start getting used to them then you understand the process it has to go through, you start adapting your own style to it also.

Due to the range of creative design processes that each user follows, creating a single pipeline interface that adapts to a user's design process requires a much more custom solution. These findings suggest that introducing bi-directional sites of exploration allows for a more iterative design process.

MetaMorphe as Co-Designer
General perceptions of the generative interface were often compared to perceptions of coding. Ideas of control similarly manifested as a user's affinity to the scripting interface. For those with more programming experience, the introducing non-deterministic actions was linked to a lack of agency:

> **D1:** I am not someone who lets random handle it. I want to figure it out on my own, I do not know if [the generative interface] is for me . . . in general I go for one thing.

In contrast, those with less affinity to the scripting interface embraced randomness as a resource, like:

> **D3:** It's always a challenge when you are working on a piece and get stuck. I get frustrated. This [generative interface] opens up a doorway to continue pushing you forward.

Straight-forward manipulation of parameters provided little agency to users. In general, the act of exploring or messing around with a design was lackluster, whereas adding in sounds or weather data made it easier to find an intention that formed a design (C1). For others, the expressibility of these interactions were surprising, random, and interesting,

> **S2:** Where as this is just modifying an alteration, for those which used my sound input, I created new dynamic forms and shapes

that don't resemble the original object. Through voice, through sound, tone, modulation, and volume, I had control of the final form. Those designs belong to me.

Perceptions of authorship encountered during the study can be divided into three general areas: 1) perception that the underlying model supersedes any artificial or superficial alteration, 2) that manipulating existing models was really a partnership and that work was a factor of a collaborative effort between the original creator of the current user, 3) and lastly that the end work was sufficiently different in context of concept, form, and as a factor of the type of data which is embedded. Notably, seven of the nine final produced models contained personal audio data or personal geographical data. Participants reported that these works were the most memorable of the process and those they felt they had contributed more to the design.

Printed MetaMorphe Artifacts as Nacent

Each participant was interviewed several days after receiving their digital model. When asked on the current location and whereabouts, two participant reported using them as functional objects (e.g. as a flower pot [C2], small pedestal [S3]). The other participants reported a more memento-type placement on a desk or workspace [S3, S3], and as a gift [C1]. Notably, the act of physically printing the object altered previous perceptions of authorship. Designs were viewed as being entirely the participant's (D2, D3). Future explorations of 3D printing were all centered on creating bespoke objects:

> D3: Symmetry is easy to make, and assymetry is accidental and more interesting. I want to make it more accidental. The Tokyo weather added some of this accidental quality.

The plastic material quality of the objects still caused many to classify them as "knick-knacks"; however perceptions of objects with subjective data is captured by C1: It is a memento but its much more than a souvenir, its real life!.

DISCUSSION

As digital fabrication continues to develop, dynamic models will become a central tenant of design. Our findings suggest that MetaMorphe enables designers to reflect on how objects can embed different histories and futures, and engage designers with renewed agency.

In his seminal 1936 text, *The Work of Art in the Age of Mechanical Reproduction*, Walter Benjamin describes how perceptions of objects changed under mechanical reproduction [2]. Among these, Benjamin identifies a ritualistic value around unique artifacts that he terms "aura" and suggests that mass manufacturing diminished this uniqueness. MetaMorphe attempts to introduce new notions of "aura" into digitally fabricated objects. Figure 9 illustrates the type of crafting around personalized artifacts that resulted from designing-with-data. Tools that integrate subjective data into digitally fabricated artifacts add new personality and meaning to objects. This has implications for sustainable design since such legacy-containing artifacts can persist as heirlooms.

In addition, increased meaning and agency in design can add an important element to STEM education. While creating highly-personal objects such as named lasercut keychains has been shown to encourage making-enthusiasm amongst young learners, these fabrication technologies become afflicted with "keychain syndrome", or the tendency to use these technologies to mass-produce trinkets instead of engendering invention [3]. More dynamic designs can allow more visibility into the process of designing and fabricating 3-D models. For instance, MetaMorphe presents both a parametric slider and its associated dynamic style, exposing the design decision and process of the original creator. While MetaMorphe specifically manipulates existing designs as opposed to starting from scratch, our user study demonstrates that many participants felt a strong connection with artifacts that embody relevant and subjective data. This increased link to authorship can be an important driving force in motivating invention.

LIMITATIONS AND FUTURE DIRECTIONS

Our objective with MetaMorphe was to find alternative ways of programming digital models that encourage metamorphic design. As such MetaMorphe is not a full-featured CAD tool; however MetaMorphe can incorporate more general purpose parametric CAD operations (e.g. tessellation, shelling, chamfering), yet non-parametric operations (e.g., brush interactions) do not have as simple an interface. Incorporating specialized markups side-by-side is a potential method for providing a heterogeneous modeling environment.

Conveying the mechanical and functional properties of a digital model was a limiting factor to how participants conceptualized which designs were modifiable. Many participants expressed a desire to specify real-world values (e.g., mm, inches) [C1, C3], or place the design in context (e.g., with a backdrop) [C2, D3]. Furthermore, the plastic material caused many to perceive printed artifacts as kitsch. Currently, MetaMorphe supports surface interactions, however designing dynamic models is more than just changing form. Under the mesh skin, structural properties like softness, flexibility, and the ability to leave impressions (e.g., leather can enhance the materiality of an artifact. As DF technologies mature integrating knowledge of material behaviors and properties in design tools can increase the diversity of designs.

CONCLUSION

Digital fabrication can promote a new class of designs that are more personal, sustainable, and dynamic. MetaMorphe provides a mechanism for enabling these behaviors in a seamless way when engaging with repositories of existing digital models. We leverage web programming metaphors to facilitate a scripted CAD and open-sharing design practice. We show that this approach supports generative, programmatic, and direct manipulation interaction styles. Participants who used MetaMorphe were able to easily explore a broad design space and create individual artifacts that embodied personal reflection, material engagement, and expressive forms.

ACKNOWLEDGMENTS

We thank Jasper O'Leary and Akhila Raju for their aid with user studies; Tim Campbell, Valkyrie Savage, Björn Hartmann, and the anonymous reviewers for their insightful comments. This research was supported by NSF Grant No. IIS-1451465, Adobe GEM, and a NSF GR Fellowship.

REFERENCES

1. Autodesk. Project Dreamcatcher, 2015.

2. Benjamin, W. The Work of Art in the Age of Mechanical Reproduction. *Visual Culture: The Reader* (1936).

3. Blikstein, P. Digital fabrication and making in education: The democratization of invention. *FabLabs: Of Machines, Makers and Inventors* (2013), 1–21.

4. Buechley, L., Rosner, D. K., Paulos, E., and Williams, A. DIY for CHI: methods, communities, and values of reuse and customization. In *CHI EA*, ACM (2009), 4823–4826.

5. Chen, X., Golovinskiy, A., and Funkhouser, T. A benchmark for 3D mesh segmentation. In *Trans. on Graphics*, vol. 28, ACM (2009).

6. Clune, J., and Lipson, H. Evolving 3d objects with a generative encoding inspired by developmental biology. *ACM SIGEVOlution 5*, 4 (2011), 2–12.

7. Follmer, S., Carr, D., Lovell, E., and Ishii, H. CopyCAD: remixing physical objects with copy and paste from the real world. In *Proc. UIST*, ACM (2010).

8. Follmer, S., and Ishii, H. Kidcad: Digitally remixing toys through tangible tools. In *Proc. CHI*, ACM (2012), 2401–2410.

9. Hiller, J. D., and Lipson, H. STL 2.0: a proposal for a universal multi-material Additive Manufacturing File format. In *Proc. Solid Freeform Fabrication Symposium'09* (2009), 266–278.

10. Hutchins, E., Hollan, J., and Norman, D. Direct manipulation interfaces. *Human-Computer Interaction 1*, 4 (Dec. 1985), 311–338.

11. Jacobs, J., and Buechley, L. Codeable objects: computational design and digital fabrication for novice programmers. In *Proc. CHI* (2013), 1589–1598.

12. Jacobs, J., and Zoran, A. Hybrid practice in the kalahari: Design collaboration through digital tools and hunter gatherer craft. In *Proc. CHI '15*, ACM Press (2015).

13. Kalogerakis, E., Hertzmann, A., and Singh, K. Learning 3D mesh segmentation and labeling. *Trans. on Graphics 29*, 4 (2010).

14. Kho, Y., and Garland, M. Sketching mesh deformations. In *ACM SIGGRAPH 2007 courses* (2007).

15. Khot, R. A., Hjorth, L., and Mueller, F. F. Understanding physical activity through 3d printed material artifacts. In *Proc. CHI '14*, ACM Press (2014), 3835–3844.

16. Kintel, M., and Wolf, C. OpenSCAD, 2011.

17. Kuznetsov, S., and Paulos, E. *Rise of the Expert Amateur: DIY Projects, Communities, and Cultures.* ACM, 2010.

18. LIA. Filament sculptures (2014).

19. McCullough, M. *Abstracting Craft : The Practice Digital Hand.* The MIT Press, July 1998.

20. Mota, C. The rise of personal fabrication. In *Proc. C&C*, ACM (2011), 279–288.

21. Mueller, R., Nieuwnhuijse, J., Bespalov, E., and Hogdson, G. OpenJSCAD, 2013.

22. Nissen, B., and Bowers, J. Data-Things: Digital Fabrication Situated within Participatory Data Translation Activities. In *Proc. of CHI '15*, ACM Press (2015), 2467–2476.

23. Oehlberg, L., Willett, W., and Mackay, W. E. Patterns of Physical Design Remixing in Online Maker Communities. In *Proc. of CHI '15*, ACM Press (2015), 639–648.

24. O'Reilly, T., DiBona, C., Stone, M., and Cooper, D. Open source paradigm shift, 2004.

25. Ovsjanikov, M., Li, W., Guibas, L., and Mitra, N. J. Exploration of continuous variability in collections of 3d shapes. In *Trans. on Graphics*, vol. 30, ACM (2011), 33.

26. Plummer-Fernandez, M. Disarming Corruptor, 2013.

27. Rosner, D. K., and Ryokai, K. Reflections on craft: probing the creative process of everyday knitters. In *Proc. C&C*, ACM (2009), 195–204.

28. Sadouma, T. Nike town 2, Jan. 2015.

29. Simon, Jr., J. Every Icon, 1996.

30. Sims, K. Evolving virtual creatures. In *Proc. Computer Graphics and Interactive Techniques* (1994).

31. Song, H., Guimbretire, F., Hu, C., and Lipson, H. ModelCraft: capturing freehand annotations and edits on physical 3d models. In *Proc. UIST*, ACM (2006), 13–22.

32. Swaminathan, S., Shi, C., Jansen, Y., Dragicevic, P., Oehlberg, L. A., and Fekete, J.-D. Supporting the design and fabrication of physical visualizations. In *Proc. CHI '14*, ACM Press (2014), 3845–3854.

33. van den Berg, D. DERRICK, Oct. 2014.

34. Vidime, K., Wang, S.-P., Ragan-Kelley, J., and Matusik, W. OpenFab: a programmable pipeline for multi-material fabrication. *Trans. on Graphics 32*, 4 (July 2013), 1.

35. Weichel, C., Lau, M., Kim, D., Villar, N., and Gellersen, H. W. MixFab: a mixed-reality environment for personal fabrication. In *Proc. of CHI*, ACM Press (2014), 3855–3864.

36. Willis, K. D., Xu, C., Wu, K.-J., Levin, G., and Gross, M. D. Interactive fabrication: new interfaces for digital fabrication. In *Proc. TEI* (2011).

37. Zhao, J., and Moere, A. V. Embodiment in data sculpture: a model of the physical visualization of information. In *Proc. DIMEA*, ACM (2008), 343–350.

38. Zoran, A., and Buechley, L. Hybrid reassemblage: An exploration of craft, digital fabrication and artifact uniqueness. *Leonardo 46*, 1 (Feb. 2013), 4–10.

39. Zoran, A., and Paradiso, J. A. FreeD: A Freehand Digital Sculpting Tool. In *Proc. CHI*, ACM (2013), 2613–2616.

Providing Timely Examples Improves the Quantity and Quality of Generated Ideas

Pao Siangliulue[1]   Joel Chan[2]   Krzysztof Z. Gajos[1]   Steven P. Dow[2]

[1]Harvard School of Engineering and Applied Sciences
Cambridge, MA USA
{paopow, kgajos}@seas.harvard.edu

[2]Carnegie Mellon University
Pittsburgh, PA USA
{joelchuc, spdow}@cs.cmu.edu

ABSTRACT

Emerging online ideation platforms with thousands of example ideas provide an important resource for creative production. But how can ideators best use these examples to create new innovations? Recent work has suggested that not just the choice of examples, but also the timing of their delivery can impact creative outcomes. Building on existing cognitive theories of creative insight, we hypothesize that people are likely to benefit from examples when they run out of ideas. We explore two example delivery mechanisms that test this hypothesis: 1) a system that proactively provides examples when a user appears to have run out of ideas, and 2) a system that provides examples when a user explicitly requests them. Our online experiment (N=97) compared these two mechanisms against two baselines: providing no examples and automatically showing examples at a regular interval. Participants who requested examples themselves generated ideas that were rated the most novel by external evaluators. Participants who received ideas automatically when they appeared to be stuck produced the most ideas. Importantly, participants who received examples at a regular interval generated fewer ideas than participants who received no examples, suggesting that mere access to examples is not sufficient for creative inspiration. These results emphasize the importance of the timing of example delivery. Insights from this study can inform the design of collective ideation support systems that help people generate many high quality ideas.

Author Keywords

Creativity, ideation, examples, collective intelligence

ACM Classification Keywords

H.5.m. Information Interfaces and Presentation (e.g. HCI): Miscellaneous

INTRODUCTION

Ideation platforms—such as Quirky.com, Innocentive.com, 99designs.com—accumulate thousands of ideas contributed

C&C 2015, June 22–25, 2015, Glasgow, United Kingdom.
Copyright is held by the owner/author(s). Publication rights licensed to ACM.
ACM 978-1-4503-3598-0/15/06 ...$15.00.
DOI: http://dx.doi.org/10.1145/2757226.2757230

by their members. Because the members can see and be inspired by each other's ideas, these collections of example ideas can serve as an important resource for creative production [8]. Ideas generated by others can help innovators working on similar problems spur new concepts by broadening their notion of the design space [19, 24, 40] and allowing for reinterpretation and recombination of ideas [19, 50, 28]. When viewing ideas for inspiration, innovators should pay attention to how to select examples [24, 45, 23, 40], and how to judge their quality [19]. This is especially important because exposure to other ideas is not always inspirational: people often transfer solution elements from other ideas even when those ideas are known to be of low quality [10, 20]. Recent research shows that even experts are susceptible to such negative effects of exposure to other ideas [26]. Other ideas can also restrict one's understanding of the solution space, for example, by limiting one's ability to see novel uses for artifacts [18, 27].

Consequently, much research attention has been devoted to understanding which properties of examples are associated with inspirational outcomes. For example, research has considered how the semantic relevance [8, 9, 13], novelty [9, 1], and diversity [15, 51, 5, 45] of examples influence ideation. However, one important question has received less attention: *when* should innovators look at examples?

A variety of theoretical perspectives suggest that the impact of examples on creative output not only depends on what examples are shown but also when those examples are delivered. Cognitive theories of creative ideation suggest that ill-timed examples can disrupt a person's train of thought [34, 33] and that people benefit most from examples when they run out of ideas [43, 36, 31]. Research on flow and interruptions also suggest that automatic example delivery can be experienced as an as interruption if not timed appropriately [3, 2, 12], thereby harming creative performance. However, the literature lacks empirical tests of these hypotheses.

In this paper, we empirically test whether people benefit more from examples when they are prepared to receive them compared to seeing those same examples delivered at fixed intervals. We conducted an online ideation experiment to test two "prepared" conditions—an *On-demand* condition, in which participants determined when to see examples, and an *On-idle* condition, in which participants were automatically presented with new examples when they had been idle for a period of time. We compared these conditions against two baselines:

a condition where no examples were provided (*None*) and a condition where the examples were provided at a regular interval (*On-interval*). The baseline conditions let us distinguish the effect of access to examples *per se* from the effect of timing of the delivery of examples.

Our results show that both prepared conditions outperform the baseline conditions, but in different ways. Participants who received examples on demand produced ideas that were deemed significantly more novel by evaluators compared to participants who did not receive any examples and to participants who received examples when idle. Meanwhile, participants who received examples automatically whenever they were idle produced a larger quantity of ideas than participants in other conditions, with no significant difference in novelty compared to ideas generated by participants in either of the baseline conditions. Finally, a follow-up content analysis of the participants' ideas showed that participants who received examples on demand used examples more (i.e., borrowed/adapted more solution elements) compared to participants who received examples when idle. These results confirm that the timing of example delivery can determine the impact of examples on creative output. From a system designer's perspective, our results suggest that, instead of giving people examples in an ad hoc way, the examples should be presented at the right moment when the user is ready to make use of those examples.

RELATED WORK

Kulkarni et al. [22] examined how the timing of examples affect creative output and concluded that early or repeated—rather than late—exposure to examples improves the creativity of generated ideas. However, Kulkarni et al. delivered examples at fixed regular intervals. This may not be optimal: intuitively, one might expect that people can be more or less "prepared" to benefit from examples at different points during the ideation process.

Several theories of example use in problem solving and creative idea generation ground the intuition that people benefit more from examples when they are primed and ready. In education, the Preparation for Future Learning perspective [42, 41] posits that learners get more out of learning resources (e.g., worked examples, lectures) if they first struggle with the concepts before being exposed to those resources. Relatedly, Kapur and colleagues have shown the value of "productive failure," a two-phase instructional strategy where students first engage in generation activities (e.g., attempting to solve problems that require knowledge of the target concepts) and then engage in consolidation/instruction, where they are exposed to the target concepts in various ways [21]. These theories of learning argue that prior problem solving can prepare learners to let go of old knowledge, and prime them to notice important features of target concepts (e.g., what problem they are trying to solve).

According to a theory of idea generation called Search for Ideas in Associative Memory (SIAM) and the subsequent empirical results, example ideas can have both positive effects (cognitive stimulation) and negative effects (cognitive interference) based on when an example is shown [34, 33]. SIAM assumes two memory systems: long-term memory (permanent with unlimited capacity) and working memory (transient with limited capacity). Long term memory is partitioned into images, which are knowledge structures composed of a core concept and its features. For example, an image can have a core concept "hotel" with features like "has rooms", "has a swimming pool", and "is cheap". When generating ideas, people run a repeated two-stage search process. First, images from long term memory are retrieved and temporarily stored in working memory. Then, in the second stage, the features of the image are used to generate ideas by combining knowledge, forming new associations, or applying them to a new domain. Retrieval of images probabilistically depends on search cues (e.g., features that are active in working memory, previously generated ideas, one's understanding of the problem). An image that is already in working memory is likely to be sampled again. SIAM, therefore, implies that seeing example ideas generally helps activate new images that would not have been accessible otherwise and thus leads to production of novel ideas. However, ill-timed examples can prematurely terminate a person's train of thought, interrupt their thinking, and cause a loss of potentially creative ideas that usually come later in the session [34, 35, 3, 2].

The Prepared Mind theory of insight offers additional insights into the optimal timing of example idea presentation. It posits that people can be more or less "prepared" to assimilate problem-relevant stimuli from the environment depending on their cognitive state [43, 36]. The theory predicts specifically that, when problem solving reaches an impasse, people maintain an open goal in memory to solve the problem, and are more motivated and better able to map problem-relevant stimuli that might have been previously ignored (e.g., because it was too semantically distant or difficult to understand/transfer). Indeed, Tseng, et al. [46] showed that people benefit more from analogically distant examples (a type of example hypothesized to be beneficial for creative inspiration [13]) during a break from problem solving after working on the problem for a significant amount of time compared to seeing the examples before working on the problem. Similarly, Moss, et al. [31] showed that people benefited more from hints after leaving a problem in an unsolved state compared to seeing the hints before working on the problem.

The shared intuition behind all of these theories is that optimal timing of example use for creative inspiration should strike a balance between allowing the ideator to queue up their own knowledge and constraints and avoiding cognitive fixation on a certain part of solution space. Therefore we predict that delivering examples *when* people run out of ideas could maximize the inspirational benefit of examples. At that point, the examples can act as external stimuli to activate new knowledge in memory to combine into new ideas. In the next section, we discuss how we might accomplish this timing of examples in an idea generation platform.

TIMING OF EXAMPLE DELIVERY

We explore two mechanisms for delivering examples to innovators when they are prepared to receive them. The first mechanism is to provide examples when people explicitly re-

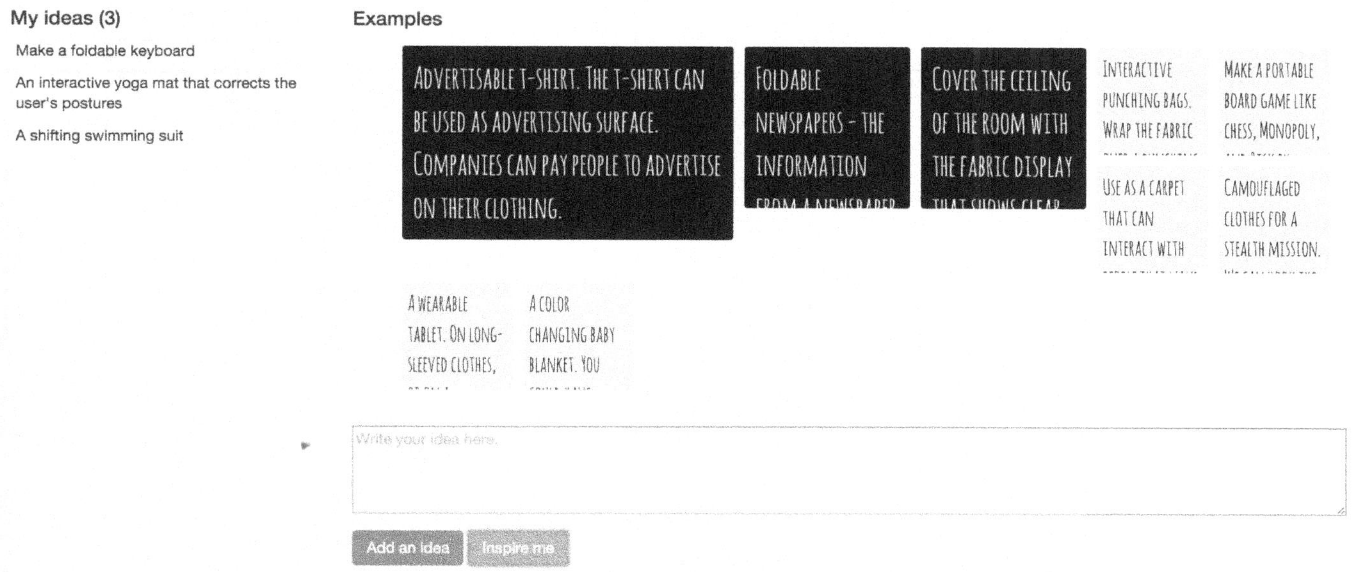

My ideas (3)

Make a foldable keyboard

An interactive yoga mat that corrects the user's postures

A shifting swimming suit

Examples

ADVERTISABLE T-SHIRT. THE T-SHIRT CAN BE USED AS ADVERTISING SURFACE. COMPANIES CAN PAY PEOPLE TO ADVERTISE ON THEIR CLOTHING.

FOLDABLE NEWSPAPERS - THE INFORMATION FROM A NEWSPAPER

COVER THE CEILING OF THE ROOM WITH THE FABRIC DISPLAY THAT SHOWS CLEAR

INTERACTIVE PUNCHING BAGS. WRAP THE FABRIC

MAKE A PORTABLE BOARD GAME LIKE CHESS, MONOPOLY,

USE AS A CARPET THAT CAN INTERACT WITH

CAMOUFLAGED CLOTHES FOR A STEALTH MISSION.

A WEARABLE TABLET. ON LONG-SLEEVED CLOTHES,

A COLOR CHANGING BABY BLANKET. YOU

Write your idea here.

Add an idea   Inspire me

Figure 1. Screenshot of the ideation interface. Participants typed their ideas in the text box. After they submitted an idea, it appeared on the pane on the left. For those in the *On-demand*, *On-idle* and *On-interval* condition, examples were shown in the example grid above the idea entry box. The most recently received examples were shown in a big black box while earlier examples were in a gray box. The "Inspire me" button at the bottom was visible only to participants in the *On-demand* condition.

quest them (the *On-demand* condition). This approach guarantees that the examples will be provided when people are receptive to new ideas [17, 43, 36, 31]. However, people might choose suboptimal strategies for requesting examples (e.g., spending too much time looking at inspiration). People might also not be aware that they are stuck in (or biased by) old patterns of thinking [29, 7, 47] and consequently fail to request examples at an opportune time.

The second mechanism automatically provides the examples when people appear to be stuck (the *On-idle* condition). In this paper, we used a simple timeout mechanism: when no activity was detected in the interface for a fixed period of time, the system automatically provided a new set of examples of ideas generated by others. Prior research provides little guidance on how idle time during ideation relates to being in a "stuck" state. Therefore, we conducted a pilot study where we observed three people generating ideas in person. We looked at big time gaps between bursts of successive idea generation. Interviews with participants revealed that during these time gaps, they ran out of ideas on one thread and then started a new train of thought. We observed that these gaps tended to be approximately 30 seconds long. Thus, we decided on a fixed idle interval of 30 seconds for the *On-idle* condition. Analyses of time gaps before example requests in the *On-demand* condition of our main experiment provide further support for this choice of idle interval.

EXPERIMENT

Participants

We recruited 120 participants from Amazon Mechanical Turk[1] (MTurk), an online micro-labor market. Three partic-

ipants did not complete the experiment and were excluded from our analysis.

We limited recruitment to workers who resided in the U.S. and who had completed at least 1,000 HITs with greater than 95% approval rate (to reduce noise from less skilled or motivated workers). Participants were paid $2.50 for their participation.

Task and Procedure

Each participant completed two idea generation tasks. In the first task, they had 3 minutes to generate as many alternative uses for rubber bands as possible. This was a warm-up task designed to familiarize participants with the system and with the example delivery mechanism. We did not include the data from this task in our analysis. In the second task, participants had 15 minutes to generate product ideas for an imaginary technology—a touch-sensitive "fabric display" that could render high resolution images and videos on any fabric through a penny-sized connector. We selected this task because it did not require extensive expertise to generate ideas, but yet was more similar to realistic design tasks than toy problems (e.g., alternative uses for a rubber band).

At the beginning of the experiment, each participant was randomly assigned to one of the four conditions:

- *On-demand*: Participants could request a new set of three examples whenever they wanted until they saw all available examples.

- *On-idle*: Participants were automatically presented with a new set of three examples when they stopped typing for 30 seconds.

[1] http://www.mturk.com

85

- *On-interval*: Participants saw a new set of three examples at the beginning of the task and on regular intervals afterward (every minute for the alternative uses task and every three minutes for the product ideas task).

- *None*: Participants saw no examples while generating ideas.

When new examples appeared, they appeared in a set of three and were shown prominently at the top of the example grid until another set of examples came. Older examples were available throughout the idea generation session, but they were less visually prominent (Figure 1). Before each idea generation session, all participants were informed about how and when they would have an access to a new set of examples. After finishing the second task, participants filled out a survey on their demographic information and their experience during the last idea generation session.

Examples
There were 9 examples available for the alternative uses task and 15 examples for the product ideas task. Examples for the alternative uses task were obtained through an Internet search. Examples for the product ideas task were obtained from a pilot round of idea generation with 12 MTurk workers generating ideas for 15 minutes each. We selected examples as follows. A trained coder (an author) evaluated the 71 potential examples for the alternative uses task and the 60 ideas collected in a pilot study of the product idea tasks. The product ideas were coded with thematic tags like "advertising" and "camouflage." We also assessed the overall quality of each idea (judging both novelty and value). We assembled sets of three ideas that comprised both high quality and diverse theme, as both example quality and diversity have been shown to improve ideation performance [37, 25, 34, 45].

Dependent Measures And Analysis
We conducted a between-subjects study with timing of example delivery (*None, On-demand, On-idle* and *On-interval*) as the sole factor.

We collected three performance measures:

- *Number of nonredundant generated ideas.* Six redundant ideas were removed by the first author. A sample (249 raw ideas by 29 participants) was also evaluated for redundancy by the second author, and the reliability was high, ICC(2,2) = 0.83.

- *Novelty* of ideas as assessed by other MTurk workers (who were not participants in the ideation study). Previous work has also used MTurk workers to evaluate creativity of ideas (e.g., [50]).

- *Value* of ideas as assessed by other MTurk workers. This measure maps onto the dimensions of appropriateness (quality) and feasibility typically used in prior studies of creativity.

To evaluate Novelty and Value, each MTurk judge rated a random sample of 25–30 ideas. The evaluators were asked to read all ideas before rating them on 2 criteria, novelty and value, each on a 7-point likert scale. For novelty, we asked them to "consider how novel, original or surprising the idea is" (1–Not novel; 7–Very novel). For value, we asked them to "consider how useful the product idea is and how practical the idea sounds assuming the 'fabric display' technology is real" (1–Not valuable; 7—Very valuable).

Each of our evaluators rated a different subset of artifacts so calculating the agreement between evaluators is not feasible. However, we have evidence from a prior reliability study that this rating approach yields satisfactory reliability. Using three different types of creative artifacts, we measured how reliability improved as we increased the number of MTurk workers assessing creativity of any one idea. We found that a panel of three raters achieved inter-panel intraclass correlation coefficient (ICC) of 0.432. Most (98.6%) of our ideas in this study were evaluated by at least three evaluators.

To address potential misalignments in absolute means and variances in scores between evaluators, we first normalized each evaluator's scores into z-scores. We then averaged the normalized (z-)scores for each idea across evaluators. A 0 z-score meant that an idea was rated average, negative z-score means that the idea was rated below average on that criterion.

To illustrate, here are examples of ideas with low novelty (z-)scores:

- *"material for a hat"* (-1.88)

- *"games"* (-1.87)

While these are ideas with high novelty scores:

- *"Curtains that make it look like people are home when they are way. as part of a security system"* (1.78)

- *"Neckties - If they spill something on it at lunch, they can change the color so it blends in and don't have to worry about anyone noticing the stain."* (1.28)

Here are examples of ideas with low value scores:

- *"A wearable table. On long sleeved clothes."* (-1.83)

- *"A color changing bra that displays your favorite apps."* (-1.60)

While these are ideas with high value scores:

- *"Use as a stealth device for soldiers to get behind enemy lines."* (1.73)

- *"Provide to underfunded schools to replace their expensive projectors in classrooms."* (1.44)

Once they finished generating ideas, participants in the *On-demand* condition answered survey questions about when and why they requested examples (Table 1).

We also recorded timestamps when ideas got submitted and when participants saw a new set of examples. Using these timestamps, we looked at how much time passed after the latest idea submission before participants requested new examples.

Adjustments to the Data

There were originally 25 participants in the *None* condition, 26 participants in the *On-demand* condition, 31 participants in the *On-idle* condition and 35 participants in the *On-interval* condition. Our random assignment mechanism did not ensure balanced numbers across conditions because some MTurk workers abandoned the tasks when the conditions were already assigned, hindering accurate counting of participants in different conditions.

We filtered out the participants who either never requested examples or requested examples only once because these participants might not have understood that they could request examples or keep requesting examples more than once. This excluded 7 out of 26 participants from the *On-demand* condition. Because evaluating ideas is costly and the numbers of participants were unbalanced, we further randomly subsampled participants in the *On-idle* and the *On-interval* conditions so that similar numbers of participants from each condition would be used in the final analysis.

We ended up with 97 participants: 25 in the *None* condition, 19 participants in the *On-demand* condition, 28 participants in the *On-idle* condition, and 25 in the *On-interval* condition. These participants (along with their 1,149 ideas) constitute the final sample for our analysis.

RESULTS

Providing examples at idle time led to more ideas

We observed a significant main effect of timing of example delivery on the number of ideas generated by participants ($F(3,93)=3.26$, $p = 0.0249$). On Average, participants in the *On-idle* condition generated the most ideas (M=13.8), followed by participants in the *On-demand* condition (M=10.94), the *None* condition (M=10.88) and the *On-interval* condition (M=8.80) (Figure 2). The pairwise Student's T comparisons show significant difference between participants in the *On-idle* condition and the *On-interval* condition. There was no difference between the other pairs.

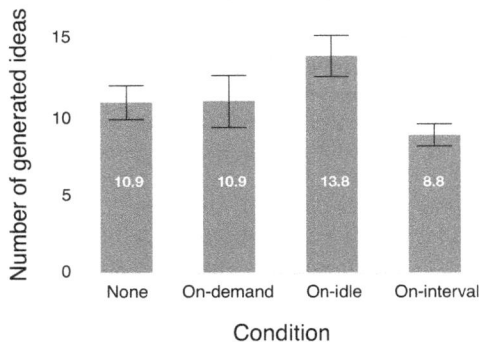

Figure 2. Participants in the *On-idle* condition generated significantly more ideas than participants in the *On-interval* condition. Error bars show standard error.

On-demand example requests led to more novel ideas

We observed a significant main effect of timing of example delivery on the average novelty of ideas ($F(3,93)=4.89$,

$p = 0.0034$). The pairwise Student's T comparisons show that participants in the *On-demand* condition (M=0.18) generated ideas that were deemed significantly more novel than those in the *None* condition (M=-0.18) and those in the *On-idle* condition (M=-0.01). The difference between the *On-demand* condition and the *On-interval* condition (M=0.05) was not significant (Figure 3).

We did not observe any statistically significant differences across conditions for the average value rating of ideas ($F(3,93)=1.18$, $p = 0.32$).

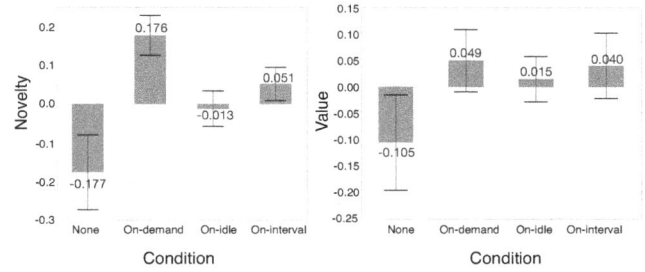

Figure 3. The mean novelty z-score for participants in the *On-demand* condition is significantly higher than for those in the *None* and *On-idle* condition. There is no statistically significant difference across conditions for the value scores. Error bars show standard error.

FOLLOW-UP ANALYSES

We conducted two sets of follow-up analyses to address questions raised by the main findings. These analyses focused on understanding why and when participants requested examples, and exploring hypotheses about why the prepared conditions (i.e., the *On-demand* and *On-idle* conditions) had different impacts on participants' creative performance.

Why and when did participants request examples?

Table 1 summarizes the survey responses of participants in the *On-demand* condition on why and when they requested examples. The responses indicate that participants primarily requested examples when they ran out of ideas. A smaller (but still sizable) proportion of participants appeared to use an alternative strategy where they looked at examples before generating ideas.

When did you request examples?	Participants N (%)
When I ran out of ideas.	15 (78.95%)
Before I started generating my own ideas.	6 (31.58%)
In the middle of coming up with new ideas.	3 (15.79%)
When I got bored.	2 (10.53%)

Table 1. When did the *On-demand* participants request examples? The majority of participants said in the post-experiment that they requested examples when they ran out of ideas.

On average, participants requested a new set of examples 31.19 seconds (SD = 44.37s) after they submitted their latest ideas (excluding example requests that came before participants submitted their first idea). This average idle time suggests that our choice of 30s delay in the *On-idle* condition was reasonable.

However, inspecting these idle time distributions across the session yields a more nuanced picture (Figure 4). First, idle times before requesting examples tend to be shorter earlier in a session: idle times for the first and second example requests tended to be shorter than 30s. Second, there was a considerable amount of variability between participants in terms of idle times: while the mean idle time is close to 30s, participants sometimes waited more than a minute before requesting examples.

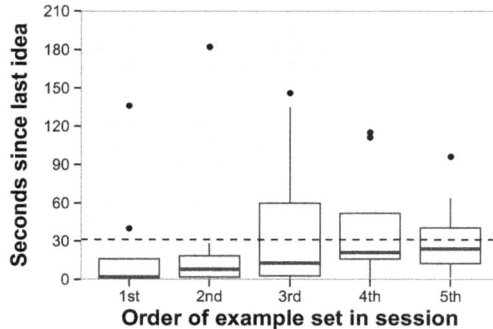

Figure 4. Boxplot of idle time before example request by order of example set in session. The mean time before requesting examples was 31.19 seconds. Participants were idle for shorter amounts of time before requesting first and second example sets than for third, fourth and fifth sets. Participants' idle times also varied considerably, with some participants waiting longer than a minute before requesting examples.

How did participants use examples?

To better understand the observed differences between the *On-demand* and *On-idle* conditions, we conducted a content analysis of the examples' impact on participants' ideas. We sampled all ideas that participants generated immediately after an example set was seen to compare against their corresponding example sets. We also included the most recent prior idea (generated within 30 seconds or less than the last seen example set) for comparison because it was common for participants to generate successive ideas within the same category or with shared functional features. In some cases, example sets were seen in succession without any ideas generated in between. In these cases, we considered the impact of the last set of examples on the next idea. This sampling procedure yielded 145 example-idea cases: 89 in the *On-idle* condition, and 56 in the *On-demand* condition. Our goal was to identify whether and how examples influenced the ideas participants generated.

The content analysis was conducted by an expert panel comprising the first and second authors. The panel separately analyzed each example-idea case to identify whether the idea appeared to be influenced by any of the examples just seen. The prior idea was included as a comparison point, since features in the idea could have plausibly been transferred/adapted from a prior idea, rather than from one or more of the examples [33]. We only considered features shared with examples that did not overlap with those of the prior idea. Specifi-

cally, we considered two kinds of example influence, following cognitive theories about example use [6, 4]:

1. Transfer of *structural features*, where the panel agreed that the idea appeared to contain mechanisms or functions (e.g., interactivity, simulation, tailoring displays to states of a system, sensing user states) also present in one or more of the preceding examples (and absent in the prior idea). For example, the idea *"Safety warnings from public institutions i.e. different colored flags on the highway that reflect Amber Alerts or how safe the roads are (a color co[d]ed system will be in place)."* shares the same mechanism of displaying the state of the systems or environment with *"Stuff animals with emotions. Make stuff animals out of this fabric. They can smile when hugged or make different facial expressions"*.

2. Transfer of *surface features*, where the panel agreed that the idea appeared to share application contexts (e.g., use for health/exercise, sports/games, learning/education) and basic features (e.g., positioning on clothing/furniture) also present in one or more preceding examples (and absent in the prior idea). For example, the idea *"To have beating organs on the outside of your clothing"* shares the same domain concept—body organ—with *"Attached with a sensor to detect body heat or heart rate, the fabric can make for clothes that detect if you are stressed out or fatigued. It will display peaceful images in soothing colors when you are stressed out"*.

Structural and surface features were considered separately to examine the possibility that participants in the *On-demand* condition were generating more novel ideas by engaging in far transfer (i.e., transferring structural features but not surface features [13]). The panel also took note of the *number* of examples that appeared to have influenced the idea.

The panel was blind to condition throughout the analysis. The panel first identified a list of features considered to be structural and surface. Then, the panel analyzed each example-idea case in an iterative manner with discussions progressing until resolution was reached. Earlier coded cases were reanalyzed in light of insights gained from later cases.

Out of the 145 example-idea cases, only 4 ideas (from 2 participants from the *on-idle* condition) were identical (or nearly identical) to the given examples. For example, a participant generated idea *"A flag that changes between various nations."* when they saw an example *"A multinational flag. Instead of having more than different flags for different nations, you can save space by having one flag that rotate showing flags of various nations."* We further inspected the ideas of these two participants and found that the copied ideas made up only a small portion of their generated ideas. The panel did not count structural or surface transfers from these copied ideas.

Figure 5 shows transfer rates for the *On-idle* and *On-demand* conditions (averaged across participants). A simple z-test for a difference in proportions yields a significant coefficient($z=3.82$, $p < .001$), indicating that transfer was observed in a statistically higher proportion of cases in the *On-demand* condition compared to the *On-idle* condition. This data suggest that participants in the *On-demand* condition used examples more often than participants in the *On-idle* condition.

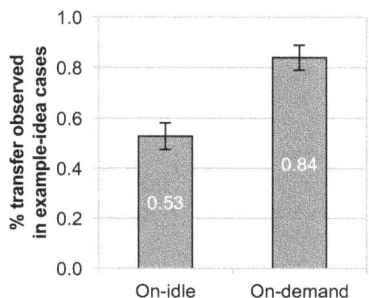

Figure 5. Participants in the *On-demand* condition used more examples to generate new ideas than those in the *On-idle* condition.

Analysis by type of feature transfer yielded similar results (see Figure 6). Transfer rates were higher for *On-demand* cases for both structural ($z=2.55$, $p < .05$) and surface features ($z=3.68$, $p < .001$). Importantly, the ratio of structural to surface transfers was similar for both conditions. These findings suggest that differences in novelty between the *On-demand* and *On-idle* conditions may be due to quantitative (i.e., more cases of examples actually influencing ideation) rather than qualitative differences (e.g., more sophisticated transfer) in how the participants used the examples.

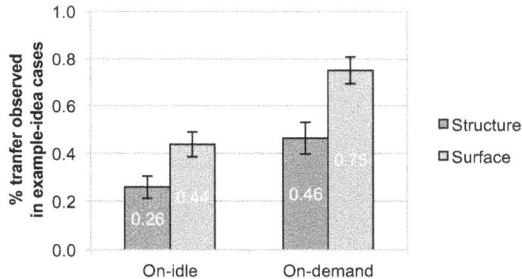

Figure 6. Participants in the *On-demand* condition transferred both structural and surface features from examples more often than those in the *On-idle* condition.

DISCUSSION

Adding to prior work showing the importance of considering *what* examples to see, our results demonstrate the importance of carefully considering *when* to see examples. Giving participants acces to examples on demand led to the highest ratings for novelty (but did not boost productivity). Automatically presenting examples to participants whenever they were idle also benefited ideation, but only for number (and not novelty/value) of ideas. In contrast, participants who received examples at regular intervals produced the fewest ideas (even fewer than participants who saw no examples at all). We now unpack these findings in more detail and draw out their implications for cognitive theories of creativity and the design of platforms for collaborative inspiration.

Why were on-demand and on-idle effects so different?

Why were there differences in the novelty of generated ideas between the *On-demand* and the *On-idle* conditions given that both interventions aimed to offer examples to people when they were stuck in a mental rut? One possible explanation may be related to our specific mechanism for automatically inferring when the person was stuck. Delivering examples when a person is idle for 30 seconds might be too simple or we might not have picked the right threshold time to infer the stuck moment. Our follow-up analyses of the idle timing data from the *On-demand* condition showed that the average waiting time was approximately 30 seconds, suggesting that, on average, our choice of idle interval was reasonable. Nevertheless, there was also variability in the wait times, both between participants and within sessions. While we do not believe the pattern of effects of on-idle examples is idiosyncratic to our choice of idle interval, future work exploring more nuanced idle intervals might yield more precise estimates of the size of these effects.

From a theoretical perspective, a more interesting alternative explanation might be that awareness is a key component of a prepared mind: that is, to benefit from inspirational stimuli, being stuck is not enough—you must also know that you are stuck. Theoretically, our results suggest that theories of creative insight inspiration (such as the Prepared Mind theory [43, 36, 31]) should pay more attention to metacognitive factors (e.g., awareness of one's own cognitive states). Practically, interventions designed to increase metacognitive awareness (e.g., mindfulness training) may help people maximize opportunities for inspiration. Future experiments might explore if on-idle inspiration delivery combined with such interventions could match the benefits of on-demand example delivery.

Alternatively, perhaps participants in the *On-idle* condition benefited less from examples because the examples were delivered while they were still productively accessing knowledge within a given category, even if they were not typing into the system. Our example sets were diverse and would probably have required participants to switch categories in order to recombine them into new ideas. SIAM theory [34, 33] predicts that switching categories requires effort, and can lead to productivity losses. Perhaps *On-idle* inspiration delivery could still be beneficial if the examples were "personalized" (e.g., coherent extensions of a user's current solution path). Such examples could activate other knowledge that is related to currently activated knowledge. Prior work has suggested that deep exploration within a category is an alternative (and often overlooked) pathway to highly creative ideas [32, 39]. Future work could develop novel mechanisms for real-time semantic analysis of participants' solution paths, and conduct experiments to test whether personalized inspiration could further help people benefit from inspirational examples.

Although participants in the *On-idle* condition produced ideas that were rated as slightly less novel than those generated by participants who received examples on demand, they were the most productive. This result suggests that we can prime people to produce more ideas by showing them examples when they are idle without sacrificing the novelty or value of generated ideas. This productivity gain might be explained by the fact that new examples were presented to them before they realized that they were stuck, allowing them to pursue a new train of thought sooner instead of wasting time waiting for new ideas. However, the follow-up analysis suggested that participants in the *On-idle* condition did not use examples to guide their ideation as often as the *On-demand* participants. An alternative explanation that is more consistent with the data is that the appearance of a new set of examples signaled to people that their performance was being monitored and thus nudged them to keep on working. Prior work has shown that people increase their rate of idea generation when they know their work is being watched or will later be evaluated [48, 30, 44]. However, there is little evidence that this increased productivity also leads to higher quality (or more novel) ideas. Indeed, people often refrain from exploring "wild ideas" if they know or perceive that they are being evaluated for their ideas, a phenomenon known as evaluation apprehension [14, 11]. Future work that explores idea generation systems with automatic example delivery mechanisms should test this alternative explanation, and carefully consider participants' perceptions of automated support when designing such systems.

Did examples really help?

One important question to consider in interpreting the results is whether the examples really helped. For example, did participants in the *on-demand* condition merely copy features from the examples? Our follow-up content analysis suggests that they did indeed use examples to guide their idea generation to a greater extent than the *on-idle* participants: does this mean then that they were not being creative? One thing we can rule out is that participants were simply copying the examples wholesale. In additional follow-up analyses of ideas generated in the *on-idle* and *on-demand* conditions, participants usually generated ideas that shared features with examples instead of simply copying them. Even in rare cases when participants submitted an idea that was almost identical to the examples, subsequent ideas were their own original ideas. We suspect that submitting ideas very similar to examples helped jolt their train of thoughts.

However, ruling out wholesale copying still leaves the question of whether ideas generated by solution transfer can be considered creative. We agree with other authors [28, 38] that solution transfer *per se* does not mean that the resulting ideas are not creative (or were not produced by a creative process). Cognitive research strongly suggests that all idea generation is inevitably structured by prior knowledge [47], and studies of real-world creative behavior underscore the central importance of building on prior knowledge [16, 19]. When this structuring and solution transfer leads to ideas that are novel and valuable, we say that the idea was "inspired by" or "built upon" the example(s) [28, 19]; in contrast, when the results are less desirable, we say that the designer was "fixated" by the examples [26, 38]. Here, the fact that the *on-demand* participants mostly generated more novel ideas (and did not

merely copy examples) suggests the former interpretation of the effects of examples is appropriate.

Further insights into the potential harm of examples

Our results also join prior work in highlighting the potential negative effects of examples. Here, we add the insight that at least some of the negative effects of examples may be due to when they are seen. Although participants in the *On-interval* condition generated ideas that were no less novel than those in the *On-demand* condition, they were the least productive (even less productive than people who saw no examples at all). One potential explanation—consistent with the SIAM model—might be that the examples were experienced as interruptions or distractions, rather than inspiration; much prior work has demonstrated that interruptions are detrimental to performance [3]. Some authors have also suggested that interruptions and distractions can be especially detrimental when one is in a state of heightened focus and concentration on a creative task [12]. While this effect might be caused by our choice of time interval, this result does demonstrate that it is possible to harm productivity with ill-timed example delivery. More in-depth examination of the effect of different length of time interval could shed some light on whether negative effects of fixed interval example delivery stem from poorly selected time intervals, or whether any fixed interval example delivery is likely to be suboptimal.

CONCLUSION

In this paper we explored the question of how the impact of examples changes depending on when they are seen during ideation. We conducted an online experiment exploring two mechanisms for delivering examples at the right moment: a system that provides examples upon request and a system that proactively provides examples when a user is idle. Our results show that people benefit most from examples when they are prepared for it. Showing examples to people when they have been idle for a period of time helps people come up with more (but not necessarily better) ideas, while showing examples on-demand helps people come up with more novel ideas. In contrast, ill-timed example delivery might harm productivity, leading to fewer ideas.

These findings help support and refine theories of creative inspiration. Future work can explore different variation of time intervals for the *On-idle* and *On-demand* conditions. The length of "stuck" time interval might vary and depend on the stage of idea generation. Our findings also point toward the benefits of personalized examples that would be most helpful to people at a specific point in time. The examples in our experiment were ideas generated by participants from the pilot study or collected from the Internet search by the authors. In more realistic settings, these examples can come from various sources such as a personal collections or existing related public idea repositories where there are thousands of ideas available. Or, if people are generating ideas in groups, these inspirations can be ideas generated by others. Once a system gathers these ideas, it can select which one to show using existing methods to select a set of inspiring examples [49, 45]

We plan to explore novel mechanisms for real-time semantic analysis of people's idea exploration to gain a deeper understanding of how to best provide them with inspiration. We hope that this line of research will lay the foundation for a new generation of intelligent idea-generation support systems that augment human creativity.

ACKNOWLEDGEMENTS

This work was funded in part by a Sloan Research Fellowship, gifts from Google and Adobe and awards from the National Science Foundation (IIS-1208382, IIS-1217096, and IIS-1122206).

REFERENCES

1. Agogué, M., Kazakçi, A., Hatchuel, A., Masson, P., Weil, B., Poirel, N., and Cassotti, M. The impact of type of examples on originality: Explaining fixation and stimulation effects. *The Journal of Creative Behavior 48*, 1 (2013), 1–12.

2. Bailey, B. P., and Iqbal, S. T. Understanding changes in mental workload during execution of goal-directed tasks and its application for interruption management. *ACM TOCHI 14*, 4 (2008), 21.

3. Bailey, B. P., Konstan, J. A., and Carlis, J. V. Measuring the effects of interruptions on task performance in the user interface. In *Proc. IEEE SMC*, vol. 2, IEEE (2000), 757–762.

4. Ball, L. J., Ormerod, T. C., and Morley, N. J. Spontaneous analogising in engineering design: a comparative analysis of experts and novices. *Design Studies 25*, 5 (2004), 495–508.

5. Baruah, J., and Paulus, P. B. Category assignment and relatedness in the group ideation process. *Journal of Experimental Social Psychology 47*, 6 (2011), 1070–1077.

6. Bearman, C., Ball, L. J., and Ormerod, T. C. An exploration of real-world analogical problem solving in novices. In *Prog. CogSci'02* (2002).

7. Bilalić, M., McLeod, P., and Gobet, F. Why good thoughts block better ones: The mechanism of the pernicious einstellung (set) effect. *Cognition 108*, 3 (2008), 652–661.

8. Chan, J., Dow, S., and Schunn, C. Conceptual distance matters when building on others' ideas in crowd-collaborative innovation platforms. In *Proc. CSCW'14*, ACM (2014), 141–144.

9. Chan, J., Fu, K., Schunn, C., Cagan, J., Wood, K., and Kotovsky, K. On the benefits and pitfalls of analogies for innovative design: Ideation performance based on analogical distance, commonness, and modality of examples. *Journal of mechanical design 133*, 8 (2011), 081004.

10. Chrysikou, E. G., and Weisberg, R. W. Following the wrong footsteps: fixation effects of pictorial examples in a design problem-solving task. *Journal of Experimental Psychology: Learning, Memory, and Cognition 31*, 5 (2005), 1134.

11. Cooper, W. H., Gallupe, R. B., Pollard, S., and Cadsby, J. Some liberating effects of anonymous electronic brainstorming. *Small Group Research 29*, 2 (1998), 147–178.

12. Csikszentmihalyi, M. *Flow and the Psychology of Discovery and Invention*. HarperPerennial, New York, NY, 1997.

13. Dahl, D. W., and Moreau, P. The influence and value of analogical thinking during new product ideation. *Journal of Marketing Research 39*, 1 (2002), 47–60.

14. Diehl, M., and Stroebe, W. Productivity loss in brainstorming groups: Toward the solution of a riddle. *Journal of Personality and Social Psychology 53*, 3 (9 1987), 497–509.

15. Doboli, A., Umbarkar, A., Subramanian, V., and Doboli, S. Two experimental studies on creative concept combinations in modular design of electronic embedded systems. *Design Studies 35*, 1 (1 2014), 80–109.

16. Eckert, C., and Stacey, M. Fortune favours only the prepared mind: Why sources of inspiration are essential for continuing creativity. *Creativity and Innovation Management 7*, 1 (1998), 9–16.

17. Friedman, R. S., Fishbach, A., Förster, J., and Werth, L. Attentional priming effects on creativity. *Creativity Research Journal 15*, 2-3 (2003), 277–286.

18. German, T. P., and Barrett, H. C. Functional fixedness in a technologically sparse culture. *Psychological Science 16*, 1 (2005), 1–5.

19. Herring, S. R., Chang, C.-C., Krantzler, J., and Bailey, B. P. Getting inspired!: understanding how and why examples are used in creative design practice. In *Proc. CHI'09*, ACM (2009), 87–96.

20. Jansson, D. G., and Smith, S. M. Design fixation. *Design studies 12*, 1 (1991), 3–11.

21. Kapur, M. Productive failure. *Cognition and Instruction 26*, 3 (2008), 379–424.

22. Kulkarni, C., Dow, S. P., and Klemmer, S. R. Early and repeated exposure to examples improves creative work. In *Design Thinking Research*. Springer, 2014, 49–62.

23. Kumar, R., Satyanarayan, A., Torres, C., Lim, M., Ahmad, S., Klemmer, S. R., and Talton, J. O. Webzeitgeist: Design mining the web. In *Proc. CHI'13*, ACM (2013), 3083–3092.

24. Lee, B., Srivastava, S., Kumar, R., Brafman, R., and Klemmer, S. R. Designing with interactive example galleries. In *Proc. CHI'10*, ACM (2010), 2257–2266.

25. Leggett Dugosh, K., and Paulus, P. B. Cognitive and social comparison processes in brainstorming. *Journal of Experimental Social Psychology 41*, 3 (May 2005), 313–320.

26. Linsey, J., Tseng, I., Fu, K., Cagan, J., Wood, K., and Schunn, C. A study of design fixation, its mitigation and perception in engineering design faculty. *Journal of Mechanical Design 132*, 4 (2010), 041003.

27. Maier, N. R. Reasoning in humans. ii. the solution of a problem and its appearance in consciousness. *Journal of comparative Psychology 12*, 2 (1931), 181–194.

28. Marsh, R. L., Landau, J. D., and Hicks, J. L. How examples may (and may not) constrain creativity. *Memory & Cognition 24*, 5 (1996), 669–680.

29. Marsh, R. L., Landau, J. D., and Hicks, J. L. Contributions of inadequate source monitoring to unconscious plagiarism during idea generation. *Journal of Experimental Psychology: Learning, Memory, and Cognition 23*, 4 (1997), 886.

30. Michinov, N., and Primois, C. Improving productivity and creativity in online groups through social comparison process: New evidence for asynchronous electronic brainstorming. *Computers in Human Behavior 21*, 1 (1 2005), 11–28.

31. Moss, J., Kotovsky, K., and Cagan, J. The influence of open goals on the acquisition of problem-relevant information. *Journal of Experimental Psychology: Learning, Memory, and Cognition 33*, 5 (2007), 876.

32. Nijstad, B. A., De Dreu, C. K., Rietzschel, E. F., and Baas, M. The dual pathway to creativity model: Creative ideation as a function of flexibility and persistence. *European Review of Social Psychology 21*, 1 (2010), 34–77.

33. Nijstad, B. A., and Stroebe, W. How the group affects the mind: A cognitive model of idea generation in groups. *Personality and social psychology review 10*, 3 (2006), 186–213.

34. Nijstad, B. A., Stroebe, W., and Lodewijkx, H. F. M. Cognitive stimulation and interference in groups: Exposure effects in an idea generation task. *Journal of Experimental Social Psychology 38*, 6 (2002), 535–544.

35. Parnes, S. Effects of extended effort in creative problem solving. *Journal of Educational psychology 52*, 3 (1961), 117–122.

36. Patalano, A. L., and Seifert, C. M. Memory for impasses during problem solving. *Memory & Cognition 22*, 2 (1994), 234–242.

37. Paulus, P. B., and Dzindolet, M. T. Social influence processes in group brainstorming. *Journal of Personality and Social Psychology 64*, 4 (1993), 575.

38. Purcell, A. T., and Gero, J. S. Design and other types of fixation. *Design Studies 17*, 4 (1996), 363–383.

39. Rietzschel, E. F., Nijstad, B. A., and Stroebe, W. Relative accessibility of domain knowledge and creativity: The effects of knowledge activation on the quantity and originality of generated ideas. *Journal of Experimental Social Psychology 43*, 6 (11 2007), 933–946.

40. Ritchie, D., Kejriwal, A. A., and Klemmer, S. R. d. tour: Style-based exploration of design example galleries. In *Proc. UIST'11*, ACM (2011), 165–174.

41. Schwartz, D. L., Chase, C. C., Oppezzo, M. A., and Chin, D. B. Practicing versus inventing with contrasting cases: The effects of telling first on learning and transfer. *Journal of Educational Psychology 103*, 4 (2011), 759.

42. Schwartz, D. L., and Martin, T. Inventing to prepare for future learning: The hidden efficiency of encouraging original student production in statistics instruction. *Cognition and Instruction 22*, 2 (2004), 129–184.

43. Seifert, C. M., Meyer, D. E., Davidson, N., Patalano, A. L., and Yaniv, I. Demystification of cognitive insight-opportunistic assimilation and the prepared-mind perspective. In *The Nature of Insight*, R. J. Sternberg and J. E. Davidson, Eds., vol. 124. MIT Press, Cambridge, MA, 1995, 65–124.

44. Shepherd, M. M., Briggs, R. O., Reinig, B. A., Yen, J., and Nunamaker Jr, J. F. Invoking social comparison to improve electronic brainstorming: Beyond anonymity. *Journal of Management Information Systems 12*, 3 (1995), 155–170.

45. Siangliulue, P., Arnold, K. C., Gajos, K. Z., and Dow, S. P. Toward collaborative ideation at scale—leveraging ideas from others to generate more creative and diverse ideas. In *Proc. CSCW'15* (2015).

46. Tseng, I., Moss, J., Cagan, J., and Kotovsky, K. The role of timing and analogical similarity in the stimulation of idea generation in design. *Design Studies 29*, 3 (2008), 203–221.

47. Ward, T. B. Structured imagination: The role of category structure in exemplar generation. *Cognitive Psychology 27*, 1 (1994), 1–40.

48. Weber, B., and Hertel, G. Motivation gains of inferior group members: a meta-analytical review. *Journal of personality and social psychology 93*, 6 (2007), 973.

49. Xu, A., and Bailey, B. A reference-based scoring model for increasing the findability of promising ideas in innovation pipelines. In *Proc. CSCW'12*, ACM (2012), 1183–1186.

50. Yu, L., and Nickerson, J. Cooks or cobblers?: crowd creativity through combination. *Proc. CHI'11* (2011).

51. Zeng, L., Proctor, R. W., and Salvendy, G. Fostering creativity in product and service development: validation in the domain of information technology. *Hum Factors 53*, 3 (6 2011), 245–70.

InkWell: A Creative Writer's Creative Assistant

Richard P. Gabriel
IBM Research
650 Harry Road
San Jose CA 95120
rpg@us.ibm.com

Jilin Chen[*]
Google
1600 Amphitheatre Parkway
Mountain View, CA 94043
chenjilin@gmail.com

Jeffrey Nichols[*]
Google
1600 Amphitheatre Parkway
Mountain View, CA 94043
jwnichols@google.com

ABSTRACT

InkWell is a writer's assistant—a natural language revision program designed to assist creative writers by producing stylistic variations on texts based on craft-based facets of creative writing and by mimicking aspects of specified writers and their personality traits. It is built on top of an optimization process that produces variations on a supplied text, evaluates those variations quantitatively, and selects variations that best satisfy the goals of writing craft and writer mimicry. We describe the design and capabilities of InkWell, and present an early evaluation of its effectiveness and uses with two established literary writers along with an experiment using InkWell to write haiku on its own.

Author Keywords

Natural language generation; creative writing; creativity; writing

ACM Classification Keywords

I.2.7 Natural Language Processing: Language generation

INTRODUCTION

> **A Snowy Evening**
>
> Deep in the dark—
> the power of snow
>   walking in the deepness
>   –InkWell

InkWell is a writer's assistant designed to help (creative) writers augment their creativity by generating a variety of revisions of a given text using a synonym-based dictionary and a wide variety of soft constraints or "influences." Because one[1] of the members of the InkWell team holds an MFA in Creative Writing, the set of constraints InkWell can handle embodies the kinds of thinking a poet or fiction writer would do—such things as the *music* of the words ("the bird's fire-fangled feathers dangle down" [1]); subtexts, moods, and connotations; subtle semantic differences created by the influence of a set of

---

[*]Author was at IBM Research when this work was done.
[1]rpg

words; a detailed language-usage model; accurate semantic senses; orthographic characteristics of words; and the notion of a spectrum from very associative word choices to very dissociative—we call this *writerly thinking*.

While designing InkWell we expected that a writer would examine the revisions, select promising suggestions, use the revisions as triggers for a better draft, and repeat this process as many times as needed to come up with a good draft. When we tested the system with two very experienced creative writers, we found another, much deeper aspect of creative writing InkWell can augment—InkWell can be a tool to help writers understand what their drafts are teaching them. Moreover, as we worked with InkWell, we discovered ways it could (almost) become a creative writer itself.

WRITERLY THINKING

Producing a work of written art requires constant discovery and guessing—because all works of art are works of exploration and discovery. MFA programs teach writers how the *craft elements* in poetry, fiction, and creative nonfiction achieve their effects—how rhyme ties ideas and images together, how images can form metaphors, how enjambment[2] creates multiple meanings and surprise, etc. And through constant practice, writers find ways to permit their drafts to teach them what those texts need in order to become art. This is not exactly like scientific, technical, and academic writing, which are about the transfer of information—though there are aspects of exploration there too. Robert Boswell, a fiction writer, puts it like this [2]:

> I have grown to understand narrative as a form of contemplation, a complex and seemingly incongruous way of thinking. I come to know my stories by writing my way into them. I focus on the characters without trying to attach significance to their actions. I do not look for symbols. For as long as I can, I remain purposefully blind to the machinery of the story and only partially cognizant of the world my story creates. I work from a kind of half-knowledge.
>
> In the drafts that follow, I listen to what has made it to the page. Invariably, things have arrived that I did not invite, and they are often the most interesting things in the story. By refusing to fully know the world, I hope to discover unusual formations in the landscape, and strange desires in the characters. By declining to analyze the story, I hope to keep it open to surprise.... The world remains half-known.
>
> ...
>
> There can be no discovery in a world where everything is known. A crucial part of the writing endeavor is to practice remaining in the dark.

---

[2]The continuation of a sentence without a pause beyond the end of a line of verse.

Even the most commercial professional writers work this way; Stephen King [3]:

> You may wonder where plot is in all this. The answer... is nowhere.... I believe plotting and the spontaneity of real creation aren't compatible.... I want you to understand that my basic belief about the making of stories is that they pretty much make themselves. The job of the writer is to give them a place to grow.

INKWELL

InkWell is designed to serve these two purposes:

- assist creativity in writing
- mimic a specific writer

InkWell takes a *template*—a specification of original text annotated with which words are variable and characteristics of those words for InkWell to consider—and produces revisions. Other writing-related constraints are written either as local bindings in the template or as global parameters and soft constraints. The example in Figure 1 shows how a writer might express a template describing Robert Frost's "Stopping By Woods on a Snowy Evening" [4]. (The original text of the poem is in the Appendix.)

InkWell In Action

Let's start by looking at what InkWell can do with the Frost poem. We will focus on the last two stanzas—here are the originals:

> He gives his harness bells a shake
> To ask if there is some mistake.
> The only other sound is the sweep
> Of easy wind and downy flake.

> The woods are lovely, dark, and deep.
> But I have promises to keep
> And miles to go before I sleep,
> And miles to go before I sleep.

The following revision was created using conservative synonym search (don't traverse far from the originally specified words), Ernest Hemingway [5] as the writer to imitate, and a preference for short words. Here is that result (changes from the original are underlined):

> He gives his harness bells a <u>cloud</u>
> To ask if there is some <u>spot</u>.
> The only other <u>music is the illusion</u>
> Of <u>worn wind and cold mound</u>.

> The <u>logs</u> are <u>good, glad, and tight</u>.
> But I have <u>words</u> to keep
> And miles to go before I sleep,
> And miles to go before I sleep.

The second variant was created using wild synonym search (go far and wide), Walt Whitman [6] as the writer to sound like ("Leaves of Grass"), and also short words:

> He gives his harness bells a <u>whip</u>
> To ask if there is some <u>end</u>.
> The only other <u>show is the push</u>
> Of <u>a couple of winds and a falling chip</u>.

> The woods are <u>clean, murky, and vigorous</u>.
> But I have <u>roots to preserve</u>
> And miles to go before I sleep,
> And miles to go before I sleep.

The last example is like the Whitman one except InkWell was directed to sound a little like Adam Smith [7] and to be a lot wilder:

> He gives his harness <u>cacabels a scramble</u>
> To <u>consult</u> if there is some <u>stumble</u>.
> The only other <u>imposition is the affixation</u>
> Of <u>counterbalanced levanter and puberulent pebble</u>.

> The <u>cocuswoods are equitable, dishonorable, and redeemable</u>.
> But I have <u>diminutives to number</u>
> And <u>millimeters</u> to go before I <u>slumber</u>,
> And <u>millimeters</u> to go before I <u>slumber</u>.

In addition, InkWell was instructed to prefer long words and to work hard on rhymes.

These are two of the haiku InkWell wrote:

> a man
>   steps out
>   of the old woman

> a puddle of water:
> as if the sun had changed

Mimicking Writers

InkWell mimics writers by using techniques including these:

- match specified (or measured) Big Five personality traits and associated personality facets [8]; match basic human values as described by Schwartz [9] and Chen [10]
- match a writer's word choices: favored words, word music, word length, favored mood
- match writing patterns: *n-grams* (2-, 3-, 4-, and 5-grams); an *n-gram* is a series of n words in a row that has appeared in a naturally occurring, existing text.

Personality-based features (originally included to support work in persuasion campaigns) turned out to be useful for creative writers—for example, to make the text more agreeable by favoring words and phrases that exhibit that personality trait or to match the personality profile of a particular writer.

Assisting Creativity

InkWell assists creativity by using techniques including these:

- use conservative or wild synonym choice (*associative* versus *dissociative* writing)—search diameter, search relevance decay rate, preference for nearby words, preference for far away words, which synonym aspects to use (hypernyms, meronyms, etc)
- obey or defy n-grams—that is, use familiar or novel phrasing
- satisfy constraints such as word-length, alternative meanings, word rhythms
- favor rhymes and echoes (similar sounding words)
- select words based on ontology (concepts) or a cluster of word-centric concepts to favor or avoid
- mimic any specified personality profile
- take into account a mood specified by a construct called a *halo*

```
(with-personality-traits (*writer-big-five*)
 (with-global-constraints ((all-echo)(all-different)))
  (with-pervasive-predicates (#'syllable-bonus-few)
   (bind ((w1 (<choose> verb-cognition :+sense [know certain]))
          (w2 (snow noun-substance :rhyme [though]))
          (w3 (<choose> adj :+sense [queer odd unusual weird demented stupid silly]))
          (w4 (or (year noun-quantity) (week noun-quantity) (month noun-quantity) (season noun-quantity)))
          (w5 (<choose> verb-motion :+sense [cause move back forth shake]))
          (w6 (<choose> noun-object  :+sense [small fragment broken break whole flake]))
          (here (here adj)) (near (near adj)) (mile (mile noun-quantity pl)) (sleep (sleep verb))
          (woods (wood noun-plant pl :+sense [forest trees plants wooded area] :-sense [wood])))
"Whose (ref woods) these are I (<choose> verb-cognition :sense think-sense) I (ref w1).
His (house noun) is in the (village noun) though;
He will not see me (stop verb gerund) (ref here :rhyme near)
To (watch verb-perception) his (ref woods) (fill verb) up with (ref w2 :different w1 :rhyme w1).
                                                  .
My (<choose> adj :sense little-sense) (horse noun-animal) must (<choose> verb-cognition :sense think-sense) it
  (ref w3 :echo w1)
To (stop verb) without a (<choose> noun :sense farmhouse-sense) (binding near :rhyme w3)
Between the (ref woods) and (frozen adj) (<choose> noun-object :sense lake-sense)
The (<choose> ask -est :sense darkest-sense) (<choose> noun-time :sense evening-sense) of the
  (ref w4 :different w3 :rhyme w3).

He gives his (harness noun) (bell noun pl) a (ref w5 :echo w3)
To (ask verb) if there is some (mistake noun :rhyme w5).
The only other (<choose> noun :sense sound-sense) is the (<choose> noun-act :sense arc-sense)
Of (<choose> ADJ :sense easy-sense) (wind noun) and (<choose> ADJ :sense downy-sense)
  (ref w6 :different w5 :rhyme w5).

The (ref woods) are (<choose> adj :sense lovely-sense), (<choose> adj :sense dark-sense), and
  (<choose>  adj :sense deep-sense),
But I have (promise noun pl) to (keep verb :rhyme sleep),
And (ref mile) to go before I (ref sleep),
And (ref mile) to go before I (sleep verb :different sleep :rhyme sleep)."))))
```

Figure 1. This is the internal template format used by Inkwell for "Stopping By Woods on a Snowy Evening." It can be edited directly by users, but is usually created using our visual template creation tool. We show this format to demonstrate the functionality of Inkwell.

Every soft constraint has an associated weight, and thus any constraint can be inverted (negated): e.g. sound like a particular writer or sound like anyone but that writer, rhyme two words or avoid rhyming them, observe n-grams or deliberately violate them. InkWell produces any number of candidate revisions, and the writer can pick and choose revisions and wordings.

The notion of a **halo** is a good example of how InkWell was designed to mimic writerly thinking. A *halo* is a mood device: specify a set of words, and InkWell starts with each of those words and fans out along synonym arcs to other words. Where several of these wavefronts hit, those words are given more weight in the revision process. Looking at Frost's poem, the line

The woods are lovely, dark, and deep

might be revised this way

The woods are bright, not very light, and high

when given this halo:

delighted, ebullient, ecstatic, elated, energetic, enthusiastic, euphoric, excited, exhilarated, overjoyed, thrilled, tickled pink, turned on, vibrant, zippy

and this way

The woods are sad, bad, and dead

when given this halo (and a preference for short words and strong rhyme):

affronted, belligerent, bitter, burned up, enraged, fuming, furious, heated, incensed, infuriated, intense, outraged, provoked, seething, storming, truculent, vengeful, vindictive, wild

Halos are an example of the strategy behind InkWell: as much as possible, use concrete words and their characteristics rather than reifications and abstractions. It's of course possible to label the two halos above as *Anger* and *Happiness*, but the actual words tell the story more directly.

InkWell uses lots of data:

- Expanded Wordnet Synonym dictionary: ~160,000 words [11] [12]
- Expanded LIWC 2001 dictionary [17]—for personality analysis
- 20,000 most common words
- CMU Phonetic dictionary: algorithmically expanded to ~220,000 words [13]—for rhymes and echoes
- Stem dictionary: ~163,000 entries (+ Porter Stemmer + Lemmatization + Wordnet's Morphy algorithm)
- n-grams: ~24m from general literature including the Google 2-grams [14] and the COCA 3-, 4-, and 5-grams [15]
- n-grams (including 1-grams) from writers; 100,000–1,000,000 per writer; currently there are about 70 writer samples to choose from (and supplying new ones is trivial)

N-grams are used to try to maintain some degree of familiarity and coherence. There are two sets of n-grams used: one from general literature (we use a filtered version of the Google 2-grams [14] but use COCA for the 3-, 4-, and 5-grams [15]), and another set of n-grams from the writer chosen to be imitated. These constraints are expressed as global variables, with separate weights possible for each of the 2-, 3-, 4-, and 5-grams. In all there are 57 different constraints that can be imposed on the revision process (not all are described in this paper).

For the Whitman- and Hemingway-influenced revisions of the Frost poem, InkWell was told to conform to the target writer's word choices and n-grams with writer 1-, 2-, 3-, and 4-gram weights of 20, 20, 30, and 40, respectively, and with a rhyme weight of 50 and an echo weight of 20. For the Adam Smith revision, Inkwell used -20, -30, and -40 for the writer 2-, 3-, and 4-gram weights, and 100 for both the rhyme and echo weights.

Synonyms and Word Senses
Synonyms in revision are tricky. It is not enough to know the part of speech or even the role of a word in a sentence—the exact sense of the word in question is essential. To revise the sentence "I like dogs" requires knowing whether by "dog" the writer means:

- *animal*: a member of the genus Canis
- *person*: a dull unattractive unpleasant girl or woman
- *person*: informal term for a man
- *person*: someone who is morally reprehensible
- *food*: a smooth-textured sausage of minced beef or pork, usually smoked
- *artifact*: a hinged catch
- *artifact*: metal supports for logs in a fireplace

Narrowing it down to an *animal* would characterize it well, but *person* and *artifact* still would leave it ambiguous. We have been working with definition-based word sets as a way to pluck good senses from synonym sets. We call these structures ***senses***, and they form the most rapidly evolving parts of InkWell.

A sense is a data structure that can be thought of as a vector of words along with associated strengths. A set of words is supplied, and using each as a starting point, InkWell visits synonyms as specified by current synonym search settings (hypernms, hyponyms, etc) out to the current synonym-search depth, and adds those words with their decayed relevance values to the vector. If a word is already in the vector, the associated relevances are summed. The vector is normalized.

InkWell can use a sense to locate words. Each word (including all its synonym senses) in the dictionary is examined along with its definition (which is just a sentence or phrase). The words in the definition are compared to the vector, and a strength computed. A subset of the strongest candidates are selected. For example, if given a sense rooted in the words "sing" and "bird," InkWell will find words like "sparrow," "lark," and "cockatoo." A negative sense can be specified as well—a sense to avoid; a full sense can be a combination of positive and negative senses.

The use of senses is seen in Figure 1 where the expression

```
(wood noun-plant pl
 :+sense [forest trees plants wooded area]
 :-sense [wood])
```

means that the word chosen to mean "wood" should be in the semantic category plant, should be made plural when rendered, should be of the same sense as the words "forest," "trees," "plants," "wooded area," and not the same sense as "wood," (that is, the material that trees are made of).

WordNet provides a variety of synonym types such as hypernyms, hyponyms, homonyms, meronyms, and variations on each. This complicates things. Which of these to consider is part of the specification InkWell uses to revise text.

On Templates
A template resembles a Lisp program whose body looks like text with parenthesized annotations. The text in Figure 1 is a template—it shows many of the mechanisms for specifying the text well enough to be effectively revised. Here are some of the highlights:

- items in parentheses are specifications of word choices; a word in the first position indicates the word whose synonyms are considered; <choose> indicates InkWell should find words that satisfy the specified word-sense description; subspecifications include:
    - the part of speech and semantic category
    - adjustments to the word when finally rendered; (pl for plural, for example)
    - words that should be the same, should be different, should rhyme, should echo
- words required to be the same are specified in the bind form
- local and global constraints are possible—short words, everything should echo, etc.
- personality traits to aim for

Creating complex templates requires tool assistance. InkWell has a template creation tool: it takes unadorned text and leads the writer through selecting adjustments, semantic categories, and the senses of words the writer intends. The tool is lightweight and visual—able to help novice writers create templates like the one in Figure 1 in less than five minutes. We are exploring ways to make this part of the process more automatic by integrating a parser (which helps only a little) and experimenting with determining the best sense for each word by looking for coherent assignments of sense in a text. For example, in a sentence like this there should be no question which sense of *dog* to use: "This dive restaurant serves amazing dogs slathered with messy, meaty chili."

InkWell Flow
Each template along with all the specified constraints and parameters is compiled into an evaluation function which returns 0 when all constraints are satisfied. InkWell selects a set of candidate replacement words and phrases, and an optimization process then selects the combination of words and phrases that best satisfy the evaluation function. The optimization process uses simulated annealing. One nice characteristic of simulated annealing is that it requires neither gradients in the evaluation functions nor any explicit staging of

the order of choices. Just add constraints and let the relatively undisciplined SA process do its thing.

For example, to evaluate how close a set of word choices is to a specified personality profile, InkWell analyzes the proposed text to (computationally) determine its exhibited personality. This is then compared to the target, and either the current text is considered a step in the right direction or a step in the wrong direction. For the personality computation, InkWell builds on the work of Tal Yarkoni [16] and uses a method which computes LIWC scores [17] for the generated text, and uses a simple, learned classification function to produce Big Five scores. Because the analyzed texts are generally pretty short, the LIWC dictionary was expanded algorithmically using the WordNet synonym dictionary, a decay function, and semantic categories derived from the LIWC categories—this expanded the LIWC dictionary from about 2300 words to about 25,000 words. The computation of personality scores needs to be fast, which is accomplished by pre-computing as much of the LIWC categories as possible and using caches. InkWell also targets *values* [10], which are computed similarly.

The overall evaluation function can be computationally intense, which is appropriate for a deliberate, creative writing task, but perhaps not for real-time language generation. For example, the template shown in Figure 1 compiles to a Lisp function $\sim$2000 lines long which is invoked 200,000 times during a typical optimization run. This means that the rhyming predicate is invoked $\sim$3.6m times. This computation is feasible through the use of parallelism and many caches.

CASE STUDIES

We performed two case studies using InkWell. One was a writer study to see how well InkWell could serve the needs of (professional) creative writers. The other was to use InkWell as a fully automated haiku generator, and to determine whether it would produce decent haiku with recognizable aesthetics.

For the writer studies we met with two established writers— a fiction writer ("Julia") and a poet ("Quinton"). One of the authors of this paper described and demonstrated InkWell to each writer (separately), and then engaged the writer in an exercise working with a draft of theirs.

The Fiction Writer

The fiction writer was first. Julia holds an MFA in Creative Writing (Fiction), and is well published in literary magazines. She also teaches writing to young adults. She was trained as a dancer and has an outgoing, extravagant personality. Much of her fiction is funny and fun. We began by inputting her text and creating a template.

> Poets bartered commodities when they were available, amended soil with their waste when they were not. Composers filled reservoirs with orchestras, music crashing through the pipes into dry fountains and apartment sinks. Farmers made bibles of seeds and left them in every nightstand drawer, hotels and residences alike.

Initial Reactions
Julia's first reaction was subdued.

The initial settings for the constraints and parameters were conservative (search to synonym depth 2, consider more general words, related words, and similar words), and thus the early revisions were close to the original. For instance, one was the following:

> Poets bartered commodities when they were available, amended soil with their waste when they were not. composers filled reservoirs with orchestras, music crashing through the pipes into dry fountains and apartment sinks. <u>Gods</u> made <u>promises</u> of seeds and left them in every nightstand drawer, hotels and residences alike.

Julia's reactions were *"kind of fun to add that stylistic layer or aesthetic"* and *"the sense... the relationship to reality has stayed the same... or is mine, still—that's how it feels."*

A Turning Point
At that point the researcher proposed making substantial changes to the settings. In particular, the synonym search was directed to look further from the original words and for more specific rather than more general synonyms. This yielded the following:

> Poets bartered <u>middlings</u> when they were <u>many</u>, amended soil with their waste when they were not. <u>Psalmists lined cisterns</u> with <u>string orchestras</u>, music crashing through the <u>lines</u> into <u>sound</u> fountains and <u>rooms</u> sinks. <u>Husbandmen made words</u> of seeds and <u>found</u> them in every <u>dresser</u> drawer, <u>courts and palaces</u> alike.

This triggered Julia's first strong reaction—a little scream and then: *"Oh, love it—so much better. Oh so interesting—so much more interesting. 'Psalmists lined cisterns with string orchestras'–that's as near the sense I was going for... only the language is much more specific. That's fun. That looks fun to me. This is a **rich** mess."* After this, the nature of the interaction changed—she was much more engaged, and suggested a number of experiments. Nevertheless, her goal was not what we anticipated. Instead of tweaking her draft, she was trying to understand or come to grips with the "structure" of her draft and the nature of its internal sense, consistency, and coherence—of the writing itself but also the world she was trying to create. Rather than seeking help with revision, she was seeking diagnostic entry points.

- *"I'm still determining the structure, the internal sense of it"*
- *"This is really interesting to me in terms of doing the 'thinking' work"*
- *"⟨the program helps figure out⟩ what's important in it, in the sense of it, where I'm creating a world that is very odd and quite intentional about the oddness, and you can get lost, really lost. It's really good for honing... focusing in on what's important."*
- *"That's the only way I can think of to do it—to see how many interesting iterations I've got, see what language sticks to my head. So I'm looking for velcro basically, and then, you know, I have the attachment piece here ⟨points to head⟩".*
- *"what's... frightening about this is that it is teasing out some things—I suppose they are in there."*

- *"I can see how you would get very familiar with the little tide pools that the language, where they come from. operating behind there. Then you would be able to say 'ok, I want to mess with it **this** way...'"*
- *"It's kind of interesting to see what it changes, so it's helping me understand what's operating"*

Julia was looking at multiple revisions ("iterations"), and because they were theoretically "close" to her original semantically—because the program looks at synonyms—the connotations and other triggers she was seeing were teaching her about what she had put on the page, and possibly how her thought processes were circling those nearby "tide pools."

Imitating Writers

Julia was also interested in some of the wilder revisions—either when InkWell was directed to look far away from the original variable words or when specific writers were targeted for imitation. The following is a revision in which the King James Bible was targeted for imitation, along with the personality traits displayed there. We also tweaked that personality by aiming it more toward disagreeableness and extraversion:

> Poets bartered <u>numbers</u> when they were <u>perverted, choked clay</u> with their <u>scrap</u> when they were not. <u>Psalmists silenced washbasins</u> with orchestras, <u>euphony</u> crashing through the <u>phone lines into naked</u> fountains and <u>teaser baptistries</u>. <u>Tillers</u> made bibles of <u>rapeseeds and gave</u> them in every <u>medicine chest knee breeches, convents and convents</u> alike.

...and this:

> Poets bartered <u>burdens</u> when they were <u>defenseless, hit sand</u> with their <u>piss</u> when they were not. <u>Psalmists cut cisterns</u> with orchestras, <u>euphony</u> crashing through the pipes into <u>outrageous</u> fountains and <u>teaser privies</u>. <u>Tillers</u> made mournings of <u>mockernut hickories and cut</u> them in every <u>vanity</u> drawer, <u>resorts and palaces</u> alike.

Her comment regarding the influence of the Bible on the otherwise wild constraint settings was *"I love it. So it takes the wildness and gives it a sort of imprimatur—something a little more solid.... And is it still mine, though? ... We've run it through filters I didn't create so much, though I ran it through my eyeball filter after that."* Her concern was that by using an aid such as InkWell, which alters her text under the influence of word-usage models of other writers, the resulting text might not be considered hers alone. She talked about how there is a similar effect when she reads another writer and there could be residual influences on what she writes after that, but that this seemed different from that.

> *"I know I wouldn't have gotten [there] that fast with 'hitting the sand with their piss' or 'choking the clay.'"*

To end the session we switched to Ernest Hemingway as the writer to imitate.

> <u>Bards</u> bartered <u>picture shows</u> when they were <u>cleanable, doctored Kitty Litter</u> with their <u>scrap metal</u> when they were not. Composers <u>filled out washbowls</u> with <u>chamber</u> orchestras, <u>euphony</u> crashing through the <u>steam pipes into liberal arts</u> fountains and <u>flat public toilets</u>. Planters made <u>content words of gentleman's-canes and called it a day</u> them in every <u>hope chest Jamaica shorts, holiday resorts and monasteries</u> alike.

Julia was taken with the phrase "doctored Kitty Litter with their scrap metal" and remarked *"That turns out to be one of those fruitful little phrase arrangements. That is teaching me something about my writing."*

Julia's Final Comments

Her final comment was as follows:

> *"So basically you're kind of channeling different voices to see 'can I mess with my syntax a little more, mess with the flavor, can I take vanilla or chocolate, my standard fare, my standard mannerisms in the written language, and mess with them?' It works for my aesthetic, certainly, because it's language driven.... and it could work for poets. I don't know with straight fiction, although it might make it a whole lot better."*

Analysis

InkWell is a complex program, and there are many dials and sliders, and to warm things up, we started with conservative settings. She initially saw only an "interesting" level of value because the revisions were not far from her original.

Once she saw the first unusual or strange revision, she became more engaged, but her thought process was a surprise to us. Instead of primarily trying to harvest the revisions for phrasing to adopt or triggers for further writerly thinking, she used InkWell as a diagnostic tool or an instrument to explore her own thinking and process—she tried to make sense of what the revisions taught her about her draft and its consistency and coherence. Another way to put it is that she was trying to analyze her draft in a way similar to a "close reading." A close reading is a deep analysis of a text, especially its use of language, in order to come to grasp its meaning and understand how it conveys that meaning. [18] [19] [20]

Only after that did she come to believe InkWell could help her "mess" with her text to explore alternative approaches—that is, to use InkWell as a direct writer's assistant—or perhaps a writing partner.

The Poet

The poet was second. Like Julia, Quinton holds an MFA in Creative Writing, and is well published in literary magazines. Quinton has a book of poetry published—his manuscript won a poetry competition whose prize was publication. Quinton primarily writes formalist poems—fixed meter and rhyme scheme. His work is directed to observing small moments in urban settings. He is close to retirement age, served in the Navy for twenty years, is church-going, and is socially conservative. He is a lawyer.

Quinton wanted to work on a poem he had just started. The fragment was quite short:

> The conic dome sluiced smartly on its tube
> Is slung across its luggage cart and docked
> in an aisle while its owner searches
> a department for...

The poem fragment is describing small missiles on a dolly in a narrow passageway on a Navy ship. As with Julia, Quinton read the first couple of conservative revisions and began analyzing them—but this time it was to understand the revision more than to understand his own draft. The following was one of the first revisions InkWell produced:

the conical dome <u>flushed</u> smartly on its <u>thread</u>
is slung across its <u>grip barrow</u> and docked
in an aisle while its owner <u>gathers</u>
a <u>number</u> for

For example, Quinton tried to make sense of the word "flushed"—how it could mean both "flush" as in clearing out with forced water as well as "flush" as in placed right up against a wall ("flush with the wall"). We continued with revisions, eventually using Herman Melville's "Moby-Dick" [21] as the piece to imitate.

A Turning Point

Again, as with Julia, we hit a turning point or *aha!* moment when InkWell produced the following:

the conic dome <u>flushed sprucely</u> on its <u>safety lock</u>
is <u>catapulted</u> across its <u>pocket pickup arm</u> and docked
in an aisle while its <u>lady of the house unlocks</u>
a <u>line of defense</u> for

Quinton let out a laugh and said *"I love that. Anything that breaks you out of that earnest, that linear thinking."* At this point he told the story of how the leader of a writing group he was in gave him the exercise to write the worst poem he could. Then after presenting that poem to the group, he was instructed to revise it to make it even worse. He said that this exercise, repeated for several poems, gave him some of the "strongest" poems he's ever written. Quinton explained as follows:

"I think part of that was giving you permission to do things that are just wild, that you don't think of as poetic and this program seems to be doing the same thing. You've got something in your head, you're describing it in a certain way, and this is just showing you all these other ways of coming at this; and not only to find a word to describe what is in your head, but kind of to blow up your head, expand it so you can in a more objective way, you can go 'wow, this whole thing that has nothing to do with what I was going after when I was starting out is actually kind of interesting.' So you might end up going in a completely different direction, and writing a completely different poem that's a hell of a lot more interesting than what you started out with. So I kind of like it as a generative tool."

Quinton believed InkWell could serve as a relentless "Dean Young in a box." Dean Young [22] has been described as a neo-surrealist, and his approach sometimes is to use surrealism to explore the imagination and to break down the border between the real and the unreal. Dean Young was one of Quinton's teachers. Quinton described Dean Young as someone whose brain is wired as a dissociative engine, and that InkWell could help poets who wanted to write that way but were too cautious or reserved.

In the end Quinton asked when InkWell would be available for his use.

Analysis

Quinton went through a similar discovery process with InkWell to what Julia did: it took an unusual, strange, and unexpected revision to move him into a more engaged exploration of what InkWell could do. We then used a variety of writers to imitate, used both conservative and wild settings, and did some variations on the personality trait settings. Quinton used it both as an instrument to explore his own draft and as a generative aid for the sorts of disconnected jumps that are hard for him to do on his own. He always circled back to the idea that escaping "earnestness" and "linear thinking" was valuable to writers. The nature of exploring his own draft was less direct than Julia's—he spent time trying to understand the mind that produced the revisions while Julia spent time trying to understand how what that mind produced revealed aspects of her own writing.

Both writers are experienced and well-trained. Both writers, when confronted with their first *aha!* revisions, displayed what could be described only as surprise and glee: Julia screamed and Quinton laughed.

InkWell as Poet

In our second study we wanted to see whether InkWell could compose decent (contemporary) haiku on its own using a fully automated, highly aleatoric process. Haiku is a good initial domain for InkWell composition experiments because syntactic sophistication is not required (haiku consist mostly of the juxtaposition of images), semantic linking of images is required, and their brevity means we can generate a lot of them to get a statistical view into InkWell's abilities.

While pursuing this study we designed a simplified template mechanism and in the process, discovered a couple of techniques for improving generated text. Figure 2 shows one of the 54 simplified templates we used for generating Haiku; such a template compiles into the more verbose form already described. Almost all the templates we used were derived from Robert Hass's translations of Bashō's haiku [23]. Contemporary Japanese and English haiku have few syllabic constraints, but in later experiments we were able to approximate the popularly understood but not quite accurate 17-syllable constraint.

Each haiku template requires InkWell to choose all the nontrivial words based on sense specifications. We supplied a set of base senses to use—for example, the *change* base sense (not used in Figure 2) was constructed from the words "change," "produce," and "yield." When a haiku is produced, each of its referenced base senses is augmented with the same randomly (and automatically) constructed other sense, as follows: a writing sample is randomly selected, and a sense is built from a randomly chosen contiguous segment of that text. For example, here is such a set of sense words selected from "Leaves of Grass": "form," "upright," "death," and "breast." The constructed sense is then combined with each base sense using the formula $b \times B + (3 - b) \times C$ where $b = R(0.1, 1.0)$ and $R(x, y)$ produces a random float between x and y, B is the base sense, and C is the randomly constructed sense. This formula describes how each base sense and randomly

```
((or a an) (young-insect noun-animal (mix-senses insect-sense-base ([larva young child] noun)))
(comma)(return) this (intense-sense noun-time) (preposition?)
(fall-sense noun-time (mix-senses season-sense-base ([season leaf fall] noun))) (return)
(remain-sense adv) not (or a an)
(old-insect noun-animal (mix-senses insect-sense-base ([adult old elder] noun)))))
```

Figure 2. One of 54 Simplified Haiku Templates Used by InkWell

constructed topic sense are to be combined—a linear combination with random coefficients to vary the relative influences of the two component senses, with the randomly constructed sense having more influence than the base sense. For example, the combined senses of the sense words selected from "Leaves of Grass" and the senses specified in Figure 2 are based on the following words:

form upright death breast larva young child insect social bee animal
form upright death breast deep central
form upright death breast leaf fall season
form upright death breast still
form upright death breast adult old elder insect social bee animal

After the thematic senses are set, all the other InkWell constraint parameters are chosen randomly except writer n-grams, which were ignored because we wanted to see whether writer-specific traits would emerge. One of the 54 haiku templates is selected, and InkWell writes that haiku.

With this process we created about 1800 haiku. We looked at two questions: Are any of the haiku good? Do any of them conform to a recognizable aesthetic?

The first thing we did was to read them—that is, to see whether any of them were actually good haiku or at least good short poems. We observed a range of quality from the demented (*a hard tick, / this round-trip light time in round-trip light time / like mad not a whitebait*) to the breathtaking (*deep in the dark— / the power of snow / walking in the deepness*) to the demonically clever (*tuned adrenalin / my music, / a beat-boogied headful*).

Because the use of the same (randomly constructed) sense to augment all the base senses in the haiku templates tended to produce related word choices, many of the haiku were thematically coherent. We used a scoring system based on n-grams and music to measure aesthetics—when asked what kind of writing they like, most people would name authors, and some would mention language use. Scoring based on n-grams measures the density of recognized n-grams in a haiku. *Normal* scoring uses the n-grams from general literature, and so measures how conventional a haiku is; *writer* scoring uses the n-grams from a particular writer, and so measures how much like that writer a haiku is. *Music* scoring measures the density of rhymes and echoes in a haiku. Here are some of the haiku that stood out.

These were in the top fifty using a combination of *music* and *normal* scoring (musical but like ordinary prose):

back in the past—
the start of the shit set piece
the ways of the world in the blue

on in the dark—
the length of the stone building
breaking in the heat

These were in the top fifty using *Walt Whitman* scoring (sound like Walt Whitman):

a maverick
troops out
of the pride of California

awake in the dark——
the edge of the water can
spread in your presence

Adam Smith:

a drop of water:
as if the bank had thought

scrupulous in the twilight—
the price of gold chases
the way of the world in power

King James Bible:

a man
passes out of
the pit

time of life issue:
a bird of prey pulls up
out of the way, into the palm

William Faulkner [24]:

a hell of pitch
as if the ring had exploded

short sight fog—
just enough to turn the face
of a man into a nag

Ernest Hemingway:

a trout
moves out of the bay

a man
steps out of the head

late in the afternoon
the glare of piss—
infernal machine sitting
in your seat

even in the afternoon
the advantage of the mother
stills the ways of the world

And some of the best ones appeared at the end of scored lists: here are the not so *normal* and *unmusical*:

a dangerous work shift interruption—
producing dumplings, we cut nasturtiums

a crooked rag day—
by myself
dunking distracted sardines

a slow circadian rhythm set:
harmonizing oysters
broke fresh foods

Although these haiku might appear quite strange, they stand up well compared to highly respected surrealist haiku from the twentieth century, such as these by the French poet, Paul Éluard [25]:

The wind
hesitating
rolls a cigarette of air

The automobile is truly fast
four matured heads
move beneath it

Grammar

The haiku experiments revealed the need for mechanisms to get simple grammar right. We had always known that n-grams would be part of the solution, but we weren't sure how to best accomplish that. We noticed right away that articles, prepositions, and determiners were sometimes wrong because the early templates explicitly mentioned them as constants. We discovered two mechanisms to address this. The first is an improved version of the `or` annotation, which indicates explicit choices. The expression

```
...(or a an) noun...
```

directs InkWell to choose the article that matches the selected noun. Some verbs take specific prepositions after them (like "run into"), so we added the form `(preposition)`, which expands to an `or` that lists all possible prepositions. But this wasn't enough. In some cases InkWell needs to decide to not choose a word. We created the construct `<null-word>` to represent a position with no word in it. The form `(preposition?)` tells InkWell to choose either the correct preposition or no preposition at all; it expands to `(or <null-word> on in under ...)`. With these, this template

```
A dog (or is are) (or a an) animal.
```

resolves to *A dog is an animal.* and this one

```
Dogs (or is are) (or <null-word> a an) animals.
```

to *Dogs are animals.*

The use of these techniques in the haiku templates made ungrammatical haiku rare—crazy, perhaps, but grammatical.

RELATED WORK

Existing tools that we are aware of broadly seem to break down into two categories: teaching the writing process and assisting in the production of complex documents. Tools that teach writing focus on two areas, teaching young children to write (e.g. [26]) and assisting English as a Second Language learners (e.g., [27]). These systems either assist in the process of developing overall content and structure, or with very low-level details of grammar and language.

Other tools assist in the construction of "complex documents," which are longer documents with lots of internal structure and many relations between different areas of the document. Mexica [28] is a system to help model the constraints of a complex document and to assist in writing based on a cognitive model of the writing process. There is great deal of work in assisting with the creation of narrative [29].

InkWell can be seen as supporting the Create phase of Shneiderman's genex model [30]. The Create phase is broken into three components: Explore, Compose, and Evaluate. Based on the results of our studies, Inkwell is currently useful for the Explore and perhaps the Evaluate components, and our eventual goal is to support Compose as well. Other work in supporting creativity for writers has examined scoring sentences for creativity based on a machine learned model [31].

Most of the work on Natural Language Generation (NLG) to this point has focused on planning the content, sentence structure, and sequencing of text. To the extent that style is considered in NLG systems, it's directed toward text generation for journalism or instruction manuals. Systems that produce stories are mainly concerned with planning and story coherence. Most of the NLG systems fall into two categories: rule-based systems and statistical systems. The former generally use handcrafted templates to generate text; the latter generally use statistical models to generate candidate utterances which are then checked for "validity," typically using n-grams. The only NLG system that is directly related to InkWell is Personage by François Mairesse and Marilyn A. Walker [32]. It's a full NLG system which also is looking at producing text exhibiting Big Five personality traits.

POTENTIALLY IMPORTANT OBSERVATION

The InkWell project started as a simple revision program designed to match personality traits as part of a research system aimed at countering malicious persuasion campaigns—it did not start as a project about creativity. In fact, InkWell's strengths as a creative partner emerged as a surprise when we noticed that using wide synonym search parameters and negative weights yielded sort-of relevant but unexpected wording changes. One way of thinking about this is that creativity is not like a module in a system, nor is it something that can be designed for—what would its requirements be, what sort of specification would it have? Creativity is a property one notices in systems.

Only in hindsight is some modicum of explanation available: InkWell is creative because its 57 parameter settings are balanced against each other during optimization, so that creative choices are possible like selecting a not-as-directly relevant word that happens to rhyme very well with some others or offsetting some agreeability with some not-so-sensible n-gram conformance.

CONCLUSION

InkWell is a tool aimed at helping deeply creative people. It has many capabilities which combine to produce a variety of revisions of a template influenced by writer-craft elements, personality traits, and writer models. InkWell is complex, but so are the facets that go into a creative writer's thought processes. Through an initial pair of writer studies we learned that InkWell can be used for exploring alternative wordings and metaphors as well as for aiding a deeper analysis of the meaning and trajectory of a writer's project. With the haiku experiment we began to observe InkWell taking the role of a writer by choosing its own words (not simply finding synonyms), and using a common "sense" overlay to work toward coherence. We also found that the haiku produced could be partitioned after the fact into aesthetic groups based on similarity to other writers, music, and distance from "normal" texts. In this work, the notion of "sense" has proven to be the most intricate and important.

A remaining challenge is syntactic transformations. For example, everyone knows Hemingway tends to use short sentences and lots of "and"s—InkWell currently cannot transform sentence structure to match Hemingway. It can do only trivial transformations after optimization.

Creativity in writing takes a couple of ingredients: being prepared to notice, wide ranging and non-judgmental production of drafts, and a selection and revision process guided by aesthetics. In a sense it's like serendipity. With InkWell we've tried to explore writerly creativity in a creative way—by letting the program emerge from a haze of half-known ideas [2].

ACKNOWLEDGMENTS
Some of this work was supported by DARPA (W911NF-12-C-0028).

REFERENCES
1. Wallace Stevens, *Of Mere Being*, "The Palm at the End of the Mind: Selected Poems and a Play," Vintage, 1990.

2. Robert Boswell, "The Half-Known World: On Writing Fiction," Graywolf Press. St. Paul, MN, 2008.

3. Stephen King, "On Writing," Pocket, New York, 2002.

4. Frost, Robert, "New Hampshire," Henry Holt, New York, 1923.

5. Ernest Hemingway, *The Complete Short Stories of Ernest Hemingway*, Scribner, 1998.

6. Walt Whitman, *Leaves of Grass*, 1855.

7. Adam Smith, *An Inquiry into the Nature and Causes of the Wealth of Nations*, 1776.

8. O. P. John & S. Srivastava, "The Big-Five trait taxonomy: History, measurement, and theoretical perspectives," in L. A. Pervin & O. P. John (Eds.), *Handbook of personality: Theory and research* (Vol. 2, pp. 102–138), New York, Guilford Press, 1999.

9. S. H. Schwartz, "Basic human values: theory, measurement, and applications," Revue Française de Sociologie, 47(4), 2006.

10. Jilin Chen, Gary Hsieh, Jalal Mahmud, Jeffrey Nichols, "Understanding Individual's Personal Values from Social Media Word Use," in Proceedings of CSCW 2014, Baltimore, MD, February 15-19, 2014.

11. George A. Miller, "WordNet: A Lexical Database for English," Communications of the ACM Vol. 38, No. 11: 39–41, 1995.

12. Christiane Fellbaum (ed.) *WordNet: An Electronic Lexical Database*, Cambridge, MA: MIT Press, 1998.

13. `http://www.speech.cs.cmu.edu/cgi-bin/cmudict`.

14. `http://storage.googleapis.com/books/ngrams/books/datasetsv2.html`.

15. Corpus of Contemporary American English, `http://www.ngrams.info/download_coca.asp`.

16. Tal Yarkoni, "Personality in 100,000 Words: A large-scale analysis of personality anfd word use among bloggers," Journal of Research in Personality, 44(3): 363–373, 2010.

17. Yla R. Tausczik and James W. Pennebaker, "The Psychological Meaning of Words: LIWC and Computerzed Text Analysis Methods," Journal of Language and Social Psychology, 29(1) 24–54, 2010.

18. `http://en.wikipedia.org/wiki/New_Criticism`.

19. I. A. Richards, *Practical Criticism: A Study Of Literary Judgment*, Mariner Books, 1956.

20. C. K. Ogden and I. A. Richards, *The Meaning Of Meaning*, Mariner Books (reissue edition), 1989.

21. Herman Mellville, *Moby-Dick: or, the Whale*. 1851.

22. `http://en.wikipedia.org/wiki/Dean_Young_(poet)`.

23. Matsuo Bashō and Robert Hass (translator), "Matsuo Bashō: Poems," `http://poemhunter.com`, 2004.

24. Wiliam Faulkner, *Collected Stories*, Random House, 1950.

25. Jeffrey Johnson, "Haiku Poetics in Twentieth-Century Avant-Garde Poetry," Lexington Books/Rowman & Littlefield Publishing Group, 2011.

26. John Halloran, Eva Hornecker, Geraldine Fitzpatrick, Mark Weal, David Millard, Danius Michaelides, Don Cruickshank, David De Roure, "The Literacy Fieldtrip: Using UbiComp to Support Children's Creative Writing," Proceedings of the 2006 Conference on Interaction Design and Children, DC '06, pp 17–24, 2006.

27. Yu-Chia Chang, Jason S. Chang, Hao-Jan Chen, Hsien-Chin Liou, "An automatic collocation writing assistant for Taiwanese EFL learners: A case of corpus-based NLP technology," Computer Assisted Language Learning, Vol 21 No 3, pp 283–299, 2008.

28. R. Pérez y Pérez and M. Sharples, "MEXICA: a computer model of a cognitive account of creative writing," Journal of Experimental & Theoretical Artificial Intelligence, Vol 13, pp 119–139, 2001.

29. Michael Mateas and Phoebe Sengers, "Narrative Intelligence," Working notes of the Narrative Intelligence Symposium, AAAI Fall Symposium Series, 1999.

30. Ben Shneiderman, "Creating creativity: user interfaces for supporting innovation," ACM Transactions on Computer-Human Interaction, Vol 7, pp 114–138, 2000.

31. Xiaojin Zhu, Zhiting Xu, Tushar Khot, "How Creative is Your Writing? A Linguistic Creativity Measure from Computer Science and Cognitive Psychology Perspectives," Proceedings of the Workshop on Computational Approaches to Linguistic Creativity, CALC '09, pp 87–93, 2009.

32. François Mairesse and Marilyn A. Walker, "Controlling User Perceptions of Linguistic Style: Trainable Generation of Personality Traits," Computational Linguistics, Volume 37 Issue 3, pp 455–488, 2011.

APPENDIX

Stopping by Woods on a Snowy Evening by Robert Frost

Whose woods these are I think I know.
His house is in the village though;
He will not see me stopping here
To watch his woods fill up with snow.

My little horse must think it queer
To stop without a farmhouse near
Between the woods and frozen lake
The darkest evening of the year.

He gives his harness bells a shake
To ask if there is some mistake.
The only other sound's the sweep
Of easy wind and downy flake.

The woods are lovely, dark and deep.
But I have promises to keep,
And miles to go before I sleep,
And miles to go before I sleep.

InspirationWall: Supporting Idea Generation Through Automatic Information Exploration

Salvatore Andolina[1], **Khalil Klouche**[1,3], **Diogo Cabral**[1], **Tuukka Ruotsalo**[2], and **Giulio Jacucci**[1,2]

[1]Helsinki Institute for Information Technology HIIT,
Department of Computer Science, University of Helsinki, Finland
[2]Helsinki Institute for Information Technology HIIT, Aalto University, Finland
[3]Helsinki Media Lab, Aalto University, Finland

ABSTRACT

Collaborative idea generation leverages social interactions and knowledge sharing to spark diverse associations and produce creative ideas. Information exploration systems expand the current context by suggesting novel but related concepts. In this paper we introduce InspirationWall, an unobtrusive display that leverages speech recognition and information exploration to enhance an ongoing idea generation session with automatically retrieved concepts that relate to the conversation. We evaluated the system in six idea generation sessions of 20 minutes with small groups of two people. Preliminary results suggest that InspirationWall contrasts the decay of idea productivity over time and can thus represent an effective way to enhance idea generation activities.

Author Keywords

Idea generation; Information Exploration; Automatic Speech Recognition.

ACM Classification Keywords

H.5.m. Information Interfaces and Presentation (e.g. HCI): Miscellaneous

INTRODUCTION

Collecting and navigating through information is an important phase in creative processes [13], which fosters associative and inspirational learning [2]. Previous work that sought to support for example brainstorming referred to the semantic network structure of human memory, where concepts feature as nodes with associative links [15]. In brainstorming, one cognitive operation to generate ideas is to retrieve concepts from associative memory. Expanding the current context of topics has been investigated through topic suggestion algorithms designed to generate candidate topics that are novel but related to the current context [9]. As brainstorming is often a collaborative practice, recent creativity systems support groups. Groups generally perform better than individuals

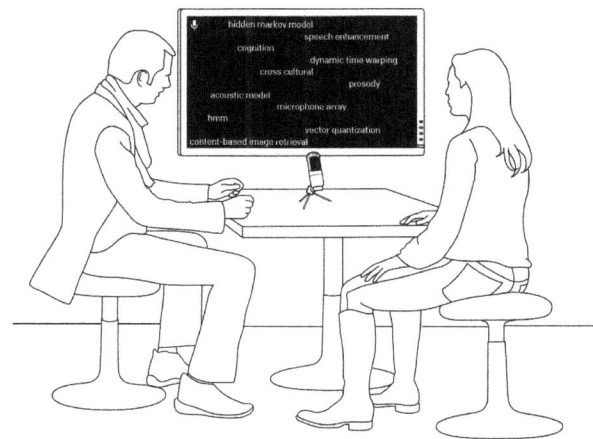

Figure 1. InspirationWall is an unobtrusive display supporting idea generation by leveraging speech recognition and automatic information exploration. It monitors users' discussion and automatically suggests keywords to support their idea generation.

in a variety of tasks [6]. Group brainstorming can be effective in generating creative ideas as suggested by cognitive approaches [3], and technology may help minimizing the effect of negative social processes [5]. A beneficial feature in group brainstorming is the ability to detect the context and content of the brainstorming through utterances of participants. Idea-Expander [14] is a tool to support group brainstorming by intelligently selecting pictorial stimuli based on the group's conversation on a chat. The pictures generally enhanced performance as measured by both originality and diversity of ideas [15]. Less investigated are face to face systems in group sessions that suggest keywords instead of pictures. Systems suggesting keywords and topics have recently been applied successfully to improve exploratory search processes [1, 10]. Such systems predict the current intent model of the user in the exploration and suggest possible explorations. These approaches have also been found useful in avoiding keyword input by selecting and manipulating suggested keywords by touch [8]. The present work investigate further alternative input modalities such as speech to text that permit the system to run in the background without interrupting the creative process but providing a continuous resource.

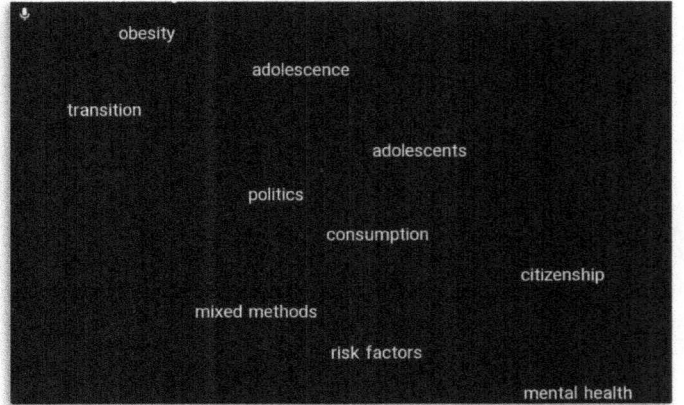

Figure 2. Left: Two participants in a brainstorming session. Right: A screen capture from the InspirationWall interface.

SYSTEM DESIGN

InspirationWall is a non-intrusive source of diverse ideas (Figure 1). It was designed as a low-key visual aid, as to not interfere with the user's idea generation process. InspirationWall continuously monitors the discussions through a conference microphone and the input to the system is recorded from users natural interaction via speech recognition. Speech recognition is performed in real-time using Googles implementation of the HTML5 Web Speech API [16].

Recognized expressions are processed by an entity-based keyword suggestion system that returns related keywords by discovering associated and novel information related to the input [11]. Returned keywords are then displayed as slowly crossing the screen from top to bottom as to allow a progressive refreshing of displayed keywords. The graphical interface of Inspiration Wall is minimal: it runs fullscreen with a black background. Keywords are displayed in white. Every two seconds providing the keyword buffer is not empty a new keyword appears at the top of the screen at a random horizontal position and falls slowly towards the bottom of the screen.

Keyword Suggestion System

As the set of potential keywords matching any part of users' discussion is likely to be much higher than what can be presented for the user, and the discussion can contain misleading cues due to the natural dialogues that the system listens, we use a centrality-based ranking of the keywords in a large knowledge-graph.

Intuitively, this approach allows the system to suggest central keywords that are related to the user input via the knowledge-graph rather than only suggesting keywords directly matching to the input. This can help discovering keywords that are highly relevant for the input, but at the same time central to the overall discussion [12]. The knowledge-graph G is undirected and labeled and consists of a disjoint union set of keywords and documents (called nodes $n \in G$) and the set of edges between the documents and the keywords. Each keyword in the graph is connected to a document it describes.

For example, an article about "relevance feedback for information retrieval" could be described with a set of keywords, such as "information retrieval", "relevance feedback", "implicit feedback", "web search", and so on. In addition, we index the text of the articles that is used to retrieve an initially relevant set of documents from which the knowledge-graph is constructed.

The user's query consists of one or more words detected via the speech recognition system. A set of keywords detected are called preference keywords $q \in G$ in the graph, where $|q| = 1$ and q_j denotes the preference for keyword j. In our case no weighting is conducted for the keywords so the preference is uniformly distributed over for the given keywords in q.

We use the personalized PageRank method [7] to compute the ranking of the nodes given the q. It can be then formalized as follows. Let an individual node be denoted as n, and by $I(n)$ and $O(n)$ denote the set of in-neighbors and out-neighbors of n in G respectively. Let A be the matrix corresponding to the graph G, where

$$A_{ij} = \frac{1}{|O_{ij} \cup I_{ij}|}$$

if the node i links to the node j or vice versa, and $A_{ij} = 0$ otherwise. For a given q, the personalized PageRank equation can be written as

$$v = (1 - c)Av + cq,$$

where $c = 0.15$ is the teleportation rate. The solution v is a steady-state distribution of random surfers, where a surfer teleports at each step to a node n with probability $c \cdot q(n)$, or moves to a random neighbor otherwise. We compute the steady distribution by using the power iteration method with 100 iterations.

The weights of the v are directly used in ranking the keywords. As the size of our knowledge-graph is hundreds of millions of nodes, the computation is not possible on-line for the complete graph. To make the PageRank computation feasible with an acceptable latency, we approximate the set of nodes to be included in the initial graph by using a language

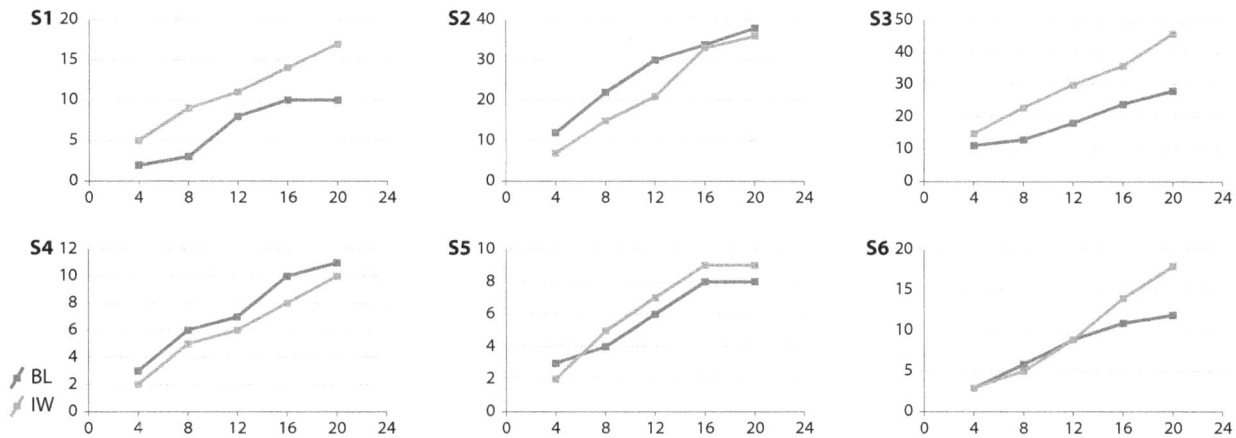

Figure 3. Accumulation of ideas per condition (BL = Baseline; IW = InspirationWall) in the different sessions S1,...,S6. On the Y-axis is the cumulative number of ideas, and on the X-axis is the time from the beginning of the session (minutes).

model approach of information retrieval [17] and select 3000 documents and the corresponding entities to be cumulatively added in the knowledge-graph at each iteration.

EVALUATION

We designed an experiment to evaluate the effect of the system on the idea generation process. The goal of the experiment was (1.) to understand if and how InspirationWall helped small groups generating more ideas, and (2.) to assess the overall effectiveness of the system as a creativity support tool using standard metrics.

Participants

The evaluation was conducted in groups of two persons (Figure 2). We recruited twelve participants (six pairs) with experience in idea generation activities from the computer science departments of two universities. Three of the participants were females and the mean age was $M = 28.33$, $SD = 3.98$. To simulate more natural discussions and brainstorming activity, we ensured that participants in the same pair knew each other. Participants were non-native English speakers from different countries and cultures (Iran, Canada, Spain, Nepal, Italy, Turkey, Sri Lanka, Rwanda, Kenya) with a similar level of proficiency in oral English. Their levels of education were: 25% PhD, 67% Master, 8% Bachelor. Participants received two movie tickets as a compensation for their participation.

Tasks

We used a within-group design, where groups were asked to perform two tasks: one with the support of InspirationWall and one without external support. We counterbalanced by changing the order in which the two tasks were performed and the order in which the groups were subjected to each condition.

The task was created to support an idea generation scenario and formulated as follows: *Imagine you have to come up with novel student projects on topic X. Please generate as many ideas as possible for new technologies, interaction techniques, methodologies, application scenarios, and so on, that* *might be used as more specific topics of the projects on topic X.* Two topics were used in the evaluation sessions: (1.) Robotics, and (2.) Wearable computing.

Metrics and Results

Quantity of Ideas

Since we were interested to check whether our application influenced the number of ideas generated, we have looked to the cumulative number of ideas considering time and session (Table 1). In total, the six groups have produced 107 ($M = 30.57$, $SD = 12.24$) ideas without external support and 136 ($M = 38.86$, $SD = 14.99$) using InspirationWall. In Figure 3, it is shown the accumulation of ideas per condition in the sessions, considering intervals of 4 minutes. In addition, video recordings obtained from the camera placed between the participants and the InspirationWall display allowed us to count the occurrences of participants looking at the screen (results shown in Figure 4). It is interesting to observe that the three groups (S1, S3 and S6) that have looked at the display the most, improved their performance with respect to the baseline condition, presenting a higher number of generated ideas and a more constant productivity.

Creativity Support Index

To measure the performance of our system in terms of creativity support, we involved participants in the assessment of the Creativity Support Index (CSI) [4].

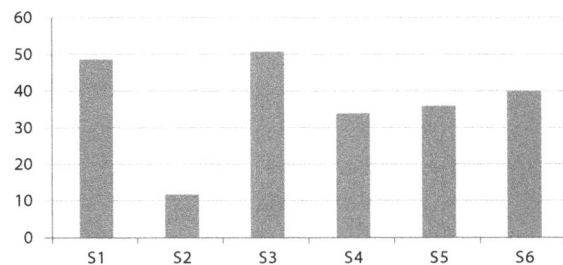

Figure 4. Number of occurrences of participants looking at the screen in sessions S1,...,S6.

Table 1. Accumulation of ideas per condition (BL = Baseline; IW = InspirationWall) at time $T = 4, 8, 12, 16, 20$ in sessions S1,...,S6. For each point in time, p-values from paired t-tests are also shown.

T		S1	S2	S3	S4	S5	S6	M (SD)	p
4	BL	2	12	11	3	3	3	5.67 (4.55)	1
	IW	5	7	15	2	2	3	5.67 (4.97)	
8	BL	3	22	13	6	4	6	9.00 (7.27)	0.61
	IW	9	15	23	5	5	5	10.33 (7.34)	
12	BL	8	30	18	7	6	9	13.00 (9.38)	0.73
	IW	11	21	30	6	7	9	14.00 (9.51)	
16	BL	10	34	24	10	8	11	16.17 (10.48)	0.23
	IW	14	33	36	8	9	14	19.00 (12.30)	
20	BL	10	38	28	11	8	12	17.83 (12.24)	0.17
	IW	17	36	46	10	9	18	22.67 (15.00)	

This index is computed from two sets of six questions and each question related with a factor. The six factors that compose the CSI are: *Collaboration, Enjoyment, Exploration, Expression, Expressiveness, Immersion* and *Results Worth Effort*. Each pair of questions are weighted based in pair wise comparisons of the factors made by each participant. The result of the CSI was $M = 53.36$, $SD = 13.35$. The most important factors for the participants were *Expressiveness* ($M = 3.58$, $SD = 1.24$) and *Exploration* ($M = 3.83$, $SD = 0.94$).

DISCUSSION AND CONCLUSIONS

Creative ideas are often triggered by unexpected associations. InspirationWall offers a quiet additional source of information to fuel the activity of collaborative idea generation. This paper presents the implementation and a preliminary evaluation of such a system. Participants were asked to generate ideas but not explicitly to use or interact with the system which was simply provided as is. Our study shows that participants that used InspirationWall more – as indicated by the count and duration of gazing occurrences obtained through video analysis – tended to generate more ideas in total and over time. Those results suggest that InspirationWall contrasts the decay of idea productivity over time typical of traditional idea generation sessions. Although the CSI does not show a high value, it is still above the median value of the scale, with the most important factors for the participants being *Expressiveness* and *Exploration*. Such results confirms the effectiveness of automatic information exploration and keyword suggestion on idea generation, opening a variety of directions for future work, including for example application to other datasets, and allowing richer interactions with the system through touch. The novel approach on idea generation support described in this paper, the simple design of our prototype and the positive results of this preliminary study are the contributions of our work to the future of digital tools for creativity support.

ACKNOWLEDGEMENTS

The data used in the experiments is derived from the Web of Science prepared by THOMSON REUTERS, Inc., and the digital libraries of ACM, IEEE, and Springer. This work has been partially supported by TEKES (Re:Know) and the Academy of Finland (278090).

REFERENCES

1. Andolina, S., et al. Intentstreams: smart parallel search streams for branching exploratory search. In *Proc. IUI*, ACM (2015).

2. Binder, T., Ehn, P., De Michelis, G., Jacucci, G., Linde, G., and Wagner, I. *Design things*. MIT Press Cambridge, MA, 2011.

3. Brown, V. R., and Paulus, P. B. Making Group Brainstorming More Effective: Recommendations From an Associative Memory Perspective. *Current Directions in Psychological Science 11*, 6 (Dec. 2002), 208–212.

4. Cherry, E., and Latulipe, C. Quantifying the creativity support of digital tools through the creativity support index. *ACM Trans. Comput.-Hum. Interact. 21*, 4 (June 2014), 21:1–21:25.

5. Diehl, M., and Stroebe, W. Productivity loss in brainstorming groups: Toward the solution of a riddle. *J Pers Soc Psycho* (1987), 497–509.

6. Hill, G. W. Group versus individual performance: Are n+1 heads better than one? *Psychological bulletin 91*, 3 (1982), 517–539.

7. Jeh, G., and Widom, J. Scaling personalized web search. In *Proc. WWW*, WWW '03, ACM (2003), 271–279.

8. Klouche, K., Ruotsalo, T., Cabral, D., Andolina, S., Bellucci, A., and Jacucci, G. Designing for exploratory search on touch devices. In *Proc. CHI*, ACM (2015).

9. Maguitman, A., Leake, D., and Reichherzer, T. Suggesting novel but related topics: towards context-based support for knowledge model extension. In *Proc. IUI*, ACM (2005), 207–214.

10. Ruotsalo, T., et al. Directing exploratory search with interactive intent modeling. In *Proc. CIKM*, ACM (2013), 1759–1764.

11. Ruotsalo, T., et al. Interactive intent modeling: Information discovery beyond search. *Commun. ACM 58*, 1 (Jan. 2015), 86–92.

12. Ruotsalo, T., and Hyvönen, E. Exploiting semantic annotations for domain-specific entity search. In *Proc. ECIR*, Springer (2015).

13. Shneiderman, B. Creativity support tools. *Commun. ACM 45*, 10 (Oct. 2002), 116–120.

14. Wang, H.-C., Cosley, D., and Fussell, S. R. Idea expander: Supporting group brainstorming with conversationally triggered visual thinking stimuli. In *Proc. CSCW*, ACM (2010), 103–106.

15. Wang, H.-C., Fussell, S. R., and Cosley, D. From diversity to creativity: Stimulating group brainstorming with cultural differences and conversationally-retrieved pictures. In *Proc. CSCW*, ACM (2011), 265–274.

16. Web Speech API. `https://dvcs.w3.org/hg/speech-api/raw-file/tip/speechapi.html`.

17. Zhai, C., and Lafferty, J. A study of smoothing methods for language models applied to ad hoc information retrieval. In *Proc. SIGIR*, ACM (2001), 334–342.

A Playful Affinity Space for Creative Research

Kam Star[1], Fotis Paraskevopoulos[2], Maria Taramigkou[2], Dimitris Apostolou[2], Marise Schot[3], Gregoris Mentzas[2]

[1]PlayGen
42 - 46 Princelet Street
London, E1 5LP, UK
kam@playgen.com

[2]National Technical University of Athens
Iroon Polytechniou 9
15780 Zografou, Greece
{fotisp, martar, dapost, gmentzas}@mail.ntua.gr

[3]Waag Society
Nieuwmarkt 4, 1012 CR
Amsterdam, Netherlands
marise@waag.org

ABSTRACT

We present a system designed with the aim to facilitate the social creativity processes underlying creative research. It provides asynchronous and synchronous facilities for multi-user interaction while leveraging creativity with computational tools for inspirational search, inspirational clue generation and problem solving advice. Initial evaluation with a small group of users indicated that the software is in-line with the creative research approach where users work together with concept developers taking on multiple roles throughout the design process.

Author Keywords

Social creativity, creative research

ACM Classification Keywords

H.5.m. Information interfaces and presentation

INTRODUCTION

Creative activity grows out of the relationship between an individual and the world of his or her work, as well as out of the ties between an individual and other human beings [3]. Social creativity arises from activities that take place in a social context in which interaction with other people and the artifacts that embody collective knowledge are essential contributors [4]. In this paper, we focus on creative research, a disruptive, practice-based, iterative and intuitive social creativity approach aiming at delivering new ideas and concepts at work. Professionals and organizations from the creative industries, such as advertising, industrial and concept design, practice creative research. We study a real use case of creative research and we present our work in progress towards providing novel computational support for enhancing the creative processes of professional concept designers embarked on creative research.

LEVERAGING CREATIVE RESEARCH

Creative research is characterized as 'practice-based' referring to the practice of making and creating [2]. Creative research is open in terms of its results while it involves a variety of stakeholders in co-creative acts; its results are practical and tangible. 'Co-creation' implies that creativity is shared by a team of people who create something collectively.

We argue that the nature of creative research and its associated practices have three drivers: originality & inspiration; (ii) expression and exploration; and evaluation and social appreciation, which we explain herein. Originality & inspiration refers to the capability of individuals to generate unique ideas or applying existing ideas to new contexts. The plethora of readily available digital content provides ample opportunities for leveraging original thinking by inspiring individuals. By discovering and injecting inspirational information in creative processes, we can boost the generation of ideas and the application of existing ideas in different contexts, effectively supporting originality [10].

Original ideas or new applications of existing ideas are of little use if they are only internalized; they need to be expressed and externalized so that other individuals with different knowledge and perspectives (so called sagacity) can understand, reflect upon, and improve them [1, 7]. To support expression and exploration, situations need to be sufficiently open-ended and complex that individuals will encounter new, unpredictable conditions, and will eventually experience breakdowns. The cognitive ability improves if individuals are offered opportunities for reflection. Participation in shared creative processes and social processes of knowledge construction can enable something new to be created and the initial knowledge to be either substantially enriched or significantly transformed during the process [4]. Collaborative spaces appear to be ideal environments to develop the divergent thinking and social interaction that are catalysts of social creativity. Such spaces should provide the affinity space in which creative researchers can interact and collaboratively prototype their ideas.

Social evaluation and appreciation refers to testing and evaluating prototyped ideas while putting users and other stakeholders at centre stage and taking advantage of the effects of social rewards, credits, and acknowledgements by others that motivate further creative activities. Game mechanics have attracted significant attention as a means to engage users in innovation-related activities. By employing game mechanics we can leverage social evaluation and appreciation of generated ideas and creative behavior at large [9].

A PLAYFUL AFFINITY SPACE FOR CONCEPT DEVELOPERS

In the context of the COLLAGE research project (http://projectcollage.eu/), we worked with a team of concept developers from the Waag Society institute for art, science and technology (www.waag.org) to elicit requirements and develop computational support for enhancing their creative research processes. Waag Society conducts creative research in close cooperation with stakeholders coming from education, healthcare, culture and other sectors. Waag concept developers generate value by building demonstrators and prototypes and evaluating them in real-life situations. In this section we outline their requirements and present the software tools developed to address them.

Concept developers envisaged an affinity place fostering an open attitude for reconsidering existing concepts and approaches in a playful way so as to promote engagement. They should be able to collaboratively be creative with other members of their team. Moreover, concept developers

should be able to search for information and receive inspiration for their projects as well as to find existing concepts and ideas, which are relevant for their projects. They asked for support in discovering relevant, trending topics from the social web by monitoring users' actions e.g., on social networks, profiling them and using this information to recommend inspirational information that may assist users in generating new ideas. Finally, concept developers enjoy reading the comments posted by others about their ideas, so they asked for feedback mechanisms to encourage them to continue submitting comments and suggestions and leverage a sense of ownership for their work.

To assist concept developers generate their own ideas, we developed HatParty. HatParty (Figure 1), a multiplayer game facilitating brainstorming sessions where project members come together to generate ideas in a fun, cooperative environment, utilizes game mechanics such as timed sessions, goals, reputation points, rating and racing to help small groups generate large number of ideas and rank them in record time. The game is based around the theme of 'a day at the races'. The first two phases of HatParty are played out as a horse race. In the Idea Generation phase users get to submit as many ideas as possible. Once the ideas have been pooled together from the first phase, the second phase, Idea Assessment, begins. Here users rate ideas based on how well they believe the idea could work in correspondence to the challenge set.

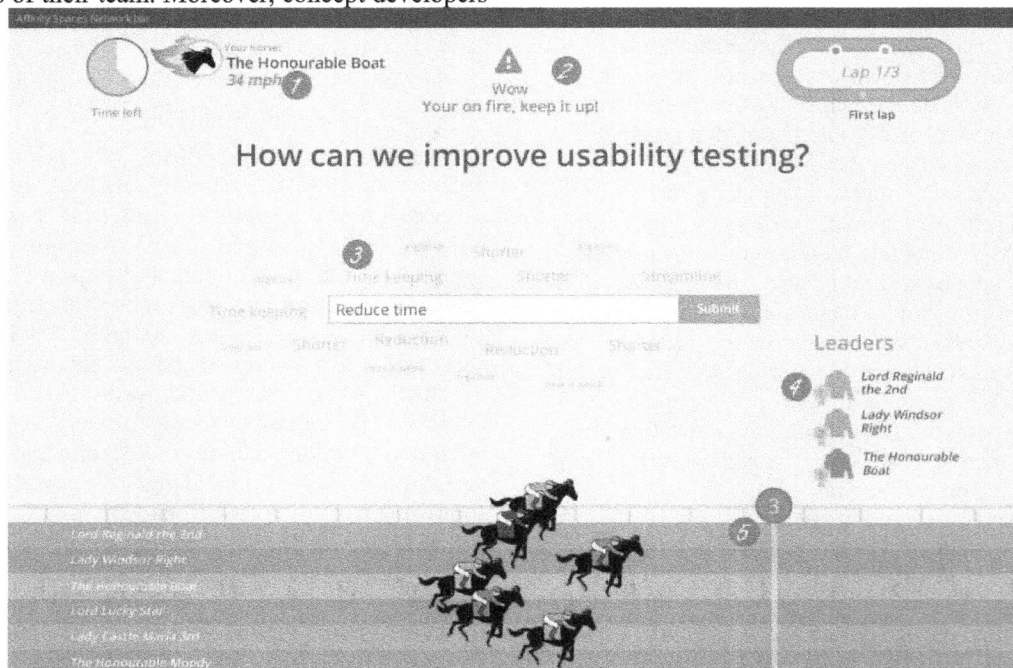

Figure 1. Hat Party (Item 1 speed indicator: while in the race there are varying levels of speed depending on how many ideas are being submitted; item 2 feedback: messages which give users feedback on their progress and what is going on in the race; item 3 inspirational clues: terms which relate to what the user types in the text box using CRUISE; item 4 leaderboard: shows the three top ranking users currently in the race; item 5 race track: helps the user keep track of their current position in the race.)

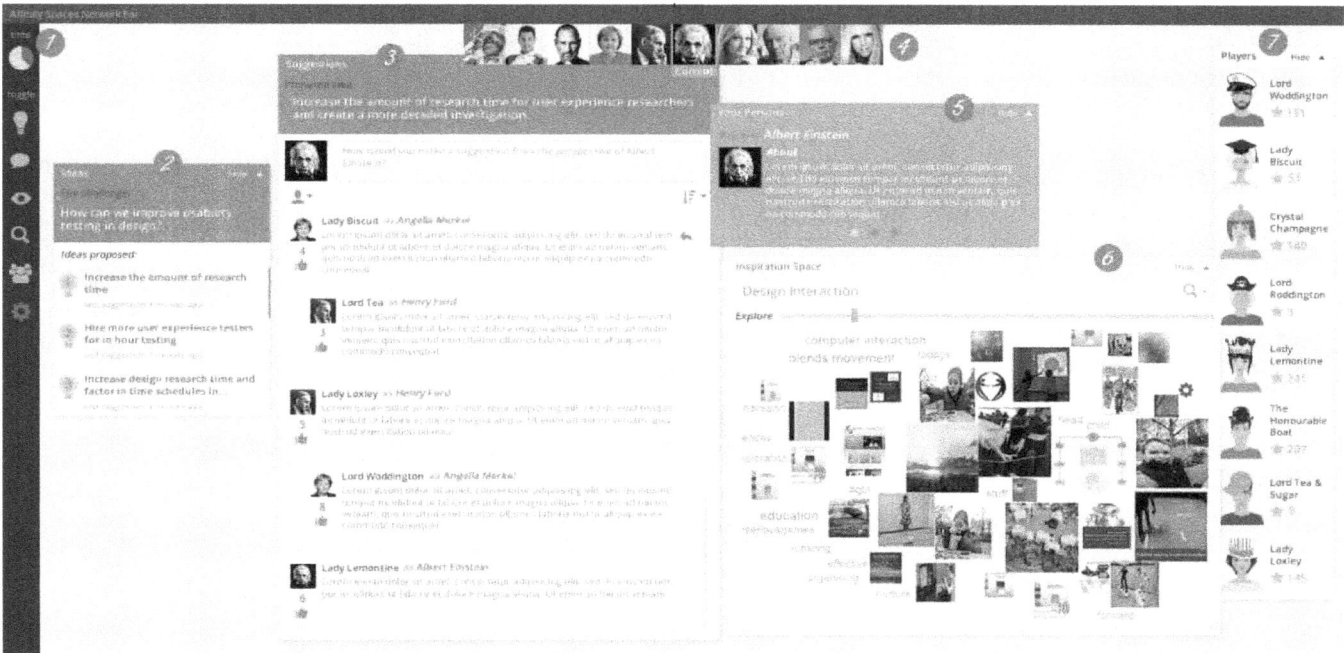

Figure 2. Idea Focus (Item 1 navigation bar: displays the current time left for the session as well as buttons to hide/show panels; item 2 ideas panel; item 3 suggestion panel: allowing users to express their opinions about the ideas in focus using the Hall of Fame technique which prompts users to respond and debate from the perspective of known personas; items 4&5 persona panels: displaying which persona the user has currently become; item 6 inspirational search: allowing the user to utilize the inspirational search service (CRUISE) by entering in a term they wish to explore and gain ideas around; item 7 player panel)

After the idea assessment phase is complete, the game progresses onto a new interface: 'Idea Focus' (Figure 2). This phase takes place as an asynchronous game with a different interface to the previous two phases. The Idea Focus can be played over the course of a few days or a week if the facilitator chooses to do so. This is to allow users enough time to explore ideas and engage in deep creative debate with their fellow colleagues.

To assist concept developers discover inspirational clues, we developed Creative User Centric Inspirational Search (CRUISE), an interactive exploratory search tool that combines diversification of content and sources with a user interface design that visualizes clues from social networks and the Web, and lets users interactively explore the Web as well as specific linked information sources such as the intranet of Waag [8, 6]. CRUISE can be used as a stand-alone tool when e.g., users want to find information to debate ideas, but it is also automatically triggered when participants, during the Ideation Phase, start typing into HatParty's idea suggestion box using the entered terms as queries for retrieving inspirational resources.

IN USE

In this section, we present our preliminary evaluation results. Specifically, seven concept developers used the software together with end users during a two-day workshop about 'Open Source Materials' with the aim 'to design and make open materials for the Fablab facility'.

Assessment statement	Day 1	Day 2
The objectives of the activity were stated clearly.	.7	.825
The user interface and navigation are intuitive.	.8	.825
The activity is relevant to my job or study.	.75	.675
I would recommend this activity to friends or colleagues.	.7	.8
My interest in the subject matter grew as I did the task.	.6	.675
As I did the activity, there were times when my curiosity was aroused.	.6	.675
Doing the activity made me curious about the subject at times.	.5	.625
There were times when my imagination was aroused.	.6	.625
As I carried out the activity I was absorbed in it.	.55	.675
I had fun interacting with my group members as we did the activity.	.65	.825
I enjoyed interacting with my group members as we did the activity.	.6	.675
Time appeared to go by quickly when I was interacting with the activity.	.4	.8
As I did the activity, I felt in control.	.45	.625
I felt that doing the activity made me more creative.	.65	.575
Doing the activity improved my insight into the subject matter.	.7	.625
Doing the activity increased my knowledge about the subject.	.7	.575

Table 1: Mean participants' responses after a two-day creative research workshop (values have been normalized such that 0 is a strong disagreement with the statement and 1 is a strong agreement with the statement)

The programme included defining 'open source material' and brainstorming what can be done with them, experimenting and making materials and developing two integrated concepts. We asked them to use HatParty as the main idea generation platform, supplemented with CRUISE to facilitate inspirational search. The software was introduced to the participants without any prior training.

The software was used with great success resulting in the generation of 240 ideas during the first session that lasted for fifteen minutes. This was deemed to be one of the highest number of ideas generated as a result of a brainstorm by the group using any related tool used in similar assignments in the past. The successful results of the first session facilitated the quick adoption of the software by the group which used it to generate ideas throughout the two-day trails. A qualitative questionnaire enquired about overall impressions, whether the software could enhance the design process and promote sharing and insight into additional features (Table 1).

Participants' feedback and perception of the software usability and usefulness improved between the initial use on Day 1 and Day 2, which is a positive indication that the software is delivering value to the participants. Positively, once users were comfortable with the software, they found it more enjoyable. Critically, the net promoter score (4th statement in Table 1) is 0.8 considered to represent a high degree of satisfaction [5] with the software as the indicator of high probability that the solution would be promoted autonomously by its users to others.

CONCLUSIONS

To address the needs of creative research, we developed software with asynchronous and synchronous capabilities for multi-user interaction while leveraging creativity with computational tools for inspirational search and inspirational clue generation. Initial evaluation with a small group of users indicated that the software is in-line with the creative research approach where concept developers work together with end users taking on multiple roles throughout the design process. Further experimentation is planned to assess the impact of the software on the creative process and outcomes. Moreover, further studies are needed to assess the fit of the software with more subtle issues underlying creative research such as leveraging of designers' empathy for the users' life stories and needs, subjectivity of interpretation of information, personal intuition, human interaction and trust. In doing so, we hope to improve our own understanding of creative research and be inspired to provide improved computational support and enhanced creativity support features.

ACKNOWLEDGEMENT

This work has been partly funded by the European Commission through IST Project COLLAGE, Grant agreement no: 318536.

REFERENCES

1. André, P., Teevan, J., & Dumais, S. T. Discovery is never by chance: Designing for (un)serendipity. In *Proc. Creativity and cognition 2009,* ACM Press (2009), 305-314.

2. Dick van Dijk, D., Kresin, F., Reitenbach, M., Rennen, E., Wildevuur, S. *Users as Designers: A hands-on approach to Creative Research*, Cip-Gegevens Koninklijke Bibliotheek den Haag, 2001, ISBN 978-90-806452-0-2.

3. Fischer, G. Individual and/versus Social Creativity (Panel). In *Proc. Creativity & Cognition 1999*, ACM Press (1999), 36-39.

4. Fisher, G. Social Creativity: Turning Barriers into Opportunities for Collaborative Design. In *Proc. Participatory Design Conference 2004*, ACM Press (2004), 152-161.

5. Keiningham, Timothy L., Cooil, B., Andreassen, W. T. & Aksoy, L. A longitudinal examination of net promoter and firm revenue growth. *Journal of Marketing 71,* 3 (2007): 39-51.

6. Paraskevopoulos, F., Taramigkou, M., Bothos, E., Apostolou, D., Mentzas, G. Creative user centric inspirational search. In *Proc. Intelligent User Interfaces 2014,* ACM Press (2014), 25-28.

7. Spink, A., Greisdorf, H., & Bateman, J. From highly relevant to not relevant: examining different regions of relevance. *Information Processing & Management, 34,* 5 (1998), 599-621.

8. Taramigkou, M., Paraskevopoulos,F., Bothos, E., Apostolou, D., Mentzas, G. Leveraging User Inspiration with Microblogging-Driven Exploratory Search. In *Proc. CAiSE Workshops 2014*, Springer LNBI 178, 238-249.

9. Wierzbicki, A. P., & Nakamori, Y. *Creative environments: issues of creativity support for the knowledge civilization age.* Springer Publishing Company, 2007.

10. Woodman, R.W., Sawyer, J.E., Griffin, R.W.: Toward a theory of organizational creativity. *Academy of Management Review*, (1993), 293–321.

The Production of Unprecedented Events

Stephen A.R. Scrivener
University College London, UK
s.scrivener@chelsea.arts.ac.uk

Abstract

What is primary in the production of new knowledge: new concepts or unprecedented events (surprising observations)? Often, when we talk about research, the focus would appear to be on the production and testing of concepts. Induction relies on observations, but its purpose is seen as being to arrive at new concepts, deductions and propositions, which when confirmed in empirical test provide grounds for belief.

Reflective thought about research has tended to focus on the nature of confirmation rather than discovery, the latter being generally accepted as inaccessible to rational analysis. However, confirmation relies on discovery and whilst some new idea might come about through the rational analysis of existing concepts, discovery tends to arise in inductions stimulated by the event of surprising or unprecedented observations.

Given the suggested significance of unprecedented events in the production of new knowledge and understanding, can we construct environments in which they can be made to happen, rather than merely waiting until we happen upon them? I will refer, in my talk, to current thinking in which experimental systems in science are conceived in this way, but will focus attention on how creative material practices, such as art and design, can also be understood as generators of unprecedented events.

ACM Classification: A.m. Miscellaneous

Author Keywords: Unprecedented events; creative material practices; knowledge production

Short Bio

Stephen Scrivener studied Fine Art at undergraduate and master levels, the latter at the Slade School of Fine Art, University College London, where he began to use the computer as a means of art production. Subsequent to the Slade, he completed a Ph.D in computer science and, thereafter, worked as a lecturer and researcher in various university computer science departments. Up to 1992 research focussed on the design and development of interactive systems for artists and designers and on how such systems are used. During this period he undertook many funded design-focussed research projects, almost all of which involved academic, commercial and industrial collaboration. He moved back into an art and design department in 1992, and his research has since focussed on the theory and practice of what is often called practice-based research, which he combines with art practice.

C&C 2015, June 22–25, 2015, Glasgow, United Kingdom.
ACM 978-1-4503-3598-0/15/06.
http://dx.doi.org/10.1145/2757226.2757258

Captured Moments: Defining a Communicative Framework for Social Photography

Robin Fogel Avni
Cornish College of the Arts
Seattle, USA
ravni@cornish.edu

ABSTRACT

As photography takes center stage on today's social media platforms, given the ease of modern capture devices (i.e. mobile phones, point and shoot cameras, tablets, etc.), the ability to produce and publish images occurs at a much quicker rate than the humble Kodak Brownie camera afforded the masses when introduced in January 1900. This enhanced ease has generated an opportunity for the everyday photographer to creatively communicate through the distribution of their images.

This paper applies research results from a qualitative visual ethnographic study focusing on the non-verbal posts of a select group of Facebook users. The Dell Hymes' SPEAKING framework was used to structure the visual data; analysis leveraged Gerry Philipsen's Speech Codes Theory and James W. Carey's Ritual Communication Theory contributes to the creation of a communicative framework for the non-verbal social media postings.

In conclusion, what emerges through the data is a visual speech code that tacitly leverages traditional photographic genres while at the same time supporting a system of meanings and symbols that enhance the instantaneous posts and communications of the day-to-day ebb and flow of life.

Author Keywords

Photography; social media; visual communication; social media communication; camera phone; mobile phone; visual ethnography; creativity; communication theory; Facebook.

ACM Classification Keywords

H.5.m. Information interfaces and presentation: Miscellaneous.

C&C '15, June 22 - 25, 2015, Glasgow, United Kingdom
Copyright is held by the owner/author(s). Publication rights licensed to ACM.
ACM 978-1-4503-3598-0/15/06...$15.00
DOI: http://dx.doi.org/10.1145/2757226.2757233

INTRODUCTON

In the 1830s, the inventors of photography endured laborious attempts, time-consuming capture techniques, and dangerous fixative processes to trap a small slice of time. Those 19th century gentlemen scientists in England and France would have found it difficult to imagine the relative ease and speed with which today's average Joe or Jill can snap, pick, and publish a picture online.

In 2013, over 500 million photographs a day were shared worldwide on Facebook, Flickr, Twitter, Instagram, and Snapchat states Mary Meeker, a renowned market analyst with Kleiner Perkins Caufield Byers. According to a recent study by the Pew Research Center's Internet & American Life Project (Duggan, 2013), 54% of U.S. internet users have posted original photos or videos to websites and 47% share photos or videos found elsewhere online.

Indeed, digital images have become the preferred medium for in-the-moment social media communication. As a result, "the changing function of photography is part of a complex technological, social, and cultural transformation." (Dijck, 2008)

What are the millions of "moments" and "selfies" (Chu, 2013) that fill our social media newsfeeds saying? What is the communicative intent behind each post and show? How do users leverage their visual creativity and expression? The goal of the "Captured Moments" project is to determine a common visual language by exploring a series of posts and patterns to establish a baseline communicative framework and answer the basic question:

What are the users who post photographs on social media expressing and sharing about their lives?

RESEARCH AND METHODOLOGY

In answer to the above question, this paper will report on the application of visual research combined with an applied ethnographic communication methodology and reference communication theory. Ultimately, a more extensive project on photographic communication will seek to determine the creative and innovative value of user-generated photography and the democratization of creativity.

Data Gathering

The goal of this first phase of the longer-term project is to explore the tracking of non-verbal, photographic social media postings and communications of non-professional photographers using the Dell Hymes' SPEAKING framework (Hymes, 1972) to structure the visual creative data; and then follow with an analysis applying Gerry Philipsen's Speech Codes Theory (Philipsen, 2004) and James W. Carey's Ritual Communication Theory (Carey, 1985) to the non-verbal communications gathered from social media.

In order to create a workable data set and effective baseline for the exploration of this first phase of data, the collection was limited to one social media platform: Facebook. The approach of gathering data from Facebook feeds successfully tested the Hymes' methodology and confirmed this approach as a viable method for analyzing non-verbal, photographic observations. For Hymes, who created the model to aid in the analysis of speech events and speech acts within a cultural context (Hymes, 1962), all communications fall under the umbrella of speech. As such the SPEAKING framework proved instrumental in the interpretation of the images throughout the compilation of data for this project, and allowed the visual elements to be coded and tagged quite easily.

Participants

To gather the visual data, the Complete Observer (Coutu, 2013) ethnographic field method was applied to three subjects, and their use of images and text, as well as number of responsive likes and comments. The Facebook observations for each individual were tracked and coded through the viewing, and capture, of their Facebook postings over a 20-day period.

Facebook Subject: Brooke Mackay Castro

Figure 1. Brooke, her husband Ricky, and their two boys.
© Brooke Mackay Castro

Brooke, mid-40s, is a higher-than-average-income, working mom with two young boys, a demanding career working at a Seattle, WA charitable foundation, who has a husband, and a house. She uses her Facebook page to share and talk about her sons most of the time; very few of her postings

have to do with her husband other than acknowledging milestones like an anniversary or a birthday. She very rarely talks about herself. All of her postings, except one, during this time period were photographs with short text blurbs. She intently documents the day-to-day activities and happenings with a pic and post. She has a large following of design friends who enjoy her images of the boys and she garners many likes. As she captures moments and marks milestones (like a new tooth) what slowly emerges is the flow of daily life with her boys.

Observation time: October 6 to October 26, 2013.

Facebook Subject: Steven Nelson

Figure 2. Selfie. © Steven Nelson

Figure 3. Thanksgiving dinner. © Steven Nelson

Steven, 50, is an Associate Professor of African and African American Art History at a Southern California university; his partner, Dana, is also in the academic world. He is well-regarded in his field and frequently travels to speak and present around the country, and the world, which he tracks on his Facebook posts. His posts are a daily mix of images, memes, comments and quips. Steven often displays his sense of humor and has a large following of friends who quip back. For example his simple post: "It's finally pretentious scarf weather" with the image of him and his scarf received 137 likes and 60 comments. Aside from his humor, Steven also displays his interest in food, sharing time with friends, and his political causes on his Facebook posts.

Observation time: November 15 to December 1, 2013.

Facebook Subject: Randee Fox

Figures 4 and 5. Randee, Jada, and Paula. Their dog (below).

© Randee Fox

Randee, 62, is a successful artist. Her partner, Paula, 55, is a retired executive who is nurturing a burgeoning music career. They live in the suburbs of Seattle. They have been together for over 25 years. Two years ago Paula's niece, Jada, came to live with them and they became her legal guardians. As evidenced by Randee's posts, creating a welcoming and stable atmosphere for Jada is paramount for her as she is the one balancing the day-to-day activities in the household. Randee frequently posts about Jada, particularly highlighting holidays such as her their dog's birthday or their first Thanksgiving or milestone moments like Jada's first day at her new school. In addition, Randee's posts are often populated with landscape photographs. She displays her interest in animals, design, craft, and showcases these types of images on her Facebook pages.

Observation time: November 9 to November 29, 2013.

Additional Subjects

In addition to the tracking of the first three participants, the incoming Facebook feed of the author was also tracked intermittently over a period of three weeks (November 18 - December 10, 2013) to monitor and examine additional photographic posting events. Some of the examples of images gathered highlighted "selfies", holidays, milestones, and memories.

Data Analysis

In the analysis of the data, Philipsen's Speech Code Theory was applied, specifically focusing on Proposition 3 which states:

"A speech code implicates a culturally distinctive psychology, sociology, and rhetoric." (Gerry Philipsen, 2004). In the case of this research, the focus of the speech code is the visual communication codes used in social media and the symbols and meanings being conveyed via each photographic post. The imagery posted conveyed its own "system of symbols, meanings, premises, and rules about communicative conduct, and these implicate a distinctive system of meanings about human nature, social relationships, and strategic conduct." (Philipsen, 2004)

In addition, the analysis also leverages Carey's Ritual Communication Theory to the non-verbal communications gathered for this project. Carey's theory is that communication is a "construction of a symbolic reality – represents, maintains, adapts, and shares the beliefs of a society in time." (Carey, 1985). The ritual view is not about the act of imparting information, i.e. such as a newspaper or broadcast, but rather looking at the communicative act as a representation of those beliefs and the "maintenance of a society." Carey defined the ritual view in terms of participating in activities, and joining in fellowship through these communicative acts. (Carey, 1985) Posting images to Facebook is a communicative act that holds symbolic meaning surrounding activities, celebrations, events, memories and moments. Taken in the context of today's dynamic, technology-enhanced and connected environment, Carey's definitions become quite powerful, and apropos, when applied to the now routine behaviors of daily social media engagement and its collective impact.

Ironically, Carey was a bit of a skeptic when it came to technology and often challenged his associates on their embrace of technology. He believed their "futuristic mentality had much in common with the outlook of the Industrial Revolution, which was heralded by many of the Enlightenment philosophers and nineteenth-century moral-

OCTOBER 14 2013 | OCTOBER 12 2013 | OCTOBER 12 2013 | OCTOBER 9 2013 | OCTOBER 8 2013 | OCTOBER 6 2013 | OCTOBER 6 2013 | OCTOBER 6 2013

POSTING — IMAGE / TEXT

	Oct 14 2013	Oct 12 2013	Oct 12 2013	Oct 9 2013	Oct 8 2013	Oct 6 2013	Oct 6 2013	Oct 6 2013
TEXT	Goggles.	Calder: "I love you very much too Mom, but I love Cela more. You	Bedtime reading.	Calder: "When I make a heart like this, (shows fingers and thumbs making a heart) it means I love you. A sideways heart means I don't want you to talk to me in a mean voice. An upside down heart means you're being loud and you have to quiet down."	States were drawn and labeled in alphabetical order. I can barely get	Teeth!	...eth!	Rice Cereal.
	LIKES: 17 COMMENTS: 0	LIKES: 42 COMMENTS: 5	LIKES: 6 COMMENTS: 0	LIKES: 33 COMMENTS: 4	LIKES: 55 COMMENTS: 15	LIKES: 30 COMMENTS: 7	...S: 30 ...MMENTS:7	LIKES: 21 COMMENTS: 6

S — SITUATION SCENE	Bath time.	Snuggling under blankets in bed.	In bed.	Instructional.	Final result of map drawing.		...owing new teeth.	Meal time.
P — PARTICIPANTS RELATIONSHIPS	Participant: Older son; Speaker: Mother	Participant: Younger son + Older son; Speaker: Mother	Participant: Older son; Speaker: Mother	Participant: Older son; Speaker: Mother	Participant: None; Speaker: Mother		Participant: Younger son; Speaker: Mother	Participant: Younger son; Speaker: Mother
E — END GOALS OUTCOMES	Take a bath.	Creating relationship.	Going to sleep.	Sharing the story.	To create a map of the United States.		document event.	Eating a meal.
A — ACT. SEQUENCE AND TOPIC	Posting during bath time with goggles	Affections.	Reading, relaxing before going to sleep.	Describing the exchange.	Draw. Label. Name.		Capturing open mouth to see new teeth.	Eat.
K — KEY AND/OR TONE	Fun. Silly.	Happy. Loving.	Attentive. Relaxed.	Humor. Relief.	Studious.			Focus.
I — INSTRUMENTALS CHANNELS	Visual + Text.	Visual + Text.	Visual + Text.	Text.	Visual + Text.		...ual + Text.	Visual + Text.
N — NORMS INTERACTION INTERPRETATION	Bath time is a regular occurrence and part of personal hygiene.	Brothers should love one another.		in between ... Son.	Learning geography.		...st teeth are a life ...ge moment for ...ung children.	Eating meals is part of daily routine.
G — GENRE OR CATEGORY	Captured moment. Portrait.	Captured moment. Portrait.		...oment.	Artifact.		...lestone moment	Captured moment.

Callout box (OCTOBER 6 2013):

Teeth!
LIKES: 30
COMMENTS:7
Showing new teeth.
Participant: Younger son
Speaker: Mother
Document event.
Capturing open mouth to see new teeth..
Joy.
Visual + Text.
First teeth are a life stage moment for young children.
Milestone moment

Callout box (OCTOBER 12 2013):

Older Son: "I love you very much too Mom, but I love him more. You used to be my favorite, but now he is."
LIKES: 42
COMMENTS: 5
The Mother has photographed the Older Son hugging the Younger Son under wool blankets and planet sheets. Both appear happy as the Older Son verbally expresses his love for his brother which the Mother dutifully records when she posts the image. This is warm and loving CAPTURED MOMENT of her two sons.

POSTING — IMAGE / TEXT (lower) & SYNOPSIS

	Oct 14 2013	Oct 12 2013	Oct 9 2013	Oct 8 2013	Oct 6 2013	Oct 6 2013	Oct 6 2013
TEXT	Goggles.	Older Son: "I love you very much too Mom, but I love him more. You used to be my favorite, but now he is."	[heart exchange text]	States were drawn and labeled in alphabetical order. I can barely get the outline of the U.S right, so I'm amazed...		...eth!	Rice Cereal.
SYNOPSIS	LIKES: 17 COMMENTS: 0. The Mother has photographed the Older Son during his bath time. He is wearing bright blue goggles sitting in a white tube. The son has a nice smile on his face and there is a funny spirit to the photograph. This PORTRAIT is also a CAPTURED MOMENT of a daily ritual of personal hygiene.	LIKES: 42 COMMENTS: 5. The Mother has photographed the Older Son hugging the Younger Son under wool blankets and planet sheets. Both appear happy as the Older Son verbally expresses his love for his brother which the Mother dutifully records when she posts the image. This is warm and loving CAPTURED MOMENT of her two sons.	...ch. But post is ...sual in it's. Perhaps ...mera ...by, but ...o capture ...r's expla... her relief.	LIKES: 55 COMMENTS: 15. The Mother has photographed the Older Son's drawing of the United States to share her amazement at his accomplishment and visual aptitude ritual while also expressing his love for his father. The photo records an ARTIFACT of his geographic knowledge.	...bration the parents' anniversary. There are no children present, not a hint. Adult silver and white table cloth. The photo documents this CAPTURED MOMENT.	...30 ...MENTS:7 Mother has photographed the ...nger Son's first ...h! Appears teething is over for now. Might be later in the day than the image at right as his bib is trimmed in a different color. First teeth are a key developmental stage in a child's life and this was captured with a happy smile. A solid CAPTURED MOMENT.	LIKES: 21 COMMENTS: 6. The Mother has photographed the Younger Son eating, perhaps spitting, rice cereal with a wide-eyed look. Part of day-to-day life revealed in this CAPTURED MOMENT.

Figure 6, 7, and 8: Example of process used to analyze and code visual imagery using the Dell Hymes' SPEAKING framework. These pages are a subset of the image captures and analysis of Brooke's Facebook postings over a 20-day period. Images © Brooke Mackay Castro

ists as the vehicle for general progress, moral as well as material." (James W. Carey, 1970) To prove the lack of credibility of his colleagues positions he wrote: "…the 'electronic revolution' and the concepts of McLuhan and others have been repeated and embraced by a coteries of advertisers and engineers, corporation and foundation executives, and government personnel." (James W. Carey, 1970) So, Carey "rejected McLuhan's belief that technology trumps human will." (Martin, 2006) Ironically, it is exactly that "human will" Carey frames in ritual communication, those "mutual roots of the commonness, communion, community, and communication" (Villi, 2012) that accurately describe the emerging visual speech codes of social media and today's social worlds of tech-enhanced communication with "almost uncanny accuracy." (Anderson, 2011)

FINDINGS

Identifying a Visual Framework

There are mounds of photographic material for research and observation with each post that is "captured and communicated in order to maintain social cohesion among a group or among individuals." (Villi, 2012) Equally as important as the opportunity to verbally chat with another via mobile phone, is the ability for individuals to visually chat with one another and as they share their in-the-moment experiences with a photo and a post through Facebook.

There is no doubt the cellphone has aided in the exponential increase of imagery being posted on social media and the frequency with which the participants in this project posted. "The online sharing of photographs has introduced a novel dimension of mass communication to personal photography, more aptly called 'publishing'. … Publishing is strongly connected to social media platforms on the web (such as Facebook, Flickr and Twitter and the growing array of mobile apps." (Villi, 2012)

Granted, these social media publishing platforms do have systemic guardrails that impact individual news feeds and streams of visual communication. These include, but are not limited to, the constraints of the format itself, the self-selection of followers/friends, and the display algorithms generated by user engagement.

However, as these "published" (Villi, 2012) images on Facebook were gathered and cataloged, The SPEAKING framework functioned extremely well as a method to track how individuals are visually engaging with their community of friends and family. The framework successfully aided in the extraction of a wealth of communicative material from the three participant's photographic Facebook postings; as well as those images that passed through the observer's Facebook newsfeed.

Once cataloged, coding began by identifying and associating related key words and descriptions and surfacing the symbols and meanings. Of particular interest, as the analysis took place, was coding the specific "Genre or Category" along with the "Act" being photographed, and then coupled with the norms of interaction. They began to form a "photographic grammar" (Villi, 2012) that eventually evolved into a basic visual communication framework for social media imagery.

In line with Carey's Ritual of Communication was the finding that the communications were frequent, and through the "ritual" of frequency created "sharing", "participation", and "fellowship" in their online community. In most cases, there was "ritual significance in creating and maintaining a world view." (Anderson, 2011)

At first pass, over seventeen categories of "Captured Moments" were identified by leveraging the descriptions that emerged through the coding. They were then aligned with one of the many available lists of classic photographic genres (Wikipedia, 2013); these lists include categories such as portraiture, landscape, fashion photography, photojournalism, etc. After several passes over the emerging genres, redundancies were eliminated, as many of the original genres that surfaced revealed to be more accurate as subsets of a larger, broader category.

For example, originally the "selfie" was identified as a separate genre/category. It seemed an easy classification given the word's recent notoriety as the Oxford Dictionary's Word of the Year (Chu, 2013), actors Tom Hanks and Steve Martin Governor's Award prank, Ellen DeGeneres's Oscar "selfie" seen round the world, and the, now infamous, U.S. President Barak Obama "selfie" at the funeral of Nelson Mandela. However, upon closer analysis, the "selfie" is at its very essence a portrait, a self-portrait to be exact, which is more about presenting/controlling an image of oneself to the world (as users don't post "selfies" they don't like since they are essentially controlling the upload). As a result, "selfie" ended up being a subset of a larger category class entitled Image Makers.

Defining the Visual Framework

Eventually, the seventeen original categories were reduced to the following seven categories to form the "Captured Moments" framework:

Image Makers

These posts are all about representing a personality, whether person or pet. Based in traditional portraiture, the representation is saying more about the personality posting than the environment or the activity; especially if it's a "Selfie". (Chu, 2013) The photo is making an image statement involving self-portrayal and observer interpretation.

Environs

The classic "wish you were here" moment where the Facebook friend is sharing an environment at the very same time they are actually experiencing one of the following: nature, landscape, travel spot, sunset, architecture, or aerial photography.

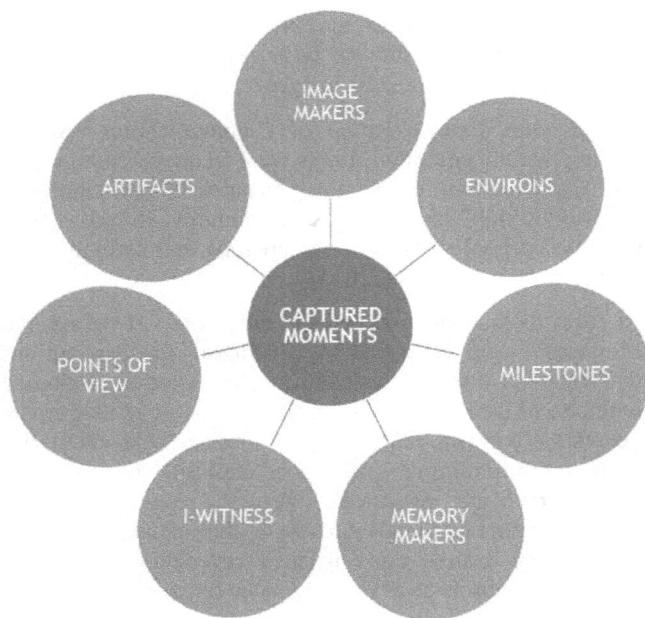

Table 1. The seven categories of the "Captured Moments" framework.

Milestones

Recurring events that are shared across a culture and/or group of people including birthdays, weddings, special events, holidays, anniversaries. There is often a cultural ritual associated with these events whether national, religious, or a specific group association. These posts are celebratory in nature.

Memory Makers

The user captures a current, precious moment-in-time for future reference and remembrance; or the user posts an existing photograph to honor or remember someone special or a moment in time past, a somber event, i.e. President of the United States John Fitzgerald Kennedy's assassination. While many of the images in these posts began life as celebratory in nature, they now have a somber side, as they are associated with times, and loved ones, that have passed.

I-Witness

Ordinary citizens, Facebook users recording extraordinary news events. Nonprofessionals now have an outlet to break news as it happens without filters (depending on where you live in the world). As a result, their photographic postings provide reportage of events and bear witness to the world. Just as with the recent images from the Boston Marathon bombing, there are plenty of posted images captured by average citizens who are ringside eyewitnesses to current world events – and are willing to start spreading the news.

Points of View

Since you are their friend and part of their community, the poster assumes you will be interested in, and share the same sentiments, about posted and pictured causes, charities, obsessions, political statements, and/or activist positions.

Artifacts

Officially, an artifact is an "object produced or shaped by human craft, but it's especially powerful when it's by the hand of a young child or an artisan chef – both of which share great popularity in Facebook picture postings. As an artifact by nature has historical interest, a.k.a. preservation, social media has become a place to display these objects, items, special keepsakes and the many meals of our lives.

CONCLUDING REMARKS

If storytelling has a beginning, middle and end, social media is bringing users back to the beginning as the constant posting of photographs creates an ongoing visual narrative throughout every aspect of their lives. They are sharing visual posts and pictures representative of their individual attitudes, personal skills, sense of self-worth, memories, and important (and not so important) life events. Users broadcast these "Captured Moments" to a far-reaching patchwork quilt of families, friends, and community.

The "Captured Moments" framework translates these postings, and ponderings, and clearly identifies a tacit communication ritual for those who opt into the Facebook social media platform. This visual speech code leverages traditional photograph genres but is enhanced by the system of meanings and symbols that graphically communicate the day-to-day ebb and flow of life.

The ease and accessibility of the camera, embedded in phones and tablets, has transformed visual communication, and enabled non-professionals to capture these photographic moments and share and participate in a larger community with a common visual language.

Each picture post has the ability to circle the word and back again; and to communicate 24/7. What was once relegated to scrapbooks and dusty shoe boxes on the top of closet shelves, is now shared with a blessing into a very public arena for all to witness and understand.

And, once upon a time? No more a single moment in time. It is a series of moments captured in Facebook postings that will last for a digital eternity.

FUTURE DIRECTIONS

This research is the first phase of a larger, more extensive project exploring social media, visual communication, and the democratization of creativity. Additional observations of the Facebook platform are needed, as well as research on the use of photography on other social media platforms.

Moving forward, the following issues will be addressed:

- Researching other social media platforms to verify the "Captured Moments" framework; specifically Instagram and Twitter.

- Expanding the literature review to enhance the individual descriptions in the visual framework.

- Interviewing photographers – both professional and non-professionals -- about creativity, the assessment of image quality, as well as explore their use of social media platforms.

- Creating, distributing, and analyzing a survey on using photographs in social media.

- Using the additional research methodologies to explore creative visual innovation on social media: lead user search, information sharing communities, crowdsourcing, and toolkits.

ACKNOWLEDGMENTS
I would like to thank those who allowed me to participate in their Facebook newsfeeds. A special thanks to Cornish College of the Arts Provost VPAA Moira Scott Payne and Design Department Chair Jeff Brice for their academic support. Additional thanks to Associate Director Lisa Coutu, Communication Leadership, University of Washington; Associate Director Anita Verna Crofts, Communication Leadership, University of Washington; and Assistant Professor Benjamin Mako Hill, University of Washington School of Communication, for encouraging my research in this emerging area of visual communication and social media.

REFERENCES
1. Anderson, H. Siblings in Cyberspace: Carey's Ritual Model of Communication in the Digital Age, *Intersect* (2011), 92-100.

2. Brandon Van Der Heide, J. D. The Effects of Verbal versus Photographic Self-Presentation on Impression Formation in Facebook. *Journal of Communication* (2012), 98-116.

3. Carey, J. W. A Cultural Approach to Communication. In J. W. Carey, Communication as Culture: Essays on Media and Society. (1985) Boston.

4. Catcher, J. (2013, December 11). 10 Legendary Selfies of 2013. Retrieved from Mashable: http://mashable.com/2013/12/11/2013-the-year-of-the-selfie/?utm_cid=mash-com-fb-main-link

5. Chu, H. Selfie: 2013's word of the year. *Los Angeles Times.* (2013, November 19) Retrieved from www.latimes.com: http://www.latimes.com/world/worldnow/la-fg-wn-selfie-2013-word-of-the-year20131119,0,1477227.story#axzz2mos3lnxD

6. Coleman, E. Ethnographic Approaches to Digital Media. The Annual Review of Anthropology, 487505. (2010)

7. Coutu, L. Communication 597: Communication Through Culture. (L. Coutu, Performer) University of Washington, Seattle. (2013, October 10)

8. Dijck, J. V. Digital Photography: Communication, Identity, Memory. Visual Communication (2008), 57-76.

9. Duggan, M. Photo and Video Sharing Grow Online. Pew Research Center, Pew Internet & American Life Project. Washington, D.C.: Pew Research Center. (2013). Retrieved from http://pewinternet.org/Reports/2013/Photos-and-videos.aspx

10. Gerry Philipsen, L. M. Speech Codes Theory. In W. B. Gudykunst, & W. B. Gudykunst (Ed.), Theorizing About Intercultural Communication (2004), 55-68.

11. Gye, L. Picture This: The Impact of Mobile Camera Phones on Personal Photographic Practices. Continuum: Journal of Media & Cultural Studies (2007), 279-288.

12. James W. Carey, J. J. The Mythos of Electronic Revolution. The American Scholar (1970), 219-241.

13. Schwarz, O. Negotiating Romance in Front of the Lens. Visual Communication (2010), 151-169.

14. Villi, M. Visual Chitchat: The Use of Camera Phones in Visual Interpersonal Communication. Interaction Studies in Communication & Culture, (2012), 39-54.

15. Wikipedia. (2013). Photography by Genre. Retrieved from Wikipedia: http://en.wikipedia.org/wiki/Category:Photography_by_genre

Strategies for Embodied Design: The Value and Challenges of Observing Movement

Sarah Fdili Alaoui*, **Thecla Schiphorst***, **Shannon Cuykendall***, **Kristin Carlson***, **Karen Studd**†, and **Karen Bradley**†

* School of Interactive Arts and Technologies, Simon Fraser University, Surrey, Canada.
† Laban/Bartenieff Institute of Movement Studies, New York, USA.
sfdilial@sfu.ca, kca59@sfu.ca, scuykend@sfu.ca, thecla@sfu.ca, karen.bradleycma@limsonline.org,
krnstudd@gmail.com

ABSTRACT

In this paper, we investigate the value and challenges of observing movement experience in embodied design. We interviewed three design researchers selected from a CHI2014 panel on designing for the experiential body. For each designer, we analyzed a publication describing their process of observing movement experience. By analyzing the interviews and publications, we studied how these researchers observe movement and how they articulate it in their design process. From our study, we contribute a set of techniques for performing movement observation inspired by somatics and body-based practices which we define as: attunement, attention, and kinesthetic empathy. We illustrate how these techniques have been applied by the selected researchers, and also highlight the remaining challenges related to articulating, translating, and sharing the felt movement experience in the context of design within HCI. Finally, we address these challenges by arguing for further exploration of movement frameworks from the fields of somatics, body-based practices, and movement studies as specific strategies that can be applied to HCI.

Author Keywords

Observation, Movement, Empathy, Interactive Systems, Design, Evaluation

ACM Classification Keywords

H.5.m. Information Interfaces and Presentation (e.g. HCI): Miscellaneous

INTRODUCTION

CHI2014 in Toronto included a panel entitled "Designing for the Experiential Body" [27]. The panelists, prominent design researchers within the CHI community, facilitated a discussion on how the community could embrace the full range of "rich body/movement-based experiences" in the design of embodied interactions [9]. The panel discussion illustrated the promising perspectives of "moving beyond treating our bodies as mere input-output machines through impoverished interaction modalities, towards richer, more meaningful interactions based on our human ways of living in the world" [27]. It also indicated that this community of knowledge and practice is facing multiple questions and challenges in bridging between such rich movement experience and the digital realm. Researchers within HCI lack common tools to describe, translate, and transmit the felt movement experience collected in self-observation and observation of others, and apply this experience to a design process.

In this paper, we seek to address the following questions: 1) How do the design researchers focusing on the experiential body observe movement? What is the nature of the action of observation? 2) How do design researchers articulate the observed movement experience? How do they describe it? And how do they implement the data collected from their observation of the 'felt' experience in order to transform their design practice?

To investigate these questions, we interviewed three design researchers that organized the CHI2014 panel titled "Designing for the Experiential Body" by discussing how they perform observation to collect movement experience, and how they articulate these experiences. We correlated their individual responses with a key publication they had each written that emphasized the use of observation in their design process. We unpack the ways in which these researchers perform and integrate movement observation into their design for movement experience. We contribute a set of techniques for performing movement observation inspired by somatics and movement studies. The techniques we highlight are: attunement, attention, and kinesthetic empathy. While our paper is based on existing techniques illustrated in our multidisciplinary literature review, we contribute by bringing them from somatics and articulating them in HCI. We show explicitly how these techniques are implicitly used by these researchers to perform self-observation and observation of others in the design for embodied movement experiences. Following this, we extract the challenges described by these researchers that relate to articulating movement experience in the context of design within HCI. We address these challenges by arguing

C&C '15, June 22 - 25, 2015, Glasgow, United Kingdom.
Copyright © 2015 ACM 978-1-4503-3598-0/15/06 ...$15.00.
DOI: http://dx.doi.org/10.1145/2757226.2757238

that the HCI community focusing on the experiential body could further explore the development of observational movement frameworks. More generally, we argue that the community would benefit from developing movement literacy and deepening its physical and theoretical movement knowledge and related design strategies. We suggest that such knowledge can come from integrating the fields of somatics and movement studies with the domain of interaction design. These fields provide experiential and analytical frameworks to perform observation and describe movement, which can provide new strategies for developing movement awareness within HCI [35].

LITERATURE REVIEW
In order to ground our study in prior works within HCI, we review the literature and present the differing approaches to observation that apply to movement experience.

Using Observation in Designing for Movement
HCI literature is rich with methodologies using objective or subjective [21] measures and other third-person perspectives, such as Cartesian observation commonly used in scientific methods. However, alternative modes of observation exist and shifting between them allows designers to attend to different qualities of the same event [35]. Schiphorst proposed an approach to observational techniques within HCI that incorporated a continuum between first, second, and third-person observation [35] as suggested by Depraz, Varela, and Vermersch in their book "On Becoming Aware" [8]. *Third-person* perspectives posit observation as objectively gathering data from the world that removes the bias of the self. *First-person* perspectives are focused on self-observation and exploration of one's own experience in developing and testing technologies. They seek interactions that afford self-connection. *Second-person* perspectives include participant observation through kinesthetic empathy. These observational methods facilitate collaboration and build a shared knowledge to connect to others' experience. Finally, Schiphorst proposes an additional technique of "observing through the self into the world", a form of second-person observation based on the "mirror of the self" technique developed by Christopher Alexander for observing relative wholeness within a situation, action, or object [1].

Third-Person Perspective
Among methods using third-person perspectives in HCI, ethnographic research methods have gained increased traction due to their ability to connect cultural and social knowledge within interaction design. They provide an interpretive description of users, environments, interactions, and the context of use. They also describe the "bias" toward understanding the use of the system from the investigator's perspective. Ethnographic methods include field work performed in natural settings deployed during the whole life cycle of development, from gathering users' needs to onsite evaluation [16]. They help make informed choices about what to study, who to observe, what activities to record, and how to analyze and integrate the data into valuable findings. Millen argues that, more than a method of field data collection, "ethnography is

rather a form of analytic reportage, with the ethnographer acting as a translator or cultural broker between the group or culture under study and the reader" [30]. Ethnographic methods have also helped to bridge the gap between third and second-person methods in interaction design through the inclusion of Cultural Probes [13].

Second-Person Perspective
Second-person perspectives include participant observation through kinesthetic empathy. This phenomenon bridges the self to others by connecting one's bodily sensations to others' experience. John Martin was one of the first to describe this phenomenon in the 1930's: "We shall cease to be mere spectators and become participants in the movement that is presented to us, and though to all outward appearances we shall be sitting quietly in our chairs, we shall nevertheless be dancing synthetically with all our musculature" [26]. Research surrounding kinesthetic empathy has grown since the discovery of mirror neurons in 1996. Mirror neurons are activated in the brain both when observing and performing movement. Neuroscientists have found that both our visual and physical familiarity with movement heightens neuronal activity when observing movement [4]. How this neuronal activity relates to one's perception and attention to movement is still unclear. However, mirror neurons may provide one possible neurological explanation for kinesthetic empathy. Qualitative studies in dance have demonstrated that movement observation can affect our bodily state by triggering physical responses [34]. Studies using eye tracking and TMS+EMG have also found that our physical and visual movement literacy play an important role in how we perceive and empathize with movement [36, 17]. This research demonstrates the importance of the body and movement literacy in the observational process.

Kinesthetic empathy research has recently been acknowledged and incorporated into design frameworks. For example, Moen developed a framework for kinesthetic movement interaction that creates pleasurable movement experiences [31]. Her framework is inspired by theories in dance developed by Blom and Chaplin [3]. It includes design considerations relating to increasing kinesthetic awareness and expressing kinesthetic empathy [31]. Fogtmann et al. developed a conceptual framework for analyzing whole-body movement interaction through outlining design themes and parameters including: *Kinesthetic Development, Kinesthetic Means,* and *Kinesthetic Disorder* [12]. *Development* refers to creating interactions that improve kinesthetic skills. *Means* refers to reaching other goals, unrelated to kinesthetic development. *Disorder* refers to the transformation of a kinesthetic sensation. Finally, Wright et al. used empathy to define characteristic of designer-user relationships when designing for user experience [37].

First-Person Perspective
Because of the often intimate nature of designing for experience, it has mostly been approached in the literature from a first-person perspective, which involves self-observation and the self as a lens to observe others' experience [29]. However, it is very difficult to gain access to experience. According to Damasio, we have access to different forms of knowledge in

different states. In order to observe, one needs to "capture" the data using one's sensorial modalities, filter it and articulate it through one's own experience [7].

In accessing experience, there is the challenge that one may not have the practiced skills of self-reflection [8] nor the adequate vocabulary to articulate one's own experience [14]. To address this difficulty, methods have been developed in the domain of cognitive science where the researcher acts as a facilitator to help articulate the subject's experience [18], using her own knowledge of the phenomena. Care is taken to construct questions using the subject's own words to avoid influencing her answers. The researcher helps the subject to achieve a mental state of re-living the experience by using "markers" in the form of statements and by focusing the questions on the physical sensations being experienced during these particular moments. This reflection allows the subject to authentically describe her process and avoid interpretations of her experience from an objective stance [33]. This is similar to the practiced reflection achieved in first-person phenomenological description [8]. Kozel proposes a methodology for first-person phenomenological observation with repeated reflection over time [19]. It consists on recording an initial, raw, visceral response to the lived experience, then letting the experience sit, revisiting the memory of that experience, and recording the new response after time has passed. Kozel suggests that evaluating phenomenological experience starts with an open and uncritical sensory information. This methodology has been applied to movement observation by Corness et al. [6]. According to Kozel, a method of evaluating experience arises from iterating such as extensive journaling and reflection.

Developing Movement Literacy

We are all expert observers of movement. All humans learn and develop the capacity to observe movement because it is fundamental to existing in the physical and social world. However, there is a difference between the observation of which there is little conscious awareness, and an articulated observation used to describe and analyze movement experience. The latter kind of observation is a skill that can be trained and practiced by developing movement literacy and deepening the physical and theoretical movement knowledge. This was found by Moen to be central when designing for a movement experience [31]. According to Moen, designers must have physical knowledge of the movement they are designing for. Moen argues that movement literacy should be gained through movement exploration and reflection on these experiences. As shown previously, the need to develop movement literacy in HCI, and particularly when designing for movement experience, correlates with recent findings in neuroscience showing that observation is influenced by our prior movement knowledge, physical, visual, and theoretical [4]. Over centuries, dance has built a strong practical and theoretical body of knowledge for performing and crafting movement. This has inspired recent works in HCI to draw upon theories in modern dance [31], and to directly collaborate with experts dancers and choreographers to formalize a movement vocabulary for interaction [10].

Other fields, such as Somatics, build acute skills of movement experience, observation, attention, and synthesis. The term somatics is derived from the Greek word "somatikos", soma: "living, aware, bodily person" and refers to body-based practices that use a first-person perspective to develop embodied awareness of body sensation and capacity as experienced and regulated from within. In *"Self-evidence: applying somatic connoisseurship to experience design"*, Schiphorst argues for the necessity of somatic connoisseurship in experience design [35]. For example, Loke and Khut utilize their somatic practice of Feldenkrais methods to design technologies that enable the users to gain awareness of the inner bodily sensation [23]. Feldenkrais methods are somatic practices that provide frameworks to describe small-scale body interactions and micro-movements [11]. Recently, researchers explored the benefit of Somaesthetics in designing for the body. This technique involves somatic introspection, meaning "an organized inward-looking inquiry by the individual about his or her bodily perception and its related affective experiences" [22]. Lee et al. used somaesthetics practice to improve the ideation process of interactive product design through a set of movement and design workshops.

Laban Movement Analysis (LMA) is a system that focuses on experiencing, observing, and articulating movement patterns. LMA per se is not viewed in the same way as practices that are primarily somatic such as Alexander Technique or Feldenkrais. It has a broader scope because it provides a rigorous use of language to analyze functional and expressive movement of any scale based on experiential knowledge and strategies. It describes movement in terms of Body (What is moving?), Effort (How is it moving?), Space (Where is it moving?), and Shape (What relationship with the environment?) [20]. In HCI, LMA was exploited to define interaction scenarios that offer the user an aesthetic exploration of movement qualities through Laban Effort [25]. Loke et al. include LMA in their "toolkit" as a way to describe movement in the design and evaluation of movement-based interactive systems [24]. Their "toolkit" offers methods and tools organized by activity, from the three perspectives of the mover, the observer, and the machine. In total, they propose 7 activities that can be used at each stage of the design process based on Investigating, Inventing and choreographing, Re-enacting, Describing and documenting, Visual analysis and representation, Exploring and mapping, and Representing machine input and interpreting movement. They use LMA to visually analyze and represent the moving bodies. Drawing upon the approach proposed by Loke et al., we suggest that LMA can be used for all of the above activities requiring an accessible form of movement experience, investigation, inquiry, and observation in design.

ANALYSIS OF THE EXPERTS' PUBLICATIONS

We selected three prominent expert peers, Kia Höök, Georges Khut, and Helena Mentis, because of their specific interests in movement experience. They are design researchers and practitioners whose research interests align with our research investigation on observation in designing for movement experience. They are among the rare design researchers whose practices are inspired by somatics, without having ever been our co-authors. They all look at movement from an experiential lens and are inspired by first and second-person methodologies in order to design body-centred interactions. We selected three specific publications from their publication record that they considered to be key illustrations of their practice, whether they are shared or single authored. The selection criteria required that the publication emphasize the use of observation in creating embodied interactive systems.

We were particularly interested in the researchers' observation process in the context of a specific design work and publication outcome. The design works that we analyzed are already published. Yet the novelty of our contribution is to highlight how the observational process implicitly encompasses our technics. Thus, our analysis of the publications advance our knowledge about the source papers and contribute to the larger field of embodied interaction.

In her paper "Transferring qualities from horseback riding to design", Kia Höök [15] analyzed her experience of learning horseback riding to understand and identify types of movement experiences. Using an auto-ethnographic approach, Höök emphasizes the need of body-centred design to better address bodily experiences. As much as ergonomics exemplifies the functionalities related to the body, interaction design should address the experience sensed and felt through the body. From her reflection, Höök extracted themes relating to her experience and showed how these might be considered in body-centred design processes. Höök describes differences in experiences between seeing her body as an object, experiencing through and in the body, and becoming a "centaur" or one with the horse. She describes the importance of finding ways to describe bodily experiences of interactions that can serve as a resource for design. However, Höök also acknowledges the challenges in translating these experiences, stating, *"Still the experiences I am trying to describe are wordless, and putting detailed descriptions of them still fails to cover the complexities and uniqueness of my embodied experience."*

Loke and Khut apply the Feldenkrais Method to explore touch and proprioception in their interactive artwork, *Surging Vertically* [23]. Loke and Khut were inspired by Feldenkrais Awareness Through Movement (ATM) lessons. In these sessions, a certified practitioner leads participants through a series of exercises designed to heighten awareness of movement sensations. Loke and Khut integrated the ATM Feldekrais lessons into their design. A ten-minute recording of an ATM lesson is played to the participant. The recording draws the participant's attention to sensations of weight throughout the body and asks her to reflect on how these sensations intertwine when moving in varying ways. After the participant has listened to the recording, a human aide pulls on a rope connected to her feet. This change in tension invites participants to rise and shift their weight forward on the balls of their feet. *Surging Vertically* allows participants to inwardly reflect on their movement experiences. The Feldenkrais Method provides a framework to invite this type of reflective, embodied interactive experience.

Mentis et al. utilized the expertise of a Certified Laban Movement Analyst to design for the body. The goal of the authors was to create a system that enables interaction based on movement qualities. They interpreted movement qualities through the lens of LMA Effort and designed a system where changes in Effort Qualities were measured using a *Microsoft Kinect* and triggered musical events. A user study was conducted to understand how participants experienced, perceived and described the interaction. The LMA expert was also interviewed to gain insight on how she identified Effort qualities in the movement. The LMA expert was able to bring a more "embodied vision" to the observational process and often she would perform the movement while observing [28]. Her observation process relied on negotiation and interpretation when viewing the whole body moving. This was achieved primarily through the expert's own body and kinesthetic engagement. One challenge in building their system, as described in the paper, was how to articulate a movement experience and sensation. LMA, as they found, is one tool to aid in this translation.

Höök, Loke and Khut, and Mentis all stress the importance of personal *experience* in their design process. Höök breaks down experience by analyzing her own process of learning horseback riding and distinguishes between outer and inner relationships in her experience. As shown by Loke and Khut, the Feldenkrais Method provides a rich framework that allows users to inwardly experience through the body with a focus on self-discovery. However, as stated by both Mentis and Höök a challenge still remains in how to connect the inner *sensing* self with the outer *thinking* self, as the process of reflecting and bringing to conscious awareness is largely a thinking practice. As Mentis found, utilizing the embodied knowledge of an LMA expert can help bridge this gap. Mentis chose to focus on the LMA Effort category in her interaction design process. While LMA Effort is one important expressive component of movement, we suggest that LMA as a whole can provide a rich observational and analytical framework allowing to access and shift between both the inner *sensing* and outer *thinking* of movement experiences, which supports creating embodied movement-based interactions.

METHODOLOGY

In this study, we interviewed the three design researchers to investigate the ways in which they observe and articulate movement experience. The interviews were performed in relationship to a specific design process that emphasizes the use of observation and that is described in their relevant publication. Our analysis of the publications was also correlated with the researcher's responses in order to support the analysis of the interviews.

Foci in Movement Observation

We define 4 main foci as important aspects of movement observation. These foci encompass 3 *observational techniques* used in somatics and LMA to observe human movement [32]; attunement, attention, and kinesthetic empathy. These techniques are concrete procedural instruments of active observation, which is the action of being consciously aware of the observational process. We developed these foci from our analysis of the literature and by articulating well-known practices of observation in the field of movement studies, and particularly LMA in which we are trained and certified as Laban Movement Analysts. Our last focus concerns the *implementation of observation in the design for movement*. Our 4 foci frame our collection and analysis of the data on the researchers' observation process.

- Observation techniques. Through our interviews, we investigated the techniques used by design researchers to observe movement experience. We were particularly interested in how they used the following techniques:

  - Attunement: The preparation to perceive sensory information in an integrated cognitive state. It's an operation in which the observer accommodates herself to another by shifting her behaviour to the situation, process, or qualities of the other [2]. Many people implicitly attune as a preparation to engage in everyday activities and to make themselves ready to receive information. Examples could include a surgeon taking a deep breath before beginning surgery or a runner closing her eyes before beginning a race.

  - Attention: The "flashlight" used to bring awareness to facets of experience. Schiphorst describes attention as the operator on experience [35]. What people pay attention to, and how they guide their attention, directly affects what they will see.

  - Kinesthetic Empathy: The phenomenon related to how the body physically responds when observing movement. What the observer's own physical response is to someone else's movements, and how it guides her attention into someone else's patterns.

- Implementation of observation. In addition to the elements used by researchers in active observation of movement, we were interested in investigating how they deployed these elements in their design practice.

Data Collection

In this study, we collected data on the observation process of the three design researchers that we selected.

Two authors of the paper performed open-ended interviews, in a room at CHI2014 venue in Toronto, at a scheduled times after the conference. We chose a conversational approach to qualitative interview techniques. Following a phenomenological methodology inspired by Depraz, Varela and Vermersch [8], we asked researchers to access the experience of movement observation, and then describe it in the context of the specific design related to the publication that we selected from their academic dissemination. All the interviews were recorded by a digital audio recorder. Each interview lasted about 40 minutes.

Our questions aimed at helping the researchers to achieve an authentic reflection about their process related to the 4 aspects of movement observation that we defined. Our questions included:

- An opening question: Can you talk about how you observe movement in your design approach [described in your paper]?

- A question about attunement: How do you prepare to observe yourself or the users' movement?

- A question about attention: What do you pay attention to?

- A question about kinesthetic empathy: If you could replay the experience [described in your paper] of observing movement, could you describe your sensations (alt: how your body feels?)?

- A question about implementation of observation: How/when/why does movement observation inform your design practice [described in your paper]?

Data Analysis

We analyzed the data collected from the interviews using a methodology inspired by grounded theory [5] that consists in the six investigators (the authors) coding the responses separately and correlating their results:

- Axial coding: All investigators listened to the interviews independently and analyzed the related publications. They extracted keywords and key concepts that define the data using the interviewees' language. The six investigators discussed all individual codes and through a member checking process formed a collaborative code.

- Selective coding: All investigators collectively extracted high-level categories (techniques, tools, etc.), during a focus group. They applied different colors to each category and then linked the data organized in the axial coding across the high-level categories using the color codes. They then compared the results across subjects. This constituted the 2D cartography of the data.

- Theoretical coding: The investigators collectively mapped the 2D cartography of the data to the 4 original observation foci used in the interviews (attunement, attention, etc.) and constructed a 3D cartography unfolding the data as shown in Figure 1.

From grounded theory, we used axial and selective coding to allow relevant and unexpected elements of observation to emerge from the analysis of the data. For example, it allowed us to articulate the remaining challenges in framing movement observation in HCI, which were not one of our foci. In the theoretical coding, we mapped our pre-defined observation foci (attunement, etc.) to the data connecting the various levels of analysis. We believe that this is a more in-depth and all-encompassing methodology that allow to unpack the researchers' observation process and extract the remaining challenges in the implementation of observation in the design for movement experience.

ANALYSIS OF THE INTERVIEWS

All three researchers stressed in the interviews the importance of the personal felt *experience* in their design for embodied technologies, which correlates with our analysis of their paper. They adopt a first-person perspective for self-observation and second- and third-person perspectives for observation of others.

In the following sections, we first present the qualities that we identified from the analysis of the interviews, that emerge from their approach to design from the felt experience. We then present the techniques and tools used by the researchers to perform observation of themselves and others, organized according to the first-, second-, and third-person perspectives that were articulated in HCI by Schiphorst [35]. The techniques that we present go beyond describing the researchers' perspectives in observation; they also illustrate their perception of their action of observation. Following that, we present the remaining challenges of movement observation and articulation in designing for the experiential body. Our findings are elaborated in a narrative way, supported by direct quotations from the interview transcripts.

The Qualities of Designing from the Felt Experience
Designing from the felt experience allows to build embodied technology that supports self-connection and affords a kinesthetic self-awareness.

The researchers that we interviewed adopt a first-person perspective to design technology that supports self-connection. For example, Georges Khut's installations displays digital media such as visuals, sound, and biofeedback that respond to the participant's physiological states captured using biosensors. They allow the participants to gain a kinesthetic awareness of their inner bodily sensations by interacting with the technology. He defined his installations as spaces in which: *"you have to feel it in your body, the nervous system and your brain, so you have an intention, then you have some feedback signal that you are hearing in the moment." (Khut)*

Designing from the felt experience opens for new embodied experiences.

Georges Khut's installation aims to provoke novel embodied experiences and *"create a costume that extends the body." (Khut)*. According to Höök, such technology opens for new embodied experiences. She suggest that researchers *"need to be open to what the digital material is giving". (Höök).*

Designing from the felt experience allows for great design qualities to emerge.

Feldenkrais methods allow Kia Höök to access her inner felt experience, which ameliorates the qualities of her design for movement experience: *"It helps to be more sensitive [...] It focuses you and it makes you land in yourself, it makes the design process way more honest, more slow and reflective and better". (Höök).*

Höök argues further that designing from an awareness of inner experience allows for such qualities to emerge in any design approach: *"It doesn't have to be that you are designing for something physical, it doesn't matter what you are designing for." (Höök)*

Similarly, Mentis acknowledges the qualities of designing from the felt experience: *"And the design is something that embodies the data that we are all mingling. Perhaps that will*

not only solve the problem but also present you opportunities, almost solving a problem that many people didn't know that they had". (Mentis).

The Techniques and Tools Used for Observation
First-person perspective
In order to develop embodied technologies, researchers pay attention to their own bodily felt experiences as a starting point.

Kia Höök's designs for the body, starting from her own body and from her embodied felt experience: *"There is a process where you are allowing yourself to go into that felt experience, and then come out of it and then you can articulate and conceptualize" (Höök)*. She engages her whole design team in gaining awareness and attending to their own bodily experience by inviting them to attend Feldenkrais sessions, that benefit the whole design cycle: *"It's a typical Feldenkrais session, 30min 40min 1h, and then for the tech testing, she [the Feldenkrais instructor] records her voice and we reuse that, or we do it without her voice and try to go through a body scan or something with the technology." (Höök)*

Khut uses as a starting point his embodied states to define those which the participants access in his interactive installation: *"As the kind of maker you are trying to find some way of drawing the technology alongside you." (Khut)*

To access their own bodily felt experience, researchers attune to themselves.

Höök is not only observing and reporting on her actions, but further gaining awareness of her own inner embodied experience by attuning to herself and to the horse. She reports on the shift in her self-observation from a remote observation of herself related to an outer attitude, to a inner observation related to an embodied felt experience of herself with the horse. *"I was looking at my body from the outside in a sense and I was re-adjusting something I was doing wrong, till I get it. So that's one experience, but another experience is once I become in sync with the horse, when we are one." (Höök).*

Khut describes how he accesses a kinesthetic awareness of himself during the conception of his installation by attuning to himself: *"I start to internalize or hear sounds or imagine some textures and think of how that would relate to a quality of breathing. It's very kinesthetic in that moment of conceiving the piece"(Khut)*. Khut also attunes to himself when testing his interactive installation, by calming down and using slow breathing: *"I had to plug myself in, keep trying it out and fine tuning it [...] And you just have to be what you want the interaction to be. Its about trying to afford this sense of focused calm and really slow breathing". (Khut)*

To observe and reflect on their own bodily experience, researchers use various tools. These can help transition between inner and outer observational states.

Höök reported during the interview on the use of video as a tool to observe and reflect on her own experience of learning horse back riding [15]: *"I did videotapes of myself and asked my teacher to look at the videos and comment on them. I*

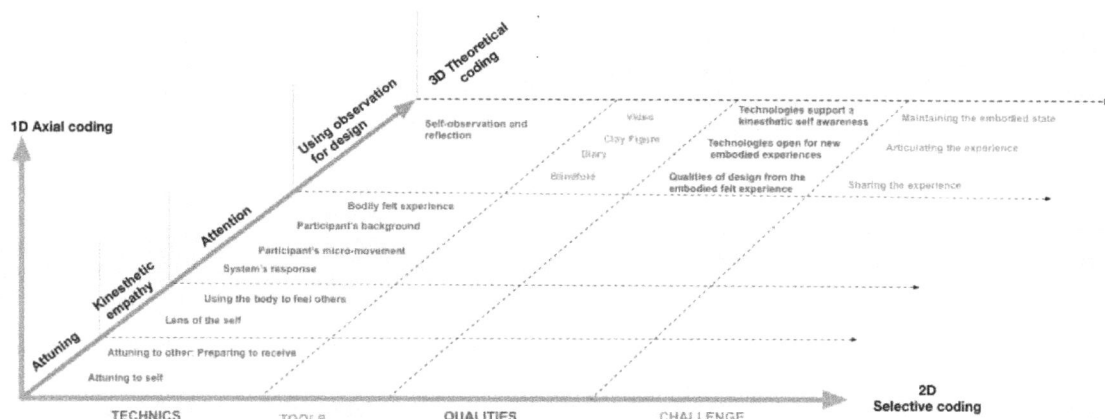

Figure 1. 3D cartography unfolding the data

took notes every time I have been riding, as detailed notes as I could. I had a camera on my helmet that was wiggling around, I put a camera on my teacher. I did everything I could think of to try and work on it." (Höök)

A diary can help an observer become aware of how she uses the lens of the self by identifying her bodily state and attuning to others. "...I wrote my own diary on the side [...] I would go and do my observations for a few hours a day and then I would come home and I would put down some of my feelings, how I felt. Things like my stress about what is going on in my own life [...] affected me as an observer." (Mentis)

Using a blindfold can help to kinaesthetically observe others by bringing attention to senses other than seeing. "...you need to be blindfolded, and then you experience materials, and other forms and articulate and elaborate about that..."(Höök). Researchers use models, such as schematic body or clay figures to transition between inner *sensing* and outer *thinking* about the movement experience: "We start by having a big sheet with a schematic body from different angles and then write down sort of what we are feeling before the Feldenkrais and then we do the Feldenkrais and then we do a reflection on the same form and then we used clay. So we do a clay figure before we do the Feldenkrais and we do a clay figure after." (Höök)

Second-Person Perspective
To observe the participants in the system, researchers attune to others by preparing to receive movement information.

According to Mentis, to observe movement, it is important to be receptive: "Observing requires us to prepare ourselves to receive the information." She describes her observational process as "just seeing" by "allowing something to happen."

Attuning is the preparation to receive information and "take in" the different patterns that emerge. Once one is able to attune to herself and to others, then empathy can allow access to an embodied understanding of others through one's own feelings and sensations. Thus the observer shifts into a state of observation of others through the lens of the self using the ability to access kinesthetic empathy.

Researchers use kinesthetic empathy; they use their body to feel the participant.

Kinesthetic empathy is defined by Mentis as a technique to feel the participant through her own body and physical sensations. Kinesthetic empathy allows to observe others through the lens of the self: ' "I am using my body to feel what other people are feeling instead of using my mind to create a story in my head to make me feel the other's story." (Mentis)

Mentis reports on how her practice of Alexander Technique allows her to develop the ability to connect her bodily sensation with the observed movement: "She [the Alexander Technique facilitator] was making these changes and yet I could feel what these changes felt like on the inside, they felt very strange and I felt very disembodied from it [...] But then she went around to work on the rest of the group and I saw! I started seeing what was happening!" (Mentis)

Researchers acknowledge the importance of the lens of the self in observation.

Mentis argues that the lens of the self is not a bias but rather a technique to observe others. "I'm observing, I'm affecting the environment and I'm being affected by the situation, I can't subtract myself from that situation. I definitely can't be objective in that environment." (Mentis)

The lens of the self allows Mentis to grasp the participant's micro-movements and "read" their emotions by connecting them to her own feelings and bodily sensations: "You feel that moment of stress, exhaustion, anxiety of the eyes [...] The tingle you feel in your body and sometimes you can't always specify what you're hearing or whats giving you that sense. [...] I should be able to read emotion and be able to see it in the work that people are doing." (Mentis)

Third-Person Perspective
To observe the participants' experience in the system, researchers pay attention to the larger patterns: the participants' backgrounds rather than their direct actions.

The participants' backgrounds reveal their experience of the interaction with the system: "The embodied part of using the *system had nothing to do with using the system. It was everything else that happened. You had a couple that came to the museum together. Are they a close couple? Are they an old couple? Do they have a history together and they want to move through the art exhibit together? Or are they just friends who are happy to separate and come back together?"* (Mentis)

Researchers pay attention to the smaller patterns: participants' micro-movements as indicators of their state.

Mentis pays attention to participants' micro-movements to observe their emotions: *"The most important thing when I am observing someone is trying to spend a lot of time not looking at his gross motor movements, which is usually what a neurologist is looking at. I am usually looking at all the small things, the little flutter across the face, the hunching of the shoulders. Someone's small hesitation."* (Mentis)

Researchers pay attention to the system's response as an indicator of the participants' state in the interaction.

Unlike Mentis, Khut's attention is drawn towards the system's response to observe the participant's inner state in his artwork: *"Its more observing the artwork [...] I'm not so sensitive to how people are, I could probably become more aware of how people are breathing, but there are a lot of people around just staring at the screen. I am just kind of observing and speculating."* (Khut)

The challenges in implementing observation in design
It is challenging to maintain the inner embodied state during the design process

Höök argues that designing from the felt experience requires to be in an inner embodied state during the design process. However, maintaining that embodied state when developing the interactive system is challenging. Höök considers that verbalizing and conceptualizing the inner felt experience into an outer design idea "loses" the embodied state. *"My feeling is that we do the Feldenkrais sessions and it is lovely and then we talk about it and the designers in the group have this urge to put some words down, because that's how they are used to do in design, you have few words, or concepts that you keep returning to in your design process. When you are evaluating design alternatives. And for me that breaks [...] I don't know how to bypass that, because it loses some of the bodily experience."* (Höök).

Khut and Mentis also raise the issue of shifting between an inner embodied state into an outer design mode. Technologies such as accelerometers are described as "rigid" because they do not maintain the embodied state that designers target: *"I feel that I can gather some really rich stories of people where they use their bodies. And then when I go to design, I'm not able to feel what I design because I feel that I am working with technology that is very rigid [...] I think that I am in it, and then I will use this accelerometer and I will use this data and then I have lost it."* (Mentis)

"You really have to consciously shift your nervous system arousal, then coming out of that and doing all that typing

again, it was very interesting to move back and forth between those two modes." (Khut)

Höök mentions that in order to overcome this issue, she is exploring the *"use of something that reminds you of the bodily experience that you have had"* during the design process.

The descriptions of the researchers show a disconnect between an inner process of *sensing* the body and an outer process of *thinking* and articulating design ideas that arise from the bodily experience. They are experiencing the inner/outer as a polarity rather than as a continuum.

It is challenging to articulate the inner felt experience using language.

According to Mentis and Höök the biggest challenge is to articulate the observed movement: *"The harder part was finding ways to articulate what I was seeing."* (Mentis)

"Once I become in sync with the horse [...] I don't think I can articulate what's going on because I am not thinking at all." (Höök)

Höök *"struggles"* to find the tools to describe the bodily experiences in order to translate them into design ideas while maintaining an authentic embodied state. *"I felt like there were so few descriptions that also include the real corporal body. You know, the sitting bones. We have been looking at Laban. I wanted to give a rich thick description of all of it and how it would all come together. I was really struggling with that. It was really difficult. This articulation process, how do you go from these experiences that happen rapidly and that are dynamically shifting, and they are in the moment and they are physical? How do you go from that into a description that can be operationalized and turn it into design ideas? And how can you be honest in your description?"* (Höök)

She argues that the existing languages to describe movement such as LMA do not provide the level of detail in the description that she needs. Moreover, using language to articulate the inner felt experience disconnects her from the authentic embodied inner state. Therefore, she does not advocate for the use of language and rather takes a detour from language and attempts to translate her inner experiences directly into design concepts: *"You don't have to conceptualize or put names on the different movements or things that you are doing because your brain is decoding these things anyways."* (Höök)

It is challenging to share the inner felt experience with participants and collaborators.

Khut's goal is to build systems that allow him to share his own intimate embodied states for participants to experience through the technology: *"It's a feeling like this sense of what would it be like if I could make this experience emerge from inside me."* (Khut).

However, there are challenges in designing systems that support sharing the intimate state with the participants through the technology. *"[...] so the design challenge is to create a sound that affords that state [the state of the designer]. And what does it mean then if you are trying to design for a tra-*

jectory, say what would it mean if you were trying to stay elevated?" (Khut)

Sharing the embodied experience is also challenging when collaborating with other designers in developing the technology: *"As a producer, and as a collaborator, you learn about how you draw those collaborators into understanding that embodied experience. A lot of the time they just don't want to do it or are resistant, they are just like tell me what you want me to do and I'll do it." (Khut)*

Although sharing one's own embodied state with collaborators remains a challenge in practice, Höök acknowledges its value in terms of building an interactive system collaboratively, departing from the shared presence and bodily experience: *"The presence of the other in the room is totally changing the experience. And so it's the only time that we [the collaborators] can talk about it and fine-tune what it is that we are trying to design for."*

DISCUSSION AND FUTURE WORKS
Our findings show that, although these researchers observe themselves and others by using **attunement**, **attention**, and **kinesthetic empathy**, they are challenged by the application of their observations to the design process itself.

The first challenge for researchers is **to stay engaged with their inner embodied insights** (those insights that emerge directly from inner felt experience) during the design process. The second challenge for researchers is to **articulate inner felt experience through language**. Articulating experience through language is elusive: there are many languages, but not all are suitable to translate inner bodily sensations to outer design concepts which arise from these experiences. The third challenge is **to share and transmit the embodied insights** with collaborators and participants. Researchers lack common tools to describe, translate, and transmit the experience collected in self-observation and observation of others and to apply it to a design process.

Our central finding is that a particular challenge for the researchers is the verbal articulation of their experiences, despite their understanding that rich embodied experiences can lead to better design of interactive technologies. In order to bridge these gaps within the HCI community, developing specific languages and techniques to organize and explicate communication of embodied insights is essential. Our expert interviewees proposed auto-ethnography, Feldenkrais Awareness through Movement, and LMA. These propositions are an initial articulation of strategies for movement observation in interaction design. We propose that building upon these languages can enrich design strategies for the experiential body within embodied interaction. The question of whether machines can learn these languages and identify components of movement in order to bridge the interface between human-centered design approaches and technologically-driven implementations remains to be seen.

In future works, we will expand the use of LMA to other activities defined within Loke et al.'s framework, including the investigation, invention, reenactment, description, and documentation of movement [24]. LMA allows one to articulate movement from an observational perspective for visually analyzing and representing human movement. It also allows one to acquire experiential data from felt sensation of movement from a first-person perspective, data that can be shared and utilized for the purpose of designing interactions based on human processes and patterns of behavior.

CONCLUSION
This paper investigates the under-explored area of observation of movement experience in interaction design in the context of HCI. We have presented a current state of the art of the existing approaches to observation. We studied the observation practices of three prominent design researchers that focus on the experiential body. We interviewed each of the researchers about how they perform observation and how they articulate the information collected. We correlated their responses with our analysis of a publication they had written that emphasized the use of observation in their design process.

Through our study, we provided two contributions to the HCI community: 1) We articulated three techniques for performing movement observation inspired by somatics and movement studies: attunement, attention, and kinaesthetic empathy. We showed how these techniques are used by these researchers to perform self-observation and observation of others in the design for the experiential body. 2) We articulated the remaining challenges related to describing and translating movement experience in design within HCI. We suggest that there remains a need to address these challenges by further exploring the application of observational movement frameworks from the fields of somatics and movement studies in the context of interdisciplinary research within HCI. However, we recognize that there are multiple techniques for performing observation and for describing movement patterns and highlight that other design researchers within HCI that focus on movement experience may be able to provide additional knowledge about their own strategies and practice.

While our paper is based on existing techniques illustrated in our multidisciplinary literature review, we contribute by bringing them from somatics and articulating them in HCI. Our set of techniques (attunement, attention and kinaesthetic empathy) is directly applicable to the design of embodied design, which has never been proposed in HCI. In further works, we will continue to pursue this work by suggesting specific methods to apply our set of techniques for direct technological implementation. We hope to contribute by further inventing ways to bridge experience and computation within HCI.

REFERENCES
1. Alexander, C. *The Nature of Order: An Essay on the Art of Building and the Nature of the Universe, Book 2.* Taylor & Francis, 2002.

2. Balzarotti, S., Piccini, L., Andreoni, G., and Ciceri, R. "I Know That You Know How I Feel": Behavioral and Physiological Signals Demonstrate Emotional Attunement While Interacting with a Computer Simulating Emotional Intelligence. *Journal of Nonverbal Behavior 38*, 3 (Apr. 2014), 283–299.

3. Blom, L. A., and Chaplin, L. T. *The intimate act of choreography*. University of Pittsburgh Press, 1982.

4. Calvo-Merino, B., Grèzes, J., Glaser, D. E., Passingham, R. E., and Haggard, P. Seeing or Doing? Influence of Visual and Motor Familiarity in Action Observation. *Current Biology 16*, 19 (Oct. 2006), 1905–1910.

5. Corbin, J., and Strauss, A. *Basics of Qualitative Research: Techniques and Procedures for Developing Grounded Theory*, vol. 14. SAGE Publications, 2007.

6. Corness, G., Carlson, K., and Schiphorst, T. Audience empathy: a phenomenological method for mediated performance. In *Proc C&C '11*, ACM (2011), 127–136.

7. Damasio, A. *Looking for Spinoza: Joy, Sorrow, and the Feeling Brain*. Houghton Mifflin Harcourt, 2003.

8. Depraz, N., Varela, F. J., and Vermersch, P. *On Becoming Aware: A pragmatics of experiencing*. John Benjamins Publishing, 2003.

9. Dourish, P. *Where The Action Is: The Foundations of Embodied Interaction*. MIT Press, 2001.

10. Fdili Alaoui, S., Caramiaux, B., Serrano, M., and Bevilacqua, F. Dance Movement Quality as Interaction Modality. In *Proc DIS'12*, ACM (2012), 761–769.

11. Feldenkrais, M. *Awareness through movement: health exercises for personal growth*. Harper & Row, 1972.

12. Fogtmann, M. H., Fritsch, J., and Aarhus, D. Kinesthetic Interaction - Revealing the Bodily Potential in Interaction Design. In *Proc OzCHI* (2008), 89–96.

13. Gaver, W., Boucher, A., Pennington, S., and Walker, B. Cultural probes and the value of uncertainty. *interactions 11*, 5 (2004), 53–56.

14. Glass, R. 8. Observer Response to Contemporary Dance. *In: Grove, Robin; Stevens, Catherine; McKechnie, Shirley. Thinking in Four Dimensions: Creativity and Cognition in Contemporary Dance*. (2005), 107–121.

15. Höök, K. Transferring qualities from horseback riding to design. *Proc NordiCHI'10* (2010), 226–235.

16. Hughes, J., King, V., Rodden, T., and Andersen, H. The role of ethnography in interactive systems design. *interactions 2*, 2 (1995), 56–65.

17. Jola, C., Abedian-Amiri, A., Kuppuswamy, A., Pollick, F. E., and Grosbras, M.-H. Motor Simulation without Motor Expertise: Enhanced Corticospinal Excitability in Visually Experienced Dance Spectators. *PLoS ONE 7*, 3 (2012), e33343.

18. Kirsh, D. Embodied cognition and the magical future of interaction design. *ACM ToCHI 20*, 1 (2013), 1–30.

19. Kozel, S. *Closer : performance, technologies, phenomenology*. MIT Press, 2007.

20. Laban, R., and Ullmann, L. *Modern educational dance*. MacDonald and Evans, 1963.

21. Latulipe, C., Carroll, E. A., and Lottridge, D. Love, hate, arousal and engagement: exploring audience responses to performing arts. In *Proc CHI'11*, ACM (2011), 1845–1854.

22. Lee, W., and Shusterman, R. Practicing Somaesthetics : Exploring Its Impact on Interactive Product Design Ideation. In *Proc DIS'14*, ACM (2014), 1055–1064.

23. Loke, L., and Khut, G. P. Surging Verticality : An Experience of Balance. In *Proc TEI'11*, ACM (2011), 237–240.

24. Loke, L., and Robertson, T. Moving and making strange. *ACM ToCHI 20*, 1 (Mar. 2013), 1–25.

25. Maranan, D. S., Fdili Alaoui, S., Schiphorst, T., Pasquier, P., Subyen, P., and Bartram, L. Designing For Movement : Evaluating Computational Models using LMA Effort Qualities. In *Proc CHI'14*, ACM (2014), 991–1000.

26. Martin, J. *Introduction to the dance*. Dance Horizons, New York, 1978.

27. Mentis, H., Hook, K., Mueller, F., Isbister, K., Khut, G. P., and Robertson, T. Designing for the experiential body. In *Proc CHI'14*, ACM (2014), 1069–1074.

28. Mentis, H., and Johansson, C. Seeing Movement Qualities. In *Proc CHI'13*, ACM (2013), 3375–3384.

29. Merleau-Ponty, M. *Phenomenology of Perception*. Editions Gallimard, 1945.

30. Millen, D. R. Rapid ethnography: time deepening strategies for hci field research. In *Proc DIS'00*, ACM (2000), 280–286.

31. Moen, J. From hand-held to body-worn: embodied experiences of the design and use of a wearable movement-based interaction concept. In *Proc TEI'07*, ACM (2007), 251–258.

32. Moore, C., and Yamamoto, K. *Beyond Words: Movement Observation and Analysis*. Gordon and Breach., (1988).

33. Petitmengin-peugeot, C., and Varela, P. The Intuitive Experience. *In The View from Within. First-person approaches to the study of consciousness* (1999), 43–77.

34. Reason, M., and Reynolds, D. Kinesthesia, Empathy, and Related Pleasures: An Inquiry into Audience Experiences of Watching Dance. *Dance Research Journal 42*, 02 (Apr. 2012), 49–75.

35. Schiphorst, T. Self-evidence: applying somatic connoisseurship to experience design. In *Proc CHI'11*, ACM (2011), 145–160.

36. Stevens, C., Winskel, H., Howell, C., Vidal, L.-M., Latimer, C., and Milne-Home, J. Perceiving Dance Schematic Expectations Guide Experts' Scanning of a Contemporary Dance Film. *Journal of Dance Medicine & Science 14*, 1 (2010), 19–25.

37. Wright, P., and McCarthy, J. Empathy and experience in hci. In *Proc. CHI'08*, ACM (2008), 637–646.

Moment by Moment: Creating Movement Sketches with Camera Stillframes

Kristin Carlson, Thecla Schiphorst, Karen Cochrane, Jordon Phillips, Herbert H. Tsang, Tom Calvert

School of Interactive Arts and Technologies, Simon Fraser University, Canada

Applied Research Lab, Trinity Western University, Canada

{kca59, thecla, kcochran, jjp1, htsang, tom}@sfu.ca

ABSTRACT

While mobile authoring applications are proliferating, choreographic tools that support the generation and transformation of user-created movement 'samples' are less readily available. iDanceForms is a novel mobile choreographic application that generates unique movement choices through a camera stillframing technique to provoke movement catalysts. In keeping with the principles of whole body interaction (and principles of 'defamiliarization'), the design of iDanceForms supports opportunities for surprise, unexpected movement choices and meaning-making. This paper presents data collected from an observational study of choreographers using iDanceForms. In the study we found that choreographers appropriated the intended functionality of iDanceForms to create highly individualized and unexpected movement sequences. They found inspiration in exploring unexpected framing of form and content, which resulted in creative explorations that produced unique movement possibilities provided by the system. Drawing from our observations we discuss possible roles that sensor-enabled mobile devices could play in movement generation through personal meaning-making, creative choreographic strategies and discovery, and in provoking whole body interaction through principles of 'defamiliarization' in the context of HCI.

Author Keywords

Movement; Choreographic Tools; Camera-Stillframing; Interactive Systems; Design; Evaluation

ACM Classification Keywords

H.5.m. Information Interfaces and Presentation (e.g. HCI): Miscellaneous

INTRODUCTION

While attention to design for felt experience and embodied interaction is growing in technology [23][18], there continues to be a lack of applications that support embodied methods of creative sketching. This paper describes iDanceForms, a mobile application that offers a unique approach to creative sketching of movement. iDanceForms allows choreographers to compose sequences of movement using their own personal movement choices. Choreographers investigate and improvise movement through the framing of the mobile tablets camera in order to select movement stillframes of still forms that they combine to create sequences of movement, holding unique meaning to the creator.

Interaction with real-time digital movement data is proliferating through an increasing range of sensing technologies including mo-cap, the Kinect, LEAP-motion, Wii-mote, vision systems, and mobile phone technologies including GPS, GSR, and accelerometers. Yet there remains a critical gap in using movement data to represent movement in the design of technology that supports creativity and movement composition. Choreographers create, explore and evaluate movement by moving. They explore movement as source material that is generated, tested and evaluated specifically through their bodies, or the bodies of their dancers. Our goal is to design creative tools for choreography, a creative artistic field that uses movement as material for creativity. These are artists and creative movement specialists who develop ideas iteratively through their embodied, kinesthetic experience: working hands-on, in situ and reflectively to explore novel ideas. The embodied process of improvisation and trial-and-error is rapidly executed in a studio in real-time. Choreographers practice, assess, evaluate and iterate new movement phrases through the bodies of the dancers participating in the choreographic process.

Figure 1. Camera Stillframing to Capture Creative Movement

Consumer technology offers a valuable opportunity for bridging the experience of creative movement composition with playful, everyday movement. Our system is a mobile platform that supports the knowledge gained through movement, felt experience, interaction with the physical world and meaning-making. Our system empowers choreographers to generate new creative ideas through their interaction with iDanceForms and a mobile device. We exploit sensors such as the camera, accelerometer and touch surface to reconsider how we can increase movement input in a simple choreographic process. The development of the iDanceForms software for mobile devices enables users to access intuitive touch screen-based interaction, to explore interface design for more complex movement procedures and to engage with physical and experiential spaces through technology.

Coughlan and Johnson stress that most of the tools available today do not provoke creative compositional choices and do not support the 'sketching process'. For example, programs such as Photoshop or Microsoft Word give artists a 'blank slate' to put their ideas on but do not assist them artistically in their practice [13]. Moreover, new design principles for creativity support tools are identified such as 1) supporting exploratory searches, 2) enabling collaboration, 3) providing rich history-keeping and design with low thresholds, high ceilings and wide walls [33]. iDanceForms explores the process of composition that choreographers may experience in everyday practice. Our goal it to design a tool that provokes playful movement exploration and reflection through 'movement sketching', rather than an archival tool that is highly detail oriented [31]. By focusing on the process of sketching we can create a space for iteration and opportunities for multiple interactions that support choreographers agency in their creative process.

Our contributions to the Creativity and Cognition community includes 1) developing a camera stillframing feature to provoke embodied methods of interaction in mobile tablets and 2) designing a platform for sketching in creative movement process. These tools provide us with a better understanding of how to support choreographers development of personal meaning-making with mobile devices.

We present results from our study with 5 choreographers who participated in a 90-minute choreographic workshop. We describe how people captured meaningful movement using camera stillframing and catalyzed new movement explorations by using the affordances of animation software on a mobile device. By drawing on principles of whole body interaction [25][30], bodily experience in technology design [18] and creativity support tools [33] we contribute design considerations for provoking playful and meaningful movement tools to support creativity.

BACKGROUND
"One can make things with it [Life Forms], one doesn't have to put things in one already knows.... one can make discoveries, and that interested me from the beginning. [29]

History of DanceForms
Using digital tools to support the creative process of choreography has a historical precedent. DanceForms (previously known as LifeForms) [10] [11] is a full animation suite designed in the 1990's to run on a desktop computer using mouse interaction for precision and specificity in designing movement. Choreographers such as Merce Cunningham used it to design movement as inspiration for constructing dances,

and for Cunningham it was particularly useful as he aged and was unable to demonstrate movement himself. Cunningham is a very special figure in the history of choreography worldwide, and a unique 'user' of the DanceForms software. He is an American choreographer who is best known for his seminal methods to consistently provoke 'new' choreographic ideas such as the use of Chance operations. Cunningham worked closed with the composer John Cage, and the visual artist Robert Rauschenberg among many others. Late in his career, Cunningham used DanceForms regularly in his process and to create multiple choreographic works by designing movement on digital dancers, manipulating the movement of joint using a mouse. He then transposes the movement decisions onto live dancers as articulated in the above quote. This process allowed him to explore movement options that he may not have otherwise considered and provoked new ways of discovering creative movement opportunities [29]. While DanceForms has been used by many choreographers over the last 20 years it has not become widely used due to the strong differences in creative processes between a personal movement experience and imagining and constructing that experience on a screen.

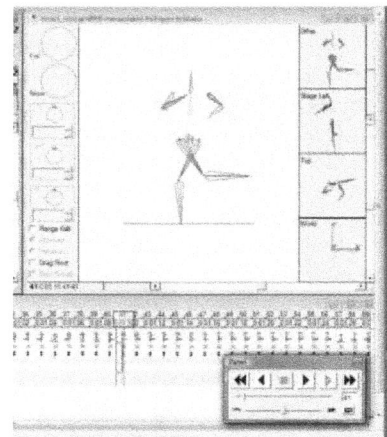

Figure 2. DanceForms Interface

DanceForms has three views: space, time, and body-position. The space view allows the user to design movement pathways as spatial patterns. The timeline allows the choreographer to design sequences and timings of movement. The body-position view allows the user to design body positions using joint manipulation or to choose codified positions from pre-designed libraries. Libraries were designed by using the corpus of standard positions that define a movement language in techniques such as ballet or modern.These Danceforms libraries have been used as source material in generative composition using a Swarm algorithm to automatically compose sequences of movement [39]. While DanceForms is the most articulate system available for computer-supported choreography, its precision-based design does not support portable, mobile, embodied or experiential forms of interaction. However DanceForms provides a rich foundation for mobile development and exploration of movement-based sensors for sketching choreography.

Related Works

While mobile applications are becoming more prevalent in playful and creative domains, many continue to rely on *traditional uses of touch-based interaction*. Touch-based interaction is becoming highly prevalent in device design, which loses an amount of precision in interaction while gaining a more tacit, direct interaction. This more tacit experience is useful in sketching applications to highlight play and creative controllers. Waern et al. design for 'play as a community value' by creating a touch-interaction based mobile application that gives beta (hints or suggestions for problem-solving) on parkour and freerunning through traditional forms of menu navigation [38]. Boring et al. designed a mobile application as a controller for creative menu navigation that included movement and touch as modalities to interact with urban media facades [9].

Mobile applications that support *innovative methods for interaction design* in playful applications do exist. Devendorf et al.'s AnyType system generates typefaces by taking photos of the world with a mobile device. AnyType is an exploration in personal meaning making by attending to the aesthetics of interaction in ways that enable users to create work from their own environment and experiences [15]. A music platform called IAMHear uses intuitive gestures from the internal gestures on the phone (in addition to the touch screen) as a controller for music performance and sound making in tabletop interfaces [21]. The Giant Steps is a music controller that uses the accelerometer in a mobile device to trigger reactive music while a user is jogging, depending on the physical activity level [3]. These systems support playful interaction and meaning-making using movement yet they do not exploit the felt experience of movement as material and as interaction for mobile creative or sketching applications.

The application of *movement as a medium in technology design* is supporting mobile application designs that explicitly explore the capture and use of human movement. Loke et al. stresses the importance of acknowledging HCI as a dialogue, by designing systems that take into account human agency that meaningfully engages with the technology through moving bodies [24]. Djajadiningrant et al. articulates bodily interaction as 'movement flow' which should be considered when designing systems for supporting the user in action in their work environment [16]. This is similar to previously discussed work by Larssen emphasizing the lack of research on the felt experience of interacting with technology [23]. Maranan et al. uses a single accelerometer for real-time capture of Laban Effort qualities of movement and articulates its application to aesthetic visualizations that provide visual feedback to movement [27]. iDanceForms creates opportunities for innovative meaning-making in movement and choreography by leveraging whole-body interaction in mobile devices.

Sketching applications that support user play and creativity are also common, but few are developed for mobile devices. Couglan and Johnson explore designs for collaborative music composition system by researching creativity based on contextual factors: interactions between people and external artifacts to articulate sketching as a core aspect of creative process [13]. Davis et al. address the Machinima programming suite of tools for video. They explore how a creativity support tool can bridge the gap between novices and experts by supporting the proper use of cinematic conventions through error reduction [14]. Zhao et al have designed the skWiki project for collaborative multimedia editing on the web that provides editing, chunking and transparent history keeping options [40]. We currently know of 20 systems that have been developed to generate choreographic sequences [35][28] or support choreographic methods [22][12][34]. A historical perspective of systems that assist in choreographic practice can be found in the paper by Fdili Alaoui et al. [2].

IDANCEFORMS

Cunningham balances the computers precise representation with the realities of human physicality, I look at some things and say, well thats impossible for a dancer to do. But if I look long enough I could think of a way it could be done. Not exactly as it's done on the screen, but it could prompt my eye to see something Ive never thought of before. [10]

iDanceForms has been designed based on the epistemology of choreography; leveraging whole-body interaction as well as the playful and creative properties of sketching to create a mobile support tool for personal meaning-making. By using an animation platform we can continue to provide an element of precision that the original DanceForms software maintains while opening to new opportunities for interaction, design and representation of movement.

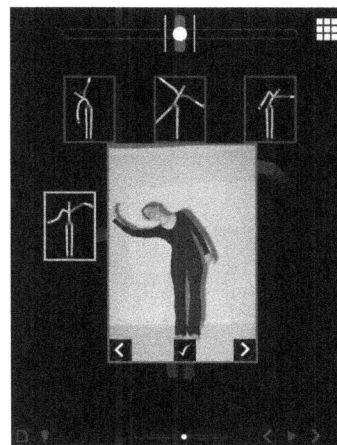

Figure 3. Movement Stillframe View

Movement Stillframing: Bridging Embodied Experience

Gromala and Bolter describe interactive art as looking either through a window or into a mirror [8]. Windows frame our vision, creating an opportunity to see the world a new, through the artwork. Whereas mirrors create reflections, presenting an image that mimics and follows the observer. The camera stillframing feature operates as a window, framing content that can be interacted with later.

When a choreographer opens the iDanceForms application on a mobile tablet, they have access to a camera function to take a photograph of a dancer. The choreographer can frame the dancer's still form (stillframe) by viewing the dancer through the device's camera, and capturing their pose as a stillframe. This enables a "moment by moment" accumulation of movement poses that produce a simple movement sketch that can be played as a movement sequence. Utilizing the 2D camera in mobile devices, the background is removed and the dancer's stillframe is compared to an existing database of images with existing skeletal data. The existing skeletal data is used to create a stillframe that can be added or reordered within a sequence of other stillfrmaes to create a movement sketch that can be further manipulated by the choreographer. This 'capture' process is an novel innovation for movement interaction which enables us to capture a wide variety of stillframe poses.

Sequencing Procedures: Touch-Based Interaction
Once the choreographer has captured still forms to use as stillframes in their animation they have options for adjusting sequencing and timing of stillframes. Touching a stillframe once will select it and enable dragging and dropping to reorder stillframes for designing creative sequences. Because we are working with stillframes, there is built-in linear interpolation that takes the shortest path to move from one stillframe to the next. This creates a unique 'movement' from the transition between a starting and ending still pose. The choreographer can control the timing of this 'movement' by adjusting the timing into and out of a stillframe with the timing bar at the top of the editing screen.

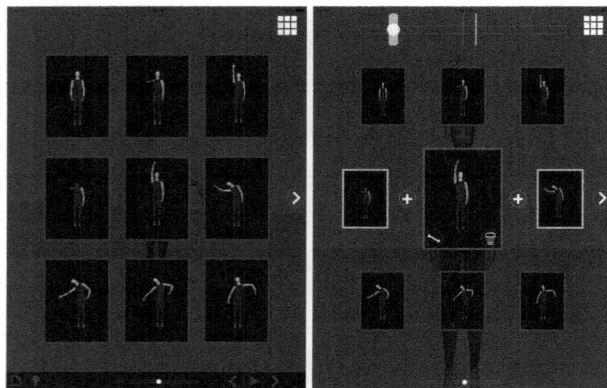

Figure 4. Editing Stillframe View

The skeleton setup and skinning techniques for the animated figure are based on the ISO standard COLLADA format [1]. The skeleton is based on a simple tree of joints with a single root while the skinning techniques are executed by assigning each vertex in a mesh of up to 4 joints with a weight value for each joint. The bind pose is baked into every transformation for efficiency while an inverse bind pose is stored to keep transformations oriented around the origin.

A linked list of stillframes are stored in the animation, which makes it easy and efficient to swap or move stillframes in the stillframe view. Each stillframe stores a pose and an integer representing the number of frames until the next stillframe.

A pose contains transformation data for each joint in the figures skeleton. Each transformation incorporates a quaternion for rotation and vectors for translation and scale. When a new frame is requested the current in-between frame is incremented. If it is greater than the current stillframes stored in-between frames, then the current stillframe is incremented. An in-between frame is calculated as the linear interpolation between two poses based on the current stillframe and current in-between. Each transformation in the poses are interpolated using slerp for the quaternion rotation. Standard linear interpolation is used on the vectors for scale and translation.

Viewing Sketches: Playback Sequences
Once the choreographer has created, sequenced and adjusted timing of stillframes they can view the animation in the playback screen. The playback screen enables the choreographer to view the animation on a 'stage' that they can move around using single finger touch to rotate around the space as well as pinch gestures to zoom. There are multiple lighting options to highlight the movement depending on creative vision of the choreography. The playback view is an important piece of the choreographic process, because it provides opportunity for viewing the animated movement, understanding the movement through the kinesthetically empathetic experience and reflection on the selection of and sequencing of still forms as stillframes. Playback is the portion of the creative process that provokes reflection and evaluation of choices made in the sketching process. Playback is the result of rapid prototyping:creating a space for choreographers to reflect in action and quickly continue working to create personal meaning.

Figure 5. iDanceForms Playback View

iDanceForms' Design Process
iDanceForms has been designed by utilizing the craft knowledge held by the participating research team, in collaboration with professional choreographers [5]. Design features for the current and future visions of iDanceForms are developed from the literature of choreographic process in addition to the researcher's craft knowledge, observations of and conversations with choreographers. This history of choreography provides frameworks and strategies for sketching, sequencing and reflecting on movement to make personal meaning

from movement material both experientially and analytically. Frameworks and strategies include Laban Movement Analysis, Viewpoints and techniques developed in disciplines such as Ballet, Modern and Improvisation [6] [7] [19] [20] [37]. These specific techniques for generating and assessing creative movement can be leveraged in technology design to support composition through new lenses, creating a tremendous amount of potential for creativity in choreography [12].

Advances in mobile devices are enabling exploration of touch and qualities of motion *in situ* that can create new spaces for creative exploration [30]. This can greatly change the opportunities for movement and technology. In a choreographer's practice, prior options for authoring movement in DanceForms or other systems required them to leave the studio, or to have a full desktop station in the studio. The separation between experientially exploring movement and analytically navigating software was difficult to bridge before mobile devices. The portability of current mobile technology with the power for natural touch interfaces, embedded sensors and cameras creates a unique tool that is easily accessible while in motion and in the moment. These new developments provide a plethora of opportunities to explore how technology can extend the existing practices of artists such as choreographers, animators, and special effect artist in order to augment their creative and compositional experiences with movement.

IDANCEFORMS STUDY: IN THE FIELD

We investigated iDanceForms in a workshop titled 'Mobile Computing as a Lens for Choreographic Perspective: Embodied, Experiential, Expressive'. Five female professional choreographers participated in the 90-minute workshop, held as part of an academic dance conference. Three of the choreographers were familiar with using technology in their choreographic process and two were not.

Data Collection and Analysis

The workshop was run as an exploratory composition course, where choreographers were asked to create short movement phrases based on their interaction with the software and their usual creative process. Data was gathered through video and audio recordings of the whole workshop. Researchers circulated between participants to gather their experience throughout their process, and held a loosely directed focus group at the end to gather any additional experiences that were not verbalized during the workshop, and to illicit group discussion around iDanceForms and choreography. The workshop data was transcribed and analyzed by using a grounded theory-inspired methodology [36] that consists of three of the researchers coding the responses separately and correlating their results. The workshop was designed around the concept of innovation: based on the cutting-edge history of contemporary dance, which rapidly evolved over the last century by continuously challenging the most recent development. We ran the workshop by asking choreographers to participate in choreographic exercises that explored three topics of composition:

Workshop Design

Still Forms and Movement: The first topic was creating still forms, or static 'poses' as opposed to the *transitions* between static poses. It is in the transitions *through* still forms that movement happens. We challenged choreographers to explore the difference between stillness and movement by creating multiple still forms and exploring how shifting the order of still forms changed how they transitioned (or moved) from one still form to another. In animation, this process would create different kinds of movement through the still forms based on linear interpolation: what the shortest pathway is between two still forms. By changing which two still forms are paired there will be a different movement pathway between them. This exploration of different movement pathways between stillness is a regular exploration of movement in choreography. The subtle shifts between the initiation of a movement and where it ends up creates very different options for a movement pathway. We explored the concept of still forms and movement pathways between still forms both through the bodily experience of movement without technology and in creating an animation in iDanceForms (as organizing a linear order of stillframes).

Sequencing: The second topic explored the act of *sequencing* through the manipulation of an existing animated movement sequence. We provided an existing animation sequence of an exercise from Cunningham Technique and asked choreographers to shift and manipulate the sequence, both on the device and in their individual movement experience. Manipulation options within iDanceForms include: exchanging and inserting stillframes of still forms, shifting the timing of individual stillframes and reflecting on the edits in the playback window. This exercise required choreographers to learn the existing movement phrase on their body, then shift back and forth between manipulating it in the software and 'trying it on' experientially. Choreographers needed to iterate between system and physical experience to attain the desired result by manipulating stillframes, reflecting on the resulting playback in the system and assessing it based on their moving experience.

Capture: The third topic explored how to use the camera stillframe function. This function uses the camera embedded in the mobile device to photograph a movement performed by a choreographer and selects the closest corresponding stillframe in the database. By capturing a still form the choreographer could create a new stillframe, and construct a sequence of stillframes populated by their own individualized movement, as it relates to the existing database. Choreographers were asked to improvise with the camera stillframing function to generate their own individualized movement, and to create a movement sequence from camera stillframes. During the workshop, choreographers were asked to use the device and explore movement through their bodily experience and choreographic lens.

While choreographers articulated their responses, experiences, and challenges throughout the workshop, they also participated in a final focus group at the end. The focus group consisted of an open discussion about choreographic experiences with the existing functionality and brainstorming about potential features and how they could support choreographic exploration and creative movement.

Results

From our study we present themes that emerged throughout the workshop and final focus group. Themes focus on aspects of the creative process, both articulated by the choreographer participants as well as were observed by the researchers. These themes detail the values that choreographers hold around their practice, and what their expectations are of technology that might play a part of their sketching process.

In-Between

Choreographers discussed 'transitions' as important aspects of movement design. Participant 2 mentioned "I am interested much less in form and shape than I am in states and dynamics. Effort is my world. Working with states and drives". The participant was referring to the concept of focusing a choreographic process on the *movement* itself. The terms 'states and drives' refer to terminology in a movement framework called Laban Movement Analysis (LMA) that articulates qualities of movement independently of and in relation to each other [37]. Participant 3 was also interesting in seeing the 'weight' of the animated figure and how the weight affected the qualities of movement. While weight has always been a difficult feature to design in animation and believable characters [17], we are researching opportunities to access 'illusions' of weight through representation. By focusing on the dynamics of movement, it does not matter what the still form or shape of the body is, how the limbs relate to each other or what the precise body's 'points in space' are. This shift of focus away from body position and onto qualities of the movement are difficult to capture in technology but are meaningful to the energy and 'essence' of a movement.

To move from the still form into movement, participant 3 explained that it "would be great to articulate where on the form the transition initiates". In real physical life, we cannot start to move by automatically shifting the entire body at the same time, as is done in animation. Through felt experience a person shifts their weight and initiates a movement from their knee, hip, head, or other body part to start the transition to move. How the movement initiates on the still form changes what the transition and quality of movement will be.

One option that would alter the linearity of transitions between still forms was addressed by participant 4, who states: "when using the iPad and connecting shapes, I was thinking that I wish I could do a half turn or quarter turn or a jump turn. So adding a quick and fun feature to connect the shapes through a turn or a jump". Adding rotation and jumping options in the *transitions* would be a novel option to manipulate the 'shortest path' between two still forms. By adding parameters for rotation and jumping many dynamics could be achieved by designing how quickly or slowly the choreographer moves into and out of a transition.

All Together

The theme 'All Together' emerged from choreographers talking about how to group stillframes together and use features

Figure 6. Participants Working Experientially

to manipulate a sequence of stillframes as a whole. Participant 1 asked if "there [was] a higher level function for grouping stillframes? So that you can group say 9 stillframes and call it a phrase, [and then] move it here". This would provide additional editing functionality, similar to how a choreographer works in the studio with dancers. This could include changing the speed of a phrase, shifting the orientation, spatial positions or the transitions between still forms. An example in a real-life studio could include a choreographer telling a dancer to take the movement sequence and perform it only using your hands, or make the whole body performance of the phrase as large as possible.

'All Together' is also a key component in designing for 'Relationships'. The compositional tool of *theme and variations* is a model for creating a core idea and developing it in different ways that are woven through a work to create a composition.

Relationships

Choreographers were interested in how to design for relationships in the software. Participant 3 discussed having 2 or more figures in the animation space that are "doing the same thing or different...[using your] history or library of movement phrases where you could add in another figure from your [personal] history". This phrase supports the importance of building relationships for meaning-making within the creative work to support evaluation in iteration. In the playback view it is useful "to rotate the stage space 360 degrees....and see it from all different angles". Having two figures, access to the history of sequences created and 360 view of spatial relationships could give perspective when dancers can't make it to rehearsal, suggested by participant 3: "sometimes they cant [come to rehearsals], so you cant see the possibilities".

Relationships also include application features such as working with two figures and having the ability to draw spatial configurations. Participant 4 mentioned that "[this] could be useful outside the studio with lots of dancers. I am always drawing pictures of how their spatial pathways should go and intersect so to be able to see broadly and test a lot of options at once, then could go into the studio knowing better what you want, what fits or what you are going for. I find that drawing pictures is really helpful because it helps you to see the broad picture of what it is". While drawing spatial pathways with multiple figures would be a useful feature and could provide 'creative situations' in the animations to be negotiated in real life by dancers, choreographers also view the iDanceForms application as a tool that could support the negotiating of multiple dancers in their live, in studio practice. Being able to 'see the possibilities' or the 'broad picture' is an important aspect of creative process, where the creator is iterating between a focus on details and broader context to ensure that the relationships they have build can bridge to meaning-making.

Additional touch interaction options that were suggested included being able to 'draw' spatial trajectories for the figure to follow or to draw a trajectory for a limb to follow. Participant 1 asked "could you give direction in space with your finger?" Working with the concept of sketching, being able to draw trajectories for both moving in space and initiating a still form to move could provide a more tacit exploration of movement on a mobile tablet. We are also exploring ways of using the internal sensors to map accelerometer data to moving a figure's limb, to play with more improvisational but embodied ways of moving figures.

Meaning-Making
The theme 'Meaning Making' emerged from choreographers discussing how to personalize movement design in iDance-Forms. Personalization was a topic in designing sequences by using music from their personal library to adjust animation in relation to was asked for to support editing choices and dynamics. Personalization was also requested in a feature to "choose images that already exist in your camera library" (Participant 1). However personalization was also discussed as the process of improvisation; how does this unique choreographer sketch? How does this unique choreographer make meaning in movement while using this mobile application? How can a choreographer be surprised through their interactions with this mobile application?

In the camera stillframing exercise the choreographers used iDanceForms in a manner that the researchers expected for about the first minute. This included taking a photo of a printout of a still form person, or photographing a live choreographer from straight-on while the subject was standing still. Taking photos in the expected way, by using a contrasting background to create a stillframe, created the exact still form stillframe that they were anticipating. However the choreographers *quickly* began exploring unique ways to take images that would produce novel results.

Choreographers were laying on the ground and taking images from above, photographing objects in the space (rather than people)(See Figure 7), and photographing multiple people at once. The choreographers who took pictures of objects and architecture located around the room were interested in what kind of movement poses random objects would generate. They didnt care if the resulting stillframes were related to the pose, or if the stillframe was shaped like an object rather than a figure. Choreographers also experimented with photographing multiple bodies in the virtual space to see what

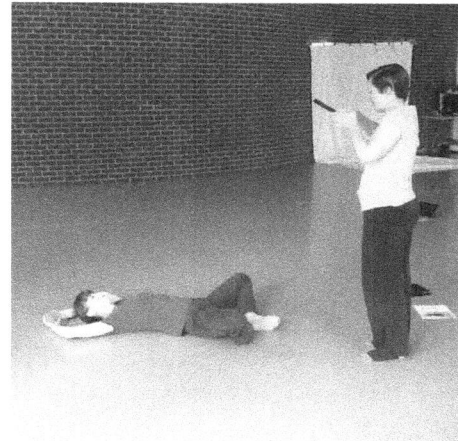

Figure 7. Participants Shifting Camera Orientation

could be generated. The camera stillframing feature was very popular because of its potential to create random or vaguely associated content from meaningful initial material.

Just like the earlier articulation of 'theme and variations', choreographers create variations based on a development of material that can be, but does not need to be, visibly connected to earlier themes. One of the researchers commented in the workshop that "[it] doesn't have to be human forms. Even the mistakes [are] really interesting". The exploratory sketching process creates meaning through the iteration and evaluation of content, based both on its personalized meaning and its novelty in relationship to the choreographer's interest.

Maneuvering
As researchers and designers we hold specific interests in designing tools to support embodied creativity by using mobile devices and the sensors they contain. The use of mobile devices in the studio by choreographers is more prevalent now than it was even 5 years ago. However, how choreographers use mobile tablets such as iPads and android devices continues to be restrained to photo and video documentation and review. To use a mobile tablet *while* dancing or choreographing takes some maneuvering. They are not as small as a phone. They will not fit in a pocket. They will not stick to skin. There are not desks or tables or furniture in a studio to place a device on while the choreographer shifts focus. Hence, how the device is held, placed and put down matters in a dance studio that contains many moving bodies.

The workshop took place in a large open room with many windows. There is a spring marley floor, a ballet barre and a piano. Throughout the workshop, choreographers were asked to shift between constructing animation on the mobile tablet and experientially moving. While this is an action that we regularly do in everyday life with our mobile phones, as we text a friend while we are walking to the train, this shift is more difficult due to the tablet's size. Choreographers were required to maneuver the devices in the space with only their own bodies, the floor and the device's case (which often functioned as a stand).

Figure 8. Choreographers Maneuvering the Mobile Devices

While choreographers sometimes sat on the ground to perform tasks with the iPad on their lap, they were often standing and holding the iPad with one hand while imitating the phrase with the rest of their body (See Figure 4). This immediate and in-situ interaction authoring option would not be possible without a light, mobile device with current processing power. Sometimes choreographers would place the iPad on the ground, using the fold-into-a-stand cover to place the iPad in a visible location to watch while they could move unencumbered. The ability for choreographers to lay on the floor or move through the space holding the iPad was an important feature to bridge and authorship system with embodied movement experience.

DISCUSSION

'By making the familiar strange, we familiarize ourselves a new with the familiar. [32]

Through the development and workshop process with choreographers we discovered 6 design goals that are important to prioritize for iDanceForms: Sketching, Catalysts, Defamiliarization, Whole-Body Interaction, Craft Knowledge and Meaning. *Sketching* creates a low-risk environment for exploration and iteration. Sketching enables rapid prototyping and is open to interpretation, creating a situation where *catalysts* for movement ideas can be provoked and developed. Every design choice in iDanceForms will be appropriated as a catalyst for creative movement because our users are so adept at thinking 'outside the box'. The open environment, sketching and catalyst design evokes playfulness, improvisation and unexpected uses.

iDanceForms is a *defamiliarization* tool because it re-invents the concept of movement and creativity for choreographers [5] [26] [4]. The creative process is separated from embodied craft knowledge and articulated a new. This requires choreographers to experience movement and think about movement differently, provoking creative opportunities in improvisation and sketching.

Whole-body interaction and a design based in the *craft knowledge* of the choreographer [5] are the critical design elements in a choreographic support tool. By engaging the expertise of felt experience [23] and designing for the affordances of mobile tablets we can create provocative, open creative environments for choreographers to explore personalized movement choices in which to create *meaning*.

Future Work

Our workshop also provided us with future design features that emerged from the discussion with choreographers. These include: Interaction with Sensors, Compositional Tools for Iteration, History-Keeping and Personalization. We describe these emerging features in more detail below, articulated in sections based on their functional, expressive and meaningful components.

Interaction: Moving Sensors

Choreographers requested methods to use touch-interaction to initiate movement from a body part, to draw pathways in space and to create relationships between figures. While these interaction methods are explicitly available and innovative to implement in a choreographic tool, we are interested in further exploring the use of embedded mobile sensors as controllers for interaction. Can a choreographer use the accelerometer to initiate a body position? Could a large walking path provide GPS data to create spatial pathways? Could devices that are within Bluetooth range create a relationship?

The process of choreography is epistemologically different from the process of animation. By engaging in the felt experience of movement and epistemological underpinnings of movement we generate more opportunities for innovation. The sketching process of trial and error is a rapid prototyping tool for quickly creating, reflecting on and assessing the value of the resulting work.

Currently, we have embedded a communication protocol similar to Open Sound Control (OSC) to connect a mobile phone and use it to control the figure in through the gyroscopic and accelerometer data. This interaction enables both precise and free form manipulation through movement. While this feature currently controls the figure in playback view we plan to soon be able to use this interaction to capture and manipulate stillframe and interpolation design in the editing view. We also plan to explore further interface design options to help us navigate through the many interaction options that we have, to enable designs that are innovative and movement based while supporting options for choreographic control. iDanceForms is committed to creating new opportunities for movement interaction by using technologies in natural user interfaces that supports the necessarily embodied and iterative choreographic creative process.

Composition: Iterative Authorship

Choreographers discussed being able to select sequences of movement to manipulate, seeing the big picture and working from dynamics. Due to the tremendous amount of movement data present in choreography, we plan to design a variety of 'levels' that can be shifted between in the application. We can currently editing joint angles on a low-level, selecting joints the axis to move on to manipulate the limb. However this continues to be very detail oriented, and we are searching for new opportunities to design for embodied interaction. Being able to 'zoom out' and see the big picture of choreographic choices was also a value. This could be addressed with different forms of representation to highlight certain qualities of movement, and could appropriated by choreographers to the 'start with the dynamics' in their creative movement process. Compositional tools that manipulate a sequence are also of interest: how do choreographers retrograde, invert, speed up, or move 'bigger' in a sequence? One opportunity we are exploring is to use a generative tool titled Scuddle to create new stillframes from a database either in iDanceForms or the choreographer's personal library [12].

History-Keeping: Functionality and Personalization
We are also working on more functional aspects of iDance-Forms to ensure that is works as a 'support tool' for choreographers. This includes designing for history-keeping and re-access of material. iDanceForms functionality also supports creative authorship by enabling access to music, existing photos in the Camera Library and sharing between collaborators.

We plan to further explore how iDanceForms can be used as a choreographic authoring tool with updated features and modes of interaction. We are planning a long-term study with a variety of choreographers to begin after the next iteration of iDanceForms development. We believe this will provide us with additional information about how choreographers work through creative ideas using felt experience in addition to understanding how iDanceForms can support and provoke their creative process.

CONCLUSION
Our design process and workshop study of iDanceForms enabled us to observe how choreographers make personalized meaning through their sketching process while continuing to engage their expertise and craft knowledge. We observed how choreographers improvised and iterated their movement choices to create opportunities for discovery and deeper engagement. Our workshop with professional choreographers illuminated the sketching process as an important tool for creative design and whole-body interaction as leveraging the epistemological underpinnings of movement. These values in design provide a rich area of inquiry towards designing for creative, felt movement experience.

We view iDanceForms as a preliminary exploration of mobile authoring tools for movement to evaluate how the affordances of such a system can support the creative values of a choreographer. We observed the playful discovery process that each choreographer experienced and began weaving into crafted movement sequences. We see potential for systems that utilize sensor-based movement to create embodied and personalized qualities of work, as opposed to designing for known creative processes using traditional interaction methods.

ACKNOWLEDGMENTS
The authors would like to acknowledge the funding support from the Social Sciences and Humanities Research Council of Canada and the Natural Sciences and Engineering Research Council of Canada.

REFERENCES
1. COLLADA.org. last accessed:, 2014.

2. Alaoui, S. F., Carlson, K., and Schiphorst, T. Choreography as mediated through compositional tools for movement: Constructing a historical perspective. In *Proceedings of the 2014 International Workshop on Movement and Computing*, MOCO '14, ACM (2014), 1:1–1:6.

3. Bauer, C., and Waldner, F. Reactive music: When user behavior affects sounds in real-time. In *CHI '13 Extended Abstracts on Human Factors in Computing Systems*, CHI EA '13, ACM (2013), 739–744.

4. Bell, G., Blythe, M., and Sengers, P. Making by making strange. 149–173.

5. Benford, S., Greenhalgh, C., Crabtree, A., Flintham, M., Walker, B., Marshall, J., Koleva, B., Rennick Egglestone, S., Giannachi, G., Adams, M., Tandavanitj, N., and Row Farr, J. Performance-led research in the wild. *ACM Trans. Comput.-Hum. Interact. 20*, 3 (July 2013), 14:1–14:22.

6. Blom, L. A. *The Intimate Act of Choreography*. University of Pittsburgh Press, 1982.

7. Bogart, A., and Landau, T. *The Viewpoints Book: A Practical Guide to Viewpoints and Composition*. Theatre Communications Group, 2005.

8. Bolter, J. D., and Gromala, D. *Windows and mirrors: Interaction design, digital art, and the myth of transparency*. MIT press, 2003.

9. Boring, S., Gehring, S., Wiethoff, A., Blckner, A. M., Schning, J., and Butz, A. Multi-user interaction on media facades through live video on mobile devices. In *Proceedings of the SIGCHI Conference on Human Factors in Computing Systems*, CHI '11, ACM (2011), 2721–2724.

10. Calvert, T. W., Bruderlin, A., Mah, S., Schiphorst, T., and Welman, C. The evolution of an interface for choreographers. In *Proceedings of the INTERCHI '93 conference on Human factors in computing systems*, IOS Press (1993), 115–122.

11. Calvert, T. W., Welman, C., Gaudet, S., Schiphorst, T., and Lee, C. Composition of multiple figure sequences for dance and animation. *The Visual Computer 7*, 2 (1991), 114–121.

12. Carlson, K., Schiphorst, T., and Pasquier, P. Scuddle: Generating movement catalysts for computer-aided choreography. In *The Second International Conference on Computational Creativity*, ACM Press (2011).

13. Coughlan, T., and Johnson, P. Understanding productive, structural and longitudinal interactions in the design of tools for creative activities. In *Proceedings of the Seventh ACM Conference on Creativity and Cognition*, ACM (2009), 155–164.

14. Davis, N., Zook, A., O'Neill, B., Headrick, B., Riedl, M., Grosz, A., and Nitsche, M. Creativity support for novice digital filmmaking. In *Proceedings of the SIGCHI Conference on Human Factors in Computing Systems*, CHI '13, ACM (2013), 651–660.

15. Devendorf, L., and Ryokai, K. AnyType: Provoking reflection and exploration with aesthetic interaction. In *Proceedings of the SIGCHI Conference on Human Factors in Computing Systems*, CHI '13, ACM (2013), 1041–1050.

16. Djajadiningra, Tom and Matthews, Ben and Stienstra, Marcelle. Interaction Relabelling and Extreme Characters: Methods for Exploring Aesthetic Interactions. 1–7.

17. El-Nasr, M. S., Bishko, L., Zammitto, V., Nixon, M., Vasiliakos, A. V., and Wei, H. Believable characters. In *Handbook of Multimedia for Digital Entertainment and Arts*, B. Furht, Ed. Springer US, 2009, 497–528.

18. Ferreira, P., and Hk, K. Bodily orientations around mobiles: Lessons learnt in vanuatu. In *Proceedings of the SIGCHI Conference on Human Factors in Computing Systems*, CHI '11, ACM (2011), 277–286.

19. Hagendoorn, I. Emergent patterns in dance improvisation and choreography. In *Unifying Themes in Complex Systems IV*. Springer Berlin Heidelberg, 2008, 183–195.

20. Humphrey, D. *The Art of Making Dances*. Princeton Book Company, 1959.

21. Kim, S., Kim, B., and Yeo, W. S. IAMHear: A tabletop interface with smart mobile devices using acoustic location. In *CHI '13 Extended Abstracts on Human Factors in Computing Systems*, CHI EA '13, ACM (2013), 1521–1526.

22. Lapointe, F.-J., and poque, M. The dancing genome project: generation of a human-computer choreography using a genetic algorithm. In *Proceedings of the 13th annual ACM international conference on Multimedia*, ACM (2005), 555–558.

23. Larssen, A. T., Robertson, T., and Edwards, J. How it feels, not just how it looks: When bodies interact with technology. In *Proceedings of the 18th Australia Conference on Computer-Human Interaction: Design: Activities, Artefacts and Environments*, OZCHI '06, ACM (2006), 329–332.

24. Loke, L., Larssen, A. T., Robertson, T., and Edwards, J. Understanding movement for interaction design: frameworks and approaches. *Personal and Ubiquitous Computing 11*, 8 (2006), 691–701.

25. Loke, L., Larssen, A. T., Robertson, T., and Edwards, J. Understanding movement for interaction design: Frameworks and approaches. *Personal Ubiquitous Comput. 11*, 8 (2007), 691–701.

26. Loke, L., and Robertson, T. Moving and making strange: An embodied approach to movement-based interaction design. 7:1–7:25.

27. Maranan, D., Fdili Alaoui, S., Schiphorst, T., Pasquier, P., Subyen, P., and Bartram, L. Designing for movement: Evaluating computational models using LMA effort qualities. In *Proceedings of the 32Nd Annual ACM Conference on Human Factors in Computing Systems*, CHI '14, ACM (2014), 991–1000.

28. Nakazawa, M., and Paezold-Ruehl, A. DANCING, dance ANd choreography: an intelligent nondeterministic generator. In *The Fifth Richard Tapia Celebration of Diversity in Computing Conference: Intellect, Initiatives, Insight, and Innovations*, ACM (2009), 30–34.

29. Schiphorst, T. *A Case Study of Merce Cunningham's Use of the LifeForms Computer Choreographic System in the Making of Trackers*. Masters Thesis, Simon Fraser University, 1993.

30. Schiphorst, T. Self-evidence: applying somatic connoisseurship to experience design. In *Proceedings of the 2011 annual conference extended abstracts on Human factors in computing systems*, CHI EA '11, ACM (2011), 145–160.

31. Schon, D. A. *Reflective Practioner: How Professionals Think in Action*. BasicBooks, 2000.

32. Sheets-Johnstone, M. *The Primacy of Movement*. John Benjamins Pub Co, 1999.

33. Shneiderman, B. Creativity support tools: accelerating discovery and innovation. *Communications of the ACM 50*, 12 (2007), 20–32.

34. Singh, V., Latulipe, C., Carroll, E., and Lottridge, D. The choreographer's notebook: A video annotation system for dancers and choreographers. In *Proceedings of the 8th ACM Conference on Creativity and Cognition*, ACM (2011), 197–206.

35. Soga, A., Umino, B., Yasuda, T., and Yokoi, S. Automatic composition and simulation system for ballet sequences. *The Visual Computer 23*, 5 (2007), 309–316.

36. Strauss, A. C., and Corbin, J. M. *Basics of Qualitative Research: Grounded Theory Procedures and Techniques*, 2nd ed. SAGE Publications, Inc, Sept. 1990.

37. Studd, K., and Cox, L. L. *Everybody is a body*. Dog Ear Publishing, 2013.

38. Waern, A., Balan, E., and Nevelsteen, K. Athletes and street acrobats: Designing for play as a community value in parkour. In *Proceedings of the SIGCHI Conference on Human Factors in Computing Systems*, CHI '12, ACM (2012), 869–878.

39. Yu, T., and Johnson, P. Tour jet, pirouette: Dance choreographing by computers. In *Genetic and Evolutionary Computation GECCO 2003*. 2003, 201.

40. Zhao, Z., Badam, S. K., Chandrasegaran, S., Park, D. G., Elmqvist, N. L., Kisselburgh, L., and Ramani, K. skWiki: A multimedia sketching system for collaborative creativity. In *Proceedings of the SIGCHI Conference on Human Factors in Computing Systems*, CHI '14, ACM (2014), 1235–1244.

Express it!: An Interactive System for Visualizing Expressiveness of Conductor's Gestures

Kyungho Lee, Donna J. Cox, Guy E. Garnett, Michael J. Junokas
Illinois Informatics Institute
University of Illinois at Urbana-Champaign
NCSA Building, 1205 West Clark, Urbana, IL 61801, USA
{klee141, donnacox, garnett, junokas}@illinois.edu

ABSTRACT

A conductor provides a single unified vision of how to interpret and perform music. However, perceiving a conductor's musical intention and expression is quite challenging as they convey information to performers with subtle, nuanced, and highly individualized gestures. This artwork visualizes the conductor's gestures in order to give the audience a better understanding of its expressivity. To represent the expressivity of the gestures, we created motion profiles over eight frames, at 30 frames per second, and compared them to previously modeled gestures using three motion factors, called Weight, Space and Time from related concepts in Laban Movement Analysis (LMA). Based on this, we have created a real-time, interactive visualization that is driven by the motion factor parameters. The visualization receives the input video stream, and it is transformed into a representation of the three motion factors extracted from the real-time conducting gestures.

Author Keywords

Visualization; expressivity; conductor's gestures; gesture recognition; music

ACM Classification Keywords

H.5.m. Information Interfaces and Presentation (e.g. HCI): Miscellaneous

INTRODUCTION

"Arms carve the air. A hand closes as if to pull taffy. An index finger shoots out. The torso leans in, leans back. And somehow, music pours forth—precisely coordinated and emotionally expressive—in response to this mysterious podium dance." [27] This quote describes how a conductor's gestures look on the stage. Just as a theater director makes various interpretive decisions with a Shakespearean tragedy, conductors study the score to find the significance they want to bring out in a performance. While leading the orchestra, conductors use their body movement as a medium to deliver musical intentions and expressions to the ensemble, indicating dynamics, tempo, articulation, balance, and general qualities of sound and performance. The art of conducting is more than just synchronization and signaling gestures: it is a fascinating—and under explored—gestural interaction model for conveying high-bandwidth qualitative and quantitative information from the conductor to sometimes hundreds of performers.

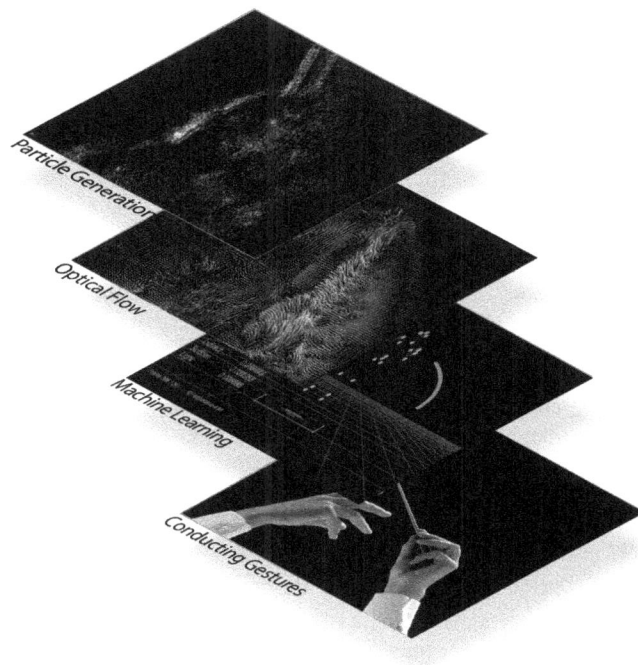

Figure 1. Express it!, a four-layer, machine-learning driven interactive visualization system.

C&C 2015, June 22–25, 2015, Glasgow, United Kingdom.
2015 ACM. ISBN 978-1-4503-3598-0/15/06$15.00
DOI: http://dx.doi.org/10.1145/2757226.2757243

Inspired by these characteristics of conducting gestures, many researchers have adopted the unique aspects of conducting gestures to develop interactive systems, driven by expressive, musical gestures. For instance, Mathew's Radio Baton is one pioneering attempt to control the musical tempo, dynamics, and expression of the music with expressive conductor-related gestures [18]. More directly, Nakra

[20] developed the Conductor's Jacket to capture and interpret physiological and motion information from musicians in order to better understand how they express affective and interpretive information while performing. Lee et al. [15] also created an interactive interface, iSymphony, that enables users to control the tempo, dynamics, and instrument emphasis of an electronic orchestra in a pre-rendered video clip by using three different baton techniques. However, little attention has been paid to quantifying, characterizing, and visualizing the expressiveness of conducting gestures themselves. Our work does exactly this: we use machine learning and other data analysis tools to drive a creative visualization of the data that is a personal yet informative reflection of the conductor's gestures and contributes to a better understanding and appreciation of the underlying meaning.

This uncharted territory is challenging due to several reasons: (i) there is no general framework for characterizing the expressive aspects of the conductor's gestures distinctly from the synchronization and signaling aspects; (ii) even given such a framework, it is not clear how to extract these expressive aspects automatically; (iii) once extracted, it is difficult to render them visually in a way that represents the key expressive features and does not merely duplicate the signaling content. In this paper, we contribute in each of these areas, but we focus on designing an interactive visualization system as an art form to represent the expressiveness of conducting gestures. We develop, inspired in part by LMA, a rudimentary framework to characterize the expressive gestures, then use a statistical template matching process to generate analytic data that is then visualized. Finally we show how it is apprehended by the audience at the exhibition.

EXPRESSIVITY IN CONDUCTORS' GESTURES

Even though conductors do not participate in producing a particular sound directly, they make a large number of diverse and often idiosyncratic physical signatures—by which we mean to include things such as facial expressions and body postures in addition to the usual hand and arm gestures—to deliver musical directions and expressions with their body movement at each moment. While some of these signatures are acquired by training in the conventional grammar of conducting—the latter including such elements as indicating beat placement and tempo through baton technique—the ways of communicating the expressive information tend to be more individual, *ad hoc*, and subjective.

Furthermore, conducting gestures, as a particular subset of musical gestures, contain intentions and the physical expressions of those intentions. Underlying these gestures are two tasks: First, the conductor maintains an inner-attitude that enables them to conceptualize their musical intention and translate it into gestures that are communicated to the ensemble musicians. Second, physical activity creates ongoing streams of information, enabling conductors to share their musical intention and to shape the playing of the orchestra. These nuanced gestures can include discrete events, such as an ictus to mark a temporal location, or continuously varying parameters, such as the moment-by-moment velocity or acceleration of the baton, etc. How does an observer, in the ensemble or

the audience, interpret these gestures? How can we describe a conductor's signatures in a way that allows us to extrapolate expressivity from them? To begin to answer these questions, we consider the conductor's gestures as existing along a continuum, such as the "Kendon's Continuum" defined by McNeil, [19]. See also [11]. In order to describe the characteristics of the gesture, many researchers in the musical domain have adapted the Kendon's Continuum to consider movement in the perspective of linguistics.

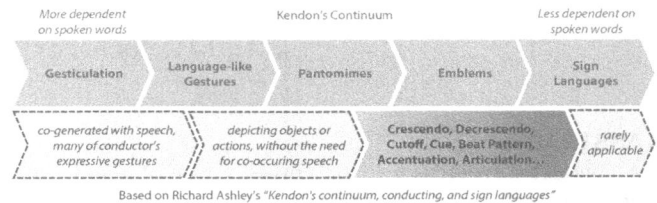

Figure 2. A diagram of the original Kendon's continuum and the musical analogue to Kendon's continuum.

Figure 2 illustrates how Kendon's Continuum can be reinterpreted in terms of expressiveness revealed in movement from the musical context [1].

This continuum proceeds from *Gesticulation* (motions that are merely related to and more-or-less synchronous with the semantic content—in McNeill's case speech, in our case music), to *Speech-framed Gestures*, to *Emblems* (which are signatures with a pre-existing conventional meaning–such as the beat patterns, accentuation, legato or staccato articulations, etc.),to *Pantomime*, to *Signs* (which are signatures with specific semantic content–such as, musically speaking, the sign for a cutoff at the end of a fermata, etc.). We focused mainly on the part of the continuum from gesticulation to emblems. While some progress has been made on very restrictive cases, we do not yet have a general theory of conducting gestures that will enable us to extract all the expressivity.

These *ad hoc* movements also incorporate a series of interrelated, yet separate streams of expression with the body. Referring to Kendon's Continuum, we can consider these types of gestures as conducting Emblems since these gestures create highly conventionalized, context-independent meanings that function as signs which can be 'read' by the musicians [7]. By using such emblemized gestures, conductors can efficiently (i.e., with little rehearsal or explaination) communicate some of their musical intentions to musicians. Simultaneously, conductors use body expressions as a medium to deliver expressive information, which is difficult to communicate solely through emblematic gestures. Revisiting Kendon's work, we can consider these gestures as having another dimension functioning as Gesticulation. According to McNeil, gesticulations are usually co-generated with speech, but having no conventional meanings and are highly dependent on context for their interpretation.

In addition to the above, we needed to keep in mind the spectrum of variability in individual conductor's approaches. For example, Lee [16] claimed that different conductors educated in different institutions and traditions, such as, Rudolf, Saito, and Green, will apply different gestural ideas, expressions, and technical principles, even for making simple 4/4 legato bean patterns. He also argued that conductors will greatly influence the orchestra and offer more nuanced and expressive performance as determined by his/her imaginative gestural interpretation. From a more practical, empirical perspective, Buck et al. pointed out that expressive musical gestures can be considered an affordance as well as a natural mediator between the mind and body movement [2]. They also believed that expressive gestures add extra-musical parameters to the audience's perception of music, creating a multi-modal experience wherein the visual affect of body movements are perceived as another means of communication. In addition, Jensenius et al. suggested the possibility of interpreting musical gestures as a body-mediated metaphor, meaning that gestures are able to function as conceptual objects that project physical movement, sound, or other types of perception to cultural topics [9].

Nevertheless, in order to extrapolate and visualize the expressiveness of conductors' gestures in a more generalized way, we needed a theory of meaning for movement that was related but distinct from the linguistic perspective of McNeil. For this, we turned to Laban Movement Analysis (LMA). For this work, we simplified and adapted elements of LMA, since it emphasizes an understanding of body movement as one aspect of a projection of an intentional process. Researchers in the field of LMA believe that the dynamics of the human body should be perceived as an outward expression of inner intent of the subject that eventually leads people to create phrases and relationships of movement that reveal personal, artistic, or cultural style.

It provides sophisticated languages and grammars that enabled us to observe and break down movement to the tiniest detail. Though LMA recognizes categories of Body, Effort, Shape, and Space (BESS), we focus here on Effort. Effort deals with the way the body moves: *"Every human movement is indissolubly linked with an effort, which is, indeed, it's origin and inner aspect. Effort and it's resulting action may be both unconscious and involuntary, but they are always present in any bodily movement."* [12]

The elements of Effort that we focus on are three of the fundamental motion factors: Space, Time, and Weight. These are each defined in terms of a continuum between two poles: Space goes from Direct at one extreme to Indirect motion at the other; Time goes between Sudden and Sustained; and Weight goes between Strong and Light. With this perspective, we created a simple low-level model of human movement that provided a baseline for representing the expressive content of the human body movement.

Charles Gambetta adopted the concept of Effort in the world of conducting in order to expose conductors to a more expansive range of movement possibilities for inspiration and exploration of their potential. In his dissertation, he used LMA to help four conductors in their training sessions. As a result, he reported that there were significant changes in movement choices [7]. With these promising results in mind, we prototyped a machine learning system to parameterize expressiv-

ity along the lines suggested by LMA, to see how elements of musical expression are represented in conductors' gestures and how they can be visualized to benefit conductors, musicians, and audiences.

DESIGNING AN INTERACTIVE SYSTEM

Motivation and Goal

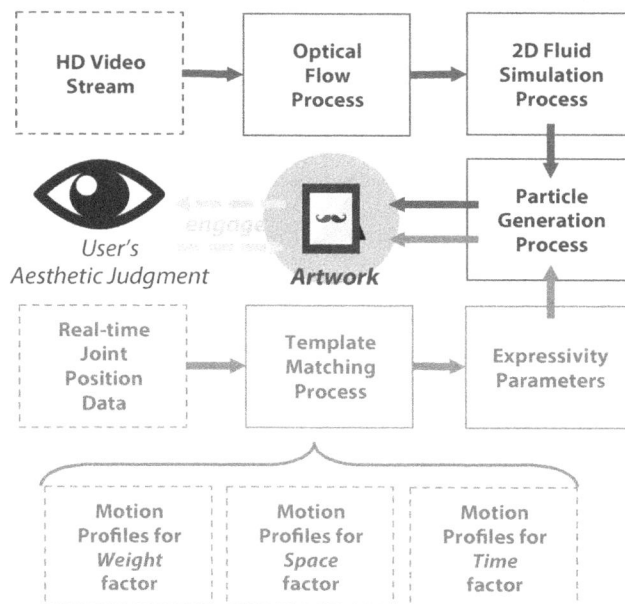

Figure 3. A flow diagram illustrating how the artwork is created by incorporating two processes, and how it is engaged with the user.

As we briefly described above, a conductor's gestures contain two different dimensions: intentions and expressions. It is difficult to discern the former from the physical manifestation of the latter. Yet, the wealth of expressive detail, combined with our intuition and personal experience of conducting, encouraged us to explore creative visual mappings of numerical data in order to evoke expressivity. We defined this interactive system as an artwork, rather than an interactive information visualization system, because our current focus is on aesthetic value rather than utility. By referring to the aesthetic value, we focused on visual style and experience as well as user input and feedback as Lau and Moere suggested in their domain model for information aesthetics [14]. We hope the artistic visualization techniques explored here facilitate the communication of meaning in a way that transcends analysis and affords the audience a deeper, intuitive appreciation of gestural interpretation. Figure 3 shows how our vision and technical specifications are intertwined in the artwork.

Design Process

We created a practical framework, as a design process, based on Camurri et al's conceptual frameworks [3], which enables capturing, processing, and visualizing expressivity in conducting gestures. Figure 4 illustrates how we built a framework on their concepts. The layers on the top show Camurri's four layered framework with our process highlighted in blue,

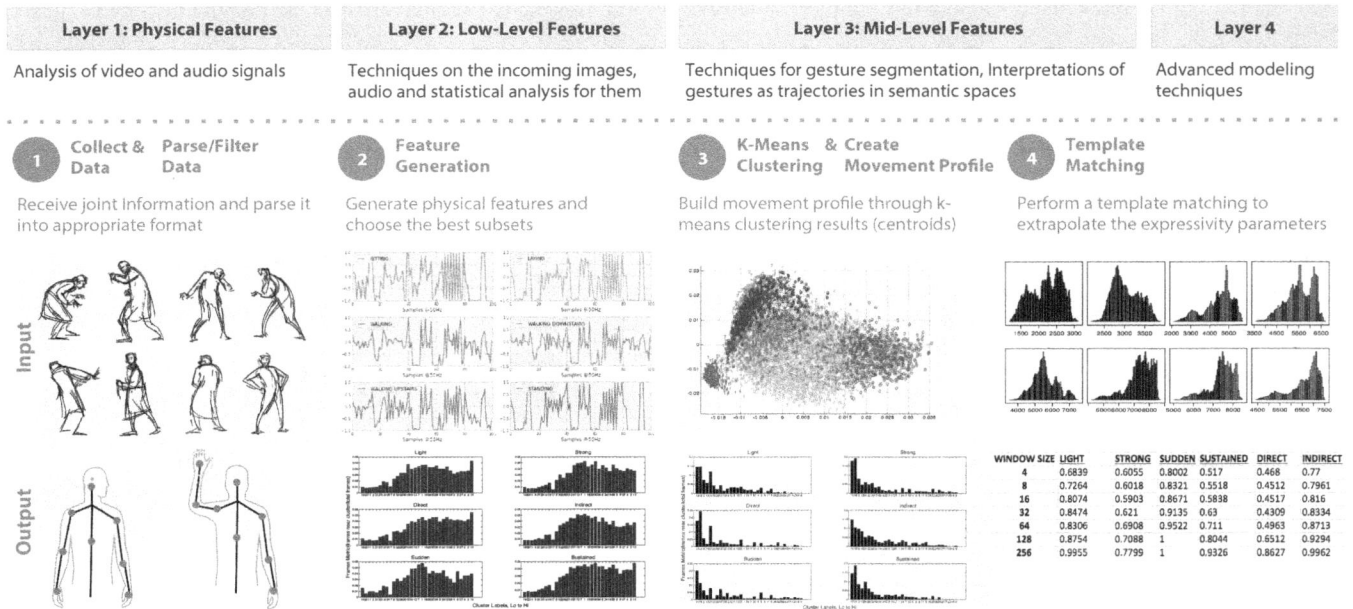

Layer 1: Physical Features	Layer 2: Low-Level Features	Layer 3: Mid-Level Features	Layer 4
Analysis of video and audio signals	Techniques on the incoming images, audio and statistical analysis for them	Techniques for gesture segmentation, Interpretations of gestures as trajectories in semantic spaces	Advanced modeling techniques

1 Collect & Parse/Filter Data Data — Receive joint Information and parse it into appropriate format

2 Feature Generation — Generate physical features and choose the best subsets

3 K-Means & Create Clustering Movement Profile — Build movement profile through k-means clustering results (centroids)

4 Template Matching — Perform a template matching to extrapolate the expressivity parameters

WINDOW SIZE	LIGHT	STRONG	SUDDEN	SUSTAINED	DIRECT	INDIRECT
4	0.6839	0.6055	0.8002	0.517	0.468	0.77
8	0.7264	0.6018	0.8321	0.5518	0.4512	0.7961
16	0.8074	0.5903	0.8671	0.5838	0.4517	0.816
32	0.8474	0.621	0.9135	0.63	0.4309	0.8334
64	0.8306	0.6908	0.9522	0.711	0.4963	0.8713
128	0.8754	0.7088	1	0.8044	0.6512	0.9294
256	0.9955	0.7799	1	0.9326	0.8627	0.9962

Figure 4. A four-layer framework for designing an interactive, machine-learning driven visualization system.

aligning each phase with Camurri's interpretation. In more detail, they proposed a conceptual, multi-layered framework for automatic expressive gesture analysis. In their work, expressive gestures are described using a set of motion features and the expressive contents from movement using advanced computational models. Inspired by Camurri's conceptual work, we built a four-phase design process: to collect data; generate features; perform k-means clustering to create a movement profile; perform template matching to extrapolate expressivity from the incoming movement data.

Building a Machine Learning Process

Winkler [28] pointed out that each part of the body has unique limitations in terms of direction, weight, range of motion, speed and force. The underlying physics of movement led us to the best representations of movement and its expressive capabilities. in this perspective, we computed basic physical features representing the conducting data by using positional coordinates extracted by the Kinect at 30 frames per second. The conductor's gesture was then denoted as an ordered sequence of these feature vectors, projected into classes by unsupervised clustering algorithm.

We clustered the data and generated characteristic templates for each motion factor from these clusters in order to design a machine learning process that enabled us to describe the characteristics of a conductor's movement. Clustering algorithms create a specified number of groups that maintain an internal coherence, yet are distinguishable from other groups. In other words, features within a cluster should be as similar as possible while features between clusters should be as dissimilar as possible. The initial clustering for our training datasets were based on velocity, the normalized dot product of successive velocity frames, and the combination of these

two features. For generating clusters, we used the K-means algorithm, which generates centroids that minimizes the average distance between features, thus grouping features with maximum similarity around these centroids [10]. We determined the cardinality of the clustering (the number of clusters; the 'K' of K-means) using a heuristic method. Empirically, we determined that 32 clusters demonstrated a good tradeoff between distinctive grouping between classes and efficient computation. The latter is important to consider in order to run the final algorithm in real time, capturing conducting gestures during a performance. Once the clusters are computed by the K-means algorithm, we arranged them from low to high velocity and generated a set of histograms. We referred to these ordered histograms as movement profiles. We then used movement profiles to perform a template matching process between training and testing data. The template matching process determined the similarity of test data based on the Euclidean distance between the learned movement profiles and the input movement profile. The input data is then classified as the movement profile that it is 'nearest' to, with distance inversely proportional to the similarity. By comparing the similarity, the computer classified the chunk of movement into one of six different categories: three motion factors of LMA in binary pairs. The template matching process is briefly visualized in Figure 6.

Creating a Generative Visualization Process

In its broadest sense, visualization is the process of making the invisible visible [4]. In more detail, Cox claims that *"The specific characteristics used to visually represent data – such as color, shape, scale, and movement, perform a semiotic function. They don't just inform; they signify."* By reflecting on that insight, we created digital representations communicating the meaning of gestures, invoking personal reflections to intensify the audience experience. From this perspective, we designed a generative visualization process which is illustrated in Figure 7.

From a design perspective, we were inspired by the visual work of tienne-Jules Marey and Gjon Mili, pioneers who attempted to capture sentient beings moving through both time and space.

Marey considered the human body an animate machine, and he dedicated his life to analyze the laws that governed its movements in a visual way. Mili used stroboscopic light to capture the motion of everything from dancers to jugglers in a single exposure. Their works depicted how the movement is being unfolded in space in one single frame. In their artwork, the subject's movement shows delicate relationships from the beginning to the end.

From a more technical perspective, were inspired by interactive artworks that adopt a generative visualization process. The optical flow algorithm (Horn-Shunk) which was used in Sand and Teller's Video Matching [23] to generate optical markers that represented the differences between two scenes acted as a primary inspiration. Shiffman's Reactive [24] was a good example of how to design a particle systems. Forbes [6] showed how interactive fluid simulation and vector visualization techniques can be utilized for media arts projects. Based on these artworks, we created a generative visualization process that enabled the audience to view the expressivity of a conductor's movement.

Our generative approach adopted a 2D fluid simulation controlled in part by video image and expressivity parameters derived from the template matching. To put energy into the 2D fluid simulation process, we first computed motion vectors (velocity and density) from the input video through the optical flow (the first row in Figure 7). Then we delivered the result to the 2D fluid simulation process to manipulate factors of the fluid (the second row). The expressivity parameters, generated from the template matching process, drive the whole visualization. In Figure 5, we can see the influence of high effort (top) and low effort (bottom) on our visualization.

Implementation

Based on this machine learning process and inspirations, we designed an interactive system using two inputs and one output for visualization. One input was from the Microsoft Kinect, tracking the movements of the two arms in order to perform the template matching process. The other was receiving video from an HD camera, capturing a base scene that was transformed into particle images.

With the Kinect input, the template matching process continuously computes histograms and generates three motion factors as expressivity parameters. At the same time, the visualization process generates particle images based on a low-resolution replication of the original video input. The parameters extrapolated from the machine learning process drive

the overall visualization system. The software was created using the Model-Viewer-Controller (MVC) design pattern [26]. This concept allowed us to separate modeling, presentation, and action easily. The model managed the behavior and data responding to requests for information about its state and instructions from the controller. The overall system was built in Max6, which was responsible for receiving data, extracting features, and performing machine learning. The visualization is composed in the Quartz Composer using OpenGL and is responsible for generating the particle system. Lastly, the controller, which interprets the conductor's movement, is designed in Visual C++ and informs the model to change appropriately using the Microsoft official Kinect SDK to receive/send the skeletal data via OSC (Open Sound Control) [29].

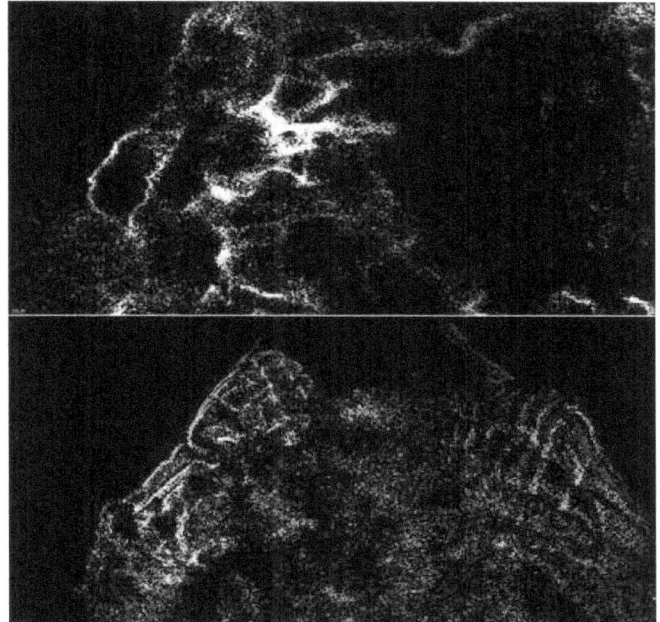

Figure 5. The screen capture of two sample visualization results: (top) the visualization with the efforts factor (strong, indirect, sustained). (bottom) the visualization with the efforts factor (light, direct, sustained).

INSTALLATION AND USER STUDIES

User Study Design

Prior attempts to observe how interactive visualizations or performances are perceived by the audience have been based on qualitative feedback from the audience, case studies, and analysis from the domain expert perspective [25][8] [13]. Starting from these evaluation methods, we evaluated the quality of our system's user experience in terms of engagement, defined by O'Brien et al. [21] as: *"desirable even essential human response to computer-mediated activities."* They suggested that engagement is heavily influenced by the user interface, its associated process flow, the user's context, value system, and incentives. In their work, they described the process of engagement as consisting of four distinct stages: point of engagement, period of sustained engagement, disengagement, and re-engagement. They explained

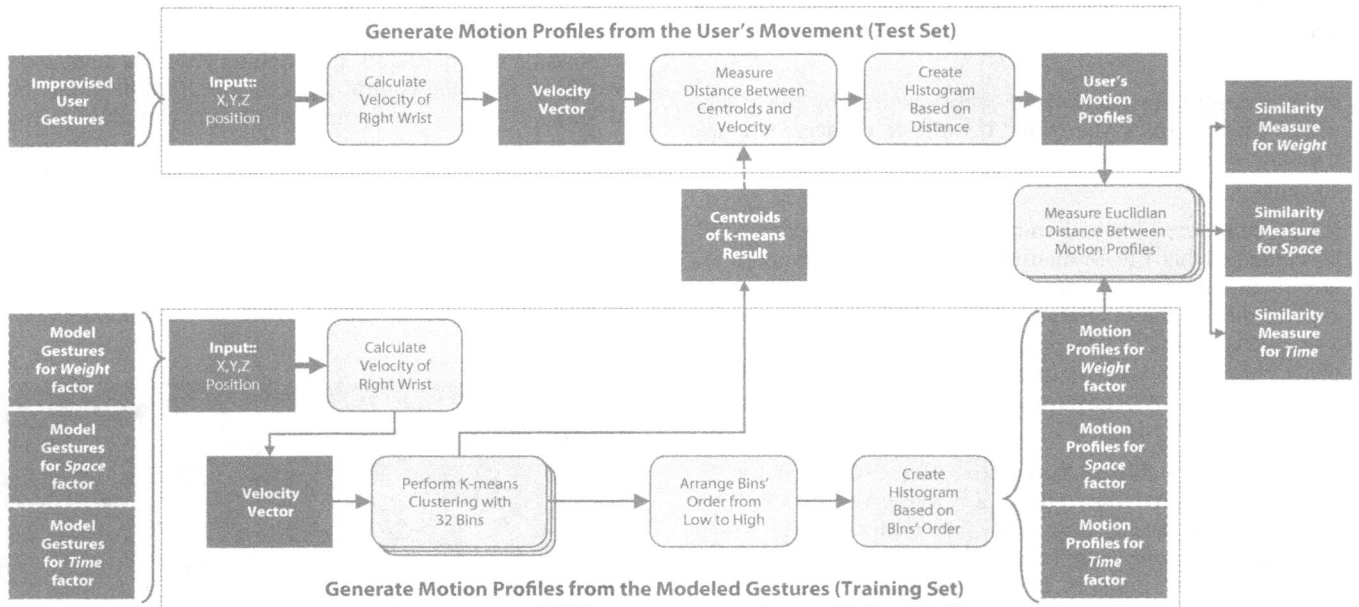

Figure 6. The flow diagram which is depicting how the template machine process is initiated, performed, and extrapolate, the expressivity as parameters to drive the visualization, from the body movement. The rounded rectangle illustrates each process while each filled rectangle represents an outcome.

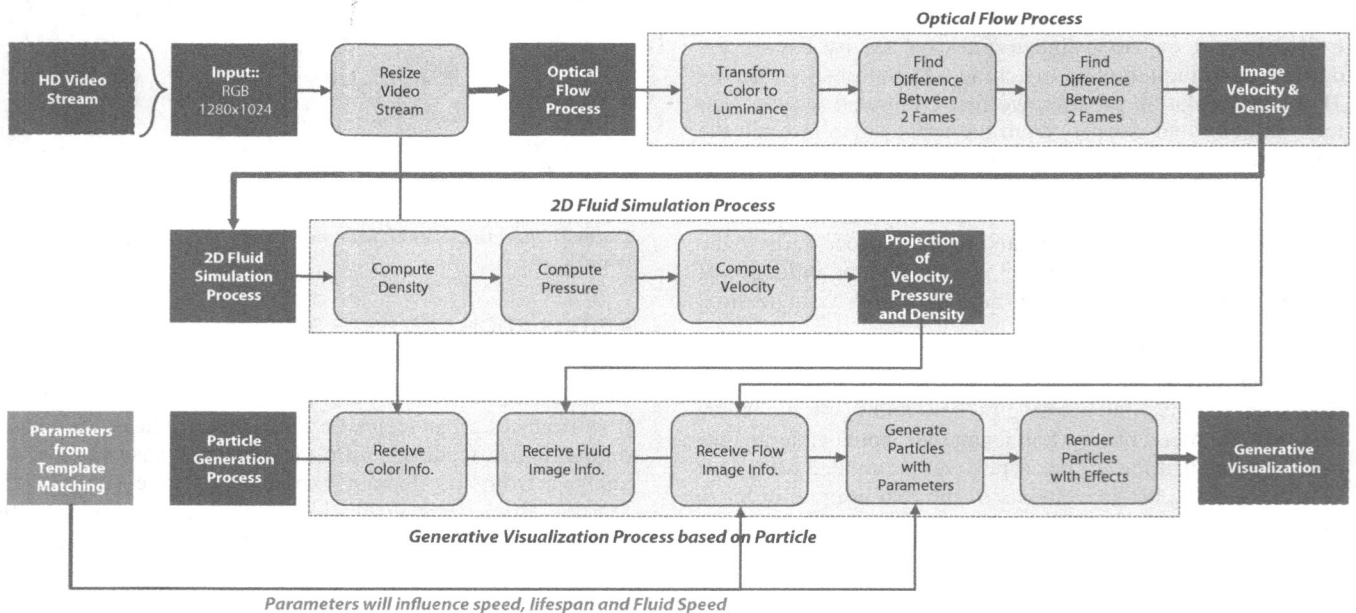

Figure 7. The flow diagram which is depicting how the generative visualization process is processed and rendered with the expressivity parameters extrapolated from the template matching process. The rounded rectangle illustrates each process while each filled rectangle represents an outcome. Note that rectangle and line colored in the dark cyan represents how the expressivity parameters intervene the generative visualization process.

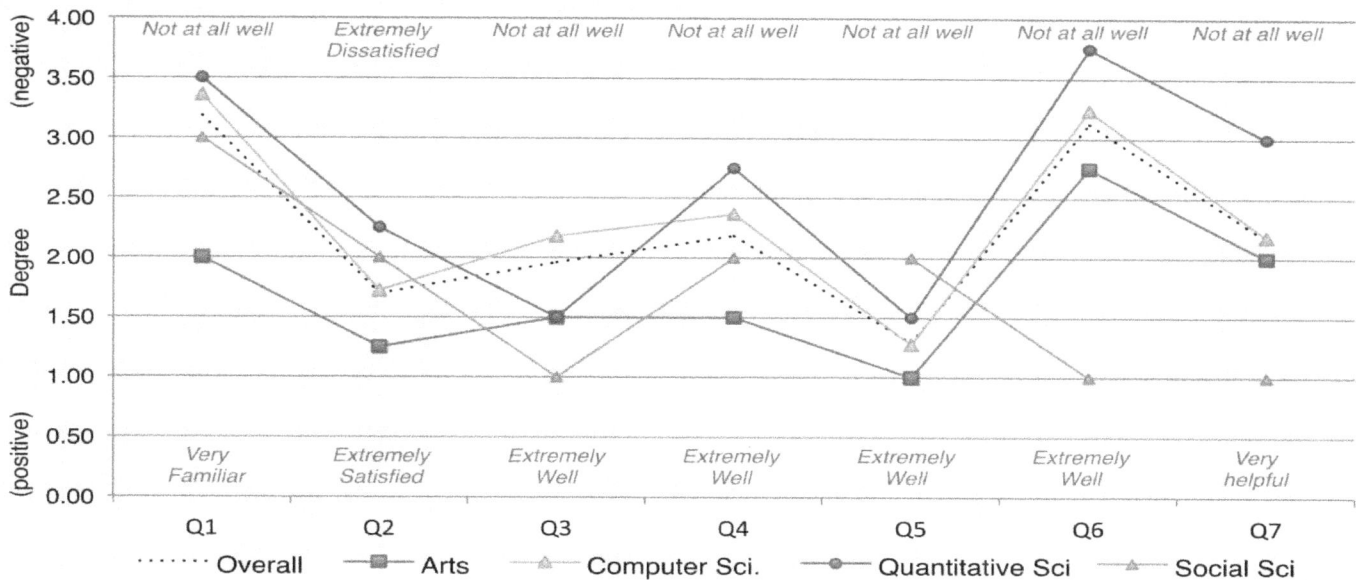

Figure 8. The responses from the different user groups. The x-axis represents the question number from 1 to 5. The y-axis represents the 5-point-scale. Each line shows how different user groups responded to each questions.

that the *point of engagement* described how participants' experiences began. They described the *period of engagement* as the participants' focus on their task and its interface. During this period, the participants' experiences the interactive system and continuously evaluates it based on the novelty of the experience, their level of interest, and their perceptions of challenge, feedback, and user control. The *disengagement* stage explains why participants stops the activity, or which factors in the participants' external environment caused them to stop or to proceed to a *re-engagement*. They suggested several attributes to evaluate these stages such as aesthetics, novelty, interest(curiosity), interactivity, or feedback. We adopted these three stages of engagement and its attributes to set up criteria for evaluating our artwork. With the notion of engagement, we designed a questionnaire of eleven questions using a 5-point scale. Q1, Q2, and Q3 were formed in order to evaluate the user's *point of engagement*, in terms of the category of the aesthetics, novelty, interests, and motivation. Q4, Q5, and Q6 were designed to address which types of engagement factors could arouse the user's engagement most. Q7 was designed to see whether the user could find any sense of utility or experiential goal while he or she was experiencing the artwork.

- Q1. How familiar are you with a conductor's role in an orchestra?

- Q2. What's your first impression to this visualization?

- Q3. Overall, are you satisfied with the visualization?

- Q4. How well, if at all, does the word "INNOVATIVE" describe this visualization?

- Q5. How well, if at all, does the word "AESTHETIC" describe this visualization?

- Q6. How well, if at all, does the word "INFORMATIVE" describe this visualization?

- Q7. How well do you feel the visualization helps you to evoke expressiveness in conducting gestures?

In the meantime, Q8, Q9, and Q10 were designed to address the attributes which might cause *disengagement* for the user. Finally, Q11 was also given to the users in order to have direct feedbacks or responses that were not covered through the survey just in case.

- Q8. If it DOES help you to evoke expressiveness in conducting gesture, what are the top two things you generally consider? Check two boxes among five selections: Abstraction of image; Fluid particle effects/motions; Interactivity (Gesture tracking via Kinect); Sound elements; The way of Installation in the venue.

- Q9. If it DOES NOT help you to evoke expressiveness in conducting gesture, what are the top two things you generally consider? Check two boxes among five selections: Abstraction of image; Complexity in fluid particle effects/motions; Lack of interactivity (need more interactivity); Lack of audio effect (need more audio); The way of Installation in the venue; Lack of explicit explanation

- Q10. If you're improving this visualization, what are the top two things you consider? Check top two things among five selections: Using more concrete/metaphorical objects (snow, fire, wind, rain, rock); Adding more concrete/metaphorical background; Adding sound/audio effects to indicate some aspect of gestures; Adding background music with the installation, Using more color and textures.

- Q11. In your own words, what are the things that you would most like to improve in this visualization?

147

User Studies at the Exhibition

In November, 2014, we exhibited our artwork at the IEEE VIS 2014 conference which was held in Paris, France to meet diverse audiences across disciplines and observe their response [17]. At the exhibition, we explained the concept and the way of experiencing the artwork briefly before the users interacted with it. After they experienced the artwork, we asked them to answer the questionnaire via Google survey anonymously. No incentives were given. We had more than 200 visitors at the exhibition. Among them, 32 participants voluntarily participated in the survey. We asked them to indicate their background in the beginning of the survey in order to analyze how different subject groups experienced the visualization. The result of the user study is shown in Figure 8.

Based on these questions, we had interesting responses from the users of different backgrounds or research interests. (Q1) the overall user group showed that they were neither familiar nor unfamiliar with the conductor's role (M=3.19, STD=1.37). Some of them were answered that they have seen the conductors on the stage or on the broad casting media. (Q2) Their first impression of the work was quite positive (M=1.70, STD=0.78). They felt extremely satisfied about the quality. (Q3) However, there was a slight disagreement from the computer science group in terms of the satisfaction measure. One of the major reasons that they showed disagreement was that they felt the visualization was too complex.

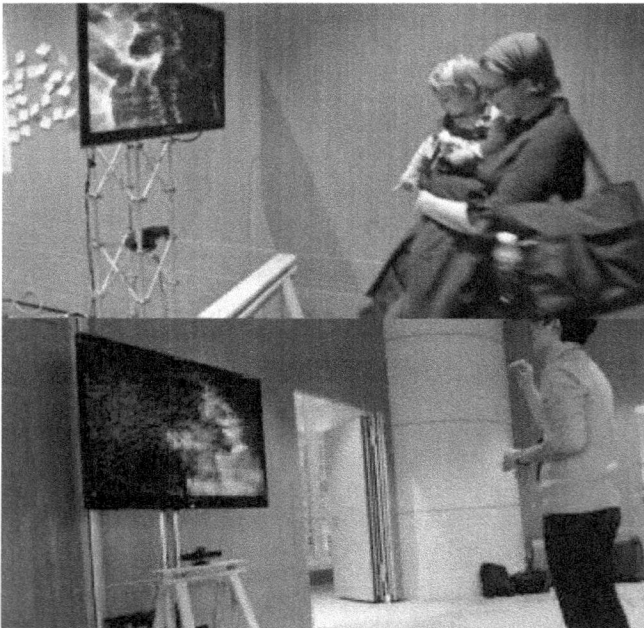

Figure 9. Users who are interacting with a relatively high level of engagement.

(Q4) Many of people showed excitement and evaluated the work as innovative approach (M=1.96, STD=1.08). However, people from the computer science group said that visualization is frequently used in their domain, so it did not seem innovative to them. (Q5) As the author hoped, all participants agreed that the work has its own aesthetic value,

Figure 10. Users who are interacting with a relatively low level of engagement.

illustrating expressivity of movement; this question showed the lowest standard deviation among all questions (M=1.29, STD=0.46). (Q6) Meanwhile, participants felt the the particle system did not provide enough information. (Q7) In general, the participants indicated that the visualization could help the audience better understanding the expressive contents in conducting gestures (M=2.16, STD=1.05). Since this question had one of the highest standard deviation, we inferred that participants experienced some conflict between the visualization's aesthetic quality and utility. Participants expressed that Fluid particle effects/motions and Interactivity (Gesture tracking via Kinect) are the most impactful factors to evoke expressiveness in conducting gestures.

(Q8) However, participants had difficulty understanding the visualization due to it being very abstract and without audio feedback. They suggested that we should use more concrete/metaphorical objects for visualization and sound/audio effects in order to indicate movement. Some asked for an explicit explanation besides the visualization.

DISCUSSION

It was our hope to design an interactive artwork that enabled the audience to witness the expressive contents in their movement through a generative visualization that used machine learning. Through the installation and the exhibition, we believe we showed how experimental interactive artworks can prompt an audience to actively investigate their movement and ponder its meaning. With the generative visualization, audiences tried to explore and make meaningful trajectories in a creative way. With the concept of user engagement and observations from the exhibition, we extracted three insights: *different levels of engagement, creative exploration with aesthetic interaction,* and *self-reflection behavior.*

As we can see in Figure 9 and 10, users from different disciplines showed different levels of engagement. According to our result, users who have an arts related background were actively engaged. They attempted to make movements that explored the limits of the visualization. These users expressed extreme satisfaction towards the artwork and showed interest in the abstract aspect of the visualization as well as its generative algorithm. Meanwhile, users who expressed a relatively low intensity were mostly focused in computer science/engineering or quantitative science backgrounds. In many cases, they seemed to try 'reading' the artwork, emphasizing its technical aspects. For this reason, we inferred that they marked relatively lower scores in the questions measuring innovativeness and aesthetic value due to the technologies not meeting their technical expectations.

Nevertheless, our audience generally expressed very high levels of satisfaction experiencing the artwork. They also showed interest in the aesthetic value of the visualization regarding creative exploration. The results confirmed that the audience was willing to engage the interactive artwork with high intensity even though the theme, concept, and utility were less clear. By exploring the artwork, the audience became more engaged with the concept, technical background, and the way of visualizing movements, asking diverse questions at the venue. Our observations and user study results support the claims of Petersen et al.'s [22] that the goal of aesthetic interaction can go beyond usability and usefulness, and it will promote curiosity, engagement, and imagination in the exploration of an interactive system. We also found that the O'Brien's model of engagement can be a good measure to observe and describe the quality of the user experience.

One last interesting implication concerns self-reflective behavior. Even though the artwork was motivated by the conductor's gestures, the audience did not use their gestures to mimic conducting. They engaged the artwork with quasi-conducting gestures but progressed to different gestures reflecting their thoughts and feelings in order to see how the visualization would reflect and transform their abstract ideas into a visual dimension. In the study of AnyType, Devendorf and Ryokai [5] suggested that their subjects tended to reflect their thoughts on capturing and creating types with the application. We observed similar behaviors at the exhibition. We tentatively conclude that the lack of control, interactivity (in terms of direct manipulation), and awareness could cause negative affects toward the work; if the user cannot create expected results within the space, they become disengaged.

CONCLUSION

Conductors put tremendous effort into gesturally communicating the imagined-ideal of a composer's intentions to an ensemble, much of which is difficult for the audience to see. In this project, we presented a creative way of visualizing the expressiveness of gestures in the form of an interactive artwork, inspired by conducting gestures. We synthesized two approaches for our work. The first approach used a generative visualization method to enable a robust amplification of expressive contents in gestures by using the optical flow and 2D fluid simulation with the particle generating system. The

second approach used template matching, which enabled us to extrapolate the expressivity from the movement and classify them into the 6 categories from the perspective of Laban Movement Analysis (LMA) theory. With the interactive visualization, an audience was invited to perform their own conducting gestures in order to witness how the expressivity in movement can be revealed visually.

As a result, our project allowed us to observe how different audiences engage interactive artwork and how they explore a creative space to generate meaningful visualizations. Based on the observations, we developed three key insights into user interaction concerning different levels of engagement, creative exploration with aesthetic interaction, and self reflection. We could see how the artwork combined with cutting-edge technologies can support individual's creative pursuits. We expect that the impact of visualization will be increased if we could: (i) collect many more movement data from subjects so that we can create more generalized movement profiles; (ii) build a more robust machine learning process that is able to provide better classification results; (iii) create a simple yet impactful mapping that will reduce the complexity in visualization.

ACKNOWLEDGMENTS
We would like to thank the researchers that participated in the MovingStories project in Canada. We also appreciate for the 2014 IEEE VISAP program since it provided a wonderful venue for selected artists to meet the best audience from related fields. We would like to thank Mohammad Amanzadeh and Yishuo Liu for their discussions and critiques.

REFERENCES
1. Ashley, R. The pragmatics of conducting: Analyzing and interpreting conductors' expressive gestures. In *Sixth International Conference on Music Perception and Cognition*, ICMPC'00 (2000).

2. Buck, B., MacRitchie, J., and Bailey, N. J. The interpretive shaping of embodied musical structure in piano performance. *Empirical Musicology Review 8*, 2 (2013), 92–119.

3. Camurri, A., Volpe, G., Poli, G. D., and Leman, M. Communicating expressiveness and affect in multimodal interactive systems. *IEEE Multimedia 12*, 1 (2005), 43–53.

4. Cox, D. J. *Astral Projection: Theories of Metaphor, Philosophies of Science, and the Art of Scientific Visualization.* PhD thesis, University of Plymouth, 2008.

5. Devendorf, L., and Ryokai, K. AnyType: provoking reflection and exploration with aesthetic interaction. In *Proceedings of the SIGCHI Conference on Human Factors in Computing Systems*, ACM (2013), 1041–1050.

6. Forbes, A. G., Höllerer, T., and Legrady, G. Generative fluid profiles for interactive media arts projects. In *Proceedings of the Symposium on Computational Aesthetics*, CA'13, ACM (2013), 37–43.

7. Gambetta, C. L. *Conducting outside the box: Creating a fresh approach to conducting gesture through the principles of Laban Movement Analysis*. D.m.a., University of North Carolina at Greensboro, 2005.

8. James, J., Ingalls, T., Qian, G., Olsen, L., Whiteley, D., Wong, S., and Rikakis, T. Movement-based interactive dance performance. In *Proceedings of the 14th annual ACM international conference on Multimedia*, MM'06 (2006), 470–480.

9. Jensenius, A. R., Wanderley, M. M., God\øy, R. I., and Leman, M. *Musical gestures: Concepts and methods in research*. Routledge, 2010.

10. Kanungo, T., Mount, D. M., Netanyahu, N. S., Piatko, C. D., Silverman, R., and Wu, A. Y. An efficient k-means clustering algorithm: Analysis and implementation. *Pattern Analysis and Machine Intelligence, IEEE Transactions on 24*, 7 (2002), 881–892.

11. Kendon, A. Do gestures communicate? a review. *Research on Language & Social Interaction 27*, 3 (1994), 175–200.

12. Laban, R. v. *The Mastery of Movement on the Stage*. Macdonald and Evans, 1950.

13. Latulipe, C., Carroll, E. A., and Lottridge, D. Evaluating longitudinal projects combining technology with temporal arts. In *Proceedings of the SIGCHI Conference on Human Factors in Computing Systems*, CHI '11, ACM (2011), 1835–1844.

14. Lau, A., and Moere, A. V. Towards a model of information aesthetics in information visualization. In *Information Visualization, 2007. IV'07. 11th International Conference of*, IV'07 (2007), 87–92.

15. Lee, E., Kiel, H., Dedenbach, S., Grüll, I., Karrer, T., Wolf, M., and Borchers, J. iSymphony: An adaptive interactive orchestral conducting system for digital audio and video streams. In *CHI '06 Extended Abstracts on Human Factors in Computing Systems*, CHI EA '06, ACM (2006), 259–262.

16. Lee, K. *Towards an Improved Baton Technique: The Application and Modification of Conducting Gestures Drawn from the Methods of Rudolf, Green and Saito for Enhanced Performance of Orchestral Interpretations*. D.m.a dissertation, The University of Arizona, 2008.

17. Lee, K. Visualizing expressiveness in conducting gestures. *Proceedings of the IEEE VIS 2014 Arts Program* (2014).

18. Mathews, M. V. The radio baton and conductor program, or: Pitch, the most important and least expressive part of music. *Computer Music Journal* (1991), 37–46.

19. McNeill, D. *Gesture and thought*. University of Chicago Press, 2008.

20. Nakra, T. A. M. Toward an understanding of musical gesture: Mapping expressive intention with the digital baton. Master's thesis, Massachusetts Institute of Technology, Program in Media Arts & Sciences, 1996.

21. O'Brien, H. L., and Toms, E. G. What is user engagement? a conceptual framework for defining user engagement with technology. *Journal of the American Society for Information Science & Technology 59*, 6 (2008), 938–955.

22. Petersen, M.G., I. O. K. P., and Ludvigsen, M. Aesthetic interaction: a pragmatist's aesthetics of interactive systems. In *Proceedings of the 5th conference on Designing interactive systems: processes, practices, methods, and techniques*, DIS'04 (2004).

23. Sand, P., and Teller, S. Video matching. In *ACM SIGGRAPH 2004 Papers*, SIGGRAPH '04, ACM (2004), 592–599.

24. Shiffman, D. Reactive. In *ACM SIGGRAPH 2004 Emerging Technologies*, SIGGRAPH '04, 22–.

25. Subyen, P., Maranan, D., Schiphorst, T., Pasquier, P., and Bartram, L. EMVIZ: the poetics of movement quality visualization. In *Proceedings of the International Symposium on Computational Aesthetics in Graphics, Visualization, and Imaging* (2011), 121–128.

26. Veit, M., and Herrmann, S. Model-view-controller and object teams: A perfect match of paradigms. In *Proceedings of the 2nd international conference on Aspect-oriented software development*, ACM (2003), 140–149.

27. Wakin, D. J. Breaking conductors' down by gesture and body part, 2012.

28. Winkler, T. Making motion musical: Gesture mapping strategies for interactive computer music. In *Proceedings of the International Computer Music Conference*, ICMC'95 (1995), 261–264.

29. Wright, M. Open sound control: an enabling technology for musical networking. *Organised Sound 10*, 3 (2005), 193–200.

#Scanners: Integrating Physiology into Cinematic Experiences

Matthew Pike
The Mixed Reality Lab
The University of Nottingham
Pike@nottingham.ac.uk

Richard Ramchurn
AlbinoMosquito
AlbinoMosquito, Manchester
Richard@albinomosquito.com

Max L. Wilson
The Mixed Reality Lab
The University of Nottingham
Max.Wilson@nottingham.ac.uk

ABSTRACT

In this paper we present #Scanners, a digital arts installation that aims to bridge the gap between digital arts and neuroscience. #Scanners is an experience in which an individual wears a wireless brain scanners whilst being presented media which is dynamically affected by the individuals physiology. A prototype system has been successfully trialled on roughly 100 users over the past 18 months and has received unanimously positive feedback. We state the minimal additional requirements for demonstrating a Higher Fidelity prototype system and argue the value of including #Scanners at C&C2015.

Author Keywords

BCI; Digital Arts; EEG; Physiology; Adaptive Media

ACM Classification Keywords

H.5.1. Multimedia Information Systems: Artificial, augmented, and virtual realities

INTRODUCTION

#Scanners is an interactive visual arts installation that aims to bridge the gap between digital arts and neuroscience. Using a wireless brain scanner, #Scanners allows the user to manipulate the displayed film and associated audio. Narratives and layers can be built that are all governed by the users concentration and meditation levels.

The motivation for this work is based on the work of Shinji Nishimoto and the writing of Walter Murch. Nishimotos et. al demonstrated the ability to reconstruct a participants visual experience (displayed patterns) using just an fMRI, and thus demonstrated the potential to visualise other visual experiences [3]. This potential provides evidence that future work may allow for an individual to view their dreams for example, which led us to thinking of how we could synthesis this experience using media. Expanding on this, Walter Murch stated, in his book"In the Blink of an Eye":

C&C 2015, June 22–25, 2015, Glasgow, United Kingdom.
ACM 978-1-4503-3598-0/15/06.
http://dx.doi.org/10.1145/2757226.2764546

"If it is true that our rates and rhythms of blinking refer directly to the rhythm and sequence of our inner emotions and thoughts, then those rates and rhythms are insights to our inner selves and therefore as characteristic of each of us as our signatures."

In addition to stating the role of blinking in expressing our inner emotions and thoughts, Murch also likens film to dream, thoughts to a shot and a blink to a cut, a set of relations we're interested in exploring with #Scanners.

Several existing works have used a similar approach of manipulating media according to an individuals physiology. Hillard et. al, for example varied a films brightness, size and continuation according to the participants physiology (measured via an EEG brain monitoring device) [1]. This form of neurofeedback with film was shown to be successful during focus and attention training for ADHD sufferers. Theta Labs[1], was an electronic arts installation by the Australian artist George Khut, in which electronic soundscapes were dynamically controlled by changes in participants Alpha and Theta brainwave activity, with the effect being likened to lucid dreaming. Similarly, Carlos Castellanos presented the "Biomorphic Aggregator"[2] a bio-responsive network data collection and visualization system where participants physiology is used to affect a data visualisation.

PROTOTYPE SYSTEM

A prototype system was developed utilising a commercially available EEG headset (Neurosky Mindwave[3]) to inform the mixing of an audio/visual based multimedia experience. The system (Shown in Figure1) comprises of a Laptop upon which the multimedia is presented and the mixing of the experience is performed, an iPad which is used to control and setup the experience (not handled by the user), a Neurosky EEG headband for blink/emotional state detection and headphones. The system uses blink, meditative and concentration data from the EEG device to affect the users experience, changing the audio mix, audio rhythm and edit points of a film accordingly.

The system was setup such that the films edit was dictated by the combination blink and concentration data. When sufficiently engaged (High Concentration) in the presented visual media , a users blinking would advance the film to the next scene. A combination of the users meditation and concentration levels and their relative changes would dictate the audio

---

[1] http://georgekhut.com/theta-lab/
[2] http://ccastellanos.com/projects/biomorphic_aggregator/
[3] http://neurosky.com/

Figure 1. The components of the prototype system (left to right), WiFi router, Portable Hardrive with multimedia, Neurosky EEG Headband, Headphones, Laptop for viewing and iPad for controlling the experience.

track played to the user. We intentionally did not classify audio tracks according to emotional states, as we wanted to give the effect of audio mixing rather than reflecting an emotional state, tracks were therefore randomly assigned but were triggered by relative changes in user state.

Deployment

The system was piloted at 4 events (W00t festival, Copenhagen 2013; Manchester University Faculty of Science open day; Anonymous Studio, Manchester and IIEX 2015), which engaged with roughly 100 individuals of a broad demographic between the ages of 12 to 60. The pilot was conducted informally as a feedback gathering exercise where participants would first engage with the system and then would informally reflect on their experience in a conversational setting with the authors.

Figure 2. A user interacting with the prototype system.

The feedback from users of the system was unanimously positive, with many likening the experience to being *"like a dream"*. One user described the experience as being hypnotic - *"It felt like I went into a hypnotic state, quite surreal but I feel quite enlightened"*, whilst others commented on the feeling of being relaxed - *"...it felt meditative like I was drifting in*

and out". Many also describe a feeling of consciousness, saying the experience *"makes you aware of your mind"* and that it *"allows you to create your own experience"* as well as being *"more immersive than Virtual Reality"* . To balance this however some users did report feeling very "involved" and described prolonged periods of high concentration without necessarily engaging with the experience.

CREATIVITY AND COGNITION

We believe #Scanners to be an appropriate demonstration of the fusion between cognitive technology and creativity. Based on the feedback from people who have already experienced the prototype system, dreaming was by far the most common comparison drawn by users of the system. Walter Murch states that aside from film, dreams are the only other time that you experience discontinuous cuts in time and space [2].

Many users wondered how the film was being composed and to what degree were they involved in the process. Some users thought they were personally responsible for the image being displayed, whereas others attempted to consciously direct the film through their emotional state. We believe that this finding identifies the importance of appropriately describing the system prior to a user engaging in an experience. We found that describing preciously how the system operated resulted in users simply using the system as an input to dictate the cut. Whereas telling users to engross themselves in the experience resulted in some users trying to infer the operation of the system, instead of experiencing the system.

Finally, there was general approval of interacting with the system. No participants reported directly feeling intimated or being uncomfortable during the experience, but further work on understanding preciously how wearing the device during such circumstances affects an individual. We can draw on the Reactivity phenomenon from Psychology for example to attempt to model how viewers may feel or react to being monitored.

REFERENCES

1. Hillard, B., El-Baz, A. S., Sears, L., Tasman, A., and Sokhadze, E. M. Neurofeedback Training Aimed to Improve Focused Attention and Alertness in Children With ADHD A Study of Relative Power of EEG Rhythms Using Custom-Made Software Application. *Clinical EEG and neuroscience 44*, 3 (2013), 193–202.

2. Murch, W. *In the blink of an eye: A perspective on film editing.* Silman-James Press, 2001.

3. Nishimoto, S., Vu, A. T., Naselaris, T., Benjamini, Y., Yu, B., and Gallant, J. L. Reconstructing visual experiences from brain activity evoked by natural movies. *Current Biology 21*, 19 (2011), 1641–1646.

[self.]: an Interactive Art Installation that Embodies Artificial Intelligence and Creativity: A Demonstration

Axel Tidemann
Department of Computer Science
Norwegian University of Science and Technology
Trondheim, Norway
tidemann@idi.ntnu.no

Øyvind Brandtsegg
Department of Music
Norwegian University of Science and Technology
Trondheim, Norway
oyvind.brandtsegg@ntnu.no

ABSTRACT

This demonstration paper describes [self.], an open source art installation that embodies artificial intelligence in order to learn, react, respond and be creative in its environment. Biologically inspired models are implemented to achieve this behaviour. The robot is built using a moving head, projector, camera and microphones. No form of knowledge or grammar have been implemented in the AI, the entity learns everything via its own sensory channels, forming categories in a bottom-up fashion. The robot recognizes sounds, and is able to recognize similar sounds, link them with the corresponding faces, and use the knowledge of past experiences to form new sentences. It projects neural memories that represent an association between sound and video as experienced during interaction.

Author Keywords

Artificial Intelligence; Interactive; Robot

ACM Classification Keywords

I.2.6 Learning: Connectionism and neural nets, Knowledge acquisition; I.2.9 Robotics

BACKGROUND

The project started out as an attempt to conceptualize what the effect of AI will have on society in the general case, and how artificially intelligent machines will interact with human beings. As an artwork, [self.] plays on the relationship between technology and humans, and relates to language, philosophy and the contemporary (over-)focus on self realization.

MATERIALS AND METHODS

Both the source code as well as building instructions have been published online[1]. The overall architecture can be seen in Figure 1. The robot was built by modifying an off-the-shelf moving head for stage lighting, stripping it for all components

---

[1] www.github.com/axeltidemann/self_dot

except the motors. A video projector, USB camera, 2 microphones and a small speaker was mounted on the remaining motorized frame. The USB camera and speaker was mounted on the projector pointing in the opposite direction of the lens. This made it possible for the person interacting with [self.] to be in focus of the camera and observe the visual output at the same time, as can be seen in Figure 1. Two microphones were mounted in a simple X-Y stereo configuration, for the purpose of sensing the horizontal position of the sound source.

The robot uses a Kalman filter to do face tracking. Sound processing is done with Csound[2]. A biologically inspired model of the inner ear [4] is used to analyze the recorded WAVE files. Since the robot also records video in addition to sound, it adds to its expressional capacity being able to project visual memories related to the interaction. In order to make the robot seem more "alive", the visual representations are an association between audio and visual input. This is achieved by using neural networks, more specifically Echo State Networks (ESNs) [3]. Motor control is inspired by Brooks' subsumption architecture [1]. There are two mechanisms that trigger movement of the robot, 1) face tracking and 2) sound. Face tracking seeks to move the robot directly in front of the person speaking to it. The sound movement triggers are based on a stereo perception of where the sound comes from.

[self.] learns a multi-modal episodic memory of each interaction, building an audio-visual memory. The robot then clusters similar sounds together. The robot also recognizes faces, which influences how new phrases are generated. The sequence of sounds and the corresponding faces builds up a web of associations that is used to create output phrases, which it contructs by finding the most similar sound in its audio-visual memory, and making combinations and associations within previous experiences.

After finding the most similar sound and generating the response, the visual response of the robot is made, created by the ESN. This yields a visual output that is almost guaranteed to never be the same; the similarity of the training sound compared to the novel sound will determine the output characteristics. For instance, a novel sound that is very similar to the original training sound will yield a sequence of images that are quite similar to the original, whereas sounds that are

---

[2] www.csounds.com

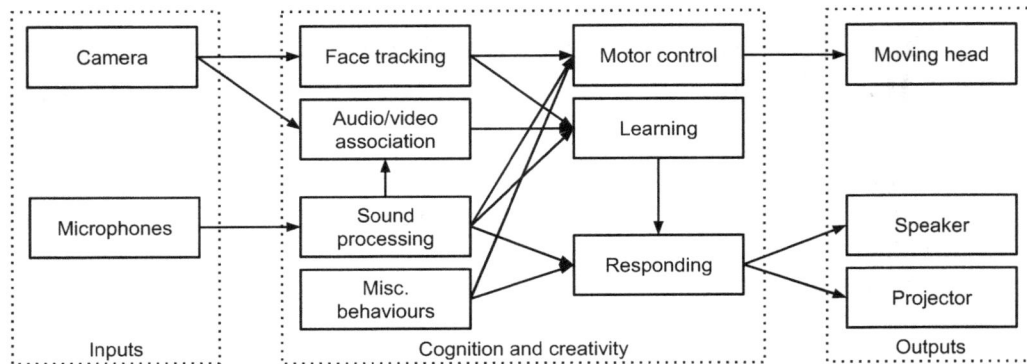

Figure 1. [self.] overall architecture. The various modules are described in the text, the signal pahts between them are indicated by the arrows.

more different will produce a sequence of images that *represent* this difference. Typically, this can be seen as effects ranging from grey blurs to flashing images.

Since the robot is an installation, it is programmed to perform certain behaviours over time to exhibit a more life-like behaviour. These can be categorized as follows: 1) *Idling:* if the robot does not see a face nor hear a sound for a certain period of time, it will start searching for face. Upon finding a face, [self.] retrieves sounds uttered by this face earlier, uses this to initiate conversation. 2) *Dream state:* at night it is programmed to go through all the memories experienced throughout the day. During the learning process, similar sounds are grouped together to form a category of sounds. Sometimes this classification might be erroneous. By calculating a sparse representation of the sounds [4], the similarity between grouped sounds can be estimated. Those found to be too different within group are discarded; this can be seen as a "mental hygiene" and consolidation process, and is called the "dream state" since this resembles what the brain does during sleep [5]. 3) *Optimization of parameters for the response mechanism:* the learning of associations between sounds, faces and their sequences yields a representation that can be used to answer in a creative way. However, there is a large parameter set that need to be adjusted in order to achieve the desired behaviour. The parameters are themselves sensitive to how many memories are stored and their inherent sequences. The robot is able to adjust these parameters itself, by optimizing the parameter settings using a genetic algorithm [2]. In other words, [self.] writes part of its own behavioural program using evolution.

PERFORMANCE

The fact that the robot is not bootstrapped with knowledge is intentional. The developers have observed how this yields an installation that not only fosters interactivity, but reinforces it, since those who interact tend to get excited by recognizing sounds/images of themselves or people they know. By implementing biological models and having a bottom-up way of learning, the goal is to implement *cognitive abilities* in the robot. Another goal is also to make this an autonomous entity that embodies *creativity*. This is most evidently shown in two places: 1) the combination of known sounds into novel

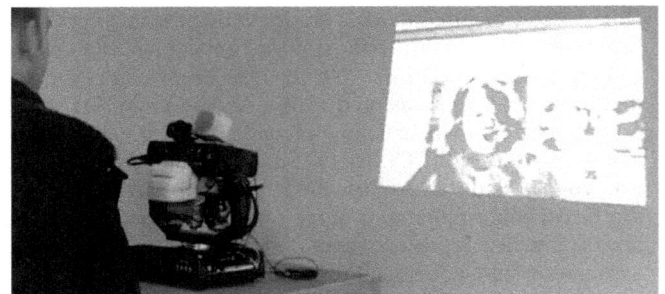

Figure 2. [self.] interacting with a person.

phrases, and 2) how this system tunes itself using evolution. Artificial evolution and computational creativity are inherently linked, since it gives a machine the possibility of finding novel combinations of previously learned concepts. Indeed, since evolution is the driving explorative mechanism in nature, and thus arguably also its *creative force*, it seems fitting to equip the robot with this functionality in order to write parts of its own behavioural program.

REFERENCES

1. Rodney Brooks. 1986. A robust layered control system for a mobile robot. *IEEE journal of Robotics and Automation* 2, 1 (1986), 14–23.

2. John H. Holland. 1975. *Adaptation in Neural and Artificial Systems*. University of Michigan Press, Ann Arbor.

3. Herbert Jaeger and Harald Haas. 2004. Harnessing Nonlinearity: Predicting Chaotic Systems and Saving Energy in Wireless Communication. *Science* 304, 5667 (2004), 78–80.

4. Richard F. Lyon, Martin Rehn, Samy Bengio, Thomas C Walters, and Gal Chechik. 2010. Sound retrieval and ranking using sparse auditory representations. *Neural computation* 22, 9 (2010), 2390–2416.

5. R. Stickgold, J. A. Hobson, R. Fosse, and M. Fosse. 2001. Sleep, Learning, and Dreams: Off-line Memory Reprocessing. *Science* 294, 5544 (2001), 1052–1057.

The Aesthetics of Activism

Michael Heidt
RTG crossWorlds
Chemnitz University of Technology, Germany
michael.heidt@cs.tu-chemnitz.de

Vicki Moulder
School of Interactive Arts + Technology
Simon Fraser University, Canada
vmoulder@sfu.ca

ABSTRACT

For this demonstration the authors intend to present the *Aesthetics of Activism* as a work-in-progress. The artwork is designed to aggregate visual material from social networks to form themed compositions that can be explored jointly within a shared interactive space. Visual elements are programmatically arranged according to formal aesthetic criteria, while motion within the exhibition space is detected via optical sensors. Artistry built into the algorithms used for creating the visual compositions and those used to present, filter and rank content within the social web are exposed for people interested in the relationships between the cultural and computer layers inherent to the system design.

Author Keywords

Interactive Art; Aesthetics; Activism; Code Literacy.

ACM Classification Keywords

H.5.m. Information interfaces and presentation (e.g., HCI): Miscellaneous.

INTRODUCTION

Interrupting our daily lives, digital platforms present us with a dizzying array of visual stimuli. Social networks and news aggregators create a torrent of content competing for our attention. The issues touched upon within these presentations range from the tremendously mundane like the advertisement for a toothbrush; to the alarmingly urgent like the impacts of climate change.

The coded infrastructures and algorithms that determine the mode and frequency of presentation remain hidden from the viewers. They thusly are not subject to reflection, public debate or negotiation on the media they are presented. Likewise, aesthetic qualities play a significant role in determining what we regard as relevant, coherent or interesting [3, 4]. Charles E. Osgood used semantic differentials to research people's response to aesthetics and claimed, 'human semantic processes are very complex, and that problems of meaning are inextricably confounded with more general problems of

human thinking or cognition" [2]. From an audience's perspective, the rules determining the aesthetic appraisals are for the most part applied subconsciously and believed to be the result of evolutionary processes. In effect, both phenomena though apparently unrelated, exhibit similar qualities. They determine how we distribute our attention without the mechanisms of their operation being transparent to us. By allowing people to jointly experience the phenomena of aesthetics and decisiveness of digital architecture, they are invited to reflect on the tacit rule-sets underlying our everyday digital interactions. In this way, we intend to demonstrate the *Aesthetics of Activism* to provoke questions such as: Is code a purely instrumental enterprise? How do we measure its misappropriation or use? And, how do digital practices affect social conditions? In the sections to follow we discuss the spatial layout and thematic structure of the demonstration model, along with details of our future work.

Spatial Layout

The proposed demo can be projected on a frosted glass or white surface at any size. As seen in figure 3 the work possesses an interactive zone situated in front of the projection, spanning an area of roughly five feet.

If two people are present, the shown projections reflect the relative positions of both bodies within the tracked radius. The system computes collages that are aesthetically juxtaposed, as well as, embodying the configuration of bodies within the interactive space. Collages are updated quicker as long as the interactive space is populated. The engendered effect of coordination invites spontaneous communication between people viewing the artwork. In the case of a single person, the distance between body and the projection alone determines the output.

Social web resources are continuously scavenged for visual content pertaining to the themes chosen by the system makers. In the absence of people or in the case of non-interactive installation, the system operates as a purely ambient display, showing aggregated content according to general formal aesthetic principles including colour harmony, typographic style and modular scale [1]. To this end continuous statistical analyses are performed on gathered material in order to prepare the collage making process.

Thematic Structure

The thematic structure of the artwork is designed so that it can spontaneously report on emerging issues. For this demonstration the artwork will project images, video and text related to Canada's Kinder Morgan[1] protest to stop a pipeline from being built at Burnaby Mountain in British Columbia, Canada as seen in figure 1.

As activists upload video and images from real-time protests, multiple views of the generative composition aggregated from social web resources are displayed. Figure 2 illustrates the compositional framework. Reflecting on the algorithmic and aesthetic aspects of the attention economy might prove especially important regarding issues such as sustainability and social change that demand a certain level of urgency. The installation thus does not want to 'admonish' its viewers. Instead, it invites playful modes of interaction that interrupt the communal experiences of everyday life.

FUTURE WORK

In this demonstration submission, we have briefly described our motivations for producing the *Aesthetics of Activism*. Our proposed demo intends to invite conference attendees to engage with an alternative image system for reporting on social change. This work is part of a larger research study that investigates the broader context of social, digital and cultural production. Our future work will continue to explore the creation of code and the detection of social media patterns as a mode of cultural production firmly rooted within the realm of aesthetic practice such as: painting, nature, or mathematics.

ACKNOWLEDGEMENTS

We gratefully acknowledge the generous support of GRAND NCE in Canada and The German Research Foundation (RTG 1780).

REFERENCES

1. Bringhurst, R. (1999). The elements of typographic style. Vancouver: Hartley & Marks.

2. Osgood, C. E. (1952). The nature and measurement of meaning. Psychological bulletin, 49(3), 197. p.318

3. Lavie, T., & Tractinsky, N. (2004). Assessing dimensions of perceived visual aesthetics of web sites. International journal of human-computer studies, 60(3), 269-298.

4. Moshagen, M., & Thielsch, M. T. (2010). Facets of visual aesthetics. International Journal of Human-Computer Studies, 68(10), 689-709

---

[1] Support Burnaby's Kinder Morgan Opposition
http://350.org/how-to-help-stop-kinder-morgan

Figure 1. The Aesthetics of Activism work-in-progress at the Surrey Central Library, BC, Canada http://interactionart.org/the-aesthetics-of-activism

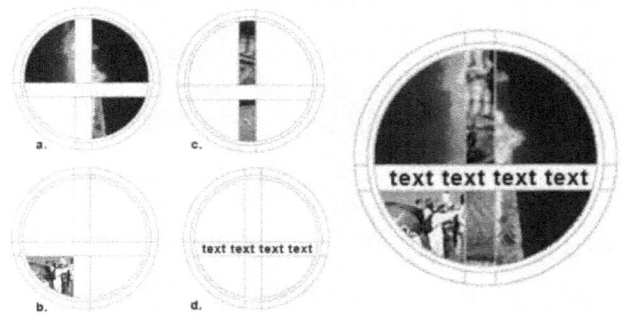

Figure 2. This illustration maps the compositional framework and placement of each layer: a) context, b) contrast, c) people protesting and d) text related to theme.

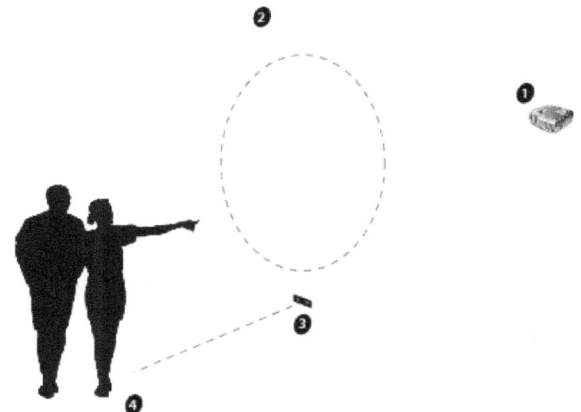

Figure 3. The demo installation can be scaled down to fit different space constraints. This illustration shows the general set-up: 1) Projector and Laptop computer, 2) Screen, 3) Kinect sensor and 4) Space for people to move in front of the sensor.

Designing Creativity Support Tools for Failure

Joy Kim, Avi Bagla, Michael S. Bernstein
Stanford University
{jojo0808, abagla}@stanford.edu, msb@cs.stanford.edu

ABSTRACT

Creative tools today strive to amplify our ability to create high-quality work. However, experiencing failure is also an important part of mastering creative skills. While experts have developed strategies for engaging in risky experiments and learning from mistakes, novices lack the experience and mindset needed to use failures as opportunities for growth. Current tools intimidate the unsure novice, as they are designed around showcasing success or critiquing finished work, rather than providing safe spaces for experimentation. To better support experiences of failure for novices, we instead propose flipping the value of failure in creativity tools from something to avoid to something to pursue actively. To do this, we develop a taxonomy of creative activities that people engage in when they aim to succeed. We then invert this taxonomy to derive a new set of creative activities where deliberate failure can provide a path towards creative confidence. Lastly, we envision possible creativity support tools as examples of the potential value of supporting activities where failure is encouraged and showcased.

Author Keywords

Creativity support tools; failure; design; novice.

ACM Classification Keywords

H.5.2. Information Interfaces and Presentation: User Interfaces — *User-centered design.*

INTRODUCTION

Creative tools today amplify success, helping creators put their best work on public pedestals. Online creative communities such as DeviantArt [3] provide online galleries for artists to showcase their work. Likewise, creativity support tool design principles developed by HCI and CSCW research communities aim to bolster creative output [16] or decrease friction in engaging in creativity [15]. The goals of such tools include preventing mistakes [17] and helping novices emulate expert work [10]. Creativity evaluation metrics also reflect this desire for success, often aiming to maximize the number of likes and remixes [31], number of completed projects [28], or scores by expert judges [19].

C&C 2015, June 22–25, 2015, Glasgow, United Kingdom.
ACM 978-1-4503-3598-0/15/06.
http://dx.doi.org/10.1145/2757226.2764542

However, this stands in stark contrast to our understanding that *failure*, rather than success, is central to mastery [24]. Writers such as Ira Glass [23] have expounded publicly on the role that repeated and purposeful failure played in their eventual success; rejected academic papers receive more citations when eventually published than those accepted on first submission [13]. Effective deliberate practice of a skill involves continuous corrective feedback to learn from mistakes [22].

However, for novices, a downward spiral forms: novices need experience in order to develop competence in a task or skill, but fear of failure prevents them from engaging in opportunities for growth. Expert creators are able to engage in an iterative process consisting of many experiments to develop the ideas and skills needed to produce a final piece [32] in order to learn both what will and won't work [9]. Novices, in contrast, tend to attribute perceived failure to lower self-worth [18], and will often perform tasks according to context-free rules they've learned in the past [11] rather than adapt their creative process as needed. Current sources of creative support suddenly become more intimidating than helpful: DeviantArt focuses on showcasing art rather than providing a safe space to experiment, critique communities only critique finished or close-to-finished works of art, and online learning communities often ignore beginner work and target feedback-giving efforts towards those who can demonstrate promise.

With this in mind, we propose *flipping the value of failure in creativity tools*: rather than viewing failure as a cost to avoid, what if creativity tools and communities viewed failure as a positive outcome?

Drawing on existing examples of creation tools and creative communities, we develop a taxonomy of common creative activities that occur when the creator's goal is to aim for success. We then derive new types of creative activities that arise when the goal is instead to aim for failure to help expand the possible design space for creativity support tools. Lastly, we envision potential tools that support some of these activities as examples of future work in this space. In this paper, we focus on novices in artistic communities surrounding domains such as drawing, painting, and music, but we anticipate our findings could apply to other domains in future work.

RELATED WORK

We focus on understanding and designing for a particular aspect of the creative process: experiencing failure (especially for novice creators). To inform our work, we look at how current tools and communities support failure as well as existing theories about how people persevere in the face of challenges.

Failure in Creative Tools and Communities

A number of tools support exploration of a creative space by supporting rapid and rough prototypes of the envisioned goal (e.g., SILK [27]). Additionally, one of the most common ways existing creator tools explicitly respond to failure is by providing an undo function [29], allowing creators to experiment, then backtrack if the attempt is judged unsuccessful. However, backtracking can often only happen linearly, such that if a new experiment is made, the old experiment is no longer accessible. Furthermore, "undo" implicitly assumes a stance that failure is mostly negative and is something to be recovered from rather than encouraged. In this paper, we explore the benefits and limitations of other possible responses to failure in creator tools through design.

Art and design education has traditionally followed the studio model [20], facilitating peer learning and social motivation by providing an open and shared environment for students to work [30] as well as helping students iteratively improve their work through public critiques from instructors and peers [32]. Online creative communities (e.g., ConceptArt.org [2]) often try to emulate this method of peer learning by providing forums where artists seeking to improve their skills can put forward their best work in order to receive feedback from a community of other skilled artists. However, such communities can sometimes discourage creativity and risk-taking by punishing those who fail to post "good" work with negative social consequences [6]. Other communities, such as Reddit's /r/sketchdaily forum [5], center around learning and practice of skills, providing drawing prompts and a central location where community members can post responses to prompts and view responses from others. However, unlike in a studio, this is often where the community's involvement in a novice creator's development ends; community members can provide critique or motivation to participate in a larger activity, but do not typically offer on-going guidance for how to understand or react to critique or how to tie what they learn from daily sketches into larger work. The novice must — somehow — figure out how to learn from their experiments and failures on their own.

The Art of Failure

Psychology distinguishes two ways in which individuals view intelligence and learning: individuals with a *fixed mindset* believe that intelligence and talent are innate abilities that are fixed from birth, while individuals with a *growth mindset* believe that intelligence and talent can be developed over time [21]. These mindsets can lead to different behaviors in contexts where opportunities for learning arise; those with fixed mindsets will avoid tasks where the risk of performing poorly is high, while those with growth mindsets will anticipate learning from challenges. Similarly, those with high *self-efficacy* (the strength of one's belief in one's own ability to complete tasks and achieve goals) exhibit a higher ability for learning and performing tasks [7], and possess robustness in the face of failure [18]. People with low self-efficacy are more likely to interpret criticism as a critique of themselves as a person rather than a critique of the work [26]. Understanding how people change from a fixed mindset to a growth mindset

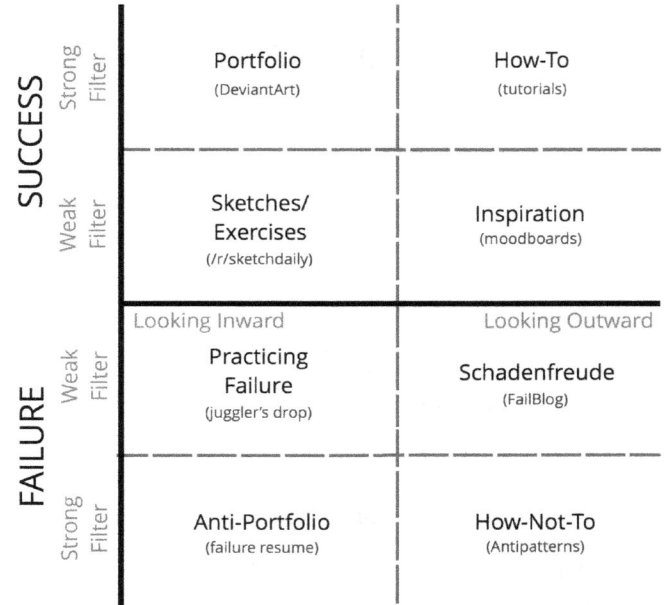

Figure 1. A taxonomy of creative activities according to how strongly they filter for success (top) and failure (bottom).

may be the key to designing tools that support novices in developing creative confidence and in responding to failures in ways that facilitate growth. Video games are an example of an activity that successfully produce high self-efficacy behavior despite repeated experiences of failure. Video games do this by designing for *flow* [25]; games are careful to only expose failures to players when next steps towards progress are clear (even if the end solution is not). Carefully measured exposure to negative experiences may produce positive changes in attitudes towards those experiences [8].

Therefore, we hypothesize that exposing or encouraging failure in a measured way may help creators (especially novices) practice developing strategies for growth and perseverance. By viewing failure as something to be encouraged rather than avoided, we open up new design spaces for the types of creativity support tools that could exist.

CREATIVE SUCCESS AND FAILURE

The attitude a creative tool or activity takes towards failure can be seen in how it asks a creator to filter what has been produced. In our taxonomy, *filtering* refers to how strictly the creator filters produced content for quality. A weak filter activity (such as sketching) tends to accept mistakes and experiments, while a strong filter activity embodies high standards of approval — only the best of what was produced remains. We also consider *where* filtering is directed: is the creator looking inwardly and filtering their own work, or are they looking outward and filtering work by others? Though other members of a community certainly also judge created work, our taxonomy of filtering takes the perspective of a creator who is making judgments of their own or others' work *during their own creative process or development*. The top half of Figure 1 shows the resulting taxonomy populated with examples of commonly practiced creative activities where a creator filters for success.

In activities where creators look at their own work with a weak filter for success, the goal is to practice certain skills. Examples of such activities usually focus on producing a large quantity of small pieces of work, and include brainstorming, prototyping, and doing daily sketches.

When creators use a strong filter for success on the work they produce, their goal is to showcase their best work. The act of creating a portfolio falls in this general area; creators perceive high risk in failing to judge their best work correctly and are thus motivated to judge their work according to a high standard.

When creators use a weak filter for success on work created by others, they usually seek inspiration. A consumer browses others' work and judges them in order to broadly explore work related to their personal tastes or a current project.

When creators use a strong filter for success on work created by others, they are able to closely study others' specific creative processes. The process is sometimes documented in some way (for example, through video recordings or tutorials) for use as a resource for learning how to do something well.

It is also possible for creators to engage in co-production. Examples of such activities are critique (where creators put forward their best work and receive feedback) and peer mentoring (where creators receive feedback on work that is not necessarily finished or polished). While not shown, it may be that these activities lie somewhere at the boundary between the left and right halves of Figure 1 — that is, the boundary between a creator and an external creative community.

Inverting the Design Space: Designing for Failure

The activities in the taxonomy above all strive towards some notion of success, differing only in how strongly a creator filters out work judged as less successful. We may be able to reveal creative activities that are not commonly supported by existing creativity tools if we instead strive to filter for failure, either by filtering out successful attempts or preserving unsuccessful attempts. We show the possible taxonomy that could result in the bottom half of Figure 1, which mirrors the taxonomy in the top half of Figure 1.

When creators view their work with a weak filter for failure, they also create quick experiments and sketches; however, instead of practicing to improve techniques or skills, these activities encourage users to practice reacting to failed attempts. An example of such an activity is the method of practicing dropping balls when learning to juggle to make failure seem more normal than success [14].

When creators view their own work with a strong filter for failure, they focus on showcasing their worst work. An example of an activity in this area might be the anti-portfolio [1], a collection of investment mistakes and missed opportunities sometimes published by large venture capital firms. A failure resume [33] is a similar document for individuals. By owning their past mistakes, creators can begin to view them as opportunities for growth rather than moments of shame.

In activities where creators use a weak filter for failure on work created by others, failures are collected for the purpose of spectating, often for humorous purposes. Movie bloopers or curated websites like FAILBlog [4], for example, fit in this part of the taxonomy.

When creators use a strong filter for failure on work by others, they also access a glimpse into others' creative processes. However, rather than focusing on how others did something correctly, creators may study failed attempts in order to learn what not to do (i.e., antipatterns [12]).

The boundary between the left and right sides of the bottom of Figure 1 also denotes activities where creators and others collaborate; however, this may involve a creator presenting failures rather than successes to others as prompts for critique or discussion.

FUTURE WORK & CONCLUSION

Focusing on what we can learn from failure, rather than fixating on how to achieve success, can change how we approach creative work. Mistakes become helpful signposts pointing our way to excellence, and failure becomes an event rather than an inherent reflection of self-worth. What would happen if creativity communities and tools helped us look for opportunities for growth rather than opportunities to maximize likes, upvotes, or reblogs?

In this work, we generated a design space centered around encouraging failure and demonstrated new opportunities for creativity support tools. For example, a tool that helps novices *practice failure* might be a community where novices are rewarded for producing a quantity of work by being able to "pay" for mentoring from experts by their show of effort. An *anti-portfolio* may point to tools that are the inverse of showcase websites such as DeviantArt, where people post work they do not like or did not finish with explanations for the failed work to aid in peer reflection and social motivation. As another example, a tool designed around *schadenfreude* might help people curate work according to what they dislike. However, rather than simply allowing people to gather generically bad work, the tool might help artists curate mindfully and purposefully, according to the artist's current project or goals (e.g., "interior designs I don't like"); even negative examples can help creators overcome design fixation [34]. A *how-not-to* tool might expose a creative process with a focus on failure; rather than producing a step-by-step guide for how to do something well, an artist might produce a step-by-step guide documenting their unsuccessful attempts at a new technique.

These examples are only a glimpse into the possible ways we may be able to fill the gaps in support for novices left by current creative tools. By explicitly designing to encourage failure in creative tools and communities, we may better enable creators to not just achieve but also grow.

ACKNOWLEDGMENTS

This material is based upon work supported by the NSF GRFP under Grant No. DGE-114747 and the NSF CAREER Grant under Grant No. IIS-1351131. Any opinions, findings, conclusions or recommendations expressed in this work are those of the authors and do not necessarily reflect those of the NSF.

REFERENCES

1. Bessemer venture partners: Anti-portfolio. http://www.bvp.com/portfolio/antiportfolio.

2. Conceptart.org. http://www.conceptart.org/forums/forumdisplay.php?59-ART-CRITIQUE-CENTER.

3. Deviantart. http://deviantart.com/.

4. Failblog. http://failblog.cheezburger.com/.

5. /r/sketchdaily. http://reddit.com/r/sketchdaily.

6. Amabile, T. M. *How to kill creativity*. Harvard Business School Publishing Boston, MA, 1998.

7. Bandura, A. Self-efficacy: The exercise of control, 1997.

8. Bandura, A., Blanchard, E. B., and Ritter, B. Relative efficacy of desensitization and modeling approaches for inducing behavioral, affective, and attitudinal changes. *Journal of Personality and Social Psychology 13*, 3 (1969), 173.

9. Bayles, D., Orland, T., and Morey, A. *Art & fear*. Tantor Media, Incorporated, 2012.

10. Benedetti, L., Winnemöller, H., Corsini, M., and Scopigno, R. Painting with bob: Assisted creativity for novices. In *Proc. UIST*, ACM (New York, NY, USA, 2014), 419–428.

11. Benner, P. From novice to expert. *AJN The American Journal of Nursing 82*, 3 (1982), 402–407.

12. Brown, W. J., McCormick, H. W., Mowbray, T. J., and Malveau, R. C. Antipatterns: refactoring software, architectures, and projects in crisis.

13. Calcagno, V., Demoinet, E., Gollner, K., Guidi, L., Ruths, D., and de Mazancourt, C. Flows of research manuscripts among scientific journals reveal hidden submission patterns. *Science 338*, 6110 (2012), 1065–1069.

14. Cassidy, J., and Rimbeaux, B. *Juggling for the complete klutz*. Klutz, 2002.

15. Cherry, E., and Latulipe, C. Quantifying the creativity support of digital tools through the creativity support index. *ACM Trans. Comput.-Hum. Interact. 21*, 4 (June 2014), 21:1–21:25.

16. Davis, N., Winnemöller, H., Dontcheva, M., and Do, E. Y.-L. Toward a cognitive theory of creativity support. In *Proc. C&C*, ACM (New York, NY, USA, 2013), 13–22.

17. Davis, N., Zook, A., O'Neill, B., Headrick, B., Riedl, M., Grosz, A., and Nitsche, M. Creativity support for novice digital filmmaking. In *Proc. CHI*, ACM (New York, NY, USA, 2013), 651–660.

18. Dodgson, P. G., and Wood, J. V. Self-esteem and the cognitive accessibility of strengths and weaknesses after failure. *Journal of Personality and Social Psychology 75*, 1 (1998), 178.

19. Dow, S. P., Glassco, A., Kass, J., Schwarz, M., Schwartz, D. L., and Klemmer, S. R. Parallel prototyping leads to better design results, more divergence, and increased self-efficacy. *ACM Trans. Comput.-Hum. Interact. 17*, 4 (Dec. 2010), 18:1–18:24.

20. Drexler, A., Chafee, R., et al. *The architecture of the Ecole des Beaux-Arts*. distributed by MIT Press, 1977.

21. Dweck, C. *Mindset: The new psychology of success*. Random House, 2006.

22. Ericsson, K. A., Krampe, R. T., and Tesch-Römer, C. The role of deliberate practice in the acquisition of expert performance. *Psychological review 100*, 3 (1993), 363.

23. Glass, I. Ira glass on storytelling, part 3 of 4. https://www.youtube.com/watch?v=BI23U7U2aUY, 2009. YouTube. Accessed: 2015-02-27.

24. Guskey, T. R. Closing achievement gaps: revisiting benjamin s. bloom's "learning for mastery". *Journal of Advanced Academics 19*, 1 (2007), 8–31.

25. Juul, J. *The art of failure: An essay on the pain of playing video games*. Mit Press, 2013.

26. Kosara, R. Visualization criticism-the missing link between information visualization and art. In *Information Visualization*, IEEE (2007), 631–636.

27. Landay, J. A. Silk: Sketching interfaces like krazy. In *Conference Companion on Human Factors in Computing Systems*, CHI '96, ACM (New York, NY, USA, 1996), 398–399.

28. Luther, K., Fiesler, C., and Bruckman, A. Redistributing leadership in online creative collaboration. In *Proc. CSCW*, ACM (New York, NY, USA, 2013), 1007–1022.

29. Myers, B. A., and Kosbie, D. S. Reusable hierarchical command objects. In *Proc. CHI*, ACM (New York, NY, USA, 1996), 260–267.

30. Reimer, Y. J., and Douglas, S. A. Teaching hci design with the studio approach. *Computer science education 13*, 3 (2003), 191–205.

31. Resnick, M., Maloney, J., Monroy-Hernández, A., Rusk, N., Eastmond, E., Brennan, K., Millner, A., Rosenbaum, E., Silver, J., Silverman, B., and Kafai, Y. Scratch: Programming for all. *Commun. ACM 52*, 11 (Nov. 2009), 60–67.

32. Schön, D. A. *The reflective practitioner: How professionals think in action*, vol. 5126. Basic books, 1983.

33. Seelig, T. L. *What I wish I knew when I was 20: A crash course on making your place in the world*, vol. 9. HarperOne, 2009.

34. Smith, S. M., Ward, T. B., and Finke, R. A. *The creative cognition approach*. MIT Press, 1995.

Choreography in the Mapping of New Instruments

Alon Ilsar
Creativity and Cognition
Studios
University of Technology,
Sydney
alon.ilsar@student.uts.edu.au

Andrew Johnston
Creativity and Cognition
Studios
University of Technology,
Sydney
andrew.johnston@uts.edu.au

ABSTRACT

This paper discusses the use of choreography in mapping sound to movement in the field of new instrument design. Using the analogy of the drum kit player utilising all four limbs in a similar fashion to a dancer, we investigate the notion of mapping movement to prerecorded sound in that order, as opposed to sound mapped to movement. In this way the mapping process becomes a type of 'choreography', where a particular piece of music is learnt to be played as the mapping is determined. We outline three main factors which must be balanced within the mapping process. We present findings from the development of a new gestural interface for electronic percussionists and several collaborations that this interface has been used in.

Author Keywords

Choreography; Mapping; New Instrument Design; Percussion.

ACM Classification Keywords

H.5.5. Sound and Music Computing; J.5. Art and Humanities: Performing arts (e.g., dance, music).

INTRODUCTION

This paper will report on the authors' experiences in designing and performing with a new gestural instrument. Over the past two years dozens of compositions and improvisations have been performed by the first author on this instrument in venues all around the world. In addition, several interviews with other musicians who have been involved have been conducted and analysed.

We begin by considering the way acoustic drum kit players 'choreograph' the way they play around the kit. We identify three main factors that affect this choreography. These three

factors cannot coexist and hence must be weighed up against each other. Using these three factors, we outline our approach to the 'mapping problem' [1] in designing a new gestural instrument for electronic percussion. We use the analogy of a dancer choreographing her/his movement to prerecorded sound in taking a compositional approach to mapping, beginning with the music and working backwards to the choreography of the movement on the gestural instrument to best fit with the music.

CHOREOGRAPHY

Choreography on the Drum Kit

The drum kit is one of the few instruments that require the coordination of all four-limbs. In this way it is similar to the art of dancing. Using this analogy, drummers, when transcribing drum kit music, often choreograph the way they play a piece of percussive music, making decisions on which of their four limbs should play each rhythm. Foot pedals have enabled drummers to play traditional hand percussion instruments like bass drums, cymbals, cowbells, woodblocks and snares with their feet to allow a different choreography of playing the kit. Interesting stickings result in dancelike choreographed drumming and when several drummers get together to perform a piece such as Steve Reich's *Drumming*, as much effort goes into the choreography as it does into the performance of the music.

Another distinguishing characteristic of the drum kit is that is it inherently adaptable. Though the standard kick, snare, hihat, crash, ride and toms can sustain a lifetime of exploration, shakers, shells, wheels, bubble-wrap, coins, anything imaginable can also become part of the kit. Even in the most experimental music, this element of deriving sounds from any material sparks interest in the more conservative audiences. 'A childlike fascination with the meticulous exploration of the sonic potential of 'things,' musical or otherwise, driven by the pleasure principle, is also common in much experimental improvised music' [2]. Since there is no way of utilising conventional harmony, melody or note duration on the drum kit, the instrument demands the musician explore rhythm and timbre to the highest degree. Drummers explore their instrument through hitting, caressing, rubbing and stroking different surfaces with different utensils, and in doing so, as in all acoustic instruments, appeal to the audience's knowledge or literature [8] of the way movement is connected to sound in the real physical world.

But how do drummers decide to choreograph their performances? We have identified three main motivating factors in the way drummers choreograph their performances. They are:

- Efficiency

- Visual performance

- Exploration

Efficiency, or ergonomics, is similar to the notion of intimacy: 'a measure of the player's perceived match between the behavior of a device and the control of that device... The ultimate goal in the process is for the player to have a high degree of intimacy such that... [the instrument] behaves like an extension of [the player] so that there is a transparent relationship between control and sound. This allows intent and expression to flow through the player to the instrument and then to the sound and, hence, create music' [3]. The most virtuosic drummers, mostly those considered as jazz drummers, use as little energy as possible in their movements to glide over the kit. Their focus is in preparing for the next movement as early as possible to have the ultimate control over the way the sound is made. This more intimate and sensual experience with the instrument leads to positive responses from audiences in smaller venues. However, in larger arenas, these subtle movements, though leading to more nuanced expression, may not lead to a transparent, visual or theatrical performance.

Audiences feel a strong connection with the large movements and **visual performance** often needed to play the drums. Exaggerated movements in the style of big rock arena exhibitionist drumming, though the least efficient way to play the drums, has its context for when more subtle playing becomes too discreet. Many styles of music have developed from the need to be more theatrical when the audience is placed further away; the best examples of this include opera and stadium rock.

The last factor of **exploration** or breaking habits is dealt with mostly in experimental music. Drummers challenge themselves by setting up their kit in unusual ways in the hope that new and different musical ideas may reveal themselves.

Choreography on the Electronic Kit

These three factors become increasingly important when facing the 'mapping problem' in designing electronic instruments. 'The basic problem of these interfaces concerns the fact that the mediation between the different modalities (basically from movement to sound) has an arbitrary component, which is due to the fact that the energies of the modalities are transformed into electronic signals. This is in contrast with traditional instruments,

where energetic modalities are mechanically mediated and where the user gets a natural feeling of the causality of the multimodal interface' [1].

Electronic pads have been used by drummers to open up more choreographic and sonic possibilities. They are just one part of an ongoing conversation between drummers and electronic beat makers. Early electronic beat makers began their art form by sampling drummers, and later cutting these samples up in various ways. This in turn led to drummers mimicking these electronically produced beats on the acoustic drum kit. As this conversation continues, acoustic drummer Chris Dave reveals that he transcribes electronic producer J Dilla's beats in his practice routine in great detail. This has led Dave to be one of the most sort after drummers in the world today, playing in some of the biggest live hip hop and nu-soul acts in the world, and doing so with a heavy electronically produced music aesthetic. He continues to reinvent the way acoustic drums are played as electronic pads struggle to make their mark.

The problem with electronic pads lies in the loss of the connection between movement and sound. This loss is mostly due to a lack of information that an electronic pad can receive from a strike as compared to the complex rippling effect that occurs when striking an acoustic drum. To overcome this, some percussionists have explored the use of 'open-air controllers' to both mimic and sonically expand the potential of a physical drum kit and 'unchain the performer from the physical constraints of holding, touching, and manipulating an instrument' [11]. We have been developing our own working prototype gestural instrument for musical expression, the *AirSticks*, using the Razer Hydra Gaming Controllers [1] as the open-air controllers. These controllers send continuous control changes of XYZ absolute position and orientation. We currently also utilise the SoftStep Foot Midi Controller [2] to incorporated foot movements in not only trigger samples but also manipulating them with various expressive moments. For more details on this instrument see previous work [4,5].

A COMPOSITIONAL APPROACH

With the *AirSticks*, the drummer is freed of restriction of needing to strike a physical surface. Her/his movement is constantly tracked and hence every movement can be choreographed and mapped to a sound. In dealing with these types of 'composed instruments' [6] we have decided to take a compositional approach, making 'a piece, not an instrument or controller' [7].

An example of this approach lies within a piece for voice and *AirSticks* entitled *Narcissus (Vocal Vacuum One)*, one

---

[1] http://www.razerzone.com/gaming-controllers/razer-hydra-portal-2-bundle

[2] http://www.keithmcmillen.com/products/softstep/

of a series of duos with various performers called *Vacuums*. Here the compositional approach started with the essential elements of the piece being composed and produced on a computer. The *AirSticks* player then turned his attention to learning to play this piece while adapting the mapping. This is the part of the process we are calling the choreography - making decisions on which movements should represent which sound, and taking into account the three factors outlined in the paper. Once the *AirSticks* player has learnt the choreography of the piece, and is comfortable enough to improvise around the piece's main structures, they can add more layers of manipulation of parameters to the mapping. The *AirSticks* player then collaborated in the rehearsal room with a vocalist and the two of them arranged the piece further as the *AirSticks* player began to integrate the live manipulation of the vocalist. It is this part of the process that the vocalist described as 'fluid,' utilising the *AirSticks* as a 'compositional tool' with which 'we perform every time we write'.

In the example above, the process begins with composition and moves to gesture mapping or choreography, then to rehearsing improvisations or playing with the written material, and finally to performing the work.

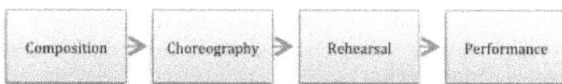

Fig 1: Composition led trajectory of the creative process

In the field of instrument design, this trajectory more commonly begins with the gesture mapping. The term choreography can only be used when it occurs after at least part of composition has been written. Though changing this trajectory does not necessarily solve the mapping problem, starting with a more complete composition can inspire different ways of mapping sound to movement, or in this more choreographic approach, movement to sound. An example of this can be found in *Dark as a Dungeon,* a live performance to silent film for guitar, electronics and the *AirSticks*. In this piece, the *AirSticks* gestures were deliberately confined to a very restricted space to represent a section of the film in which men were going down a mineshaft. This was juxtaposed against the choreography of another section which use much larger, more open gestures to represent the vastness of a mountainous landscape.

In an interview after the performance, the collaborator mentioned that 'it was great to have that visually [the choreography of the *AirSticks*] as part of the performance.' This approach allows the instrument designer to more comprehensively weigh up the importance of visual performance against the other two mapping factors. Without starting with some degree of composition, it is difficult to imagine the connection between visual performance and the yet to be heard music. Indeed the first

author has often been told that when improvising on the *AirSticks*, even though he looks connected to the instrument, and plays with great expressivity, certain key visual elements of the performance are missing, as opposed to the very stylised approach taken in playing the instrument when the music is pre-composed. Being aware of the constant tension between the concepts of efficiency, visual performance and exploration in the mapping of a new gestural instrument can lead to more informed decision-making throughout the process.

CHOREOGRAPHY ON THE AIRSTICKS

The *AirSticks* explores the role of 'metaphor for improving the amount of expression possible with a device. Metaphor depends on a literature, which forms the basis for improving transparency' [8]. With the *AirSticks* this literature is the movements made by performers on a traditional drum kit. Using drumming as a metaphor for mapping the *AirSticks* also helps lower the entry level of the instrument, allowing experienced drummers to transfer their motor skills from playing the traditional acoustic drum kit to this new instrument [9]. In designing the *AirSticks* special consideration is given to how confidently and easily an expert percussionist could play the instrument on her/his first attempt. A practice regime has been created for the new instrument with a tutorial style guide for learning to play the *AirSticks*. This guide breaks down all the layers of mapping possibilities by starting from the metaphor of an electronic drum kit.

Distinct from a 'conceptually complete' instrument like the drum kit, piano or Theremin which can be explored within its physical and sonic constraints, new instruments undergo 'a constant series of revisions, redesigns and upgrades' [10]. The performer must constantly ask herself/himself whether to keep practicing a difficult passage or simply design the instrument in a way that allows an easier playing of this passage. In other words, does the designer put efficiency above visual performance and exploration in order for the passage to sound the way the performer or composer want it to sound?

Exploration becomes a greater factor in the choreography of new instruments compared to that of a drum kit. Since it is very easy to dramatically change a mapping of a new instrument, the exploration of movement and sound can shadow the concerns of efficiency and visual performance. One example of this occurred when, after an improvised performance of the *AirSticks* with an acoustic bass player, an audience member suggested that a certain movement made on the *AirSticks* looked uncomfortable and visually unpleasing. This particular movement, an overextension of the wrist towards the underarm, was made by the performer to attain a desired sound within the improvisation, even though the movement was an uncomfortable one to make. For the next performance the movement was remapped so that the sound could be attained and explored without discomfort. Exploring a mapping with these other concepts in mind can lead to great breakthroughs in making a mapping more efficient and/or visually appealing. A similarly uncomfortable movement could be desirable in pushing the body to the limits to get some sort of physical feedback.

FUTURE WORK

We have begun to design the hardware and software for the next incarnation of the *AirSticks*, taking into consideration the concepts discussed in this paper. Our next version of the instrument addresses the 'mapping problem' in three ways.

- We are working on a morphing algorithm to allow more exploration of sounds within the mapping

- We are designing hardware with haptic feedback that feels more like a real drum kit.

- We will utilise the controllers themselves further in the mapping process, alleviating the need to use the keyboard and mouse of the computer to choreograph movement to sound.

CONCLUSION

In this paper we have described an approach to new instrument design which puts greater emphasis on the choreography of movement. In this approach, the composition of parts of the music takes place in advance of the design of the mappings between gesture and sound. We argue that this approach can improve the visual impact of performance and provide a new perspective on composition and design that leads to a blurring of boundaries between dance and live music performance.

REFERENCES

1. Maes, P.-J., Leman, M., Lesaffre, M., Demey, M., and Moelants, D. From Expressive Gesture to Sound, *Journal on Multimodal User Interfaces*, 3, 1-2 (2010), 67-78.

2. Arias, R. I Know It's Only Noise but I like It: Scattered Notes on the Pleasures of Experimental Improvised Music', *Leonardo Music Journal*, 12 (2002), 31-32.

3. Fels, S. Designing for Intimacy: Creating New Interfaces for Musical Expression, *Proc. IEEE 2004*, 92, 4 (2004), 672-685.

4. Ilsar, A., Havryliv, M., and Johnston, A. The AirSticks: A New Interface For Electronic Percussionists, *SMC'11 2013*, (2013) 220-226.

5. Ilsar, A., Havryliv, M., and Johnston, A. Evaluating the Performance of a New Gestural Instrument Within an Ensemble, *Proc. NIME 2014*, (2014) 339-342.

6. Schnell, N., and Battier, M. Introducing Composed Instruments, Technical and Musicological Implications'. *Proc. NIME 2002*, (2002) 1-5

7. Cook, P.R. 'Music, Cognition, and Computerized Sound: An Introduction to Psychoacoustsics, The MIT Press (2001).

8. Fels, S., Gadd, A., and Mulder, A. Mapping Transparency Through Metaphor: Towards More Expressive Musical Instruments', *Organised Sound*, 7, 2 (2002) 109-126.

9. Mulder, A. Towards a Choice of Gestural Constraints for Instrumental Performers, *Trends in Gestural Control of Music* (2000) 315-335.

10. Ostertag, B. Human Bodies, Computer Music, *Leonardo Music Journal*, 12 (2002) 11-14.

11. Rovan, J., and Hayward, V. Typology of Tactile Sounds and Their Synthesis in Gesture-Driven Computer Music Performance, *Trends in Gestural Control of Music*, (2000) 297-320.

Creativity and Goal Modeling for Software Requirements Engineering

Jennifer Horkoff, Neil Maiden, James Lockerbie
Centre for Creativity in Professional Practice, City University London
{horkoff, neil.maiden.1, james.lockerbie.1}@city.ac.uk

ABSTRACT

In order to be successful, software (applications) must be both useful and innovative. Techniques for determining the requirements (functions and qualities) of software have traditionally focused on utility, with a prominent body of work using graphical goal modeling and analysis to ensure that system functions meet the needs (goals) of users. However, these techniques are not designed to foster creativity, meaning that resulting systems may be functionally useful but not sufficiently innovative. Further work has focused on creativity workshops for finding and developing software requirements. However, creative outputs are not grounded in user goals, are not amenable to decision support techniques, and cannot be easily captured by non-experts. In this work we report initial progress on a project aiming to combine goal modeling and creativity techniques for enhanced software Requirements Engineering (RE). We apply our methods to a historical case in air traffic control, providing example outcomes, illustrating the benefits of a creativity- and goal-oriented approach to early software development.

Author Keywords

Creativity Support; Requirements Engineering; Goal Modeling; GORE; Software Engineering.

ACM Classification Keywords

D.2.1. Requirements/Specifications: Elicitation Methods

INTRODUCTION

It is essential that software (applications) are both useful, meeting the needs of users, and innovative, providing a competitive advantage. Existing work in Software Engineering has focused primarily on software utility, introducing systematic methods such as goal-oriented conceptual modeling and analysis to ensure that the requirements (functionalities and qualities) implemented by a software system meet user needs. Work within the last decade has focused more on the latter goal – ensuring that developed software is innovative –

via the application of creativity techniques as part of software requirements analysis. In this paper, we aim to support the development of software which is both useful and innovative by finding synergistic combinations between conceptual goal modeling and creativity techniques, as applied in determining software system requirements.

Existing creativity work has identified a large number of creativity techniques (e.g., [10]). Creativity can be transformational, changing boundary rules to consider transformative ideas, possibly in another paradigm [4], exploratory, exploring a space of possibilities, or combinatorial, combining together creative output. Each creativity technique can be classified along these dimensions (see the BeCreative Tool for example classifications [2]).

The past decade has seen the application of creativity techniques to software Requirements Engineering (RE), typically in the form of multi-day workshops (e.g., [9, 8]). These workshops gather domain experts and, with the help of experienced facilitators, apply a number of creative activities (e.g., Round Robin, Creativity Triggers, Assumption Busting) in order to elicit creative ideas concerning new software.

Although these workshops have been successful in generating more creative requirements, feeding into the design and construction of innovative systems, challenges exist. Workshop output is captured in a very free and open format (text, use cases). Although this freedom enables capture of creative output, it makes it difficult to transfer these outputs to a format with is more precise and unambiguous, more amenable for downstream development and for transformation into software code. The free-form nature of the creative output makes it difficult to perform any sort of systematic analysis of alternative ideas, with rationale for the rejection or acceptance of certain ideas often lost. Furthermore, creativity workshops for RE (Requirements Engineering) require much guidance and expertise by facilitators, making it difficult to replicate such workshops in different contexts. *Overall, there is a need for methods which capture creative output in a more structured form, facilitating idea selection, making the creative RE process more methodological and applicable by non-experts.*

Goal-Oriented Requirements Engineering has advocated for the use of high-level, graphical models to capture the needs and interactions which underlie system requirements (see [13, 12] for example frameworks). Such models focus on modeling systems from a socio-technical perspective, capturing both software and people in their various roles. Goal

C&C'15, June 22-25, 2015, Glasgow, United Kingdom
ACM 978-1-4503-3598-0/15/06. http://dx.doi.org/10.1145/2757226.2764544

models are particularly amenable to systematic analysis of goal satisfaction, allowing modelers to evaluate and choose between alternative system functionality, analyzing tradeoffs between system qualities (e.g., security vs. usability) [6]. Such analysis helps to make decision-making rationale explicit, preserving rationale for future system changes.

Although GORE has been advocated and used as part of several industrial projects [1], challenges remain. In order to drive such purpose-driven analysis, one must ask: where do system and stakeholder goals come from? Experience has shown that users are more task and process oriented, and often have trouble articulating their motivations [11]. One of the benefits of GORE is the ability to evaluate and choose between functional alternatives (e.g., encrypt communication or add extra password control?). But where do these alternatives come from? How can we ensure that alternatives are sufficiently innovative? *There is a need for methods to incorporate creativity into goal-oriented modeling and analysis.*

In this paper we describe the initial outputs of a research project aiming to exploit the synergies between creativity techniques and goal modeling for RE. Specifically, this paper focuses on the combination of creativity techniques with the structure of goal models, using the contents of the model to facilitate creative thought and exploration, with outputs incorporated back into the model. We illustrate these ideas concretely by returning to a past case study involving air traffic control conducted by the second and third authors. We use the models and domain knowledge from this case to understand how the application of creativity techniques would have produced new ideas, changing project outcomes. We present these changes through a series of examples, demonstrating the combination of techniques.

In the rest of this paper, we provide more detail on creativity and goal modeling for RE, describe our illustrative air traffic case, provide examples of the method combination for this case, then present conclusions and outline future work.

ILLUSTRATIVE EXAMPLE: AIR TRAFFIC CONTROL
The second and third authors conducted an industrial RE analysis for the UK's National Air Traffic Service (NATS). The project aimed to evaluate pre-existing requirements for the Controlled Airspace Infringement Tool (CAIT), which provided air traffic controllers with timely warnings of air traffic infringements. For example, NATS had issues with hobby fliers skirting the controlled airspace, or in one case even flying over a major airport in confusion, believing it was their local airfield. In order to evaluate the effects of the CAIT requirements on the entirety of the system, the team created a large i* (goal model) using input from a series of workshops. The model helped to validate the safety of the software requirements for CAIT over the entire socio-technical system, see [7] for more details of the original study.

Although the analysts were able to apply i*, they did not apply creativity techniques to this case. As a pilot study testing the technique combinations proposed in this work, we return to the NATS study, particularly the large i* model (Figure 2),

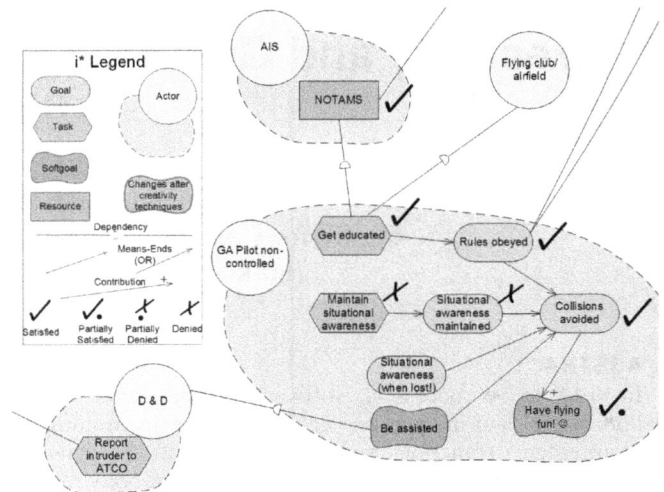

Figure 1. Part of the Requirements (i*) Model for the CAIT (Air Traffic Control) System focusing on the non-controlled General Aviation Pilot.

using this model in conjunction with creativity techniques, reporting selected results.

BACKGROUND
In this section we provide more background on goal-oriented modeling and creativity workshops for software Requirements Engineering (RE).

Goal-Oriented Requirements Engineering
Goal models (e.g., [13, 12]) capture stakeholder goals, refining goals into more detailed goals, or into operational tasks or requirements. The i* framework, for example, contains both software and system actors (applications, stakeholders), goals, tasks, alternative solutions, and dependencies between actors. These models use the concept of a softgoal to capture important system qualities or "non-functional requirements" such as performance, usability, or customer satisfaction [13]. Figure 1 shows a view of part of the i* model built for our illustrative air-traffic control case. Here, the GA (General Aviation) non-controlled Pilot actor wants to, for example, achieve the goal Rules obeyed, which requires him/her to perform the task Get educated. The actor depends on the AIS (Aeronautical Information Service) for the resource NOTAMS (Notice to Airmen). In order to show the complexity and richness of these types of models, we show a high-level view of the entire i* model in Figure 2.

The underlying semantics of these models allows us to evaluate alternative functionality, e.g., Maintain situational awareness vs. Get educated. Qualitative evaluation over i* models lets users explore the level of goal achievement given a particular alternative, asking what if? and is this possible? questions [6]. For example, what if the GA Pilot Got Educated, but did not Maintain situational awareness? The output of this type of analysis is shown in Figure 1.

Creativity Workshops in Requirements Engineering
Several papers have reported experience applying creativity techniques in an RE workshop setting as part of the RESCUE process (e.g., [9, 8]). This approach has been applied

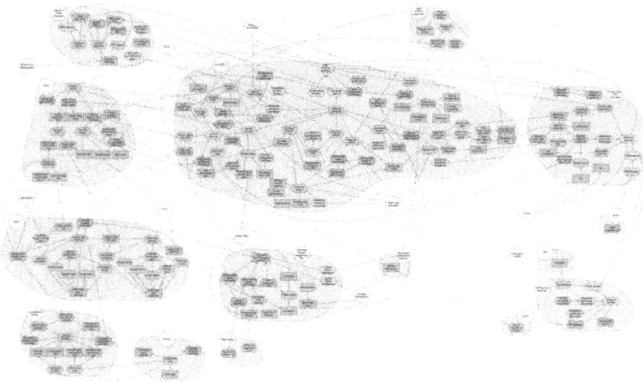

Figure 2. High-level view of the Requirements (i*) Model for CAIT.

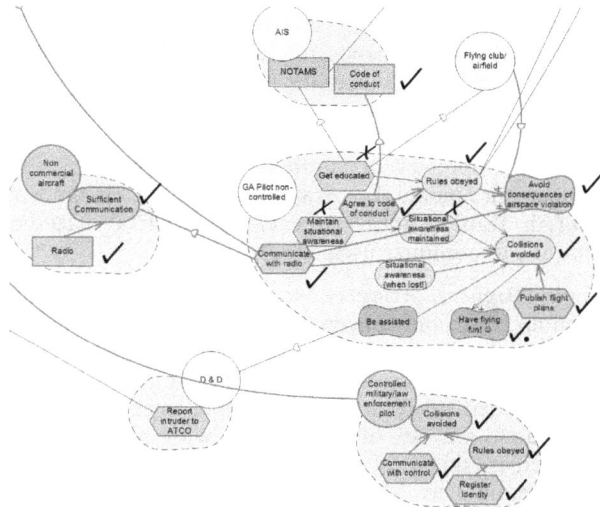

Figure 3. Changes to the i* model (purple) after performing Creativity Activities, focusing on the non-controlled General Aviation Pilot.

in settings such as Air Traffic Control, work-integrated learning, and food traceability. Workshops typically involve several stages, each of which can be mapped to a particular type of creativity: Round Robin (exploratory), Scoping (transformational), Creativity Triggers (exploratory), Constraints (transformational), Ideas from presented design features (exploratory), and Storyboarding (combinatorial). Inputs to workshops included use cases, context, and rich picture models. Workshop outputs included collages using pictures, storyboards, idea cards placed on pin boards, and mock-ups. Although these artifacts were very expressive, they did not explicitly allow for the capture and evaluation of alternatives. Outputs were converted manually by analysts into lists of ideas, requirements, and/or software use cases.

CREATIVITY TECHNIQUES AND GOAL MODELING

We have used the expertise of the authors in both creativity and goal modeling to select creativity techniques which have promising synergies with goal modeling. We select techniques in all categories, with the intention that multiple techniques will be applied in succession. We recommend that starting with transformatory techniques, moving to exploratory creativity, combinatorial creativity, then a period of reflection and evaluation. This order may be adjusted depending on the flow of ideas and needs of the domain.

Transformational Creativity

Customer Journey Maps. This technique encourages modeling or sketching the user's journey through touchpoints, interacting with various system components. In the NATS case, the journey of the uncontrolled pilot initially seems simple, take off, fly, possibly violate airspace, be notified of violation, correct, and land. However, the creation of this map challenges the system boundaries. Does the pilot's journey really start at take off and end and landing? Can the prevention of air space violation begin with training, education or some form of registration? Who provides this training and registration? Does the journey really end when the plane lands? Are air space violations reported and are their negative consequences? For the pilot? The pilot's flying club? Some aspects of these ideas (e.g., Get educated) were captured in the original i* model, but further ideas, such as the consequences of airspace violation, are missing and can be added

to the model. We show the cumulative additions made to the i* model in purple in Figure 3, with the new softgoal Avoid consequences of airspace violations and dependency from the Flying club/airfield added as a result of this particular creative activity.

Hall of Fame/Bright Sparks. The Hall of Fame technique encourages users to make use of famous figures as personas, adopting the mindset of a particular person, and asking how they would use a system. In our case we focus again on the primary problematic actor, the uncontrolled pilot. We can use the Bright Sparks tool to randomly suggest a famous persona, listing relevant creativity questions [3]. For example, the Bright Sparks tool suggests "Daredevil", the man without fear – a blind superhero with radar senses who fights crime. What if Daredevil was our uncontrolled pilot? Examining the goals of the i* actor, such a pilot would no longer aim to achieve the Rules obeyed goal, and would instead rely on his radar senses for enhanced situational awareness, likely avoiding assistance, even when offered. How can the system deal effectively with such Daredevil pilots? One idea may be harsh consequences for airspace violations, another may be some sort of special status for those involved in sanctioned law enforcement, perhaps with classification similar to military aircraft. How are such aircraft registered and identified? Again, we can capture these ideas in the revised i* model, adding a further kind of pilot actor with differentiated goals and dependencies (bottom of Figure 3).

Exploratory Creativity

Assumption Busting. In this technique, underlying domain assumptions are identified and then "busted", exploring the solutions space. Goal-oriented modeling allows for the explicit modeling of assumptions in the model. In the NATS example, satisfaction arguments were collected but were incomplete. For example, there was an assumption that the boundaries of controlled airspace were strict, and aircraft was either in or out; however, that assumption was not explicitly captured in the model. By including this assumption explicitly, we can explore the consequences of removing the assumption, adding resulting ideas back to the model. For example, if the airspace boundary was instead controlled in a more gradual way, for example, with various zones of violations producing gradually more severe warnings, this would have effects across the entire model. For example, this may help the Civil ATCO (Air Traffic Control Officer) to better Prioritize their actions, and to minimize escalations sooner.

Creativity Triggers. Triggers such as service, participation, connections, trust and convenience are used to provoke creative ideas. Applying these to the NATS goal model, connection and trust resonate particularly. Considering again the uncontrolled pilot, many of the challenges in the system are due to the lack of connectivity with this actor. One way to increase this level of connection would be to increase communication between this actor and other actors, perhaps via mandatory radio communication, something which is not currently enforced. Such ideas put constraints on non-commercial airplanes, now added to the i* model, requiring they have sufficient communication devices. In this way, the Civil ATCO could increase connectivity with the non-controlled pilot, working together to achieve Collisions avoided and to avoid consequences of airspace violation.

Similarly, applying the trust trigger to the model generates several ideas. Fundamentally, the system is driven by mistrust of the uncontrolled pilot. If trust can be increased, via education, publishing flight plans, or agreeing to a code of conduct before flying, more infringement incidents could be avoided and safety could be better ensured. These ideas are reflected in purple in Figure 3.

Combinational Creativity

Pair-wise Comparisons. This technique intends to combine generated ideas, narrowing the space of possibilities. Applying it to the i* model, we can consider the combination of various goals or actors, either to merge concepts, or to generate further connections. In the NATS case, we have made modifications to the non-controlled pilot which lead to us explicitly representing the Non-commercial aircraft in the model. We can consider whether this actor may be merged with the pre-existing Aircraft actor, now that both actors require means to communicate with the system, in this case it would mean that Non-commercial aircraft would have to provide information to the Surveillance sensor.

Our changes are summarized in Figure 3. Further consideration of these ideas grounded in the model may produce further changes. Overall, these ideas, if applied, would lead to a system which is more innovative, but still useful, introducing creative solutions while addressing system goals.

Reflection and Evaluation

We can use systematic goal model analysis to evaluate the effectiveness of our ideas, and help chose between alternative ideas. Sample analysis results are shown in Figure 3.

CONCLUSIONS AND FUTURE WORK

We have provided specific examples of the ways in which creativity techniques can be combined with goal modeling for creative requirements engineering. This combination provides the following benefits: **1)** helps to elicit richer goals and more creative alternatives as part of the system design space, **2)** takes advantage of the semi-automated trade-off analysis and reasoning tools (e.g., [6] supporting decision making over alternatives **3)** captures creative output in a form which is more amenable to downstream system development (i.e., architecture, code), **4)** makes the creative RE process more concrete, methodological and visual, better facilitating application by non-experts.

Future plans include further exploration of the combination of creativity techniques with goal modeling, including additional domains and further synergistic creativity techniques (e.g., brainsketching, role play). Future efforts will focus on providing tool support, guiding users through a distributed process of creative thinking and modeling (see [5] for an overview of our tooling plans). Finally, we plan to apply our modeling and techniques to new industrial cases, understanding the benefits and challenges of our method in practice.

ACKNOWLEDGMENTS
This work is supported by an ERC Marie Skodowska-Curie Intra European Fellowship (PIEF-GA-2013-627489) and by a Natural Sciences and Engineering Research Council of Canada Postdoctoral Fellowship (Sept. 2014 - Aug. 2016).

REFERENCES
1. iStar Showcase'11: Exploring the goals of your systems and businesses, practical experiences with i* modeling. `http://www.cs.toronto.edu/km/istar/iStarShowcase_Proceedings.pdf`.
2. BeCreative. `http://becreative.city.ac.uk/index.php`, 2014.
3. BrightSparks. `http://brightsparks.city.ac.uk/`, 2014.
4. Boden, M. A. *The Creative Mind.* London: Abacus, 1990.
5. Horkoff, J., and Maiden, N. Creativity and conceptual modeling for requirements engineering. In *CreaRE: Fifth International Workshop on Creativity in Requirements Engineering* (2015).
6. Horkoff, J., and Yu, E. Interactive goal model analysis for early requirements engineering. *Requirements Engineering* (2014), 1–33.
7. Lockerbie, J., Maiden, N., Engmann, J., Randall, D., Jones, S., and Bush, D. Exploring the impact of software requirements on system-wide goals: a method using satisfaction arguments and i* goal modelling. *Requirements Engineering* 17, 3 (2012), 227–254.
8. Maiden, N., Jones, S., Karlsen, K., Neill, R., Zachos, K., and Milne, A. Requirements engineering as creative problem solving: A research agenda for idea finding. In *18th IEEE International Requirements Engineering Conference (RE10)* (2010), 57–66.
9. Maiden, N., Ncube, C., and Robertson, S. Can requirements be creative? experiences with an enhanced air space management system. In *Software Engineering, 2007. ICSE 2007. 29th International Conference on* (May 2007), 632–641.
10. Michalko, M. *Thinkertoys: A Handbook of Creative-Thinking Techniques.* Potter/TenSpeed/Harmony, 2010.
11. Rolland, C., Souveyet, C., and Achour, C. B. Guiding goal modeling using scenarios. *Software Engineering, {IEEE} Transactions on 24*, 12 (1998), 1055–1071.
12. van Lamsweerde, A. *Requirements Engineering: From System Goals to UML Models to Software Specifications.* Wiley, Mar. 2009.
13. Yu, E. Towards modelling and reasoning support for early-phase requirements engineering. In *3rd IEEE International Symposium on Requirements Engineering*, IEEE (1997), 226–235.

Decreasing the Effect of Verbal Noise in Analyzing Cognitive Activity of a Design Process

Mina Tahsiri
University of Nottingham
Department of Architecture &
Built Environment, University
of Nottingham, Nottingham,
UK. NG7 2RD
mina.tahsiri@nottingham.ac.uk

Jonathan Hale
University of Nottingham
Department of Architecture &
Built Environment, University of
Nottingham, Nottingham, UK.
NG7 2RD
jonathan.hale@nottingham.ac.uk

Chantelle Niblock
University of Nottingham
Department of Architecture &
Built Environment, University
of Nottingham, Nottingham,
UK. NG7 2RD
chantelle.niblock@nottingham.ac.uk

ABSTRACT

In studying cognitive activity in design it is common practice to use designers' verbalizations during a design process to elicit the reasoning behind design actions. These verbalizations are segmented in order to enable a quantifiable analysis of the cognitive processes. Researchers have shown how Shannon's entropy can be applied to coded verbal data to provide a measure of creativity of those processes. We applied this method to a pilot study, investigating the effects of different design tools on creativity in the context of architectural design. Participants had to design three tasks of isomorphic nature, each with a different tool, in one design session. As shown a significant number of verbal comments were repetitions of already established ideas. Such comments brought nothing new to the sequence of activities but affected the value of information carried within that process which biased the measure of creativity. The paper regards these utterance as verbal noise. It proposes the use of corpus linguistic tools together with a coding scheme that can depict the hierarchical relationship of cognitive patterns used in the process to eliminate verbal noise from analysis. The method was applied to one participant's data, which shows a promising step in increasing the veracity of using verbal data in analyzing cognitive activity.

Author Keywords

Design process; cognitive activity; creativity; verbal noise

INTRODUCTION

In a protocol study, verbalizations are segmented based on the intention of the designer and then coded using a coding scheme. Each segment represents an idea and because design is known to be a reflection-in-action process, an idea

C&C '15, June 22-25, 2015, Glasgow, United Kingdom
ACM 978-1-4503-3598-0/15/06.
http://dx.doi.org/10.1145/2757226.2764545

may reoccur in different forms at different points within the process. The semantic connection leads to a linked network of ideas. In any cognitive system all of the segments (ideas) have the potential to be linked together depending on the conditions such as the external stimuli or characteristics of the designer.

Nevertheless, for every given idea the more links that can be made to ideas in succession, the richer that system is in terms of idea generation. Also the more able the system is in linking distant segments (ideas) together increases the integration of links and the cohesiveness of the creative system. Kan and Gero [6] use the terms forelinks to describe the former and horizonlinks for the latter, and suggest that a creative cognitive system is one that reaches an equilibrium between the number of generated ideas and their cohesiveness. In this context, segments represent information, each of which bears different values for that system. Therefore Kan and Gero suggest employing Shannon's entropy for measuring the sum value of these different link categories as a measure of creativity. Accordingly, if every idea is linked to every other idea, then the outcome of that system is known and there is no degree of uncertainty, therefore the entropy measures 0. This is also the case where an idea fails to make any connections, however unlikely. Maximum entropy of 1 is reached when each segment can make half of its potential links [6].

When a certain idea reoccurs or a semantically similar related idea is generated, a link with the original idea is made and the entropy of the cognitive system increases. So a verbal comment, however inferior in the number of links it makes, can affect the measurement of creativity. Imagine the case, where you are asked to solve a problem. If it is your first encounter with such a problem, although you may not find the answer, but you often find yourself exhausted after many seemingly discrete trial and errors of ideating. However if you had some adequate familiarity with the concepts involved to solve that problem, although you may never have solved it before, you tend to be able to provide a more coherent presentation of your answer in the same time frame. In the second case, you would probably provide

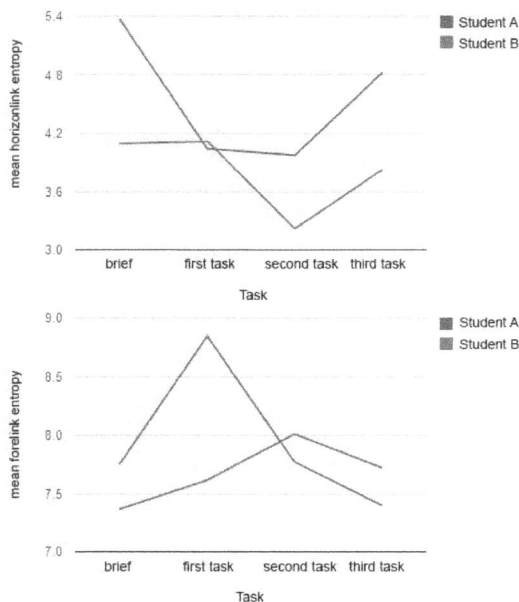

Figure 1: The mean dynamic entropies of student's cognitive process during each task stage of the design session

more verbal comments as you are actually less engaged with the actual solving of the problem. You may find yourself repeating yourself without necessarily needing to do so as an effort to show you are producing thought. Such utterances are deemed as noise in this paper. Now, in two process where we can argue in favor of expecting similar patterns in the entropy of the cognitive system, but graphs depicting dynamic changes indicate otherwise; the viability of our proposed method for eliminating noise can be assessed in how well the graphs of dynamic entropies of the two process map onto (or close to) each other.

PILOT PROTOCOL STUDY

A pilot study was conducted to compare the effect of three different design tools (Rhinoceros 3D and SketchUp as Computer Aided Design tools and freehand sketching) on the distribution of cognitive activity and creativity for two architecture students with similar problem solving approaches. Each student engaged in three successive design tasks of isomorphic structure in one design session with only one tool assigned to that task and they were required to think aloud.

The analysis proceeded by using the Function-Behavior-Structure coding scheme (developed by Gero) [3] to code the data and then by linking the segments twice and arbitrating the results using the Delphi method. The linkoder [4] software was then used to calculate the mean dynamic entropies for each process. As shown in figure 1, in comparing the mean dynamic entropies of different tasks, both students displayed a significant drop in the forelink entropy of the last task but rose to their highest measure of horizonlink entropy in this task.

Further examination of the processes shows parallel graphs in changing from the second task to the third between the students, although either student used a different tool in their third task. This indicates that as the project develops the students become less reliant on the tool and more reliant on their mental imagery to shape a concept. Therefore by this stage much of the students' verbalizations were a result of previously conceived ideas. In other words, the outcomes of the third task revealed the effect of learning successive tasks have on one another.

Moreover the approach and succession of reasoning in the final task seemed to portray a close resemblance to that of the brief reading stage. Some of the verbal comments were identical to ideas provided earlier on and in some instance they were repeated more than a couple of times within the course of the final task. An example of such is student A's comment:"but it was like towards the[..]creation of mirrors, you will reflect all the flames, like onto the pavilion", "but it was like towards the[..]creation of mirrors, you will reflect all the flames, like onto the pavilion", "and then you would have like a couple of mirrors. All the inside of these walls that will be reflecting like all these flames."

In regards to creativity and idea generation involved when designing, using tools such as sketching or designing based on mental imagery alone, Bilda et al [2] concluded no significant difference between these two. Their study was done on professional designers. Other studies indicate that experienced designers tend to address design based on their preconceived ideas, a breadth first depth later approach [8,10] and therefore the design tool acts as a peripheral aid to cognition. At a smaller scale, a similar conclusion can be made in case of less experienced designers like students, who gather experience during the course of a task and become less dependent on their external utensils in design thinking as the task proceeds.

The expectancy was therefore, to be able to see a similar pattern in the structure of forelink and horizonlink entropy graphs between the brief reading stage and the final task, yet this was not the case. And so it was conclude that a considerable number of the verbal comments were noise.

PROPOSITION FOR REDUCING VERBAL NOISE

In order to reduce the amount of verbal noise, the following necessities were recognized: 1- to identify semantically similar ideas via a concordance tool used in corpus linguistic analysis called *AntConc* [1]; 2- To investigate their significance in the succession of events, by considering their pattern structure and their role in the distribution of cognitive information across internal and external constructs of the cognitive system.

Antconc enables the extraction of keywords from a reference corpus in order to distinguish between semantic concordances within a target corpus/text. For this research, the verbal comments of the brief reading stage formed the reference corpus and the ones from the final task, were the target corpus. The method for eliciting pattern structure was derived by tailoring Zhang and Norman's [12] method in analyzing the effect of representations in distributed cognitive tasks, for design processes. The proposed method enabled the decomposition of the cognitive process into its internal and external components so that the different functions of internal and external representations can be identified. It also illustrated the hierarchical relationship between the patterns and ideas derived from them and allowed for a parallel analysis to that done via the F-B-S coding scheme.

Distributed cognition and representational analysis

Distributed cognitive theory, describes cognition as an aggregation of functions constructed by internal and external constructs of a cognitive system [5]. On this basis, Zhang and Norman discuss that the internal and external representational spaces together form a distributed representational space which is the representation of the abstract task space. Tasks which are isomorphic (structured the same with different representation) will have a similar structure when analyzed at the level of abstract task space but the distribution of patterns across the two spaces and their integrations may be different. To be able to analyze this they show that information that a person has to remember to solve a problem is homed in the internal task space, whereas the information in the external task space are those implicitly derived from the internal information or which the problem solver produces unconsciously.

The cognitive pattern structure of a design process

In design studies, a brief may provide the initial set of information needed for problem solving but a respectful number of information is produced as a result of evaluation and reflection in action. This fact is demonstrated by studies that use coding schemes, categorizing coded segments into new and old [11]. The modification and regeneration of ideas denotes a hierarchical order for cognitive patterns contributing to the idea. Similar to pattern recognition in the neocortex (refer to [9]), information in the brief acts as a corpus of primary patterns, which prepares the mind for recognition of higher level patterns that are a combination of the primary ones. The more a particular pattern is used and the more the designer becomes conscious of it, the higher possibility of its contribution to higher level patterns. The patterns which have homed in in the conscious part of memory can be communicated verbally.

Therefore in the pilot study conducted, a keyword generator was used to extract the main primary patterns at the center of attention to the designer in the brief reading stage. What the designers directly takes on from the brief and tries to memorize is their internal patterns and what they infer from it depending on other experiences is their external ones. Consequently there are three groups of patterns: primary, modified and generated. So where other coding schemes which code at the level of the artifact in production and

Category	Name	Description
Analysis (the formulation of the task space)	Primary Internal Pattern (IRpe)	Patterns created directly from reading the design brief for the first time, without any drawing taken out
	Generated Internal Pattern (IRg)	Patterns created as a result of reformulation
	Modified Internal Pattern (IRm)	Patterns from the previous move modified as a result of reformulation
	Primary Expected External Pattern (ERpe)	Implicit patterns in the design brief, driven from the primary internal patterns. (patterns other than the internal patterns which justify the designer's proceeding action)
	Generated Expected External Pattern (Erg)	Implicit patterns created as a result of reformulation
	Modified Expected External Pattern (ERm)	Implicit patterns from the previous move modified as a result of reformulation
Synthesis (Drawing/ Depicting action)	Applied Structural External Pattern (ERs)	Drawing actions leaving a mark on the representational medium as patterns
	Potential Structural External Pattern	Drawing action or bodily actions (eye movement/hand movement) not leaving a mark
Evaluation (Reformulation actions)	Transformed Image evaluation (ERs'₁)	When no new pattern is added to the task space but an action is executed, such as deleting. (no drawing action is executed as a result of this pattern)
	Primary Image evaluation (ERs'₂)	When no new pattern is added to the task space but a drawing action is executed on the current shape
	Task Space evaluation (ERs'₃)	When new patterns are introduced to the task space or old patterns refined as a result of transforming actions such as rotation.

Table 1.Categories of a pattern of cognition in design

analyze the structure of the abstract task space, this research's method of coding provides an insight into the distribution of patterns and the cognitive complexities involved in producing the artifact. Table 1 describes the different pattern categories used in this research.

Reducing verbal noise for student A's final task

Student A's verbal comments from the brief reading stage were fed into AntConc as a reference corpus and a series of keywords were produced based on the likelihood of their use. Amongst these, keywords which referred to a functional, behavioral or structural considerations of the design were extracted. These words in the order of their likelihood are [sketchup, stuff, flames, see, mirror, corner, floor, opening, slab, wall, center, glass, geometry, material, organic, weaving, stairs, triangle, bricks, comfort, covered, movement, reflection and window]. The concordances for each keyword were then looked into.

Figure 2 shows that the word "see", as an example, had 23 hits in the final task. Hits 9, 10 are the student's comment

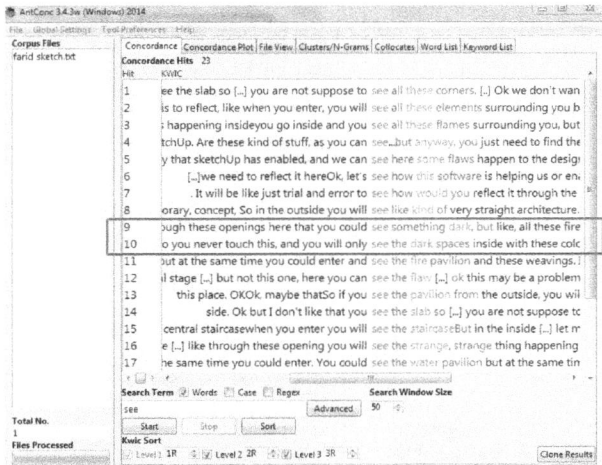

Figure 2: Concordances of Student A's verbalization for the search term "see"

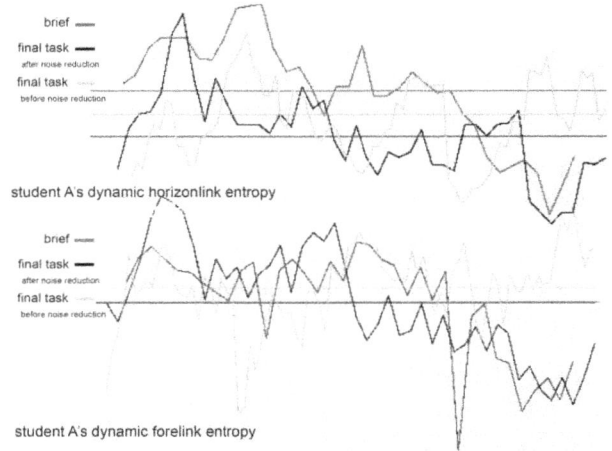

Figure 3: Student A's comparison of dynamic forelink/horizon link entropies at brief reading and the final task pre and post verbal noise reduction

about "seeing something dark in the inside". Both of these hits, related to segments which had received the same F-B-S code (Bs). Each segment was analyzed in relation to the pattern structure of its preceding and successive segments. Both segments (hits) use the same distribution of internal-external patterns (IRm9+IRm14/ERpe17). The pattern, IRm14 was newly generated in hit 9 and that segment affects the pattern structure of the segment in its succession. However hit 10 uses no new pattern and has no effect on the next segment. In the case of hit 10, IRm14 was also used in the preceding segment, and so the reuse of that pattern combination was expected and added no significant value of the succession of event; hence regarded as noise.

In total 58 verbal noises were identified and eliminated from the data. The link relationship between the remaining data was once again revised, for which forelink and horizonlink entropies were calculated and graphs drawn. As shown in figure 3 the pattern of change in dynamic entropies after noise reduction displays a closer resemblance to that of the brief reading stage. This outcome, suggests the proposed method a promising approach for eliminating confounding variables from protocol studies.

CONCLUSION AND FURTHER WORK
Although verbalization may be criticized as a way of understanding genuine cognitive activity, it is still a main tool for creating a general image of what goes on in the mind. Therefore it is important for analysis methods that use verbal data to be refined. This study displayed the relevance of an understanding of pattern structure and their internal-external cognitive distribution as an aid in distinguishing between genuine verbal data and noise. However, the method in itself needs to be refined and tested with a larger study group. In particular, for both eliminating noise and revising links, a less subjective, more automated approach should be sought after. Relevant to this and in another study Kan and Gero [7] reduced subjectivity in linking segment by developing a LISP program that uses an

English language corpus to make semantic links. Therefore integrating corpus linguistic methods and cognitive pattern recognition is a step in a promising direction.

REFRENCES
1. Anthony, L. AntConc (version 3.4.3). Waseda University, Tokyo, Japan, (2014).
2. Bilda, Z., Gero, J.S., Purcell, T. To sketch or not to sketch? That is the question. *Design Studies*, 27(2006), 587–613.
3. Gero, J.S., Mc Neill, T. An approach to the analysis of design protocols. *Design Studie*s. 19 (1998), 21–61.
4. Gero, J.S., Pourmohamadi, morteza. Linkographer: An analysis tool to study design protocols based on FBS Coding scheme. In *proc. ICED 11*(2011), 1–10.
5. Hutchins, E. Cognition in the wild. MIT Press, Cambridge, (1995).
6. Kan, J., Gero, J.S. Acquiring information from linkography in protocol studies of designing. *Design Studies*, 29 (2008), 315–337.
7. Kan, J., Gero, J.S. Using entropy to measure design creativity: Using a text based analysis tool on design protocols, *Rigor and Relevance in Design,* International Association of Design Research Societies, (2009).
8. Kavakli, M., Gero, J.S. Sketching as a mental imagery processing. *Design Studies*. 22 (2001), 347–364.
9. Kurzweil, R. How to create a mind: The secrets of human thought revealed. Viking Penguin, (2012)
10. Ozkan, O., Dogan, F. Cognitive strategies of analogical reasoning in design: Differences between expert and novice designers. *Design Studies*. 34 (2013), 161–192.
11. Suwa, M., Purcell, T., Gero, J.S. Macroscopic analysis of design processes based on a scheme for coding designer's cognitive actions. *Design Studies*. 19 (1998), 455–483.
12. Zhang, J., Norman, D.A., 1994. Representations in distributed cognitive tasks. *Cognitive Science*. 18 (1994), 87–122.

[self.]: an Interactive Art Installation that Embodies Artificial Intelligence and Creativity

Axel Tidemann
Department of Computer Science
Norwegian University of Science and Technology
Trondheim, Norway
tidemann@idi.ntnu.no

Øyvind Brandtsegg
Department of Music
Norwegian University of Science and Technology
Trondheim, Norway
oyvind.brandtsegg@ntnu.no

ABSTRACT

This paper describes [self.], an open source art installation that embodies artificial intelligence (AI) in order to learn, react, respond and be creative in its environment. Biologically inspired models are implemented to achieve this behaviour. The robot is built using a moving head, projector, camera and microphones. No form of knowledge or grammar have been implemented in the AI, the system starts in a "tabula rasa" state and learns everything via its own sensory channels, forming categories in a bottom-up fashion. The robot recognizes sounds, and is able to recognize similar sounds, link them with the corresponding faces, and use the knowledge of past experiences to form new sentences. It projects neural memories that represent an association between sound and video as experienced during interaction.

Author Keywords

Artificial Intelligence; Interactive; Robot

ACM Classification Keywords

I.2.6 Learning: Connectionism and neural nets, Knowledge acquisition; I.2.9 Robotics

INTRODUCTION

This paper describes the early stages of an open source art installation that implements various AI techniques to govern its behaviour. The motivation is to raise questions of what are the implications as AI becomes a greater part of our lives, and how people react to an entity that they form in their own image. [self.] is much like a child, since its vocabulary (both visually and auditive) is dependent on what it learns from the people interacting with it. The creators have deliberately avoided pre-programming the system, so the resulting behaviour emerges from the interaction it experiences. This makes the entity evolve over time.

BACKGROUND

The project started out as an attempt to conceptualize what the effect of AI will have on society in the general case, and how artificially intelligent machines will interact with human beings. The original intent was to explore a biologically inspired architecture that would strive towards the ultimate goal in AI; consciousness. The ability to learn and categorize concepts learned from interaction with the environment without a prior knowledge base is an example of such a design choice. As an artwork, [self.] plays on the relationship between technology and humans, and relates to language, philosophy and the contemporary (over-)focus on self realization.

MATERIALS AND METHODS

This section describes how the robot has been implemented. Both the source code as well as building instructions have been published online[1]. The overall architecture can be seen in Figure 1. The following text will describe the various building blocks of the architecture. The aim of the project is thus to combine well-known techniques from sound processing and AI to create an entity that is entirely open in design and implementation. The robot was built by modifying an off-the-shelf moving head for stage lighting, stripping it for all components except the motors. A video projector, USB camera, 2 microphones and a small speaker was mounted on the remaining motorized frame. A picture of the final installation can be seen in Figure 2.

Inputs

The robot has two forms of input: video (USB camera) and audio, where two microphones were mounted in a simple X-Y stereo configuration, for the purpose of sensing the horizontal position of the sound source.

Cognition and creativity

The robot uses its sensory input to learn. The signals are sent to three different modules; these are face tracking (video), audio/video-association (audio and video) and sound processing (audio). The outputs of these modules (as well as that of "Misc. behaviours") are propagated to more higher-level functions ("Learning" and "Responding") as well as low-level motor control, before being sent to the output layer modules.

Face tracking

The module searches for faces in the stream of images coming from the camera. Since the robot is built for interaction with people, the closest face is selected in case of multiple

C&C 2015, June 22–25, 2015, Glasgow, United Kingdom.
ACM 978-1-4503-3598-0/15/06.
http://dx.doi.org/10.1145/2757226.2764549

---

[1]www.github.com/axeltidemann/self_dot

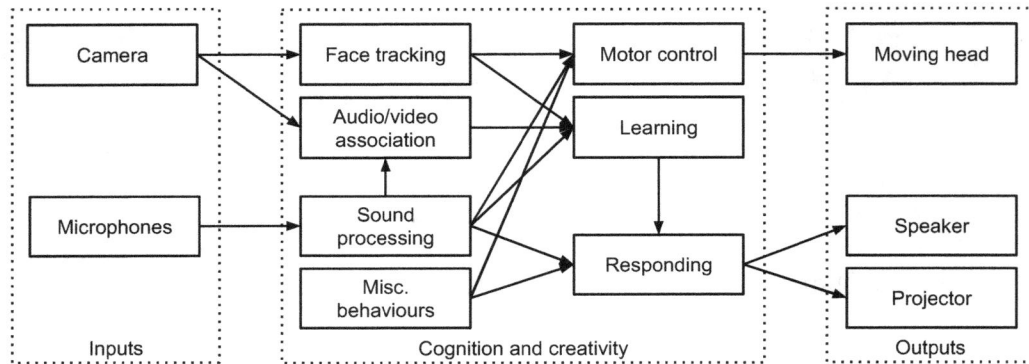

Figure 1. [self.] overall architecture. The various modules are described in the text, the signal paths between them are indicated by the arrows.

faces. OpenCV[2] is used to do face extraction. The face extraction done by OpenCV is sensitive to rotations of the face; it works best when people stare directly into the camera. In order to do face *tracking*, a Kalman filter [9] is implemented. It performs online state estimation of the face position, allowing for smooth face tracking. This is beneficial in situations where OpenCV intermittently fails to find a face, even though a face is present in an image. The face tracking influences motor control, since the estimated position of the closest face is used to move the robot so that the face is in the center of the image.

Sound processing

Audio input and output is done via Csound[3]. Automatic calibration of the input signal level and capture of a background noise image is done at startup and during runtime. The input signal is analyzed for transients and this is used as a crude segmentation marker. Transient detection is based on amplitude slope and as such is independent of the absolute amplitude. Audio recording starts when a transient is detected, and continues until the signal level has dropped below a threshold (typically 6 dB below the signal level at the initial transient). Silent (or noisy) parts of the recording is stripped before passing on the audio to other parts of the system.

A biologically inspired model of the inner ear [10] is used to analyze the raw WAVE files created by Csound. The model performs sound analysis based on a bio-mimetic cascade of asymmetric resonators with fast-acting compression. This is a biologically inspired model of the cochlea, and the output is called a neural activation pattern (NAP). What separates it from a Fourier spectrum is that the NAP has features that correspond to auditory physiology. The NAP is used for both learning and building an association between audio and video, as described in the following sections.

Audio/video association

Since the robot also records video in addition to sound, it adds to its expressional capacity being able to project visual memories related to the interaction. In order to make the robot

seem more "alive", the visual representations are an association between audio and visual input. This is achieved by using neural networks, more specifically Echo State Networks (ESNs) [8], a relatively novel neural network architecture that is characterized by its huge hidden layer and fast training algorithm. When a certain interaction segment is to be learned, the corresponding NAP and image sequence are learned by an ESN, which represents an audio-video *transformation*.

Motor control

Motor control is inspired by Brooks' subsumption architecture [3]. There are two mechanisms that trigger movement of the robot, 1) face tracking and 2) sound. Face tracking seeks to move the robot directly in front of the person speaking to it. The sound movement triggers are based on a stereo perception of where the sound comes from. One can describe the face tracking as higher level cognitive function, and the sound movement trigger as lower level. This is where the subsumption architecture comes into play; a sound can inhibit the face tracking motor control. This typically happens if someone is standing in front of the robot but not speaking to it, the robot will then turn to another person that starts talking.

Learning

Learning is the core element of [self.]. As described above, [self.] learns a multi-modal episodic memory of each interaction, building an audio-visual memory. The robot then clusters similar sounds together, based on the length and the similarity of the NAPs. The clustering is based on the Hamming distance [6] between the sounds of roughly the same length. This module also learns to recognize faces, since the "Face tracking" module outputs the extracted face. The facial recognition is done by a Support Vector Machine [4]. The various techniques implemented are chosen based on empirical experimentation.

The recorded audio segments are analyzed with regards to the contexts in which the sound was perceived. This creates a set of quality dimensions for each sound and [self.] uses these as modes of association when it creates an output statement. One such context is the face recognition ("who said what"), another is the context of the sentence in which the sound was perceived. The position of the sound in a sentence (e.g. in the

---

[2]opencv.org
[3]www.csounds.com

182

beginning or end) is also recorded, and there are also contexts for longer time spans (e.g. sounds perceived within a couple of minutes or within an hour). Sound duration is recorded, and also a similarity measure (Hamming distance) to other classes of sounds, used as yet another such context or quality dimension. In this manner, a multi-dimensional web of associations is built, where a dynamic weight can be applied to each. The balancing and weighting of the different associations is done in a manner inspired by fuzzy logic, where an item can have partial membership in each of the different relevant contexts. The most significant (loudest) sound in an input sentence is flagged, and this is used as the seed for the associations of [self.] when generating a response.

Responding

When a new sound (i.e. the NAP) reaches the responding module, the most similar sound in the audio-visual memory is retrieved, based on the Hamming distance to the other sounds of roughly same length. Using the most significant sound in the latest input sentence, [self.] looks for associations to this sound, to create a response sentence. The associations are created by looking up the different contexts as described above. It can for example look for sounds that are similar, sounds uttered by the same face and sounds perceived within the same sentence or time span. In this manner a chain of associations is created, and this is used as a repository of sounds to construct a response. The position in a sentence each sound was perceived in is also used as a filter for selection of sounds in a responding statement.

After finding the most similar sound and generating the response, the visual response of the robot is made. This is the output of the corresponding audio-visual ESN when given the NAP of the new sound as input. This yields a visual output that is almost guaranteed to never be the same; the similarity of the training sound compared to the new sound will determine the output characteristics. For instance, a new sound that is very similar to the original training sound will yield a sequence of images that are quite similar to the original, whereas sounds that are more different will produce a sequence of images that *represent* this difference. Typically, this can be seen as effects ranging from grey blurs to flashing images. The sound-to-image association creates a visual collage-like series of images, representing the memory of which person [self.] has learned each sound from. As such this gives a direct insight into the learning process the AI has gone through when interacting with its environment.

Memories that are not recalled ("refreshed") when [self.] is responding will fade away as time passes.

Misc. behaviours

Since the robot is an installation, it is programmed to perform certain behaviours over time to exhibit a more life-like behaviour. These can be categorized as follows: 1) *Idling:* if the robot does not see a face nor hear a sound for a certain period of time, it will start searching for face. Upon finding a face, [self.] retrieves sounds uttered by this face earlier, and uses these to initiate a conversation. Similarly, if the robot has not said anything for a certain period of time, it will say something on its own. 2) *Dream state:* at night it

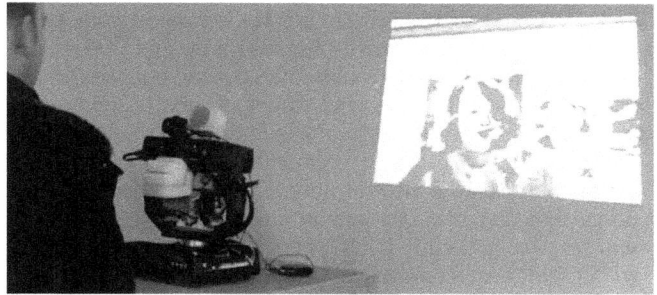

Figure 2. [self.] interacting with a person.

is programmed to go through all the memories experienced throughout the day. During the learning process (see above), similar sounds are grouped together to form a category of sounds. Sometimes this classification might be erroneous. By calculating a sparse representation of the sounds [10], the similarity between grouped sounds can be estimated. Those found to be too different within a group are discarded; this can be seen as a "mental hygiene" and consolidation process, and is called the "dream state" since this resembles what the brain does during sleep [11]. 3) *Optimization of parameters for the response mechanism:* the learning of associations between sounds, faces and their sequences yields a representation that can be used to answer in a creative way. However, there is a large set of parameters that need to be adjusted in order to achieve the desired behaviour. The parameters are themselves sensitive to how many memories are stored and their inherent sequences. The AI is able to adjust these parameters itself, by optimizing the parameter settings using a genetic algorithm [7]. In other words, [self.] writes part of its own behavioural program using evolution.

Outputs

To produce sound output, a speaker is mounted on top of the projector. Csound is used for the playback of recorded sound segments. The output sounds are transformed slightly, using granular [2] and spectral[4] transformation techniques. These transformation are subtle, aiming to retain the voice characteristics of the originally perceived sound, while also providing a distinct own voice for [self.]. This is intended as a means of connecting each output sound to the person [self.] has learned this sound from, much in the same manner as can be perceived from the ESN-based video output. The projector mounted on top of the moving head is used to display the ESN generated images from the "Responding" module; this is not simply playback of a video recording, but a visualization of the neural memory of the learned interaction.

DISCUSSION

The developmental focus of [self.] has been on using biologically inspired models in order to create an artificially intelligent entity, where its entire knowledge base comes from experience. The intention of its developers is to not bias

---

[4]www.csounds.com/manual/html/SpectralRealTime.html

the robot, and therefore it is not bootstrapped with knowledge. The developers have observed how this yields an installation that not only fosters interactivity, but reinforces it, since those who interact tend to get excited by recognizing sounds/images of themselves or people they know. Furthermore, the responses of [self.] is influenced not only by what the person says, but also for how long this person says something. For instance, if a person utters a simple word, [self.] will respond accordingly. If a person makes a long sentence, [self.] will form a response of roughly equal length, with corresponding sounds and images that make sense to the robot. This feedback loop further encourages interaction.

By implementing biological models and having a bottom-up way of learning, the goal is to implement *cognitive abilities* in the robot. Another goal is also to make this an autonomous entity that embodies *creativity*. This is most evidently shown in two places: 1) the combination of known sounds into novel phrases, and 2) how this system tunes itself using evolution. Artificial evolution and computational creativity are inherently linked, since it gives a machine the possibility of finding novel combinations of previously learned concepts. Indeed, since evolution is the driving explorative mechanism in nature, and thus arguably also its *creative force*, it seems fitting to equip the robot with this functionality in order to write parts of its own behavioural program. In other words, the robot is programmed to be creative without being told *how* to do so, or *what* to do.

[self.] is not just an interactive art installation, due to its open nature it can also be thought of as a research *platform* when it comes to human-computer interaction, cognition and creativity. This is facilitated by sharing the code and the design plans.

This paper has described the first implementation of [self.]. However, the authors are very aware that the system is far from being a truly sentient AI. Even though the robot learns like a child, it currently does not have the possibility to grow into an adult in terms of reasoning power and deeper knowledge of its surroundings. These limitations are also partly due to the state of AI research. On the other hand, this serves as a motivation to continue implementing models of human cognition to get closer to this goal, as described in the next section.

FUTURE WORK
The goal is to develop [self.] into an AI with higher levels of cognition. To enable this while preserving the principle of not giving [self.] a pre-programmed knowledge base to start from, it seems necessary to first delve into lower levels of perception to create a finer granularity of the learned items. This would allow for more flexible recombination when generating output. One of the possibilities to enhance the recognition of sounds is to implement more sophisticated machine learning techniques. An interesting (and traditional) approach is to use Hidden Markov Models [1]; newer developments include deep learning with neural networks [5]. The motor capabilities of [self.] has the potential to convey *emotions*, since it has been observed that people interacting with [self.] tend to empathize with the way it moves its head, e.g. being sad if

the head is pointing downwards. This is purely unintentional at the current stage, but reveals the possibility of making the robot even more expressive in a way that is intuitive to humans.

ACKNOWLEDGMENTS
The authors would like to thank the Arts Council Norway, Trondheim Muncipality and the Norwegian University of Science and Technology for financial support. Special thanks to Stefan Gemzell of Ljusdesign for giving us for free the first moving head to experiment on, and to Robin Støckert of Soundscape Studios for providing us with the rest of the hardware for the robot. We would also like to thank curator Anne Gro Erikstad inviting us to create the artwork [self.] for its first exhibition at Trøndelag Senter For Samtidskunst in November 2014.

REFERENCES
1. Leonard E. Baum and Ted Petrie. 1966. Statistical Inference for Probabilistic Functions of Finite State Markov Chains. *Ann. Math. Statist.* 37, 6 (1966), 1554–1563.

2. Øyvind Brandtsegg, Sigurd Saue, and Thom Johansen. 2011. Particle synthesis – a unified model for granular synthesis. In *Linux Audio Conference*.

3. Rodney Brooks. 1986. A robust layered control system for a mobile robot. *IEEE journal of Robotics and Automation* 2, 1 (1986), 14–23.

4. Corinna Cortes and Vladimir Vapnik. 1995. Support-vector networks. *Machine Learning* 20, 3 (1995), 273–297.

5. Alex Graves and Navdeep Jaitly. 2014. Towards end-to-end speech recognition with recurrent neural networks. In *Proceedings of the 31st International Conference on Machine Learning (ICML-14)*. 1764–1772.

6. R.W. Hamming. 1950. Error detecting and error correcting codes. *Bell System Technical Journal, The* 29, 2 (1950), 147–160.

7. John H. Holland. 1975. *Adaptation in Neural and Artificial Systems*. University of Michigan Press, Ann Arbor.

8. Herbert Jaeger and Harald Haas. 2004. Harnessing Nonlinearity: Predicting Chaotic Systems and Saving Energy in Wireless Communication. *Science* 304, 5667 (2004), 78–80.

9. Rudolph E. Kalman. 1960. A new approach to linear filtering and prediction problems. *Journal of Fluids Engineering* 82, 1 (1960), 35–45.

10. Richard F. Lyon, Martin Rehn, Samy Bengio, Thomas C Walters, and Gal Chechik. 2010. Sound retrieval and ranking using sparse auditory representations. *Neural computation* 22, 9 (2010), 2390–2416.

11. R. Stickgold, J. A. Hobson, R. Fosse, and M. Fosse. 2001. Sleep, Learning, and Dreams: Off-line Memory Reprocessing. *Science* 294, 5544 (2001), 1052–1057.

Drawing Apprentice: An Enactive Co-Creative Agent for Artistic Collaboration

Nicholas Davis, Chih-Pin Hsiao, Kunwar Yashraj Singh, Lisa Li, Sanat Moningi, Brian Magerko

Georgia Institute of Technology
School of Interactive Computing
{ndavis35, chsiao9, kysingh, lisa_li, smoningi3, magerko}@gatech.edu

ABSTRACT

This paper describes a co-creative web-based drawing application called the Drawing Apprentice. This system collaborates with users in real time abstract drawing. We describe the theory, interaction design, and user experience of the Drawing Apprentice system. We evaluate the system with formative user studies and expert evaluations from a juried art competition in which a Drawing Apprentice submission won the code-based art category.

Author Keywords

Computational Creativity, Creativity Support Tools, Art, Collaboration, Cognitive Science

ACM Classification Keywords

H.5.m. Information interfaces and presentation (e.g., HCI): Miscellaneous.

INTRODUCTION

During collaboration, ideas mix, fuse, and combine to form unexpected results [4]. The feedback offered in collaboration helps individuals iterate and refine ideas through time, often leading to more creative outcomes [4]. Collaboration therefore offers a compelling mechanism to enhance the creative process and stimulate creative engagement through time.

The Drawing Apprentice is a co-creative drawing agent that collaborates with human users in real time artistic collaboration. It is aimed at supporting the creative process of users by inspiring and pushing their creative boundaries similar to a human collaborator (as opposed to the typical focus of creativity support tools: *improving the creative product* [5]).

The system is designed to stimulate the user's creativity by introducing unexpected contributions at the right time in the creative process. However, determining when to make an expected or an unexpected contribution is difficult to know

C&C '15, June 22-25, 2015, Glasgow, United Kingdom
ACM 978-1-4503-3598-0/15/06.
http://dx.doi.org/10.1145/2757226.2764555

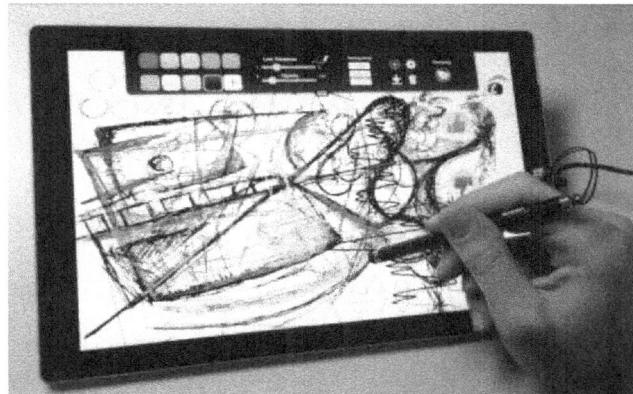

Figure 1. User collaborating with the Drawing Apprentice web application.

without understanding what the user is thinking as they draw. The Drawing Apprentice system analyzes each of the user's lines as they are drawn in real time. The agent develops a dynamic model of the user's creative behavior through time to generate and modify creative actions.

RELATED WORK

There are many effective methods to model creativity and collaboration, such as shared mental models [2] and turn taking [6]. However, many approaches face a similar knowledge engineering bottleneck in open-ended creative contexts. The complexity and unpredictability of human creativity presents a challenge to many approaches in artificial intelligence.

Recent advances of interactive machine learning (IML) [3] present a potential solution to some of those knowledge engineering requirements. In IML, agents observe humans and form models of their actions. According to the agents' demonstrations, users can provide feedback to facilitate learning [3]. In this approach, knowledge is acquired through real-time interaction rather than offline knowledge engineering. Implementing IML systems in meaningful creative contexts presents a new set of challenges surrounding social coordination and interaction dynamics.

DRAWING APPRENTICE INTERACTION DESIGN

To facilitate interactive machine learning in artistic collaboration, the Drawing Apprentice interface features several forms of feedback to help train the system's algorithms. The interaction design of the system is inspired by the ideas of participatory sense-making in the cognitive science theory of enaction [1]. For example, the system features up/down voting buttons to inform the system whether the user liked the last contribution (shown on the right side of Figure 1). To teach the system about meaningful relationships in the drawing, we enable an additional form of 'line grouping' feedback. Once users click the grouping button, they can lasso several lines on the canvas to 'group' them. Once grouped, the agent can interact with this entire group of lines as if it were one shape object, i.e. draw inside vs. outside the shape, redraw the entire shape, modify part of the shape, etc.

SYSTEM EVALUATION

Our system evaluation includes informal demonstrations (~30 users), formative user studies (6 novice users), and expert evaluation at a juried art competition. During semi-structured interviews, users report that Drawing Apprentice motivates them to continue their artistic task to explore how the agent responds. Users were both impressed and puzzled by the agent's line responses because the agent sometimes appeared to understand their intention while it obviously violated it at other times. Often, the user's mental models seemed to attribute a greater degree of 'intentionality' and 'creativity' to the Drawing Apprentice system than researchers predicted.

The most common request from users was better pattern recognition. For example, several users wanted the system to complete simple patterns, such as a filling in the missing petals on a flower. Users report some emotional connection to the agent anchored by the character used to represent the Drawing Apprentice on the drawing canvas. We predict animating this character will serve as helpful feedback to increase this emotional connection and help facilitate more effective collaborations.

Figure 2 shows a Drawing Apprentice collaboration that won the code-based art category of the Clough Art Competition. The juror provided an evaluation of the system and artwork, "The act of collaboration between a person and the enactive agent (presented live or through video documentation) is a visually exciting back-and-forth exchange worth watching, or perhaps even participating in yourself. Stepping Stones excellently demonstrates the way technology can partner in an artist's creative process, as well transform passive viewers into collaborators themselves" [7]. The submission was evaluated based on the image in Figure 2 and a video demonstration (refer to ACM digital library to see the video).

CONCLUSIONS

This paper introduced a co-creative drawing agent called the Drawing Apprentice. This system collaborates with users in real time on abstract drawings. Our approach

Figure 2: Drawing Apprentice submission to the Georgia Tech Clough Art Competition in code-based art category titled 'Stepping Stones to Enactive Computing' [7].

extends the recent work on interactive machine learning designed to reduce the knowledge engineering requirements for building creative agents. We present the interaction design and initial evaluation of the system based on expert evaluation and user feedback.

REFERENCES

1. Fuchs, T. and De Jaegher, H.Enactive intersubjectivity: Participatory sense-making and mutual incorporation. *Phenomenology and the Cognitive Sciences 8*, 4 (2009), 465–486.
2. Fuller, D. and Magerko, B.Shared mental models in improvisational performance. *Proceedings of the Intelligent Narrative Technologies III Workshop on INT3 10*, (2010), 1–6.
3. Gillies, M., Kleinsmith, A., and Brenton, H.Applying the CASSM Framework to Improving End User Debugging of Interactive Machine Learning. *Proceedings of the 20th International Conference on Intelligent User Interfaces*, (2015), 181–185.
4. Sawyer, R.K. and DeZutter, S.Distributed creativity: How collective creations emerge from collaboration. *Psychology of Aesthetics, Creativity, and the Arts 3*, 2 (2009), 81.
5. Shneiderman, B.Creativity Support Tools: Accelerating Discovery and Innovation. *Commun. ACM 50*, 12 (2007), 20–32.
6. Thomaz, A.L. and Chao, C.Turn-taking based on information flow for fluent human-robot interaction. *AI Magazine 32*, 4 (2011), 53–63.
7. Film/Graphic Art/Code-based Art. http://m.gatech.edu/w/artcrawl/c/#/app/2015/catego ries/film-graphic-art-code-based-art/141.

Psychogeographical Sound-drift

Ivan Chaparro
Professor
Jorge Tadeo Lozano University
Cra 4 # 22–61, Bogota, Colombia
ivanf.chaparrom@utadeo.edu.co
(+57) 319 2573243

Ricardo Duenas
CTO
Resoundcity Art Lab
Cra 4 # 22–61, Bogota, Colombia
info@resoundcity.com
(+57) 317 8436111

ABSTRACT
This demo is one of the results of a practice-based research, which explored the generation of interactive experiences based on the cooperative collection of data for ethnographical purposes. In this case, a collection of soundscapes from Stockholm has lead to some experiments where the audio clips gathered are controlled in real-time according to a brain computer interface and a set of rules that determines a real time composition.

One of the most significant inputs at this point has been the theory of Psychogeography, which posits that the territory and its transformation can be understood as an psychological and emotional setup, susceptible of being understood by means of different kinds of dynamic measurements and modes of representation.

The result described here is an experimental performance and sound-video installation in which the visitors can 'stroll' through a data archive, according to their brain activity, and by means of a brain scan device. The measurement of specific brain waves creates a sound and video synthesis related to the media collection.

This demo seeks to expose the concept and technological implementation behind the result and also to perform the interactive sound experience at the event.

Author Keywords
Sound art; archive; biosignals; performance; interaction.

INTRODUCTION
The increasingly ease of access to technologies for measuring physiological and biological signals have enabled artists and designers to explore the wide range of possibilities of sensor-based interactions and devices. In the case of sound art, the musical performance has been enhanced with the possibilities of real-time signal processing and the improvements of Human-Computer Interaction systems, Digital Audio Workstations, interactive methods of sound synthesis and so forth.

C&C '15, June 22-25, 2015, Glasgow, United Kingdom
ACM 978-1-4503-3598-0/15/06.
http://dx.doi.org/10.1145/2757226.2764559

In one hand it is possible to consider the developments of interactive and digital media in relation to sound and in the other it is possible to weight correspondingly the improvements and recent accessibility to Brain-Computer Interfaces and similar technologies for measuring biosignals.

According to proprioceptive processes and information related to states of concentration, attention and bodily input, the project explored, initially, means of auditory representation of such processes, and ultimately the possibility for interrelating brain activity with external phenomena by means of a system of rules and equivalences.

STATEMENT
The project started with a conceptual exploration of 'walking in the city as an aesthetic practice' and an experimentation and technical research related to sound, digital recording, postproduction and interactive archives.

The intention was to bring together a theoretical and narrative study of walking from a socio-cultural perspective of history and a technological survey of sound as an artistic possibility and a tool of analysis for understanding public space and the specificity of a given urban scenario.

The main referent of the theoretical research was the account of Paris from the poet Charles Baudelaire as a *flâneur*, namely, a walker, a detached observer who wanders the city being simultaneously part and apart from the crowd, a stroller[1].

The approach of this project involved the experience of walking as an acoustic practice, which implied to understand the city from the perspective of sound, a hectic aural scenario that provides all sorts of rhythms and frequencies, an audible set-up, that can be captured in the form of short fragments, a collection of intangibles that generated an archive as spread dots on a massive web.

The practical aim of the research was to create an experimental and interactive navigation through an archive of sound. Metaphorically speaking we intended compare a specific city with a human mind by means of computer programming and digital sensing devices of human biosignals.

Performance–Installation Description and technical details

City, Sound and Emotion[2] is an installation and performance that connects a person's brainwaves with an archive of sounds of Stockholm, gathered while walking aimlessly in the city and its surroundings for over ten months. The result is a unique sound composition created by each guest according to his response to the experience. The intention of this installation is to find the way in which the visitor connects a series of acoustic fragments creating a soundscape, allegorically seen as a resonance with the city.

Three channels of sound interact with the brain activity of one guest at a time; the rest of the audience would presence the particular composition, mediated by a neural impulse actuator[3], also known as brain computer interface.

The device used has been designed to interact with computer software using biosignals, in other words, electrical pulses recorded by three electrodes, from the user's brain, through his forehead. These potentials are amplified by the device and translated into frequency ranges that are assigned into different channels. The measurement of the brain waves of a person listening to the archive would be translated into commands that would control the selection of the sequence of files.

The device in question translates the combined reading of brainwaves, eye and muscle movements into numerical data. The biosignals measured by the actuator are specifically electrical potentials that "include *electro-myogram*, *electro-encephalogram* and *electro-oculogram*, all of which are electrical signals generated by activity patterns in muscles, brain and eye, respectively"[4]. These potentials are amplified and de-convoluted into different frequency components.

The device allows to measure the activity and excitation levels of the eye movement, the "*alpha*" and the "*beta*" spectrum of the brain and also the muscle tension; all divided by channels (*Glance, Alpha 1, Alpha 2 Alpha 3, Beta 1, Beta 2 Beta 3* and *Muscle*)

The "*alpha*" spectrum refers to the measuring of the alpha waves in the brain activity. They are in the frequency range of 8 to 12 Hz. This kind of brain activity predominantly originates in the occipital lobe and is related to the visual cortex activity. The "beta" spectrum refers to the measuring of the beta brain waves and its rhythm is associated with active and busy thoughts in a normal awake conscious state and also sensory feedback. They are divided into three ranges, every one of them measured separately by the actuator.

SOFTWARE

For data acquisition we used the software *NIA* release 4.01.12[5], which is the original software bundled with the headset. For audio processing we used Pure Data (Pd): an open source visual programming language specialized in audio processing.

The *NIA* software directly reads the headset data and generates keystrokes on the window of the active application, in this case the Pd program. The application starts detecting the keystrokes related to certain brain activity, assigning one or more audio files according to the interval and a system of equivalences. These audio files are added to the sound composition and mixed in real time, every single time there is a change in the brain activity of the person who has the actuator connected. The resulting audio signal is sent separately to four powered speakers, which are located at the four corners of the space, allowing the *spatialization* of audio files and the simulation of motion and displacement.

Please take a look at the trailer of a previous performance carried out in Stockholm:

http://www.resoundcity.com/human-mind-as-a-city/

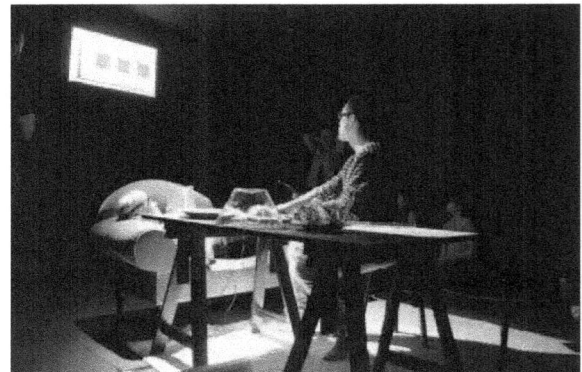

Figure 1. Performance session, Stockholm Sweden.

References and Citations

[1] Jerry Saltz, "Modern Machinery", *New York Magazine*, May 9th, 2011.

http://nymag.com/news/intelligencer/49958/

[2] Ivan Chaparro and Ricardo Dueñas. Accessed June 13, 2014, http://www.resoundcity.com/human-mind-as-a-city/

[3] "OCZ's Neural Impulse Actuator." Accessed June 13, 2014, http://techreport.com/articles.x/14957

[4] "NIA Manual" Accessed June 13, 2014, http://www.ocztechnology.com/res_old/files/misc_products/NIA_complete_English.pdf

[5] "NIA game controller" Accessed June 13, 2014, http://www.ocztechnology.com/drivers/OCZ_nia_Game_Controller/

Between the Bottle Cap and the Battery: An Investigation of Interrupted Gameplay

Jesús Ibáñez[1], Yoram Chisik[1,2], Monchu Chen[1,2]
[1]Madeira Interactive Technologies Institute and [2]University of Madeira
Caminho da Penteada, 9020-105 Funchal, Portugal
jesus.ibamar@gmail.com, ychisik@gmail.com, monchu@gmail.com

ABSTRACT

In this paper we present the initial results of a pilot study designed to explore the reactions and actions of children who experience a power failure while playing a hybrid physical/digital game. We wanted to see whether we can maintain the engagement of the children with the game if the digital component of the game (a tablet based game) ceases to function and if so whether they will continue from where they left off in the digital game or whether they will start a new round of gameplay. Early results suggests that the power failure and the resultant interruption to gameplay did not hamper the children engagement with the game but provided them with the opportunity to re-engage with the physical elements of the game. This suggests new directions for exploring the design of hybrid physical/digital games.

Author Keywords

Games; play; gameplay; children; interaction design; game design, HCI4D; Inventame.

ACM Classification Keywords

K.8.0 [Personal Computing]: General---games

INTRODUCTION

The relative low cost of tablets and thus their high availability coupled with a simple mode of interaction and high level of responsiveness allowing even the smallest of toddlers to interact effectively with a tablet have turned tablets into a popular platform for the development of games for children.

However while the screen offers high levels of response coupled with high-resolution images and high-pitched sounds it offers a very limited set of interactions centered on a small screen. This runs contrary to the way children

C&C '15, June 22-25, 2015, Glasgow, United Kingdom
ACM 978-1-4503-3598-0/15/06.
http://dx.doi.org/10.1145/2757226.2764551

think and explore with their hands [1] and thus has turned the attention of researchers and developers to hybrid approached that capitalize on the affordances of physical and digital technologies [4, 8]. There is however another aspect to digital technology that has remained largely unexplored due to the fact that it is largely taken for granted. Digital devices are dependent on a constant flow of electricity to preserve their functionality and sustain the flow of experiences that maintains the engagement of the player with the game. However a constant flow of electricity is not something that can be taken for granted in many parts of the world leading to interrupted experiences and shattered expectations.

Most of the investigations of hybrid digital/physical applications or tangible user interfaces have explored how the elements work together [7,9] or what are the differences when users use one modality as opposed to another [3]. Little work has been done on developing hybrid games that actively support the maintenance of gameplay through a failure of a supporting infrastructure, e.g. electricity, network connectivity, etc.

In *Flow: The Psychology of Optimal Experience*, Csikszentmihalyi [2] notes that in order to maintain a flow state, i.e. a state of engagement with an activity (which in our case is playing a game) one must have perceptible ability to continue with the activity. Hybrid games comprised of both physical and digital elements provide such ability. Our aim in this project is to explore the ways in which children switch between digital and physical variants of a game during a simulated power failure as a means of understanding how we can create hybrid games that continue to engage the interest of players in the event the digital components of the game are rendered useless by a power failure.

GAME AND PLATFORM USED FOR THE STUDY

To facilitate the investigation we are exploring how children play *Las chapas* a traditional physical game based on bottle caps in its physical form and in a digital form created using *Inventame*.

Inventame

Inventame [5, 6] is an Android application designed to facilitate the creation of videogames from handcrafted scenarios constructed using traditional materials such as pens, pencils, colored blocks, etc. Inventame works by allowing users to assign visualizations, behaviors and interactions to digital representations of their handcrafted scenarios.

To create a new game users load an image into the invention screen (Figure 1). The picture can be one they have just taken of their scenario or one stored in the device gallery of photos.

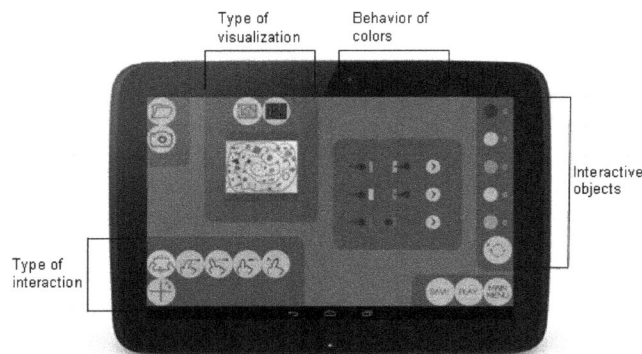

Figure 1: The *Inventame* game creation screen

Once an image has been loaded *Inventame* processes the image and produces an interactive surface to which users can ascribe behaviors and add interactive objects.

Inventame is able to distinguish between three distinct colors in an image (red, green and blue) and provides the user with the ability to associate specific behaviors to specific colors. The available behaviors are: *collide,* when an object reaches an area of the interactive surface with that color it will collide with it, i.e. it will not be able to pass through it; *modify,* when an object reaches an area of the interactive surface with that color it will pass through and change its colour to a predefined color (at the moment only grey and pink are defined as options); *pass over,* when an object reaches an area of the interactive surface with that color it will pass over it without any effect. These behaviors act as feedback mechanisms through which various game semantics can be conveyed to a player.

Users are able to add or remove interactive objects by dragging any of the 5 colored circles to the interactive surface, a larger view of the surface is provided by interactive objects editor screen (Figure 2). The location where the user places the interactive object will be their initial position when the game is started. The availability of several colors enables the creation of multiple representations, e.g. for multiple players, or for a player and a ball. The exact number of interactive objects will be determined by the user based on the specific game he wishes to create. For example, a football like game will require the addition of several objects while a labyrinth puzzle game may require only one.

Once the surface and objects have been set the user can choose between a number of interactions which can be used to move the objects on the surface. These include: *tilt* (tilt the device so that the interactive objects fall as if gravity would affect it); *push* (tap, hold and pull forward to throw the object); *slingshot* (tap, hold and pull back to slingshot the object); *follow the finger* (tap the screen and the ball starts moving towards the finger location) and *direct location* (tap the object, hold and directly slide your finger on the screen towards the location where you want to locate the object).

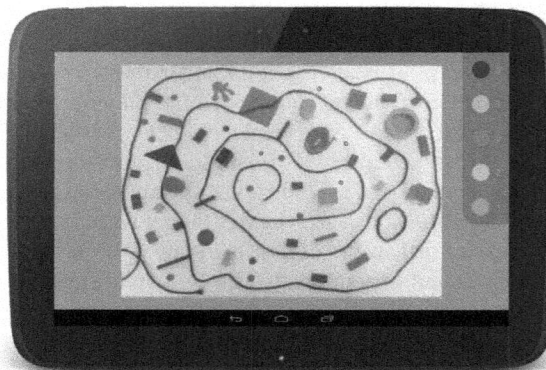

Figure 2: The Interactive objects editor screen

Las chapas

"Las chapas" (Figure 3) is a traditional street game that used to be popular in Spain and is still played in the physical education classes of some schools. The game consists of bottle caps (chapa in Spanish), and a circuit drawn by the players. Traditionally the circuit was drawn on the sidewalk using chalk, but nowadays adhesive tape affixed to the classroom or gym floor is the more popular solution.

In essence, the game is a bottle cap race. First, all the bottle caps (one per child) are put on the start line. Then, the children take turns hitting their bottle cap with their index finger (following a pre-defined order). If a bottle cap goes outside the circuit, it should be put back on the point from where it left the circuit. The first bottle cap to reach the finish line is the winner.

Figure 3: A child playing *las chapas*

PILOT EVALUATION

As a trial run for a bigger study we conducted a pilot evaluation with three pairs of boys in the ages of 5 and 7, 6 and 7, and 8 and 10 in Barcelona, Spain. For each pair we followed the following steps twice:

1. The children were provided with instructions on how to construct the physical track and how to play the game. They then proceeded to construct and play the game by themselves using the materials provided (two blue cords with a length of 7.5 meters and a diameter of 8 millimeters and a number of bottle caps). We used cords as opposed to chalk or adhesive tape in order to support rapid reconfiguration of the track.

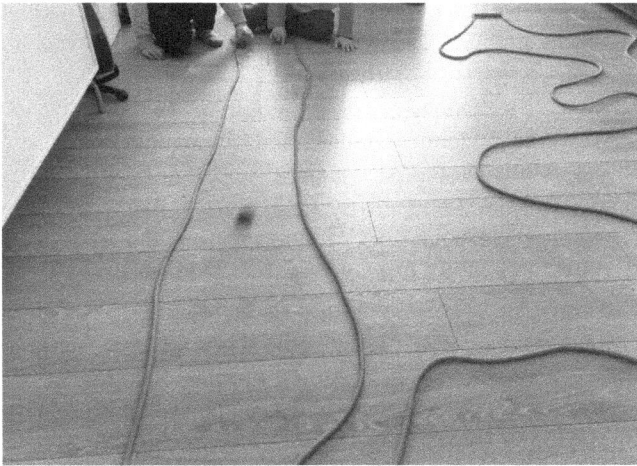

Figure 4: One of the pairs constructing their track

2. The children were then provided with a Google Nexus 10 tablet with *Inventame* installed on it and instructed on how to create and play a digital version of the game. They then proceeded to create and play the game on the tablet. Figure 5 depicts a version of one of the digital tracks created by the children. The game mimics the physical game in that the blue lines act a solid objects preventing the interactive cap from crossing the blue lines. The red line acts as a finishing line and will change its color to grey when pass over by an interactive cap.

Figure 5: A *Las Chapas track on Inventame*

3. When the moderator noticed the children were engrossed in the game and have traversed more than 2/3 of the track, he sent an invisible signal to the tablet, which caused it to shut off mimicking a power failure. We then observed the reaction and actions taken by the children with the aim of answering the following questions:

R1: How would the children react to a power failure that prevents them from continuing to play with the digital game on a tablet?

R2: Would the children return to playing the physical game?

R3: If so, would they continue the current game (by locating the bottle caps at the same locations they had in the digital circuit at the moment the battery ran out)? Or would they start a new game?

As noted above we followed this sequence of steps twice. In the first instance we kept the physical circuit on the floor in the way the children left it, in the second instance we dismantled the track and wound the cords once the children started to play the digital game. In both cases we allowed the children to return to the physical game whenever they wished to do so.

INITIAL OBSERVATIONS AND REFLECTIONS

The cords proved to be well suited for the task of track creation and the children found the task both easy and enjoyable. Two of the pairs designed typical circuits with a few curves while the third pair designed a highly curved track with a number of narrow sections.

The creation of the digital game proved to be equally engaging with all three pairs experimenting with a number of the available interaction options before settling on one. Two of the pairs chose the slingshot option while the other chose the push option.

When the children experienced the power failure during the first session of digital play (with the original physical track still intact) they went back to playing the physical game. Two of the pairs positioned their bottle caps at their respective locations when the tablet stopped working, i.e. they continued the same round of play while the remaining pair started a new round. All three pairs maintained the same physical track.

After the power failure during the second round of digital play (with the original track dismantled) the children again returned to the physical game. In all 3 pairs there was some discussion on whether they should try to recreate the original track or construct entirely new ones? However, once started they all opted to improve on their original designs. Once the new tracks were completed two of the pairs started a completely new round, while the other pair started a new round but maintained the relative positioning they had in the interrupted digital game.

Our initial observations suggest that the physical game provided not only an engaging alternative to the digital game once the power ran out (and there was nothing to do but wait till the power returns or the battery charges up) but also a challenging addition to the overall interaction with the game. One of the children described the experience of having to rebuild the physical track in order to continue playing as "moving to a new level in the game" and another echoed a similar sentiment by saying he enjoyed the challenge of creating trickier tracks. This anecdotal evidence is further bolstered by the fact that once told the battery was charged and they can continue to play with the tablet, the children did not want to continue playing their "old" games with the tracks they have previously created but wanted to transfer the new tracks to the tablet and continue playing using the new tracks.

CONCLUSION AND FURTHER WORK

In summary, we can say that the power failure and the resultant interruption to digital play did not hamper the children's engagement with the game but provided them with the opportunity to re-engage with the physical elements of the game. Although the game is competitive by nature (being a race) the children easily switched from a competitive mode while playing the game to a cooperative mode while constructing the tracks. They actively discussed their designs and collaborated in the construction of the track and were to reach consensus in spite of having contradictory preferences.

We intend to carry out further studies with the following objectives. 1. Validating of the findings of the pilot study. 2. Explore ways in which power interruptions (real or simulated) can be used as an integral element of the mechanics of a game in order to create more emergent forms of gameplay.

REFERENCES

1. Antle, A. (2013). Exploring how children use their hands to think: an embodied interactional analysis In *Journal of Behaviour & Information Technology* 32(9), 938-954. Taylor and Francis.

2. Csikszentmihalyi, M. (2008). *Flow: The Psychology of Optimal Experience.* Harper Perennial Modern Classics.

3. Esteves, A., van den Hoven, E., & Oakley, I. (2013). Physical games or digital games?: comparing support for mental projection in tangible and virtual representations of a problem-solving task. In *Proc. of TEI '13*, 167-174. ACM.

4. Hinske, S., Langheinrich, M. & Lampe, M. (2008). Towards guidelines for designing augmented toy environments. In *Proc. of DIS '08*, 78-87. ACM.

5. Ibanez Martínez, J. (2014) Craft, click and play: crafted videogames, a new approach for physical/digital entertainment. In *Proc. of IDC '14*, 313-316.

6. Inventame (2015). http://inventame.org/.

7. Mazalek, A., Nitsche, M., Rebola, C., Wu, A., Clifton, P., Peer, F. & Drake, M. (2011). Pictures at an exhibition: a physical/digital puppetry performance piece. In *Proc. of C&C '11*, 441-442. ACM.

8. Osmo (2015). www.playosmo.com

9. Ryokai, K., Lee, M. J., and Breitbart, J. M., (2009). Children's storytelling and programming with robotic characters. In *Proceeding of C&C '09*, 19-28.

Playable Art: Physical Art with a Playable Digital Counterpart

Jesús Ibáñez
Madeira-ITI, University of Madeira
9020-105 Funchal, Madeira, Portugal
jesus.ibamar@gmail.com

ABSTRACT

This paper contributes an approach to create playable art consisting of physical art with a playable digital counterpart. We propose the use of *Inventame*, an App that allows the user to focus on the creative and artistic part. He crafts his own game in the real world with his preferred physical materials (pencils, markers, coloured wooden blocks, etc.). Then, he takes a picture of his creation, configures a few options in the App, and the picture becomes playable. This paper also describes four examples that illustrate the creation of playable art from several different kinds of art, using different materials and with different functions and playability.

Author Keywords

Playable Art; Crafting; Games; Interaction Design; Apps.

ACM Classification Keywords

K.8.0 [Personal Computing]: General---games.

INTRODUCTION

The discussion of whether games can be considered a form of art has been lately in the air. Defenders and detractors have exposed their views, especially since the New York's MoMA (Museum of Modern Art) acquired several games for its design collection. Beyond that discussion, Game Art is being established as a new emergent discipline. Game Art, as defined by Matteo Bittanti, is any art in which digital games played a significant role in the creation, production and/or display of the artwork [1]. Games have been appropriated by artists such as Cory Arcangel, Natalie Bookchin, Eddo Stern, Bill Viola, Anne-Marie Schleiner, Julian Oliver and Mathias Fuchs (among others), who have used games as a medium of expression. Strategies utilized by game artists include modding, hacking and hardware modification.

In this paper, we describe an approach to create playable art consisting of physical art with a playable digital counterpart. We propose the use of Inventame, an App that allows the user to focus on the creative and artistic part. By using that tool anyone can create a piece of playable art without worrying about the technical aspects. The user/artist can craft his own game in the real world with his preferred physical materials (pencils, markers, coloured wooden blocks, etc.). Then, he takes a picture of his creation, configures a few options in the App and the picture becomes playable. This paper also describes four examples that illustrate the creation of playable art from several different kinds of art, using different materials and with different functions and playability.

INVENTAME

The technology we have employed for the work presented in this paper is an Android App named *Inventame* [2]. The App is available on Google Play[1]. Further information (including video) can be found on the App website[2].

Inventame allows the creation of new video-games from pictures of crafted scenarios. In short, the user can add any number of moveable **interactive objects** that are displayed as small coloured circles. There are several different **interactive mechanisms** available to move the interactive objects. The user can choose between two different **kinds of visualization**. *Inventame* is able to recognise a number of **colours** in the scenario. For each of the three recognisable colours, the user decides what happens when an interactive object reaches a zone of the scenario that has that colour.

Next we show in more detail how a new game can be defined in *Inventame*. Once a picture is loaded (whether the user has picked it from his gallery or he has just taken it with the camera), the invention screen (see Figure 1) is the key screen for creating a new game.

---

[1] https://play.google.com/store/apps/details?id=org.inventame.inventame

[2] http://inventame.org/

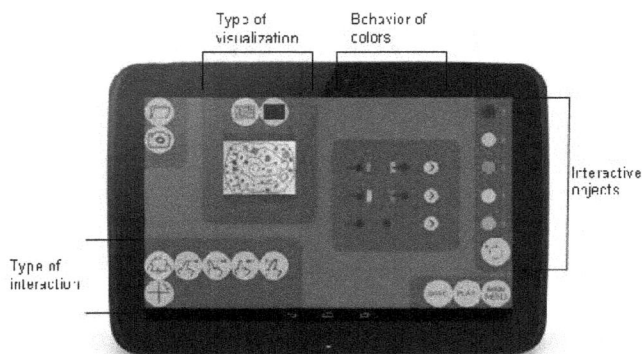

Figure 1. The invention screen.

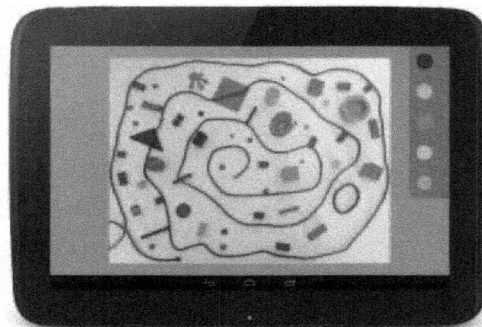

Figure 2. The interactive objects screen.

Type of visualization. The App allows the user to choose between two different kinds of visualization. He can toggle between displaying the original picture/scenario and displaying the picture/scenario as recognized by *Inventame*.

Type of interaction. There are several different interactive mechanisms available to move the interactive objects: tilt (tilt the device so that the interactive objects fall as if gravity would affect it), push (tap, hold and pull forward to throw the object), slingshot (tap, hold and pull back to slingshot the object), follow the finger (tap the screen and the ball starts moving towards the finger location) and direct location (tap the object, hold and directly slide your finger on the screen towards the location where you want to locate the object).

Behavior of colors. Inventame recognises a number of colours (red, green and blue) in the picture/scenario. For each of the three recognisable colours, the user decides what happens when an interactive object reaches a zone of the picture/scenario that is in that colour. He can choose among these options: the coloured zone behaves as a solid element (that is, the interactive object collides with that zone), the colour of the zone changes to a grey colour, the colour of the zone changes to a pink colour, and the object passes over the zone without causing any effect to it. Thus, when designing his game, the user should decide the roles in his game, the colours he employs for representing elements with that role, and their behaviour. For instance, the user could have elements with roles positive and negative in his game. He could use, for example, green and red colours for representing respectively those roles. Then he can decide provide visual feedback (for instance change to pink colour and change to grey colour respectively) to show when a positive or negative element in the scenario is reached by an interactive object. Note that this is just visual feedback. The semantic meaning of this action is given by the user and it depends on the particular game/scenario.

Interactive objects. By pressing the bottom button of the interactive objects area, the user is redirected to the interactive objects screen (see Figure 2) where he can add/remove interactive objects to/from his game. The location where he adds an interactive object will be its initial location. The numbers beside the colored circles indicate the number of interactive objects of each color in the game. Since there are five different colors of interactive objects, different kinds of objects can be considered (for instance, different teams). Note that the appropriate number of interactive objects depends on the kind of game being created. For instance, for a football-like game, the user would add several interactive objects (one object per player plus an additional one for the ball). However, in a labyrinth game, one interactive object could be enough.

EXAMPLES

In this section, we describe four examples that show the potential of our approach for the creation of playable art from several kinds of art, using different materials and with different function and playability.

Urban Art (Split the Colours)

The case we present in this section exemplifies how serendipitous scenarios can be converted into games. You could fortuitously pass by a scene you love for your game. The graffiti used in this example was found on a wall on a street in Vilanova i la Geltrú (Barcelona). We took a picture of it and converted it into a game. The goal of the game is to split the interactive balls in two different graffiti letters depending on their colour. The user can move the balls by tilting the device. Same coloured balls should be placed into the same graffiti letter.

Figure 3 displays the configuration of the game. The first screen shows the initial positions of the interactive objects. The second one shows the rest of parameters. Note that the behaviours of colours in the scenario are: the interactive objects pass over green and red zones without causing any effect to it; blue zones behave as solid elements, that is, the interactive objects collide with those zones. Note that the edges of the letters in the graffiti are blue.

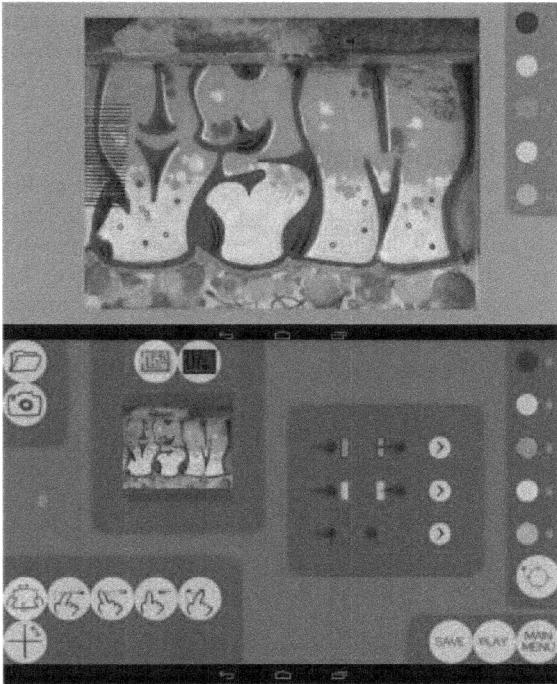

Figure 3. Configuration of the "Split the Colours" game.

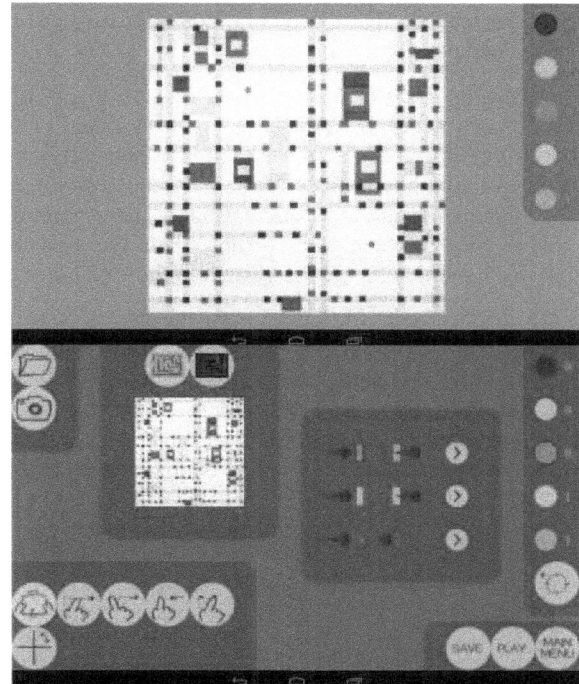

Figure 4. Configuration of the "Tag in Broadway" game.

Painting (Tag in Broadway)

Paintings can be used as game scenarios. The user can create his own paintings or he can use existing paintings by other painters. In the case we show here, we employed *Broadway Boogie-Woogie*, a painting by Piet Mondrian completed in 1943. This painting was inspired by the city grid of Manhattan, and the boogie woogie music to which Mondrian loved to dance. For the game, we used a photograph we downloaded from the wikipedia [3].

We designed a game for two users, represented as green and blue interactive balls, initially located at different zones of the painting. The game is a variation of the popular tag game. The players take turns shooting their interactive ball, trying to impact the opponent's ball. The first that impacts the opponent wins the game. In each turn, each player shoots his ball once. However, if the ball touches a red rectangle, the player can shoot again. Moreover, the interactive balls bounce with the blue rectangles of the painting. The balls are shot by using the *slingshot* type of interaction.

Figure 4 displays the configuration of the game. Note that the behaviours of colours in the scenario are: blue zones behave as solid elements, that is, the interactive objects collide with those zones; the color of a red zone changes to a grey colour when it is reached by an interactive ball. It provides visual feedback indicating when a player can shoot again.

Protest Art (Catch the Corrupt)

In this section we show an example of playable protest art. The piece is intended to denounce the impunity of corruption in Spain. The concern of society is enormous, after a spate of scandals in political parties, the royal family and banking. News about corruption appear and are discussed everyday on the media. The general perception of society is that corruption, in Spain is unpunished. This is specially painful in a country where the economic crisis has produced an enormous degree of unemployment and there are several hundred evictions per day.

In this case, we use an article published on *El País* (the highest-circulation daily newspaper in Spain) on 25 February 2015. The news headline highlights that heads of the CAM have been acquitted by the scandal of diets. The article explains how 18 members of the supervisory board of the CAM (a savings bank that had to be nationalized) spent 1.3 million euros in diets and the court has acquitted them (despite the request of prosecutors).

In order to create the game, we wrote the word "corrupt" in red (on top of the area where the article mentions the 18 members of the CAM board) and drew several blue lines. Then we took a picture and defined the game in *Inventame*. We added 5 interactive balls representing elements of society that try to catch the corrupt. The player can move the balls by tilting the device. The balls collide with the blue lines.

The goal of the game is to reach the word "corrupt" with the interactive balls. However, when a player tries to reach

---

[3]   http://en.wikipedia.org/wiki/Broadway_Boogie-Woogie

the goal, he realizes that there is no apparent way to reach him. The corrupt is protected by the blue lines.

The interesting point is that the only chance to catch the corrupt, in this game, is to edit the game itself and change the behaviour of the blue color so that the interactive balls can pass over the blue lines. Thus, this game sends a clear message against impunity of corruption: If the system does not allow you to catch the corrupt, then the system is corrupt. You should change the system in the first place.

Figure 5 displays the configuration of the game. Note that the behaviours of colours in the scenario are: blue lines behave as solid elements, that is, the interactive objects collide with those lines; the color of a red zone changes to a grey colour when it is reached by an interactive object. It provides visual feedback indicating that the corrupt have been caught.

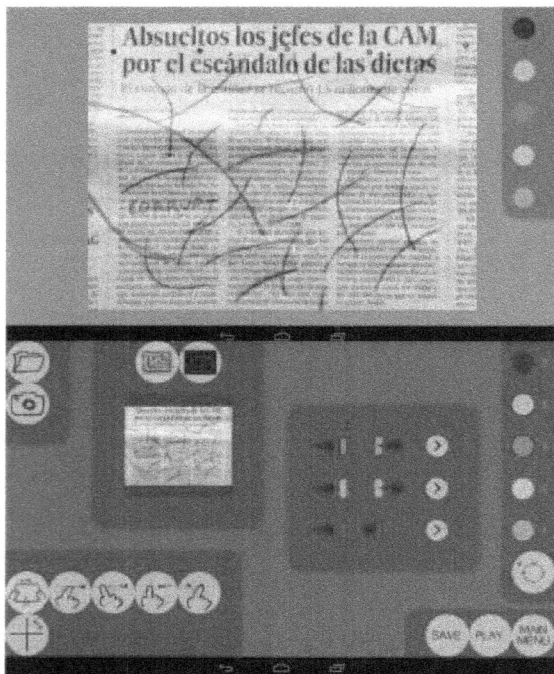

Figure 5. Configuration of "Catch the Corrupt" game.

Crafted Gift (Happy Birthday)
Users can create personalized playable crafted gifts for their loved ones. We illustrate this case with a happy birthday card. It was the 40th birthday of our beloved friend Bea. We drew a birthday cake with candles on a piece of paper. We also wrote a congratulatory message (in Spanish). Then we added decorative blue and green thin plastic tubes. We took a picture of this creation and designed a simple game.

By using *Inventame*, we added four interactive objects balls on top. The goal of the game is to blow out the candles by touching the candles' fire with the interactive balls. The user can move the balls by tilting the device. The balls collide with the blue and green elements. Thus, in order to "win", the user should be able to take (at least) one ball to the red

fire of the candles, dodging the obstacles. The challenge presented by this game is solvable in a short time but it requires the user effort, just as it happens with the act of blowing real candles.

Figure 6 displays the configuration of the game. Note that the behaviours of colours in the scenario are: blue and green zones behave as solid elements, that is, the interactive objects collide with those zones; the color of a red zone changes to a grey colour when it is reached by an interactive object. It provides visual feedback indicating that the candles are blown out.

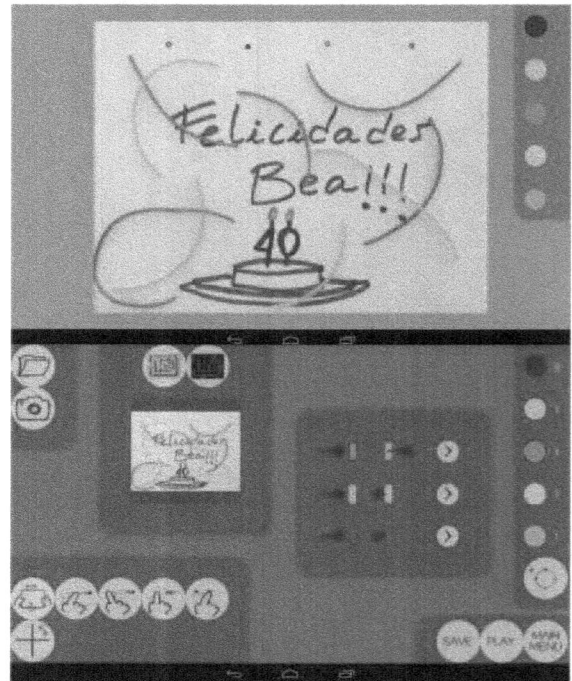

Figure 6. Configuration of the "Happy Birthday" game.

CONCLUSION
We have proposed an approach to create playable art consisting of physical art with a playable digital counterpart. It has been shown how the App *Inventame*, facilitates the creation of this playable art. The potential of our approach has been demonstrated by showing four examples of creation of playable art from several different kinds of art, using different materials and with different function and playability.

REFERENCES
1. Bittanti, M. Game Art (This is not) A Manifesto (This is) A Disclaimer. In *GameScenes: Art in the Age of Videogames*, eds. D. Quaranta & M. Bittanti, Johan and Levi, Milan, (2006), 7-14.

2. Ibanez Martínez, J. Craft, click and play: crafted videogames, a new approach for physicaldigital entertainment. In *Proceedings of the 2014 conference on Interaction design and children (IDC '14)*, ACM Press (2014), 313-316.

Remote Control of Complex Interactive art installations

Andrew Bluff
University of Technology, Sydney
Sydney, Australia
bluffy@rollerchimp.com

Dr Andrew Johnston
University of Technology, Sydney
Sydney, Australia
andrew.johnston@uts.edu.au

ABSTRACT
Movement based interactive artworks are capable of instantly engaging audiences by reacting to physical motion consistently with real-world physics. Sustaining this engagement, however, requires a constant alteration of both the output and interaction aesthetics. Mobile devices (such as the iPad or iPhone) can be used to control the often-overwhelming plethora of parameters found in many interactive systems. The effect that mobile control of these parameters has on the inception, refinement and live performance of two separate art works is examined. An open-source dynamic remote control system is being developed to further facilitate the creative development and performance of interactive artwork as demonstrated by these case studies.

Author Keywords
Remote Control; Mobile Device; Interactive Artwork; Presets; OpenFrameworks; iPad; iPhone; TouchOSC;

ACM Classification Keywords
H.5.2. Information Interfaces and Presentation (e.g. HCI): Input devices and strategies

INTRODUCTION
Developing interactive artworks that are engaging to both participants and passive audience members is a difficult task. Interactivity can provide instantaneous engagement but a plethora of different visual states and interaction aesthetics are often needed to maintain engagement for extended periods. When designing visual states for artworks that involve interactive graphics, the iPad becomes an invaluable creative tool. The development of two separate interactive artworks with iPad controls are examined. Within these works, the mobile control allowed the artistic director more creative control, facilitated rapid content development and produced a more nuanced audience interaction.

Simulations of real-world physics can be used to transform real-time motion capture data into complex and engaging audio visual works[4]. These systems can sense physical movement of the participants to create reality-based interactions that are easily understandable to even the novice participant[3]. However, the continued use of a single motion mapping for extended period of time is likely to induce audience fatigue and engagement will subsequently decline over time. To combat this, Salter et al [7] postulate that dramatic or narrative arcs can be introduced to the system at a higher level to keep the interactions fresh and maintain interest in the piece. Chadabe[1] argues that it is preferable to have a system with a large number of parameters to alter the mapping from motion into the system, although with an increase in the number of parameters comes a decrease in the ability to coherently manipulate all of these parameters. The two artworks examined utilise real-world physics simulations and each had a large number of parameters that could alter the way the system responds to motion by introducing physical phenomena such as mass, viscosity and gravity effects. Combinations of these settings were stored as high level presets that allowed simple but meaningful manipulation of all parameters simultaneously. Choreographing these presets enabled a narrative arc to develop over time, helping to sustain audience engagement.

Control over these low-level parameters and high-level presets was added to a remote control device (iPad) to facilitate a rapid and more creative development. Mobile devices, such as iPads, iPhones and Android tablets, have been used to control many real time installations and musical instruments. They can offer the user a malleable interface that is specifically tailored to the needs of the job at hand. The first widely successful touch screen based mobile control was the JazzMutant Lemur [5]. It contained a range of user programmable virtual buttons and sliders with the sole purpose of controlling other equipment from a semi remote location. Since the introduction of the iPhone and iPad, software developers have been able to replicate the Lemur functionality at a significantly lower price. TouchOSC[1] is one of the more successful applications to mimic remote control in a fashion similar to the Lemur.

Although easy to use, TouchOSC requires the user to manually create layouts in order to interface with the target device. Recently, a number of apps have been developed to automatically generate these layouts with minimal manual effort. *Mira* is a remote app suite that auto generates layouts based on Max/Msp user interfaces[9]. *Control* is a similar technology which expands on the concept by allowing advanced script-

C&C '15, June 22-25, 2015, Glasgow, United Kingdom.
ACM 978-1-4503-3598-0/15/06.
http://dx.doi.org/10.1145/2757226.2764553

[1]http://hexler.net/software/touchosc

ing on the device for complex interactions between the virtual sliders, knobs and buttons[6] .

The two artworks examined reveal that the creation and refinement of high level presets from a mobile device can enhance both the development and operation of interactive artworks. A prototype software solution capable of generating and manipulating high-level presets for OpenFrameworks applications is also presented[2].

CHOREOGRAPHED PHYSICAL THEATRE

Encoded[3] is a one hour interactive physical theatre show by *Stalker Theatre* including dance, aerial acrobatics, projection mapping and interactive graphics. The interactive graphics are generated in real-time by a complex particle system that uses optical motion tracking and fluid simulation to react naturally to the movement of the performers. The fluid simulation system was created using OpenFrameworks.

The first stage of the project development involved a series of physical workshops that focused on improvisation of both physical movement and interactive graphical states. The multitude of fluid simulation controls were manipulated to create a palette of interesting high-level presets that worked well with different types of physical movements. These presets were given semi-descriptive names such as 'strings', 'snowman' and 'water-wall' which enabled the artistic director to request certain reactive scenes which could then be choreographed, stating that "One of the challenges with this technology is that there is so many variables that being able to do the snapshot of the scene is the first big step".

Providing remote control of these named presets with the TouchOSC app running on an iPad (see figure 1) had a seemingly profound effect on the development of the show. The interactive system soon became a known and controllable entity in which desired states could be recalled at will. The artistic director of *Encoded* was given a copy of the TouchOSC layout on his own personal iPad so that he possessed simple but immediate control over the reactive fluid system via selection of these predefined presets. Despite some initial scepticism regarding the workflow, he quickly warmed to the remote control system stating that "It allowed for a much more responsive creative environment because it was immediate. It allowed for a refinement and subtlety of development process because everything was at your fingertips"

Giving the director control during rehearsals meant that he could easily see the available palette of predefined presets and quickly select which looks would match a given movement choreography. Before the introduction of the iPad to *Encoded's* development, any changes to the system were by way of a loud verbal command from the director on the stage to the interactive technician at the back of the theatre. The iPad control largely removed the need for these distracting interactions and enabled the director to pay more attention to the performers on stage. This direct control also freed up the digital projections operator to focus on other development

Figure 1. The TouchOSC layout used to operate the reactive graphics for the physical theatre performance, *Encoded*. Blue buttons operate presets in the fluid simulation graphics, while the red buttons control the VJ software and vision mixer

tasks like creating and refining traditional projection mapping graphics. The remote control of the fluid simulation was so successful that the vision mixing and pre-rendered video playback was also controlled by the TouchOSC layout.

INTERACTIVE INSTALLATIONS

Creature[4] is an interactive artwork inviting audience participation and was developed over a much shorter time frame than the two year *Encoded* project. The system borrowed considerable knowledge and technology from the *Encoded* project, but we opened up the system to the audience and expanded on the existing technology considerably. *Creature* was created for an outdoor art and science event exploring the theme of biodiversity. Local fauna was 3D modelled for the piece while local flora was photographed and texture-mapped onto simple geometric particle shapes. The interactive states found a balance between interactivity and narrative by morphing between abstract movement based particle graphics and simple 3d-modelled imagery. A considerable amount of new presets were created for the event to ensure that the interactive component remained a satisfying experience while the entire piece contained a diverse visual palette.

The TouchOSC solution used in the *Encoded* development provided an easy show operation environment and allowed the artistic director to build scenes by selecting from a palette of pre-defined presets. The solution was quite simplistic, however, and did not help with the initial development period of building presets, or allow any deviation or refinement from these predetermined presets.

---

[2]http://www.openframeworks.cc/
[3]https://vimeo.com/55150853

[4]https://vimeo.com/108033499

When designing creativity support tools, such as a remote control for interactive artworks, Shneiderman[8] suggests that it should be simple for novices to start using the device, while still allowing flexibility for advanced users to achieve all that they desire. The high-level preset functionality presents the users with an easy way to recall 'look's that are already known to work well, while the low-level parameter interface allows advanced users exact control over every single element of the system. To satisfy both the remote control requirement and the importance of preset creation and recall on creative development, a new software application (codenamed ioStorm) has been developed. This app will automatically generate control layouts from OpenFrameworks software and allows the user to access low level parameters and generate their own presets from the one remote mobile app.

ioStorm - Remote Control System Description

When opened for the first time, the remote ioStorm application will connect to the ioStorm enabled applications via UDP protocols over any available wireless network. The host app automatically respond to the presence of the remote app by sending all of the parameter names, types and acceptable values to the remote device. The ioStorm app generates a simple user interface for these parameters which mimics the user interface found in the host applications. By generating a user interface on the fly, the system alleviates the time associated with setting up the remote layout design in TouchOSC. As the system mimics the user interface of the desktop app, familiarity with the system is also ensured. Upon change to either of the desktop apps or the app running on the remote device, the values are immediately synchronised via OSC commands to ensure all user interfaces are always up to date.

Presets can be triggered, created and edited from the remote iOS application, enabling the user simple and easy control over the system. The control can be at a high level via pre made presets, such as with the TouchOSC *Encoded* setup, or at a low-level giving access to the entire system via the parameter slider interface. All communications use the OpenSoundControl format which allows external programs (such as TouchOSC, Max/Msp or Puredata) a simple interface for recalling presets or even manipulating specific parameter values.

Development of Interactive States

When working in-situ at a venue the system is usually hidden away from the interaction zone so as to not break the immersive 'magic' of the installation with technological clutter. For *Creature*'s first outing the main computer system was awkwardly placed underneath a bank of make-shift scaffolding with the projector and infrared camera placed at the top of the scaffold tower. The physical distance and barrier between the technology and interaction zone made it very difficult to create and refine new interaction states.

With *Creature*, there were no designated performers or choreographed movements to build the interactive states around. Building this type of interaction suggested an iterative trial and error approach where neither graphics, interaction or

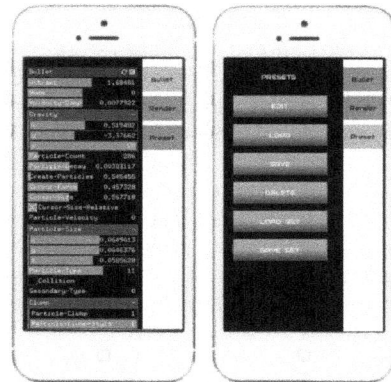

Figure 2. The ioStorm auto-generated layout for the *Creature* installation, displaying both low-level parameter control (left) and high-level preset control (right)

movement were predefined. This development of the interaction aesthetic was where the remote control became incredibly useful. The system could be altered, refined and tweaked, all whilst being up and close to the action. By physically participating in the interaction the digital artist could fully experience the system's shortcomings and strengths and instantly make adjustments as needed. Actually interacting with the system personally is the best way to make sure that the interaction aesthetic 'feels' right and that the piece is engaging to use. The preset system that is built into the ioStorm code makes it possible to then quickly store and test presets all whilst being immersed in the interactive installation. The ioStorm remote software made it possible to fine tune all of the interactive states in the *Creature* installation under a tight deadline (due to rain delays) and without any extra man power needed to constantly simulate the potential movements of the audience.

OPERATION OF INTERACTIVE WORKS

The installation was initially controlled from the tech box where the computers and projector were setup. It was possible to see that quite a number of the audience (around 30 at a time) were engaging with the system by waving their hands in the air to move the projections around. A selection of pre-made presets were sporadically selected and the crowd appeared to enjoy each change in both visual and interaction aesthetics.

Upon grabbing the mobile iPad controls and joining the crowd the true nature and breadth of interactions with the system became observable. From the control box, it appeared that the crowd was bunched closely up against one another and more or less just waving their hands. From the vantage point of the interaction zone, it became apparent that the crowd was not actually all bunched up but in groups of two or three coming back from the projection surface by up to 5-10 meters. Each group had positioned themselves with a decent amount of space in which to move about. It was very much a family event and many of the parents were standing back from the wall where they would occasionally wave their hands to interact with the system, all whilst still keeping a keen eye on their children who were playing closer to the projection wall. Many of the children of all ages were not only jumping and waving to interact with projections, but were performing cart-wheels, hand stands and occasionally hopping to mimic the natural movement of the local animals like kangaroos and frogs. On a few occasions it would turn into a game whereby a group of children would compete to see how much of the image they could affect and what patterns they could create by scrambling up the vertical projection wall as high as possible. These different interactions were only observable from within the crowd and the remote control device allowed the system to be tweaked from this vantage point. This allowed a much more refined control over the artwork where the system could become highly tuned for the movement of individual members of the audience. The operator of the show was able to experience the interactions at the same time as controlling them. New presets were even created and refined whilst operating amongst the crowd as the operator was able to immediately see the affect of each parameter change on the interaction and ultimately engagement of the audience. It was very obvious to understand when an interaction state was not responding pleasingly from this vantage point. The influence of mobile operation was noticed by the director of the work, who stated that "when the operator is also part of the audience... that line between objective and subjective kind of blurs. It's a new creative environment that is emerging with this technology. It's less removed, more experiential".

CONCLUSION

During the development of both *Encoded* and *Creature* it became evident that the ability to quickly save the state of the system in a preset was a vital part of the creative process. Once these presets had been created the show could then be storyboarded in high-level chunks to create a narrative arc to the piece. Mobile remote control of the interactive system presented many benefits:-

- Promoted creative choreography of established presets
- Reduced operational needs during rehearsals
- Rapid development of interactive states
- Refined nuance of the interaction aesthetic
- Experiential operation tailored to specific audience interactions

Future work

The ioStorm remote control app was very successful in controlling the OpenFrameworks software behind the interactive *Creature* installation and facilitated the rapid development and refinement of interactive content. The software is still in early prototype and needs several improvements before releasing to the Opensource community. A zero-config network system, like Bonjour, should be added to allow automatic communication to any ioStorm compatible server running on the network. Recent work on the 'Storm' software suite has also seen the addition of preset morphing as a creative way to control the system. Adding a simple and intuitive method to morph between presets could add significant scope for improvisation and creative operation of interactive installations.

Given the success of the projects to date, addressing these outstanding issues to the ioStorm software suite should provide a streamlined solution to facilitate the development of future movement based artworks utilising the power or mobile devices. Ground Theory [2] methods can then be used to further evaluate the impact of using ioStorm to remote control interactive art installations.

ACKNOWLEDGMENTS
Thanks to the artistic director of the Stalker Theatre Company, David Clarkson for continued support.

REFERENCES

1. Joel Chadabe. 2002. The limitations of mapping as a structural descriptive in electronic instruments. In *Proceedings of the 2002 conference on New interfaces for musical expression*. National University of Singapore, 1–5.

2. Barney G Glaser and Anselm L Strauss. 2009. *The discovery of grounded theory: Strategies for qualitative research*. Transaction Publishers.

3. Robert JK Jacob, Audrey Girouard, Leanne M Hirshfield, Michael S Horn, Orit Shaer, Erin Treacy Solovey, and Jamie Zigelbaum. 2008. Reality-based interaction: a framework for post-WIMP interfaces. In *Proceedings of the SIGCHI conference on Human factors in computing systems*. ACM, 201–210.

4. Andrew Johnston. 2013. Fluid simulation as full body audio-visual instrument. In *Proc. Of Conf. on New Interfaces for Musical Expressions, Daejeon*. 132.

5. Charles Roberts. 2011. *Control: Software for end-user interface programming and interactive performance*. Ann Arbor, MI: MPublishing, University of Michigan Library.

6. Charles Roberts, Graham Wakefield, and Matthew Wright. 2012. Mobile controls on-the-fly: An abstraction for distributed NIMEs. In *Proceedings of the 2012 Conference on New Interfaces for Musical Expression (NIME 2012)*.

7. Christopher L Salter, Marije AJ Baalman, and Daniel Moody-Grigsby. 2008. Between mapping, sonification and composition: responsive audio environments in live performance. In *Computer Music Modeling and Retrieval. Sense of Sounds*. Springer, 246–262.

8. Ben Shneiderman. 2007. Creativity support tools: Accelerating discovery and innovation. *Commun. ACM* 50, 12 (2007), 20–32.

9. Sam Tarakajian, David Zicarelli, and Joshua Kit Clayton. 2013. Mira: Liveness in iPad controllers for Max/MSP. In *Proceedings of the International Conference on New Interfaces for Musical Expression, Daejeon, Korea*.

How Space and Tool Availability Affect User Experience and Creativity in Interactive Surfaces?

Michail N. Giannakos[1], Ioannis Leftheriotis[1,2]
[1]Department of Computer and Information Science
Norwegian University of Science and Technology
Trondheim, Norway

[2]Department of Informatics
Ionian University
Corfu, Greece
mgiannakos@acm.org, iolef@acm.org

ABSTRACT
As computing increasingly deals with our complex daily experiences, designers are challenged with new methods and ways of implementing complex interactions in limited user space and tools, but without hindering user experience and creativity. In this paper, we present the results of an empirical investigation regarding the effect of space and tool availability on user experience and creativity. The goal is to understand whether and how space and tool availability allow users to be more creative and improve their overall experience. To do so, we developed a connect-the-dots drawing multi-user application with a focus on having certain restrictions in size and specific tool availability. Based on this application, we conducted an empirical study with 38 users. For the evaluation, surveys, photos and observations were recorded and used in our analysis. The results showed that: (a) tool availability does not affect user creativity and experience and (b) space availability affects user creativity, collaboration and hedonic motivation (pleasure). Although our results are early, provide insights that tools' limitation does not hinder users' ability to be creative; and space availability is of great importance in creative activities.

Author Keywords
Multi-touch; creativity; size; tools; user experience; collaboration; hedonic motivation;

ACM Classification Keywords
H.5.m. Information interfaces and presentation (e.g., HCI): Miscellaneous.

INTRODUCTION
During the last years, larger interaction surfaces such as tabletops or larger vertical Multi-Touch (MT) screens have been studied in order for the researchers to investigate

C&C '15, June 22-25, 2015, Glasgow, United Kingdom
ACM 978-1-4503-3598-0/15/06.
http://dx.doi.org/10.1145/2757226.2764554

devices' affordances and the novel interaction techniques the users have been able to apply.

Reasonably, due to the larger space they provide and thus the larger interaction area, most studies have been focused on multi-user collaboration strategies and their group-work support. Increasing the physical size and resolution of displays has several benefits [7]. Even in traditional windows, icons, menus, pointer (WIMP) environment, the larger surfaces allows for larger number of windows, and with a larger number of windows multiple users are able to work in parallel, co-creating artifacts or co-experiencing the interaction. For example, Czerwinski et al. [3] demonstrate that users are significantly more productive and more satisfied when carrying out complex, multiple window tasks across larger display surfaces. According to Mahey et al. the study of human creativity, among others, tends to focus on the environment or situations in which creativity is facilitated [9]. However, in a creative context/task, what is the impact of the larger available space of larger MT screens to the users, remains an unanswered question that motivates this study.

Furthermore, compared to other traditional indirect-mapping input devices (such as mouse for example) MT surfaces provide better user experience. As Leftheriotis et al [8] demonstrate in their experiment, using a MT screen gives a higher "flow" to the users (derived from concentration, unambiguous feedback and control) and even when their performance is lower with the MT, it seems that this does not affect their perceived usability, or the enjoyment. Watson et al [11] also exhibits that users are happier and more engaged while using MT.

In this work, we take advantage of the larger space and the higher user experience quality that the MT surface offers, in order to understand how the size or the tools that are given to the users impact their self-expressed creativity. According to Battarbee et al [1], creativity is enabled and constrained by technological possibilities. In addition, Erickson [4] claims that even when there are spatial constraints, activity might be generated. And since activity is closely coupled with at least lower level of creativity [10], we believe that there is a need to investigate whether there is a correlation between availability in space or tools and creativity aspect in the context of MT screens. Motivated by the above we:

Investigate the effect of space and tool availability on user experience and creativity

METHODOLOGY

The MT Drawing Application

In order to be able to investigate our research question, we developed a connect-the-dots - drawing MT application with a focus on using specific size and tools for the user. The idea is simple and intuitive: Users have to draw inside their personal window (Figure 1b), with the given drawing tools (Figure 1a). Users were able to move their personal windows. By using a pinch gesture, they were able to change the size of the window to an extent. The maximum window size was 500x500px while the analysis of the 27 inches screen size was 1920x1080px and there were four brush types: a) thick black line, b) bold black line, c) thick colored line, d) bold colored line.

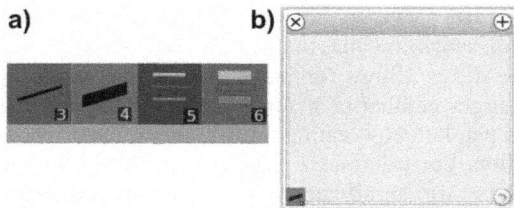

Figure 1. a) The available actions (thin line, thick line, thin colored line, thick colored line). b) Personal windows inside which users were able to draw.

Procedures

In the beginning, there was an exploratory phase of the application where the users got acquainted with the MT technology in general. In the next phase, we demonstrated to the users the connect-the-dots - drawing application and explained to them how to articulate the multi-finger chords in order to use the appropriate personal window. We showed the users how to draw inside their window and we also explained them the relation among the number of the finger that had to be touched on the screen and the respective action that would occur. We let the users to work and understand how the system works for five to ten minutes until they would have felt confident with the interactions.

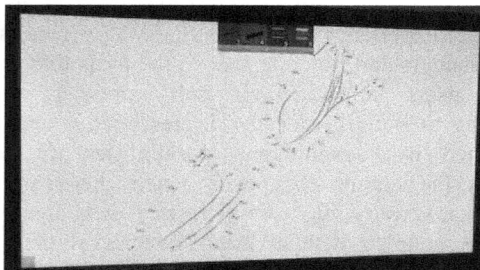

Figure 2. Beginning of the task

The experimental task begins with a number of dots and some additional black lines that represent a flower on a white background (Figure 2). The task was simple: We asked from the children to connect the dots and then draw inside the flower with the colors and brushes they wanted. Based on creativity classification by Sanders [10], this task combines two levels of creativity: the connect-the-dots subtask can be considered as *making* (there is some guidance from the system with the initial dots and lines) and the drawing subtask can be considered as *creating* (express users with the absent of a predetermined pattern). In Figure 3, some screenshots from the experiment are shown.

Figure 3. Experiment screenshots

Users worked in pairs and were told that they can draw together on the MT screen. However, they were free to choose the collaboration strategy they wanted. There was no limit to their imagination or their time since we wanted to investigate whether and how they collaborate and their strategies while using chord interaction and personal windows technique in a creative content, so we had a variety of creative results (Figure 4).

Figure 4. Final drawing screenshots

Participants

Of the 38 participants, 20 were males and 18 were females. All of the students who participated in the experiment were 17-20 years old, enrolled in the third grade of high school, or first/second year in the university. The experiment took place during an extracurricular activity in Trondheim, Norway and Corfu, Greece.

Data Collection
A wide range of data was collected to address our research questions including surveys and observations. During all the experiments one of the researchers was present to observe. By the end of the activity we implemented a survey based on measures related to size and tool availability and users' experience with the application. In particular, in Table 1 the items/questions used to measure each construct are described. In all cases, 7-point Likert scales were used to measure the variables.

Construct	Questions Used
Size Availability	Did the size restrict your painting activity?
Tools Availability	Did the available tools restrict your painting activity?
Creativity	Did the painting activity allow me to be creative?
Utilitarian Motivation* (UM)	The application was: a) Effective, b) Helpful, c) Functional, d) Practical, e) Necessary
Hedonic Motivation* (HM)	The application was: a) Fun, b) Exciting, c) Delightful, d)l Enjoyable, e) Thrilling
Intention to Use* (IU)	a) I will regularly use it the future b) I intend to use it in the future c) I will think about using it
Collaboration	I was able to collaboratively perform the task

*mean values of the questions were used for the analysis

Table 1: Constructs and questions used

EARLY RESUTS
As a first step, we employed Spearman's correlation coefficient between the factors, which is about quantifying the strength of the relationship between the variables. Spearman's test suggests that some of the factors are related, in some cases relatively strongly (Table 2). More precisely, the available size is related with creativity, hedonic motivation and collaboration. Tools availability is related only with collaboration. There is also a relation on users' hedonic and utilitarian motivation with their intention to use the application in the future.

Spearman (p)	Avail. Tool	Avail. Size	Creativity	UM	HM	IU
Size	0.024					
Creativity	0.222	0.344*				
UM	0.232	0.134	0.211			
HM	0.242	0.431**	0.402*	0.593**		
IU	0.195	0.060	0.290	0.336*	0.506*	
Collaboration	0.325*	0.521*	0.594**	0.163	0.365*	0.190

Correlation is significant at the ** 0.01 and * 0.05 level.

Table 2: Spearman's correlation coefficient between factors.

To examine our research question regarding space's and tool's availability impact of users' experience, we divided users two times. The first time we divided them to those who were satisfied/unsatisfied with the available tools (inside their personal window) and then to those who were satisfied/unsatisfied with the available space of the window. Then a t-test was conducted, in which the two independent variables (Space Availability, Tools Availability) and the five dependent variables (UM, HM, IU, Creativity, Collaboration) were included. As the outcome data in Table 3 (top of the next page) illustrates, space availability has indicated a significant effect on users' HM, creativity and collaboration. On the other hand, tools availability has no impact on users' experience.

CONCLUSIONS
Interactive surfaces, like tabletops or wall-size displays, closely resemble real-world work surfaces [5]. In this study, we employed a well-known task from real world - a drawing/dot-to-dot task - in order to explore whether there is a connection between tools and space availability on users' experience and creativity in an interactive surface.

Multi-touch interfaces allow for multi-user collocated work despite limitations such as the restrictions in space (due to multi-user interaction and the possible collisions between the users). According to [3], more display space allows multiple windows to be displayed simultaneously, which can result in increased performance and user satisfaction. Based on the results of our study, space availability affects not only hedonic motivation (pleasure) and collaboration, but also users' creativity. Our results are in accordance to Catala [2], who claims that in terms of creativity traits, interactive surfaces seem promising as groups working in such digital platforms show significantly more performance in fluency of thinking, being more motivated, and novel.

	Mean (S.D.)		t (p)	Mean (S.D.)		t (p)
	Sufficient space	Need more space		Sufficient tools	Need more tools	
UM	5.73 (1.00)	5.46 (0.94)	0.82 (.420)	5.79 (1.08)	5.43 (0.84)	1.10 (.279)
HM	6.07 (0.80)	5.24 (1.04)	**2.71 (.010)***	5.91 (1.00)	5.49 (0.97)	1.29 (.207)
IU	5.08 (1.50)	4.90 (1.40)	0.36 (.716)	5.12 (1.33)	4.87 (1.57)	0.52 (.610)
Creativity	5.85 (1.27)	4.82 (1.59)	**2.18 (.036)***	5.21 (1.58)	5.56 (1.42)	0.67 (.491)
Collaboration	6.25 (1.33)	4.91 (1.79)	**2.61 (.013)***	5.39 (1.48)	5.89 (1.88)	0.89 (.378)

S.D. Standard Deviation; *p < 0.05

Table 3: Testing the effect of space and tool availability on user experience and creativity

On the other hand, we show that tool availability does not affect user creativity and experience in interactive surfaces. We believe that our result has to do with the affordances of the MT interactive surface. In literature, there are many tools or toolkits with which creativity is facilitated. For example, Greenberg [6] suggested that the use of toolkits for novel and perhaps unfamiliar application areas by programmers enhance the creativity. Programmers, instead of focusing on low-level implementation they concentrate on creative designs. However, previous studies [8, 11] demonstrate that in the case of an interactive surface, it is the low-level implementation – the direct touch interaction technique – that augments user experience and thus making the users express their creativity. In this sense, users seem to disregard the use of additional tools as a mean to foster their creativity. Besides, in the higher level of creativity, creating relies on the use of raw materials [10].

ACKNOWLEDGMENTS
We would like to thank all the participants of the study. We also thank A. Angeletaki, K. Chorianopoulos, L. Jaccheri, and G. Papastefanou for their extremely helpful assistance. This work was partially funded by ARK4 project of the National Library of Norway and the NTNU UB.

REFERENCES
1. Battarbee, K., and Koskinen, I. Co-experience: user experience as interaction. CoDesign, 1, 1 (2005), 5-18.

2. Catala, A., Jaen, J., van Dijk, B., and Jordà, S. Exploring tabletops as an effective tool to foster creativity traits. In Proc. of TEI 2012, ACM Press (2012), 143-150.

3. Czerwinski, M., Smith, G., Regan, T., Meyers, B., Robertson, G., and Starkweather, G. Toward characterizing the productivity benefits of very large displays. In Proc. of INTERACT 2003, Springer (2003). 9–16.

4. Erickson, T. From interface to interplace: The spatial environment as a medium for interaction. In Proc. of Spatial Information Theory A Theoretical Basis for GIS Springer (1993), 391-405.

5. Geyer, F., Pfeil, U., Höchtl, A., Budzinski, J., and Reiterer, H. Designing reality-based interfaces for creative group work. In Proc. of C&C 2011, ACM Press (2011), 165-174.

6. Greenberg, S. Toolkits and interface creativity. Multimedia Tools and Applications, 32(2), (2007), 139-159.

7. Jakobsen, M. R., and Hornbæk, K. Up close and personal: Collaborative work on a high-resolution multitouch wall display. ACM Transactions on Computer-Human Interaction (TOCHI), 21, 2 (2014).

8. Leftheriotis, I., and Chorianopoulos, K. User experience quality in multi-touch tasks. In Proc. of EICS 2011, ACM Press (2011), 277-282.

9. Maher, M. L. Evaluating creativity in humans, computers, and collectively intelligent systems. In Proc. of DESIRE Network Conference on Creativity and Innovation in Design. ACM Press (2010), 22-28.

10. Sanders, E. B. N. (2006). Scaffolds for building everyday creativity. Design for Effective Communications: Creating Contexts for Clarity and Meaning. Jorge Frascara (Ed.) Allworth Press, New York.

11. Watson, D., Hancock, M., Mandryk, R. L., and Birk, M. Deconstructing the touch experience. In Proc. of the ITS 2013, ACM Press (2013). 199-208.

Examining the Association Between Users Creative Thinking and Field Dependence-Independence Cognitive Style through Eye Movement Components

Efi A. Nisiforou
Multimedia and Graphic Arts
Cyprus University of Technology
30 Archbishop Kyprianou Str. 3036, Lemesos
Cyprus
efi.nisiforou@cut.ac.cy

ABSTRACT

This eye tracking study investigated the association between individuals' field dependence - independence cognitive style and level of creative thinking based on users' eye movement behaviour while interacting with a set of visual perceptual tasks. Subjects FD-I cognitive style and creativity were measured with the use of the Hidden Figures Test (HFT) and Torrance Test of Creative Thinking (TTCT). The psychometric methods and the eye tracking-derived data were statistically examined demonstrating a relationship between users' cognitive style, creativity attributes and eye gaze behaviour. This research study adds further to the evidence and theory base of Human-computer interaction for applications in the user-centred design and suggests future directions for research.

Author Keywords

Field dependence-independence; eye-tracking; eye gaze; visual stimuli; Hidden Figures Test; Torrance Test of Creative Thinking.

ACM Classification Keywords

H.5.2 User Interfaces User-centered design; I.5.2 Design Methodology (e.g. Feature evaluation and selection, Pattern analysis).

INTRODUCTION

This study was an investigation towards an on-going project that aims to provide guidelines for the design of adaptive environments by understanding how users of different cognitive types interact with various tasks [1]. The idea that individuals differ in the way they solve or approach tasks

C&C 2015, June 22–25, 2015, Glasgow, United Kingdom.
ACM 978-1-4503-3598-0/15/06.
http://dx.doi.org/10.1145/2757226.2764556

has provided a central underpinning for research in the field of the applied cognitive dimensions. Currently, there is an escalation of studies that examine individuals' cognitive components in correlation to visual perception. In order to accomplish the aforesaid long term vision of the research, there is a need for some premise indicators to be considered. Therefore, the purpose of the current work is to look for any possible connections between the eye gaze pattern and individuals' cognitive characteristics such as featural processing style and creativity.

Creativity involves the capacity to spontaneously shift back and forth between analytic and associative modes of thought according to the situation [2]. These types of thought demonstrate individual differences in how visual information is perceived. One of the most widely used tests to assess associative thinking (divergent or local processing styles) and analytic thinking (convergent or global processing styles) is the Hidden Figures Test [3]. Besides, focusing on specific patterns activates memory that supports divergence or convergence [4]. Thus, a question arises as to whether people who process information in a more analytic way, are more creative than those who look at the whole image/ object embedded in a scene. Finally, the notion that field independent people have been found to be more creative than the field dependents remains vague.

Earlier studies have proposed that the use of ambiguous stimuli may in some way be associated with degrees of creativity [5, 6, 7]. Additionally, tolerance of ambiguity is believed to contribute to the creative process because it enables the exploration of new, uncommon or complex stimuli [8]. These lines of work suggest that the more individuals can tolerate ambiguous objects, the more creative they become.

Thus, the purpose of the designed research is twofold. Firstly it seeks to identify the association between users' Field dependence-independence cognitive style and creative thinking, and secondly to examine individual differences in eye movement patterns during a computer-based visual perceptual task processing between the three different cognitive groups of users [i.e. Field Dependent (FD), Field Neutral (FN) and Field Independent (FI)].

Specifically the study seeks to address the following research questions:

Q1. Is there any association between users' Field Dependence-Independence cognitive type and their level of creative thinking?

Q2. What are the differences between users' cognitive groups (FD, FN, and FI) and eye movement behaviour?

THEORETICAL BACKGROUND

Field dependence - independence cognitive style
The field dependence-independence (FD-I) is among the most widely used cognitive style dimensions appearing in the literature [9, 10]. These dimensions are formed based on the individual's reliance on the context to extract particular meaning and describe three contrasting ways of processing information (FD, FN, FI) [1]. Participants' level of field dependency is measured with the use of the Hidden Figures Test [4]. The HFT contains 32 questions divided into two parts. The test presents five simple figures and asks learners to find one of the five simple figures embedded in a more complex pattern. The field dependents find it difficult to identify a simple geometric figure that is embedded in a complex shape while field independent learners can identify the separate parts of a whole. FD learners, take longer to detect a simple figure than FI students, or they may not be able to find it at all [1, 10]. FI individuals, are therefore, more likely to be influenced by internal than external cues and be selective in their information input [1, 2].

Creative thinking
Creativity has been defined as the process of incorporating seemingly unrelated and irrelevant information to solve problems [12]. Creative thinking is often thought to involve divergent thinking; that is being able to consider a solution in many different ways rather than converging on a single answer [13]. One of the broadest used assessments of creativity is the Torrance Test of Creative Thinking (TTCT) [14, 15]. It is based on widespread analyzes; thus it can be determined that the TTCT is the best creativity test currently exist [16]. The TTCT is available in two versions; the TTCT-Verbal and the TTCT-Figural, each one consists of Form A and B [17]. Both forms are concerned with four principal cognitive processes of creativity: (a) fluency of relevant responses; (b) flexibility as referred to a variety of answers; (c) originality entails considering novelty responses; and (d) elaboration as stated to the number of details used to provide an answer. However, in the scope of this review, only the TTCT-Figural was used.

Eye tracking and eye movement data
Eye tracking studies try to investigate and understand user behaviour and offer information on issues such as cognitive activity [18]. The use of eye tracking has long been established in Psychology as a technique for analyzing user attention patterns in information processing tasks [18]. These attention patterns of eye movement data are very informative in revealing evidence about the cognitive processes [17]. A previous study examined the potential of eye tracker as a tool for detecting users' cognitive dimensions with respect to the FD-I classification. The study identified differences between the three cognitive styles and search tasks time completion [1]. Although current studies have provided valuable insights into how different tasks affect a user's eye gaze behaviour, further research needs to examine individual differences in eye movement components in terms of other cognitive features such as creative thinking and featural processing styles.

METHOD

Participants
The target audience of the study consisted of thirty one normal vision students with average age 19, 61 years (SD = 1.874) recruited from the school of Psychology at a private University in the U.K.

Procedure and Materials
Users' interaction and cognitive behaviour were examined with the aid of the eye tracker technology during perceptual processes involved in the interpretation of ambiguous figures. The design of the environment was programmed through the iView SDK software development (kit-interface). A number of twenty (20) ambiguous images (10 images per ambiguous category) were scaled to the same dimension and equalized for intensity. The exploration was conducted in three parts, using the following research tools: a) Hidden Figures Test- HFT; b) Torrance Test of Creative Thinking – TTCT), and, c) eye movement components analysis through eye tracking.

Part A - Hidden Figures Test (HFT)
Participants' level of field dependence was measured with the use of the Hidden Figures Test and participants had a 24 minutes time limit to complete the test. It consists of 32 questions divided equally into two parts. The test presents five simple figures and asks learners to identify which of the five simple figures is embedded in the complex pattern. Individuals who scored 10 or lower are categorized as FD; those who possess a score from 11 to 17 are classified as FM or FN, and as FI those who score 18 or higher [1].

Part B - Torrance Tests of Creative Thinking (TTCT) (Figural Test Form A)
The researcher administered the TTCT to the participants as a way to measure their level of visual creativity. The TTCT-Figural contains three non-verbal activities: (a) Picture Construction, (b) Picture Completion and (c) Lines

(repeated figures). Ten minutes were required to complete each activity with a total working time of 30 minutes. The figural test comprises of three activities designed to measure five cognitive characteristics (fluency, originality, abstractness of titles, resistance to premature closure and elaboration) and thirteen creative strengths.

Part C – Eye movements' gaze analysis using the iViewX model of the eye-tracking device.
Students were asked to perform perceptual visual tasks while viewing ambiguous figures (images with more than one meaning). Their task was to press keyboard buttons every time they see the picture changing into something else, coupled with eye gaze recordings.

RESULTS AND DISCUSSION

Field Dependence-Independence cognitive style
Eye tracking metrics revealed statistically significant differences between the three different cognitive groups of learners and their level of creative thinking. The findings of the study are discussed in terms of the association between field dependent, field neutral and field independent cognitive groups and the level of creativity during a visual search task process. As previously mentioned, the Hidden Figure Test (HFT) was used to define users' FD-I current cognitive type (e.g. FD, FN and FI). Participants' score on the test was calculated as the difference between the numbers of questions answered correctly minus the number answered incorrectly. The participants were classified into their cognitive type as follows: 16 field dependent, 8 field neutral and, 7 field independent. The testing activity involved in the HFT is a reliable and widely used approach for determining the FD-I cognitive dimension.

Level of creative thinking
The results from the Torrance Test of Creative Thinking (TTCT) indicated participants' level of creative thinking. The scoring scales measure the five norm-referenced totals (Fluency, Originality, Elaboration, Abstractness of Titles and Resistance to Premature Closure) and the 13 criterion-referenced scores, which compose the Creative Strength total. The cut off scores procedure of the three levels of creativity (Low, Moderate, and High) was based on previous studies measurements taking into account the standard deviation and mean of the Creativity Index [2]. Participants were classified as 6 Low creative thinkers, 21 moderate creative users, and 3 high creative thinkers.

Eye movement comparisons of FD, FN, and FI users
Figure 1 demonstrates the scan paths of the field dependent, field neutral, and field independent subjects as a result of their interaction in one of the thirty visual stimuli of the experiment. The eye tracking scan paths reflect the users' eye gaze patterns while performing the perceptual visual tasks. It was hypothesized that individuals FD-I cognitive

style will affect their degree of creative thinking. Specifically, it was assumed that the FI will produce a higher level of creativity, contrary to the FN and FD users who might exemplify a moderate and a lower creativity level respectively.

These eye gaze patterns demonstrate that the field dependents produce a greater number of fixations and saccades, showing disoriented eye movement behaviour. In contrast, the field independents' and field neutrals' eye gaze activity exemplified a more oriented navigation, resulting in less number of fixations and saccades.

Figure 1. Example of the ambiguous figure displayed in the experiment demonstrating FD, FN and FI users scan paths (from left to right), My Wife and Mother-in-Law © W. E. Hill

One-way Anova
A one-way ANOVA was conducted to examine the association between the field dependence-independence cognitive style and users' level of creative thinking on the visual stimuli employed. There was a significant correlation of the level of field dependency on creative thinking at the $p<.05$ level for the three cognitive groups $F(2, 28) = 4.21$, $p = .025$. Post hoc comparisons using the LSD test indicated that the mean score for the field dependence cognitive group (M = 0.13, SD = 0.23) was significantly different from the field independence group (M = 0.68, SD = 0.24). Moreover, the field neutral users' (M = 0.13, SD = 0.23) were significantly different from the field independents. Overall, these results suggest that individuals' level of field dependency affects their level of creative thinking. Specifically, the field dependent individuals exemplify lower levels of creative thinking, whereas, the field independents were classified as higher creative thinkers. The field neutral group showed a moderate creativity level compared to the FI group. However, it should be noted that there were no statistically significant differences between the field dependence and field neutral cognitive groups ($p = .58$).

Thereby, why does looking at the whole suggest more creativity than looking at the specific? These findings in turn are greatly accentuated by the capacity to shift between associative and analytic thinking as a medium to be creative. The different processing modes are typical of creative thinking and can be explained based on Gabora's cognitive theory of memory activation [2]. This approach is related to what we know about the different ways individuals' process and perceive visual stimuli.

CONCLUSION

The eye tracking technique was employed to examine the association between the Field Dependence-Independence cognitive style and creativity during perceptual processes involved in the interpretation of ambiguous figures. This paper moved one step beyond creativity and cognition studies by adding an eye gaze behaviour empirical study. The findings yielded that the field independence group of individuals; who allocated less number of fixations in the visual stimuli of the experiment, resulted in higher levels of creative thinking than when related to the field dependence group. Besides, the field neutral group showed a moderate creativity level compared to the FI group. This finding proposes that paying attention to stimulus features rather than the ensemble suggest more creativity. Therefore, a contribution to Creativity and Cognition can be made by better understanding that certain types of people (as measured by the HFT) are probably more creative (as measured by the TTCT).

Currently, further research is under progress that will take the above study on its next phase combining behavioural and electrophysiological methods. The forthcoming work aims to investigate the mechanisms that underlie the association between FD-I cognitive style, eye gaze patterns, and creative thinking. As a final point, this work will contribute to the long term vision for the design of personalized environments that can reflect users' cognitive needs and characteristics.

REFERENCES

1. Nisiforou, E. A., and Laghos, A. Do the eyes have it? Using eye tracking to assess students' cognitive dimensions. *Educational Media International, 50*, 4, (2013), 247-265.

2. Gabora, L. Revenge of the 'neurds': Characterizing creative thought in terms of the structure and dynamics of memory. *Creativity Research Journal 22*, 1, (2010), 1-13.

3. Ekstrom, R. B., French, J. W., Harman, H.H., and Dermen, D. *Manual for Kit of Factor-Referenced Cognitive Tests*. Educational Testing Service, Princeton, New Jersey, 1976.

4. Gabora, L. Toward a theory of creative inklings. In R. Ascott (Ed.), *Art, Technology, and Consciousness, Intellect Press*, Bristol, UK, (2000), 159-164.

5. Wiseman, R., Watt, C., Gilhooly, K., and Georgiou, G. Creativity and ease of ambiguous figural reversal. *British Journal of Psychology, 102*, 3, (2011), 615-622.

6. Urban, K. K. Toward a Componential Model of Creativity. In D. Ambrose, L. M. Cohen, and A.J. Tannenbaum (Eds.), 2003. *Creative Intelligence: Toward Theoretic Integration.* Hampton Press Inc: Cresskill, NJ.

7. Dove, G., and Jones, S. Using data to stimulate creative thinking in the design of new products and services. In *Proceedings of the 2014 conference on Designing interactive systems* (pp. 443-452). ACM.

8. Zenasni, F., Besançon, M., and Lubart, T. Creativity and tolerance of ambiguity: An empirical study. *The Journal of Creative Behavior, 42*, 1, (2008), 61-73.

9. Witkin, H., A. Individual Differences in Ease of Perception of Embedded Figures. *Journal of Personality, 19*, 1, (1950), 1–15.

10. Guisande, M., Pramo, M., Tinajero, C. Y., and Almeida, L. Field dependence-independence (fdi) cognitive style: An analysis of attentional functioning. *Psicothema 19*, 4, (2007), 572–577.

11. Runco, M. A., Millar, G., Acar, S., and Cramond, B. Torrance tests of creative thinking as predictors of personal and public achievement: A fifty-year follow-up. *Creativity Research Journal, 22*, 4, (2010), 361-368.

12. Medin, D. L., Ross, B. H., and Markman, A. B. *Cognitive psychology.* (3rd ed.) Forth Worth, TX, Harcourt College, 2001.

13. Sternberg, R. J. The nature of creativity. *Creativity Research Journal, 18*, 1, (2006), 87-98.

14. Torrance, E. P. *The Torrance Tests of Creative Thinking-Norms-Technical Manual Research Edition-Verbal Tests, Forms A and B- Figural Tests, Forms A and B.* Princeton, NJ, Personnel Press, 1974.

15. Razumnikova, O. M., and A. U. Zagainova. The significance of motor asymmetry and hemispheric characteristics for effective convergent and divergent thinking during information identification. *Journal of Asymmetry, 7*, 2 (2013).

16. Kim, K. H. The APA 2009 division 10 debate: Are the Torrance Tests of Creative Thinking still relevant in the 21st century? *Psychology of Aesthetics, Creativity and the Arts, 5*, (2011), 302-308.

17. Rayner, K. Eye movements in reading and information processing: 20 years of research. *Psychological bulletin, 124*, 3, (1998), 372.

18. Rayner, K. Eye movements and cognitive processes in reading, visual search, and scene perception. *Studies in Visual Information Processing, 6*, (1995), 3-22.

Scranvas: Gamified Forum for Amateur Designers to Share Creative Work and Generate Constructive Feedback

Abhishek Chakraborty
Industrial Design Centre, Indian Institute of Technology Bombay
Powai, Mumbai - 400076
abhishek.mech011@gmail.com

ABSTRACT
Feedback is important for cultivating creativity. Constructive feedback on design is crucial for helping design students and amateur designers iterate towards better solutions. However most of the current platforms don't promote honest design feedback and are primarily used only for self-promotion. This paper proposes Scranvas, a community for students and non-experts to encourage sharing of creative work and generate constructive feedback. Users interpret the designs based on the context and goals stated by the designer and share feedback through annotations.

Author Keywords
criticism; community; design feedback; gamification; evaluation

ACM Classification Keywords
H.5.m. Information interfaces and presentation (e.g., HCI): Miscellaneous.

INTRODUCTION
Feedback is a crucial aspect of the creative design process [7, 9]. Feedback exposes gaps between what the user intends and what others perceive in a design [6], which, if not addressed can generate adverse results [3]. Knowing where the gaps exist is therefore critical to help designers iterate toward more effective solutions [4].

From a creative cognition perspective, feedback can foster insight or unblock creativity because the feedback serves as retrieval signals that activate new memory items and thought production [12]. This, in turn, can spark new understanding of a design, new solution approaches, or new perspectives on the design problem. Designers who receive feedback during iterative design process produce higher quality outcomes than those who do not [4]. Sharing

multiple designs with others helps in increased communication, improves design exploration and the final outcome as well [5].

However, the user may feel uncomfortable showing his or her design to others due to the fear of criticism [2] or may not prefer interruption in their work [8]. Fear of negative feedback is a common problem, which often negatively affects the work and thus, creativity [1]. Also, studies have shown that little actionable feedback is generated in design communities (e.g. Behance) and the quality does not exceed beyond comments such as "Good work!" [17]. These platforms are mainly for self-promotion and are means of growing one's network. Making strong criticism of someone else's work openly might deter the chances of being appreciated by the designer and his peers as well. It is often awkward to give bad feedback publicly. Also, the expertise of the person in that domain heavily influences the perception towards his or her feedback.

Apart from getting feedback on work, designers also have to be encouraged to share and discover creative work. If there are no works, there is no scope for feedback. Even non-designers do hobby design related works, but they are awkward to post it in design communities as these are targeted towards professionals and experts, not at casual designers.

BACKGROUND RESEARCH AND DESIGN PROCESS

Design Feedback from Amateurs
Design is a complex task and researchers have investigated many directions for how a non-expert crowd can aid design. For example, Dow et al. studied how crowd technologies can aid each phase of the design process such as collecting preferences on variations of a design (AB testing) [4]. Others have utilized crowds for rating ideas in innovation competitions [18] and testing interfaces based on task performance [10]. Crowd-based usability Web sites can also be used to collect feedback on designs. For example, when using Fivesecondtest, a user can pose free-form questions to the crowd about a design and the site returns a word cloud from the responses.

But there is no method of providing coordinated views for analyzing the association between the crowd's perception of a design and the visual elements within it. There is also no proper way to generate specific feedback (e.g. on the user's goals) not directly provided by different Usability

Testing sites. Though the question format of the sites are helpful, the user would still need to conceptualize and phrase the questions in a way that yields desired and consistent responses.

Various Methods of Receiving Design Feedback

There are at least two approaches for computationally generating feedback on designs. One approach, software critics, is to encode and apply domain-specific knowledge in the form of rules to generate feedback on designs. The limitation of this approach is that it cannot consider the unique goals of the user or nuances of the design problem.

A second approach is to build computational models to predict aesthetics and affect, complexity and colorfulness [14], or perceptual groupings using the visual features of a design. But since the feedback is not synthesized from human input, it cannot include explanations and inspiration for improvement.

Besides software tools, a user can use social approaches to receive feedback on designs such as organizing critiques, informally asking peers, and participating in online design communities.

Contextual Enquiry

A critical challenge for generating design feedback via internet users is to identify what type of feedback is desirable to the user, yet can be generated by non-experts. To address this challenge, we conducted interviews with thirteen participants. Eight were graphic design students while the other five are either hobby designers and had no formal training in design.

Interviews were semi-structured. After breaking the ice by asking about their ongoing design projects, questions were asked probing the importance of feedback in the design process, what methods are used to receive feedback and from whom, what makes feedback effective, and what type of feedback might be desired. Additional questions pursued interesting points raised by the participants.

Following qualitative analysis methods, we had three main findings from the interviews. First, all of the participants emphasized the importance of receiving feedback during the design process. Echoing prior work [15, 16], participants reported that feedback helps them better understand what is or is not being communicated in the design, inform design choices, and remove creative blocks. They start thinking in a different way after getting good feedback.

Second, participants struggle to receive the feedback desired using existing methods. Participants reported that feedback received from peers is often optimistic and usually lacks clear direction for improvement. Peers usually know how much work has been put into the work and they might not want to hurt the designers' feelings. Participants who leveraged online communities such as Behance and Dribbble complained the feedback received was too little and lacked depth. It is not very often that one gets very constructive feedback on these sites. It's also a follower based community. So a person with fewer followers won't get much feedback. Moreover, these sites are targeted towards professionals and not necessarily design students. Feedback from those knowledgeable about design is deemed useful but not typically available outside of scheduled critiques or studio work, or if one's peer network does not include designers. Requesting feedback is therefore considered a limited resource that must be used judiciously.

Finally, all of the participants expressed that feedback from a non-expert crowd would be useful for comparing the perceptions of the crowd to their own expectations. Trained designers see things in certain ways. But if one can get non-designers or amateurs to understand the concept that means the design work is done very well. Participants also felt that it's easy to get caught inside the design bubble. "A lot of times, if you are surrounded by designers, you only design for designers."

From the responses, we also identified four types of design feedback that would be desirable. One type of feedback relates to assessing the visual hierarchy of a design: What is the first thing people see in a design? Does it stand out? What do they first read? What do they first see? What do they think they are going to see?

A second type of feedback mentioned is capturing first impressions when the design is viewed: What are people's initial impressions of it? What's the reaction to this or what does this make the user think of? Is that the reaction that the designer wants them to perceive?

A third type of feedback is whether the crowd understands the communicative goals of the design: Does the design convey the right message to the audience? How is the mentioned goal coming across to the audience? How well do the concepts read?

A fourth type of feedback tacitly mentioned is assessing a design relative to design guidelines, e.g. contrast, proximity, and alignment. This feedback was inferred from many responses expressing the need for technical insights about a design and clear direction for how to improve it: "I want highly technical feedback and constructive feedback. What's wrong and how to fix it? Do the colors clash or complement each other? Are there any distractions?"

Community and Forums

Communities and forums thrive on creation of content. If there is no sharing of creative work, then there is no scope of feedback either. Also, what the designer does with the feedback and how it is incorporated in the next iterations is more important than the feedback itself. Mamykina et al [11] claimed that both intrinsic and extrinsic motivators underlie the users' contributions in forums and communities.

However, extrinsic motivation and intrinsic motivation might function differently. In gamification schemes, users extrinsically motivated by earning points tend to lose their enthusiasm once they reached a certain level, and only those users who are driven by their intrinsic motivators would maintain their activeness. Although Quora does not incorporate such a point system, users still have several extrinsic motivators for participation, namely building a reputation and social capital.

Reciprocity is relatively neglected but it is often the foundation of lots of intrinsic motivation to contribute such as altruism. Reciprocity means that users contribute because they have benefited from the community, or because they anticipate that they will benefit in return. If users get good feedback on their works from a community, they might be motivated to share more work thereby enabling others to discover good designs.

Furthermore, Nowak and Roch et al [13] also pointed out the importance of gratitude. They proposed that when the recipients of altruistic behaviors experience gratitude, they tend to be inclined to help either the contributor or a third person. Gratitude and reciprocity will encourage continued altruistic cooperation, which is ideal for any community.

PROBLEM STATEMENT
The primary users of portfolio sites like Behance and Dribbble are design professionals. Their main purpose is to connect with potential clients or firms for jobs. They share finished and polished works, so there is no possible way to know the study and explorations behind them. Currently, there are not many ways to share hobby and casual works, learn from others and grow. Any kind of community for hobby designers and design enthusiasts to share their works and learn from their peers is absent. Most platforms are majorly targeted to professionals. The peer review mechanism in most platforms has reduced to mere back-patting and appreciations.

SCRANVAS

Introduction
This paper proposes a gamified community system for receiving feedback called Scranvas. In contrast to the getting feedback through sites likes Behance, Scranvas relies on design goals set by the users to generate feedback that surpasses simplistic statements.

Inside the community there are different forums called Houses (see Figure 1) with specializations (e.g. Graphic Design, UI Design). Members in the houses can make two kinds of post: a) their own work for creative feedback from others. They have to provide the context and thought behind the design along with the design goals, or b) Design case studies or critiques they have written on someone else's work (e.g. Critique on the logo design of Fitucci). Non-experts can learn a lot even by reading critiques on someone else's work.

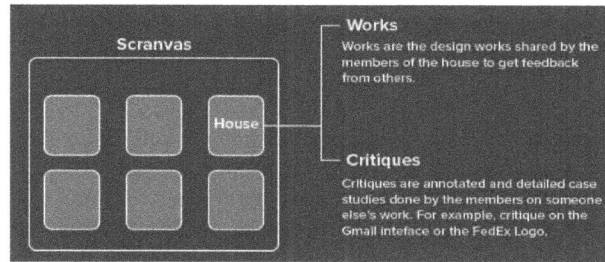

Figure 1: Conceptual Model of Scranvas

Feedbacks are single blind. The creator will not know who has given feedback on his work and thus judge the feedback only by its content and not get influenced by the level of expertise of the user.

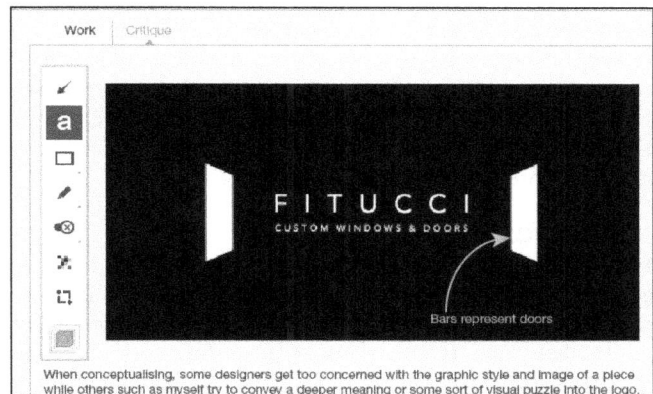

Figure 2: Annotations help in pointing at certain areas.

The annotation tool is used to point at certain areas in the design while giving feedback (see Figure 2). Annotations are helpful in pointing out areas which are standing out or need to change; or identify the visual hierarchy. Text is used to further emphasize how the mentioned goal is coming across to the audience, suggest improvements or share sources of knowledge and inspiration.

Retake

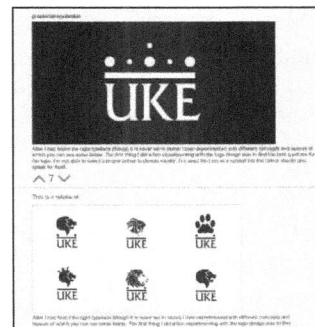

Figure 3: Retake is an iteration of the original work

After getting feedback, a member can submit an improved version of his work which is called a 'Retake' of the original work (see Figure 3). A retake is a means of showing what he or she has taken into account from the feedback.

Imitate
A lot can be explored through imitation as well, other than studying case studies or reviewing someone else's work. If a novice designer likes someone's work he can choose to 'Imitate' it and upload his own version or interpretation and connect it with the original work. Imitations allow novices to practice design and give credit to the original inspiration as well.

Scoring Points
Members of the house can upvote or downvote posts and comments thereby keeping only the good and relevant ones on top. Members get points when their posts and comments are voted up. Their scores also increase when they do retakes, or someone imitates their work. The scores may indicate the quality of their work and also their contribution to the community. The scores act as motivation factors for the members to contribute to the community and thereby practice more creative work.

EVALUATION AND CONCLUSION
Initial user testing has been done using a Wizard of Oz approach where seven users (design students) were asked to post design works using a shared Google Docs document while they also (anonymously) gave feedback on each other's works. The evaluation happened at a stretch of three days.

Users praised the idea of 'retake' and 'imitate' stating that these might motivate users to improve upon their work. They liked the idea of blind review as it saves them from any kind of feedback anxiety, but also felt that it deterred them from networking with the reviewers.

Scoring points act as a motivation factor for the members to create more designs. The voting system curates contents; therefore users see only the best contents for creative inspiration. This may also motivate users to create good content so that they may reach the front page with upvotes.

Future plans include developing and deploying a working prototype (website) for testing the system with a large number of users and investigation of the effects of feedback on motivation level and creativity.

REFERENCES
1. Amabile, T.M. How to kill creativity. Harvard business review 76, September-October (1998), 76-87.

2. Diehl, M. and Stroebe, W. Productivity Loss in Brainstorming Groups: Towards the Solution of a Riddle. Journal of Personality and Social Psychology, 53, 3, (1987), 497-509.

3. Does This JC Penney Tea Kettle Look Like Hitler?, NBC's Today.com, http://www.today.com/news/does-j-c-penney-teakettle-look-hitler-6C10100642, Retrieved on May 28 2013.

4. Dow, S.P., Heddleston, K., & Klemmer, S.R., The Efficacy of Prototyping Under Time Constraints. In Creativity & Cognition, (2009), 165-174.

5. Dow, S.P., Fortuna, J., Schwartz, D., Altringer, B., & Klemmer, S., Prototyping Dynamics: Sharing Multiple Designs Improves Exploration, Group Rapport, and Results. In CHI, (2011), 2807-2816.

6. Elkins, J. Art Critiques: A Guide. New Academia Publishing, Washington DC, 2012.

7. Feldman, E.B. Varieties of Visual Experience: Art as Image and Idea. Prentice-Hall, Englewood Cliffs, N.J., 1981.

8. Fogarty, J., Hudson, S.E., Atkeson, C.G., Avrahami, D., Forlizzi, J., Kiesler, S., Lee, J.C., et al. Predicting Human Interruptibility with Sensors. TOCHI, 12, 1, (2005), 119-146.

9. Hundhausen, C.D., Fairbrother, D., & Petre, M. An Empirical Study of the "Prototype Walkthrough": A Studio-Based Activity for HCI Education. TOCHI, 19, 4, (2012), 1-36.

10. Komarov, S., Reinecke, K., & Gajos, K.Z., Crowdsourcing Performance Evaluations of User Interfaces. In CHI, (2013), 207-216.

11. Mamykina, L., Manoim, B., Mittal, M., Hripcsak, G., and Hartmann, B. Design Lessons from the Fastest Q&A Site in the West. Proceedings of CHI 2011, 2857-2866.

12. Nijstad, B.A. and Stroebe, W. How the Group Affects the Mind: A Cognitive Model of Idea Generation in Groups. Personality and Social Psychology Review, 10, 3, (2006), 186-213.

13. Nowak MA, Roch S. (2007). Upstream reciprocity and the evolution of gratitude. Proceedings of the Royal Society B: Biological Science, 274 (1610), 605-609.

14. Reinecke, K., Yeh, T., Miratrix, L., Mardiko, R., Zhao, Y., Liu, J., & Gajos, K.Z., Predicting Users' First Impressions of Website Aesthetics With a Quantification of Perceived Visual Complexity and Colorfulness. In CHI, (2013), 2049-2058.

15. Schön, D.A. Designing as Reflective Conversation with the Materials of a Design Situation. Knowledge-Based Systems, 5, 1, (1992), 3-14.

16. Tohidi, M., Buxton, W., Baecker, R., & Sellen, A., Getting the Right Design and the Design Right. In CHI, (2006), 1243-1252.

17. Willett, W., Heer, J., & Agrawala, M., Strategies for Crowdsourcing Social Data Analysis. In CHI, (2012), 227-236.

18. Xu, A. and Bailey, B.P., A Reference-Based Scoring Model for Increasing the Findability of Promising Ideas in Innovation Pipelines. In CSCW, (2012), 1183-1186.

Sketch-Play-Learn - An Augmented Paper Based Environment for Learning the Concepts of Optics

Bhawna Agarwal
Indian Institute of Technology Guwahati
India
bhawna2109@gmail.com

Richa Tripathi
Indian Institute of Technology Guwahati
India
richatpt@gmail.com

ABSTRACT

In this paper, we introduce Sketch-Play-Learn, an augmented paper-based tabletop system to support students learning of the principles of light behaviour. This project emphasises the use of the most ubiquitous and inexpensive learning medium, which is paper. Students engage themselves in completing a goal-based task sketched by the teacher on paper and observing the visual feedback on the same paper. We argue that augmenting the paper with digital information while providing a tabletop setup provides a novel and appealing approach to learning for classroom use. In this paper, we discuss the motivations for our project and describe the design and implementation our system. We also describe an initial evaluation with children and outline future research goals.

Author Keywords

tangible interaction; augmented paper; light; reflection; colors; learning; design

ACM Classification Keywords

H.5.2. Information Interfaces and Presentation (e.g. HCI): User Interfaces

INTRODUCTION

The potential of tangible user interfaces (TUIs) to support education and learning is enormous [8]. Research has demonstrated that tangibles can increase learners motivation by high levels of engagement [1]. One area that might benefit from the application of this technology is that of optics. Paper has physical characteristics, called affordances, that affect how it is used. Not only is it lightweight and flexible, but it is easy to annotate and personalize [7]. Being tangible, paper provides a cheap, easy way to attach virtual elements to reality. Sketch-Play-Learn augments the physical paper and we believe that this interactive paper has the potential to offer the best aspects of both physical paper and electronic documents, by making the paper the user interface.

In this paper, we describe the design and implementation of Sketch-Play-Learn, an augmented tabletop system with

C&C 2015, June 22–25, 2015, Glasgow, United Kingdom.
ACM 978-1-4503-3598-0/15/06.
http://dx.doi.org/10.1145/2757226.2764558

paper based input and tangible interaction means for children aged 11-14 years to support their learning of the principles of light behavior, particularly the laws of reflection and the color of objects. We emphasize the use of paper which is an integral medium of learning. Students engage themselves in completing a goal-based task - sketched by the teacher on paper - by using tangibles. Furthermore, they can see the light travel on the same paper as well as the popups which give information about the angles and explain the concept of color of objects. Because of the tabletop system, the collaboration between children is less constrained and less formal.

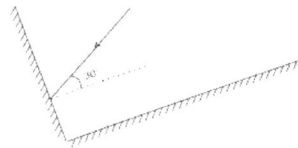

15. Two mirrors meet at right angles. A ray of light is incident on one at an angle of 30° as shown in Fig. 16.19. Draw the reflected ray from the second mirror.

Figure 1. An optics problem given in class 8th textbook

RELATED WORK

Price et al. [9] developed a system using literal physical correspondence metaphor to promote understanding of light behavior on real world objects. However, the paper presented issues that arise when designing using a physical correspondence metaphor in tangible learning environments. Despite using real objects children did not tend to extend or generalize their models of understanding to real context. At school level, light is usually represented by straight lines and diagrams on paper indicating directions and angles. We are interested in providing children with an exploratory and interactive system while keeping them as close as possible to the conventional, school level representations. We argue that this would help them in applying the concepts learned for actual problem solving which is done majorly on paper (Fig. 1). Because students are mostly familiar with drawing ray diagrams on paper, this system would complement rather than replace the typical paper environment. Paper is already situated and integrated in the classroom environment and its practices. In addition, paper is cheap to produce, yet persistent and malleable to adapt to the dynamics of the classroom which encourages better teacher-student learning system. Manipulation of paper interfaces opens a wide range of interaction styles that a user can perform [5] [2]. Dillenbourg et. al. observed that paper based interfaces can be easily adopted into traditional classroom practices [3] [4]. They designed a tabletop system to facilitate geometry learning, seamlessly integrating it with conventional geometry tools.

Wellner's seminal paper [12] on linking digital documents with their paper counterpart, marks an early attempt to use augmented reality for working transparently on a digital document and its physical copy. We draw inspiration from this work, particularly the aspect of augmenting paper for feedback. We build on this earlier work by exploring the benefits of augmented paper in the context of learning. We are more interested in using pen and paper for input in contrast to integrating the physical paper into computer applications. Sketch-Play-Learn aims at leveraging the benefits of pen and paper for learning, involving intuitive interactions while providing visual feedback in the same, co-located environment.

Glassified [10] explores paper augmentation by supplementing paper/pen strokes with virtual graphics. We took inspiration from Glassified's representation where physical pen/paper strokes and digital feedback are present on the same plane of paper. We intend to build on this co-located, digital representation by extending the benefits of paper-based augmentation to table-top environment for active collaboration, where students engage themselves in completing the assigned task in a classroom setting. Sketch-Play-Learn supports goal-based directed learning approach facilitated by teacher-learner interaction.

The key contribution of this paper is that it proposes an augmented reality tabletop interface that is seamlessly merged with a traditional, commonly used medium of learning.

SKETCH-PLAY-LEARN DESIGN

Design and Prototyping

The goal while designing the interface (Fig. 2) was to keep it simple involving intuitive interactions, which is appealing and understandable to the children, both in terms of the information as well as the colors and fonts used. After doing a thorough literature research to find out the concepts which were given in the science books of class 7 and class 8, we made a list of these concepts and refined it to finalize what we aim to teach. Special attention was given to the figures and diagrams of the experiments given in the book which was used in designing the elements of the interface. The design elements used for the concepts are:

- General instructions: Instructions are printed on the left side of the table as well as the goal is labeled

- First law of reflection (angle of incidence = angle of reflection): Color coding of each angle is done and the law is printed at the bottom of the table with the same color codes

- Color of objects: On each reflection from a surface, a popup image, unique to each surface, is shown to explain the concept of selective absorption and reflection from smooth colored surfaces

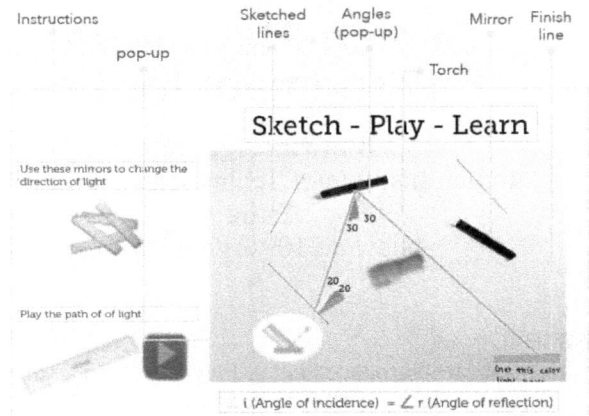

Figure 2. Interface of Sketch-Play-Learn.

The design and selection of appropriate physical representations is a very important aspect of tangible interface design [11]. The light ray travels on the paper and the information is projected adjacent to the sketch (co-located). Adding a separate screen for displaying information diverts the attention of the users. Hence, the physical paper was augmented with digital information so as to provide a better user engagement.

We implemented our system using the Processing language (Fig. 3). An overhead camera captures the image of the tabletop using JMyron library for processing. Image processing was used to detect the lines and colors using the OpenCV library for processing. Additionally, we used the reacTIVision technology [6] to identify the markers (play and pause). The markers were tagged with fiducials and tracked using an additional camera kept at the bottom. Thus the system uses two cameras and a projector for displaying the path of light and other information.

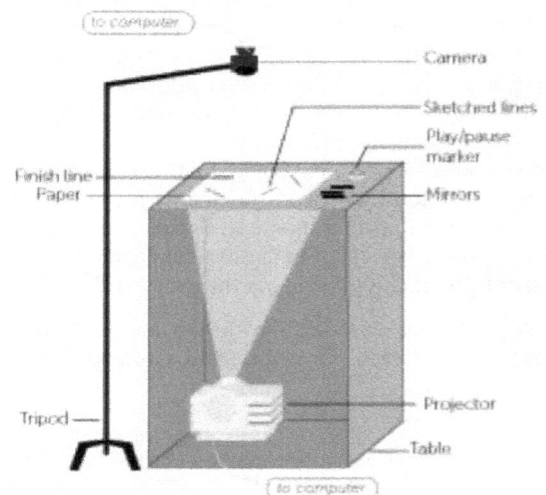

Figure 3. Schematic diagram of the initial, rough prototype

Working

We explain the working of Sketch-Play-learn in two parts i.e. the role of the teacher and the role of the student.

The teacher: The task to be completed is sketched by a teacher on paper (Fig. 4). For this, the teacher is provided with an A4 sheet printed with the outline of finish box at the bottom right corner of the paper. Then he sets up a combination of red, blue and green colored smooth surfaces for the student by drawing straight colored lines. He then fills up the finish box with either red, blue, green color or leaves it blank. He also specifies the initial direction of white light by rotating the torch kept in the middle.

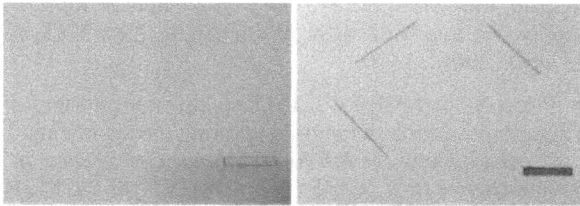

Figure 4. Initial A4 sheet provided to teacher (left); setup drawn by the teacher(right)

The student: This setup is now given to the student. The goal is that the student has to place a maximum of three mirrors and direct the light to the finish box. The color of the final light should be that of the finish box (if the box is filled with red, blue or green color) or white (if the box is left blank). The goal is projected on the paper below the finish box. For example, for the green colored box, Get GREEN colored light here is projected. The student places the tangible mirrors in a way which, according to him, would be a correct arrangement to achieve the goal. Then, he places the Play marker on the paper. On placing the play marker, white light starts travelling in the direction of the torch and gets reflected by the colored surfaces and mirrors in its path. On each reflection, the normal to the surface is drawn and the incident and reflected angles are shown (using color coding). A popup image at the same location is also projected to explain the concept behind the color of objects. For example, for reflection from the plane mirror, the image projected shows all the seven colors of white light getting reflected and for reflection from the red colored surface, the image shows only red color being reflected while the other six colors are absorbed. If the goal is achieved, a text is displayed above the finish box as Correct! otherwise it shows Incorrect!. If the goal is not achieved, the student places a Pause marker on the paper. This removes the path of the light ray while the goal and the normals are still projected. The student can move the mirrors to change the arrangement and the normals would aid him in doing so. On placing the Play marker again, the path of the light is projected according to the new arrangement.

PRELIMINARY EVALUATION

Preliminary evaluation (Fig. 5) was carried out with 14 eighth grade students in the classroom environment at a local school. The goal of the investigation was to identify the usability problems and to get a basic sense of students reaction to the tabletop system. Students showed a great interest and curiosity towards the tabletop setup kept in front of the class. A quick question answer session was carried out to brush up the concepts of light taught in their previous classes. Groups of two to three pupils were invited to explore the interface at a time. For the purpose of evaluation, the students were given tasks on paper and were assigned 15-20 minutes to complete the given task. Sessions were video recorded and quick observations were made while they were interacting among themselves and with the interface. The investigation provided encouraging evidences that the paper-based augmented environment can be a viable tool for classroom based learning activities. For example, some students were able to complete the task after few trials even without being aware of the concepts of light. Few other students, after seeing that a paper based task is given to them, brought in their rulers/pencils to predict the path of light. There were also examples of active discussions leading to achieving a common goal. One student - curiously watching other students use the system - solved the task on paper. Thus, he could easily connect to and make sense of the system rather than trying to understand the representations.

Figure 5. Initial evaluation of Sketch-Play-Learn at a local school.

DISCUSSION AND FUTURE WORK

For initial prototyping, we have used an overhead camera and projector system. However, in order to reduce the bulkiness and to be able to make the product commercially available, we would like to explore other technologies, for instance, using the camera of an iPad. It should be possible to allow continuous adjustment and easy alteration of the optical parameters, which is required for learning the optical concepts by simulation.

For the initial evaluation, we did not include the teacher for assigning the tasks. In next stages, we would like to improve the existing prototype and conduct more formal evaluations in a classroom environment by involving the teacher, to check the usefulness as well as assess the degree of collaboration, engagement and learning among students. We want to see if our approach has been effective in educating the concepts in an efficient manner. We would like to focus on measuring the difference in learning outcomes at individual and group levels between students using two learning methods: the traditional classroom based chalk-and-talk approach and paper-based tabletop environment. To achieve this, we intend to explore the dependencies of learning outcomes on key factors like task type, task difficulty, system instructions, tangible input, interface, group size and prior knowledge and experiences of the user.

REFERENCES

1. Bakker, S., Vorstenbosch, D., van den Hoven, E., Hollemans, G., and Bergman, T. Tangible interaction in tabletop games: Studying iconic and symbolic play pieces. In *Proceedings of the International Conference on Advances in Computer Entertainment Technology*, ACE '07, ACM (New York, NY, USA, 2007), 163–170.

2. Bonnard, Q., Jermann, P., Legge, A., Kaplan, F., and Dillenbourg, P. Tangible paper interfaces: Interpreting pupils' manipulations. In *Proceedings of the 2012 ACM International Conference on Interactive Tabletops and Surfaces*, ITS '12, ACM (New York, NY, USA, 2012), 133–142.

3. Bonnard, Q., Verma, H., Kaplan, F., and Dillenbourg, P. Paper interfaces for learning geometry. In *Proceedings of the 7th European Conference on Technology Enhanced Learning*, EC-TEL'12, Springer-Verlag (Berlin, Heidelberg, 2012), 37–50.

4. Cuendet, S., Bonnard, Q., Kaplan, F., and Dillenbourg, P. Paper interface design for classroom orchestration. In *CHI '11 Extended Abstracts on Human Factors in Computing Systems*, CHI EA '11, ACM (New York, NY, USA, 2011), 1993–1998.

5. Do-Lenh, S., Kaplan, F., Sharma, A., and Dillenbourg, P. Multi-finger interactions with papers on augmented tabletops. In *Proceedings of the 3rd International Conference on Tangible and Embedded Interaction*, TEI '09, ACM (New York, NY, USA, 2009), 267–274.

6. Kaltenbrunner, M., and Bencina, R. reactivision: A computer-vision framework for table-based tangible interaction. In *Proceedings of the 1st International Conference on Tangible and Embedded Interaction*, TEI '07, ACM (New York, NY, USA, 2007), 69–74.

7. Mackay, W. E., and Fayard, A.-L. Designing interactive paper: Lessons from three augmented reality projects. In *Proceedings of the International Workshop on Augmented Reality : Placing Artificial Objects in Real Scenes: Placing Artificial Objects in Real Scenes*, IWAR '98, A. K. Peters, Ltd. (Natick, MA, USA, 1999), 81–90.

8. Piper, A. M., O'Brien, E., Morris, M. R., and Winograd, T. Sides: A cooperative tabletop computer game for social skills development. In *Proceedings of the 2006 20th Anniversary Conference on Computer Supported Cooperative Work*, CSCW '06, ACM (New York, NY, USA, 2006), 1–10.

9. Price, S., and Falcão, T. P. Designing for physical-digital correspondence in tangible learning environments. In *Proceedings of the 8th International Conference on Interaction Design and Children*, IDC '09, ACM (New York, NY, USA, 2009), 194–197.

10. Sharma, A., Liu, L., and Maes, P. Glassified: An augmented ruler based on a transparent display for real-time interactions with paper. In *Proceedings of the Adjunct Publication of the 26th Annual ACM Symposium on User Interface Software and Technology*, UIST '13 Adjunct, ACM (New York, NY, USA, 2013), 21–22.

11. Ullmer, B., and Ishii, H. Emerging frameworks for tangible user interfaces. *IBM Syst. J. 39*, 3-4 (July 2000), 915–931.

12. Wellner, P. Interacting with paper on the digitaldesk. *Commun. ACM 36*, 7 (July 1993), 87–96.

The Haggle-O-Tron: Re-inventing Economic Transactions in Secondhand Retail

Siobhan Magee
School of Informatics
University of Edinburgh
siobhan.magee@ed.ac.uk

Fionn Tynan O'Mahony
Edinburgh College of Art
University of Edinburgh
fionntom@gmail.com

Martin De Jode
CASA
University College London
m.dejode@ucl.ac.uk

Mark Hartswood
School of Informatics
University of Edinburgh
mjh@inf.ed.ac.uk

Eric Laurier
School of Geoscience
University of Edinburgh
eric.laurier@ed.ac.uk

Chris Speed
Edinburgh College of Art
University of Edinburgh
c.speed@ed.ac.uk

ABSTRACT

Secondhand retail in the UK charity sector plays a number of important social and economic roles: charity shops are community focal points; money is generated for good causes; and goods are re-circulated that might otherwise be discarded as abject and unwanted. However, like much of the UK high street, the prosperity of charity shops is under significant threat from the rise of internet shopping. Access to online markets via smart phones equips customers to check prices for secondhand items, some customers then deploy information, usually from eBay, to attempt to haggle with shop staff. The *Haggle-o-Tron* playfully subverts both normative and emerging secondhand retail valuation practices by revealing secondhand goods' financial, moral, social and aesthetic properties. This paper reports on how we employ vibrant yet uncomplicated design interventions that embed the charity's values and ethos to reconfigure store-based economic transactions.

Author Keywords

Second hand retail; economic transactions; reflective design; ludic design;

ACM Classification Keywords

H.5.m. Information interfaces and presentation (e.g., HCI): Miscellaneous.

INTRODUCTION

This short paper reports initial findings from an ongoing project within the UK's Digital Economy, Research in the

Wild programme. The aim of the project is to explore how design can be used to probe and surface the practices and resources in the secondhand market. Although we draw upon design's more playfully creative side we do this with the serious intent of inquiring into extending the circulation of goods with its consequences for sustainability. The paper introduces the changing context of UK high street charity shops that sell secondhand items and the implications that secondhandedness has for calculating and agreeing the value of one-off items. It is within this frame that we show the creative process that brought together ethnographic study, design exercise and disruption. The ethnography identified techniques that consumers used to establish, and, sometimes, attempt to, negotiate the value of items with shop staff. Developing a playful physical prototype turned upon responding to and reimagining the role of secondhand things in practices of secondhand bargaining. Returned to the setting, the prototype disrupted the everyday cognition of price thereby allowing the investigation of value in relation to price.

CONTEXT - THE SECOND HAND OXFAM

The research is carried out in Oxfam's high street shops in the UK that operate as a place for the public to both donate as well as purchase secondhand items. Donating, buying, selling and receiving secondhand goods creates a complex space of consumption, distribution and value [5]. Oxfam has developed expertise on the markets in this complex space,– to give one example – secondhand clothes' flow from in-shop purchases, redistribution to international aid programmes or reconstitution from rags into new clothes. Tracking and tracing systems that offer consumers more insight into the trajectories of products remain limited in the secondhand sector. While the current economic downturn is a difficult period for consumers and industry to invest in sustainable initiatives, secondhand markets, which are inherently more sustainable, are booming. This places pressure on the charity sector as surplus items are now traded for cash in the high street. Unsorted clothes can fetch on average 90pence per kilo. By contrast Oxfam can sell unwanted clothes at up to £9.30 per kilo in their shops. Consequently Oxfam require solutions to boost the quantity of donations they receive and ensure goods are sold in their shops (rather than sold on to the rag trade). Here we will concentrate on shop sales, though our larger study also examines secondhand things' circulation through other sectors.

In exploring the space, materials and practices that comprise retail charity and find a picture that has a more complex moral geography than might be found in first hand retail settings [5]. It is a materially distinct setting comprised of many 'one-off' items rather than the mass-produced brands and lines that simplify the ascription of value to first hand items. This has consequences for the strategies that customers and retailers alike can legitimately use to establish the relationship between value and price. In the next section we turn to our ethnographic study of secondhand retail practices, exploring some of these issues in more detail.

OXFAM AND 2ND HAND RETAIL

At various points between May and July 2013, the research team carried out an ethnographic study that informed the development of an intervention. Through participant observation, conversation and semi-structured interviews with shop managers, volunteers, and customers in five Oxfam shops in urban, suburban, and rural parts of the North of England, the project team learned about (amongst other topics) instances in which shoppers contested the price of goods. Some shoppers attempted to 'haggle down' the price of a good, by, for instance, unfavourably comparing in-store prices to those on eBay and Amazon. Oxfam staff and volunteers would counter this with information that showed the value of the item beyond its price: its rarity; how convenient it was to be able to 'walk away it now', and its economic worth for Oxfam aid programs. Acquiescing to customer requests for price reductions was against Oxfam's policy.

eBay and Amazon Marketplace's accessibility via smartphones- making low-price goods visible 'on the go'- significantly enhances shoppers' equipment to rebalance the asymmetry of calculative resources identified by Callon & Muniesa [3]. The study revealed that online market places put significant pressure on Oxfam's pricing strategy for certain items (especially books) as well as providing a basis for the customer to contest Oxfam's pricing. Haggling itself as a practice made apparent criteria for setting a fair price. This practical problem became the focus of the research team's intervention.

Below we spell out how this informed the development of a design intervention that enabled customers to negotiate a lower price. The design drew upon the sequences of haggling re-imagining them through the existing 'things' found in secondhand retail environments such as kitchen objects, papers receipts and gift cards that donated Oxfam charity (e.g. goats, schools, healthcare)..

IMAGINING ALTERNATIVE ECONOMIC TRANSACTIONS THROUGH DESIGN

When questioning how we could disrupt calculative practices within Oxfam, we had a number of aims:

- To explore how in the face of low prices online, the balance of legitimacy in value calculation could be shifted back toward high street retail.
- To explore the sorts of resources that Oxfam can use in its value calculations, some of which trade upon charity retail's moral capital.
- To seek playful engagement with Oxfam customers in order to disrupt norms and conventions, enabling shopping practices to be both investigated and re-imagined.
- To surface and reflect back customers' and retailers' secondhand retail valuation practices as a basis for re-imagining how these might be performed in future.

Our design approach was creative in the mixing and tailoring of three existing design paradigms toward disruption rather than requirements. Ethnography uncovered existing practices within their setting via the 'thick description' commonly used to inform interaction design. At this initial stage we revealed unusual and emergent economics-in-action within charity retail that framed our design briefs rather than the design of a concrete object.

We turned the process of 'reflective design' [7] toward provoking both Oxfam staff and shoppers to reflect upon their own values and practices through disrupting them. This drew us to question how haggling could be brought back into the conventional repertoire of marketplace practices used in an Oxfam store. Haggling was a *emergent* practice in our study - one that a minority of shoppers were leaning towards but that staff had yet to accommodatec. Haggling deviates from normative UK retail practices where prices are typically non-negotiable beyond discounts in quite particular circumstances, and so often feel awkward or transgressive. Reintroducing haggling provided us with a disruptive element to enable shoppers' and retailers' to refashion their normative valuation and price-analysis practices. Simultaneously we aimed to 're-equip' Oxfam to establish provenance, stories and histories of secondhand items by turning the price into an extended interaction in which past and future 'value chains' would be made visible and used as bargaining tokens in the haggling process. For instance, what a particular price would contribute to aid projects, or the provenance of an item as a rare and cared-for thing. The final part of the mix was Gaver's 'ludic' [4] design, because we wanted our to have our intervention appeal to peoples' sense of fun, to be enjoyable, and in this atmosphere of playfulness to create a space where conventional notions of retail can be suspended and new forms of engagement explored. This led us to the idea of imbuing an everyday secondhand object with peculiar interactional properties if also familiar and unfamiliar technologies. We will now explore the rationale for the concept of a *Haggle-o-Tron* that draws together these different design approaches.

DESIGNING THE HAGGLE-O-TRON

We settled upon a teapot as the physical form for our *Haggle-o-Tron* for a number of reasons. One was practical: it has an internal space that could accommodate the haggling mechanism. The second was that it avoided being anthropomorphic, instead the kind of mundane secondhand object that evokes the the domestic. This also avoided the strong pre-existing cultural connotations that would be implied by a cartoon or toy robot. Thirdly, by making it an 'agent' it lessened the inhibition of haggling with a human spokesperson (e.g. a shop manager). Instead the teapot presented something (somewhat) 'blank' because our expectations of it as an agent are culturally undefined. This 'blankness' would allow participants freer rein to explore assessment and pricing practices. The design resonated with our interest in the playful possibilities presented by giving objects human retail roles found during the ethnographic study. Thus we equipped the teapot with squeaks, grunts and whistles by which it could respond to customers, a camera lens and a printout 'mouth' redolent of a till receipt that captures the haggle in real time, and playfully subverts the traditional role of the receipt.

Figure 1 The first iteration of the Haggle-o-tron in situ at an Oxfam shop in the North of England. © Fionn Tynan-O'Mahony

The first iteration of the *Haggle-o-Tron* involved a researcher engaging with shoppers through the video camera and microphone installed in the teapot. The researcher communicating with the shopper by its sounds and by printing out short messages on its paper roll.

Figure 2 Cartoon reconstruction of a haggle. © Eric Laurier

This receipt also displayed the agreed price of the object and acted as a memory of the transaction.

The deployment took place over two days during which an estimated 8 customer interactions (haggles) took place leading to 6 actual sales. The number of people who engaged with the intervention was, however, much greater as it included couples and families and those who engaged with the Haggle-o-tron without haggling, as well as shoppers, volunteers, and staff who were caught in the change in atmosphere that the intervention created. For example, the Haggle-o-tron was an additional conversation point between volunteers and shoppers.

DISCUSSION

The haggling practices with the *Haggle-o-Tron* surfaced accounts of the thing's value through its original manufacturer, its potential recipients and its appearance. Offers (e.g. '£3' in fig. 1) were not always accompanied by accounts and could be just given as minimal counter-offers.

Our initial trials have provided insight not only into haggling practices but into how customers are hailed to initiate a retail encounter. What we had overlooked in our original scenario was the importance of soliciting potential hagglers. The *Haggle-o-Tron* whistled and greeted potential hagglers by making inferences from their proximity, their movement and whether they were carrying items. It became clear that shoppers' work is also about ignoring or avoiding being hailed. Shoppers only initiated haggling once they were minimally committed to bargain for items.

In making sense of the strange agent, customers brought their familiar practices with retail barcode scanners and with Skype cameras to interacting with the Haggle-o-Tron. There are then showing-to-camera skills that brought to dealing with autonomous retail agents. For instance, once in view of the camera, hagglers expected to be able to point at features of their object, hold up fingers for value, smile to reinforce a plea and so on. This raises the ongoing problem of computer vision being able to recognize gestures, though within the logic of haggling as sequences of actions.

One unexpected positive quality of the *Haggle-o-Tron* was its immobility. Unlike the intrusive 'can I help you?' of sales-work, the device required customers to approach it in response to its solicitations. There are then clear possibilities for using proximity and motion sensors to make inferences about customers' openness to beginning a haggle. Subsequently, in the second autonomous prototype, objects for sale were tagged with Bluetooth® Low Energy proximity tags that triggered a branching narrative, unique to that item. It moved through levels of value with the customer through printing more information. The customer was able to suggest higher or lower prices in response to the 'haggle'.

Snippets of information imparted in the haggle were used to construct value chains from the past in to the future, such as **past**: stories of provenance similar to those found in the Shelflife / Tales of Things project [1], where the item was made or found; **present**: current prices on eBay, current Oxfam campaigns; and **future**: how many goats the product will allow Oxfam to give, or for forthcoming events.

CONCLUSIONS
In this paper we have investigated both how people value things in material settings that have conventional pricing practices and explored haggling that draw upon alternate price establishment practices. In our study we use a playful design approach to provide a creative response to the secondhand market through 're-equipping' an Oxfam shop to encourage and explore haggling. The intervention begins to rebalance shoppers' access to global online markets with local inquiries into future, current and past value in order to secure the pricing of particular items. The *Haggle-o-tron* blends together ethnographic study, disruptive intervention and prototype developing in order to provide a creative response to secondhand retail transactions. The study provided insight for Oxfam and others in the secondhand market into the potential for delegating pricing practices to non-human, yet domestic and playful agents.

ACKNOWLEDGEMENTS
The Internet of Secondhand Things project was funded by a UK Engineering and Physical Sciences Research Council, Research in the Wild grant (EP/K012819/1) and Oxfam UK. Many thanks to Oxfam staff and customers.

REFERENCES
1. Barthel, R., Leder Mackley, K., Hudson-Smith, A., Karpovich, A., de Jode, M., Speed C. An internet of old things as an augmented memory system. Personal and Ubiquitous Computing, 17, (2013), 321-333.

2. Cochoy, F. A sociology of market-things: on tending the garden of choices in mass retailing. The sociological review 55, s2, (2007), 109-129.

3. Callon, M. and Muniesa, F. Economic markets as calculative collection devices. Organisation Studies 26, 8 (2005), 1220-1250.

4. Gaver, W. Designing for Homo Ludens, Still. In (Re)searching the Digital Bauhaus. Binder, T., Löwgren, J., and Malmborg, L. (eds.). London: Springer, 2009.

5. Gregson, N. & Crewe, L. Second-hand cultures. Berg 3PL, (2003).

6. Miller, D. A Theory of Shopping. Cambridge and Oxford: Polity Press, (1998).

7. Sengers, P., Boehner, K., David, S. and Kaye, J. 'J'. Reflective design. In *Proceedings of the 4th decennial conference on Critical computing: between sense and sensibility* (CC '05), ACM Press, (2005), 49-58.

Creative Language in a Student-generated Bioorganic Chemistry Wiki Textbook

Andrea Tartaro
Furman University
3300 Poinsett Hwy.
Greenville, SC 29613 (USA)
andrea.tartaro@furman.edu

Brian C. Goess
Furman University
3300 Poinsett Hwy.
Greenville, SC 29613 (USA)
brian.goess@furman.edu

Mike Winiski
Furman University
3300 Poinsett Hwy.
Greenville, SC 29613 (USA)
mike.winiski@furman.edu

ABSTRACT

We describe an approach to analyzing student-created content on wiki systems based on identifying creative linguistic content. We apply this approach to wiki entries written by students in an advanced chemistry course. We illustrate creative linguistic forms, how they change over time, and, based on in-depth student interviews, their value to student producers and consumers of wiki content.

Author Keywords

Creativity; language; wiki; student-centered learning

ACM Classification Keywords

H.5.m. Information interfaces and presentation (e.g., HCI): Miscellaneous.

INTRODUCTION

What happens when college students are empowered to write their own intermediate-level, scientific, wiki-based textbook? Previous research argues that similar collaborative learning activities develop students' critical thinking as well as creativity (e.g., [1,2]). In this paper, we look at one aspect of student creativity by analyzing the language students use when they create and edit a wiki textbook chapter. While previous research has investigated the *types* of edits students make on a collaborative wiki (e.g., adding sentences, editing content within sentences) [3], we detail the linguistic form of student contributions – the creative language used to describe complex scientific content – and how it evolves as subsequent students edit the initial content. Using in-depth interviews, we also examine students' own reflections on learning from student-created content. Throughout the wiki we found numerous examples of creative language use, including: metaphorical phrases, figures of speech, colloquial forms, and puns. While creative language use was abundant in the initial creation of

the wiki chapter, subsequent student editors frequently replaced these sections with more formal prose. However, powerfully evocative creative language forms that may enhance and enrich an understanding of the underlying science best persisted through numerous rounds of editing by subsequent students. Our contributions include a new approach to analyzing student-created content on wiki systems based on identifying creative linguistic content (rather than types of edits) and the application of that approach to student-generated content written on scientific topics that are more advanced than has been previously studied. These contributions provide a necessary foundation for future studies that will examine the relationship between creative language use, technical specificity, and student understanding of complex scientific information within the context of student collaboration via production and consumption of wiki content.

BACKGROUND

Learning sciences and wiki research is increasingly documenting the benefits and drawbacks of collaborative student wikis and similar collaborative activities. The research is framed in Social Constructivism theory, which emphasizes the relationship between social aspects of learning and individual cognitive processes [e.g.,1,2].

When considering the potential benefits of student-created wiki textbooks, it is also important to remember that language creativity is not restricted to the literary arts, but rather is present in everyday interactions [4] and plays an important role in social interaction [5]. Carter argues that creativity can act as a uniting force to help establish and maintain interpersonal relationships [5], and that there is a corresponding need for further research that examines "critical or salient moments in discourse when creativity… is a key component of social interaction" [5].

The valuable role creative language use plays in establishing, maintaining, and building social relationships, combined with the role social interaction plays in collaborative learning environments like wikis, suggests creative language in wikis may support collaborative student learning in important ways. This may be especially true in challenging science courses where student-to-student cooperation and communication can substantially enhance learning outcomes. We saw an opportunity to utilize these strategies when developing a new course in organic chemistry, an intermediate-level chemistry course that is required for a variety of natural science majors and students interested in health-related fields.

In order to better address the needs of pre-medical students taking the new Medical College Admissions Test (MCAT) beginning in 2015, the chemistry department at Furman University redesigned its traditional sophomore-level, two-course sequence in organic chemistry and launched a new two-course sequence in 2008 consisting of one accelerated course in traditional synthetic organic chemistry followed by a new course in biological organic chemistry [6]. The novelty of this new, second course presented a unique challenge – lack of an existing textbook related to the course material. Given the likely benefits described above of an entirely student-created wiki textbook, we created a bio-organic wiki textbook space coincident with the launch of the new course and asked students to create the content.

METHODS

We created a wiki space using a WSYWIG wiki editing platform. Students were made aware that the only instructor-generated content on the wiki would be a home page consisting of links to individual "chapters" corresponding to each lecture in the course. In the first offering of the course (Fall 2008), each student was tasked to create one wiki chapter based on the associated course materials and lecture. These students created an initial draft of online content starting from a blank slate, which was then anonymously peer-reviewed by a classmate. Students then modified their chapters based on those comments. The final product was graded based on effort alone; style and accuracy were not a component of the assigned grade.

In subsequent course offerings (2009-2010), students served as an editor/contributor for a specific wiki chapter. Again, their revisions were graded based on effort alone. In recent course offerings (2011-2014), the existing wiki textbook was made available to students, but no related assignment was given. Therefore, these students participated in the wiki as content consumers only.

We selected volunteers from amongst two groups of wiki participants for compensated in-depth interviews regarding their experience with the wiki. Six students from a producer group (Fall 2009) were interviewed within one year following their graduation from college. Ten students from one of the consumer groups (2011-2014) were interviewed immediately following completion of the course. These interviews were transcribed and coded to facilitate analysis.

ANALYSIS

We traced the evolution of the textual content of one chapter of the bioorganic wiki textbook over time in order to develop a method for examining creative language use in student-created content. The particular chapter chosen is one that is unusually rich in both creative language use by the original author as well as in edits by subsequent contributor/editors, and its topic is one that can be made comprehensible to non-specialists. The chapter discusses how specific enzymes break apart protein bonds in a fraction of a second, which, in the absence of such an enzyme, would instead take a decade or more.

We identified specific forms of linguistic creativity used by the initial producer of the chapter content. Previous research has identified various relevant forms of linguistic creativity such as wordplay, metaphor, figures of speech, and parallelism [4]. Expanding on these established forms, we used a data-driven approach [7] to identify and describe a wide range of creative language use and how that language changes over time through the actions of three subsequent contributor/editors. In addition, we identified passages in the interview transcripts where students discuss their views on these topics.

RESULTS

Creative Language Forms

Students used a variety of creative language forms in their wiki compositions and edits, including: metaphorical phrases, figures of speech, anthropomorphisms, colloquial forms, parallelism, cultural references, words of encouragement, humor, fun phrases, and puns. Representative examples are presented in Table 1.

While figures of speech or colloquial forms may not be considered creative in many contexts, they are creative when used in new, metaphorical contexts. Quote 1 of Table 1 uses one such metaphor to emphasize the value of the broken-down products. Other metaphors anthropomorphize actors in the reactions by attributing emotion or intention, for example "angry" in Quote 2 draws attention to the negative charge of the oxygen. Colloquial forms can be used to signify specific meaning, for example, "went and forgot" is often used to signify a speaker's disapproval, as in Quote 3, which when combined with "silly person" is signaling something "stupid" [8], and emphasizes the importance of a specific concept (chemical resonance). Parallelism is a creative form used for emphasis [4,5]. For example, Quote 4 uses parallelism to emphasize the increased speed of enzymatic reactions relative to a typical reaction. Notably, these linguistic forms, along with cultural references (Quote 5), encouragement (Quote 6), fun phrases (Quote 7), puns and other humor, represent use of the student's natural voice and stand in contrast to the voice typically used by experts when writing a textbook.

Editorial Changes Analysis

We identified twenty-six elements of linguistic creativity in the wiki chapter of nearly 1500 words created by the producer student in Fall 2008. Subsequently, three student

No.	Quote	Creative Language Description
1	The body must break [them] down **to get to the juicy center.**	Figure of speech
2	...[1]**offer up their hydrogens as a sacrifice** to the [2]**very angry,** mostly negatively-charged…oxygen.	[1]Figure of speech [2]Anthropomorphizing metaphor
3	After all, we would rather prefer not turning into [1]**puddles of goo** because some silly person [2]**went and forgot** about the resonance.	[1]Metaphor [2]Colloquial form
4	Chemists **can overcome this** [long half-life]… **by employing a days worth of** acid or base catalyst. Nature **can overcome this by employing one thousandth (or less) of a second's worth** of enzyme action.	Parallelism
5	We as lowly humans trying to imitate **God/evolution/flying spaghetti monster/whatever suits your pleasure**	Cultural reference
6	The mechanism seems scary, I know… but don't worry.	Encouraging words
7	Too bad scientists cannot be as awesome as enzymes.	Fun phrase
8	…a typical serine protease immediately after its **strike** on the carbonyl carbon…	Anthropomorphism
9	…**chain gang partnership** of the catalytic triad.	Metaphor
10	…**slams** back down to … bond and **throw** serine back where it came from.	Anthropomorphism

Table 1: Examples and descriptions of creative language use

contributor/editors were assigned the task of improving the page in any way they saw fit. We analyzed the ways in which the original elements of linguistic creativity changed over time as well as any new elements of linguistic creativity that were introduced by the new authors. Of the twenty-six original elements, eleven were ultimately replaced with more scientific prose, seven were deleted entirely, five were modified slightly, and three survived unedited. Of the next two contributor/editor's sixteen new elements, five were changed or deleted, and the rest remained unmodified.

Three interesting observations emerge from this analysis. First, the greatest use of creative language arose from the original producing student, who started from a blank slate. Second, the vast majority of these original instances were ultimately deleted or replaced entirely with more scientific prose. For instance, the text of Quote 2, while vivid and interesting to read, was recognized by the first contributor/editor as unhelpfully vague and deleted in its entirety. Eventually, the second and third editing authors installed new text with a much longer, more scientific explication of the same process. As a result of this and other similar edits, over time the chapter evolved towards a more textbook-like presentation style. Finally, most of the elements that persisted fell into three categories: (1) asides that offered words of encouragement to readers (e.g., Quote 6); (2) fun phrases that did not detract from understanding the basic scientific processes involved (e.g., Quote 7); and (3) those that, in the opinion of the course instructor, are not only based on a strong scientific foundation but use powerfully evocative creative constructions to aid comprehension (e.g., Quotes 8-10). For example, Quote 8 calls to mind the strike of a snake on its prey, which is a remarkably vivid (and accurate) way of internalizing how the enzyme behaves towards its target. Quote 9 is a clever metaphor illustrating how three specific parts of the enzyme work together to accomplish the overall reaction. Like a chain gang is linked together at the feet to enforce cooperation, the "catalytic triad" of the enzyme is linked together through chemical bonds. Quote 10 uses active verbs to create in the reader's mind an image of a sequence of chemical events that is linked together through actions more commonly found in sports narratives.

Interview Excerpts and Analysis
During the interviews, producers and consumers provided a number of comments that highlight and reflect on the creativity of the wiki authors (all quotes are from the consumer group unless indicated otherwise). Some interviewees specifically discussed how creativity and humor in the wiki made the course more fun and the wiki easier to read. Others valued student linguistic creativity that is distinct from the language used by the course instructor and the more formal prose found in traditional textbooks:

"Students put their own personality into the wiki. They put it almost in layman terms and they throw in some humor sometimes, which makes the course more fun. And it's always great to hear quotations from movies."

Many students felt another student could explain things in a different way that may be more understandable, or simplify challenging material using less formal language:

"Sometimes students can explain things in a way that other students can understand… I feel like there's a good balance of putting things in the way [the professor] puts it and then putting it the way students would do it."

"The wiki uses simpler language, where it can be used, but also uses… correct terminology where it fits"

"You can visualize things easier… with the more conversational language."

One producer commented that the process of being creative specifically helped his learning:

"[it helped my learning] to present it in a way that's a little bit unique from just what you heard in class… you could [develop] a tip or trick so that you can remember something. I think… coming up with those definitely helped my learning."

CONCLUSION

Creative language use may enhance learning in student-created wiki textbooks and similar collaborative environments because these environments leverage social aspects of learning [1,2] and because creative language builds and maintains social relationships [4,5]. In this paper, we analyzed the creative language students use to describe complex scientific content when writing and editing a wiki chapter as well as students' own comments on the creativity of student-created content. We identified a number of creative forms, including metaphors, humor and words of encouragement, that reflect the students' natural voices and contrast the voice of a typical textbook. Interviews confirmed that producing students learned from creatively presenting material, and consuming students appreciated the student-centered language used throughout the wiki. While some of the creativity is likely used to mask a lack of fundamental scientific understanding of the material, there are numerous examples of evocative creative language that enrich the descriptions of the underlying science. These examples tended to persist through numerous rounds of editing.

We also found creative language examples were most abundant for the original producing student and that most of these instances were deleted or replaced by more scientific prose. This seems to contradict the students' stated preference for more student-centered language, which we take as an indication of the powerful effect of their pervasive exposure to traditional textbook writing styles. Encouragingly, Emigh and Herring [9] note that while the design of the public editing features of wikis often leads to a more standardized and formal style over time, there are other designs for collaborative spaces that lead to better preservation of linguistic diversity.

Our findings suggest that many creative language forms may have been edited out over time in service of greater technical specificity despite students' stated preference for student-centered language. The methods developed in this paper provide the means for analyzing additional wiki content to evaluate and refine this hypothesis. Is it generally true that creative linguistic forms tend to be replaced over time by more standard scientific prose? Are there specific linguistic forms for which this is more true than others? Is there a correlation between the use of certain forms of creative language and a lack of scientific rigor, and is this correlation consistently recognized by subsequent student editors in a way that results in their replacement by more standard prose?

These answers are valuable only inasmuch as they help us understand which creative linguistic forms truly enhance student learning outcomes. For instance, when students' co-construction of knowledge differs stylistically from the presentation of knowledge in traditional textbooks, are learning outcomes improved? What role does students' linguistic creativity play in the relationship between the social and individual cognitive processes of learning? And, ultimately, can the wiki editing features be redesigned to encourage the persistence and enhancement of creative linguistic forms that are most valuable to enhancing learning outcomes? An increased understanding of the relationship between linguistic creativity, scientific rigor and student understanding may inform the design of systems and assignments supporting learning of complex scientific content.

REFERENCES

1. Hamer, J., Purchase, H.C., Luxton-Reilly, A. and Sheard, J. Tools for "Contributing Student Learning." In *Proc. ITiCSE-WGR '10*, ACM Press (2010), 1-14.

2. Forte, A. and Bruckman, A. Constructing Text: Wiki as a Toolkit for (Collaborative?) Learning. In *Proc. WikiSym '07*, ACM Press (2007), 31-41.

3. Chu, E.H.Y, Notari, M., Chen, K., Chan, C.K., Chu, S.K.W. and Wu, W.W.Y. A triangulated investigation of using wiki for project-based learning in different undergraduate disciplines. In *Proc. WikiSym '13*, ACM Press (2013), Article 40, 7 pages.

4. Maybin, J. and Swann, J. Everyday Creativity in Language: Textuality, Contextuality, and Critique. *Appl. Linguist.*, Oxford University Press (2007), 29 (4): 497-517.

5. Carter, R. Response to Special Issue of Applied Linguistics Devoted to Language Creativity in Everyday Contexts. *Appl. Linguist.*, Oxford University Press (2007), 29 (4), 597-608.

6. Goess, B.C. Development and Implementation of a Two-Semester Introductory Organic-Bioorganic Chemistry Sequence. *J. Chem. Educ.*, ACS Publications (2014), 91, 1169-1173.

7. Weingart, L.R. How Did They Do That? The Ways and Means of Studying Group Processes. *Res. Organ. Behav.*, JAI Press Inc. (1997), 19, 189-239.

8. Stubbs, M. Sequence and Order: The neo-Firthian tradition of corpus semantics. In Hasselgård, H., Ebeling, J. and Ebeling, S.O. (eds). *Corpus Perspectives on Patterns of Lexis*. John Benjamins Publishing Company (2013), 13-34.

9. Emigh, W and Herring, S.C. Collaborative Authoring on the Web: A Genre Analysis of Online Encyclopedias. In *Proc. HICSS '05,* IEEE (2005), page 99.1.

Creativity Support to Improve Health-and-Safety in Manufacturing Plants: Demonstrating Everyday Creativity

Konstantinos Zachos, Neil Maiden
City University London
Northampton Square, London
EC1V 0HB, UK
kzachos@soi.city.ac.uk

Sergio Levis
FCA Group
Via Nizza, 250, 10126
Turin, Italy
sergio.levis@fcagroup.com

Kasia Camargo,
Gianluca Allemandi
CNH Industrial, Cranes Farm Road,
Basildon SS14 3AD, UK
kasia.camargo@cnhind.com

ABSTRACT

This paper reports the development and deployment of digital support for human creativity in a domain outside of the creative industries – health-and-safety management in manufacturing plants. It reports applied research to extend a risk detection and resolution process at a world-class manufacturing plant that produces tractors with creativity techniques and new digital support for the plant employees to use these techniques effectively as part of the risk detection and resolution process. The development of the digital support was constrained by the plant's processes, resources and manufacturing culture, and the new digital support reported in this paper was designed for quick use across the plant with minimum training or management overhead. The paper reports the development, implementation and early evaluation of the creativity techniques and digital support in the plant as a demonstrator for the wider application of creativity techniques and digital support tools.

Author Keywords

Creativity; health-and-safety; risk management; mobile

ACM Classification Keywords

D.5.2 [User Interfaces]: User-centered design, voice I/O
General Terms
Design, human factors

INTRODUCTION

The last decade has seen considerable advances in the use of digital support for human creative activities in arts and design – disciplines already recognized as creative such as music, and film and television. However, this focus on the creative industries has sometimes acted as a barrier to creativity research to explore and develop support for human creativity in disciplines not generally perceived as creative. For example, there is little explicit teaching or uptake of creativity techniques and methods in engineering, although few would disagree that engineering practice necessitates creative problem solving. Other disciplines, however, are not even perceived to have a role for creative thinking, even

though the work undertaken in them seeks to produce outcomes that are novel, useful and surprising [23]. Examples include nursing and transport planning, and most of these disciplines provide no explicit support for human creativity, in spite of the potential benefits that could accrue from more creative thinking by their professionals. In this paper, we argue for and develop support to deliver human creativity in one important activity not treated as creative – health-and-safety management in manufacturing plants – as a demonstrator for the wider application of creativity methods, techniques and digital support tools.

Increasing the health and the safety of citizens continues to be an important aim for organisations and governments. In the United States, for example, there were 4,500 workplace deaths in 2010, 250,000+ work-related injuries and illnesses in 2011 [20], and in the European Union almost 2.5 million workplace incidents resulting in at least 3 person-days off work occurred in 2012 [9]. New legislation and management systems have resulted in improved worker health and safety through the introduction of systematic processes, however notable numbers of deaths and injuries continue to occur. Now, to reduce these numbers further, some organizations are exploring different approaches to complement systematic processes. One of these organizations is CNH Industrial, a global leader in the capital goods sector, and the new approach is creative thinking.

CNH Industrial's current systems for occupational health-and-safety management and lean manufacturing involve all of its employees in the detection, reporting and resolution of health-and-safety risks. To support employees to think more creatively in this risk detection, reporting and resolution process, the EU-funded COLLAGE project has extended it with support for creative thinking about risk resolutions and, more significantly, developed new digital support for this creative thinking. This paper reports the development and piloting of digital creativity support for employees in one CNH Industrial manufacturing plant outside of London that produces tractors. In particular, it describes how advanced natural language parsing and information retrieval techniques were combined to design new digital support for human creative thinking in an environment with little digital expertise and resources.

The next sections of the paper report related work and the current risk resolution process in use in the CNH Industrial plant. Subsequent sections describe the creative risk resolution process that was developed for use by plant employees, the digital solution implemented to support employees to undertake the process, and early results from pilot use in the plant of the process and digital support. The paper ends with first lessons for the uptake of creativity techniques and digital support tools outside of the creative industries.

RELATED WORK

Most research to develop digital support for human creativity has been undertaken in industries in which people receive creative skills and training. Examples of industries for which research was undertaken in the last ACM Creativity and Cognition conference include the performing arts, music, and film and television. However, beyond the creative industries, creativity support research has been limited. The science and engineering domains have been a focus of limited digital support, for example with new tabletop visualizations to support biological discoveries [26], social media to support collaborative creativity in education [3] and integrations of creativity techniques into complex engineering processes [8]. Moreover, although business activities have been a common target for creativity and innovation research, most has sought to support human creativity through new problem solving methods (e.g. [12]), techniques (e.g. [17]) and creative collaboration spaces (e.g. 7]).

Healthcare is one domain that has been the target of creativity research. Creativity is often treated as an important precondition for technology innovation, for example to develop new medical devices [6] and assist stroke patients [5]. Some researchers have also made the case to treat healthcare as creative work, for example to encourage creative problem solving by nursing administrators who set the tone in a work unit, and how others undertake creative work [2]. Houts et al. [11] proposed a prescriptive creative problem-solving model to help family carers deliver care to people with chronic diseases discharged from hospital. The model was tailored to the healthcare domain from the Osborn-Parnes creative problem-solving model [19], and distinguished situations in which creative problem solving could be used from situations in which advice needed to be sought from experts. More recently, care for older people with dementia has been framed as creative work, and new creativity support technologies have been developed for use by carers, and shown to be effective in care settings [15]. Digital support tools have also been produced to support medical volunteers to think creatively to resolve non-routine medical work during emergencies.

However, in general, little research to develop digital support for human creativity outside of the creative industries has taken place, and we are unaware of applications of creativity research to improve health-and-safety work.

RISK RESOLUTION IN MANUFACTURING

CNH Industrial employs more than 71,000 people in 62 manufacturing plants worldwide. Each of CNH Industrial's brands focuses on one industrial sector, for example *Iveco*

on commercial vehicles, *Heuliez Bus* on buses, and the focus of this paper, *Case IH*, *New Holland Agriculture* and *Steyr* on tractors. The CNH Industrial plant east of London covers 40 hectares, employs 1,000 people and produces 133 different models of 20,000 tractors per year in the 110-270 horsepower range with 10,000 possible machine configurations at a rate of 1 every 4 minutes. Given the nature of this manufacturing process and its products, the plant treats the health and safety of all of its employees with the utmost importance – it is OHSAS 18001-certified, recorded zero non-conformities in the 2014 audit, and leads safety culture change using world-class manufacturing techniques.

The plant's existing risk detection and resolution processes are primarily paper-based and driven by levels of perceived risk. Whenever an employee encounters a serious incident or near-miss, s/he reports it verbally to an occupational health representative who uses the information to complete a *Safety Emergency Work Order* form that structures information about the incident or risk with 6 headings – *what, when, where, who, which* and *how* – and a human body chart. An example of this form is shown on the left of Figure 1. The representative emails the completed form to the relevant team leader who completes it using a predefined classification of root causes for the incident, suggests the implementation of corrective actions, and submits it to the plant and health-and-safety managers for approval. If serious injuries occur, these are reported to the enforcing Health and Safety Executive via the UK's National Incident Centre, and a member of the plant's health-and-safety team then initiates an investigation to discover root causes for the incident, analyze resolutions that can prevent reoccurrence and review procedures related to the occurrence of the incident. Each implemented resolution to the risk is then documented on the action part of the *Safety Emergency Work Order* form, copies of which are printed and posted on health-and-safety noticeboards. In contrast, whenever an unsafe act or condition is encountered, the employee who discovers it completes the *Unsafe Act and Condition* paper form and places it in one of the return boxes placed around the plant. An example of this form is shown on the right of Figure 1. A member of the health-and-safety team then collects all completed forms from the boxes, reviews them and transfers the form content using a desktop computer to a *Sharepoint* database used to assign individual incidents to managers or team leaders, and on a *MS-Excel* spreadsheet that is used for further data collection and trends analysis.

This current risk detection and resolution process implements systematic processes that place a strong emphasis on root cause analytic and structured techniques to discover the immediate, underlying and root causes of a risk. These analytic techniques, although fit for purpose, provide little scope or support for creative thinking. Furthermore, the current process offers little support for sharing effective risk resolution practices between CNH Industrial plants. Most risk resolution information is shared within a plant by printing and placing it on health-and-safety notice boards such as the one in Figure 2.

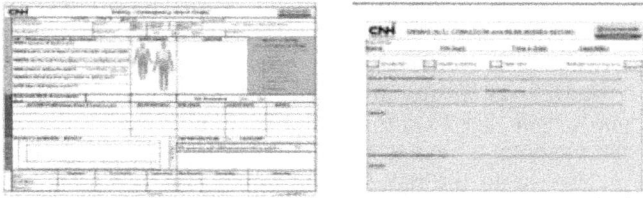

Figure 1. Two forms from the current health-and-safety procedures in the plant – the Safety Emergency Work Order form (left) and Unsafe Act and Condition form (right)

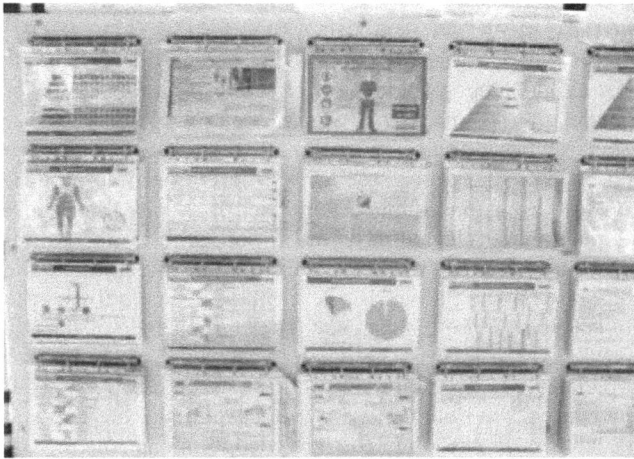

Figure 2. A typical noticeboard for sharing risk resolution information amongst plant employees

In contrast, the plant management anticipated that new digital technologies could not only increase employee engagement in the risk resolution process, but also increase cross-plant communication and creative collaboration and provide more effective management oversight of the process. Therefore, new research was undertaken to enhance the plant's process with creativity support for risk detection and resolution, and to design and implement a new form of digital support for human creativity as part of the process. The next sections describe the enhanced process and the digital support that was implemented.

CREATIVITY SUPPORT FOR RISK RESOLUTION

The plant's manufacturing process imposed significant constraints on our extension to the risk detection and resolution process with creativity support. It involved employees who work on the production lines in shifts and cannot stop their work on demand to undertake creative tasks. Moreover, due to shift rotations, even pre-planned time to participate in the process was limited to a maximum of 30 minutes per risk. In addition, most employees had little or no experience of using creativity techniques, the nature of most manufacturing work was repetitive and did not foster creative thinking, and the focus on the continuous manufacture of tractors generated a culture that was solution-oriented. This context, very different to most creative industries, provided several

challenging constraints on our development of effective new creativity support for risk resolution. The digital support needed to be simple to learn and to use, not consume too much worker time, and deliver one or more candidate resolutions that could be implemented by the end of the process.

In response to these constraints a simple *diverge-converge* creative process to risk detection and resolution was developed and provided as input to a user-centred design process that was undertaken by a small design team with stakeholders including the plant manager, health-and-safety captains and health-and-safety supervisor. At the start of the process the designers observed the plant's risk detection and recording process and analyzed its paper-based and digital information artefacts, an analysis which led to the identification of a set of bottlenecks and potential barriers to creative thinking in the process. The designers, health-and-safety supervisor and some captains then collaborated in a simple co-design process to determine possible different digital interventions during risk detection and resolution processes that would be made using mobile devices available on the plant floor and desktop computers in offices. They redesigned the process to remove duplicate information about risks, replace paper-based information flows with email document exchanges, and generate a new online risk repository to store these digital documents. Once these architecture decisions had been made, a series of increasingly sophisticated prototypes of a new software application were developed and made available for formative evaluation by stakeholders. First versions of the prototype were demonstrated to the stakeholders for feedback in controlled settings, then later versions were made available to stakeholders for trial use in the plant over a period of week, to enable thorough testing and refinement through report-back sessions with the designers. The outcome of this user-centred design process was a functioning, usable and robust software application to provide support for creative thinking during risk detection and resolution processes.

The input to each instance of the new *diverge-converge* process using the application was a detected and documented risk, and the anticipated outputs were one or more resolutions to the risk that one or more members of a team composed to resolve the risk would consider novel and useful [23]. Each instance of the process was planned to last for no more than 20 minutes. To *diverge* from an input risk to generate new ideas with which to resolve it, a team uses 2 creativity techniques. The first is the S*uperhero* technique [17], with which the team selects one well-known superhero at a time, then applies the superpowers of that hero to generate new ideas about how the risk can be resolved. Each team is guided through this process with a predefined set of well-known superheroes and their special powers. The second technique is the *Seen-it-before* creativity technique. The team is encouraged to review similar previous risks that have been resolved, and to generate new ideas about how to resolve the current risk from resolutions to the previous risks. Then, to *converge* from the set of new ideas about how to resolve the risk to one resolution to implement, each team uses a third creativity technique that is a variation on the *TRIZ* method [1] adapted to the manufacturing plant environment. The technique, called *Creative Clues*, defines a set of desirable characteristics and qualities of novel risk resolutions to risks. The team selects one clue at a time and seeks to generate and evolve new ideas into risk resolutions with the stated characteristic or quality. The resulting risk resolution is documented in the existing plant forms as part of the wider health-and-safety management procedures. The overall process, and its fit within this health-and-safety management process, is depicted graphically in Figure 3.

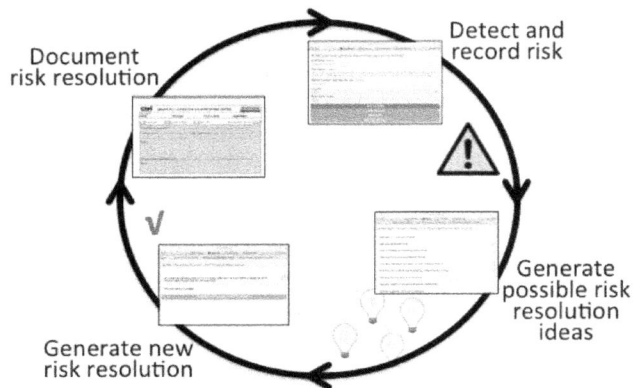

Figure 3. The new diverge-converge creative process for risk detection and resolution that was implemented in the plant

As part of the user-centred design process, a paper-based version of this creative risk resolution process was piloted in 2 one-hour training sessions at the CNH Industrial plant attended by a total of 18 team leaders and health-and-safety captains. During each session, researchers introduced the process and examples of creative problem solving in practice, then presented a previous serious incident in which a worker received a superficial cut to the head when a duckboard, which he sat on in order to view the underside of a tractor to check for oil leaks, moved unexpectedly. The team leaders and health-and-safety captains were divided into teams of 3 and asked to generate new resolutions to the risk using the new process. In the *diverge* phase each team spent 15 minutes generating new ideas using the *Superheroes* technique supported by visual images of 12 superheroes. In the converge phase each team spent a further 10 minutes evolving the new ideas into a resolution to the risk using a small number of *Creative Clue* cards such as *place one object inside of another*.

The plant management deemed the training sessions a success – all team leaders and health-and-safety captains were able to use the techniques with limited training in a short period of time. Most of the teams identified the potential benefits of the use of these techniques to resolve risks, and most of the teams generated risk resolutions that were no-

ticeably different to the original resolution that was applied. For example, the use of the *Superhero* technique generated ideas such as *raising the tractor in the air to avoid the need to lie down* (superhuman strength), *sensor devices beneath the tractor to automate the current manual check* (x-ray vision), and *coloring the oil so that it can be seen without going under the tractor* (radioactive man). Likewise, use of the *Creative Clues* technique guided the teams to generate resolutions to the risk such as *having workers wear hats during inspections* (from the desirable characteristic of having one object inside another) and *mixing oil with other liquids to make it more visible* (from the desirable characteristic of mixing elements with liquid or air).

DIGITAL SUPPORT FOR CREATIVE RISK RESOLUTION
The user-centred design process sought to address 2 overarching challenges to develop effective digital support for risk resolution. The first was to determine an effective means with which to deliver digital technologies to replace and enhance the paper-based risk recording on the production line. Desktop computers in fixed locations throughout the plant were rejected in favor of more mobile tablet computing devices that workers could take to the incident site and complete an online risk description form, equivalent to the previous *Safety Emergency Work Order* and *Unsafe Act and Condition* forms. The second was to determine how to implement effective digital support for each creativity technique in an environment with limited digital expertise and no additional resource for knowledge management. To overcome this challenge we decided that each component of the digital support would need to be either a predefined software component that will not require plant resources to be managed or a software component that can automatically process the language of employee communication in the risk detection and resolution process – written natural language English.

Therefore, to implement the digital support for the *Superheroes* technique, the user-centred design process extended an existing web application called *Bright Sparks* [14]. The *Bright Sparks* application is a digital implementation of the *Hall of Fame* creativity technique [17] that retrieves information about well-known personas from the Internet and presents it to users to stimulate creative thinking about a problem. To extend it to support CNH Industrial's creative risk resolution process, the researchers implemented a version that did not require management by the plant and presents information about superheroes and guides users to generate new ideas based on the superpowers of each. An example of use of *Bright Sparks* is shown in Figure 4.

To implement the digital support for the *Seen-it-before* creativity technique, the user-centred design process resulted in a new web application called *Risk Hunting* to exploit the one digital resource already available in the plant – the natural language data that had been digitally recorded about 5000+ detected and resolved risks in CNH Industrial's existing *Sharepoint* database. The application was implemented with a set of computational mechanisms developed to make sense of, match and generate new creative content from the unmanaged natural language resource to present to employees to encourage creative thinking about resolutions to a current risk. And to implement the digital support for the *Creative Clues* technique, researchers codified the set of desirable characteristics and qualities of novel resolutions to risks so that employees using the *Risk Hunting* application receive automatically generated creative ideas that are both possible resolutions to the risk and guidance to discover the risk resolution.

Figure 4. Digital support for the Superheroes technique with the Bright Sparks application

The *Risk Hunting* Application

The *Risk Hunting* application was developed for use by health-and-safety teams in creative sessions lasting a maximum of 20 minutes. It was implemented with the 4 software components: (1) a front-end web application that employees interact with to describe a risk, receive creative guidance to resolve the risk and document new resolution ideas; (2) a digital repository of descriptions of previous risk-resolution cases; (3) a computational software service that automates the *Seen-it-before* technique to discover and retrieve creatively similar risks and their resolutions; and (4) a computational software service that automates the *Creative clues* technique to generate clues automatically from descriptions of detected risks and retrieved risk resolutions. One further component implements the *Bright Sparks* application as part of the *Risk Hunting* application, but it is not reported further in this paper.

The application was developed to support human-centred creative cognition [13], an activity in which idea generation takes place concurrently with information finding. The application supports members of a health-and-safety team to search for and generate ideas in the 3 search spaces depicted graphically in Figure 5. The first search space is formed by the 8000+ previous risk-resolution cases described in the digital repository, and the creative search service searches this space of cases automatically to discover similar risk-

resolution cases as part of the implementation of the *Seen-it-before* technique. The second space is the search space of possible new risk resolutions to be generated from each retrieved resolution. The application guides members of the health-and-safety team to undertake exploratory creativity to generate new ideas through information finding in this space. The third space is the search space of new risk resolutions that result from the combination of previous risk resolutions and the desirable qualities and characteristics of resolutions to risks in manufacturing plants codified in the *Creative Clues* technique. The creative clue generation service searches this space automatically in order to generate possible risk resolutions that the application presents to the team members to guide their idea generation process. As such, members of the health-and-safety team are directed to undertake a guided creative cognition activity through the search of 3 different search spaces in order to find relevant information and discover and generate new risk resolution ideas from it.

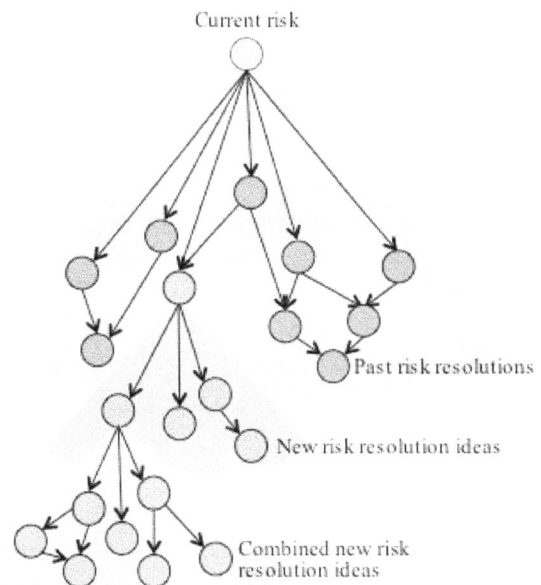

Figure 5. The spaces of previous risk-resolutions and resolution ideas that creative search strategies support navigation of

The front-end web application supports this human-centred creative cognition by accepting unrestricted natural language input and tick-box selections from plant employees. More visual interactions were rejected in order to ensure the application use by the widest range of employees. At the start of a new risk resolution session, one or more team members enter key information about the detected risk – a risk description, location and risk to different human parts – into the application that is extracted from the *Safe Emergency Work Order* or *Unsafe Act and Condition* forms. Each risk is described using unstructured natural language – it does not require explicit tagging with predefined terms – constraints that might inhibit the required creative flow during the session. Use of the application to document information about the moving duckboard risk, reported earlier in the paper is shown in Figure 6. As well saving or editing this new risk description, the team members can request the application to find similar risks.

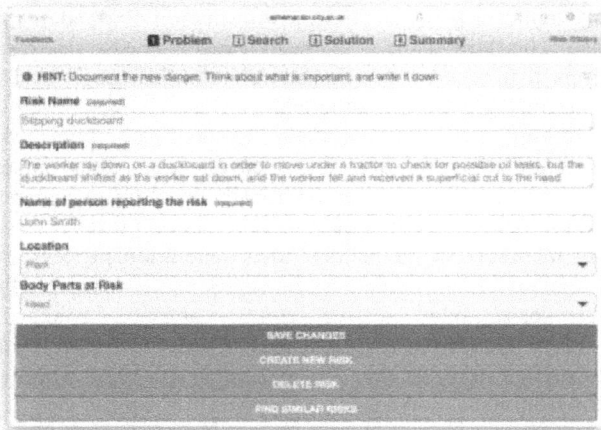

Figure 6. Entering a natural language new risk description into the *Risk Hunting* application.

The team members then browse simple descriptions of previous recorded risks that are retrieved by the application as similar to the detected risk and select one or more to review further. For each retrieved risk, the team members can review the original resolution(s) that were applied successfully to resolve the risk and request creative clues that the application generates automatically from retrieved information about risk resolutions. Examples of retrieved previously-resolved risks shown on the left of Figure 7 include an *oil leak from a tractor unit, an extractor fan that fell from its mounting,* and *an extruding object such as a bar axle.* Some creative clues to resolve the current risk based on the previous risk resolution related to an *extractor unit* shown on the right of Figure 6 include *think about deactivating the unit, think about either trying to put holes in the unit or to fill holes in the unit,* and *think about how to make the unit self-sustaining, so that it uses all of its waste.* The team members can also request the application to generate creative clues from information that the team members enter directly about the detected risk. Examples of the creative clues that the application generates for the current risk example in the bottom right of Figure 7 include *think about if it is possible to regenerate the leaks, think about whether you can balance the worker with something else,* and *think about doing the opposite of what is expected with the leaks.*

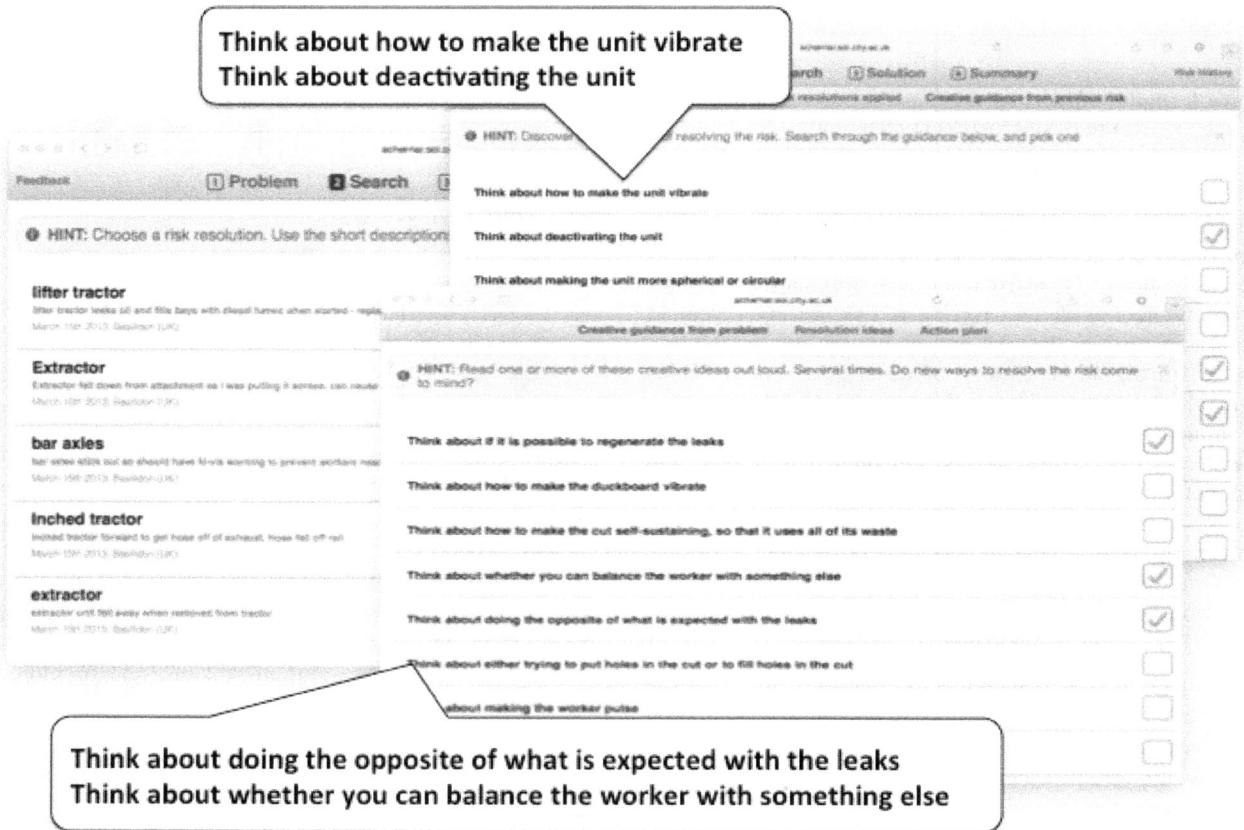

Figure 7. Creative guidance for resolving a risk based on computationally generated creative clues from selected previous risk cases and the current risk information

The team members might use these clues to generate ideas such as seeking to replicate and discover oil leaks with specialist equipment in order to detect risks, develop a mechanism that takes the worker's weight and support them to spot oil leaks in relative safety, and in response to doing the opposite of what is expected, postpone the detection of oil leaks until a later, more effective stage in the production process.

The Digital Repository of Risk Resolutions

The digital repository is implemented using eXist, an open source native XML database featuring index-based XQuery processing that the creative search service queries using XQuery, a query language designed for processing XML data. It stores natural language descriptions of previous risks and their resolutions in XML based on the structure of CNH Industrial's *Sharepoint* database of risks. The current version of the digital repository implemented in the plant maintains a record of more than 8000 detected risks and their resolutions. Each risk-resolution case and its attributes are specified in 3 parts. The first part describes the detected risk and specifies attributes such as a natural language description of the risk situation, employee body parts that were at risk, and details of the location of the risk. The second part describes the resolutions that were applied successfully to resolve the risk, and specifies attributes such as corrective actions and future recommendations. The third part describes all other information about the risk-resolution and specifies a larger number of attributes that include the incident short code and persons involved in the incident. As reported earlier, no ontology or tags are specified to provide semantic information about each case.

The Creative Search Service

The service was implemented to discover and retrieve risks and their resolutions that are similar to the current risk. To do this it implements 3 different creative search strategies to generate new content about: (1) objects or actions described in the new risk description, for example new resolutions associated to objects such as the *duckboard* or actions such as *slipping*; (2) the wider classes of object or action described in the risk description, for example all classes of action in which someone or something falls over, and; (3) objects and actions that are indirectly associated with the original risk description, for example about *accidents*, an event that is indirectly related to the action *slipping*. The creative search service was developed to use natural language parsing and information retrieval techniques. It automatically disambiguates each term in an entered risk description with its most probable meaning, then extends queries generated from the risk description with additional terms based on the disambiguated meanings that implement each of the above creative strategies to match to terms in previous risk-resolution cases [27]. These creative search service capabilities are implemented in 4 software components shown in Figure 8.

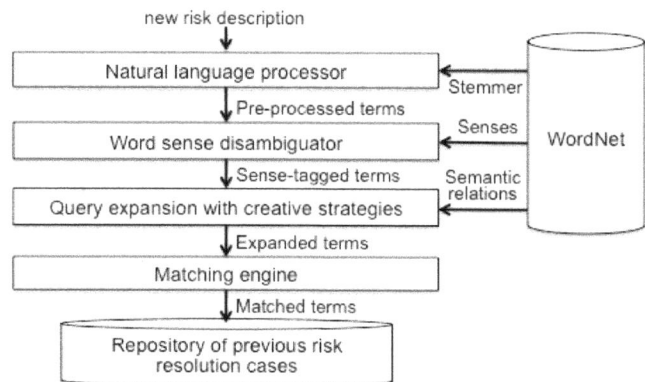

Figure 8. The algorithm of the Creative Search Service

In the first component the detected risk description is divided into sentences then tokenized, part-of-speech tagged and modified to include each term's morphological root (e.g. *shifted* to *shift*, *leaks* to *leak*) using the Brill Tagger [4]. In the second component the service applies increasingly sophisticated procedures to disambiguate each term by discovering its correct sense and tagging each term with that sense using context knowledge from other terms in the query (e.g. defining a *leak* to be *an accidental hole that allows something (fluid or light etc.) to enter or escape* rather than *unauthorized (especially deliberate) disclosure of confidential information*). In the third the service implements the creative search strategies by expanding each term with other terms that have similar meaning according to the tagged sense to discover previous risk-resolution cases with different forms of similarity to the input risk description (e.g. the term *leak* is synonymous with the terms *opening, gap and space* which are then also included in the query based on the creative strategy). In the fourth the service matches all expanded and sense-tagged query terms to a similar set of terms that describe each case in the repository in 2 steps: (1) XQuery text-searching functions to discover an initial set of case problem descriptions that satisfy global search constraints, and; (2) traditional vector-space model information retrieval, enhanced with *WordNet*, to refine and assess the quality of the candidate risk-resolution case set. WordNet is an on-line lexical database based on psycholinguistic theories of human lexical memory [22] that divides the lexicon into nouns, verbs, adjectives and adverbs. The meanings of words, called senses, for each are organized into synonym sets, or synsets for short, which represent concepts, and each synset is followed by its definition or gloss that contains a defining phrase, an optional comment and one or more examples. Senses are also structured using semantic relations between them to link concepts.

As such, the creative search service uses *WordNet* word sense and definition data to generate and direct creative searches. Expansion of a query with new terms that are semantically different to the original terms will enlarge the search space of risk-resolution cases compared with expansion of the query with new terms that are semantically more similar. Each strategy was designed to generate new content about an object or action described in the new risk description, the wider class of object or action that is described in the risk description, or about objects and actions indirectly associated with the original risk description. To implement these directions, the service uses different types of ontological information from *WordNet* to discover semantically related terms to each term:

1. *Synset expansion*: each original term is replaced with its synset, for example the term *shift* is replaced with its synset for sense #2 [*shift, dislodge, reposition*]. As such, the strategy expands the query to retrieve then generate new content about each object or action described in the new risk description using synsets;

2. *Hypernym expansion*: each original term is augmented by its WordNet direct hypernym, for example the hypernym of *leak* is *hole* so the revised query includes both terms. This strategy expands the query to retrieve then generate new content related to the classes of each object or action described in the new risk description using hypernyms;

3. *Gloss words expansion*: each term is augmented with all of the terms in its gloss *specified in WordNet*. For example the sense#1 definition of the term *leak* is *an accidental hole that allows something (fluid or light etc) to enter or escape*. Hence the terms *hole, fluid, light, enter* and *escape* are extracted and included in the extended query. This strategy expands the query to retrieve then generate new content related to each object or action using the gloss definitions from *WordNet*.

The resulting query of expanded terms is transformed into a XQuery that is fired at the equivalent risks resolved previously described in the digital repository. At the end of each invocation, the service returns an ordered set of the descriptions of the five highest-scoring cases that are presented to the employees, as shown on the left of Figure 7.

The Creative Clue Generation Service
The creative clues technique is implemented as also shown in Figure 7 using a second computational service that automatically generates instances of creative clues based on the TRIZ method [1] with names of objects extracted from descriptions of detected risks and retrieved risk resolutions. The set of classes of creative clues was selected from a wider set of qualities and characteristics associated with creative outcomes developed as part of the TRIZ [1] creative method. A total of 85 different classes were selected according to the relevance and feasibility of its quality and characteristic in the pilot CNH Industrial plant, then ranked by the paper's authors for its perceived usefulness to creative thinking about risk resolutions, and based on this ranking, a multiplier was attributed to that class to increase its presence in the creative clues that are generated by the service at run-time. A subset of the creative clue classes and their multipliers are listed in Table 1 to demonstrate the range and different forms of the classes. Some of the classes are specified to generate creative clue instances about mechanical objects named in risk and resolution descriptions, others about the actions and behaviours named in these risk and resolution descriptions. The service will, on average, generate an instance creative clue to think about dividing a mechanical object up 9 times more frequently than it will generate one about putting the mechanical object in a vacuum.

To generate each creative clue presented by the Risk *Hunting* application, the service also parses the natural language descriptions of the risk and resolution descriptions to extract (1) *objects* in the forms of nouns and proper place names; and (2) *activities* in the form of verb phrases determining the active verbs and all text through to the next punctuation/conjunction word. To do this, the service's algorithm splits the text into sentences and applies a part-of-speech tagging process to mark up words in each sentence as belonging to each lexical, part-of-speech category using information about both its definition and its context in the text. The algorithm then applies a natural language processing technique called *shallow parsing* that was developed to generate machine understanding of the structure of a sentence without parsing it fully into a parsed tree form. The output of this shallow-parsing process is a division of the text's sentences into a series of words that, together, constitute a grammatical unit. Finally, to select candidate objects and actions from these grammatical units, the algorithm applies lexical extraction heuristics on a syntax structure rule-tagged sentence to extract content words relevant for the generation of one or more objects. Returning to our example, the service returns the following objects: *worker; walkway; leak; engine,* and one activity: *slip on a walkway due to a small oil leak from an engine.* The service uses these identified objects and activity to automatically generate creative clues.

Creative clue class	Multiplier
Think about dividing the [mechanical-object] up	9
Think about how to make the [mechanical-object] move and adjust	8
Think about how to introduce feedback to the [action] action	7
Think about whether it is possible to make the [mechanical-object] an irregular shape	5
Think about how to continue to [action], rather than stopping the action	4
Think about putting the [mechanical-object] in a vacuum	1

Table 1. Example creative clue classes and their attributed multipliers for creative clue generation

DEPLOYMENT AND EARLY EVALUATION OF *THE RISK HUNTING* APPLICATION
The described version of the *Risk Hunting* application was deployed for 4 months in the tractor plant to enable its formative and summative evaluations by the health-and-safety team, primarily using mobile tablet devices as depicted in Figure 9. Early summative evaluation results have revealed both successful application use and some barriers to its widespread uptake in the plant. Both are reported here.

Figure 9. Use of the *Risk Hunting* application on mobile tablet devices in the tractor plant

Analysis of the data collected about application use over the first 21 working days of the summative evaluation reported in Table 2 revealed that team members using the application documented, on average, more than 2 new risks per day. Moreover, on average for each new risk, the team used the application to retrieve and select 4 different previous risks, selected 5 creative clues and document just over 2 new ideas with which to resolve each risk. The 6 health-and-safety captains and 2 supervisors documented most of these risks, while some production line supervisors accounted for the remaining documented risks.

Total numbers of ...				
new risks described	retrieved risks browsed	creative clues viewed	superheroes explored	resolution ideas generated
46	180	210	67	98

Table 2. Totals of use of different Risk Hunting application features over first 21 working days of summative evaluation

Some of the 46 resolved risks documented in the application revealed evidence of possible creative thinking. Two examples are presented in Table 3. The first reported the danger from boxes that might fall due a forklift truck driver placing them in the wrong place, and the documented resolution revealed some evidence of transformational creativity – rather than just have the boxes stocked correctly, use of the selected creative clues led to a resolution that proposed to rethink the space in which the boxes are stored.

Risk	Risk description	Risk resolution
1	Boxes from prop shaft kitting area have been stocked by the flt driver outside of the designated lines, so therefore overharg into agv buggy route location e8.	Make the boxes move and adjust-area needs to be moved around to insure all boxes are situated within the lines.
2	Risk of being struck by falling object.	Clear driveline of any excess parts prior transit to pedline.

Table 3. Two examples risks and their resolutions documented in the *Risk Hunting* application

However, other risks were given simple resolutions that revealed little or no evidence of creative thinking. For example the second risk in Table 3 reports a simple risk and resolution to avoid the risk of being struck by falling objects. One reason given for such simple risk resolutions was that not all risks required creative thinking to resolve them – some risks had effective and known resolutions.

Furthermore, focus groups with members of the health-and-safety team revealed several barriers to use of the application as intended. As well as a small number of application usability problems to be overcome with small software redesigns and additional user training, these focus groups revealed that the teams considered that 20 minutes was too much time to find to think creatively and collaboratively about discovered risks. Therefore, to overcome this barrier, we redesigned the plant's roles and workflow to encourage active involvement of new creativity champions who users will be able to approach to encourage creative thinking with the application during the resolution of a new risk. A second change will be the running of 1-hour creative risk resolution sessions, once a fortnight to review risks documented and resolved in that fortnight, that can be resolved more effectively – the team of health-and-safety captains will work collaboratively to re-resolve these risks as needed, to improve the risk resolutions, all using the application.

CONCLUSIONS AND FUTURE WORK

In this paper we argue for and report new digital support for human creative cognition in the management of health-and-safety in a world-class manufacturing plant as a demonstrator for the use of creativity techniques and digital support tools outside of the creative industries. A simple *diverge-converge* creative process that invokes the use of 3 different creativity techniques was developed and piloted in sessions with plant employees. Based on the success of the pilot sessions, new digital support for these creativity techniques was implemented to operate within the constraints of the complex, time-limited manufacturing environment. The *Risk Hunting* application was developed to support human-centred creative cognition through the navigation of 3 different risk resolution search spaces. It provides deliberately simple forms of creativity support based on the outcomes of computational manipulation of untagged natural language descriptions of current and previous risks and their resolutions. The deployment and formative evaluation of the application in the plant has been successful – the employees are able to use the application, although the evaluation has revealed some socio-technical barriers that we are currently addressing through further training development and evolution of the software. A second web application called *Bright Sparks* has been developed to support the use of the super-heroes creativity technique in the plant.

Our next stage in this project is to complete the summative evaluation of both applications once lessons from the formative evaluation have been implemented. This evaluation will take place over a minimum of 3 months through the spring and summer of 2015, and involve the rigorous analysis and comparison of the novelty and value of risk resolutions generated in the plant with the existing risk detection and resolution process and the new creative risk resolution process with its digital support. We look forward to reporting this further work in a future publication. In this more technical research paper, we hope that it offers encouragement and guidance to researchers to develop new digital support for human creative thinking in the many disciplines outside of the creative industries that have the potential to benefit from increased creative competences.

ACKNOWLEDGEMENTS

The research reported in this paper is supported by the EU-funded FP7 COLLAGE project 318536.

REFERENCES

1. Altshuller G., 1999, 'The Innovation Algorithm: TRIZ, Systematic Innovation, and Technical Creativity', Worcester, MA: Technical Innovation Center.

2. Arbesman M., Puccio G., 2001. Enhanced Quality Through Creative Problem Solving. Journal of Nursing Administration 31(4), 176 -178.

3. Aragon C.R., Poon S.S. & Aragon A. M-H. D., 2009, 'A Tale of Two Online Communities: Fostering Collaboration and Creativity in Scientists and Children', Proceedings 7th ACM conference on Creativity and Cognition, ACM Press, 9-18.

4. Brill E., 1992, 'A simple rule-based part of speech tagger', Proc., Third Conference on Applied Natural Language Processing, ACL, Trento, Italy.

5. Correia de Barros A. & Duarte C., 2009, 'Assistive Devices: Stroke Patients' Design, Proceedings 7th ACM conference on Creativity and Cognition, ACM Press, 79-86.

6. Davidson J. & Jensen C., 2013, 'Participatory Design with Older Adults: An Analysis of Creativity in the Design of Mobile Healthcare, Proceedings 9th ACM Conference on Creativity & Cognition, ACM Press, 114-123.

7. Doorley S. & Witthoft S., 2012, 'Make Space', Wiley, Hoboken, New Jersey.

8. Eckert C., Wyatt D. & Clarkson J., 2009, 'The Elusive Act of Synthesis: Creativity in the Conceptual Design of Complex Engineering Products', Proceedings 7th ACM conference on Creativity and cognition, ACM Press, 265-274.

9. Eurostat 2014, available at: appsso.eurostat.ec.europa.eu.

10. Hinsch M.E., Stockstrom C. & Lüthje C., 2014, 'User Innovation in Techniques: A Case Study Analysis in the Field of Medical Devices', Creativity and Innovation Management 23(4), 484–494.

11. Houts, P.S., Nezubd, A.M., Magut Nezubd, C, Bucherc, J.A., 1996, 'The prepared family caregiver: a problem-solving approach to family caregiver education', Patient Education and Counselling, 27(1), 63-73.

12. Isaksen, S.G. Brian, K. Dorval, Treffinger, D.J. 2011, Creative Approaches to Problem Solving: A Framework for Innovation and Change. Sage Publications, Inc; Third Edition.

13. Kerne, A., Koh, E., Smith, S. M., Webb, A., Dworaczyk, B., 2008, 'combinFormation: Mixed-Initiative Composition of Image and Text Surrogates Promotes Information Discovery', ACM Transactions on Information Systems, 27(1), 1-45.

14. Lockerbie J. & Maiden N.A.M., under submission, 'Using the Bright Sparks Software Tool During Creative Design Work', submitted to Collaboration in Creative Design, Springer-Verlag.

15. Maiden N.A.M., D'Souza S., Jones S., Muller L., Panesse L., Pitts K., Prilla M., Pudney K., Rose M., Turner I. & Zachos K., 2013, 'Computing Technologies for Reflective and Creative Care for People with Dementia', Communications of the ACM 56(11), 60-67.

16. McCarthy D., Koeling R., Weeds J., Carroll J., 2004, 'Using Automatically Acquired Predominant Senses for Word Sense Disambiguation', In: Proceedings of the ACL 2004 Senseval-3 Workshop Barcelona, Spain.

17. Michalko, M., 2006. 'ThinkerToys: A Handbook of Creative-Thinking Techniques', Second Edition. Ten Speed Press, New York.

18. Miller K., 1993, 'Introduction to WordNet: an On-line Lexical Database' Distributed with WordNet software.

19. Osborn A.F., 1953, 'Applied Imagination: Principles and Procedures of Creative Problem Solving', Charles Scribener's Sons, New York.

20. OSHA, 2014, 'All about Occupational Safety and Health Administration', US Department of Labor, accessible from https://www.osha.gov/Publications/all_about_ OSHA.pdf

21. Salton G., Wong A. and Yang C.S., 1975, 'A vector-space model for information retrieval', Journal of the American Society for Information Science 18,13-620.

22. Simpson, T., 2005,. Wordnet.net. opensource.ebswift. com/WordNet.Net.

23. Sternberg, R. J. (Ed.), 1999, 'Handbook of creativity', New York, Cambridge University Press.

24. Stevenson M., Wilks Y., 2001, 'The Interaction of Knowledge Sources in Word Sense Disambiguation' Computational Linguistics, 27(3), 321-349.

25. Webb M. Linder R. & Kerne A., Lupfer N., Qu Y., Poffenberger B. & Revia C., 2013, 'Promoting Reflection and Interpretation in Education: Curating Rich Bookmarks as Information Composition', Proceedings 9th ACM Conference on Creativity & Cognition, ACM Press, 53-62.

26. Wu A., Yim J.B., Caspary E., Mazalek A. Chandrasekharan S. & Nersessian N.J., 2011, 'Kinesthetic Pathways: A Tabletop Visualization to Support Discovery in Systems Biology', Proceedings 8th ACM Conference on Creativity and Cognition, ACM Press, 21-30.

27. Zachos K., Maiden N.A.M., Zhu X. & Jones S., 2007, 'Discovering Web Services To Specify More Complete System Requirements', Proceedings CaiSE'2007, Springer-Verlag Lecture Notes on Computer Science LNCS 4495, 142-157.

Critiki: A Scaffolded Approach to Gathering Design Feedback from Paid Crowdworkers

Michael D. Greenberg
Segal Design Institute
Northwestern University
Evanston, IL USA
mdgreenb@u.northwestern.edu

Matthew W. Easterday
Segal Design Institute
Northwestern University
Evanston, IL USA
easterday@northwestern.edu

Elizabeth M. Gerber
Segal Design Institute
Northwestern University
Evanston, IL USA
egerber@tnorthwestern.edu

ABSTRACT

Feedback is important to the creative process, but not everyone has a personal crowd of individuals they can turn to for high-quality feedback. We introduce and evaluate Critiki, a novel system for gathering design critiques on crowdfunding project pages from paid crowdworkers. Stemming from previous research on crowdfunding project creators and their need for early-stage design feedback, we design and build a working system which fits the need of this population: rapid and inexpensive feedback. To solve issues with critique quality we describe a scaffolding technique designed to assist crowdworkers in writing high-quality critiques. We evaluate Critiki with two field deployments: 1) A randomized controlled experiment with 450 crowdworkers to evaluate the efficacy of the scaffolding technique and 2) A user study with 31 crowdfunding project creators to determine usability and user satisfaction. We contribute to research on Creativity and Cognition by demonstrating a working creativity support system, empirically evaluating the system, and describing how scaffolding approaches can be designed for other crowdsourced tasks.

Author Keywords

Crowdsourcing; Design; Scaffolding; Feedback; Crowdfunding; Mechanical Turk

ACM Classification Keywords

H.5.m. Information Interfaces and Presentation (e.g. HCI): Miscellaneous

INTRODUCTION

Online crowdfunding, the act of asking a crowd of supporters to each contribute a small amount of funds towards a larger monetary goal, has emerged as disruptive new way for creative ventures to start and establish communities of supporters [7, 20]. Since 2008, Kickstarter, the largest of the crowdfunding platforms has raised over $1.1 billion for new creative ventures [2]. In addition to coordinating the collection and transfer of funds, the Kickstarter platform provides a page

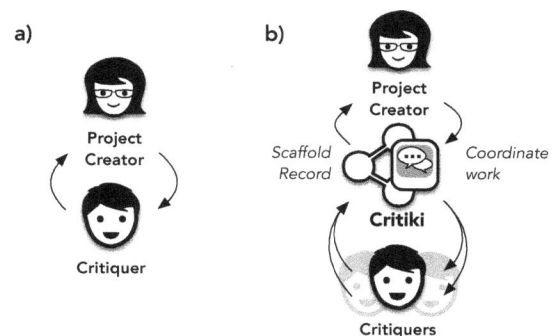

Figure 1. (a) Traditional critique and (b) Critiki: a scaffolded approach to critique. Critiki assists with the process of feedback by acquiring feedbackers, scaffolding the process and presenting results.

for each project where the creator communicates the need for funds through a title, video and description text. As such, the way that people communicate their project's goals through this page content has a direct effect on crowdfunding success [17, 13]. However, not every project creator creates a succinct, effective pitch.

Previous research has shown that while the quality of the page content can effect the outcome of the campaign, many crowdfunding project creators do not get feedback on their pages before they launch [15]. This research has shown that the creators of projects are reluctant to ask their personal social network for feedback, are too busy to coordinate a feedback process, and are uncertain how to frame feedback questions [20]. Some project creators don't even have a group of effective feedbackers they can turn to. However, this same research found that people who do muster the time and courage to gather feedback find feedback to be extremely useful in clarifying their pitch and improving their campaign [20].

To address this need, we built Critiki: a system for gathering design critiques on crowdfunding pages from paid crowdworkers (Figure 1). Critiki allows crowdfunding project creators to quickly (<2 days), and inexpensively ($5) gather design feedback with low effort (<5 minutes) on their part. Critiki manages the process of designing effective feedback tasks, posting tasks on paid crowdwork platforms, and collating the feedback so that project creators can use the feedback to revise their project page.

Beyond crowdfunding, the Internet has sparked a generation of individuals who increasingly collaborate on creative work online. As researchers of creativity, we are interested in building new computational systems which support the creative process. In this paper we focus on creative support in the form of feedback, which has been shown to increase the quality of creative work [18, 4]. However, not everyone has access to a crowd of experts who might give high quality feedback. To this end, we're interested in supporting feedback processes, by lowering the barriers to accessing feedback, in domains where people are doing creative work online.

Leveraging paid crowdworkers for feedback however, presents challenges since crowdfunding pages are thematically diverse and have many parts. For example, crowdworkers may not know that the quality of the video on a crowdfunding page is more important than the project description text [17]. In addition crowdworkers might not have the vocabulary to elicit an effective critique. Since the range of themes and possible critiques on crowdfunding pages is diverse, open-response feedback prompts, rather than rubrics or more rigid structures might be an appropriate approach. However, previous research has shown that there are serious issues present with asking crowdworkers open-response questions as well [21].

Critiki addresses issues with open-response questions by doing the following: 1) We use a scaffolding approach from learning sciences to guide crowdworkers through the steps of an effective critique. 2) We provide examples of high-quality critiquing points to crowdworkers to provide them with a vocabulary necessary to elucidate high-quality critiques.

We evaluate Critiki with two field deployments. In the first deployment we show the effectiveness of a scaffolding approach by comparing the quality of scaffolded feedback responses with general open-ended responses in a randomized controlled experiment. In the second deployment, we deploy Critiki with creators of 31 crowdfunding projects and show how they find it useful and easy to use.

This work provides four distinct contributions to Creativity and Cognition: 1) a description of the design and implementation of a system that gathers high quality feedback for crowdfunding project pages, 2) a scaffolding approach for gathering feedback, 3) a set of principles for the design and implementation scaffolded tasks with paid crowdworkers, 4) in the context of crowdfunding we empirically demonstrate that our scaffolding technique is superior to open-response approaches.

RELATED WORK

In this section we review relevant work from crowdfunding, and crowdsourcing as well as related work from the learning sciences on design feedback and scaffolding approaches.

Crowdfunding

Crowdfunding has emerged as a new means for novice creatives to collect funding to do new creative work. Crowdfunding supports creatives by providing a platform to collect funds for and assemble a community around their creative projects in public and in enterprise settings [16, 30]. Previous social computing research on crowdfunding has shown that elements of the campaign page, phrasing of the pitch and updating backers can play a significant role in the success of campaigns [17, 29, 38]. Despite the growing popularity of crowdfunding, few tools have been built that incorporate these findings to assist new project creators with the process of crowdfunding.

In general, design critique and feedback are crucial to all creative success [18, 35]. However, novice creatives, especially those who are running their first crowdfunding campaign often do not have access to experts for critique, nor might they have the time, motivation, or expertise to source high-quality feedback [20]. If we can create a platform to efficiently and inexpensively crowdsource design critique then we can serve this open need. However, crowdsourcing open-response critique presents challenges in achieving complex work.

Open-response Approaches to Crowd Feedback

Significant work has been done in the area of crowdsourcing feedback for creative work. Many commercial systems such as Behance and Dribbble exist for designers to get simple, open-response feedback from an unpaid crowd. Previous research on Dribbble however, has shown that using the site for "showing-off", rather than for gathering feedback is how users attain and grow status in the community [28]. Prior to these online feedback systems, there is a significant body of literature related to automated feedback systems (eg. [14]). While we acknowledge the computational approaches to feedback, in this paper we focus on crowdsourcing as a method of gathering design feedback.

In the area of crowdfunding, Kickstarter has recently implemented an open-response feedback mechanism on their website. However the Kickstarter feedback interface relies on the project creator having an established community of feedbackers s/he could turn to. If project creators eschew the Kickstarter feedback system and attempt to gather feedback off the platform, these creators may not have crowds ready to critique, the time necessary to design critique tasks, nor the expertise to ask effective feedback questions. Asking paid crowdworkers for feedback (as opposed to personal social connections), might solve these issues in gathering design feedback.

Task Design for Crowdwork

An open question in crowdsourcing research is *how to improve crowdwork quality on complex tasks* [22]. The "find-fix-verify" and "shepherding" approaches involve algorithmically dispatching workers to either locate errors or grade the work of other crowdworkers [8, 12]. These approaches work best for tasks which can be easily broken down into independent sub-parts. While many have attempted to improve the quality of crowdwork through algorithmic approaches, a handful of researchers have examined how the design of tasks affects work quality. Previous research has focused on designing for usability [25], and there is a small but growing body of empirical work on how the design of tasks can affect the quality of crowdwork output. Research has shown that easier to comprehend and cognitively designed tasks result in better quality work [19, 3].

Scaffolding

One alternative to algorithmic and design based approaches is an approach based on scaffolding: guiding individuals through smaller subtasks in sequence that, in turn, have them complete a larger complex task [32]. Unlike many crowdsourced tasks in which many workers collaborate on one canonical answer, design critique involves independent work. Design critique also involves many steps: observing, knowing what to critique, and expressing the critique in a logical format [26]. Scaffolding, an approach studied by the learning sciences, is widely used across domains such as paper writing, where it has been shown to improve the quality and quantity of student feedback to expert levels [10, 9]. However, challenges remain for crowdsourcing feedback since crowdworkers often lack (1) contextual knowledge, and (2) domain understanding [5]. Drawing from learning sciences research, we use scaffolding to address both of these challenges.

Scaffolding Responses Online

Several projects from Social Computing research have implemented scaffolding approaches with crowds. Kokkalis introduced the idea of taskplans, short checklists of tasks to be done, which helped workers to finish tasks faster and more accurately [23]. Kulkarni and Klemmer take a scaffolding approach to peer grading in MOOCs. In this work they describe how structured peer training and grading mechanisms can perform at the level of expert graders and achieve high levels of agreement with previously established answers [24].

One approach to structuring crowd critique tasks without established answers is Voyant. The Voyant system breaks down the task of critiquing a visual design into several domain-specific sub-tasks, such as determining the focus point, and recording visceral impressions [37]. Voyant is focused on gathering rapid user impressions as a form of critique, and does not focus on text-based critiques. This system works well for visual design tasks, but subtasks in Voyant are inextricably tied to idiosyncratic features of visual design tasks.

Another approach to scaffolding crowd critique is the CrowdCrit system described by Luther [27]. Similar in approach to the Voyant system described above, CrowdCrit is highly specialized to visual critique, with a focus on judging content based on agreed upon principles of high quality graphic design. The process of eliciting critiquing points is supported by the system, but does not support critique of multimedia content such as webpages. In parallel to previous work, our goal with Critiki is to design scaffolding for open-response feedback tasks for crowdworkers where there is no set of established answers. As crowdworkers are potentially novices in giving design feedback [33], we apply scaffolding to guide them through the process of giving high quality design critiques. We hypothesize that scaffolded critiques will be higher quality than open-response critiques (*H1*).

Scaffolding with Examples

While scaffolds can be used to guide workers through the steps of a complex tasks, a challenge remains that paid crowdworkers may not have the domain knowledge necessary to compose a good critique. In other work on crowd critique and peer critique, the peers who are critiquing work have also completed a version of the task for their own submission [10, 24]. Even though these individuals may not be experts in critique, they will most likely be familiar with the assignment or task, as they have previously completed the task at hand. Paid crowdworkers however, do not have this contextual knowledge. Therefore the final challenge in crowdsourcing critique is informing the crowdworkers of relevant contextual information so that they can construct a quality critique.

How then can we quickly educate people about topics for good critique? One approach takes inspiration from how students learn to mirror the behaviors of their teachers [11, 5]. In classrooms it is often observed that language used by teachers is quickly adopted by students [5]. We hypothesize that we can encourage mirroring behavior through the use of examples. Giving crowdworkers example terminology to adopt in each feedback prompt will encourage mirroring behavior and therefore improve the quality of critiques (*H2*). Overall, while crowds have proven to be an effective tool for gathering an anonymous, unbiased opinion on tasks like visual design, and as peer assessors in MOOCs, challenges still remain in crowdsourcing complex, creative work like text-based critique. In this paper we demonstrate how a properly designed scaffolding approach can improve the quality of crowdsourced feedback in the domain of crowdfunding.

Design Rationale

We argue that in order to encourage crowdworkers to give higher quality feedback: (1) the crowdwork platform needs to use scaffolded tasks and guided feedback prompts, (2) crowdworkers need to be briefed on relevant contextual information through examples, and (3) the critiquing system needs to be easy to adapt and extensible, so scaffolded tasks may be iteratively designed and adapted to other domains. Previous research indicates that scaffolded tasks work to produce quality feedback from novices, and that a scaffolding approach can brief individuals on relevant contextual information [10]. The scaffolding approach should solve the challenge of assisting paid, novice, crowdworkers with performing critiques in domains in which they are non-experts. We expect this technique to perform higher quality feedback than open-response prompts.

CRITIKI

Critiki is a scaffolded feedback system powered by crowdwork platforms, such as Amazon Mechanical Turk or MobileWorks. Critiki consists of several interfaces for submitting feedback tasks, performing critiques, and viewing critiques:

Task Creation: the creator of the crowdfunding campaign can submit a crowdfunding project page for critique. See Figure 3.

Task Interface: the crowdworkers view the crowdfunding page to be critiqued, constructs their critique and submits the task. See Figure 4.

Critique Compilation: the creator of the campaign can see all the critiques presented on one page.

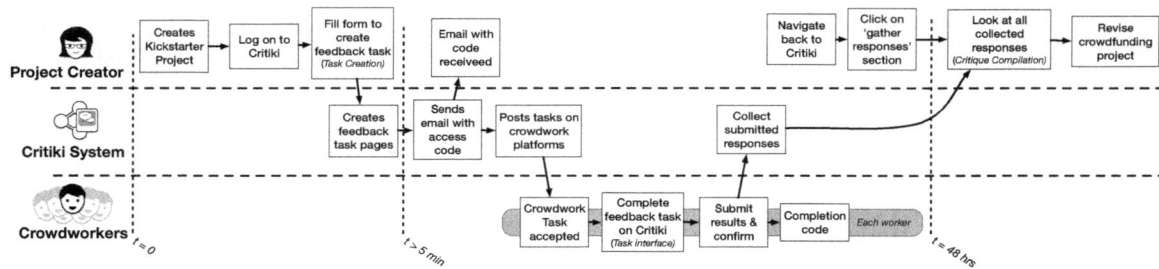

Figure 2. Map of interactions on Critiki

Figure 3. The task creation interface on Critiki. Creators answer three questions to create feedback tasks for their crowdfunding project

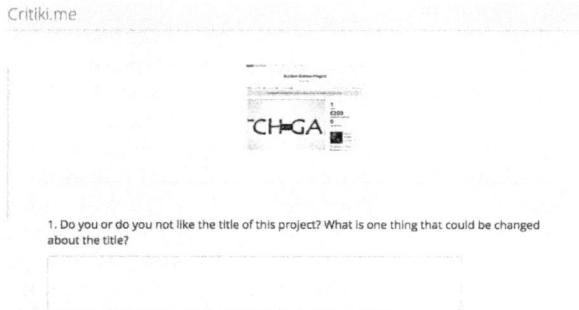

Figure 4. A task on Critiki. The content to be critiqued is on the top. The first two scaffolded questions are at the bottom. Thumbnail can be clicked to open in a new tab.

We use Critiki to gather design critiques on the title and video of crowdfunding campaigns. Critiki was iteratively designed and deployed from April 2013 to January 2014. Critiki facilitates the workflow of the feedback process (Figure 2), from the sourcing of critiques, to the presentation of assembled critiques. This process proceeds as follows:

1. Creator creates campaign content on Kickstarter.
2. Creator submits their crowdfunding page for critique (Figure 3).
3. Feedback Tasks are created on crowdwork platforms.
4. Crowdworkers are recruited on MobileWorks or MTurk [31, 1] and are brought to the task interface (Figure 4).
5. Crowdworkers answer six open-response critique questions, specifically designed to scaffold the critiquing process.

6. Steps 4, 5 and 6 are repeated until all tasks are completed.
7. Creator views feedback. A unique link provides access to a page on Critiki to view aggregated feedback.

Critiki coordinates all of the above steps. A user who is requesting feedback on Critiki needs to provide only three pieces of information to create a task: 1) their email, 2) the location of their project page (a Kickstarter.com URL), and 3) an access code we provide to them (to prevent abuse). Creating a task on Critiki should take under 5 minutes. In contrast, consider the knowledge and time involved in posting a request for work on a crowdwork platform like MTurk. One must first create and fund an account. Next the individual would need to design an unbiased and useful feedback task. One must also know the right amount to pay per task and the proper way to advertise the task on the MTurk. Errors in any of these steps might lead to poor results or no results at all [21]. Platforms like MTurk are certainly valuable resources, but the barrier to entry is often high. With Critiki we aim to lower the barrier to accessing high quality critiques.

In addition, consider the potential social costs for posting feedback tasks on personal social networks. Previous research has shown that people are reluctant to ask their personal social networks for questions that might be personal, and that individuals are reluctant to ask too much of their personal crowds [34]. As such, having an inexpensive tool for gathering high quality feedback quickly could reduce the burden on personal social crowds.

We designed Critiki to be an easy-to-use interface to crowdwork platforms like Mechanical Turk and to avoid the social costs of asking friends and family for feedback. As such, we have both research and usability goals for Critiki. For the user we have designed Critiki to be easy to use, and useful. The research goal for Critiki, however, is to show the efficacy of a scaffolding approach to improve feedback quality.

STUDY DESIGNS
We present two studies with the Critiki system: 1) To empirically evaluate the quality of feedback gathered by Critiki, and 2) To evaluate the usability and usefulness of the system with crowdfunding project creators.

STUDY 1: CRITIKI EVALUATION STUDY
The first study focused on evaluating the quality of feedback between three different feedback task designs. With this study we test our two hypotheses:

H1: Scaffolding tasks will return higher quality critiques than open-response tasks.

H2: Scaffolding with examples will encourage workers to use example terminology.

Study 1: Participants

To evaluate the scaffolds, we recruited workers on MTurk to critique 3 projects. The projects came from the Fashion, Product design and Technology categories on Kickstarter. 150 workers critiqued each project, 450 critiques in total. MTurk workers could critique multiple projects but not allowed to critique one project more than once. MTurk workers were paid $0.25 per response (US workers only). MTurk workers averaged just under 5 minutes on each task. Data collection took place over 10 days. We also recruited two crowdfunding experts to critique each of the three projects. Each expert had launched multiple successful crowdfunding campaigns, raising between $3,000 to over $110,000. Themes of their projects included: poster design, urban gardening, and photography. The experts were thanked for their time with $20 gift cards.

Study 1: Experimental conditions

To determine the efficacy of the scaffolding technique for gathering better critiques, responses on Critiki (step 5 in the above procedure) were framed in one of three ways: Open-Response, Scaffolded, and Scaffolded with Examples. We used a randomized, controlled 3-group between subjects design for this experiment. Below we describe each of the experimental conditions:

Condition 1: Open-Response

In this condition, crowdworkers were asked to give a design critique and were only asked one question. The question asks the crowdworker to "Give feedback on the title and video of the project page." This condition was included as a baseline condition for comparison. This condition is also similar to feedback prompts on popular design feedback platforms online such as Behance and Dribbble as well as the feedback system built into Kickstarter. Our expert responses were also collected in this condition.

Condition 2: Scaffolded

In this case crowdworkers are asked to critique a crowdfunding page by answering 5 questions which scaffold the process of giving a critique. Each question asks the crowdworker to focus on a single element of the campaign and describe what they liked, didn't like and would change about the element. The questions were intended to walk the crowdworker through the process of critique by highlighting important sections of the page. These questions were informed by previous research on page elements which are important to success, [17] and were iteratively designed. These questions focus on the title, video narrative, video length, and video quality. For example, the question about the title asks "Do you or do you not like the title of this project? What is one thing that could be changed about the title?" We hypothesized that scaffolded critique will result in higher quality critiques than open response (H1). We recognize that a common definition of scaffolding includes the concept of "fading," where the scaffolds are gradually removed as skills improve [36]. Our approach does not use fading since we cannot know whether the crowdworker has previously performed tasks. Our approach in this condition is to present the same scaffold to every crowdworker.

Condition 3: Scaffolded with Examples

In the third case we have added a series of examples of high quality critiques to the scaffolded questions. Each question is paired with 4 examples of potential pitfalls which can be critiqued. These examples are also sourced from previous research on effective crowdfunding campaigns and communication design. For example, the question which asks about video quality informs the crowdworkers that: "In good videos: 1) Scenes are well lit, 2) Transitions between scenes are smooth, 3) The volume on voices is even, 4) The camera is not shaky" This condition tests whether crowdworkers will use examples if they are provided. We hypothesize that workers assigned to this case will discuss the themes presented in the hypotheses with a greater frequency (*H1*), and will provide higher quality critiques than the open open-response (*H2*).

Evaluating Critique Quality

To evaluate the quality of the feedback we adopted a technique similar to that used by Cho in previous research on evaluating the quality of scaffolded critique [9]. First, feedback was divided into idea units, which are defined by Cho as "a self-contained message on a single problem" [6], in essence a singular thought or idea. Once the critiques were broken into idea units they were coded into one of 8 categories to separate high-quality critique elements from low-quality critique elements. Table 1 shows examples of idea units and their corresponding codes.

We used a modified version of the Cho and Schunn coding scheme due to differences in our tasks. The Cho and Schunn task is focused heavily on gathering suggestions, while our task is designed to gather suggestions, praise and critique. As such, Cho and Schunn make a distinction between high-quality and-low quality suggestions; they use the terms "directive" and "non-directive" respectively. We use the terms "Nuanced Suggestion" and "Suggestion" to describe the same concept. Since we are looking to evaluate quality we need a distinction between high and low quality praise and critique in addition to suggestions. This coding scheme is designed to flag aspects of positive critiques: 1)Statements telling an individual what to change (Nuanced Suggestions), 2) Statements telling an individual specifically what people like (Nuanced Praise), 3)Statements describing issues people had with specific page elements (Nuanced Critique).

These codes follow 2 of Hattie's "3 Feedback Questions," which must be answered in high quality feedback [18]. Hattie lists these questions as 1) How am I going? (Praise & Critique), and 2) Where am I going? (Suggestions).

A high quality critique will therefore have a higher number of idea units coded as Nuanced Critique, Nuanced Praise and Nuanced Suggestions. We sum the number of idea units coded as $NC + NP + NS$, and assigned this value as the number of "High Quality Units" (HQ). Conversely, the number of

Code	Explanation	Example Responses
NC	Nuanced Critique	"I didn't like the hand motions the speaker was using, it was very distracting." "The main issue is that the volume is waaaay(sp) too high in the beginning"
C	Critique	"The video is low quality." "I don't like the title"
NP	Nuanced Praise	"I really liked that the lighting was bright and you could see the actors." "The video does a good job of telling the audience the point–better quality sneakers."
P	Praise	"The video is good." "Great video."
NS	Nuanced Suggestion	"You should use a pointed microphone to capture better audio" "Generally, I dont́ think videos of this sort should last any more than 2 minutes."
S	Suggestion	"The audio should be improved." "Fix the video."
I	Indifference	"The title is OK." "I have no suggestions"
SUM	Summarization	"This is a Kickstarter project." "You are asking people for money"
OT	Other	"Good luck!" "N/A"

Table 1. Critique quality codes

"Low Quality Units" (LQ), was defined as the sum of the remaining codes: $C + P + S + I + SUM + OT$. We define higher quality critiques as having a higher quantity of high quality units than low quality units.

Evaluating the use of Examples

One coder coded each of the idea units for example theme use. Idea units were flagged if they matched the theme of example text. For example, a comment about "lots of camera movement" was coded as a use of the example: "shaky camera". However, if the theme of the comment did not match one of the examples then the idea unit was not coded as such.

Study 1: Results

We used Critiki to gather feedback on three different Kickstarter projects. We gathered 450 critiques (150 per project) from workers on Mechanical Turk. Two crowdfunding experts critiqued each of the three projects for a total of 456 critiques. Each of these critiques was divided into idea units. Two coders who were experts in design critique divided 10% of the data set (46 critiques) into idea units. The coders agreed on their idea units ($ICC(A, 1) = 0.965$), and one coder was tasked with dividing the remaining critiques into idea units. This process resulted in 4447 individual idea units. Each of these idea units were coded by two coders into the eight codes listed above. Two coders again coded a subset of 10% of the data into these eight categories, after two rounds of training the inter-rater reliability for the raters was found to be $\kappa = 0.71$ ($p < 0.001$). One coder coded the remaining 90% of the dataset. Coded data was then summed into *HQ* and *LQ* responses. Table 1'' lists the average number of idea units per response that fell into the High Quality and Low Quality categories by condition.

	Average number of Idea Units			
	High Quality	Low Quality	Example	Total
Open Response	3.42	0.94	0.55	4.36
Scaffolded	9.18	3.66	1.57	12.84
Scaffolded w/ Ex.	9.50	3.93	2.44	13.43
Expert 1	6.67	0.67	1.00	7.33
Expert 2	10.00	3.67	2.00	13.67

Table 2. Summary of study 1 results (Average number of idea units per response).

We find that the length (number of characters) of critiques was longer in the scaffolded and scaffolded with examples cases (4.36, 12.84 and 13.43 idea units on average in the open-response, scaffolded and scaffolded with examples cases respectively, see Table 2). Figure 5 shows a box plot of the total number of idea units by conditions. In general we see higher number of idea units in both the scaffolded and scaffolded with examples conditions than in the open-response condition. A pairwise t-test with the Bonferroni correction showed a significant result in each case ($p < 0.001$). There was no significant difference between the scaffolded and scaffolded with examples conditions.

In addition, we find that critiques completed in both the scaffolded conditions produced a higher quantity of idea units coded as High Quality units. This is consistent with *H1*. Figure 6 shows a box plot of the High Quality idea units across conditions. A pairwise t-test with the bonferroni correction showed a significant result between cases the open response

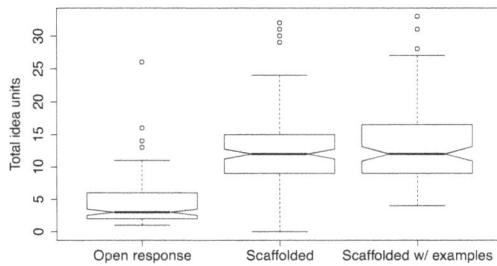

Figure 5. Box plot of the total number of idea units across conditions. Note that both scaffolded cases return more idea units (longer critiques) than the open-response case.

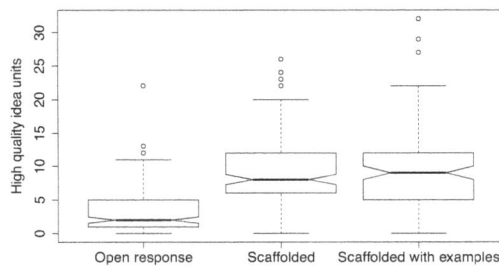

Figure 7. Box plot of number of Low Quality idea units across conditions. Note that both scaffolded cases have a higher number of low quality units.

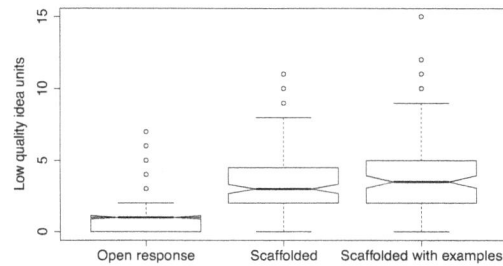

Figure 6. Box plot of number of High Quality idea units across conditions. Note that both scaffolded conditions produce responses with a higher number of high quality idea units.

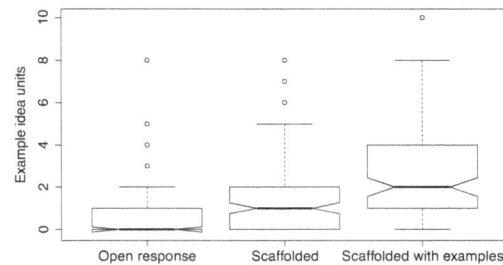

Figure 8. Box plot of number of example idea units across cases. Note increasing trend as we move from open-response to scaffolded and scaffolded w/ example cases.

case and each of the scaffolded cases ($p < 0.001$ in each case). There was no significant difference between the scaffolded and scaffolded with examples conditions.

We also find that both the scaffolded conditions produced a higher quantity of Low Quality idea units as well. Figure 7 shows a box plot of the Low Quality idea units. Pairwise t-tests with the bonferroni correction show a significant difference between the open response and both the scaffolded and scaffolded with examples conditions ($p < 0.001$ in each case). There was no significant difference between the scaffolded and scaffolded with examples conditions.

We also observe people using the examples more in the scaffolded with examples case than in any other condition. This is consistent with *H2*. Figure 8 shows a boxplot of this distribution as well. In general we see an increasing trend, with the open-response condition providing the lowest average number of example idea units (0.55), more in the scaffolded condition (1.55) and the most in the scaffolded with example condition (2.44). Pairwise t-tests with the bonferroni correction show a significant result between each pair of conditions ($p < 0.001$ in each case).

As a test for robustness and generalizability, a one-way ANOVA was used to test for differences in feedback quality between the three projects in high quality units. The number of high quality feedback units did not differ signifi-

cantly across the three different projects, $F(2, 300) = 0.265$, $p = .768$.

We find mixed results from the two crowdfunding experts. One expert performed roughly at the level of a scaffolded crowdworker, while the other expert performed at a level between crowdworkers in the open-response and scaffolded conditions. Experts were asked to critique in an open-response manner so it is important to note that an expert performed better than the average crowdworker in the open-response condition. Table 2 reports the average number of idea units per response from each of the three conditions as well as the average response of each of the two experts.

STUDY 2: USER STUDY
In this study we evaluate the efficacy and usability of Critiki by testing with actual crowdfunding project creators. We expect that Critiki will be easy to use and will be useful in the crowdfunding process.

Participants
To determine the usability and efficacy of Critiki we tested it with 31 crowdfunding project creators. These creators were recruited by contacting projects off of the Kickstarter "recently launched" page. To be clear, these were projects that had already launched, not creators in the process of designing campaigns. 186 project creators were contacted, and 46 individuals agreed to participate; however, only 31 actually

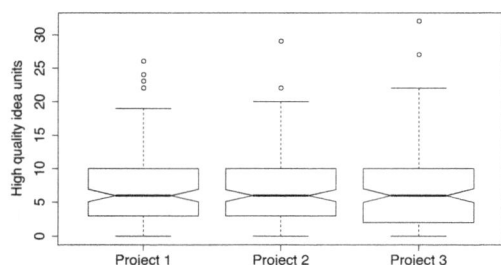

Figure 9. Box plot of number of high quality idea units across projects. Note the lack of variation between different project categories.

followed through created a task on Critiki. Of the 31 creators, 6 were female, 14 were male and 11 projects were run by groups of two or more individuals. Projects came from 8 of the 12 categories on Kickstarter.

For the second study we recruited workers from Mobile-Works. For each critique task, 20 individuals were recruited and paid $0.25 (a total of $5 per project) for a critique. Project creators did not pay to use the Critiki system. However, creators were asked to fill out a short survey about their use and impressions of the system.

Study 2: Data Collection and Analysis
We collected qualitative and quantitative data throughout the month-long deployment. To evaluate the usefulness and efficacy of Critiki, we monitored the quality of the feedback from Critiki and surveyed users for their impressions of the system. The survey asked the users to grade the feedback that was gathered using a rubric for quality, to grade the usability of Critiki, and to grade the usefulness of the system.

Study 2: Results
We facilitated 31 creators of crowdfunding projects to gather feedback on their campaigns using the Critiki tool. 595 individual pieces of feedback were collected; an average of 19.2 responses per project. The full critique was returned to the project creator in around 48 hours.

Feedback Quality
Overall the quality of the critiques spanned from low to high quality, based on an informal appraisal. High quality critiques were often lengthy:

> "It took me a couple times to figure out what it was about. In the description it is trying to be too much. I think it should focus on the story or art, OR focus on the mental health issues addressed but not both and most importantly naming the reviewers on the first page there does not give it credibility but rather it seems to be trying to [sic] hard to prove something."

But other feedback was less specific and actionable, such as general suggestions: *"Show the device detecting bad air quality with cigarette smoke or diesel fumes."*, vague suggestions: *"Vedio [sic] is ok but the description needs some changes."*, and incomprehensible responses: *"ZKZJME"*.

Project Creator Impressions
We distributed a survey to the 31 project creators who tested Critiki with their crowdfunding project, 12 of whom responded (38.1%). Project creators were asked to rate the ease of use for creating and viewing results as well as the helpfulness of Critiki on a 7-point likert scale. 7/12 reported that Critiki was easy to create tasks on and that Critiki was easy to view feedback with . 10/12 respondents reported that they would use Critiki again, and 6/12 reported that they would recommend it to a friend.

Project creators were also asked to rate the usefulness, specificity and comprehensibility of Critiki feedback on 5-point likert scales. We also asked for open-ended thoughts about the Critiki system. Most of the respondents reported that the feedback was useful (7/12), specific (8/12), and comprehensible (10/12). Most respondents felt that Critiki should be used earlier in the crowdfunding process (8/12). When asked, one project creator wrote:

> "I didn't use it until after my campaign had launched, though, so my ability to make changes was low." (P1)

When asked about the helpfulness of Critiki in creating campaign material, respondents cited the value of outside opinions, and the objectivity of critiques as benefits. Several respondents did claim that irrelevant and low-quality responses were distracting. One respondent did not understand that Critiki was not going to provide financial contributions to his campaign. However several project creators highlighted the strengths of crowdsourcing feedback. One person wrote:

> "It offered me the perspective of the client as opposed to the perspective that is inherently mine. It was a good way to see what other see, honestly and with helpful ideas ... The person that helped me was great. He gave me some incredible feedback and I used several of his ideas." (P4)

Our small field deployment validated the need for the Critiki system by deploying with actual crowdfunding project creators. While our survey response sample size is small and potentially skewed by the "good subject effect," we found that crowdfunding project creators generally viewed Critiki as useful. In the future, testing with crowdfunders who are *preparing* campaigns, rather than individuals who have already launched campaigns will better validate whether Critiki helps project creators to succeed at crowdfunding.

DISCUSSION
Across two field deployments we evaluated Critiki with both actual crowdfunding project creators and in a randomized controlled experiment. In the first study we show how a properly designed scaffold can be applied to elicit a higher quantity of quality critiques than comparable open-response critiques (validated *H1*), despite there also being a higher quantity of low-quality critiques as well. We feel confident that while scaffolding produces more critiques (both high and low quality), that the benefits of more high quality critique outweigh the potentially negative experience of sifting through more low-quality critique. In our coding scheme the low quality critiques aren't necessarily bad advice, but rather are just

phrases to be skipped over before reaching specific feedback. In addition, we discuss later in this section some potential future approaches to removing low-quality feedback.

We also find that crowdworkers use example terminology when given in the question prompt (validated *H2*). We contribute to the crowdsourcing literature by describing the design and implementation of an effective system and demonstrating empirically how the design of tasks can lead to higher quality critiques. We see this work as a parallel thread to existing, algorithmic, crowdwork approaches [21, 22].

While we showed in the first study that scaffolded crowdworkers perform roughly at the level of crowdfunding experts, we find several other benefits of asking an anonymous crowd of workers for feedback. As we know from previous research, one potential benefit of asking a crowd of individuals for feedback is the ability to gather a wide range of responses [21]. We see this benefit in our study as well. Based on an informal evaluation, we find that all of the themes which experts brought up in their critiques existed somewhere within the 50 responses from MTurk workers. While not every critique discussed every theme, the crowdworkers more than spanned the thematic space that the experts discussed. In addition, crowdworkers bring a diverse set of opinions and provide more opportunities to find smaller mistakes. For example, in one of the projects one crowdworker discussed how the hand gestures the presenter was using were "incredibly distracting". While this is an obscure and possibly minority opinion, this critique might not have surfaced unless many individuals were consulted.

Another benefit of asking a crowd (as opposed to an expert) is the ability to quickly gather consensus [21]. While experts can have gravity attached to their judgments, the same can be given to many individuals saying the same thing. For example, in one of the projects, 22 out of the 50 crowdworkers mentioned that the lighting in the video was too dark. When reviewing all the feedback, this mistake emerges as a common theme. While we did not analyze the feedback for theme consensus within our feedback, we suggest that an interface which presents common critiques (rather than Critiki's current approach of presenting all the feedback, unfiltered) could be an interesting addition to the Critiki design.

In the second study we validated both the need and the efficacy of Critiki by deploying with 31 crowdfunding project creators. While we were not able to recruit people who were actively developing crowdfunding projects, we were able to test with people who had recently launched their project. However, this allowed us to further validate the need for a tool like Critiki in the early stages of crowdfunding planning, as several of the people we recruited claimed that Critiki would have been more useful earlier on in the campaign process. Interestingly, one of the experts we recruited actually inquired about using Critiki to gather feedback on his next crowdfunding project.

Scaffold Design
Due to the malleability of scaffolds and the success of scaffolds in many domains within the learning sciences [10], we feel that scaffolding techniques can be used to used to crowdsource critique in other online domains such as website design and presentation design. However, designing a quality scaffold is not quite as simple as asking a few general questions. Through the design process for Critiki we discovered that our best scaffolded questions for feedback asked for specific contributions as well as specific changes to be made.

When designing an effective scaffold it is also important to first understand the limitations of the system to be critiqued and potential pitfalls in critique. For example, in early iterations of the Critiki system, our scaffolds did not specify exactly what segment of the page was up for critique. This led to some critique opinions which might be valid, but not high quality suggestions. For example, some early critiques we gathered critiqued the "green color scheme" on the page. Unfortunately, on a Kickstarter page, this is not an editable element. To this end, scaffolds must be designed to guide the workers towards giving suggestions that are both relevant to the page and relevant to constraints of the design space.

Testing scaffolding with the crowd gives an opportunity to iteratively test and alter their scaffold. This is in contrast to deploying scaffolds with students in classrooms, where there is effectively only one opportunity to implement the scaffold correctly (the iteration cycle is at the semester or year level). However, with crowds we can rapidly test scaffolds to determine which parts are effective and which parts are not. This process was crucial to the success of the scaffolds we deployed with Critiki.

Limitations & Future Work
One limitation in our approach is data presentation. We currently present all the feedback that Critiki gathers grouped by question. This interface presents the answers to each question in a bulleted list, as opposed to a narrative or a thematic consensus. One major focus of additional work in this area will be to learn how to automatically separate high-quality critiques from low-quality ones, and to aggregate high quality critiques by theme. This might be an area where a crowdsourcing approach like find-fix-verify, or an algorithmic approach like natural language processing might help to separate and curate critiques into a narrative or checklist.

Future work will focus on implementing an iterative design for the overall task. Currently we ask all 20 crowdworkers to answer the same set of scaffolded questions. We do not know at what point there exist diminishing returns due to the potential thematic repetition in answers. If we understand the point of diminishing returns then it might be possible to design a series of different scaffolded tasks to fill the 20 responses, rather than one task for all 20.

CONCLUSION
We built and evaluated Critiki, a system for gathering design feedback for crowdfunding project creators. This research suggests that with proper design a crowdsourcing system can be built to provide a useful service (design feedback), to a population in need (crowdfunders), for a small amount of money ($5.00). Critiki lowers the bar to accessing high-quality critique, and in doing so it has the potential to help novice designers get critiques before they develop a personal

network of high-quality critiquers. We look forward to developing and deploying more Critiki-like tools and to continuously make it easier to access high quality critiques.

ACKNOWLEDGMENTS

We would like to thank all members of the Delta Lab for their helpful feedback through the process of this project. Special thanks to Darren Gergle and Haoqi Zhang for their detailed critiques along the way. This work was supported by the Segal Design Institute, NSF GFRP and NSF Grants IIS-1320693 & IIS-1217225.

REFERENCES

1. Amazon mechanical turk - welcome. https://www.mturk.com/mturk/welcome.

2. Stats kickstarter. http://www.kickstarter.com/help/stats.

3. Alagarai Sampath, H., Rajeshuni, R., and Indurkhya, B. Cognitively inspired task design to improve user performance on crowdsourcing platforms. CHI '14, ACM (New York, NY, USA, 2014), 3665–3674.

4. Amabile, T. M., Collins, M., Conti, R., Phillips, E., Picariello, M., Ruscio, J., and Whitney, D. Creativity in context: Update to the psychology of creativity, 1996.

5. Ambrose, S. A., Bridges, M. W., DiPietro, M., Lovett, M. C., and Norman, M. K. *How learning works: Seven research-based principles for smart teaching.* John Wiley & Sons, 2010.

6. Artemeva, N., and Logie, S. Introducing engineering students to intellectual teamwork: The teaching and practice of peer feedback in the professional communication classroom. *Language and Learning across the Disciplines 6*, 1 (2002), 62–85.

7. Belleflamme, P., Lambert, T., and Schwienbacher, A. Crowdfunding: Tapping the right crowd. *Journal of Business Venturing* (2013).

8. Bernstein, M. S., Brandt, J., Miller, R. C., and Karger, D. R. Crowds in two seconds: Enabling realtime crowd-powered interfaces. In *UIST 2011* (2011), 3342.

9. Cho, K. Commenting on writing: Typology and perceived helpfulness of comments from novice peer reviewers and subject matter experts. 260–294.

10. Cho, K., and Schunn, C. D. Scaffolded writing and rewriting in the discipline: A web-based reciprocal peer review system. 409–426.

11. Clark, R. Design document for a guided experiential learning course. *Final report on contract DAAD* (2004), 19–99.

12. Dow, S., Kulkarni, A., Klemmer, S., and Hartmann, B. Shepherding the crowd yields better work. CSCW '12, ACM (New York, NY, USA, 2012), 10131022.

13. Etter, V., Grossglauser, M., and Thiran, P. Launch hard or go home!: predicting the success of kickstarter campaigns. In *Proceedings of the first ACM conference on Online social networks*, ACM (2013), 177–182.

14. Fischer, G., Nakakoji, K., Ostwald, J., Stahl, G., and Sumner, T. Embedding computer-based critics in the contexts of design. In *Proceedings of the INTERACT'93 and CHI'93 Conference on Human Factors in Computing Systems*, ACM (1993), 157–164.

15. Gerber, E. M., and Hui, J. Crowdfunding: Motivations and deterrents for participation. *ACM Transactions on Computer-Human Interaction (TOCHI) 20*, 6 (2013), 34.

16. Gerber, E. M., Muller, M., Wash, R., Irani, L. C., Williams, A., and Churchill, E. F. Crowdfunding: an emerging field of research. In *CHI 2014*, ACM (2014), 1093–1098.

17. Greenberg, M. D., Pardo, B., Hariharan, K., and Gerber, E. Crowdfunding support tools: predicting success & failure. In *CHI'13 Extended Abstracts on Human Factors in Computing Systems* (2013), 18151820.

18. Hattie, J., and Timperley, H. The power of feedback. *Review of educational research 77*, 1 (2007), 81–112.

19. Huang, S.-W., and Fu, W.-T. Systematic analysis of output agreement games: Effects of gaming environment, social interaction, and feedback. 61801.

20. Hui, J. S., Greenberg, M. D., and Gerber, E. M. Understanding the role of community in crowdfunding work. CSCW (2014).

21. Kittur, A., Chi, E. H., and Suh, B. Crowdsourcing user studies with mechanical turk. In *Proceedings of the twenty-sixth annual SIGCHI conference on Human factors in computing systems* (2008), 453456.

22. Kittur, A., Nickerson, J. V., Bernstein, M., Gerber, E., Shaw, A., Zimmerman, J., Lease, M., and Horton, J. The future of crowd work. In *Proceedings of the 2013 conference on Computer supported cooperative work* (2013), 13011318.

23. Kokkalis, N., Huebner, J., Diamond, S., Becker, D., Chang, M., Lee, M., Schulze, F., Koehn, T., and Klemmer, S. R. Automatically providing action plans helps people complete tasks. In *Proceedings of the 4th Human Computation Workshop, HCOMP*, vol. 12 (2012).

24. Kulkarni, C., Wei, K. P., Le, H., Chia, D., Papadopoulos, K., Cheng, J., Koller, D., and Klemmer, S. R. Peer and self assessment in massive online classes. *ACM Transactions on Computer-Human Interaction (TOCHI) 20*, 6 (2013), 33.

25. Lasecki, W., Miller, C., Sadilek, A., Abumoussa, A., Borrello, D., Kushalnagar, R., and Bigham, J. Real-time captioning by groups of non-experts. In *Proceedings of the 25th annual ACM symposium on User interface software and technology*, ACM (2012), 23–34.

26. Lawson, B. *How designers think: the design process demystified.* Routledge, 2006.

27. Luther, K., Tolentino, J.-L., Wu, W., Pavel, A., Bailey, B. P., Agrawala, M., Hartmann, B., and Dow, S. P. Structuring, aggregating, and evaluating crowdsourced design critique. In *Proceedings of the 18th ACM Conference on Computer Supported Cooperative Work & Social Computing*, CSCW '15, ACM (New York, NY, USA, 2015), 473–485.

28. Marlow, J., and Dabbish, L. From rookie to all-star: Professional development in a graphic design social networking site. In *Proceedings of the 17th ACM Conference on Computer Supported Cooperative Work & Social Computing*, CSCW '14, ACM (New York, NY, USA, 2014), 922–933.

29. Mitra, T., and Gilbert, E. The language that gets people to give: Phrases that predict success on kickstarter. CSCW (2014).

30. Muller, M., Geyer, W., Soule, T., and Steven, D. Grassroots innovation and collaboration through enterprise crowdfunding. In *Seventh International AAAI Conference on Weblogs and Social Media* (2013).

31. Narula, P., Gutheim, P., Rolnitzky, D., Kulkarni, A., and Hartmann, B. MobileWorks: a mobile crowdsourcing platform for workers at the bottom of the pyramid.

32. Reiser, B. J. Scaffolding complex learning: The mechanisms of structuring and problematizing student work. *The Journal of the Learning Sciences 13*, 3 (2004), 273–304.

33. Ross, J., Irani, L., Silberman, M., Zaldivar, A., and Tomlinson, B. Who are the crowdworkers?: shifting demographics in mechanical turk. In *CHI'10 Extended Abstracts on Human Factors in Computing Systems*, ACM (2010), 2863–2872.

34. Rzeszotarski, J. M., and Morris, M. R. Estimating the social costs of friendsourcing. In *Proceedings of the SIGCHI Conference on Human Factors in Computing Systems*, CHI '14, ACM (New York, NY, USA, 2014), 2735–2744.

35. Shute, V. J. Focus on formative feedback. *Review of educational research 78*, 1 (2008), 153–189.

36. Van Merriënboer, J. J., and Kirschner, P. A. *Ten steps to complex learning: A systematic approach to four-component instructional design.* Routledge, 2012.

37. Xu, A., Huang, S., and Bailey, B. Voyant: Generating structured feedback on visual designs using a crowd of non-experts. In *Proc. CSCW, 2014* (2014).

38. Xu, A., Yang, X., Rao, H., Fu, W.-T., Huang, S.-W., and Bailey, B. P. Show me the money! an analysis of project updates during crowdfunding campaigns.

A Modular Approach to Promote Creativity and Inspiration in Search

Alice Thudt
InnoVis Group, University of
Calgary, Canada
alice.thudt@gmail.com

Uta Hinrichs
SACHI Group, University of
St Andrews, UK
uh3@st-andrews.ac.uk

Sheelagh Carpendale
InnoVis Group, University of
Calgary, Canada
sheelagh@ucalgary.ca

ABSTRACT

When searching through collections of books or written texts, the efficient yet limiting query paradigm is still the most dominant entry point. Previous work characterizes search processes in various contexts and describes them as integral and closely related to creative endeavours. We revisit this work from a design perspective, proposing guidelines for versatile search interfaces that are based on a modular approach to search. Inspired by aspects of search in physical environments, our recommendations address learning, creativity, inspiration, and pleasure as positive aspects of (book) search. Based on in-depth interviews with library patrons about search practises in physical and digital environments and drawing from previous work on search behaviour, we discuss search patterns as modular constructs consisting of micro-strategies. We illustrate how the structure of these patterns is highly flexible. Much like creative processes, they fluidly evolve based on learning and ideation during search, particularly in physical environments. This modular perspective provides a basis for designing interfaces that facilitate creative approaches to search in digital environments.

Author Keywords

Book Search; Creativity; Search Interface; Qualitative Study

ACM Classification Keywords

H.5.m. Information Interfaces and Presentation (e.g. HCI): Miscellaneous

INTRODUCTION

With the transition of many information services to the digital realm, search is no longer just the domain of knowledge workers—it directly impacts everyday life. Search interfaces have become the go-to point for finding books, articles, recipes, and people with shared interests, and are also used for inspiration and ideation. This has led to an expanding interest in the nature of search from a wide variety of fields.

Research in library and information sciences has recognized search as a complex and fluid process that cannot be satisfied by simple query-response paradigms [3, 28, 47, 53]. A large

body of literature has investigated information behaviour in professional [1, 2, 3, 6, 14, 31, 32] and leisure contexts [10, 18, 30, 42]. Research has also considered search as part of creative processes [24, 32, 46] as well as a creative process in itself [28, 29]. Furthermore, exploratory search [35, 53] and search for pleasure (e.g., [22]) have been discussed, alongside design considerations for versatile interfaces that go beyond targeted search [21, 46, 32, 51, 53, 56].

Despite this, people still predominately face query-based interfaces that hamper the fluid, complex, and creative nature of search endeavours when searching through book collections online. In this paper we discuss the characteristics of search strategies and processes from a design perspective, bridging insights from information sciences, information retrieval, creativity and design research, and HCI. Similar to Lee et al., we consider search to be a creative process [28, 29] inherent in everyday creativity and individual knowledge construction [4, 23]. We therefore investigate how knowledge about book search can facilitate the design of interfaces that promote versatile and complex search processes and, as part of this, learning, inspiration, social endeavours, and pleasure.

We interviewed library patrons about their approaches to book search as an activity performed frequently in professional and leisure contexts, as well as using digital and physical search environments. Participants described a broad range of search behaviours, influenced by the characteristics of the digital or physical information space. They describe their search endeavours as flexible, often complex, search processes that fluidly evolve as learning, ideation, and creative thinking take place. We illustrate how these *search processes* can be supported through four *micro-strategies*: querying, linking, scanning, and assessment. While similar strategies have been discussed in previous work [1, 3, 14, 28, 32], we propose these four strategies as the core modules that compose many different forms of book search. We illustrate how considering their composition directly informs the design of flexible search interfaces, merging the advantages of digital and physical search environments. Based on this modular approach to search, we provide guidelines for supporting fluidity in search processes through continuous navigation, search histories, thus promoting sensuous search experiences.

BOOK SEARCH AS A COMPLEX CREATIVE PROCESS

Search has long been recognized as a special case of problem solving [33], the "problem" being a need for certain information. However, with the increasing predominance of search activities conducted in many contexts ranging from professional to everyday scenarios, recent research has begun to consider search and exploration as positive activities that can (and should) be pleasurable in order to promote creative discovery and sensemaking [12, 51]. In fact, research suggests that search is closely related to creativity and ideation [28, 29, 24] where tactics are fluidly applied, combined, and adjusted in order to reach a certain goal [1, 21, 29].

Based on our interviews that focused on book search in professional and leisure contexts as well as in digital and physical environments, we describe how flexible and creative search processes are formed by four basic micro-strategies. We discuss implications for design suggested by this modular view on search. Our work builds on a vast body of research that has investigated human information behaviour including cognitive and affective aspects, information needs and processes, as well as creativity as it relates to information seeking.

Models of Search Behaviour

A number of models of search behaviour have been developed based on the analysis of knowledge workers' information seeking (see [21, chpt. 3] for a comprehensive overview). These models can be distinguished based on the goals and granularity in which they classify search behaviours. Some of these models reflect on stages of the iterative process of search, from the identification of an information need, to the query formulation, to the result review [25, 36, 45, 50]. Others have investigated higher-level strategies [3, 14, 25, 34, 32], including, for instance, *chaining* [14], *footnote chasing*, and *citation searching* [3] to find related resources.

Bates introduced one of the earliest facilitation/teaching models for professional reference search that distinguished four categories of low-level tactics with 26 individual tactics in total, including, e.g., *correcting* the formulation of a search request, *surveying* possible search terms, or *reducing* the number of search terms to expand the number of search results [1]. Based on this model, further research investigated search tactics in professional contexts [7, 31, 32, 48, 55]. Similar tactics and strategies are reflected in our research, however, we expand on previous work by exploring search processes from a design perspective. Our work focuses on the flexible formation and composition of micro-strategies which is driven by the search purpose and guided by ideation and learning.

The Context of Search

Previous research typically distinguishes between professional and leisure search contexts. Professional search is conducted by domain experts and knowledge workers [1, 6, 40], while leisure search is characterized by personal goals such as pleasure or mastery [22, 30, 39, 42]. A range of literature has investigated professional search behaviours and processes [1, 2, 6, 9, 11, 14, 17, 25, 26, 31, 32], e.g., bibliographic and reference search [1], search in digital libraries and on the internet [6, 37, 48], video search [55], and search in creative professions such as architecture [32]. Studies have found that leisurely search, more than professional search, follows personal curiosities [10, 18, 20, 30], however, most research on leisurely information search (e.g., fiction reading) focuses on selection strategies rather than search processes [43, 44, 49]. For instance, while some studies have investigated how people search for fiction books [40, 43, 44, 49], insights do not go beyond broad strategy categories such as "known-item search" or "browsing". Considering both digital and physical search environments, our work contributes the investigation of search processes as they evolve as part of book search in general. We aim at informing the design of search interfaces that can support a large variety of activities as part of both professional and leisurely book search.

While search patterns may differ depending on the context [40, 55], our findings indicate that people do not necessarily consciously distinguish between professional and leisure book search. Therefore, we focus on how the characteristics of the search environment (i.e., its digital vs. physical context) influence search and how people experience this as part of their search endeavours.

Search & Creativity

Previous research has highlighted parallels between search and creative processes. Shneiderman considers search as part of the creative process and describes how software tools can support creative tasks [46]. Kaufman and Beghetto introduced "mini-c" as an aspect of creativity that focuses on "the dynamic, interpretative process of constructing personal knowledge and understanding" [23, p.3]. They highlighted the relationship between learning and creativity [4]. Information seeking as a process of individual knowledge construction can therefore be considered as an instance of "mini-c". Lee et al. have investigated the relationship between creative and information seeking processes more closely and coined the term "creative information seeking" [28, 29]. Combining models describing the creative process [19] and information seeking behaviour [14], they propose a six-stage model, where individual stages can be combined depending on the complexity of the search task [29]. Expanding on this idea of creativity as a characteristic and *driver* of information seeking activities [32], we define micro-strategies as modules of search processes that, through interface design, can be supported and combined in versatile ways to enable opportunities for learning, creativity, and ideation.

Designing Search Interfaces

Alongside research on search behaviour and its relation to creative processes, a range of considerations on how to design search interfaces exist. Shneiderman argues for visual search interfaces that highlight relations between search results, promote new associations and exploration through filtering, and support of search histories [46, 47]. On a more concrete level, Hearst provides general design guidelines for digital search interfaces. Building upon search behaviour models, her guidelines address design aspects such as the importance of supporting versatile queries and query refinement, showing document details within the search result list, highlighting the relation between query terms and search results, and integrating search and the navigation of search results [21]. She also discusses the importance of visual and interaction aesthetics to promote pleasurable and prolonged search activities. Distinguishing four categories of search interface features (input, control, informational, and personalizable features), Wilson provides a feature-centric approach to designing search interfaces [56]. His 26 design recommendations largely overlap with Hearst's guidelines. White and Roth's design recommendations focus on *exploratory* search interfaces in particular [53]. While several of these recommendations overlap with those by Hearst and Wilson, the latter particularly emphasize the importance of supporting learning and sensemaking through the search interface design to help people tailor and steer their exploration into relevant directions.

While existing design guidelines are fairly concrete when it comes to supporting particular aspects of search such as query refinement, others, such as "supporting learning and understanding", or "offering visualizations to support insight/decision making" [53], remain at a more abstract level. Given the flexible and diverse character of search activities, we propose a new approach to designing search interfaces that aims at supporting versatile search processes by developing design considerations directly from the micro-strategies that form these processes. In this way, a large variety of search scenarios and purposes can be supported, and individual search activities can be dynamically revised and refined as new knowledge and ideas develop during search.

STUDY METHODOLOGY
Our interview-based study focused on book search as it occurs in both digital and physical environments. Our interview questions were deliberately kept broad and open-ended to tease out people's experiences in different search contexts. For instance, we asked participants about their general approach to book search, that is, activities that they typically apply to find books and textual information for work-related and personal interests, in both digital and physical spaces. We asked them to describe search strategies in detail based on examples, the factors of digital and physical information spaces they appreciated or found annoying, and their general experience and attitude toward search endeavours.

Study Setup & Participants
The study was conducted at a university library, where we interviewed patrons about their book exploration habits. Ten library patrons were invited ad-hoc for a spontaneous interview (quoted as A#, five female). In addition, ten participants were recruited and invited to the library for an interview (quoted as R#, three female). Recruitment allowed for in-depth interviews and expanded our participant population beyond visitors of the university library. Recruited participants' ages ranged from 20–60 years; six of them were university students from different disciplines and all had used computers for more than five years. No demographic data was collected from library patrons in order to limit their time commitment.

Data Collection & Analysis
All 20 interviews were audio recorded and transcribed. The transcripts were coded independently by two researchers following a thematic analysis approach [5]. Two coding passes were applied. In the first pass we coded participants' statements about specific search and exploration approaches, how they manifest in different contexts, and their motivations for book searches. We further coded for experiences and problems in the different (digital and physical) search environments. The codes from this first pass were often quite specific, and were collaboratively analyzed to extract individual strategies, compound processes, and motivations that drive participants' search habits. Through this analysis, higher-level categories emerged: common strategies, including querying, linking, scanning, following recommendations,

and reading book previews; desired search outcomes, satisfying a particular reading experience, or locating material on a topic of interest; and complex search processes that are a combination of low-level search strategies.

The resulting final coding schema was applied in a second coding pass. A subsequent analysis resulted in a modular view on book search under the following themes: *Micro-Strategies*, *Search Purposes*, and *Search Processes*. We discuss our findings in the following three sections.

FINDINGS
To set the context for discussing participants' search strategies and processes in-depth, we first report on the general scenarios in which our participants conduct their searches.

Search Contexts. In our interviews we deliberately encouraged a free contemplation of book search. We found that 95% of our participants described their processes independent of the search context (professional vs. leisure). While participants stated that their search processes may differ depending on the contexts, only one participant clearly separated between professional and personal book search. Our design considerations therefore address both work-related and leisure book search, rather than contrasting them.

Environments. Participants commented on a variety of search environments including public and academic libraries, bookstores and common digital search environments (library catalogues, online book stores, academic and general purpose search engines). While all participants mentioned the use of digital book search engines, only one used *exclusively* digital environments. Our findings show how micro-strategies and processes manifest in digital and physical environments and highlight their problems and benefits.

In the following three sections we deconstruct search into its basic components. We describe micro-strategies that we identified through our interviews. We outline search and exploration purposes and illustrate in sample scenarios how these purposes drive the fluid composition of micro-strategies into complex search processes. We then discuss the design space that this modular approach to search opens up.

MICRO-STRATEGIES
There is a large body of work that discussed lower-level activities of information search processes (e.g. [1, 3, 14, 25]). As part of this work, different terminologies were used. Bates defines the term search *tactics*, i.e., low-level *moves* that are applied to further and revise a search [1]. The terms "search tactic" and "moves " have been used relatively consistently to describe low-level search activities [48, 55], however, Fidel introduces "moves" as part of search tactics and strategies [15]. The term *search strategy* is used in various ways, sometimes for the search as a whole [1] and sometimes to describe activities that are less specific than search tactics, but are still at a relatively low level of granularity [3, 14] (e.g., area scanning, author searching, and citation searching as search strategies [3]). While some discussions of search strategies suggest their sequential character [25], others highlight that, depending on the search tasks, they can be combined in different ways, and often iteratively [14, 28, 29].

Our interviews revealed search strategies that are similar to the ones discussed in previous literature. We define *micro-strategies* as components from which a search process is composed. Micro-strategies are (1) *abstract* and thus apply to a variety of scenarios, (2) *consistent* in their level of granularity, and (3) sufficiently *descriptive* to imply interface design guidelines. We describe these micro-strategies in the light of previous literature and emphasize how each of them is supported in digital and physical environments—an aspect that our interview analysis contributes to the field.

QUERYING, i.e, issuing an inquiry (e.g, a question, keyword, title, or author name) to a system, person, or other point of reference was mentioned by all participants. This does not come as a surprise—querying as part of search has been extensively discussed in previous literature [1, 8, 34, 35]. Most digital search interfaces support querying well: typing a term into a text field produces a list of results. Querying can be further facilitated through design, e.g., by suggesting related terms (see [21, chpt.1] for more details). Seven of our participants also described querying in bookstores or libraries by asking a staff member to help them find a book or section.

Queries for specific books are typically performed by title and/or author.

Less targeted queries by topic or keyword can produce much larger result sets.

LINKING describes strategies in which the information seeker is led from a "seed item" to one or more related items. Kwasnik describes digital browsing as *"movement in a connected space"* [26] guided by links. This can be either *item-to-item linking* between individual books, or *item-to-set linking*, connecting a single book to a book collection.

Item-to-item linking has been discussed, e.g., as *forward* and *backward chaining* [14, 28] and *citation searching and footnote chasing* [3]. Participants' statements confirm that citation linking is applied digitally and physically. People also follow other links between individual books in a physical space by browsing adjacent books on a bookshelf. Digitally, recommender systems can provide item-to-item links based on peoples browsing or purchasing behaviour.

In *item-to-set linking*, an individual book leads to a *set* of books, for instance, by the same author or about a related topic. In physical environments the location of a specific book on a shelf can be considered as a connection to related adjacent material. Our participants mentioned the use of a variety of such linking features in digital search environments, for example, the use of author and keyword links to find related books sets.

SCANNING describes strategies in which a set of books is skimmed visually or through physical movement to gain an overview in preparation for selecting particular items. In contrast to assessment strategies (see next paragraph), scanning focuses on visual aspects of books that are readily

available without further interaction (e.g., title and author visible on the book spine or in a digital result list). For example, the book's title alone can provide an idea about its topic to enable quick pre-selection. Besides textual features, visual and aesthetic characteristics of books can act as eye catchers. Participants also mentioned an attraction to books that evoke personal associations or visually stood out from the rest of the collection. They highlighted the importance of the spatial layout of items to allow taking in their visual cues, and particularly lauded physical environments for their visual richness.

Scanning has been discussed in the context of browsing [9, 14, 34], e.g., when trying to locate a known book in a collection, (*linear and selective scanning* as part of *search browsing* [34]), getting an overview of a collection (*semi-directed* or *general purpose browsing* [34]), or for more open-ended explorations (*serendipity* or *casual browsing* [34, 35]). *Area scanning* has been referred to as an activity in which the searcher looks at adjacent books [3].

ASSESSMENT describes strategies in which an individual item is inspected for its relevance to the search purpose. Similar strategies have been previously discussed as *differentiating*, *evaluation* or *exclusion/negation*, in which particular items are ruled out [35], or *selecting*, in which useful items are chosen [31]. Our participants frequently mentioned assessment strategies as part of their book search. In contrast to *scanning* (gaining an overview and identifying books of potential interest, see above), assessment strategies include a qualitative judgement of individual items to make an informed choice. While Makri discusses assessment as a high-level strategy that includes *selecting*, *distinguishing*, *browsing*, and *extracting* [32], we consider assessment as a micro-strategy that can include meta-level and content-level investigation of found items, similar to what Buchanan and McKay discuss as "closed book" and "open book" assessment [8].

Meta-level assessment is based on a book's metadata (e.g., title, author, abstract or citation rank). When using digital search interfaces, participants stated that they assess items based on their position in a result list, where the ordering of search results acts as a measure for relevance of the book content. Participants further mentioned that the "look and feel" of a book influences if they acquire it or not. In particular, physical criteria can hint at a particular reading experience.

Content-level assessment considers the book's content or writing style, e.g. by skimming through it. While physical books provide direct access to their content, book previews provided by some digital platforms fulfill a similar purpose. Reading reviews is another content-level assessment strategy. Participants particularly value reviews if selection criteria are difficult to assess through the book's metadata.

Scanning and assessment can be considered as components of what Marshall and Shipman have coined as *"information triage"* [37]. With our design-oriented approach to deciphering search in mind, we aimed at providing more specific distinctions between different strategies that fall into this category.

SEARCH & EXPLORATION PURPOSES

Previous research has suggested that search can consist of fluid, sometimes iterative processes depending on the search purpose [29]. Our research expands on this by illustrating the diversity and complexity of such processes based on our micro-strategies. Our findings confirm that book explorations cover a range of purposes beyond well-defined information needs, as indicated in previous research on exploratory search and everyday life information seeking [8, 22, 35, 39, 53]. Specifically, we identify four search purposes that go beyond finding a known book: finding books within constrained criteria, discovery of new topics, knowledge and understanding, and a rewarding, inspirational exploration experience.

Constrained Criteria

Similarly to Buchanan and McKay [8], we found searches for new books within more or less specific criteria to be common in both leisure and professional contexts. The relation to a known book can help to specify the nature of the desired book: *"I want a book that is related to this [known book] but I don't know exactly what I want."* [R6]. Library classification systems support this purpose by organizing books based on content similarity. Searches with broader criteria (e.g. topic or genre) are experienced as more difficult, especially with common query approaches that can lead to an abundance of results: *"If I was looking for something like non-academic literature it is hard. I get all kinds of websites, non-relevant searches and stuff, just because a keyword overlaps. I can't read in there, it's too much. [...] I give up."* [A11].

Participants also described searches for books that encompass a particular reading experience. Such criteria are particularly difficult to express in a query and our participants experienced these searches as cumbersome in digital environments: *"Let's say I want to read a book for pleasure, but where do I start? Which author? What language? What subject?"* [A8].

Topic Discovery

An even more open-ended purpose of book search is the discovery of books on new, unknown topics. Here, the purpose is to be inspired; to identify new topics of interest and to discover related books: *"I'm really enthusiastic to find that kind of untouched areas."* [R3]. The driver of such open-ended exploration is a general *"curiosity, I guess, or just thirst for more. I don't know, I just want to keep discovering."* [R10].

Participants described such open-ended explorations for "something different" as better supported in physical libraries or bookstores than in digital search interfaces: *"I really didn't know what keywords I should put in to find what I wanted, because the thing is, I really didn't know exactly what I wanted. So this is the problem—if you know, [what you are looking for] it's easy, but if you don't, if you just want to read something different, it's kind of hard."* [R6]. Participants bemoaned a loss of opportunities for open-ended explorations and serendipitous discoveries with the transition of book collections to the digital realm: *"So that kind of sense of digging through the shelves, looking for hidden treasures [...] seems to be just going away."* [R10].

Knowledge & Understanding

Some book explorations that participants described follow the purpose of gaining an understanding or furthering knowledge about a particular topic, rather than locating one or multiple books. In these searches, books become a portal to the desired information but are not the actual target of the search: *"I would also like to have a digital copy, so I could search for things [within the book] easily, to find stuff that I'm looking for."* [R6]. The focus is on the information bits hidden within books, not necessarily on the books themselves.

Another search outcome may also be information toward a broader question: *"I have my research question. That is my query, and then I always have a thing I want to prove in mind. [...] And then I go with that book that really fits, what I want to prove. And then I go and I'll say: 'Oh this would be really great backup information or this would be something to add to it.'"* [R7]. Physical books lend themselves to quickly getting a content overview and, hence, to learn about a topic: *"When you have it in your hand, it is easier to flip through it, it's like you can [adjust] the speed or the slowness with which you go through it. [...] Whereas online previews are like clicking one page, one page, one page."* [R5].

Exploration Experience & Inspiration

Our interviews also pointed to a form of book exploration where the purpose is neither acquisition of books nor furthering knowledge. Instead, the exploration experience can be rewarding in itself, especially if the environment or collection is inviting: *"For the joy, yes. I do that [going to a bookstore] for the joy."* [R4]. *"So just finding a whole group of them [comics] and just being 'Oh wow, let's go through all these...', yeah, there's something to that."* [R10].

Participants usually turned to physical environments such as bookstores when aiming for a rewarding stroll through a book collection: *"Sometimes I wish libraries were kind of more like bookstores. If you go into [bookstore name] you'll always see signs saying 'Adult Fiction'. [...] In academic libraries I feel like, sometimes I go in there and it's always just call numbers. And that's great for librarians, because they know what that means, but I'm just a user, so I don't know what that means."* [R7]. The focus on efficiency in digital interfaces neglects the support of exploration solely for *"joy"* [R4] as the following statements points out: *"I guess the idea of like a shopping expedition to go look for something, like that kind of fun is gone. But I guess it's more efficient to just have everything at your fingertip at home."* [R10].

CONSTRUCTION OF COMPLEX SEARCH PROCESSES

The purposes described above drive the combination of micro-strategies into search processes. Our interviews indicate the fluidity and complexity of some search processes where even the initial purpose can change on the fly. In the following, we illustrate the construction of a range of processes from micro-strategies according to scenarios extracted from our interviews. We further discuss learning, social aspects and pleasure as concepts that are an integral part of search as a creative endeavour.

Process Composition by Example

The exploration processes we extracted from our interviews indicate a range of complexity. Targeted search purposes (→*Known Book* or *Constrained Criteria*) are based on straightforward processes with a simple combination of micro-strategies. The more open-ended the purpose of a book search (→*Topic Discovery* or *Knowledge & Understanding*), the more complex and iterative the search process becomes.

Known-book search is the simplest type of search and often accomplished by *querying*. Targeted search processes with the purpose of satisfying *Constrained Criteria* typically require a combination of micro-strategies as illustrated in Scenario 1: *"When I read in the train, I really know what I want to read, and I read almost every time the same kind of book. So I know which author I like, or which kind of book I want. [...] I pick the book because I know the author, or it's just a new best-seller. I pick the book, I read the summary. Probably, I look into the book on two or three pages, if I like how the author writes, and then I buy it or not."* [R9].

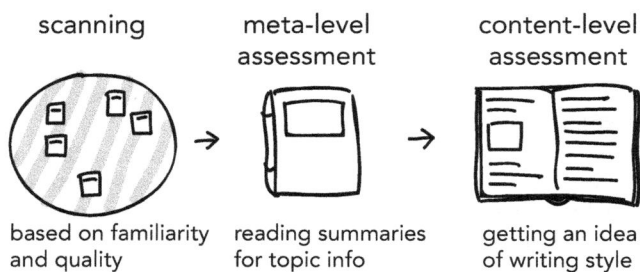

scanning	meta-level assessment	content-level assessment
based on familiarity and quality	reading summaries for topic info	getting an idea of writing style

Scenario 1. Finding books within certain criteria.

This participant has a clear idea of the type of book she wants to read in a particular context (the train) without having a particular title in mind. She first *scans* available sources for books that promise a certain reading experience. Familiarity drives her scanning activity as she has a habitualized understanding of what she is looking for. She then performs a *meta-level assessment* of the topic by reading a book's blurb, followed by a *content-level assessment* of the writing style to determine if the book matches the desired reading experience. This process can be repeated until one or several books with the desired criteria are located. Note that *scanning*, *meta-*, and *content-level assessment* are often applied in sequence, as part of more complex search processes.

Search processes aimed at *Topic Discovery* or *Knowledge & Understanding* are often characterized by more complex and iterative combinations of micro-strategies. The fluidity of such exploratory searches has been described in the context of knowledge work [17, 29, 34, 53] and everyday information seeking [39]. Based on our interviews, we have identified patterns of *narrowing* and *expanding* as part of these search processes, similar to elaboration and reduction applied in creative design processes to arrive at the most promising result [27]. For example, when talking about a typical search process in the professional context, one participant described how he iteratively specifies queries as he learns from previous query results: *"When I have a topic, and I probably have little idea of what the topic is about, and [when] I start to look for it, I look for the topic in general, and then there are books showing up. So I go through the summaries, so I start to learn something about the topic, and there are a lot of little ideas what I can pick pretty fast. And if I found something what is*

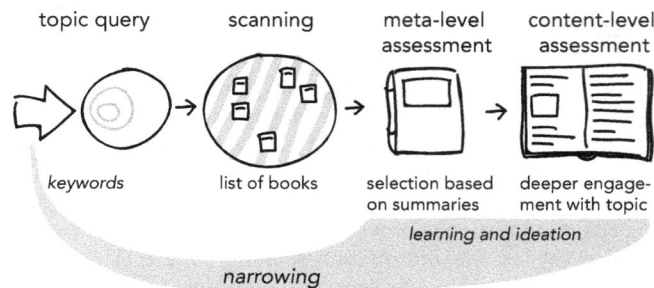

Scenario 2. Iteratively refining and narrowing queries.

more the focus what I have to write about or whatever, then I can go deeper into it, and I can pick other keywords." [R9].

As illustrated in Scenario 2, the search starts with a topic *query* and *scanning* of the result list. The following *meta-* and *content-level assessment* of books leads to ideas for more specific keywords to initiate new queries. This process allows the participant to slowly hone in on his topic of interest.

Other examples we found can be understood as inversions of the previous scenario, where participants started by *querying* for a particular book, but from there expanded their search by *linking* to related books by the same author or with related keywords (see Scenario 3). In this process, the purpose of the search changes from a *Known Book* search to a search by *Constrained Criteria*, or even for *Topic Discovery*: *"Sometimes I follow, because they have keywords, so if it [the book] is in the subject area and I need to expand my search, I'll put in the specific author and then I'll find out what kinds of areas they are listed under. And then I can click on that link and then find out what else is available. So again it's clicking through the links, that are already supplied."* [A9].

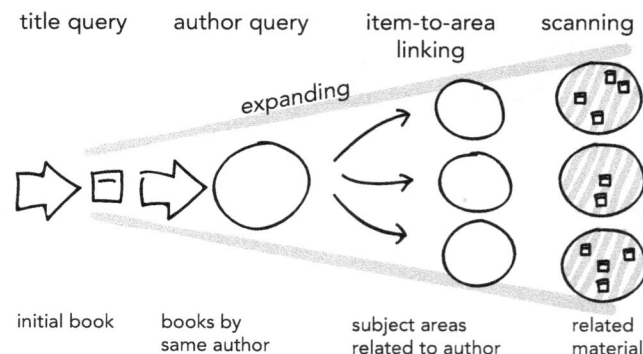

Scenario 3. Expanding the search criteria.

Participants reported on these types of search processes when using digital tools as well as in libraries and bookstores: *"I'll have my specific target [when I go to a library] like I said, but then I'll always go and find more stuff as I'm there."* [R7]. Search processes in which the result space is expanded by linking to related books or topic areas, and in which the purpose of the search shifts away from the initial target, are often accompanied by serendipitous discoveries. Participants described these search experiences as quite positive: *"I appreciate being able to be pleasantly surprised, I appreciate being shown things that I might not otherwise be looking for.*

But I'm also worried of being taken too far off course." [R5]. This statement suggests that search expansions can also be accompanied by hesitation to move too far away from the initial purpose of the search and a fear of getting lost. Interestingly, our participants expressed these negative feelings typically with regard to digital search tools: *"[You] get lost in the database and then do not really know where you are as far as what you've searched. It's kind of hard to look back."* [A3].

Participants also described types of fluid search processes which they understand as a linear exploration of a book collection on a path from one book to the next (see Scenario 4): *"It's like you search for one thing and it leads you [down] a path. And sometimes I spend half an hour looking for something when I found what I needed in the first five minutes, but I ended up continuing, [...] just like seeing what else there was that was related or connected."* [R5].

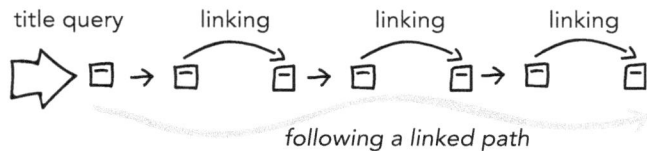

topic query   scanning   assessment

opening links   overload of information

Scenario 5. Separate collecting and learning process.

title query   linking   linking   linking

following a linked path

Scenario 4. Following a linked exploration path.

Our findings further demonstrate the creative nature of exploratory search processes including their relation to learning, social aspects, and rewarding experiences.

Search as a Creative Learning Process

Our analysis shows that iterative and evolving searches [3] are often intertwined with learning and ideation. Assessing search results leads to increasing knowledge about a search topic, which, in turn, results in new ideas on how to refine or expand the search (see Scenarios 2 & 3). It is the *early* assessment that aids the learning and ideation process, however, the instantaneous character of digital environments can invite search behaviours that do not include early assessment: *"On the internet, I put things into a search engine, [and] I end up following the links. That's usually how I find stuff. The problem with that though is, there are sometimes so many links that I never spend enough time actually looking at the results that come up. [...If] I just stopped and looked at the results and read some more in detail, [...] I would probably get some deeper information and understand it better [...] You click on links because it's so easy. And you end up collecting so many. And sometimes they are just repeats or they aren't actually that useful. And then you just have an overload of information. [...] Electronically things are instantaneous: you can get so much [...] but if you don't process it, that's as good as not getting information at all."* [A9].

In this linear process search and learning are separate. The participant starts her search by *querying*, *scans* the results, and collects items for further *assessment* (see Scenario 5). While she is aware that an early content-level assessment could inspire further explorations and benefit learning, she does not assess the items until the collection is complete. Digital tools encourage this behaviour which leads to an overwhelming amount of potentially irrelevant collected sources.

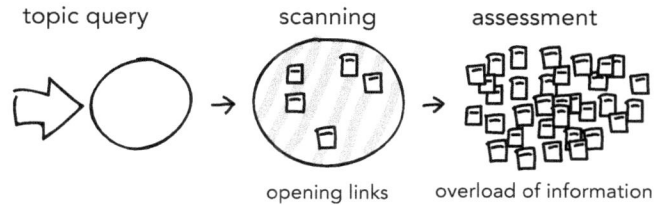

The same participant stated that, in contrast, in a physical library, her search process is more intertwined with learning (comparable to Scenario 2): *"It's the physical weight of things and the physical distance between things that slows you down. That's not a bad thing necessarily. It gives you time to really think about: 'Do I need this information? Is the information useful?' And it forces you to stop and first look at it before you go to the next one. [...] If you are forced to take the physical steps to get to the place and then look at the book and really think about it, then that makes you more efficient than a whole bunch of hits."* [A9]. In physical libraries the weight of books practically enforces a content-level assessment as part of the search process, promoting information processing and learning. As the statement indicates, the time that it takes to walk up to bookshelves, physically moving through the information space, is actually appreciated as *incubation time* that promotes thinking and ideation [19, 28]. While digital search engines facilitate fast and convenient access to vast information sources, they do not promote content assessment. This comes at the expense of learning and ideation processes.

Social Aspects of Search

Social influences on exploratory search have been previously mentioned [30, 35, 46, 47, 53]. Similarly, our participants talked about seeking out resources curated by individuals or groups with particular domain knowledge or status: *"When I want to find things that are more specific, I usually look for a source, or a collection point, or a blog, or somebody who tweets about it, that I can follow."* [R5]. Curated resources are particularly useful as starting points for finding books on specific topics, or defined by "soft" characteristics that are difficult to specify, e.g., concerning a particular reading experience: *"I think, what I've done before [is] find a group of people that I know are interested in that type of literature and then I look at their website."* [A11]. Recommendations by friends or colleagues are considered most trustworthy and relevant: *"I'm usually advised to look at these books, so by my supervisor, or, you know, my friends."* [R4].

Annotations in physical books encountered during content-level assessment can also enhance search as a social experience: *"There is one book in this library, that people have written in, and there is, like, different notes, that people have made. And you can see the hand writing of several different readers—I've even written in it. [...] and that's part of like the heritage of that book."* [A9]. Such handwritten annotations make visible how people have explored a book. They leave evidence which information pieces other people found important and help the knowledge building process.

Search as a Rewarding Experience

The most open-ended book explorations are driven by the purpose of engaging in a rewarding *exploration experience*. Participants describe these types of searches as highly opportunistic, serendipitous, and driven by curiosity without implying a particular order of strategies. While generally similar types of micro-strategies are applied, they are carried out with a focus on visual and sensory aspect of the books.

During experience-driven explorations, participants described *assessment* strategies, such as content skimming and looking at book covers, that are also common in targeted book search. However, in this context, the focus is not on pre-defined criteria. Instead, books can catch people's attention based on visual aspects: *"Sometimes the really funny looking covers are what attracts me in the first place. They don't look like a good book, they are like the two cent cheap novels, but I think that the covers are really funny so I'll take them off the shelf. And there's like, you know, books from the 1920s that have a different feel than the books from 2011. So, I don't know, there is something different about it."* [A9]. Here, a book's content or credibility, even the anticipated reading experience is of secondary relevance. Instead, the experience value lies in its visual appearance (e.g., a *"funny cover"* [A9]), or its physical appeal or even smell: *"What I like is the smell of a new book."* [R9]. The exploration experience itself takes priority and applied criteria opportunistically form, evolve, and change as part of the exploration.

In searches when the main purpose is a pleasurable and inspiring exploration experience, the visual presentation of a book collection plays an important role. A layout that enables scanning and meta-level assessment of visual and tangible characteristics of books as well as the aesthetic appeal of the search environment can inspire and enhance the exploration experience, as the following statements illustrate: *"If you're going through the stacks, it's harder to browse, cause they are, like, closer together, and you have to look closely at the titles. But if they're just laid on a table in front of you it's easy to kind of just scan your eye over them, and then if something catches your eye you grab it. [...] I really like to browse by colour, that's something that I feel like, when I'm at the library for real. I'm looking at different colours, things that catch my eye. [...] It's like aesthetically pleasing, it's kind of nice to look at, so you want to explore that more."* [R7].

Our interviews indicate that physical spaces offer a more appealing environment for pleasurable and rewarding explorations. In addition to their visual richness, libraries and bookstores provide manageable collection sizes and a sense of continuity. This makes the exploration experience comfortable and rewarding by aiding navigation while avoiding the feeling of being overwhelmed or *"getting lost"* [A3]—a common experience in digital information spaces. *"When I look for books I mainly, since it [the physical space] is categorized by sections, it's really easier to find where you are, what you are looking for. For instance, I look for, I don't know, books about music and books about, let's say, cooking even. And then I, since it's a targeted area, I know that all they have is here. So either I find it here or not."* [R4].

DESIGNING MODULAR SEARCH INTERFACES

Our findings show the fluidity in which micro-strategies are composed into complex search processes. Now, how does the deconstruction of search and knowledge about the composition of search processes that are driven by creativity, ideation, and learning inform the design of digital search interfaces? As discussed earlier, a number of valuable high- and low-level guidelines for designing digital search interfaces already exist [8, 21, 24, 35, 32, 46, 51, 53, 56]. We revisit and synthesize these with the modularity of search processes in mind. If search is composed of the four micro-strategies we propose in this paper, this can directly inform the design of versatile search interfaces that promote creativity and learning. As Makri and Warwick argue, "it is possible to support creativity, albeit indirectly, by ensuring that electronic resources are designed to support the lower level behaviours [...] in ways that might lead to creativity" [32, p.1767].

Supporting Individual Micro-Strategies. As our search scenarios show, *querying* is often integrated in iterative search processes where the goals are ill-defined. It is therefore important to support dynamic querying [47, 53], query by example [21], and a tight coupling of the query and results [35].

When it comes to displaying a collection of books—be it before or after a query has been issued—it is important to visually highlight different characteristics and/or facets of the collection. This can promote thinking by free association which, in turn, can support ideation, creativity, and learning during search processes [46]. This aspect in particular must be considered when designing for *linking*. Digital search interfaces can provide a range of different types of links, and thus present a "well-connected space and navigational aids" that supports browsing [26]. The key is to make these linking branches visible to guide the exploration [46]. Inspired by research on information-based ideation [24], we suggest providing visual previews of the thematic area behind a link to promote curiosity and foreshadow directions of potential exploration paths, which can further minimize the fear of getting lost in the collection. As Kerne et al. suggest, the presentation of rich (visual) links within and across collections can also help to provide stimuli to overcome fixation or getting stuck [24].

Visual overviews of a subset or the entire book collection are also important to facilitate *scanning*. Whitelaw suggests "generous interfaces", in which rich collection overviews are provided without requiring people to issue a query first [54]. Along these lines, websites such as Pinterest have been found to promote creativity and ideation [30]. Visual overviews can be item-based or include abstract visualizations [35, 51] to inspire new exploration paths. In *assessment* strategies, characteristics of the individual book and its content play an important role [8]. Making high-level information about a book available, as well as its content (including keyword searches within the book), can improve *assessment* [53, 54] and thus integrate learning into the search process.

Fluidity Through Continuous Navigation. Our findings show that a sense of continuity is a valuable aspect when exploring physical information environments. It is important to maintain the context and avoid abrupt switches between different search stages/views. In digital search, participants expressed anxiety over "getting lost" when navigating away from result lists to item views, which is generally detrimental to creative thinking and ideation [28]. Furthermore, a disconnect of assessment strategies from the overall search process (see Scenario 5) compromises the integration of learning and search. Related work suggests easing the transition from overviews to detailed perspectives as well as displaying resources in context of their collection [13]. Enabling continuous navigation supports the fluid combination of micro-strategies. If screen real estate permits, such fluid transitions can be realized by providing all-in-one views of the collection/results, item meta-data, and previews. Other more compact solutions include layering these components so that a sense of presence of the collection/result list is provided at all times; even during the examination of a single item.

Histories and Exploration Trails. Our research confirms the importance of search histories [38, 46, 53] to encourage exploration and fostering people's understanding of an information space or a collection, while minimizing the fear of losing focus or getting lost. One way of doing this is to make exploration paths that lead to a particular item explicit, for instance, through visual breadcrumbs, illustrating queries or highlighting visited links. While common search websites support the "browser history" feature, visualization-based interfaces often do not. Supporting this type of history can increase peoples willingness to explore beyond initial search goals, enable sharing results, and consult previous searches at a later point in time to find more related or similar material.

Offering Curated Collections. Curated sub-collections can provide starting points for less directed, experience-oriented explorations or for searches with hard-to-define criteria (e.g., a particular reading experience). The support of knowledge sharing has been recommended in the context of collaboration and creativity [46, 53]; the curation of content can be considered as beneficial for creative ideation [30, 24, 38]. Integrating such features from digital creative communities [1] where people make collections of hand-picked items available for others to browse into search interfaces can help to support the creative aspects and outcomes of search. The key here is to present such items in visual rather than textual ways, which provides a rich overview into the content the item represents.

Playfulness and Rich Interaction. Playful representation and interaction approaches to digital collections promote explorations where the experience is a reward in itself. In physical environments people engage in sensory experiences that are driven by visual cues and curious discoveries. Previous research highlights the importance of supporting serendipity [16, 51] through unexpected juxtaposition of items [26, 51] and by enticing curiosity and promoting playful explorations [51]. Play has also been discussed as an important facilitator for creativity and inspiration [41, 52]. More concretely, this can be achieved by highlighting outliers, by supporting organic animations and transitions, and by providing rich visual cues that invite discovery and further exploration.

---

[1] https://www.etsy.com/; http://www.pinterest.com/

Furthermore, digital technology, such as direct-touch displays can promote a playful approach to information exploration.

CONCLUSION

We have presented an in-depth qualitative analysis of people's book search habits in professional and personal contexts and in a large spectrum of digital and physical book search environments. Our findings reflect that book search can be considered as a complex process that is constructed from four basic micro-strategies: querying, linking, scanning, and assessing. Depending on the search purpose, these processes can take on highly unique and diverse forms where creativity, ideation and learning are an outcome and driver of the search process. As such social, sensory, and visual aspects play an important role in rewarding information explorations. Based on these insights, and by revisiting and synthesizing previous research on search and creativity, we have introduced a modular perspective on search. Our work informs the design of search interfaces that promote and facilitate creative and versatile search endeavours. Future research will investigate the generalizability of our model beyond book search.

ACKNOWLEDGEMENTS
We would like all our study participants for sharing their approaches to search with us. We also thank Jagoda Walny and Lindsay MacDonald who provided useful feedback on this paper. Last but not least we thank our funding agencies—NSERC, SurfNet, AITF, Grand, Smart Technologies—that made this research possible.

REFERENCES
1. Bates, M. J. Information Search Tactics. *Journal of American Society for Information Sciences 30* (1979), 205–214.
2. Bates, M. J. An exploratory paradigm for online information retrieval. In *Proc. of Information Science* (1985), 91–99.
3. Bates, M. J. The design of browsing and berrypicking techniques for the online search interface. *Online Information Review 13*, 5 (1989), 407–431.
4. Beghetto, R. A., and Kaufman, J. C. Toward a Broader Conception of Creativity: A Case for "mini-c" Creativity. *Psychology of Aesthetics, Creativity, and the Arts 1*, 2 (2007), 73–79.
5. Boyatzis, R. *Transforming Qualitative Information: Thematic Analysis and Code Development.* Sage Publications, 1998.
6. Buchanan, G., Cunningham, S. J., Blandford, A., and Rimmer, J. Information Seeking by Humanities Scholars. In *Research and advanced technology for digital libraries.* 2005, 218–229.
7. Buchanan, G., and Loizides, F. Investigating document triage on paper and electronic media. In *Research and Advanced Technology for Digital Libraries*, vol. 4675 LNCS. 2007, 416–427.
8. Buchanan, G., and Mckay, D. In the Bookshop : Examining Popular Search Strategies. *Proc. of JCDL'11* (2011), 269–278.
9. Chang, S.-J., and Rice, R. E. Browsing: A Multidimensional Framework. *Annual review of information science and technology* (1993), 231–276.
10. Chang, S.-J. L. Information Research in Leisure: Implications from an Empirical Study of Backpackers. *Library Trends 57*, 4 (2009), 711–728.
11. Choo, C. W., B, D., and Turnbull, D. Information Seeking on the web: An integrated model of browsing and searching. *First Monday 5*, 2 (2000), 1–13.
12. Dörk, M., Carpendale, S., and Williamson, C. The information flaneur: A fresh look at information seeking. In *Proc. of CHI'11* (2011), 1215–1224.

13. Dörk, M., Carpendale, S., and Williamson, C. Fluid views: a zoomable search environment. In *Proc. of AVI* (2012), 233–240.

14. Ellis, D. A behavioural approach to information retrieval design. *Journal of Documentation 45*, 3 (1989), 171–212.

15. Fidel, R. Moves in Online Searching. *Online Review 9*, 1 (1985), 61–74.

16. Ford, N., Miller, D., Alan, O., Ralph, J., Turnock, E., and Booth, A. Information Retrieval and creativity: Towards support for the original thinker. *Journal of Documentation 55*, 5 (1999), 528–542.

17. Foster, A. A nonlinear model of information-seeking behavior. *Journal of the American Society for Information Science and Technology 55*, 3 (Feb. 2004), 228–237.

18. Fulton, C. The pleasure principle: the power of positive affect in information seeking. *Proc. of Aslib 61*, 3 (2009), 245–261.

19. Gabora, L. Cognitive Mechanisms Underlying the Creative Process. In *Proc. of Creativity and Cognition* (2002), 126–133.

20. Hartel, J. Information activities and resources in an episode of gourmet cooking. *Information Research 12*, 1 (2006), 54–57.

21. Hearst, M. A. *Search User Interfaces*. Cambridge University Press, 2009.

22. Kari, J., and Hartel, J. Information and Higher Things in Life : Addressing the pleasurable and the profound in information science. *Journal of the American Society for Information Science and Technology 58*, 8 (2007), 1131–1147.

23. Kaufman, J. C., and Beghetto, R. a. Beyond big and little: The four c model of creativity. *Review of General Psychology 13*, 1 (2009), 1–12.

24. Kerne, A., Webb, A. M., Smith, S. M., Linder, R., Lupfer, N., Qu, Y., Moeller, J., and Damaraju, S. Using Metrics of Curation to Evaluate Information-Based Ideation. *ACM Transactions on Computer-Human Interaction 21*, 3 (2014), 1–48.

25. Kuhlthau, C. C. Inside the search process: Information seeking from the user's perspective. *Journal of the American Society for Information Science 42*, 5 (June 1991), 361–371.

26. Kwasnik, B. H. A Descriptive Study of the Functional Components of Browsing. In *Proc. of Engineering for HCI* (1992), 191–203.

27. Laseau, P. *Graphic Thinking for Architects and Designers*. John Wiley and Sons, 1980.

28. Lee, S.-S., Theng, Y.-L., and Goh, D. H.-L. Creative information seeking Part I: a conceptual framework. *Proc. of Aslib 57*, 5 (2005), 460–475.

29. Lee, S.-S., Theng, Y.-L., and Goh, D. H.-L. Creative information seeking: Part II: empirical verification. *Proc of Aslib 59*, 3 (2007), 205–221.

30. Linder, R., Snodgrass, C., and Kerne, A. Everyday ideation: all of my ideas are on pinterest. In *Proc. of CHI'14* (2014), 2411–2420.

31. Makri, S. *A Study of Lawyers' Information Behaviour Leading to the Development of Two Methods for Evaluating Electronic Resources*. PhD thesis, University College London, 2009.

32. Makri, S., and Warwick, C. Information for Inspiration: Understanding Architects Information Seeking and Use Behaviors to Inform Design. *Journal of the American Society for Information Science and Technology 61*, 9 (2010), 1745–1770.

33. Marchionini, G. Information-seeking strategies of novices using a full-text electronic encyclopedia. *Journal of the American Society for Information Science 40*, 1 (1989), 54–66.

34. Marchionini, G. *Information seeking in electronic environments*. Cambridge University Press, 1997.

35. Marchionini, G. Exploratory Search: From finding to understanding. *Communications of the ACM 49*, 4 (2006), 41–46.

36. Marchionini, G., and White, R. W. Find What You Need, Understand What You Find. *Journal of Human-Computer Interaction 23*, 3 (2008), 205–237.

37. Marshall, C. C., and Shipman, F. M. Spatial hypertext and the practice of information triage. *Proc of HYPERTEXT '97* (1997), 124–133.

38. m.c. Schraefel. Building Knowledge: What's beyond Keyword Search? *IEEE Computer 42*, 3 (2009).

39. McKenzie, P. J. A model of information practices in accounts of everyday-life information seeking. *Journal of Documentation 59*, 1 (2003), 19–40.

40. Mikkonen, A., and Vakkari, P. Readers' Search Strategies for Accessing Books in Public Libraries. In *Proc. of Information Interaction in Context* (2012).

41. Russ, S. W. *Affect and creativity: The role of affect and play in the creative process*. Psychology Press, 1993.

42. Savolainen, R. Everyday life information seeking: Approaching information seeking in the context of "way of life". *Library & Information Science Research 17*, 3 (1995), 259–294.

43. Sheldrick Ross, C. Finding without seeking: the information encounter in the context of reading for pleasure. *Information Processing & Management 35*, 6 (Nov. 1999), 783–799.

44. Sheldrick Ross, C. Making Choices: What Readers Say About Choosing Books to Read for Pleasure. *The Acquisitions Librarian 13*, 25 (2000), 5–21.

45. Shneiderman, B. Clarifying search: A user-interface framework for text searches. *D-Lib Magazine* (1997).

46. Shneiderman, B. Creating creativity: user interfaces for supporting innovation. *ACM Transactions on Computer-Human Interaction 7*, 1 (2000), 114–138.

47. Shneiderman, B. Creativity Support Tools: Accelerating Discovery and Innovation. *Communications of the ACM 50*, 12 (2007), 20–32.

48. Smith, A. G. Internet search tactics. *Online Information Review 36*, 1 (2012), 7–20.

49. Spiller, D. The provision of fiction for public libraries. *Journal of Librarianship and Information Science 12*, 4 (1980), 238–266.

50. Sutcliffe, A., and Ennis, M. Towards a cognitive theory of information retrieval. *Interacting with Computers 10* (1998), 321–351.

51. Thudt, A., Hinrichs, U., and Carpendale, S. The Bohemian Bookshelf: Supporting Serendipitous Discoveries through Information Visualizaiton. In *Proc. of CHI'12* (2012), 1461–1470.

52. Vandenberg, B. Play, problem-solving, and creativity. *New Directions for Child and Adolescent Development 1980*, 9 (1980), 49–68.

53. White, R. W., and Roth, R. A. Exploratory Search: Beyond the Query-Response Paradigm. *Synthesis Lectures on Information Concepts, Retrieval, and Services 1*, 1 (Jan. 2009), 1–98.

54. Whitelaw, M. Towards Generous Interfaces for Archival Collections. Presented at ICA, Brisbane, 2012.

55. Wildemuth, B. M., Oh, J. S., and M, G. Tactics Used When Searching for Digital Video. In *Proc. of Information Interaction in Context* (2010).

56. Wilson, M. *Search-User Interface Design*. Morgan & Claypool Publishers, 2011.

Creating a Collaborative Space for Creativity through a Pervasive User Experience

Deborah Maxwell
Design Informatics,
Edinburgh College of Art,
University of Edinburgh
d.maxwell@ed.ac.uk

Chris Speed
Design Informatics,
Edinburgh College of Art,
University of Edinburgh
c.speed@ed.ac.uk

Karl Monsen
Design Informatics,
Edinburgh College of Art,
University of Edinburgh
karl.monsen@gmail.com

Diego Zamora
Design Informatics,
Edinburgh College of Art,
University of Edinburgh
diego.zamora1@gmail.com

ABSTRACT

This paper explores the potential of a pervasive user experience to inspire, provoke and support creative thinking amongst participants in an intensive ideation workshop. The pervasive experience used a iPad-based virtual narrator to guide groups of participants around a physical and digital environment. It took place towards the start of a three-day workshop and the playful, self-directed nature of the experience was designed to align with subsequent workshop activities. This paper describes the user experience, presenting observations and findings through the lens of space (facilitation, augmentation and story), considering how the experience related to and supported the overall workshop aims of ideation and creative thinking. We conclude by examining some of the tensions that emerged, namely; 1) the disconnect between researcher and participant expectations, 2) the potential trade off between 'authentic' outputs and participant engagement, and 3) bridging the knowledge within the workshop with the world outside the workshop.

Author Keywords

Creativity support tools; design methods; reflection on design processes; storytelling; narrative; games and play.

C&C '15, June 22 - 25, 2015, Glasgow, United Kingdom © 2015 ACM.
ISBN 978-1-4503-3598-0/15/06...$15.00 DOI:
http://dx.doi.org/10.1145/2757226.2757234

ACM Classification Keywords

H.5.m. Information interfaces and presentation (e.g., HCI): Miscellaneous.

INTRODUCTION

Increasingly, design and creative thinking is being heralded as an attitudinal shift and approach that can solve societal and economic problems, moving beyond the tradition craft and design (product, user experience (UX)/user interface (UI)) provinces [31,43]. Social media as well as mass media is awash with articles advising readers of techniques to improve their and their companies innovation and creative capacity through design. This is mirrored by a call for design, computing and engineering education to adopt similar transferable, problem solving approaches [8, 20, 21].

At the same time, universities are increasingly encouraged by government and funding bodies, particularly in the arts and humanities, to show the value of research activities through interdisciplinary knowledge exchange across academia, industry, and third sector. The model of the sole genius artist or designer is dead. Fast ideation in groups, we argue, is rapidly becoming the norm, and a proliferation of service and UX design toolkits (e.g. IDEO, Nesta) have emerged to support such activities. Creating collaborative spaces for creativity therefore is also increasingly sought after, yet successful crafting of design and creative thinking environments can be challenging.

The workshop or sandpit [26] as a learning and thinking space has become a dominant paradigm. Maxwell & Williams [29] note that significant challenges can occur in facilitation and ownership in ideation workshops, whereby compliant participants, 'privileged' to be part of the workshop, are content to be led through workshop processes unquestioningly. Similarly, there is the danger of groupthink [24], particularly in intensive, pressurised workshop scenarios, such as the workshop that forms the focus for this paper.

This paper explores the potential of a pervasive user experience, the *Broonie Experience*, that was developed as a bespoke activity to inspire, provoke and support creative thinking amongst participants within one of these relatively conventional ideation and 'design thinking' workshops. The *Broonie Experience* was conceptualised in response to the challenge of introducing workshop participants from different backgrounds to service design methods and a range of digital technologies. The research question for this work was then: How might an interactive, technology-driven group experience support creative thinking for participants at an ideation workshop?

RELATED WORK & MOTIVATION

The *Broonie Experience* was created as an attempt to address the challenges of 'hothousing' participants in a workshop and as a way to mitigate against groupthink [24]. Service design tools appear to offer a route to empathetic design, and the use of personas [18] in HCI and design is well documented as a means to externalising and considering end users. Whilst often cited, the relevance of personas is not universally acknowledged – Chang et al's [17] study observed how practitioners actually use personas in their work, discovering that this is not always as originally intended, but rather they "might be generated based on designers' own thoughts and experiences, instead of on user research results" [p 442]. In order to pre-empt this stereotyping and insular thinking, the *Broonie Experience* drew on existing empirical data (VisitScotland's visitor market segmentation report [37]) to provide a framework for personas that groups of participants would progressively annotate during the *Broonie Experience*.

Persona design [18] is just one example of the storytelling techniques employed across research processes as well as outputs [30]; for instance as visual storyboarding, animatics, scenario design [15] as well as setting up user experiences [41], role playing [10], and user enactments [33], where users 'act' out "loosely scripted scenarios" [p338] on existing and new technology concepts. The use of personas beyond collaged or text-driven formats have been explored, e.g. Shyba and Tam [38] consider convergence points between theatre art and Cooper's personas and Goal-Directed Design, offering a means of embodying and experiencing a persona through acting and creative writing exercises. Given 'design thinking' context of the workshop described in this paper, we decided to employ a collaborative persona activity that drew on research from pervasive user experiences and HCI to create a blended digital-physical experience that through embodied play would encourage participants to develop empathy for their created persona characters. This approach, as realised largely through digital technology, would introduce participants to a range of technologies in a non-threatening playful environment and would, we felt, be engaging and spark creative thinking between participants.

In order to support creative thinking and flow (Csikszentmihalyi's [19] notion of 'flow' is the intense state when "people are so involved in an activity that nothing else seems to matter; the experience itself is so enjoyable that people will do it even at great cost, for the sheer sake of doing it,"), we considered carefully the trajectory [5] of the user experience and journey. By conceptually situating the *Broonie Experience* as a pervasive technologically-mediated experience, with a richly constructed underlying rationalised narrative from folklore, we attempted to create a complex user experience such as those described in Benford et al's work on pervasive gaming and experiences [5, 6, 25], but applied to creative thinking and design tools. Spence et al [40] identify characteristics of such performative experience designs, characterising three key strands, including Staging with multiple users and one device, where the "focus here is often on interaction and/or movement in public settings" [p 2052], and the *Broonie Experience* most closely fell into this category.

We sought then to explore the potential of a multi-layered narrative, attempting to blur the boundaries between digital and physical, fact and fiction, as described by Stenros et al [42] and incorporating elements of gamification [22]. The pervasive user experience, the *Broonie Experience*, made use of Scottish folklore (seldom employed in interactive narratives or pervasive games) to construct a meta-narrative and narrator that determined the design, implementation, and orchestration of the experience. Folklore forms part of the traditional oral culture of storytelling in Scotland that exists to this day [39], and within the tourism and cultural heritage theme of the workshop it was natural to embed folkloric elements within the experience. The accessibility and familiarity of storytelling and narrative structures through childhood and media (e.g. films, novels, folktales, even the structure of news articles) further supports this. Indeed, many interactive narratives (e.g. [13, 36]), closely aligned to pervasive user experiences, have often drawn on narrative frameworks (e.g. Propp's Morphology of the Folktale [35], Georges Polti's The Thirty-Six Dramatic Situations [34], Labov and Waletzky's functional narrative analysis [27], and Campbell's Monomyth [14]) to develop algorithms and computational models.

METHODS

The *Broonie Experience* described in this paper was conceptualised and developed as part of a larger residential workshop, which took place in Edinburgh, UK, in February 2014, as part of the Design in Action research project. The overall workshop brought individuals together from different backgrounds, including designers, academics and business, using creative thinking as a catalyst to generate

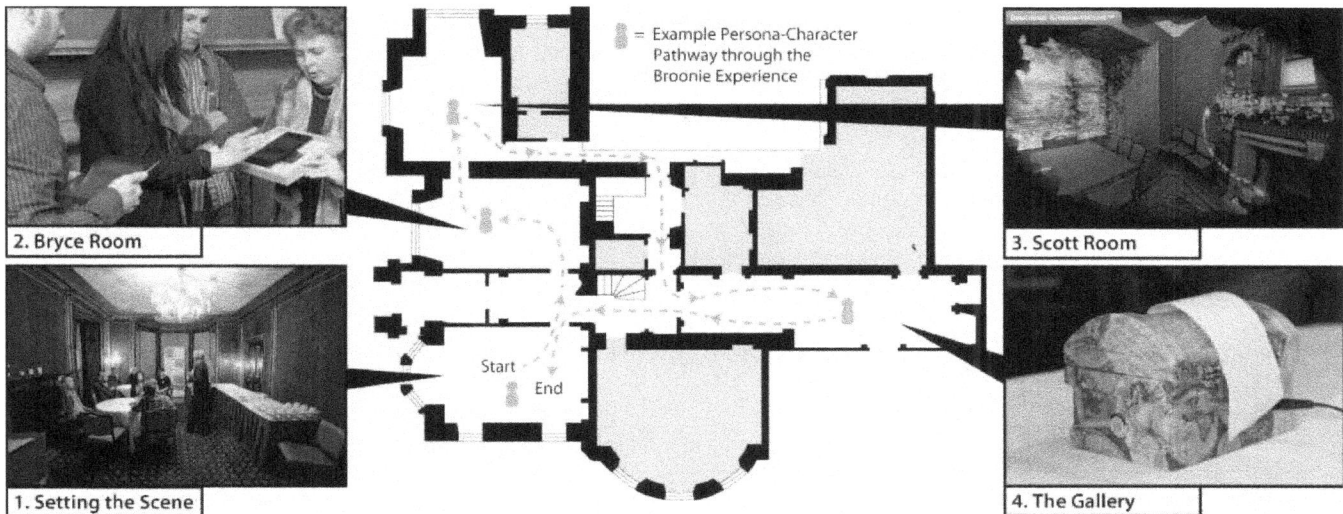

Figure 1: Pathway through the Broonie Experience with images indicating some of the technology and environment in each room.
©Deborah Maxwell

new business ideas around a central topic. Post-workshop, seed funding was available to support these new business ideas. Participants were introduced to service design tools as an alternative way to approach problems, whilst also networking and working collaboratively with other participants. It is worth noting that the workshop was not intended as a codesign process, as participants were not necessarily stakeholders nor end users of the business ideas they developed.

The workshop referred to in this paper was centred on new technologies in tourism and cultural heritage in Scotland. 20 participants were selected following an online application process and with few exceptions had never met each other before. By intention, they encompassed a wide range of backgrounds: computing academics and developers, digital publishing start ups, museum and heritage consultants, and product and graphic designers.

The *Broonie Experience* was conceived as an experimental activity that would support the ideation and creative thinking process of the overall workshop, providing a means for informal story sharing and group bonding amongst participants.

Data Gathering

The *Broonie Experience* was designed as a one-off event; this meant that there was essentially one opportunity to gather data. Therefore, to both mitigate risk and maximise data triangulation, a variety of qualitative data gathering techniques were employed to capture the multimodal experience, namely: 1) visual documentation by a photographer, 2) audio recordings of participant dialogue during the experience, 3) written researcher observations, documented immediately following the experience, and 4) individual semi-structured interviews with six participants conducted 2-3 weeks after the workshop. All participants

completed ethics forms agreeing to data gathering methods and interviews. All sources were collated and analysed using an open coding scheme to enable thematic findings to emerge from the data.

The Broonie Experience

The central concept of the *Broonie Experience* for participants was to support the fleshing out of four characters using a digital narrator that would enable self-direction through a physical, digital, and story environment, incrementally revealing narrative information. To facilitate this, we employed a central trickster narrator character drawn from Scottish folklore, a Broonie. The experience was introduced and told through Jack the Broonie, a little known creature from Scottish folklore (reworked in contemporary fiction as 'house elves' in J. K. Rowling's Harry Potter series). Broonies are reclusive creatures, never seen and easily offended, who typically live in farmsteads, doing chores in return for a bowl of cream and some cake. Jack was a modern day Broonie, au fait with social media that allowed him to have a social life without having to interact face to face with people. Jack is also a trickster [3], disruptive, evasive but, hopefully still entertaining and in some ways endearing. This was delivered through a conversational, sometimes cheeky, dialect presented as both on-screen dialogue and audio [2] via an iPad.

In the *Broonie Experience*, each of the four persona-characters played by participants had lost an object, see Figure 2 (i.e. an old mobile phone, guidebook, glove, or map). To find their missing object each persona-character team (or player) had to undergo a quest [12] through the hotel public rooms, gradually building up the character's persona along the way, guided by the dubious trickster narrator, Jack the Broonie.

Inspiration for the aesthetic of the experience came in part from the affordances of the hotel and their marketing brochure, which included a floor plan that was reminiscent of a board game (i.e. Cluedo). This map layout manifested into the primary navigation metaphor of the HTML5 app that participants used to negotiate the physical environment (see figure 1 for example map). This material formed the underlying framework for the experience, providing clear opportunities for the participants to develop character personas through text fields on an iPad.

Design Approach

The implementation of the *Broonie Experience* was informed primarily by a second person scenario script that was written by one of the paper authors to convey the concept to the rest of the research team. The scenario, which walked through an idealised version of the *Broonie Experience*, presented the story arc as well as envisaging how a range of digital technologies might be embedded in the physical space;

[...]the researcher closes the door behind you, and the next iPad screen encourages you to look around for Alice's missing map. You notice that the mantelpiece is thick with dust and that there is a saucer of cream and a small honey-covered sponge cake on the main table, with a 'not for the consumption of hotel guests' admonishing note placed strategically alongside them. [...] The iPad room plan seems to indicate that there is something of interest near the window [...] on a table there is a small box containing a receipt printer, highlighted by a table lamp, which begins to print. You and your team go over and rip the print out from the box [...]

This scenario guided the flow of the *Broonie Experience* in terms of plot, interactive elements, and physical movement round the space. It served as the starting point for the paper authors to develop a set of discrete digital media components, including the core HMTL5 Web App, complemented with an augmented reality panorama, a Raspberry Pi driven thermal receipt printer and a Near Field Communication (NFC) web-linked photograph frame. The transition from text-based scenario to working prototype evolved through an informal development process, that included in-depth discussions, storyboard sketches, and walk-throughs amongst the research team.

What Actually Happened?

The *Broonie Experience* took place on the first evening after dinner following participants' arrival late that afternoon. Two groups of participants (4 in each) simultaneously took part in a first round of the narrative, each following a slightly staggered pathway through the space (see figure 1), followed by a second round of two groups (6 in each), so that all 20 participants were involved in total.

Participants self-selected into two groups and were verbally introduced to the activity by a researcher. Each group had an iPad and was issued with a small laminated physical profile card that provided information on their persona type, as characterised by VisitScotland's visitor market segmentation [30], e.g. Younger domestic explorer, average age 42, above average income, holiday motivations: escape from routine, convenience, love UK breaks. Through on-screen prompts and text fields, participants named and provided background information on their persona-character (e.g. where they lived and who they lived with) and 'met' Jack the Broonie through Twitter like visual interactions and audio. They were made aware of their character's lost object (see Figure 2) and were invited to begin their search through the hotel by following the iPad onscreen map.

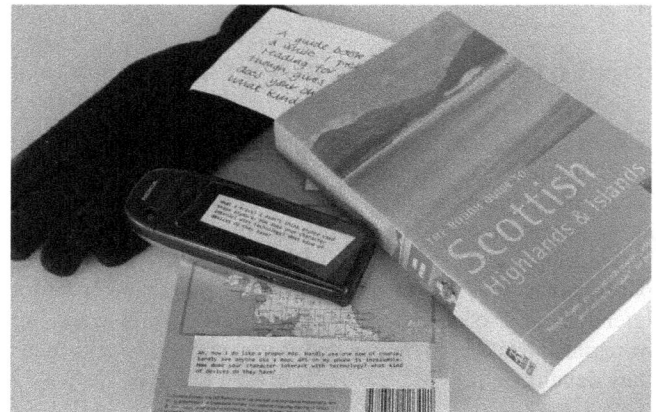

Figure 2. The quest objects, showing typed and written character prompts. ©Deborah Maxwell

In each subsequent room, participants were introduced to an additional technology or prop, each of which prompted the groups to consider their persona-character and input their answers into the iPad app. For instance, a Raspberry Pi computer connected to a thermal receipt printer. On pressing the button (Figure 1) it printed:

Gosh, this is a cosy space, those sofas look like they'd never let you go. I'd love to relax on holiday and just do nothing (no printing at all), go totally off-grid. What about your persona? What do they like to do on holiday? What is their most important factor in choosing a holiday destination? [Hint: Press the button again for more info]

On pressing again statistical information from visitor surveys was printed. Additional information was provided upon repeatedly pressing the button.

The quest concept was continued throughout the rooms, moving between physical and digital environments; for instance an augmented image of one of the rooms overlaid a 'Broonie trail' to the mantelpiece (Figure 1). As the iPad was moved so the stitched panorama also rotated to reveal more of the room, according to the accelerometer (see Figure 3). In the physical room, participants found a scrunched up piece of paper where the 'Broonie trail' indicated, containing the prompt question for their persona-character along with supplementary written and visual information about the role of Scottish culture to visitors.

Figure 3. Using the iPad to see the 'Broonie Vision'. ©Deborah Maxwell

In addition, in an attempt to bridge the digital and physical interactions and avoid a 'heads down' focus on a screen, 'Easter Eggs' in the form of additional background information were placed around the hotel. For example, a saucer of cream and a cake with honey (a folklore reference to the only reward a Broonie might accept) was set up one of the rooms.

Upon both groups being guided by Jack the Broonie to the starting point, they discovered that each group had found the other's missing object, whereupon they swapped objects and completed the quest.

FINDINGS

We here consider the findings grouped within the broader concept of space, that is, how the *Broonie Experience* was navigated through: 1) facilitation space, 2) augmenting space, and 3) story space. Following this, we consider how far these facets of space support the notion of developing a collaborative space for creativity for participants.

Space through Facilitation

Critical to the design of the *Broonie Experience* was a handing over of control from the research and facilitation team to the participants themselves. The central task of the experience was for each participant group to develop a design persona; for this to work effectively we believed that participants should take ownership of their group's persona-character. This began with a physical handing over of an iPad device to each team, with no restriction or direction about how or who should take charge of them. This 'stepping back' was afforded by the distributed (i.e. digital and physical artefacts placed in different rooms of the hotel) and self-directed nature of the experience, with the iPad-based Broonie character guiding participants through

on-screen text, visuals, and accompanying audio to explore and engage with the technology and props in each room to build up their persona. The role of the researcher team then was primarily as observers, not leaders or directors.

This intentional deferring of control and opening up of facilitation was mirrored by subsequent workshop activities. For instance, midway through the workshop on the following day, teams were assigned their 'first group task', where teams were explicitly given permission to make their own decision about what to do over the next hour. This activity served to alter the pace and provide a change of scenery, as well as afforded significant intergroup networking and conversation around the ideas from earlier discussion sessions.

In an attempt to mitigate potential power dynamics that may have emerged through the use of a central iPad, the *Broonie Experience* extended beyond the screen based device (e.g. search for a physical key to open a chest, receipt printer, physical objects, Jack the Broonie audio comments), thereby encouraging all team members to be involved. Even with this approach however, the use of an iPad meant that one person was predominantly driving the interactions; some of the groups varied this role, rotating who held and inputted response into it, while other groups did not. The research team did not attempt to influence control of the device, merely observe.

Space through Augmentation

The hotel environment provided the physical space for the experience, offering a series of interlinking rooms and blank canvas for augmentation with both lo-fi and digital props. The use of multiple rooms in the hotel afforded lots of short movements, which have been shown to promote creative thinking [4, 9] but could be construed as problematic in terms of required levels of organising and planning. However, pervasive gaming experiences, which "extend the gaming experience out into the real world" [6], require significant planning, performativity, and orchestration [6]; the *Broonie Experience* described in this paper was no exception.

The importance of movement and space was a recurrent theme of the workshop, with follow on activities making use of the rooms to 'force' participants to move, e.g. to get coffee, hear keynote talks, find pre-allocated seats at different tables for mind mapping etc. All of this required informal participant negotiation.

The physical space lent itself to a pervasive experience or game. It was a blank canvas with marble and carved wooden fireplaces and large tables that could be easily populated with props and technologies. Unlike some of the painstakingly crafted Nordic live action role-playing games (e.g. [44, p1550]), we did not seek to create a 'Three-Sixty Illusion' [44], rather to provide just enough tangibility to situate technologies and encourage group interaction by reducing the predominance of a single person holding an iPad. The props were therefore in some cases quite subtle, and not necessarily picked up on by all participants as they looked quite incongruous. For instance, a bowl of cream and honey cake set out for the 'Broonie' was unnoticed, and even the documenting photographer did not realise that this was part of the set up.

A key challenge within intensive ideation workshops (such as sandpits) is recognising that the knowledge and expertise contained within the workshop, whilst considerable, is finite. This is particularly pertinent for design-led workshops such as the example described in this paper, and therefore awareness of and empathy for context-led ideas and solutions is paramount. The *Broonie Experience* offered a means to ground the workshop in a wider setting, using empirical published data about user markets and encouraging participants to think outside the physical and mental spaces of the workshop. This shifting of perspective parallels with the notion of *immediacy* of media; that is, the ability of media to open a window into another reality, for example, a film attempting to put the viewer inside the action. Bolter & Grusin [11] describe what they call the 'double logic of remediation'. New forms of media seek to provide such immersion with the content that the medium itself 'disappear[s] from the user's consciousness.' That is, 'the logic of immediacy dictates that the medium itself should disappear and leave us in the presence of the thing represented: sitting in the race car or standing on a mountaintop.' [11, pp. 3] O'Neill [32] explains immediacy through the useful analogy of looking through a window. The main focus is of the view outside the window rather than the window itself.

This was echoed through some of the technology employed; the implementation of the custom built augmented reality HMTL5 panorama controlled by the iPad's accelerometer was quite novel, however no participants, even mobile developers, commented on this in any way. The relative invisibility of these components and props is indicative of the appropriateness of the inventions within the game mindset of the participants;

"It's not just that the technical underpinnings of theatrical performance are unimportant to audience members; when a play is "working," audience members are simply not aware of the technical aspects at all." [28, p15]

We could argue therefore that the Broonie was in some ways an immersive experience, opening a window out onto the 'real' world, as afforded by the technology and interaction mechanisms and through the persona technique. However, as a counterpoint to this, in pervasive gaming and media terms, the prototype nature of the experience meant that the *Broonie Experience* was a seamful design experience [16] where the underlying technology intentionally showed through. We could have used more of a Wizard of Oz approach relying on the research team as human agents, however given a desire within the wider workshop aims to open up discussion and awareness of new

technologies this was deemed inappropriate. In general participants were very forgiving of the prototype nature of the *Broonie Experience*; this may have been in part due to the way the research team presented the experience as an exploratory activity.

Space for Story

The *Broonie Experience* was not a typical interactive narrative or pervasive game (e.g. [25]). Groups did not follow a multi-branched path, nor were they able to dictate the course of the experience or influence the scripted dialogue between their persona-character and Jack the Broonie. They were on a Quest [12], yet the conventional dramatic structure [1, 13] of conflict-diversion-resolution (in this case finding their persona-character's missing object, which had been stolen by the Broonie) was downplayed in favour of exploring the environment and developing their persona-character. Therefore, despite nominally following a simple story arc through the meta-narrative, character creation was the primary goal, a pre-story activity, with a potential next step in a user-centred design process being to create scenarios for the persona-characters to inhabit [15].

The meta-narrative in the *Broonie Experience* was in some ways quite subtle and underplayed; rather it served the role of directing action and suspending disbelief. The development by the research team of the narrator's (Jack the Broonie) backstory was important in design decisions when planning the experience, but this central importance was not carried through into the execution; rightly, the focus was on creating the persona-characters. Similarly, the quest objects served their purpose in driving action forward but were not of primary importance, also suggesting that they worked well as a mechanism. Participants saw the experience as a game, but without any elements of competition; this is reflected in the variable and relaxed pace that each group took – groups did not display any urgency to complete the 'game' first or race to find their persona-character's lost object first. This was therefore experienced as intended, the objects were devised to create the incentive to explore the physical space, taking the both the persona-character and the participant groups on a 'trajectory' [5], maintaining a coherent narrative within which rich discussions could take place.

The understated story arc within the persona-character process provided space for participants to layer into the story content by adding somewhat irreverent persona-character conflict and undercurrents. For instance, out of the four persona-characters, two were secretly gay (one male, one female) unbeknown to their fictitious partners, and a third (male financial manager) loved ballroom dancing but dreamt of becoming a belly dancer. These backstories became increasingly elaborate throughout the experience, and scenarios were created without prompting as reasoning for their persona-characters' preferences in holiday choices, attitudes towards technology. For instance, here one group collaboratively discusses the gadgets their character owns:

[Group debating the fitness and tech gadgets their character has. Group laughter and all talking at same time.]

ParticipantF7: *What about cooking gadgets?*

ParticipantM8: *I think he's quite old fashioned, he kind of leaves that down to the wife.* [All laugh] *I'm thinking Hugh earns enough money that maybe his wife does all that for him.* [Group laughter]

ParticipantF7: *Something for blood pressure?*

ParticipantM5: *That heart thing you run with.*

ParticipantM8: *Pacemaker?!* [Group laughter]

ParticipantM5: *Heart monitor.*

ParticipantM9: *50's a bit young for that!*

ParticipantM5: *It's been a stressful life!* [Group laughter]

As the above extract demonstrates, group discussions were not dominated by one individual, all group members contributed, indicating the accessibility of the experience (see Figure 4).

Creating immersive experiences is challenging yet participants certainly appeared to suspend their disbelief whilst taking part. The introduction of Jack the Broonie as trickster narrator immediately set the scene as other worldly, placing it firmly in the fairy tale or fantasy world. Consequently, we argue, the premise of the missing objects, or MacGuffins, was unchallenged, and further set the experience as outwith the previous networking and workshop setting into a more playful domain (i.e. that of a Quest [12]). As soon as participants began to input information into the iPad about their persona-character (name, hometown, lives with) they interpreted the experience as a game. Whilst the authors would not define the *Broonie Experience* as a game, it does contain game design elements [22, p12], i.e. game design patterns (time constraint and resources) and game models (challenge, fantasy, curiosity), and so according to Deterding et al. [22] could be classified as Gameful Design or Gamification.

In addition, participants quickly began to enter into the spirit of the activity, talking back to the Broonie character, e.g. ParticipantM4: "Hi Jack!" [Group laughter]; and even trying to intertwine their own reality into the persona-character:

[In a discussion about persona-character and what kinds of activities they might enjoy and where they might visit in Scotland...]

ParticipantF3: *The Wickerman Festival then? Lots of gay people there.*

ParticipantF10: *Right the Wickerman Festival then. My God you're persuasive.*

ParticipantF3: *I want her [Character] to go near me you see, I'm always trying to attract people.* [Participant ran a guesthouse near the festival location.]

Figure 4. Showing group interaction and laughter. ©Deborah Maxwell

Despite the mixed responses to personas as a design tool, discussion around their characters was rich and appeared to create genuine empathy, with groups debating at some length (and good humour) the types of interactions and motivations that their characters had. For instance, one group created a fictitious dog for their persona that determined his travel requirements when booking hotels, and also led to the use of various wearable gadgets to monitor his fitness whilst out walking the dog. Another group had to eventually compromise on their character's personality due to increasingly heated but good natured debate:

ParticipantF3: [Reading] *What will the year of homecoming mean for your character? Will they visit Scotland, make the most out of the 430 events or deliberately avoid the crowds? I think they'll deliberately avoid the crowds.*

ParticipantM4: *Noo! She's a-*

ParticipantF3: *She's a quiet-*

ParticipantM4: *She's a senior sales-*

ParticipantF3: *She's fed up with all the hubbub.*

ParticipantM4: *No she's going to – she wants to be at the opening ceremony of the Commonwealth Games. There's definitely something for her to go to.*

ParticipantF3: *Where does she live? She lives in London, she wants to escape the crowds.*

ParticipantM4: *No, she's used to the crowds. The Commonwealth Games? That's no crowd for her!* [Group laughter] *She can easily handle that, you know.*

As can be seen from the above quotes, the *Broonie Experience* enabled participants who had only recently met to learn more about each others' attitudes and personalities, as group dynamics and strong characters emerged. This was an unintended side-effect of the Experience that was valuable for the wider workshop and later group formation.

Summary of Findings

Space for Story, Space for facilitation, and Space through Augmentation all illustrate the ways in which participants collaboratively negotiated the *Broonie Experience* and how it helped to scaffold this pop-up community of practice. Erden et al. [23] argue that knowledge creation and innovation, primary aims of the larger workshop environment that forms the context of this paper, is often "not the product of a single person but a collective work of a group of people or a team" [p5]. This "group tacit knowledge (GTK)… is socially complex and difficult to imitate" [p5]. They identify four levels of quality of GTK, from Groups as Assemblages with "nearly no shared experience", through to Collective Improvisation where groups develop "a collective mind which leads not only to coordination in certain situations but also to collective intuition". Whilst it is unrealistic to expect that group dynamics would develop to the level of Collective Improvisation, we did hope that the *Broonie Experience* would go some way towards developing a sense of shared memory amongst participants. ParticipantF1, on being asked whether she had used their *Broonie Experience* persona during an interview post-workshop, indicated that it had formed part of a shared history between her and a fellow participant;

ParticipantF1: …*when we were thinking about our avatars, we were thinking about making personas for them. […] Because I think two of us, yeah,* [participant name] *was in that group with us as well, so we, you know, we just talked about George* [persona-character], *or we talked about the line dancing. So that just made it fun.*

It is clear that the gamification and fantasy or folklore elements embedded in the experience were taken as permission to 'play' with the persona-characters. In addition, despite the limited usage of the persona-characters in the overall residential workshop, they were memorable, with all interviewees able to recall (some with striking clarity) the persona-character that they had developed 2-3 weeks previously. Additional, though anecdotal, evidence was a conversation between a researcher and a participant who had missed the first evening (and therefore the *Broonie Experience*) who confided that she felt she had missed out on a significant 'group bonding' experience after hearing about it from other participants. Therefore, the perception was that it had been a valuable shared group experience.

TENSIONS

The *Broonie Experience* described in this paper brought to light several tensions, namely 1) the disconnect between researchers' expectations and participants' perceptions of the experience as a game, and how this was negotiated, 2) the apparent trade off between 'authenticity' and

engagement in this context, with the creation of engaging and outlandish stories that deviated from more conventional realistic, arguably more 'authentic', persona-characters, and 3) providing a bridge to consider not only the knowledge and experience contained in the workshop environment, but the experience and wide world out with the workshop.

The inherent 'game' like quality of The Broonie meant that participants treated it as such, and so the character-personas, whilst raising discussion and indicating what kind of material might be included in them, had limited value in and of themselves as tools for informing design. The specific character-personas were not used explicitly during the rest of the workshop by participants in their wider design processes; although personas as a method were independently initiated and employed by several of the workshop groups that emerged over the following two days. It was clear from follow up interviews that participants enjoyed the *Broonie Experience*,

"*I actually thought it was more of a get to know you exercise which is breaking down barriers* […] *we just enjoyed ourselves*" [ParticipantF1]; and "*I thought that was cool yeah. It was like Crystal Maze. [laughs] That was fun. […] I think everyone else, it helped them relax a bit as well 'cos we were kind of moving around and talking to each other*". [ParticipantF7]

On reflection therefore, the primary value of the Broonie Experience was as a means to provoke discussion around technology and encourage the formation of working groups.

CONCLUSIONS

The development process for the *Broonie Experience* was motivated by rethinking the way in which 'hothousing' workshop participants leads to limitations on the creative process, such as groupthink. The research aimed to demonstrate that through embodied play, groups may seek to extend the narratives of specific character personas given their experiences within those personas, using empathy as a creative catalyst. The work brought to light several tensions as noted above, but let us consider the *Broonie Experience* in terms how an interactive, technology-driven group experience support creative thinking for participants at an ideation workshop.

Firstly, the *Broonie Experience* was deployed as a session within an overall workshop as a deliberate contrast to the intense, 'hothouse' atmosphere of the event, where participants were aware that they had to ideate, self-select into groups, develop, and pitch a business concept in under 48 hours. The *Broonie Experience* provided an early reminder that the workshop challenges should be considered in a wider frame, opening a virtual window onto the world outside the workshop, in this instance, through data about cultural heritage and visitors to Scotland. This opening up discouraged the circular 're-cooking' of ideas, and groupthink, as was evidenced by the wider workshop.

Secondly, the manner in which participants immediately and instinctively engaged with the experience as a game, recognizing playful and narrative elements led to the embroidery of elaborate backstories for their persona-characters, demonstrating creative thinking. In Scottish oral tradition, the only 'rule' for a storyteller when asked about an aspect of the story by a listener is that the answer can never be, 'I don't know.' In a similar manner, participants justified their persona-character responses to questions (e.g. the places their persona-character would want to visit) by elaborating on the backstory, thereby creating plausible reasons for their character's behavior, and arguing for the validity of their response to the rest of the participant group.

Third, and finally, as discussed in the Findings section, discussions and participant groups that emerged during the *Broonie Experience* did, at least to some degree, translate to the rest of the workshop, evidence that the legacy of the experience extended beyond its duration. This suggests that the experience supported participants' ideation and creative thinking process throughout the extended workshop.

The role of technology within the *Broonie Experience* worked well as a neutral actor; had the research team taken on the role of the narrator through role play, given the wider ideation workshop context, participants would not have engaged in the same way. The Broonie character as realized through an iPad was distinctive, and we argue, helped to suspend disbelief and immediately situated the experience as a 'game'. In addition, the range of technology provoked debate and peer learning across the groups, as those with more technical experience explained technology (such as Raspberry Pi) to others.

The *Broonie Experience* had significant value in sparking group discussion on and around persona-characters and technologies, working well to generate a shared experience and group history. In particular, unanticipated persona-character elaborations into short stories within the wider metanarrative of the Broonie demonstrates the potential for future development of this type of design-led experiences.

Design and HCI practitioners and researchers may want to consider therefore the potential of rich, embodied user experience journeys, as augmented with digital media, as collaborative and/or empathic tools within design processes. Future work, we suggest, lies in investigating the optimum interaction framework for such experiences, i.e. ranging from fully constructed preexisting persona-characters to be explored through for instance geo-tagged media, to more open frameworks that allows participants to construct and populate with personas and scenarios on-the-fly. These design tools and approaches, we posit, may be particularly valuable when working with and across diverse groups of participants and stakeholders as a non-threatening way of provoking rich discussions and reflections.

ACKNOWLEDGMENTS
The research was part of Design in Action (Arts and Humanities Research Council AH/J005126/1). The authors would like to thank our participants for agreeing to be part of the interactive narrative experience and for being interviewed. Photography credits Lindsay Perth.

REFERENCES
1. Appan, P., Sundaram, H., and Birchfield, D. 2004. Communicating everyday experiences. *Proc. SRMC 2004*, ACM Press (2004), 17-24.

2. Aylett, M. P., and Pidcock, C. J. The CereVoice characterful speech synthesiser sdk. *Proc. AISB 2007*, 174-178.

3. Barbara Babcock-Abrahams, B. "A Tolerated Margin of Mess": The Trickster and His Tales Reconsidered. *Journal of the Folklore Institute*, 11, 3 (1975), 147-186

4. Beatty, E. L. & Ball, L. J. (2011). Investigating exceptional poets to inform an understanding of the relationship between poetry and design. *Conference Proceedings: DESIRE 11*.

5. Benford, S., Giannachi, G., Koleva, B., and Rodden, T. From interaction to trajectories: designing coherent journeys through user experiences. *Proc. CHI 2009*, ACM Press (2009), 709-718.

6. Benford, S., Magerkurth, C., and Ljungstrand, P. Bridging the physical and digital in pervasive gaming. *Communications of the ACM* 48, 3 (2005), 54-57.

7. Benyon, David, Oli Mival, and Serkan Ayan. "Designing blended spaces." *Proceedings of the 26th Annual BCS Interaction Specialist Group Conference on People and Computers*. British Computer Society, 2012.

8. Big Beacon Manifesto [Accessed on 12 January 2015] http://bigbeacon.org/big-beacon-manifesto.pdf

9. Blanchette, D. M., Ramocki, S. P., O'del, J. N., & Casey, M. S. (2005). Aerobic Exercise and Creative Potential: Immediate and Residual Effects. Creativity Research Journal, 17 (2 & 3), pp. 257-264.

10. Boess, S., Saakes, D., and Hummels, C. When is role playing really experiential? Case studies. *Proc. TEI 2007*, ACM Press (2007), 279-282.

11. Bolter, J. D. & Grusin, R. A. (1999) Remediation : understanding new media, Cambridge, Mass. ; London, MIT Press.

12. Booker, C. *The Seven Basic Plots: Why We Tell Stories*. Bloomsbury Publishing, 2004.

13. Brooks, K. M. Do story agents use rocking chairs? The theory and implementation of one model for computational narrative. *Proc. MULTIMEDIA 1996*, ACM Press (1996), 317-328.

14. Campbell, J. *The Hero with a Thousand Faces*. Fontana Press, 1993.

15. Carroll, J. M. *Making Use: Scenario-based Design of Human-Computer Interactions.* MIT Press, 2000.

16. Chalmers, M., and Galani, A. Seamful Interweaving: Heterogeneity in the Theory and Design of Interactive Systems. *Proc. DIS 2004*, ACM Press (2004), 243-252.

17. Chang, Y. N., Lim, Y. K., and Stolterman, E. Personas: From Theory to Practices. *Proc. NordiCHI 2008,* ACM Press (2008), 439-442.

18. Cooper, A., and Saffo, P. The Inmates are Running the Asylum. Sams, Indianapolis, 2004.

19. Csikszentmihalyi, M. *Flow: The psychology of optimal experience.* Harper & Row, New York, 1990.

20. Denning, Peter J. "The whole professional." *Communications of the ACM* 57.12 (2014): 24-27.

21. DesignX: A Future Path for Design. The Design Collaborative. [Accessed on 12 January 2015] http://www.jnd.org/dn.mss/designx_a_future_pa.html

22. Deterding, S., Dixon, D., Khaled, R., and Nacke, L. From Game Design Elements to Gamefulness: Defining "Gamification". *Proc. MindTrek 2011,* ACM Press (2011), 9-15.

23. Erden, Z., von Krogh, G., and Nonaka, I. The Quality of Group Tacit Knowledge. *Journal of Strategic Information Systems*, 17, 1 (2008), 4-18.

24. Esser, J. K. (1998). Alive and well after 25 years: A review of groupthink research. *Organizational behavior and human decision processes*, *73*(2), 116-141.

25. Fosh, L., Benford, S., Reeves, S., Koleva, B., and Brundell, P. See me, Feel me, Touch me, Hear me: Trajectories and Interpretation in a Sculpture Garden. *Proc. CHI 2013,* ACM Press (2013), 149-158.

26. Giles, J. "Sandpit initiative digs deep to bring disciplines together." *Nature* 427.6971 (2004), 187-187.

27. Labov, W., and Waletzky, J. Narrative analysis: oral versions of personal experience. *Sociolinguistics: The essential readings* (2003), 74-104.

28. Laurel, B. *Computers as Theatre.* Pearson Education, 1993.

29. Maxwell, D., Williams, A. 2014. Pragmatics, Plasticity, and Permission: A Model for Creativity in Temporary Spaces. *Proc. 19th DMI: Academic Design Management Conference* (London, UK, September 02 - 04, 2014).

30. Maxwell, D., Woods, M., and Abbott, D. StoryStorm: A Collaborative Exchange of Methods for Storytelling. *Proc. DIS 2014*, ACM Press (2014), 207-210.

31. Norman, D. *State of Design: How Design Education Must Change* [Accessed on 12 January 2015]

https://www.linkedin.com/pulse/20140325102438-12181762-state-of-design-how-design-education-must-change

32. O'Neill, S. *Interactive media : the semiotics of embodied interaction.* London, Springer (2008).

33. Odom, W., Zimmerman, J., Davidoff, S., Forlizzi, J., Dey, A. K., and Lee, M. K. A Fieldwork of the Future with User Enactments. *Proc. DIS 2012*, ACM Press (2012), 338-347.

34. Polti, G. *The Thirty-Six Dramatic Situations.* JK Reeve, Boston, 1954.

35. Propp, V. *Morphology of the Folktale.* University of Texas Press, 1968.

36. Robertson, J., Luckin, R., and Gjedde, L. *Inside stories: A Narrative Journey.* Lulu.com, 2008.

37. Scotland: An Insight into our Customer Segments, VisitScotland Report, 2011. [Accessed on 12 January 2015] http://www.visitscotland.org/pdf/An%20Insight%20into%20our%20Segments%20updated.pdf

38. Shyba, L., and Tam, J. Developing Character Personas and Scenarios: Vital Steps in Theatrical performance and HCI Goal-Directed Design. *Proc. CandC 2005,* ACM Press (2005), 187-194.

39. Smith, Donald. *Storytelling Scotland: a nation in narrative.* Interlink Publishing Group, 2001.

40. Spence, J., Frohlich, D. M., and Andrews, S. Performative Experience Design. *Proc. CHI EA 2013*, ACM Press (2013), 2049-2058.

41. Stappers, P. J., Saakes, D., and Adriaanse, J. On the Narrative Structure of Virtual Reality Walkthroughs. *Proc. Computer Aided Architectural Design Futures 2001*, Springer Netherlands (2001), 125-138.

42. Stenros, J., Montola, M., and Mäyrä, F. Pervasive Games in Ludic Society. *Proc. Future Play 2007*, ACM Press (2007), 30-37.

43. Verweij, L. *We are coming to view design more as a mentality than a skill.* [Accessed on 12 January 2015] http://www.dezeen.com/2014/03/25/opinion-lucas-verweij-design-education/

44. Waern, A., Montola, M., and Stenros, J. The Three-Sixty Illusion: Designing for Immersion in Pervasive Games. *Proc. CHI 2009,* ACM Press (2007), 1549-1558.

Emotion and Creativity: Hacking into Cognitive Appraisal Processes to Augment Creative Ideation

Alwin de Rooij
Centre for Creativity
City University London
Northampton Square, London
EC1V 0HB, UK
alwinderooij@city.ac.uk

Philip J. Corr
Department of Psychology
City University London
Northampton Square, London
EC1V 0HB, UK
philip.corr.1@city.ac.uk

Sara Jones
Centre for HCI Design
City University London
Northampton Square, London
EC1V 0HB, UK
s.v.jones@city.ac.uk

ABSTRACT

Creativity thrives when people experience positive emotions. How to design an interactive system that can effectively make use of this potential is, however, still an unanswered question. In this paper, we propose one approach to this problem that relies on hacking into the cognitive appraisal processes that form part of positive emotions. To demonstrate our approach we have conceived, made, and evaluated a novel interactive system that influences an individual's appraisals of their own idea generation processes by providing real-time and believable feedback about the originality of their ideas. The system can be used to manipulate this feedback to make the user's ideas appear more or less original. This has enabled us to test experimentally the hypothesis that providing more positive feedback, rather than neutral, or more negative feedback than the user is expecting, causes more positive emotion, which in turn causes more creativity during idea generation. The findings demonstrate that an interactive system can be designed to use the function of cognitive appraisal processes in positive emotion to help people to get more out of their own creative capabilities.

Author Keywords

Affective Computing; Cognitive Appraisal; Creativity; Creativity Support Tools; Emotion; Idea Evaluation; Idea Generation; Interactive Systems; Natural Language Processing; Positive Computing.

ACM Classification Keywords

H.5.2 Information interfaces and presentation: User interface; J.4 Social and Behavioral Sciences: Psychology.

INTRODUCTION

Positive emotions can help adapt the way people think and act such that creativity during idea generation is augmented [3]. Interactive systems that aim to influence emotion can, therefore, be designed to help people to get more out of their own creative capabilities. However, not many approaches exist that have successfully targeted this relationship between emotion and creative ideation [9]. The rarity of such systems is surprising because creativity is often heralded as a unique and valuable human skill, one that is at the heart of wellbeing, innovation, and culture [8, 28].

In this paper, we describe the conception, making, and experimental evaluation of an interactive system that is designed to hack into the cognitive appraisal processes that form part of positive emotions, with the goal to augment creative ideation. Based on experimental and theoretical findings from psychology [3, 32, 35], and our own previous studies [9, 11], we argue that the degree to which ideas generated are appraised as original causes positive and negative emotion over time, and that this can influence creative ideation.

On the basis of this argument, we created an interactive system, which autonomously estimates the originality of the user's ideas, and presents these estimates as feedback to the user. This system is designed to be able to manipulate this feedback in a way that conveys that the user's ideas are less original, the same, or more original than people might typically expect, so that we are able to vary the likelihood that people appraise their own ideas as more or less original, and cause positive and negative emotion accordingly.

We hypothesize and experimentally demonstrate that our interactive system can influence the way users appraise the originality of their own ideas, and that making the ideas look more original than they are causes more positive emotion, which augments creativity during idea generation tasks. Thus, the contribution of the research presented in this paper is a demonstration that an interactive system can be designed to use the function of cognitive appraisal processes in positive emotion, to help people perform better on idea generation tasks that require creativity.

EMOTION AND CREATIVITY

Emotions are responses to events that help adapt the way we think and act in support of our own and other's wellbeing [26, 32, 35]. Emotions consist of adaptive changes in a number of components, including: the appraisal of events (e.g. this is appealing); action tendencies that prepare and guide taking action (e.g. a tendency to approach); somatic and neuroendocrine responses that support and guide evaluation and action (e.g. dopamine release in reward pathways); motor expressions that make up the physical actions that occur in response to an event (e.g. smiling and approaching movements); and feelings, the aspects of these components that can be subjectively experienced (e.g. feeling joyous) [35].

Creative ideation refers to the generation of novel and effective ideas. Ideation is an integral part of the creative process, where it facilitates the generation of sufficient original material from which effective ideas can be developed [8, 28]. Creative ideation involves two major components, a generative component which enables the integration of features and concepts from already procured knowledge into ideas, and an evaluative component which appraises the generated ideas [25]. Creativity during ideation is influenced by the flexibility with which information is made available to the generative process, by the functioning of working memory, and by motivational factors that ensure an increased investment of resources to attain the goals of an idea generation process [3, 25, 28].

The link between *emotion and creative ideation* can be explained by the adaptive change that forms part of an emotion, and its influence on the execution of the idea generation process [10]. Typically two aspects of emotions augment creative ideation. First, there is a link between *positive emotion* (e.g. joy, pride) and the *flexibility* with which a flow of information is made available to the generative process, such that increased flexibility increases the likelihood that original ideas are generated [1, 2, 3]. In addition, there is a link between emotions such as joy or anger that associate with an approach action tendency (i.e. the tendency to pursue something positive), and increased effort investment and engagement [3, 34], such that increases in effort and engagement ensure sufficient cognitive and motivational resources are invested to enable creativity during idea generation. In this paper, we focus exclusively on the link between positive emotion and creative ideation.

Interactive systems designed to target the emotion-creativity link are relatively rare. First, there is a line of research that focuses on emotion induction (or mood induction), which typically implements techniques developed for experimental purposes on digital platforms [24, 27]. For instance, showing positive rather than negative pictures during creative problem solving and idea generation tasks enabled creativity on a crowdsourcing platform [24]. Second, there is a line of research aimed at developing interactive systems that help regulate the emotions that are caused during a creative activity [9, 11, 29]. For instance, systems that impose using arm gestures designed based on motor expressions that associate with positive rather than negative emotions, and approach rather than avoidance action tendencies, up-regulate positive emotion, and augment creativity during idea generation and insight problem solving [9]. However, no interactive systems exist that explicitly attempt to *cause* emotion, rather than induce emotion in a more indirect manner, to influence the emotion-creativity link. In this paper we develop such a technology.

CAUSING EMOTION

Cognitive appraisal theory describes the way in which appraisals, or perceptions, of events cause emotional responses [26, 32, 35]. These appraisals typically drive the changes in other components of an emotion, which shape its adaptive response (Figure 1). According to this theory, appraisals that imply *goal-conduciveness* and *goal-obstruction* differentiate positive from negative emotions. Goal-conduciveness and goal-obstruction refer to the way in which an event influences the progress toward attaining the individual's goals. That is, if the event implies that the current situation can lead to or led to attaining the individual's goals, positive emotion is elicited, but when it implies the reverse, negative emotion is elicited. Other appraisals (e.g. of cause, coping potential, and norm violation) further differentiate the type emotion that unfolds (e.g. the difference between the positive emotions of joy and pride). See [26, 32, 36] for overviews.

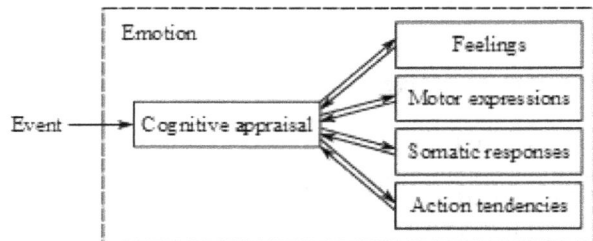

Figure 1 Appraisal-centered interpretation of emotion (after [26, 36]). Bi-directional arrows represent feedback relations among the emotion components.

There are, however, two additional factors that need to be taken into account to enable these appraisals to lead to a sufficiently strong emotional response to impact the link between emotion and creative ideation. We believe that both these two factors need to be taken into account when designing our interactive system.

First, *interactions between appraisals* moderate the intensity of an emerging emotion [5, 41]. So, in addition to the influence of appraised goal-conduciveness or -obstructiveness on positive or negative emotion, the appraised *goal-relevance* of an event, i.e. the evaluation of how strongly the event affects the individual's current goals, moderates the *intensity* of the resulting positive and negative emotions [22, 30]. For instance, when primed with achievement goals, performance feedback that is positive (success) and negative (failure) can elicit positive and negative emotions whose intensity varies according to the appraised goal-relevance of the feedback [22]. This suggests that an event should be perceived as both goal-relevant and goal-conducive to increase the intensity of the emotion caused.

Second, feedback connections among appraisal processes and among other emotion components (Figure 1), can create a temporary disposition to have the same emotion that was initially caused when they were first manipulated [23, 35, 38]. Thus, appraising an event in a particular way increases the likelihood that subsequent events will be appraised in a similar manner [38]. It follows that when appraisals of a certain kind happen more closely together, this enables the emergence of the associated emotional response [32]. For instance, if there are only a few goal-conducive events over a period of time, one might feel slightly positive, but when something obstructive happens, one's emotional state might be prone to change. However, if the rate of goal-conducive events increases, positive emotion will emerge in a way that is more intense, and less prone to negative influences [23, 32]. Therefore, a certain *rate of goal-conducive events* is likely also to be necessary to cause a sufficiently strong emotional response for our approach to be effective.

Interactive systems designed to model, recognize, and communicate emotions are becoming increasingly pervasive [36]. However, technologies designed to intentionally cause emotion are relatively rare. Recent work includes priming using digital media [17], adaptive music selection [43], and affective mirrors [37]. However, most research has focused on invoking emotion by mimicking social and affective interactions between a user and an interactive system, such as an avatar or robot [36]. The work presented in this study is more closely related to technologies, such as gaming technologies that target reward [21]. Similarly, technologies for behavior change and persuasion [15], and the more recent positive computing, which focuses on supporting well-being and human potential [6], incorporate cognitive appraisal theory implicitly or explicitly. Technologies that explicitly target appraisal processes, with the goal to cause emotion, however, are rare. In this paper we develop such a technology, by manipulating the cognitive appraisal processes that happen during creative ideation.

CAUSING EMOTION TO AUGMENT CREATIVITY

The existence of an evaluative component in the creative ideation process, as mentioned above, implies that appraisals form an integral part of this process [25, 28]. We assume that a cognitive appraisal theory of emotion [32, 35], can also be applied to the appraisals that form part of the ideation process [25, 28], and that a technology that is designed to influence the appraisals that form part of positive and negative emotion, can therefore help to intentionally cause positive and negative emotions during creative ideation.

Events that are *goal-relevant* within the context of creative ideation can be found by examining the function of ideation in the creative process as a whole. Typically, the function of the generative component of creative ideation is to come up with sufficient *original* material during the early stages of a creative process, whereas other goals, such as developing effective ideas, become more important during later stages [8, 28]. This is reflected in people's judgment of creativity, in which originality can weigh stronger than effectiveness for ideas developed in a creative ideation task [cf. 16]. This indicates that within the context of creative ideation, the appraised originality of an idea has at least some goal-relevance.

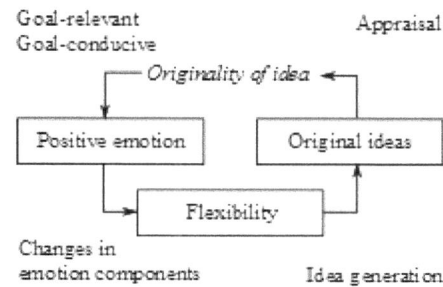

Figure 2 Impression of the hypothesized link between positive emotion, flexibility, and the generation of original ideas.

It follows from the above that generating original rather than unoriginal ideas is *goal-conducive* rather than *goal-obstructive*. Indeed, the amount of original ideas [11], and the percentage of ideas that are original [9], rather than the total amount of ideas, or the variety of the semantic concepts used in the ideas, have been shown to correlate positively with the intensity of positive emotion during idea generation. This indicates that generating more original ideas increases the prevalence and the intensity of positive emotion, whereas generating more unoriginal ideas increases the prevalence and the intensity of negative emotion. We conjecture that an increase or decrease in *the rate of appraised original ideas* can thus drive a positive feedback loop between appraising originality, positive emotion, and generating original ideas (Figure 2), which enables the emergence of a sufficiently strong positive emotion to lift both emotion and creativity simultaneously, and robustly.

An *interactive system* that targets the rate at which original and unoriginal ideas are produced can therefore be assumed to target the link between positive emotion and creative ideation. This would be the first interactive system that explicitly targets the way emotions are caused during a creative task [cf. 9, 11, 24, 27, 29]. Next we describe the implementation of such a system.

INTERACTIVE SYSTEM

To evaluate our conjectures, we developed an interactive system that is designed to influence the appraisal processes underlying positive and negative emotion during creative ideation. First, the system is capable of estimating the originality of an idea in a human-like way, in real-time. Second, the system is designed to manipulate feedback on the originality of an idea in such a way that the user's ideas appear less, the same, or more original than they really are. Finally, the system enables textual input of ideas, and presents the manipulated feedback on those ideas after typing, so that this can help the user to appraise his or her own ideas, with the aim of influencing the user's appraisals of their ideas and thereby increasing their creativity.

Estimation of originality

We operationalize originality as the statistical infrequency of an idea [31]. It follows that the frequency of an idea in a large collection of ideas about a particular subject might indicate the originality of that idea. Calculating originality thus requires a way of 1) representing ideas, 2) representing the space of ideas about a particular subject, and 3) using that idea space to estimate the originality of a new idea. See [16, 20] for related approaches.

Idea representation

In our system, an idea is represented as an unstructured collection (set) of word senses and related concepts. To generate this representation, the system takes an idea in natural language, disambiguates the part-of-speech of the words in the ideas [19], extracts the verbs and nouns, and then disambiguates the word sense of these verbs and nouns [4]. We assume that most of an idea's meaning is contained in the verbs and nouns in that idea. To make this approach less sensitive to different ways of phrasing the same idea, the IS-A (e.g. a house is a building) and PART-OF (e.g. a room is part of a house) relations of the extracted senses are retrieved from WordNet [13] to form a concept network for each idea.

Idea space generation

To be able to estimate the originality of an idea the system requires an idea space. This is created by taking a large collection of ideas, extracting the word senses from these ideas as previously described, and storing and counting the frequency of all these word senses. For this study we used the ideas that had been generated in previous studies using the same idea generation task that we will use in this study. These were kindly donated by [9, 18, 39, 40] (Table 1). This enabled us to generate three idea spaces, representing ideas about using a brick, a paperclip, and a knife.

Estimation of originality

To estimate the originality of a new idea the system extracts the concepts from this idea and retrieves the frequencies of these concepts from the idea space representation. For each idea the system summarizes the frequencies of the extracted

concepts, or senses (including the associated senses) by computing the grand mean. That is, the mean of the means for each of the senses and their associated concept networks. This is done to insure that the contribution of each sense is not strongly dependent on the amount of semantically related senses found in WordNet, and to reduce the dependency of the scores on the amount of verbs and nouns that are present in an idea. The system then computes the percentile rank of the grand mean relative to the grand means of all the ideas used to generate the idea space for a particular subject. This yields a ranked originality estimate that ranges between 0 (=very unoriginal) to 100 (=very original). This is the system's estimate of originality that is used in the study.

Subject	n-people	n-ideas	Taken from
Brick	409	3504	[9, 18, 39, 40]
Paperclip	210	2128	[18]
Knife	242	1698	[39]

Table 1 Characteristics of the idea collections.

Pre-study: Human-likeness of the systems estimates
To investigate whether the system's estimates corresponded with human estimates we asked people to estimate the originality of 45 ideas (15 for each subject in Table 1). We asked people to use a Likert scale from 0 to 10 (0=very unoriginal, 10=very original) to 1) estimate how original they thought each idea was, and 2) state what was the lowest and the highest score that they felt could reasonably be given for each idea. Thirty-one people (16 females, 15 males, M_{age}=34.6, SD_{age}=9.87) rated the ideas in this way. These people were students and employees of a UK and a Dutch university, and did not participate in the main experiment. The same set of ideas was also rated by the developed system.

To test the consistency of the human ratings of originality and compare these with the system's ratings we first calculated the mean correlations between the participants' ratings (averaged using Fisher's z-transform). The results showed that the originality estimates by the participants correlated on average weakly to moderately to each other, $.260 < \bar{r} < .673$, with $\bar{r}$=.526. The mean correlation between the system's estimates and the estimates of the participants was similar, $\bar{r}$=.453. This indicates that people rate the originality of ideas in a manner that has limited consistence, and subsequently, so does the interactive system. This supports our assumption that a collection of ideas about one subject can be used to estimate the originality of an idea in a manner that is consistent with human estimates.

Feedback manipulation

For our experimental purposes we enable the system to manipulate the feedback it provides on ideas so that it seems to users that their ideas are 1) less original than they might expect (*negative*), 2) similar to what they expect (*neutral*), or 3) more original than they expect (*positive*). To make sure that these *feedback manipulations* are believable (e.g. not too positive that the user would not take the feedback seriously anymore), we used the data from the pre-study described above to fit three mapping functions (Table 2) that could map the originality of an idea as calculated by the system to an appropriate rating for use in the positive, neutral or negative conditions, as described below.

All the functions were generated using curve fitting (without an intercept). For the neutral manipulation we fitted the systems unmanipulated estimates, with the human estimates. The resulting function maps the system's unmanipulated estimates to approximate to the originality appraisals that people usually expect. To obtain the negative and positive mappings we fitted the human estimates with the lowest and highest scores the participants felt could reasonably be given, using a quadratic function. The resulting functions map the estimates that are processed by the neutral mapping, to originality estimates that are worse or better than people typically expect.

Feedback	Mapping function
Negative	$f(x) = .441x + .004x^2$
Neutral	$f(x) = .814x$
Positive	$f(x) = 1.794x - .008x^2$

Table 2 Generated mapping functions for the negative, neutral, and positive feedback manipulations.

We assume that if users take the manipulated feedback into account as part of the evaluative component of their idea generation process, then these manipulations should influence the way they appraise their ideas, and therefore the link between positive emotion and creative ideation, as explained above.

Feedback presentation

To enable basic textual input of ideas and effectively communicate the feedback on those ideas we developed a user interface. Users can type in their ideas in text blocks using the English language. Upon pressing ENTER the system estimates the originality of an idea, and maps this score to an output value using the pre-specified negative, neutral, or positive feedback manipulation. The resulting output is presented as informational feedback about the idea the user just generated (Figure 3). The feedback is presented by using a colour code (red= unoriginal, orange= somewhat unoriginal, amber= somewhat original, green= original), and numerically using the manipulated ranked estimate of originality.

We assume that presenting the feedback right after each idea is generated, collides with the moment that the user

will anyway tend to evaluate his or her idea, so that the system can inform the user's appraisals of the originality of his or her own ideas, which may then target the hypothesized link between positive emotion and creative ideation.

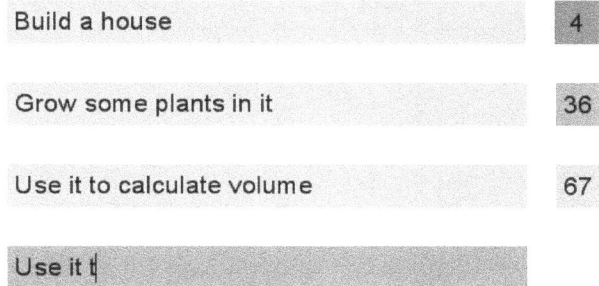

Figure 3 A screenshot of the way feedback is presented showing text entry (left), and feedback (right). The ideas and feedback shown here are responses to the brick as a subject, with the negative feedback manipulation.

Hypotheses

To put our theoretical conjectures and developed interactive system to the test, we experimentally test the following four hypotheses (Table 3).

#	Hypothesis
H1	*Positive, rather than neutral or negative manipulation of computational feedback augments creativity during idea generation.*
H2	*Positive, rather than neutral or negative manipulation of computational feedback causes positive emotion.*
H3	*Negative, rather than neutral or positive manipulation of computational feedback causes negative emotion.*
H4	*Positive, rather than neutral or negative manipulation of computational feedback causes positive emotion, which augments creativity during idea generation.*

Table 3 Hypotheses

METHOD

To test our hypotheses we used an experimental within-subject design. Each participant did three idea generation tasks using the interactive system. For these three tasks the *negative, neutral, and positive* feedback manipulations described above were used, for the brick, paperclip, and knife subjects. The manipulations and the subjects that were used were randomized to prevent research bias, and we used a cover story so that participants were not aware that the feedback was manipulated. In total, 49 people (25 women, 24 men, M_{age}=30, SD_{age}=8.38) participated in our study. Two participants guessed the purpose of the study and five people reported to have tried to game the interactive system by typing in bizarre ideas to gain high originality scores during one or more of the tasks. We removed these cases from further analysis to ensure that these possible extraneous sources of variation did not influence testing the hypotheses. This resulted in 134 usable cases. All participants were students or employees of City University London.

Idea generation tasks

To measure the participant's momentary creative ideation abilities we used the commonly administered alternative uses task (AUT) [33]. The AUT requires participants to generate as many as possible original, creative uses for a common object within a specified amount of time (4 minutes in our study). Participants used the interactive system to do the AUT three times, with the brick, paperclip, and knife as a subject, in random order.

Assessment of originality

We used the system's own originality estimates to calculate an originality coefficient for each participant after each task as follows. Any idea scoring above the 75th rank, according to the unmanipulated estimate calculated by the system, was counted as an original idea (26% of the ideas in this study). For each participant, we divided the number of original ideas by the total number of ideas generated during a task to obtain the participant's originality coefficient for that task. This approach is shown to have more external validity than other common objective ways of assessing originality [31].

Assessment of emotion

At the end of each task, the participants used Likert scales with emotion words on opposite ends to rate feelings of satisfaction (1=not satisfied, 9=very satisfied) and frustration (1=not frustrated, 9=very frustrated) they had experienced during the task. We assumed that these would reflect the type of negative and positive emotions typically associated with goal-conduciveness and goal-obstruction while pursuing a goal under time pressure in this way [32, 35]. Note that feelings only reflect aspects of the emotion components that can be subjectively experienced [35]. Therefore, these measures are a proxy to assess positive and negative emotion.

Manipulation checks

It is conceivable that the feedback manipulations could have made the system's estimates less believable, rather than having the intended effects. To check whether the feedback manipulations in fact led to the intended influences on appraised originality of ideas, the participants used a Likert scale to rate their own creative performance after each task (1=worse, 9=better than expected), as well as how reliable the participants thought that the feedback was (1=very unreliable, 9=very reliable).

Procedure

Upon arrival the participants were seated at the computer and introduced to the study. We used a cover story that informed the participants that we were testing "... *the efficacy of using computer supported idea evaluation,*" but withheld information about the actual experimental conditions until the end of the experiment. Informed consent was signed, and the participants filled in a brief questionnaire to collect personal data. We then explained that they would do three AUTs during which our interactive system would provide feedback about the originality of their ideas. For the AUTs we emphasized that "...*the goal is to come up with as many original, creative, uses of a common object as possible*". For the system's feedback we emphasized that participants should "... *use the feedback as a guide that helps you during your idea generation process.*" A picture of the subject used during each AUT was shown just before each task. Each task took exactly 4 minutes during which time participants could type in their ideas. After each task, participants filled in a questionnaire that was used to assess emotion and enable the manipulation checks described above, and also included filler questions about the way they used the system. After the experiment ended, the true purpose of the study was explained, and we gauged whether the participants had guessed this purpose, had tried to game the feedback by typing in bizarre ideas, or had problems using the system otherwise. To compensate the participants, we handed them a £5 voucher for a large online retailer, and a chocolate bar.

Analysis

To analyze the data from our study, we used linear mixed model (LMM) analysis with two levels [14]. The feedback manipulations were entered as the repeated measures fixed effects at level-1, with random intercepts for the participants nested at level-2. To obtain a suitable covariance structure we entered the data with different covariance structures and minimized the -2 Log likelihood (-2LL) and the model's degrees of freedom. We only accepted models with more degrees of freedom when the decrease in -2LL significantly differed from a simpler model given the χ^2 distribution [14]. For each of the dependent variables we arrived at the scaled identity covariance structure as the best fit, which is used to report our results in the following section.

RESULTS

To make sure that the feedback manipulations targeted the way participants appraised the originality of their ideas as intended, we first carried out two manipulation checks. LMM analysis showed that the effect of feedback manipulations on perceived creative task performance was significantly different in the different conditions, $F(2, 87.86)=55.19$, $p<.001$. However, the perceived reliability of the system's feedback was not significantly different, $F(2, 87.91)=.554$, $p=.577$. This indicated that the feedback manipulations had the intended effect, which helps validate this study within our theoretical framework about the link between originality and cognitive appraisal processes.

To check whether positive and negative emotion influenced creativity across the tasks, we correlated the originality, satisfaction (positive emotion), and frustration (negative emotion) data. Because the data were repeated measures, person-mean centering was used to remove between-person variance [cf. 12]. The results showed that there was a significant positive correlation between satisfaction and originality, and a significant negative correlation between frustration and originality (Table 4). These findings indicated that across all tasks there was a relationship between positive emotion, negative emotion, and creative ideation, which helps validate this study within the context of our theoretical framework about the link between positive emotion and creative ideation.

DV	1.	2.	3.
1. Originality	-		
2. Satisfaction	.382**	-	
3. Frustration	-.438**	-.733**	-

Table 4 Pearson correlation coefficients between the dependent variables originality, satisfaction, and frustration (variables were person-mean centered). *p<.05, **p<.001.

IV	Originality	Satisfaction	Frustration
Negative	.225 (.142)	3.42 (1.71)	5.87 (1.70)
Neutral	.254 (.119)	4.80 (1.70)	5.13 (1.77)
Positive	.292 (.145)	6.14 (1.50)	3.80 (1.89)

Table 5 Means and standard deviations (between parentheses) of the dependent variables for each treatment.

IV	Originality	Satisfaction	Frustration
Negative	-.067* (.026) [-.120 -.015]	-2.70** (.29) [-3.28 -2.11]	2.07** (.31) [1.46 2.67]
Neutral	-.036 (.026) [-.088 .016]	-1.32** (.29) [-1.90 -.73]	1.33** (.31) [.72 1.93]
Positive	.ᵃ	.	.
Intercept	.292* (.021) [.249 .334]	6.12** (.24) [5.65 6.61]	3.81** (.27) [3.29 4.34]

Table 6 Estimates of fixed effects of the feedback manipulations on satisfaction, frustration, and originality. Unstandardized estimates, standard errors (between parentheses), 95% confidence intervals (between square brackets). *p<.05, **p<.001. ᵃData relative to the positive condition, as modelled by the intercept.

The means and standard deviations of the dependent variables originality, satisfaction, and frustration for the

three feedback manipulations are presented in Table 5. To test whether the feedback manipulations influenced originality, satisfaction, and frustration we performed LMM analysis on each of these variables individually (Table 6).

Estimates of fixed effects showed a significant difference between the mean originality coefficients for the feedback manipulations, $F(2, 89.74)=3.33$, $p=.040$. Compared to the positive condition (which corresponds to the intercept shown in Table 6), participants were less likely to generate original ideas in the neutral condition, and even less in the negative condition. Note however, that despite this trend, only the difference between the negative and the positive conditions was significant. The findings indicate that positive, rather than neutral or negative manipulation of computational feedback augments creativity during idea generation. This supports hypothesis H1.

Estimates of fixed effects also showed a significant difference between the mean satisfaction ratings for the feedback manipulations, $F(2, 89.86)=42.27$, $p<.001$. Compared to the positive condition, participants reported significantly less satisfaction in the neutral condition, and even less satisfaction in the negative condition. The findings indicate that positive, rather than neutral or negative manipulation of computational feedback causes positive emotion. This supports hypothesis H2.

Finally, estimates of fixed effects showed a significant difference between the mean frustration ratings for the feedback manipulations, $F(2, 89.94)=23.55$, $p<.001$. Compared to the positive condition, participants reported significantly more frustration in the neutral condition, and even more frustration in the negative condition. The findings indicate that negative, rather than neutral or positive manipulation of computational feedback causes negative emotion. This supports hypothesis H3.

	Originality	Satisfaction	Frustration
Repeated measures	.015** (.002) [.011 .020]	1.90** (.29) [1.41 2.55]	2.05** (.31) [1.53 2.75]
Intercept (subjects)	.005* (.002) [.002 .012]	.73* (.30) [.33 1.65]	1.06* (.38) [.52 2.13]

Table 7 Estimates of covariance for the LMMs. Unstandardized estimates, standard errors (between parentheses), 95% confidence intervals (between square brackets). *p<.05, **p<.001.

In terms of model quality, the estimates of covariance showed that the feedback manipulations (repeated measures, Table 7) represented the majority of variability. However, in all cases the variance for the random intercepts (participants) was significant as well (intercept, Table 7), which shows that there were variables that could explain differences between the individuals in the relationship between the feedback manipulation, and originality, satisfaction, and frustration, that we did not measure.

IV	ACME	ADE	Total effect
Feedback manipulation → Satisfaction → Originality			
Negative	-.075** [-.119 -.037]	.007 [-.053 .068]	-.068* [-.123 -.017]
Neutral	-.037** [-.058 -.017]	.004 [-.027 .037]	-.033* [-.060 -.006]
Positive	.[a]	.	.
Feedback manipulation → Frustration → Originality			
Negative	-.037* [-.070 -.008]	-.031 [-.083 .026]	-.068** [-.117 -.020]
Neutral	-.018* [-.034 -.003]	-.015 [-.042 .012]	-.034* [-.057 -.008]
Positive	.[a]	.	.

Table 8 Multilevel causal mediation analysis of the influence of the feedback manipulations on satisfaction and frustration on subsequent originality. ACME = Average Causal Mediation Effects, ADE = Average Direct Effects. 95% Confidence intervals (between square brackets). *p<.05, **p<.001. [a]Data relative to positive condition.

To add to this, and in particular to test our fourth hypothesis concerning the role of emotion in mediating the effect of our feedback manipulations on creative ideation, we carried out a multilevel causal mediation analysis [42]. The results of this showed that, when the participant's feedback was manipulated to be neutral or more negative, they were less likely to generate original ideas than when the feedback was manipulated to be more positive. Thus the effect of the feedback manipulations on originality was mediated by the increase in satisfaction that was caused by the feedback manipulation (ACME, Table 8 top half), and the decrease in frustration that was also caused by the feedback manipulation (ACME, Table 8, bottom half). The influence of feedback manipulation on originality could only be explained by the caused differences in satisfaction and frustration, as no significant direct effects of feedback manipulation on originality were found (ADE, Table 8). In terms of the differences between the ways in which the two mediation models explained the relation between emotion and creative ideation, we found that the total effect (Total effect, Table 8) for the satisfaction model was similar to the ACME, with only little variation explained by the ADE, whereas the total effect for the frustration model was explained partly by the ACME and partly by the ADE (although not significant in the latter). This provides evidence for a causal relationship between the feedback manipulations, satisfaction, and the generation of original ideas. That is, positive, rather than neutral or negative manipulation of computational feedback causes positive emotion, which augments creativity during idea generation. This supports hypotheses H4, as well H1, H2 and H3.

DISCUSSION AND FUTURE WORK

Our findings demonstrate that an interactive system can be designed to hack into the function of cognitive appraisal processes in emotion, positive emotions in particular, and that this can be used to augment creative ideation. The findings indicate that the feedback from our interactive system influenced the way in which users appraised the originality of their own ideas. The system's manipulation of the feedback influenced satisfaction (positive emotion) and frustration (negative emotion), where providing feedback that made the user's ideas look more original than they really were, rather than the same or worse, helped cause more positive emotion, and less negative emotion (H1 and H2), and helped people to generate more original ideas (H3). The influence of the feedback manipulations on positive emotion, in this case satisfaction, explained most of the impact on creative ideation (H4).

There were also some inconsistencies in the data. Although the impact of our system on positive and negative emotion was effective, not all results for originality differed significantly. Although there is a clear trend that matches our hypotheses, the standard deviations and confidence intervals show that there is also a clear overlap between the conditions. On the one hand we can argue that using the system's estimates of originality as a measure introduces unnecessary noise into the data, which makes the rejection of the null hypothesis less likely. This is to be expected due to the limited consistency with which people, and in the same way, the interactive system, estimates originality. On the other hand, this overlap is likely to be inherent in the way the interactive system is designed to manipulate the feedback. That is, the feedback the user receives depends on the user's own ideas, which can be manipulated only so much without jeopardizing its believability. It is, therefore, likely that the system could in some cases not increase the feedback enough to increase the rate of goal-conducive events to generate a sufficiently strong positive emotion.

Another limitation is that with our experimental setup it is not possible to prove that there is a reciprocal relation between the appraised originality of someone's ideas, positive emotion, and the actual generation of original ideas, which was assumed when conceiving our approach. This leaves the results open for alternative interpretations. For instance, it could be that more negative feedback is simply more inhibiting than positive feedback. Many creativity techniques emphasize that less inhibition (e.g. deferring judgment) is key to creativity [cf. 8, 28]. It is conceivable that people experience positive and negative emotion accordingly, without any impact on a reciprocal link between emotion and creativity. However, theory [23, 32], and our own findings about the causal relation between the feedback, positive emotion, and originality are in fact more in line with our own explanation.

Overall, this study offers a novel contribution to theoretical work about the emotion-creativity link, the design of creativity support tools, and more generally to the design of interactive systems that are intended to cause emotion. From a theoretical perspective, our experimental findings corroborate existing findings on the link between positive emotion and creative ideation [1, 2, 3], and extend these findings by showing a direct causal link between positive emotion and creative ideation, within subjects. Moreover, our research provides, for the first time, concrete evidence for a link between cognitive appraisal processes, positive emotion, and originality within the context under investigation.

From the perspective of technology our approach contributes to creativity support tools by providing a novel way in which such tools can influence the emotion-creativity link [cf. 9, 24, 27, 29]. Moreover, the developed interactive system is one of the first to target creative ideation, by supporting its evaluative component [cf. 16, 20]. Note that using this particular implementation of the interactive system, beyond its experimental purpose, would require it to have a more active and sophisticated way in which it can acquire and relate ideas, to meet the variety of subjects people can generate ideas about. If such a system can be designed, then this potential promises application in different types of creativity support tools, in particular those that enable an active human-machine creative collaboration.

More generally, our approach contributes to interactive systems that are designed to help cause emotion [cf. 17, 37, 43]. In particular, this approach can be valuable in such systems because it is shown to not just influence the feelings that we associate with emotions, but also other adaptive change that associates with emotion, see [7]. This potential promises application beyond creativity support, and may extend to other situations where the adaptive potential of emotion can help people, be it to assist them in performing better at other tasks, or to enable them to support their own wellbeing [6, 15, 21, 36].

Future work will focus on explicitly targeting other cognitive appraisal processes that can be used to help cause emotions to support other aspects of creativity and the creative process in addition to ideation. For instance, a system based on our principles could attempt to explicitly target uncertainty, which forms part of anxiety, and has been linked to deep and analytic processing of information, which can help select ideas that are effective [10]. Moreover, we can extend our approach to other events that are relevant to other goals that may arise during creative ideation, such as the goal to generate effective ideas, which increases the scope of where systems such as ours can be used [8]. Focusing on temporal ways of assessing emotion [e.g. 22] could help explain how the rate of appraisals over time might be used to guide the intensity of an emotion, which could be effective since intensity in particular might hold the key to further augmenting task performance [1].

Given these positive results, we consider this study as a first step toward a novel line of interactive technologies that aim to use the function of cognitive appraisals in emotion, as a way to intentionally cause emotion, with the goal to help people to get more out of their own creative capabilities.

REFERENCES

1. Akhbari Chermahini, S. and Hommel, B. More creative through positive mood? Not everyone!. *Frontiers in Human Neuroscience 6*, (2012), article 319.

2. Ashby, F.G., Isen, A.M., and Turken, A.U. A neuropsychological theory of positive affect and its influence on cognition. *Psychological Review 106*, 3 (1999), 529-550.

3. Baas, M., De Dreu, C.K.W., and Nijstad, B.A. A meta-analysis of 25 years of mood-creativity research: Hedonic tone, activation, or regulatory focus?. *Psychological Bulletin 134*, 6 (2008), 779-806.

4. Banerjee, S. and Pedersen, T. An adapted Lesk algorithm for word sense disambiguation using WordNet. In *Proc. CICLing '02*, (2002), 136-145.

5. Brans, K. and Verduyn, P. Intensity and Duration of Negative Emotions: Comparing the Role of Appraisals and Regulation Strategies. *PLoS ONE 9*, 3 (2014), e92410.

6. Calvo, R.A. and Peters, D. *Positive computing: Technology for wellbeing and human potential.* MIT Press, Cambridge, MA, USA, 2014.

7. Chiew, K.S. and Braver, T.S. Dissociable influences of reward motivation and positive emotion on cognitive control. *Cognitive, Affective & Behavioral Neuroscience 14*, 2 (2014), 509-529.

8. Cropley, A. In praise of convergent thinking. *Creativity Research Journal 18*, 3(2006), 391-404.

9. de Rooij, A. and Jones, S. (E)Motion and creativity: Hacking the function of motor expressions in emotion regulation to augment creativity. In *Proc. TEI '15*, (2015).

10. de Rooij, A. and Jones, S. Mood and creativity: An appraisal tendency perspective. In *Proc. C&C '13*, (2013), 362-365.

11. de Rooij, A. and Jones, S. Motor expressions as creativity support: Exploring the potential for physical interaction. In *Proc. BCS HCI '13*, (2013), article 47.

12. Enders, C. K. and Tofighi, D. Centering predictor variables in cross-sectional multilevel models: A new look at an old issue. *Psychological Methods 12*, (2007), 121-138.

13. Fellbaum, C. (Ed.) *WordNet: An electronic lexical database.* MIT Press, Cambridge, MA, USA, 1998.

14. Field, A. *Discovering statistics using IBM SPSS statistics - 4th edition.* Sage Publications, Thousand Oaks, CA, USA, 2013.

15. Fogg, B.J. Persuasive technology: Using computers to change what we think and do. *Ubiquity*, (2002), 5.

16. Forster, E.A. and Dunbar, K.N. Creativity evaluation through latent semantic analysis. In *Proc. CogSci '09*, (2009), 602-607.

17. Giannoulis, S. and Verbeek, F. The happiness cube paradigm; eliciting happiness through sound, video, light and odor. In *4th Int. Workshop on Emotion and Computing, KI '09*, (2009).

18. Griffin, G. and Jacob, R. Priming creativity through improvisation on an adaptive musical instrument. In *Proc. C&C '13*, (2013), 146-155.

19. Halácsy, P., Kornai, A., and Oravecz, C. Hunpos - an open source trigram tagger. In *Comp. Proc. ACL '07*, (2007), 209-212.

20. Harbison, J.I. and Haarmann, H. Automated scoring of originality using semantic representations. In *Proc. CogSci '14*, (2014), 2327-2332.

21. Koster, R. *Theory of fun for game design*. O'Reilly Media, Inc., 2013.

22. Kreibig, S.D., Gendolla, G.H., and Scherer, K.R. Goal relevance and goal conduciveness appraisals lead to differential autonomic reactivity in emotional responding to performance feedback. *Biological Psychology 91*, 3 (2012), 365-375.

23. Lewis, M.D. Bridging emotion theory and neurobiology through dynamic systems modeling. *Behavioral and Brain Sciences 28*, 2 (2005), 194-245.

24. Lewis, S., Dontcheva, M., and Gerber, E. (2011). Affective Computational Priming and Creativity. In *Proc. CHI '11*, (2011), 735-744.

25. Lyer, L.R., Doboli, S., Minai, A.A., Brown, V.R., Levine, D.S., and Paulus, P.B. Neural dynamics of idea generation and the effects of priming. *Neural Networks 22*, (2009), 674-686.

26. Moors, A. On the causal role of appraisal in emotion. *Emotion Review 5*, 2(2013), 132-140.

27. Morris, R.R., Dontcheva, M., Finkelstein, A., and Gerber, E. Affect and creative performance on crowd-sourcing platforms. In *Proc. ACII '13*, (2013), 67-72.

28. Mumford, M.D., Medeiros, K.E., and Partlow, P.J. Creative thinking: processes, strategies, and knowledge. *The Journal of Creative Behavior 46*, 1 (2012), 30-47.

29. Nakazato, N., Yoshida, S., Sakurai, S., Narumi, T., Tanikawa, T., and Hirose, M. Smart Face: enhancing creativity during video conferences using real-time facial deformation. In *Proc. CSCW '14*, (2014), 75-83.

30. Nyer, P.U. A study of the relationships between cognitive appraisals and consumption emotions. *Journal of the Academy of Marketing Science 25*, 4 (1997), 296-304.

31. Plucker, J.A., Qian, M., and Wang, S. Is originality in the eye of the beholder? Comparison of scoring techniques in the assessment of divergent thinking. *The Journal of Creative Behavior 45*, 1 (2011), 1-22.

32. Roseman, I.J. Emotional behaviors, emotivational goals, emotion strategies: Multiple levels of organization integrate variable and consistent responses. *Emotion Review 3*, 4 (2011), 434-443.

33. Runco, M.A. (ed.) *Divergent thinking*. Ablex Publishing Corporation, Norwood, NJ, USA, 1991.

34. Salamone, J.D. and Correa, M. The mysterious motivational functions of mesolimbic dopamine. *Neuron 76*, 3 (2012), 470-485.

35. Scherer, K.R. The dynamic architecture of emotion: Evidence for the component process model. *Cognition & Emotion 23*, 7 (2009), 1307-1351.

36. Scherer, K.R., Bänziger, T., and Roesch, E. (eds.) *A blueprint for affective computing: A sourcebook and manual*. Oxford University Press, Oxford, UK, 2010.

37. Shahid, S., Krahmer, E., Neerincx, M., and Swerts, M. Positive affective interactions: The role of repeated exposure and copresence. *IEEE Transactions on Affective Computing 4*, 2 (2013), 226-237.

38. Siemer, M. Mood congruent cognitions constitute mood experience. *Emotion 5*, (2005), 296-308.

39. Silvia, P.J., Winterstein, B.P., Willse, J.T., Barona, C.M., Cram, J.T., Hess, K.I., Martinez, J.L., and Richard, C.A. Assessing creativity with divergent thinking tasks: Exploring the reliability and validity of new subjective scoring methods. *Psychology of Aesthetics, Creativity, and the Arts 2*, 2 (2008), 68-85.

40. Slepian, M.L. and Ambady, N. Fluid movement and creativity. *Journal of Experimental Psychology: General 141*, 4 (2012), 625-629.

41. Sonnemans, J. and Frijda, N. The structure of subjective emotional intensity. *Cognition & Emotion 8*, (1994), 329-350.

42. Tingley, D., Yamamoto, T., Hirose, K., Keele, L., and Imai, K. Mediation: R Package for Causal Mediation Analysis. *Journal of Statistical Software 59*, 5 (2014), 1-38.

43. van der Zwaag, M.D., Janssen, J.H., and Westerink, J.H.D.M. Directing physiology and mood through music: Validation of an affective music player. *IEEE Transactions on Affective Computing 4*, 1 (2012), 57-68.

An Enactive Characterization of Pretend Play

Nicholas Davis, Margeaux Comerford, Mikhail Jacob, Chih-Pin Hsiao, Brian Magerko
Georgia Institute of Technology
School of Interactive Computing
{ndavis35, m.e.comerford, mikhail.jacob, chsiao9, magerko }@gatech.edu

ABSTRACT

This paper presents the results of an empirical study of 32 adult dyads (i.e. groups of two people) engaged in pretend play. Our analysis indicates that participatory sense-making plays a key role in the success of pretend play sessions. We use the cognitive science theory of *enaction* as a theoretical lens to analyze the empirical data given its robust conceptual framework for describing participatory sense-making. We present here five enactive characteristics of pretend play that appear to be necessary and sufficient for the emergence and maintenance of successful pretend play – mental preparation, meaning building, narrative enaction, narrative deepening, and flow maintenance. This enactive formalization is used to propose a computational model of pretend play that can be used to inform the design of an agent capable of playing in real time with human users.

Author Keywords

Pretend Play; Creativity; Computational Creativity; Co-Creative Agents

ACM Classification Keywords

H.5.m. Information interfaces and presentation (e.g., HCI): Miscellaneous.

INTRODUCTION

Play is a fundamental aspect of human existence. Although play predates any concept of human culture or society [14, 22] – animals engage in play as children and adults without any formal cultural context – it is an important part of the human condition within familial and social groups. Play serves to strengthen social ties within groups, increase affect between individuals, and allow meaningful learning and practice at creative problem solving [7]. While play has been categorized by multiple efforts, it has yet to be formally understood in terms of the processes and actions participants execute to create a story world together, make stories, and establish shared meaning. Studying the fine grained behaviors of individuals engaged in pretend play

C&C '15, June 22 - 25, 2015, Glasgow, United Kingdom
© 2015 ACM. ISBN 978-1-4503-3598-0/15/06...$15.00
DOI: http://dx.doi.org/10.1145/2757226.2757254

can therefore inform us both about play at a deeper level as well as provide insight into how to formally represent such behaviors in computational systems. These formal representations can in turn help the design of various technologies to support, facilitate, and teach playful behavior.

This article describes our current efforts to characterize successful playful behavior between adult dyads (groups of two people) with an aim towards informing intelligent agents that are capable of playing with human collaborators for entertainment, learning, and play therapy. Our current specific focus is on studying the socio-cognitive capabilities involved in third person pretend play between adult dyads (i.e. play between two participants who physically control objects and characters) [26,29,32]. We present a theory of pretend play based on our empirical observations viewed through the lens of the *enactive theory of cognition*.

The enactive approach in cognitive science emphasizes the "social and intersubjective nature of human understanding" [23]. While our analysis may have employed other cognitive theories, such as embodiment, distributed cognition, situated action, social cognition, or information processing, enaction provides a framework that unifies elements of each of these approaches together, which helps provide a systemic perspective of pretend play. In particular, enaction emphasizes the role that emergent and dynamic social coordination plays in guiding and facilitating perception and action [28]. We leverage the robust conceptual framework and vocabulary of enaction to formally represent participatory sense-making in the domain of pretend play.

Enactive cognition explains *interaction dynamics*, striving primarily to understand how perception and action are coordinated with the environment and other agents in that environment through emergent and continuous interaction known as *structural coupling* (or simply *coupling*). In this theory, stable relationships between perception and action characterize co-constructed meaning in the environment (i.e. the 'rules of the game' that help guide behavior and frame expectations to facilitate successful interaction) [13].

In his work detailing the enaction paradigm, Vernon [30] describes sense-making as the process by which "emergent knowledge is generated by the system itself [as] it captures some regularity and lawfulness in the interactions of the system, i.e. its experience." Our empirical study of play, as described in this paper, suggests that the primary process or mechanism that drives dyadic pretend play can be described as participatory sense-making (multiple agents engaged in coordinated sense-making), per the enactive theory of cognition [13].

We contend that successful pretend play requires players that are willing to a) co-construct shared meaning, b) enact a narrative based on that shared meaning, and c) deepen the narrative in a coordinated manner to maintain the flow of the emergent play experience. There are many communication, interaction, and cognitive strategies and processes recruited in successful pretend play, but our primary contention is that *participatory sense-making is the fundamental phenomenon that gives rise to successful dyadic adult pretend play.*

This article begins by briefly reviewing research on pretend play and similar technical projects in other creative domains working towards developing co-creative agents that improvise with humans in real time. It then describes our empirical investigation into dyadic pretend play and presents our enactive characterization of pretend play. Qualitative examples are provided throughout the characterization to demonstrate the utility of the enactive concepts to account for the success or failure of play. Finally, it presents a visual convention for representing the interaction dynamics of participatory sense-making. We describe how data collected using this novel convention can inform a computational model of pretend play.

RELATED WORK

A multitude of empirical studies of play have revealed its fundamental importance for development, in terms of cognition, communication, and emotion [6,19,24]. However, as Sutton-Smith has argued, the next step to understanding play is the development of detailed processual accounts of play [29] - of which there are few. Indeed, formal models of the socio-cognitive processes involved in play are fewer still. Zook et al. previously presented a formal computational model of pretend object play, but focused almost entirely on the process of substitution between real and pretend objects as opposed to any interactional aspects of play [32]. Bello presented a formal model of pretense as counterfactual logical reasoning within the PolyScheme cognitive architecture [3]. Nichols and Stich also offer an architectural model of pretense referring to a Possible Worlds Box as a separate mental workspace used during pretense [20]. However, all three models differ fundamentally from the work presented here by relegating interactions between agents playing pretend to future work. In contrast, our work focuses strongly on the interaction between agents engaged in pretend play.

While some researchers in the field of social robotics have begun to look into how robots can interact with humans to collaborate in socially appropriate and meaningful ways, this work remains outside the field of play research [1]. Outside of social robotics, the majority of agents capable of creative collaboration with human partners have come from studies of music improvisation [4,12,18], collaborative drawing [11], contemporary movement improvisation [16], and theatrical improvisation [17]. Magerko et al.'s Digital Improv Project employs the concepts of offers, iconicity, and shared mental model negotiation in order to create agents capable of playing improv games, such as Three Line Scene and Party Quirks [2,21]. Davis et al.'s Drawing Apprentice takes an enactive approach similar to the one advocated in this paper to implement an enactive co-creative agent that is able to collaborate on a drawing in real time with human users [11]. All of these agents demonstrate a capacity for creative collaboration to build an artifact, either a piece of music or performance, but fail to address many of the larger problems involved in creating an agent capable of interacting effectively in open ended interactions, such as pretend play.

EXPERIMENTAL DESIGN

We conducted an observational experiment to investigate pretend play during which we recruited adult dyads (i.e. groups of two) to play together in different conditions. Overall, 32 dyads were recruited, with a total of 64 participants. Recruiting advertisements specified to bring a partner to the study (i.e. participants were not playing with strangers). Participants were recruited from the student population of the Georgia Institute of Technology (age range 18-24; n=33 male, n=31 female). Of the 32 pairs, 16 consisted of male/female pairings, and the other 16 were pairings of the same gender (male/male, female/female).

Before beginning their experimental play sessions, participants were asked to complete three warm-up activities to get them into a playful mood and comfortable in the play space provided: *Zip-Zap-Zop* (a fast paced language game), *One Word Story* (players take turns adding one word to a story), and *Animalistics* (acting out an animal using a toy without talking). Next, participants completed two pretend play sessions lasting five minutes each, which were recorded, resulting in 64 play sessions to analyze. As shown in Figure 1, the play sessions took place on a large play-mat laid out over tables to allow players to stand while playing. Toys were kept in a box on the edge of the table containing primary-colored foam blocks and a varied selection of toys, such as those shown in Figure 1.

Participants were randomly assigned one of four scenario prompts to guide their play. To determine what the most popular scenarios would be given the toys we provided, an Amazon Mechanical Turk study was conducted. The four most common play scenarios suggested from that study were "Drag Race", "Car-Smash-A-Thon", "Monsters Attack", and "Zoo Visit".

During the first play session both participants were given the same (randomly-selected) prompt to guide their play, while during the second session, their prompts differed (referred to as session A and B in data analysis, respectively). Half of the 32 dyads groups were asked not to talk (sound effects were permitted) during their sessions in order to investigate the effect of verbal communication on pretend play. In all conditions (talking and non-talking), participants were encouraged to play together and find a way to use both of their prompts in the same play story. After each session, we administered a retrospective protocol analysis during which participants were shown their filmed play session and asked to describe their motivation, intention, and general thoughts on the actions they took during the play session.

Figure 1: Experiment setup of toys and play mat with two participants from the adult dyad study.

DATA ANALYSIS

Since relatively little is formally known about the sociocognitive processes of pretend play, we designed our data analysis method as an exploratory investigation to characterize playful behavior. We utilized a grounded theory [14] approach to the data analysis that began by reviewing the video records from the pretend play studies and coding the data to identify prominent concepts and categories. Initially, we framed our analysis purely in terms of identifying all the observable behaviors involved in human dyadic pretend play to embrace the bottom-up, data-driven approach of grounded theory. Through gradual iteration, we devised a categorization and coding scheme that described actions and related concepts at a fine level of granularity. Example categories included: Player, Object Type, Object Role, Play Action, Communication, Narrative Development, and Milestones.

Within each category, there were often many nuances and subcategories. Communication and narrative development had the most compelling and complex subcategories. Communication, for example, had several elements, such as whether the communicative act was verbal versus non-verbal, performed in character (diagetic) versus breaking character (non-diagetic), and the context of communication, i.e. whether the communicative act was utilized as a play offer, acceptance, or negotiation. The motivation for selecting a communication strategy seemed to be related to previously established co-created meanings, which subsequently helped guide the narrative going forward. It

was therefore not as productive to look at individual actions as much as at the flow of actions and interactions through time (i.e. the interaction dynamics of the players).

As our analysis continued, it became clear that the dynamic and flowing nature of participant interactions could not be explained by any one action or combination of actions. The success of play appeared to be correlated to some emergent property of multiple factors. After comparing our empirical play data to the processes described in enactive literature on sense-making, we hypothesized that pretend play and participatory sense-making feature a similar process of social coordination utilizing the history of interactions, negotiated meaning, and feedback from verbal and non-verbal communication. With this observation and insight from the initial coding set, we iterated on our coding scheme once more by leveraging the concepts of participatory sense-making in enaction that help describe interaction dynamics.

We scoped our research question as a means of operationalizing our data-driven insights and reframed the investigation to ask: *what are the minimal requirements to enable an agent to successfully play?* To answer this question, we framed our analysis using concepts from the theory of enaction and focused primarily on a) continuously evolving interaction (rather than discrete actions and cognitive scripts) and b) different ways of coupling and coordinating interaction between agents to build meaning in a way that leads to successful play.

This type of analysis required an event level description of what types of perceptions and actions players used to make sense of the current interaction throughout the play session. This included a description of what actions the players performed and what analysts inferred they were trying to achieve with those actions given the current and historical context. To acquire this data, we performed an event level textual description of all the videos by carefully watching and transcribing an *intentional description* of what analysts inferred participants were trying to accomplish, a *behavioral description* of the how participants performed the actions to accomplish their intention, and an *evaluation* examining how this particular interaction related to the perceived success or failure of the play session.

Examining the data through the lens of enaction theory - in particular the concepts describing the sense-making process – facilitated our conceptualization of what could be happening during play. We composed a list of core and causal mechanisms controlling key sense-making processes during pretend play. We then employed these enactive characteristics observed in successful pretend play to further quantify the relative success of each of the sessions. We assigned a score of 3 if all 5 characteristics were present, a score of 2 for 3 if 4 of the characteristics present, and a score of 1 for 1 to 2 of the characteristics present.

Two analysts independently scored the data, achieving an inter-rater reliability score of .80 (joint probability agreement) with a Cohen's Kappa of .69 (substantial agreement). Of 64 total sessions, approximately 18 sessions were given a score of 3, 29 sessions were given a score of 2, and 20 sessions were given a score of 1. We performed a t-test (alpha of) to compare the success rates of talking and non-talking sessions. A t-test revealed there was no significant difference between the evaluation scores of talking and non-talking sessions (alpha of < 0.05; t-value of 0.36). A second t-test was performed on the scores for different vs. same play prompts. No statistically significant difference was found in the scores for sessions in which the experimental task involved the same play prompt and different play prompts (alpha .05; t-value of 0.80).

ENACTIVE CHARACTERIZATION OF PRETEND PLAY

Our data suggests that there are five critical ingredients required for two agents to successfully play: 1) Enter into a 'playful mindset,' willing to engage in imagination; 2) Negotiate a set of rules and roles that constitute a nucleus activity; 3) Embody characters and interact through them in a shared narrative world; 4) Introduce creative actions and elements to make the narrative more interesting; 5) Ensure coordination by negotiating timely additions to the narrative. Each of these ingredients is described in detail below referring to empirical data from the play session, as it is helpful to describe the characteristic. The play sessions are numbered 1-32 and denoted with an A or B depending on whether they were the first or second play session of the experiment, respectively.

Prepare the Mind

Enter into a 'playful mindset' to frame the interaction and set expectations. While pretend play typically comes easily to children, adults may feel self-conscious and perhaps even silly playing with toys and creating an imaginary story world. For play to be successful, participants should be open and willing to 'suspend their disbelief' and work to fully immerse themselves in the narrative world. Preparation strategies observed in the data include taking on the persona of a character and beginning to interact with the environment through that character. Actions that signal a player is attempting to 'embody' the persona of a character provide evidence of mental preparation. For example, participants often lowered their voice and moved more slowly when controlling large monster characters, such as Godzilla.

Players who failed to prepare themselves during the warm-up activities also tended to fail to immerse themselves in play, as was the case for Session 25. During Session 25, Player 1 appeared uninterested in playing, as evidenced by minimal participation in the warm-up games; that player attempted to gloss over each game by doing the bare minimum required to finish the game or let the timer run out. Based on our observation, this player was not open and

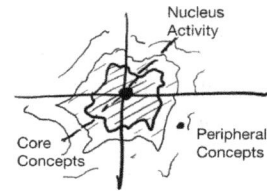

Figure 2: Depiction of nucleus activity

willing to become immersed and play in an imaginary world. The data indicates that the more immersed players become, the easier it is to generate actions to perform, which can lead to more successful play (as shown in examples in the next subsection).

Build Meaning

Negotiate a set of rules and roles that constitute a nucleus activity and shape interaction. Players co-construct a new reality, a shared narrative world, by physically and conceptually structuring the environment in meaningful ways, taking control of characters, and providing details and specifications of characters that help enact the narrative [27]. Without a basic foundation of shared meaning, the participants don't know the 'rules of the game,' so to speak, and therefore cannot enact a narrative and successfully pretend play. We define this minimal seed of shared meaning as a *nucleus activity*, which is the most clearly defined and agreed upon elements of a story world and their most prototypical associations (i.e. prototype theory of categorization [25]). By definition, nucleus activities contain at least one role for each player and one rule to guide and shape interaction in some manner (see Figure 2).

The nucleus activity consists of a solidly negotiated core with peripheral concepts that are tangentially related for either participant. The strategies participants use to build meaning and co-construct nucleus activities vary drastically. The number of elements used to add onto the nucleus activity and build the narrative world, for example, does not seem to necessarily correlate with the success of the play session (as one of our initial hypotheses suggested). Rather, the quality or depth of meaning attached to each of those elements influences success. Assigning more details to further specify the role of their characters facilitates a deeper character embodiment. As players become more deeply immersed in the narrative world, they subsequently interact more naturally through that character.

Session 24A provides a good example of a nucleus activity serving as the seed from which complex interactions emerge. The players in this session initially worked together to construct a tower and other structures while making casual dialogue about the construction process. Then, Player 1 quickly grabs Tiger the toy box and performs a large jumping motion while roaring, and said "Giant Tigger. Giant Tigger attacks!" Her dialogue suggests that she specified a more detailed role for her character as a *giant* Tigger, a particular type of Tigger, that has the tendency to attack, which is the first ingredient for a nucleus activity. Player 2 acknowledges the attack (a precondition for negotiating a solid nucleus activity) when he said, "…and everyone is dead already…" Player 2 then goes in the box to retrieve a large character of his own and says, "Now, what do the monsters do?" Player 1 exclaims: "They fight each other!" and Player 2 responds, "Of, course!" and he laughs, indicating he agrees and is entertained and engaged by the decision. That sequence of dialogue sets up the 'monsters fight each other' nucleus activity that grows and transforms throughout the rest of the play session. Next, they added an additional rule to the nucleus activity of characters 'dying' after they are attacked by the monster. After a character died, the players would go to the box to recruit the next character for battle. Each time a new character was brought in front of Player 1's Tigger character, she would have it attack that character, including multiple pounces and roars.

There were several interesting narrative developments that were born from the simple nucleus activity identified here. Each action was rationalized with respect to the 'monsters fighting each other' nucleus activity as well as the individual capabilities and nuances of each character.

This example demonstrates that the quality of meaning that is co-constructed and applied to elements in the play space is more influential that the number or type of elements used in the play session. Individuals that were obviously not immersed in the narrative tended to have less qualitatively meaningful elements in the narrative world, which suggests that *preparing the mind and being consciously open and willing to immerse oneself in an imaginary world is correlated with the depth and complexity of meaning co-constructed in the narrative world.*

Enact the Narrative

Embody characters and interact through them in a shared narrative world. Once a nucleus activity is well established, players perceive the real objects of the environment (i.e. blocks and toys) through a 'perceptual logic' [10,11] that filters perception with respect to the co-created meaning structures of their nucleus activity. Examples of perceptual logic that could account for interaction patterns in pretend play include character motivations, character play affordances, narrative trajectory, environmental constraints (e.g. the setting), and feedback (e.g. other players).

Actions are not generated solely from a narrative or cognitive script. Rather, actions emerge through embodying and taking on the persona of a character and performing actions that make sense for that particular character in that particular narrative world (which may happen to draw upon previously learned cognitive scripts). Character definitions, motivations, and tendencies are adjusted based on feedback from their play partner. Narrative is an emergent quality of pretend play that arises as players work together to make sense of their respective actions (both retroactively and proactively) in the context of meaning structures established thus far in the play session. We propose that this "social coordination through interaction" is a form of participatory sense-making and a key component of describing pretend play.

For example, once the players in Session 24A defined the nucleus activity of 'monsters fighting each other' it was easy for them to focus on interacting with each other and creating interesting and funny variations on that initial nucleus activity. One type of variation on a 'rule' in the nucleus activity involved varying the type of action used in this particular type of monster fight, which was largely dominated by Tigger during the first half. As a result of Tigger's tendency to bounce, the monster fighting was generally accomplished in a bouncy and circular type path. At one point, when Player 2 is controlling a small plastic Godzilla, the participants form a tightly coupled action loop where Player 2 would try to jump on top of Tigger; Player 2 would then bounce Tigger on top of Godzilla.

The pattern repeated as participants laughed and made comments about it. Player 1 remarked, "You can't keep a Tigger down!" and player 2 replied, "You can! I just haven't bounced on his tail yet!" Player 2's last statement suggests the formation of a new rule in the nucleus activity that relates Tigger's tail to his ability to bounce. According to this logic, damaging Tigger's tail should limit his ability to jump, thus leading to a 'winning' scenario for Player 2's character. Player 2, however, cannot think of a way for his Godzilla character to reasonably damage the tail of Tigger at this point in the play session. He allows Godzilla to be defeated and returns to the box to find another candidate.

Later, Player 1 finds a super hero, and introduces it to the play session, "…wait…wait…a super hero!...I guess it's wolverine or something…come to save the day!...even though the people are already dead, but…" At this point Player 2 takes over Tigger, while Player 1 controls the Wolverine character she just took from the box. When Player 2 controls Tigger, he tries to further specify the character saying "He is made of rubber, so you can't stab him." However, Player 1 disagrees he is made of rubber and thinks he can be stabbed. Player 2's assertion that Tigger as 'rubber' makes sense given Player 2's initial contention that the only way to hurt Tigger was by damaging the tail.

Both participants generally agreed upon the basic nucleus activity of 'monsters fighting' and its rules about characters dying, but through the process of enacting the narrative participants explore the search space of the nucleus activity and pushed its boundaries. When participants disagreed, it was because there was a further specification that was assumed by one player given the agreed upon nucleus activity, but that assumption was not shared by the other player. This was evidenced by the disagreement about the circumstances under which the Tigger character can be defeated. Disagreements typically spur negotiations that provide opportunities to deepen the narrative and make it more engaging.

Deepen the Narrative

Introduce creative actions and elements to make the narrative more interesting. Purely enacting a basic narrative is engaging for a short period of time. To maintain creative engagement for an extended period of time, it seems necessary for players to add additional details and elements to the story world. This aspect of participatory sense-making no doubt has different strategies. We observed one strategy in particular that appears to be a recipe for success.

First, a nucleus activity is negotiated during initial setup. That nucleus activity can contain different amounts of complexity and detail. It can be negotiated using a variety of methods, but it minimally involves a definition of rules and roles. Those rules and roles have relevant knowledge associated with them, which should be considered as being included in a 'shared conceptual search space' of the co-constructed nucleus activity. Each action players perform has a certain semantic distance (degree of relatedness between concepts) from the core of this nucleus activity. Actions that are further away from the core are defined as more creative.

Creative actions require more explicit forms of negotiation because they might fundamentally change the nucleus activity and narrative world based upon it. When distant creative actions are not successfully negotiated, "siloed" play may occur as each player's mental model of the narrative world diverges. Successfully negotiating creative actions expands the core of the nucleus activity, as shown in nucleus activity expansion phase of Figure 4. Since the conceptual space of the nucleus activity is by definition a shared search space, its expansion increases the possibilities for relevant interactions, which tends to make it easier for individuals to play successfully.

Questions and actions that help clarify and add specificity to elements of the nucleus activity help to enact a narrative. For example, as players in 33A walked their character around the zoo, they questioned how the animals were caught, which provided an opportunity to provide an interesting back-story. Player 1, as his Godzilla character asked, "How did you manage to catch this giant tiger?" Next, Player 2 responded with a witty retort, "With a lot of cat nip…" When players rationalize their selections with respect to the nucleus activity, they tend to help make the narrative world more robust, interesting, and creative.

Maintain the Flow

Ensure coordination by negotiating timely additions to narrative. The creativity of participants and the actions they perform must be paired with the ability to maintain the flow of the play session through time. Successful sessions typically featured players that were attentive to their partner and strived to include them in a meaningful way.

Depending on the demands of the situation, this can include subtle gestures, such as seeking feedback using eye contact. More active attempts maintenance activities involve explicitly engaging their partner, such as directing actions and dialogue toward them, or asking their partner questions to prompt elaboration. Social skills such as collaboration and empathy are important factors here.

Good players maintain a healthy respect for the rules of the nucleus activity, and will defend actions that violate those rules in some way (while still remaining open to negotiation). When players take creative actions that could be classified in the distant periphery of the nucleus activity, sometimes negotiation is required to ensure the nucleus activity expands properly. For example, in the Session 24A we described earlier, the participants have an interesting negotiation analyzing whether or not Tigger is made of rubber and therefore immune to 'claw' attacks. Player 1 acts as the Wolverine character and stabs Player 2's Tigger character, repeating "…stab, stab, stab…" Player 2 responded, saying "Nope…he is made with rubber so he cannot be sliced through with the claws." Player 1 objected, saying "Yeah he can!"

At this point, the physical play activity slowed down and players faced toward each other to continue the dialogue (while still performing the same attack actions, but with less vigor). Player 1 defends her point by saying, "Rubber can totally be cut with claws, especially when they are hard like him." Player 2 elaborates his initial 'rubber Tigger' addition to the nucleus activity to negotiate further, saying "Well…it self-heals, mostly…" Player 1 is not satisfied, and responded "Pffft, not really…besides-- [Player 1 performs slicing action from her Wolverine character on Tigger's tail]…cut off your tail!"

This turn of events ties back into one of the earliest rules added to this nucleus activity when Player 2 himself defined Tigger's tail as the special damage point that would render the character immobile. Player 1 takes a lead role throughout the negotiation and relies on a previously established part of the core nucleus activity to add a creative twist to the narrative.

Once Tigger's tail is cut off, Player 2 laments, "Oh no! Now Tigger is land-bound and must crawl around like a *normal* tiger, and he tries to eat wolverine, but wolverine is…" Player 1 then finishes Player 2's statement "…wolverine just slashes him up…" Next, Player 1 takes a lead role again and suggests the formation of a new nucleus activity, saying "Time to rebuild the town..." Player 2 agrees, and he continues on that trajectory by saying 'OK, and now wolverine rebuilds the town…' Player 2 interjects, "by himself…amongst all the dead people," referring to the initial play action that started the nucleus activity, i.e. Tigger destroying the town and all of the people dying.

The above example illustrates how Player 1 is guiding the play session and leading the interaction while still allowing

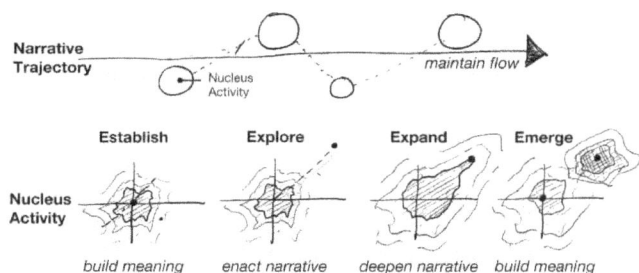

Figure 4: A narrative trajectory emerges from making sense of the current and previous nucleus activities

and encouraging contributions from the other player. Similar to how a good conversationalist knows when a topic is becoming stale, good players consciously maintain the flow of the play experience. Players engage in a coordinated dance of building on and subverting their partner's intentions in the shared narrative world by modulating between enacting and deepening the narrative. This skill involves knowing when to add depth to the narrative world and how to include your partner in that process. Through time, creative activities expand nucleus activities into new domains that might require slightly more rule definition and specification, eventually forming an independent nucleus activity, as shown in emergent nucleus activity phase in Figure 4.

Successful play sessions tend to have relatively well defined leader/follower roles that naturally switch over time as players come up with new ideas and strive to implement them in the story world. Oftentimes, the most successful play sessions involved players who handed off leadership to each other as their narratives progressed. Players that exhibit leadership in play tend to work to 'make sense' of both their and their partner's play actions by developing a common thread tying together the various nucleus activities constructed throughout the play session, termed the 'narrative trajectory' and shown in Figure 4.

AN ENACTIVE MODEL OF PRETEND PLAY
Enaction helps provide concepts like participatory sense-making that are useful for producing the above descriptions of successful pretend play, but how do we transition from this framework to a formal representation that informs the design of an intelligent agent that can play with humans? In the following section, we formalize the ideas of participatory sense-making to develop a computational tractable model of interaction dynamics in pretend play.

Interaction Dynamics of Participatory Sense-Making
As part of our ongoing analysis, evaluation, and formalization of the enactive characterization of pretend play, we developed a visual convention for graphing the interaction dynamics of social coordination in participatory sense-making. A graphical convention to represent the interaction dynamics would support comparative analysis of

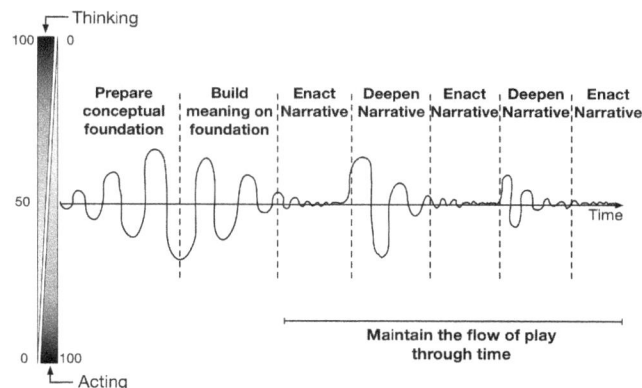

Figure 3: The enactive characteristics of pretend play mapped onto a sense-making curve

multiple pretend play sessions to further formalize our enactive characterization of pretend play. For example, determining how well participants worked together to *maintain the narrative* involves understanding several temporally contingent factors, such as the fluid nature of turn taking and leadership (i.e. whether players actively worked to include their partner), the degree to which participants are immersed in a shared narrative world, and what type of cognitive processing players employ throughout their interactions. From these empirically derived features, we devised the following requirements for graphing interaction dynamics in pretend play. The visual representation should:

1. Distinguish between neatly delineated turns and fluid coordination

2. Distinguish between high and low degrees of cognitive effort

3. Distinguish the approximate type of cognitive processing a player is engaged in, i.e. whether the player is devoting attention resources to mental activity (i.e. developing mental models and forming hypotheses to *build meaning*) or physical activity (i.e. performing and adapting actions to *enact the narrative*).

4. Represent the temporal distribution of these three features through time in a quantifiable manner

Figure 3 shows a sense-making curve using the graphical convention we developed for modeling interaction dynamics in pretend play. When the sense-making curve is plotted through time, the direction and manner of its progression characterizes the approximate narrative trajectory or flow of narrative experience through time.

The horizontal axis shows the progression of time during a play session, while the vertical axis corresponds to the distribution of the agent's limited attention resources at that point in time, i.e. the agent's cognitive load. The top quadrant corresponds to the general category of cognitive processing associated with thinking, while the bottom quadrant corresponds to the type of cognitive processing emphasized during performing actions.

As the player expends more cognitive resources thinking (i.e. building narrative meaning by forming models and hypotheses about co-constructed narrative elements), this curve would rise above the horizontal axis. Conversely, as the agent attends to their environment during the performance and negotiation of actions (i.e. performing the rolling motion associated with driving a toy car), the curve would fall below the central line.

The magnitude of the deviation in either the top or bottom quadrants corresponds to the approximate degree of cognitive effort exerted by the agent. Our graphing convention defines the zero points for the two vertical scales of thinking and acting at the top and bottom of the graph, respectively. This convention creates an inverse relationship between two overlapping scales. This method is preferred over two distinct linear processes with zero beginning at the central horizontal line given the fundamental assumption of enaction that humans think through action and act in order to facilitate thinking [13]. With this convention, the central horizontal line represents a roughly 50% distribution of cognitive resources between thinking and acting. For example, in session 24A (see Maintain the Flow section) players generated new modifications to their characters (i.e. imbuing Tigger with the quality of 'rubber' to deflect incoming attacks) at the same time as performing actions with those characters. In this circumstance, we might find several instances where the player's cognitive load could be described as 70% action and 30% thinking or some fluctuation thereof.

A section of the sense-making curve would correspond roughly to Csikszentmihalyi's definition of *creative flow* [9], where an individual is 'in the zone' and does not have to think or plan their creative contributions. Rather, Csikszentmihalyi reports that individuals experiencing flow often report an effortless execution of task and complete immersion in the activity. Conversely, an agent actively making sense of their environment would fluctuate around the central line in a slow percept-action feedback loop, as seen in preparation and building sections of the sense-making curve in Figure 3.

Modeling interaction dynamics using sense-making curves also helps formalize the role an agent might play in participatory sense-making in the context of pretend play. For example, the data shows how nucleus activities gradually grow in an organic and emergent manner through coordinated negotiations (described in the Maintain the Flow section). However, the question remains as to the exact processes and procedures utilized during this sense-making procedure. The sense-making curve provides a tool to make quantifiable predictions and hypotheses about the types of interaction dynamics and negotiation strategies that are observed to influence successful pretend play.

Nucleus Activities as a Shared Search Space

The empirically derived concept of nucleus activities suggests a design principle for conceptual search spaces that can potentially increase the feasibility of designing an agent that effectively 'plays' in real time. Based on our enactive characterization, we propose an approach to knowledge acquisition and learning in a pretend play agent by defining several nucleus activities over time that each serves as a separate conceptual search space for the agent. While a narrative thread connects these nucleus activities, the agent's computational processing (i.e. action recognition, action selection, and action modification) can be constrained to each individual nucleus activity as an independent search space during that particular phase of the pretend play session.

Within the confines of each individual nucleus activity, the agent can perform a constraint satisfaction process to generate and adapt actions in real time. Below are four initial constraints in the pretend play domain based on unique features of play (i.e. toys, partners, narrative, etc.) as well as features that were helpful in analyzing interaction dynamics in the pretend play data.

1. The literal physical constraints and affordances of the environment based on the player's body (i.e. how easily grasped toys are, the plushness of their texture, etc.).

2. The pretend constraints and affordances of the environment and the characters the players are actively using (i.e. whether a player's character can climb over, see, or reach various elements in the play world).

3. The narrative trajectory and flow of the play experience, i.e. bias search results toward those interactions that would somehow extend the current nucleus activity or link to previously defined nucleus activities.

4. Partner feedback, such as verbal communication, turn rhythm, eye contact, smiles, laughter, and looks of confusion or boredom.

The difficult and interesting computational challenge in this context is defining how an agent might be able to successfully negotiate a seemingly incongruous object into the narrative through negotiation and in real time. Given the observations from the pretend play data, successful negotiation includes gradual negotiation of an idea, including modification and elaboration of the seed idea. Negotiation includes multiple strategies that could be modeled using algorithms specializing in combinatorial creativity [5,8,31]. To account for the largely distinct type of actions generated during the building and enacting phases of pretend play, it is useful to delineate separate constraint satisfaction processes for co-creative pretend play agents.

The first constraint satisfaction process can be employed to determine a seed idea. This constraint satisfaction process corresponds roughly to the enactive characteristic *building meaning*. It deals large with constraints 1-3 identified above. Next, the agent works to negotiate that new idea into the existing nucleus activity or start a new nucleus activity. The initial seed action itself can be relatively simple, but the agent needs to be equipped with strategies and skills that enable negotiation and participatory sense-making. For example, the agent should be able to 'test out new ideas' through experimentation.

Encoding a large knowledge base for the agent to search through to select seed actions is less important than providing the agent with the ability to modify actions effectively. We see evidence of tightly coordinated and successful play interactions that evolved from relatively basic nucleus activity and seed idea. For example, Session 24A began with the seed idea of 'Business Man Zoo Visit.' The selection of 'business man' and 'zoo' played less of a role in constraining action selection than subsequent modification, elaborations, and specifications of the nucleus activity, as described in the Maintain the Flow section. Interactions that leverage existing nucleus activities fall into the category of enacting the narrative. While a co-creative agent is actively engaged in enactive the narrative, resources should be dedicated to interpreting feedback and social cues from the play partner for use in the modification and elaboration of elements of the nucleus activity.

Thus, the ideal co-creative pretend play agent should be capable of learning to: 1) select appropriate seed actions to build new meaning; 2) modify and elaborate seed action through real time negotiation and interaction; and 3) employ 1 and 2 at the appropriate time to help maintain the flow of the play session. These high level system needs demonstrate how the enactive characteristics can be employed to inform the design of co-creative pretend play agents.

FUTURE DIRECTIONS

The next steps in our research agenda include further quantification of our empirical play data by manually graphing each play session using the conventions of the sense-making curve presented earlier. Multiple analysts will be recruited to review each session to plot a sense-making curve for each player describing their approximate interaction dynamics throughout the play session. The granularity and the precision of the graph can change based on the needs of the analyst and the stage of analysis. For example, in early stages of data analysis, researchers can sketch rough depictions of the entire session at a low resolution for coarse-grained analyses and comparisons. In particular, this procedure benefitted the authors given the particular complexity of open-ended creative tasks and the large number of interconnected variables that all subtly influence the creative process.

The current method of manually plotting sense-making curves by hand is slow and imprecise. We are currently developing a research tool to optimize the process of producing sense-making curves from data in real time. This tool presents video data from the play studies along with a joystick interface and a real time plot of the joystick output visualized in a sense-making curve. This tool will enable researchers to rapidly produce sense-making curves to support exploratory and comparative data analysis.

The sense-making curve data will enable us to evaluate hypotheses generated by our enactive characterization of pretend play. For example, given the prevalence of participatory sense-making, we predict that turn frequency would gradually increase as participants solidified a shared activity. Further, each new nucleus activity could spawn another participatory sense-making process during which users work to gradually assimilate the new contribution to the narrative world. We plan to conduct another round of coding using the sense-making curves

Concurrently, we have begun implementing a co-creative play agent that attempts to build nucleus activities through negotiation and feedback, as observed in the pretend play studies. As the results from the sense-making curve analysis are formalized, these insights will be leveraged to help answer hypotheses generated from our enactive characterization of pretend play. These results will help further formalize and model the interaction dynamics of participatory sense-making in pretend play. This degree of formalizing will help inform what type of interaction dynamics and machine learning algorithms might be effective in co-creative pretend play agents.

CONCLUSIONS
This paper reports on an empirical investigation into pretend play between adult dyads. We used the cognitive science theory of enaction as a lens to analyze our empirical data and developed an enactive characterization of pretend play. In particular, we propose five characteristics of play that all rely on participatory sense-making: preparing the mind, building meaning, enacting the narrative, deepening the narrative, and maintaining the flow of the play session. The enactive concept of participatory sense-making was proposed as the key mechanism of pretend play. We developed a novel graphical convention called sense-making curves to model and represent interaction dynamics over time. Our future work includes conducting another round of data analysis to plot sense-making curves for all the pretend play sessions. This data will help evaluate the predictions and hypotheses generated by our enactive characterization of pretend play.

ACKNOWLEDGEMENTS
This work is supported in part by NSF IIS grant #1320520.

REFERENCES

1. Bartneck, C. and Forlizzi, J.A design-centred framework for social human-robot interaction. *Robot and Human Interactive Communication, 2004. ROMAN 2004. 13th IEEE International Workshop on*, (2004), 591–594.

2. Baumer, A. and Magerko, B.Narrative development in improvisational theatre. In *Interactive Storytelling*. Springer, 2009, 140–151.

3. Bello, P.Pretense and cognitive architecture. *Advances in Cognitive Systems 2*, (2012), 43–58.

4. Beyls, P.Interaction and Self-organisation in a Society of Musical Agents. *Proceedings of ECAL 2007 Workshop on Music and Artificial Life (MusicAL 2007)*, (2007).

5. Boden, M.A.*The Creative Mind: Myths and Mechanisms*. Weidenfeld & Nicolson, London, 1990.

6. Brown, S.L.*Play: How it shapes the brain, opens the imagination, and invigorates the soul*. Penguin, 2009.

7. Caillois, R.*Man, play, and games*. University of Illinois Press, 2001.

8. Colton, S., López de Mantaras, R., and Stock, O.Computational Creativity: Coming of Age. .

9. Csikszentmihalyi, M.*Flow*. Springer, 2014.

10. Davis, N., Do, E.Y.-L., Gupta, P., and Gupta, S.Computing harmony with PerLogicArt: perceptual logic inspired collaborative art. *Proceedings of the 8th ACM conference on Creativity and cognition*, 2011, 185–194.

11. Davis, N., Popova, Y., Sysoev, I., Hsiao, C.-P., Zhang, D., and Magerko, B.Building Artistic Computer Colleagues with an Enactive Model of Creativity. *International Conference on Computational Creativity*, AAAI (2014).

12. Eigenfeldt, A. and Pasquier, P.Negotiated content: generative soundscape composition by autonomous musical agents in coming together: freesound. *Proceedings of the Second International Conference on Computational Creativity, Mexico City*, (2011), 27–32.

13. Fuchs, T. and de Jaegher, H.Enactive intersubjectivity: Participatory sense-making and mutual incorporation. *Phenomenology and the Cognitive Sciences 8*, 4 (2009), 465–486.

14. Glaser, B.G., Strauss, A.L., and Strutzel, E.The discovery of grounded theory; strategies for qualitative research. *Nursing Research 17*, 4 (1968), 364.

15. Huizinga, J.*Homo Ludens: A study of the play - element in culture*. Routledge, 1950.

16. Jacob, M., Coisne, G., Gupta, A., Sysoev, I., Verma, G.G., and Magerko, B.Viewpoints AI. *AIIDE*, (2013).

17. Magerko, B., Manzoul, W., Riedl, M., et al.An Empirical Study of Cognition and Theatrical Improvisation. *Proceedings of the Seventh ACM Conference on Creativity and Cognition*, ACM (2009), 117–126.

18. McCormack, J.Eden: An Evolutionary Sonic Ecosystem. In J. Kelemen and P. Sosík, eds., *Advances in Artificial Life SE - 13*. Springer Berlin Heidelberg, 2001, 133–142.

19. Morgenthaler, S.K.The meanings in play with objects. *Play from birth to twelve and beyond: contexts, perspectives, and meanings*, (1998), 359–367.

20. Nichols, S. and Stich, S.P.*Mindreading: An integrated account of pretence, self-awareness, and understanding other minds*. Clarendon Press/Oxford University Press, 2003.

21. O'Neill, B., Piplica, A., Fuller, D., and Magerko, B.A Knowledge-Based Framework for the Collaborative Improvisation of Scene Introductions. In M. Si, D. Thue, E. André, J. Lester, J. Tanenbaum and V. Zammitto, eds., *Interactive Storytelling SE - 10*. Springer Berlin Heidelberg, 2011, 85–96.

22. Pellegrini, A.D. and Smith, P.K.Physical Activity Play: The Nature and Function of a Neglected Aspect of Play. *Child Development 69*, 3 (1998), 577–598.

23. Popova, Y.B.Narrativity and enaction: the social nature of literary narrative understanding. *Frontiers in psychology 5*, (2014), 895.

24. Power, T.G.*Play and exploration in children and animals*. Psychology Press, 1999.

25. Rosch, E.Cognitive representations of semantic categories. *Journal of Experimental Psychology: General 104*, 1975, 192–233.

26. Sawyer, R.K.*Pretend play as improvisation: Conversation in the preschool classroom*. Psychology Press, 1997.

27. Sawyer, R.K.*Improvised dialogues: Emergence and creativity in conversation*. Greenwood Publishing Group, 2003.

28. Stewart, J.R., Gapenne, O., and Di Paolo, E.A.*Enaction: Toward a new paradigm for cognitive science*. MIT Press, 2010.

29. Sutton-Smith, B.The role of toys in the instigation of playful creativity. *Creativity Research Journal 5*, 1 (1992), 3–11.

30. Vernon, D.*Artificial Cognitive Systems*. MIT Press, 2014.

31. Wiggins, G. a.A preliminary framework for description, analysis and comparison of creative systems. *Knowledge-Based Systems 19*, 7 (2006), 449–458.

32. Zook, A., Magerko, B., and Riedl, M.Formally Modeling Pretend Object Play. *Proceedings of the 8th ACM Conference on Creativity and Cognition*, ACM (2011), 147–156.

Beyond Slideware: How a Free-form Presentation Medium Stimulates Free-form Thinking in the Classroom

Rhema Linder, Nic Lupfer, Andruid Kerne, Andrew M. Webb,
Cameron Hill, Yin Qu, Kade Keith, Matthew Carrasco, Elizabeth Kellogg
Interface Ecology Lab
Department of Computer Science and Engineering
Texas A&M University, College Station, Texas USA
{rhema,nic,andruid,andrew,cameron,yin,kade,matthew,elizabeth}@ecologylab.net

ABSTRACT

We investigate how presentation in a free-form medium stimulates free-form thinking and discussion in the classroom. Most classroom presentations utilize slideware (e.g. PowerPoint). Yet, slides add intrusive segregations that obstruct the flow of information. In contrast, in a *free-form medium of presentation*, content is not separated into rigid slide compartments. Instead, it is visually arranged and transformed in a continuous space.

We develop a case study that investigates student experiences authoring, presenting, viewing, and discussing free-form presentations in a graduate seminar class. We analyze interviews, present a sampling of student presentations, and develop findings: free-form presentation stimulates free-form thinking, spontaneous discussion, and emergent ideation.

Author Keywords

Presentation; slideware; new media; education

ACM Classification Keywords

H.5 Information Interfaces and Presentation (e.g. HCI)

INTRODUCTION

This work investigates how classroom presentation in a free-form medium stimulates free-form thinking and discussion among students and the instructor. Presentation is a major component of classroom education. *Slideware* presentation media, such as PowerPoint, organize content into discrete elements, chained into linear sequences. Tufte criticizes PowerPoint as harmful to cognition because it, "Slices and dices evidence into arbitrary compartments" [35].

In contrast, in a *free-form medium of presentation*, content is not separated into rigid slide compartments. Instead, it is visually arranged and transformed in a continuous space. We

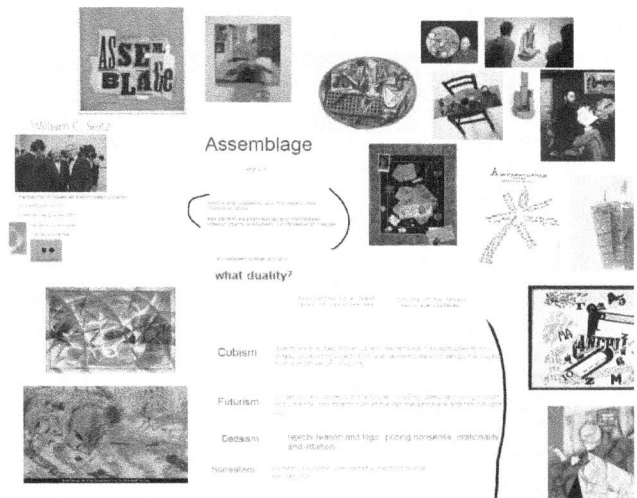

Figure 1. A multi-scale information composition, created and presented in class by a student instructor, on the Art of Assemblage, by William Seitz. View online: `http://ideamache.ecologylab.net/v/x2unOPmLEC/`

develop a case study investigating student experiences authoring, presenting, viewing, and discussing free-form presentations in a graduate seminar class.

Illich motivates the importance of free expression and thought in education [13]. Free-form thinking is spontaneous and unrestricted. We define *free-form thinking* as involving: (1) improvisational exploration of associations; (2) the emergence of new ideas, generated through building on previously known associations; (3) divergent wanderings to unexpected places; and (4) spontaneous synthesis of new understandings, relationships, and ideas.

To author free-form presentations, students engaged in web curation using the *IdeaMâché* system [14, 23]. The present research follows the conceptual model of the art world, where curation has become a mode of discourse involving the spatial arrangement of exhibition forms, using conceptual strategies of information systems [26]. Lupfer identifies the processes of *curation* as gather, assemble, annotate, and exhibit [23].

IdeaMâché supports curation and presentation in the medium of *information composition*, in which elements are gathered from web pages, and assembled to form a visual semantic whole, which is intended to stimulate creative cognition of relationships [16]. The elements of curation are text, image, video, and sound clippings. The forms of annotations are text and sketch. Processes of curation are performed in a web browser. Curations are stored in the cloud, enabling authoring and presenting from anywhere.

We identify IdeaMâché's form of composition as a *free-form medium*, both of web curation—as users gather, assemble, annotate, and exhibit content—and of presentation, when they exhibit their curations in the classroom. Sketch annotation enables unconstrained markings to be incorporated in curations, while text annotation enables open exposition. Elements can be positioned anywhere relative to each other, as the user performs assemblage on a continuous 2½D canvas. They can be positioned, scaled, and rotated. A zoomable user interface enables organizing and presenting content at different levels of magnification, comprising a medium of *multi-scale information composition*. During authoring and presentation, the camera, can be positioned anywhere in the 2½D space.

Students in the graduate seminar course, *Curation and Ideation meet Social Media* (CISM), adopted IdeaMâché as a presentation tool (see Figure 1). The situated context of the classroom provides an ecologically valid environment for investigating the impact of free-form presentation on education. Graduate students in a seminar course are expected to engage in a high level of scholarship, asking critical questions and meaningfully contributing to class discussions.

Our research question investigates, *How does IdeaMâché's free-form medium of curation and presentation impact student and instructor experiences in the classroom?* We suspected that free-form presentation would have advantages, based on prior findings in the fields of visual thinking [2], art [4], and creative cognition [9].

We conducted semi-structured interviews to gain insight on the impact of using a free-form presentation medium in a discussion oriented course. We asked students to explain their experiences and processes as authors, presenters, and audience members. We analyzed interview data using grounded theory methods [34], forming four conceptual categories: *free-form assembly*, *curation and presentation practice*, *presentation improvisation*, and *as the audience*.

Our findings show how a free-form medium of presentation stimulates free-form thinking, improvisation, spontaneous discussion, and emergent ideation. Based on our findings, we discuss opportunities for advancing pedagogy and implications for the design of presentation tools for education.

RELATED WORK

Slideware
Slideware is a category of presentation support software which use slides to author and deliver presentations. A slide is set of information contained in a single view. Typically, a slide contains formatted text, an image or two, and may include video or audio media. During the performance of a presentation, a slideware deck shows a sequence of slides, which functions as a visual aid while the presenter speaks. Popular slideware includes Microsoft PowerPoint and Apple Keynote.

Tufte argues that the limitations of slideware result in mistakes [35]. The medium's ready-made bullet point lists promote confusion. When presenting, the relatively low resolution encourages using shorthand phrases instead of nuanced articulation. He berates PowerPoint as inappropriate for serious work after an analysis of templated Colombia Space Shuttle slides:

> [R]igid slide-by-slide hierarchies, indifferent to content, slice and dice the evidence into arbitrary compartments, producing an anti-narrative with choppy continuity.

In Tufte's view, the sequential and rigid slide-by-slide and line-by-line animations in PowerPoint create obnoxious transitions in a low-fidelity pigeonholed format. Instead of PowerPoint presentations, he prescribes using handouts. He rejects Miller's Magical Number Seven [24] as justification for the six words by six lines practice of PowerPoint. Instead, he suggests Miller's work motivates that building on *context* increases how many elements can simultaneously be understood.

Presentation Support Software
Prior research has addressed the shortcomings of slideware by transforming how the information presented and navigated. Criticisms of slideware has led researchers to explore ZUI media [11, 12, 21, 27], flexible ordering of slides [33], virtual blackboards [30], and multiple screens [5].

Zoomable user interfaces (ZUIs) enable the user to manually control the scale of the view, using continuous changes in scale as a fundamental interaction technique [3]. Good and Bederson developed CounterPoint, a ZUI presentation medium with paths that connect content for presentation [11]. They argued that ZUIs address problems with linear presentation software by providing a non-linear sequence during presentation delivery, maintaining multiple sequences through a presentation, and allowing different levels of details in context. They reported that CounterPoint provided better visual queues to prompt questions from their audience [12]. Fly [21] and Prezi [27] also implement ZUI presentation media, but the sequence of prepared views is linear, rather than hierarchical. Prior ZUI presentation tools use planned paths, rather than live navigation though pan and zoom. Rigid linear progression does not support improvisation, which enriches discussion oriented classes.

Spicer et al. addressed time constraints in presentation, creating a system that alters slide sequences based on importance [33]. NextSlidePlease automatically generates a slide sequence, including detailed slides for long presentations and overview slides when less time is available. In a study, participants re-created PowerPoint presentations, finding NextSlidePlease helped mange time constraints. We report on students skipping content in free-form presentations to manage time.

Lanir et al. observed differences in the dynamics and spontaneity between how presenters used slideware and blackboards [19]. Presenters rarely returned to previous slides, but often drifted back and forth between ideas when using the blackboard. To support a larger visual space and enable non-linear presentations, researchers have developed systems which make use of multiple displays [20, 5]. MultiPresenter enables displaying two slides simultaneously, or one slide along with a finite space in which the presenter can clip content from any slide, arrange, and annotate [20]. Bligh and Coyle observed use of a multi-display presentation system in architecture education critiques [5]. They found creative benefits for both students and instructors as serendipitous discoveries emerged through drawings to elaborate ideas and unforeseen juxtapositions of content from the use of multiple displays. Free-form presentations juxtapose information in a continuous view, furthering this line of inquiry.

Curation and Appropriation

In the most broad sense, curation is a selective human process of choosing and combining items that provide value for a specific context [29]. Processes of curation creates wholes which have value beyond their individual elements. Curation enables generating and expressing ideas [16, 22]. People can consciously work with information as a means to generate and better articulate ideas [16]. For example, people use Pinterest to find and combine Pins from others, creating unique sets of image bookmarks [22] that address everyday, personal needs. This work explores free-form curation for authoring and delivering presentations in the classroom.

Popular digital curation tools, such as Pinterest and Tumblr, are designed for distributed viewership. In contrast, in-person presentations are visual aids for a live audience. Like slideware, Pinterest, Tumblr, and other curation tools use linear boards to store content [16], and so compartmentalize. In a free-form curation medium, however, content elements are visually transformed and arranged in a continuous space. Students in CISM used multi-scale information composition to create free-form presentations.

The process of curation is beneficial to personal learning because it provokes reflection and interpretation [37]. Webb et. al describe curation as an iterative, cyclic process, which helps people reflect, interpret, and construct relationships among ideas and content. We investigate curation as a means to author and exhibit in person presentations, in anticipation of the audience's needs.

Visual Thinking and Cognition

Presentations and their media are visual aids and support external cognition [31]. There are many approaches to describing how people perceive and utilize vision in cognition.

Arnheim argues that human processes of perception and thinking are difficult to separate [2]. Instead, thinking and perception both occur through the same cognitive mechanisms. For example, a person can both look (perceive) and close their eyes and imagine (think) to perform a number of operations: selection, abstraction, synthesis, combination, separation, and contextualization. These operations help people recognize and generate patterns from phenomena, helping form concepts for productive thinking.

Berger frames analysis through art, how we see paintings and other visual media [4]. He notes that children look and recognize before they speak. To *see*, one must purposefully choose to give something attention and attempt to recognize context. The meaning of an image depends on its context, that is what is seen immediately before, after, and along with it.

Finke explores visualization in the mind's eye as a means of invention [9]. Finke's experiments showed that people can imagine simple shapes and combine them to form emerging designs, e.g. the letters O and V can be manipulated to form an ice-cream cone. Experiments have shown the usefulness and novelty of designs started from images in the mind's eye. Spatial and visual cognition tends to use combinations and operations as creative stepping stones. The eventual solution is often not planned, but emerges from combinations who's value may only be recognized in hindsight. He calls these non-immediately useful combinations *pre-inventive structures*.

Tversky shows how visual communication is selective and relies on context from the world to enable practical interpretation [36]. For example, abstract maps can support navigating a city. She argues that visual communication involves telling a larger 'truth' by being selective and distorting details.

IDEAMÂCHÉ: FREE-FORM WEB CURATION

Students used the IdeaMâché system to curate media and perform presentations. IdeaMâché is designed to support expression and creativity online through a free-form medium of curation. The system's zoomable curation canvas supports gathering and assembling clippings, annotating with sketch and text, and a range of expressive visual and spatial transformations on all elements. Curated elements in IdeaMâché are represented as *rich clippings*. The system automatically captures each clipping's context in the web, as a metadata summary, using the type system developed by Qu et al. [28].

Zoomable Curation Canvas: Multi-Scale Assemblage

IdeaMâché provides a zoomable canvas for curating rich clippings and annotations. This supports organization of curated elements in the medium of *multi-scale information composition*, creating relationship which span across multiple levels, extending the tradition of the Eames' Powers of Ten [8].

IdeaMâché's zoomable curation canvas is a practically infinite 2½D space. Users are able to pan indefinitely and arrange elements of curation as close or far away as they like. This enables assemblage of content across position and scale.

In our study, students and the professor used IdeaMâché to assemble multi-scale curations. Subsequently, to perform a presentation, they moved the camera manually across and into their curations, to navigate among views (using the present IdeaMâché). The cognitive and neuromuscular effort involved in this navigation was non-trivial. Participants learned to navigate presentations effectively, despite this effort.

Annotation capabilities afford exposition, which involves labeling, explaining, expounding, connecting, and illustrating. IdeaMâché supports annotations in forms of text and sketch. Sketch annotations enable expression through drawing. The roles of sketch annotations include textural, relational (e.g., arrows and boxes), literal (drawings of objects), and abstraction. Text annotations enable labeling the whole curation and subsets of elements. They thus support explicit categorizing, as well as expression through writing. Basic text editing, styling, and formatting are supported.

IdeaMâché supports visual transformation of clipping and annotation elements. The user can freely position, scale, rotate, layer, and blend elements. Through the use of visual transformations, users create engaging and emergent information compositions, juxtaposing concepts and telling stories.

STUDY: CURATION AND IDEATION MEET SOCIAL MEDIA

Curation and Ideation Meet Social Media (CISM) was a graduate seminar course taught during the Fall 2014. The course was open to students from a variety of disciplines, including, arts, humanities, social sciences, computer science, and engineering. Of the 12 students enrolled, 2 were undergraduate students. An additional 3 students audited the course. Thus, there were a total of 15 students, 12 male and 3 female.

The charter of CISM was to consider what curation is, how it serves human needs for engagement in ideation, and actual and potential involvement of social media. Students were asked to imagine future personal and social forms of curation and ideation, and roles for people and computing. They investigated contemporary curation and ideation practice, with reference to art contexts, empirical theories of creative cognition, graphical presentation, and social media.

In this seminar course, students were expected to participate at an advanced level. The course schedule included a comprehensive set of research readings, individual assignments, and a final project. Final projects involved curation, design, systems, information visualization, studies, and writing.

Participant Observer Methodology

We took a participant observer approach in our investigation. Participant observation is a thoroughly accepted method of ethnography, because it has been shown that all ethnographies inherently represent the perspectives of the ethnographer(s), as well as subjects [7]. In developing this research, our positions as researchers, students, and instructors overlap. Thus, we invoke a ethnographic methodology of first-person thick description, as advanced by practitioners such as Geertz [1].

We introduced IdeaMâché at the beginning of the semester of CISM. For the first class, the instructor, a co-author of this work, presented a course overview using IdeaMâché. In the next class, the *student instructor*, another co-author, presented a tutorial about how to use IdeaMâché. He also used IdeaMâché as the presentation medium.

We followed our evolving research protocol, as IdeaMâché has been used in various courses during various semesters. We ask students to participate in a study. We give students consent forms that allow us to gather their curations and ask them for interviews. We emphasize that participation in the study was optional and that it would not affect grades. In practice, in this stage, we are unsure as to if we will analyze a course's data and perform any further study.

Student Presentations

The instructor gave few presentations. Instead, student presentations on the course's primary readings led discussion and learning in class. The Research Literature Presentation assignment specified distilling and connecting significant research contributions from a set of readings, then contextualizing these vis-a-vis others across the curriculum and more broadly, in the fields of HCI, CSCW, and creative cognition. It further specified, "Make your slides (Powerpoint, Prezi, Sheets, ...) visually support and complement what you will say verbally." Of 22 total, 3 research literature presentations were given by the instructor, 4 by the student instructor, and 17 by other students. In practice, all of these research literature presentations used IdeaMâché. This was apparently influenced by the precedent set by the instructor and student instructor who gave the first four presentations with IdeaMâché.

Students also made presentations as part of two specified projects: (1) Curation: Analysis | Synthesis (individual), and (2) Final Project Cycle (team-based).

1. *Curation: Analysis | Synthesis* involved writing a short essay on a set of readings, authoring a curation, writing another short essay in response to the curation, and presenting and discussing the curation in class. This project was assigned twice, for different sets of readings. In regard to the medium of curation, the assignment specified: "IdeaMâché, Pinterest, Buzzfeed, Tumblr, or propose another platform and get [the instructor] to agree."

2. Presentations in the final project cycle were made once at the proposal stage, once in the middle, and once at the end. No specification was made about presentation medium.

As the end of the semester neared, we realized that almost all of the presentations in the course had been made with IdeaMâché. While we had anticipated some use from students, the level of adoption far exceeded our expectations. We sensed that an interesting educational process had been engaged and body of work created through presentations in the course. Thus, we decided to investigate further. Our main research question was: *How does IdeaMâché's free-form medium of curation and presentation impact student and instructor experiences in the classroom?*

Visual Data

We develop and present *visual data*. By this, we mean that the curation products stand as themselves, as aesthetic, conceptual, and communicative works, for direct interpretation by researchers. In this way, visual data sits alongside of qualitative and quantitative data, in mixed methods.

We collected students' free-form presentations, which were turned in as part of course assignments. In total, students and instructor created 44 free-form presentations using IdeaMâché. We present this significant body of work as a visual dataset, through an online spreadsheet [http://goo.gl/O4qpTb]. The spreadsheet features links to each of the 20 research literature and 24 Analysis | Synthesis presentation curations, for viewing in IdeaMâché. Free-form expression, visual explanation, and non-linear connections are clearly visible.

Student	Background	Gender
P1	PhD student. Works in industrial engineering and process management.	M
P2	PhD student with EE background. Works in same lab as P1.	M
P3	Part time Masters student. Software developer.	M
P4	Masters student graduating this semester with recently funded startup.	M
P5	PhD Student. Prior masters degree was in computer engineering. Now working in HCI.	F
P6	PhD Student in HCI. Works in same lab, but not on IdeaMâché.	M
P7	PhD Student in HCI. Works in same lab, but not on IdeaMâché. A co-author of this work.	M
P8	Undergraduate in Computer Science. IdeaMâché developer and co-author of this work.	F
P9	Undergraduate in Computer Science. IdeaMâché developer and co-author of this work.	M
P10	Student instructor, co-author of this work.	M

Table 1. We interviewed 10 of the 12 students registered for CISM.

Qualitative Data

We interviewed 10 of the 12 students (Table 1) who were enrolled in the course. Two of these were undergraduates. The instructor was not present for interviews. Semi-structured interviews ranged from 30 minutes to slightly over an hour. We recorded audio from each interview and later transcribed results. Two co-authors, who participated as students and tutors in CISM, led interviews.

Semi-structured interviews began with general questions about each student's background. We asked about experiences in authoring, presenting, and observing IdeaMâché use in class. We asked each student to contrast to prior experiences with slideware. For the first half of the interview, two researchers and an interviewee sat around a table without looking at the student's presentation. This allowed the participant to reflect from memory.

Next, we asked participants to login to IdeaMâché and show us their work. Gathered around a large display, we continued the dialogue, contextualized by the visual data, information compositions they had authored and used in presentations. This elicited participants to reflect on specific elements of their work, in the context of the course.

Using grounded theory methods [34], we investigated student experiences and perspectives. We initially transcribed four interviews and performed open coding. This produced more than 50 unique code labels, such as "macro shape", "great presenters" and "detours". Using these open codes, we formed and analyzed four conceptual categories: *free-form assembly*, *curation and presentation practice*, *presentation improvisation*, and *as the audience*. We recoded the first four interviews and coded the remaining six from this perspective. Using this framework, we also drew on prior literature to form theory and present findings.

FINDINGS

We report on findings from the student interviews. Students employed *Free-form Assembly* to create continuous structures of information. Classroom interactions helped foster a *Curation and Presentation Practice* which encouraged experimentation and helped students develop skills organizing and presenting. Students responded to questions and class discussions with *Presentation Improvisation*. Finally, they participated and recognized high quality work *As the Audience*.

Free-form Assembly

In their interviews, students explained that the free-form medium supported them in displaying and connecting a large amount of information. The medium of information composition of clippings imposes fewer constraints on the scale and position of information compared to those of slideware. Students gathered and assembled clippings, manipulating the position, scale, and other visual features of clippings and connected ideas with sketch and text annotations.

Students reported that multi-scale information composition was more effective for associating content elements, as compared to PowerPoint. Students were able to think about and express relationships though positioning clippings and using sketch annotations. They spatially grouped related clippings to form 'clumps'. P8 talks about her process of organizing her presentation.

> P8: Even when I was planning the presentation I was able to put thoughts down and arrange them in clumps and groups, rather than having them on different slides in a specific order and not allowing me to be more flexible with how I arranged everything.

P8's experience coincides with prior findings on cognitive processes that arise through curating and categorizing. Curation requires human qualitative reasoning and critical thinking [29]. Lakoff and Johnson [18] assert categorization is essentially an experimental process. In P8's view, the free-form medium of presentation supports her improvisation in thinking as she arranges clippings to test different relationships.

The visual and conceptual connectedness supported by free-form assembly extends beyond creating 'clumps' to the information composition as a whole. Through the use of scale and zoom, multi-scale information composition enables presenting relationships across levels of scale. We call this multi-scale organization. P9 highlights the holistic connectedness of the medium and how it contrasts with PowerPoint.

> P9: It feels like there's this place where you're putting everything and you're making [different clippings] bigger and smaller, but it all feels like its one big connected thing. Whereas PowerPoint feels like you've chopped up a lot of stuff.

P9's critique of PowerPoint, as "chopped up", mirrors Tufte's [35] assessment that slides segregate information. In comparison, free-form presentation extends cognition by connecting related items together in 'chunks' [24]. The zoomable and near-infinite canvas provides ample space for expressing and articulating complex relationships. P9 continues:

> P9: It's the difference between having a bunch of stuff on notecards and like having a bunch of stuff on a piece

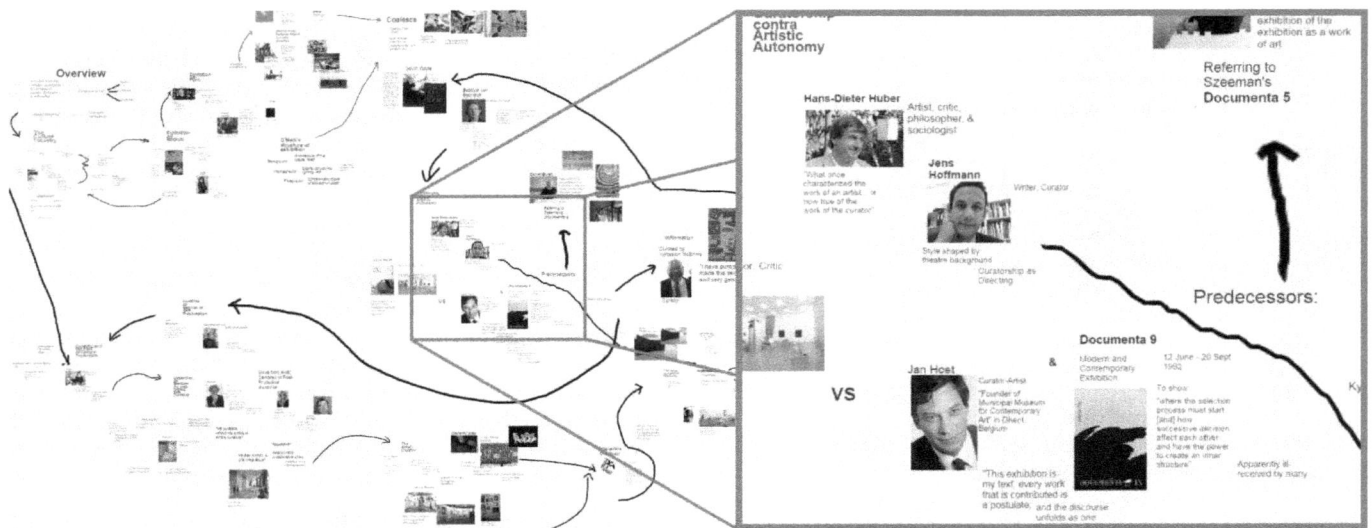

Figure 2. A student presentation, authored by *Trey Roady*, shown as a zoomed out view on the left with a detailed view of a specific area on the right. Viewable online: `http://ideamache.ecologylab.net/v/WclWQvZdTT/`.

of paper. [Information] on the notecards [is] all still in the same stack, but its all on different pieces of paper.

Alongside the use of position and scale, students used sketch annotations to articulate relationships between clippings and chunks of clippings (e.g., Figure 2). For example, P1 describes his use of sketching in his presentation, and P3 explains how sketches help structure information.

> P1: I use the drawing tool for arrows, to try and provide connections over how things flow through the structure, what path I'm taking through it so people can see where I'm going next. I also use those arrows to point back and show where new material points back to old material.

> P3: Well the nice thing about lines is that they direct your attention. ... Having lines, arrows, things like that, provide additional structure to the entire presentation.

> P7: It would be much harder to do [my presentation like this in] PowerPoint. [With PowerPoint], you have headers and section headers, and maybe sections. ... I think it's much harder to show the relationships and structure in Powerpoint.

The visual medium of presentation, that is, slideware or free-form, impacts a students ability to perform associational thinking. The medium may may help or hinder students connecting, conceptualizing, articulating, and understanding information. The free-form medium of multi-scale information composition helped students understand and create relationships among ideas.

Curation and Presentation Practice

The use of IdeaMâché was not required, but through the emergent culture of the classroom, it became the dominant tool used in the course. Most students did not have prior experience with IdeaMâché. However students felt comfortable using it, following the instructors' examples. Students learned the capabilities of the medium by participating in the class and experimenting outside.

P4 describes how seeing other students give their research literature presentations helped him learn the course expectations.

> P4: Seeing other presentations definitely helped me understand that I needed a little more ... prior work, specifically.

Students lead the majority (17 of 22 total) of research literature presentations. After seeing the professor, student instructor, and others' used IdeaMâché for course presentations, students grew comfortable in using it in lieu of slideware. While this was not required, they chose to use IdeaMâché for all research literature presentations and Curation: Analysis | Synthesis assignments. P3 saw the high level of student involvement as a way to make the course engaging. P2 notes his motivation for choosing to use IdeaMâché.

> P3: [CISM has] a different format of students actually engaging in lectures and presenting the lecture material.

> P2: It is to the professor's taste. The class is emphasizing IdeaMâché. ... [I thought], maybe it fits this class.

While students recognized the value of a free-form medium for presentation in the classroom, they saw PowerPoint as more formal. The look of IdeaMâché seemed informal to P3 and P4. One source for this perception may be the overwhelming popularity of slideware media. For contexts such as P4's start up investment and P6's conference presentations, an "executive look" can be crucial.

> P3: So [IdeaMâché] was overall an easier experience. It didn't look as professional, but ... [it is] more suited to brainstorming activities [and]... informal presentations.

> P4: Prezi is not a formal way of presenting at all. Microsoft nails it when it comes to formal presentation,

because of their enterprise roots. ...Prezi came into it late, compared to PowerPoint. ...We did try Prezi with a couple of investors, and trust me feedback wasn't really good. ...We went back to PowerPoint. You meet so many investors, but at the end of the presentation, you kind of gauge how the audience has understood it.

P6: I don't trust myself to fly by the seat of my pants [at internship and conference presentations]. Which, if I was doing something with IdeaMâché for those cases, I might be a little bit more worried if I still do a professional presentation with less structure.

While P4 was willing to try different presentation media, his audience did not receive it well. P6's view is that strong, non-improvised presentations are more appropriate for conference presentations. The context of CISM was more receptive of informal styles and alternate presentation media.

Students both observed presentations from class and browsed free-form presentations in IdeaMâché to familiarize themselves with how the medium could be used. They drew from examples to learn to better articulate ideas through information composition of clippings. While P4 emulates great work, P2 avoids pitfalls.

P4: I basically bookmark and keep [great work]....it gives you a better perspective of how you would use the tool. ...Presentations were much cleaner and much more precise and well designed than the first set.

P2: I liked the clear structure of IdeaMâché. ...There are a lot of freedoms in IdeaMâché ...if the structure is too complex, I feel like that might not be a good thing.

IdeaMâché's free-form medium requires ongoing critical thinking to effectively organize and structure information. P2 critiques overly complex design. P4 notes student presentations became better organized and more precise with practice.

Presentation Improvisation

Students describe their experience of presenting with IdeaMâché as planned, while leaving room for improvisation. By leveraging free-form presentation structures, presenters were able to manage audience attention. The free-form medium supported presenter improvisation, enabling them to embed details in presentations. without knowing if they would get covered. Students used the medium to help respond to spontaneous class discussion. In contrast, with typical slideware, presenters add in-depth details after the 'last' slide. P1 calls this strategy "hidden slides".

P1: You know that someone is going to ask you about this heavy data slide, but you don't have the time. What you'll do is put it at the end ...as a *hidden slide*. When you scroll through during presentation mode, it doesn't show up, but the moment that somebody asks, you can pop out, pull out the hidden slide and say, "here."

We contrast this interaction with how P3 answered a question.

P3: I was talking about social and cognitive causes ...and then the question came up about some additional

causes that were similar and touched on in the other paper. So I zoomed out from this area over here and refocused that. And then, after that, I simply went back.

The free-form medium enables connecting details to an overview, using scale. Connected concepts are positioned in lateral relationships. Students, such as P2 and P3, panned and zoomed through these spatial structures, taking on the role of a discussion conductor, who guides the attention of the audience to cover the main points of a presentation, while supporting free-form thought.

P3 compares free-form presentation to "choose your own adventure" games, in reference to a classic genre of non-linear children's books (e.g. [25]). In his presentation, P3 included more details than he expected to present.

P3: I covered about 75 percent of [my presentation], but there was another 25. ...And then, I just covered whatever was appropriate during the presentation and whatever direction the questions went or wherever the interest was. It's kind of like a *choose your own adventure*.

...You have the content that you expect to cover that you are intending to cover ...but there were all these possibilities that I could see branching off.

P2: [Panning and zooming is] a way to guide their attention. ...Conceptually I think I built some smooth connections around these digital objects.

To P6, guiding audience attention is important. He describes a tradeoff between slideware and free-form presentation:

P6: With a Powerpoint, ...it's easier to make sure they don't see what's coming up next. So I have more control over the experience. Whereas with this, it is really hard for me to keep people from looking ahead, which I may or may not want depending on how I want to present the material. ...I feel like it helps me fluidly focus on different ideas during the presentation. I can bring in ...different media from different places which ...sort of facilitates discussion during the presentation.

Free-form presentation, while offering less total control, helps the audience look ahead, stimulating spontaneous discussion. P6 also highlights heterogeneous kinds of media that can be curated. His presentations juxtaposed scholarly media with entertaining and relevant videos.

Manipulating precise views over a free-form presentation can be challenging.

P2: part of [IdeaMâché's] worth is that its flexible, but when I present, I'm not be very good at controlling IdeaMâché. Sometimes ...I zoom out too fast. So, maybe the audience will be a little bit confused.

While free-form presentation is flexible, supporting spontaneous discussion, transitioning from view to view smoothly can be difficult.

As the Audience

Students from CISM were presenters and audience members. We asked students to characterize their experience as audience members. In general, presentations were understood and stimulated class discussion. Certain presentations (see Figure 2) stood out to students as beautiful and effective.

In some cases, students produced disorderly presentations. This may have been due to time limitations, unfamiliarity with the medium, or design skills. A free-form medium is not a panacea. Without proper design, presentations can appear muddled. P1 suggests a technique of 'signposts' for visualizing themes to help mark progression through a presentation.

> P1: Some people had difficulties knowing what they wanted to say next, what they wanted to say about a topic, they had to explore the space when they were up there. ...A couple of people did not know exactly [what came next] if they didn't signpost it themselves.

As an audience member, P6 recalls being "entranced" by the visual material, rather than the presentation.

> P6: I remember specifically [in one] that I found it hard to focus on what he was currently talking about ...I was sort of entranced by [the content].

Students noticed high quality work. The attributes of strong work included clear relationships among elements, creative presentation, and visually distinct arrangement.

> P8: There were a couple that were really good. ...I thought that one showed the relationships between things very well. It was a creative way to set it up. [I]t got the point across that he was trying to say.

Overall, spontaneous discussion in CISM added depth and emergent ideas. P4 notes how free-form presentations stimulated questions how material was related, which P9 and P8 saw answered with new ideas for meaningful connections.

> P4: [Free-form presentation] helps you question how things are related; and the more open a presentation is, the more questions you get.

> P9: [Some were] not really relevant ...But, then again, there were a lot of really good [discussions] ...[that] brought a lot of information into the class.

> P8: People would bring up related papers or related experiments to compare and contrast and go more in depth.

P10 describes his presentations as unscripted, relying on the content of the presentation to help draw out discussion. As P7 notes, in CISM, questions from presenters stimulated discussion that produced little-c creative ideation.

> P10: I feel like it's extremely appropriate for everyone to get out the most information and learning they can out of a presentation whether or not the presenter was prepared for it. ...I hadn't rehearsed this - I didn't have any script I was going off of. ...I would ask people, "Does anyone have any thoughts about this?" ...[I'm] trying to share the wealth of knowledge of all the students in the classroom.

> P7: Often when the presenter asks, initially there's a period of silence. Then someone says something, some initial thought. ...In that case, almost all [students] will respond. People collectively come together and answer.

While P7 and P9 note some tangents, by and large, presentations informed CISM participants and stimulated engaging discussions.

IMPLICATIONS FOR DESIGN

We develop implications of design for pedagogy and the design of presentation tools to support creativity. Our findings show that a free-form presentation medium stimulates associational thinking, improvisation, and spontaneous discussion.

Continuous Views Connect Ideas

We observed that students associated ideas and concepts in new ways. They created their own perspectives, extended their understanding, and connected ideas. Burleson argues creative learning tools should enable showing multiple points of views to foster the imagination [6]. Panning and zooming the ZUI canvas can create an infinite number of viewpoints. During a presentation, students create and encounter new and emergent views. Contrast this with the finite number of n slides in a PowerPoint presentation. Tufte prefers high fidelity paper to slideware because its form is continuous, rather than 'sliced and diced' [35]. P9 remarked that, with free-form presentation, *It feels like you're still in the same conceptual space ...[instead of PowerPoint's] flipping through all these different images.* Continuous views better connect ideas.

We observe that imposing predefined frames on a presentation medium 'slices and dices' information. This is true not only of slideware, but also with ZUI's like CounterPoint [12] and Prezi [27]. CounterPoint uses a slide metaphor, but allows slides to be freely arranged. However, information must still be contained in rigid rectangular frames. In the same way, Prezi requires information to be placed within rectangular frames to enable presentation transitions. While these systems possess advantages over PowerPoint, such as smooth transitions and better connected content, the frames separate content, in comparison with IdeaMâché's free-form medium.

The free-form medium enabled showing multiple perspectives through continuous and non-linear assembly and annotation of information. Students used the medium to experiment with relationships among elements. P3 connected ideas by arranging clippings and associating them with arrows, *"Having lines, arrows, things like that, provide additional structure."* These implicit structures and free-form assembly of clippings enable associational thinking.

Promote Improvisation

In CISM and other discussion driven courses, improvisation is crucial to education. Fisher and Amabile propose a model for improvisational creativity: *"In improvisational creativity, a large number of well-learned facts and routines that are readily available, accessible, and flexibly organized are important to prior action [10]."* Improvisational creativity relies on a 'vocabulary' of small chunks of actions, for example, 'licks' in jazz. Encouraging experimentation, accepting mistakes, and promoting action facilitates improvisational creativity.

Students assembled their own vocabularies for improvisation using clippings. In CISM, students gathered their vocabularies from prior research and recent news. Through the free-form medium of information composition, students organized their clippings into flexible visual structures. Students relied on their prepared vocabularies to present.

As the course culture matured, students became more adept at preparing for improvisation. As P4 saw it *"[presentations were] much more precise and well designed [the second time around] than the first set."* P1 developed a technique he called 'signposts'. A signpost is a large clipping which denotes a major theme in the presentation. He used these signposts to direct audience attention and help him navigate the ZUI to dynamically react to questions. P1 and P3 both included information in their presentation that they planned on skipping over, unless asked about specifically. The informality created by the improvisational presentation style encouraged spontaneous discussion, learning, and experimentation. As Burleson notes, a constructionist approach to education favors student intuition over formal instruction [6]. Students used the flexible structures and self-created vocabularies to improvise as presenters. As P3 described it, he guided his presentations in a kind of 'choose your own adventure' style.

Enable Scripted Presentation with Improvisation
Students' free-form presentations were unscripted. For classrooms, improvisation and discussion was seen as appropriate. However, scripted presentations with an "executive look" are commonly expected. P2 expressed anxiety about panning and zooming IdeaMâché during presentations. In formal presentations, P6 was leery of poor outcomes from unscripted presentation. The risk of potential failure can be exacerbated by the high cognitive load needed while presenting. In the present version of *IdeaMâché*, users had to manually control pan and zoom while presenting. The implication for design is that new free-form curation media should enable scripted presentation, which automates panning and zooming, while also allowing for improvisation.

Stimulate Creative Ideation: Emergence
Creative ideation, learning, and self-actualization are synergistically connected [6]. In Kaufman's et al.'s model of creativity, personal insight is a necessary precursor to more eminent creative products [15]. Thus, personal insight and learning initially constitute *mini-c* creativity. When it is externally expressed and communicated, these insights become *little-c*, shared everyday innovations. They label innovation that reaches the professional leves as *Pro-C* creativity, while using *Big-C* creativity for innovations that impact society. Authoring free-form presentations in CISM stimulated mini-c ideation. These mini-c ideas took on little-c creative function, as students shared them through class discussions, papers, and final projects. Inasmuch as students publish ideas developed through the course, these ideas developed through free-form presentation take on a Pro-C role. For example, P5

crystalized her thesis topic through authoring and presenting in CISM using the free-form medium. This paper is another example of Pro-C creativity developed through free-form curation and presentation.

A free-form medium provides opportunities for creative ideation. Panning and zooming an information composition presents curation elements in a series of contexts. Presenters and audience members are stimulated to reflect on relationships among these combinations of clippings and annotations. Finke argues that intermediate combinations, which do not immediately appear useful, function as precursors to useful ideas; these are known as *preinventive structures* [9]. Free-form presentations, by presenting many views, display perspectives that can inspire ideation. By seeing objects in new contexts, presenter and audience engage in visual thinking via gestalt experimental categories [18], contexualized perception [2], and relational and artistic meaning making [4].

P5 developed a presentation on how biracial identities, such as her own, become impinged on by prevailing either-or mentalities on race. She initially curated clippings, such as one of the Blue Man Group, simply because she liked them. In practice, these functioned as preinventive structures, which stimulated emergent ideation. For example, *P5: I pulled different pieces together ... I talked about the Blue Man Group ... Blue is a natural color, the color of the sky and the ocean. As far as skin tone, it has no connotation or associations with race or emotion.* Through recontextualization in the contexts of the composition as a whole and of her presentation in class, P5's Blue Man Group clipping came to stand for blended identity, extending beyond expected categories of race.

CONCLUSION
Free-form curation provides preinventive structures, which, through free-form presentation, stimulate free-form thinking, mini-c and greater creativity, and emergent ideation in the classroom. Krueger uses *responsive environment* to describe an iterative series of contexts, established by an interactive computing system, and transformed by participants' actions through the interface [17]. We found that in the classroom, the presenter continuously interprets the needs of the class, expressed through discussion, in response to a series of contextualizing views of a multi-scale information composition. The presenter responds iteratively by speaking and revising the view. The rest of the class iteratively responds by speaking. Free-form thinking is stimulated. Ideation happens. The use of IdeaMâché thus constituted a responsive environment of free-form presentation and spontaneous discussion.

Students in CISM curated clippings and annotations, forming preinventive structures that stimulated free-form thinking. In presenting, they explored associations improvisationally, presenting a series of unscripted contexts. Students connected and recontextualized information from research literature, social media, and their own experiences. These recontextualizations frequently attained mini-c, individual, and little-c, classwide, levels. Moving beyond the classroom, contributing to theses and to publications such as this, ideation stimulated by the free-form medium of curation and presentation subsequently attains the level of Pro-C creativity.

Presentations that involve improvisation better support learning and ideation than scripted monologues. While slideware "slices and dices" information into fixed slides, free-form curation provides a continuous space for connecting ideas. The continuous space better supports experimental categorization [18] in the authoring process. In class, the series of contexts provides diverse views, which help overcome fixation [32]. The ability to improvise with pan and zoom in presentations creates an infinite space of potential perspectives, producing new opportunities for ideation. Unscripted presentations can better respond to situated emergent contexts in the classroom. They can effectively build on emergent ideas that arise through spontaneous discussion.

Our investigation takes a participant observer approach. The researchers were involved in the course and in the design and development of IdeaMâché. Co-authors of this paper served as active participants, as creators, exemplars, teachers, developers and observers. We thus instantiate the first-person tradition of ethnography in HCI. Students and researchers spontaneously participated in a process of creative ideation. We iteratively created a body of scholarly and artistic work, which in turn, through free-form presentation, stimulated free-form thinking and improvisational discussion.

We were surprised by students' level of adoption of multiscale information composition, by the quality of their presentations. We invite the reader to experience the wonderful body of work created by the participants of CISM [`http://goo.gl/O4qpTb`]. Free-form thinking and presentation are critical for the current and next generation of thinkers who continuously co-create and transform the world. We identify IdeaMâché's free-form medium of curation and presentation, multi-scale information composition, as a means for stimulating spontaneity and creative ideation in a range of courses throughout STEM, arts, and humanities education at secondary school and university levels.

ACKNOWLEDGEMENTS
This material is based upon work supported by the National Science Foundation under grants IIS-074742 and IIS-1247126. Any opinions, findings, and conclusions or recommendations expressed in this material are those of the authors and do not necessarily reflect the views of the NSF.

REFERENCES
1. *The Interpretation of Cultures*. Basic Books.

2. Arnheim, R. *Visual thinking*. Univ of California Press, 1969.

3. Bederson, B. B., and Hollan, J. D. Pad++: A zooming graphical interface for exploring alternate interface physics. In *Proc UIST*, ACM (1994).

4. Berger, J. *Ways of seeing*, vol. 1. Penguin UK, 2008.

5. Bligh, B., and Coyle, D. Re-mediating classroom activity with a non-linear, multi-display presentation tool. *Computers & Education 63*, 0 (2013), 337 – 357.

6. Burleson, W. Developing creativity, motivation, and self-actualization with learning systems. *International Journal of Human-Computer Studies 63*, 4 (2005).

7. Clifford, J., and Marcus, G. E. *Writing culture: The poetics and politics of ethnography*. Univ of California Press, 1986.

8. Eames, C. Powers of ten, 1977.

9. Finke, R. *Creative Imagery: Discoveries and Inventions in Visualization*. L. Erlbaum Associates, 1990.

10. Fisher, C. M., and Amabile, T. Creativity, improvisation and organizations. *The Routledge companion to creativity* (2009), 13–24.

11. Good, L., and Bederson, B. B. Zoomable user interfaces as a medium for slide show presentations. *Information Visualization* (2002).

12. Good, L. E. Zoomable user interfaces for the authoring and delivery of slide presentations.

13. Illich, I. *Tools for conviviality*. World perspectives. Harper & Row, 1973.

14. Interface Ecology Lab. Ideamache. `http://ideamache.ecologylab.net/`, 2015.

15. Kaufman, J. C., and Beghetto, R. A. Beyond big and little: The four c model of creativity. *Review of General Psychology 13*, 1 (2009), 1.

16. Kerne, A., Webb, A. M., Smith, S. M., Linder, R., Lupfer, N., Qu, Y., Moeller, J., and Damaraju, S. Using metrics of curation to evaluate information-based ideation. *ACM Trans. Comput.-Hum. Interact. 21*, 3 (2014).

17. Krueger, M. W. Responsive environments. In *Proc ACM National Computer Conference* (1977), 423–433.

18. Lakoff, G., and Johnson, M. *Metaphors we live by*. University of Chicago press, 2008.

19. Lanir, J., Booth, K. S., and Findlater, L. Observing presenters' use of visual aids to inform the design of classroom presentation software. In *Proc CHI* (2008).

20. Lanir, J., Booth, K. S., and Tang, A. Multipresenter: A presentation system for (very) large display surfaces. In *Proc ACM Multimedia* (2008).

21. Lichtschlag, L., Karrer, T., and Borchers, J. Fly: A tool to author planar presentations. In *Proc CHI*, ACM (2009).

22. Linder, R., Snodgrass, C., and Kerne, A. Everyday ideation: All of my ideas are on pinterest. In *Proc CHI* (2014).

23. Lupfer, N. Beyond the feed and board: Holistic principles for expressive web curation. Master's thesis, Texas A&M University, 2014.

24. Miller, G. A. The magical number seven, plus or minus two: some limits on our capacity for processing information. *Psychological review 63*, 2 (1956), 81.

25. Montgomery, R. A., and Granger, P. *Journey under the sea*. No. 2. Bantam Books, 1979.

26. O'Neill, P. *The Culture of Curating and the Curating of Culture(s)*. MIT Press, 2012.

27. Prezi - Ideas matter. `http://prezi.com/`.

28. Qu, Y., Kerne, A., Lupfer, N., Linder, R., and Jain, A. Metadata type system: Integrate presentation, data models and extraction to enable exploratory browsing interfaces. In *Proc ACM EICS* (2014).

29. Rosenbaum, S. *Curation Nation: How to Win in a World Where Consumers are Creators*. McGraw-Hill, Feb. 2011.

30. Rößling, G., Trompler, C., Mühlhäuser, M., Köbler, S., and Wolf, S. Enhancing classroom lectures with digital sliding blackboards. *ACM SIGCSE Bulletin 36*, 3 (2004).

31. Scaife, M., and Rogers, Y. External cognition: How do graphical representations work? *Int. J. Hum.-Comput. Stud. 45*, 2 (Aug. 1996), 185–213.

32. Smith, S., Ward, T., and Schumacher, J. Constraining effects of examples in a creative generation task. *Memory & Cognition 21* (1993), 837–845. 10.3758/BF03202751.

33. Spicer, R., Lin, Y.-R., Kelliher, A., and Sundaram, H. Nextslideplease: Authoring and delivering agile multimedia presentations. *ACM Trans. Multimedia Comput. Commun. Appl. 8*, 4 (2012).

34. Strauss, A., and Corbin, J. M. *Grounded theory in practice*. Sage, 1997.

35. Tufte, E. R. *The cognitive style of PowerPoint*, vol. 2006. Graphics Press Cheshire, CT, 2003.

36. Tversky, B. Visualizing thought. *Topics in Cognitive Science 3*, 3 (2011), 499–535.

37. Webb, A. M., Linder, R., Kerne, A., Lupfer, N., Qu, Y., Poffenberger, B., and Revia, C. Promoting reflection and interpretation in education: Curating rich bookmarks as information composition. In *Proc Creativty and Cognition* (2013).

Creative and Opportunistic Use of Everyday Music Technologies in a Dementia Care Unit

Kellie Morrissey
School of Applied Psychology
University College Cork
k.morrissey@ucc.ie

John McCarthy
School of Applied Psychology
University College Cork
john.mccarthy@ucc.ie

ABSTRACT

This paper describes everyday technologies in use in a long-term dementia care ward, and ways in which these technologies facilitated creative expression for residents within. Drawing on ethnographic research focusing on participation in creative activities for people with dementia living in care, the paper details how residents engaged with technologies (such as television) in a passive way (spending hours sitting in front of the TV without engaging with others around them), and in an active way (singing and dancing to music played via stereo and record player). Findings from this research emphasise the importance for interaction design for dementia in appreciating the role of active creative participation in sustaining personhood in dementia. Given a lack of both time and resources in publicly-funded care homes, we also highlight the value of opportunistic design in the field.

Author Keywords

Ethnography; music technologies; everyday technologies; elderly; dementia; care; quick and dirty design.

ACM Classification Keywords

H.5.m. Information interfaces and presentation (e.g., HCI): Miscellaneous.

INTRODUCTION: CREATIVITY IN THE CARE HOME

Often suffering from a lack of funding, staffing, and general resources, publicly-funded dementia care wards can be experienced by people with dementia as unstimulating spaces [5, 8]. The transition from life at home to life in care can be difficult both for family who must make this decision as well as the person with dementia themselves: awakening each morning in an unfamiliar space; surrounded by strangers and by carers who (are obliged to) intervene in matters of hygiene and health, and often experiencing extended periods without meaningful activities in a (perceived to be) strange environment, this shift in lifestyle occurs at a time when the person is already experiencing significant changes in their own sense of

personhood, and it is a shift that can be very distressing for the person with dementia.

Extant research [2, 9] has indicated that rich and varied environments contribute towards neuroplasticity and are of potential help in supporting memory and through this, a coherent sense of self- and personhood. Many care homes provide art or music activities or therapy, and although these services are potentially beneficial for residents, in publicly-funded homes they can be difficult to procure. Moreover, many residents of care homes are unable to tell carers about themselves explicitly: without this communication, the activities these residents engage with may be unsuitable or inappropriate despite the best efforts of staff. The aim of the project that this paper begins to report is to understand how interaction design can contribute to identifying and supporting appropriate creative activities in residential dementia care.

Killick & Craig [4] offer some ideas on what it means to be creative in a dementia context. Creativity for people with dementia must give pleasure; this does not mean that we can ignore the very real struggles that come along with creating art in this context – issues with movement, with perception and organisation – but that these feelings must not be the overriding ones. The activity that involves creativity must be pursued and enjoyed for its own sake. Running concurrently with this is that creativity involves a making process. It may be an appropriation of raw materials – paper and paint into a portrait, flour and eggs into a cake – but the process must be pursued for its own end and also result in a 'something'. In making something, the authors write that another vital characteristic of creativity is that it is expressive:

"Many people with dementia need constant reassurance that their selfhood is intact, and the exploration of feeling-states is helpful to that process." (Killick & Craig, 2012, p. 14)

Killick & Craig differentiate between what they call 'big C creativity', where someone has spent much of their life devoting themselves to their craft and so identifies as an artist, and 'small C creativity', relatively everyday instances of creativity which every individual shows and which can be enhanced and brought out further by activities such as painting, singing and storytelling. This paper discusses instances of what Killick & Craig call 'small C creativity' which were observed during a year-long ethnographic study into a publicly-funded care home in the south of Ireland. These instances of creativity were notable due to the fact that they occurred not during creative activity sessions, but during the course of the day in the unit – despite the relatively impoverished space in the care unit itself. The space created by and during these 'creativities' was mediated by residents' engagement with everyday technologies on the ward: notably the television, the radio, and a stereo player. The ultimate aim of this project is the generation of ideas for design to support creativity in dementia care, and this paper demonstrates how everyday interactions with these technologies might help us do just that.

METHODOLOGY

Design and analysis

This study used ethnographic methods in order to capture an 'insider's view' of life with dementia in care. These ethnographic methods involved the lead author in a period of observation and constant involvement in the life of the research setting - entering the care setting 1-2 times a week for 4-6 hours across a period of 12 months. In these settings, observations were made of daily life, carers were informally interviewed, and creative workshops were held within the unit.

Field notes were taken briefly on-site and then written out in detail later that evening, and casual interviews and 'chat' were also transcribed later. Emergent data was analysed in the dementia care unit study using a method of Grounded Theory as laid out by Charmaz [1], where initial coding influenced iterative stages of the ethnography as the research itself narrowed down over a period of months and data saturation was reached.

Setting

The dementia care setting was a dementia-specific ward in a public community hospital ("St Eithne's"). The ward consisted of two large 'day rooms', two outdoor gardens and two communal dormitories where residents slept. Throughout the course of the ethnography, 8-10 full-time residents lived in the unit, with 3-5 day residents visiting for 6-8 hours a day, 2-3 days a week. Residents of St Eithne's had to have received a diagnosis of dementia, and had to be ambulatory, in order to be placed in the ward.

Ethics

This study was reviewed and granted approval by the School of Applied Psychology's Ethics Committee. Consent was assessed and gained using guidelines laid out by the Mental Capacity Act of 2005, and the Code of Professional Ethics of the Psychological Society of Ireland.

THE TEXTURE OF CREATIVITY IN CARE

The following sections will highlight how creative expression in the unit unfolded, mediated through the presence of, and engagement with, everyday technologies

in the unit itself. We will also detail an instance of low-level design in the unit. Finally, we will present a list of considerations and possible design spaces that are indicated by these instances of engagement.

Passive engagement: television as a 'nanny'

Following a communal breakfast each morning, residents were led by carers into the day room. The day began with a Catholic mass, which residents watched on television. This mass was 'piped-in' from a chapel on the site of the community hospital situated less than 20 metres from the main door of St Eithne's. Residents rarely engaged with the mass, and indeed most spent this time dozing in their seats, though still some others spoke the correct responses and blessed themselves at the right time. Most mornings, following this mass, were passed watching television – carers would rotate through a collection of about 5-7 DVDs, mostly old films, documentaries on old Ireland, or concerts. The effect of this was that each day was passed watching the same small selection of media. Carers also switched the television to terrestrial channels, and during this time residents could watch the news or soap operas. Although activities were scheduled for residents each day, these did not occur as per the schedule and so the main source of stimulation for residents was typically the television itself. Residents did not tend to engage with everyday TV – they would sit and seem to be watching, would not be able to comment on what they were watching when asked - but were often roused by the musical media.

In being roused by the musical media, residents engaged in creative ways within this creative space. In selectively responding to certain media above others, they expressed their own preferences, made their own choices and seemed to experience a sense of joy, participation, and pleasure that allowed them to (in creative ways) connect both to other people in the unit as well as to a past sense of self.

Connection through music: dance and touch

As a researcher in the context seeking 'ways in' to the experience of others, observing residents' interactions with music allowed the lead author to identify the music which each resident particularly enjoyed. She was then able to turn this music around and use it as a way to connect to residents who were otherwise somewhat unresponsive or reserved. Moreover, residents themselves could connect to one another and perform during these moments as well. These moments were just that – opportunistic and immediately creative – and were made possible by residents' willingness to engage with technologies such as the radio and the television in the unit. The following subsections detail these moments in greater detail.

Claire and Ben: dancing to a script

One day in July, residents were seated in the day room watching a DVD the lead author had brought in of 'Singin' in the Rain.' Beside her, resident Claire was tapping her feet and whooping along to the music when she suddenly stopped, grinned, and pointed at another resident, Ben, a few chairs away.

'That man,' she exclaimed, 'should get up and dance!'

Ben looked over, nonplussed. The lead author joked with the two that they should get up and dance together. Ben acquiesced, held out his hand to Claire, and the two performed a nimble two-step around the room before collapsing on the couch, laughing at each other.

This opportunistic engagement occurred suddenly for the two residents who, hitherto, had not even spoken to each other. Not only did the musical space (created by a familiar film and familiar music on the television) allow for the two to express themselves via dance, it allowed them to connect via an implicit 'script'; here, the two were not residents, patients, sufferers – they were dance partners. Unlike the very demonstrative art sessions residents sometimes attended, this, like Killick & Craig, above, detail, was an opportunistic activity that was engaged in for its own sake – though in the end it allowed for a connection none of the participants and onlookers might have thought possible.

Valerie: touch and ritual
Modes of communication would shift during engagement with music and while verbal communication would wane, other modes of intersubjective communication would become prominent – for instance, movement, sway, tapping and touch rose to the forefront during these sessions. This shift in communication was one which was often more creative and expressive than the pleasant 'chit-chat' residents with which residents were often engaged.

Sitting and listening one day to an old record of Irish ballads, resident Valerie took the lead author's hand and the two swayed from side-to-side half-singing the songs. After a while this swaying turned into a dance as Valerie guided her hand in a sort of a twirling, twisting pattern in the air in rhythm to the music. The two paused after each song to applaud the singers, but Valerie reached for the lead author's hand immediately afterwards. At one point Valerie simply held her hand very tightly as they watched the television or chatted, or observed the people around them. Valerie squeezed her hand very tightly and ran her fingers over her knuckles. The lead author let her guide her hand again and she brought it very close to her face, rubbing it gently over her cheek and chin.

Valerie's initial reaction in reaching out for the lead author's hand seemed to be to guide it in a sort of dance to music, but eventually finishes with her interacting with her hand (and the author herself) as something soothing, something calming and yet communicative. Valerie was someone who carried around several keepsakes – rosary beads, a small book of poems – and would often take out these items and run her fingers through the pages or the beads. Here, she interacted with the hand in that same way: first as a communicative and responsive object in a dance, and then as a connective 'talisman' of sorts. Again, the

familiar music from the record player facilitated this seemingly emotional and yet wordless connection by which Valerie (and the author) were soothed.

'Entering' media: dementia and 'delusions'
Dementia can bring along with it instances of hallucinations and delusions which can be distressing both for the person with dementia and the caregiver/family alike. However, one resident in St Eithne's, Maggie, experienced these delusions in a way which allowed her to interact deeply with the media with which she engaged – for example, presenting Maggie with a magazine about children would often see her interact with the pictures of the babies within, carrying out conversations with them and, if approached, would tell stories about the times she and the child had had together.

This immersion was even more marked when Maggie watched television. Early on in the ethnography, Maggie fell and broke her leg. Carers needed to ensure Maggie would not move around too much on her broken leg, and so placed her on a moveable armchair fitted with a pressure alarm. Noting that Maggie 'came alive to music', they placed this seat close to the television and switched on her favourite concert DVD – Daniel O'Donnell. Observing Maggie during this time, she began to act as though enchanted and in a reverie – she sat, smiling widely at the screen with rapt attention as well as adoration. As the song finished, she would applaud loudly and wave to the smiling singer onscreen, blowing kisses. As I sat beside her, she began to tell me that she and the singer were friends.

'He came to visit me last summer,' she said. 'His wife is a lovely woman.'

The delusions and hallucinations which come with dementia are often listed as a negative characteristic of the disease; here, however, they acted as a way for Maggie to both make sense of her experience retroactively, as well as a conduit into media that clearly gave her a sense of pleasure.

LOW-LEVEL DESIGN IN THE UNIT: A SONGBOOK
The previous observations have constructed a picture of St Eithne's as a place in which residents received good medical care, but where residents' creativities were self-constructed in and through a space mediated by music-playing, everyday technologies. Given the lack of resources in the unit and in many other units in the UK and Ireland, personalised creative care and design may be unlikely. Opportunistic or 'quick and dirty' design in settings such as St Eithne's have the potential to be valuable as long as they are guided by a commitment to key values – here, 'small c' creative values such as experiencing pleasure and creating a 'something' where there was previously nothing – but also an acknowledgement of, and respect for, the personhood of the other.

Therefore, we offer the following observation as a jumping-off point for situational, low-level design in dementia care to support creativity and connection to self. In principle, this is not limited to music – in the earlier observations, we saw residents engaging meaningfully with television as well – however, in this paper we will concentrate on the role of music due to the rich potential it offered residents.

Bill and the songbook

Bill's difficult transition to living in care resulted in the formerly talkative man withdrawing almost entirely into himself, becoming disinclined to participate in talk and in group activities. Nurses and carers did not know what to do with Bill – they knew a little about his life outside the unit, but he was not as easily prompted into storytelling as he had been. This resulted in a sort of depersonalisation of Bill; day after day, the lead author would come into the unit to see him sitting, often sleeping, on a sofa in the parlor as others around him chatted or watched television.

Remembering that Bill used to love to sing, and prompted by a chat with him one day in which he spoke deprecatingly about himself, the lead author created a basic songbook for Bill and filled it with his favourite songs. This meant that activities with Bill in the future were enriched due to the presence of this personalised songbook. However, even in authors' absence, the presence of this book meant that carers who interacted with Bill still had a portal or a 'way in' to his experience. 'He carries that book around the whole time,' carer Libby remarked. The ward occasionally rotated carers from other wards, which meant that residents did not always have a fixed set of carers to interact with, and thus this songbook could say something about Bill which he, in his present state, could not. Music that has been selected by residents, in this way, can act as a signal or a beacon to others who cannot find a way in, and through even low-level design, it can give a voice to an experience that is presently voiceless.

OPENING THE DESIGN SPACE & OTHER CONSIDERATIONS

The authors intend for this paper to begin to open several possible design spaces in dementia care wards. In particular, we have highlighted the following:

1. Media selection is important for participants with dementia, and a well-stocked media library can be enriching;

2. Particular music can transform and create spaces through activities performed within (e.g., Claire and Ben's dance);

3. Design surrounding music in dementia should incorporate movements and gestures, both explicit and performative (e.g., dance, tapping) and personal or soothing (e.g., Valerie's seeking to hold hands).

4. Although 'designing for deficit' is potentially inappropriate, design should be cognisant of cognitive and perceptual abnormalities (e.g., Maggie's 'delusions')

inherent to dementias, and work to include considerations of these into design research.

5. Basic design, if informed by a well-developed and respectful knowledge of our participants, can be enriching, connective, and communicative.

Although we do not intend these considerations to constitute formal guidelines for design research in the area, they represent areas of possible research and innovation in the area of dementia, design, and creativity.

CONCLUSION

This paper presents observations from an ethnographic study that found that many creative interactions on dementia care residents' behalf were mediated through engagement with music technologies. The importance of music for people with dementia has often been noted [6, 5], and engagement with music can be something which is intensely personal, evocative of one's own past and yet by another turn, playful and social. These observations of everyday creativities point to the potential inherent even in existing technologies (such as television) to become an active, immersive and creative technology in the setting of a dementia ward, as well as describing the kinds of enriching interactions that can arise from their use.

ACKNOWLEDGEMENTS

We thank the Irish Research Council for funding this research.

REFERENCES

1. Charmaz, K. (2014). *Constructing Grounded Theory*. London: Sage Publications.

2. Cowl, A. L., & Gaugler, J. E. (2014). Efficacy of creative arts therapy in treatment of Alzheimer's Disease and dementia: a systematic literature review. *Activities, Adaptation & Aging*, 38(4), 281-330.

3. Hara, M. (2011). Music in dementia care: increased understanding through mixed research methods. *Music and Arts in Action*, 3(2), 34-58.

4. Killick, J., & Craig, C. (2011). *Creativity and communication in persons with dementia: a practical guide*. London: Jessica Kingsley Publishers.

5. McDermott, O., Crellin, N., Ridder, H. M., & Orrell, M. (2013). Music therapy in dementia: a narrative synthesis systematic review. *International Journal of Geriatric Psychiatry*, 28(8), 781-794.

6. Reed-Danahay, D. (2001). 'This is your home now!': conceptualizing location and dislocation in a dementia unit. *Qualitative Research*, 1(1), 47-63.

7. Leuty, V., Boger, J., Young, L., Hoey, J., & Mihailidis, A. (2013). Engaging older adults with dementia in creative occupations using artificially intelligent assistive technology. *Assistive Technology*, 25(2), 72-79.

Tightly Coupled Agents in Live Performance Metacreations

William Marley
Digital Media and Arts Research Centre
CSIS Department
University of Limerick
William.Marley@ul.ie

Nicholas Ward
Digital Media and Arts Research Centre
CSIS Department
University of Limerick
Nicholas.Ward@ul.ie

ABSTRACT

We consider how the application of AI in digital musical instruments might maximally support exploration of sound in performance. Live performance applications of AI and machine learning have tended to focus on score following and the development of machine collaborators. In our work we are interested in exploring the development of systems whereby the human performer interacts with a reactive and creative agent in the creation of a single sonic output. The intention is to design systems that foster exploration and allow for greater (than with acoustic instruments) opportunities for serendipitous musical encounters. An initial approach to the integration of autonomous agency, based on gesture reshaping schemes within the Reactable performance system, is first outlined. We then describe a simple platform based on the non-player characters within Pacman, which serves as a test bed for guiding further discussion on what musical machine collaboration at this level may entail. Pilot studies for both systems are outlined.

Author Keywords

Digital Music Systems; TUI; Autonomy; Agency; Machine Collaboration; Reactable; AI; Pacman.

ACM Classification Keywords

H.5.2 Information Interfaces and Presentation (e.g. HCI): User Interfaces; H.5.5 Information Interfaces and Presentation (e.g. HCI): Sound and Music Computing; I.2.11 Artificial Intelligence: Distributed Artificial Intelligence.

INTRODUCTION

Current research examining the role of intelligent music systems in our creative endeavours has not yet fully addressed the importance of high-level musical features, specifically the role of instrumental movement and a music

systems artificial reactiveness to this, in their design considerations. Yet, without such an understanding, we believe that we are left with an inadequate foundation upon which to discover the true potential of intelligent music systems in our musical explorations.

We are ultimately focusing on two main principles in the design of creative digital musical instruments (DMI's). Firstly, our systems should be body-centered, with physicality and the role of the body remaining a central theme. This concept is aligned with those expounded within the New Interfaces for Musical Expression (NIME) community where we see a focus on tangible user interfaces and body-centered instruments. In the work presented here and in much of the work displayed by NIME, the notion of instrumental movement has guided consideration of how the performer interacts with an interface. Secondly, our systems exhibit creativity, dependent upon and reactive to user input. We are interested in exploring the interagency of performer and instrument, where human and artificial agents collaborate in the creation of a single sonic output. The growing field of Musical Metacreation (MUME) presents interesting approaches to the design of creative music systems, and it is within MUME that our work positions itself.

BACKGROUND
Musical Metacreation

The objective of metacreation is to equip machines with the capacity to be creative. MUME is concerned with autonomy and agency in composition and performance [3]. MUME is a multidisciplinary approach, utilizing tools from Artificial Intelligence (AI), Artificial Life (AL) and Machine Learning (ML). The practice aims to develop metacreations - artificially creative music systems inspired by human creativity with possibilities beyond human capabilities. MUME practitioners aim to explore computational creativity through the development of interactive systems and interfaces for use by musicians and artists. As proposed by Eigenfeldt et al [3], metacreative systems fall under the categories of improvisational systems (online) and compositional systems (offline). A focus toward online systems takes precedence in this research, as it is more concerned with how the system interacts with a live performer in real time. A taxonomy of metacreative systems has been outlined by Eigenfeldt et al [3] as a means of classifying metacreative applications in terms of human designer/composer control over musical output. Their taxonomy consists of seven levels, ordered from least machine-autonomous to most:

1. Independence – any process on a musical gesture that is beyond the control of the composer.
2. Compositionality – the use of any process to determine the relationship between pre-defined musical gestures.
3. Generativity – the generation of musical gestures.
4. Proactivity – system/agents are able to initiate their own musical gestures.
5. Adaptability – a) Agents behave in different ways over time due to their own internal evolution; b) agents interact and influence one another.
6. Versatility – Agents determine their own content without predefined stylistic limits
7. Volition – Agents exhibit volition, deciding when, what, and how to compose/perform.

George Lewis' Voyager system (1985) is an example of a highly complex, multi-agent metacreation [4]. This system functions through the analysis of musical input provided by an improviser. This analysis triggers an improvising program that displays a proactive, highly independent level of musical interaction. Voyager displays a high level of autonomy in that it does not need human input to function. Omax [2] uses on-the-fly statistical learning for virtual improvisation generation and stylistic model archiving. Omax is a reactive system, involving a process of systematically re-sending mirror images of a performance back to a performer. The work of William Hsu [6] also involves analysis of human input, focusing mainly on improvised acoustic sources. In the case of [6], the level of autonomy is lower than previous examples, with the user maintaining a large quantity of control over the systems functionality.

A commonality among such metacreative systems is an emphasis on score following, audio analysis and musical accompaniment. In contrast to this, our research is concerned with control data generated by a performers physical interaction with an instrument. We are not concerned with the design of a system that analyses the notes we play or the score we supply it. Instead, we wish to focus on how we physically interact with the instrument and the process of constructing musical output. We do not consider the artificial agent as accompaniment to our musicianship, but as the instrument itself that must be navigated and explored to produce a single sonic voice.

Toward these ends, we developed two systems in which artificial agents respond and react to the user in different ways. In the first work, the Gestroviser, we take the classic paradigm whereby the system imitates a second performer improvising or accompanying the main performer. In this case, the human player is performing **with** an artificial instrument. The Gestroviser was implemented in the Reactable, a popular tabletop DMI (briefly discussed in the next section). In the second work, PacEQ, we move on to explore the notion of performing **on** a system with artificial intelligence. Again, like the Gestroviser, we develop a system that takes physical gesture data as input. Here we want to consider what happens when this physical input guides the configuration and reaction of the system resulting in only one sonic voice.

The development of these systems involved an iterative design methodology. Outlined below are our initial prototypes and pilot studies of both systems, with algorithm refinement currently ongoing. The purposes of our pilot studies were to test the basic functionalities of the systems and our users understanding of them. These goals are formed from a human-centered view of interaction design in computational creativity. We second Bown [7] in how the nature of the interaction between humans and creative systems is a primary concern. We sought to construct empirical evidence of a users comprehension of the processes displayed in a DMI endowed with varying levels of creativity. However, we also acknowledge Bowns [7] point that using human responses about a system alone are not sufficient, and further studies on behavior are necessary.

REACTABLE
The Reactable is an electronic musical instrument with a table-based tangible user interface (TUI) used for control and visual-feedback. The instrument is heavily inspired by the analogue modular synthesizers of the 60's [1], and does in fact employ the same modular synthesis format by creating signal chains of multiple generator, effect and control modules. The Reactable functions with the use of acrylic pucks on a translucent circular sheet of perspex, with the pucks representing these modules, and their rotation, table-position and proximity to other connected modules. The instrument utilizes the users physical expressivity, with the movement and manipulation of these modules directly corresponding to sonic alterations.

GESTROVISER
At its simplest, the functionality of Gestroviser could be likened to the recording of automation data for a musical parameter and then playing it back. However, we were interested in extending this functionality by endowing the system with agency whereby it modifies the input. This led to the design of the 'call-and-response' scheme of the Gestroviser. The Gestroviser would virtually link to another object (host) where it would capture input data generated as the user rotated the host. Following this, the system would then playback its interpretation of this gesture to the host, artificially imitating a simple, improvising co-player.

For reasons of simplicity we initially chose to focus on the rotation data produced when the player rotates a Reactable puck (host). This continuously streamed data represents the reorientation of the tangible blocks situated upon the table.

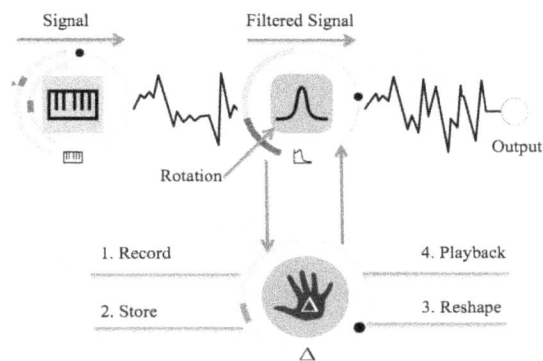

Figure 1: Basic Reactable signal flow and Gestroviser data capture process

In the standard Reactable software the main function of this rotation data is to communicate audio-signal alterations (effects etc.) to the synthesis engine. In our case the data stream is bifurcated, applying filtering to the original signal while being sent to a 'sample-record-store' function within the Gestroviser. This procedure is activated through the virtual 'linking' operation between objects (fig. 1). This stored data represents a users physical gesture, which is then to be processed for playback to the host object. We segment the input stream in real-time by feeding the sampled data consecutively into eight storage buffers. The rationale behind this method is twofold: we wish to minimize the quantity of data points to be processed at one time, while also allowing the re-organization of segments for playback generating new gestures similar to the original. Four playback modes were implemented. These modes are selected using the finger slider on the Gestroviser. An internal timer activates a probability function that considers the position of the slider in relation to the next mode. As the user moves the slider closer to the next mode, the probability of that mode being activated increases. We implemented this function to enhance the variability of the output gesture on the host. The first mode triggers the unaltered gesture. The second mode triggers the unaltered gesture from two segments behind the first mode. The third mode triggers a new gesture consisting of data generated by a Markov Chain algorithm on each consecutive segment, using the original data as input. The fourth mode triggers this same data, but randomly shuffles the segments for output.

PILOT STUDY 1

We gathered five users to test the Gestroviser. The users had experience in using DMI's, all with varying expertise. Three users had live public performance experience, while two stated they had used DMI's before. They were given ten minutes to test the system, and were given no prior information on how to use it. Each user was observed individually, with only the user and observer present. The users were supplied with pre- and post-test Likert scale questionnaires to complete, with five answers ranging from

'Fully Disagree' to 'Fully Agree'. The pre-test questions were as follows:
1. I have experience making laptop and/or electronic music
2. I am familiar with the Reactable and how it works
3. I tend to improvise when making music
4. I employ experimentation when making music

The post-test questions were as follows:
1. I knew what was happening
2. Give a brief description of what was happening
3. I was in control of what was happening
4. I enjoyed using the test object
5. I think this feature is useful for music performance

The pre-test questionnaire showed four users having a working knowledge of the Reactable itself, which was an obvious advantage when approaching this test. The same number of users showed a preference for improvisation and experimentation when making music. One user answered on the lower end of the scale for all pre-test questions, leading us to assume they were an outlier in the group and may not be properly suited to the task. Questions 1 and 3 of the post-test questionnaire specifically focused on the users understanding of the system. Three users answered that they did not know or have control of what was happening, while two users were simply not sure. Interestingly, three users enjoyed using the Gestroviser and found it useful for music performance, despite not understanding what was happening or having control of the system. The users then supplied feedback on their experience, one user stating that they "really liked the idea of the computer being able to sensibly improvise" and commented on the "sense of surprise" while testing. Two users made specific comments on their lack of understanding of the system, suggesting visual feedback for guidance and more instruction prior to the test would be beneficial. Despite some positive feedback, the initial 'call-and-response' concept behind the design of the Gestroviser became its main drawback. Indeed there was agency displayed in its artificial gestures. However, performing with it required the user to stand and watch these gestures, unable to act until the Gestroviser had completed its routine. This level of interaction seemed stunted, and not ideal for our design purposes.

PacEQ

The concept for PacEQ grew as a direct response to the shortcomings of the Gestroviser, in specific its 'call-and-response' interaction scheme. We wished to investigate the possibility of endowing creative agents with personality, and how this may benefit the design of a more collaborative and reactive system. We narrowed our focus further toward a more collaborative interaction between human and computer, whereby both would work simultaneously to produce a single sonic output.

PacEQ is a graphically presented multi-agent system that controls a 28-band EQ filter for pre-composed sound sources. The function of the user (represented onscreen by a yellow node) is to guide four agents across a 2-dimensional interface using a mouse or track-pad. This 2D space represents the EQ filter. The controllable filter bands are not visible to the user, with filter alterations being controlled by the movement of the artificial agents. For example, an agent is located at the bottom left of the screen therefore a frequency in the lower range (eg. 50Hz) is attenuated. The guiding of multiple agents by the user ensures timbre variability and suitably interesting sound alterations for testing. Agent behaviour is based on the AI routines of the non-human characters in the classic videogame Pacman. Pittmans [5] detailing of the character personalities and behaviours formed the basis for the programming of these agents in PacEQ. The following are brief descriptions of their personalities:

- Agent 1: Tracks the user quicker and more directly
- Agent 2: Always situated ahead of user movements
- Agent 3: Unpredictable movements around the user
- Agent 4: Retreats to furthest location when close to user

The behaviour of these agents is also determined by certain nuances in the users interaction. For example, when the user does not interact then agent 1 becomes the guide and moves quicker and more erratically encouraging the other three agents to do likewise. The objective with this feature is to encourage the user to stay active on the system (or inactive, depending on the users sonic preferences). The agents also slow down when the user moves to the bottom of the screen, i.e. the area where most frequency attenuation takes place. These interactive functions were programmed to challenge the test user further in their navigation of the system in an attempt to produce a desired output.

PILOT STUDY 2
Four users took part in this pilot study. Similar to our initial study, these users had experience working with DMI's. Each user was given a laptop, mouse and headphones to use for the experiment, and asked to use the system for ten minutes in whatever way they deemed suitable. The users could see the agents onscreen in addition to an audio switch that turned on the overall sound. We used the same pre- and post-test questionnaire as in our previous study but without the questions regarding the Reactable. Unsurprisingly, the user group showed little comprehension of the role of the agents. They did, however, realise the implications on the audio output if not their control over it. Similar to the users of the Gestroviser, the users seem to gain pleasure from performing with PacEQ despite their lack of understanding of its controls. User experience comments included:

- "As I was unable to get fully to grips with the software I am eager to get back to it and learn how to use it. I am interested to know how it could be useful to me in the future."

- "Really interesting! Took me a while to figure out I could move the yellow node!"
- "I feel like more control over the output sound could be afforded to the user."
- "I had no idea what to even expect and I thoroughly enjoyed using it."

Aside from obvious issues regarding user comprehension of the system, we are encouraged by these experiments in assigning novel behaviours to multiple agents.

DISCUSSION
It is evident from both pilot studies that while we can move forward in the design of creative systems that can react to the user in increasingly complex ways, it is also necessary for the designer to consider the users ability to comprehend the processes and behaviour of the creative system in equal measure. In the development of the Gestroviser and PacEQ we have learned that one can engage with a creative system without knowing what is happening or how to control it. However we believe that a more intelligible connection between user input and system response will enhance our engagement with creative systems. Future work will incorporate the machine learning of a users physical interaction with a system and the development of engaging AI responsiveness to maximally support exploration of sound in performance.

REFERENCES
1. Jordà, S. The Reactable: Tangible and Tabletop Music Performance. *CHI '10,* ACM (2010), 2989-2994.

2. Assayag, G., Bloch, G. and Chemillier. M. Omax Brothers: a Dynamic Topology of Agents for Improvization Learning. ACM (2006).

3. Eigenfeldt, A., Brown O., Pasquier, P. and Martin, A. Towards a Taxonomy of Musical Metacreation: Reflections on the First Musical Metacreation Weekend. AAAI (2013).

4. Lewis, GE. Too Many Notes: Computers, Complexity and Culture in Voyager. MIT Press (2000), 33–39.

5. Pittman, J. *The Pac-Man Dossier.* 2011. http://home.comcast.net/~jpittman2/pacman/pacmandossier.html#Chapter_4.

6. Hsu, W. Using Timbre in a Computer-based Improvisation System. *Proceedings of International Computer Music Conference* (5-9) (2005)

7. Bown, O. Empirically grounding the evaluation of creative systems: incorporating interaction design. *Proceedings of the Fifth International Conference on Computational Creativity* (2014)

Biological Citizen Publics: Personal Genetics as a Site of Scientific Literacy and Action

Stacey Kuznetsov[1], Aniket Kittur[1], Eric Paulos[2]

Human-Computer Interaction Institute[1]
Carnegie Mellon University
Pittsburgh, PA, USA
{stace, nkittur}@cs.cmu.edu

Electrical Engineering and Computer Sciences[2]
University of California
Berkeley, CA, USA
paulos@berkeley.edu

ABSTRACT

Low-cost genetic sequencing, coupled with novel social media platforms and visualization techniques, present a new frontier for scientific participation, whereby people can learn, share, and act on data embedded within their own bodies. Our study of 23andMe, a popular genetic testing service, reveals how users make sense of and contextualize their genetic results, critique and evaluate the underlying research, and reflect on the broader implications of genetic testing. We frame user groups as citizen science *publics*— groups that coalesce around scientific issues and work towards resolving shared concerns. Our findings show that personal genetics serves as a site for public engagement with science, whereby communities of biological citizens creatively interpret, debate, and act on professional research. We conclude with design trajectories at the intersection of genetics and creativity support tools: platforms for aggregating hybrid knowledge; tools for creative reflection on professional science; and strategies for supporting collaborations across communities.

Author Keywords

Genetics, scientific literacy, biological citizenship, publics

ACM Classification Keywords

H.5.m. Information interfaces and presentation (e.g., HCI): Miscellaneous.

INTRODUCTION

Since the completion of the Human Genome Project [19], an international research effort that mapped the human DNA in its entirety in 2003, genetic research and its underlying technologies have advanced in radically new and unexpected ways. The cost of genetic sequencing has decreased exponentially over the past decade. Affordable genetic testing services and intuitive visualizations of the

C&C '15, June 22 - 25, 2015, Glasgow, United Kingdom
© 2015 ACM. ISBN 978-1-4503-3598-0/15/06···$15.00
DOI: http://dx.doi.org/10.1145/2757226.2757246.

results are increasingly turning personal DNA into an object an inquiry. This creates a new frontier for scientific participation, in which people can make sense of, share, and act on information embedded within their own bodies. Little is known about this space within creativity literature: how do people interact with and make sense of the underlying scientific information, and how does the understanding of personal genetics influence their sense of self and their daily lives?

We present a study of 23andMe [1], a low-cost ($99), online service and community for personal genetic testing. While the DNA testing itself is done in professional laboratories, 23andMe serves as a site for sense making "from below": forum and community features enable participants to share experiences, narratives, and intuitions about their results. Similar to other citizen science efforts [e.g. 5, 13, 28], 23andMe relies on lower-cost sensing (genetic sequencing) and increased computational power (for processing genetic information), as well as new social media tools to support the emerging communities of participants. However, public participation in personal genetics also presents a shift from people 'as sensors'—*i.e.*, gathering information about external environments—to communities who collect, make sense of, and act on information embedded within their own bodies. Thus, participation in genetics is often motivated by and brings about a host of new concerns, from discovering personal and intimate information about oneself to understanding patterns in human migration and evolution. These issues reflect opportunities and challenges arising from the convergence of biology and computation [27].

Research contributions

We frame 23andMe participant communities as citizen science *publics*—groups that coalesce around scientific issues and work towards resolving shared concerns [7].

Figure 1. 23andMe spit kit.

Drawing on concepts of biological citizenship [24] and biosociality [21], we first reflect on how services such as 23andMe serve as sites for creative sense-making around biological traits and concerns. We then detail our analysis of 23andMe forum threads and a qualitative study of six individuals who joined and used the service over the course of 3 months. Our findings reveal why participants joined 23andMe; how they contextualized the data within their lives and environments; how they critiqued and evaluated the underlying research; and their reflections on the broader implications of genetic testing. We conclude with a discussion of *biocitizen publics* and suggest three opportunity areas for Creativity and Cognition: 1) tools that creatively visualize genetic information along with self-reports and human experiences; 2) technologies that support creative reflection on scientific research; and 3) feedback systems whereby members of the general public can contribute to and influence professional research.

BIOLOGICAL CITIZENSHIP AND SCIENCE PUBLICS

The concept of biological citizenship was first discussed in the context of people's claims to welfare for biological damages (i.e., Chernobyl Nuclear Power Plant workers who demanded compensation for the 1986 disaster) [21]. Of course, biology has, in some ways, always been intertwined with ideas of citizenship: from the pragmatic association with where one is born, to the more contentious questions of national identity being shaped by race and family lines. Globalization has arguably blurred geographic boundaries by increasing connectivity between cultures, economies, and community practices [24]. Advancements in genetics contribute to this trend by offering new information regarding personal, family, and cultural backgrounds. These developments bring the concept of citizenship as a purely national concept into question [24] and give rise to new types of agency that can be exercised by biological citizens.

Genetic information can serve as both an individuating and a collectivizing force [22]. On one hand, it reveals unique features of individuals (*e.g.*, distinct ancestral backgrounds or unusual biological traits). At the same time, people are collectively making sense of and sometimes act on shared genes or genetic conditions [22]. This *biosociality*—the forming of communities around biological characteristics—leads to new types of activism [20, 24]. For instance, groups formed around genetic conditions (e.g., Huntington's disease[1]) influence professional science, both by contributing their own tissue samples and medical data to research, as well as by shaping the research itself through advocacy, funding, and public awareness campaigns.

Citizen science publics and interaction design

Building on existing trends in quantified-self [e.g., 14], interaction design will soon be addressing personal sensing beyond step counts, blood pressure, *etc.* and considering

personal DNA. Our study is among the first to examine personal and collective interpretations of this data, and can be seen as parallel to prior research in eHealth [e.g., 13, 17]. Unlike 23andMe participants, however, eHealth users are relatively sure of their diagnosis, and their discussions focus on treatments, preventative action, and social support [13]. Genetic data, on the other hand, has a higher degree of uncertainty—genes are viewed as potentials for traits rather than definite indicators. Moreover, while eHealth sites tend to focus on diseases [ibid], 23andMe also offers data about physical and mental abilities and ancestry. Users are therefore interested in understanding themselves and fulfilling their potential through their genes.

The resulting communities can be viewed as citizen science publics: participants collectively interpret, critique, and make impact on professional research. Other citizen science efforts [5, 13, 28, and others] rely on low-cost sensing to support publics around ecological concerns. In the context of personal genetics, concerns are deeply intimate and idiosyncratic, often made more unique by people's specific environments, lifestyles, and physical bodies. Genetics publics thus draw on heterogeneous methods and materials, including sensing technologies, social media tools, and the human bodies themselves to construct, communicate, and pluralize scientific knowledge [24].

Prior studies show a limited public understanding of science, often due to mixed messages from television shows and science fiction movies, as well as pre-existing mental models of genetic tests, diseases, and kinship [3, 18, and others]. While scientific literacy has been a major focus within HCI [*e.g.*, 23, 25, 26, 28], research has not explored scientific literacy in the context of genetic publics. Tools that enable collective sense-making around genetic concerns are reminiscent of politically-oriented approaches to link people through their actions [11, 15]. For instance, DiSalvo proposed *tracing* to expose hybrid "networks of materials, actions, concepts and values that shape and frame an issue over time" as a design strategy for supporting publics [8]. We contribute to this research by focusing on knowledge production and agency within a personal genetics community.

ABOUT 23ANDME

Founded by Linda Avey and Anne Wojcicki in 2006, 23andMe is a biotech startup aimed at providing low-cost genetic testing. The service offers "a comprehensive genetic scan of a subset of the SNPs (single nucleotide polymorphisms, or DNA variations) in your genome which correspond to the SNP data being studied by the research community" [1]. 23andMe works as follows: user can order a 'spit kit' online, which arrives a week later; 2) the kit is used to collect and preserve the participant's saliva sample, and is mailed back to 23andMe; 3) after a 4-6 week processing period, the results are viewed and shared online.

---

[1] E.g., Huntington's Disease Society of America; hdsa.org.

At the time of research, the service offered genetic health results—from one's ability to taste bitter flavors, to hereditary illnesses such as Parkinson's disease—as well as genetic ancestry. Shortly after our study, the FDA ordered 23andMe to stop offering health results to new users, and this order is currently under negotiation with the service. The health results profile over 240 conditions, ranging from multiple sclerosis, to Alzheimer's disease, cystic fibrosis, or sarcoma, as well as traits such as alcohol flush reaction, hair curl type, lactose intolerance, smoking behavior, photic sneeze reflex, and drug response—sensitivity to coumadin, phenytoin, warfarin and others. Ancestry results include maternal and paternal line haplogroups (genetic populations that share a common ancestor), overall composition broken down by geographic region, and percentage of Neanderthal DNA. The site also provides social networking tools: relative finder, which connects users based on shared DNA; forums, whereby users can discuss topics such as health, ancestry, specific haplogroups, Alzheimers disease, or general questions about the 23andMe service.

A platform for citizen-driven genetic research

23andMe links its results with corresponding academic publications, enabling users to learn how the findings were produced and 23andMe's confidence in its data. Some 23andMe results are improved through surveys and questionnaires on the site. These cover ancestral and health history, and personal traits such as computing one's empathy quotient, determining if one's personality is planned or spontaneous, or smoking behavior. The site also provides surveys that lead to discoveries—helping scientists identify genetic variants that are associated with traits such as dimpled chin, freckling, or earlobe type. In addition, 23andMe invites community members to propose their own research projects. Members can submit research proposals, which are evaluated by 23andMe committees of professional scientists [1]. Upon approval, members can design studies, recruit respondents, and analyze the data through 23andMe. Ongoing projects aim to identify SNP's that might be associated with specific traits, including Parkinston's disease, sarcoma, and Alzheimer's.

RESEARCH METHODS

Our research includes several strands of investigation. We began by reviewing and coding public 23andMe forum posts. Our research covers both the initial posts and the corresponding responses within 150 threads from Labs, Measures of Intelligence, Health, Relative Finder, and Hereditary forum topics. We identified 238 themes, which were affinity diagrammed into topical categories. These high-level groupings served as focal points for our in-depth qualitative study of 23andMe users. The study followed six individuals as they joined 23andMe and interacted with the service over the course of 3 months. Participants completed initial semi-structured interviews about their motivations for joining 23andMe, prior knowledge of genetic testing, as well as their personal health, family history, personality and

intelligence. After the initial interview, participants signed up for the 23andMe service with private accounts (that are not accessible to the researchers) and completed the spit kits on their own. Participants attended follow-up interviews when their data became available online, probing their reactions to and understanding of the results, whether or not their expectations were met, and how the information might impact their lives in the future.

Data from the first two interviews, along with the themes derived from the forums, was synthesized into two co-design activities for our third set of interviews. These final interviews were conducted about a month after participants' data was first made available on 23andMe, probing how the service affected their lives over the past month, and asking them to complete the co-design activities. In a concept generation phase of this interview, participants were prompted to envision future genetic services, what types of organisms might be tested, and for what factors/traits. Photographs (cards) presented a range of settings (e.g., home, park, restaurant), organisms (plants, pets, other humans), and types of sensing (scanning, swabbing, drawing fluid). After this brainstorming, participants were asked to talk through several scenarios where they might use one of the sensing methods to test a particular organism in a specific context. Participants were asked to speculate on issues such as comfort level, data sharing, privacy, and implications of these types of testing. Participants were compensated $10 per hour for their time during the interviews, and reimbursed for the 23andMe service. Data from the interviews was transcribed and coded to themes.

Ethics and privacy

Due to the sensitive nature of genetic testing, our research engaged with a range of ethics and privacy issues. On one hand, we introduced users to 23andMe given the risk of the service revealing information that could drastically impact individuals' understanding of themselves and their families. The effects of personal and community interactions with genetic data is highly debated: direct-to-consumer genetic tests have been shown to motivate healthy behavior as well as cause health anxiety [e.g. 12], and this is also reflected by the site's negotiations with the FDA. Moreover, there is also a possibility of the service itself having a breach in privacy and/or using participants' information towards undesirable research. We mitigated these issues by being transparent: our recruitment and consent materials stated that there were potential risks of privacy loss as well as the genetic results being surprising and/or upsetting. We emphasize that all work in personal genetics must consider and engage with such possible unwanted consequences.

About the participants

Participants were recruited with flyers posted at local bulletin boards, coffee shops, gyms, and restaurants, and pre-screened to ensure a range of ages, backgrounds, and family situations, as well as a gender balance. Our study included 6 participants (ages 24-64, 3 male): five completed all interviews, and one completed only the first two due to a delay caused by a 23andMe DNA processing error. Participants' occupations included a massage therapist, an engineer, a federal contractor, a musician, a project assistant, and a retired music teacher. None of the participants had a genetics or related background, and only P1 had used genetic testing before the study to find out her ancestry. We continue by detailing our findings across four themes: i) motivations for joining 23andMe; ii) contextualizing 23andMe data; iii) validating 23andMe results; and iv) the broader implications of genetic testing.

MOTIVATIONS FOR JOINING 23ANDME
Participants and forum contributors cited health, ancestry, identity, and community as key motivations for joining 23andMe. What often set these apart from motivations of other citizen science communities is the highly personal and intimate nature of the information being sought after.

Health
All participants described themselves as health conscious, and linked health with a combination of environmental, lifestyle, and genetic factors. Three of the participants were interested in 23andMe primarily for health reasons. P1, for instance, wanted to learn if breast cancer, which ran in her family, was caused by genetics:

I'd love to see the health side of my background. Both my grandmothers had breast cancer. My maternal grandmother died from it my paternal grandmother had them removed and she survived. But none of my aunts have had it. So I wonder if it was genetic or if it was something environmental. (P1)

Similarly, P2 wanted to learn about drug responses, and whether they were linked with his ethnicity. P1, P2 and P6 were interested in *'actionable information'* to reduce the risks of developing genetic diseases. It's important to note, however, that two of the participants, P4 and P5, were more skeptical of the role their genes play in their health.

I just think that we have so much more control over our health than geneticists and most people lead you to believe... I just wouldn't be too concerned about anything that indicated like oh you have an elevated risk for this cancer or that or this because I just feel like I know that the way I live my life has way more to do with it than just some genes. (P4)

Above, P4 believes that her lifestyle influences her health over genetics. P4 and P5 both stated that they would not be concerned about their health risks on 23andMe.

Ancestry
All six participants were interested in their ancestry, and had their family histories passed down to them by word of mouth, birth and marriage certificates, or comprehensive written family trees and genealogies. To varying degrees, all participants described mysteries or disagreements about their pasts, and were hoping to lear more through 23andMe:

I'd like to know whether what I've been told by relatives you know how accurate it is 'cause I know they traced the family tree of my mother's mother's mother's family but the rest of it you kinda go by family tales. (P5)

The unknowns included inconsistencies in documents such as birth certificates, as well as questions about specific family members' backgrounds. Participants also wanted to rectify disagreements about the ethnic and geographic composition of their ancestors, such as, for instance *"rumors about Chinese ancestors"* (P2) or whether or not her paternal side, which has been believed to be pure English, has any *"Irish blood"* (P5). Moreover, participants were interested in early migrations (*"information about where my ancestors migrated from"*, P2; *"what different migrations of people out of Africa you're most closely related to and that really interests me"*, P4). These motivations were also reflected by the Ancestry and Paternal/Maternal Line forum postings (e.g., *"I'm adopted (the reason why I joined 23andMe) so I really don't know much about my family or relatives."*[2]).

Personal identity
While health and ancestry were cited as the primary motivations, participants also tended to link genetic information with ideas about personal identity.

I like exploring existence and just the mind and body and just curious. Just understanding more and more about myself (P6)

I'm just interested in finding out about my genetic code and what part of that plays into who I actually am. (P3)

In the excerpts above, participants express a desire to learn more about themselves through the use of 23andMe. These comments highlight the ways participants view their genes as playing a key role in who they are. To different extents, this idea was reflected by all participants, who discussed 23andMe as a resource to learn more about oneself.

Community and connectedness
Finally, several participants also highlighted the value of 23andMe as a community tool. For example, P3 was interested in the *"less clinical"* aspects of genetic testing:

You can like see different people in the community and see who you're related to and it seems less clinical I guess than if I were to just test for diseases and be like oh I'm a carrier for this.

Similarly, P4 suggested that the service might be *"fostering a sense of community and interconnectedness within human beings"*. Forum posts, especially in the Community category, reflected this idea as well:

Who would ever join this thread if they didn't want to find out something about people who are genetically similar to them, especially when they have rare, or rare-ish combinations? That's why I joined 23andMe...[3]

---

[2] https://www.23andMe.com/you/community/thread/15124/
[3] https://www.23andMe.com/you/community/thread/12766/

Interestingly, individual genes were often used as "pivots" on which to find other users that had similar traits or conditions (e.g., *"Is There Anyone Else with 2Copies of the Gene for Intelligence?"*). However, these connections were not motivated by forming social bonds such as making friends, but rather for informational reasons (*e.g.*, to learn about the experiences, backgrounds, and health problems of those with similar traits, disease risks, or ancestry).

To summarize, participants and forum contributors cited a host of personal and intimate reasons for joining 23andMe including mitigating personal health risks, rectifying discrepancies in family histories, reflecting on personal identity, and connecting with other 23andMe users.

CONTEXTUALIZING AND LINKING GENETIC DATA

Participants expressed a range of initial reactions to their data, from feeling like she won a *'genetic lottery'* (P1) and describing the information as *'futuristic'* and *'cool'* (P3, P6), to being somewhat disappointed with a lack of specificity in the ancestry data (P2, P4). Over time, participants tended to link their genetic data with various aspects of their lives, as well as environmental factors, and cultural and historic knowledge. These links often served to determine causality—to explain why or how participants came to be who they are, as well as to make sense of their surrounding world. The links also served to alter lifestyle and behavior, as well as predict implications for future relationships, and generations. We detail several of these connections and their implications below.

Past experiences

The study participants, as well as the forum contributors, compared 23andMe results with personal experiences, inferring the genetic data to be correct when these matched. For example, P1's odds of post-operative illness were consistent with her prior experience with anesthesia and her non-verbal intelligence results on 23andMe matched earlier SAT test scores. Similarly, P2 linked his odds of developing keloids with past injuries, while P3 associated his genetic 'inability to taste bitter flavors' with his preference for bitter foods such as coffee or beer. Posts across the Health forums expressed similar connections (*e.g.*, *"My 23andMe health risks does state I have a high risk for asthma... I am sensitive to certain things like wood smoke, some flower fragrances and some perfumes."*[4]).

Background and family history

Similar to drawing on their personal experiences, 23andMe users also linked their genetic data with what they knew of their family histories and backgrounds, and in many cases, used these comparisons to validate the 23andMe results. It was not uncommon to observe participants cross-referencing their high-risk traits with specific family members who experienced those conditions (e.g., *"I know*

people in my family who've had a lot of these so it seems like to match up"*, P3). For instance, P4 noted that intolerance of cumadin and eye degenration, which 23andMe showed her at risk for, run in her family; while P1 associated her Eastern European background, as shown on 23andMe me, her dad's side *"because there's Lithuanian and some other things over there"*. These findings were consistent with our forum analysis, which showed other examples of traits being linked with family histories (e.g., *"I am a carrier (for hemochromatosis) and my Aunt died from the disease."*[5]; *"I've found synasthesia to be genetically linked on the maternal side of my family.*[6]).

Resolving unknowns about the past

In addition to associating 23andMe data with known family facts, participants also tried to use the service to resolve inconsistencies and unknowns. For instance, P1 speculated that her surprising Ashkenazi heritage, as shown by 23andMe, might explain a mysterious name change in the family. Likewise, forum posts included links between ancestry results and specific family members.

It may clear up the question of her race. I have found Jacob Cassell, which may confirm the Cherokee rumor in my family.[7]

Other attempts to explain background questions were less successful, especially in cases when 23andMe results did not provide enough detail. P2, for instance, could not infer whether his background included Chinese ancestry, because his heritage was shown broadly as "South East Asian". Similarly, P5 could not determine if her paternal side contained Irish heritage based on the "European" category. Moreover, all female participants were disappointed with the fact that the service could not profile their paternal side.

Lifestyle and behavior changes

Five participants also linked 23andMe results with changes in day-to-day behaviors. For example, P2 who was shown to have a high chance of blood clots by 23andMe, planned to get an exercise ball and walk more, P3 noted that his increased risk of developing a heart condition, as suggested by 23andMe, *"reminds me that I should be healthy... eat healthy and it can be avoided"*. P6 also reconsidered his diet and exercise based on his inherited traits:

Like the fact that I'm likely [lactose] *intolerant—that made me interested in realizing maybe I should stay stay away from milk cause I've noticed if I drink a lot of milk I get a little stuffy. The muscle type, that I'm likely not a sprinter that made me think about how I should exercise.*

Forum threads also showed a host of similar examples, whereby results influenced participants' behaviors:

Since the 23 & Me results I am reducing my fat intake.[8]

---

[4] https://www.23andMe.com/you/community/thread/8777/

[5] https://www.23andMe.com/you/community/thread/563/

[6] https://www.23andMe.com/you/community/thread/14056/

[7] https://www.23andMe.com/you/community/thread/18896/

My take-away from this is: stop eating meat. It has a high correlation with stomach cancer and if you are potentially at a higher risk it is in your best interest on so many levels to minimize risk.[9]

However, although the majority of participants and many forum posts linked genetic risks with lifestyle changes, P4 was less concerned about the role her genes play in her health. Throughout the interviews, P4 emphasized that environmental factors influence her disease risks more than her genes do, and she was therefore not planning to make any changes based on the 23andMe results.

Cultural and historical context

Finally, participants also contextualized their genetic information within their broader understandings of history, culture, religion, and evolution. For example, historical knowledge was used to speculate on and explain unexpected 23andMe results:

So it says 0.7% South Asian, which I can see that because you know just historically there's a lot of trade between south Asia and the Philippines there's a kingdom down there. (P2)

In the above excerpt, P2 notes that his South Asian heritage, as shown on 23andMe, could be explained by ancient trade routes. Similarly, P4 associates her surprising Balkan lineage with a broader view of fluidity across cultures:

It did show that I had some Balkan ancestry… it kinda goes to show how you know we think of there being some kind of stability with like ethnic groups of people but of course all kinds of people have been migrating all over for a really really long time… there's just a lot more fluidity.

Interestingly, some of the results were also associated with cultural stereotypes (e.g., "*I don't have the alcohol flush reaction, which is usually I thought was mostly Asian people who have that*", P3; "*I'm an Asian that's bad at math*", P2, based on measures of intelligence results).

Evolution

Similar to placing genetic results in a historical or cultural context, participants and forum contributors also linked genetic information with their ideas about evolution. P5 speculated about how evolution might have played a role in creating the gene that prevents people from tasting cilantro, while forum posts hypothesized about evolutionary causes of certain genetic traits or mixing with Neanderthal DNA:

Is it something that millennia ago that people were in a certain area and it was lifesaving to them to—you do not touch the cilantro. (P5)

I have 3.1% Neanderthal genes, which puts me in the top 98th percentile of all humans. Since evolutionary biologists and geneticists believe the Neanderthal and modern human mixing occurred in southern Europe, that could explain it.[10]

These excerpts exemplify how 23andMe users linked genetic test results with potential evolutionary causes.

To summarize, this section highlighted how 23andMe results were contextualized within and linked to users' environments, lifestyles, family backgrounds, and broader cultural and historical knowledge.

MAKING SENSE OF PERCEIVED INACCURACIES

While contextualizing 23andMe data within aspects of their lives, participants and forum contributors found instances where they did not agree with the results—from traits such as eye color, photic sneeze reflex, or smoking behavior, to their ancestry such as haplogroup information that did not reflect their country of origin. Although most participants (5 out of 6) appreciated being able to see the studies 23andMe drew upon to present the data, they also tended to cross-check information with other genetic testing services, as well as sources such as Wikipedia, Mayoclinic, Webmd, and friends who they considered to be experts. Oftentimes, these inquiries led to users to question, debate, or refute scientific information. Many factors—from environmental influences, to study limitations and biases—were drawn upon to determine whether the genetic data was reliable. Below, we detail how participants made sense of and interpreted discrepancies between their perceptions of themselves and their external world, and the genetic data that reflected the invisible information within their bodies.

Nature vs. nurture

All of our participants, as well many of the forum posts we analyzed, discussed genetic testing as an indicator that has a degree of uncertainty. It was not uncommon to hear our participants refer to 23andMe traits and conditions as a "propensities", or "not definites". To varying degrees, all participants acknowledged 23andMe results as predispositions rather than guarantees (e.g., "*whether they're activated has to do with a lot of factors*" P4). Participants and forum posters emphasized the role that environment and lifestyle plays in gene expression:

This risk is not taking into account me, but only my genes. (P3)

It's always going to be a complex interplay of nature and nurture; genetic factors or predispositions probably (at least IMO) going hand in hand with environmental / cultural factors, *individual* predispositions, etc.[11]

These excepts show that, while in many cases, participants did not doubt the accuracy of the genetic tests per say, they attributed inaccuracies in their results to the influences of environmental and lifestyle factors.

---

[8] https://www.23andMe.com/you/community/thread/10116/
[9] https://www.23andMe.com/you/community/thread/9664/

[10] https://www.23andMe.com/you/community/thread/11378/
[11] https://www.23andMe.com/you/community/thread/15866/

Small datasets and preliminary research

In other cases, 23andMe users critiqued the results for being based on small (inconclusive) datasets. It was not uncommon to hear participants refer to 23andMe results as based on *"preliminary research"* (P3), or findings that are constantly changing based on new or incoming data (P1).

There's more studies more research going on so I guess within the framework of the limited knowledge that we have now and our understanding of things now as a snapshot I guess I trust this as much as you can [trust] what we know now. (P2)

Above, P2 notes that 23andMe results are dependent on *'what we know now'*, and may change as new data comes in. P6 and P3 also pointed out that 23andMe tests for a small subset of genetic mutations. For instance, P3 commented that the service *"only tests for 3 of 100s of possible mutations you might have in the BRCA [breast cancer] gene"*; while P6 also critiqued the 23andMe service for not taking into account how different genes might interact with each other.

Limitations and biases of supporting studies

In some cases, participants and forum contributors also identified limitations and biases in the underlying research. It is important to note that even prior to joining 23andMe, all participants expressed a skepticism towards scientific publications—from questioning data that is *"constantly changing"* (P2), to suggesting that findings may be influenced by corporations, researchers' *"pre-conceived ideas"* (P4), or financial and political motivations (P5). Given participants' initial skepticism towards scientific research, it is not surprising that they also identified limitations in studies cited by 23andMe. Most commonly, they noted that that the related studies did not apply to their gender, ethnicity, or age group (e.g., *"this health risk assumes I'm European and of a different age"*, P3; *"maybe if I was that group it would be accurate"*, P2). Furthermore, participants also pointed out that many of the sample sizes were too small (e.g., a study of 139 people), or had un-accounted variables (e.g. *"who are you studying will skew results"*, P4).

In addition, several forum discussions expressed concerns over potential biases in the underlying research.

In many fields it is rare for a person to strive for the truth ahead of getting published, getting tenure, or other renown.[12]

I think the test has a major flaw in that all the people are white... So would it not make sense that white people would do better on this test than Asians, Mexicans or African-Americans?[13]

These excerpts illustrate potential research biases that were of concern to 23andMe users: ulterior political or financial motives of the underlying studies, and racial bias.

Inaccurate 23andMe survey responses

Finally, participants and forum contributors questioned the accuracy of some of the 23andMe results that were based on the site's surveys. For instance, P5 noted that she guessed her survey answers when she could not remember her family history, and was worried that others might be doing the same, thereby skewing the data. Moreover, P3 pointed out that there was no mechanism for changing one's survey responses if they were accidentally entered incorrectly. Several forum posts expressed similar concerns (e.g., *"I really have to question the effectiveness of some of their [23andMe] research questionnaires"[14]*).

To summarize, this section outlined several ways by which participants and forum contributors made sense of instances when their 23andMe results did not match with what they believed to be true about themselves. Among the discussed factors were the influence of environment and lifestyle over genetics, as well as lack of data, limitations of supporting studies, and inaccuracies in 23andMe survey responses.

BROADER IMPLICATIONS OF GENETIC TESTING

Finally, our forum analysis and discussions with participants revealed ways that 23andMe users reflected on the broader implications of genetics. Below, we detail users' speculations about potential positive and negative consequences, and new ways of seeing that might emerge as genetic testing becomes more widespread.

Potential positive consequences

All participants emphasized that genetic testing poses unprecedented opportunities for healthcare.

I think it just would be empowerment for people to be able to watch out for their own health. I think it would be on a societal basis ... I would think people would take a little better care of themselves or at least would know what to watch out for. (P1)

Above, P1 highlights how access to genetic testing might empower people to mitigate disease risks and/or take better care of personal health. To varying degrees, all participants also highlighted opportunities for improved preventative care and diagnostics, and drugs being designed to suit individuals based on their genes. Participants also pointed out that services such as 23andMe could *'advance scientific knowledge'* for researchers and the general public (P1, P2), or serve as an *'educational tool'* to show how *'humanity is evolving'* (P4).

More broadly, several participants also commented on the implications of large communities forming around shared ideas rooted in genetics.

It brings people together with all this medical information already tied to them... so it's a good method of inquiry for a group because this group already exists and they have this huge pool of data. (P3)

---

[12] https://www.23andMe.com/you/community/thread/538/

[13] https://www.23andMe.com/you/community/thread/13697

[14] https://www.23andMe.com/you/community/thread/8139/

I guess just like one thing with the internet is it does like bring together large groups of people instantaneously pretty much so you knows it's good that there's always at least the availability at least to start like a massive movement almost at the drop of a hat where you can rally people around an idea. (P4)

These excerpts illustrate how participants viewed 23andMe as resource for bringing people together to learn new information or to work towards changing the status quo.

Potential negative consequences
Alongside these envisioned positive outcomes, participants also discussed a range of privacy and ethics concerns associated with genetic information being aggregated by companies such as 23andMe and available online. These ranged from questions of data ownership and discrimination by employers or insurance companies, to more extreme visions of dystopian futures where people might be disempowered or separated into cast systems based on genetics. Interestingly, all participants also agreed that the potential benefits of genetic testing outweighed the possible negative consequences. Despite their privacy concerns, for instance, all participants were not too worried about a breach of security to the 23andMe site, which was noted in the 23andMe terms of use, and likened this possibility to someone stealing their credit card information.

New ways of seeing
Finally, participants also reflected on future genetic testing technologies as not necessarily a means to a scientific end (*i.e.*, diagnosing a disease), but also as a new way of seeing or understanding the world. For instance, when asked to envision the implications of rapidly sequencing any genetic material, P4 discussed the value of *seeing* or knowing things more intimately:

It's not because you're tying to find something out its the act of knowing like you know something more intimately because you've seen a different side of it. (P4)

Here, P4 reflects on widespread genetic testing as an opportunity to observe living and organic materials differently. To varying degrees, other participants expressed similar ideas, noting that tools for rapid genetic sequencing might help identify surrounding organisms or learn more about the world ("*it would be easier to figure out what things were made of*", P4; "*it might be really neat for findings things*", P1).

To summarize, this section highlighted participants' perspectives on the bigger implications of genetic testing, which ranged from positive consequences for healthcare and bringing people together, to questions about ethics and privacy, as well as new ways to see the world differently.

BIOCITIZEN PUBLICS
Thus far, we detailed our study of 23andMe, including users' motivations, practices, challenges and reflections on the broader implications of genetic testing. Our findings are, in many ways, aligned with Rose et al.'s analysis of biological citizenship [24], particularly by showing how widely accessible genetic data contributes to the blurring of citizenship as a purely national concept grounded in geographic boundaries. Indeed, learning about ancestry was a key motivation for joining 23andMe, and this information resulted in feelings of 'connectedness' to other community members. Most directly, these trans-national connections were made evident through 23andMe's relative finder, which revealed genetic kinship ties across the world; as well as forum features, whereby users interact with others who are, as one member put it, 'genetically similar'. More broadly, the service showed trends in evolution and human migrations, which in the words of one participant suggested 'fluidity' rather than 'stability' between ethnic groups.

With ideas about biological citizenship thus rooted in global inter-connectedness, users of 23andMe coalesce around scientific findings not as passive consumers of data but as active, trans-national participants who interpret, contest, and/or validate their results. New practices, centered around contextualizing and making sense of genetic data are giving rise to sub-communities or *publics*. Similar to other citizen science groups arising out of shared concerns (e.g., local air quality), 23andMe publics are predicated on pressing questions of personal identity, personal health, or family history. Also, like the traditional citizen science efforts to gather local and professional knowledge, 23andMe users share and reflect on personal experiences, lifestyle choices, environmental factors, and cultural beliefs along with scientific (genetic) data. These heterogeneous information sources are aggregated across the 23andMe platform, whereby users draw on the site's research and social tools to create hybrid assemblies of personal narrative, pluralistic discourse, and academic research.

Finally, when these assemblies of hybrid knowledge reveal discrepancies between genetic test results and what participants know about themselves and their world, users collectively contest the underlying data. The emerging dialogues critique the biases, methodology, and scope of professional research: from identifying unfair funding influences, to speculating about the importance of environmental factors that may have been overlooked by studies, or pointing out limitations in participant pools. With this framing of 23andMe users as active science communities, there are many opportunities for HCI to support and sustain the resulting biocitizen publics. Not unlike HCI's involvement with other citizen science groups, future design trajectories might include: platforms for aggregating different types of knowledge; tools for contesting and legitimizing scientific research; and enabling agency within and across genetics communities.

Interactive systems for visualizing hybrid information
Our findings suggest that genetic test results were rarely, if ever, considered in isolation. Instead, participants entangled 23andMe data with personal experiences, family narratives, lifestyle changes, and cultural/historic information. C&C

can support this creative sense-making of hybrid information through new visualizations and sharing tools.

One opportunity lies in treating genes as *informational pivots* that creatively aggregate information about environments, lifestyles, and backgrounds across users. For example, future interactive systems could use graph visualizations: genes can be presented as nodes with which users associate personal experiences, family histories, or cultural and historic knowledge. In addition, systems can link personal narratives and experiences with genetic test results. While the 23andMe service currently only supports text-based input across forums, future systems can enable rich multi-modal metadata to be attributed to specific genes. For instance, users may want to share visual or audio experiences (photos, videos) of living with certain genes.

Considering personal genetics as a first-class organizing principle throughout online services also has the potential to change the way we organize, seek, and share information. With connectedness being a key value for 23andMe users, this approach could more intuitively reveal links between biology, people, and environments. Interfaces with genes as pivots could support DiSalvo's concept of *tracing* [8] to enable fluid navigation between scientific data and other factors such as local history, morals, and personal relationships. Building on 'politics of scale', such platforms can also enable people to become connected not only through their actions [11] but also through their genes.

Tools for creative reflection on scientific research
Aggregating diverse forms of knowledge along with genetic data led participants to critique the underlying research. Our findings show that participants actively problematized or validated 23andMe results. Here, C&C is presented with opportunities to support creative and critical reflection on scientific research. Most directly, sharing mechanisms could enable people to discuss and evaluate the underlying work. For example, future personal genetic systems could enable users to comment on and rate study size, data quality, biases, claims, and other aspects of the research that is drawn upon to present the genetic results. In addition, systems could also more deeply engage people with the scientific method, enabling members of the general public to effectively formulate hypotheses, explore the underlying data, and validate the results. These approaches could embrace *agonistic pluralism* to create productive conflict and people to contest the status quo [9].

Of course, tools for contesting professional research raise questions about the scientific literacy of participants. Earlier research has commented on the limitations of more traditional tools to codify and transfer scientific knowledge [*e.g.*, 16] and services such as 23andMe present new opportunities for disseminating information to people with varying degrees of expertise. The service already supports scientific literacy by communicating information in a variety of ways, from short layman summaries or star confidence ratings, to extensive excerpts from academic publications. Citizen science systems in other domains (e.g., environmental monitoring) could adopt similar or new visual techniques to make scientific data more transparent and legible. For instance, systems focused on factors such as air quality or phenology could more transparently present aspects of the contributing research, such as sample size, duration of studies, reproducibility, or funding sources.

In parallel, creativity support tools can more deeply engage members of the general public in discourse around bioethics, healthcare, and public participation in science. For instance, work in tangible interaction can overtly reveal recent trends in biotechnology research by incorporating genetic information and organic materials into tangible artifacts. New interactive experiences might highlight different biological aspects of the living world. Enabling people to see more intimate information within their bodies and the living systems around them (i.e., new ways of seeing) might bring about new forms of reflection, discussion, and action within and across groups.

Supporting new forms of activism
Finally, as 23andMe users made sense of their results, they inevitably commented on the broader implications of genetic testing. From the potential improvements to public healthcare and ways to bring large groups of people together, to the possibilities of seeing the world in new ways, or concerns about ethics and privacy, 23andMe users engaged with the larger issues around genetics. For creativity systems, this presents opportunities to support new collaborations and activism across communities. With critique of genetic research being a prevalent practice throughout 23andMe, interactive technologies can enable groups to more directly impact professional science work. For example, new tools might allow 23andMe users to create and contribute to advocacy initiatives around genetics research that is relevant to their lives. This could take on the forms of public awareness campaigns to nudge science agendas, tools to encourage more people to participate in science studies, or platforms for raising money to fund new research projects more directly. New systems can also serve to democratize science by interfacing genetic research with related healthcare and policy debates and decisions.

CONCLUSION
As genetic testing continues to become more accessible, communities of participants will grapple with increasingly complex scientific information. This creates opportunities to re-envision how people engage with the intimate data embedded in their own bodies and the living systems around them, and support the emerging citizen science *publics* as they debate and act on genetic research. As a first step, our work examined the practices of 23andMe users, focusing on how participants contextualize their genetic results, critique and evaluate the underlying research, and

reflect on the broader implications of genetic testing. Our findings revealed new research areas for creativity and cognition: platforms for aggregating and visualizing hybrid knowledge; tools that enable creative reflection on scientific research; and systems for supporting collective action within and across genetic communities. These directions can enable broader scientific participation and support citizen science publics at the intersection of genetics and interaction design.

ACKNOWLEDGEMENTS

This work was supported by NSF IIS-1211047.

REFERENCES

1. 23andMe. https://www.23andMe.com/

2. Andrews, L., Dorothy, N. 2001. Body Bazaar: The Market for Human Tissue in the Biotechnology Age. Crown, 1st ed.

3. Bates, B. R., Lynch, J. A., Bevan, J. L., & Condit, C. M. 2005. Warranted concerns, warranted outlooks: A focus group study of public understandings of genetic research. Social Science & Medicine, 60, 331-344

4. Bonney, R., Cooper, C. B., Dickinson, J., Kelling, S., Phillips, T., Rosenberg, K. V., & Shirk, J. 2009. Citizen Science: A Developing Tool for Expanding Science Knowledge and Scientific Literacy. BioScience, 59(11), 977-984.

5. Burke, J., Hansen, M., Parker, A., Ramanathan, N., Reddy, S., Srivastava, M. B. 2006. Participatory Sensing. WSW'06 at SenSys, Boulder, CO, 117-134.

6. Cosley, D., Frankowski, D., Kiesler, S., Terveen, L., Riedl, J. 2005. How oversight improves member-maintained communities. CHI '05. ACM, New York, NY, USA, 11-20.

7. Dewey, J. The Public and Its Problems. NY: Holt, 1927.

8. DiSalvo, C. 2009. Design and the Construction of Publics. Design Issues (MIT) 25, no. 1.

9. DiSalvo, C. Design, democracy, and agonistic pluralism. Proceedings of the Design Research Society Conference 2010, Montreal, 2010, 6.

10. DiSalvo, C., Lukens, J., Lodato, T., Jenkins, T., Kim, T. 2014. Making public things: how HCI design can express matters of concern. CHI '14, 2397-2406.

11. Dourish, P. 2010. HCI and Environmental Sustainability: The Politics of Design and the Design of Politics. DIS'10, 1-10.

12. Egglestone C., Morris A., O'Brien A. 2013. Effect of direct-to-consumer genetic tests on health behaviour and anxiety: a survey of consumers and potential consumers. J Genet Couns. 2013 Oct;22(5):565-75.

13. Frost, J. H., & Massagli, M. P. (2008). Social uses of personal health information within PatientsLikeMe, an online patient community: what can happen when patients have access to one another‚Äôs data. Journal of Medical Internet Research, 10(3).

14. Li, I., Dey, A., Forlizzi, J. 2010. A stage-based model of personal informatics systems. CHI '10, 557-566.

15. LeDantec, C. A., Christensen, J. E., Bailey, M., Farrell, R.G., Ellis, J. B., Davis, C. M., Kellogg, W. A., Edwards, W. K. 2010. A Tale of Two Publics: Democratizing Design at the Margins. In Proc of. DIS'10

16. Lee, S., & Roth, W. M. (2003). Of traversals and hybrid spaces: Science in the community. Mind, Culture, & Activity, 10, 120–142.

17. Maloney-Krichmar, D., & Preece, J. (2005). A multilevel analysis of sociability, usability, and community dynamics in an online health community. ACM Transactions on Computer-Human Interaction (TOCHI), 12(2), 201-232.

18. Michie S., Smith J.A., Senior V., Marteau T.M. 2003. Understanding why negative genetic test results sometimes fail to reassure. American Journal of Medical Genetics, 119A:340–347.

19. National Human Genome Research Institute. All about the Human Genome Project. http://www.genome.gov/

20. Neuhauser, D. 2009. Biosocial Citizenship: Community Participation in Public Health. cwru.edu/med/epidbio/mphp439/Biosocial_Comm.pdf

21. Petryna, A. 2002 Biological citizenship: science and the politics of health after Chernobyl, Princeton NJ: Princeton University Press.

22. Rabinow, P. 2008. Artificiality and Enlightenment: From Sociobiology to Biosociality. Anthropologies of Modernity: Foucault, Governmentality, and Life Politics. Jonathan Xavier Inda (ed.), pp. 181-193.

23. Rogers, Y., Price, S., Fitzpatrick, G., Fleck, R., Harris, E., Smith, H., Randell, C., Muller, H., O'Malley, C., Stanton, D., Thompson, M., Weal, M. 2004. Ambient wood: designing new forms of digital augmentation for learning outdoors. Interaction design and children: building a community, p. 3-10.

24. Rose, N., and Novas, C. 2005. Biological Citizenship. In Global Assemblages: Technology, Politics, and Ethics as Anthropological Problems, Ong, A., and Collier, S. J. eds. Blackwell Publishing, pp. 439-463.

25. Shaer, O., Kol, G., Strait, M., Fan, C., Grevet, C., Elfenbein, S. 2010. G-nome surfer: a tabletop interface for collaborative exploration of genomic data. CHI '10. ACM, New York, NY, USA, 1427-1436.

26. Shaer, O., Mazalek, A., Ullmer, B., Konkel, M. 2013. From big data to insights: opportunities and challenges for TEI in genomics. TEI '13. ACM, NY, 109-116.

27. Taylor, A. S., Piterman, N., Ishtiaq, S., Fisher, J., Cook, B., Cockerton, C., Bourton, S., Benque, D. 2013. At the interface of biology and computation. CHI '13, 493-502.

28. Willett, W., Aoki, P., Kumar, N., Subramanian, S., Woodruff, A. 2010. Common sense community: scaffolding mobile sensing and analysis for novice users. Pervasive'10, 301-318.

Making Magic:
Designing for Open Interactions in Museum Settings

Robyn Taylor[1], John Bowers[1], Bettina Nissen[1], Gavin Wood[1], Qasim Chaudhry[1],
Peter Wright[1], Lindsey Bruce[2], Sarah Glynn[2], Helen Mallinson[2], Roy Bearpark[2]

[1]Culture Lab, Newcastle University,
Newcastle upon Tyne, UK
initial.surname@ncl.ac.uk

[2]Great North Museum: Hancock,
Tyne and Wear Museums, Newcastle upon Tyne, UK
initial.surname@twmuseums.co.uk

ABSTRACT

This paper describes three interactive artefacts created for a children's exhibition intended to encourage creativity and allow educational opportunities to emerge naturally through playful exploration. We describe five sensibilities that were used to inform our designs: considering artefacts as resources and scaffolds for imaginative engagement, rewarding extended investment, facilitating requisite unpredictability, encouraging an imaginative orientation to participation, and permitting multiple loci for interaction. Based on observation of how our interactives were used by the public, we discuss how our approach facilitated 'open interactions' in a manner that was sensitive to the museum context, favoured a mix of materialities, and manifested a subtle mix of participation and designer autonomy.

Author Keywords

Digital art, digital interactives, research through design, museum, gallery interpreter, creative play, heritage

ACM Classification Keywords

H.5.2 User Interfaces (D.2.2, H.1.2, I.3.6)

General Terms

Design

INTRODUCTION

The Victoria and Albert Museum's *Magic Worlds* was a child-oriented exhibition that invited visitors to explore fairy tales, fantasy literature, and the origins of magic and illusion. Drawing from the museum's national childhood collection, a touring version of V&A's Magic Worlds was presented in several British museums in 2013 to 2014. Each host museum was able to make local design enhancements to complement and augment the touring exhibition.

In 2014, our research team designed and crafted bespoke interactive digital content that was used as part of a three-month installation of Magic Worlds at the Great North Museum:Hancock (GNM), located in Newcastle upon Tyne. Working together with the exhibition designer, educational director, and the museum manager over a period of several months, we created three digital artefacts for the exhibition: an interactive witch's cauldron that responded with audio-visual feedback when children cast spells by throwing ingredients into the cauldron, and two magic mirrors that displayed fantastical reflections and optical effects. These artefacts were carefully placed within the overall spatial design of the exhibition so as to create possibilities for story-telling and dramatic play within the setting. The GNM's presentation of the Magic Worlds exhibition was extremely popular, receiving 154,655 visitors during the three months it was open to the public – making it the museum's most well-attended exhibition since its reopening in 2009.

Figure 1. Helen, the Gallery Interpreter, plays with the Magic Cauldron alongside a child visiting the exhibition

In this paper we explore how the Magic Worlds exhibition provided us with an opportunity to design interactive pieces intended to support a children's museum in facilitating open-ended enquiry and creative exploration. We built our approach upon current research surrounding the use of digital interactives in museum settings [14], the exploration of playful design [13] strategies in HCI and how the experience of interactive technology is shaped by and shapes the overall design of the setting [10]. We define a series of *design sensibilities* that helped inform the making of three compelling digital interactives that were congruent with the stylistic and educational goals of the exhibition, and discuss several interesting phenomena we observed arising from their use. We follow an orientation to Research through Design which recognizes that there is a mutual refining of the designed artefacts and the detailed sense we give to our sensibilities as the design process unfolds (c.f. [3,12]) Overall, we characterize our work as situated, favouring a mix of materialities, and manifesting a mix of participation and designer autonomy. Taken together this makes a contribution to how museum design can be reimagined as a resource for designing open interaction.

THE MUSEUM AND EXHIBITION CONTEXT

There exists a substantial and varied body of literature in human computer interaction (HCI) and computer supported cooperative work (CSCW) addressing the complexity of designing for modern museum and related cultural spaces. [11] and [10] describe some early explorations of the use of ubiquitous computing and mixed reality technologies in, respectively, a castle and a personal collection, giving particular attention to the design of trajectories through multiple interactive 'loci' – an emphasis given further analysis by [2]. [8] has been particularly concerned to draw upon 'place geography' in design work in museum and heritage sites to create characterful and meaningful hybrid digital artefacts within them. Heath, Hindmarsh, vom Lehn and colleagues in an extensive body of work [e.g. 14, 15] have analysed the details of social interaction within museum and related settings, drawing out a number of implications for design and research agendas in HCI and CSCW more broadly. To give a final example of work in such settings, Nissen and colleagues [19] explore how fabrication technologies can be used to create bespoke souvenirs based on individuals' experience of an exhibition.

This research literature is an essential context for our work. So, equally, are the specific contingencies associated with the opportunities we had. As a touring exhibition, Magic Worlds was already organized around the V&A's own design commitments but these left much undetermined. Local museums hosting the exhibition could not only add items from their own collections but also give the overall architecture of the exhibition space a specific character. Equally, our digital artefacts were not produced 'to brief'. We had creative licence with them under the overall aegis of relevance to the Magic Worlds theme. Indeed, the local design of the exhibition space was developed mindful of the fact that digital artefacts were under development and, as their form began to emerge, particular locations in the exhibition were selected for them and the local context in which these artefacts would appear was shaped to maximize visitors' potential appreciation of them. As such, Magic Worlds presented a fascinating occasion to explore the complex 'entanglements' and 'meshwork' involved in

making [1,17] and the different constraints and enablements which configure design spaces.

The Layout and Visit Trajectory of Magic Worlds

Magic Worlds was installed in a 500m^2 gallery space in the GNM that was divided into three major rooms, each themed in accordance with the V&A's selection of artefacts around a different aspect of magic and folklore: fantasy, illusion, and enchantment. The 'Fantasy' room featured materials relating to fairy tales and fantasy literature, 'Illusion' showcased the history of magicians and magic-as-spectacle, as well as examples of classic optical devices and trickery. The third room, 'Enchantment' focused on magical creatures and beings such as dragons, fairies and elves. In each of the exhibition's rooms, familiar scenes and settings from literature and folklore were staged in child-size miniature. Visitors to the 'Fantasy' room, for example, encountered a variety of themed play areas such as a child-sized gingerbread house from Hansel and Gretel, and a walk-in wardrobe space from The Lion, the Witch and the Wardrobe, while the 'Enchantment' area was styled as a magical meadow populated by fairies and dragons. Each area and referenced story corresponded to artefacts and educational materials situated nearby.

Much emphasis was placed on the importance of crafting visitors' trajectories of experience through the exhibition [cf. 2]. As the gallery was divided into several spaces, each themed space was made visually and sonically distinct with the goal that visitors would thoroughly explore and engage with one space before progressing through to the next. To encourage a flow of movement throughout the exhibition, transitions between the major themed areas were carefully crafted, stimulating the senses through appealing staging and set design (notable transitions included a tree-lined canopy leading into 'Fantasy' and a vintage-styled hall of mirrors welcoming visitors into the world of 'Illusion') in order to tempt visitors onward to find out what came next. It was intended that this journey – a winding path of exploration and discovery – would add to visitors' enjoyment of and engagement with the exhibition.

The Exhibition 'Interactives'

The GNM wanted the experience of visiting Magic Worlds to differ from a traditional museum visit, in order to challenge any lingering perception of museums as stilted, inaccessible places where visitors are only permitted to look but not touch. As the museum manager put it in a recorded group discussion: "we want people to care about the venue, to care about the objects. If you constantly put barriers between them and the stories and the objects, it becomes very difficult for them to [care]". To encourage visitors to engage with the exhibition content through hands-on activity, many pieces were physically accessible to the patrons. The designers of Magic Worlds provided an extensive array of costumes and props, and encouraged the children to touch, wear and use them as they visited, explored, and play-acted inside the exhibition space.

We created three digital interactives for the exhibition – two 'magic mirrors' (one residing in the 'Fantasy' room, and one in the 'Illusion' room) and a 'magic cauldron' situated in a small room of its own next to the 'Enchantment' space, and styled in the theme of literary witches and witchcraft. The digital interactives as well as the expanded collection of costumes and props were intended to encourage children to play-act and engage with the story-based spaces. It was hoped that, by providing numerous opportunities for hands-on, interactive play, the exhibition content would inspire social exchange and provide creative stimulation for further discovery. Later in this paper we will explore how successful our strategies were.

Enquiry-Based Learning Through Hands-On Activity

Magic Worlds did not present curriculum-based educational content in a traditional manner, but rather exhibited an open-ended collection of materials intended to support and stimulate children's creativity and curiosity by presenting classic literature and folklore in an accessible fashion. The museum's educational goal was to encourage 'enquiry-based learning' [18] whereby educational opportunities were allowed to grow naturally out of playful visitor experiences. The GNM's learning officer elaborated on the museum's belief that open ended enquiry and exploration would lead to learning, citing the work of Piaget, Vygotsky and Bruner [e.g. 23] on cognitive and social constructivism. The learning officer explained that their vision for Magic Worlds was to enable visitors to craft their own individual journey through the experience. Educational opportunities or avenues for discovery would arise as visitors constructed their own knowledge through firsthand explorations with artefacts – encounters mediated by parents or Gallery Interpreters or through peer-to-peer interaction and play.

Anticipated Visitors

While many school groups toured and visited the exhibition, the GNM also wanted to target family groups comprising individuals from different age groups, and provide avenues for family members to interact with and alongside one another. The design of the interactives – both the traditional (such as costume pieces and cozy family reading spaces) as well as the digital – intended to challenge and stimulate older children while simultaneously engaging younger family members as well. The GNM also wanted to make sure that the exhibition would encourage families to make repeat visits, with the intention being that the exhibition should be enjoyable on multiple levels. Entry to the museum was free, and it was hoped that children whose first visit consisted primarily of discovering and playing in the space might engage more thoughtfully with specific artefacts or interactives on subsequent visits. These concerns of the museum relate very strongly to the contributions of Heath and his colleagues [e.g.14, 15] which emphasize how visits are typically made within small groups who manifest quite characteristic patterns of interaction – for example, animating exhibits for each other, comparing perceptions, adults facilitating the engagement of children, and so forth – and all of this done in the presence of other such groupings.

The Role of the Gallery Interpreter

To facilitate and support social interaction in the exhibition, the GNM brought in Helen, a specially trained Gallery Interpreter. While also being responsible for ensuring museum safety and performing daily routine operational tasks, Helen's function as a Gallery Interpreter differed from that of a traditional 'invigilator' or 'docent'. While she was available to protect and provide knowledge about the exhibition artefacts if needed, her primary role was to scaffold social interactions amongst the families visiting the space. She was encouraged to mediate the visitor experience by stimulating and even modeling role-play and creative, educational interaction, functioning in a manner similar to the role of 'orchestrator' described by Benford and Giannachi [2]. Joining alongside visitors to take part in creative play (see Fig. 1) allowed Helen to function as what Heath et al. term a co-participant [14], able to influence visitors' experience simply by visibly engaging with the exhibition herself. Helen worked on-site six days a week during the entirety of Magic Worlds' run. Later in this discussion we will explore how her situated understanding of the experience was helpful when evaluating and making sense of the way our interactives were used by the public.

DESIGNING THE DIGITAL INTERACTIVES

We began exploratory design work on potential digital interactives several months before the GNM exhibition's launch. Through collaborative discussion with museum stakeholders (including the exhibition designer, the educational director and the museum manager) the digital designers in our team explored how interactive digital content could enrich the visitor experience.

Design Sensibilities

Alongside engaging in a variety of design activities, we began to formulate design sensibilities on the basis of some of the above concerns of the museum, our own past work and creative practices, and other relevant contributions within HCI and CSCW, such as the works of Heath, Hindmarsh and vom Lem (e.g. [14] [15].) In addition, we consider the work of Humphrey and Gutwill, whose discussion of 'Active Prolonged Engagement' (APE) [16] extensively explores how educational value is obtained through deepening visitors' interactions and personal processes of meaning-making rather than simply by measurably increasing their canonical knowledge. Humphrey and Gutwill further distinguish APE from what they term 'planned discovery' [16] in which encounters with museum content are carefully orchestrated to maximize the discoverability of educational content. Accordingly, rather than deterministically directing exactly what it would be that visitors were intended to learn from their own participation, we identified five design sensibilities to create a design space in which play and discovery were emphasized in a manner consistent with the GNM's goals for the exhibition. These provided initial orientations for our design activity that were subsequently refined as our design work unfolded.

1) Resourcing and scaffolding. In contrast to firmly enshrining a story or meaning into the technology, whatever is designed should instead enable and inspire creative storytelling and acting out, allowing children to imagine and discover the content of their play. In this way, technologies serve as a resource for interaction, rather than mandate what should occur [cf. 17, 20]. This approach allows the Gallery Interpreter to appropriate the interactives rather than merely enact what their 'rules' require. Where constraint is designed into the artefact, it should be for the purposes of configuring participation rather than restricting visitors' creative choices and/or forcing them down a path of 'planned discovery' [16]. In this way, adults might be able to 'scaffold' the activities of children, to use Bruner's term [6], rather than tell them what to do.

2) Rewarding extended investment. Artefacts should be designed such that prolonged or repeated exposure should yield deepening engagement, whether through revealed complexities, or by encountering a greater breadth of creative stimuli [13]. While extended engagement should uncover more of interest, we did not want casual encounters to somehow feel incomplete. Accordingly, we concerned ourselves with artefacts which manifested a variety of behaviours, any one of which might offer some intrigue, but where extended curiosity uncovered more of the picture, without there being a sense that there was a hidden goal, which might frustrate if not discovered [see also 3].

3) Robustness yet requisite unpredictability. Artefacts should maintain an acceptable level of (physical and interactive) robustness, while introducing a requisite level of unpredictability in order to stimulate engagement through mystery. Dalsgaard terms this as designing for 'inquisitive use' [9]. Bowers [3] in his analysis of the work of designs such as the drift table [13], argues that they are appealing because they have interactivity which combines the right kind of unpredictability (so users 'steer' the pieces, rather than control them) with known states that are easy to get (back) to or recognise if troubles occur.

4) Encouraging imaginative orientation to participation. To design technology that exists at the intersection of multiple potential users and permits a multiplicity of footings from which it can be encountered, design should be mindful that participation with the artefact could take many forms [14,16,21,22]. So exactly *how* one should participate with the technology should be a matter for flexible, imaginative appropriation too.

5) Multiple loci for interaction, trajectories and placements. As we have described, any digital interactive we were to build would need to coexist with many other things. It would not be appropriate for digital pieces to overshadow the other exhibition content, nor require ways of engaging with them which were out of keeping. Thus we avoided artefacts that were recognisably interactives favouring an embedded computing and sensor-based approach. Also, by carefully placing a number of devices through the exhibition, we aimed for each piece to afford a 'locus for interaction' [10] within the visit trajectory [2].

The Design Process
Identifying and finalizing the particular digital interactives was done through a collaborative process that saw our digital interaction researchers meet several times with the museum manager, exhibition designer, and the educational director. In between these meetings, our digital designers met independently to brainstorm and generate ideas. This allowed us to address the museum's needs and desires, while still maintaining some autonomy over our own design practice and digital research goals. Correspondingly, as design ideas emerged, the museum designers were able to anticipate the best locations for the pieces and to ensure that their surrounding contexts promoted the intended experience of them.

The initial meeting with the whole team allowed us to share the museum's vision for the exhibition, identifying several aspects of the Magic Worlds national content that could benefit from digital enhancement. In a half-day workshop, our digital design team began by discussing, exploring and elaborating the design sensibilities we hoped to embody in our interactive artefacts. With these design sensibilities in mind, we held a freeform brainstorming session whereby we suggested and debated numerous ideas for artefacts we hoped would fit well with the museum's interests while remaining aligned with our creative vision for interaction design. Some twenty proposals were offered. We then critically evaluated this array of initial ideas, in terms of their clarity, feasibility, relevance to the exhibition, the degree of collective enthusiasm shown for them amongst the digital designers, and a general anticipation of their research value. A long short-list of six proposals was discussed together with the museum stakeholders. We further examined the practicalities and logistics of realising each proposal, as well as the educational potential and thematic congruence each idea would contribute to the Magic Worlds exhibition as a whole. Three interactive digital artefacts were mutually agreed upon as particularly suitable.

CRAFTING THE INTERACTIVE ARTEFACTS
The first two artefacts we built were *magic mirrors*. The first one would be situated in the 'Fantasy' area, where children were encouraged to try on an array of playful fairytale costumes and examine their reflections in a magic

mirror augmented with digital technology. The second magic mirror was to be placed in the 'Illusion' area, which had previously been identified as an aspect of the exhibition that would benefit from the inclusion of interactive reference points for young children to engage with. The third digital artefact would be a *magic cauldron*, with digital technologies used to make children's interactions generate audio-visual response and provide a scaffolding resource for stories and play-acting around casting spells.

Magic Mirrors

The mirrors were implemented using 42-inch flatscreen monitors that were mounted in portrait orientation on the walls of the exhibition space. To disguise the monitors and make them coherent with the exhibition's physical aesthetic, we fashioned elegant antiqued-gold picture frames (made from lightweight wood and firmly attached to each monitor's casing) that concealed the plastic monitor bezels. Mounted in the top of each picture frame was a digital camera whose field of view was trained upon the space in which a visitor would stand if looking at the framed monitor. Displaying a horizontally flipped stream of the live camera feed on the monitor display allowed the visitor to see him/herself as if in a mirror (see Fig. 2.) While both mirrors were physically identical, they functioned in two distinctly different ways, with one 'magic' mirror transforming time, and the other manipulating space.

Delay Mirror

The Delay Mirror's 'magic' trickery was based upon manipulating the temporality of how a visitor saw his/her mirrored reflection. At times the Delay Mirror behaved like a normal mirror, showing a live feed of the visitor's reflection. However, after several seconds the visitor might observe a subtle surreality as the video image gradually time-shifted or reversed the camera feed.

Figure 2. Costumed girls dance in front of the Delay Mirror

Layering and overlaying time-delayed image feeds, and varying the playback speed and playback direction of the video in an unpredictable fashion produced complex visual effects. A visitor might catch sight of his/her own reflection in the mirror, seconds later only to notice a time-delayed video recording of his/her original entrance into the frame, accelerating through time to catch up seamlessly and merge back into the live feed, leaving him/her to observe a simple 'mirror image' once more. This gave the impression of a

ghost of one's past-self occasionally being visible alongside one's current self, from time to time entering and leaving one's current body. Visitors were unable to predict exactly what would happen next, or even verify what in fact they had just indeed seen – the time-shifted overlays replaying the visitor's previous behaviours were intentionally bewildering. Just when a visitor thought s/he had figured out what the mirror was doing, the mirror's behaviour would change. In keeping with our previously identified design sensibility valuing *requisite unpredictability*, we hoped that this type of ephemeral, unrepeatable interaction would engender enchantment and engagement through its very mystery, and in addition, that the mirror would *reward extended investment* with deepening knowledge. Visitors who persisted in exploring the mirror's functionality could learn to react to and exploit the layering algorithms to produce pleasing visual effects.

Kaleidoscope Mirror

As the second mirror was located in the 'illusion' space, the intention was to tie its functionality to the other artefacts in that part of the exhibition – optical illusions and classic magical trickeries. To do this, the mirror's 'magic' was enacted by manipulating the spatial orientation of the visitor's mirrored reflection. Visitors looking into the mirror could see their images dissected into shards reflected like the spirals of a traditional kaleidoscope, or bisected and reflected, making them appear a one eyed Cyclops, or in possession of two heads. Thus the Kaleidoscope Mirror referenced vintage Hall of Mirrors experiences, alongside other exhibits exploring classic magic tricks and illusions.

Placing, Encountering and Playing with the Magic Mirrors

When designing the mirrors, we were mindful of their placement within the exhibition's trajectory of discovery. The Delay Mirror was situated in the 'fantasy' room, which included a large array of fairytale costumes for dressing up so that the wearing of costumes would naturally prompt the children to seek out the mirror and discover it's functionality. Being located in the 'illusion' room, the Kaleidoscope Mirror's constantly moving and eye-catching imagery would attract the attention of children in the space. As both of the mirrors had narrow fields of view, and their 'reflections' were partially obscured when people stood in front of them, the experience of using the mirror was relatively private. As in [22], our design allowed the visitor some control over what aspects of the interaction s/he chose to reveal.

Magic Cauldron

The Magic Cauldron resided in its own witchcraft-themed small room adjoining the 'Enchantment' space dedicated to magical creatures. While most of Magic Worlds had a charming, friendly feel, the cauldron chamber had a darker, spookier atmosphere. The Magic Worlds national collection had originally contained a simple cauldron, associated with several two-dimensional painted wooden objects (such as spiders and toads) that children could throw into it in order to play at casting magic spells. When one of our design team observed the Magic Worlds exhibition in Liverpool, it was apparent that even this very basic prop appealed to children's imaginations – although it did nothing in response, small children were enthusiastic in their willingness to don witch's robes and play around it.

We were eager to explore how we could encourage even greater engagement by augmenting the cauldron's functionality with responsive audible and visual behaviours. As children threw each item or combination of items into the cauldron, we wanted to reward them with interesting audio-visual effects, in the hopes that by exploring the feedback their actions could trigger, they would be motivated to develop ever more complex play-acting 'spells' – ideally by drawing upon the age-appropriate examples of literary and cultural witches and witchcraft that were presented as part of the Magic Worlds content. In keeping with our previously identified design sensibilites, we wanted the cauldron to be a *resource that would scaffold* creative, theatrical, 'acting out' behaviour. We needed to design an interaction system that could support *multiple orientations to participation*, as a successful feedback mapping would need to respond satisfyingly to children old enough to role-play more elaborate, nuanced games with the cauldron artefact, as well as engage and entertain younger, less sophisticated children at a simpler level. In addition, we had to anticipate that the cauldron would be used in a very challenging environment – the system we created would have to be *robust* enough to accommodate rough handling, accepting of the inevitability that the toys and objects thrown into in the cauldron would vary over the exhibition's lifespan as items went missing or were broken and replaced.

Designing a Weight-Responsive Self-Calibration Algorithm

For these reasons we had to think very carefully when designing the algorithm which mapped the children's actions to audio-visual responses. We had initially considered working with a fixed set of 'ingredients' that could be combined to produce a finite number of predefined 'spells'. This idea was rejected for reasons both practical and pedagogical. Logistically, we acknowledged the likelihood that items would routinely go missing, and that it might be difficult to find exact matches for their identical replacement. Equally, from a pedagogical perspective, we were aware that this form of interaction could overly constrain children's natural creativity.

Instead, we devised a weight-responsive, self-calibrating, self-mapping algorithm that would respond to any number of items, thrown in in any order. The cauldron was outfitted with a weight-sensing mechanism by situating 6 Phidget load sensors under a platform that sat inside the cauldron to catch the items as they were thrown in. Significant changes in the mean weight picked up by the sensors were recorded and a histogram of their distribution was computed, normalized and used as a transfer function to map any given input to an output state in a manner inspired by techniques of histogram-based normalization in computer graphics.

Overall, the algorithm had the effect of ensuring that any given set of inputs would be remapped automatically to fill the available range of outputs approximately evenly. Although this meant that processing could take a little time and produce some 'false positives' and 'misses', as we shall argue further, this is consistent with our overall philosophy of *requisite unpredictability*.

Aesthetics of the Cauldron Interaction

We needed the cauldron's visual feedback to be striking in order to make its presence visibly impressive. We hid flat LED light panels under the translucent acrylic panel that registered the weights of the items thrown in, making it appear that a ghostly glow was emanating from the surface of the cauldron itself. The bubbling and burbling lighting evoked an eerie roiling cauldron whose flickering glow immediately drew visitors' attention upon entering the chamber. The lighting effects intensified as children threw objects into the cauldron while play-acting at spell-casting. We wanted to imbue the cauldron with a 'witchy' personality, making it seem as if it was 'hungry', wanting to 'eat' the objects thrown inside. To convey this, the audio soundscape we created for the cauldron consisted entirely of 'mouth' sounds – chewing, swallowing, gulping and groaning – increasing in volume and intensity as more items were 'fed' to the cauldron.

The items provided as 'ingredients' for the spells were carefully chosen for their sensory as well as conceptual qualities – including furry rats and scaly snakes and a giant friendly rubber toad. Children so inclined could revel in what the exhibition designer referred to as "the ick factor" of the grosser items, while younger or more tentative ones could enjoy the soft squidgy textures of the cuter creatures.

Facilitating Educational Play with the Magic Cauldron

A number of design choices made to help shape encounters with the cauldron were intentionally done to stimulate learning through creative play. Firstly, the cauldron room featured a large glass display case that contained a curated collection of taxidermy animals and fossils drawn from the GNM holdings and archives. This macabre collection evoked traditional witchcraft, and while the items contained were too delicate to actually touch, their presence in the space was intentionally situated to provide material to stimulate children's imaginations when play-acting at spell casting. Secondly, one wall of the chamber was decorated with a variation upon the Macbeth text, *"Hubble bubble, toil and trouble..."* the intention being that this reference might encourage children to incorporate literary concepts or references into their creative play. Additionally, several of the items that could be thrown into the witch's cauldron specifically related to thematic material featured in other exhibitions found throughout the museum in order to spark children's recollections and encourage self-driven reflection and creativity. Finally, as previously mentioned, Helen, the Gallery Interpreter was on hand to assist children in using and exploring the piece.

OBSERVATIONS

During the exhibition's three-month run, our research team was able to observe our artefacts being used in-situ, taking detailed notes of the encounters that took place, and discussing the experiences with the public. In addition, we had ample opportunity to share experiences and work alongside the museum staff, most notably with Helen. Her long-term, situated exposure to the daily goings-on of Magic Worlds proved an invaluable resource when trying to make sense of how our interactive content was experienced by the public. 'Living with' the exhibition for an extended duration and incorporating the artefacts into her creative practice availed her a unique vantage point from which to understand the experience [cf. 21].

Inspired by Ciolfi's walkthrough methods in which she encouraged docents to share their knowledge while physically traversing an exhibition space [7], we conducted three 45-minute walkthroughs with the staff: one with Helen, one with a front-of-house staff member, and one with the museum's exhibition designer. In addition, we were able to conduct a debriefing session that brought the entire team together to discuss our experiences. Upon examination of the data, several high-level themes emerged that helped us characterize the nature of the public's experience with the digital interactives. These were prominent throughout our data but for space reasons we can only illustrate each with a few clear examples.

Telling Stories and Acting Things Out

In our interviews with parents and families, the vast majority of the parents we approached indicated that the interactive content was the primary reason for their repeat visits to Magic Worlds. Our cauldron provided a key opportunity for children to dress up and 'act out', and it was hoped that by providing children with the spooky cauldron room – effectively a theatrical set – and themed costume pieces and props, creative, educational play would naturally take a theatrical turn.

Let us give a characteristic example of this type of play. A school group of nine year old girls put on the witches' costumes, and began experimenting with throwing items into the cauldron and remarking upon the increased audio-visual feedback in return. They spent some time investigating how the cauldron worked, remarking upon the various effects they could trigger by throwing large items in versus small ones, or multiple items at once. Eventually the girls ceased their play, and began conferring with one another, with much emphasis being placed on discussing the text painted on the wall, *"Hubble bubble, toil and trouble..."* The girls called their teacher over to confer with her as to what they should do next. We asked the teacher

what had been discussed, and she told us that the girls had been asking her for additional lines of text from Macbeth that they could use to create a small performance for the parents who had accompanied them on their trip. After some rehearsal time during which they assigned each other lines and decided upon an order of items to be thrown into the cauldron for maximum effect, the parents were summoned and assembled. The girls presented a brief excerpt from Macbeth, using the audio-visual functionality of the cauldron to punctuate their dialogue as they took turns throwing objects into the cauldron (see Fig. 3.)

Figure 3. Schoolchildren use the Magic Cauldron to act out a scene from Shakespeare's Macbeth

This type of behaviour exemplifies the creative learning our digital interactives were intended to provoke. Interviewing the exhibition designer, she told us she loved "the fact that it was their idea, before they called [their teacher] over to say *'Look what we've been doing!'* ...I was really pleased with that." The children observed in this incident used the cauldron as a *resource for acting out* – and a true stimulus for child-led educational creativity. The digital content, experienced cohesively situated within the exhibition context, had sparked a learning opportunity – the girls took initiative in researching and engaging with the story of Macbeth.

Scaffolding the Skilled Storyteller

We were pleased to see how our cauldron interactive facilitated the activities of the Gallery Interpreter, and helped scaffold the storytelling and play-acting activities she used to encourage children to engage with the exhibition. We spent a substantial amount of time with Helen, watching her interact with the children. It was intriguing to observe how she made use of the cauldron artefact in her practice, because rather than directly instructing the children with regards to how the cauldron worked, her manner of encouraging and helping children often took the form of inviting them to join her in improvisational play. She would invite them to help her cast a magic spell, and as part of the process of doing so would exaggeratedly pause to observe and remark upon what kinds of magic effects were triggered after each item was thrown in – intentionally drawing their attentions to the audio-visual feedback programmed into the cauldron artefact. All the while she maintained the children's focus on the experience of play-acting at casting a spell. In this way, rather than directly instructing them on how to use the cauldron, she could model for the children how to best explore its responsivity in a creative, playful way. Her willingness to play-act alongside the children (see Fig. 1) modeled the type of creative play the exhibition designers hoped to encourage. In addition, Helen's storytelling and play-acting skills helped her to encourage younger or more timid children to experiment with the cauldron. Helen would try to coax shyer children into joining her, and if they still found the skulls and brains too frightening, she could engage them in discussion about the rubber toad – sometimes convincing them to play-act as toads themselves, hopping and jumping with her around the space.

Helen found the very mouth-like, human vocal sounds we had designed for the cauldron helped support an anthropomorphic approach to explaining any technical vagaries that might crop up when engaging with it in view of the public. For example, if too many objects were thrown in at once, or the weighing platform became misaligned or dislodged, causing the weight-sensing algorithm to behave erratically, she could explain that the cauldron "wasn't behaving itself properly today." She could then remove the objects and firmly settle the weighing platform, patting it into place "so it could calm down" – an easily accessible 'return-to-start' that we had designed for and our algorithms support. The conceit that it was an entity capable of obstinacy or misbehavior helped Helen reduce the need to break character, allowing her to maintain the play-acting scene being developed. Her ability to use the nuances of the cauldron's *functionality as a scaffold* upon which to build a creative context allowed her to seamlessly accommodate 'glitches' in her method of practice or even be usefully inspired by them

Experience Sharing amongst Families

The Magic Cauldron often provided opportunities to observe family groups playing together, as its interface clearly facilitated multiple users. The two magic mirrors also provided us with opportunities to watch how families and groups shared their playful experiences. The Delay Mirror was designed to both delight and teasingly frustrate visitors due to its ever-changing method of layering real-time and time-delayed video streams. Its behaviour would unpredictably switch from displaying a 'normal' mirror image, to suddenly displaying surreal time-lapsed footage. We had ample opportunity to observe how this functionality stimulated interesting social interactions amongst family groups. Typically, one member of a family would notice the Delay Mirror's weird, time-lapsed imagery, and would then try to draw another family member's attention so that they

could share the experience. As the mirror's behaviour shifted between augmented imagery and 'normal' mirror functionality, it was quite often that by the time the summoned family member arrived to see the supposedly 'magic' mirror, s/he was greeted by nothing more interesting than his/her own reflection, to the consternation of the family member who had been insisting that something interesting had been going on. This often resulted in animated discussions amongst the family groups. In addition, children playing and dancing in front of the mirror often attracted the attention of their parents, spurring the children to engage in even more performative behaviour knowing they had an attentive audience.

The Kaleidoscope Mirror also produced opportunities for parents and children to interact with one another – particularly parents with smaller children that could be lifted and held. The repetitive, pattern based imagery of the Kaleidoscope was able to hold small children's attentions, and both ourselves and Helen regularly witnessed parents lifting their little toddlers to eye level with the Kaleidoscope, pointing out and identifying the child's own image as it was fragmented and replicated in geometric patterns in the moving display.

Connecting to the Wider Museum

The Magic Cauldron provided an interesting stimulus for visitors to make connections between the Magic Worlds exhibition and the rest of the museum. Some of the toy items used as spell ingredients opened up an opportunity space to establish connections with other exhibitions concurrently running in the GNM. We often noticed children showing a particular fascination with a large rubber skull and a pink rubber brain of corresponding size. Children could regularly be seen trying to compress the rubber skull to push the brain into the appropriate place inside the cranium. When we asked Helen about this behaviour, she laughed, and asked the nearby child to tell me why she was trying to press the brain into the skull. The child explained that she knew "from the Egypt [exhibition]" (held downstairs as part of the museum's permanent collection) that brains were pulled out of the noses of bodies as part of the mummification process. Helen told us that that she often used this discussion as an opportunity to educate children about how bodies were prepared as part of traditional Egyptian mummification practices. Helen also told us that a large rubber toad used as a prop for the cauldron often found its way to various other places in Magic Worlds, sometimes being treated as a potential prince to be kissed in the 'Fantasy' room's fairytale settings, or taken as a guest to the Mad Hatter's Tea Party. On multiple occasions, children snuck the toad out of Magic Worlds altogether, whereupon staff would eventually find him – often having been returned to his natural habitat in the area of the museum's permanent collection exhibiting reptiles and amphibians.

DISCUSSION

In this paper we have described our work on Magic Worlds, a touring exhibition of the UK's Victoria and Albert Museum, to which we added playful, interactive digital artefacts. Our work was informed by research on interaction in museum and related cultural settings in HCI and CSCW and involved extensive consultation between museum stakeholders and digital designers. As our exploratory design work developed, we formulated a number of design sensibilities to configure the design space we were working in and created three digital artefacts which were carefully placed within the exhibition environment. We have discussed how those artefacts were engaged with and, in particular, how they could be used playfully and casually, yet also in a manner which supported concerted activities of potential pedagogical value, including curiosity into their own technical operation. Through this, wider connections to the exhibition and the museum context could be made. Let us now draw out some more general contributions.

Resources For Open Interactions

The richness and nuanced complexity of behaviours around interactives in cultural settings have been noted by many authors [e.g. 2,10,11,14,15,19,21,22]. The interactions we have observed around our pieces are radically *open* in at least two senses. First, they are *open to variable participation*: it is not defined in advance exactly who the users might be in any particular encounter with an exhibit. Second, they are *open-ended*: it is not defined in advance when exactly their encounter should start and when it should stop – people can carry on indefinitely if what they are acting out continues to amuse. This makes it highly problematic to define interaction around a sense of the 'session' or of given 'user-identities'. It is more appropriate to design technologies which are open to the (rest of their) world, yet offer enough to be appropriable for a variety of purposes, many of which might be unknown in advance to designers – technologies which serve as *resources* for action and interaction. While these arguments might be familiar from students of Suchman [20] onwards, we feel that we have outlined some design sensibilities and given some specific examples of this approach in concrete design action. We have taken the idea of creating resources for open interactions 'down' to the level of computational algorithms for calibrating and mapping sensor data.

While the idea of supporting interactivity in this way is often called upon, digital interactives in museum environments – including some of the most impressive design work in HCI – often still require considerable buy-in to make them work. For example, much of the research reviewed by Benford and Giannachi [2] still involves conspicuous technologies even if they are embedded or ubiquitous (e.g. an RFID tagged object which has to be held just so for a tag reader to detect it, a handheld device needing network coverage) – often with a cover story to help participants suspend disbelief. In our case, we feel we have gone some way to reverse this picture. Our pieces do not require anything other than ordinary action (stand and watch, put a toy in a pot) to come alive, thereby enabling participants to develop their own stories, with any accounts of the behavior of the artefacts being easy to incorporate within ongoing play rather than something that requires a suspension of disbelief or detailed instructions at the outset.

Interaction Far Beyond The 'Interface'

It is important to realize, though, that this is achieved only through the concerted influence of the overall context of the exhibition. The design of the various rooms in Magic Worlds, the positioning of our interactives in them and in relation to other exhibits, the overall design quality of the whole exhibition, their presence in a museum which has an amphibian section (even), all – in various ways – contribute to what success we have in designing for open interactions.

Important also is the role of the Gallery Interpreter in further scaffolding playful engagement. In a more general sense, participants to our setting can be regarded as *performing technologies,* incorporating them into some performed activity but also giving sense to them through that. For some time, critical thinkers in HCI have been arguing that "the interface reaches out" and that it is perhaps better to speak of the activity of *interfacing* than the idea that an interface is a fixed object [5]. Our work convinces us that these points need to be pushed to quite a radical extreme. Human computer interaction exists in a heterogenous context, with a mix of materialities in play. In making up a story around the cauldron, children equally avail themselves of the writing on the wall, their teacher's knowledge of Shakespeare, the skillful performance of Helen, the costumes and props, and put it all together to make their own coherence. Clearly, one cannot anticipate all possible such ad hoc 'assemblages'. However, we feel our sensibilities for the design of open interactions go someway to giving a hint of where to start in making things which are open to these possibilities and so give participants a desirable *creative latitude.*

An Entangled Design Process

The approach we took also enabled us to organize a design process that did justice to the complex entanglements that can be involved in engaging with cultural settings. As we have noted, Magic Worlds lay at *the intersection of multiple constraints and enablements*. The Museum worked within what had been curated by another institution, yet enhanced it with local design work and contributions from local collections. The digital designers in our team were not making things 'to brief' but were concerned to explore configurations of human-computer interfaces through their work. It was important to develop a *reciprocal accommodation* of the interactives which were made to the setting in the exhibition and of aspects of that setting to the interactives. This required design work that entangled different expertises (the digital, exhibition building, performance). We feel that our patterned mix of design autonomy and wider organizational consultation suggests a *'third way' in HCI between design research and participatory and co-design tendencies.* Building multiple pieces that could resource open interactions with a requisite unpredictability and robustness facilitated this. At the other extreme, proposals for a unitary work requiring considerable organizational and end-user buy-in or asserting an independent aesthetic would have been badly suited to such an entangled context.

Making Magic: Ludic Design For Real
Design research in HCI commonly advocates a principle of 'ludic design'. In a number of papers, Gaver and colleagues [13] have counterposed playful, ludic design with functional design where particular purposes are designed for. However, the context of Magic Worlds puts this opposition in some crisis as here *the purpose is play*. However, the issue is perhaps not between what is playful and what is not, but rather where a commitment to purposes is made by designers. Designing to support a particular function, as much early HCI sought to, requires some definition or knowledge of purposes in advance of design that will then meet those 'requirements'. In contrast, we have sought to support open interactions (open to varied participation, open-ended in terms of activity and outcome) through design processes of a particular character and with artefacts which behave and intrigue in a particular kind of way, co-existing in settings with many other kinds of materiality. That, for us, is making magic.

ACKNOWLEDGEMENTS
This research is part funded by the UK's Arts & Humanities Research Council as part of the Creative Exchange knowledge exchange hub between Newcastle and Lancaster Universities, and the Royal College of Art. It is also part funded by the Natural Sciences and Engineering Research Council of Canada postdoctoral fellowship programme.

REFERENCES
1. Barad, K. Meeting the Universe Halfway: Quantum Physics and the Entanglement of Matter and Meaning. Duke University Press, 2007.

2. Benford S., Giannachi G. Performing mixed reality. The MIT Press, Cambridge. 2011

3. Bowers, J. "The logic of annotated portfolios: communicating the value of' research through design'." *Proc of DIS,* ACM, 2012.

4. Bowers, J., Bannon, L., Fraser, M., Hindmarsh, J., Benford, S., Heath, C., Taxen, G., Ciolfi, L. From the Disappearing Computer to Living Exhibitions: Shaping Interactivity in Museum Settings. In *The Disappearing Computer.* Springer LNCS, 2007.

5. Bowers, J. and Rodden, T. Exploding the interface: Experiences of a CSCW network. InterCHI'93, 255–262, 1993.

6. Bruner, J. S. The culture of education. Harvard University Press, 1996.

7. Ciolfi, L. Taking a walk: investigating personal paths in the museum space. *Conf. on Creative Inventions, Innovations and Everyday Designs in HCI,* 2007.

8. Ciolfi, L. and Bannon, L. Space, place and the design of technologically enhanced physical environments. *Space, Spatiality and Technology,* Springer. 217-232, 2005.

9. Dalsgaard, P. Designing for inquisitive use. In *Proceedings of* DIS '08, 2008.

10. Fraser, M.,Bowers, J., Brundell, P. *et al.* Re-tracing the past: mixing realities in museum settings. *Proc. of Advances in Comp. Entertainment,* 3-5, 2004.

11. Fraser, M., Stanton, D., Kher Hui, N. *et al.* Assembling History. *ECSCW* 179-198, 2003.

12. Gaver, W. What should we expect from research through design? In *Proc CHI '12* pp. 937-946, 2012.

13. Gaver, W.W., Bowers, J., Boucher, A. *et al.* "The drift table: designing for ludic engagement." In *Proc. CHI'04* pp. 885-900, 2004.

14. Heath, C., Luff, P., Vom Lehn, D., Hindmarsh, J., Cleverly, J. Crafting participation: designing ecologies, configuring experience. *Visual Comm., 1*(1), 9-33, 2002.

15. Hindmarsh, J., Heath, C., vom Lehn, D., and Cleverly, J. Creating Assemblies in Public Environments: Social Interaction, Interactive Exhibits and CSCW. *Comput. Supported Coop. Work* 14, p.1-41, 2005.

16. Humphrey T., Gutwill, J. Fostering Active Prolonged Engagement: The Art of Creating APE Exhibits. The Exploratorium, 2005

17. Ingold, T. Making: Anthropology, archaeology, art and architecture. Routledge, 2013.

18. Kahn, P., and O'Rourke, K. Understanding enquiry-based learning. In *Handbook of enquiry and problem-based learning.* Galway, Ireland: CELT, 1-12, 2005.

19. Nissen, B., Bowers, J., Wright, P., Hook, J., and Newell, C. Volvelles, Domes and Wristbands: Embedding Digital Fabrication within a Visitor's Trajectory of Engagement. Proc. DIS 2014, 825-834

20. Suchman, L. Human-machine reconfigurations: Plans and situated actions. Cambridge University Press, 2007.

21. Taylor, R., Schofield, G., Shearer, J., Boulanger, P., Wallace, J., Wright, P., Olivier, P. Designing from Within: humanaquarium. In Proc. CHI '11, 1855-1864.

22. Taylor, R., Schofield, G., Shearer, J., Wright, P., Boulanger, P., Olivier, P. Nightgallery: Theatrical Framing and Orchestration in Participatory Performance. Personal and Ubiquitous Computing, February 2014.

23. Wood, D. *How Children Think and Learn.* 2nd edition. Oxford: Blackwell Publishers Ltd., 1998.

Architecture by Tools: The Syntax of Drawing and the Creativity of Thought

Mina Tahsiri
University of Nottingham
Department of Architecture &
Built Environment, University
of Nottingham, Nottingham,
UK. NG7 2RD
mina.tahsiri@nottingham.ac.uk

ABSTRACT

This short paper summarizes a PhD research in progress as titled in the heading. The research investigates the effect that design tools have on the method of drawing and creativity in early stages of architectural design with an intention of contribution to the procurement of CAD tools. Currently into the second year of the PhD, pilot protocol studies have been executed and new propositions for coding schemes and method of analysis are being tested.

Keywords

Drawing; creativity; CAD tools; protocol study

INTRODUCTION

Based on the premise that there is a connection between the bodily act of drawing, conceptualization and creativity, there have been two kinds of approaches in designing Computer Aided Design (CAD) tools that bring drawing by CAD closer to drawing by hand. One approach is concerned with the physical experience of free hand drawing and takes into account, the speed and liberated movements that can be applied. This approach has led to the development of pen-based input tools such as the digital napkin [,4]. Another approach which focuses on simulating a similar cognitive experience to free hand drawing, emphasizes on sustaining ambiguity and imprecision through the process. This approach has mainly led to developments in shape grammar and improving tools to recognize patterns of emerging shape [2]. This research searches for an alternative approach to inform the design of CAD tools by understanding how freehand drawing compared to CAD tools structures the distribution of information in a creative process. In particular it focuses on computer based drawing tools which are increasingly being used in early stages of architectural concept development and their affordance for

C&C '15, June 22-25, 2015, Glasgow, United Kingdom
ACM 978-1-4503-3598-0/15/06.
http://dx.doi.org/10.1145/2757226.2764762

creative reasoning is debatable. For this comparison, cognitive structures under the influence of a NURBS based tool, Rhinoceros 3D, and a geometric modeling tool SketchUp will be compared to freehand sketching. The research questions the relationship between the syntax of drawing and creativity. It understands design actions (verbal and physical) as patterns that are connected together in a hierarchical order, for which the sequence of their occurrence in a process, can affect the possibilities of access to higher order patterns within that cognitive system. This in return should change the amount of information each pattern carries and the designers' ability in both generating ideas and cohesively making links between them; hence a measure for creativity.

Currently the coding schemes used in current research suggests the effect of design medium on creativity to be rather insignificant [1,6]. In particular since design is considered as a reflective in action process and related studies have valued the situatedness of cognition, a gap in the method of analyzing and coding data from protocol studies was identified in this research. There forth attention is drawn towards distributed cognitive theory, which describes cognition as an aggregation of functions constructed by internal and external constructs of a cognitive system [5]. In this sense tools as part of the external construct are not mere peripheral aids to cognition but part of the structuring of cognition. Zhang and Norman [7], in their seminal study on 'representations in distributed cognitive tasks' had identified a similar gap in cognitive studies. They assert on the necessity of decomposing the representation of a task into its internal and external components so that the different functions of internal and external representations can be identified. Accordingly the internal and external representational spaces together form a distributed representational space, which is the representation of the abstract task space. In the case of this research the assumption is that current coding schemes analyze design activity at the abstract level of cognition and therefore cannot elicit the direct effect of external/internal variables on creativity. The research therefore intends to employ Zhang and Norman's approach to develop a scheme which expresses the process in terms of a series of internal and external patterns which could be useful in the procurement of future CAD tools.

METHODOLOGY

Central to the research is a protocol design study which records design actions (verbal and physical) in controlled lab conditions for a specific study group to compare their behavior through segmenting and coding the data. The theoretical framework which tailored an understanding of the theory of distributed cognition and representational analysis to design studies was developed in the first year of the PhD and led to the following structure for the protocol study:

- Protocols to be recorded by concurrent verbalization. The process of verbalization to be instructed such that the generation of patterns within either internal/external constructs can be easily distinguishable and subjectivity in coding minimized;

- Participants to be from same educational background and of equal design and tool operating skills;

- Tasks to be of isomorphic structure.

Two pilot studies with different groups of students have been carried out so far to test the appropriateness of the task and experimental structure and to reduce the effect of confounding variables such as learning effect. At this stage, the pilot studies mainly focused on analyzing the processes at the abstract level and so forth used the FBS (Function-Behavior-Structure) [3] coding scheme. Based on the results, the research is assessing the potential of its proposed scheme (at early stages of development) and has developed a modified step-by-step protocol study plan for the main study. The results of the pilot study will be further discussed; meanwhile the modified plan is as follows;

- Participants: nine architecture students from the University of Nottingham to be studied in three groups of three by undergoing three isomorphic tasks with two weeks intervals in between.
- The order of tasks within each group is as follows
  Group A: freehand-SketchUp-Rhino
  Group B: Rhino-Freehand-SketchUp
  Group C: SketchUp-Rhino-Freehand
- For each task:
  1. A short movie of the sites is shown which reads the brief. Participants are then given two minutes to recite any information remembered from the brief. This acts as an indication of patterns housed in the internal construct.
  2. The brief and some images of the site are given to the student to re-read and to discuss the importance and relevance of those information and any initial ideas, to elicit the primary patterns within the external construct.
  3. The participants engage in the act of design with the sole use of the provided tool for 40 minutes and no reference to the brief.

RESULTS

In the pilot studies, the design tasks were successive and executed in one design session. The tasks were sub-tasks of one design brief. Results from one study with two students showed highest measure of creativity in the third task, although different tools were used. As a result, less new patterns are generated and the cohesiveness of the external construct increased. However using the FBS scheme, this change in distribution was not explicit. Moreover no significant difference between the distribution of design issues that deal with the formal structure of the design was seen throughout the processes when analyzed by the latter scheme. Students also designed their first task with different tools which comparatively affected performance in the second task for which the tool used was the same. The student who freehand sketched in their first task displayed a weaker idea generation but stronger cohesiveness in their second task. The pattern structures helped in explaining the reason for this outcome. Despite similar number of patterns for both student in the second task, the student who hadn't freehand sketched in the first task, produce twice as more new patterns in this task. This student was also able to show a higher frequency of internal activity and although his frequency of external activity was similar to the other student, he produced three times the number of patterns that the other student had externally.

NEXT STEP

1- In pilot studies: To calculate the amount of information each pattern carries in the cognitive system and deduct a relationship between design actions specific to a tool and the probability of occurrence of patterns. To demonstrate how a particular sequence of patterns affects the complexity of internal/external constructs. Investigate the possibility of creating algorithms simulating students' cognitive activity.
2- Make a conclusion on the most suited method of segmenting and coding main study.

REFERENCES

1. Bilda, Z., Gero, J.S., Purcell, T. To sketch or not to sketch? That is the question. *Design Studies*. 27(2006), 587–613.
2. Gero, J.S., Jun, H.J. Getting computers to read the architectural semantics of drawings. In *proc. ACADIA'95* (1995), 97-112.
3. Gero, J.S., Mc Neill, T. An approach to the analysis of design protocols. *Design Studies*. 19 (1998), 21–61.
4. Gross, M.D., Yi-Luen Do, E. Demonstrating the Electronic Cocktail Napkin: a paper-like interface for early design. In *proc. CHI '96* (1996), 5–6.
5. Hutchins, E. Cognition in the wild. MIT Press, Cambridge, (1995).
6. Yu, R., Gero, J.S., Gu, N. Impact of using rule algorithms on designers' behavior in a parametric design environment: Preliminary results from a pilot study. *Global Design and Local Materialization*. 369 (2013), 13–22.
7. Zhang, J., Norman, D.A. Representations in distributed cognitive tasks. *Cognitive Science*. 18 (1994), 87–122.

Researching Design Fiction With Design Fiction

Joseph Lindley
HighWire Centre for Doctoral Training
Lancaster University
joseph.lindley@gmail.com

ABSTRACT

The term design fiction was first used in 2005 by Bruce Sterling [18:30] and in 2009 Julian Bleecker built on the idea by combining it with various other characterisations [cf. 1,2,10] and catalysed a step change in design fiction discourse. Since then design fiction has gained significant traction across academic contexts; at symposia and conference events; and through its practice within commercial design studios and industry. Despite becoming a popular way of framing speculative design, the characterisation of design fiction as research approach still remains "up for grabs" [19:22] as it is "enticing and provocative, yet [...] remains elusive" [7:1]. In 2013 Bleecker remarked in terms of his studios own practice "I don't think we've figured it out" and that "studying it, understanding it and trying to devise some of the principles - of what we're calling design fiction - is what we're trying to do" [1]. Adopting a research through design approach [5,6], this doctoral research intends to shed light on the questions raised by Bleecker by researching design fiction, *with* design fiction.

Author Keywords

Design fiction, design theory, diegetic prototyping

ACM Classification Keywords

H.5.m. [Information interfaces and presentation]: Miscellaneous – Design;

CONTEXT

Technology and network effects pervade society [11] as Toffler's notion of "future shock" [20] becomes more tangible in that we struggle to keep pace with technological change, or as Feenberg puts it "we are more than ever aware of both the promise and the threat of technological advance, [yet] we still lack the intellectual means and political tools for managing progress" [4]. With these points in mind it is understandable why approaches that encourage designers to "act as catalysts

for public debate and discussion about the kinds of futures people really want" [3:6] become increasingly attractive and relevant. Futurism and design futures are by no means new concepts and have existed in varying forms, ranging from fascist Italian futurism, through early science fiction, to radical design [cf. 3]. However, design fiction exhibits a strong interdisciplinary grounding that covers the social sciences [2], media studies [10], fine art [3] and the corporate world [8,9]. These theoretical underpinnings are combined with accessible and evocative ways of communicating them (oftentimes with film, though frequently straying into other media as well). This combination of a strong and diverse theoretical grounding, along with compelling communication tools, makes design fiction a powerful and flexible tool that can open up discursive spaces. Design can meaningfully utilise these spaces in order to move society towards more preferable futures.

RESEARCH THROUGH DESIGN

This project adopts a research through design approach to making a contribution to knowledge about design fiction. Being a relatively new term with only a handful of texts referring to design fiction theory, the corpus of literature on the subject is not sufficient to build meaningful rhetoric based on discourse alone. Instead this research builds on the work for Frayling [5] and considers the multidimensional, and reciprocal, relationship that research, art, science, and design have with each other. Relevant and available discourse is considered in terms of research *into* design fiction while contextual searches for individual instances of design fiction practice are incorporated in terms of research *for* design fiction.

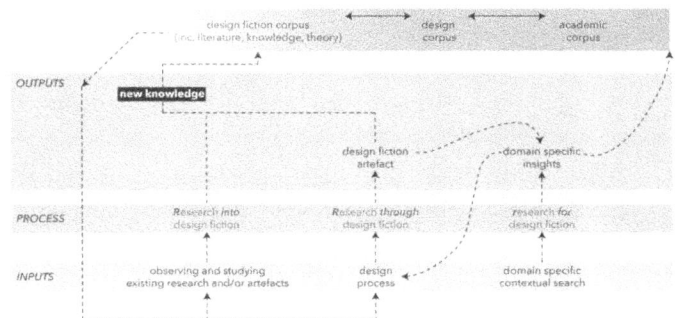

Figure 1. Research through, into and for design fiction.

Research *through* design fiction is adopted as the primary means of knowledge production [6,16] and indeed is considered as an epistemic stance in its own right [17]. Reconciling different formulations of research through design with a range of practice is a challenge here. Reflective practice is central to insight generation, however precisely what constitutes suitably rigorous reflective practice is hard to delineate. Similarly, articulating how produced artefacts relate to reflection, and how both relate to 'new knowledge' is difficult to reconcile with scientised perspective of design.

PROGRESS SO FAR AND CHALLENGES TO COME

With 18 months remaining to consolidate this research into a doctoral thesis, progress is positive although significant challenges remain. Research through design outputs have included: *Heating Britain's Homes* [12]; *A Machine. Learning.* [13]; and *Care For A Robot* (a forthcoming documentary film for Ethicomp 2015). Alongside these practical explorations, complimentary theoretical work has been produced: rhetorical arguments for using design ethnography to make sense of design fictions under the banner "anticipatory ethnography" [14]; reviews of literature in order to disambiguate design fiction rhetoric and provide a "pragmatics framework" [16]; an *application* of anticipatory ethnography [15]. However two issues broadly cut across these outputs: first, is the challenge of reconciling differing perceptions on research through design as epistemology, a task made more complex by the diversity of design fiction's potential forms [16]. The second challenge relates to the nature of doctoral theses. Should *this* thesis reflect the topic and *be* fictional itself? How would being fictional impact upon rigour? How can the reflexivity, central to the research through design, be incorporated meaningfully? As an 'inter-discipline' how should design fiction research negotiate disciplinary silos?

ACKNOWLEDGEMENTS

Many thanks for Paul Coulton's supervision and for the valuable review comments. This work is funded under the RCUK Digital Economy Programme (Grant Reference EP/G037582/1).

REFERENCES

1. Bleecker, J.Design Fiction: A short essay on design, science, fact and fiction. *Near Future Laboratory*, (2009).

2. Dourish, P. and Bell, G."Resistance is futile": reading science fiction alongside ubiquitous computing. *Personal and Ubiquitous Computing 18*, 4 (2014), 769–778.

3. Dunne, A. and Raby, F.*Speculative Everything.* The MIT Press, London, 2013.

4. Feenberg, A.*Transforming technology: A critical theory revisited.* Oxford University Press, 2002.

5. Frayling, C.Research in Art and Design. *Royal College of Art Research Papers 1*, 1 (1993), 1–9.

6. Gaver, W.What should we expect from research through design? *Proceedings of the 2012 ACM annual conference on Human Factors in Computing Systems - CHI '12*, (2012), 937.

7. Hales, D.Design fictions an introduction and provisional taxonomy. *Digital Creativity 24*, 1 (2013), 1–10.

8. Johnson, B.Science Fiction Prototypes Or: How I Learned to Stop Worrying about the Future and Love Science Fiction. *Intelligent Environments*, (2009).

9. Johnson, B.D.*Science Fiction Prototyping.* Morgan & Claypool, 2011.

10. Kirby, D.The Future is Now: Diegetic Prototypes and the Role of Popular Films in Generating Real-world Technological Development. *Social Studies of Science 40*, 1 (2010), 41–70.

11. Lanier, J.*Who owns the future.* Simon and Schuster, 2013.

12. Lindley, J. and Coulton, P.Modelling Design Fiction: What's The Story? *StoryStorm Workshop at ACM Designing Interactive Systems 2014*, (2014).

13. Lindley, J. and Potts, R.A Machine. Learning: An example of HCI Prototyping With Design Fiction. *Proceedings of the 8th Nordic Conference on Human Computer Interaction*, (2014).

14. Lindley, J., Sharma, D., and Potts, R.Anticipatory Ethnography: Design fiction as an input to design ethnography. *Ethnographic Praxis in Industry Conference*, (2014).

15. Lindley, J. and Sharma, D.An ethnography of the future. *Strangers in Strange Lands*, (2014).

16. Lindley, J.A pragmatics framework for design fiction. *European Academy of Design Conference (In press)*.

17. Ramirez, R.An epistemology for research through design. *Proceedings of the ICSID Design Education Conference*, (2009), 1–14.

18. Sterling, B.*Shaping Things.* The MIT Press, 2005.

19. Tanenbaum, J.Design fictional interactions. *Interactions 21*, 5 (2014), 22–23.

20. Toffler, A.*Future Shock.* Random House, 1990.

Intelligent Systems to Support Large-Scale Collective Creative Idea Generation

Pao Siangliulue
Harvard School of Engineering and Applied Sciences
Cambridge, MA USA
paopow@seas.harvard.edu

ABSTRACT

In recent years, it has become possible for large groups of people to collaborate and generate ideas together in ways that were not possible before. However, the large number of ideas and participants in this setting also pose new challenges in helping people find inspiration from a large pool of ideas, and coordinating the collective effort. My research aims to address the challenges of large scale idea generation platforms by developing methods and systems for helping people make effective use of each other's ideas, and orchestrate collective effort to reduce redundancy and increase the breadth of generated ideas.

INTRODUCTION

Emerging large online innovation platforms like OpenIDEO.com, My Starbucks Idea and Quirky promise an unprecedented torrent of ideas, harvested from minds of thousands. The strengths of these platforms lie not only on the sheer number of contributors but also on the diversity of thinking, expertise, and knowledge of all contributors as a whole. Idea exchanges in such settings—often in the form of inspiration—bring about novel ideas that none of the contributors would have thought of alone.

But the large-scale idea generation paradigm also introduces new challenges. First, the large number of ideas reduces the chance of a contributor finding non-redundant inspiring ideas. Contributors usually have to wade through a large number of ideas with no effective way to find inspiring sets of ideas. Second, there is no existing mechanism to coordinate effort among a large number of contributors in idea generation. Instead of working together, contributors generate ideas alone without knowing how to best contribute. This lack of coordination produces redundant common ideas and limits the breadth of exploration of new ideas [11].

To help a large community of ideators make full use of its size and diversity, we need new methods and tools that enable them to make effective use of each other's ideas, and orchestrate collective effort to explore diverse possibilities.

HELPING PEOPLE FIND INSPIRING IDEAS

Idea exchanges on large innovation platforms often occur when contributors get inspired by each other's ideas. The ideas people see and when they see them affect the ideas they generate [4, 8]. An effective approach therefore should help a contributor find inspiring ideas from a large pool at an appropriate time.

Selecting a diverse set of ideas

Prior research suggests that a set of inspiring ideas consists of diverse ideas [6]. However, there is no robust scalable method to identify a diverse set of ideas. Asking human experts to look at all ideas and keep track of how each idea relates to others does not scale. When the number of ideas rises to several hundreds, the task becomes difficult

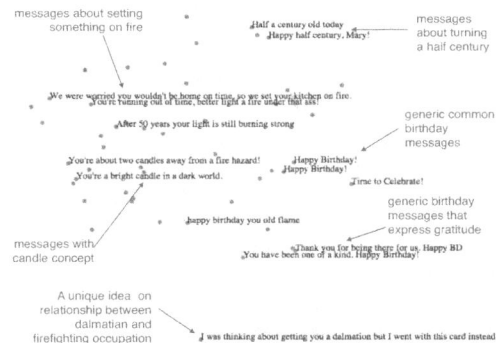

Figure 1. An idea map of birthday messages to a 50-year-old female firefighter. Similar ideas are placed close to each other and dissimilar ideas are kept far apart. See emergent clusters of ideas around different themes and sentiments

In our recent work [7], we developed a crowd-powered method for constructing an abstract spatial "idea map" (Figure 1) from simple human's judgement on similarity between ideas ("Is idea A more similar to B or C?"). We built our method on prior work on multidimensional scaling and active similarity learning techniques [10, 9] to embed ideas in an idea space with as few human queries as possible. From the idea map, we can algorithmically extract diverse sets of examples at scale. In contrast to some existing methods [1], our approach is applicable to any creative artifact and not is limited to textual ones. We also demonstrated that people generate diverse ideas when they see a set of diverse ideas selected by our algorithm.

Extracting information from user natural interactions
So far, we have outsourced human computation tasks necessary for idea map generation to micro-task marketplaces like Amazon Mechanical Turk. Instead of relying solely on outside labors, we look for solutions that enable users to contribute without disrupting their idea generation. User contribution could be more reliable. Plus, they do not incur extra financial cost. Prior work in online education has shown methods that extract information from learners by embedding the tasks into activities that learners find intrinsically motivating [3, 12]. Likewise, we can provide ways for users to bookmark ideas for their own references as a part of information discovery process [2]. By aggregating what each person's bookmarks are and how they organize them, we can derive an input to the algorithms used for selecting inspiring ideas.

Suggesting ideas that inspire individual contributors
We should provide ideas that fit individual's idea generation process. Different people find inspiration in different ideas. In a pilot study, we found that people are more receptive to inspirations that are different but still share some properties with their own ideas. This finding agrees with prior finding that people generate better ideas when they integrate ideas that are conceptually closer rather than farther from each other [1]. If we can identify ideas that are similar to the contributors' ideas so far yet different in an interesting way, we might inspire them to come up with more interesting ideas. One possible approach is to place generated ideas on an idea map and suggest ideas of certain distant from these ideas. Other approaches such as selecting inspirations based on user-generated labels would be worth exploring as well.

Choosing appropriate time to show inspirations
Once we find a set of inspiring ideas, we have to select the right moment to present them. Recent work has demonstrated that not just the choice of examples, but also the timing of their delivery can impact creative outcomes [5]. We have explored two timing mechanisms: (1) participants can request ideas on demand, and (2) a system automatically infers when participants are stuck and provides ideas at that moment. Our results show that people who requested examples themselves generated the most novel ideas and people who received ideas automatically when idle produced the most ideas [8]. These results can inform the design of ideation support systems that aim to help people generate many high quality ideas.

COORDINATING EXPLORATION OF IDEA SPACE

As the number of contributors increases, the more crucial and difficult it becomes to coordinate the community efforts. Without coordination or some guidance from the system, people may not know how to best contribute. They could end up generating redundant ideas that are very similar to one another instead of exploring a broader range of ideas in the idea space. However, too much communication overhead can be overwhelming.

We are still drafting the plan to explore different mechanisms that reduce idea redundancy and widen the breadth of ideas generated while minimizing communication overhead. I would love to hear suggestions on which of various directions I should take for my thesis. One possible mechanism is to identify which parts of the idea space have not been explored and direct more people to generate ideas in those unexplored regions of the space. This mechanism can be integrated into a system as a form of an explicit todo list [13] or as a subtle nudge through inspiration suggestion. Another approach is to provide people with an overview of the state community's idea generation along with an effective way for contributors to inform others of their plan so that they don't interfere with each other.

CONCLUSION

Large ideation platforms promise a huge opportunity for innovation, but are limited by lack of appropriate methods and tools that helps people discover inspiring ideas and coordinate their effort. By synthesizing knowledge human computation and machine learning, we can create an intelligent system that addresses the existing challenges and improves collective idea generation at scale.

REFERENCES

1. Chan, J., Dow, S., and Schunn, C. Conceptual distance matters when building on others' ideas in crowd-collaborative innovation platforms. In *Proc. CSCW'14*, ACM (2014), 141–144.

2. Kerne, A., Koh, E., Dworaczyk, B., Mistrot, J. M., Choi, H., Smith, S. M., Graeber, R., Caruso, D., Webb, A., Hill, R., et al. combinformation: a mixed-initiative system for representing collections as compositions of image and text surrogates. In *Proc. JCDL'06*, ACM (2006), 11–20.

3. Kim, J., Guo, P. J., Cai, C. J., Li, S.-W. D., Gajos, K. Z., and Miller, R. C. Data-driven interaction techniques for improving navigation of educational videos. In *Proc. UIST'14*, ACM (2014), 563–572.

4. Kohn, N. W., and Smith, S. M. Collaborative fixation: Effects of others' ideas on brainstorming. *Applied Cognitive Psychology 25*, 3 (2011), 359–371.

5. Kulkarni, C., Dow, S. P., and Klemmer, S. R. Early and repeated exposure to examples improves creative work. In *Design Thinking Research*. Springer, 2014, 49–62.

6. Nijstad, B. A., Stroebe, W., and Lodewijkx, H. F. M. Cognitive stimulation and interference in groups: Exposure effects in an idea generation task. *Journal of Experimental Social Psychology 38*, 6 (2002), 535–544.

7. Siangliulue, P., Arnold, K. C., Gajos, K. Z., and Dow, S. P. Toward collaborative ideation at scale—leveraging ideas from others to generate more creative and diverse ideas. In *Proc. CSCW'15* (2015).

8. Siangliulue, P., Chan, J., Gajos, K. Z., and Dow, S. P. Providing timely examples improves the quantity and quality of generated ideas. In *Proc. Creativity and Cognition'15* (2015). To appear.

9. Tamuz, O., Liu, C., Belongie, S., Shamir, O., and Kalai, A. T. Adaptively Learning the Crowd Kernel. *arXiv.org* (May 2011).

10. van der Maaten, L., and Weinberger, K. Stochastic triplet embedding. *Machine Learning for Signal Processing (MLSP), 2012 IEEE International Workshop on* (2012), 1–6.

11. Ward, T. B., Patterson, M. J., Sifonis, C. M., Dodds, R. A., and Saunders, K. N. The role of graded category structure in imaginative thought. *Memory & Cognition 30*, 2 (2002), 199–216.

12. Weir, S. A. Learnersourcing subgoal labels for how-to videos. In *CHI'14 Extended Abstracts*, ACM (2014), 945–950.

13. Zhang, H., Law, E., Miller, R., Gajos, K., Parkes, D., and Horvitz, E. Human computation tasks with global constraints. In *Proc. CHI'12*, ACM (2012), 217–226.

SolidSketch - Toward Enactive Interactions for Semantic Model Creation

Chih-Pin Hsiao
ACME Lab, GVU Center
College of Architecture
Georgia Institute of Technology
chsiao9@gatech.edu

ABSTRACT

SolidSketch is a solid and parametric modeling program that enables users to rapidly construct 3D parametric and semantic models through sketch and multi-touch input. The interaction design principles of SolidSketch are based on the cognitive science theory of enaction. We argue enactive interactions would support design creativity by enabling rapid iteration and continuous feedback throughout a flexible design exploration. SolidSketch infers the intention of the user by continuously analyzing the surrounding context and user's behavior. This paper briefly introduces the enaction theory, the interaction designs as well as the implementations of SolidSketch.

Author Keywords

Sketch Interactions; Multi-touch Interactions; Enaction; Embodiment; Design Cognition; 3D Modeling

ACM Classification Keywords

H.5.m. Information interfaces and presentation (e.g., HCI): Miscellaneous.

General Terms

Human Factors; Design; Theory.

INTRODUCTION

It is widely accepted that sketching is a critical part of the design process [4]. It encourages designers to rapidly and flexibly express their ideas, which helps develop, explore, and validate those designs. Without sketching, much of this interpretation, analysis, and creative work would otherwise have to take place in the designer's mind, which in most cases would be extremely difficult given the complexity designers often face.

When sketching, designers offload many of these cognitive processes onto the physical environment, which helps facilitating design thinking. Given this constant interaction with the materials in the environment, design researchers,

such as Donald Schön, describe design as a "conversation with the materials of a design" [4]. Physical and tangible tools, such as pen and paper, are so familiar and flexible that they allow designers to 'speak' fluently as they converse with the materials, i.e. gradually creating and examining sketches. However, some digital tools, such as CAD programs, are rich in specialized and powerful features, but often lack this dynamic feedback loop that gives rise to the 'conversation with materials.' In this paper, we use the new cognitive science theory of enaction to describe the cognitive mechanisms involved throughout the dynamic 'conversation' that emerges between a designer and the materials in their environment. We then take this cognitive feature into considerations for creating a solid and parametric modeling program to facilitate the design process.

THE ENACTION PARADIGM

In the enaction theory [3], these "conversation-like" activities are referred to as a sense-making process that often requires humans to perform tangible interactions to gain insights and understand how the things work. Enaction is a newly established cognitive theory that describes how perceptions and actions influence each other continuously in a percept-action feedback loop. This dynamic feedback loop helps coordinate and guide the interaction [3]. This process of gradual negotiation through interaction with the environment aligns perfectly with what Schön was referring to as a conversation with the materials of a design. From enaction theory, we have built a dynamic model of creative sense-making [1] and identified a set of cognitive characteristics in our design thinking process.

Sense-Making: During sense-making, cognitive systems playfully interact with their environment to learn how it works. These experimental interactions help the agent develop a dynamical model of the current environment to help guide and coordinate real time interaction.

Autonomy: Cognitive systems have dynamically changing intentions and needs that vary based on their context. Design support tools should embrace that autonomy rather than trying to impose artificial structures upon the creative process.

Embodiment: Humans think by interacting with the environment around them. Direct physical manipulations provide continuous real time feedback that informs experimental interactions and helps individuals make sense of their overall directive and intention.

Emergence: In enaction, cognition continually emerges as humans organically interact with their dynamically changing environment. All interaction and creativity are viewed as inherently improvisational and based on real time negotiation. Tasks emerge through interaction, they are not always pre-defined. Creative interactions should help users discover, explore, and redfine problems, questions, and goals in a flexible manner.

Figure 1. The five sketch gestures used in the system

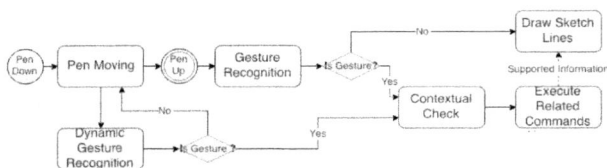

Figure 2. The pipelines for contextual bounded filter algorithm used for gesture recognition

SYSTEM DESIGN

Our goal is to build a program that enables users to interact with models in an enactive manner through sketch and multi-touch while still retaining the power of CAD tools. The system should facilitate continuous percept-action feedback loop with the digital environment while analyzing the sketch and trying to understand the intentions and meanings of these interactions. Thus, we propose SolidSketch in which the users can freely create parametric and semantic models on canvas using freehand sketching and multi-touch input. With a minimum amount of GUI components, the user can create geometries with relationships, while maintaining the user's continuous interaction flow.

Sketch Interaction and Recognitions

SolidSketch tries to recognize the user's intentions of drawing straight or curved lines, as well as sketch gestures. We start from sketch feature extractions for completing these tasks. While conventional programs require users to click on buttons or type in commands, SolidSketch enables users to perform sketch gestures on the desired location, which helps maintain the continuous interaction flow. However, since this is a program for creating 3D content, the strokes drawn on a tablet can be projected to infinite locations in a 3D virtual space. We adopt a contextual bounded filter algorithm (CBFA) to solve this issue. Figure 2 illustrates the pipeline of how the algorithms are used in the system.

Pen and Multi-Touch Inputs

The major difference between pen and multi-touch input is the granularity level the user can control. Pen input usually can give more detailed controls while touch input has less granularity. Thus, in SolidSketch, pen is used for sketching lines and applying detailed constraints while touch is for shape relationship manipulations and space navigations.

Building Constraints through Interactions

In design studies, constraint settings are important procedures for embedding knowledge into a design [2]. It is also a way for letting the computer know the designer's intentions. As mentioned, sketch gestures are used for assigning constraints, especially those gestures with the forms of symbols, such as angle gesture, tick gesture, and circle gesture. We use these gestures for setting constraints between sketch components, such as line segments and angles. After passing the sketch gestures through CBFA, the system will decide what constraint from selected candidate sketch components and where to set it. After making a decision, it will present animated transitions between the geometries without and with the constraints.

'Prototype' operation is used for generating models from a set of constraints. To choose a 'prototype' operation, the user will need to click on the only UI component in SolidSketch showing on the left of the system. One simple built-in prototype operation is the 'extruding' operation to generate 3D solid models from profiles. The user can enter the prototyping mode to add new prototypes. While in this mode, the system relates the operations to the existing constraints depending on the surrounding contexts. One example is that the user can dynamically create an array of geometries on an existing geometry that has well defined constraints based on the contexts surrounding with the manipulating area. The system will create another set of constraints in addition to the original constraints for this operation. If the user chooses to apply these constraints while drawing a new sketch line, the system will dynamically generate the geometry for the user.

FUTURE WORK

We have done our first formal user study. We found different interaction patterns while using the prototype comparing to the traditional GUI program. We would like to conduct the next study to understand whether these different behaviors affect their sense making process and thus make exploratory adjustments based on the continuous representations from the system.

REFERENCES

1. Davis, N., Hsiao, C.-P., Popova, Y., and Magerko, B. An Enactive Model of Creativity for Computational Collaboration and Co-creation. *Creativity in the Digital Age*, Springer-Verlag, London, 2015, 109-133.
2. Gross, M.D. and Habraken, N.J. Design as Exploring Constraints. *Ph.D Dissertation*, 1986, 169.
3. Hanne De Jaegher. *Enaction: Toward a New Paradigm for Cognitive Science.* MIT Press, 2010.
4. Schön, D.A. Designing as reflective conversation with the materials of a design situation. *Knowledge-Based Systems 5*, 1 (1992), 3–14.

Pen + Touch Diagramming to Stimulate Design Ideation

Andrew M. Webb
Interface Ecology Lab
Department of Computer Science and Engineering
Texas A&M University
andrew@ecologylab.net

ABSTRACT

Ideation, the process of generating new ideas, is central to design where the goal is to find novel solutions around a set of requirements. Designers engage in diagramming, creating external representations of ideas. Diagramming connects the body and creative cognitive processes, as the hands transform physical media to explore ideas. HCI researchers need to leverage body-based interaction to support creativity. My Ph.D. research develops a new body-based diagramming environment to stimulate design ideation.

Author Keywords

diagramming, design, ideation, body-based interaction

ACM Classification Keywords

H.5.1 Information interfaces and presentation: HCI.

INTRODUCTION

Generating new ideas is critical for design. Design processes are supported by embodied representations, including gestures, tangibles, and diagrams, which have been found to help people think [9, 8]. A *diagram* is a design thinking tool that stimulates imagination [1]. The process of diagramming mediates exploration of relationships between concepts, using ambiguity to foster multiple interpretations. Designers explore ideas by transforming physical diagrams (e.g. cutting, folding, sketching over) using their hands (with tools). The proliferation of sensory modalities, such as multi-touch, pen, and computer vision, enables cost-effective development of new forms of body-based interaction that can support expressive diagramming. We hypothesize that making diagramming more based in the body will promote exploration of diverse transformations, stimulating ideation.

We develop a new diagramming environment to investigate how body-based interactions impact creative cognitive processes. We derive new bimanual pen + touch interactions for diagramming on personal surfaces. We evaluate our new environment in landscape architecture education.

BACKGROUND

We ground design of our environment in embodied cognition. Cognitive models, including those associated with creativity, are based in the body [2]. Tversky et al. demonstrate that gestures help people not just to communicate meaning, but further, to remember and to understand complex ideas [10]. Of particular value are iconic gestures, whose shapes map directly to what they mean, metaphoric gestures, that use spatial representation to convey relationships, and embodied gestures, which encode knowledge motorically, as images and diagrams encode pictorially. These species of gestures provide us with cognitive guidance for how to develop body-based interfaces that will help designers diagram and form new ideas.

We seek to embody gestural interaction with diagrams through bimanual pen + touch techniques. Guiard developed one of the first models of bimanual interaction, the kinematic chain [5]. In a kinematic chain, the non-preferred hand (NPH) acts to define a reference frame for the actions of the preferred hand (PH). When drawing on paper, this is equivalent to the NPH positioning and rotating the paper in conjunction with the PH making marks with a pen. We design pen + touch interaction techniques using the kinematic chain model.

DIAGRAMMING ENVIRONMENT

We are developing a new diagramming environment to investigate how bimanual pen + touch interactions can support design processes. Through iterative design, we are evaluating impact on design ideation in architecture education.

Information Composition + Sketching

Our diagramming environment integrates information composition with sketching in an infinite zoomable space. Information composition, a medium for representing a personal information collection as a connected whole, supports reflection when performing information-based ideation tasks [11]. Designers engage in information-based ideation tasks, using information as support for generating new ideas [7], such as investigating how properties of different materials will impact a design. In our diagramming environment, designers gather images and text while sketching out ideas and exploring relationships amidst the collected information (see Figure 1).

Sketches act as interactive imagery [3]. Strokes are drawn, re-drawn, drawn over, and erased, transforming ideas. Design ideation environments should support abstraction, ambiguity, and imprecision in sketching [4]. Through integrating information composition with sketching, we support ambiguity and varied interpretations in diagramming.

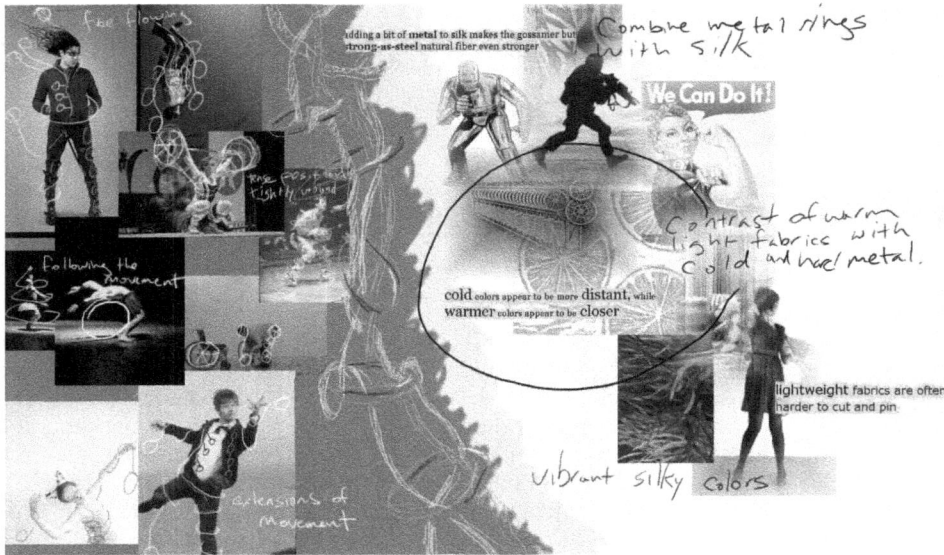

Figure 1: Example information composition + sketching diagram created by a hypothetical student for a fashion design assignment. Student searched for information on materials, such as textiles, and collecting resources. She developed idea of warm vibrant silk contrasting with cold dark metal (right). Circle shapes inspired design of metal rings with silk strands. Ideas were explored by sketching over these images.

Body-based Diagramming: Pen + Touch Interaction

We seek to provide pen + touch interactions that are intuitive, expressive, and more directly connect designers to diagrams. The goal is not simply to make diagramming easier, but to aid designers in forming abstractions and investigating ambiguous representations through body-based experiences. While diagrams vividly convey spatial relationships and ideas, much of the thinking and mental models of the author are encoded in body-based creative processes of transformation. We define diagram transformation as any operation that changes a diagram to encode meaning, e.g.: adding and removing elements, affine transforms, color-space transforms, cropping, and distortion. Just as a designer uses her hands to transform physical diagrams (e.g. rotating, folding, or bending material), body-based interaction techniques are needed for transforming our new diagramming medium.

As recommended by Hinckley et al. [6], the pen, when used by itself, makes marks. The exception is when kinematic chains are created. When pen input is combined with touches, that act as modifiers, commands are invoked. We develop new bimanual pen + touch interaction techniques for diagram transformation, including cropping, layering, rotating with 3D perspective, and brush styling. Designers fluidly switch between sketching ideas and transforming diagram elements. Designers investigate varied ideas through transformations, while using a NPH undo gesture to iteratively revert changes.

Evaluation: Landscape Architecture Education

As a context for evaluating effects of body-based diagramming on design ideation, we are engaging in field studies in architecture education. Student teams in two design studios have used a preliminary version of our diagramming environment on course assignments. We collected the diagrams they created, video recorded their body-based interactions while working in the environment, and interviewed several participants. We are in the process of analyzing this data, both in terms of quantitative ideation metrics [7] and qualitative coding of video and interview data.

CONCLUSION

HCI researchers have the opportunity to transform design processes with the development of new body-based interactions. Digital environments enable creation and exploration of large information spaces that can be dynamically transformed. Interactions with these environments need to be expressive to support diverse transformations. Simultaneous pen and multi-touch input will support such expressive transformations. Developing pen + touch interaction techniques that use kinematic chains will help designers think about how elements are transformed and the relationships between elements and transformations.

REFERENCES

1. Deleuze, G., and Guattari, F. *A Thousand Plateaus: Capitalism and Schizophrenia.* University of Minnesota Press, 1987.

2. Glenberg, A. Why Mental Models Must Be Embodied. *Advances in Psychology 128* (1999), 77–90.

3. Goldschmidt, G. The Dialectics of Sketching. *Creativity Research Journal 4*, 2 (1991), 123–143.

4. Gross, M. D., and Do, E. Y.-L. Ambiguous intentions: a paper-like interface for creative design. In *Proc. UIST* (1996), 183–192.

5. Guiard, Y. Asymmetric division of labor in human skilled bimanual action: The kinematic chain as a model. *Journal of motor behavior 19* (1987).

6. Hinckley, K., Yatani, K., Pahud, M., Coddington, N., Rodenhouse, J., Wilson, A., Benko, H., and Buxton, B. Pen + touch = new tools. In *Proc. UIST* (2010).

7. Kerne, A., Webb, A. M., Smith, S. M., Linder, R., Lupfer, N., Qu, Y., Moeller, J., and Damaraju, S. Using metrics of curation to evaluate information-based ideation. *ACM Trans. Comput.-Hum. Interact. 21*, 3 (June 2014), 14:1–14:48.

8. Kim, M., and Maher, M. Comparison of designers using a tangible user interface & graphical user interface and impact on spatial cognition. In *Proc. Human Behaviour in Design* (2005).

9. Suwa, M., and Tversky, B. What do architects and students perceive in their design sketches? a protocol analysis. *Design Studies 18*, 4 (1997), 385 – 403.

10. Tversky, B., Heiser, J., Lee, P. U., and Daniel, M. P. *Explanations in gesture, diagram, and word.* Oxford University Press, Oxford, 2009, 119–131.

11. Webb, A. M., Linder, R., Kerne, A., Lupfer, N., Qu, Y., Poffenberger, B., and Revia, C. Promoting reflection and interpretation in education: Curating rich bookmarks as information composition. In *Proc. Creativity and cognition* (2013).

Public Online Failure With Crowdfunding

Michael D. Greenberg
Northwestern University
Delta Lab
2133 N. Sheridan Rd
Evanston, IL 60652, USA
mdgreenb@u.northwestern.edu

ABSTRACT

Kickstarter is a growing online crowdfunding platform where individuals attempt to raise funds for creative projects by leveraging their personal social networks for small financial contributions. Crowdfunding platforms like Kickstarter are actively growing, with thousands of individuals attempting projects each month. While other scholarly research and the popular press has focused on the success stories from crowdfunding, the fact remains that a majority of projects fail. Little attention has focused on the majority of individuals who have run failed projects and experienced a publicly embarrassing event in the process. We see crowdfunding platforms as a unique opportunity to study and understand how individuals react to online embarrassment.

Author Keywords

Failure; Persistence; Crowdfunding; Kickstarter

ACM Classification Keywords

H.5.m. Information Interfaces and Presentation (e.g. HCI): Miscellaneous

INTRODUCTION

In the Spring of 2013, Chris Dickens, an entrepreneur from California raised over $2,989 via contributions from 72 people on Kickstarter.com to fund the production of "The Vigilante Project," an independent comic. However, this was not Chris's first attempt at fundraising on Kickstarter. Just 2 months prior, an earlier iteration of the same project failed to meet its funding goal, gathering contributions from only 35 people. Chris was undeterred after his first failure. Bolstered by social support from peers, he committed to the mission of the project by keeping his supporters updated on his progress as he prepared to try again. And after his second project attempt was successful, Chris has remained an active member of the Kickstarter community by financially supporting the projects of 9 others. Chris's case is atypical for participants on Kickstarter, as only 3% of failed projects creators attempt

C&C '15, June 22-25, 2015, Glasgow, United Kingdom.
ACM 978-1-4503-3598-0/15/06.
http://dx.doi.org/10.1145/2757226.2764767

to relaunch their project [5]. We position crowdfunding platforms like Kickstarter as a unique location to study how individuals react to the experience of online failure.

Theoretical Framing

Since failure is often part of a longer creative process, this begs the following question: what might motivate people like Chris who have failed to return to crowdfunding? While the process of creative expression is often characterized by a series of failures on the way to an eventual success [1], we have observed through previous work that Kickstarter actively does not support the process of iterative failure necessary for creative work [5]. On Kickstarter, roughly 50% of projects fail, however only 3.8% of failed projects eventually relaunch and try again [5] If platforms like Kickstarter represent the way that individuals will get started with creative work in the future, then we have a responsibility to understand the public experience of failure on these platforms and to design for it.

The future of online creative entrepreneurship and creative work might hinge on supporting failure within these platforms more effectively, since the failures are highly visible to social networks and persist even after the project has ended. Related work from entrepreneurship studies has described a theory of how entrepreneurs persistence through failure through a solitary process [7], however the online environment is highly social and provides numerous avenues for feedback from peers [3]. So while participating in these platforms might be cheaper in the sense of monetary costs to participate, failure is potentially more costly in the sense of social costs [2]. Therefore we are doubly concerned with supporting failure within these platforms; not only is failure a critical part of the creative process, if not handled correctly, it can have severe detrimental effects in an online environment. We argue that in order for Kickstarter and other, future creative work platforms like Kickstarter to avoid stagnating user growth, they must be designed with the experience of iterative failure in mind.

It is inevitable on platforms like Kickstarter, or any creative platform for that matter, that some people will experience a failure before an eventual success. While previous research on crowdfunding showed that failure was seen as a positive experience for project creators, the overwhelming majority of failed project creators do not return to their project [5]. We wonder then, why do people fail to return in any form? While in some extreme cases, failure can lead to stigmatization from further participation, a failure to design for the experience of failure might result in user retention issues. This in turn might lead to a decline in participation on these platforms.

While Internet platforms allow anybody the opportunity to start creative work, they especially help novices who may not have existing networks of supporters. As these novice users represent the future of participants on these creative platforms, it is important to support them as they begin to participate, so as not to marginalize them before they become experienced community members. So while platforms like Kickstarter have emerged where people engage in creative ventures online, we know little about why creators fail to return and what can motivate individuals to come back after a failure event. Chris Dickens is an outlier in a community of abandoned projects, and we know very little about what makes his case different from the majority of project creators. We address this gap.

PREVIOUS RESULTS

Our previous work has shown that people find the experience of failing with crowdfunding to be difficult, yet rewarding at the same time [5]. In this work, where we interviewed 11 individuals who ran failed crowdfunding campaigns, everyone responded that at least some part of the failure experience was positive. At the extremes, one individual described the experience of failure with crowdfunding as deeply disturbing:

> "Oh my god, I lost confidence in myself and .... I was really disappointed. It became too personal for me..."

After three failure events this person was unwilling to attempt crowdfunding again, however they did report that they learned important skills in the process of failure. At the other end of the spectrum, others had largely positive experiences with failure events:

> "I dont want to be cheesy but it made me stronger. It made me stronger in that I found different ways to connect with my audience... So, hopefully people are learning. People that fail learn and reevaluate, I know I did."

This individual used the embarrassing experience of failure as a learning experience and eventually launched a successful next campaign.

While participating in these online venues might not make an individual famous, or wealthy, there are clear professional and social benefits to participating. The project creator often gains professional skills in marketing and communicating which can be easily transferred to other domains [6]. Furthermore, the continued production of innovative, creative work on platforms like Kickstarter has value beyond the personal social level, as it has value from a cultural and economic perspective.

If systems like Kickstarter can better support creative projects that fail, then everyone who might consume or enjoy these cultural goods stands to benefit. To better understand the dynamics of failure on Kickstarter, we wonder then, why so few failed crowdfunding projects relaunch? What motivates

people to return? One simple explanation is social support. While the community plays a large role in determining a success of a campaign [4], it is unclear how the social support from community members can affect creators of campaigns that have failed.o

FUTURE WORK

In my dissertation work, I will study user retention after failure on Kickstarter as, I am broadly interested in why people return after creative failure online. We posit that HCI can contribute to this important problem by testing and designing interfaces which promote both social encouragement and individual persistence, both of which might help individuals to continue participating after and failure.

My dissertation work will encompass several, smaller projects. First, I will investigate the demographics of the crowdfunding population. Since there is a large body of literature on the demographics of failed entrepreneurs, this will give us a baseline population to compare to. The second study will expand my previous work on motivations and deterrents to relaunching crowdfunding projects [5]. This chapter will focus on expanding the previous interviews to better understand why people are motivated to relaunch. The third study will quantitatively analyze the motivations for relaunching by analyzing trace data on projects from Kickstarter. Finally the last study will be a design intervention with failed project creators where we apply and test the design principles we derived from the previous three studies to see if our designs can motivate more people to relaunch.

ACKNOWLEDGEMENTS
Thanks to the NSF GFRP for supporting this work.

REFERENCES
1. Barron, F., and Harrington, D. M. Creativity, intelligence, and personality. *Annual review of psychology 32*, 1 (1981), 439–476.

2. Burke, M., Kraut, R., and Marlow, C. Social capital on facebook: Differentiating uses and users. In *CHI 2011*, ACM (2011), 571–580. 00159.

3. Burke, M., Marlow, C., and Lento, T. Feed me: motivating newcomer contribution in social network sites. In *CHI 2009*, ACM (2009), 945–954.

4. Etter, V., Grossglauser, M., and Thiran, P. Launch hard or go home!: predicting the success of kickstarter campaigns. ACM Press (2013), 177–182.

5. Greenberg, M. D., and Gerber, E. M. Learning to fail: Experiencing public failure online through crowdfunding. CHI '14, ACM (New York, NY, USA, 2014), 581–590.

6. Hui, J. S., Greenberg, M. D., and Gerber, E. M. Understanding the role of community in crowdfunding work. CSCW '14, ACM (New York, NY, USA, 2014), 62–74.

7. Singh, S., Corner, P. D., and Pavlovich, K. Failed, not finished: A narrative approach to understanding venture failure stigmatization. *Journal of Business Venturing 30*, 1 (Jan. 2015), 150–166.

Distributed Affect as a Framework for Analyzing Creative Collaboration

Taylor Jackson Scott
University of Washington
423 Sieg Hall
Seattle, WA 98195
omni@uw.edu

ABSTRACT

Historically, the study of affect has been intimately tied to theories of both cognition and creativity, and there are still unexplored connections between these related phenomena. This paper discusses research to expand and refine the formulation of distributed affect as a theoretical framework for analyzing and understanding creative collaboration. I elaborate on parallels between theories of cognition that extend beyond the individual as the unit of analysis and the text-based chat communication of affect between members of a distributed group who utilize creative problem solving to achieve their goals. Directions for future research are also discussed. A better understanding of the way in which distributed affect operates will have a significant impact on research into collaborative creativity as well as implications for the design of interfaces to support this type of distributed work.

Author Keywords

Distributed affect; creative collaboration; distributed groups; computer-mediated communication

ACM Classification Keywords

H.5.3 Group and Organization Interfaces: Computer supported cooperative work

INTRODUCTION

As core components of our mental faculties, affect and cognition play integral roles in almost everything that humans do. A large body of ongoing research has attempted to describe the interplay between them [5, 12, 13]. Recent theoretical perspectives have explored the view that cognition can be distributed beyond the individual [15]. However, there is less work on how affect could operate beyond the individual as the unit of analysis. Similarly, there has been much recent attention given to the role that affect plays in the creative process [13], but only some initial attempts to describe how affect operates in a distributed group that is carrying out creative work [2].

Building on work by Aragon and Williams [2] and Hutchins [10], the primary goal of my work is to provide an expanded formulation of *distributed affect* as a framework for understanding how affective states, through collaborative interaction in a dynamic system, extend beyond the individual in persistent and pervasive ways and the influence this has on group dynamics and creative problem solving. While Hutchins' theory of distributed cognition [10] accounts for how cognitive states are shared and stored among people and artifacts within a group, it does not account for the equally important role of affect in such a system. Aragon and Williams' [2] complex systems model can help researchers study the critical role of affect in creativity, yet stops short of providing a comprehensive framework for studying distributed affect as it occurs in more general forms of collaboration. It is these gaps in knowledge that my dissertation research plans to address.

DISTRIBUTED AFFECT

As Hutchins illustrated in his seminal work on distributed cognition, *Cognition in the Wild*, groups achieve complex cognitive tasks via the "propagation of representational states across a series of representational media" [10]. This model of distributed information coordination and sharing across a system of people and artifacts plays a crucial role in the problem solving capabilities of a group, and is necessarily included in the unit of analysis when examining the cognitive properties of this system. Similarly, I posit that the sharing of affective states between members of a group is equally important. It has also been established that creativity, problem-solving and cognition are heavily influenced by and intimately tied to affect [11, 13].

In studies of complex cognition in the real world, focusing only on the individual as the unit of analysis neglects the larger cognitive ecosystem. Aragon and Williams note that Hutchins focused his analysis of the cognitive system on knowledge that did not reside in any one individual, but that his analysis "did not explicitly call out the emotional states that drove the collaborative problem-solving process" [2]. I argue that it is important to look beyond the individual where affect is concerned, as well. As previous studies [1, 7] have shown, affect does not take place inside of a vacuum, detached from the environment and interactions with others—it is distributed across, and influenced by others. In service of this notion, I have identified four distinct features of distributed affect that provide the mechanism for understanding DA's operation within a group context. These are: *transference, resonance, pervasiveness,* and *persistence*. These features emerge from existing theories of distributed affect [2], distributed cognition [10], emotional contagion [3, 8], as well as from the qualitative analysis of chat data as described in previous work [4, 14]. I will briefly define these features below:

Transference is concerned with how affect is transferred and shared between the members of the group, as well as between other representational tools and media within the group.

Resonance describes how the affective states can build, one on top of the other, in a kind of positive or negative feedback loop between members of the group.

Pervasiveness refers to the spread of one or more affective states throughout the entire group as a unit of analysis and is concerned with the dynamics of the group as a whole.

Persistence refers to the temporal duration of affective states in the group, and stands in contrast to the relatively short-lived and interruptive experiences typically associated with an individual emotion.

CURRENT RESEARCH

My ongoing research in this area has focused on the text-based expression of affect found in the chat logs of the Nearby Supernova Factory (SNfactory), an astrophysics collaboration of approximately 30 core members. The group operates their telescope remotely three nights per week; during operation, numerous critical decisions must be made quickly and collaboratively despite the group not being collocated. Online chat is the team's primary means of communication during telescope operation, where the expression of affect is still a prominent and important occurrence [6] Their work has resulted in a chat log corpus with approximately 485,000 messages sent over a period of four years.

These logs have been previously coded for the expression of affect [4, 14], and I am moving on to a second phase of coding and analysis. Now that the features of distributed affect previously described have been formulated, I am in the process of operationalizing them so that portions of the chat logs can be coded for instances of these features at play within the group. These coded logs will be analyzed using computer-mediated discourse analysis (CMDA), a method that is ideally suited to the text-based medium and empirical goals of this research [9]. Through this analysis, I plan to answer questions concerning how the features of distributed affect interact with one another and how this dynamic interaction contributes to the creative problem solving that the group displays.

I posit that distributed affect plays a critical role in the way collaborative teams work, and this framework will provide scholars with the scaffolding to enable them to identify and analyze it in their own data. It will also result in implications for the design and evaluation of systems to support this type of creative collaboration. I hope to ultimately show that this framework of distributed affect can move beyond text-based communication and be generalized to other forms of creative collaborations in a wide variety of contexts.

ACKNOWLEDGMENTS
I would like to thank my collaborators and my advisor, Cecilia Aragon, for her guidance on this work.

REFERENCES

1. Aragon, C. R., Poon, S., et al. A Tale of Two Online Communities: Fostering Collaboration and Creativity in Scientists and Children. C&C '09. ACM, (2009), 9-18.

2. Aragon, C.R. and Williams, A. Collaborative Creativity: a Complex Systems Model with Distributed Affect. CHI '11. ACM, (2011), 1875-1884.

3. Barsade, S. G. The Ripple Effect: Emotional Contagion and its Influence on Group Behavior. *Administrative Science Quarterly. 47*, 4 (2002), 644-676.

4. Brooks et al. Statistical Affect Detection in Collaborative Chat. CSCW '13. ACM. (2013), 317-328.

5. Eich, Eric, et al. *Cognition and Emotion*. Oxford University Press, New York, 2000.

6. Hancock, J.T., Landrigan, C., Silver, C. Expressing Emotion in Text-based Communication. CHI '07. ACM, (2007), 929-932.

7. Hancock, J.T. et al. I'm Sad You're Sad: Emotional Contagion in CMC. CSCW '08, ACM, (2008), 295-298.

8. Hatfield, E., Cacioppo, J. T., and Rapson, R. Emotional Contagion. *Current Directions in Psychological Science, 2*, 3 (1993), 96-99.

9. Herring, S. Computer-Mediated Discourse Analysis: an Approach to Researching Online Behavior. *Designing for Virtual Communities in the Service of Learning* (2004), 338-376.

10. Hutchins, E. *Cognition in the Wild*. MIT Press, Cambridge, Mass, 1995.

11. McLeod, Douglas B. The Role of Affect in Mathematical Problem Solving. In Douglas B.McLeod and Verna M. Adams. eds. *Affect and Mathematical Problem Solving: A New Perspective*. Springer-Verlag, New York, 1989, 20-36.

12. Ortony, Andrew, Gerald L. Clore, and Allan Collins. *The Cognitive Structure of Emotions*. Cambridge University Press, 1990.

13. Russ, S.W. *Affect and Creativity: the Role of Affect and Play in the Creative Process*. L. Erlbaum Associates, Hillsdale, N.J., 1993.

14. Scott, Taylor Jackson et al. Adapting Grounded Theory to Construct a Taxonomy of Affect in Collaborative Online Chat. SIGDOC '12, ACM (2012), 197-204.

15. Stahl, Gerry. *Group Cognition: Computer Support for Building Collaborative Knowledge*. MIT Press, Cambridge, Mass, 2006.

Tools for Wools: An Interactive Urban Knitting Installation and Creative Research Method

Janis Lena Meissner
Vienna University of Technology
A-1040 Vienna, Austria
janis.meissner@tuwien.ac.at

ABSTRACT

Urban knitting (also known as yarn bombing, knitted graffiti and guerilla knitting) is a globally occurring street art trend which uses traditional craft techniques to modify objects in urban space. It is the chosen tool of present-day craftspeople for creative expression in public. However, the personal narratives woven into the installations usually remain inaccessible for the broad audience. This paper presents my Master's thesis work on "Tools for Wools", an interactive prototype which integrates physical wool panels, touch sensors and an information device with intent to fill the identified information gap. The subsequent evaluation allowed insights on the manifold reasons for urban knitters to engage in this particular form of everyday creativity. I therefore suggest that such prototype projects can also serve as a qualitative research tool to reveal motivations underlying creative craft practices.

Author Keywords

Urban knitting; interactive art; creative research methods

ACM Classification Keywords

H.5.2. User Interfaces (D.2.2, H.1.2, I.3.6): Prototyping; Theory and methods; User-centered design

INTRODUCTION

Research on creativity is split: While some studies analyse the high-end creative genius of renowned individuals, others focus on everyday creativity of the rather average person. "Big C" is opposed to "little C" when it comes to decide what creativity is and what it is not [1]. Gauntlett [4] criticises the definition of creativity by Csikszentmihalyi for being too exclusive and suggests to shift the focus from the creative product and its socio-cultural validation towards the immanent process of creation. Peter Dormer who published a collection of essays exploring craft philosophies sees a similar problem in separating the Arts from the Crafts which ultimately results in the marginalisation of the latter [2].

One of the traditional crafts which has been highly marginalised is knitting. In contrast to painting, sculpting and other classic activities attributed to the Fine Arts, handicraft techniques have traditionally been associated with the domestic sphere of practical chores [6]. Their creative potentials in terms of design and expressiveness have been largely undermined. Nonetheless, the craft technique has survived, and after being ill-reputed as a housewife duty for some decades, it recently regained new popularity among young emancipated women (and men as well). In times when buying off-the-shelf clothes is often cheaper than producing it oneself, knitting practices become increasingly detached from its original practical purposes. Many of todays knitters rather seem to focus on the process of knitting than on the final product, however to date this is largely seen as a process that is separate from technology concerns.

URBAN KNITTING

My Master's thesis is dealing with urban knitting which I would like to describe here as a very specific form of "everyday creative" handicraft. It is a textile form of street art where fabric pieces of knit, crochet or embroidery are installed in public places. Urban knitters skip traditional craft notions of self-reliance in favour of personal expressiveness by leaving individual woolly traces in shared urban environments which don't serve any other practical purposes. Their installations vary a lot in colours, materials, craft techniques and size. It can involve one single knitter or hundreds of knitters collaborating together on one project.

Even though they form a global street art trend all together, each urban knitter has a different motivation to engage in it. For some it might be a feminist attempt to make the formerly invisible domestic work of housewives visible. For others it might be a comprehensive "craftivist" method to address other political and social issues. Urban knitting is therefore often very meaningful in terms of its inherent symbolism. It consists of carefully produced physical artefacts which don't only emerge from the opinions, thoughts and emotions of their creators but also serve as their public comments.

The problem is that the resulting artwork often isn't self-explanatory and subject to the individual interpretation of the spectator passing by. This is of course a problem shared with other forms of Fine Art, since art is most of the time far from self-evident. A key difference though is that, when exhibited in a gallery or museums, there is usually infrastructure to explain it, such as labels or exhibition catalogues. Building on related work such as [5] which uses technology to reveal the provenance of knitted artefacts and to capture aspects of their

C&C 2015, June 22-25, 2015, Glasgow, United Kingdom
ACM 978-1-4503-3598-0/15/06.
http://dx.doi.org/10.1145/2757226.2764769

creation process, my Master's thesis aims to provide a smart informative equivalent for urban knitting.

PROTOTYPE

With the intention to make the messages and creative processes behind urban knitting more visible, an interactive prototype was built which provides information on each piece of an exemplary installation. The first proof-of-concept version comprises five pieces of knitting and crochet produced by different artists. These components differ in applied craft technique as well as in material, colour, size and design. Still each crafted piece is big enough to place a flat hand on it. Next to the urban knitting arrangement, an information device is mounted in a frame.

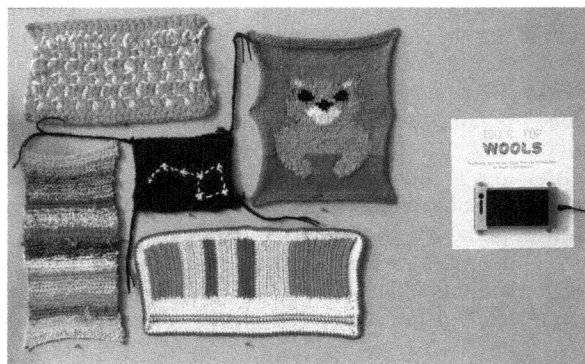

Figure 1. Front view on the "Tools for Wools" prototype.

Capacitive touch sensors are attached behind the textile pieces and remain invisible for the interested spectator. Touching any part of the installation triggers a signal which is first processed by an Arduino microcontroller and then sent to the Android-operated information device for displaying the according information. So whenever someone touches any of the panels, the screen shows the title and artist name as well as a description text and a photo of the knitter with her piece.

CREATIVE RESEARCH METHOD

Besides the classical computer science aspect of information accessibility it is also worth noting how the construction of such a prototype can be used as a qualitative research method. In fact, all of the Android application content uses first-hand information provided by the participating artists themselves. The idea was that they should explain their contributions in their own words and present themselves to the installation spectators in any form they wanted. In this way the participants did not only explain their work to outsiders but also provided rich data for further analysis. Apart from that three of the knitters agreed to be interviewed after seeing the prototype as a whole. As a consequence they started to reflect on their own contributions once again. While being primarily concerned with how their explanations could be optimized, they also reached a new meta-level to elaborate on their urban knitting practices. The project procedure can therefore be interpreted as an instance of creative research methods as introduced by Gauntlett [3] which, to summarise, comprises the engagement of the participants in a creative practice and subsequent reflection on the meaning of the outcome.

Even though the study involved only five urban knitters, its results already pointed out several factors which seem to be important sources of motivation for them. Since different facets of similar background stories were told, the variety of individual incitements can be categorized into four basic types in relation to the following aspects:

Urban space: Urban space is reclaimed as a shared place of action and intervention which is used to pursue a personal mission within a social but non-personal environment.

Ideals and values: The participants depicted themselves as caring fellow citizens with strong believes who want to express this part of their identity. Of course these statements are not always totally clear in expressing their creator's ideas but they definitely indicate topics which are valued by them, such as their wishes for collective happiness. With a little wool they seek to democratize urban space while giving their local peers a little colourful break from "grey" everyday-life.

Craft: While urban knitters produce crafted artefacts for committing it to the public, they give up on any individual use of their physical creations and to some extent even a personal connection to it. Instead their main relatedness pertains to the process of its making. This shift in focus highlights the knitters common appraisal for aspects inherent to the applied crafting techniques.

Material: Urban knitters often don't pay so much attention on their choice of materials and in many cases just use what they have at hand. Using left-over yarn is not perceived as a restrictive factor in their design, though. On the contrary, it is often reported to result in stimulating craft experiments.

Further discussion of the categories is needed. My ongoing research therefore involves building a next version of the prototype comprising a larger installation and a more representative user study in the wild. Whether or not the results will answer the question if such a system succeeds in making urban knitting more accessible to outsiders, it is worth discussing what we thereby can learn about the practices of urban knitters and in which way their everyday creative capacities might also be relevant for other citizen activities in urban space.

ACKNOWLEDGMENTS

I would like to thank my student peers Farzaneh Yegan and Michael Treml for working with me on the prototype, and Geraldine Fitzpatrick for her support and supervision.

REFERENCES

1. Cropley, A. J. Definitions of Creativity. *Encyclopedia of Creativity 1* (2011), 126–135.

2. Dormer, P. *The Culture of Craft.* Studies in design and material culture. Manchester University Press, 1997.

3. Gauntlett, D. *Creative Explorations: New Approaches to Identities and Audiences.* Routledge, London, 2007.

4. Gauntlett, D. *Making is connecting.* Polity Press, Cambridge, 2013.

5. Rosner, D. K., and Ryokai, K. Spyn: Augmenting the creative and communicative potential of craft. In *Proc. of CHI'10*, ACM (New York, 2010), 2407–2416.

6. Turney, J. *The Culture of Knitting.* Berg, 2009.

Assessing the Creativity of Designs at Scale

Christopher J. MacLellan
HCII, Carnegie Mellon University
Pittsburgh, PA
cmaclell@cs.cmu.edu

ABSTRACT

How best to assess the creativity of a large number of designed artifacts remains an open problem. The typical approach is to have experts answer likert questions about individual artifacts. This process typically requires a substantial amount of training to ensure the judges achieve an acceptable level of agreement. Consequently, the approach does not scale well as it is infeasible to have multiple experts regularly evaluate the creativity of a large number of designs. The current work explores an alternative approach that uses both individual and pairwise judgements from novice crowd workers to support reliable and scalable assessment of creative designs. This approach, which we call TrueCreativity, can operate over a set of evaluations from a large number of judges and appropriately weights their evaluations based on their past reliability and agreement with other judges. We show that this approach produces results that strongly correlate with another measure of creativity.

Author Keywords

Empirical Methods, Quantitative; E-Learning and Education; Machine Learning and Data Mining; Crowdsourcing

ACM Classification Keywords

H.5.3 [Information Interface and Presentation]: Group and Organization Interfaces – Evaluation/methodology.

INTRODUCTION

The ability to assess the creativity of designed artifacts in a scalable way has implications for both design research and instruction. Scalable techniques for creativity assessment might be used to conduct larger-scale empirical studies into creativity, facilitating the process of scientific discovery. Further, techniques for the scalable assessment of artifact creativity have implications for how design is taught. For example, Scott Klemmer recently launched a massive open online course on Human-Computer Interaction. A key component of this course was getting grades on designed artifacts from peers [1]. Peer grading allowed students in the course to get feedback in situations where it would be infeasible for the instructors to grade every design. A scalable technique for measuring the creativity of designed artifacts might be used to facilitate this peer grading process.

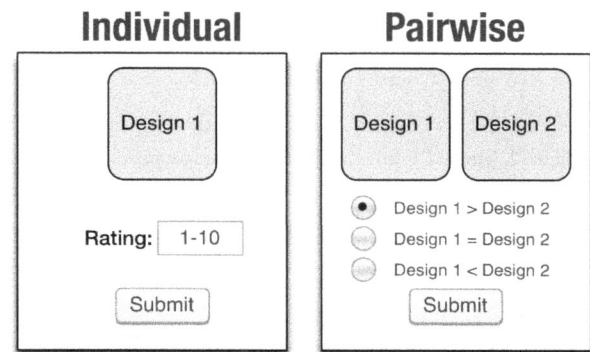

Figure 1. Simplified depictions of the rating formats used in the individual and pairwise rating schemes.

Despite the benefits, there is no clear approach to assessing the creativity of designs at scale. Traditionally, design creativity is assessed by a panel of experts using a likert measure. Scaling this approach consists of having novices, instead of experts, complete the same measures [1]. However, there are several criticisms against this approach [2]. In particular, each judge may award higher or lower ratings on average or they may award the same average rating, yet discriminate more finely amongst the designs. The typical approach to overcoming these difficulties is to train the judges until they achieve acceptable agreement, and to regularly retrain them to prevent rater drift. However, this is infeasible when using a large number of raters (e.g., mechanical turk workers or peers from an online class). Recent approaches have explored the use of reference items to correct for judge bias [5], but this approach still does not account for differences in judge discrimination abilities and it is unclear how the selection of reference items impacts the estimation of judge bias.

TRUECREATIVITY

To overcome these challenges we developed TrueCreativity, a Bayesian method for reliably assessing the creativity of designed artifacts using novices from the crowd. To apply this method we collect both individual creativity ratings (we used a 10 point scale) and pairwise creativity ratings (i.e., asking a judge to determine which of two designs is more creative or if they are equal) from crowd workers. Figure 1 depicts the rating formats we had judges use. These ratings are then combined into a single estimation of each design's latent creativity using a statistical model that estimates and corrects for judge bias and discrimination in both rating formats. We chose to support pairwise ratings because they do not suffer

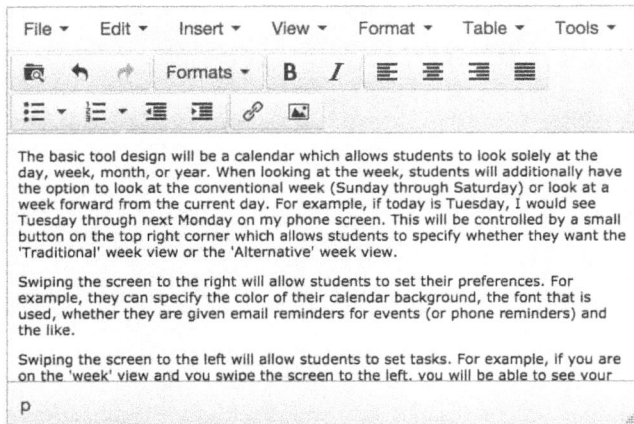

Figure 2. TinyMCE interface with an example participant design.

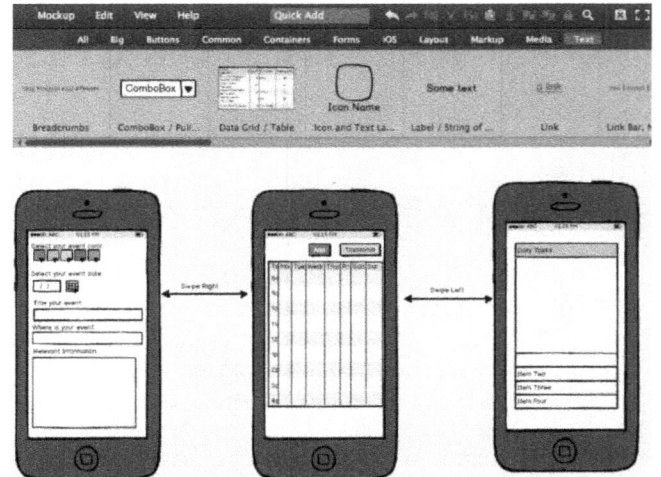

Figure 3. Balsamiq interface with an example participant design.

from the same criticisms as individual ratings (i.e., pairwise ratings are scale independent) and because research indicates that ordinal rating is easier and more reliable for novices [3]. To combine both formats of ratings we first specified the likelihood of each rating given the item and judge parameters. We modeled the likelihood of the individual ratings using a linear model that has a parameter for each item (i.e., TrueCreativity) and two parameters for each judge (i.e., bias and discrimination). For the pairwise ratings, we modeled the likelihood of each rating using a multi-class logistic regression that has one parameter for each item being compared (i.e., TrueCreativity) and three parameters for each judge (i.e., their lower and upper thresholds for rating items as equal and discrimination). After specifying the models, we used Markov Chain Monte Carlo optimization to compute the most likely TrueCreativity, bias, and discrimination values given all of the ratings in both formats. This method extends prior approaches that correct for judge bias [5]. In particular, we eliminate the need for reference items by using all of the ratings to jointly estimate judge parameters and item parameters. In essence, we use all overlapping ratings across both models to estimate and correct for judge bias and discrimination abilities.

PRELIMINARY RESULTS

As a preliminary evaluation of our approach we assessed the creativity of two sets of smart phone time management application designs. One set consisted of wireframes created using Balsamiq (http://www.balsamiq.com). The other set consisted of textual designs produced using a word processor. Figures 2 and 3 shows an example design in each format. For each design we had an existing creativity measure that was based on the number of unique features present in the designs. This "feature count" measure was produced by two expert coders who first generated a list of 18 unique features by studying the designs and then independently coded the designs in terms of the features they contained. For each feature the agreement of the coders was high (Cohen's $\kappa > 0.7$). This approach is similar to the ideation quantity measures used in other studies of creativity [4].

To compute the TrueCreativity scores we had 36 workers from Amazon Mechanical Turk and 6 researchers from our

lab independently judge the creativity of the designs using both rating schemes. For each wireframe we collected 6 individual ratings and 18 pairwise comparisons. For each textual design we collected 3 individual ratings and 9 pairwise comparisons. After computing the TrueCreativity measure using these ratings, we found that it was strongly correlated with the feature count measure (Pearson's $\rho = 0.5, p < 0.01$ for the wireframes and Pearson's $\rho = 0.72, p < 0.01$ for the textual designs). This agreement suggests that the measures have good convergent validity. While it took approximately one month to develop and achieve a reliable coding scheme for the feature count measure, it only took two days to collect the ratings necessary for computing the TrueCreativity scores. Given these results, future work will focus on rigorously assessing the reliability and validity of this approach.

ACKNOWLEDGEMENTS
This work is advised by Ken Koedigner and Steven Dow and supported by IES (R305B090023) and NSF (IIS-1208382 and IIS-1217096).

REFERENCES
1. Kulkarni, C., Wei, K. P., Le, H., Chia, D., Papadopoulos, K., Cheng, J., Koller, D., and Klemmer, S. R. Peer and Self Assessment in Massive Online Classes. *TOCHI 9*, 4 (2014), 131–168.

2. Pollitt, A. Comparative judgement for assessment. *International Journal of Technology and Design Education 22*, 2 (2012), 157–170.

3. Raman, K., and Joachims, T. Bayesian Ordinal Peer Grading. In *L@S '15* (2015), 149–156.

4. Shah, J. J., Kulkarni, S. V., and Vargas-Hernandez, N. Evaluation of Idea Generation Methods for Conceptual Design: Effectiveness Metrics and Design of Experiments. *JMD 122*, 4 (2000), 377–384.

5. Xu, A., and Bailey, B. P. A Reference-Based Scoring Model for Increasing the Findability of Promising Ideas in Innovation Pipelines. In *CSCW '12* (2012), 1183–1186.

Feminist Hackerspaces as Sites for Feminist Design

Sarah Fox
Human Centered Design & Engineering
University of Washington
Seattle, USA
sefox@uw.edu

ABSTRACT

This paper describes the work I have conducted with colleagues in and around feminist hackerspaces — workspaces that support the creative and professional pursuits of women. Through action research, interviews, and participant observation, I have explored the motivations, activities, and ideals of people organizing feminist hackerspaces. Additionally, I have begun to investigate what feminist design of technology might look like through the facilitation of a series of design workshops in two of these spaces. Through this work, I examine the feminist ideals that develop in these spaces as both discursive and material phenomena that shed new light on what counts as hacking, technology and collaboration.

Author Keywords

Hacking; making; craft, design; hackerspaces; feminism; STS.

ACM Classification Keywords

H.5.m. Information interfaces and presentation (e.g., HCI): Miscellaneous.

INTRODUCTION

Over eighteen months in Northern California and the Pacific Northwest, colleagues and I have pursued study of women-oriented and feminist hackerspaces — workspaces that support the creative and professional pursuits of women. These spaces developed in 2013, most prominently in the Pacific Northwestern United States, to make room for values, goals and practices that do not sit easily within existing sites of technical production. In designing how the spaces should look, feel, and run, members reframe activities seldom associated with technical work (e.g., weaving, identity workshops) as forms of hacking. Using interviews, design workshops, and participant observation, we trace how the reimagining of everyday space — how it might look, feel, and interact with society — became a

C&C '15, June 22-25, 2015, Glasgow, United Kingdom
ACM 978-1-4503-3598-0/15/06.
http://dx.doi.org/10.1145/2757226.2764771

means of grappling with the alignments and disconnects between familiar infrastructures and the unfamiliar symbolic work feminist hackers hope to engender [3].

OBSERVATIONS

Since their inception in 2012, feminist hackerspaces have offered local residents a place to gather, share ideas, learn creative techniques, and grow professional partnerships. Sophie Toupin, a feminist scholar and member of a feminist hackerspace in Montreal, describes these sites as the "spatial manifestation of the feminist hacker, maker and geek culture" [7]. Though all different in their implementations, these spaces share a core tenant that women and other marginalized people should be welcomed to perform technical practice without being subjected to discrimination or abuse. Liz Hendry, co-founder of Double Union in San Francisco, notes that feminist hackerspaces, like many other hackerspaces, focus not only on making, but also teaching and learning. Where they start to diverge is around the values they aim to uphold and the activities they serve to promote. Noting difference, Hendry adds, "[ours] is starting with a few extra values: intersectional feminism, support for feminist activism and strong respect for personal boundaries" [4]. As a safeguard against harassment, these spaces established codes of conduct intended to communicate institutional values. Without these codes, members might face the burden of having to continually explain their viewpoints. As Toupin notes, "When feminist and anti-oppression politics are not explicitly part of the ethos of a space whether virtual or physical, the burden of education will often be placed upon the people who are living these oppressions" [6].

At first glance, many tools within these sites seem at home in a conventional hackerspace. We observed resources for hardware hacking such as soldering irons, laptops, and what one member called a "documentation station," a tripod-mounted webcam with a microscope and light positioned over an electronics workbench for digitally capturing and sharing video of microelectronics tinkering. Analogue tools sat next to these devices. For instance, during workshops in Seattle Attic we saw knitting and crocheting tools, a variety of looms, button making supplies, a 19th century, industrial sewing machine, and associated restoration materials. Such juxtapositions call into question the kinds of activity identified as 'technology' in line with common definitions of do-it-yourself culture that contest mainstream technology development. Through material and discursive engagement, members of these spaces contest widely understood forms of hacking and technology development.

WORKSHOPS

During the first several months of research, our focus was on observational study of feminist hackerspaces in Seattle (Seattle Attic) and Portland (Flux). In preparation for a field visit to Double Union in San Francisco, one of the co-founders asked us to facilitate a design workshop in the space. In moving beyond a purely observational position, into one that might be more interventionist, we took the workshop event as an opportunity to speculate on the types of things that might inform and generate ideas for the participating members. We were particularly interested in a design agenda that could extend members' personal and collective concerns, recognizing their organization of the space as a productive act, enacting particular values and ideas in relation to a broader technology cultures. Our workshops used these concerns to investigate the shape and character of a feminist approach to design. Central in this project was an infrastruturing of design decisions: recognizing how inverting our perspective — highlighting the sociotechnical assemblages underlining our design projects — could offer possibilities for rethinking technology design.

Seeing the development of these spaces as instances of feminist activist work, we invited members to continue their intervention by interrogating other spaces they move through and tools they use regularly. For the first workshop, we built on Dunne and Raby's speculative approach by asking members to interpret values embedded in the built environment with an eye toward design potentials that might exist in the future or an alternative present [2]. Members individually engaged in a weeklong photo elicitation exercise prior to the meeting, which became the basis for the workshop's main activity of producing low-fidelity design proposals. In a later workshop, held at Seattle Attic, we asked both members and guests to consider how the infrastructure of their daily lives might have been designed with certain values in mind [1].

In each of the workshops, participating members and guests were asked to break out into groups of two or three to re-design a space or tool they found problematic in someway. In the first workshop, with space as the focus, members examined a corporate technology office, a shared kitchen in a cooperative house, a BART transit station, and Danielle Steele's mansion. In the second workshop, members and guests elected to reimagine Soylent (the food replacement startup), an accessible crosswalk, paywalls (mechanisms preventing users from accessing certain information without paying a fee), "dick pics" on Tinder, and a signup survey for a local bike sharing service.

Through these workshops, we saw that when design becomes part of emphasizing a feminist encounter with technology, it must confront the variety of feminisms at play. Entanglements of feminisms and design processes in practice transformed people's ways of knowing and enacting their views. They revealed feminism and design as co-constitutive: transforming one another through their interaction.

CONCLUSION

In focusing on feminist forms of collaborative work in hackerspaces, this paper follows a renewed interest in the role feminist epistemologies and methods might play in research on social and collaborative systems. Stemming from the field of Science and Technology studies, a somewhat radical body of feminist scholarship has engaged with design and technology development through the lens of new materialism [5]. This work offers a critique of conventional technology and gender studies in which scholars treat technology as 'open to interpretation' but gender as stable. For example, Joanna Sefyrin explored the practices behind accounts of IT development, suggesting that women get systematically excluded from these accounts. By following women participating in an IT design project in a Swedish government agency, Sefyrin shows how the substantive contributions women make go unacknowledged. She notes, "[…] the question of whether women can be considered insiders or outsiders of IT design also has to do with how 'IT design' is defined" [5]. Perhaps one can see how questions like this start to complicate the story of 'access' as a means for 'getting more women into technology.' Much like this work, investigating the mutual-construction of gender and technology as an intervention into social studies of IT, I offer analysis of feminist hackerspaces as interventions into design and development methods.

REFERENCES

1. Bowker, G.C. and Star, S.L. *Sorting Things Out: Classification and Its Consequences*. The MIT Press, Cambridge, Mass., 2000.
2. Dunne, A. and Raby, F. *Speculative Everything: Design, Fiction, and Social Dreaming*. The MIT Press, Cambridge, Massachusetts ; London, 2013.
3. Fox, S., Ulgado, R.R., and Rosner, D. Hacking Culture, Not Devices: Access and Recognition in Feminist Hackerspaces. *Proceedings of the ACM 2015 conference on Computer Supported Cooperative Work* (2015).
4. Hendry, L. The Rise of Feminist Hackerspaces and How to Make Your Own. *Model View Culture*, 2014. https://modelviewculture.com/pieces/the-rise-of-feminist-hackerspaces-and-how-to-make-your-own.
5. Sefyrin, J. Entanglements of Participation, Gender, Power and Knowledge in IT Design. *Proceedings of the 11th Biennial Participatory Design Conference*, ACM (2010), 111–120.
6. Toupin, S. Feminist Hackerspaces as Safer Spaces? *dpi*, 27 (2013).
7. Toupin, S. Feminist Hackerspaces: The Synthesis of Feminist and Hacker Cultures » Journal of Peer Production. *Journal of Peer Production*, 5 (2014).

Visualizing Computer Activity to Support the Resumption of Long-term Creative Work

Adam Rule
Design Lab, UC San Diego
9500 Gilman Drive, La Jolla, CA 92093
acrule@ucsd.edu

ABSTRACT

Creative projects can span weeks, months, or even years. Working on these timescales can be difficult due to the need to restore context — a task's physical, digital, and mental resources — after each break. Prior research on using computers to restore context has focused on *digital context*, reopening collections of documents or visualizing interactions with a single program. My research explores how visualizing system-wide activity can help people restore the *mental context* of creative work.

Author Keywords

cues; context reinstatement; distributed cognition; information visualization

INTRODUCTION

Creative projects are rarely finished in one sitting but routinely span weeks, months, or even years. Resuming these activities after a break can be difficult due to a loss of context: those physical, digital, and mental resources needed to complete a task. Today, much creative work is mediated by computers and researchers have naturally looked in their direction for help with context reinstatement. One approach has been to restore collections of programs and files to their previous arrangement on one's screen [1, 8]. While restoring this type of context is helpful, it does not guarantee the restoration of the thoughts that guide and motivate creative work.

This is partly because mental context is an evolving collection of ephemeral thoughts. While this evolution leaves some traces on artifacts, it is more clearly seen in the actions that produce them. In this vein, tools like Chronicle and YouPivot have made it easier to review how an application or document was used over time [4, 5]. However, these tools cannot visualize activities that span multiple applications and are optimized for finding documents and commands rather than cueing memory.

C&C '15, June 22-25, 2015, Glasgow, United Kingdom
ACM 978-1-4503-3598-0/15/06.
http://dx.doi.org/10.1145/2757226.2764772

People have extremely detailed visual memory [2] and viewing screen recordings of past work helps them remember off-screen details such as constraints or the presence of coworkers in their office [3]. The associative nature of memory makes this possible; seeing an image that one has seen before makes memories associated with that image easier to retrieve. While abstract summaries and timelines support searching, they are not the most effective cues of mental context because they were not visible when that context was formed.

My research explores how visualizing computer-mediated work can help people restore the mental context of creative activities. Specifically it seeks to:

1. Describe context reinstatement as a distributed cognitive process

2. Evaluate various cues for recalling mental context

3. Build tools that help creative practitioners restore mental context

MENTAL CONTEXT AS DISTRIBUTED COGNITION

Cognition is not limited to the brain but is a process of coordinating mental activity with external resources, such as physical artifacts and other people, over time [6]. Due to human's associative memory, viewing interactions with digital artifacts helps them recall what they were thinking at the time of the interaction. Our first study asked which interactions and static screen elements cue which types of memory. In the study, students watched week-old screen recordings of their own computer work and described what they were doing at the time of recording. These auto-confrontation interviews revealed that: 1) people draw mental context from a wide range of on-screen cues including text, images, window movement, and mouse activity, 2) these cues prompt recall of motivations and strategies, not just the name of the activity, and 3) people rely on a combination of cues *and* self-knowledge to reconstruct context, rather than reading it directly from the cues. These results support the notion that context reinstatement is a distributed cognitive process aided by viewing work as it unfolds over time.

To observe context reinstatement in the wild, we are currently having creative practitioners record their computer work for two weeks. In interviews after each week of recording, participants walk through moments when they were restarting long-term projects. We have collected data from eight web developers and are currently recruiting writers and visual artists.

Our results are preliminary but suggest that: 1) dependencies between project components, deadlines, and constraints are commonly sought aspects of context, 2) context of different granularity is intentionally externalized onto different artifacts such as scratch pads, todo lists, and whiteboards, and 3) context is not always intentionally sought out but is often cued by stumbling upon an artifact, like and email, and then elaborated with details from internal memory. These results suggests that context reinstatement involves an ecosystem of physical, digital, and mental resources that are opportunistically assembled.

FINDING THE MOST EFFECTIVE CUES

While visual cues drawn from screen recordings help people restore mental context, the question remains of which cues are most effective. Prior research has found that people recognize websites from small thumbnail images [7] and remember elaborate details about prior work while watching screen recordings [3]. Rather than study the recognition of well defined pages or use videos to cue memory, we asked if static thumbnails or short animations could cue elaborate memories of ill-defined activities such as writing or data analysis. We had six graduate students record their work for two weeks. After each week, we showed them static or animated thumbnails of their computer activity that week and asked them to describe as much as they could remember about the recorded moment. Comparing several types of thumbnails we found that 1) static images cue more accurate memories than short animations, and 2) thumbnails showing a small area around a user's mouse cued as elaborate of memories as thumbnails showing the entire desktop (though these snippet thumbnails had to be large enough for text to be legible). These results suggest that showing less may actually prompt more elaborate and accurate recall of mental context.

BUILDING USABLE TOOLS

While reviewing static images of computer activity may help restore mental context, a number of design decisions need to be made before implementing a robust tool for recording and reviewing creative activity. Figure 1 shows an early interactive visualization we developed that lets users see various representations of their activity on a timeline and in the frame of their desktop. We are still in the early stages of tool building and are exploring questions such as: What privacy concerns do people have with tracking their creative activity? How might users unobtrusively annotate their activity as they are working to assist with context reinstatement? Should visualizations be organized around time, documents, high level activities, or some other unit? We plan to answer these questions through contextual inqueries and iterative prototyping.

CONCLUSION

My research demonstrates the value of reviewing screen recordings for restoring the mental context of computer-mediated work. Using associative memory and salient cues, people are able to reconstruct thoughts they had while previously working. My thesis will further explore which representations of computer activity prompt robust recall and explore the social and design factors that may hamper or promote the recording, reviewing, and sharing of creative work.

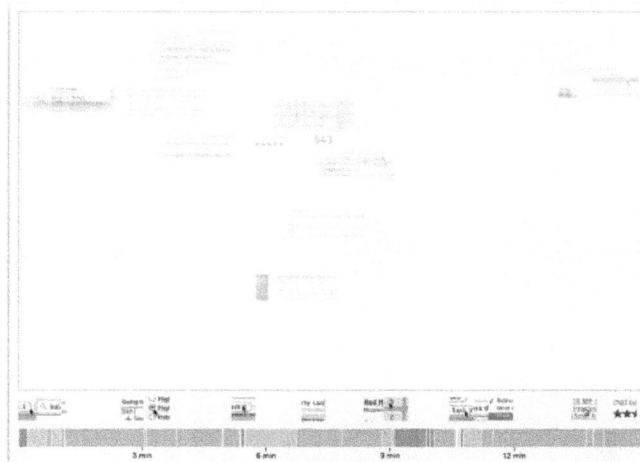

Figure 1. One activity visualization prototype showing snippets of screenshots along a timeline and arrayed in the frame of a "desktop"

ACKNOWLEDGMENTS
I would like to thank my advisor Jim Hollan, co-advisor Aurélien Tabard, and collaborators Jonas Kemper and Karen Boyd. This research was funded by NSF grant #1319829.

REFERENCES

1. Bardram, J., Bunde-Pedersen, J., and Soegaard, M. Support for activity-based computing in a personal computing operating system. In *Proceedings of the SIGCHI conference on Human Factors in computing systems*, 211–220.

2. Brady, T. F., Konkle, T., Alvarez, G. A., and Oliva, A. Visual long-term memory has a massive storage capacity for object details. 14325–14329.

3. Cangiano, G. R., and Hollan, J. D. Capturing and restoring the context of everyday work: A case study at a law office. In *Human Centered Design*. Springer, 945–954.

4. Grossman, T., Matejka, J., and Fitzmaurice, G. Chronicle: capture, exploration, and playback of document workflow histories. In *Proceedings of the 23nd annual ACM symposium on User interface software and technology*, 143–152.

5. Hailpern, J., Jitkoff, N., Warr, A., Karahalios, K., Sesek, R., and Shkrob, N. YouPivot: improving recall with contextual search. In *Proceedings of the SIGCHI Conference on Human Factors in Computing Systems*, 1521–1530.

6. Hutchins, E. *Cognition in the wild*. MIT Press.

7. Kaasten, S., Greenberg, S., and Edwards, C. How people recognise previously seen web pages from titles, URLs and thumbnails. In *People and Computers XVI-Memorable Yet Invisible*. Springer, 247–265.

8. Rattenbury, T., and Canny, J. CAAD: an automatic task support system. In *Proceedings of the SIGCHI conference on Human factors in computing systems*, 687–696.

An Enactive Approach to Facilitate Interactive Machine Learning for Co-Creative Agents

Nicholas Davis
Georgia Institute of Technology
ndavis35@gatech.edu

ABSTRACT

This paper introduces a novel approach to developing co-creative agents that collaborate in real time creative contexts, such as art and pretend play. Our approach builds upon recent work in computational creativity called interactive machine learning (IML). In IML, agents learn through demonstration, interaction, and real time feedback from a human user (as opposed to offline training). To apply IML to open-ended creative collaboration, we developed an enactive model of creativity (EMC) based upon the cognitive science theories of enaction. This paper introduces our enactive approach to building co-creative agents within the broader field of interactive machine learning by describing the theory, design, and initial prototypes of two co-creative agents.

Author Keywords

Computational Creativity, Creativity Support Tools, Collaboration, Cognitive Science, Human Computation

ACM Classification Keywords

H.5.m. Information interfaces and presentation (e.g., HCI): Miscellaneous.

INTRODUCTION

The field of computational creativity can broadly be categorized into three domains: (1) *Creativity support tools* (CSTs) that enhance the creative product, such as Photoshop; (2) *Generative computational creativity* systems that autonomously produce creative artifacts, such as The Painting Fool [1]; and (3) *Computer colleagues* that collaborate with human users as a partner in the creative process [5]. Computer colleagues blend the first and second methods of computational creativity identified above to support the creative process through direct collaboration.

Collaborative creativity research points to significant benefits of collaboration for the creative process, such as inspiration, increased motivation, and synthesis of ideas [6]. Real time improvisation presents a unique collaboration context due to the continuous and varied feedback offered

by different styles of turn taking and shared contribution. However, developing an agent that can interact effectively in open-ended creative applications is difficult due to the computational complexity of knowledge engineering and real-time adaptation.

While there are many approaches of developing co-creative agents, we selected the cognitive science paradigm of enaction that emphasizes how meaning gradually emerges through dynamic interactions and negotiations in a process referred to as sense-making. To formalize the theory, we developed the enactive model of creativity (EMC) that begins to apply this framework to model how agents dynamically co-construct meaning by using feedback to coordinate real time interactions [2]. Before we introduce our co-creative prototypes, Drawing Apprentice and PlayPartner, we will briefly introduce the field of interactive machine learning and delineate the proposed contribution of our enactive approach.

CREATIVE ARTIFICIAL INTELLIGENCE

The field of artificial intelligence and robotics still face a large unsolved problem: AI does not perform well in open-ended situations that required flexible adaptation [3]. The knowledge engineering requirements are too large. This problem is particularly relevant for computational creativity because collaborative creativity is perhaps the most open-ended domain possible.

The field of interactive machine learning attempts to mitigate this knowledge engineering bottleneck by creating agents that interact with human users and learn through demonstration, imitation, and feedback [4]. The approach advocated here extends the work being done on interactive machine learning by introducing EMC to enhance the design of interaction dynamics and feedback. Once we have a reliable method to model these features of interaction, we can potentially increase the efficiency of the interactive machine learning algorithms and increase the flexibility and robustness of co-creative agents interacting in unpredictable and open-ended creative contexts.

CO-CREATIVE ENACTIVE AGENTS

The goal of an enactive agent is to facilitate successful and compelling interaction in a real time context. This evaluation metric distinguishes our enactive approach from other IML approaches that employ interactions primarily as a method to increase the computational efficiency of the learning algorithms. The evaluation metrics for a successful co-creative agent are defined by a subjective evaluation from the user. Ideally, the human should perceive the agents as having a certain degree of competency and understanding of the creative collaboration. However, an enactive agent is not necessarily expected to 'understand' the meaning of its actions from a human perspective, i.e. the user's knowledge and the agent's knowledge are grounded in different experiences.

For the enactive agent, its knowledge of the world comes from its own set of experiences, which are strictly constrained to the input of the user, including demonstrations, interactions, and feedback. Thus, when the agent performs the appropriate action and appears to be 'creative' or 'intelligent' from the perspective of the user, the agent does not have the same type of knowledge representation as the user. Since enactive agents learn exclusively through experience, the approach advocated here includes pairing a human user with an enactive agent in a collaborative game to increase user engagement, acquire more users, and ultimately increase the creativity of the agent through human computation. Next, we describe two prototype systems employing an enactive approach to interactive machine learning.

SYSTEM DESCRIPTIONS

Drawing Apprentice is a co-creative drawing agent that collaborates with human users in real time abstract art collaboration. It learns through decomposing the user's lines, analyzing their styles, and learning the user's preferences based on the real-time interaction data. User feedback on successive interactions, such as 'liking' or 'disliking' the agent's reactions, help the agent hone its model to a level of detail and granularity appropriate for the current interaction. Since creative intentions dynamically grow and transform throughout the course of an artwork, the system's model of the user evolves dynamically throughout the course of collaboration. The Drawing Apprentice system is implemented on a web-based application shown in Figure 1.

PlayPartner is a co-creative pretend play agent that is able to dynamically define, modify, and generate actions based upon a co-constructed core activity. The system is meant to inspire, enhance and teach playful behavior to children. Similar to Drawing Apprentice, the PlayPartner employs the EMC to engage users in a process of participatory sense-making. The interactive machine learning algorithms in this system rely solely on perceptual information from the users performed actions in continuous real time interaction. The system is implemented in a virtual environment where players demonstrate play activities and interact with the system to refine and validate its knowledge.

CONCLUSIONS

This paper introduced an enactive approach to interactive machine learning. We describe two co-creative agents developed with our enactive model of creativity. This model formalizes the ideas of participatory sense-making

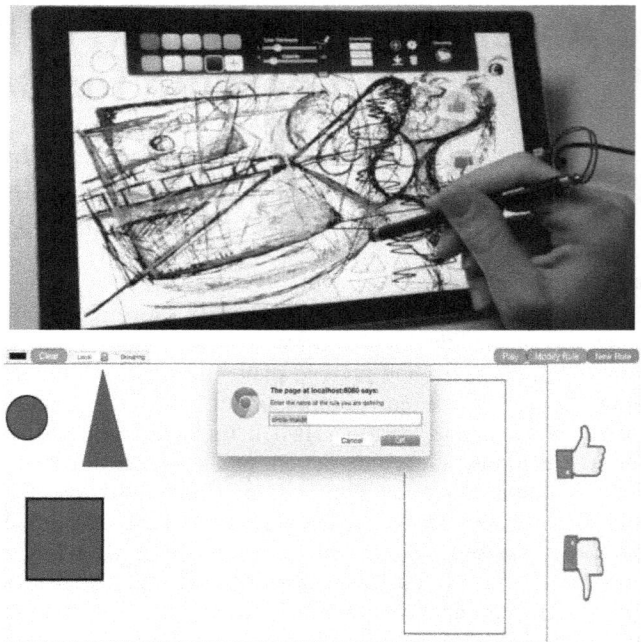

Figure 1: Top: Drawing Apprentice web application. Bottom: PlayPartner user interface.

in the recent cognitive science theory of enaction. Leveraging human users as a teacher and the system as a learner in these creative contexts reduces the overhead of authoring content for co-creative agent significantly. After explaining our novel approach to IML in the broader context of the field, we describe two co-creative prototype systems in the domain of collaborative drawing and pretend play.

REFERENCES

1. Colton, S., Wiggins, G.A., and others.Computational creativity: The final frontier? *ECAI*, (2012), 21–26.
2. Davis, N.M., Hsiao, C.-P., Popova, Y., and Magerko, B. An Enactive Model of Creativity for Computational Collaboration and Co-creation. In N. Zagalo and P. Branco, eds., *Creativity in Digital Age*. Springer-Verlag, London, 2015, 109–133.
3. Froese, T. and Ziemke, T.Enactive artificial intelligence: Investigating the systemic organization of life and mind. *Artificial Intelligence 173*, 3 (2009), 466–500.
4. Gillies, M., Kleinsmith, A., and Brenton, H.Applying the CASSM Framework to Improving End User Debugging of Interactive Machine Learning. *Proceedings of the 20th International Conference on Intelligent User Interfaces*, (2015), 181–185.
5. Lubart, T.How can computers be partners in the creative process: Classification and commentary on the Special Issue. *International Journal of Human-Computer Studies 63*, 4-5 (2005), 365–369.
6. Sawyer, R.K.Improvisational Cultures: Collaborative Emergence and Creativity in Improvisation. *Mind, Culture, and Activity 7*, 3 (2000), 180–185.

Leveraging Online Communities for Novice Designers

Julie Hui
Segal Design Institute
Northwestern University
Evanston, IL
juliehui@u.northwestern.edu

ABSTRACT

While universities teach students how to build new products, few students choose to further implement their work due to limited resources and mentorship. Theories of learning and innovation describe the importance of working in a social context to acquire resources from peers. While HCI researchers have built recommender and expert routing systems to identify help givers, novice designers still fail to contact expert peers for various psychological reasons, such as fear of contacting someone older or more experienced. By designing online tools and platforms that encourage and scaffold that act of help-seeking, we can connect more designers with informal mentors who can help them improve and implement their work as a professional product. The goal of my dissertation is to support help-seeking among novice designers by 1) developing an emergent model of help-seeking behavior in the context of crowdfunding, and building a tool that 2) recommends potential help-givers from one's social network and 3) presents their information in a way that encourages reaching out for advice.

Author Keywords

Crowdfunding; Help-seeking; Novice designers; Entrepreneurship; Mentorship.

ACM Classification Keywords

H.5.3. [Group and Organizational Interphases]: Design

INTRODUCTION

While novice designers have begun to seek resources through online communities, such as crowdfunding [2,8,9] and social media platforms [7], these practices are fairly nascent and not well supported. *I propose that designing online communities that promote help-seeking will encourage more novice designers to seek relevant knowledge, skills, and dispositions from experienced peers.* Help-seeking is considered a short in-depth transaction, such as a

C&C '15, June 22-25, 2015, Glasgow, United Kingdom
ACM 978-1-4503-3598-0/15/06.
http://dx.doi.org/10.1145/2757226.2764774

video call or series of email conversations, to learn how to perform a single or small group of tasks [1], such as figuring out what material is best for a certain product design or how to connect and converse with an overseas manufacturer. Help-seeking is more time consuming than generic social media Q&A, such as asking on Facebook, "What restaurants are good in Chicago?", but less time consuming than formal mentorship, which typically requires repeated lengthy one-on-one sessions over many months or years.

While much research has been performed on identifying experts and question answerers on social networking platforms and Q&A sites [5,11], few have focused on the practice of help-seeking and the help-seeker perspective, particularly in the design context. We argue that even if an ideal help-seeker/helper pairing is produced, information is not exchanged if the help-seeker does not make contact as the help-seeker typically initiates contact in a professional setting. By understanding how, why, and from whom novice designers are comfortable seeking help, we can build tools that support more help-seeking transactions that help novice designers further improve and implement their work.

CROWDFUNDING AS A SUPPORT TOOL FOR DESIGN WORK

My research seeks to understand and design tools that support the day-to-day responsibilities and psychological experience of designers using online communities to create and implement new products. My previous work provides an empirical understanding of how the social and public nature of crowdfunding, online platforms that allow people to seek funding from the crowd often in exchange for a reward [2], has changed the work of professional creatives. For instance, we find that designers and other creative professionals are motivated to crowdfund to expand awareness of their work and form connections with like-minded others [2,8], build entrepreneurial self-efficacy by receiving public validation [4], and acquire professional skills by communicating with a wider range of people [6,9].

Through these studies, we identified the emergent practice of how designers communicate with and observe peer crowdfunders to learn new skills. Initial findings suggest that *direct communication* follows a help-seeking process [1] where crowdfunding designers determine that they need help, identify someone who can provide help, then reach out with a request, such as through email or a crowdfunding platform message. Through *indirect communication*, designers observe online artifacts of others' work, such as studying written project descriptions of successful crowdfunders. Transferred skill knowledge includes skills to create the campaign material, such as videography, skills to publicize one's work, such as how to use social media effectively, and skills to follow through with project goals, such as identifying reliable manufacturers. The sharing of knowledge between crowdfunders sets the basis of my dissertation work, which is to further understand and create tools that support help-seeking among novice designers.

ONLINE HELP-SEEKING FOR NOVICE DESIGNERS
I plan to continue this research by 1) developing an emergent model of help-seeking for novice designers who use crowdfunding, 2) identifying and ranking help-giver attributes that encourage help-seeking, and 3) using those attributes to design and test a help-giver system.

I have begun to build an emergent model of help-seeking for novice designers who use crowdfunding to carry out their work. I plan to interview 45 more designers who launched projects on crowdfunding platforms about how they perform help-seeking. Data will be analyzed following structured qualitative analysis [12] to identify codes inspired by Nelson-Le Gall's original help-seeking model [1]. In addition, I will also inquire which technologies were used throughout their help-seeking process to identify opportunities for design interventions.

I will then rank help-giver attributes novice designers consider when deciding whether to initiate contact. For instance, when do novice designers rank homophily attributes, such as similar age and same gender, over skill attributes, such as years of professional product design experience? I will perform a factorial design [3] to test which attributes are more important than others when choosing a help giver, and whether different types of people tend to prefer certain attributes over others. I will then use these attributes to create a system that ranks and presents potential help givers from one's extended social network. An initial version of this system will be deployed in Northwestern's entrepreneurial design courses. The system will be evaluated through interviews and surveys by comparing help seeking practices between students who were and were not introduced to the tool.

THEORETICAL AND PRACTICAL CONTRIBUTIONS
I contribute to literature on design work and designing online communities. We know little about the mechanisms by which novice designers build connections with informal mentors. Understanding how novice designers seek help online and why they choose certain people will help educators create instruction that caters to novice motivations. Furthermore, because the growth and health of online communities rely on people forming new connections [10], expert recommender systems should also take into consideration features associated with help-seeker willingness to reach out for help.

CONCLUSION
Online help-seeking among novice designers represents only one of many ways people have begun to leverage social technologies to access the vast amount of resources available in online communities and social networks. My previous and continuing work aims to build a rich understanding of how novice designers seek help from informal mentors through online communities in order to develop tools that supports this behavior.

REFERENCES
1. Gall, S.N.-L. Help-seeking behavior in learning. *Review of research in education*, (1985), 55–90.
2. Gerber, E.M. and Hui, J. Crowdfunding: Motivations and Deterrents for Participation. *ACM Transactions on Computer-Human Interaction 20*, 6 (2013), 34:1–34:32.
3. Gergle, D. and Tan, D. Experimental Research in HCI. In J. Olson and W. Kellogg, eds., *Ways of Knowing in HCI*. Springer, New York, 2014.
4. Harburg, E., Hui, J., Greenberg, M., and Gerber, E. The Effects of Crowdfunding on Entrepreneurial Self-Efficacy. *Proc. of the Conference on Computer Supported Cooperative Work and Social Computing*, ACM (2015).
5. Horowitz, D. and Kamvar, S.D. The anatomy of a large-scale social search engine. *Proc. of the International World Wide Web Conference*, ACM (2010), 431–440.
6. Hui, J. and Gerber, E. Crowdfunding Science: Sharing Research With An Extended Audience. *Proc. of the Conference on Computer Supported Cooperative Work and Social Computing*, ACM (2015).
7. Hui, J., Gerber, E., and Dow, S. Crowd-Based Design Activities: Helping Student Connect with Users Online. *Proc. of the Conference on Designing Interactive Systems 2014*, ACM.
8. Hui, J., Gerber, E., and Gergle, D. Understanding and Leveraging Social Networks for Crowdfunding: Opportunities and Challenges. *Proc. of the Conference on Designing Interactive Systems*, ACM (2014), 677–680.
9. Hui, J.S., Greenberg, M.D., and Gerber, E.M. Understanding the Role of Community in Crowdfunding Work. *Proc. of the Conference on Computer Supported Cooperative Work and Social Computing*, ACM (2014), 62–74.
10. Kraut, R.E. and Resnick, P. *Building Successful Online Communities*. The MIT Press, 2012.
11. McDonald, D.W. and Ackerman, M.S. Expertise recommender: a flexible recommendation system and architecture. *Proc. of the Conference on Computer Supported Cooperative Work*, ACM (2000), 231–240.
12. Miles, M.B. and Huberman, A.M. *Qualitative Data Analysis*. Sage Publications, Thousand Oaks, CA, 1994.

Designing Crowdsourcing Techniques Based on Expert Creative Practice

Joy Kim
Stanford University HCI Group
jojo0808@stanford.edu

ABSTRACT
Current crowdsourcing workflows comprise of discrete tasks that guide the crowd towards predetermined goals. However, this approach is ill-suited towards supporting massively collaborative open-ended creative work, which often involves an exploration of possible end results and revision of creative goals. My dissertation explores how existing expert creative practice can inform new crowdsourcing techniques that allow the crowd to collaborate on complex creative tasks such as writing short stories.

INTRODUCTION
Creative collaboration on the web can draw together diverse viewpoints to support goals such as songwriting, animation and remixing. Furthermore, crowdsourcing platforms such as Amazon Mechanical Turk have made it possible for hundreds of people to collaborate at massive scale on complex activities such as captioning classroom lectures in real-time [7] or singing a note-by-note re-interpretation of the song *Daisy Bell* [6].

However, many crowdsourcing workflows today consist of a highly structured series of small tasks that lead towards a predetermined goal [5]. This works well when enforcing a specific standard of quality for contributed work or producing something rapidly at scale, but inherently limits the scope of contributions workers can make. In the Daisy Bell project, for example, workers sang individual notes for a song, but did not help design the overall structure of the project. Similarly, the role of the crowd in supporting creative work has often been to give feedback [9, 11] rather than engage in direct collaboration. These projects end up complete, but are only as good as the original creator's individual vision; because of these workflows are designed with a particular output in mind, the quality of the end result relies heavily on the way a single project designer incorporates crowd contributed work.

In contrast, experts engaging in open-ended creative work iteratively explore possible outcomes and constantly revise creative goals. The creative processes that expert creators already use are an untapped source of reliable creative strategies that may help us understand how the crowd could also achieve complex creative projects. We know, for example, that experts reflect during practice [10], split creative responsibility when working collaboratively [2], make use of past well-worn approaches through patterns [1], and continually create and revise constraints to develop purpose for their work [3]. Rather than focusing on generating expert-level *outcomes*, designing strategies for enabling the crowd to follow an expert-like *process* may enable them to coordinate with more freedom and generate higher quality work.

My research focuses on adapting expert creative practice into social computing and crowdsourcing environments. Specifically, I re-imagine the strategies that experts use to collaborate with others, develop ideas, and reflect on their work to create new crowdsourcing techniques that enable the web to collaborate at scale on complex creative goals. Such techniques may allow the crowd to create and revise their own creative objectives and inform the design of tools that favor a thoughtful and reflective creative process over attractive but trivial shortcuts.

ENSEMBLE: CREATIVE STRENGTHS OF THE CROWD
Many successful storytelling collaborations already separate creative leadership from more general participation [8]. In Ensemble [4], we reflected this practice by structuring collaborative roles around the complementary creative strengths of the crowd and a creative expert. Ensemble is an online collaborative story-writing platform based on an approach where a leader directs the high-level vision for a story and articulates creative constraints for the crowd. Using this platform, we ran a month-long short story competition where over one hundred volunteer users on the web started over fifty short stories.

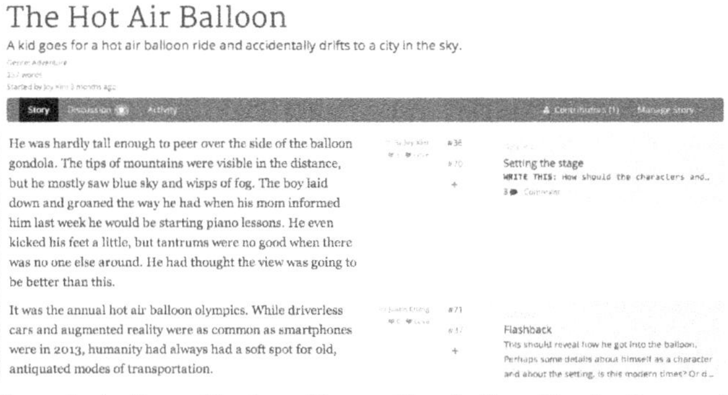

Figure 1. An Ensemble story. The working draft, written by the crowd (left), reflects the outline structure provided by the story leader (right).

C&C 2015, June 22–25, 2015, Glasgow, United Kingdom.

http://dx.doi.org/10.1145/2757226.2764775

We found that leaders used the platform to direct collaborator work by establishing creative goals, and collaborators contributed meaningful, high-level ideas to stories through specific suggestions. This work suggested that asymmetric creative contributions may support a broad new class of creative collaborations, and pointed towards the broader idea of using existing expert practice to inform the design of creative crowdsourcing workflows.

MECHANICAL NOVEL: EVOLVING CREATIVE VIEWS

While the crowd was able to make meaningful contributions to short stories through Ensemble, their influence relied on individual leaders that evaluate and merge these contributions. Rather than splitting the responsibilities of low-level work and high-level structure between the crowd and a leader, how could we allow the crowd to influence the direction of their own work?

To explore this idea, we developed Mechanical Novel, an online crowdsourcing platform built on top of Amazon Mechanical Turk that guides the crowd through the process of developing a short story idea into written text. Past work has shown that allowing the crowd to iterate on its own work results in higher quality contributions [12]; we extend this idea by introducing *flip-flopping*, where workers alternately iterate on 1) low-level contributions based on the high-level structure so far, and on 2) high-level structure based on ideas being explored in low-level contributions. Preliminary results suggest that this provides workers with the opportunity to challenge the constraints of a complex creative project as they work.

ART+FAILURE: SUPPORTING PROCESS, NOT OUTCOME

Although experiencing failure is an important part of the creative process, creative tools today strive to amplify our ability to output high-quality work by helping us avoid mistakes. While experts have developed strategies for learning from missteps, novices lack the experience and mindset needed to use failures as opportunities for growth, and may find themselves intimidated by tools that are designed around showcasing success. To better support experiences of failure for novices, we instead propose inverting the value of failure in creativity tools in order to encourage novices to actively pursue experimentation and risks. For example, an online community where people post work they do not like or did not finish could help novices practice failure through social motivation to reflect on their efforts. Another tool might expose a creative process with a focus on failure; rather than producing a step-by-step guide for how to do something well, artists could collaborate on a step-by-step guide documenting their unsuccessful attempts at a new technique. We are currently designing and iterating on such online communities. Focusing on what we can learn from failure, rather than fixating on how to achieve success, may change how we approach creative work.

CONCLUSION

My dissertation research connects understandings of expert creative processes with social computing and crowdsourcing systems. First, this research will contribute practical techniques for crowd-supported creative work. Because we are designing for a massive number of non-experts working towards a common creative goal, these techniques may grant new insight into how to support massive online collaborative work in general. Second, this work explores the implications of designing creativity support tools to help the crowd emulate expert *process* rather than expert *results*. The crowd may be able to create high-quality output while maintaining creative independence. But how will attribution work? Can we compare the success of crowdsourced creation with that of traditional processes? In addition to contributing a new method of approaching creative work, this thesis will also open avenues for wrestling with the questions that come with a new creative form.

REFERENCES

1. Alexander, C., Ishikawa, S., and Silverstein, M. Pattern languages. *Center for Environmental Structure 2* (1977).

2. Collins, S. Who really runs things, November 2007. `http://articles.latimes.com/2007/nov/23/entertainment/et-channel23`.

3. Flower, L., and Hayes, J. R. A cognitive process theory of writing. *College composition and communication* (1981), 365–387.

4. Kim, J., Cheng, J., and Bernstein, M. S. Ensemble: Exploring complementary strengths of leaders and crowds in creative collaboration. In *Proc. CSCW*, ACM (New York, NY, USA, 2014), 745–755.

5. Kittur, A., Smus, B., Khamkar, S., and Kraut, R. E. Crowdforge: Crowdsourcing complex work. In *Proc. UIST*, ACM (New York, NY, USA, 2011), 43–52.

6. Koblin, A., and Massey, D. Bicycle built for 2000, 2009. `http://www.bicyclebuiltfortwothousand.com/`.

7. Lasecki, W., Miller, C., Sadilek, A., Abumoussa, A., Borrello, D., Kushalnagar, R., and Bigham, J. Real-time captioning by groups of non-experts. In *Proceedings of the 25th Annual ACM Symposium on User Interface Software and Technology*, UIST '12, ACM (New York, NY, USA, 2012), 23–34.

8. Luther, K., and Bruckman, A. Leadership in online creative collaboration. In *Proc. CSCW*, ACM (New York, NY, USA, 2008), 343–352.

9. Luther, K., Pavel, A., Wu, W., Tolentino, J.-l., Agrawala, M., Hartmann, B., and Dow, S. P. Crowdcrit: Crowdsourcing and aggregating visual design critique. In *Proc. CSCW Companion*, ACM (New York, NY, USA, 2014), 21–24.

10. Schön, D. A. The reflective practioner. *London: Temple Smith* (1983).

11. Xu, A., Huang, S.-W., and Bailey, B. Voyant: Generating structured feedback on visual designs using a crowd of non-experts. In *Proc. CSCW*, ACM (New York, NY, USA, 2014), 1433–1444.

12. Yu, L., and Nickerson, J. V. Cooks or cobblers?: Crowd creativity through combination. In *Proc. CHI*, ACM (New York, NY, USA, 2011), 1393–1402.

Glitching

Beverley Hood

School of Design, Edinburgh College of Art,
University of Edinburgh
Lauriston Place, Edinburgh
b.hood@ed.ac.uk

ABSTRACT

Glitching is a digital installation and performance project led by artist Beverley Hood, that attempts to re-describe the movement derived from characters in contemporary sports and action computer games. Based on the premise of home entertainment dance and fitness training games, it uses the motion-sensor controller, Microsoft Kinect, and large-screen display to create a digital installation for the public to interact with. The exhibition visitor is invited to step into the digital shoes of the 'lead dancer', and attempt to follow the awkward and intricate, glitch choreography performed by the dancing troupe on screen.

Author Keywords

Glitch, art, installation, performance, digital, kinect, technology, design, interactive

INTRODUCTION

Glitching is an interactive installation and performance project inspired by malfunctions in movement, or glitches, derived from characters in contemporary sports and action computer games. Glitching uses Microsoft Xbox Kinect, a pseudo game interface and large-screen display, to create a full-body, skeletally controlled, interactive experience.

There are two versions of the Glitching project: an interactive installation, presented within galleries, symposiums and festivals; and a live performance, presented within theatrical venues, which uses the interactive installation as reference and backdrop, and features the dancers Tony Mills, Hannah Seignior and Felicity Beveridge. For ACM Creativity & Cognition 2015, I am proposing to present the interactive installation.

As the gaming world grows ever more sophisticated and ubiquitous, the movements of digital characters become more and more 'realistic' and convincing, thanks to

constant improvements in software and hardware. Often derived from the real (using motion capture and body scanning of professional sports players for example), gaming characters of the 21st century have an extraordinary embodiment, fluidity of movement and naturalness. However, there are always imperfections, glitches and divergences, and it is these disruptions that I am interested in. Whether through unexpected programming errors or the users' inability to control the characters in seamless game-play (resulting in bumping into walls, misfiring, etc.) there is still the potential for awkwardness between spells of perfection.

Fig 1. Glitching 2012 Game interface

Glitching focused on the artificial nature of these malfunctions by employing highly trained real bodies to re-stage them, in this case professional dancers including Tony Mills, a world champion Breakdancer with an extraordinary ability to interpret and create fluid, awkward and extreme movements. In Glitching I explore how this physically re-enacted choreography can be embedded and re-imaged within a 'live' digital environment, for an audience to interact with. Using the premise of home entertainment dance and training games (such as Just Dance and Dance Central), Glitching employs the motion-sensor controller, Microsoft Kinect, and large-screen display to create a digital installation for the public to interact with. The exhibition visitor is invited to step into the digital shoes of the 'lead dancer', and attempt to follow the awkward and intricate, glitch choreography performed by the dancing troupe on screen. As the user attempts to follow the digital choreography onscreen, another layer of disturbance occurs, because an encounter with the Kinect is in itself rife with interference, resistance and glitches. Due to skeletal limitations and the (mis)interpretation and unreliability of the data from the sensor, so the users own movements are distorted and transformed.

Glitching explores the potential of a convergent approach to physicality, attempting to construct a new, mixed presence vocabulary. At the same time this is a highly divergent pursuit, both pushing the limits of the human body and reveling in the artificial, alterity, absurdity, and the unstable.

Fig 2. Glitching 2014 Interactive installation

The development was funded by an Artist's Commission, from the Scotland & Medicine partnership, for the exhibition Human Race: inside the history of sports medicine (with additional funding from a Creative Scotland, Visual Artist Award and Edinburgh College of Art). This exhibition was part of the London 2012 Cultural Olympiad's 'The Scottish Project', touring public-funded museums and galleries throughout Scotland during 2012-2013. It was also presented at the ON COLLABORATION II 2013 conference at Middlesex University, London and at the New Technological Art Award 2014 - Update_5, Zebrastraat Museum, Ghent, Belgium.

TECHNICAL AND LOGISTICAL REQUIREMENTS
- PC laptop
- Large flatscreen (e.g. 46 inches)
- Microsoft Kinect
- Kinect power and extension
- Kinect stand
- 'Game Zone' floor vinyl.

N.B Please note all equipment can be provided by the artist except for flat screen and 'Game Zone' floor vinyl.

Using the premise of home entertainment dance and training games, Glitching employs the motion controlled 'Kinect' sensor, PC (windows 7) laptop, large flat-screen display (46" – 50"+) and a 'game zone' floor matt to define players position. The overall exhibition space required is approx. 190cm (approx. height of flat screen) x 370cms (to rear of 'game zone' matt). The image above provides documentation of the work installed. For ACM Creativity & Cognition 2015, I would anticipate wall mounting the flat-screen and Kinect, with the PC laptop ideally being placed out of sight.

The piece has a holding screen (silent), from which the viewer triggers the choreography they can follow, during which plays an audio track. At the end of the 'game' the project reverts to the holding screen and silence. Please note that Glitching works in a variety of lighting conditions but the Kinect sensor is disrupted by direct sunlight and very strong spotlights.

PROJECT DOCUMENTATION
Project Blog - http://glitchchoreography.wordpress.com/
Interface Documentation - http://vimeo.com/99935216
Installation Documentation - https://vimeo.com/114281999

ARTIST'S BIOGRAPHY
Beverley Hood is a media artist, researcher and lecturer. Her research practice over the past 15 years has studied the impact of technology on relationships, the body and human experience, through the creation of practice-based projects and writing.

Beverley studied Sculpture and Electronic Imaging at Duncan of Jordanstone College of Art, Dundee and Nova Scotia College of Art & Design, Halifax, Canada. A longstanding research interest is live performance using technology, participatory media art projects and collaboration. Current projects include Eidolon, a collaboration with the Scottish Clinical Simulation Centre (SCSC), at the Royal Forth Valley Hospital, Larbert, a state-of the-art multi-professional training facility, which undertakes simulation based medical education (SBME). She was Co-Investigator on Moving Targets, a £3 million Scottish Funding Council project (2010-13) bringing together universities, agency, audience and industry and is also a member of the CIRCLE research network (Scottish/UK researchers and practitioners developing collaborative creative environments).

She is also a lecturer and researcher in the School of Design, Edinburgh College of Art, University of Edinburgh. Teaching included postgraduate studio and context courses, undergraduate studio courses and PhD students, across the School of Design.

ACKNOWLEDGMENTS
Thanks go to all the performers, technologists and organisational staff for their contribution to this project. Thanks go to the Scotland & Medicine partnership, Creative Scotland and the University of Edinburgh for their funding and New Media Scotland for their support in kind.

Dreams of Mice

Vicky Isley
boredomresearch
Bournemouth University
Poole, UK
visley@bournemouth.ac.uk

Paul Smith
boredomresearch
Bournemouth University
Poole, UK
psmith@bournemouth.ac.uk

ABSTRACT

Dreams of Mice explores a changed understanding of sleep brought about by networked technologies. A contemporary world of instant messaging and 24/7 connectivity encourages us to remain permanently available. Using computer modeling, recorded neurological data and game engine technology, boredomresearch http://www.boredomresearch.net ask if we can afford to disconnect; questioning the importance of the non-productive third of our lives we spend asleep. Brain activity during sleep reveals that far from downtime, sleep is complex and beautiful. Developed from research exploring the interaction between environmental factors effecting sleep and human neurological disorders - *Dreams of Mice* considers the increased control, management and disruption of sleep behaviours. Collaborating with a neuroscientist at the University of Oxford, capturing and recording the dreams of laboratory mice, boredomresearch have revealed the intriguing beauty of slumber in a real-time artwork driven by the firing neurons of dreaming mice (see Fig.1). When we go to sleep we disconnect from our social networks and perpetual status updates, entering the last remaining sanctuary from the demands of a permanently connected and networked society. But is the space of dreams at risk from the relentless encroachment of connective technologies?

Author Keywords

Sleep; neuroscience; moving image; dreams; mice; game engine technology; data; computer animation; societal issues; sound acoustic; artistic research; computational aesthetics.

SHORT DESCRIPTION

Evocative visual expression of neural activity recorded in a dreaming mouse, rendered in real-time, using a 3D game engine. An art and science collaboration with a visual artist and neuroscientist.

ARTISTIC CONCEPT

As I type this opening paragraph the documents brilliant white background confuses my biological clock. The light from my laptop signals that its time to wake, just before I set off up *'the wooden hills to Bedfordshire'*, interfering with the natural process of sleep. Sleeps relationship with light is just one insight coming from research centred on slumber. Our introduction into sleep research came from Dr Peter Oliver from the Department of Physiology, Anatomy and Genetics of the University of Oxford http://www.dpag.ox.ac.uk/research/oliver-group where he is researching the interaction between sleep disturbance, circadian rhythms and issues of mental health. Oliver showed us sleep data taken from mice both exhibiting normal and abnormal sleep/wake behaviour. The sleep behaviour of healthy mice is clear. Mice are active during darkness, switch on the light and they immediately snuggle up in their nests and go to sleep. It's as though they fall asleep at the flick of a switch. Mice exhibiting neurological disorders are not so predictable with periods of activity and sleep occurring more randomly.

For many, sleep is fragile and if things go wrong it can have serious implications for wellbeing. The Sleep and Circadian Neuroscience Institute (SCNi) has provided many insights into the magical domain of sleep, profoundly antithetical to those who advocate the notion that sleep is for wimps. In contrast there is evidence to support that our ability to come up with novel solutions to complex problems is hugely augmented by healthy sleep with some estimates suggesting over a threefold increase in creativity. Unfortunately, many of these recent insights are failing to penetrate into contemporary culture. As the lure of 24/7 connectivity increases, we are permanently tempted by perpetual status updates and tweets. More worrying is the dissolving boundary between work and rest with many working into the night responding to a never ending barrage of emails and texts, all demanding our immediate attention. Increasingly employers and colleagues will contact staff out of hours interrupting the sanctity of family life. As yet the only sanctuary from digital connectivity is the sacrosanct domain of sleep - but for how long?

Fascinated by Oliver's research we went to visit his lab in Oxford where we were introduced to the mice. Unlike humans, mice have not developed an addiction to technology, preferring a strict fitness regime. Like pet mice the world over, the lab mice spend a vast amount of their

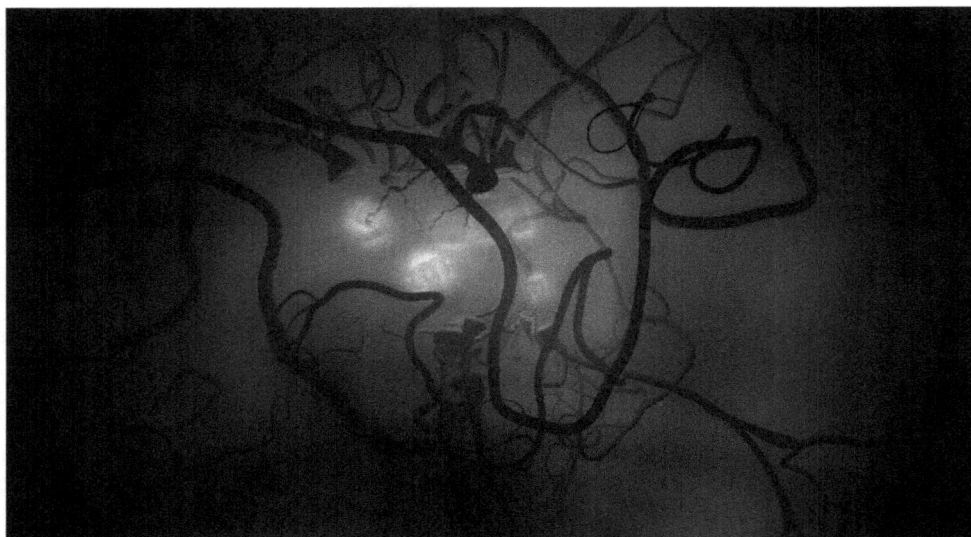

Figure 1. Screen image from development version of 'Dreams of Mice' (2015) depicting the firing neurons through light. Image: courtesy of boredomresearch and DAM Gallery, Berlin.

waking time running in a wheel. The wheels in the lab are attached to counters that keep track of sleep/wake behaviour. In one corner we came across some mice with small bumps on their heads. These were implants recording the activity of individual neurons. Following our tour of the lab we were introduced to Dr Vladyslav Vyazovskiy http://www.vvlab.org a neuroscientist researching the dynamics of brain activity during sleep. He was delighted to show us the neuron data he has been collecting from sleeping mice. At first glance this data is unremarkable, appearing like a noisy sound wave in an audio editing package. However, discussing the research at length it became clear that Vyazovskiy was intimately connected with the data, pointing out specific changes that mark the transition to and from REM (rapid eye movement) sleep. Vyazovskiy talked about his ideas about what might be happening during sleep, highlighting significant points where many neurons fire simultaneously or inhibit one another. Despite a shared fascination with the amount and richness of activity during sleep, it is safe to say that the aesthetic principles of arts and science differ considerably. We were keen to get hold of some data from Vyazovskiy to create an expression that was more evocative of the delicate nature of dreams.

On parting company with Vyazovskiy, we casually reassured him that there was no real hurry for the data, before returning to our studio where we obsessively checked email in anticipation of its arrival. Soon we had our first tests running in the game engine and sat spellbound, watching the most private, fluttering and gentile trembling of a mouse's dream. What we show in *Dreams of Mice* is different to the insights of science. Using similar principles of computation and visualization we reveal the delicate fragility of what we have - "*Tread softly because you tread on my dreams*" W. B. Yeats.

ARTIST BIOGRAPHY

boredomresearch have long held a fascination with the creative potential of contemporary technologies using these to explore facets of present day culture. In opposition to technologists speed obsessed pursuit of efficiency, boredomresearch propose an alternative expression favouring the pursuit of serenity. Their highly aesthetic, computational artworks have received worldwide media attention including: BBC, New Scientist, TIME magazine, Discovery Channel Canada. boredomresearch's artwork has been exhibited worldwide including: KUMU Art Museum in Tallinn, Estonia; House of Electronic Arts, Basel; Today Art Museum, Beijing; LABoral Centro de Arte y Creacion Industrial, Gijón and Instituto Itaú Cultural, São Paulo. Their work is held in a number of internationally significant collections including British Council and Borusan Contemporary Art Collection, Istanbul.

ACKNOWLEDGMENTS

We thank Dr Vladyslav Vyazovskiy and Dr Peter Oliver from the Dpt of Physiology, Anatomy and Genetics, University of Oxford for allowing us to use their data within this project. It has been a pleasure to collaborate with them. Thanks also to the National Centre for Computer Animation for supporting boredomresearch's practice-led research at Bournemouth University, UK. The artwork is exhibited courtesy of DAM Gallery, Berlin. Vyazovskiy would like to thank his team for their help with collecting the data: Dr Simon Fisher, DPhil students Nanyi Cui and Laura McKillop. The data has been collected with financial support from The Wellcome Trust Strategic Award to the Sleep and Circadian Neuroscience Institute (SCNi) and Marie Curie Career Integration Grant to Vyazovskiy.

Crypto Heater: A Design Fiction

Joseph Lindley
HighWire Centre for Doctoral Training
Lancaster University
United Kingdom
joseph.lindley@gmail.com

PROPOSAL ABSTRACT

This proposal is to exhibit the work named *Crypto Heater* which is part of a design fiction [c.f 1,5,8:30] series intended to explore a near future world in which cryptographic currencies such as Bitcoin [6] have become commonplace. This work opens up space for discussion about the activities of the distributed peer-to-peer network of so-called 'miners' that ensure the security of the Bitcoin network and regulate the supply of new currency in the Bitcoin economy.

The physical part of the work (the heater itself) is set within a fictional near-future reality. In this reality, Bitcoin has become central to our financial service industry, and 'mining' in domestic settings is promoted by the government, as a means of heating our homes and to ensure security of the network. A 'story world' is constructed using devices such as promotional materials from the UK Government's *Ministry of Crypto Currency;* technical specifications; customer testimonials; and the heater itself.

The main element of the exhibit is a fully working *Crypto Heater* prototype. This device *is* (in the fictional world, and the real world) part of the distributed network of Bitcoin miners. Through computation, it converts electrical energy into cryptographic currency. Uniquely *Crypto Heater* dissipates the heat energy (a by-product of the computational effort required to be a Bitcoin miner) through a standard household radiator. By offsetting the value of the cryptographic currency produced, against the cost of electricity used, the heater provide subsidized domestic heating.

Author Keywords
Design fiction, Bitcoin, Diegetic Prototypes

ACM Classification Keywords
H.5.m. Information interfaces and presentation: Design

BIOGRAPHY

I am a doctoral candidate at the HighWire CDT (Lancaster University). My PhD research is centred around producing knowledge about design fiction, by research through design [c.f 3,7,10].

Outside of an academic context I have a variety of experience. From 2002 to 2006 I worked as an ICT professional, writing code, doing systems analysis and managing projects. In 2006 I joined Manchester School of Art & Design in order to study Interactive Arts, obtaining a 1st class BA (Hons). During the same period I made a living as an artist, photographer and musician, completing a number of commissions, exhibitions, and publishing/performing music for Creaked Records (Lausanne) under the moniker Joe Galen. Between 2010 and 2012 I managed the Interpretation and Translation Service for Central Manchester Hospitals (UK National Health Service), leading the team staff through a comprehensive modernization programme.

NOTES ON THE WORK

This proposal describes an iteration of a pre-existing work[1]. Previously the concept pivoted on a story world that was told and created using fictitious newspaper headlines [4]. This second iteration crafts the story more passively, utilising promotional and technical materials as a means to ask the audience to participate in the fictional world in an embodied mimetic mode, as opposed to the purely diegetic mode [1]. Producing knowledge through designing, making, and practical experiments, forms an integral part of the research through design approach that my doctoral research is focused on.

This work comprises of two elements, one is the story world and the materials needed to construct it. The second is the prototype heater. In the case of this work the prototype is a standard personal computer that has two GPU devices cooled by water. For this iteration presentation of the heater is revisited in order to make the heater seem less prototypical and appear more

---

[1] Previously exhibited at Synergize 2014 (Lancaster University) (http://www.synergize2014.org/ and #include2 (Edinburgh College of Art)

production-ready, with the intention of improving the work's ability to suspend disbelief [9].

Figure 1. An illustration showing the first iteration of the crypto heater.

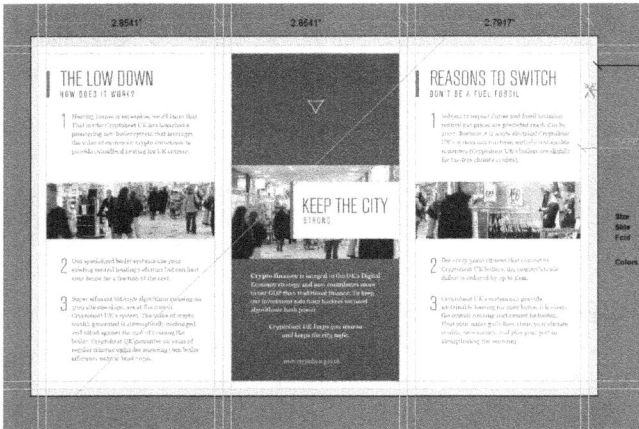

Figure 2. Draft promotional material for the (fictional) Ministry for Crypto Currency.

RESEARCH SIGNIFICANCE

This work is part of a wider body of doctoral research that hinges around a research through design approach to conducting research [3,7,10], as such the academic contribution is inherently contingent and reflexive. Proposed discussion points include:

- Nuances of the Bitcoin electronic cash system (that make this concept plausible)

- Commenting on how this work opens 'a discursive space' [2:6] and what emerges from it

- How the original incarnation of this work lead to the conception of a three-layer model for design fiction [4]

- What lead the move away from diegetic (telling) narration of the story world to a mimetic induction (showing) of story world – does this have implications for design fiction?

- Discussing what this work is *for*, for instance can design fiction work like this help us move towards "preferable" [2:5] futures?

ACKNOWLEDGEMENTS
Many thanks to Paul Coulton, Simon Atwood and to the HighWire Centre for Doctoral Training. This work is funded under the RCUK Digital Economy Programme (Grant Reference EP/G037582/1).

REFERENCES

1. Bleecker, J. Design Fiction: A short essay on design, science, fact and fiction. *Near Future Laboratory*, (2009).

2. Dunne, A. and Raby, F.*Speculative Everything.* The MIT Press, London, 2013.

3. Gaver, W.What should we expect from research through design? *Proceedings of the 2012 ACM annual conference on Human Factors in Computing Systems - CHI '12*, (2012), 937.

4. Lindley, J. and Coulton, P.Modelling Design Fiction: What's The Story? *StoryStorm Workshop at ACM Designing Interactive Systems 2014*, (2014).

5. Lindley, J. A pragmatics framework for design fiction. *European Academy of Design Conference (In press)*.

6. Nakamoto, S. *Bitcoin: A peer-to-peer electronic cash system.* 2008.

7. Ramirez, R. An epistemology for research through design. *Proceedings of the ICSID Design Education Conference*, (2009), 1–14.

8. Sterling, B. *Shaping Things.* The MIT Press, 2005.

9. Sterling, B. Bruce Sterling Explains the Intriguing New Concept of Design Fiction (Interview by Torie Bosch). *Slate*, 2012. http://www.slate.com/blogs/future_tense/2012/03/02/bruce_sterling_on_design_fictions_.html.

10. Zimmerman, J., Stolterman, E., and Forlizzi, J. An Analysis and Critique of Research through Design : towards a formalization of a research approach. *Proceedings of DIS 2010*, (2010).

How to Catch a Cloud

Minka Stoyanova
City University Hong Kong
Hong Kong, China
theartist@minkaart.net

ABSTRACT

For the digitally tethered, life is defined at the intersection of the virtual and the physical. Our experience is necessarily tempered by a stream of simultaneous meta interactions, each an archive, an extension, and a reflection of some experienced reality. "How to Catch a Cloud" is a tool, a web-based application for the communal creation of such a stream. It also results in a democratically rendered, visual archive of experiences and impressions. But, more than either of these it is a proposition, an invitation, and an experiment.

We manifest our existence through a process of obsessive archival. By referencing the parallel associations inherent in the use of the term, "cloud," this work proposes the possibility of capturing that which exists, but cannot be located, the climate. Finally, it wonders what we are truly collecting/creating in this manic cycle of perpetual archival. What are we placing in this uncontrollable and ephemeral space, this cloud? Is it, perhaps, that equally indescribable idea of "the soul," or is it merely another representation, perpetually updated but always at a remove... never able to come fully into synchronicity with the experience it represents.

Author Keywords

Climate; Data; Cloud; Interaction; Archive; Social

ACM Classification Keywords

J.5

DESCRIPTION OF WORK

"How to Catch a Cloud" is an internet based application (mobile friendly) that functions as a tool for individuals' interaction with and archival of their communal experiences. The application prompts users to draw a cloud (or any image) as a report on or reaction to their ongoing experience. The application also allows users to view a continuous stream (in real time) of the images being produced by other users. In an exhibition setting, this stream is projected onto a wall or via another display technology, thus exhibition visitors are able to view images being added to the system in real time. In this way, the exhibited portion becomes an ongoing archive of the experience of the event as a whole.

Figure 1. Screenshot of the user interface when displaying user generated content in real time.

INTRODUCTION

As cited by Nassim Nicholas Taleb in his book The Black Swan [1] (and others), recent social and economic experience has begun to challenge a potent but enduring myth. This myth, that the vagaries and vicissitudes of human experience can potentially be understood (and possibly forecasted) if only we are able to collect enough data, has been perpetuated and strengthened in the digital age. The rise of an industry focused solely on the collection and analysis of data exemplifies the enduring potency of this myth. However, in our relentless struggle to finally capture enough, we are perpetually thwarted by the enigmatic phenomenon of our own perception. As revealed in the recent internet phenomenon of "the dress" [2], the search for truth remains lost in the (albeit clichéd) philosophical question of the very existence thereof; "can anything be truly known if we can only know what we perceive?"

ARTWORK/EXPERIMENT

Drawing upon data collection methodologies from social science, we can understand that the "truth" or "fiction" of much data is of relatively little importance. Social scientists – in attempts to understand or just capture complex cultural or social systems – often collect qualitative data (narrative, perception, anecdote and experience). These perception-based data points paint a picture which is arguably of equal (or greater) truth than that which can be viewed through sole reliance on quantitative data (raw statistics/numbers). For many,

C&C '15, June 22-25, 2015, Glasgow, United Kingdom
ACM 978-1-4503-3598-0/15/06.
http://dx.doi.org/10.1145/2757226.2757369

truth is not found in that which can rigorously proven, but instead in the collected beliefs and perceptions of a community. "How to Catch a Cloud" reflexively, experimentally, and critically applies this outlook to the problem of capturing the indescribable – specifically, the social climate.

By creating a playful interface that prompts users to draw (visually represent) their immediate feelings about an ongoing activity or event, the work becomes an ongoing archive of perceptual experience. However, the analysis and curation of the data collected is also left to the user as the application presents the whole of the collected data, in a continuous stream. In order to represent that which is un-representable the work captures not only what is intentionally reported by the user, but also what is unintentionally recorded. By removing the primacy of textual representation and instead asking users to present their reactions in a visual format, the collected data becomes an archive of personal symbolic representations and individual artistic gestures (micro-performances of making).

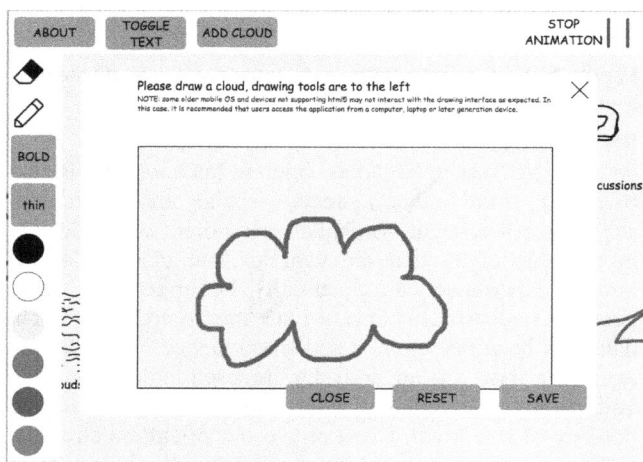

Figure 2. The drawing input interface. Users are allowed to add 40 characters of text after submitting a drawing (as seen in the scrolling interface).

The repeated application of weather-based terminology further reinforces the enigmatic nature of that which is being captured by the work while also referencing the associations that are inherent in our use of weather-based language to describe both the internet and analog social systems. All of these systems (weather, internet, society) are both ubiquitous and ephemeral, everywhere and nowhere, necessary and terrifying. They cannot be truly represented as a whole, but are only represented through the presentation of various individual data points (average temperatures, average connection speeds). However, these statistics do not describe the actual experience of this ubiquitous phenomenon's effect. Nor do they capture the phenomenon in its entirety. The common terminological thread which is repeated in our descriptions of these systems ('the cloud' or 'the climate') reinforce our parallel experience of these systems as exceptionally relevant but frustratingly indescribable.

CONCLUSION

This work proposes a tool for archiving our communal experience, but perhaps more importantly it presents a question regarding the very nature of the data we are compelled to collect. Each image is itself a data point, made up of digital (computational) data. However, each image is also a collection of the intended and unintended reports of an individual. As a whole, the images become an abstract representation of a communal experience which is essentially indescribable. While the total work is (in fact) an archival representation, it is also decoupled; it creates a secondary layer of discourse which can become only marginally connected to the originating experience. In doing so, it not only references the futility of describing these indescribable phenomenon, but also (hopefully) reinforces the very real spaces that can emerge spontaneously from our discursive attempts to create those descriptions.

NOTES AND REFERENCES
[1] Nassim Nicholas Taleb. 2007. The Black Swan: the impact of the highly improbable. Random House.

[2] The dress meme (Feb/March 2015) was an internet phenomenon and debate caused by an optical illusion resulting from specific lighting conditions in an image of a dress. The dress, which in reality was blue and black appeared to a significant part of the population as white and cream in the image. The variation in perception of the dress color (between blue and black and white and cream) was actually the result of perceptual differences in individuals' unconscious interpretations of the given lighting conditions.

Skin Music (2012): an Audio-Haptic Composition for Ears and Body

Lauren Hayes
Arts, Media and Engineering
Herberger Institute for Design and the Arts
Arizona State University
laurensarahhayes@gmail.com

ABSTRACT

Skin Music (2012) is a musical composition that is experienced as a private, multisensory installation by one person at a time. By lying on a piece of bespoke furniture, the listener perceives the music both through the usual auditory channels, as well as by different types of haptic sensation, through their body. The piece addresses the shared perceptual experiences of sonic and haptic sensation through an exploration of vibrational feedback.

Author Keywords

Haptics; composition; multimodality; vibrotactile feedback

ACM Classification Keywords

H.5.5 (Sound and Music Computing): Methodologies and techniques

INTRODUCTION

The link between sound and touch is inherent: hearing is, essentially, "a specialized form of touch" [2]. Profoundly deaf musician Evelyn Glennie asserts a view that is the grounding premise for this work. Her statement could be explained in physical terms by the fact that sound is the rapid vibration of molecules in the air, which excite the membranes, hair and fluid inside of our ears, allowing us to hear. Moreover, our perception of sound goes beyond just the penetration of the auditory canal, and in fact is felt by our whole body, through vibrations within the organs and the bones [8].

Over the last eight years I have explored the relationships between sound and touch by developing bespoke digital musical instruments (DMIs) using haptic technology [4]. My research has also examined the possible applications of vibrotactile technology in deepening the performer's engagement with her instrument [3, 5], as well its ability to provide cues and aid communication during musical improvisation [6].

C&C 2015, June 22–25, 2015, Glasgow, United Kingdom.
ACM 978-1-4503-3598-0/15/06.
http://dx.doi.org/10.1145/2757226.2757370

On furthering this research through the creation of numerous live electronic and electro-instrumental compositions, I discovered that not only was the vibrotactile technology useful during performances, but that it also allowed me to access multisensory information during the compositional process itself. I was able to experience the *feel* of a piece of music during its creation. This motivated me to explore how music might also be experienced physically by an audience.

AUDIO-HAPTIC COMPOSITION

Skin Music (2012) is an intimate work that explores the relationships between sound and physical sensation from the listener's perspective. While a piece of music can touch us by arousing the emotions or triggering a memory, music also touches us physically, through vibrations in the air, which our ears perceive as sound, but which are felt, often subconsciously, by the entire body.

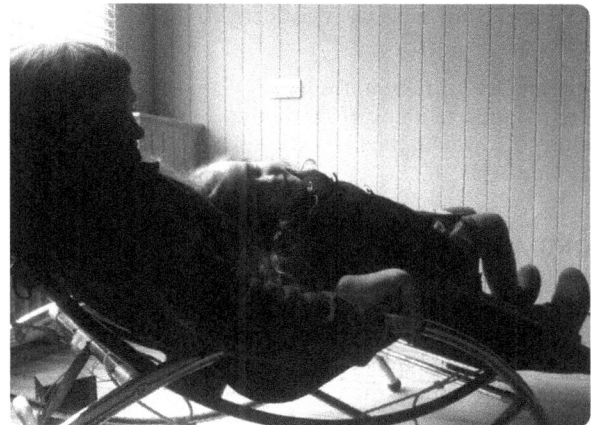

Figure 1. Participants experiencing *Skin Music*.

To experience *Skin Music*, the audience member is asked to lie on a chaise longue (see Figure 1). The piece begins and the music is transmitted through loudspeakers placed underneath the piece of furniture, and also through the listener's body directly from the structure of the chair.

Technical Development

Six vibration motors were embedded in the chair (see Figure 2). By utilising the pulse-width modulation pins of an

Arduino via Max/MSP, different intensities of targeted vibration can be felt. Additionally two tactile transducers were attached below the chair. These can deliver targeted low frequency audio signals (60-70 Hz) to the feet and spine areas. This allows for two main sources of tactile sensation to be used and combined within the piece.

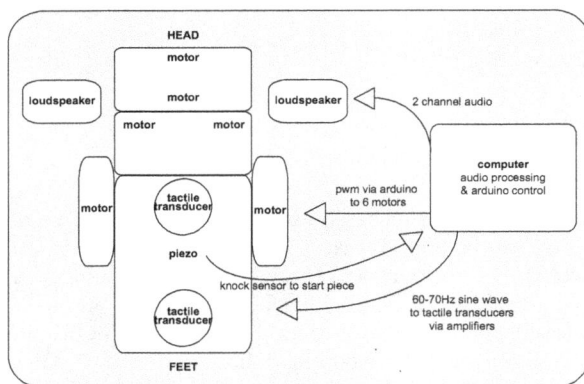

Figure 2. Routing and haptic placement in *Skin Music*.

Compositional Framework
The work draws on previous research by Chang and O'Sullivan [1] who use audio-visual theories, such as temporal linearisation, synchronisation, and masking in order to develop ways of linking the tactile and auditory sensations. I also implemented various arrangements of *vibrotactile apparent movement* [7]. This allowed me to create haptic trajectories, where a sensation could be perceived as moving, for example, up from the shoulders, to the neck and onto the head area.

Additionally, different frequency ranges within the audio were mapped to areas of the body. At certain points within the piece, lower pitched sounds will be felt lower on the body, and vice versa.

CONCLUSION
This potential new art form [3] falls within an area of composition that is largely unexplored and deserves more investigation, particularly in light of recent developments within the field of embodied music cognition. *Skin Music* was first exhibited at the Summerhall gallery, Edinburgh for six weeks of private view. *Skin Music II* is currently in development in collaboration with the school of Arts, Media and Engineering, Herberger Institute for Design and the Arts, Arizona State University.

BIOGRAPHY
Lauren Sarah Hayes is a composer and performer from Glasgow, Scotland, whose practice explores new strategies for live electronic music performance by investigating the performer's physical relationship with the digital realm. She seeks to deepen this through the modality of touch. She is a regular improviser, collaborating in duos/trios (Mùstek,

FHM) and also performing with large-scale ensembles (Edimpro). For many years she has given multisensory workshops for various groups, including those with sensory impairment, learning difficulties, and autism. These workshops use vibration and music, and often result in custom built instruments designed specifically for a client.

She enjoys performing her music around the world and has been supported by artistic residencies at EMS (Stockholm) in late 2011, in which she gave a live performance for Sveriges-Radio P2, and also at STEIM (Amsterdam) in 2012. In 2012 she directed the Inventor Composer Coaction, which facilitated collaboration between composers in Edinburgh and inventors of new digital musical instruments. She is a founding member of LLEAPP (Laboratory for Laptop and Electronic Audio Performance Practice), a yearly roving research forum for sonic arts. In 2012 she became an associate of the New Radiophonic Workshop and she is currently Visiting Assistant Professor in Sound Studies at Arizona State University.

ACKNOWLEDGMENTS
I would like to thank Tobias Feltus for his assistance in crafting the chair, as well as Paul Robertson for supporting this project at Summerhall, Edinburgh.

REFERENCES
1. Chang, A., and O'Sullivan, C. An Audio-Haptic Aesthetic Framework Influenced by Visual Theory. In *Haptic and Audio Interaction Design*, T. I. Workshop, Ed. (Jyväskylä, Finland, September 2008).

2. Glennie, E. Hearing essay. `http://www.evelyn.co.uk/Resources/Essays/Hearing%20Essay.pdf` [accessed 23rd August 2013], 1993.

3. Hayes, L. Vibrotactile feedback-assisted performance. In *Proceedings of the 2011 Conference on New Interfaces for Musical Expression*, NIME (Oslo, 2011).

4. Hayes, L. Performing articulation and expression through a haptic interface. In *Proceedings of the 2012 International Computer Music Conference.*, ICMA, Ed. (Ljubljana, 2012).

5. Hayes, L. Haptic augmentation of the hybrid piano. In *Contemporary Music Review*, vol. 32:5. Taylor and Francis, 2013.

6. Hayes, L., and Michalakos, C. Imposing a networked vibrotactile communication system for improvisational suggestion. In *Organised Sound*, vol. 17(1). Cambridge University Press, 2012, 36–44.

7. Niwa, M., Yanagida, Y., Noma, H., Hosaka, K., and Kume, Y. Vibrotactile apparent movement by dc motors and voice-coil tactors. In *Proceedings of The 14th International Conference on Artificial Reality and Telexistence (ICAT)* (Seoul, Korea, 2004), 126–131.

8. Waters, S. Performance Ecosystems: Ecological approaches to musical interaction. In *Proceedings of the 2007 Electroacoustic Music Studies Network* (Leicester: De Montfort, 2007).

Viewpoints AI

Mikhail Jacob
Georgia Institute of Technology
Atlanta
USA
mikhail.jacob@gatech.edu

Brian Magerko
Georgia Institute of Technology
Atlanta
USA
magerko@gatech.edu

ABSTRACT

The Viewpoints AI installation [2, 3] attempts to create an interactive movement-based art experience that has almost no predefined instantial content. As opposed to focusing on designer-created content that reflects their specific view of an interactive experience, we have instead created a movement-based play space where interactors can freely dance with a virtual AI-based character named VAI, teaching it as they interact. VAI analyses interactor movements through procedural representations of the Viewpoints movement theory (from theatre and dance) [1] and improvises responses as an equal collaborator from its past experience with people. VAI uses this procedurally and experientially realized content to present an engaging movement-based experience that any audience member can walk up to and immediately begin dancing with.

The Viewpoints AI installation uses shadow theatre as inspiration for creating a liminal space for the projected AI character and an interactor's shadow to co-exist within a real / virtual space. Interactors step in front of a spotlight that projects their shadow onto a large muslin screen. VAI is also projected onto that same space. Viewpoints AI, thus builds on ancient and new media forms, creating an experience that is a playful - but coherent - expression between both the interactor and VAI.

Author Keywords

Movement Improvisation; Interactive Art Installation; Viewpoints; Co-creativity; Learning Through Interaction.

ACM Classification Keywords

I.2.6. Artificial Intelligence: Learning – Knowledge acquisition. J.5. Computer Applications: Arts and Humanities – Performing arts (e.g., dance, music).

INTRODUCTION

The Viewpoints AI installation [2, 3] is both an audience-facing performance piece and a participatory interactive

C&C '15, June 22-25, 2015, Glasgow, United Kingdom
ACM 978-1-4503-3598-0/15/06.
http://dx.doi.org/10.1145/2757226.2757400

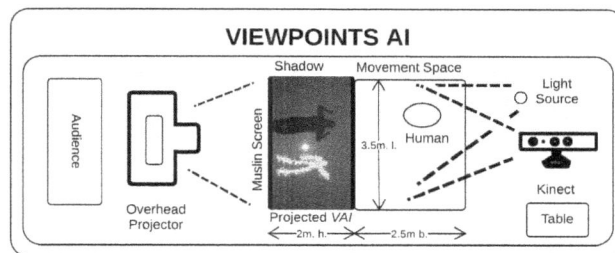

Figure 1: The Viewpoints AI installation.

experience. Interactors can walk up and improvise a movement-based narrative with a virtual AI-based character named *VAI*. It does this by utilizing Viewpoints movement theory [1] in order to systematically analyze rhythmic movement in terms of various Viewpoints dimensions. These include properties of the movement such as tempo, energy and smoothness among various others. These allow VAI to both find appropriate responses as well as to transform the remembered movements along Viewpoints dimensions for coherent novelty.

THE VIEWPOINTS AI INSTALLATION

The Viewpoints AI installation projects the VAI avatar onto a screen and simultaneously casts the human interactor's shadow onto the same screen. This can be done in two ways. Using a point source of illumination in order to cast an analog shadow onto the projection screen, and rendering a digital shadow captured by the installation's Microsoft Kinect depth sensor. The analog shadow theatrical version is described in this article.

The installation uses a translucent screen in order to front-project the virtual character from the direction of the audience and rear-project the analog shadow from behind the screen. The usage of both sides of the projection screen presents the audience (and the interactor) with an unobstructed view of the human's shadow and virtual character interacting on screen. Figure 1 illustrates the installation in this configuration. In this version of the installation, audience members view the installation from the front and interactors walk behind the screen in order to interact with VAI using their shadow.

Interactors can improvise dance or rhythmic movement with VAI by doing repeated rhythmic movements (Figure 3). The interactor's movements are captured using a Microsoft Kinect depth sensor that is placed either behind the interactor or in front of the interactor depending on the configuration. This depth sensor captures the interactor's

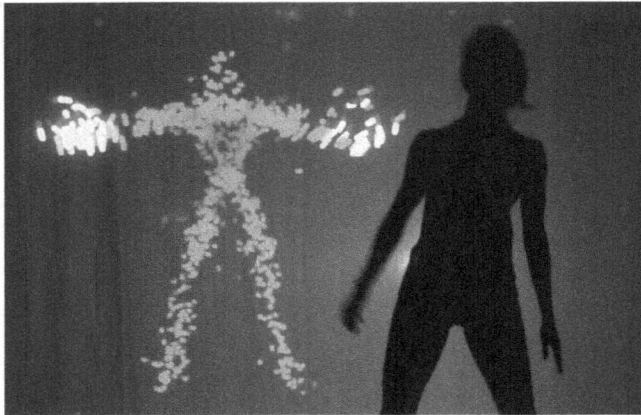

Figure 3: VAI improvising dance with an interactor.

Figure 2: VAI providing a novel offer to the interactor.

movements and VAI derives additional Viewpoints information about the movements. This Viewpoints information captures a subset of the Viewpoints dimensions of tempo, duration, repetition, spatial relationship, gesture, topography, and shape. VAI starts responding by mirroring the human's movements in real time. When the human attains a detectable rhythm, VAI's heart will start to glow in time. It learns that rhythmic movement.

It can then choose to respond to the interactor's movement (Figure 2) by choosing from a number of strategies or response modes. These include *repetition* of the interactor's movement, *transformation* of the interactor's movement using Viewpoints information or acontextual functional transformations, *novel movement* remembered from memory (using Viewpoints information to ensure similarity and appropriateness), *interaction pattern application*, and *emotional responses*. Interaction pattern application refers to usage of action - response pairs that VAI learns from observing how interactors respond to its own movements. Emotional responses refer to emotionally coherent reactions to portrayed emotional content detected in the interactors movements, such as responding with fear when portrayed anger is detected in the interactor's movement.

Responses are then executed by VAI for as long as the interactor keeps moving in rhythm. When the interactor stops moving or changes to another rhythm, VAI responds accordingly. VAI itself, is visualized as a sentient cloud of fireflies or motes of light. VAI's visualization changes according to the various Viewpoints information, for example the color changes according to the energy of VAI'smovement.

ARTIST BIO

Dr. Magerko is an Associate Professor of Digital Media and Director of the Adaptive Digital Media (ADAM) Lab at the Georgia Institute of Technology. He received his B.S. in Cognitive Science from Carnegie Mellon in 1999, and his M.S. and Ph.D. in Computer Science from the University of Michigan in 2001 and 2006 respectively. He has been a pioneer in the field of interactive narrative technologies,

developing AI-based technologies for interactive narrative such as IDA, ISAT, and the Digital Improv Project. Dr. Magerko's research in digital media lives within the space of computation, creativity and cognition, which delves into understanding more about humans as creative beings to enable the creation of new digital media experiences. He has been PI on over $2 million of federally-funded research and has authored over 60 peer reviewed articles related to creativity and computation. His work has been featured in such venues as the Chicago Improv Festival, The Tech Arts Festival at Georgia Tech, the DAEL Window Project in downtown Atlanta, and at multiple AI conferences (e.g. AAAI and AIIDE).

Mikhail Jacob is a Ph.D. student at the Georgia Institute of Technology. He received his B.E. in Computer Science Engineering from the Manipal Institute of Technology in 2011, and his M.S. in Computer Science from the Georgia Institute of Technology in 2013. He has developed AI-based technologies in areas such as pretend play, improvisational contemporary movement, improvisational theater, generative visual art and procedurally generated video games. He is interested in researching socio-cognitive models of creativity in artistic or expressive domains and his current research is on computationally modeling pretend play with objects and toys. His work has been featured at venues such as the ICIDS 2014 Art Exhibition titled "Remembering/Forgetting" in Singapore, Tech Arts Festival at Georgia Tech, the DAEL Window Project in Atlanta, the Autumn School on Computational Creativity in Porvoo (Finland), the Georgia Game Developers Association in Atlanta, and at the AIIDE conference.

REFERENCES

1. Bogart, A. and Landau, T. *The viewpoints book: a practical guide to viewpoints and composition.* New York: Theatre Communications Group, 2005.

2. Jacob, M., Coisne, G., Gupta, A., Sysoev, I., Verma, G. G., and Magerko, B. Viewpoints AI. In *Proc. AIIDE 2013*, AAAI Press (2013).

3. Jacob, M., Zook, A., and Magerko, B. Viewpoints AI: Procedurally Representing and Reasoning about Gestures. In *Proc. DiGRA 2013*, DIGRA (2013).

COTree – scripting the truth

Lasse Steenbock Vestergaard
The Alexandra Institute Ltd.
Aarhus, Denmark
lasse.vestergaard@alexandra.dk

Joakim Old Jensen
201209440@post.au.dk

Christina Exner
201209667@post.au.dk

Agnete Horup
201308556@post.au.dk

Anna Lindebjerg
201308550@post.au.dk

Kirstine West Andersen
201308540@post.au.dk

Nikolaj Christian Mikkelsen
201308531@post.au.dk

Aarhus University
Aarhus, Denmark

ABSTRACT
COTree is a physical interaction design installation shaped as a climbing plant. COTree is composed of smart materials, and electronic design tools like Arduino. The installation has leaves that change shape and color depending on CO_2 concentrations in the surrounding environment. When the audience experiences a plant withering caused by too much CO_2, they become aware that pollution is happening all around us – the audience is breathing the same air as the plant! How do you get away from the pollution, and where should you go?

Author Keywords
COTree; energy; carbon dioxide; critical design; physical interaction design; smart materials; thermochromic; muscle wire.

ACM Classification Keywords
H5.m. Information interfaces and presentation (e.g., HCI): Miscellaneous.

INTRODUCTION
In this paper we are presenting the art installation COTree. COTree is a physical interaction design built with smart materials [2], and leveraging from existing design tools like the Arduino platform [3]. COTree is evolving around the human perception of the world. Natural life cycles, everyday pollution, and human perception are core

elements that are intertwined and explored in this installation.

COTREE AS INSTALLATION
COTree is a climbing plant that responds to CO_2 levels in the surroundings, by either withering (become brown/yellow and crumble) or blossom (stretch and become green) [5]. From a more technical and practical perspective, the movements and color changes happens through the use of specific smart materials. We use thermochromic ink [16] for coloring (becomes transparent at 30 degree Celsius), and muscle wire [14] for making the leaves crumble and stretch.

COTree exists in the same world as the onlooker – it's not a screen of pixels. You can touch, and see the plant wither and blossom before your eyes. Initially the audience will be surprised by the unnatural behavior, they will quickly be aware that the installation is reacting to CO_2 in the environment, and they will start wonder - what should you do when experiencing a plant dying before your eyes? If the plant can't breath because of toxic air, then it might not be healthy for me either - where should I go?

With COTree we script the understanding of the invisible surroundings, and apply our own interpretation. This interpretation gives the installation a personality – it's a fragile individual existing in our world, and it's being subject to the same chemicals, inputs, and relations as us. By creating an installation that responds to the physical environment, and is close to the audience, we investigate and question whether we should believe everything we experience, and take algorithmic results as true answers. Additionally, we want to make awareness of the human carbon footprint – even though we think we are being green, we are still breathing out CO_2, using Internet, and driving our car to work.

BIOGRAPHY OF DESIGNERS

COTree is created by the art collective Rum13 [15], and each of the members have been involved in different projects through out the recent years. We have been participating in creating an electronic toolkit for interaction designers [11], we have created a simplified library for the Arduino where it has become easier for designers to use sensor data in their prototypes [4], we have participated in research projects at the University of Aarhus, Denmark. Here we have been involved in the interactive literary installation Ink [9], and the pop up installation Instant Kafé [10]. Furthermore, we were engaged in the media architecture biennale in Aarhus 2012 [12], where we installed 5500 RGB LEDs on the city hall tower [13]. Finally, we have been working with COTree for some years now, and it has been exhibited at a few events around Aarhus [6, 7, 8].

SPACE FOR COTREE

The installation is designed as a climbing plant, and it therefore requires a surface large enough for it to spread out. In our experience, a vertical pillar is an extremely good surface for showing off COTree. Additionally, working in three dimensions (ex. around the pillar) has great impact as well – the installation becomes more integrated into the surface thereby giving a more organic look and feel.

Figure 1. Showing suggestion for where to setup COTree [1]

When we saw the images of the exhibition area, we instantly fell in love with the concrete pillars that holds the entire construction in place. In Figure 1 we have inserted a red oval where COTree would fit perfectly. We will place a wooden box/chair at the foot of the pillar, and from there the branches of the climbing plant will crawl upwards. The total height will be around four meters.

The installation is composed of two main branches that are flexible (essentially just electric cords), and therefore it is quite adaptable – it can be bend in different shapes, and we can change height and width of the used space quite easily.

EQUIPMENT FOR THE INSTALLATION TO WORK

COTree will be augmented directly on the existing architecture, and therefore does not require much equipment. Since the installation can be up to four meters tall, it is relevant to use a ladder for mounting. Additionally, the installation requires access to electric power (100-240 volts depending on what is available), and can manage with a single power plug.

REFERENCES

1. ACM creativity and cognition. http://cc15.cityofglasgowcollege.ac.uk/content/artworks.

2. Minuto, A., Nijholt, A. Smart material interfaces as a methodology for interaction: a survey of SMIs' state of the art and development. In *Proceedings of the second international workshop on Smart material interfaces: another step to a material future* (2013), 1-6.

3. Arduino. http://arduino.cc.

4. ArduinoMax_InOut_forDummies. http://playground.arduino.cc/interfacing/MaxMSP.

5. COTree. http://cotree.dk.

6. COTree at Aarhus festuge. http://kognitionsdesign.dk/projects/cotree.

7. COTree at MAB14. http://mab14.mediaarchitecture.org/exhibition/exhibits/cotree.

8. COTree at Sustain festival 2014. http://cotree.dk/cotree-pa-godsbanen-d-15-17-maj.

9. Ink. http://www.inkafterprint.dk/?page_id=45.

10. Instant Kafé. http://darc.imv.au.dk/instantkafe/.

11. Brynskov, M., Lunding, R., Vestergaard, L. S. The design of tools for sketching sensor-based interaction. In *Proceedings of the Sixth International Conference on Tangible, Embedded and Embodied Interaction* (2012), 213-216.

12. Media architecture biennale 2012. http://mab12.mediaarchitecture.org.

13. Media architecture institute. http://www.mediaarchitecture.org/city-hall-tower-aarhus.

14. Muscle wire. http://www.musclewires.com/AboutMuscleWires.php.

15. Rum13. http://rum13.dk.

16. Kaihou, T., Wakita, A. Electronic origami with the color-changing function. In *Proceedings of the second international workshop on Smart material interfaces: another step to a material future* (2013), 7-12

Hudson Valley Muddy Waters: Using AR to Reveal Microscopic Life in the Macroscopic Forest

Cynthia Beth Rubin

Critic	Artist in Residence
Foundation Studies	Menden-Deuer Lab
Rhode Island School of Design	Graduate School of Oceanography
Providence, RI, USA	University of Rhode Island
info@cbrubin.net	Narragansett, RI, USA

ABSTRACT

Hudson Valley Muddy Waters makes visible the microscopic life that is key to the health of our forests and streams. The work demonstrates how Augmented Reality and creative imaging can expand the role of the artist in facilitating deeper public connections with the material of science and the macro/microscopic environment.

The artist reverses the usual AR relationship of "real" to "aesthetically mediated" by presenting a painterly digital image as point of departure onto which "reality" is layered, rather than the other way around. Using the app Aurasma, the viewer is prompted to experience the thrill of discovering microscopic life in water via short videos of an actual stream and video micro-captures from the same site..

Author Keywords

Augmented Reality; Art; Microscopy; Video; Digital Imaging; Plankton; Environment; Water

ACM Classification Keywords

H.5.M, • Human-centered computing~Scientific visualization • Computing methodologies~Mixed / augmented reality • Computing methodologies~Perception

SCIENCE AS AESTHETIC EXPERIENCE

One of the motivating factors was to bring the excitement of microscopic imaging and discovery to the public viewer. Collecting water samples and subsequently discovering living, swimming organisms while looking under the microscope is simply an awesome experience. Is it possible for artists trained in the visual language of creative imaging and digital enhancement to employ aesthetic techniques in bringing this experience to a broader audience? How can this be done within the context of a non-site specific installation that can be accessible on any wall anywhere?

Figures 1 & 2 User viewing videos of microscopic life through interactive Augmented Reality.
See video of interaction: https://vimeo.com/126021640

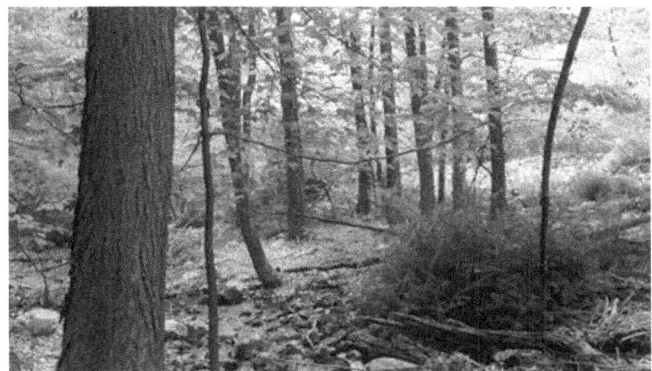

Figure 3: View of the original site Hudson Valley, NY, USA

Figure 4: Hudson Muddy Waters, C.B. Rubin, digital print for AR installation, variable dimensions, 2014. Composited from multiple drawings and photographs of a single site in a forest in the Hudson Valley, New York State, USA [1]

Figure 5: QR code directing users to Aurasma channel.

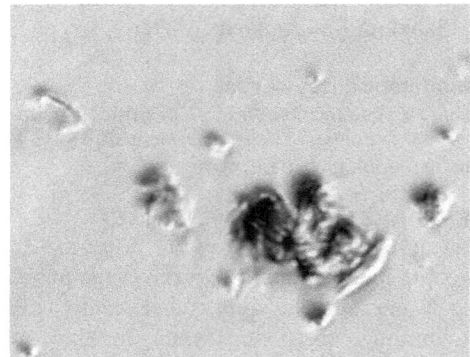

Figure 6: Video still from sequence of freshwater plankton revealed through interactive AR. Micro-video by C. B. Rubin

ACKNOWLEDGMENTS

This project was funded in part by the Rhode Island Science and Technology Advisory Council Collaborative Research award; thanks to the researchers in the Menden-Deuer lab, Graduate School of Oceanography, University of Rhode Island, who provided information on plankton and thoughtful insights on communicating the aesthetics of science through engaging dialogues on the depiction of the real and the mediated. Thanks also to Art Kibbutz for the artist residency which began the project, and to the Nature Lab at the Rhode Island School of Design, which provided microscopic equipment through the EPSCoR grant EPS-1004057, and valuable expertise on micro-imaging.

NOTE

1. An earlier version of *Hudson Muddy Waters* was presented as a poster entitled Sensing Science: the Microscopic Environment, at ISEA 2014, in a session on Public Space (proceedings forthcoming).

Dream Vortex: Artwork in Interactive 3D

Meredith Tromble
San Francisco Art Institute
San Francisco, California, USA
mtromble@sfai.edu

Dawn Sumner
University of California, Davis
Davis, California, USA
dysumner@ucdavis.edu

ABSTRACT

Dream Vortex is a virtual art installation with interactive 3D objects, developed for a CAVE, Oculus Rift, or 3D monitor by artist Meredith Tromble and scientist Dawn Sumner. The central structure is an interactive vortex of hand-drawn dream images that appear in 3D space before the viewer, accompanied by a sound environment. A viewer interacts with the vortex by selecting dream emblems with a game controller. With it, the viewer has the ability to "touch," move, and compose the images, much like picking up physical objects and moving them around. Once a dream is selected, the vortex disappears; the chosen dream and a suite of related dreams fade into view. For the time span of a typical dream (a few minutes) the viewer can interact with them, moving, resizing, and arranging them in new patterns. The dreams are contributed by the research community at UC Davis, so conceptually the work links "opposites": subjective and objective knowledge; 2D and 3D space; and our oldest and newest art-making media.

Author Keywords

Art and science; CAVE; collaboration; dream drawing; interactive art; interactive 3D objects; Oculus Rift.

ACM Classification Keywords

J.5. Fine Arts.

INTRODUCTION

Dream Vortex is an interactive, 3-D virtual art installation that geobiologist Dawn Sumner, a co-founder of the KeckCAVES 3D imaging facility at the University of California, Davis (UCD), and I have been developing for the past three years with assistance from physicist Jim Crutchfield of the Complexity Sciences Center at UCD.

The central structure of the work is a vortex of images that appear in the air before the viewer. With a controller, the

C&C '15, June 22-25, 2015, Glasgow, United Kingdom
ACM 978-1-4503-3598-0/15/06.
http://dx.doi.org/10.1145/2757226.2757374

viewer has the ability to "touch," handle, and move them, much like entering a room with physical objects and moving them around. Participants can arrange the elements in their own tableaux, although a dream-appropriate degree of surprise is provided by a hidden network of associations built into the programming. In the same way that the work bridges old and new technologies of art, it connects the subjective and objective sides of human experience because the elements, such as dogs, houses, and cars, originate in dreams contributed by the scientist community at Davis. The intent is cultural rather than psychological, to create an imaginative space of play in the research environment as well as an aesthetic experience for viewers.

INTERACTIVE SCENES

In Scene 1, fleeting images of dreams spiral up out of the floor in a vortex. [Figure 1] The viewer glimpses them, but they are elusive, as when one is waking and trying to recall the dream world.

Figure 1. *Dream Vortex* (2011-) Still, Scene 1

Colorful sprites provide extra light and trigger soft sounds that complement a background soundtrack of noise – often David Dunn's bark beetles.

Special emblems representing specific dreams occasionally float upward in the center of the vortex: a shoe, glasses, a sphere, the letter C... When the dreamer chooses one of these emblems, it starts to slowly float downward toward the floor as the vortex continues upward. The dream associated with the emblem emerges on the floor in place of the vortex and absorbs the emblem.

As Scene 2 emerges, ghosts of other dreams appear around the focus dream. [Figure 2]. These dreams, which are linked to the chosen dream through one of seven types of association, can be arranged and overlapped by the viewer to create visual patterns. (The categories of association are action, animal, color, emotion, environment, place, and profession of the dreamer.) They appear and disappear at random, as new dreams fades slowly in. There is an illusion of control, but as viewers play with the piece they must accept a degree of chance.

After some time, the focus dream fades away and fleeting images and sprites begin to emerge from the floor in a spiral. Ghosts of the associated dreams persist for a while, but disappear one at a time until the vortex dominates the return to Scene 1. The dreamer can only get back to Scene 2 by choosing another emblem, when one finally appears.

Figure 2. *Dream Vortex* (2011-), Still, Scene 2

ART AND RESEARCH

The mission of KeckCAVES is to "provide an intellectual and computational framework for the visual exploration...of data and models...using visualization tools to gain insights into problems that are difficult to address using other techniques." It is an interdisciplinary center with ongoing work in biology, geology, mathematics, physics and other fields. Sumner and Crutchfield have both previously collaborated with other artists and found their questions and projects useful in developing scientific tools.

As an artist, Tromble has envisioned new possibilities for the programming that enrich her work but which also expand the tools available to the scientists. The first *Dream Vortex* prototypes were made in Mycelia, a network visualization program created at UCD, to which Sumner added new imaging and movement capabilities required for the *Dream Vortex*. These augmentations include displaying images at the nodes of an interactive network and the ability to control the movement of the entire network in 3D space. The current version uses Vroom and PyVrui, also developed at UCD. The personal 3D viewing technology Oculus Rift became available for research when the Complexity Sciences Center acquired a developer kit; adapting the piece for Oculus Rift provided a test case for the lab to work with the new equipment.

CONCLUSION

Historically, the availability of affordable video equipment stimulated the development of a new field of art. With the increasing availability of affordable 3D equipment, we are on the cusp of a new surge in virtual, 3D art. The emerging possibilities of integrating virtual and physical installations in art spaces, with mobile equipment, make this a critical moment to pursue bringing a liminal, mixed-reality world into being.

Dream Vortex, as a collaboration between an artist and a scientist, dissolves the boundaries between seemingly opposite activities. It unites human's oldest and newest image-making technologies, charcoal drawing and programming, and brings subjective questions into an objective research environment. It is also a beautiful visual and aural experience, a harbinger of the new art forms that will emerge as 3D tools become widely available to artists.

ACKNOWLEDGEMENTS

We thank Jim Crutchfield, godfather of the *Dream Vortex*, for his support at all levels; Joe Dumit for brainstorming and technical insight; Christopher Ellison, Oliver Kreylos, and Jordan Van Aalsberg for their programming; Leonardo/ISAST and the Djerassi Artist Residency for the gift of time, and all the dreamers for their dreams. Tromble gratefully acknowledges support for the project from the San Francisco Art Institute and Anwyl McDonald.

System Self Assembly: The Self in the City

Andrew Welsby
60 North Hanover Street
Glasgow, G1 2BP
andy.welsby@me.com
andrewwelsby.com

ABSTRACT

System Self Assembly (2015) is an installation that is the result of a year long auto-ethnographic study. The work explores performative concepts of the self, agency, and the redundancy of the modern medium.

Author Keywords

System; art; performative; assembly; interactive; ethnography.

INTRODUCTION

System Self Assembly (2015) is a floor based physical installation. Viewers are invited to participate with the construction of the artwork as it evolves. The work comprises 364 wooden triangles measuring on average 40cm x 30cm each. The triangles interlock creating a seemingly amorphous 3-dimensional shape. However, the continuing evolution of the shapes is in fact procedural.

PROCESS

System Self Assembly (2015) is the final physical manifestation of a one year process of situating myself at the center of an anthropological investigation of Glasgow's landscape. The intention was to focus on my surroundings in new and different ways by creating a system for observing, and feeding back observed information. Thus creating a visual based analysis of my surroundings.

Part of the feedback process was to take a photograph from my exact location, at mid-day (or as close to as was possible) facing precisely north, drawing upon observer-as-participator research methodology [1]. Historically, cameras have provided anthropologists with an invaluable tool to collect and present social reality differently. Photography therefore allows researchers to ask different questions, and represent findings in new ways [2].

One such representation used a Processing sketch (a self authored computer program) to statistically sample sixteen equidistant points in each photograph.

Figure 1. RGB – XYZ transformation for 3 consecutive weeks

This technique obtained accurate colour information as it was distributed about the photograph. The system dictated that the colour information for each of the sixteen points should be converted to a red (R), green (G) and blue (B) hex value. Each value had a numerical attribution between 0 and 255. Once the data was collected and stored, the values were converted to points on an XYZ axis: R became X, G became Y, and B became Z. This process was repeated for all of the sixteen points, where a single line creates a vertex shape connecting the coordinates.

The vertex shapes have informed the fabrication of a physical system. Viewers are asked to interact with the work by looking beyond the medium of the piece, to reflect on the degree of performative agency that individuals have within their surroundings.

Figure 2: 10 pieces assembled – a sample instance of the installation.

The intention of the work is to minimise the materiality of the piece, thus encouraging the apprehension and interrogation of the systems process. The form of the 364 pieces is flexible, suggesting the work can never be complete. Instead the work has states of iteration as viewers contribute to its continually changing arrangement.

CONCLUSION

This artwork rejects materiality to explore a systems based process reflecting the performative agency we all have with our lived environments. Using myself as the point of departure encourages users to consider the work using 3 main points: The historical perspective, the contemporary discursive perspective and the contemporary practice perspective [3].

BIOGRAPHY

I am a visual artist based in Glasgow, currently working with video, performance, systems and machine made art. I hold a Master of Research degree from Glasgow School of Art, a PGDip in Electronic imaging and a BA (hons) Fine Art, both from Duncan of Jordanstone College of Art, Dundee.

I am interested in the construction of identities within local, national and global communities, using a theoretical framework drawn from Cybernetics and Postcolonial theories. Specifically I focus on the construction of asymmetrical identity relationships where hegemony and myth are the constructing orders. My current practice creates autonomous systems and drawing machines, often from modified and re-purposed children's toys, found wood and plastic. My work draws upon theories of 'post-expert' and detournement, making visible the deconstruction of traditional power structures and asking where the 'self' is situated in comparison to the 'other'. Using a system based approach, my systems make works that either help visualise the Cybernetics or Postcolonial theories found in my research, or suggest parallel courses of investigation.

REFERENCES

1. Bryman, A. *Social Research Methods*, OUP, Oxford. 2004.

2. Leavy, P. *Method Meets Art*, The Guildford Press, NY. (2009) 230.

3. Halsall, F. Systems Aesthetics and the System as Medium, *Systems Art Symposium,* Whitechapel Art Gallery, UK. 2007.

'Sense-a-Ball' Pong

Dr Mark Palmer
Department of Computer Science and Creative Technologies
UWE Bristol
Bristol
Avon
United Kingdom
Mark.Palmer@uwe.ac.uk

ABSTRACT

The attraction of classic computer games wasn't their verisimilitude. Games like *Battlezone* and *Elite* blended perception and action through interactivity that flowed around the immateriality of the game object; cinematic tropes then emphasised this in films like *Tron* and *Minority Report*.

Arguably this reveals a facet of perception we have passed over in favour of the fixed outlines of objects. But if this is a part of perception per se rather than being limited to the screen, shouldn't we be able to experience this within the physical world?

Sense-a-Ball Pong explores this by making the classic computer game of Pong 'physical'. A grid of vanes will orientate themselves towards the 'ball' *implying* its position whilst it will be invisible. Utilising distance sensors player's will then use their hand to play with the ball. If perception does flow around the object it should become evident in this work.

Author Keywords

Perception; Immateriality; Physicality; Interactivity.

ACM Classification Keywords

K.8.0 Games; J.5 Fine Arts

THE BODY, THE VIRTUAL AND PERCEPTION

What constitutes our embodied experiences is still something that is subject to debate across a range of disciplines, nevertheless its importance in shaping the mind is becoming increasingly recognised [1]. Having worked on

a Body Image Tool for people with Complex Regional Pain Syndrome (CRPS) (fig 1) Palmer has recognised the plasticity of perception [2] and the way it is deeply embedded in context and action. Building on prior research addressing the Rubber Hand Illusion [3,4,5,6] this has led to an involvement with further research examining the use of Kinect and varying representations of the body which has begun to show that it is possible to affect our perceptions of our body through the way it is represented on screen.

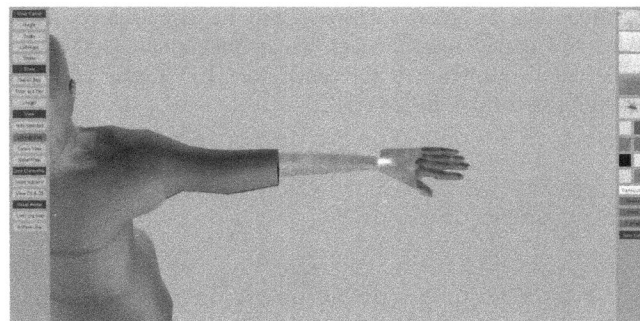

Figure 1. Image generated by a patient of their CRPS affected limb.

Given these factors, it appears that the virtual is not just a means to create alternative realities, but an opportunity to question the nature of experience itself. But how might the opportunity to do this be approached? The problem is that systems such as the Wii, which have been important in allowing a more embodied approach to interaction, have also led to a startling re-enforcement of a particular kind of physicality. This has been illustrated through the unfortunate injuries that have occurred when users have accidently hit other players and objects around them. Perhaps more worryingly there have been cases of hyperextension injuries as users strike at virtual objects that offer none of the resistance that their physical counterpart would provide [8]. If it the case that the mixing of physical action and the virtual representation of the real leads to these problems if we wish to examine the underlying aspects of perception that concern the 'immaterial' we need to alternative ways for our bodies to engage with the immateriality that attracted many of us to the digital in the first place.

Whilst our tendency towards a particular kind of physicality brings one set of issues, the digital often brings other assumptions that can be equally as problematic. One of the most challenging of these has been the propensity to assert notions of the transcendental when talking of the virtual. If we examine perception's ability to sense 'more than' the harsh outlines of the objects we find in the world, it does not mean this has to be accounted for through a move to another 'reality', in fact this can take us away from the very thing we wish to examine as we fall back on the dualities that have plagued philosophy and science. Rather the subtlety of perception needs to be understood in this world, but without assumptions that can cloud our understanding of perception. We need to develop an understanding of what the virtual has gifted us in developing our understanding of perception and to begin to realize what alternative approaches to embodied interactivity may have to offer. *Sense-a-Ball Pong* has been created to explore these phenomena, asking players to physically interact with a ball that cannot be seen.

In order to achieve this, a grid of 'vanes' will be created that will turn 'bill boarding' themselves towards the ball's position (fig 2). Each of these will be constructed from balsa and doped tissue, much as model planes used to be constructed, allowing a reference to CAD forms and the intangibility of the digital (fig 3).

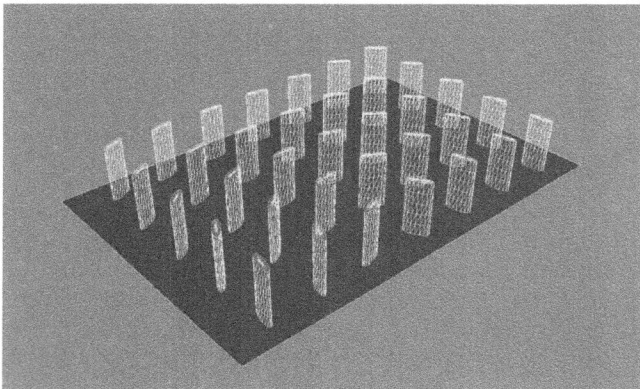

Figure 3. Vane

Figure 2. Bill boarded forms orientated towards the virtual ball's position.

REFERENCES

1. Gallagher, S. *How The Body Shapes The Mind*. Oxford University Press (2005).

2. Turton, A. Palmer, M. et al. Evaluation of a prototype tool for communicating body perception disturbances in complex regional pain syndrome *Frontiers in Human Neuroscience*. Vol 7. Article 517

3. Botvinick, M. and Cohen, J. Rubber hands 'feel' touch that eyes see. In *Nature*, 391 pp. 756.

4. Slater, M. Perez-Marcos, D. Henrik Ehrsson, H. and Sanchez-Vives, M.V. Towards a digital body: the virtual arm illusion. In *Frontiers in Human Neuroscience*, Vol 2, Article 6

5. Yuan, Y. and Steed, A. Is the rubber hand illusion induced by immersive virtual reality? In *Virtual Reality Conference(VR) 2010 IEEE*, pp. 95-102.

6. Kilteni, K. Normand, J.M. Sanchez-Vives, M.V. and Slater, M. Extending body space in immersive virtual reality; a very long arm illusion. In *PloS One,*7(7) pp.e40867.

7. Jalink, M.B., Heineman, E. Pierie, J-P.E.N. and Hoedemaker, H. Nintendo related injuries and other problems: review. In *BMJ* 2014; 349:g7267.

City | Data | Future: Envisioning Interactions in Hybrid Urban Space

Michael Smyth
Edinburgh Napier University
10 Colinton Road
Edinburgh, UK
m.smyth@napier.ac.uk

Ingi Helgason
Edinburgh Napier University
10 Colinton Road
Edinburgh, UK
i.helgason@napier.ac.uk

Ivica Mitrović
Arts Academy
University of Split
Split, Croatia
ivica@umas.hr

ABSTRACT

The City | Data | Future installation is a collection of "design fiction" video scenarios that speculate about the experience of urban life and how it might change in the near future.

These visions were collaboratively created over the course of an interdisciplinary summer school, exploring the emergent field of urban interaction design. The focus of this field is public space and the relationships between people – with and through technology. Cities in the future will contain a tangled mesh of interlocking data streams, and this complexity is increasingly forming the backdrop to human activities. The installation presents a series of works that invite the viewer to consider how technology might shape the city of the future and subsequently, our relationship with the city, and with each other.

The works have been created as part of the UrbanIxD project, which ran between 2013-14 and was funded under the EU FP7 FET Open initiative.

Author Keywords

Urban interaction design; design fiction; critical design; installations.

ACM Classification Keywords

H.5.m. Information interfaces and presentation (e.g., HCI): Miscellaneous.

INTRODUCTION

The installation, presented at Creativity & Cognition in 2015, is an extract of the full City | Data | Future exhibition. A full description of the exhibition and the venues where it has been shown can be found at: www.citydatafuture.eu.

C&C '15, June 22-25, 2015, Glasgow, United Kingdom
ACM 978-1-4503-3598-0/15/06.
http://dx.doi.org/10.1145/2757226.2757380

This exhibition, which travelled to several European venues during 2014 and 2015, presents a series of visions depicting what it might be like to live in a near future city, saturated with data. Each exhibition piece questions our changing relationship with the city and its citizens.

What might it mean to live in a city where everything is measured, and crowdsourced opinion holds sway? How might this affect our own judgment in the face of such quantification, and what does this mean for the creation and consumption of personal data? Will the city of the future protect us or will it monitor us? Will it provide shelter so that we can decide with whom we share our most intimate thoughts? As we reflect on the value we place on data, what new rituals might emerge around our need to share?

Welcome to the Hybrid City of all our futures.

Figure 1. Images from the design fiction videos

Presenting the installation

The exhibition was designed to be flexible for presentation at many types of venues and events. For Creativity & Cognition 2015, the exhibit comprised of the following elements, which were designed to be adjusted or altered according to the available space.

- 1 or 2 large video projections onto screens, walls or hangings. This displays a collection of the design fiction videos (*Figure 1*). Examples of the design fiction videos can be seen at www.citydatafuture.eu/category/works

- 1 smaller monitor screen or projection, presenting a showreel video explaining the making of the design fictions at the UrbanIxD summer school. (*Figure 2*) (The UrbanIxD Summer School showreel: www.vimeo.com/78513943)
- 1 tabletop display for a small physical prototype artifact, and supporting printed materials, postcards and reference copies of the exhibition catalogue. (*Figure 3*)

Figure 2. Still from UrbanIxD showreel

Figure 3. Exhibition catalogue

BIOGRAPHIES

The work presented in this installation is truly the result of collaboration, both in the generation of the concepts and in the creation of the works themselves. These works emerged from the creative activities of the UrbanIxD project Summer School held in 2013 in Split, Croatia. UrbanIxD was a Coordination Action project, that ran from 2013-2014, for the European Commission under the Future and Emerging Technologies programme. This Coordination Action defined a multidisciplinary research community working in the domain of technologically augmented, data-rich urban environments, with particular focus on the human activities, experiences and behaviours that occur within them. Project website: www.urbanixd.eu

All 40 of the summer school participants, their atelier leaders, and atelier coordinators contributed to the concepts that informed the works. The production of the final versions of the works was managed by Ivica Mitrović and Oleg Šuran at the University of Split, Croatia.

Author biographies
Michael Smyth was the Coordinator of the UrbanIxD project that is funded under the EU FP7 programme, part of the FET Open initiative (www.urbanixd.eu). He has worked in the fields of Human Computer Interaction and Interaction Design since 1987 and during that period has published over 60 academic papers in refereed journals, books and conferences. In addition he has had interactive installations exhibited at both UK and international conferences and arts & design festivals. He is co-editor of the book entitled Digital Blur: creative practice at the boundaries of architecture, design and art, Libri Publishing.

Ivica Mitrović is an assistant professor in the design and visual communications department at the Arts Academy in Split, where he teaches subjects related to design, and interactive design in new media. He received his Ph.D. at the University of Split. He has been mentor and co-mentor of numerous exhibited and awarded student projects in national and international juried design exhibitions. He curated retrospective exhibitions of the interactive design workshops titled "Interactions 2004 - 2012", and a review of the Croatian scene in the field of new media design, exhibited in the gallery HDD in Zagreb. He is the author of the book "Designing New Media, Design and New Media - Croatian Context (1995 - 2010)", and is vice president of the Croatian Design Association.

Ingi Helgason is a research fellow and part-time lecturer at Edinburgh Napier University, where she is studying towards a PhD in Interaction Design. She also teaches interaction design and technology innovation at the Open University. She has worked as a researcher on EU FP6 and FP7 projects, including UrbanIxD. She was a member of the executive committee of the Create series of interaction design conferences. She is one of the organisers of This Happened Edinburgh, a series of events focusing on the stories behind interaction design.

Lichtsuchende:
A Society of Cybernetic, Phototropic Sunflowers*

Dave Murray-Rust
School of Informatics
University of Edinburgh
d.murray-rust@ed.ac.uk

Rocio von Jungenfeld
School of Design
University of Edinburgh
rocio.von-jungenfeld@ed.ac.uk

ABSTRACT

Lichtsuchende is an interactive installation, built using a society of biologically inspired, cybernetic creatures who exchange light as a source of energy and a means of communication. Visitors are invited to engage with the installation using torches to influence and interact with the phototropic robots. The embodied algorithms give rise to emergent behaviours with communicative and emotional resonance, allowing a duet between the humans and the cybernetic beings.

Author Keywords

Cybernetics; Interaction design; Actor Network Theory

INTRODUCTION

Biologically inspired artworks have the potential to feel alive, creating an interplay of needs between the visitors and the system. When people experience digital algorithms associated with the physical structures of artificial creatures, there is a tendency to anthropomorphise, to project ideas of emotion and behaviour, and to empathise with them. There is a vibrant history of swarm behaviour and artificial life within the world of computational art. To highlight some influences on this work: Blackwell's SwarmMusic [2] paired a digital swarm with a skilled human improviser to create musical duets and rAndom International's *Audience* piece works with the idea of static robot swarm directing their attention to visitors which they find in some sense 'interesting' [1]. Finally, there is a clear relation to Ihnatowicz's seminal *Sound Activated Mobile*[2], one of the earliest cybernetic kinetic sculptures.

Lichtsuchende engages with the relation between embodied algorithms and emotional responses, the ways in which we may socialise with robots [3]: how the internal state is performed and understood, how activity is organised, and what gives rise to the underlying dynamics of action and response. This draws on Barlow's modal action patterns—recognisable behaviours with clear preconditions underpinning theories

[1] http://www.chrisoshea.org/audience
[2] http://www.senster.com/ihnatowicz/SAM/sam.htm

C&C 2015, June 22–25, 2015, Glasgow, United Kingdom.
ACM 978-1-4503-3598-0/15/06
http://dx.doi.org/10.1145/2757226.2757381.

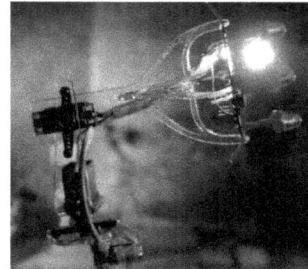

Figure 1. The head of a robot, consisting of a PCB mounted on an armature composed of transparent acrylic and servo motors.

of animal communication such as zones of safety [1], and Maslow's organisation of human needs into a hierarchy of dependance with the requirement to satisfy base needs before more rarefied desires are considered [5].

Another area of interest is the relation between digital creatures and their environment, in particular Uexküll's *Umwelt*—the perceptual life-world which gives rise to the creatures' biosemantic view of their environment: "Every subject spins out, like the spiders threads, its relations to certain qualities of things and weaves them into a solid web, which carries its existence" [6, p. 53].. The environments in which these creatures exist, however, are often created alongside their inhabitants, developed in dialogue with the ways in which the creatures practise and perform their behavioural routines. This creates a symbiotic relation, where the environment and its organisms shape and influence each other [4, p. 20], an ecosystemic network between the emerging lifeforms, their creators, and their visitors.

DESCRIPTION OF THE WORK

Lichtsuchende is an interactive installation, comprising a society of cybernetic creatures. The creatures base their interaction on the exchange of light, using it both as a source of energy and a means of communication. Visitors to the installation can interact with the creatures using torches to influence their behaviour (Figure 2). A video showing an early version of the robots can be found here: http://bit.ly/1HFOod8.

The creatures resemble sunflowers to some extent: they are fixed to the floor, and rotate their heads to track light. They have a relatively curtailed set of basic capabilities for sensing and affecting their environment (Figure ??): actuators to angle their heads; 5 ambient light sensors arranged in a cross allow them to sense the intensity and gradient of the light

Figure 2. Lichtsuchende installed in the Hidden Door Festival, Edinburgh, 2014. Photo credit Chris Scott @chrisdonia

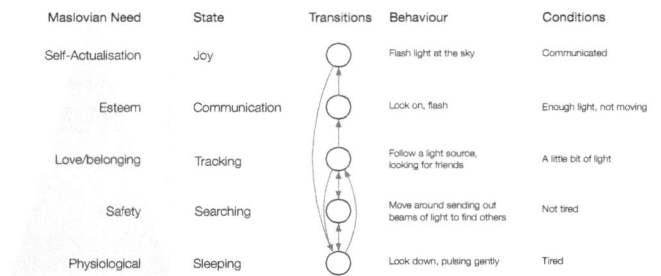

Figure 3. Behavioural states of the robots with their activation conditions, and a relation to the Maslovian hierarchy of needs.

field in front of them; and cluster of superbright LEDs emit a strong, narrow beam of light in the direction that they are facing, with variable intensity 1.

This means their *Umwelt* is built on an extremely pared down set of basic inputs: knowing their position, and sensing part of the structure of the light field around them. This allows them to turn their attention towards sources of light, and to project light in the direction of their attention as a means of engaging, connecting their inner world to that of their fellows and any visitors in the installation environment.

As previously noted, the central characteristic of the creatures is their fascination with light, their immediate enrapturement and constant alignment with any source of photons. As well as their fascination wiht light, the creatures navigate a graph of behavioural states (Figure 3), which are arranged in a rough parallel with Maslow's hierarchy of needs [5]. Taken in increasing priority, the states, their conditions and the associated observable activities are as follows:

Sleeping occurs when a flower lacks energy, looking downards, pusling gently and regaining energy.

Searching involves moving by small, random amounts, and then sending out a slow pulse of light in that direction to see if anything responds.

Tracking happens when ther is sufficiently bright light source and involves turning towards the sensor giving the highest reading. When tracking, the robot outputs a strong beam of light, to allow itself to be tracked by whatever is producing the light. Tracking consumes a lot of energy, meaning that often the flower will go to sleep if the light source is lost.

Communication is enabled when a robot has seen a bright light, for a certain amount of time, with minimal movement, indicating that it has found a fellow flower. The physical effect is that the robot freezes in place, and flashes rapidly, as a placeholder for exchange of information.

Joy occurs when communication is successfully completed: the flower points at the sky, emits a few bright flashes of light. It then goes back to sleep, exhausted.

Some physical behaviour is unplanned, resulting from their embodiment and situation: if a person reaches out to touch a flower which is tracking light, their hand casts a shadow on the sensor, and the robot will turn away. This can happen abruptly, and has been interpreted as shyness, or a nervous reaction. We are interested firstly in how the robots' internal state can be communicated to visitors, the relation between display and interpretation and matching conceptual ideas to anthropomorphic readings. Secondly, how can the network of states be constructed to give rise to pathways of behaviour that are understandable and plausible in the context of creaturehood.

The behaviours above provide a link between the individual and the social, and these interrelationships provide fertile ground for emergent behaviour. At one level, there are the effects of having several autonomous, embodied entities sharing a space: communication may occur or not; if it does, it may be subject to misinterpretation, or interrupted by the actions of others. There is the possibility of cascades of behaviour change throughout the space, a positive feedback as each robot activates others, spreading excitation.

We are interested in the question of what it takes to design an 'interesting' robot society, which exhibits a range of behaviour, which reacts to visitors but has its own internal dynamics, and which doesn't exhibit pathological complete failure modes.

REFERENCES

1. Barlow, G. W. Modal action patterns. In *How Animals Communicate*, T. A. Sebeok, Ed. Indiana University Press, 1977, 98–136.

2. Blackwell, T. Swarm Music: improvised music with multi-swarms. In *2003 AISB symposium on AI and Creativity in Arts and Science* (2003), 41–49.

3. Fong, T., Nourbakhsh, I., and Dautenhahn, K. A survey of socially interactive robots. *Robotics and autonomous systems 42*, 3 (2003), 143–166.

4. Ingold, T. *The Perception of the Environment: Essays on livelyhood, dwelling and skill*. Routledge, 2000.

5. Maslow, A. H. A theory of human motivation. *Psychological Review 50*, 4 (1943), 370–396.

6. Von Uexküll, J. *A foray into the worlds of animals and humans*. University of Minnesota Press, 2010.

Lucid Peninsula: DreamScope:
An Interactive Physical Installation

Mara Dionisio, Paulo Bala, Rui Trindade, Valentina Nisi, Julian Hanna
Madeira Interactive Technologies Institute
{msgdionisio, paulo.bala, rui.antero.trindade, valentina.nisi,
julianhanna}@gmail.com

Time's Up
Time's Up
tina@timesup.org

ABSTRACT

In this paper we present Lucid Peninsula, an interactive installation designed to immerse participants in a dreamlike, post-apocalyptic story world. The goal of the installation is to offer a way for people to experience the future through a physical interactive installation. To achieve this aim we designed and developed the interactive DreamScope device, while the Time's Up collective designed and built the physical installation. On one side with the Dreamviewer binoculars users will be able to see the world outside and absorb data relating to factors such as air quality, presence of plant and other life forms, etc. On the other side of the installation, the audience will be able to borrow mobile devices (Dreamcatchers) and venture into the actual landscape of the city, in order to 'catch' the dreams of the inhabitants of the peninsula, which are mixed with memories of the world before it was transformed.

Author Keywords

Interactive Installation; Physical Installation;Virtual Reality

ACM Classification Keywords

H.5.1 Multimedia Information Systems

INTRODUCTION

Lucid Peninsula is an interactive installation designed to immerse participants in a dreamlike, post-apocalyptic storyworld where changes to the Earth's atmosphere have led to the emergence of new species, conditions, and ways of life. Fragments of memories and dreams belonging to the inhabitants of the previous era still linger in this new world, hovering over certain locations. The Lucid Peninsula storyworld where the lucid dreaming takes place emerged from a future scenario planning activity undertaken by artists and designers from the FoAM and Time's Up collectives in June 2014. We worked closely with these artists to create the Lucid Peninsula interactive physical

C&C '15, June 22-25, 2015, Glasgow, United Kingdom
ACM 978-1-4503-3598-0/15/06.
http://dx.doi.org/10.1145/2757226.27573827,5

installation. Lucid Peninsula is a part of Future Fabulators, an EU-funded project that aims to explore and prototype possible futures within a cultural framework. [1]

The goal of the installation is to offer a means for people to experience the future by bringing to life a storyworld the audience can interact with, reflect on, and interrogate with questions such as: Could I live in this world? Could this really happen? How would I adapt?

LUCID PENINSULA STORYWORLD

The Lucid Peninsula is a futuristic world that feels familiar, yet strange: an eternal twilight of dreamlike metaphors and shape-shifting beings. Environmental living conditions have radically changed and the search for green plants has become crucial for survival. The outside air is toxic: not immediately lethal, but requiring special gear and treatment after exposure.

PHYSICAL INSTALLATION AND DREAMSCOPE MOBILE APPLICATION

To give the public a chance to experience the Lucid Peninsula firsthand, we designed a physical installation and an interactive environment. A special device called a DreamScope, comprised of Dreamviewer binoculars and a mobile Dreamcatcher, will guide people in the discovery of this world. The equipment will be located in a special room, dedicated to the detoxification and recovery of air force pilots who sweep the peninsula in search of rare green plants and need to undergo a special purification treatment before they can fly the next mission.

We designed and developed the interactive DreamScope device, while the Time's Up collective designed and built the recovery room. On one side of the installation, the Dreamviewer binoculars will be positioned at a window so that users will be able to see the world outside and try to gauge the viability of venturing outside again, taking into account data such as air toxicity, availability of plants, other life forms, etc. On the other side of the installation, the audience will be able to borrow mobile devices (Dreamcatchers) and venture into the real streets of Glasgow, in order to 'catch' the dreams of the inhabitants of the peninsula, which are mixed with memories of the world before it was transformed into the dry and toxic Lucid Peninsula that it has become.

Physical Installation

As long as people continue to travel to the Lucid Peninsula, a place to rest and recover before the next leg of the journey will be necessary. As travellers rest or sleep through the recovery process, the capacity to dream is vital: to be lucid, to share and live in dreams, is a necessity. Dreaming is an important part of life in this future world sustained by memories of a time when things were different.

The physical installation recreates this special environment with an air purifying machine, medical gear necessary for the healing process, a machine to archive dreams and memories, and the interactive DreamScope, comprised of the viewer and the catcher (explained in the next section).

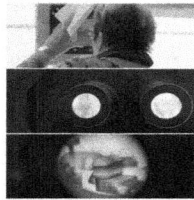

Figure 1- DreamScope Viewer

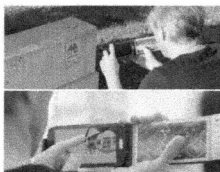

Figure 2 - DreamScope Catcher

DreamScope Mobile Application

Lucid DreamScope: Viewer

The Dreamviewer enables the audience to glimpse life in the Lucid Peninsula. The device is used by pilots in the recovery room to check outside conditions (temperature, humidity, visibility), make sure it is safe to exit the room, and find locations with heightened dream activity.

With the Dreamviewer, visitors can enjoy a 180-degree panoramic view of the outside world, as if they are looking through a window of the room. The 3D world depicts a desert-like landscape with orange sky and large red sun. The 3D landscape simulates the landscape outside the recovery room, highlighting buildings that the user can explore in the city. Users can zoom in on buildings in the landscape to apprehend more details of the structure. This is possible through the use of a Google cardboard virtual reality kit. [2] The software was built using the Unity game engine and receives input from the compass and the accelerometer in order to show the virtual environment of the Lucid Peninsula.

Lucid DreamScope: Catcher

With the Dreamcatcher visitors will discover the dreams of Lucid Peninsula inhabitants. A poster in the fictional recovery room alerts users that they can encounter and experience fragments of dreams through the mobile Dreamcatcher device. This device has an Android application built using the Unity game engine and it features image recognition to trigger the virtual environments of characters' dreams.

In order to retrieve dream fragments the visitor borrows a mobile device in exchange for an ID card at the front desk of the exhibition venue. Then a mobile phone and physical map of the surrounding area is delivered to the visitor, highlighting where the dreams are located.

When the visitor gets to a place where a dream is available, s/he will find a special icon (see top of Fig. 2) indicating dream presence and scan it. An interactive view of the Lucid Dreaming world appears on the screen of the mobile device.

By tapping the screen users can create circular viewing portals that show what the Lucid Peninsula world looked like at a different time. An audio narration recounts the dream mixed with memories from the dreamers. The dreams themselves focus on the past and how the world once was (our current world) and the nostalgia the present inhabitants feel about such distant times, mixed with stories of their present lives.

CONCLUSION

The Lucid Peninsula was successfully exhibited in Austria and Romania, in the context of the exhibition Intime Raume 2014 by IMA [3] and Future Fabulators exhibition by AltArt [4]. The diverse audience found the Dreamscope entertaining and thought-provoking. We would like to exhibit the Dreamscope interactive installation at the C&C in order to probe the audience through exposure to future scenarios as well as engaging them in a pleasurable, interactive and dreamlike experience.

ACKNOWLEDGMENTS

We wish to acknowledge Future Fabulators, EU Culture Funds (2013-1659/001-001 CU7 COOP7) for sponsoring our investigation, our fellow researchers at all partner institutions, M-ITI, Time's Up, and FoAM for their help and contributions, and the LARSyS (PEst-OE/EEI/LA0009/2013) research group for support and funding.

REFERENCES

[1]http://futurefabulators.m-iti.org;

[2] http://www.google.com/get/cardboard/

[3] http://ima.or.at/lucid-peninsula/?lang=de

[4]http://www.altart.org/?p=1322

Statuevision: Glasgow

Ali Momeni
Carnegie Mellon University
School of Art / IDEATE
CFA 300 - 5000 Forbes Ave
Pittsburgh, PA
momeni@cmu.edu

Claire Hentschker
Carnegie Mellon University
School of Art / IDEATE CFA
300 - 5000 Forbes Ave
Pittsburgh, PA
chentsch@andrew.cmu.edu

ABSTRACT

Statuevision is an interactive public projection performance that engages citizens in conversations about urban histories. *Statuevision: Glasgow* invites participants to explore Glasgow's history through its iconic statues and monuments. This performance employs interactive technologies that enable participants to animate three-dimensional renderings of the cities statues while learning about the lives of the figures.

Author Keywords

Art; Technology; Projection; Intervention; Public Space; Animation; Modeling

ACM Classification Keywords

H.5.m. Information interfaces and presentation (e.g., HCI): Miscellaneous.

BACKGROUND

Statuevision was debuted in October of 2014 as part of the 5x5 project, a Washington DC program of contemporary, temporary public art, dedicated to exploring new perspectives on the District. Through 5x5, the DC Commission on the Arts and Humanities sought out five curators to commission publicly accessible works of art. As part of 5×5, artist Ali Momeni developed *Statuevision* to celebrate local monuments and national histories in a public and participatory video projection performance. The performance in DC consisted of six mobile carts beaming animated images of the district's statues on DuPont Circle at night. This collaborative project brought local history teachers and historians, young students from Capital Hill Montessori, students from Carnegie Mellon University and everyday DC history buffs together in narrating the lives and achievements of historical figures commemorated in statues around the district. In developing the project the university students worked with seven and eight year olds to rehearse the performance while learning about world

C&C '15, June 22-25, 2015, Glasgow, United Kingdom
ACM 978-1-4503-3598-0/15/06.
http://dx.doi.org/10.1145/2757226.2757383

history though statues. The piece explored the past and future of historic movements, and DuPont Circle as the site for intergenerational assembly in celebration of public statuary and the history it embeds. The one-night performance began at dusk in DuPont Circle surrounding Chester French's statue. The event assembled approximately 500 DC citizens and visitors to experience live, real-time interactive projections based on 3-dimensional models of District statues.

The process of creating *Statuevision* produced several hardware, software and social instruments that are extensible. An archive of scanned 3D models of DC statues, custom software for real-time animation, and gestural control suited for seven to eight year old students were produced as part of the project. *Statuevision: Glasgow* is an adaptation of the original work for Glasgow, its statues and its history. During the conference the artists will create a site-specific projection performance that will bring the magic of augmented puppetry and historical story telling to a new city.

CONTENT

Using existing and freely available technologies, the Statuevision team creates accurate 3D models of Glasgow's public statues. The 3D models are made using the free and online 123D Catch tool by AutoDesk, which allows users to generate a 3D model of an object with just a few dozen still images taken from various angles around the object. These models are further refined using MeshLab, another freely available and open source tool. During the performance, custom software allows the public to animate and move video projections of the statues in ways akin to puppetry. The process of creating *Statuevision: Glasgow* will generate an archive of 3D models will be shared publicly through SketchFab, a free and accessible online resource that allows social sharing and downloading of 3D models, and media content about the historical significance of each statue and monument represented will be shared with the public.

HARDWARE AND SOFTWARE

Statuevision employs custom software implemented in Max, openFrameworks, and OpenGL Shaders. Several overarching goals guide Statuevision's software development: 1) an intuitive and gesturally controlled system for animating 3D models in real time, 2) a performative storytelling rubric with well defined rolls for the speaker, the audience and the assistant. 3) platforms and technologies that be embedded in future versions of the project, thereby removing the need for laptops in future performances.

Figure one shows the mobile projection units designed for the DC.

An adjustable, incandescent lamp attaches to each cart providing the participants with a spotlight as they manipulate the projections. The Projector remained firmly mounted to the cart with a Magic Arm and clamp. The lighting, projector, speaker and computer receive power from a battery fastened to the inside of the cart that remains hidden by white paneling, bearing the branded *Statuevision* name and logo. The bottom of each cart glows with a RGBWW controllable strip light lining the base. These carts were designed and assembled specially for the *Stautevision* project.

CONCLUSION

As an art project, *Statuevision: Glasgow* proposes to transform the familiar, often unheeded, presence of historic monuments into a catalyst for public discourse and amusement. The performance will highlight Glasgow's legacy as a site bridging past political identity and present popular culture, spanning generations and social strata, encouraging playful congregation and vibrant public exchange throughout the course of the event. As a one night experience, *Statuevision* aims to create a space where the familiar is rendered unfamiliar, pedestrians become puppeteers, and art works of a distant past are imbued with renewed significance and impact. All in all, the project desires to forge a community through shared experience and appreciation for the rich history embedded in the monuments of Glasgow, and people who walk amongst them.

BIOS

Ali Momeni is an artist and educator, exploring dynamic systems and moving targets. He works with kinetics, electronics, software, sound, light, people, plants and animals. His creative output ranges from sculptures and installations, to urban interventions and music theater performance. Momeni currently teaches in the School of Art at Carnegie Mellon University and oversees CMU ArtFab.

Claire Hentschker is studying art and media design at Carnegie Mellon University. She is interested in augmenting realities, and exploring technology as a platform for community building.

Video documentation: https://vimeo.com/117190296

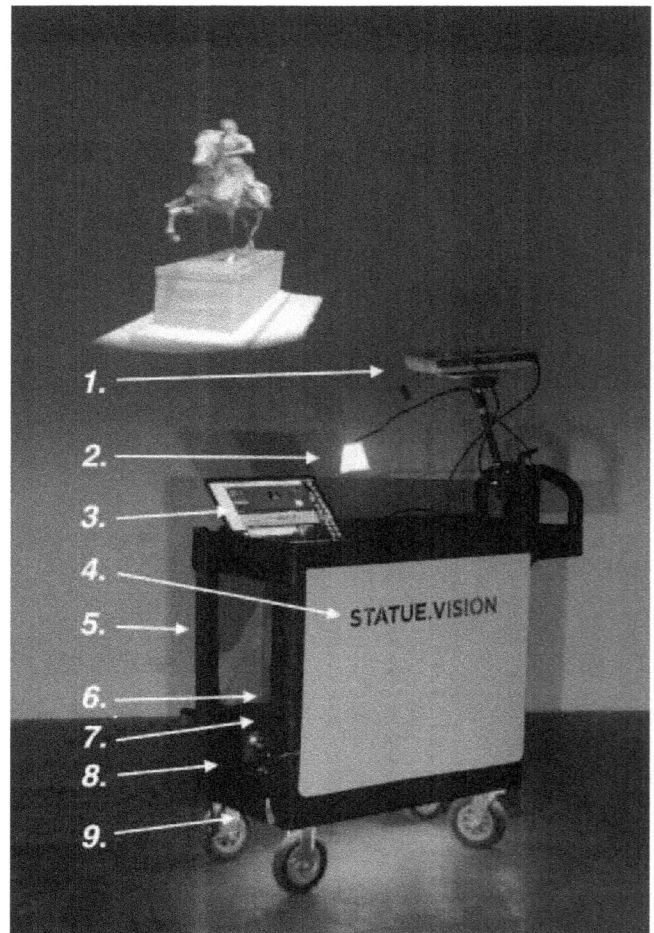

Figure 1.

1. **Projector: Dell HD700 3000 Lumin Projector,**

2. **Top Lighting: 12V incandescent overhead lighting with hand-made lampshade,**

3. **Laptop: Macbook or Macbook Pro,**

4. **Side Panels: Lasercut 0.006" polystyrene with Statuevision logo,**

5. **Rubbermaid Heavy-Duty Utility Cart**

6. **Battery: LiFO4 100 Amp Hour,**

7. **Inverter: 1000 Watt,**

8. **Speaker: Mackie amplified 150 Watt public announcement system,**

9. **Bottom Lighting: RGBWW remote-controllable strip lighting**

SIGCHI Conference Proceedings Format

Michael Denton
Artist, composer
6 Hazel Court, Stonestile Lane, Hastings, E
Sussex TN354PE
art@overlap.co.uk
01424 755315

Anna McCrickard
Artist, editor, animator
6 Hazel Court, Stonestile Lane, Hastings, E
Sussex TN354PE
anna@overlap.co.uk
01424 755315

SUMMARY OF WORK:
Aquatint

Live audiovisual event. Duration: 30 to 70 minutes. Venue: single screen/ cinema. **Music & Imagery Overlap**

Overlap have developed a style outside film, TV and video art - a way of abstracting and combining imagery that has a musical or painterly logic rather than a narrative based or conceptual one. A visual take on serialism - wallpaper with conceits.

Recent works explore the relationship between still and moving imagery through systems of implied motion within transitions, use of discreet picture planes and obscuration techniques. The view is in movie time but limited to flat photographic space, through a perceptual keyhole more akin to memories and dreams. Experiments with sound and image are distilled into single screen pieces - Lazy Wave, Cloud Edged, Forest Tree, Returning - forming useful components for live mixing, audiovisual polyphonies for installations and performances.

Aquatint is a mesmeric dance of shapes, lights and abstract imagery on the cusp of the recognizable, reflecting the emotional response we experience in powerful natural environments. Atmospheric, complex, sensual and earthy, yet delivered through a systematic patterning within a synthetic void.

In a world of ubiquitous, immediately interpret-able imagery and information, perhaps a crucial purpose for abstraction is a kind of universal yet personal sensory mapping. Whilst referencing a traditional art form through painterly, processed delivery, Aquatint is at once romantic and analytical, closer to memories and dreams than cinema: prompting thoughts about portrayals of beauty and the quasi-religious reverence that landscape can trigger. Elemental, technological, dramatised, abstraction.

BIO:

Michael Denton and Anna McCrickard formed Overlap in 1999 as a platform for music, electronic art and music industry, festival and gallery activities including single screen pieces, VJing, audiovisual performances and installations. Overlap's music is created alongside their imagery. Current work explores the relationship between still and moving imagery through systems of implied motion within transitions, use of discreet picture planes and obscuration techniques.

Recent activity:- *Forest Tree* selected for the STRP Eindhoven Biennale 2015; *Cloud Edged* premiere, Light Fantastic exhibition Frieze Art Fair 2015; a celebration of 100 Years of Electronic Music with live projections at the National Portrait Gallery London; *Trespass* audiovisual "painting" installation for the National Trust's Fenton House, Hampstead; *The Lost Houses* atmospheric audiovisual portrait of the decline of the English country house for the National Trust/ Calke Abbey; opening the Arquiteturas Film Festival in Lisbon with the *Places that Dance* audiovisual performance; short films *Returning* and *Switch* awarded special mentions at the Avanca and EMAF film festivals; an audiovisual performance in the British Ambassador's Residence in Beijing; a visual remix of the Beatles' Magical Mystery Tour for the film's gala premier at London's BFI.
See
http://www.overlap.co.uk/Overlap_About_Events&Releases.htm

Author Keywords
Audiovisual performance; abstraction; fine art; serialism; minimalism; Vjing; electronica; cinema; moving image art; landscape

C&C '15, June 22-25, 2015, Glasgow, United Kingdom
ACM 978-1-4503-3598-0/15/06.
http://dx.doi.org/10.1145/2757226.2757359

Torrrque – Augmented Drum-Kit

Christos Michalakos
The University of Edinburgh
Alison House, 12 Nicolson
Square, Edinburgh, EH8 9DF
cmichalakos@gmail.com

ABSTRACT

Torrrque is an improvised piece of music with the Augmented Drum-Kit, a bespoke electro-acoustic instrument comprising of a traditional acoustic drum-kit, embedded speakers, microphones, motors, solenoids, DMX[1] lights and live electronics. The setup is controlled by a Max/MSP[2] patch, which works with a combination of machine-listening techniques, timed events, and direct intervention by the performer.

Author Keywords

Music; improvisation; interaction; gesture; new instruments for musical expression; live electronics; sound art; sound.

ACM Classification Keywords

J.5 [Arts and Humanities]: Sound and music computing.

INSTRUMENT

The first version of the Augmented Drum-Kit was developed from September 2009 to August 2013 as part of the author's doctoral studies at the University of Edinburgh. The instrument has been used in a plethora of works, including solo and group albums, improvisations, performances, and workshops on bespoke instrument design. As of November 2014 and the "What Is Sound Design?" Symposium at the University of Edinburgh, DMX light control has been incorporated to the instrument's capabilities in order to afford a unified audiovisual performance experience, where sound, light and space are complementary. The extended instrumental space can now be shaped and visually altered with light, through physical gestures on the drum-kit, using similar techniques with the ones employed for the electronic sound control.

PAST PERFORMANCES

Works with the instrument have been presented in various conferences and festivals, including the International Symposium on Electronic Art (Albuquerque 2012), New Interfaces for Musical Expression (Oslo 2011, London 2014), International Computer Music Conference (Ljubljana 2012), Sonorities (Belfast 2011) and Gap in the Air (Edinburgh 2015).

Figure 1. *Torrrque* performed as part of Gap in the Air Festival of Sonic Art

RECORDINGS

The Augmented Drum-Kit is featured on the following releases[3]:

- Christos Michalakos - *Frrriction*
- Christos Michalakos – *Long Distance*
- Mŭstek – *Signal Powder*
- Mŭstek – *Node / Antinode*
- Better a Broken Bone – *Better A Broken Bone*

---

[1] http://interactive-online.com/what-is-dmx (Accessed April 2015)

[2] https://cycling74.com/ (Accessed April 2015)

C&C '15, June 22-25, 2015, Glasgow, United Kingdom
ACM 978-1-4503-3598-0/15/06.
http://dx.doi.org/10.1145/2757226.2757360

[3] The Reid label: http://reidid.bandcamp.com/ (Accessed April 2015)

Sarlacc

Shawn Lawson
Rensselaer Polytechnic Institute
lawsos2@rpi.edu

Ryan Ross Smith
Rensselaer Polytechnic Institute
ryanrosssmith@gmail.com

ABSTRACT

Sarlacc, an audio-visual performance, features visuals live coded within the OpenGL fragment shader, that are reactive to incoming audio frequencies parsed by band, beats per minute, and Open Sound Control data. The sound component is performed using Ableton Live and analog synthesis.

Author Keywords

OpenGL; shaders; live coding; performance; audio-visual; Open Sound Control

ACM Classification Keywords

J.5. Arts and Humanities: Arts, Performing arts. D.2.6. Programming Environments: Interactive environments. I.3.6. Computer Graphics: Methodology and Techniques: Interaction techniques.

INTRODUCTION

Sarlacc, the second audio-visual performance piece created by the authors, was developed during a short, intense residency period where iterative improvisational sessions became the foundation of the creative process, and ultimately, the final work. This paper will briefly discuss tool design and interaction, aesthetic concerns, and the creation process of *Sarlacc* in general.

TOOLS

Sarlacc was developed and is performed using both author-developed software and consumer-available software and hardware.

Visuals

The visual component of *Sarlacc* is created in an integrated development environment (IDE) that runs as a webpage in the Google Chrome web-browser (see figure 1). The IDE, from top layer to bottom layer, includes: an interface written in JavaScript with JQuery, a text editing area using the ACE library, and lastly a 3D canvas element for WebGL rendering [1, 2, 3].

Live coding is, generally speaking, software editing in real-time, generally at a low-level [4]. The live coding of *Sarlacc's* visuals occur within the aforementioned text editor of the IDE. The text editor contains OpenGL fragment shader code associated with a timer set to automatically compile the shader code every 200 milliseconds [5]. If the code is compiled without errors, it is loaded onto the graphics card and used to draw the imagery in the canvas layer. To this end, successful edits to the shader code are seamlessly reflected in the visuals, without the need for compile, play, or execute buttons. Coding errors are highlighted, while the most recent successful edit will continue generating the visuals.

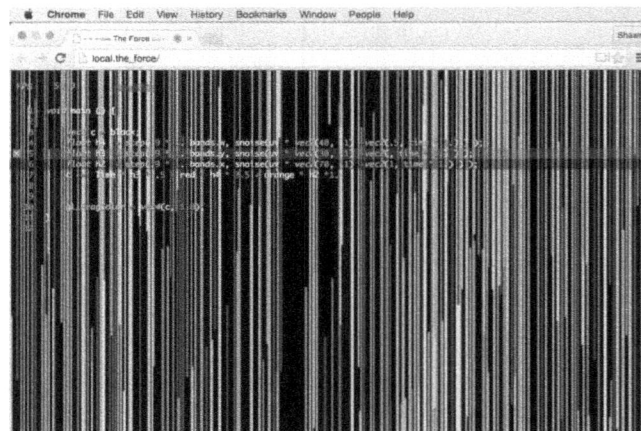

Figure 1. IDE for performing visuals runs as a webpage in Google Chrome.

The WebKit web-browser engine contains functionality for accessing any audio/microphone input to the computer [6]. The IDE uses this audio input and WebKit's frequency analysis tools to create four frequency bands: low, middle-low, middle-high, and high. This frequency band data, supplied by the audio performer, is passed into the OpenGL shader, providing a steady stream of variable control data.

For further integration with the audio an Open Sound Control (OSC) network is created between the audio performer and the visual performers computers [7]. The audio performer synchronizes sample and scene launch from Ableton Live with a Max/MSP application to send triggers synchronized to beats per minute (BPM) over the OSC network. The visual performer's IDE parses these OSC packets and makes the BPM data accessible from within the OpenGL shader.

Finally, an additional OSC network is created between a device (phone or tablet) that is running a custom-designed slider interface created with Lemur, and the visual performer's computer [8]. The Lemur app virtualizes on screen a conventional MIDI-like input device, including a set of sliders, knobs, and buttons. The visual performer uses this interface to facilitate direct control over time-sensitive visual modifications, smooth blending of on screen elements, and to *fine tune* the aesthetic feel.

Audio

The audio component features a set of pre-composed elements available for localized and global triggering, from one-shots to entire sequences, with those most salient elements available for real-time modification. The audio component also features the use of analog synthesis and other outboard gear for use as a transitional supplement, noise source, and to provide direct access to the visual element through the instantiation of discrete, discernable frequencies.

AESTHETICS

The aesthetic goals of *Sarlacc* were to construct an audio and visual build-narrative merging elements of EDM, J-Pop, Gif-Culture and mechanical and electronic-inspired audio and visuals.

The visual aesthetic experience is unequal parts pop-culture, abstract expressionism, and glitch-art. Specific to the creation of *Sarlacc*, the capability to draw sprite sheet animations was implemented into the IDE. This add-on allows the visual performer to use animated sprites, as source material in the performance. This expanded the capability of the visual imagery to include the iconic image of the *nyan cat* (see figure 2).

PROCESS

The sustained creative focus of the one-week-residency used to create *Sarlacc* revealed a new and exciting process for the authors: iterative-improvisation.

Prior to the residency the authors' process was to create small parts independently, before meeting to create short bursts of audio-visual mashups toward the discovery of audio-visual combinations that fulfilled our aesthetic goals, facilitated performance flow from one section to the next, and provided a sequential logic of sorts; a non-narrative story arc.

The constraints of the residency led to the iterative-improvisation method out of necessity, while still framed by several previously-agreed upon *aesthetic* constraints. The authors would improvise together with a single visual and audio segment until it was collectively felt that the segment had solidified into a singular audio-visual entity. Once all segments had been completed, sequence and transitions were subjected to a similarly improvisatory method.

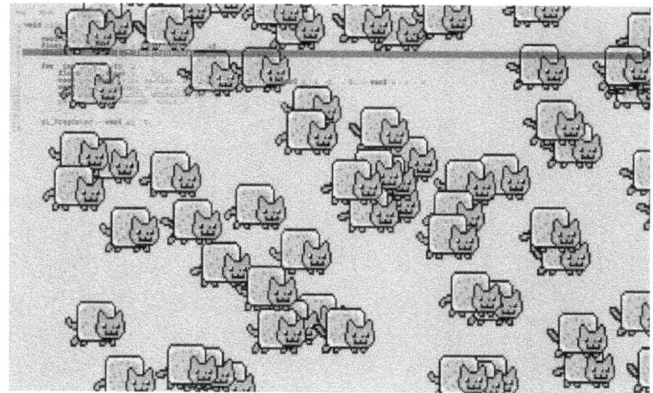

Figure 2. Example of Gif-Culture, sprite sheet animation.

CONCLUSION

Portions of the IDE were very much in play during the development of *Sarlacc*. The points at which these technologies turned from roadblocks to opportunities allowed for the iterative-improvisation method to flow smoothly.

At the end of the residency, the authors noted that the iterative-improvisation method shortened the development time of the performance work from two months to three days, and the sustained one-on-one creative contact forced a continued reflexive feedback ultimately resulting in a stronger, more cohesive work.

ACKNOWLEDGMENTS

Large thank you to CultureHub in New York City for providing us the time and space to experiment and create *Sarlacc* [9].

REFERENCES

1. JQuery library for Document Object Model (DOM) manipulation of html. http://jquery.com.

2. ACE library for text editing in a web-browser. https://github.com/ajaxorg/ace.

3. WebGL library of OpenGL for drawing graphics in a web-browser. https://www.khronos.org/webgl/.

4. TopLap, home of live coding. http://toplap.org/about/.

5. OpenGL library for drawing graphics. https://www.khronos.org/opengl/.

6. WebKit the web-browser engine in Google Chrome. https://www.webkit.org.

7. Open Sound Control (OSC) communication protocol common to music/media performance. http://opensoundcontrol.org.

8. Lemur, for creating and using OSC interfaces https://liine.net/en/products/lemur/.

9. Culture Hub, incubator for arts and technology. http://www.culturehub.org

Playing with InMuSIC: an Interactive Multimodal System for Improvised Composition

Giacomo Lepri
Institute of Sonology - STEIM
Royal Conservatory of The Hague
Juliana van Stolberglaan 1 2595 CA The Hague
The Netherlands
leprotto.giacomo@gmail.com

ABSTRACT

InMuSIC is a real-time interactive musical system conceived to be used in a context related to the practice of electro-acoustic free improvisation. By integrating the observation of both non-verbal expressive behavior cues (motion tracking) and several sonic parameters (audio stream analysis) the system is able to identify, during the performance, relevant expressive musical properties. The real-time measurements control different digital sound processes through the correlation of different mapping strategies. The generated audio interventions should then be perceived as a consolidated sonic integration of the improvised performance. The research is based on the belief that human behaviors and their ambiguity must be taken into consideration in order to design and shape meaningful and sustainable technologies.

Author Keywords

Computer music; improvisation; real-time interaction; non-verbal expressive behavior.

ACM Classification Keywords

J.5. Arts and Humanities: Performing arts

THE INTERACTIVE PARADIGM

InMuSIC is a real-time interactive musical system conceived to be used in a context related to electroacoustic free improvisation. Music practice is often the result of a wide range of expressive requirements and technical skills. Based on this, the research aims to intuit, observe and measure some of the most relevant aspects related to musical affective intentions during a music performance. In this framework improvisation is therefore conceived as a complete musical act, synthesis of an intricate creative process involving physicality, movement, cognition, emotions and sound. The key intuition of the research relies on the implementation of a set of affective interactions by identifying and processing relevant expressive

C&C '15, June 22-25, 2015, Glasgow, United Kingdom
ACM 978-1-4503-3598-0/15/06.
http://dx.doi.org/10.1145/2757226.2757375

musical hints of a performer through the observation of both embodied motion cues (motion tracking) and sonic parameters (audio stream analysis). Due to the implementation of a complex paradigm of musical relations the system and the performer should then establish a deep connection based on mutual exchanges. The central nodes of the interactive model developed are based on a multilevel correlation between motion and sound. In other words, the idea is to provide the system with an adaptive nature inspired by the human ability to focus, act and react differently in relation to diverse musical conditions.

SYSTEM ARCHITECTURE

From a practical point of view, given a musician playing a freely improvised session, the system performs four main tasks. Each task is assigned to a specific unit. The individual units themselves are constituted by several sub-units. The overall architecture of the system is characterized by a modular approach, the four components are implemented in different environments and they communicate through a standard Open Sound Control (OSC) protocol. Therefore is possible to run the units on different machines connected by a network. A description of the four modules and their functions is now presented.

- **Audio analysis** - the module detect and filters the raw audio data comparing various analysis executed through different techniques for real-time extraction of audio features (i.e. amplitude/loudness, onsets/event [6], variation of pitch [3], noisiness/roughness [5], and spectral centroid/brightness). During the performance the incoming musical information is constantly interpreted and shaped. By matching and evaluating the outputs of the different algorithms, the system chooses between several analysis strategy. A simple example is the onset detection: three algorithms for onset detection are implemented, the system selects one of the three available outputs in relation to the information coming from the amplitude analysis algorithm (each onset detection algorithm is more reliable in specific dynamic ranges). This approach allows an adaptive detection and classification of the musical features previously listed. A microphone is used to detect the sound produced by the musician. The audio analysis algorithms are implemented using the software Max/Msp.

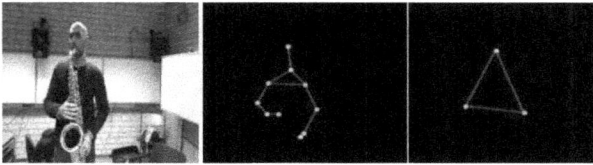

Figure 1. The detected skeleton of a musician playing the saxophone.

- **Movement analysis** - through the use of techniques for real-time extraction and interpretation of full body movements [4] of the improviser the system computes an analysis of different expressive gestural features. Considering a reduced amount of visual information: 3D position, velocity, and acceleration of the musicians head and hands (see Figure 1). Three expressive features are extracted: smoothness (degree of fluidity, continuity or impulsiveness), contraction index (degree of posture openness) and kinetic energy (overall quantity of motion). The notion of expressive movement taken into account implies behavioral features pertinent to a large range of gestures and not restricted to specific types of movements. Certainly each instrument (traditional or related to new technologies) carries a specific apparatus of gestural affordances. Moreover each musician develops a personal manner to physically interact with it. The challenge of this procedure consist of detecting abstracted high level information that can be representative of an open sphere of possible expressive motions. A qualitative approach to upper-body movement for affect recognition is here adopted [2]. The 3D sensor used for the movement detection is Microsoft Kinect, the movement analysis is implemented using the software EyesWeb [1].

- **Mapping and interactions design** - this unit is the kernel of the system; it handles the most abstract compositional level of the interaction through the use of multilevel mapping strategies and decision making algorithms. The function of this module is related to the generation of new musical information and satisfying musical feedback (i.e. development of musical structures and real time sound reactions/interactions). The module computes a constant correlation between the information coming from the audio and movement modules. By detecting and memorizing the conditions that mostly occurs during the performance, the system creates a database on the fly. This adaptive catalog is one of the main sources for the development of new musical material. The module is implemented in order to execute processes related to two different time windows: short time scale reactions 2-4 seconds (real time) and long time scale reactions 2-4 minutes (formal time). The reference paradigm refers to studies on the human auditory memory [7] (short-term and long-term memory).

- **Sound generation** - by performing various Digital Signal Processes (DSP) the module should produce heterogeneous sound materials. The techniques implemented are live sampling, granulation, Fast Fourier Transform (FFT) analysis and re-synthesis and additive/subtractive synthesis. The intention is to develop a constant dialogue between acoustic and electronic sound materials (e.g. fusion, separation, imitation, variation). The management of the

generated sound materials is based on several criteria that coordinate the distribution of the energy over the spectrum. The generated audio interventions should be perceived as a consolidated sonic integration/innovation interconnected with the improvised performance.

THE PERFORMANCE

The performance proposed consists in a free improvised session with the InMuSIC system: clarinet and live electronics. The software is tuned be sensible to a specific vocabulary of full body movements related to the clarinet practice. The performance is based on a mutual musical exchanges between the system and the musician. During the improvised session the platform will balance different degrees of adaptiveness, autonomy and imitation/variation in relation to the information analyzed. The notion of interaction here conceived implies the possibility of establish and develop an intense process of interchange. Then this procedure can potentially modify the behavior and, to some extent, the musical perception/awareness of the actors involved. The notion of interaction here conceived implies the possibility of establish and develop an intense process of interchange. From an aesthetic point of view InMuSIC is conceived to be used in musical contexts related to a specific electroacoustic improvisational tradition. However, the system is intended to perform a music which is concerned with spectral qualities and flexible fluctuations in time rather than actual melodic/harmonic progressions and metrical tempo.

REFERENCES
1. Camurri, A., Hashimoto, S., Ricchetti, M., Ricci, A., Suzuki, K., Trocca, R., and Volpe, G. Eyesweb: Toward gesture and affect recognition in interactive dance and music systems. *Computer Music Journal 24*, 1 (2000), 57–69.

2. Camurri, A., Lagerlöf, I., and Volpe, G. Recognizing emotion from dance movement: comparison of spectator recognition and automated techniques. *International journal of human-computer studies 59*, 1 (2003), 213–225.

3. De Cheveigné, A., and Kawahara, H. Yin, a fundamental frequency estimator for speech and music. *The Journal of the Acoustical Society of America 111*, 4 (2002), 1917–1930.

4. Glowinski, D., Dael, N., Camurri, A., Volpe, G., Mortillaro, M., and Scherer, K. Toward a minimal representation of affective gestures. *Affective Computing, IEEE Transactions on 2*, 2 (2011), 106–118.

5. MacCallum, J., and Einbond, A. Real-time analysis of sensory dissonance. In *Computer Music Modeling and Retrieval. Sense of Sounds*. Springer, 2008, 203–211.

6. Malt, M., and Jourdan, E. Real-time uses of low level sound descriptors as event detection functions using the max/msp zsa. descriptors library. *Proceedings of the 12th Brazilian Smposium on Computer Music* (2009).

7. Snyder, B. *Music and memory: An introduction*. MIT press, 2000.

'AirStorm,' A New Piece for AirSticks and Storm – Gestural Audio-Visual for Electronic Percussionists

Alon Ilsar
University of Technology,
Sydney
alonilsar@gmail.com

Andrew Bluff
University of Technology,
Sydney
bluffy@rollerchimp.com

ABSTRACT

'AirStorm' is a semi-improvised short 10-min piece for solo AirSticks and physical model visualisation performed by Alon Ilsar and Andrew Bluff respectively. It will be made up of a drum synth, drum samples, other selected samples and room feedback triggered and manipulated by Ilsar on this newly built interface for electronic percussionists. The piece will display some of the capabilities of the AirSticks along with Ilsar's dedication to practicing and composing for this new interface. *'AirStorm'* will be based around the conferences theme of 'Computers, Arts and Data' through the choice and samples and ways are played.

The movement data from Ilsar's Airsticks is processed in real-time by Bluff's physics based visualisation engine, *Storm*. Particles are pushed around a virtual 3D world in response to the movements of the AirSticks and rigid body collision adds a sense of real-world authenticity and complexity. The system responds to drums and movements of the AirSticks with a combination of different visual and physical effects. The real-time visualisations exemplify the movement and sonic complexity of Ilsar's AirSticks performance, providing a visually stimulating and highly synesthetic element to the piece.

THE PROPOSED PERFORMANCE

This performance by Alon Ilsar will display some of the capabilities of the AirSticks, a new interface for electronic percussionists. The AirSticks allows the performer to trigger and manipulate sounds in a 3D virtual space, using various hand, finger and foot movements. This virtual space is completely fluid, with sounds morphing from to another. As the AirSticks tilt past a trigger point, they send a MIDI signal which is then mapped to a sound. This sound may remain on until the AirSticks are brought back above the triggering tilt angle and manipulated in various ways using several different hand, finger and feet movements. We believe this attention to note length and the ability to add

expressivity after a note is triggered gives the AirSticks a great advantage over other electronic percussive instruments. This plethora of one-to-one mappings leads to an intimate and transparent instrument; one that can react to musical situations as quickly as an acoustic instrument. Indeed the hope is that an experienced acoustic drummer will be able to learn the AirSticks quickly, but take years to master.

For this performance, the AirSticks will be interacting with Bluff's *Storm* application to provide real-time visualisations. The movement, drum triggers and controller information are piped to the *Storm* application by various MIDI messages. The position and velocity of Ilsar's hands injects particles and forces into a rigid body collision engine. These virtual particles can collide with each other in a realistic manner to add a sense of realism and complexity to the visual representation. There is a constant force applied to the particles on the z-axis forcing them to either fade into the background or fly out towards the audience. This provides a small time-line effect where you can see a short history of movement tracing Ilsar's physical trajectories.

A many-to-many mapping is used to transform the position and orientation of the AirSticks into various forces on the virtual physical system as visual effects are also applied to the rendering of the particles. The many-to-many mapping is created by continually morphing a set of system wide presets. This allows the visuals to respond to each parameter of the AirSticks, combining subtle and high impact visual states. An example of a subtle visual state might be small changes in colour, gravity or blur while high impact states change the particle types from lines to squares or spheres. Drum sounds triggered by the AirSticks also affect the visuals by triggering a set of visuals post processing effects such as RGB-shift, depth blurs and toon shaders.

The complex combination of the many positional and triggered visual effects with the motion generated particles creates a constantly evolving and highly engaging visual tapestry that conveys a powerful synesthetic link to the gestural movements and sonic output of the live AirSticks performance.

C&C '15, June 22-25, 2015, Glasgow, United Kingdom
ACM 978-1-4503-3598-0/15/06.
http://dx.doi.org/10.1145/2757226.2757376

Author Keywords
Gestures; interfaces; percussion; mapping

ACM Classification Keywords
H.5.2. Information Interfaces and Presentation (e.g. HCI): Input devices and strategies

Biographies
Alon Ilsar is an instrument designer, electronic producer, experimental percussionist and composer. He is currently doing a practice-based research PhD at UTS in designing a new interface for electronic percussionists. He completed his Bachelor of Arts majoring in Music and Philosophy and continued on to complete his Honours in Music on creative online collaboration. He has also been heavily involved in theatre and film as drummer, composer and sound designer. His diverse projects include The Sticks, Kirin J Callinan, Brian Campeau, Keating! the Musical, Eddie Perfect, Meow Meow, Tim Minchin, Circus Monoxide, The Colors Tribute Band, Gauche, Trigger Happy, Darth Vegas, Silent Spring and Malarkey. For more info please visit www.alonilsar.com

Andrew Bluff is a new media artist with commercial software development experience in the creative media industries. Currently undertaking doctoral studies at the University of Technology in Sydney, Andrew pushes the boundaries of creative and interactive technologies to explore new sonic territories, visual motifs and performance modalities.

Incorporating interactive theatre, mobile computing, concatenative synthesis and new music instrument design, Andrew's recent exploits have seen him install interactive works into the Bachhaus in Germany, collaborate with the Chicks on Speed for their latest 'Scream' exhibition, pick up a prize for Crowd Art at the prestigious ZKM AppArtAwards in Germany and perform large-scale outdoor interactive projections in South Korea, Mexico and Australia. For more info please visit www.rollerchimp.com

Additional Information

Recordings

For an excerpt of AirStorm see

https://vimeo.com/121327080

For other works with the AirSticks see

http://alonilsar.com/airsticks/

For Bluff's other works involving Storm and particle based simulations see

http://www.rollerchimp.com

Performance: *Constellation Theory of Knowledge*
Electronic Music and Philosophical Metaphor

Scott L. Simon
CCS / University of
Technology,
Sydney, Australia
scott.simon@uts.edu.au

ABSTRACT

This short paper describes a performance in the Artworks section of the Creativity and Cognitions conference 2015. The artwork makes use of the author's research into creating a dialog between the fields of music and philosophy. Specifically the artwork is a multimedia piece that structures a philosophical text as a metaphor realized as electronic musical shape and process. The piece is entitled: *Constellation theory of knowledge*. Utilizing the philosophical concept of the "constellation" (an idea that Theodor Adorno and Walter Benjamin both made use of) the work seeks to first describe the idea and then articulate it in metaphorical form. This process is an extension of earlier modes of composition that utilized ideas in music via symbolic abstraction. R. Strauss and R. Wagner both made use of this form – the procedure has not been developed further and offers interesting possibilities in terms of orienting motion processes within electronic music.

Author Keywords

Philosophy; Electro-Acoustic Music; Multi-Media Artwork.

ACM Classification Keywords

Performance; Algorithms; Computation

INTRODUCTION

The concept of utilizing philosophy in relation to music is one that has a long history. Pythagoras theorized about the nature of the cosmos in its fundamental relation to musical ratio and the overtone series [3]. In the present context research is in process that extends the lexicon of composers like R. Strauss and R. Wagner in relation to their connection to philosophical ideas. It is well documented that these composers utilized philosophy (Nietzsche and Schopenhauer in particular) in their compositional process

[4, 8].

The manner in which a text can come to "mean" something precise within a piece of music is an issue that is contentious: it is generally denied that instrumental music can point to a direct signified that will be understood by different subjects univocally [5]. Music has been regarded as a non-representational form of art in influential philosophies (for example Schopenhauer) [6]. How then can one make use of Philosophy within music?

The rationale behind the "program music" of the 19th Century was one in which music was to become more than the "play of tones" – music was to become a full cultural sphere in its own right [2]. This sphere would make possible the realization of poetic and textual elements within music, elements that would be recognized as such by the audience. This would allow music to take its place at the top of the artistic tree – above poetry. Franz Brendel, a musical theorist of the 19th Century and editor of the *Neue Zeitschrift für Musik*, believed that the next step from classical symphonic forms was program music [7]. Composers such as R. Strauss integrated formal abstractions that symbolized philosophical ideas into their work [8].

The use of relational and interactive forms of art makes the structuring of meaning and the synchronizing of mental topography within music possible. Certainly some purely instrumental works already make use of this "external" component in the form of a written text that accompanies the performance of a work. The manner however that the different textual components are realized as musical form will often only be understood casually or in a different way from person to person. When things become a too obvious "tone painting" the effect is one that has been (generally) regarded as losing that all important *ineffability* of the musical form. The problem then is how to create a shared mental topography without compromising the sphere of music in its prototypically relevant shape.

PERFORMANCE PIECE

The performance is a 10 minute electronic piece that will involve improvising within various guidelines that are established by the philosophical metaphors. The title of the work *Constellation theory of knowledge* gives an insight into the kind of metaphors that will be generated. I will briefly set out here the different elements in that regard.

Let it be noted at this point that one of the claims to significance of the research practice (connected to the performance) is the theorizing of the entire process of connecting philosophy to music. Thus we have examples of earlier music that make use of a musical shape to symbolize an idea but we do not have a complete theory that articulates (1) the focus of the metaphor (intervallic, architectonic, spectral etc.) (2) the theorization of a relational component in the music (thus the music becomes a way of working between music and philosophy as a dialog between people) (3) the sequencing of musical shapes that reflect the temporal unfolding of a philosophical idea and (4) the use of the philosophical metaphor to define the types of synthesis algorithms that will be produced. This last point shows that one is not producing a "pleasing" sound or tone that will be then made use of, rather the structure of the synthesis is in part defined by the criteria defined by the metaphors.

Specific to this work and the content it is dealing with we have three or four basic structures. The main theme is one that focuses upon the manner in which knowledge is generated and the manner in which that knowledge is processed. The three stages: (1) systematic articulations (2) the fragmentation of systems (3) the constellation theory of knowledge. Systematic articulations are represented by diatonic chordal structures. The fragmentation of the system is represented by these chords breaking into their harmonic partials (each note breaking into its respective harmonic partials). The constellation theory of knowledge is represented by a shaping process: an algorithm was written to create rhythmically coherent shapes (subjectively organized) from the note fragments and organize them in space.

The basic structure of the piece is one in which the performer plays some chords into the DAW (Ableton Live) and then manipulates them according to a scored timeframe. In the present case the piece is a live improvisation – the choice of timeframe is not strictly predetermined. The chords are then fragmented with a Max/MSP patch that allows for the chords to be broken into their respective notes and recorded as a midi sequence. This sequence will then be passed through a Harmonic synth *Polyver* that can deal with each of the partials within each of the "note fragments" individually. This is the process of fragmentation. The final step is the re-assembling of the fragments into coherent groups and shapes that will be organized around the metaphorical "object" of knowledge. In this case the shapes (symbolic forms) will be perceptually guided in relation to a metronomic kick drum. This has the advantage of making

sense of the shapes within the standard metric conventions of Western music culture.

The philosophical idea and the manner in which this idea is represented as metaphor are present as a visual program for the audience. A video is triggered by the performer as the work is performed that contains the text / metaphorical ideas.

The performance reflects research into the creation of a dialog between music and philosophy undertaken at the Creativity and Cognitions Studio (University of Technology, Sydney). Significance is claimed in respect to its extension of the musical lexicon that was established by earlier practitioners. The multi-media aspect of the art reflects not merely an "expression" of the artist but also a relational component that is embedded in the work. The work is understood to bring together various conceptual components that serve to develop meaning creation within music. One of the central components here is the emphasis upon human centered dialog in establishing the trajectory of compositional algorithm. This is understood by the artist to be a way of establishing conversation and communication with a philosophical / sociological structure in addition to those conversations that are focused only upon the technical. This fusion of the philosophical with the computational allows human concerns to be constantly brought into the programming environment at a level that fosters structures that might be marginalized in purely technical environments.

ACKNOWLEDGMENTS
The author wishes to thank Ernest Edmonds and Sam Ferguson for input into the algorithms and thought processes that make up the present study.

REFERENCES
1. Adorno, T. *Negative Dialektik*, Suhrkamp, Frankfurt, 1966.

2. Dahlhaus, K. *Esthetics of Music.* Cambridge University Press, Cambridge, 1982

3. Litt, D. *The Music of the Spheres.* Powerpoint Presentation. Stanford University, 2013. .

4. Magee, B. *The Philosophy of Schopenhauer.* Oxford University Press, Oxford, 2002.

5. Nattiez, J.J. *Music and Discourse: toward a semiology of music.* Princeton University Press, Princeton, 1990.

6. Schopenhauer, A. *The World as Will and Representation.* (Trans. E. F. J. Payne), Dover Publications, New York, 1966.

7. Taruskin, R. *Music in the 19th Century: The Oxford History of Music.* Oxford University Press, Oxford, 2011.

8. Williamson, J. *Strauss: Thus Spake Zarathustra.* Cambridge University Press, Cambridge, 1993.

Creativity in Collaborative Design

Monica Landoni
Faculty of Informatics, Università della Svizzera
italiana, CH6904Lugano, Switzerland
Monica.landoni@usi.ch

Paloma Diaz
Computer Science Department
Universidad Carlos III de Madrid, 28911
Leganes, Madrid (Spain)
pdp@inf.uc3m.es

ABSTRACT
With this half-day workshop we will offer a venue to colleagues in Arts and Humanities, designers and computer scientists at large for sharing their experiences about raising creativity levels when running collaborative design sessions. We will target researchers interested in collaborative design involving different types of users including adults, children, teenagers and senior citizens, as much as truly intergenerational experiences. We will hear about the challenges they face in terms of keeping participants engaged and stimulate their individual and social creativity. We will aim at discussing the practicalities of setting up a collaborative design study that are so crucial to its success but rarely reported in literature. There will also be time for exploring more theoretical issues such as when a stimulus is genuinely thought provoking and when instead it becomes overpowering. We will debate on how to measure creativity in this setting and whether it is possible to relate and attribute it to specific activities and roles played by participants.

Author Keywords
Collaborative Design; Children; Measures; Activities, Stimuli.

ACM Classification Keywords
D.2.2 Design Tools and Technique, H.5.2 User Interfaces.

INTRODUCTION
Collaborative design is a subset of Participatory Design, a theory born in Scandinavian countries. Its core principle is that users should have a central role in the design of tools and procedures for them to use. In particular users and designers can mutually learn from each other by sharing users' expertise on work practices and designers' knowledge of the many opportunities provided by technology. Participatory Design has moved from being used with adult workers to a variety of other scenarios and one of the most promising is that of designing for children

C&C '15, June 22-25, 2015, Glasgow, United Kingdom
ACM 978-1-4503-3598-0/15/06. http://dx.doi.org/10.1145/2757226.2767187

with children. Other interesting groups that raise specific challenges are senior and intergenerational groups.

Collaborative Design or co-design as we have referred to it above, is a method for designers to work with a target audience in order to solve a problem. In co-design users are actively involved in designing a solution and this is a crucial difference with other user-centred approaches. While applying the co-design approach researchers explore different methods and techniques in order to stimulate participation, engagement and creativity in participants. We propose in this workshop to focus on the role creativity, both individual and social, plays in this process starting from, but also going beyond, the ideation element of design and how creativity can be both influenced and measured by researchers. We would like this workshop to provide a venue for discussing, sharing and raising issues related to creativity in collaborative design as this technique has gained popularity in the HCI community and can greatly benefit from the wealth of expertise gathered around this Cognition and Creativity event.

Running of the event
We propose a format that we feel will be conducive of sharing and exchanging experiences and opinions in a constructive and productive way by following a number of paradigms. These include: "speed-dating" for a quick get to know each other and "round tables" for dealing with recognized challenges. We will start by inviting each participant to submit, before the event, a one-page statement where they will declare their interest, experience, position and purpose in attending the workshop. In the first part of the event, participants will speed-date with each other to further discuss their profiles and find out similarities of interests, purposes and intents. Later on, round tables will be set up in order to discuss the main challenges as these emerged from this profiling exercise. Each table will have a "champion" that will motivate discussion and report the core of their discussion to the rest of the participants.

We would expect participants from the Human Computer Interaction community and from its Children Design sub-group since they have embraced collaborative design while contribution from colleagues designers and researchers with a background in Arts and Humanities will be most welcome as extremely beneficial and stimulating for the creativity level of our workshop. We will use DBWorld and CHI lists to promote this event. There will be no specific venue requirements, simply a re-adjustable space for having pair and group discussions and an overhead projector for reporting groups' achievements. We would expect the event to last half a day. The findings will be gathered in a white paper for all participants to contribute.

Proposers

Monica Landoni is a senior researcher at the faculty of Informatics, Università della Svizzera italiana. Her project HEBE, sponsored by the Swiss National Science Foundations, focused on co-design with children that produced guidelines for the design of innovative children e-books. These findings have been published at the 2013 and 2014 editions of International Conference of Design for Children.

Paloma Diaz is Professor of Computer Science at Universidad Carlos III de Madrid and head of the Interactive Systems Research group (dei.inf.uc3m.es). She led the urThey project that involved children in the co-design of games to support informal learning experiences.

Supporting Creative Design Processes in Blended Interaction Spaces

Peter Dalsgaard
Kim Halskov
Aarhus University
Aarhus, Denmark
dalsgaard@cavi.au.dk
halskov@cavi.au.dk

Wendy Mackay
Universite Paris-Sud
Paris, France
Wendy.Mackay@lri.fr

Neil Maiden
City Univ. London
London, UK
neilmaiden@me.com

Jean-Bernard Martens
Technische Universiteit
Eindhoven
The Netherlands
J.B.O.S.Martens@tue.nl

ABSTRACT

Creative processes involve a repertoire of digital devices ranging from mobile phones over tablets and desktop computers to electronic whiteboards and wall-sized displays. While some integration across multiple devices is supported more sophisticated kinds of integration that connect devices and amplify their potential are limited. Many creative practices also rely on physical materials and tools. This will workshop investigate how the combination of physical and digital artifacts can support creative work practices. In this context, we propose to examine: Individual and social creative activities; Creativity methods; Emergence and transformation of design ideas; Generative design materials; Design constraints.

Author Keywords

Design processes; creativity; design materials; design environments; constraints.

ACM Classification Keywords

H.5.m. Information interfaces and presentation: Miscellaneous.

INTRODUCTION

Today, more and more forms of human activity involve a repertoire of digital devices ranging from mobile phones over tablets and desktop computers to electronic whiteboards and wall-sized displays. While some integration across multiple devices is supported by access to shared data, e.g. via cloud computing services, more sophisticated kinds of integration that connect devices and amplify their potential are limited. Interestingly, many creative practices such as design and architecture, to a large extent still rely on physical materials and tools like for instance pen and paper, Post-It notes and whiteboards,

C&C '15, June 22-25, 2015, Glasgow, United Kingdom
ACM 978-1-4503-3598-0/15/06.
http://dx.doi.org/10.1145/2757226.2767184

which are not connected to nor supported by digital means. Blended Interaction has emerged as a promising approach for conceptualising interaction in physical environments augmented by ICT to blend the power of digital computing and the physical environment. Blended Interaction seeks to combine the virtues of physical and digital artifacts in a complimentary way [6]. This approach is well suited for developing digital support for creative work practices that acknowledge the benefits of current analogue tools and practices, so that the desired properties of each are preserved. This workshop, will investigate how Blended Interaction Spaces (BIS) can support, augment and potentially transform creative work practices.

Specifically we examine the following themes to advance research on IT supported creative practices:

- Individual and social creative activities
- Creativity methods
- Emergence and transformation of design ideas
- Generative design materials
- Creativity constraints

INDIVIDUAL AND SOCIAL CREATIVE ACTIVITIES

While creativity research has historically focused on the individual lone-genius creator that notion has recently been challenged by researchers arguing for team-based creativity [9]. We pose the thesis that the individual vs. social creation dichotomy is artificial: real-life creativity almost always takes place in both spheres, albeit at different times, leading to the research question: *how can Blended Interaction Spaces facilitate seamless integration of individual creative sessions (e.g. using iPads and mobile phones) with collaborative ones (e.g. using wall sized displays in combination with iPads), hereby allowing for ideas to travel across platforms and contextual boundaries?*

CREATIVITY METHODS

A number of interaction design methods support ideation and creativity [1] e.g *Future Workshops* [7] and *Inspiration Card Workshops* [4]. However, few traditional creativity methods are supported by digital means. We wish to explore the potential for doing so, as well as discuss the pros and cons of using it to support creativity methods, leading us to these questions: *how, and to which extent, can creativity methods be supported and/or augmented by Blended Interaction Spaces, and how can new methods harness the potentials of Blended Interaction Spaces?*

EMERGENCE AND TRANSFORMATION OF DESIGN IDEAS

Design ideas often emerge from specific sources of inspiration, and are shaped through negotiation and transformation mediated by design artefacts [5]. While ideation is central to the development of novel interaction concepts that pervade the CHI community, little has been done to examine how ideation and concept development can be supported via IT. Likewise, there are few digital tools that can help researchers explore the emergence and transformation of ideas through a design process and thus provide richer data for understanding the creative process, which in turn could lead to the development of more fruitful methods and tools to support it. This leads to the questions: *how can we develop Blended Interaction Spaces to support creativity methods, and how can we track and analyse the emergence of design ideas and the transformation of design ideas across devices in Blended Interaction Spaces?*

GENERATIVE DESIGN MATERIALS

Schön [10] coined the term *generative metaphors*, generative in the sense that "it generated new perceptions, explanations, and inventions" (ibid 259). Based on experiences from our own work, and supported by insights from the field of creativity studies, we suggest extending the concept to *generative design materials*, i.e. digital and physical artifacts that, when employed in a design process, support the development and refinement of design concepts. This leads to the questions: *how can generative design materials, digital as well as physical, spur ideation and create momentum in a creative process? What are the differences between using digital and physical materials for this end, and how can we combine the two in meaningful ways?*

CREATIVITY CONSTRAINTS

Leading creativity scholars argue that constraints are integral to the creative process; in spite of this, research into constraints has been limited and it will therefore be at the vanguard of future creativity research [11]. Although constraints act as obstructions in a process by determining what cannot be done [8], they also give rise to new opportunities and inspire creative breakthroughs [1] [12], which leads to the questions: *what is the nature of creativity constraints and how can they be balanced and managed in a creative process?*

ACKNOWLEDGEMENTS
This research has been support by Innovation Fund Denmark grant 1311-00001B (CIBIS): www.cavi.au.dk/CIBIS.

REFERENCES
[1] Biskjær, M.B. and Halskov, K.: Decisive constraints as a creative resource in interaction design. *Digital Creativity* vol 25, 1, 2014, 27-61.

[2] Biskjaer, M., Dalsgaard & Halskov, K. : Creativity methods in interaction design. In the proceedings of DESIRE 2010.

[3] Fruchter, Renate, et al. (2007). Collaborative design exploration in an interactive workspace. AI EDAM-Artificial Intelligence Engineering Design Analysis and Manufacturing 21.3, 279-294.

[4] Halskov, K. & Dalsgaard, P. (2006). Inspiration Card Workshops. Proceedings of DIS 2006, 2006, 2-11.

[5] Halskov, K., Dalsgård, P. The Emergence of Ideas: The interplay between sources of inspiration and emerging design concepts. Journal of CoDesign, 3 (4), 2007, 185–211.

[6] Jetter, H. C., Reiterer, H. & Geyer, F. 2014. Blended Interaction: understanding natural human-computer interaction in post-WIMP interactive spaces. Personal Ubiquitous Comput. 18, 5 (June 2014), 1139-1158.

[7] Jungk, R. & Müllert, N. Future Workshops: How to create desirable futures. Institute for Social Inventions, London, 1987.

[8] Onarheim, B. (2012). Creativity under Constraints: Creativity as Balancing 'Constrainedness' Doctoral dissertation (PhD). The PhD School of Economics and Management, Copenhagen Business School.

[9] Sawyer, K. (2012). Explaining creativity. The science of human innovation. 2nd edition. Oxford University Press.

[10] Schön, D. (1979): Generative Metaphor: A perspective on Problem-Setting in Social Policy. In Ortony, A. (ed) (1979): Metaphor and Thought. Cambridge: Cambridge University Press (254-283).

[11] Sternberg, R. J. & Kaufman, J. C. (2010). Constraints on creativity: Obvious and not so obvious . In J. C. Kaufman & R. J. Sternberg (Eds.), The Cambridge Handbook of Creativity. (pp. 467-482). Cambridge, UK: Cambridge University Press.

[12] Stokes, P. D. (2006). Creativity from Constraints: The Psychology of Breakthrough. New York: Springer Publishing Company.

Psychogeographical City: The City Understood as an Emotional Scenario

Ivan Chaparro
Professor
Jorge Tadeo Lozano University
Cra 4 # 22–61, Bogota, Colombia
ivanf.chaparrom@utadeo.edu.co
(+57) 319 2573243

Ricardo Duenas
CTO
Resoundcity Art Lab
Cra 4 # 22–61, Bogota, Colombia
info@resoundcity.com
(+57) 317 8436111

BACKGROUND AND DESCRIPTION

This workshop is the result of a practice-based research, which explored several interrelated elements: first the theory of Psychogeography, applied to the creative representation of urban environments from a multilayered approach and from an emotional and psychological perspective; second, the exploration of sound and acoustic theory, as research tools and artistic possibilities, directed towards the analysis of public space, its documentation and understanding in relation to processes of identity, intangible patrimony and storytelling. And finally, an experimentation and technical research related to audio postproduction, real-time data visualization, processing and interaction. This exploration lead altogether to the design of a persuasive experience that sought to communicate the research outcomes to a broader audience by means of an experimental performance and sound installation presented initially in several cities in the north of Europe.

AIM

The main aim of the workshop is to illustrate the way in which the city, understood as a multifaceted system, can be abstracted and represented in relation to human emotions and therefore as an psychological-auditory scenario.

Different ways of walking through the city mean different narratives and perspectives and consequently different ways of thinking urban spaces.

APPROACH

The Workshop is divided in 5 stages as follows:

1. Introduction to the concept of Fragmentality (1 hour): namely, a form of urban exploration and documentation that involves walking by foot the streets of a given city collecting fragments in order to generate a posterior dialectical image through several methods of analysis. This initial stage is highly influenced by the practice of flânerie from the poet Charles Baudelaire, the work of the philosopher Walter Benjamin, the theory of Psychogeography, the Situationist techniques and recent inter and transdisciplinary practices carried out mainly in the north of Europe. All of them taken as conceptual basis that outline the acts of walking and collecting as social and aesthetic disciplines.

2. The Derive (2.5 hours): Based on the conceptual basis outlined in the 1st stage, in the second step, the workshop participants have to stroll the streets in groups, following a simple set of rules while documenting their impressions with short text entries and sound clips. In order to capture the latter it is a requirement from the participants to have smartphones with GPS-logging and audio-recording features.

- Sound collection: right after the workshop participants get back from their 'Derive', the organizers would collect and organize the audio files they collected in a collective archive, which would be the raw material for the final interactive experience.

3. Analysis and Storytelling (1 hour): the Derive carried out in the previous step is followed by a group discussion in which the impressions are shared and contrasted. Through several ideation techniques the goal is to generate a few collective narratives out of the short fragments of text collected during the walks.

4. Socialization and narrative crowd-ideation (1 hour): at this stage the different groups share the result of their impressions in the form of narratives, graphics, images, videos and so forth. Thereafter, the idea is to create a single narrative out of the stories presented by the different groups.

5. Interactive sound-experience (30 mins): following the overall concept, the final stage is an experimental performance in which the audio-clips provided by the participants become the fragments in a collective and interactive composition, where the resulting soundscape responds to different kinds of visualization and sonification.

C&C '15, June 22-25, 2015, Glasgow, United Kingdom
ACM 978-1-4503-3598-0/15/06.
http://dx.doi.org/10.1145/2757226.2767186

By using different kinds of visualizations and representations, the concept of the final experience illustrates metaphorically the core of Psychogeographical theory, that is, a 'topographical model', which compares the human psyche with an imagined space, in order to make its complexity understandable. We intend to do the opposite, to create a sound-imagined space out of urban fragments, out of the fragments gathered collectively. It will be like thinking of a map from a given territory which helps us to understand its geography, which, both like a mind or a city, has conscious, subconscious and unconscious areas.

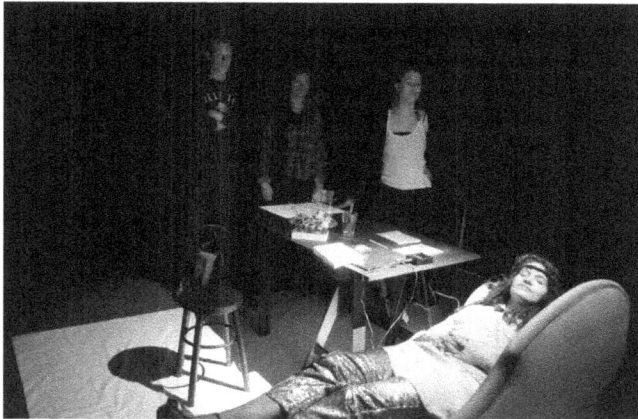

Figure 1. Workshop session,2013, Stockholm, Sweden.

Figure 2. Workshop session, 9th Design & Emotion Conference 2014, Medellín, Colombia.

INTENDED NUMBER OF ATTENDEES (MAXIMUM AND MINIMUM)
Min 10, max 30

PLANNED LENGTH OF THE WORKSHOP
(5 - 6 hours)

EQUIPMENT NEEDED TO CONDUCT THE WORKSHOP.
1. A room for a screening, following debate and sound-performance:
2. Necessary equipment
   - Projector
   - 4 studio sound-monitors (speakers) similar to these ones: http://amzn.to/1fQJBb6
   - Wires and connectors suitable to distribute them along the room, preferably in each corner (the idea would be to simulate the perception of spatial movement through a quadraphonic sound system)

Materials and special requirements needed for the workshop.
The assistants require the following equipment and tools:

1. A smartphone suitable for recording sound-clips in wav format

2. Headphones

3. Drawing materials: color-pencils, color-pens, markers. (paper and other required elements would be provided)

Please take a look at the trailer of the result of a previous workshop carried out in Stockholm:

http://www.resoundcity.com/human-mind-as-a-city/

Mind's Ratchet: Ecologies of the Artificial: Transverging Cognition and Creativity

Marcos Novak
Media Arts and Technology/CNSI/Art
University of California, Santa Barbara
marcos@mat.ucsb.edu

Abstract

How can we, in the 21st century, understand creativity and cognition is a way that is at once consonant with both the "sciences of the artificial" and with the "ecology of mind"? Given our accelerating advances in the understanding of mind as mechanism, and given our evident aim to imbue autonomous machines with artificial life, artificial intelligence, and artificial consciousness, and, given that the built world is always and necessarily the mirror of our choices and values, by what ethics can we guide our technics, and by what means, and to what ends?

Transvergence is an evolving framework for research, pedagogy, and creative production. Among its aims is "transformation the leads to speciation" — of works, ideas, disciplines, and everything else that might be brought together to combine into new formations. Motives and mechanisms drawn from nature and culture are extended through technology into means by which to explore a broader spectrum of the possible than might otherwise be attainable.

As with natural systems, this effort must convert noise into life, thought, and beauty.

ACM Classification

F. [Theory of Computation]; F.1.1 [Theory of Computation]: Models of Computation--- self-modifying machines, unbounded-action devices; F.1.2 [Theory of Computation]: Modes of Computation---interactive and reactive computation; F.4.2 [Theory of Computation]: grammars and other rewriting systems; H.1.1 [Information Systems]: systems and information theory; H.5.1 [Information Systems]: multimedia information systems---artificial, augmented, and virtual realities; H.5.5 [Information Systems]: sound and music computing--- signal analysis, synthesis, and processing; I.1.0 [Computing Methodologies] cognitive simulation, philosophical foundations; I.2.11 [Information Systems]: Distributed Artificial Intelligence; J.3 [Computer Applications]: Biology and Genetics; J.4 [Computer Applications]: Social and Behavioral Sciences; J.5 [Computer Applications]: Arts and Humanities; J.6 [Computer Applications]: Computer-Aided Engineering; K.4.1 [Computers and Society]: Public Policy Issues---ethics

C&C '15, June 22-25, 2015, Glasgow, United Kingdom
ACM 978-1-4503-3598-0/15/06.
http://dx.doi.org/10.1145/2757226.2785731

Author Keywords: Transvergence; perforated systems, liquid architectures; transarchitectures; archimusic; navigable music; worldmaking; transactivity; speciation; creativity; cognition; cybernetics; artificial life; artificial consciousness; ecology.

Short Bio

Marcos Novak is the founding Director of the transLAB at UCSB, where he is Professor and Vice Chair of MAT (Media Arts and Technology), and is also affiliated with with CNSI (California NanoSystems Institute) and Art. He is an artist, theorist, and transarchitect, and a pioneer of algorithmic design in architecture. In 2008, *"Transmitting Architecture"*, the title of his seminal 1995 essay, became the theme of the *XXIII World Congress of the UIA (Union Internationale Des Architectes)*, the largest architectural organization in the world.

His projects, theoretical essays, and interviews have been translated into over twenty languages and have appeared in over 70 countries, and he lectures, teaches, and exhibits worldwide. He is a Fellow of the World Technology Network, a Distinguished Affiliated Scholar of the Alexander Fleming Biomedical Sciences Research Center, and serves on the editorial boards of several journals. Deeply interested *worldmaking*, the future, and the avant-garde, he is also the fortunate recipient of a classical education in Greece, where he grew up. In 2000, he represented Greece at the Venice Biennale, and has participated in numerous art and architecture biennials since, both in Venice and elsewhere

Performing Digital Media Design

Jocelyn Spence
Digital World Research Centre
School of Arts
University of Surrey
j.c.spence@surrey.ac.uk

ABSTRACT

This workshop explores a novel design practice and the methodology behind it in an entirely hands-on way. Participants will create a performance centring on their own personal digital media using *Collect Yourselves!* – a two-phase online system that guides the selection, sharing, and live performance of digital photos. Through using the system and briefly analysing the results, participants will gain first-hand understanding of the potential for using performance to extend interactions with technology into an emotionally and aesthetically charged space. The workshop will then cover the basics of the methodology used to create this system, leading to a brainstorming session for how to use Performative Experience Design to interrogate and enhance each participant's own research interests. Participants in this workshop will create and experience a compelling and potentially transformative engagement with digital technology, then use this experience and the methodology behind it to pursue the unique aesthetics of performance in their own work.

Author Keywords

Performative Experience Design; interaction design; performance; autobiography; digital media

ACM Classification Keywords

H.5.m. Information interfaces and presentation (e.g., HCI): Miscellaneous.

General Terms

Human factors; Design; Theory.

PERFORMANCE SUMMARY: *COLLECT YOURSELVES!*

This workshop explores intermedial [4] autobiographical performance, mediated and structured by a browser-based application called *Collect Yourselves!* A *Collect Yourselves!* performance consists of two phases. In the first phase, participants log in and upload personal photos in response to several prompts crafted to invoke the properties of autobiographical performance: self-making, situatedness, 'heightened attention', and the 'aesthetics of the event' [5, 2]. In the second phase, the participants come together in a shared time and space, where *Collect Yourselves!* guides them through the live performance of the personal photos they have uploaded and the stories behind them. Previous incarnations of this system have established that these participatory performances succeed in generating the aesthetics of performance in a private space (and there will be no external audience for this workshop). *Collect Yourselves!* nudges participants towards an engagement with their own personal digital media in a way that has so far resulted in increased risk, vulnerability, connection, intimacy, comfort, and challenge.

Design-oriented (Performance) Research

Collect Yourselves! came about as the first prototype in a process known as Performative Experience Design. This is a sub-field positioned directly between design-oriented research [1] and performance studies. Design-oriented research and much of the research in performance studies rely on the production and analysis of novel designs that lead to insights about interaction and experience. In the case of Performative Experience Design, the unit of analysis is not the technology itself, but rather the experience shared among those people who are brought together by their interactions with digital media.

Workshop Aims

This workshop proposes to give participants a thorough, hands-on experience of how performance aesthetics can extend interactions with technology. It also explores the methodology behind this experience, giving them the tools to apply this approach to their own work in a creative, collaborative session. The workshop will provide the basics of background and approach, leaving as much time as possible for group discussion and contributions.

Designer/deviser Biography

The system's main designer (in HCI terms) or deviser (in performance terms) is Jocelyn Spence, a Research Fellow at the University of Surrey. *Collect Yourselves!* formed the core of Jocelyn's completed doctoral thesis, an interdisciplinary work situated in both interaction design and performance studies. She is also a performance practitioner with the company *Would-be Nuns and Cowboys*, exploring intermedial autobiographical

C&C '15, June 22-25, 2015, Glasgow, United Kingdom
ACM 978-1-4503-3598-0/15/06.
http://dx.doi.org/10.1145/2757226.2789213

performance from a more straightforwardly theatrical perspective.

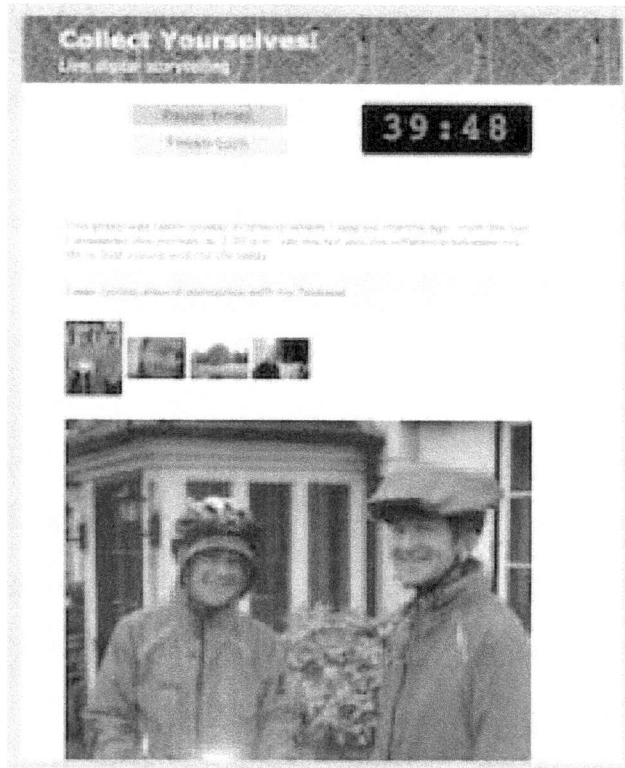

Figure 1. Sample display in the performance phase.

Participatory Performance
Although the performance is shaped by the *Collect Yourselves!* system, the content is provided by the participants. They should bring a device capable of uploading selected personal photos to the system during the workshop, and will be given time in the morning to make these selections (the 'devising phase'). They will also be encouraged to take photos at the conference for use in the workshop. Participation will be capped at eight people.

The Devising Process – Timing is Everything
Time is of central importance to this performance. First, participants must engage in a form of devising process [3] in which they engage with their personal digital photos – whether stored in the cloud or on their smartphones, tablets, or laptops – and choose one photo in response to each of five prompts. This is a reflective and often gratifying process in itself. Devising has proved to be key to the performance outcomes, even when participants spend as little as a quarter of an hour on it. For this reason, the workshop allows plenty of time for devising in the morning, then conducts the performance after lunch.

The Prompts
The performance involves selecting photos and telling the stories behind them in response to prompts on the following topics: 1) a photo you forgot you had taken; 2) the photo taken nearest in time to a particular event; 3) a photo of something you think no one else has noticed at this conference event; 4) a photo representing something you wish you could research; and 5) a photo that you tell a story about – which is a lie or fiction.

Technical Requirements
Beyond requiring participants to bring their own laptop, tablet, or smartphone for uploading (and possibly taking) photos for the devising phase, the workshop will require reliable and speedy WiFi access. It will also require a power supply, projector, projector screen, flipchart, a relatively quiet space in which eight participants can move about freely, and lighting that can be dimmed to allow projected photos to be seen clearly without restricting performers' ability to be seen and to move about safely.

CONCLUSION
The *Collect Yourselves!* workshop aims to give participants a dynamic, hands-on experience with intermedial autobiographical performance and the Performative Experience Design methodology. It offers enough background to be practically useful, while leaving ample time for participants to share their own interests and insights with each other. I hope to capture people's imagination and give them tools for expanding their future research or practice, using a specifically performative aesthetic to inform and expand the possibilities of a creative engagement with interactive technologies.

REFERENCES
1. Fällman, D. Design-oriented human-computer interaction. In *Proc. CHI '03*, ACM Press (2003), 225-232.

2. Fischer-Lichte, E. *The transformative power of performance: A new aesthetics*. Routledge, London, 2008.

3. Heddon, D. and Milling, J. *Devising performance: A critical history*. Palgrave Macmillan, Basingstoke, 2006.

4. Nelson, R. Introduction: Prospective mapping. In: S. Bay-Cheng, C. Kattenbelt, A. Lavender and R. Nelson, eds. *Mapping intermediality in performance*. Amsterdam University Press, Amsterdam (2010), 13-23.

5. Spence, J., Frohlich, D. and Andrews, S. Performative experience design: Where autobiographical performance and human-computer interaction meet. *Digital Creativity 24*, 2 (2013), 96-110.

Author Index

www.ingramcontent.com/pod-product-compliance
Lightning Source LLC
Chambersburg PA
CBHW080655220326
41598CB00033B/5214